# COMPANY LAW

# COMPANY LAW

*Fifth Edition*

## BRENDA HANNIGAN, MA, LLM

*Professor of Corporate Law*
*Law School*
*University of Southampton*

# OXFORD
## UNIVERSITY PRESS

Great Clarendon Street, Oxford, OX2 6DP,
United Kingdom

Oxford University Press is a department of the University of Oxford.
It furthers the University's objective of excellence in research, scholarship,
and education by publishing worldwide. Oxford is a registered trade mark of
Oxford University Press in the UK and in certain other countries

Second edition 2009
Third edition 2012
Fourth edition 2015

Impression: 1

Published in the United States of America by Oxford University Press
198 Madison Avenue, New York, NY 10016, United States of America

British Library Cataloguing in Publication Data
Data available

Library of Congress Control Number: 2018939626

ISBN 978–0–19–878770–9

Printed in Great Britain by
Bell & Bain Ltd., Glasgow

# Preface

Since the last edition, there has been the UK decision by referendum to leave the European Union. At the time of writing, there is little clarity about how such an exit might happen. It follows that there is uncertainty about the impact of any such exit on Company Law where the EU *acquis* is deeply embedded. Issues which will require resolution include, *inter alia*, the impact on freedom of establishment, on cross-border mergers, on accounting and audit, on prospectuses, on regulated markets, on the implementation of the Shareholder Rights Directive amendments, and the consequences of no longer being within the scope of the EU Insolvency Regulation. Given the uncertainty as to the direction of travel, the text reflects the current world where the UK is a member of the European Union.

Legislative matters then await a position on Brexit, but fortunately, we have a rich seam of demanding jurisprudence on matters of everyday concern to companies and their stakeholders to distract us from the wider uncertainties.

Throughout the text, the significant company law cases since the last edition are addressed, cases such as *R v Boyle Transport (NI) Ltd* (addressing corporate veil and one-man company issues); *Bilta (UK) Ltd v Nazir* (on attribution); *Eclairs Group Ltd v JKX Oil & Gas plc* (on proper purpose doctrine); *First Subsea Ltd v Balltec* (on corporate opportunities and remedies); *Cullen Investments v Brown* (on derivative claims); and *Burnden Holdings v Fielding* (on limitation). The new edition reflects the proposed 2018 UK Corporate Governance Code (the final text was not available at the time of going to print so please check the text against the final version once it is available) and the 2016 Green Paper on Corporate Governance Reform and Government Response, together with EU developments, especially on freedom of establishment and the recast EU Insolvency Regulation 2015/848.

As ever, my sincere thanks to the editorial and production teams at OUP for their attentive professional help at every stage of this work.

The law is stated as of 1 February 2018.

Brenda Hannigan
Professor of Corporate Law
Law School
University of Southampton

# New to this edition

**Recent decisions which are considered include:**

- *R v Boyle Transport (NI) Ltd* (addressing corporate veil and one-man company issues);
- *Bilta (UK) Ltd v Nazir* (on attribution);
- *HRH Okpabi v Royal Dutch Shell* and *Lungowe v Vedanta Resources plc* (parent liability for torts of subsidiaries);
- *Re Charterhouse Capital Ltd* and *Staray Capital Ltd v Yang* (PC) (alteration of articles);
- *BTI 2014 LLC v Sequana SA* (distributions and duties to creditors);
- *Polbud v Wykonawstwo* (freedom of establishment);
- *Eclairs Group Ltd v JKX Oil & Gas plc* (proper purpose doctrine);
- *First Subsea Ltd v Balltec* (corporate opportunities and remedies);
- *Cullen Investments v Brown* (derivative claims);
- *Burnden Holdings v Fielding* (limitation and remedies);
- *LRH Services v Trew* (improper distributions).

**Legislative and policy measures and initiatives which are considered include:**

- the proposed 2018 UK Corporate Governance Code (the final text was not available at the time of going to print so please check the text against the final version once it is available);
- the 2016 Green Paper on Corporate Governance Reform and Government Response together with the HC BEIS Committee report on Corporate Governance (Third Report, session 16–17);
- the recast EU Insolvency Regulation 2015/848.

# Outline contents

## Part IV  Corporate Finance—Share and Loan Capital

## Part V  Corporate Liquidation

# Contents

## Part II Corporate Governance—Directors' Roles and Responsibilities

## Part V Corporate Liquidation

# Table of cases

# Table of legislation

**United Kingdom Statutory Instruments**

# Table of European legislation

## Regulations

## Recommendations

# PART I
# The Corporate Structure

# 1

# Formation, classification, and registration of companies

## A Introduction

### Registered companies

**1-1**    Companies registered under the Companies Act 2006 (CA 2006) and its predecessors are the focus of this book. In this initial chapter we consider the mechanics of formation and registration and the various types of companies which may be formed, as well as looking briefly at alternative vehicles for business. Before looking at these matters, an overview of the process of formation and the key players in a registered company may be helpful for the student reader at whom this book is aimed.

### An overview of the formation of a registered company

**1-2**    To form a registered company under the CA 2006, all that is required is one person and a lawful purpose (s 7). Some brief documentation must be submitted (either electronically or on paper) to the registrar of companies (located at Companies House, Cardiff) together with a registration fee of £10 (if electronic) and £40 (if paper). Once the formalities are completed correctly, the registrar of companies issues a certificate of incorporation whereupon the company comes into existence (s 16(2)). This process typically takes less than a week (if paper-based) and it can be completed in a single day if speed is important. The process is simple, quick, and inexpensive.

**1-3**    Imagine that A and B wish to form a registered company to run a printing business. A alone could form a company since, as noted earlier, only one person is required, but for these purposes we will assume A and B wish to form a company together. In fact, Companies House statistics show that the average number of shareholders per company is two.[1] There are a few initial decisions which A and B have to make. First, they have to decide how they are going to split the ownership of the company. Assume they agree that they will split the ownership of the business 70 per cent and 30 per cent to reflect the contributions that they are going to make to it. The division of ownership is entirely a matter of choice for them, obviously, as is the number of shares to issue. They may decide to issue:

- 1,000 £1 shares with A taking 700 of the shares, putting £700 into the company's finances in the form of share capital, and B taking 300 shares, putting £300 into the share capital; or
- 100 £1 shares with A taking 70 (£70) and B taking 30 (£30); or

---

[1]    Companies House Statistical Release, Companies Register Activities 2016–17, Table A7.

- 100 1p shares with A taking 70 (70p) and B 30 (30p); or
- 10 1p shares with A taking seven shares (7p) and B taking three shares (3p).

**1-4**  Share capital is considered in detail later. For the moment it suffices to appreciate that A and B have complete flexibility as to the amount of money that they put into the company in the form of share capital and the value, called the nominal value, they wish to assign to the shares. They have complete flexibility as to the number of shares they issue and the same ownership division can be achieved by issuing 10 or 100 or 1,000 shares. Shares typically carry one vote per share so, on any of the examples given in **1-3**, A has 70 per cent of the votes and B has 30 per cent of the votes. Most matters within a company can be decided on a simple majority vote so A has effective control of the company with B as a minority shareholder, a position which may prove uncomfortable, as we shall see. Depending on the circumstances, A and B might prefer a 60/40 split of the shareholdings, or a 90/10 split, or even a 50/50 split, but a 50/50 split has an in-built deadlock problem if the two shareholders disagree so it is not advisable. As can be seen, it is possible to form a company with very little capital, though in the case of a public company wishing to carry on business, there is a minimum share capital requirement of £50,000 (CA 2006, s 763, see **1-46**). For the moment, though, we will concentrate on private companies. The distinction between public and private status is discussed later in the chapter.

**1-5**  As the shareholders of the company, A and B appoint the directors who will manage the business. Given his voting control, A could impose his choice of directors, but frequently it will have been agreed that A and B will be the directors. The result is that A and B are the shareholders and A and B are also the directors of the company, a form of structure which is very common.

**1-6**  Equally, A and B may decide to bring other members into the business and issue further shares to them and/or appoint them to the board. With additional shares issued, the shareholders might be A, B, C, and D with only A and B being directors; or A and B might be the only shareholders with the board made up of A, B, C, and D; or A and B may be the only shareholders while C and D are the only directors. In other words, while uniformity of identity between the shareholders and the directors is very common in small companies, that need not be the case. Indeed, one of the advantages of incorporation is that it allows the ownership of the company to be separated from the management of the business. It is possible to be a shareholder without being a director and vice versa and, of course, in the largest companies with hundreds of thousands of shareholders, there can be no question of the shareholders being the directors, and the directors usually have only minuscule shareholdings compared to the total number of shares in issue.

**1-7**  Now we have the key players as far as company law is concerned, the directors and the members or shareholders (for the most part, the terms 'members' and 'shareholders' are synonymous). Collectively, the members or shareholders own all of the share capital of the company and control the company through their shareholdings. A key responsibility of the shareholders is to appoint, by a majority vote, the directors who provide the management of the company. For the many companies where there are only two shareholders who are also the directors, formal distinctions between the role of the shareholders and the directors (which in law are separate functions with separate obligations) are often meaningless. As a matter of law, as we shall see, the company owns the business and its assets (and is responsible for its liabilities), but in a two person company, with a small business, where the same people are the directors, shareholders, and employees, those two people often regard themselves and describe themselves as the owners of the company. In addition to the directors and shareholders, many other constituencies, or stakeholders, also have a

role to play in the company. Employees and creditors come instantly to mind. Their relationships with the company are primarily a matter of employment law, contract law, and
insolvency law whereas the focus of company law is the company and its shareholders and
directors. A contentious issue now is the extent to which the directors should take account
of stakeholder interests, especially in larger companies; see the discussion in Chapter 10.

**1-8**    Returning to A and B, they must also decide on the type of company that they want
to form. The CA 2006 provides for various types of company, but the most commonly
adopted form is the private company limited by shares. A company is a company limited
by shares if the liability of its members is limited by its constitution to the amount, if any,
unpaid on the shares held by them (CA 2006, s 3(2)).

**1-9**    Let us imagine that A has taken 70 £1 shares and B has taken 30 £1 shares, the £100 company being a very common structure. With only £100 of share capital, the company will
initially seek to finance its activities through bank financing and so it must arrange
loans and overdrafts with the bank. The company, the separate entity formed on incorporation, will acquire employees and premises, the company will enter into contracts,
and the company will incur debts. If the company incurs, say, debts of £25,000 and
collapses into insolvency, the company owes the creditors £25,000, but the members'
liability is limited to the amount unpaid, if any, on the shares held by them (s 3(2)). The
liability of A is limited to the £70 due on his shares and B's liability is limited to the £30
due on his shares. Assuming that A and B paid for their shares at the time the company
issued the shares to them, as would be typical, A and B have already paid the sums due
and no further payments can be required from them to meet the company's liabilities
to its creditors. The only caveat being that, in some cases, A and B may have been pre-
vailed upon by one or more creditors (typically, the company's bank) to give personal
guarantees and security over personal assets which the bank can call upon in the event
that, on insolvency, the company's assets are insufficient to meet the company's debts
due to the bank.

**1-10**    For the purposes of the discussion to date, it was assumed that the parties wishing to
register a company will put together the documentation and submit it to the registrar of companies. It is also common to purchase a company from a company formation agent. Company formation agents can provide useful assistance and advice
for those wishing to form a company who are uncertain about the formalities, and
most companies continue to be formed (electronically) by them. In due course, it is
expected that there will be a simple online formation procedure available to all. As a
company does not exist prior to the issue of the certificate of incorporation, any debts
incurred by A and B in obtaining premises, hiring equipment, etc prior to that point
are incurred personally.

**1-11**    For similar reasons, A and B may opt for same-day incorporation where the registrar
processes all the documentation and issues the certificate of incorporation on the same
day as the application for registration is made.[2] Same-day incorporation may also make
sense where there is a need to secure a particular name for the company since, once registered, no other company can have the same name, or even a name considered 'too like'
that name (CA 2006, ss 66, 67).

**1-12**    Having incorporated, A and B, as the directors and shareholders, have taken on new legal
roles and responsibilities, the discharge of which is the subject of the remainder of this

---

[2] The same-day incorporation fee is £100 (if paper) or £30 (if electronic).

book. Sometimes, the ease and speed of incorporation can obscure these legal realities and it is often the case that the parties themselves have only a minimal understanding of their changed legal status and potential liabilities. In part, this lack of understanding is due to the fact that incorporation, either directly or by the purchase of a company from a formation agent, can be achieved without any professional advice being sought or required. The result can be a failure on the part of the incorporators to appreciate the duties and responsibilities of directors including their obligations to the company's creditors, the need for the company's affairs to be run in a manner which takes account of minority shareholder interests and does not unfairly prejudice them, and the ongoing (often minimal) obligations which companies have with respect to filing information with the registrar of companies so as to ensure that the public register is up to date and accurate. This is not to say that access to limited liability should be restricted, but rather that all concerned need to appreciate the legal responsibilities attached to acquiring corporate status.

**1-13**     Of course, A and B are not compelled to incorporate and there are some other options open to them which are worth considering before we look at the formation of registered companies.

## Alternative structures to the registered company

**1-14**     Conducting a business through the mechanism of a registered company has the particular advantages of the separate legal personality of the company (see **1-37**), the limited liability of the members, and the possible separation of ownership and management of the company. Where these attributes are either not important or not attainable (for example, because of the small scale of the business), then a registered limited company may not be the most appropriate legal structure for that business given that incorporation brings with it a changed set of legal roles and responsibilities which the parties may not wish to bear.[3]

### A sole trader

**1-15**     One option is for an individual to act as a sole trader and with very large numbers of companies having no more than two members and an issued share capital of (at most) £100, it is debatable whether some of those businesses might not be conducted more appropriately as sole traders. A sole trader is simply that—an individual carrying on business as an individual. The disadvantage is that the sole trader has unlimited liability, but many shareholders in small companies obtain only partial limited liability in any event, as they may have given personal guarantees to major creditors of the company, such as banks. The main advantage in being a sole trader is privacy as there is no obligation to register any information as to the business or its financial position with a public registry.[4]

### Partnership

**1-16**     Partnership is the relation which subsists between persons carrying on a business in common with a view to profit.[5] Partnerships are governed by the Partnership Act 1890, but most partnerships draw up their own partnership agreements which override the Act. English partnerships are not separate legal entities and partners do not have limited liability. The

---

[3] See BEIS, *Business Population Estimates for the UK and Regions 2017* (November 2017) Figure 4, which shows that, at the start of 2017, 60 per cent of private sector enterprises were sole proprietorships, 30 per cent were companies, and 7 per cent were partnerships.

[4] See n 3, there were an estimated 3.4m sole proprietorships in the UK at the start of 2017.

[5] Partnership Act 1890, s 1.

advantage of this structure is that the business affairs of a partnership are entirely private and there is no obligation to register financial or partnership information at a public registry.[6]

## Limited partnership

**1-17** Limited partnerships are governed by the Limited Partnership Act 1907[7] and must be registered at Companies House. A limited partnership allows for limited partners alongside general partners with unlimited liability (though a company can be a general partner and so limited liability may be secured for the general partner in that way). The liability of a limited partner for the debts of the partnership is limited to the amount of their contribution to the partnership, but a possible disadvantage of this structure is that a limited partner must be excluded from all management functions. On the other hand, a limited partnership is a useful business vehicle for investors who are content to allow the general partners to manage the assets, particularly as financial privacy is ensured, given there is no obligation to file accounts with Companies House. This structure is used throughout the venture capital investment industry and so the limited partnership has evolved into a somewhat specialised business vehicle.[8] In January 2017, the Department for Business, Energy and Industrial Strategy issued a call for evidence with respect to use of the limited partnerships.[9] Subsequently, a new type of investment limited partnership called a Private Fund Limited Partnership was introduced as of 6 April 2017.[10]

## Limited liability partnership

**1-18** Limited liability partnerships (LLPs) are something of a hybrid between a company and a partnership. A limited liability partnership is a body corporate with legal personality separate from that of its members which is formed by being registered at Companies House. LLPs are governed by the Limited Liability Partnerships Act 2000 and related regulations including, in particular, the Limited Liability Partnership (Application of the Companies Act 2006) Regulations 2009 which apply many provisions of the CA 2006 to LLPs with appropriate modifications.[11]

**1-19** To register an LLP, there must be two or more persons associated for carrying on a lawful business with a view to profit.[12] Details of the registered office and of the members (an LLP does not have a share capital, so there are no shareholders) must be provided. There must be at least two designated members who are named members with

---

[6] See n 3, there were an estimated 414,000 partnerships in the UK at the start of 2017.

[7] In 2008, the Government consulted on plans to modernise and simplify the law on limited partnerships in line with recommendations previously made by the Law Commission; see BERR Consultation Document, *Reform of Limited Partnership Law, Legislative Reform Order to repeal and replace the Limited Partnerships Act 1907* (August 2008), URN 08/1153 and the Law Commission Report, *Partnership Law* (Law Comm No 283), November 2003. These plans were dropped subsequently and only some modest amendments were made to the 1907 Act by SI 2009/1940.

[8] There were 15,244 on the register as of March 2017 (figures for England and Wales), but 29,709 in Scotland, reflecting their particular value to the investment industry based in Scotland, see Companies House *Companies Register Activities Data Tables 2016–17*, Table B2.

[9] BEIS, *Review of Limited Partnership Law: a call for evidence* (January 2017). BEIS then issued a further consultation document, 'Limited Partnerships: reform of limited partnership law' (30 April 2018).

[10] See the Limited Partnerships Act 1907 as amended by the Legislative Reform (Private Fund Limited Partnerships) Order 2017 (SI 2017/514).

[11] SI 2009/1804. See generally *Palmer's Limited Liability Partnership Law* (3rd edn, 2017). LLPs were introduced following intense pressure from accountancy firms which were concerned that partnership (with its unlimited personal liability of the partners) was an unattractive business vehicle for the profession. But when the legislation was enacted, it was decided to make it available to all rather than restrict it to the professions. [12] LLPA 2000, s 2(1)(a).

particular responsibilities such as with respect to signing and delivering accounts to the registrar of companies. The constitution of the LLP, the members' internal agreement dealing with such matters as the division of management powers and profits, is not registered. To that extent, members of an LLP retain some of the essential privacy of a partnership. An LLP is required to file annual accounts and a confirmation statement[13] (at least once every 12 months). The liability of the members is limited, in this case to such amount as they have agreed internally to contribute to the debts of the LLP. On insolvency, all the corporate insolvency regimes are available and applicable to an LLP which remains liable to its creditors to the full amount of its assets. As can be seen, therefore, the LLP is a hybrid creation straddling the line between partnerships and companies. As of March 2017, there were 52,001 LLPs (figures for England and Wales) registered with Companies House.[14]

### An unlimited company

**1-20**  One other option to note is the unlimited company, i.e. a company without any limit in its constitution on the liability of its members (CA 2006, s 3(4)). This status might appear an unattractive option, given the open-ended commitment by the members to meet the company's liabilities, yet there were 3,625 on the register at 31 March 2017.[15] The advantage which an unlimited company has over other forms of registered company is that generally there is no obligation to file accounts with the registrar of companies (s 448). Where privacy is a major consideration, therefore, and the risk of insolvency is remote (for example, because the company is not trading but holding investments), unlimited liability may be attractive. On the other hand, the accounting disclosure requirements have been significantly reduced in recent years for small limited companies[16] so this advantage may not be as attractive as it once was. There may be taxation reasons, however, why an unlimited company may be advantageous.

**1-21**  Overall, the popularity of these other mechanisms such as the LLP (52,001 on the register, figures for England and Wales), the limited partnership (15,244 on the register), or the unlimited company (3,625) has to be put in the context of a register of 3,408,366 companies,[17] the vast majority of which are companies limited by shares combining a separate legal entity with limited liability for the members.

## B  Company formation—companies limited by shares

**1-22**  The most common type of registered company is the company limited by shares so, assuming that A and B wish to register a company limited by shares, they must draw up certain documents and submit them to the registrar of companies together with the registration fee (see **1-2**).[18]

---

[13]  Confirmation statements replace the annual return (since 30 June 2016) and confirms information about the LLP's registered office, members, and people with significant control.

[14]  See Companies House *Companies Register Activities Data Tables 2016–17*, Table B4.

[15]  Companies House *Companies Register Activities Data Tables 2016–17*, Table B2. Of course, the member could be a limited company.

[16]  See CA 2006, s 444 and the thresholds for this category are quite high, see s 382. See also **18-25**.

[17]  Companies House *Companies Register Activities Data Tables 2016–17*, Table A1.

[18]  The fee is low out of concerns that otherwise it might be seen as an indirect tax on capital raising, see Drury, 'The "Delaware Syndrome": European Fears and Reactions' [2005] JBL 709 at 726–7. There is also a limited web-incorporation service where the fee is £12.

## Memorandum of association

**1-23**  An application for registration must be accompanied by a memorandum of association (CA 2006, s 9(1)). The memorandum is a short prescribed document[19] stating that the subscribers wish to form a company under the CA 2006 and agree to become members of the company and, in the case of a company with a share capital, they agree to take at least one share each (s 8(1)). The memorandum is intended to be of merely historical significance indicating the initial founding of the company. Previously, the memorandum of association was an important external-facing document telling the outside world the key facts about the company: its name, its status as a public company (if that was the case), the jurisdiction in which it was registered, the company's objects, that the members' liability was limited, and setting out the amount and division of the company's authorised share capital. Now the memorandum simply records the identity of the original founders of the company and indicates how many shares they took on formation. In many cases, the original founders will be formation agents (see **1-10**) and so the document will have no continuing relevance.

## Application for registration

**1-24**  The company's application for registration must state:

- the company's proposed name;
- whether the registered office is to be situated in England and Wales, Wales, Scotland, or Northern Ireland;
- whether the members' liability is to be limited and, if so, whether by shares or by guarantee;
- whether the company is to be a public or a private company (CA 2006, s 9(2)).

The application must contain:

- a statement of capital and initial shareholdings (if a company limited by shares) or a statement of guarantee (if a company limited by guarantee);
- a statement of the company's proposed officers, including the proposed company secretary (if the company is a public company or where a private company chooses to have a company secretary);
- a statement of initial significant control;
- a statement of the intended address of the company's registered office;
- a copy of any proposed articles of association unless the intention is to rely on the model default articles, discussed at **1-30** (CA 2006, s 9(4), (5)).

### Statement of capital and initial shareholdings

**1-25**  The statement of capital and initial shareholdings must state:[20]

- the total number of shares and the aggregate nominal value of the shares to be taken on formation by the subscribers to the memorandum;

---

[19] The memorandum of a company with a share capital must be in the form set out in the Companies (Registration) Regulations 2008, SI 2008/3014, reg 2(a), Sch 1.

[20] The statement of capital and initial shareholdings also must contain the name and address of each subscriber to the memorandum of association: CA 2006, s 10(3); the Companies (Registration) Regulations 2008, SI 2008/3014, reg 3.

- the aggregate amount (if any) to be unpaid on those shares (whether on account of their nominal value or by way of premium);
- for each class of shares, prescribed particulars of the rights attached to them, the total number of shares of that class, and the aggregate nominal value of those shares (CA 2006, s 10(2)).

**1-26**  The statement of capital provides important information as to the share structure of the company as (1) it establishes how much share capital has been raised and how much is paid and unpaid and (2) it identifies the rights attached to the shares where there are classes of shares. Most companies have only one type of share, an ordinary share, such as the £1 share noted at **1-9** held by A and B, and class rights are irrelevant in such a company. Classes of shares are discussed at **16-19**. As from the date of incorporation, the subscribers to the memorandum become holders of the shares specified in the statement of capital and initial holdings (CA 2006, s 16(5)).

### Statement of the proposed officers

**1-27**  Particulars of the initial director(s) of the company[21] must be delivered with the application for registration and the statement of the proposed officers must include a statement by the subscribers to the memorandum of association that each of the persons named as a director has consented to act in the relevant capacity (CA 2006, s 12(1), (3)).[22] If the company is a public company, or where a private company chooses to appoint a secretary, particulars of the proposed secretary of the company must also be given together with a statement that the person named has consented so to act. From the date of incorporation, those persons so named as directors and company secretary are deemed to have been appointed to office (s 16(6)).

### Statement of initial significant control

**1-28**  This statement of initial significant control delivered to the registrar must state whether, on incorporation, there will be anyone who will count for the purposes of the register of people with significant control over a company as a person whose particulars would be required to be entered in the company's PSC register.[23] As to the PSC register, see CA 2006, s 790M and the discussion at **16-91**.

### Statement of the address of the company's registered office

**1-29**  Every company must have a registered office (CA 2006, s 86) which essentially is meant to be the administrative office of the company and all business letters, order forms, and websites of the company must give the address of the registered office[24] which may be a service address. The registered office is the location at which members and others may consult the various registers which the company is obliged to maintain,[25] such as the register of members (see **16-73**). The registered office is also the place where documents must be

---

[21] A private company must have at least one director, a public company must have at least two: CA 2006, s 154.

[22] As soon as reasonably practicable after registering this statement of proposed officers, the registrar of companies must send a notice to each person so named stating that they have been so named and including such information relating to the office and duties of a director (or details of where information of that sort can be found) as the Secretary of State may from time to time direct the registrar to include: CA 2006, s 1079B(3).    [23] CA 2006, s 12A.

[24] The Companies (Trading Disclosures) Regulations 2008, SI 2008/495, reg 7.

[25] Companies may choose a single alternative inspection location instead of the registered office, see CA 2006, s 1136 and The Companies (Company Records) Regulations 2008, SI 2008/3006, reg 3.

deposited, such as the statement by the company's auditor on ceasing to hold office (s 519), and where legal documents may be served on a company. It is also the address with which the registrar of companies corresponds so it is important that any change of address of the registered office is notified promptly to the registrar.

### Copy of articles of association

**1-30**    The application for registration must contain a copy of the proposed articles of association (CA 2006, s 9(5)). If, on formation, articles are not registered or, if articles are registered, in so far as they do not exclude or modify the relevant model articles, the relevant model articles form part of the company's articles automatically (s 20(1)). Model forms of articles are provided for public and private companies limited by shares and for companies limited by guarantee and any company may adopt all or any of the provisions of the relevant model articles for that type of company.[26] The articles of association are a key element of the company's constitution and set out the rules governing the internal running of the company. The matters typically covered in the articles include the conduct of meetings and voting procedures; capital matters including share transfer and transmission; the appointment and removal of directors and their powers; and the declaration of dividends. A detailed account of the articles can be found in Chapter 5.

## Statement of compliance

**1-31**    In order to minimise the amount of checking which needs to be done by the registrar of companies, a statement of compliance (i.e. a statement that the requirements as to registration have been complied with) signed by every subscriber to the memorandum must be delivered to the registrar of companies with the registration application (CA 2006, s 13(1)). It is an offence to make a false statement of compliance (s 1112).

## The company name

**1-32**    Care must be taken as to the choice of company name for various reasons but essentially because a name may be rejected by the registrar on a variety of grounds and there may be problems with other persons and businesses who may claim goodwill in the same or a similar name. With respect to the latter issue, the CA 2006 makes provision in ss 69–74 for a procedure whereby a person may object to a registered name on the ground that it is the same as a name associated with the applicant in which he has goodwill or that it is sufficiently similar to such a name that its use in the UK would be likely to mislead by suggesting a connection between the company and the person objecting. Objections are considered by a company names adjudicator[27] and, if an objection is upheld, the company will be required to change its name (s 73). Detailed rules as to company names are set out in CA 2006, Pt 5, ss 54–85 and related statutory instruments.[28] In addition to complying

---

[26]  CA 2006, s 19(3). See the Companies (Model Articles) Regulations 2008, SI 2008/3229. It is the model articles in force at the time of the company's registration which apply: CA 2006, s 20(2); and subsequent amendments of the model articles do not affect a company registered before the amendment takes effect: s 19(4). Many companies on the register of companies remain subject to the 1985 Table A articles and some are still governed by the 1948 Table A articles.

[27]  See CA 2006, ss 70–74 and the Company Names Adjudicator Rules 2008, SI 2008/1738. The names adjudicator role was created by the CA 2006. The adjudicators are based at the UK Intellectual Property Office rather than at Companies House and they sit as a Company Names Tribunal to determine these disputes.

[28]  See the Company, Limited Liability Partnership and Business (Names and Trading Disclosures) Regulations 2015, SI 2015/17; Company, Limited Liability Partnership and Business (Sensitive Words and Expressions) Regulations 2014, SI 2014/3140.

with those requirements, the directors need to consider any risk of the company being sued for passing off by other businesses and any possibility of an infringement of an existing trade mark. A company may trade under a business name and, in that case, it must also comply with the business name regulations (s 82).

**1-33**    Essentially, the scheme governing company names is as follows:

- Certain designations or their alternatives are required unless the company meets the criteria for exemption.[29] The required designations are 'ltd' or 'limited' for a private company and 'plc' or 'public limited company' for a public company (or their Welsh equivalents).[30]

- A company must not be registered with a name if, in the opinion of the Secretary of State (i.e. the registrar of companies), its use by the company would constitute an offence or it is offensive.[31]

- The use of certain other 'sensitive' names requires the consent of the Secretary of State or some other designated body.[32]

- A company must not be registered with a name which is the same as another name appearing in the registrar's index of company names.[33]

**1-34**    A company must display its registered name at its registered office and any other location at which the company's records are available for inspection and at any other location at which it carries on business.[34] A company must also disclose its registered name on a wide range of business documentation and correspondence and on its websites.[35] The company name must be engraved on the company's seal, if it has one.[36] In addition to its name, on registration a company is allotted a registered number[37] which is important in distinguishing between companies.

**1-35**    A company may alter its name by special resolution or by any other means (such as an ordinary resolution or resolution of the directors) allowed by the company's articles.[38] It may be directed to change its name in certain circumstances, as where it is 'too like' an existing name.[39] There are also restrictions on the use of certain names by former directors of a company which has gone into insolvent liquidation.[40]

---

[29] CA 2006, ss 60–63. The conditions for exemption are in SI 2015/17, reg 3.     [30] CA 2006, ss 58–59.

[31] CA 2006, s 53.

[32] CA 2006, ss 54–56. 'Sensitive' words include words such as 'Royal', 'University', 'Chartered' which suggest some status or association and which could be used improperly to mislead people, see SI 2014/3140.

[33] CA 2006, s 66(1), subject to SI 2015/17, reg 8 which allows for the use of the same names in a group context.

[34] CA 2006, s 82; see SI 2015/17, Pt 6 Trading Disclosures. There is an exemption for a location which is primarily used for living accommodation designed to assist small companies which carry on business from the directors' homes, see SI 2015/17, reg 22(3).

[35] CA 20006, s 82; and see SI 2015/17, regs 24 and 25. The categories of document which must disclose the registered name include business letters; bills of exchange, promissory notes, endorsements and order forms; cheques purporting to be signed by or on behalf of the company; orders for money, goods or services purporting to be signed by or on behalf of the company; and, crucially, a catch-all category of 'all other forms of its business correspondence and documentation', see reg 24(1).

[36] CA 2006, s 45(2). A company is not required to have a company seal, s 45(1), but may choose to do so.

[37] CA 2006, s 1066.

[38] CA 2006, s 77(1) and see s 77(2). A special resolution requires a 75 per cent majority while an ordinary resolution requires a simple majority: see ss 282, 283.     [39] CA 2006, s 67; see also ss 75, 76.

[40] See IA 1986, s 216; IR 2016, Part 22; see the discussion at **15-42**.

### The certificate of incorporation

**1-36**  Once all the required documents are submitted together with the registration fee, and assuming there has been proper compliance with the formalities and no problems about the company name, the registrar issues a certificate of incorporation of the company which is conclusive evidence that there has been compliance with the requirements of the CA 2006 in respect of registration (CA 2006, s 15). From the date of incorporation mentioned in the certificate, the subscribers to the memorandum, together with such other persons as may from time to time become members of the company, are a body corporate (s 16(2)).

**1-37**  Once incorporated, the company is a separate legal entity from the shareholders which means that it is the company which conducts the business, owns property, hires employees, incurs debts, makes profits, etc. The separate existence of the company means that the membership may be constantly changing, as shareholders transfer or sell their shares, but the business of the company is unaffected. The members enjoy limited liability, as noted at **1-9**, and are not required to participate in the management of the company which is a matter for the directors. These many advantages, in particular the separate legal status of the company, the limited liability of the members, and the separation of ownership and management of the company, ensure that the registered company limited by shares is an immensely popular and successful vehicle for the conduct of business in this jurisdiction.

## C  Company formation—companies limited by guarantee

**1-38**  A company limited by guarantee is a company having the liability of its members limited by its constitution to such amount (usually very small, £1 or £5) as the members undertake to contribute to the assets of the company in the event of its being wound up.[41] Such a company does not have a share capital (no contribution is required until winding up) and so these companies have members and not shareholders. Given the absence of share capital, such companies must necessarily be private and not public companies[42] (the distinction between private and public companies is discussed at **1-42**). While there is no prohibition on trading by companies limited by guarantee, such companies are predominantly found in the not-for-profit sector and are widely used for community and sporting groups, local associations, flat management companies, and for educational and charitable purposes.[43] The advantages of incorporation for such organisations lie in legal personality and limited liability so facilitating the ownership of property and the contracting of obligations despite a fluctuating membership and without exposing the members to personal liabilities.

**1-39**  The incorporation process for these companies is identical in most respects to a company limited by shares, save for necessary modifications, for example, a statement of guarantee is required instead of a statement of capital and initial shareholdings (see **1-25**). Membership of a company limited by guarantee is governed by the articles of association.

---

[41]  CA 2006, s 3(1), (3).

[42]  See CA 2006, s 4(2). The formation of companies limited by guarantee with a share capital has been prohibited since 22 December 1980.

[43]  See Companies House *Companies Register Activities Data Tables 2016–17*, Table C1, which shows 105,429 private companies limited by guarantee on the register with no issued share capital (figures for England and Wales).

The model form of articles, if adopted, provides that new members may not be admitted unless approved by the directors, membership is not transferable and ceases on death, and a member can withdraw on giving seven days' notice.[44]

## D  Private and public companies

### Introduction

**1-40**  For those forming a company, a further choice is whether to register as a private or a public company. In practice, the vast majority of companies are formed as private companies limited by shares. As of March 2017, there were 3,408,366 companies (figures for England and Wales) on the register of which 3,402,554 (99.8 per cent) were private companies and 5,812 (0.2 per cent) were public companies.[45] Even those companies which are public companies are usually formed initially as private companies and subsequently re-register as public companies (re-registration is discussed at **1-52**).

**1-41**  As to the definition of a public and private company, CA 2006, s 4 states that a 'private company' is a company which is not a public company and a 'public company' is a company limited by shares or by guarantee and having a share capital,[46] whose certificate of incorporation states that it is a public company, and which has complied with the requirements of the Companies Acts in relation to public companies.

### Differences between public and private companies

**1-42**  On many issues the CA 2006 imposes quite different requirements on public and private companies and the general regulatory approach is that the statutory requirements with respect to public companies are more onerous than those imposed on private companies. For example, public companies do not qualify for the many accounting and audit exemptions available to private companies.

**1-43**  CA 2006, s 4(4) draws attention to what it describes as 'the two major differences' between public and private companies, namely the prohibition on private companies offering their securities (for our purposes, essentially shares) to the public (s 755) and the requirement for a trading certificate (s 761) but it is the former which is the key distinction. Other distinctions, noted below, would relate to the company name, accounting and audit requirements, officer requirements, and corporate formalities.

### Private companies and public offers

**1-44**  The key distinction between public and private companies is that a public company may offer its securities to the public (although it is not obliged to do so) and a private company is prohibited from offering its securities to the public. While there is no longer a criminal sanction attached to a breach, a private company may be subject to an order restraining a contravention of the prohibition, a requirement to re-register as a public company or even an order for the compulsory winding up of the company (CA 2006, ss 755–760).

---

[44]  See The Companies (Model Articles) Regulations 2008, SI 2008/3229, reg 3, Sch 2, arts 21 and 22.

[45]  See Companies House *Companies Register Activities Data Tables 2016–17*, Tables A1, A2, A3.

[46]  As of 22 December 1980, such companies cannot be formed: CA 2006, s 5(1), so the vast majority of public companies are companies limited by shares.

**1-45** As noted, the general approach is that the regulation of public companies is stricter than that for private companies. The reason why stricter regulation is imposed is because of the possibility that a public company may offer its shares to the public. The additional requirements (minimum capital, fuller accounts, more formal corporate governance structures, etc) could be imposed on a private company, but Parliament chooses not to do so, because a private company does not cross the threshold which would justify and require additional regulation. The threshold that does justify additional regulation is the possibility that the company may offer its shares to the public. This is not an arbitrary threshold, rather it is the precise point at which the public interest intrudes into the classification debate. Corporate self-interest in raising capital meets the public interest in the protection of investors. Investor protection requirements form a package which consists of more than mere prospectus requirements (a prospectus is the formal public document offering shares for sale) and includes the accounting requirements, the corporate governance requirements, more formal decision-making, etc which are characteristic of a public company. See the discussion of public offers by private companies at **21-96** et seq.

### Trading certificate and share capital

**1-46** A public company formed as such cannot commence trading without a trading certificate issued by the registrar of companies which he may only do if satisfied that the nominal value of the company's allotted share capital is not less than the authorised minimum (CA 2006, s 761), which is £50,000 or the prescribed euro equivalent, €57,100 (s 763).[47] There is no minimum share capital for a private limited company hence the ability of A and B to set up a private company with very small amounts of capital (see the example at **1-3**) and a private company can trade immediately on incorporation without any need for a trading certificate. In general, the rules governing payment for share capital and dealings in share capital are stricter for public companies, as is discussed in Chapters 21 and 22.

### Company name

**1-47** The most visible distinction between a public and a private company lies in the name which, in the case of a public company, must end in 'public limited company' or its abbreviation 'plc' (or Welsh equivalent) while the name of a private company must end in 'limited' or its abbreviation 'Ltd' (or Welsh equivalent).[48] In certain circumstances, a private company may be exempted from ending its name with the word 'limited'.[49]

### Accounting and audit requirements

**1-48** A public company cannot qualify for the accounting exemptions (discussed in Chapter 18) available to small or medium-sized companies[50] or the audit exemption available to small companies.[51] Public companies also have a shorter period (six months rather than nine months) within which to deliver their accounts to the registrar of companies (CA 2006, s 442(2)) and the penalties for late filing are more substantial for a public company.[52]

---

[47] See the Companies (Authorised Minimum) Regulations 2009, SI 2009/2425, reg 2.
[48] CA 2006, ss 58, 59.      [49] See CA 2006, ss 60, 61.      [50] See CA 2006, ss 384(1)(a), 467(1)(a).
[51] See CA 2006, s 478(1)(a).
[52] CA 2006, s 453(2) and the Companies (Late Filing Penalties) and Limited Liability Partnerships (Filing Periods and Late Filing Penalties) Regulations 2008, SI 2008/497, reg 2.

### Officers and members

**1-49**  A public company must have at least two directors while a private company requires only one (CA 2006, s 154). A public company must have a company secretary (ss 270, 271).

### Corporate formalities

**1-50**  A public company must hold an annual general meeting (CA 2006, s 336) and may not use written resolutions (s 281(2)). In recognition of the informal manner in which many private companies conduct their business, private companies are not required to hold annual general meetings and are expected to use written resolutions rather than hold meetings of any sort (s 281(1)).

### Publicly traded companies

**1-51**  Public companies can be further classified depending on whether their securities (shares for our purposes) are traded on a market. The questions for public companies are: (a) whether they wish to offer their shares to the public at all (they are not required to do so); (b) whether they wish also to be admitted to trading (which usually goes hand in hand with a desire to offer their shares to the public since the public will only be willing to buy the shares if they can then trade them); and (c) the type of market on which they wish to be traded. The usual option in the UK is that larger established public companies look for a listing on a regulated market which means essentially on the Main Market run by the London Stock Exchange (LSE), hence 'listed' companies. Smaller, perhaps more speculative, companies look to be admitted to trading on the Alternative Investment Market (AIM) also run by the LSE. There were 5,812 UK public companies on the register of companies as at 31 March 2017, just 0.2 per cent of the UK register.[53] As of December 2017, there were 942 Main Market UK listed companies and there were 960 UK companies trading on AIM[54] so roughly 33 per cent of public companies are traded on one or other market, but only 16 per cent of public companies are listed public companies. See further at **21-100**.

## E  Re-registration of companies

**1-52**  It is possible for a company to alter its status by re-registration in accordance with CA 2006, Pt 7. The most common alterations of status are when a private company decides to re-register as a public company[55] and when a public company decides to re-register as a private company.[56]

---

[53]  See Companies House, *Statistical Tables on Companies Registration Activities 2016–17*, Table A3.

[54]  Monthly statistics on Main Market (listed) companies and on AIM companies can be found on the LSE website. Another term commonly but erroneously used as synonymous with listed company is 'quoted company'—this area is bedevilled by confusing terminology. UKLA uses 'quoted company' to describe companies traded on a MTF in which case it is not a listed company while, in the CA 2006, the term 'quoted company' has a precise meaning with respect to certain disclosure requirements. For the purposes of the CA 2006, s 385, a quoted company is a company whose equity share capital is officially listed in the UK or in an EEA State or is admitted to dealing either on the NYSE or Nasdaq (i.e. the main American stock exchanges).                                                                                                 [55]  See CA 2006, ss 90–96.

[56]  See CA 2006, ss 97–101. It is also possible for a private company to re-register as unlimited (ss 102–104) and for a public company to re-register as an unlimited company (ss 109–110), but for obvious reasons of liability, those options are rarely exercised.

**1-53**  As noted at **1-40**, a private company re-registering as a public company is the most common way in which public companies are formed. A detailed re-registration procedure is laid down in the statute, but in essence the company must secure the consent of its shareholders,[57] alter its name and its articles to reflect its new status, and comply with the share capital requirements for public companies.[58] Assuming that the documentation is correct, the registrar of companies issues a certificate of incorporation altered to meet the circumstances of the case, i.e. to show that the company is now a public company—the entity continues, but its status is changed (CA 2006, s 96). There are a number of reasons why a company might seek a change of status. The change may be driven by economic growth which the directors and shareholders feel should be reflected in the more closely regulated legal structure of a public company. It may be that the company needs to raise share capital and wants to offer its shares to the public and the original owners may wish to realise some of the value of their holding in the company by selling out to the public. It may be that the owners have no interest in raising capital, but wish simply to secure the more prestigious status of being a public company.

**1-54**  Just as companies may decide to move 'up' to the status of a public company, others may wish to 'retreat' from being a public company to being a private company. This change may be because the need for capital (and therefore the facility of offering their shares to the public) is no longer a priority for the company. In that situation, the company is incurring the burden of the additional regulation which is imposed as a consequence of public company status for no purpose and it makes sense to re-register. In many cases, this move backwards is achieved by the original founders of the company buying back the shares of the company in the hands of the public and returning the company to its former private status and ownership. Unless there are tangible benefits from being a public company, many directors and shareholders prefer the lighter regulation of private companies. There is also much less media attention on private companies. The detailed procedure is laid down in CA 2006, ss 97–101, but in essence the company must secure the consent of its shareholders[59] and alter its name and articles of association to reflect its new status. Assuming that the documentation is correct, the registrar of companies issues a certificate of incorporation altered to meet the circumstances of the case, i.e. to reflect the fact that the company is now a private company (s 101).

## F  Groups of companies

**1-55**  Of course, businesses are not confined to operating through one company and it is common for larger enterprises to organise their affairs through a group of companies made up of a holding company and subsidiaries and myriad combinations thereof.

**1-56**  The CA 2006, s 1159(1) defines a company as a 'subsidiary' of another company, its 'holding company', if that other company:

(a)  holds a majority of the voting rights in it, or

(b)  is a member of it and has the right to appoint or remove a majority of its board of directors, or

---

[57]  See CA 2006, s 90(1)(a), a special resolution is required (a 75 per cent majority, see s 283).
[58]  See CA 2006, s 90(2), (3).
[59]  See CA 2006, s 97(1)(a): a special resolution is required (a 75 per cent majority, see s 283).

(c) is a member of it and controls alone, pursuant to an agreement with other share-holders or members, a majority of the voting rights in it, or if it is a subsidiary of a company which is itself a subsidiary of that other company.[60]

**1-57**   This provision identifies three mechanisms by which a company may be a subsidiary of another company so where Company A meets these criteria with respect to its control of Company B, Company B is a subsidiary of Company A. Equally, if Company B meets these criteria in respect of Company C, Company C is a subsidiary of Company B and of Company A. The effect of the definition is that, on this example, Company A is a holding company and its subsidiaries are B and C while B is also a holding company with a subsidiary, C. Each company is a separate legal entity and is formed under the CA 2006 in accordance with the formalities discussed earlier in this chapter with the only difference being the presence of corporate shareholders rather than individuals.

**1-58**   The requirement in CA 2006, s 1159(1)(a) is that the holding company holds a majority of the voting rights in the subsidiary company for, as noted earlier, it is voting power which gives control of a company. Equally, the person who controls the board in practice has control of the company so s 1159(1)(b) recognises that situation. Section 1159(1)(c) expands the definition further to ensure that the situation where a member does not have control of a company on paper but does have control as the result of some agreement with other shareholders or members is also encompassed by the definition. The application of the equivalent CA 1985 provision (CA 1985, s 736) was considered by the Supreme Court in *Enviroco Ltd v Farstad Supply A/S*[61] which highlights that CA 1985, s 736(1)(c), now CA 2006, s 1159(1)(c), requires that a company be a member of the subsidiary company and have control in the way outlined in the provision. In this instance, the company in question had charged its shares in the other (would-be subsidiary) company as security to a bank and, in accordance with Scots law, the company had had to register those shares in the name of the bank with the result that it was no longer a member of the other company (membership is dictated by the entries on the register of members, see **16-1**). In those circumstances, the Supreme Court ruled that, as it was no longer a member of the other company, the company could not claim that the other company was its subsidiary on the basis of the application of what is now CA 2006, s 1159(1)(c).[62] A company is a 'wholly-owned subsidiary' (see s 1159(2)) where Company A is the only shareholder in Company B— B is a wholly-owned subsidiary. This is an advantageous structure for Company A for it avoids any difficulties arising from any minority interests within Company B which might otherwise affect the way in which Company A may run Company B.

**1-59**   There are many good business reasons (and often tax reasons) why a company chooses to expand and/or divide its activities through subsidiary companies. It may be administratively convenient and economically efficient to divide activities between subsidiaries. It may make geographic sense depending on the nature of the company's business. It may be financially appropriate, allowing assets and liabilities to be allocated efficiently and it may facilitate external borrowings. The business and practical reasons for proceeding through a variety of subsidiary companies within a group structure in this way are clear

---

[60] The meaning of each of the categories is expanded upon in CA 2006, Sch 6.

[61] [2011] 2 BCLC 165. The case concerned certain obligations and exemptions under a charterparty and the charterparty expressly defined the term 'subsidiary' for the purpose of the charterparty as having the meaning assigned to it by the statute (then CA 1985, s 736, now CA 2006, s 1159).

[62] The company could not rely on what is now CA 2006, s 1159(1) or (2) because it did not have control in those ways.

but the relationship between the individual companies within the group can give rise to some interesting legal issues. These are considered in Chapter 3.

## G  The registrar of companies and the public registry

**1-60**  Disclosure has always been seen as the price to be paid by incorporators in return for the conferring of limited liability which, as noted at **1-9**, insulates the shareholders' personal fortunes from the reach of the company's creditors (unless the shareholders have been persuaded to give personal guarantees). To redress the balance, Parliament has required the disclosure of information by companies in a variety of ways, of which the most important is to the registrar of companies based at Companies House in Cardiff. In addition, disclosure is required at the company's registered office and, for public companies, at annual general meetings. Traded companies are obliged by listing and stock exchange rules to keep the markets informed. Increasingly, companies make extensive use of their websites to maintain ongoing disclosure with their shareholders and, in the case of quoted companies, they are obliged to use their websites for this purpose, as noted at **17-7**. The information disclosed typically relates to the financial position of the company (for example, its annual accounts) as well as information about those persons involved with it as directors and shareholders (for example, the composition of the board and details of shareholdings). The merits of disclosure can be debated in terms of economic value but the justifications for imposing wide-ranging disclosure requirements centre particularly on the provision of information: to assist creditors in assessing the risks of dealing with a limited company; to assist shareholders to monitor the quality and conduct of the company's management and the economic performance of the company; and generally for the efficient operation of the capital markets. Disclosure is discussed in Chapter 18.

# 2

# The framework of company law

## A The statutory framework

### Background

**2-1**   The subject of this work is the law governing registered companies, that is companies registered under the Companies Act 2006 (CA 2006) and its predecessors.

**2-2**   Incorporation by registration was first made possible by the Joint Stock Companies Act 1844. At that time, limited liability was unknown and it was not introduced until the Limited Liability Act 1855. The pattern of company law, thereafter, was of major consolidating legislation at regular intervals, such as the Companies Act 1908, the Companies Act 1929, and the Companies Act 1948. Prior to the CA 2006, the most recent consolidation was the Companies Act 1985 (CA 1985), subsequently amended, in particular, by the Companies Act 1989 and by the Companies (Audit, Investigations and Community Enterprise) Act 2004. More discrete material was to be found in the Company Directors Disqualification Act 1986 and the Business Names Act 1985.

**2-3**   Insolvency matters were hived off initially to the Insolvency Act 1985, a major piece of reforming legislation introduced in response to the Cork Committee Report on Insolvency Law and Practice (1982).[1] The Insolvency Act 1985 was then consolidated with elements of the Companies Act 1985 in the Insolvency Act 1986 (IA 1986). Limited technical amendments to insolvency law followed in the Insolvency Act 1994 and the Insolvency (No 2) Act 1994. More significant reforms were effected by the Insolvency Act 2000 and the Enterprise Act 2002. The increasing importance of cross-border insolvency issues was recognised by the EC Regulation on Insolvency Proceedings No 1346/2000,[2] now recast as Regulation 2015/848 on Insolvency Proceedings,[3] and by the Cross-Border Insolvency Regulations 2006.[4]

**2-4**   In addition to these company and insolvency statutes which are of central importance to this book, there are other substantial statutes elements of which intrude on company law matters, such as the Financial Services and Markets Act 2000, Pt VI, dealing with the listing of securities, public offers of shares, and prospectuses.

**2-5**   The three legislative pillars prior to the Companies Act 2006 then were the Companies Act 1985, the Insolvency Act 1986, and the Financial Services and Markets Act 2000 (FSMA 2000). The IA 1986 and FSMA 2000 were the product of major reviews in those subject areas which left the CA 1985 as most in need of reform, especially as it had been subject to much piecemeal amendment over the years. In March 1998, the Department of Trade and Industry (DTI), now the Department for Business, Energy and Industrial

---

[1] *Report of the Review Committee on Insolvency Law and Practice*, Cmnd 8558 (1982).
[2] OJ L 160/1, 30.6.2000.     [3] OJ L 141/9, 5.6.2015.     [4] SI 2006/1030.

Strategy (BEIS), decided that the time was right for a comprehensive three-year review of company law.[5]

## The Company Law Review

**2-6** Launching the initial consultation document,[6] the DTI acknowledged the numerous problems with the CA 1985. The legislation was drafted in excessive detail, it used over-formal language, it over-regulated some issues (such as capital maintenance), while other matters were inadequately provided for or needed legal underpinning (such as the duties of directors and the conduct of meetings).[7] The Government's intention was stated as being that new arrangements should be devised to provide a more effective, including cost-effective, framework based on principles of consistency, predictability, and transparency.[8] The task of reviewing the existing arrangements and suggesting the way forward fell to the Company Law Review made up of a Steering Group, comprised essentially of businessmen and lawyers, and numerous working groups from which emerged a stream of consultation documents.[9] The Company Law Review (hereinafter CLR) produced its Final Report in 2001 which concentrated on the following issues:[10]

- For small and private companies,[11] the recommendations centred on simplified decision-making and streamlining internal administration. There should be no need for such companies to hold general meetings or to appoint a company secretary. They should have a simplified constitution; shareholders should be encouraged to use mediation and arbitration to resolve their disputes instead of litigation; the rules on share capital should be relaxed and the financial reporting and audit requirements of these companies should be reduced.[12]

- On directors, the key recommendation was for the inclusion in the statute of a statement of directors' duties.[13]

- On shareholders' rights and remedies, there were recommendations for the creation of a statutory derivative action and measures to enhance the exercise of shareholders' rights at meetings.[14]

---

[5] See DTI, *Modern Company Law for a Competitive Economy* (1998). For a comprehensive account of the Review process, see Rickford, 'A History of the Company Law Review' in De Lacy (ed), *The Reform of United Kingdom Company Law* (2002).    [6] DTI, *Modern Company Law for a Competitive Economy* (1998).

[7] See DTI, *Modern Company Law for a Competitive Economy* (1998), paras 3.2, 3.4, 3.7.

[8] See DTI, *Modern Company Law for a Competitive Economy* (1998), para 3.1.

[9] The most important documents, all of which go under the title *Modern Company Law for a Competitive Economy*, were *The Strategic Framework* (February 1999), URN 99/654; *Developing the Framework* (March 2000), URN 00/656; and *Completing the Structure* (November 2000), URN 00/1335. Some topics were the subject of specific consultations, see *Company General Meetings and Shareholder Communication* (October 1999); *Company Formation and Capital Maintenance* (October 1999); *Reforming the Law Concerning Oversea Companies* (October 1999); *Capital Maintenance: Other Issues* (June 2000); *Registration of Company Charges* (October 2000).

[10] See CLR, *Modern Company Law for a Competitive Economy, Final Report*, vols I and II (2001), URN 01/942.

[11] Research carried out for the CLR showed that 70 per cent of companies had only one or two shareholders and 90 per cent had fewer than five shareholders: CLR, *Developing the Framework* (2000), URN 00/656, para 6.9.

[12] See CLR, *Modern Company Law for a Competitive Economy, Final Report*, vol I (2001), URN 01/942, Chs 2 and 4; *Completing the Structure* (2000), URN 00/1335, Ch 2; *Developing the Framework* (2000), URN 00/656, Chs 6 and 7.

[13] CLR, *Modern Company Law for a Competitive Economy, Final Report*, vol I (2001), Ch 3; *Completing the Structure* (2000), Ch 3; *Developing the Framework* (2000), paras 3.12–3.85.

[14] *Developing the Framework* (2000), Ch 4.

- On accounting and audit requirements, a significant recommendation was for larger companies to publish an operating and financial report. No changes were proposed to auditors' duties of care.[15]

**2-7**   The CLR considered briefly whether it would be preferable to opt for a separate free-standing limited liability vehicle for small companies with separate legislation, but it rapidly concluded that the main obstacles to that approach would be definition problems and transition difficulties as companies grow.[16] An integrated Companies Act, but one focused on small rather than larger companies, was its preferred approach.[17] On reflection, it also considered that the focus of the legislation should be on private companies, as it is the private/public distinction which is crucial,[18] as noted at **1-40**, and it was appropriate to deregulate private companies across the board rather than attempting to define some new category of small company.[19] In other words, the CLR thought that the legislation should reflect reality, which is that the register of companies is made up predominantly of small private companies, though the CA 1985 envisaged a register dominated by large public companies. This 'think small first' approach has now become something of a tenet of regulation, both domestically and at the European level.

**2-8**   The Government responded to the CLR Report with a White Paper entitled *Modernising Company Law*,[20] published in July 2002, which broadly adopted the Review's recommendations[21] and this was followed by a further White Paper, *Company Law Reform*,[22] in March 2005 before, at last, a Company Law Reform Bill was introduced in November 2005.

**2-9**   At that stage the intention was to retain substantial elements of the Companies Act 1985 alongside the CLR Bill, but eventually the Government was persuaded that the most sensible way forward was to bring those parts of the CA 1985 which were not being repealed into the CLR Bill. As there was no time for further review, those provisions of the CA 1985 which were brought into the Bill were merely restated so as to ensure that their drafting was consistent with the plain English used in the Bill, but no substantive changes were made to the CA 1985 provisions. The result is the CA 2006, which is a mixture of new and old, though the old has been restated in plain English so that, at least, it looks new![23] As a result of the addition of the CA 1985 provisions to the Bill, its title was changed to the Companies Bill and it received Royal Assent on 8 November 2006 as the Companies Act 2006, some eight and a half years after the launch of the Company Law Review.

---

[15] CLR, *Modern Company Law for a Competitive Economy, Final Report*, vol I (2001), Ch 8.

[16] See CLR, *Developing the Framework* (2000), URN 00/656, para 6.19; *The Strategic Framework* (1999), URN 99/654, para 5.2.          [17] See CLR, *The Strategic Framework* (1999), URN 99/654, para 5.2.

[18] See CLR, *Final Report*, vol I (2001), URN 01/942, para 2.7.

[19] See CLR, *Completing the Structure* (2000), URN 00/1335, Ch 2; *Developing the Framework* (2000), URN 00/656, Chs 6 and 7. On the deregulation of company law with respect to the small private company see, generally, Hannigan 'Public Interest in the Regulation of the Small Private Limited Company—the Dwindling Role of Mandatory Rules in English Company Law' in Watson (ed), *The Changing Landscape of Corporate Law in New Zealand* (2017).

[20] CM 5553-I, 5553-II (2002). See Goddard, 'Modernising Company Law: The Government's White Paper' (2003) 66 MLR 402.

[21] Legislative time had been diverted to strengthening audit regulation in the wake of the collapse of the American energy group, Enron, with billion dollar losses; see the Companies (Audit, Investigations and Community Enterprise) Act 2004.                              [22] Cm 6456 (2005).

[23] There is always the risk when restating a provision that the result is a change in the law which may create an interpretation conundrum for the courts when faced with wording which alters the meaning of a provision but a declared legislative intent merely to restate. For example, CA 2006, s 40(1) restates CA 1985, s 35A(1), but the wording is altered and the consequence is that the law has been altered, see discussion at **9-28** et seq.

## The Companies Act 2006

**2-10**   At the time of its enactment, the Companies Act 2006 was the largest statute ever passed by Parliament. It has 1,300 sections and 16 Schedules. Commencement of the legislation took place piecemeal between 6 April 2007 and 1 October 2009. It is fully in force (with a few minor exceptions).[24] Despite its length, many Parts of the Act rely on secondary legislation to supplement the statutory framework which is part of a deliberate strategy to create some flexibility to accommodate future developments.

## B  The European framework

### Overview of the European agenda and approach

**2-11**   As the limited liability company is the main vehicle for private industry across Europe, it was understood from the earliest days of the European Community that at least some measure of harmonisation of national laws would be required to ensure a common or single market, given that the legal structures of companies vary significantly across the Member States. Hence the European Parliament, Council, and Commission in order to attain freedom of establishment must act:[25]

> 'by coordinating to the necessary extent the safeguards which, for the protection of the interests of members and others, are required by Member States of companies or firms[26] ... with a view to making such safeguards equivalent throughout the Union.'

### Harmonisation

**2-12**   The European Commission (hereinafter the Commission) proceeded initially by way of a Company Law harmonisation programme which resulted in the adoption of a series of numbered directives[27] (The First Company Law Directive, The Second Company Law Directive, and so on). Some of the Directives concern relatively discrete (and technical) matters, such as the Eleventh Directive on disclosures by branches of overseas companies.[28] Others are of broader significance, such as the Second Company Law Directive which lays down many of the share capital rules for public limited

---

[24] A subsequent evaluation of the Companies Act 2006 for the Department for Business, Innovation and Skills found relatively high levels of awareness of the legislation with small private businesses welcoming the flexibility provided for them by measures such as the removal of the requirement for private companies to hold AGMs and the greater use of written resolutions: see ORC International, *Evaluation of the Companies Act 2006* (August 2010); also BIS Memorandum to the Business, Innovation & Skills Select Committee, *Post-Legislative Assessment of the Companies Act 2006*, January 2012, Cm 8255.

[25] Treaty on the Functioning of the European Union (TFEU) (Consolidated version) OJ C 326/47, 26.10.2012, art 50(2)(g).

[26] That is companies or firms within the meaning of the second paragraph of art 54 of TFEU which defines 'companies or firms' as meaning companies or firms constituted under civil or commercial law, including cooperative societies, and other legal persons governed by public or private law, save for those which are non-profit-making.

[27] Some of the proposed Directives have fallen by the wayside (for example, nos 5, 9, and 14) leaving Company Law Directives numbered 1–4, 6–8, 10–13, many of which have now been codified into Directive 2017/1132 while others such as the 4th and 7th Directives on Accounts have become a new Accounting Directive 2013/34.

[28] Eleventh Council Directive (EEC) 89/666, now consolidated as Directive 2017/1132, OJ L 169/46, 30.6.2017.

companies.[29] This harmonisation stage lasted roughly from 1968 to 1989 but it then more or less stalled, in part because other areas, such as financial services, took centre stage, in part because it was difficult to garner support for this type of highly technical harmonisation. The result was that from the mid-1990s until early 2000 there was little activity on the company law front.[30]

### Modernisation

**2-13**  In September 2001 a High Level Group of Company Law Experts (HLG) was formed to review the need for the modernisation of company law in Europe. The impetus came in part from the need to implement the Financial Services Action Plan which aimed to ensure an integrated capital market by 2005. There were concerns that corporate scandals and collapses (including Enron in the US, but also the collapse of the Italian company, Parmalat) had damaged investor confidence which is central to the successful and efficient operation of capital markets. The collapse of Enron with billion dollar losses brought a speedy (and severe) legislative response by the American authorities, notably through the Sarbanes-Oxley Act.[31] The European authorities were anxious to show an equally positive and identifiable European response which, with an emphasis on transparency and accountability, would ensure high standards of corporate governance and restore investor confidence. Added urgency was given to the situation by the imminent accession (in May 2004) of new Member States, many of them Eastern European countries with a limited history of open corporate markets, given the post-war Soviet occupation of their countries. A further impetus for change was the general globalisation of trade and increase in cross-border economic activity and a concern that the EU had to be proactive in facilitating that trade. The HLG published a consultation document and a report in 2002[32] and the Commission responded in May 2003 with an Action Plan for Company Law which identified a number of priorities for reform.[33] The guiding criteria in drawing up the Action Plan were the need to respect subsidiarity and proportionality; the requirement for flexible application based on firm principles; and the need to shape international regulatory developments.[34]

**2-14**  The short-term priorities of the 2003 Action Plan focused on securing a Shareholder Rights Directive,[35] a Recommendation on directors' remuneration and on the role of non-executive directors, the creation of a European Corporate Governance Forum, and amendments to the Accounting Directives to ensure greater transparency and accountability. This phase ran (roughly) from 2001 to 2006 and was driven by a need to modernise company law across the Member States. There was less of an emphasis on harmonisation and a greater emphasis on framework Directives so leaving Member

---

[29] Second Council Directive (EEC) 77/91, now consolidated as Directive 2017/1132, OJ L 169/46, 30.6.2017.

[30] See generally Wouters, 'European Company Law: Quo Vadis?' (2000) 37 CMLR 257.

[31] For an interesting overview of the Sarbanes-Oxley Act 2002, see Canada, Kuhn, and Sutton, 'Accidentally in the Public Interest: The Perfect Storm that Yielded the Sarbanes-Oxley Act' (2008) 19(7) *Critical Perspectives in Accounting* 987.

[32] See Report of the High Level Group of Company Law Experts, *A Modern Regulatory Framework for Company Law in Europe* (November 2002) which was preceded by a consultation paper of the same name in April 2002.

[33] See European Commission Communication, *Modernising Company Law and Enhancing Corporate Governance in the European Union—A Plan to Move Forward*, COM (2003) 284, 21.5.2003. For an overview, see Baums, 'European Company Law after the 2003 Action Plan' (2007) 8 EBOR 143.

[34] See Commission Action Plan, COM (2003) 284, pp 4–5.

[35] Directive 2007/36/EC, OJ L 184/17, 14.7.2007.

States more leeway in addressing their particular circumstances. Such Directives may be easier to negotiate, an important consideration now that there are 28 Member States, but may encourage divergence between Member States rather than harmonisation. The Commission also made greater use of Recommendations and Communications which are not legally binding (so-called 'soft-law') especially to encourage coordination and convergence on corporate governance measures. The advantage in proceeding in this way is that measures can be agreed swiftly by the Commission and, by identifying and setting standards of best practice, market forces can compel convergence, in effect, on such standards. This sudden spurt of activity from 2001 onwards came to a somewhat abrupt end in 2006 when, at the broader political level, it became apparent that there was some resistance to further EU integration generally (as seen in the resistance to the adoption of a European Constitution).[36] There was more than an element of regulatory fatigue for all concerned and a backlash against what was seen as burdensome EU-derived regulation, a flame fuelled by opportunist Eurosceptics who chose to ignore the extent to which domestic Governments generated bureaucratic regulation and gold-plated European requirements.

## Simplification

**2-15** Though good progress was made on the short-term priorities identified in the 2003 Action Plan, the Commission decided in December 2005 to hold a further consultation to determine whether to proceed with the remaining elements of the Plan.[37] The outcome was a shift in focus from generating initiatives to simplification measures, a greater focus on cross-border matters and on a reduction of regulatory burdens.[38] Against this backdrop, the Commission found support for possible simplification across the whole range of Company Law Directives,[39] the goal being to create a 'simplified business environment' starting from a 'think small first' position which recognised the central role that SMEs (small and medium-sized enterprises) play in the EU economy.[40] That goal provided the framework for many of the EU initiatives on company law and was reflected in the Small Business Act (SBA) adopted by the Commission in 2008. The SBA is not a piece of legislation, but the overarching framework for EU policy on SMEs which is focused on facilitating SME access to finance and markets, reducing administrative burdens, and promoting entrepreneurship. For example, since 2012 all legislative proposals have to be based on the

---

[36] See Hartley, *The Foundations of European Union Law* (8th edn, 2014), pp 9–12.

[37] See European Commission, *Consultation on Future Priorities for the Action Plan on Modernising Company Law and Enhancing Corporate Governance in the European Union* (December 2005).

[38] This move was in keeping with a broader exercise which the Commission had commenced in 2005 which had identified Company Law as one of the priority areas for simplification. See Commission Communication, *Implementing the Community Lisbon Programme: A strategy for the simplification of the regulatory environment*, COM (2005) 535, OJ C 309/18, 16.12.2006; also Commission Communication, *Better Regulation for Growth and Jobs in the European Union*, COM (2005) 97, 16.3.2005. This strategy now is developed under the banner of 'smart regulation'.

[39] See Commission, *Communication on a simplified business environment for companies in the areas of company law, accounting and auditing*, COM (2007) 394, 10.7.2007. There was general support for simplification of the Directives rather than outright repeal which it was thought would only generate further costs and uncertainties.

[40] There are around 23.8m SMEs in the EU representing 99.8 per cent of all enterprises, employing 93m people and accounting for 66.6 per cent of total employment: see European Commission, *SME Performance Review, Annual Report on EU Small and Medium-sized Enterprises, 2016/2017* (2017), Table 2. In the UK, SMEs account for 99.3 per cent of all 5.7m private sector enterprises and provide around 60 per cent of all employment in the private sector: see BIS, *Business Population Estimates for the UK and Regions 2017* (November 2017).

premise that micro-entities should be excluded unless a case can be made for their proportionate inclusion.[41] The Commission issued a further 'Action Plan' in December 2012 which outlined that the focus of the Commission's continued initiatives would lie along three main lines: enhancing transparency between companies and investors; encouraging long-term shareholder engagement; and improving the framework for cross-border operation of companies.[42]

**2-16**    As, by their very nature, European measures are integral to and form part of substantive domestic law, the content of a particular measure is discussed in the chapter dealing with the substantive law on that issue, hence the capital requirements for public companies are discussed in Chapter 21, the substantive accounting and audit requirements are discussed in Chapter 18, and so on. The rest of this chapter focuses on an overview of the measures taken or planned in order to give the reader a sense of the extent of EU involvement in the development of company law. Three major (overlapping) themes emerge:

(1) an emphasis on disclosure and transparency—these are the standard regulatory tools of any jurisdiction dealing with limited entities—the aim is primarily but not exclusively creditor protection;

(2) a focus on corporate governance in publicly traded companies aimed primarily at shareholder engagement and protection and at investor confidence; and

(3) a focus on structures/restructuring and corporate mobility which is consistent with the underlying rationale of the development of an integrated internal and now capital market across the European Union.

More recently, there has been an emphasis on making sure that the company law framework in each Member State is compatible with the framework of the digital single market, specifically with regard to the interconnection of business registers and the provision of online incorporation. To that end, the Commission has brought forward a proposal for a Directive as regards the use of digital tools and processes in company law.[43]

### Disclosure/creditor protection

**2-17**    Transparency and disclosure are key themes in the domestic Member State regulation of limited liability companies and it is not surprising therefore that many of the European company law measures have focused on these issues.[44] Indeed, transparency was one of the themes of the First Company Law Directive[45] which, amongst other things, requires companies to publish certain documents (for example, the constitution and accounts) and particulars (for example, of directors) on a public register. That information must be accessible to the public and copies must be available at a price not exceeding the administrative cost of providing the information—the public register meeting these requirements is maintained here by Companies House, as discussed at **1-60**. The Eleventh Company

---

[41]  See European Commission, *Minimizing regulatory burden for SMEs, Adapting EU regulation to the needs of micro-enterprises*, COM (2011) 803 final, 23.11.2011, para 4, also **2-19**. On micro-entities, see n 54 and **18-27**.

[42]  Commission Communication, '*Action Plan: European company law and corporate governance—a modern legal framework for more engaged shareholders and sustainable companies*' COM (2012) 740 final, 12.12.2012.

[43]  COM (2018) 239 final, 25.4.2018.

[44]  Such as the Prospectus Regulation 2017/1129, OJ L 168/12, 30.6.2017, replacing Prospectus Directive 2003/71/EC, OJ L 345/64, 31.12.2003, which provides for extensive financial disclosures for current and prospective shareholders, creditors, and the wider securities markets.

[45]  First Council Directive 68/151/EEC, OJ L 65, 14.3.1968, p 8, now consolidated as Directive 2017/1132, OJ L 169/46, 30.6.2017. See Edwards, *EC Company Law* (1999), Ch II.

Law Directive[46] augments these requirements by imposing disclosure requirements in respect of branches opened in a Member State by companies from another Member State. The intention is to ensure that companies cannot avoid disclosure requirements in another Member State by opening branches rather than subsidiary companies. Further, a Business Registers Interconnection System (BRIS) has been created to facilitate the access to information on EU companies for the public and to ensure that all EU business registers can communicate with each other electronically in a safe and secure way in relation to cross-border mergers and foreign branches. The ultimate aim is to enhance confidence in the single market through transparency and up-to-date information and to reduce unnecessary burdens on companies.[47]

**2-18** Of course, the most important disclosure required of limited entities is disclosure of their financial position as evidenced by their accounts and it is with respect to accounting disclosures that the EU influence has been greatest. The accounting disclosure requirements were prescribed for decades by the Fourth and Seventh Company Law Directives dealing with the presentation and content of a company's individual accounts[48] and group accounts,[49] respectively. The Fourth and Seventh Directives were replaced by the Accounting Directive 2013/34/EU.[50] Another significant accounting step was the adoption in June 2002 of a Regulation on the application of International Accounting Standards (IAS)[51] which, since 1 January 2005, requires listed companies to draw up their consolidated accounts in accordance with IAS (now IFRS—International Financial Reporting Standards) rather than standards derived from accounting practice in individual Member States.[52] This Regulation was a transformational measure which necessitated a general overhaul of the accounting framework in the EU for companies falling within the scope of the Regulation. These measures together (the Accounting Directive and the Regulation on IAS) are designed to ensure the highest standards of transparency (compatible with the economic size of the company) and comparability for accounts of companies formed in the Member States.

**2-19** The Accounting Directive introduces a modified specific regime for small companies while, for medium and large companies, the intention primarily is to reduce the number of accounting options available so as to improve the comparability of their accounts.[53] With respect to small companies, the aim is to reduce overall the regulatory burden, for example, by allowing them to prepare a simpler profit and loss account and balance sheet, by limiting disclosures in the notes to the accounts, and by removing any EU requirement for an audit (UK small companies are already exempt from any audit requirement, see **18-55**). A further Directive 2012/6/EU on micro-entities allows for minimal accounting disclosures by these companies.[54] All of these matters are discussed in Chapter 18.

---

[46] Eleventh Council Directive (EEC) 89/666, now consolidated as Directive 2017/1132, OJ L 169/46, 30.6.2017. See Edwards, *EC Company Law* (1999), Ch VIII.

[47] BRIS is based on Directive 2012/17/EU, OJ L 156/1, 16.6.2012, on the interconnection of business registers, see recital 6, and the Implementing Regulation (EU) 2015/884, OJ L 144/1, 10.6.2015.

[48] Fourth Council Directive (EEC) 78/660, OJ L 222/11, 14.8.1978.

[49] Seventh Council Directive (EEC) 83/349, OJ L 193/1, 18.7.1983.      [50] OJ L 182/19, 29.6.2013.

[51] Regulation (EC) No 1606/2002, OJ L 243/1, 11.9.2002; and see the European Commission Press Release, IP/02/827, 7 June 2002.

[52] International Accounting Standards were issued by the International Accounting Standards Committee which has since been replaced by the International Accounting Standards Board (IASB) which issues International Financial Reporting Standards (IFRS).      [53] See COM (2011) 684 final, 25.10.2011.

[54] OJ L 81/3, 21.3.2012; and see CA 2006, s 384A: a micro-entity is a company which satisfies at least two of the following three criteria: balance sheet total of not more than £316,000, turnover not more than £632,000, and a maximum of 10 employees.

**2-20**   Of course, disclosure of accounting information alone is insufficient without assurance as to the quality of that information which comes from the requirement that the accounts be audited. Audit issues are governed by the Eighth Company Law Directive 2006/43/EC[55] which made comprehensive provision for all matters pertaining to the statutory auditor, his qualifications, role and independence, as well as providing for disciplinary processes, quality assurance, and public oversight of the audit profession. In the light of the financial crisis of 2007–08, the Commission made significant amendments by way of an amending Directive 2014/56/EU[56] and Regulation 537/2014,[57] addressing the audit of public interest entities (i.e. entities such as listed companies, credit institutions, insurance undertakings, and entities designated as public interest entities by Member States), see **18-48**.

**2-21**   The Accounting Directive and the Audit Directive have a major role to play in terms of creditor protection, of course, since they are intended to ensure the provision of comparable accounts backed up by high quality audits which give creditors the information they need to assess the risk of dealing with limited companies. The other traditional protective device is the use of capital maintenance rules to ensure that companies cannot return capital to their shareholders ahead of a winding up other than in accordance with statutory procedures designed to protect creditors. Capital maintenance revolves around two types of provisions, payment rules and return of capital rules, and these issues were addressed in the Second Company Law Directive (EEC) 77/91 which provides for the formation of public limited companies and the maintenance and alteration of their share capital.[58] The focus was on public companies because of their economic significance and the fact that their activities could be expected to extend beyond national boundaries. Given those features, the preamble to the Directive notes the importance of ensuring minimum equivalent protection throughout the EC for both creditors and shareholders of such companies.

**2-22**   The Second Directive, now consolidated as Directive 2017/1132,[59] is one of the most significant European company law measures for it prescribes in detail the capital rules applicable to public companies, especially with respect to capital maintenance and the rules governing distributions to members. The drawback with the Second Directive has always been the level of prescription imposed by it and there has been pressure in the past on the Commission for reform, if not outright repeal, of the Directive.[60] However, a feasibility study conducted on behalf of the Commission on an alternative regime to the capital maintenance regime,[61] published in January 2008, concluded that in fact the Second Directive is flexible in many ways and its requirements do not cause significant operational problems for companies.[62] Subsequently, limited changes have been made

---

[55] Directive 2006/43/EC, OJ L 157/87, 9.6.2006; which replaced an earlier version, Directive (EEC) 84/253, OJ L 126/20, 12.5.1984.          [56] OJ L 158/196, 27.5.2014.

[57] OJ L 158/77, 27.5.2014.          [58] See generally, Edwards, *EC Company Law* (1999), Ch III.

[59] OJ L 169/46, 30.6.2017.

[60] See BERR, Note and Consultation on European Commission Consultation on Simplification of EU Company Law etc, August 2007.

[61] See KPMG, 'Feasibility study on an alternative to the capital maintenance regime established by the Second Company Law Directive 77/91/EEC of 13 December 1976 and an examination of the impact on profit distribution of the new EU accounting regime' (January 2008).

[62] The Commission concluded therefore that 'no follow-up measures or changes in the Second Company Law Directive are foreseeable in the immediate future', see Response of the Commission to the results of the external study on the feasibility of an alternative to the Capital Maintenance regime of the Second Company Law Directive and the impact of the adoption of IFRS on profit distribution.

to the Directive as part of the simplification programme.[63] These capital matters are discussed in detail in Chapters 21 and 22.

## Corporate governance

**2-23** Corporate governance is a much used term which can mean different things depending on the context but essentially the focus is on how boards of companies operate and the relationship between the directors and the shareholders. The European Commission has acted relatively cautiously on these matters taking something of a backseat role to the Member States, with a consultation paper on the EU Corporate Governance Framework in 2011,[64] followed by a broader consultation on the future of European company law in February 2012.[65] The direction of travel on corporate governance matters has been mainly consistent with and in the wake of UK developments (see Chapter 6).

**2-24** In 2002 the Commission initiated a review of corporate governance codes across the EU, but quickly concluded that there was no need for a European corporate governance code, given that the review found that practically every Member State had at least one code and all the codes had very similar characteristics.[66] The European Commission proceeded on corporate governance issues thereafter mainly by way of Recommendations, such as its 2005 Recommendation on the role of non-executive directors[67] and its 2009 Recommendation on the remuneration of directors of listed companies.[68] Corporate governance issues featured in various Directives, such as the requirement in the Eighth Company Law Directive for certain companies to have an audit committee. The most substantive corporate governance measure adopted was the Shareholder Rights Directive 2007/36,[69] implemented here by way of amendments to CA 2003, Pt 16 on Meetings (meetings are discussed in Chapter 17). The Directive sets out detailed minimum requirements with respect to the notice to be given of general meetings, the information to be provided to shareholders, the right to ask questions and receive answers at meetings, the right to add items to the meeting agenda, voting procedures including electronic participation, proxy rights etc. In other words, the focus is on the process of shareholder engagement, especially in the cross-border context.[70] Amendments to Directive 2007/36 have been made by Directive 2017/828 with a view to enhancing further shareholder participation rights, particularly to facilitate cross-border voting, to require greater engagement by institutional investors and asset managers. The amendments also strengthen shareholder control over directors' remuneration and over related party transactions These matters are discussed in Chapter 6.

---

[63] See Directive 2006/68/EC amending Directive 77/91/EEC, OJ L 264, 25.9.2006, p 32. See Government Response to consultation on implementation of amendments to the Second Company Law Directive (2007), URN 07/1300; also DTI, 'Implementation of the Companies Act 2006' (2007), URN 07/666, Ch 6.

[64] European Commission Green Paper, *The EU Corporate Governance Framework*, COM (2011) 164, 5.4.2011. This Green Paper followed an earlier focus on financial institutions, see European Commission, *Corporate governance in financial institutions and remuneration policies*, COM (2010) 284, 2.6.2010, and accompanying Commission Staff Working Document, SEC (2010) 669.

[65] See Commission Press Release IP/12/149, 20.2.2012, 'European Company Law: what way forward?'

[66] See Commission *Communication on Modernising Company Law*, COM (2003) 284, 21.5.2003, para 3.1; Weil, Gotshal, and Manges, *Comparative Study of Corporate Governance Codes Relevant to the European Union and its Member States* (January 2002).

[67] Commission Recommendation on the role of non-executive or supervisory directors of listed companies and on the committees of the (supervisory) board (2005/162/EC), OJ L 52, 25.2.2005, p 51.

[68] C(2009) 3177, 30.4.2009.  [69] Directive 2007/36/EC, OJ L 184/17, 14.7.2007.

[70] See COM (2014) 213, final, 9.4.2014.

**2-25**  A more controversial governance initiative involved a wide-ranging debate on voting rights in publicly traded companies, especially on proportionality between capital and control, and the principle of one share, one vote. While one share, one vote is the standard structure in this jurisdiction, many other Member States are accustomed to more complex and opaque structures, with voting control commonly retained by small numbers of shareholders, often reflecting long-standing family holdings. Basically, the argument is that if a company wants to accept shareholders' capital, it should be prepared to give them voting rights proportionate to the capital contributed and allow them a say in the conduct of the company's affairs through the mechanism of the general meeting. This ensures a powerful shareholder voice as a brake on the board of directors which might otherwise enjoy a cosy relationship with the key shareholders leading to a sharing between them of private benefits not available to the other shareholders. The countervailing argument runs along the lines that these are pure contractual matters and that shareholders purchasing shares in these companies contract on the basis that they will have limited voting rights and that limitation is (a) accepted by them voluntarily and (b) reflected in the price that they pay for their shares. It is also suggested that these structures are embedded in different corporate cultures which accept and respect long-standing family control and there is no demand for change. If there was a concern, the market would reflect that concern by marking down the share value of companies with restricted voting rights, but no such write-downs occur which suggests it is not a matter of concern to investors. The discussion of these matters came to a slightly abrupt end in October 2007 when Commissioner McCreevy announced that, following a review of a study on proportionality in the EU[71] and an impact assessment of the issue of proportionality, no further action would be taken on the matter. In part, the decision came about because the empirical evidence available to the Commission did not provide sufficient evidence of the existence and extent of private benefit extraction resulting from a lack of proportionality.[72] There was also significant political opposition to any change, especially from the Nordic countries where such concentrated shareholdings are commonplace. If there is to be movement on the matter, it will have to come from pressure by market participants on individual companies.[73]

## Corporate restructuring/mobility

**2-26**  A variety of measures have been adopted to facilitate mergers and takeovers as companies seek to expand through acquisitions and also to provide a range of corporate structures so as to facilitate operations across the internal market.[74]

---

[71] *Report on the Proportionality Principle in the European Union* carried out by ISS Europe, ECGI, Shearman & Sterling for the European Commission (May 2007).

[72] See Commission Impact Assessment on the Proportionality between Capital and Control in Listed Companies, SEC (2007) 1705, 12.12.2007.

[73] See the interesting paper by Khachaturyan, 'Trapped in Delusions: Democracy, Fairness and the One-Share-One-Vote Rule in the European Union' (2007) 8 EBOR 335 who argues that the case for ISIV being made mandatory has not been made out and that ISIV is not as valuable as is assumed and that it is neither a sufficient nor a necessary condition for shareholder democracy in general or shareholder empowerment in the EU in particular. See also OECD Report on the issue, 'Lack of Proportionality Between Ownership and Control: Overview and Issues for Discussion' issued by the OECD Steering Group On Corporate Governance, December 2007.

[74] We can note in passing the Twelfth Company Law Directive, Directive 89/667 EEC, OJ L 395/40, 30.12.1989, codified as Directive 2009/102, OJ L 258/20, 1.10.2009, which allows for the formation of one-member private companies and the CA 2006 permits public and private companies to have a single member (CA 2006, s 7).

**2-27**  The most significant European contribution in terms of mergers and takeovers is the Thirteenth Company Law Directive, more commonly called The Takeover Directive 2004/25/EC, which applies to takeover bids for securities of a company governed by the law of a Member State where all or some of the securities are admitted to trading on a regulated market.[75] Seventeen years elapsed from the initial proposal to the Directive coming into force on 20 May 2006.[76] The Directive lays down a framework of principles which govern takeovers and requires offers to be made to all shareholders. There are detailed rules as to the conduct of the bid and the documentation which must be provided to shareholders, though the requirements are watered down by a variety of Member State opt-outs. Nevertheless, given the history of the Directive, it was an achievement at least to have secured a framework for the conduct of takeovers throughout the EU. The Directive was implemented by CA 2006, Pt 28. The position under the Directive to a large extent reflects the UK position on takeovers as set out in the Takeover Code.

**2-28**  The Third and Sixth Company Law Directives are concerned with mergers and divisions of public companies within a single Member State.[77] They apply to mergers by way of the transfer of assets and liabilities from one company to another. The package is completed by the Tenth Company Law Directive 2005/56/EC on cross-border mergers[78] which facilitates mergers of companies from different Member States and was implemented by the Cross-Border Mergers Regulations 2007.[79] The three merger and divisions Directives have been consolidated as Directive 2017/1132.[80] The Commission has now put forward a proposal for a comprehensive overhaul of these cross-border provisions as well as the introduction of rules dealing with cross-border conversions, see **2-46**.

## Freedom of establishment

**2-29**  As discussed, there has been a measure of Commission activity in the area of corporate restructuring etc, but the greatest impetus to corporate mobility has come, not from the Commission, but from the Court of Justice. A practice had developed of businesses from other Member States incorporating in the UK, driven by the absence of minimum capital requirements for private companies and the speed, ease, and low cost of incorporation (see Chapter 1). This practice was not welcomed by the (original or true) 'home' Member States of those businesses which sought to challenge or hinder such business then from operating in that Member State. This raised issues as to freedom of establishment under (then) arts 43 and 48 of the EC Treaty, now arts 49 and 54 TFEU,[81] which were addressed by the European Court in a series of notable cases.

---

[75]  OJ L 142/12, 30.4.2004.

[76]  The first proposal for a Directive on Takeovers was put forward by the European Commission in 1989: see OJ C 64/8 14.3.1989. It was revised in 1990: see OJ C 240/7, 6.9.1990; in 1996: see COM (95) 655, 7.2.1996; in 1997, see OJ C 378, 13.12.97; followed by a new proposal in 2002, see OJ C 45 E, 25.2.2003, p 1.

[77]  Third Company Law Directive 78/855/EEC concerning mergers of public limited liability companies; Sixth Company Law Directive 82/891/EEC concerning the division of public limited liability companies, now consolidated as Directive 2017/1132, OJ L 169/46, 30.6.2017.

[78]  OJ L 310/1, 25.11.2005, now consolidated as Directive 2017/1132, OJ L 169/46, 30.6.2017

[79]  See The Companies (Cross-Border Mergers) Regulations 2007, SI 2007/2974.

[80]  OJ L 169/46, 30.6.2017.

[81]  The Treaty on the Functioning of the European Union (Consolidated version) OJ C 83/47, 30.3.2010: art 49 provides for freedom of establishment and art 54 requires companies formed in a Member State to be treated in the same way as natural persons who are nationals of Member States.

**2-30**    In *Centros Ltd v Erhvervs-og Selskabsstyrelsen*, Case C-212/97[82] a Danish couple set up and registered a private company in England (which never carried on any activities in England) and then applied to the Danish authorities for permission to operate a branch in Denmark so circumventing the stricter minimum capital requirements imposed on Danish private companies. The Danish authorities refused to register the branch on the basis that the couple were carrying on their principal establishment in Denmark in breach of national law. The issue was referred to the European Court which concluded that it is contrary to the right of freedom of establishment for a Member State to refuse to register a branch of a company in these circumstances.

**2-31**    The Treaty provisions on freedom of establishment are intended, the Court said, specifically to enable companies formed in accordance with the law of a Member State and having their registered office, central administration, or principal place of business within the Community, to pursue activities in other Member States through an agency, branch, or subsidiary. Member States are entitled to take measures to prevent their nationals from attempting, under cover of Treaty rights, improperly to circumvent their national legislation or from improperly or fraudulently taking advantage of Community provisions. The fact that a national of a Member State chooses to form a company in the Member State whose company law rules seem the least restrictive and to set up branches in other Member States does not, in itself, however, constitute an abuse of the right of establishment, even if no activities are then conducted in the Member State of incorporation.

**2-32**    This position was strengthened by the ruling in the *Uberseering*[83] case where the European Court confirmed that Member States must recognise companies incorporated in other Member States without further formality and without any need for the Member States to enter into conventions concerning the mutual recognition of companies. In *Uberseering* the company had been incorporated in the Netherlands but came to conduct all of its activities in Germany and all its shareholders were German. When the company tried to sue on a civil matter in Germany, it was denied *locus standi* on the basis that it had no legal capacity in Germany, not having been incorporated there. The European Court held that the failure to recognise the company's standing and effectively to require its reincorporation in Germany was an infringement of and incompatible with the freedom of establishment.[84]

**2-33**    A strategy which some Member States adopted to maintain some control over these companies (sometimes described as pseudo-foreign or formally foreign companies) was not to deny recognition to the entity validly incorporated under the law of another Member State, but to impose additional constraints on them when the formally foreign company carried on all or most of their activities in their Member State (as in *Centros*). In *Inspire Art Ltd*[85] the European Court concluded that such measures also infringe the right of freedom of establishment.

**2-34**    In *Inspire Art* the company was incorporated in England but its sole director was based in, and all its activities were conducted in, the Netherlands. The Dutch authorities tried to subject this formally foreign company to disclosure and minimum capital requirements which would put it on a footing similar to companies incorporated in the Netherlands. A failure to comply would result in personal liability for the directors so denying them the

---

[82]  [2000] 2 BCLC 68.
[83]  *Uberseering BV v Nordic Construction Co Baumanagement GmbH (NCC)* [2005] 1 WLR 315.
[84]  See note 77.
[85]  *Kamer van Koophandel en Fabrieken voor Amsterdam v Inspire Art Ltd* [2005] 3 CMLR 34.

protection of limited liability despite the business having been incorporated as a limited liability company. The court considered this attempt to impose capital requirements to be a breach of freedom of establishment in that it made it restrictive and therefore less attractive. In so far as disclosure requirements could be imposed, the European Court held, they were limited to the requirements of the Eleventh Company Law Directive on disclosure by branches which adequately protected the interests of creditors in the Netherlands by ensuring that they were aware of the status and nature of the foreign company.

**2-35** The European Court accepted, as it had in *Uberseering*,[86] that in certain circumstances and under certain conditions the protection of creditors, minority shareholders, and employees[87] and the preservation of the effectiveness of fiscal supervision and the fairness of commercial transactions may justify measures restricting the freedom of establishment.[88] But measures restricting the fundamental freedoms must fulfil four conditions: they must be applied in a non-discriminatory manner; they must be justified by imperative requirements in the general interest; they must be suitable for securing the attainment of the objective which they pursue; and they must not go beyond what is necessary in order to attain it.[89] In *Uberseering*, creditor protection did not demand measures beyond disclosure.

**2-36** The next stage in this jurisprudence was the decision in *Re Sevic Systems AG*[90] where the German authorities refused to register a merger between a Luxembourg company and a German company on the basis that the German registration provisions applied only to mergers between two German companies. The European Court held that a difference in treatment of mergers according to whether they were internal within a Member State or of a cross-border nature between a company formed in one Member State and a company formed in another was a measure likely to hinder cross-border mergers and to deter the exercise of the freedom of establishment. The result in *Sevic* has been overtaken by the adoption of the Tenth Company Law Directive on cross-border mergers[91] which requires Member States to recognise such mergers and determines how such mergers are to be conducted.

**2-37** The result of these cases is that businesses have freedom to choose where to incorporate and where to carry on their main activities. Once properly incorporated in Member State A: (i) that company must be recognised as such in all other Member States, even if it conducts no business in the state of incorporation (*Uberseering*); (ii) that company can choose to operate in another Member State either through a subsidiary, branch, or agency (*Centros*); and (iii) where the choice is to act through a branch, the Member State cannot impose obligations on the branch equivalent to those imposed on businesses incorporated in that Member State (*Inspire Art*).

**2-38** One consequence of the *Centros* line of authorities has been that some Member States moved to liberalise their domestic requirements and speed up their formation processes

---

[86] See [2005] 1 WLR 315 at [92].

[87] As to whether measures to protect employee rights of co-determination, as in Germany, might be acceptable, see Johnston, 'EC Freedom of Establishment: Employee Participation in Corporate Governance and the Limits of Regulatory Competition' (2006) 6 JCLS 71.

[88] [2006] 2 BCLC 510 at [28].

[89] [2006] 2 BCLC 510 at [23]; also *Gebhard v Consiglio dell'Ordine degli Avvocati e Procuratori di Milano* (Case C-55/94) [1995] ECR I-4165 at [37].

[90] [2006] 2 BCLC 510, ECJ; and see Siems, 'Sevic: Beyond Cross-Border Mergers' (2007) 8 EBOR 307.

[91] Directive 2005/56, now consolidated as Directive 2017/1132, OJ L 169/46, 30.6.2017. See The Companies (Cross-Border Mergers) Regulations 2007, SI 2007/2974.

in order to compete with this jurisdiction which is seen as having the lowest entry requirements with minimum formalities (Chapter 1) and, of course, no minimum share capital requirement for private companies. In France, for example, the minimum capital requirement for SARLs (a type of company equivalent to a private company here) was removed while Germany modernised its law governing private limited companies (GmbH).[92]

**2-39**  These cases involved a company incorporated in one Member State and wishing to remain so incorporated seeking to exercise rights of establishment elsewhere in the EU. Litigation then moved on to a further permutation on mobility, namely the ability to transfer an entity from Member State A to Member State B and so effect a change of governing law without liquidation of the business. The issue arose in *Re Cartesio Oktató*[93] where a Hungarian partnership wanted to transfer its seat to Italy while retaining its incorporation in Hungary, though Hungarian law required the seat of the company to be in Hungary. The European Court accepted that the Hungarian authorities were entitled to refuse permission for this transfer. Reiterating a point made previously by the Court, it is for the state of incorporation to determine the necessary connections to that State which will entitle the entity to the status of a company incorporated in that jurisdiction and subject to its company laws. A Member State can provide, therefore, that a company incorporated under the law of that Member State may not transfer its seat to another Member State whilst retaining its status as a company governed by the law of the Member State of incorporation.[94] Following the decision in *Cartesio*, much debate followed as to the meaning of a particular dictum in the case where the court indicated that a home Member State cannot prevent an entity from seeking to convert to an entity in another Member State 'to the extent that it is permitted under that law to do so'.[95] It was not entirely clear whether this meant that it was up to the host Member State to determine the basis and extent to which it would accept incoming, cross-border, conversions. The issue was taken up again by the European Court in the *VALE* judgment.[96] In this instance, an Italian company wished to transfer its real seat to Hungary and to that end completed all the formalities in Italy and was removed from the commercial register in that country. It then completed the required Hungarian formalities to continue its activities in that country, but when it asked for the record to indicate that the Italian company was the predecessor in title to the Hungarian company, the Hungarian authorities refused on the basis that Hungarian law allowed for the recognition of the predecessor in title only in the case of domestic companies. The European Court took this opportunity to explain the dictum in *Cartesio*, pointing out that, while companies have the right to exit from their jurisdiction of initial incorporation, it does not mean that the host Member State may determine the basis on which it will receive them, free of all EU constraints derived from the freedom of establishment. The host Member State may determine the rules governing incoming conversions, but they must be rules which are compatible with the freedom of establishment and so they cannot discriminate as between domestic and foreign companies. Of course,

---

[92] The reformed GmbH Act also provides for a new category of GmbH (an UG in German), popularly known as the 'mini-GmbH', which can be started with a capital of just €1. The UG must put aside one quarter of annual profits to allow its share capital to grow to the GmbH level (€25,000). Once this level has been reached, the accumulated capital can be converted into share capital and the UG can then change its name to a GmbH. For an interesting account of the adaptation of national law to the *Centros* jurisprudence, see Bratton, McCahery, and Vermeulen, 'How Does Corporate Mobility Affect Lawmaking? A Comparative Analysis,' in Prentice and Reisberg (eds), *Corporate Finance Law in the UK and EU* (2011).

[93] [2010] 1 BCLC 523.      [94] [2010] 1 BCLC 523 at [110].

[95] [2010] 1 BCLC 523 at [112]. See Morsdorf, 'The Legal Mobility of Companies within the European Union Through Cross-Border Conversion' (2012) 49 CMLR 629.

[96] *VALE Építési Kft* (Case C-378/10) [2013] 1 WLR 294.

in the absence of EU legislation on the matter, each Member State will have its own laws on conversions, but those laws must adhere to the general requirement that they must not be less favourable to foreign companies from other Member States than to domestic companies and they must not be such as to render the exercise of the right impossible or excessively difficult so as to indirectly restrict the exercise of the right. It is therefore possible, under this jurisprudence, for any company (whether formed in a Member State which adheres to the incorporation or real seat theory of incorporation) to exercise its right of freedom of establishment and convert itself into an entity governed by the company laws of another Member State, provided it adheres to the national rules governing such conversions, and provided such national rules in turn are compatible with the freedom of establishment.

**2-40** In *Polbud* the Court of Justice confirmed that articles 49 and 54 TFEU must be interpreted as meaning that freedom of establishment is applicable to the transfer of the registered office of a company formed in accordance with the law of one Member State to the territory of another Member State, for the purposes of its conversion (in accordance with the conditions imposed by the legislation of the other Member State including the conditions to determine the connection of the company to the national legal order), into a company incorporated under the law of the latter Member State, when there is no change in the location of the real head office of that company. A Polish company wished to transfer its registration to Luxembourg while still retaining all of its activities in Poland. The Polish authorities refused a request to remove the company from the Polish commercial register because the company had not been liquidated in Poland. The Court of Justice ruled that the original home Member State may not require a transferring company to be liquidated in order to be removed from the register. A national measure of that nature would be liable to impede, if not prevent, cross-border conversions and therefore constitutes a restriction on freedom of establishment which is permissible only if it is justified by overriding reasons in the public interest including the protection of the interests of creditors, minority shareholders, and workers. Accordingly, arts 49 and 54 TFEU do not, in principle, preclude measures of a Member State intended to ensure that the interests of creditors, minority shareholders, and employees of a company that has been incorporated under the law of that Member State, and is to continue to carry on business in the national territory, are not improperly affected by the transfer of the registered office of that company and its conversion into a company under the law of another Member State. The result is that companies can choose to leave their original jurisdiction to seek incorporation elsewhere without interruption of their activities, so long as the transfer does not seek[97] to adversely impact on creditor, or employee or minority rights in the original Member State. A change of jurisdiction to enjoy a more favourable legislative regime is not, in itself, an abuse.

**2-41** Directors need to take heed though when exercising their rights of freedom of establishment. In the *Kornhaas* case,[98] a company established under the law of England and Wales was the subject of insolvency proceedings opened in Germany under Insolvency Regulation 1346/2000, now recast as Insolvency Regulation 2015/848, where it was carrying on an establishment. The German liquidator was entitled, on the basis of a national

---

[97] *Polbud* (Case C-106/16) [2018] 2 CMLR 5; *Re Sevic Systems AG* (C-411/03) [2006] 1 CMLR 45; *AGET Iraklis* (C-201/15) [2017] 2 CMLR 32.

[98] *Kornhaas v Dithmar* (Case C-594/14, CJEU) [2016] BCC 116. See Szydio, 'Directors' Duties and Liability in Insolvency and the Freedom of Establishment of Companies after Kornhaas' (2017) 54(6) CML Rev 1853; Ringe, 'Kornhaas and the Challenge of Applying Keck in Establishment' (2017) 42(2) EL Rev 270.

provision, to seek reimbursement of payments made by the company's managing director before the opening of the insolvency proceedings but after the date on which the insolvency of that company was established. Such proceedings are derived directly from the insolvency proceedings and closely connected with them such that, according to the CJEU, they are governed by the law of the insolvency proceedings (and not the law of the place of incorporation). As the application of a provision of national law in this way does not concern the formation of a company in a given Member State or its subsequent establishment in another Member State, because the provision is only applicable after the company is formed and only once it is considered to be insolvent, the Court of Justice ruled that application of the national provision did not affect freedom of establishment under arts 49 and 54 TFEU.

**2-42**    Welcome though these decisions are, as Biermeyer has noted, we are left with a 'legal jungle of rules' in which 'it is easy to get lost'.[99] It is not clear for example what the position is on cross-border conversions in the UK, given that the CA 2006, while allowing in Pt 7 for conversions for domestic companies from private to public status and vice versa and from limited to unlimited and vice versa, makes no specific provision, unsurprisingly, for cross-border conversions. This is true of more than half the Member States where there is no specific provision for cross-border conversions.[100] There may be a right under this European jurisprudence to convert from, say, a Polish company into a UK company, but there are no procedural mechanisms in place to determine how such a process might occur.

**2-43**    The net result of this activist jurisprudence from the Court of Justice is that there is a considerable measure of corporate mobility within the EU,[101] so much so that the European Commission decided in 2007 not to proceed with a proposed Fourteenth Company Law Directive allowing for the cross-border transfer of the registered office of limited companies.[102] At the moment, the same result can be achieved by other mechanisms, especially by the use of a cross-border merger whereby the company which wishes to move to another jurisdiction can now set up a company in that other jurisdiction, merge the existing company into that new company, and dissolve the first company, so effecting a transfer of the business and the registered office to the new jurisdiction without liquidation.[103] Indeed, it is possible to use the cross-border merger provisions to merge, even when a group is comprised entirely of UK companies and one dormant company from another Member State, as the Court of Appeal confirmed in *Re Easy Global Services Ltd*.[104] The court ruled that it would be a material restriction on the right of establishment if the UK's cross-border mergers regime made it more difficult to proceed where the proposed merger included a foreign subsidiary of a UK company in another Member State which was dormant or had smaller scale operations, as compared with a merger involving a more substantial foreign subsidiary. Such a restriction could deter UK companies from

---

[99] See the excellent note by Biermeyer on *VALE*, 'Shaping the Space of Cross-border Conversion in the EU. Between Right and Autonomy: VALE' (2013) 50 CMLR 571.

[100] See COM (2018) 241 final, p 3.

[101] See, generally, Johnston and Syrpis, 'Regulatory Competition in European Company Law after Cartesio' (2009) 34 EL Rev 378; Armour and Ringe, 'European Company Law 1999–2010: Renaissance and Crisis' (2011) 48 CMLR 125.

[102] For a contrary view, see Johnston and Syrpis, 'Regulatory Competition in European Company Law after Cartesio' (2009) 34 EL Rev 378.

[103] See Siems, 'Sevic: Beyond Cross-Border Mergers' (2007) 8 EBOR 307; Papadopoulos, 'EU Regulatory Approaches to Cross-border Mergers: Exercising the right of establishment' (2011) 36 EL Rev 71;

[104] [2018] EWCA Civ 10.

setting up small-scale or dormant subsidiaries in other Member States to maintain flexibility in organising their affairs. It could effectively impose a practical requirement to set up subsidiaries which were capitalised or expected to trade at a significant level, as a price for such flexibility. There was nothing, the court said, in the Directive to indicate an intention to permit the introduction of such restrictions.[105]

**2-44** Despite the scope of this jurisprudence on freedom of establishment and the flexibility now evident, critics argued that companies should not need to use such 'detour' mechanisms but did need a straightforward mechanism for the transfer of the registered offices and for mergers and divisions.[106] The Commission has decided therefore to proceed with a proposal for a Directive on cross-border conversions, mergers, and divisions.[107] The intention is to create a framework to conversion, as the Court indicated in *Polbud* would be desirable, looking to member, employee, and creditor protections and the Commission is also taking the opportunity to improve the cross-borders mergers Directive in the light of experience, particularly by introducing a fast track procedure for straightforward cases while adding extra protection measures for shareholders and creditors, where discrepancies between Member States remain. The objectives, as stated by the Commission, are to enable companies, particularly small companies, to convert cross-border in an orderly, efficient, and effective manner while protecting the most affected stakeholders such as employees, creditors, and shareholders in a suitable and proportionate manner.[108] This will enable companies to convert cross-border by changing their legal form of one Member State into a similar legal form of another Member State, while keeping their legal personality throughout the process. The opportunity will also be taken to address some of the procedural complexities surrounding the Cross-Border Merger Directive[109] while introducing a harmonised legal framework for cross-border divisions, given that many Member States have no national law on divisions and the legal position is therefore very uncertain.

## C  European structures

**2-45** In addition to facilitating movement between Member States and takeovers across jurisdictions, the Commission has also looked to create new European structures. An example is the European Economic Interest Grouping (EEIG) which can be established between two or more trading entities based in different Member States.[110] It is of limited appeal

---

[105] It is also possible for a European Company, subject to detailed formalities, to transfer its registered office, see Council Regulation 2157/2001, OJ L 294/1, 10.11.2001, art 8. A major limitation on the process is that the SE's registered office and head office must be in the same Member State (see art 7); also Ringe, 'The European Company Statute in the Context of Freedom of Establishment' (2007) 7 JCLS 185.

[106] See Gerner-Beuerle, Mucciarelli, Schuster, and Siems, 'Cross-border Reincorporations in the European Union: The Case for Comprehensive Harmonisation' (2017) 18 JCLS 1; Morsdorf, 'The Legal Mobility of Companies within the European Union Through Cross-Border Conversion' (2012) 49 CMLR 629. Also Wymeersch, 'Is a Directive on Corporate Mobility Needed?' (2007) 8 EBOR 161; Mucciarelli, 'Company "Emigration" and EC Freedom of Establishment: Daily Mail Revisited' (2008) 9 EBOR 267. See also Wisniewski and Opalski, 'Companies' Freedom of Establishment after the ECJ *Cartesio* Judgment' (2009) 10 EBOR 595; Lombardo, 'Regulatory Competition in Company Law in the European Union after Cartesio' (2009) 10 EBOR 627.        [107] COM (2018) 241 final, 25.4.2018.

[108] Com (2018) 241 final, 25.4.2018.        [109] Directive 2005/56 replaced and codified by Directive 2017/1132, OJ L 169/46, 30.6.2017.

[110] See Council Regulation EEC/2137/85, OJ L 199/1, 31.7.1985; and the European Economic Interest Grouping Regulations 1989, SI 1989/638. See generally Keegan, 'The European Economic Interest Grouping' [1991] JBL 457.

because its activities have to be ancillary to the activities of its members (so it is confined to areas such as research, marketing, or training) and it cannot be profit-making in its own right. There are just 294 on the register.[111]

### The European Company (SE)

**2-46**   After decades of discussion,[112] agreement was reached in 2001 on the European Company, the Societas Europaea (SE), with a Council Regulation providing for the European Company Statute[113] while a Council Directive supplements the statute and makes provision for the involvement of employees.[114]

**2-47**   An SE may be formed in one of four ways:

- by the merger of two or more existing public limited companies from at least two different EU Member States;
- by the formation of a holding company promoted by public or private limited companies from at least two different Member States;
- by the formation of a subsidiary of companies from at least two different Member States;
- by the transformation of a public limited company which has, for at least two years, had a subsidiary in another Member State.

**2-48**   An SE must have a minimum share capital of €120,000. The board of directors can be organised either on the basis of a supervisory and a management board or as a unitary board. The registered office of an SE must be in the same Member State as its head office and the registered office can be transferred to another Member State without the need to wind up the company. The provisions contained in the accompanying Directive on worker involvement are complex, given that they are the result of decades of negotiations designed to accommodate the very differing views on this issue across the Member States. Essentially, levels of worker participation in the pre-existing entities must be replicated in the SE but, if there were none, the SE need not make provision for any such participation, though there are default rules as to the provision of information to and consultation with employees.

**2-49**   The laws applicable to the SE are those laid down in the Regulation and Directive and where no provision is made (and no provision is made on matters such as capital maintenance, directors' duties, shareholders rights, and insolvency), the matter is governed by the laws applicable to public companies of the Member State in which the SE has its registered office. The result is an element of uncertainty as to the applicable law and, given the significance of the matters governed by the law of the Member State of the registered office, these entities begin to look like national public companies which is a long way from the concept of a European company as originally envisaged.

---

[111] As of 31 March 2017, see Companies House, *Companies Register Activities Data Tables 2016–16*, Table C1.

[112] For the history of the proposal, see Edwards, *EC Company Law* (1999), pp 399–404. First proposed by the Commission in 1970, discussions over the years were dogged by controversy over issues such as the interface between national and European law, the appropriate taxation regime, and, most particularly, by an inability to reach agreement on the provisions for employee involvement.

[113] Council Regulation (EC) No 2157/2001, OJ L 294/1, 10.11.2001, implemented by The European Public Limited-Liability Company Regulations 2004, SI 2004/2326.

[114] Council Directive 2001/86/EC, OJ L 294/22, 10.11.2001.

**2-50**  It is also the case that the SE has been somewhat overtaken by other developments, such as the breadth of the freedom of establishment articulated by the European Court, discussed at **2-29** et seq, and the ease of transfer between Member States as a result of the Tenth Company Law Directive 2005/56/EC, now Directive 2017/1132,[115] on Cross-Border Mergers, noted at **2-43**. The Commission has made considerable strides also in devising a package of uniform obligations with respect to publicly traded companies, not just in terms of disclosure and corporate governance as discussed, but with regard to other matters, such as the Prospectus Regulation 2017/1129 governing public offers of shares,[116] see **21-109**. The result is that the existing structures may facilitate operations across the EU without the need for a European Company. Certainly, the SE has not proved attractive in this jurisdiction although it has been used to some extent in other Member States.[117] In 2010, the Commission reviewed the operation of the SE Statute.[118] It found that the positive aspects of an SE are the European image and supranational character of the SE and the possibility it offers of transferring the registered office and using the SE to reorganise and restructure groups, but the drawbacks identified were that the process of setting up an SE is seen as costly, time-consuming, and complex, especially with regard to employee participation. Overall, the Commission concluded that the application of the SE Statute poses a number of problems in practice, noting that:

> 'the SE Statute does not provide for a uniform SE form across the European Union, but 27 different types of SEs. The Statute contains many references to national law and there is uncertainty about the legal effect of directly applicable law and its interface with national law. Furthermore, the uneven distribution of SEs across the European Union shows that the Statute is not adapted to the situation of companies in all Member States.'[119]

While acknowledging these findings, the Commission does not plan to revise the SE Statute in the short term, noting the complexity of the discussions which would then ensue, so instead the focus is on improving the awareness of companies and their legal advisers about the SE.[120]

**2-51**  The complexity of the European Company means that it is unlikely to prove attractive to SMEs and it was never envisaged that it might be appropriate for such entities. Instead, for many years it was mooted that the Commission should consider a European Private Company Statute and the Commission did conduct a feasibility study on the issue in 2005.[121] The results were divided but the idea gathered some momentum and the Small Business Act announced by the Commission in June 2008 (see **2-15**) included a proposal

---

[115]  OJ L 169/46, 30.6.2017.

[116]  OJ L 168/12, 30.6.2017, replacing Prospectus Directive 2003/71/EC, OJ L 345/64, 31.12.2003.

[117]  At 31 March 2017, there were 50 SEs on the register at Companies House: see *Companies Register Activities Data Tables 2016–17*, Table C1. The European Trade Union Institute maintains a SE data base for worker participation purposes and, at February 2018, it showed 2,943 SEs across the EU.

[118]  See Report from the Commission on the application of Council Regulation on the Statute for a European Company (SE), COM (2010) 676 final, 17.11.2010, and related Commission Staff Working Document, SEC (2010) 1391 final, 17.11.2010.

[119]  See COM (2010) 676 final, 17.11.2010, section 6.

[120]  See European Commission, *Action Plan: European Company Law and Corporate Governance*, COM (2012) 740 final, 12.12.2012, para 4.6. In reality, this initiative has amounted to little more than some information on SEs being gathered together on the Commission website.

[121]  See European Commission, *Feasibility Study of a European Statute for SMEs* (2005).

for a Regulation on the Statute for a European Private Company.[122] The key elements of the Societas Privata Europaea (SPE) were to be that it would be a private company limited by shares, with a minimum share capital of €1 and a name ending in 'SPE' which could be formed from scratch or created from another form and by one or more persons. It might be registered in any Member State and its registered office and centre of activities might be in different Member States. It would be able to transfer its registered office without winding up. It would not need initially to have any cross-border activities or connections. The legal framework for the SPE would be provided by the Statute so ensuring uniform rules across the EU, but the detailed regulation of the internal working arrangements within the SPE would be a matter for the articles. For matters not governed by the Statute or the articles, the law of the Member State in which the SPE is registered would apply.

**2-52**     As with the SE, it was not clear that there was demand for this structure given, as the European Commission itself conceded, that most small businesses have no interest in cross-border trading and are reasonably content with the range of business vehicles offered by their domestic jurisdiction.[123] It might have been attractive to businesses from jurisdictions with high minimum share capital requirements but many jurisdictions have reformed their laws in recent years to abolish or significantly reduce the minimum share capital required. After some initial enthusiasm for this project, political support for the proposal diminished and the SPE proposal was withdrawn.[124]

## The Single Member European Private Company (SUP)

**2-53**     In 2014, the European Commission brought forward an alternative proposal, for a Societas Unius Personae (SUP), a single-member private limited liability company.[125] The Commission considers that SMEs (small and medium-sized enterprises) find it difficult to engage in cross-border activities and, if they do so at all, then they do so by forming subsidiaries in other Member States but that is costly, especially if the intention is to operate in a number of Member States, each of which applies different laws to the subsidiary. The Commission considered, therefore, that its proposal for a single-member private limited liability company would address some of the obstacles facing SMEs and would facilitate group structures. The objective is to make it easier and less costly to set up companies across the EU and to encourage SMEs to do so. The proposal differs from the European Company in that this is not a European form of company; the intention is that Member States will provide in their legal systems for a national company law form that would follow the same rules in all Member States and would have an EU-wide common name,

---

[122] See the *Proposal For A Council Regulation On The Statute For A European Private Company*, COM (2008) 396, 25.6.2008; also Drury 'The European Private Company' (2008) 9 EBOR 125. A leading proponent of the idea, Drury comments (at 130) that, amongst its attractions, the SPE would provide a uniform structure for a Europe-wide group of companies, would facilitate inward investment by providing a vehicle that can operate in and move to any part of the Union under a single set of rules, and would give a European identity to businesses for marketing purposes.

[123] The UK Government was supportive of the proposal, but thought it was complex and that it was unlikely that many UK companies would choose to form an SPE rather than a UK private limited company, see HC, European Scrutiny Committee, 38th Report, Session 2010–12 (HC 428), paras 2.12–2.20.

[124] See annex to COM (2013) 685 final, p 9.

[125] Commission proposal for a Directive on single-member private limited liability companies COM (2014) 212 final, 9.4.2014, again an online consultation in 2013 preceded the proposal. See also Commission Memo/14/274, 9.4.2014. There is an existing Directive on single-member private companies, codified in Directive 2009/102/EC, but it is a modest measure merely recognising that single-member private companies are permissible, and that Directive would be replaced by this proposal.

Societas Unius Personae (SUP). The common elements would be as to manner of registration (simple online), uniform articles of association, a minimum capital requirement of €1, and adequate protection of creditors via solvency requirements before distributions to members.[126] It would be limited to single members and there would be no scope for dividing the shareholding or for issuing more than one share. A SUP that wanted to increase its number of shareholders would have to convert into some other national company form. The proposals was robustly rejected by the key European Economic and Social Committee[127] in September 2014 on numerous grounds including the lack of a substantial minimum capital, the ability to separate the registered office from the administrative headquarters, the absence of employee participation requirements, the lack of a restriction to SMEs, and the inadequate protection of creditors and consumers. In the face of such objections, the proposal did not advance and in its Work Programme 2018, published on 24 October 2017, the Commission announced that the proposal will be withdrawn.

**2-54**   Finally, it is worth noting a further private initiative to develop a European Model Company Law Act (EMCA) along the lines of the American Model Acts. The purpose is to provide a model law which national legislatures would be free to adopt in whole or in part. The EMCA presents a structure based on broadly acceptable uniform rules, building on the common legal traditions of the Member States and the existing *acquis* and drawing on best practice in the various Member States.[128]

---

[126]   See generally Wuisman, 'The Societas Unius Personae' (2015) 15 EC Law 34; Teichmann and Frohlich, 'Societas Unius Personae (SUP): Facilitating Cross-border Establishment' (2014) 21 Maastricht J Eur & Comp L 536.                                                                      [127]   OJ C 458/19, 19.12.2014.

[128]   The Act can be accessed on the SSRN website at https://papers.ssrn.com/sol3/papers.cfm?abstract_id=2929348. See Andersen, 'The European Model Company Act (EMCA): A New Way Forward' in Bernitz and Ringe (eds), *Company Law and Economic Protectionism—New Challenges to European Integration* (2010); also Baums and Andersen, 'The European Model Company Act Project' in Tison et al (eds), *Perspectives in Company Law and Financial Regulation* (2009). Further information on this project is available at http://law.au.dk/en/research/projects/european-model-company-act-emca/.

# 3

# Corporate personality

## A A separate legal entity

### The *Salomon* principle

**3-1**    On incorporation, a company becomes a legal entity separate and distinct from its share-holders and it is not the agent of those shareholders, not even if it is a one-man company with one shareholder controlling all its activities. This fundamental principle of company law was established by the House of Lords in *Salomon v Salomon & Co Ltd*.[1]

**3-2**    In this case, Mr Salomon sold his shoe business to a company which he had set up for the purpose under the Companies Act 1862. The formalities under the Act (very simi-lar to those still required today) were completed and the members of the company were Salomon, Mrs S, and five of their children (a minimum of seven members being required at that time).[2] As part of the consideration for the sale of the business to the company, Mr Salomon received fully paid-up shares and also debentures to the value of £10,000 which he subsequently assigned to another party. In effect, the debentures meant that initially Mr Salomon, and subsequently the assignee, were creditors of the business with first claim on the remaining assets should the company go into liquidation, as indeed happened. The company became insolvent and was unable to meet the full claim of the assignee or to meet at all the claims of the other (unsecured) creditors. The liquidator attempted to hold Mr Salomon liable for the debts of the company on a variety of grounds including that the whole transaction was a fraud on the company's creditors from which Salomon should not be allowed to benefit and that the company was simply his agent and therefore he should indemnify the company (and its creditors) with respect to the debts incurred by the company.

**3-3**    At first instance, the court agreed that the company was merely an agent of Salomon and therefore, as principal, he was liable to indemnify the agent (the company) for its debts.[3] The Court of Appeal rejected Salomon's appeal and concluded that the formation of the company and the issue of the debentures was a mere scheme to enable Salomon to carry on business in the name of a company with limited liability contrary to the true intent and meaning of the Companies Act 1862. In essence he was a sole trader screening himself

---

[1] [1897] AC 22, HL. See generally Grantham and Rickett (eds), *Corporate Personality in the 20th Century* (1998).

[2] The CA 2006 permits single member private and public companies, see s 7. A public company must have two directors, however, while a private company need have only one director (s 154) who can be, and often is, the sole member.

[3] See *Broderip v Salomon* [1895] 2 Ch 323.

from liabilities and as such it was a device to defraud creditors.[4] Lopes LJ noted that 'it would be lamentable if a scheme such as this could not be defeated'.[5]

**3-4**  On a further appeal by Salomon, the House of Lords concluded that there was nothing untoward with the formation and operation of the company and it reversed the decision of the Court of Appeal. The company had been duly formed and registered and was not the mere alias or agent of or trustee for Mr Salomon. As Lord Herschell noted, in a popular sense a company may be said to carry on business on behalf of its shareholders, but it certainly does not constitute an agency relationship between them or render the shareholders liable to indemnify the company against the debts which it incurs.[6] There was no sham or fraud, the formation and operation of the company were not contrary to the true intent and meaning of the Companies Act 1862, and Mr Salomon was not liable to indemnify the company against the creditors' claims.

**3-5**  Lord Macnaghten noted that when the memorandum[7] is duly signed and registered, a body corporate is formed[8] and it cannot lose that status by issuing the bulk of its shares to one person. He went on:[9]

> 'The company is at law a different person altogether from the subscribers to the memorandum; and, though it may be that after incorporation the business is precisely the same as it was before, and the same persons are managers, and the same hands receive the profits, the company is not in law the agent of the subscribers or trustee for them. Nor are the subscribers as members liable, in any shape or form, except to the extent and in the manner provided by the Act.'[10]

**3-6**  As for the description of these companies as 'one-man companies', Lord Macnaghten said that if that phrase was intended to convey that a company under the absolute control of one person was not a legally incorporated company, it was inaccurate and misleading.[11] Lord Herschell noted that he was 'at a loss to understand what is meant by saying that A Salomon & Co Ltd is but "an alias" for A Salomon. It is not another name for the same person; the company is ex hypothesi a distinct legal persona.'[12] Likewise, Lord Halsbury emphasised that the sole guide to matters was the statute which did not enact requirements as to the extent or degree of interests which may be held by the subscribers to the memorandum of association.[13] The House of Lords had little sympathy for the unsecured creditors who had only themselves to blame, having had full notice that they were no longer dealing with an individual.[14]

**3-7**  The result was that the House of Lords affirmed that, once the company is legally incorporated, the company must be treated like any other independent person with rights and

---

[4] See [1895] 2 Ch 323 at 338–9, per Lindley LJ. The Court of Appeal dissented from the lower court's view that the company was to be regarded as the agent of the appellant, rather they considered the relationship to be one of trustee and cestui que trust.       [5] [1895] 2 Ch 323 at 340–1.

[6] [1987] AC 22 at 43, see too at 31 (Lord Halsbury), 51 (Lord Macnaghten), 56 (Lord Davey).

[7] See CA 2006, s 8 and **1-23** as to the memorandum of association. As Kerr LJ commented in *J H Rayner v Dept of Trade* [1989] Ch 72 at 188: 'That rejection [in *Salomon*] of the doctrine of agency to impugn the non-liability of the members for the acts of the corporation is the foundation of our modern company law.'

[8] See CA 2006, s 16(2).       [9] [1897] AC 22 at 51, HL.

[10] That liability, in the case of a company limited by shares, is limited to the amount, if any, unpaid on the shares held by them, see CA 2006, s 3(2) and **3-13**; also IA 1986, s 74(1)(d).

[11] [1897] AC 22 at 53.       [12] [1897] AC 22 at 42.

[13] [1897] AC 22 at 29–30; and see Lord Watson at 38–9.

[14] See [1897] AC 22 at 53, per Lord Macnaghten at 45, per Lord Herschell at 40; per Lord Watson at 45–6.

liabilities of its own.[15] The mere fact that a person owns all the shares in a company does not make the business carried on by that company his business.

**3-8**     A further illustration of this point can be found in *Gramophone & Typewriter Co Ltd v Stanley*[16] where an English company owned all of the shares in a German company. At issue was whether the business of the German company was really the business of its English shareholder since, if it was, that exposed the shareholder to a greater tax liability. Given that there was factual evidence that the German company was a real company with a real business and not a sham or pretence, the question was whether the German company was the agent of its English shareholder. The Court of Appeal was agreed that, as laid down in *Salomon*, merely holding all of the shares is insufficient to create an agency relationship.[17]

**3-9**     The position is the same today as in those early cases and a modern day Mr Salomon is entitled to expect the courts to apply the *Salomon* principle in the same way. In *MacDonald, Dickens & Macklin v Costello*[18] a couple set up a company to undertake a building contract with a construction company. At every stage of the process, it was clear that the building project was being undertaken by the company, the company hired the builders, paid the invoices etc, though, of course, the company was managed and run by the couple who were the only shareholders and directors. The company became insolvent and failed to pay the builders. The court accepted that the contract was between the builders and the company, but nevertheless the court made an order for restitution against the couple, on the basis that they had been unfairly enriched by being in receipt of the benefit of the building work. On appeal, the Court of Appeal quashed the order, saying it undermined the contractual arrangements entered into between the builders and the company which was the mechanism which the parties had used to allocate the risk involved in the project. Most pertinently, the Court of Appeal noted that the obligation to pay the builders was contractually confined to the company and if a claim was permitted directly against the couple (who were the shareholders and directors, it will be recalled), 'it would shatter that contractual containment' and alter the usual consequences of the company's insolvency which was one of the risks assumed by the builders in contracting with a company.[19] A direct claim against the couple would improve the builders' position over the company's other unsecured creditors.[20] Had the builders wanted to limit their risk, they could have sought personal guarantees from the couple which they had not done. In effect, the court was not prepared to let a restitution order undermine the corporate and contractual structure which the parties had transparently adopted and which the claimants had appreciated throughout.

**3-10**    In legitimating the one-man company, the decision in *Salomon* also legitimates the group concept with each subsidiary company being a separate and distinct entity and not the agent of its controlling or sole shareholder, its parent company.[21] The relationship between a parent and a subsidiary company is the same as between Mr Salomon and his company. The parent company (i.e. the corporate shareholder in the subsidiary) and the subsidiary

---

[15] [1897] AC 22 at 31, per Lord Halsbury.
[16] [1908] 2 KB 89; see also *Tunstall v Steigmann* [1962] 2 QB 593; *Ebbw Vale UDC v South Wales Traffic Area Licensing Authority* [1951] 2 KB 366.          [17] [1908] 2 KB 89 at 96, 100, 105.
[18] [2011] 3 WLR 1341.     [19] [2011] 3 WLR 1341 at [21].     [20] [2011] 3 WLR 1341 at [21].
[21] *Salomon v Salomon & Co Ltd* [1897] AC 22; *The Albazero* [1977] AC 774 at 807, HL, per Roskill LJ; *Bank of Tokyo Ltd v Karoon* [1987] AC 45 at 64, CA; *Adams v Cape Industries plc* [1990] BCLC 479 at 513–15, 519–20. The definition of holding (parent) and subsidiary company is set out in CA 2006, s 1159, and see the discussion of corporate groups at **1-55** et seq.

company are separate legal entities and each company is entitled to expect that the court will apply the *Salomon* principle in the ordinary way and respect the separate identity of each company in the group.[22]

### An exceptional agency

**3-11**   Although *Salomon v Salomon & Co Ltd*[23] establishes that a company is not, per se, the agent of its shareholders, exceptionally, it may be possible to establish that an agency relationship does exist between a company and its shareholders,[24] as it may arise between any two legal entities, but it must arise from circumstances other than mere control of the company or ownership of its shares.[25] Whether such circumstances exist involves the court in a detailed factual examination in order to determine whether the intention of the parties was to create a relationship of principal and agent and, as Toulson J has noted, ordinarily the intention of someone who conducts trading activities through the vehicle of a one-man company will be quite the opposite,[26] something which can equally be said of those who set up subsidiary companies.[27] Unsurprisingly, then, examples of an agency relationship are rare. In *Re FG (Films) Ltd*[28] a company claimed that it had made a film which was therefore a British film and so entitled to certain tax advantages. The company had a capital of £100, no premises other than its registered office, and no staff. The financing of the film (some £80,000) was provided by an American company which through a nominee held 90 per cent of the company's shares. The court concluded that it could not be said in any real sense that this 'insignificant' company had made the film, its participation was so small as to be practically negligible, and it had acted, in so far as it had acted at all, merely as the agent and nominee of the American shareholder. In *Smith, Stone & Knight Ltd v Birmingham Corp*,[29] on unusual facts, the court accepted that a subsidiary did carry on business as agent for the parent to whom the business and the profits of the business belonged.

---

[22]   *Adams v Cape Industries plc* [1990] BCLC 479 at 520, CA; *Ord v Belhaven Pubs Ltd* [1998] 2 BCLC 447 at 458, CA.     [23]   [1897] AC 22, HL.

[24]   *Salmon v Salomon & Co Ltd* [1897] AC 22 at 55; also *Gramophone & Typewriter Ltd v Stanley* [1908] 2 KB 89 at 96. See Ottolenghi, 'From Peeping Behind the Corporate Veil to Ignoring it Completely' (1990) 53 MLR 338 at 345–6, who notes that the court, in the agency cases, is constructing or imputing an agency relationship as a result of first lifting the corporate veil to see who is behind the company and then declaring that the relationship between the controller and the company is an agency relationship, which he describes as a 'special method of penetrating the corporate veil'.

[25]   *Yukong Line Ltd of Korea v Rendsburg Investments Corp of Liberia* [1998] 2 BCLC 485 at 494. See too Tomlin J in *British Thompson-Houston Co Ltd v Sterling Accessories Ltd* [1924] 2 Ch 33 at 38: 'If [the controller] is to be fixed with liability as principal, the agency of the company must be established substantively and cannot be inferred from the holding of director's office and the control of the shares alone.'

[26]   *Yukong Line Ltd of Korea v Rendsburg Investments Corp of Liberia* [1998] 2 BCLC 485 at 496.

[27]   See *Atlas Maritime Co SA v Avalon Maritime Ltd, The Coral Rose (No 1)* [1991] 4 All ER 769 at 779.

[28]   [1953] 1 All ER 615. See also *Firestone Tyre and Rubber Co Ltd v Llewellin* [1957] 1 All ER 561 (an assessment of tax upheld where business of parent and subsidiary carried on by the subsidiary as agent for the parent).

[29]   [1939] 4 All ER 116 (parent company took over a partnership, incorporated it as a wholly-owned subsidiary, and ran it really as a department of the parent company with a manager, the parent was in effectual and constant control; see at 119 for the unusual facts of this case). But see Toulson J in *Yukong Line Ltd of Korea v Rendsburg Investments Corp of Liberia* [1998] 2 BCLC 485 at 495–6, who criticises this decision of Atkinson J as coming close in effect to the approach of the Court of Appeal in *Salomon* which was rejected by the House of Lords; see also Day [2014] LMCLQ 269 at 287. In *JH Rayner Ltd v Dept of Trade* [1989] Ch 72 at 189, Kerr LJ noted that the facts in *Smith Stone & Knight Ltd v Birmingham Corp* were so unusual that they cannot form any basis of principle.

**3-12**    More commonly, an agency argument is rejected.[30] For example, in *Adams v Cape Industries plc*[31] it was argued that certain US subsidiaries were agents of an English parent company such that the English parent company was conducting business in the US. The presence of the English company in the US was necessary if a US court judgment was to be enforced against it. As is clear from the authorities, if the agency argument is to prevail, it is necessary for the court to look in detail at the relationship between the English parent company and the US subsidiaries. With respect to one particular subsidiary, the evidence was that it leased premises, employed people, and carried on activities on its own account as principal. It earned profits, paid its taxes, and had its own debtors and creditors. For all the closeness of the relationship with the English parent company whose products it marketed, it had no power to bind the parent company to any contractual obligation and it never did effect a transaction in a manner such that the parent company became subject to any contractual obligations to any person. The Court of Appeal concluded that it was indisputable that a substantial part of the business carried on by the subsidiary was in every sense its own business.[32] There was no agency relationship with the parent company. Theoretically, then, an agency relationship may exist between a company and its controlling shareholder, but it takes exceptional facts to establish such a relationship.

### Consequences of *Salomon*

**3-13**    As a legal entity, separate and distinct from its shareholders, the company must be treated like any other independent person with rights and liabilities appropriate to itself.[33] It is the company which conducts business, it is the company which enters into contracts and incurs debts, and the shareholder's only obligation in respect of such debts in a company limited by shares is to contribute to the company's assets such amount, if any, unpaid on the shares held by them (CA 2006, s 3(2)).[34] The company can own property and its property is not the property of its main shareholder (not even if he owns all the shares), who cannot insure it,[35] but who can be charged with stealing from the company.[36] As Rimer LJ crisply put it, 'it follows from the fact of the company's separate identity that its property belongs beneficially to the company itself and in no sense belongs, either in law or in equity, to its shareholders, who have no interest of any nature, whether proprietary or

---

[30] For example, see *Re Polly Peck International plc (No 3)* [1996] BCLC 428 at 434, 441 (despite a subsidiary company having negligible capital, no separate management, and the most minimal role in certain bond issues, the court did not accept that it was an agent of its parent company).

[31] [1990] BCLC 479.

[32] The subsidiary in this case was NAAC; see the discussion at [1990] BCLC 479 at 520–2. With regard to another subsidiary (CPC), see [1990] BCLC 479 at 523–4, the court thought the facts were even weaker in that it was not a wholly-owned subsidiary but was an independently owned company. While the English company had provided funding for it, it carried on business on its own account and not as agent for the English company.

[33] *Salomon v Salomon & Co Ltd* [1897] AC 22 at 30, HL, per Lord Halsbury; also *Maclaine Watson & Co Ltd v International Tin Council* [1989] 3 All ER 523 at 531.

[34] See also IA 1986, s 74(1)(d). If the shares are fully-paid, the shareholders have no further liability as shareholders. Typically, shares are issued fully-paid (see **21-15**) and the model articles for private companies, if adopted, require the shares (other than shares taken on formation by the subscribers to the memorandum) to be fully-paid, see Companies (Model Articles) Regulations 2008, SI 2008/3229, reg 2, Sch 1, art 21.

[35] *Macaura v Northern Assurance Co* [1925] AC 619 at 626–7, HL; '… the corporator, even if he holds all the shares, is not the corporation … ' at 633, per Lord Wrenbury.

[36] *A-G's Reference (No 2 of 1982)* [1984] QB 624, CA.

otherwise, in its assets'.[37] The two sides of the coin can be described in 'asset partitioning' or 'entity shielding' terms, meaning that, as a consequence of separate legal personality, the entity's assets are shielded from the shareholders' creditors and, as a consequence of limited liability, the shareholders' assets are not available to meet the company's debts.[38] The company can employ people and can employ its controlling shareholder.[39] The company has perpetual existence and succession and this continuity is important and convenient. The membership may be constantly changing but the entity continues until steps are taken to bring it to an end through winding up. The company can sue and be sued in its own name and this is advantageous to third parties who do not have to concern themselves with identifying who are the shareholders at any given moment. Ultimately, it is the company which may go into insolvency.

**3-14** Sometimes the fact that the company is a distinct legal entity works to a shareholder's disadvantage and the courts are unwilling to allow a shareholder to elect to have the benefits without the disadvantages of incorporation. This is particularly true with regard to attempts by shareholders to claim for what is termed reflective loss, i.e. losses suffered by shareholders which are only reflective of loss suffered by the company and in respect of which the company should sue. In keeping with the separate legal personality of the company, the rule in *Foss v Harbottle*[40] establishes that where a wrong is done to the company, the company is the proper plaintiff in respect of it. It follows that a personal claim by a shareholder in respect of the diminution in value of his shareholding as a result of a wrong done to the company (for example, where the company has a claim in negligence against a third party) is misconceived and will be struck out. The shareholder's loss is merely reflective of the loss suffered by the company and that loss will be fully remedied if the company enforces its full rights against the wrongdoer.[41] This principle respects company autonomy and ensures that a party (the shareholder) does not recover compensation for a loss suffered by another (the company).[42] This issue of reflective loss is discussed in detail in Chapter 20, as is the rule in *Foss v Harbottle*.

**3-15** While the fundamental principle is that a company is an entity distinct from its shareholders, there are exceptions to the principle, for example a statute, typically for reasons of taxation and financial transparency, may require the separate legal entity to be disregarded, as where parent companies are required to prepare consolidated group accounts

---

[37] *Prest v Prest* [2013] 1 All ER 795 at [101]. A standard freezing order does not bring within the definition of a defendant's assets, the assets of a company which he controls: *Lakatamia Shipping Co Ltd v Su* [2015] 1 WLR 291 at [31]–[35], [41]–[42], [51]; *Group Seven Ltd v Allied Investment Corp Ltd* [2014] 1 WLR 735, though the order will prevent the defendant from diminishing the value of his assets which consist in part of his direct or indirect holding in the company. See Aitken, '"Ownership", "Control" and the Freezing Order' (2015) 131 LQR 26.

[38] See Kraakman et al, *The Anatomy of Corporate Law* (3rd edn, 2017), pp 6–10; also Hansmann and Kraakman, 'The Essential Role of Organizational Law' (2000) 110 Yale LJ 387.

[39] See *Lee v Lee's Air Farming Ltd* [1961] AC 12 where a controlling shareholder was a 'worker' for workers' compensation purposes when he was killed in the course of his work. A controlling shareholder of a company can be an employee of the company for the purposes of redundancy payments under the Employment Rights Act 1996, s 182, but whether such an employer/employee relationship exists in a particular case is a question of fact: the court must inquire as to whether a true contract of employment exists and the degree of an employee's shareholding and control of the company, even if total, is not ordinarily relevant to that inquiry: *Neufeld v Secretary of State for Business, Enterprise and Regulatory Reform* [2009] 2 BCLC 273.

[40] (1843) 2 Hare 461.

[41] *Prudential Assurance Co Ltd v Newman Industries Ltd (No 2)* [1982] 1 All ER 354 at 366–7; *Johnson v Gore Wood & Co* [2001] 1 BCLC 313, HL; see **20-73**.

[42] *Johnson v Gore Wood & Co* [2001] 1 BCLC 313 at 338, per Lord Bingham, HL.

showing the affairs of the parent and subsidiary undertakings.[43] More importantly, there is a discretionary jurisdiction whereby, in a variety of circumstances, the court may disregard or pierce or lift the corporate veil and look to those controlling the entity.

## B  Piercing the corporate veil

### Background

**3-16**  To understand the debate on the jurisdiction to pierce the corporate veil, some consideration of the background is needed.[44] Until recently, it was considered that there was a discretionary jurisdiction to pierce the corporate veil where special circumstances existed indicating that the company was a mere façade concealing the true facts, an articulation of the piercing doctrine stated by Lord Keith in *Woolfson v Strathclyde Regional Council*[45] which was much cited and endorsed, including in the Court of Appeal,[46] albeit on an obiter basis. There was a subsequent elaboration of the concept of 'mere façade' in *Adams v Cape Industries plc*.[47] Equally, the case law showed that the jurisdiction was quite limited[48] and, as Munby J pointed out in *Ben Hashem v Ali Shayif*[49] ' ... reported cases in any context where the claim has succeeded are few in number and striking on their facts'. There has always been a judicial concern not to create commercial uncertainty and undermine the benefits of incorporation. Having incorporated, shareholders have a legitimate expectation, as do those who deal with the incorporated entity, that the courts will respect the status of the entity and apply the principle of *Salomon v Salomon & Co Ltd* in the ordinary way.[50] To the extent that a piercing jurisdiction existed, the authorities on piercing which were commonly cited included *Gilford Motor Company v Horne*;[51] *Jones v Lipman*;[52] *Gencor ACP Ltd v Dalby*,[53] and *Trustor AB v Smallbone*;[54] though whether they were genuine veil-piercing cases was and is often disputed, as we shall see.

---

[43] See CA 2006, ss 399, 403–406. Other provisions, such as IA 1986, s 214 (liability for wrongful trading), are sometimes described as examples of statutory piercing of the corporate veil, but they are merely provisions which impose liabilities on directors as a consequence of their involvement in the running of a company and do nothing to undermine the company as a separate legal entity.

[44] The material which follows on piercing the corporate veil is derived in part from Hannigan, 'Wedded to *Salomon*: Evasion, Concealment and Confusion on Piercing the Veil of the One-Man Company' (2013) 50 Irish Jurist 11.

[45] (1979) 38 P & CR 521, HL. See generally Rixon, 'Lifting the Veil between Holding and Subsidiary Companies' (1986) 102 LQR 415.

[46] *Re H (restraint order: realisable property)* [1996] 2 BCLC 500 at 511; *Adams v Cape Industries plc* [1990] BCLC 479 at 515; *Ord v Belhaven Pubs Ltd* [1998] 2 BCLC 447 at 457; *Trustor AB v Smallbone* [2001] 2 BCLC 436; *Yukong Ltd of Korea v Rendsburg Investments* [1998] 2 BCLC 485. See also *Dadourian Group International Inc v Simms* [2006] EWHC 2973; *Lindsay v O'Loughnane* [2012] BCC 153. The issue of piercing the veil was also addressed in a number of family law authorities which are discussed in detail by Munby J in *Ben Hashem v Ali Shayif* [2009] 1 FLR 115; and by Rimer LJ in the Court of Appeal in *Prest v Prest* [2013] 1 All ER 795 at [111]–[150].

[47] [1990] BCLC 479, essentially that a 'façade' involves use of a corporate structure by a defendant to evade limitations on his conduct imposed by law or such rights of relief as third parties already possess against him, at 519.          [48] See *Ord v Belhaven* [1998] 2 BCLC 447 at 457.

[49] *Ben Hashem v Ali Shayif* [2009] 1 FLR 115 at [221].

[50] See *Adams v Cape Industries plc* [1990] BCLC 479 at 520; *Ord v Belhaven Pubs Ltd* [1998] 2 BCLC 447 at 457; *Ben Hashem v Ali Shayif* [2009] 1 FLR 115 at [221]; *Macdonald v Costello* [2011] 3 WLR 1341 at [23] and [32].          [51] [1933] Ch 935, CA.

[52] [1962] 1 All ER 442, Ch D.     [53] [2000] 2 BCLC 734, Ch D.     [54] [2001] 2 BCLC 436, Ch D.

**3-17** In *Gilford Motor Company v Horne*[55] a director of a company (Horne) was subject to a restraint of trade provision on leaving the company. Subsequently, he wished to carry on a competing business in breach of that contractual provision and he did so through a company set up with his wife and an employee as directors and shareholders. The court held that the company was formed as a device to mask the carrying on of business by Horne in breach of his pre-existing legal duty and an injunction was granted against him and the company, prohibiting each of them from acting in breach of the defendant's contractual obligations.

**3-18** In *Jones v Lipman*,[56] in an attempt to evade an order for specific performance, the defendant (Lipman) transferred a property to a company which he set up and of which he and a clerk of his solicitors were the only shareholders and directors. The court made an order for specific performance against the defendant and the company noting that the company was merely a mask used by the defendant to try to evade his pre-existing obligation to convey the property to the prior purchaser, the plaintiff.

**3-19** In *Gencor ACP Ltd v Dalby*[57] a director in breach of his fiduciary duty had profited personally by diverting to himself business opportunities which came to him as a director of the company. The company sought to recover the proceeds which had been paid to an offshore company wholly owned and controlled by the director, who tried to argue that he had not profited personally. Rimer J found that the offshore company had no staff or business and its only function was to receive these profits. In essence, the court said, it was no more than the director's offshore bank account. Rimer J considered that such a creature company was quite insufficient, in his words, to prevent equity identifying it with the director and he ordered that the company and the director were each accountable for the profits.[58]

**3-20** In *Trustor AB v Smallbone*[59] almost £39m had gone missing from the claimant company with £20m ending up in a company, I Ltd, which was essentially a front for S, the former managing director of the claimant company. The claimant sought summary judgment that S was jointly and severally liable with I Ltd which required that the corporate veil be pierced to establish that receipt by I Ltd was receipt by S.[60] Applying the test laid down in *Woolfson v Strathclyde Regional Council*,[61] Sir Andrew Morritt V-C, held that I Ltd was a device or façade used for the receipt of the claimant's money which had been misapplied by S. For piercing, he said, there must be impropriety linked to the use of the company structure to avoid or conceal liability for that impropriety.[62] The company was the means by which S committed unauthorised and inexcusable breaches of his duties as a director of the claimant company[63] and, on that basis, S had no defence to the claim that he had received the £20m.

**3-21** These authorities were summed up by Munby J in *Ben Hashem v Ali Shayif*[64] as follows:

> '... in each of these cases the wrongdoer controlled the company, which he used as a façade or device to facilitate and cover up his own wrongdoing—in the first two cases [*Gilford, Jones*] as a means of breaching his contract, in the latter two cases [*Gencor, Trustor*] as a means of receiving money for which he was accountable. In other words, in each of these cases there were present the twin features of *control* and *impropriety*.'

---

[55] [1933] Ch 935, CA.     [56] [1962] 1 All ER 442.     [57] [2000] 2 BCLC 734.
[58] [2000] 2 BCLC 734 at 744. As the Court of Appeal noted in *VTB Capital v Nutritek International Corp* [2012] 2 BCLC 437 at [70], the company was being used by Dalby as a mask or device to conceal his own interest in the secret profits for which he was accountable.     [59] [2001] 2 BCLC 436.
[60] [2001] 2 BCLC 436 at [13].     [61] (1979) 38 P & CR 521.     [62] [2001] 2 BCLC 436 at [22].
[63] [2001] 2 BCLC 436 at [25].     [64] [2009] 1 FLR 115 at [171].

While it was possible to impose some sort of order on the authorities, as Munby J suggested, there was also much criticism of the overall incoherence of the position reached[65] which was summed up by Lord Neuberger in *Prest v Petrodel Resources Ltd*[66] in the following terms:

'It is … clear from the cases and academic articles that the law relating to the doctrine is unsatisfactory and confused. Those cases and articles appear to me to suggest that (i) there is not a single instance in this jurisdiction where the doctrine has been invoked properly and successfully, (ii) there is doubt as to whether the doctrine should exist, and (iii) it is impossible to discern any coherent approach, applicable principles, or defined limitations to the doctrine.'

**3-22**  In *VTB Capital plc v Nutritek International Corpn*[67] Lord Neuberger drew attention to the fact that Lord Keith's views in *Woolfson v Strathclyde*[68] were obiter, brief, and his alone, and he pointed out that there was nothing to suggest that Lord Keith's position had been affirmed or approved by the House of Lords, merely an indication that the House of Lords was prepared to assume that the power to pierce the corporate veil existed. The *VTB Capital* case sparked renewed debate about the existence, nature, and extent of any doctrine of piercing the corporate veil.[69]

**3-23**  Fortuitously, the Supreme Court had an opportunity to address the doctrine shortly afterwards in *Prest v Petrodel Resources Ltd*[70] where the issue was the ability of the court in divorce proceedings to make orders in favour of a wife requiring companies wholly owned or controlled by the husband to transfer assets held by the companies[71] to the wife on the basis that this was property to which the husband was 'entitled in possession or reversion' for the purposes of the Matrimonial Causes Act 1973, s 24(1)(a).

**3-24**  The UK Supreme Court did hold in favour of the wife, overruling the Court of Appeal, which had dismissed her claim,[72] but it did not do so on the basis of piercing the veil, there

---

[65] See, for example, Tham, 'Piercing the Corporate Veil: Searching for Appropriate Choice of Law Rules' [2007] LMCLQ 22; Moore, '"A Temple Built on Faulty Foundations": Piercing the Corporate Veil and the Legacy of Salomon v Salomon' [2006] JBL 180; Lord Cooke of Thorndon, *Turning Points of the Common Law* (1997), Ch 1, 'A Real Thing: Salomon v A Salomon & Co Ltd'; Ottolenghi, 'From Peeping Behind the Corporate Veil to Ignoring it Completely' (1990) 53 MLR 338. See also Davies, *Introduction to Company Law* (2010), p 33 who suggests that no single explanation of the cases will be found and that company lawyers will not often have much to contribute to these debates, essentially because the true question is what is the purpose of the rule which it is alleged requires the veil to be pierced and does it require that the corporate personality be disregarded.      [66] [2014] 1 BCLC 30 at [64], and see too at [77].

[67] [2013] 1 BCLC 179 at [121].      [68] (1979) 38 P & CR 521.

[69] See Hare (2013) 72 CLJ 280; (2013) 34 Co Law 248; and n 70.

[70] [2013] 3 WLR 1, see Pey Woan Lee, 'The Enigma of Veil-piercing' (2015) 26 ICCLR 28; Tan Cheng-Han, 'Veil Piercing—a fresh start' [2015] JBL 20; Tjio, 'Lifting the Veil on Piercing the Veil' [2014] LMCLQ 19; Lim, 'Salomon Reigns' (2013) 129 LQR 480; Hare, 'Family Division, 0; Chancery Division,1: Piercing the Corporate Veil in the Supreme Court Again' (2013) 72 CLJ 511; Hannigan, 'Wedded to *Salomon*: Evasion, Concealment and Confusion on Piercing the Veil of the One-Man Company' (2013) 50 Irish Jurist 11; Rose, 'Raising the Corporate Sale' [2013] LMCLQ 566; Grantham, 'The Corporate Veil: An Ingenious Device' (2013) 32 Univ of Queensland LJ 311.

[71] An order in favour of the wife with respect to the husband's shareholdings (which were, obviously, his property) in these companies was not considered a useful option as neither the companies (incorporated in the Isle of Man) nor the husband were resident in the UK and it was considered that any order requiring him to transfer his shareholdings to her would have been unenforceable, hence the focus on obtaining orders with respect to properties in the UK.

[72] See [2013] 1 All ER 795 for a magisterial review of the *Salomon* principle by Rimer LJ.

being no use of the companies to evade a legal obligation of, or to frustrate the enforcement of, an existing legal right against the husband.[73] Rather, the way in which the companies acquired and paid for those assets meant, the court held, that they were held on resulting trust for the controller of the companies, i.e. the husband.[74] For the purposes of the Matrimonial Causes Act 1973, s 24(1)(a), therefore, the assets were assets to which he was 'entitled in possession or reversion' and against which orders could be made in the wife's favour.[75] This ruling raises the question whether creditors of a one-man company must consider the manner in which the company has acquired its assets, and from whom, and for what price, and must consider whether any of the company's assets are being used as the matrimonial home (it is not clear how a creditor would be in a position to ascertain whether this is the case or even whether the company is a one-man company[76]). It may be that assets which appear to be available to the company's creditors may be held instead on resulting trust for the shareholder and his/her creditors.[77]

**3-25** Leaving those matrimonial/creditor issues aside, our concern is with the approach taken by the Supreme Court to the veil-piercing jurisdiction. The leading judgment in *Prest* was given by Lord Sumption and, while all the justices were agreed on the outcome of the case, there were varying degrees of endorsement of Lord Sumption's views on piercing the corporate veil, as is discussed later. Strictly speaking, those views are obiter given that the case was decided on the basis of the assets being held by the companies on resulting trust for the husband. Nevertheless, it is clear that they will be influential in, if not determinative of, the future development of the law on this issue.

## The jurisdiction to pierce the corporate veil, *Prest v Petrodel Resources Ltd*

**3-26** As to the scope of the piercing jurisdiction, and therefore the exception to the *Salomon* principle that a company is a legal entity distinct from its shareholders, in *Prest v Petrodel Resources Ltd*[78] Lord Sumption stated the position in the following terms:

---

[73] The assets were held by the companies for tax planning and financial reasons and had been acquired by the companies years before the marriage was in difficulty.

[74] *Prest v Petrodel Resources Ltd* [2014] 1 BCLC 30 at [48]–[52], [57], [84], [97], [103], and [104].

[75] Lord Sumption went on to suggest, tentatively, that 'in the case of the matrimonial home, the facts are quite likely to justify the inference that the property was held on trust for a spouse who owned and controlled the company' see [2014] 1 BCLC 30 at [5], a view supported by Lady Hale, who suggested that it would often be the case that the companies will be mere nominees holding property on trust for the husband, at [93]. No other members of the court commented on this point regarding the matrimonial home. See *M v M* [2014] FLR 439 (properties held by companies were held on resulting trust for the husband).

[76] See comments by Rimer LJ in *Prest v Prest* [2013] 1 All ER 795 at [107]. Lord Sumption criticised the trial judge for making an order requiring the transfer of the properties, which in effect made the wife a secured creditor to the discomfort of the unsecured creditors of the companies with no knowledge of the state of the shareholder's marriage, at [41], but a finding of a resulting trust is to like effect.

[77] The decision may equally be confined to the facts, especially the failure of the husband and the companies to engage with the court proceedings and provide any explanation for the manner in which the assets were held, see [2014] 1 BCLC 30 at [4], [43]–[47]. It may be rare for the facts to support a resulting trust in this way and, even when they do, the trust is restricted to the family home, so it may have little overall impact on the assets held by companies in this scenario, see George, 'The Veil of Incorporation and Post-divorce Financial Remedies' (2014) 130 LQR 373; also George, 'Family Finances and the Corporate Veil' [2013] Fam Law 991.

[78] [2014] 1 BCLC 30 at [35]. He avoided the language of 'façade' and 'shams' which he thought unhelpful, see at [28]. On the powers of the family courts, the Supreme Court agreed wholeheartedly with the Court of Appeal and confirmed that there is no different or broader veil-piercing jurisdiction in the Family Division. As Lord Sumption commented, '… courts exercising family jurisdiction do not occupy a desert island in which general legal concepts are suspended or mean something different', at [37].

'I conclude that there is a limited principle of English law which applies when a person is under an existing legal obligation or liability or subject to an existing legal restriction which he deliberately evades or whose enforcement he deliberately frustrates by interposing a company under his control. The court may then pierce the corporate veil for the purpose, and only for the purpose, of depriving the company or its controller of the advantage that they would otherwise have obtained by the company's separate legal personality.'

Furthermore, piercing will be possible only if there is no other remedy available to the claimant for, Lord Sumption said, if it is not necessary to pierce, then it is not appropriate to do so because then there is no public policy imperative to justify piercing the veil.[79] Lords Neuberger and Clarke, in agreement with Lord Sumption, stressed that all other, more conventional, methods must have proved of no assistance if the court is to allow piercing.[80] Alternative remedies available to claimants would include, for example, in a case like *Yukong Line Ltd of Korea v Rendsburg Investments Corp of Liberia*[81] using powers in the Insolvency Act 1986 to challenge asset transfers between companies and the conduct of directors/controllers in authorising the transfers.[82] In other situations, it may be possible to impose a personal liability in tort on company controllers without the need to pierce the corporate veil to reach them. For example, in *VTB Capital plc v Nutritek International Corp*,[83] Lord Neuberger noted that piercing the veil was not needed to enable the claimant bank to get redress as, subject to jurisdictional issues, they were able to claim against the controllers of the company in deceit and conspiracy, the allegation being that the controllers were parties to a common design to defraud the bank.[84] In cases such as *Gilford Motor Company v Horne*[85] and *Jones v Lipman*,[86] ancillary relief orders can be sought.[87]

**3-27** Lord Sumption also considered that, when speaking of piercing the corporate veil, we should only be speaking of 'those cases which are true exceptions to the rule in *Salomon v A Salomon and Co Ltd* …, i.e. where a person who owns and controls a company is said in certain circumstances to be identified with it in law by virtue of that ownership and control'.[88]

---

[79] See Lord Sumption [2014] 1 BCLC 30 at [35]; and see at [96] (Lady Hale, with whom Lord Wilson agreed); at [97], [100] (Lord Mance). One of the notable features of the Supreme Court judgment in *Prest* is that there is remarkably little discussion of any policy basis from which the exception or exceptions to *Salomon* are to be derived, Lord Sumption merely noting, at [8], that companies have been the principal unit of commercial life for more than a century and that their separate legal personality and property are the basis on which third parties are entitled to and do deal with them; and, at [41], emphasising that that separate personality and property is crucial to the protection of the interests of the company's creditors. See Grantham, n 70, at 315 who notes the legalistic, formalistic, and technical approach of the Supreme Court which he says resonates clearly with that of the House of Lords in *Salomon*.

[80] See *Prest v Petrodel Resources Ltd* [2014] 1 BCLC 30 at [62] and [103], respectively. For a discussion of possible alternatives, see Day, 'Skirting around the Issue: The Corporate Veil after *Prest v Petrodel*' [2014] LMCLQ 269.     [81] [1998] 2 BCLC 485.

[82] See *Ord v Belhaven Pubs Ltd* [1998] 2 BCLC 447 at 458.

[83] [2013] 1 BCLC 179. See also *Alliance Bank JSC v Aquanta Corp* [2013] 1 All ER (Comm) 189 at [40], CA: a perfectly orthodox cause of action in that case lay, the court said, in an implied contract or in tort without any need to consider piercing the corporate veil.

[84] [2013] 1 BCLC 179 at [5] and [146]. See also *Lindsay v O'Loughnane* [2012] BCC 153; *Dadourian Group International Inc v Simms* [2006] EWHC 2973.     [85] [1933] Ch 935, CA.

[86] [1962] 1 All ER 442.

[87] It would have sufficed in *Jones* to have made the order for specific performance against Lipman, requiring him to procure the company, through his control of it, to convey the property; and for the injunction against Horne to restrain him, his servants and agents, see *VTB Capital plc v Nutritek International Corp* [2012] 2 BCLC 437 at [79]; also Lord Neuberger's comments in *Prest v Petrodel Resources Ltd* [2014] 1 BCLC 30 at [71]; and see Lim, 'Salomon Reigns' (2013) 129 LQR 480 at 483–4.     [88] [2014] 1 BCLC 30 at [16].

## Deliberate evasion

**3-28**  The evasion must be of some pre-existing obligation of X owed to Y which exists independently of the company's involvement[89] and piercing must not merely attempt to hold X liable for what in truth is an obligation of the company; the question is whose obligation is being evaded. In *Yukong Line Ltd of Korea v Rendsburg Investments Corp of Liberia*[90] a company wrongly repudiated a charterparty and the director and controller of the company (X) immediately moved the contents of the company's bank account to another entity with a view to putting those funds beyond the reach of any claim for wrongful repudiation by the ship-owner. It was argued that the corporate veil of the repudiating company should be pierced to make X a party to the charterparty and therefore personally liable in damages for the wrongful repudiation. Toulson J rejected any jurisdiction to pierce the corporate veil to make the controller of the company personally liable for the company's debts.[91] The wrong here is a breach of contract by the company for which the company is liable, there is no existing obligation of X with respect to the charterparty. In *VTB Capital plc v Nutritek International Corporation*,[92] the Supreme Court, applying *Yukong Line*, rejected a claim that the corporate veil might be pierced to render the company's controller party to and personally liable on loan agreements entered into between the company and the claimants.[93] As Lord Sumption noted, the fundamental objection to the argument in *VTB Capital plc* was that piercing the corporate veil was being invoked so as to create a new liability that would not otherwise have existed.[94] There must be an evasion of existing obligations, rather than potential future liabilities, for the management of future risk is the common purpose of incorporation.[95]

**3-29**  The interposed company must be controlled by X, directly or indirectly, since the improper use alleged is the interposition of the company to defeat some duty or obligation owed by X to Y. For example, in *Gilford Motor Co v Horne*[96] the company was considered to be controlled by X though the directors and shareholders were X's wife and an employee; in *Trustor v Smallbone*[97] the company was owned and controlled by a Lichtenstein trust of which X was a beneficiary; in *Jones v Lipman*,[98] X and a clerk of his solicitors were the shareholders and directors of the company; in *Gencor ACP Ltd v Dalby*,[99] the company was wholly owned and controlled by X. Conversely, the presence of

---

[89] [2014] 1 BCLC 30 at [28]. See Tjio 'Lifting the Veil on Piercing the Veil' [2014] LMCLQ 19 at 23–4 who supports the approach in *Prest* on the basis that it allows for piercing where persons try to use the separate entity to protect assets from their own creditors or to escape some immediate liability pressing on them but withhold piercing where the issue is liabilities arising from a business that is owned by the company, as in *VTB Capital plc v Nutritek International Corpn* [2012] 2 BCLC 437, for example. On this basis, he considers that the decision will bring some certainty to this area.           [90] [1998] 2 BCLC 485.

[91] Incidentally, it would have been appropriate to have pierced the veil of the recipient company in *Yukong Line* to follow assets which had been transferred away in that case, but that relief was not sought.

[92] [2013] 1 BCLC 179, aff'g [2012] 2 BCLC 431.

[93] To have held to the contrary would amount to a jurisdiction to subject parties to contractual obligations under a contract to which neither they, nor the only undisputed parties to the contract, had ever agreed or intended they should be subject, as Lloyd LJ put it in the Court of Appeal, see [2012] 2 BCLC 437 at [95].

[94] See *Prest v Petrodel Resources Ltd* [2014] 1 BCLC 30 at [34]. See too *Ord v Belhaven Pubs Ltd* [1998] 2 BCLC 447, where an attempt to make the shareholders liable for the company's acts (by substituting the company's shareholders, as defendants, for the company in certain litigation) was decisively rejected. As the court noted, if the claimants wanted to sue the shareholders, in effect they would have to find a new cause of action against a new party; also *MacDonald Dickens & Macklin v Costello* [2012] QB 244, CA (there was no basis for providing a remedy in restitution directly against the shareholders of a company because of the company's breach of contract).                    [95] See *Adams v Cape Industries plc* [1990] BCLC 479.

[96] [1933] Ch 935.        [97] [2001] 2 BCLC 436.        [98] [1962] 1 All ER 442.

[99] [2000] 2 BCLC 734.

unconnected shareholders means that the veil cannot be pierced, for then the company cannot be identified with its controller.[100] The company need not be set up for the purpose of evasion, though that is often the case; it suffices if it is being used for evasion at the time of the transactions in issue.[101] The motive behind the use (not necessarily the incorporation) of the company must be a deliberate evasion of obligations or liabilities of X or the deliberate frustration of enforcement measures against X.[102] The focus is on the dishonest use of the company for an evasive purpose.[103]

**3-30**   The decision in *Prest v Petrodel Resources Ltd* constrains the piercing jurisdiction within such narrow confines that it could have been abolished as being of little consequence, it would seem, and indeed Lords Sumption and Neuberger considered abolition, but they concluded in favour of retaining the jurisdiction in order to have some flexibility for novel situations not yet envisaged,[104] though it must be doubtful that it will be called upon.

### Evasion v concealment

**3-31**   In defining the principle, Lord Sumption drew what he said was a critical distinction between evasion and concealment, while conceding that many of the cases involve both elements. He said:[105]

> 'The concealment principle is legally banal and does not involve piercing the corporate veil at all. It is that the interposition of a company or perhaps several companies so as to conceal the identity of the real actors will not deter the courts from identifying them, assuming that their identity is legally relevant. In these cases the court is not disregarding the "facade", but only looking behind it to discover the facts which the corporate structure is concealing. The evasion principle is different. It is that the court may disregard the corporate veil if there is a legal right against the person in control of it which exists independently of the company's involvement, and a company is interposed so that the separate legal personality of the company will defeat the right or frustrate its enforcement. Many cases will fall into both categories, but in some circumstances the difference between them may be critical.'

**3-32**   Lord Neuberger agreed with this 'evasion-piercing' versus 'concealment-lifting' analysis,[106] noting that a similar point had been made by Staughton LJ in *Atlas Maritime*

---

[100]   *Trustor v Smallbone* [2001] 2 BCLC 436 at [14], [20]. For example, in *Ben Hashem v Ali Shayif* [2009] 1 FLR 115 the presence of genuine third party shareholders with real minority interests was one of the grounds on which the court refused to pierce the corporate veil, see at [193]. Of course, the court will have regard to the extent of the unconnected interests and, where they are de minimis, the court may still identify the company with its controller.

[101]   This point was made by Munby J in *Ben Hashem v Ali Shayif* [2009] 1 FLR 115 at [164], [165], approved in all material respects by the Court of Appeal in *VTB Capital plc* [2012] 2 BCLC 437 at [78]; it was repeated, without qualification, by Lord Sumption in *Prest v Petrodel Resources Ltd* [2014] 1 BCLC 30 at [25]; and see [2013] 1 All ER 795 at [145], CA. This point seems to have been misunderstood in *R v Sale* [2014] 1 WLR 663 at [39].

[102]   *Prest v Petrodel Resources Ltd* [2014] 1 BCLC 30 at [35]; a point which the Court of Appeal had emphasised in *Adams v Cape* [1990] BCLC 479 at 516, 518.

[103]   *Prest v Petrodel Resources Ltd* [2014] 1 BCLC 30 at [18], [89]; see also *VTB Capital plc v Nutritek International Corpn* [2012] 2 BCLC 437 at [80].

[104]   See [2014] 1 BCLC 30 at [27] (Lord Sumption), at [79]–[80] (Lord Neuberger). See also Pey Woan Lee, n 70, at 30, 32, who notes that defining piercing by reference to evasion renders the jurisdiction otiose and extraordinarily narrow in scope.       [105]   *Prest v Petrodel Resources Ltd* [2014] 1 BCLC 30 at [28].

[106]   *Prest v Petrodel Resources Ltd* [2014] 1 BCLC 30 at [60]–[61].

*Co SA v Avalon Maritime Ltd, The Coral Rose (No 1)*[107] who considered 'lifting' to involve having regard to the shareholdings for some legal purpose. Lord Neuberger considered that evasion is the *only* basis for piercing the corporate veil, though he undermined his apparent support for a veil-piercing jurisdiction at all by saying that the approach may just be an example of the general principle that fraud unravels everything,[108] or possibly just an application of agency or trusteeship law.[109] Lord Mance agreed on evasion as the basis for piercing,[110] but considered that there may be other exceptions to the *Salomon* principle, before also noting that the strength of the *Salomon* principle and the other tools available to the law mean that any other exception would be novel, very rare, and difficult to establish,[111] a point with which Lord Clarke agreed.[112]

**3-33**  The question is whether the pivotal distinction which Lord Sumption drew between concealment and evasion is justified, with lifting permissible in concealment cases but piercing permitted only in the limited evasion context discussed earlier. Despite what Lord Sumption says, lifting the veil, looking behind the company to see who the 'real actors' are, where their identity is legally relevant,[113] seems little different in effect to piercing the veil to identify whether there is an evasion of rights or frustration of enforcement by the 'real actors'.

**3-34**  There would be a distinction if piercing the corporate veil resulted in the controllers of the entity becoming liable for the company's obligations but, as discussed at **3-28**, in *VTB Capital plc v Nutritek International Group plc*[114] the Supreme Court emphatically rejected (as the lower courts had) any suggestion that veil piercing, even if granted, could have the consequence that the puppeteers might be made party to the puppet's contracts and liable

---

[107] [1991] 4 All ER 769 at 779.

[108] *Prest v Petrodel Resources Ltd* [2014] 1 BCLC 30 at [83], though in Lord Neuberger's view, if the piercing doctrine goes wider than that 'fraud unravels all', it should be a matter for Parliament. Lord Sumption, too, seems to support the view that piercing is an aspect of the fraud principle: see at [18]. See too Rimer LJ in the Court of Appeal, *Prest v Prest* [2013] 1 All ER 795 at [156], who similarly sees the piercing jurisdiction as 'perhaps a relative of the principle that a wrongdoer cannot ordinarily be allowed to profit from his own wrong'. See also Beatson LJ in *Antonio Gramsci Shipping Corp v Lembergs* [2013] 4 All ER 157 at [66], on the difficulty of further common law development of the law in this area in the absence of agreement in the Supreme Court on an underlying principle or principles.

[109] *Prest v Petrodel Resources Ltd* [2014] 1 BCLC 30 at [81]–[83], agency or trusteeship because of the words 'under his control' in Lord Sumption's statement of the principle, at [35], set out in the text at **3-26**.

[110] Lady Hale (with whom Lord Wilson agreed) did not express a clear view on the restriction of the piercing jurisdiction to evasion, commenting merely that she was not entirely sure that all the cases can be classified as evasion or concealment cases, and suggesting that the 'piercing' case law might just be seen as examples of the law preventing people who operate limited companies from taking unconscionable advantage of those with whom they do business, see [2014] 1 BCLC 30 at [92]. In so far as the latter point is a variant on the argument that the corporate veil can be pierced in the interests of justice, that basis has been rejected by the courts repeatedly: see *Adams v Cape Industries plc* [1990] BCLC 479 at 512–13; *Trustor AB v Smallbone* [2001] 2 BCLC 436 at [14], [21]; *Ord v Belhaven Pubs Ltd* [1998] 2 BCLC 447 at 457; *Yukong Line Ltd of Korea v Rendsburg Investments Corp of Liberia* [1998] 2 BCLC 485 at 497.

[111] *Prest v Petrodel Resources Ltd* [2014] 1 BCLC 30 at [97]–[100], [102].

[112] *Prest v Petrodel Resources Ltd* [2014] 1 BCLC 30 at [103]. Lord Walker, at [106], limited himself to commenting that in his view there is no doctrine or principle at all of piercing the corporate veil, the term being merely a descriptive label, often used indiscriminately, to describe the disparate occasions on which some rule of law produces apparent exceptions to the principle of the separate juristic personality of a body corporate reaffirmed by the House of Lords in *Salomon*.

[113] *Prest v Petrodel Resources Ltd* [2014] 1 BCLC 30 at [28].

[114] [2013] 1 BCLC 179, aff'g [2012] 2 BCLC 437, CA and Ch D.

accordingly.[115] This unanimity of view in *VTB Capital plc* that there is no question of contractual obligations of the company being extended to the controllers means that the piercing doctrine in England poses no threat to *Salomon* and the linked principle of limited liability. As Warren J vividly put it in *Dadourian Group International Inc v Simms*,[116] the court in *Gilford Motor Co v Horne*[117] did not make Mr Horne liable for the company's electricity bill. The consequence of piercing is merely to address the particular wrong which merits the court exercising the jurisdiction in the first place.[118] For example, when the court pierces the veil because a company is being used to evade a contractual obligation, as in *Gilford Motor Co v Horne*,[119] the consequence is the enforcement of that contractual obligation, or, if the veil is pierced because the company is being used to hide assets, as in *Trustor v Smallbone*,[120] the consequence is an order for the recovery of the assets. Piercing is a limited operation with limited consequences rather than a wholesale disregard of the fact of incorporation. The consequence of piercing will depend therefore on the nature of the wrong which warrants piercing in the first place. As Lord Sumption stated, piercing the corporate veil is for the purpose of depriving the company or its controller of the advantage they would have obtained by the company's separate legal personality,[121] but lifting the corporate veil is usually for the same reason—to identify the shareholders so as to attach some consequence to them which typically denies them an advantage they or the company would have obtained from the company's separate legal personality.

**3-35**   On Lord Sumption's analysis, he considered only *Gilford Motor Co v Horne*[122] and *Jones v Lipman*[123] to be piercing cases, with *Gencor v Dalby*[124] and *Trustor v Smallbone*[125] being lifting or concealment cases. *Gilford* is a true piercing case, in Lord Sumption's view, because the employer had a legal right which he could enforce against Horne who interposed a company so as to defeat the right or frustrate its enforcement. Piercing deprived Horne of the benefit which he might otherwise have derived from the separate legal personality of the company.[126] Likewise in *Jones v Lipman*,[127] where the plaintiff's right to specific performance would have been frustrated unless the company was treated as

---

[115] See also *Linsen International Ltd v Humpuss Transportasi Kimia* [2011] EWCA Civ 1042 at [12], aff'g [2011] 2 Lloyd's Rep 663. There is no support for such a position in the authorities other than the now discredited decisions of Burton J in *Antonio Gramsci Shipping Corp v Stepanovs* [2012] 1 BCLC 561 and *Alliance Bank JSC v Aquanta Corp* [2012] 1 Lloyd's Rep 181: see *Antonio Gramsci Shipping Corp v Recoletos Ltd* [2012] 2 Lloyd's Rep 365 at [54]–[55].

[116] [2006] EWHC 2973 at [682].      [117] [1933] Ch 935.

[118] *VTB Capital plc v Nutritek International Corp* [2013] 1 BCLC 179, aff'g [2012] 2 BCLC 437. See Munby J in *Ben Hashem v Ali Shayif* [2009] 1 FLR 115 at [164]: once the requirements for piercing are satisfied, 'the court will pierce the veil only so far as is necessary to provide a remedy for the particular wrong which those controlling the company have done'. Also Warren J in *Dadourian Group International Ltd v Simms* [2006] EWHC 2973 at [682]: '... if the veil is to be lifted, it is to be lifted for the purposes of the relevant transaction.' See also *La Générale des Carrières et des Mines v FG Hemisphere Associates LLC* [2013] 1 All ER 409, PC.

[119] [1931] Ch 935. See Tham, 'Piercing the Corporate Veil: Searching for Appropriate Choice of Law Rules' [2007] LMCLQ 22 at 29–31, who argues that this case and also *Jones v Lipman* [1962] 1 WLR 832 should not be seen as veil-piercing cases at all but as examples of equitable relief for breaches of contract or conduct inducing breaches of contract.      [120] [2001] 2 BCLC 436.

[121] *Prest v Petrodel Resources Ltd* [2014] 1 BCLC 30 at [35]. Relief can be granted against the company on the basis of an anterior wrong by the controller of the company who is using the company to immunise himself from liability and the relief against the company can be justified as an exercise by the court of a discretionary jurisdiction to do what is convenient in the circumstances: *VTB Capital plc v Nutritek International Corpn* [2012] 2 BCLC 437 at [92], [94], CA.

[122] [1933] Ch 935, CA.      [123] [1962] 1 All ER 442.      [124] [2000] 2 BCLC 734.
[125] [2001] 2 BCLC 436.      [126] *Prest v Petrodel Resources Ltd* [2014] 1 BCLC 30 at [29].
[127] [1962] 1 All ER 442.

being under the same obligation as Lipman to convey the property to the plaintiff.[128] Lord Neuberger, for his part, thought that neither *Gilford* nor *Jones* provides much direct support for piercing the corporate veil[129] and, for him, *Gilford* is a case of concealment,[130] so illustrating the difficulties of applying this categorisation. Arguably, both *Gilford* and *Jones* can be seen as cases in which the court lifted the corporate veil to see whether Horne and Lipman were behind the relevant companies and were therefore in breach of their existing legal obligations.

**3-36**  Turning to *Gencor v Dalby*[131] and *Trustor v Smallbone*,[132] for Lord Sumption the true legal relationship between the controllers and their interposed companies in these cases was that the companies never held the money (secret profits/misappropriated funds made/ taken by their controllers in breach of their duties as directors of third companies) in their own right, but as agents for their controllers.[133] Hence receipt by the company gave rise to ordinary equitable remedies against both the company (as a third party involved in a breach of duty) and the controller (for breach of duty). The crucial point for Lord Sumption was that neither controller had used the company's separate legal personality to evade a liability they would otherwise have had,[134] and hence they are concealment cases. True, Dalby and Smallbone each remained liable for breach of duty, but in each case the interposed company was intended to frustrate enforcement measures against the interposed company's controllers by concealing the whereabouts of the secret profits/ misappropriated funds. On that basis, applying Lord Sumption's analysis and contrary to his conclusions, *Gencor v Dalby* and *Trustor v Smallbone* arguably are piercing cases. Equally, they can be seen as lifting cases, where the court has lifted the veil of incorporation of the companies in question to identify the company's shareholders as Dalby and Smallbone and find their receipt of the secret profits/misappropriated funds, so denying them the advantage of the recipient company's corporate personality.

**3-37**  If we turn to some other examples of lifting the veil, we can see that the consequence is often to deny the controller the advantage of legal personality. For example, in *Atlas Maritime Co SA v Avalon Maritime Ltd, The Coral Rose (No 1)*[135] the consequence of lifting the corporate veil was to identify a creditor of a company subject to an asset freezing order

---

[128]  *Prest v Petrodel Resources Ltd* [2014] 1 BCLC 30 at [30].

[129]  *Prest v Petrodel Resources Ltd* [2014] 1 BCLC 30 at [69], a view he had expressed previously in *VTB Capital v Nutritek International Corp* [2013] 1 BCLC 179 at [134]–[135], essentially seeing *Gilford* as an agency case and *Jones* as a case where the order there made could have been made against any third party, whether a company or the defendant's wife would have made no difference; alternatively, he suggested that the sale in *Jones* could have been regarded as a sham transaction.

[130]  [2014] 1 BCLC 30 at [70].     [131]  *Prest v Petrodel Resources Ltd* [2000] 2 BCLC 734.

[132]  [2001] 2 BCLC 436.

[133]  The relevant factors in the agency were the ownership and control of the company, the circumstances and source of the receipts, and the nature of the company's other transactions if any: see *Prest v Petrodel Resources Ltd* [2014] 1 BCLC 30 at [32].

[134]  *Prest v Petrodel Resources Ltd* [2014] 1 BCLC 30 at [33]. Lord Sumption, at [33], also distinguishes these cases from *Gilford* and from *Jones* on the basis that, in those cases, Horne and Lipman had a liability which arose independently of the involvement of the company, but so did Dalby and Smallbone (a liability for breach of duty to their companies), so it is difficult to follow this argument.

[135]  [1991] 4 All ER 769. See also *Daimler v Continental Tyre Co* [1916] 2 AC 307 at 345, where the House of Lords considered that, although a company was incorporated as an English company, it might be appropriate in some circumstances to look at the enemy character of the shareholders, lift the veil in effect, with the result that the company, though English in form, might be an enemy alien with whom trading was illegal. Also *Re H* [1996] 2 BCLC 500, CA (veil lifted to prevent defendants using corporate structures to hide their assets from receivers appointed by HMRC); also *BCCI v BRS Kumar Bros Ltd* [1994] 1 BCLC 211.

as the parent company and 100 per cent shareholder of the company, which enabled the court to conclude that the company should not be allowed to make a payment to its 'creditor' in the ordinary course of business, the transfer being intended to evade the purpose of the asset freezing order by allowing assets to be put beyond the reach of the beneficiary of the freezing order. In *Aveling Barford Ltd v Perion Ltd*[136] the court lifted the corporate veil so as to reveal that an apparent sale of assets to a company at an undervalue was in fact an unlawful distribution of assets by the vendor company to its controlling shareholder who was also the controller of the purchasing company. In *R v Sale*[137] X had paid bribes to help secure contracts for his wholly owned company which proceeded to carry out the contracts in an entirely satisfactory way. The court lifted the veil of the company to identify X with the company for the purpose of quantifying X's liability to account for benefits obtained by him from his criminal conduct.

**3-38**  These cases are examples of lifting the veil to see if a transaction with company Y, which X could not enter into or does not wish to appear to enter into, is in fact with or for the benefit of X where that fact is legally significant. It is possible then to distinguish piercing and lifting scenarios, but the consequence of each exercise is the same, to deny X an advantage which he would dishonestly have obtained from the use of a corporate structure.

**3-39**  It is clear, looking at the authorities, that the line which Lord Sumption has drawn between lifting and piercing, between evasion and concealment, is difficult to apply consistently and objectively, even if the factual scenarios can be distinguished. Concealment is inherent in many evasion cases, indeed evasion is commonly achieved through concealment, as Lord Sumption acknowledged.[138] Also, the language of lifting and piercing is used interchangeably as Lord Neuberger accepted in *VTB Capital plc v Nutritek International Corp*,[139] suggesting that, in truth, there may be little difference between 'piercing' and 'lifting' the corporate veil. Yet, following *Prest*, there is a narrow, defined, basis for piercing the corporate veil, while the basis for lifting the veil is not determined, although it would seem implicit in Lord Sumption's description of the concealment principle (and therefore the lifting jurisdiction) as 'legally banal',[140] that he sees it as an unconstrained jurisdiction to look through the company to identify the real actors when legally relevant to do so.[141] Lord Clarke alone in *Prest* rejected the distinction between evasion and concealment and the restriction of piercing to evasion cases, noting that it had not been discussed in argument and should not be adopted until the court has heard detailed submissions about it.[142] It would seem that, as the piercing jurisdiction withers into obsolescence, the debate as to the extent of exceptions to the *Salomon* principle continues with

---

[136] [1989] BCLC 626.

[137] [2013] EWCA Crim 1306, [2014] 1 WLR 663; and see *R v Boyle Transport (Northern Ireland) Ltd* [2016] BCC 746 at [111], agreeing that *R v Sale* is a concealment case. See also *Airbus Operations Ltd v Withey* [2014] EWHC 1126 (corporate veil could be lifted where the companies in question had been used to conceal the receipt of secret commissions by the companies' controllers in breach of duty).

[138] *Prest v Petrodel Resources Ltd* [2014] 1 BCLC 30 at [28].

[139] [2013] 1 BCLC 179 at [118]–[119]. See also *La Générale des Carrières et des Mines v FG Hemisphere Associates LLC* [2013] 1 All ER 409, PC at [30] (dealing with a state-owned entity) where Lord Mance likewise seemed to suggest that there is no distinction, the question in that context being whether it 'would be appropriate to look through or past the entity to the state, lifting the veil of incorporation'. In *Prest* in the Court of Appeal, Rimer LJ in his magisterial review of the law refers throughout, interchangeably, to piercing and lifting, see [2013] 1 All ER 795 at [122], [132], [140]–[143], [154].

[140] *Prest v Petrodel Resources Ltd* [2014] 1 BCLC 30 at [28].

[141] See *R v Boyle Transport (Northern Ireland) Ltd* [2016] BCC 746.

[142] *Prest v Petrodel Resources Ltd* [2014] 1 BCLC 30 at [103].

just a change in terminology, the question now being as to the scope of the jurisdiction to lift the corporate veil coupled with greater use of agency, trust, tort, and the criminal law etc, i.e. some other legal basis for the allocation of liabilities.[143]

**3-40**   The Privy Council had the opportunity to apply *Prest* in *Persad v Singh*[144] where a lessor sought to pierce the veil of a corporate lessee in order to attach personal liability to the sole shareholder and director when the lessee defaulted on its obligations under the lease. The lessor had negotiated the lease with the individual, but the lease was executed by the company, a fact that was appreciated by the lessor. The Privy Council overruled the courts in Trinidad and Tobago and refused to pierce the corporate veil. Lord Neuberger noted that the facts did not begin to justify piercing the veil, relying on *Prest*. In this case, the individual was not under any relevant legal obligation or liability to the lessor at the time when the company executed the lease. The fact that the company was a one-man company (which seemed to have been regarded as crucial by the local courts) was also considered. On this issue, Lord Neuberger said:[145]

> 'The fact that [the company] was a "one man company" is also irrelevant: see *Salomon v A Salomon and Co Ltd* ... which famously established the difference between a company and its shareholders. That case also exposes the fallacy of the notion that the court can pierce the veil where the purpose of an individual interposing a company into a transaction was to enable the individual who owned or controlled the company to avoid personal liability. One of the reasons that an individual, either on their own or together with others, will take advantage of limited liability is to avoid personal liability if things go wrong, ... If such a factor justified piercing the veil of incorporation, it would make something of a mockery of limited liability both in principle and in practice.'

### The evolving jurisdiction post-*Prest*—lessons from confiscation

**3-41**   These lifting/piercing veil issues can be usefully examined in the context of confiscation orders under the Proceeds of Crime Act 2002. Essentially, an individual who is convicted of a crime can be the subject of confiscation order which is intended to recover the benefit received by the wrongdoer from the criminal activity and a receiver can be appointed to recover the amount from the realisable property of the individual. In *Salomon* terms, the question is whether a benefit received by a company is received by the individual shareholder who has been convicted of some wrongdoing and whether assets held by a company owned by the shareholder are realisable property of the individual. The point can be illustrated by *R v Sale*[146] where bribes were paid by X, a director, in order to secure contracts for his company which was 100 per cent owned by him. The Court of Criminal Appeal accepted that the profit made by the company on these contracts was the benefit received by X. Other examples would include *Jennings v Crown Prosecution Service*[147] where the company was used as a vehicle for a fraud and the two controllers (Jennings being one—he was an employee, not a shareholder or director) were convicted. The benefit received by the company was treated as the benefit received by Jennings.

**3-42**   The issue was considered in detail by the Court of Criminal Appeal in *R v Boyle Transport (Northern Ireland) Ltd*[148] which offers a valuable discussion, post-*Prest*, of the lifting and

---

[143]   See Pey Woan Lee, n 70, at 32.        [144]   [2017] BCC 779.        [145]   [2017] BCC 779 at [20].

[146]   [2014] 1 WLR 663.        [147]   [2008] 1 AC 1046.

[148]   [2016] BCC 746. See Laird, 'Piercing the Corporate Veil in Confiscation Proceedings' (2017) 133 LQR 217; Fortson, '*R v Boyle*' [2016] Crim LR 658–64; Liptrap (2016) 37 Co Law 345.

piercing jurisdiction. The company was a haulage company which had operated for many years on the basis of tachograph tampering which meant that their drivers were able to drive for hours well beyond the legal limits, so significantly increasing the profits of the business. It was a family business and the father and a son were described as 'the operating mind'. They were the sole directors and held 50.1 per cent of the shares. Other family members (wife and two sons) held the remainder of the shares, but they were not directors. When the law closed in, the assets of the 'old' company were transferred to a 'new' company under the same ownership. Confiscation orders initially were made by consent and the lower court treated the turnover and net assets of the company (old and new) as, respectively, the benefit received by, and the realisable property of, the father and son. A receiver was appointed over the new company's assets which successfully appealed to have the order set aside, on the basis that it was not justifiable to treat the turnover of the company as benefit obtained by the individuals or to treat the assets of the company as realisable property of the individuals.

**3-43**    The Court of Criminal Appeal reverted to orthodox *Salomon* principles. On the basis of *Salomon*, the court said, to conclude that the turnover or a major part of it was benefit obtained by the individuals personally would be an 'unjustified departure ... from established principles of company law and an unjustified application of the doctrine of lifting or piercing the corporate veil'[149] (note the court using the terms interchangeably). Any benefit obtained by the individuals should have been assessed, counsel submitted (and the court considered his arguments essentially correct), by reference to the extra remuneration, dividends, and any other benefits or pecuniary advantages accruing to them personally, occasioned by the enhanced profitability of the company by reason of it being operated in an illegal way.[150] The court noted that the rules on piercing identified in *Prest* apply to criminal and civil proceedings and apply in the same way in all contexts, whether they are family disputes, contracts, confiscation proceedings etc.[151] The Court of Criminal Appeal acknowledged that, in a number of confiscation proceedings, the court appeared to equate the individual with the company, but the court said these decisions can be explained on the basis of (a) concessions by the defendants, and (b) the fact that criminality was involved and often there was concealment of that criminality. The companies involved could be described as facades or shams or alter egos and, the court said, 'many of the cases of this kind are clear examples of the concealment principle',[152] such as *Jennings*[153] and *Sale*.[154] In cases of criminality of this nature, the confiscation order should reflect the gross takings of the criminal enterprise.[155] In cases where the business is legitimate, but has been conducted illegally, as in *Boyle*, a different calculation may be needed, focused on the benefit received or obtained by the individual.[156]

**3-44**    The Court of Criminal Appeal also noted that, in many of the confiscation cases, such as *R v Sale*, the wrongdoer has been the sole shareholder, but that fact is not a conclusive fact, since the very essence of *Salomon* is that merely being a sole shareholder does not make the company his alter ego.[157] Decisions which seem to put a great stress on the fact that

---

149    [2016] BCC 746 at [85].        150    [2016] BCC 746 at [82], [85].        151    [2016] BCC 746 at [91]–[92].
152    [2016] BCC 746 at [94].        153    [2016] BCC 746 at [94], [109].
154    [2016] BCC 746 at [94], [111]. Laird, n 148, makes the point that the decision in *Boyle* seems to point prosecutors to establishing (other than by 100 per cent control) that the company is an alter ego, since then a confiscation order can extend to all the turnover and assets, but the decision gives no guidance on the facts which will result in the company being categorized as the alter ego of its controller.
155    [2016] BCC 746 at [95].        156    [2016] BCC 746 at [127], [128].
157    [2016] BCC 746 at [96], [115], [117].

the individuals were sole shareholders must not be taken as an invitation to the courts in confiscation cases to regard sole ownership and control of a company as necessarily and always sufficient *of itself* to justify treating the company as the alter ego of the defendant.[158] Rather these cases should be confined to their facts and, if need be, the court should apply the concealment principle and lift the veil to identify the benefit received by individuals.[159]

**3-45**   Returning to the facts in *R v Boyle Transport (Northern Ireland) Ltd*, no case either for lifting or for piercing the corporate veil had been made out.[160] The company was not the alter ego of the individuals. It was a company with a business and an existence of its own with other shareholders, so there was no basis for equating its turnover and assets with benefit received by the individual wrongdoers. The matter was remitted to the lower court to reassess the benefit received by the individuals.

**3-46**   Another authority to note is *R v Powell*[161] where a company was in breach of waste regulations and was convicted of criminal offences. A director and significant shareholder (Powell) was also convicted on the basis that she consented to or connived in the company's offence, which is a common basis for holding directors criminally liable at the same time and on the same basis as the company. A confiscation order was made against her with respect to salary and other direct benefits accruing to her in her individual capacity. Significant clean-up costs arose consequent on the company's breach of the law but the judge ruled that Powell could not be held liable for the company's pecuniary advantage in avoiding the costs involved in cleaning up the site. The Crown appealed that refusal. Applying *Boyle*, the Court of Criminal Appeal noted that the company had a legitimate business, Powell was not the sole shareholder, her liability was based on connivance or consent (i.e. not a primary liability, but parasitic on the company's offence), and she had made a considerable investment in the business. The business was lawful until it became unlawful through breach of the regulations. There was no facade or concealment by hiding behind the company's structure in a way which abused the corporate shield. It was neither a case of concealment nor evasion, rather the facts pointed away from it being a case where a benefit obtained by a company should be treated in law as a benefit obtained by the individual criminal.[162]

## C  The corporate group—separate entities or single unit

### Separate legal entities

**3-47**   As noted, the decision in *Salomon v Salomon & Co Ltd*[163] legitimated the one-man company and from that evolved the modern phenomenon of the corporate group with subsidiary companies owned by corporate shareholders.[164] The English courts have been robust

---

[158] [2016] BCC 746 at [119]. If there is a concern that some benefit is not within reach of an order, the solution, to capture all of the benefit, is to charge the company and then apply confiscation proceedings to the company while acknowledging that a corporate prosecution is often not possible for various reasons including insolvency, at [120]–[121]; and see Laird, n 148.            [159] [2016] BCC 746 at [119].

[160] [2016] BCC 746 at [108].        [161] [2016] EWCA Crim 1043, [2017] Env LR 11.

[162] [2016] EWCA Crim 1043, [2017] Env LR 11 at [32].        [163] [1897] AC 22, HL.

[164] As the Reflection Group Report noted, the international group of companies has become *the* prevailing form of European large-sized enterprises, based on the optimal combination of central control exercised by the parent company and local autonomy granted to subsidiaries, a feature which regulation should not ignore: see *Report of the Reflection Group on the Future of EU Company Law* (April 2011) (Expert report to European Commission).

in their application of the *Salomon* principle in this group context. As the Court of Appeal commented in *Adams v Cape Industries plc*:[165]

'[S]ave in cases which turn on the wording of particular statutes or contracts, the court is not free to disregard the principle of *Salomon v Salomon & Co Ltd* merely because it considers that justice so requires. Our law, for better or worse, recognises the creation of subsidiary companies, which though in one sense the creatures of their parent companies, will nevertheless under the general law fall to be treated as separate legal entities with all the rights and liabilities which would normally attach to separate legal entities ...'

**3-48**　It is sometimes suggested that this adherence to a strict *Salomon* approach, affording separate legal status to each entity, is inappropriate in the modern business world where much commercial activity is carried on in corporate groups in a way which could not have been envisaged in 1897. Various alternative approaches have been proposed from time to time such as, for example, that the courts should allow the corporate veil to be pierced more freely in the group context. More fundamentally, it is argued that the law should develop a mechanism whereby obligations and responsibilities could attach to the group and not to individual companies. In this way, the law would reflect the economic reality which is that these companies trade as a group, raise capital as a group, and are considered by those dealing with them to be a group.

**3-49**　While some support for the development of a group enterprise law was offered by Lord Denning MR in *DHN Food Distributors Ltd v Tower Hamlets LBC*,[166] it was robustly rejected by the House of Lords in *Woolfson v Strathclyde Regional Council*[167] which doubted whether the Court of Appeal had applied the correct principle in *DHN*. Generally, the English courts have shown a strong determination not to embark on any such development.[168] In *Adams v Cape Industries plc*[169] Slade LJ noted:

'There is no general principle that all companies in a group of companies are to be regarded as one. On the contrary, the fundamental principle is that "each company in a group of companies (a relatively modern concept) is a separate legal entity possessed of separate legal rights and liabilities": see *The Albazero* [1975] 3 All ER 21 at 28, [1977] AC 774 at 807 per Roskill LJ.'

**3-50**　Slade LJ went on:[170]

'We agree ... that the observations of Robert Goff LJ in *Bank of Tokyo Ltd v Karoon* [1986] 3 All ER 468 at 485, [1987] AC 45 at 64 are apposite:
　　"Counsel suggested beguilingly that it would be technical for us to distinguish between parent and subsidiary company in this context; economically, he said, they were one. But we are concerned not with economics but with law. The distinction between the two is, in law, fundamental and cannot here be bridged." '

---

[165] [1990] BCLC 479 at 513. See too Flaux J in *Linsen International Ltd v Humpuss Transportasi Kimia* [2011] 2 Lloyd's Rep 663 at [38]–[39]; the closeness of companies and commonality of directors within a group are not enough to justify the disregarding of the corporate structure.

[166] [1976] 3 All ER 462 at 467, CA. The other judges decided the case on a narrower basis.

[167] (1979) 38 P & CR 521.

[168] The position is different in the context of EU competition law where liability may indeed arise on the basis of parent and subsidiaries forming a single economic group; see the valuable discussion by Hughes, 'Competition Law Enforcement and Corporate Group Liability—adjusting the veil' (2014) 35 ECLR 68.

[169] [1990] BCLC 479 at 508.　　[170] [1990] BCLC 479 at 514.

**3-51**  Pressed to regard a group of companies as a single economic unit in *Re Polly Peck International plc (No 3)*,[171] Robert Walker J rejected that submission, noting that the separate legal existence of group companies is particularly important when creditors become involved.[172] In *Ord v Belhaven Pubs Ltd*,[173] the court rejected an attempt by the plaintiffs to substitute, for the original defendant subsidiary company, either its parent company or another wholly-owned subsidiary in the group which the plaintiffs wanted to do as, following a restructuring of the group, the original defendant no longer had substantial assets. The Court of Appeal noted that the trial judge (who had permitted the substitution) appeared to have viewed the whole group as an economic entity and therefore thought substitution was appropriate. Hobhouse LJ emphatically rejected this approach, noting:[174]

> 'The approach of the judge in the present case was simply to look at the economic unit, to disregard the distinction between the legal entities which were involved and to say: since the company cannot pay, the shareholders who are the people financially interested should be made to pay instead. That of course is radically at odds with the whole concept of corporate personality and limited liability and the decision of the House of Lords in *Salomon v Salomon & Co Ltd* [1897] AC 22.'

**3-52**  The true position, Hobhouse LJ said, is that companies are entitled to organise their affairs in group structures and to expect the courts to apply the principles of *Salomon v Salomon & Co Ltd* in the ordinary way.[175] As Slade LJ noted in *Adams v Cape Industries plc*[176]

> '[W]e do not accept as a matter of law that the court is entitled to lift the corporate veil as against a defendant company which is the member of a corporate group merely because the corporate structure has been used so as to ensure that the legal liability (if any) in respect of particular future activities of the group (and correspondingly the risk of enforcement of that liability) will fall on another member of the group rather than the defendant company. Whether or not this is desirable, the right to use a corporate structure in this way is inherent in our corporate law.'

**3-53**  Counsel had argued that the veil should be pierced because the purpose of the group structure in *Adams* was that the English parent company could trade in the US through subsidiaries without running the risk of tortious liability with respect to its asbestos business. Slade LJ acknowledged that this might indeed be the purpose of the structure adopted, but he went on:[177]

> '[I]n our judgment, Cape [the English company] was in law entitled to organise the group's affairs in that manner and … to expect that the court would apply the principle in *Salomon v Salomon & Co Ltd* [1897] AC 22 in the ordinary way.'

**3-54**  At one time, the European Commission had ambitions for a Directive on Groups,[178] but discussions never progressed very far and in 2002 the Commission accepted the

---

[171] [1996] 1 BCLC 428.

[172] [1996] 1 BCLC 428 at 444; and see Flaux J in *Linsen International Ltd v Humpuss Transportasi Kimia* [2011] 2 Lloyd's Rep 663 at [19], [126], the single economic unit argument forms no part of English law.

[173] [1998] 2 BCLC 447, CA.    [174] [1998] 2 BCLC 447 at 457.    [175] [1998] 2 BCLC 447 at 458.

[176] [1990] BCLC 479 at 520. See Grantham, n 70, at 314 who reminds us that the shifting of risk is not an unintended consequence of incorporation, but its purpose.

[177] [1990] BCLC 479 at 520. See too *Ord v Belhaven Pubs Ltd* [1998] 2 BCLC 447, CA.

[178] There had been some discussions in the 1970s and 1980s with respect to draft proposals for a Ninth Company Law Directive on Groups based on complex German provisions, but no progress was made, see Edwards, *EC Company Law* (1999), pp 390–1.

recommendation of the High Level Group of Experts on Company Law that any plans in that direction should be abandoned.[179] There have been occasional further initiatives such as the suggestion to the EU Commission that it should consider adopting a Recommendation recognising the interests of the group which would both allow the board of the parent company to manage the group in the interests of the group and allow the board of a subsidiary to rely lawfully on the interests of the group in reaching their decisions.[180] In 2016, an informal company law expert group drew up a report for the Commission on group interest, but no further progress has been made at the time of writing.[181] Even without a group law, there has long been an emphasis on the need for greater transparency from groups,[182] especially when they include listed companies, so ensuring that creditors are well informed as to the risks they run in contracting with such structures. There are requirements for group accounts (see **18-30**), the notes of which must give information about subsidiary companies and identify the parent and the ultimate parent company, and the Transparency and Takeover Directives respectively require disclosure of controlling shareholdings to the markets[183] and in the company's annual report.[184]

**3-55**   The Company Law Review (CLR) was unconvinced of the need for particular reforms with respect to group law, pointing out that contract creditors can protect themselves by contract terms and pricing mechanisms from the risks of trading with an insolvent subsidiary,[185] and concluding that there was no evidence before it of abuse of corporate status by parent companies to avoid tort liabilities.[186] The CLR did put forward a modest proposal, later dropped, for an elective regime allowing parent companies to avoid some disclosure requirements in return for accepting liability for a subsidiary's acts.[187] A somewhat similar position is reached by CA 2006, s 479A which allows qualifying subsidiary companies to be exempt from mandatory audit provided certain conditions are met including a parent company guarantee of subsidiary liabilities (see s 479 C and **18-55**). It is not clear to what extent parent companies have taken advantage of this option and, of course, it only protects creditors of the subsidiary if the parent company is able ultimately to make good on the guarantee.

---

[179] See the Report of the High Level Group of Company Law Experts entitled *A Modern Regulatory Framework for Company Law in Europe*, 4 November 2002, Brussels, Ch V of which is devoted to Groups.

[180] See *Report of the Reflection Group on the Future of EU Company Law* (April 2011), Ch 4 on Groups of Companies.

[181] See Informal Company Law Expert Group, *Report on the Recognition of the Interest of the Group* (October 2016). See too a paper by a different informal group of European Company Law Experts, 'A Paper for Reforming Group Law in the European Union—Comparative Observations on the way forward' (October 2016) available at www.ssrn.com. See also Sorensen, 'Groups of Companies in the Case Law of the Court of Justice of the European Union' (2016) 27 EBL Rev 393.

[182] See Communication from the Commission to the Council and the European Parliament, *Modernising Company Law and Enhancing Corporate Governance in the European Union—A Plan to Move Forward*, Brussels, 21.5.2003, COM (2003) 284.

[183] See the FSA Handbook, *Disclosure and Transparency Rules* (DTR), rule 5.

[184] While there are a lot of disclosure requirements which provide information on group structures, the information is scattered through a variety of documents and it remains difficult for investors and others to have a clear picture of the main features of a company's group structure. The Reflection Group Report, n 164, pp 68–75, suggests that it might be worth considering whether investors in listed companies would benefit from easily accessible information on the group structure set out in the company's corporate governance statement.

[185] See Company Law Review, *Modern Company Law for a Competitive Economy, Completing the Structure* (2000), paras 10.20; 10.58.

[186] See *Completing the Structure* (2000), paras 10.58–10.59.

[187] See *Completing the Structure* (2000), at paras 10.19–10.57; *Final Report*, vol 1 (2001), at para 8.26; Boyle (2002) 23 Co Law 35

**3-56**  While the use of groups is well established, and the basic legal structure is well under-stood, issues of interest would include the position of the creditors of a subsidiary company (including tort creditors), the duties of directors of a subsidiary, and the protection of minority interests in a subsidiary,[188] each of which is considered briefly in what follows.

## Creditor issues

**3-57**  The primary legal reason for the use of a group structure is risk management, to further limit liabilities,[189] since ultimately, as Templeman J memorably put it in *Re Southard Ltd*,[190] a parent company can discard the runt of the litter. He noted:[191]

> 'A parent company may spawn a number of subsidiary companies, all controlled directly or indirectly by the shareholders of the parent company. If one of the subsidiary companies, to change the metaphor, turns out to be the runt of the litter and declines into insolvency to the dismay of the creditors, the parent company and other subsidiary companies may prosper to the joy of the shareholders without any liability for the debts of the insolvent subsidiary.'

**3-58**  Of course, as a matter of good business practice, many parent companies will not insist on their strict legal right to walk away from the liabilities of their subsidiaries, but will meet a subsidiary's obligations, particularly if the subsidiary's creditors are also creditors and suppliers of the parent company and other companies in the group. A concern for its business reputation may also make a parent company meet a liability which legally it could otherwise disown. Once the scale of liabilities is significant, however, a parent company is unlikely voluntarily to accept the liabilities of the subsidiary since its own shareholders and creditors will be endangered by such action.[192]

**3-59**  It is important therefore that creditors of a group company identify the precise subsidiary with which they are dealing and appreciate that *Salomon* will prevent their having a claim against assets elsewhere in the group. It may be the case that the subsidiary has a share capital of £100 and no assets of its own. Of course, this could equally be the position where a creditor deals with a company with individual rather than corporate shareholders, so the position is not peculiar to corporate groups.

**3-60**  If the creditors are to protect their position and extend their reach to the assets of the parent company and/or other companies in the group, they must use contractual devices to do so, recognising that the superior negotiating power of financial institutions may mean that the ordinary contract creditor has little bargaining power. Creditors such as banks, on the other hand, will be in a position to ensure that they have cross-guarantees and security from all the companies in the group. Typically, a bank will require each subsidiary company to provide security and guarantees that it will meet its own liabilities to the bank and the liabilities of any other company in the group to the bank. These contractual

---

[188] See generally, Dine, *The Governance of Corporate Groups* (2000); Blumberg, *The Multinational Challenge to Corporation Law* (1993). Much of the literature focuses on the problem of group insolvency, see Mevorach, *Insolvency within Multinational Enterprise Groups* (2009).

[189] There are numerous business reasons why businesses want to use a group structure, such as diversification, geographical spread, and administrative convenience.

[190] [1979] 3 All ER 556.     [191] [1979] 3 All ER 556 at 565.

[192] For example, in *Re Simon Carves Ltd* [2013] 2 BCLC 100 the parent company did stand behind a subsidiary for many years as losses mounted before throwing in the towel once losses exceeded £200m.

devices ensure that the bank is able to ignore the separate legal entities and, in effect, to lend to the group and to recover from the group. The consequence for the creditors of an individual subsidiary company may be that difficulties elsewhere in the group will force the bank to call in the cross-guarantees resulting in all probability in the collapse of the entire group.[193]

**3-61**    For creditors without the bargaining power to secure cross-guarantees, the most that they may be able to extract is a letter of comfort from the parent company. An illustration can be found in *Kleinwort Benson v Malaysia Mining Corp*.[194] Here a bank intended to lend several million pounds to a subsidiary company and sought some protection against the risk of default by the subsidiary from the parent company. The most the parent company was willing to give was a letter of comfort which stated: 'it is our policy to ensure that the business of the subsidiary is at all times in a position to meet its liabilities to you'. When the subsidiary collapsed, the parent company denied any liability to the creditor under the letter of comfort. The Court of Appeal agreed that this letter had no contractual effect. The court concluded that the concept of a comfort letter to which the parties had resort when the parent company refused to accept liability was known by both sides to amount to the parent assuming, not a legal liability to ensure repayment of the liabilities of the subsidiary, but a moral responsibility only. In *Re Simon Carves Ltd*,[195] the relevant letter of comfort from the parent company said 'we confirm that we shall provide the necessary financial and business support to the company to ensure that the company continues as a going concern'. The company had been balance sheet insolvent from 2008 onwards and continued to trade until July 2011 when it went into administration and then liquidation with a deficiency of £290m, approximately. A creditor owed £12m on construction work for the company tried to establish that the comfort letter was legally binding, but the court rejected the claim. The parent company carefully addressed the letter of credit to the directors of the subsidiary and did so in the context of the directors preparing the company's annual accounts for which purpose the directors needed to be reassured that the company was a going concern (which it was with the support of the parent company). The letter served no wider purpose and was not legally binding.[196]

**3-62**    Nevertheless, in the absence of a guarantee, creditors still seek letters of comfort in the hope that the parent company will, for business reasons, decide to honour that moral responsibility. A letter of comfort given dishonestly to induce another party to provide funding would be actionable, as would a letter of comfort which on closer analysis proves to be a binding contractual obligation, so care must be exercised in the giving and drafting of such letters.

**3-63**    It is also possible that, on insolvency, a liquidator may be able to establish that the parent company has exercised such control over the subsidiary as to render the parent company a

---

[193] For an example of these arrangements, see *Facia Footwear Ltd v Hinchcliffe* [1998] 1 BCLC 218.

[194] [1989] 1 All ER 785; a subordination agreement is another possibility for creditors to consider, see for example *Re SSSL Realisations (2002) Ltd* [2007] 1 BCLC 29 at [66] (group of companies entered into a subordination agreement that no group company would prove for an inter-company debt in the liquidation of any group company until a principal creditor had been paid in full), disapproved on other grounds, [2012] 1 BCLC 227. Subordination agreements are permissible, see *LB Holdings Intermediate 2 Ltd v Lehman Bros International (Europe)* [2017] BCC 235 at [66].

[195] [2013] 2 BCLC 100.

[196] The court noted that it would be remarkable if, by virtue of a brief letter, the parent company would have committed itself contractually to the discharge of all of the subsidiary's huge liabilities, see [2013] 2 BCLC 100 at [36].

shadow director of the subsidiary so opening up potential civil liability as a shadow director for matters such as wrongful trading by the subsidiary company.[197] In practice, such
potential liability is a remote prospect. Shadow directors are discussed at **7-21**; wrongful
trading is considered at **15-18**.

**3-64**    As for tort creditors of a subsidiary company, it is often argued that the application of the
*Salomon* principle is particularly unfair in their case since they are involuntary creditors.[198] It is clear from *Adams v Cape Industries plc*,[199] see **3-52**, however, that the English
courts see no need to regard such creditors as deserving of any particular flexibility in
terms of applying the *Salomon* principle. The claimants in that case were tort creditors.
They were employees of US subsidiaries who had suffered asbestos-related illness as a
result of their employment but *Adams* is a strong reaffirmation by the Court of Appeal
of the *Salomon* principle. Far from showing a willingness to pierce the veil because the
claimants were tort creditors, the Court of Appeal emphasised that the use of a group
structure in this way to insulate the rest of the group from future liabilities of a particular
subsidiary is inherent in English company law.[200] That is not to leave tort creditors unpro-
tected, for commonly they will be protected by insurance cover held by the subsidiary.

**3-65**    Given particular circumstances, it may also be possible that a parent company, as a separate legal entity, may owe a duty of care directly to the employees of a subsidiary. In
*Chandler v Cape plc*[201] the Court of Appeal confirmed that, while a parent company owes
no duty of care to the employees of a subsidiary company by reason only of being the
parent company, a parent company may be found to have assumed a duty of care towards
the subsidiary's employees, not in all respects necessarily but, as here, a duty to advise or
ensure that employees in a subsidiary company have a safe system of work.[202] The parent
company was liable in damages to an injured employee, not as a consequence of piercing
the veil,[203] not on the basis of being an economic unit with its subsidiary, but on the basis
that two separate entities each undertook obligations to the employee.

---

[197] See *Re Hydrodam Ltd* [1994] 2 BCLC 180, and note CA 2006, s 251(3), see **7-29**.

[198] See Muchlinski, 'Holding Multinationals to Account: Recent Developments in English Litigation and
the Company Law Review' (2002) 23 Company Lawyer 168.

[199] [1990] BCLC 479, CA.        [200] [1990] BCLC 479 at 520, per Slade LJ.

[201] [2012] 3 All ER 640, CA. See Petrin, 'Assumption of Responsibility in Corporate Groups' (2013) 76
MLR 603; Day, 'Negligence and the Corporate Veil: Parent Companies' Duty of Care to their Subsidiaries'
Employees' [2014] LMCLQ 454; Grusic, 'Responsibility in Groups of Companies and the Future of
International Human Rights and Environmental Litigation' (2015) 74(1) CLJ 30; Goudkamp, 'Duties of
Care and Corporate Groups' (2017) 133 LQR 560.

[202] See [2012] 3 All ER 640 at [80] where Arden LJ (with whom Moses and McFarlane LJJ agreed) summarises the factors which influenced the court in finding a duty of care, namely that (i) the companies were in
the same line of business; (ii) the parent company's long experience in the industry gave it superior knowledge of health and safety issues; (iii) the subsidiary's system of work was unsafe as the parent company knew
or ought to have known (it had previously operated from the same premises); and (iv) the parent company
knew or ought to have foreseen that the subsidiary or its employees would rely on the parent company
using its superior knowledge for the employees' protection. It sufficed on (iv) that there was evidence that
the parent company was in the practice of intervening in the trading operations of the subsidiary and it was
not necessary to show that the parent company was in the practice of intervening on the health and safety
policies of the subsidiary. But these factors are illustrative, rather than exhaustive, of when a duty of care
may arise: *Thompson v The Renwick Group plc* [2014] 2 BCLC 97 at [33].

[203] See [2012] 3 All ER 640 at [69] where Arden LJ emphatically rejected any suggestion that the court
in this case was in any way concerned with piercing the corporate veil. But see Pey Woan Lee, n 70, who
makes the point, at 33, that whatever the court's protestations, it is obvious that the liberal imposition of tort
liabilities could make significant inroads into the separate entity rule.

**3-66**  The decision reinforces *Salomon* while solving for the employee the adverse consequences of the separate legal status of his employer distinct from its (parent company) shareholder. If the outcome reduces the value to the parent company of the separate legal status of the employing subsidiary company, it has only itself to blame since it was its own failure to observe that separate status, intervening in the trading operations of the subsidiary, which gave rise to the duty of care. In most parent company scenarios, this will not be the case. In *Thompson v The Renwick Group plc*[204] the court rejected a claim that a duty of care had arisen, noting that the facts were far removed from *Chandler v Cape plc*. Merely because the companies in that case were operating as a division of a group carrying on a single business did not mean that the legal personality of the subsidiary companies had not been retained and respected. Tomlinson LJ noted that the co-ordination of operations as between subsidiaries is just that, without it being demonstrated that the group holding company assumed control in such a manner as to demonstrate an assumption of duty to the employees of the subsidiaries.[205] Tomlinson LJ considered that the approach in *Chandler v Cape plc* could be distilled into a two-fold test of whether: (i) the parent company is better placed, because of its superior knowledge or expertise, to protect the employees of subsidiary companies against the risk of injury and whether, because of that feature, (ii) it is fair to infer that the subsidiary will rely upon the parent deploying its superior knowledge in order to protect its employees from risk of injury.[206] It would seem that the small window of obligation which may have opened up in *Chandler v Cape* is indeed quite narrow.

**3-67**  The issues of parent company liability have been considered on a number of occasions recently by the Court of Appeal in jurisdictional disputes where tort claims have been brought usually because the (overseas) subsidiary is insolvent, but the parent company is resident in the UK and the issue is one of forum.[207] These jurisdictional disputes nevertheless provide an opportunity for the courts to consider whether a duty of care might arise. In *HRH Okpabi v Royal Dutch Shell*[208] the Court of Appeal by a majority concluded that the evidence in that case did not demonstrate a sufficient degree of control by the parent company over the subsidiary's operations to establish the necessary degree of proximity at trial to support a claim that the parent company owed a direct duty of care with respect to environmental damage caused by an operating subsidiary in Nigeria. The holding company was the ultimate holding company of the Shell group of more than 1,000 companies. It had no employees, no operations, no licence to operate in Nigeria and only indirectly held shares in the operating subsidiary which was autonomous with considerable income and assets. On the *Caparo* criteria, neither proximity nor reasonableness would be met. Vos J noted that ' ... it would be surprising if a parent company were to go to the trouble of establishing a network of overseas subsidiaries with their own management structures if it intended itself to assume responsibility for the operations of each of those subsidiaries. The corporate structure itself tends to militate against the requisite proximity.'[209] Sales LJ dissented, being of the view that control by the parent company of

---

[204] [2014] 2 BCLC 97, CA. See Day, n 201.     [205] [2014] 2 BCLC 97 at [36], CA.

[206] [2014] 2 BCLC 97 at [37]. See criticism by Goudkamp, n 201, at 564 of this approach as a distraction from the application of the *Caparo* criteria (essentially, foreseeability of the type of harm which has arisen, proximity between claimant and defendant, and that the imposition of a duty is fair, just, and reasonable in the circumstances) which determine generally whether a duty of care arises between A and B, whether A and B are individuals or companies.

[207] On forum issues, see Chan, 'The Jurisdictional One-Two Punch' [2017] LMCLQ 190.

[208] [2018] EWCA Civ 191; see Goudkamp, n 201, for commentary on the first instance decision in *Okpabi*.

[209] [2018] EWCA Civ 191 at [196].

important aspects of the management of the pipeline and facilities, specifically in relation to the risk of oil spills, meant it was well arguable that there was a proximate relationship between the parent company and the claimants.[210]

**3-68**   The state of play is usefully summed up by the Court of Appeal in *Lungowe v Vedanta Resources plc*[211] where the court accepted that it was arguable that a parent company owed a duty of care to local residents near to a polluting mine run by a subsidiary company when the parent company seemed to have operational control over the mining subsidiary. Simon LJ noted:[212]

> '... that certain propositions can be derived from these cases which may be material to the question of whether a duty is owed by a parent company to those affected by the operations of a subsidiary. (1) The starting point is the three-part test of foreseeability, proximity and reasonableness. (2) A duty may be owed by a parent company to the employee of a subsidiary, or a party directly affected by the operations of that subsidiary, in certain circumstances. (3) Those circumstances may arise where the parent company (a) has taken direct responsibility for devising a material health and safety policy the adequacy of which is the subject of the claim, or (b) controls the operations which give rise to the claim. (4) *Chandler v Cape Plc* and *Thompson v The Renwick Group Plc* describe some of the circumstances in which the three-part test may, or may not, be satisfied so as to impose on a parent company responsibility for the health and safety of a subsidiary's employee. (5) The first of the four indicia in *Chandler v Cape Plc* requires not simply that the businesses of the parent and the subsidiary are in the relevant respect the same, but that the parent is well placed, because of its knowledge and expertise to protect the employees of the subsidiary. If both parent and subsidiary have similar knowledge and expertise and they jointly take decisions about mine safety, which the subsidiary implements, both companies may (depending on the circumstances) owe a duty of care to those affected by those decisions. (6) Such a duty may be owed in analogous situations, not only to employees of the subsidiary but to those affected by the operations of the subsidiary. (7) The evidence sufficient to establish the duty may not be available at the early stages of the case. Much will depend on whether ..., the pleading represents the actuality.

**3-69**   The lesson for parent companies and fellow subsidiaries is that the courts will respect the separate legal entities so long as the companies do so. An arm's length relationship (possibly reinforced by holding the shares indirectly) ensures no duty of care will arise while integrated operations and a control relationship of superior knowledge and experience on the one hand and reliance on the other run the risk, more so vis-à-vis employees than others, of a duty of care being imposed.'

## Directors' duties

**3-70**   Where a company is a subsidiary company within a group of companies, the directors must act, as required by s 172(1), in good faith, to promote the success of that subsidiary company as a separate legal entity with its own separate creditors and whose interests are distinct from the interests of other companies in the group.[213] The absence of evidence of actual separate consideration of the interests of the company is not necessarily indicative

---

[210] [2018] EWCA Civ 191 at [172].     [211] [2017] BCC 787, CA.     [212] [2017] BCC 787 at [83], CA.
[213] *Re Capitol Films Ltd, Rubin v Cobalt Pictures Ltd* [2011] 2 BCLC 359 at [50]; also *Re Polly Peck International plc (No 3)* [1996] 1 BCLC 428 at 440.

of bad faith on the directors' part, rather the question to be asked in those circumstances is whether an intelligent and honest man in the position of a director of the company concerned could, in the whole of the existing circumstances, have reasonably believed that the transaction was for the benefit of the company,[214] substituting an objective test for the normal subjective test applicable under s 172(1),[215] see **10-9**. At a practical level, the two issues are likely to be intertwined since what promotes the success of the group may be relevant to promoting the success of the company.[216]

**3-71**    For example, it may be appropriate for a solvent subsidiary to provide financial support for the rest of a group, though the group is in financial difficulty, when the continued prosperity and the very existence of the subsidiary may depend on the group remaining in business, as is commonly the case. The problem arises because, as noted at **3-60**, banking arrangements typically require each subsidiary to guarantee the indebtedness of all the other companies in the group with the result that the insolvency of one company in the group can trigger the collapse of the remaining companies as well. These arrangements commonly are in the interests of the subsidiary company, as much as the interests of the group, because the subsidiary gets access to a level of borrowing and on more favourable terms than would otherwise be possible on its own account.

**3-72**    The difficulty in separating group interests and the company's interests is illustrated by *Facia Footwear Ltd v Hinchcliffe*[217] where a cash-rich subsidiary had entered into cross-guarantees whereby the subsidiary guaranteed the indebtedness of the group.[218] At issue were million-pound payments made to other group companies by the directors of the subsidiary two months prior to the subsidiary going into administration at a time when the whole group, and the subsidiary as an individual company, were in very serious financial difficulties.[219] The administrators sought summary judgment against the directors on the grounds that making these payments in disregard of the interests of the creditors of the subsidiary at that time was a breach of the directors' duties to the subsidiary company (see CA 2006, s 172(3), and **10-41**).

**3-73**    The application for summary judgment was refused.[220] The directors in their defence had maintained that the payments were in the normal course of implementation of group treasury arrangements and there was no suggestion that the payments were for private purposes or in breach of any statutory obligation or were otherwise than for the trading purposes of the recipient companies. Most importantly, if the group of companies collapsed, the subsidiary would collapse also under the weight of the cross-guarantees. Moreover, the court found that the directors were intent on keeping the group afloat as they believed a refinancing scheme was a serious possibility.

[214] *Charterbridge Corpn v Lloyds Bank* [1969] 2 All ER 1185 at 1194, per Pennycuick J.

[215] *Colin Gwyer & Associates v London Wharf (Limehouse) Ltd* [2003] 2 BCLC 153 at [73].

[216] In *Nicholas v Soundcraft Electronics Ltd* [1993] BCLC 360, for example, the directors of a subsidiary company were not in breach of their duties to the company when they failed to take action to recover debts owed to it by the parent company. The parent company was the sole distributor of the subsidiary's products and was in serious financial trouble and it was in the interests of the subsidiary company that the parent should not go into liquidation.                                                    [217] [1998] 1 BCLC 218.

[218] No challenge was made to the propriety of the decision as to the subsidiary's participation in the security arrangements which facilitated other beneficial arrangements for the subsidiary: see [1998] 1 BCLC 218 at 223–4.                                                                          [219] [1998] 1 BCLC 218 at 228.

[220] This outcome does not mean that the court would not have found against the directors in a full hearing, but simply that the case against them was not so convincing that the court would grant a summary judgment. In the event, the administrators did not pursue the case.

**3-74** Sir Richard Scott acknowledged the difficulties facing the directors of the subsidiary. It was clear, he said, that in continuing trading in those final months, the directors were taking a risk; clear too that, given the parlous financial state of the group, the directors had to have regard to the interests of creditors. But, he noted, the creditors of the group, and of the subsidiary in particular, would clearly have been best served by a refinancing that could support a continuation of profitable trading. The cessation of trading followed by the disposal of the assets of the companies on a forced sale basis would lead, it was always realised, to heavy losses for the creditors. The creditors' only chance of being paid in full lay in a continuation of trading. In his opinion, it was, therefore, not in the least obvious that in continuing to trade in those final two months, the directors were ignoring the interests of the creditors of the subsidiary.[221]

**3-75** A failure to respect the separate legal identity of a subsidiary in an insolvent situation may merit, subsequently, a finding of unfitness and disqualification as a director. In *Secretary of State for Business, Innovation and Skills v Doffman*[222] the court was particularly critical of two directors who disregarded the separate interests of individual companies within a group of companies of which they were the sole shareholders and transferred assets between the companies without regard to the interests or often the solvency of the transferor. Finding the directors to be unfit and disqualifying them, the court noted that those who take advantage of the corporate entity's separate legal personality also have to recognise the concomitant duties which arise,[223] citing with approval Lewison J's comments in *Secretary of State for Trade and Industry v Goldberg*[224] that '… respect for the separate legal personality of each company, and recognition of a director's duty to exercise his powers in the best interests of the particular company of which he is a director are essential attributes of fitness to be concerned in the management of a company'. In *Re Genosyis Technology Management Ltd, Wallach v Secretary of State for Trade and Industry*[225] the directors of a subsidiary company entered into a settlement agreement with a defaulting debtor which involved the debtor making a significant payment to the parent company rather than to the subsidiary. The subsidiary had stood to gain €1.25m from earlier drafts of the settlement but, under the version actually signed, payment was direct to the parent company which undertook to make payments to the subsidiary amounting to £166,000. In disqualification proceedings against the two directors of the subsidiary, the court noted that the company was insolvent at the time of the agreement, therefore the interests of the creditors intruded, and the directors owed a fiduciary duty to act in their interests. But there was no evidence that the directors, who were also directors of the parent company, at any time considered the separate interests of the subsidiary and of its creditors. The directors were culpable in not doing so and were disqualified for five years.

### Minority shareholders

**3-76** Not all subsidiary companies are wholly-owned subsidiaries and there may be minority shareholders who may find themselves in a difficult position if the parent company acts

---

[221] [1998] 1 BCLC 218 at 228.      [222] [2011] 2 BCLC 541.      [223] [2011] 2 BCLC 541 at [251].

[224] [2004] 1 BCLC 597 at [29]. See also *Re Mea Corporation Ltd, Secretary of State for Trade and Industry v Aviss* [2007] 1 BCLC 618 at [109]–[112], where two directors were disqualified for seven and 11 years respectively. At a time when each of the group companies was insolvent and under pressure from creditors, these two directors (who had insisted on the adoption of a group treasury policy) allowed such cash as was available and collected centrally, to be paid out to other companies in which one of the two directors had substantial interests, in disregard of the interests of the creditors of the individual companies.

[225] [2007] 1 BCLC 208.

as if the subsidiary is wholly-owned and in disregard of the interests of the separate legal entity. The problem can be illustrated by *Scottish Co-operative Wholesale Society Ltd v Meyer*.[226] In this case the majority shareholder no longer had any need for the subsidiary so ran down its business to the point where it had no business. The minority shareholders petitioned for relief under CA 1948, s 210. The House of Lords concluded that the affairs of the subsidiary had been conducted by the controlling shareholder (through its nominee directors) in an oppressive manner and ordered the majority to buy out the minority shareholders on a valuation basis which presupposed that no oppressive conduct had occurred. The equivalent, but more generous, jurisdiction for modern shareholders is CA 2006, s 994 (see Chapter 19) which allows for petitions by a member on the basis that the company's affairs are being conducted in an unfairly prejudicial manner. The Court of Appeal in *Re Citybranch Group Ltd, Gross v Rackind*[227] accepted that, in an appropriate case, the conduct of a holding company towards a subsidiary company may constitute the conduct of the affairs of the subsidiary in an unfairly prejudicial manner so as to merit a petition by a shareholder in the subsidiary and, vice versa, a shareholder in a holding company may petition that the conduct of the affairs of the subsidiary can be regarded as part of the conduct of the affairs of the holding company; see further at **19-28**. Also, a derivative claim may be brought by a shareholder in a parent company with respect to a breach of duty by a director or directors of the subsidiary company where the parent and subsidiary company are under the same wrongdoer control which prevents the company suing in respect of such a wrong;[228] see further at **20-16**. In other words, in an appropriate case, the courts will not allow the separate legal entity principle to be used (or abused) to defeat the legitimate interests of minority shareholders.

---

[226] [1959] AC 324, HL.

[227] [2004] 4 All ER 735 at [26], at least where the subsidiaries are wholly owned and have boards substantially similar to the parent company; see also *Scottish Co-operative Wholesale Society Ltd v Meyer* [1958] 3 All ER 66.

[228] *Universal Project Management Services Ltd v Fort Gilkicker Ltd* [2013] 3 WLR 164, [2013] 3 All ER 546.

# 4

# Rules of attribution—corporate acts and liabilities

## A Corporate acts and liabilities

**4-1** In the previous chapter, we considered the circumstances in which, as an exception to the separate legal entity rule in *Salomon v A Salomon and Co Ltd*,[1] the courts might pierce the corporate veil so as to identify a person with a company by virtue of his ownership thereof for the purpose of giving effect to existing rights or remedies against that person. In this chapter we look at a further issue linked to the concept of the company as a separate legal entity and that is how to identify which acts of the human agents involved in the separate legal entity are the acts of the company for the purposes of determining the rights and liabilities of the company. Decisions of the board or of the shareholders acting in general meeting are acts of the company, but formal decisions of that nature are relatively rare and in the context of a disputed matter unlikely to be present. There are several distinct sets of rules which may assist in this context. As Moore-Bick LJ noted in *Man v Freightliner Ltd*,[2] there are rules of attribution which determine that some acts are the acts of the company; there are agency rules which determine that the acts are the acts of an agent for which the company is liable; and there are vicarious liability rules which determine that the acts are the acts of an employee for which the company is deemed liable. Our concern is with rules of attribution which determine whose acts are the acts of the company for which the company should be liable and, in that context, as Moore-Bick LJ explained, '... these rules do not involve so much the attribution of one person's state of mind to another as the identification of the natural person or persons who are to be regarded as representing the juridical person for the purposes of the substantive rule in question.'[3]

**4-2** Problems are limited in respect of contract and tort where agency and statute (in the case of contracts) and vicarious liability (in the case of torts) provide the answers to questions of whose acts are the acts of the company for the purpose of liability. A company is liable for the wrongful acts of an agent or employee acting within the scope of his authority or in the course of his employment,[4] as is the case with any principal or employer. But sometimes agency and vicarious liability rules may not resolve an issue in a civil context, for

---

[1] [1897] AC 22, HL.     [2] [2005] EWHC 2347 at [154].
[3] *Man Nutzfahrzeuge v Freightliner Ltd* [2005] EWHC 2347 at [154].
[4] *Lloyd v Grace, Smith & Co* [1912] AC 716. The term 'ordinary course of employment' has an extended scope for these purposes to include acts so closely connected with the acts that the employee was authorised to do that for the purpose of liability they can fairly and properly be said to be done by the employee while acting in the ordinary course of his employment: *Lister v Hesley Hall Ltd* [2001] 2 All ER 769, HL; *Dubai Aluminium Co Ltd v Salaam* [2003] 1 BCLC 32, HL.

example as to how a company might be liable for knowing receipt[5] or knowingly being a party to fraudulent trading[6] or in deciding whether the acts of a dominant manager and shareholder can be attributed to a company so as to prevent the company relying on an insurance policy which excludes liability for deliberate acts of the company,[7] or whether perjured evidence can be attributed to a company so that a judgment procured by such evidence can be set aside.[8] In the criminal context, vicarious liability plays only a limited role and generally *mens rea* must be established ('knowingly', 'recklessly', 'intentionally', etc). In these situations, it will be necessary to rely on rules of attribution to determine whether the mental state of an individual or individuals should be attributed to the company. As the need for specific rules of attribution is greatest in the context of criminal liability, the discussion of the rules of attribution is set out at **4-33** et seq dealing with criminal liability, but it should be borne in mind, as noted, that those rules may also be needed in a civil context. Typically, the courts have cited authorities from both civil and criminal jurisdictions in a particular case, but, as we shall see, more recently there has been something of a divergence of approach between criminal and civil cases.[9]

## B **Corporate liability in contract**

**4-3**   Parties wishing to enforce contractual obligations entered into by companies must ensure that:

>   (1)   the commitments made are within the capacity of the company and the authority of the executing officer or employee as agent, although much statutory protection is provided to ensure that this is the case; and
>
>   (2)   any due formalities of execution have been observed (see CA 2006, ss 44 and 46). A company may enter into a contract in writing under its seal (if it has one)[10] or, more commonly, a contract may be made on behalf of the company by a person (such as a director or manager) acting under its authority, express or implied (s 43).

**4-4**   Issues of capacity are of ever-decreasing significance (see discussion at **5-13**) so the essential contractual issues revolve around the authority of the contracting agent and whether it suffices to bind the company. Those issues of authority involve the application of the rules of agency as to the actual or apparent authority of the agent acting for the company. These agency rules are bolstered by statutory provisions (CA 2006, ss 39 and 40) designed to minimise the risk to third parties of any lack of authority. A further complication may be that the agent has authority to enter into the transaction but is acting for an improper purpose. All of these matters are discussed in Chapter 9. A key point to note is that contractual liabilities attach to the company as the contracting party and not to the agent

---

[5]   See *El Ajou v Dollar Land Holdings plc* [1994] 1 BCLC 464.

[6]   See *Re BCCI (No 15); Morris v Bank of India* [2005] 2 BCLC 328.

[7]   See *KR v Royal & Sun Alliance plc* [2007] BCC 522 (company could not rely on an insurance policy which excluded liability for deliberate acts of the company; the acts in question were the acts of the company's controlling shareholder and managing director who was, the court said, the company's directing mind and will; his acts were to be attributed to it with the result that the company was unable to claim on the policy).          [8]   See *Odyssey Re (London) Ltd v OIC Run-off Ltd* [2001] 1 Lloyd's Rep IR 1.

[9]   This may mean that it is not appropriate to cite the criminal authorities any longer in the civil context. See Lord Walker, in *Moulin Global Eyecare Trading Ltd v Commission of Inland Revenue* [2014] HKEC 419, HKCFA at [106]. See *Odyssey Re (London) Ltd v OIC Run-off Ltd* [2001] 1 Lloyd's Rep IR 1.

[10]   Companies are not required to have a company seal and documents executed by signature in accordance with CA 2006, s 44 have the same effect as if executed under seal.

who negotiates on behalf of the company, though exceptionally an agent may be sued for breach of warranty of authority.

## C Corporate liability in tort

**4-5**  A company is entitled to sue in respect of torts committed against it and it can be sued for a tort committed by it. As the company is an artificial legal entity, all torts of a company (even torts of omission) are committed through human agents. As noted, a company is vicariously liable for the acts of an agent or employee acting within the scope of his authority or in the course of his employment. The agent or employee is liable personally and the company vicariously and they are joint tortfeasors (each joint tortfeasor being liable for the entire loss caused). The position was explained in *Lloyd v Grace, Smith & Co*[11] as follows:

> '[T]he general rule [is] that the principal is liable to third persons in a civil suit "for the frauds, deceits, concealments, misrepresentations, torts, negligences, and other malfeasances or misfeasances, and omissions of duty of his agent in the course of his employment, although the principal did not authorise, or justify, or participate in, or indeed know of such misconduct, or even if he forbade the acts, or disapproved of them."'

**4-6**  Corporate liability is straightforward and it is possible for a director who commits a wrongful act to be personally liable on this basis, as an agent acting within the scope of his authority and, as we shall see, the House of Lords now favours that straightforward approach. There has been some debate as to whether it is more appropriate, given the company is a separate legal entity, that wrongful acts by a director should be attributed to the company so only the company is liable. This approach is sometimes referred to as the 'disattribution' theory whereby, if an act is attributed to the company on this basis, it is 'disattributed' to the director personally.[12]

**4-7**  This question of the personal liability of a director is particularly important where the company is a one-man company or the company is insolvent and the only person able to meet any liability in damages is the director personally (or his insurers), but there are conflicting policy issues here.[13] On the one hand, a willingness to hold a director liable personally for torts (vicariously) committed by the company runs the risk of disregarding the corporate entity contrary to the principle in *Salomon v Salomon & Co Ltd*[14] and, where the director is the controlling shareholder, denying the protection of limited liability conferred by incorporation.[15] The general approach is that a director is not automatically to

---

[11] [1912] AC 716 at 737, HL.

[12] A leading advocate of this approach is Grantham, see, in particular, Grantham and Rickett, 'Directors' Tortious' Liability: Contract, Tort or Company Law?' (1999) 62 MLR 133, and Grantham, 'Company Director's Personal Liability in Tort' (2003) 62 CLJ 15. For a robust rejection of the disattribution idea, see Campbell and Armour, 'Demystifying the Civil Liability of Corporate Agents' (2003) 62 CLJ 290. For a response, see Grantham, 'The Limited Liability of Company Directors' [2007] LMCLQ 362.

[13] See generally Noonan and Watson, 'Directors' Tortious Liability—Standard Chartered Bank and the Restoration of Sanity' [2004] JBL 539; Grantham [2007], n 12.   [14] [1897] AC 22, HL.

[15] See *Williams v Natural Life Health Foods Ltd* [1998] 1 BCLC 689 at 698, HL; also the dissenting judgment of Sir Patrick Russell in *Williams v Natural Life Health Foods Ltd* [1997] 1 BCLC 133, CA. But see Shapira, 'Liability of Corporate Agents: *Williams v Natural Life*' (1999) 20 Co Law 130 at 135, who makes the point that imposing liability on directors does not nullify the many other benefits of limited liability and incorporation.

be identified with his company for the purpose of the law of tort, for enterprise must not be discouraged by subjecting directors to such onerous personal obligations without due regard to the part the director plays personally in respect of the acts complained of.[16] On the other hand, the courts are concerned that an individual should not be able to avoid liability for tortious acts committed by him by sheltering behind the corporate veil.[17] For that reason, where a director commits a tort personally, his status as a director should not (and does not) confer any immunity from personal liability.[18] Of course, deciding whether the director has committed the tort personally is the difficulty, given that his argument is that he is not acting personally but acting on behalf of the company. As we shall see, the courts are working towards a pragmatic compromise between the twin policy concerns of maintaining the protection of incorporation and enforcing the personal liability of those who commit a tort, recognising that the corporate liability is vicarious and the actual wrongdoer is the relevant employee and as such must be held responsible.

## Personal liability for torts committed by a director

**4-8** The debate as to whether a director should be personally liable where he commits a tort has been clearly answered in the affirmative by the House of Lords in *Standard Chartered Bank v Pakistan National Shipping Corpn (No 2)*.[19] The facts essentially were that the managing director of a shipping company presented false shipping documents that resulted in the company obtaining payment of $1.1m from a bank. The bank subsequently sued the company and the director in deceit. The company was held liable, but the Court of Appeal allowed an appeal by the director against a finding of personal liability concluding that he had made the fraudulent representation on behalf of the company and not personally.[20] The bank appealed successfully to the House of Lords.

**4-9** Lord Hoffmann noted that the director made a fraudulent misrepresentation intending the bank to rely upon it and the bank did rely on it. The fact that, by virtue of the law of agency, his representation and the knowledge with which he made it would also be attributed to the company would be of interest, Lord Hoffmann said, in an action against the company.[21] However, this did not detract from the fact that they were his representations and his knowledge.[22] Lord Hoffmann noted that the director was not being sued for the company's tort. He was being sued for his own tort and all the elements of that tort were proved against him. He was liable, not because he was a director, but because he committed a fraud.[23]

**4-10** Lord Rodger, concurring, noted that someone who commits a tortious act is liable for their consequences; whether others (such as a company) are also liable depends on the circumstances.[24] All the ingredients of the tort of deceit (false statement made knowingly or recklessly intending another party to rely on it to his detriment) were made out

---

[16] *C Evans and Sons Ltd v Spritebrand Ltd* [1985] BCLC 105 at 115, per Slade LJ; see also *Rainham Chemical Works Ltd (in liq) v Belvedere Fish Guano Co Ltd* [1921] 2 AC 465 at 488; also *Trevor Ivory Ltd v Anderson* [1992] 2 NZLR 517 at 524–8.

[17] See Chadwick LJ in *MCA Records Inc v Charly Records Ltd* [2003] 1 BCLC 93 at [47].

[18] *Standard Chartered Bank v Pakistan National Shipping Corp* [2003] 1 BCLC 244 at [40], per Lord Rodger.

[19] [2003] 1 BCLC 244, HL. See Noonan and Watson, n 13; Todd, 'Assuming Responsibility for Tort' (2003) 119 LQR 199; Grantham, 'Company Director's Personal Liability in Tort' (2003) 62 CLJ 15.

[20] See [2000] 1 All ER (Comm) 1, CA.    [21] [2003] 1 BCLC 244 at [20].

[22] [2003] 1 BCLC 244 at [20].    [23] [2003] 1 BCLC 244 at [22].    [24] [2003] 1 BCLC 244 at [40].

against the director. That being so, there was no conceivable basis on which the director should not be held liable for the loss suffered by the bank.[25] His status as a director when he executed the fraud could not invest him with immunity[26] and he was liable in deceit.[27]

**4-11** The decision in *Standard Chartered* shows a shift in emphasis or indeed a return to first principles.[28] Instead of approaching the issue by attributing acts to the entity so establishing a corporate liability and then looking at the possibility of some basis for a personal liability, the first consideration is to establish whether the director committed the tort. If he did, a personal liability ensues which brings with it a vicarious liability on the part of the company for the acts of its agent.

**4-12** For whatever reason, perhaps because of the welcome clarity brought to these issues by the decision in *Standard Chartered*, perhaps because of the increasing availability of directors' and officers' liability insurance, perhaps because, in hard times, every avenue is worth pursuing if it increases the claimant's chances of actual recovery, there appears to be something of an increase in claims in deceit against individual directors.

**4-13** In *GE Commercial Finance Ltd v Gee*[29] the executive chairman of a group of companies (who was also the 80 per cent shareholder) and the group's finance director were liable in deceit and in conspiracy to the tune of £16m following an orchestrated and substantial fraud on the claimant involving the raising of false debts under a debt financing arrangement. The finance director knew that the figures communicated to the claimant were false, and the court found that his intention in making the false representations was to induce the claimant to make and to continue making the payments they did make. The court found that the executive chairman knew and encouraged what the finance director was doing.

**4-14** In *Contex Drouzhba Ltd v Wiseman*[30] an action in deceit lay against a director who signed on behalf of the company a document containing a fraudulent misrepresentation. The Court of Appeal found that his signature was not only that of the company but also his personal signature making him a person who made a fraudulent misrepresentation. The facts were that the company entered into an agreement with a supplier that payments would be made to the supplier within 30 days of the shipment of the goods. The agreement was signed by the defendant as managing director of the company. The court found that, at the time he signed the agreement, the defendant knew that the company would be unable to make payment for the goods at all, let alone within 30 days of invoice or a reasonable period thereafter. The court found that the director had made that representation knowingly and with no reasonable belief in its truth. In these circumstances, the director was personally liable.

**4-15** The Court of Appeal noted that it is clear, following the decision in *Standard Chartered Bank v Pakistan National Shipping Co*,[31] that, even if a company is liable for a deceit carried out by its director, the director also has a personal liability for his own fraud. Where a document contains a fraudulent representation made by a director, there is no reason, the court said, why his signature on the document should not render him personally liable.

---

[25] [2003] 1 BCLC 244 at [40].     [26] [2003] 1 BCLC 244 at [40].
[27] See also *Daido Asia Japan Co Ltd v Rothen* [2002] BCC 589; *Noel v Poland* [2001] 2 BCLC 645; *Edgington v Fitzmaurice* (1885) 29 Ch D 459.     [28] See Campbell and Armour, n 12; also Shapira, n 15.
[29] [2006] 1 Lloyd's Rep 337.
[30] [2008] 1 BCLC 631, CA, aff'g [2007] 1 BCLC 758. See also *UBAF Ltd v European American Banking Corp* [1984] 2 All ER 226.     [31] [2003] 1 BCLC 244.

The court agreed that not every contract signed by a director would contain implied representations by the director. Each case would depend on its own facts. But a director signing a document which contains a promise of payment on certain terms may be making an implied representation about the ability of the company to pay since there is, by implication, a representation that the company has the capacity to meet the payment terms. Here the defendant had made a fraudulent representation in writing as to the credit or ability of the company and he was liable.[32]

**4-16** In cases where the claim is based on deceit, it is clear that the relevant policy considerations favour personal liability given the deliberate nature of the wrongdoing and the courts are anxious to prevent directors from avoiding this liability by hiding behind their companies.[33] On the other hand, there is possibly a greater reluctance to hold a director liable personally for negligent misrepresentations made by his company.

**4-17** This issue was addressed by the House of Lords in *Williams v Natural Life Health Foods Ltd*[34] which concerned negligent advice given by what was essentially a one-man company. M was the managing director and principal shareholder of a company which held itself out as having the expertise to provide advice on running health food shops, expertise derived from M's experience in running his own shop. The plaintiffs had relied on financial projections negligently produced by the company in opening their health shop which had collapsed leaving them with significant losses. The company was liable for the negligently produced figures, but it had been dissolved. The question was whether M could be personally liable.[35] The lower courts thought so,[36] but the House of Lords disagreed.

**4-18** Their Lordships agreed with the dissenting judge in the Court of Appeal that the fact that, in a one-man company, the functions of the company must necessarily be centred on this individual does not make him personally liable.[37] A director could only be personally liable to third parties for loss which they suffer as a result of negligent advice given to them by the company if he assumes personal responsibility for that advice and the plaintiffs rely on that assumption of responsibility.[38] It is not sufficient that there be a special relationship between the injured party and the company. There must be an assumption of responsibility such as to create a special relationship with the director himself and that will depend on things said and done by or on behalf of the director.[39] Moreover, the test

---

[32] The Court of Appeal noted counsel's point that this route of suing in deceit offers creditors a possible direct remedy against directors which is more advantageous to them than liquidators bringing claims against directors for fraudulent or wrongful trading where any recovery is a collective one for the benefit of all the creditors: see [2008] 1 BCLC 631 at [7].

[33] See Noonan and Watson, n 13, also Grantham [2007], n 12.

[34] [1998] 1 BCLC 689, HL. There are numerous commentaries on this case, see Payne, 'Negligent Misstatement—A Healthier Decision for Company Directors' (1998) CLJ 456; Griffin, 'Company Director's Personal Liability in Tort' (1999) 115 LQR 36; Grantham and Rickett, n 12; Shapira, n 15; Todd, n 19; Reynolds, 'Personal Liability of Company Directors in Tort' (2003) 33 Hong Kong LJ 51.

[35] It had not been pleaded that the director was a joint tortfeasor with the company, see **4-23**, but even if it had been pleaded, it would have failed since, as Lord Steyn pointed out, the basis for a claim for negligent misstatement is a special relationship between the parties giving rise to an assumption of responsibility. Joint tortfeasor liability is based on procuring etc others to act so there cannot be any special relationship between the parties and therefore joint tortfeasor liability could not be relevant to liability for negligent misstatement: see [1998] 1 BCLC 689 at 698.

[36] The Court of Appeal decision is reported at [1997] 1 BCLC 131; the first instance judgment at [1996] 1 BCLC 288.      [37] [1998] 1 BCLC 689 at 697. See also *Trevor Ivory Ltd v Anderson* [1992] 2 NZLR 517.

[38] [1998] 1 BCLC 689 at 695, but see Todd, n 19.

[39] [1998] 1 BCLC 689 at 695. See also *Noel v Poland* [2001] 2 BCLC 645.

of reliance is not simply reliance in fact but whether the plaintiffs can reasonably rely on the assumption of responsibility.[40] On the facts in *Williams*, their Lordships found that there were no personal dealings between M and the claimants, he never crossed the line to assume a personal responsibility towards them, and he was not personally liable.[41]

**4-19**    The decision in *Standard Chartered Bank v Pakistan National Shipping Corp*[42] has clari-fied that where all of the elements of a tort claim can be established against an individual director, such as where fraudulent misrepresentations are made by a director, the fact that he is a director does not and should not act to bar his personal liability. There is no incon-sistency between that decision and the decision in *Williams*. If the elements of negligent misstatement had been established in *Williams*, the individual director would have been liable, but they were not, and so the director was not personally liable. On the other hand, what *Williams*[43] does show is that only in exceptional cases would a claim for negligent misstatement succeed against an individual director.[44] If in a one-man company, such as *Williams*, there was no assumption of responsibility and therefore no liability, it is dif-ficult to imagine an assumption of responsibility by directors in other contexts.[45]

**4-20**    This outcome in respect of economic loss caused by negligence, reached through an appli-cation of tort law, in effect reinforces *Salomon v Salomon & Co Ltd*[46] by leaving liability to fall on the entity, if at all. Liability for economic loss from negligent misstatements is precisely the type of business risk which incorporation is used to manage. This out-come ensures the effectiveness of incorporation in those circumstances and is especially important in the context of small or one-man companies which provide advice and ser-vices.[47] On the other hand, there is no justification for allowing individuals to use corpo-rate structures to avoid liability in tort for deliberate wrongdoing by them individually.[48]

**4-21**    The balance struck in *Williams* and in *Standard Chartered* can be seen as a display of judicial dexterity to resolve the uncertainties which were beginning to gain ground in this area. The decisions are welcome at every level: doctrinally it is important that tort law should apply to directors in the same way as anyone else; pragmatically because the policy issues have been resolved in a practical way which does not allow directors to evade their personal responsibilities while equally ensuring that a director is not always per-sonally liable for all torts arising in the course of a business. The courts are essentially

---

[40]  [1998] 1 BCLC 689 at 696.

[41]  See criticisms of this finding of fact by Shapira, n 15, 133. For an exceptional case where the line was crossed, see *Fairline Shipping Corp v Adamson* [1974] 2 All ER 967 where a director involved himself per-sonally with a customer of the company to such an extent that it was clear that he regarded himself, and not the company, as concerned with the storage of the customer's goods. The director had therefore assumed a duty of care to the customer.                                                     [42]  [2003] 1 BCLC 244, HL.

[43]  [1998] 1 BCLC 689, HL.

[44]  The Court of Appeal has subsequently noted the 'difficult' and 'problematic' nature of a claim for negligent misrepresentation '… since in a company context representations by directors are almost always considered to be made on behalf of their companies': see *Foster v Action Aviation Ltd* [2014] EWCA Civ 1368 at [34].

[45]  See Campbell and Armour, n 12, 301 who make the point that this difficulty in establishing an assump-tion of responsibility will make it difficult to bring a successful claim against any agent acting on behalf of a principal, not just company directors.

[46]  [1897] AC 22, HL.

[47]  See Payne, n 34. Noonan and Watson, n 13, 548 make the point that the very act of incorporation will often be an effective disclaimer of personal liability by a director giving advice on behalf of the company.

[48]  See Grantham (2007), n 12, who makes the point that, when expressing concerns about allowing those engaged in business to shift the risk of their endeavours to others, we must not forget that that is actually the purpose of the legislation allowing for the incorporation of limited liability entities.

determining whether, as a matter of policy, in the particular context, it is appropriate for the entity (negligence) or the entity and the individual (deceit) to bear the liability.

**4-22**    In bringing much needed clarity to this difficult area, their Lordships have taken the opportunity to assert or reassert the primacy of vicarious liability (and so reduce the importance of other specific rules of attribution) in this context with their Lordships asserting in *Williams v Natural Life Health Foods Ltd*[49] and in *Standard Chartered Bank v Pakistan National Shipping Corp*[50] that the matter is an agency matter, one of the personal liability of the agent and corporate vicarious liability for the wrongs of that agent.[51]

## Director's liability for procuring wrongdoing

**4-23**    The discussion to date has centred on the situation where a director personally commits a tort. Another way of imposing liability on a director is to hold a director liable as a joint tortfeasor with the company where, though he has not committed the act himself, the director has authorised, directed, or procured the wrongful act.[52] For example, if an employee of the company makes a fraudulent misrepresentation on behalf of the company, a director could be personally liable if he procured the making of the false statement.[53]

**4-24**    The difficulty is defining the nature and extent of the participation of the director in the tortious act which renders him personally liable on this basis. This is an elusive question, as Slade LJ described it in *C Evans and Sons Ltd v Spritebrand Ltd*,[54] but important guidance was provided by the Court of Appeal in *MCA Records Inc v Charly Records Ltd*.[55] The facts in the case were relatively straightforward. At issue was the liability of Y who did not hold the office of director but who was described as the controller of C Ltd which had infringed the copyright vested in the claimants with respect to certain recordings. Y appealed against a finding that he was personally liable as a joint tortfeasor in respect of the infringement by the company.

**4-25**    The Court of Appeal emphasised that a director is not liable as a joint tortfeasor with the company if he does no more than carry out his constitutional role in the governance of the company, i.e. by voting at board meetings (likewise a controlling shareholder is not liable merely if he exercises control through use of his voting powers).[56] But, if a director or controlling shareholder chooses to exercise control otherwise than through the constitutional organs of the company, and the circumstances are such that he would be liable if he were not a director or controlling shareholder, the court thought that there was no

---

[49] [1998] 1 BCLC 689, HL.       [50] [2003] 1 BCLC 244, HL.

[51] See Lord Hoffmann in *Standard Chartered Bank v Pakistan National Shipping Corp* [2003] 1 BCLC 244 at [20]; Lord Steyn in *Williams v Natural Life Health Foods Ltd* [1998] 1 BCLC 689 at 694.

[52] *Rainham Chemical Works Ltd (in liq) v Belvedere Fish Guano Co Ltd* [1921] 2 AC 465 at 488, HL; *Performing Right Society Ltd v Ciryl Theatrical Syndicate Ltd* [1924] 1 KB 1; *C Evans and Sons Ltd v Spritebrand Ltd* [1985] BCLC 105.       [53] See *Daido Asia Japan Co Ltd v Rothen* [2002] BCC 589 at [32].

[54] See [1985] BCLC 105 at 117.

[55] [2003] 1 BCLC 93, CA. See Ho, 'Liability of Directors as Joint Tortfeasors' [2009] JBL 109; see also *SEI Spa v Ordnance Technologies (UK) Ltd (No 2)* [2008] 2 All ER 622 (managing director and sole shareholder of a company liable as joint tortfeasor with the company having shared a common design that the acts complained of, the infringement of design rights, should take place; the director encouraged or procured the breach by the company's engineers).

[56] [2003] 1 BCLC 93 at [49]. See the valuable discussion by Hughes, 'Competition Law Enforcement and Corporate Group Liability—Adjusting the Veil' (2014) 35 ECLR 68, of potential tortious liability on the part of individual directors and controlling shareholders where they act unconstitutionally.

reason why he should not be liable with the company as a joint tortfeasor.[57] The issue is whether A would be liable as a joint tortfeasor with the primary infringer B, whether or not the relationship between A and B is that A is a director of B.[58]

**4-26**　Chadwick LJ emphasised that the relevant enquiry is whether the individual has been personally involved in the commission of the tort to the extent sufficient to attract liability as a joint tortfeasor. The director must be concerned with the company in a joint act done in pursuance of a common purpose so as to attract liability.[59] But, Chadwick LJ went on:[60] 'if all that a director is doing is carrying out the duties entrusted to him as such by the company under its constitution, the circumstances in which it would be right to hold him liable as a joint tortfeasor with the company would be rare indeed.'

**4-27**　Returning to the dispute in *MCA Records Inc v Charly Records Ltd*,[61] the court noted that, in the context of intellectual property, liability as a joint tortfeasor might arise where the individual intends and procures and shares a common design that the infringement take place. On the facts, Y induced the company to copy the recordings and to issue them to the public, he planned the exploitation of the recordings, and intended that the company should continue to do so for as long as possible. He was rightly liable, the court held, as a joint tortfeasor.[62]

**4-28**　The position on liability as a joint tortfeasor is now governed by the Supreme Court decision in *Fish & Fish Ltd v Sea Shepherd UK*[63] where the Supreme Court ruled that, in order to be liable with a principal tortfeasor, it has to be proved that a defendant combined with the principal tortfeasor to do, or to secure the doing of, acts which constituted the tort and this requires proof that the defendant acted in a way which furthered the commission of the tort by the principal tortfeasor and that the defendant did so in pursuance of a common design to do, or to secure the doing of, the acts which constituted the tort. In *National Guild of Removers and Storers Limited v Luckes*,[64] applying those principles, the court found a company had committed the act of passing off (by including certain information on its website), but its two directors were not liable as joint tortfeasors when it turned out that they did not know of the information wrongly included on the website. As the court noted, an alleged joint tortfeasor cannot have actively co-operated to bring about the relevant act of the primary tortfeasor if he (the alleged joint tortfeasor) did not know about that act.

**4-29**　Clearly a factual analysis of the director's conduct is needed in each instance and, in essence, where the director acts appropriately and seeks to ensure that the company's

---

[57] [2003] 1 BCLC 93 at [50].　　[58] [2003] 1 BCLC 93 at [41].

[59] [2003] 1 BCLC 93 at [37], applying *The Koursk* [1924] P 140. To be liable with a principal tortfeasor, a defendant has to be proved to have combined with the principal tortfeasor to do, or to secure the doing of, acts which constitute the tort; that requires proof that the defendant acted in a way which furthered the commission of the tort by the principal tortfeasor and that he had done so in pursuance of a common design to do, or to secure the doing of, the acts which constitute the tort; whether the matters relied on had any significance to the commission of the tort would depend on the circumstances of the case: *Fish & Fish Ltd v Sea Shepherd UK* [2015] 2 WLR 694, S Ct.　　[60] [2003] 1 BCLC 93 at [49].

[61] [2003] 1 BCLC 93, CA.

[62] See also *Koninklijke Philips Electronics NV v Prico Digital Disc GmbH* [2004] 2 BCLC 50 (defendant director was in charge of the day-to-day running of the defendant company which infringed the claimant's patent. Held: the director's close involvement with the day-to-day actions of the company, and his independent authority in respect of those actions, were sufficient to render him liable as a joint tortfeasor with the company).　　[63] [2015] UKSC 10, [2015] AC 1229.

[64] [2017] EWHC 3176.

agents and employees conduct themselves in accordance with the law, personal liability is unlikely. The importance of potential liability as a joint tortfeasor, however, is that it ensures that a director cannot easily evade liability by the device of ensuring that another agent or employee carries out wrongful acts at his direction.

## D  Criminal liability of the company

**4-30**  A company is subject to the criminal law in the same manner as any other person although, as an artificial legal entity, there are some offences which a company is deemed unable to commit such as bigamy or offences of assault and some offences for which it cannot be convicted as the only penalty is imprisonment, such as murder.[65] Otherwise, the requisite *actus reus* and *mens rea* can be sought in the relevant officer, agent, or employee and the fact that there is a *mens rea* requirement is no obstacle to corporate liability. Thus, a company can be held liable for offences involving an intent to deceive;[66] for conspiracy to defraud;[67] and for filing false tax returns.[68]

**4-31**  As far as criminal law is concerned, in general vicarious liability or agency will not be relevant and an employer or principal is not criminally liable for an offence committed by his employee or agent (assuming the employer has not aided or procured the commission of the offence in some way), even though it is committed in the course of the employment or agency, though there are statutory exceptions where an absolute liability is imposed on the employer or principal (including a corporate employer or principal) for the wilful acts or default of a servant or employee.[69] Hence, as a matter of criminal law, it will often be necessary to apply rules of attribution to determine whether a criminal act by a director or employee should be attributed to the company so as to make the company also a criminal.

**4-32**  What those rules of attribution are was explored in detail by Lord Hoffmann in *Meridian Global Funds Management Asia Ltd v Securities Commission*[70] where he attempted to set the law on this issue on a new purposive basis different from the then prevailing 'directing mind and will' approach. That directing mind and will approach required 'the identification of the natural person or persons who are to be regarded as representing the juridical person for the purposes of the substantive rule in question',[71] those persons who are the embodiment of the company itself such that their acts are the acts of the company.[72] The relationship between *Meridian* and the directing mind and will doctrine remains controversial, as is discussed in what follows.

---

[65]  See generally Wells, *Corporations and Criminal Responsibility* (2nd edn, 2001).
[66]  *DPP v Kent and Sussex Contractors Ltd* [1944] 1 All ER 119.
[67]  *R v ICR Haulage Ltd* [1944] 1 All ER 691.    [68]  *Moore v I Bresler Ltd* [1944] 2 All ER 515.
[69]  *Mousell Bros v London and North-Western Rly Co* [1917] 2 KB 836 at 845; *G Newton Ltd v Smith* [1962] 2 All ER 19. See *R v British Steel plc* [1995] 1 WLR 1356; *National Rivers Authority v Alfred McAlpine Homes East Ltd* [1994] 4 All ER 286; *Re Supply of Ready Mixed Concrete (No 2), Director General of Fair Trading v Pioneer Concrete (UK) Ltd* [1995] 1 BCLC 613, HL.    [70]  [1995] 2 BCLC 116, PC.
[71]  *MAN Nutzfahrzeuge AG v Freightliner Ltd* [2005] EWHC 2347 (Comm) at [154], per Moore Bick LJ.
[72]  *Lennard's Carrying Co Ltd v Asiatic Petroleum Co Ltd* [1915] AC 705 at 713–14, per Viscount Haldane, HL.

## Rules of attribution

**4-33** Rules of attribution are necessary then to determine whose acts count as the acts of the company and the issue is dominated by the speech of Lord Hoffmann in *Meridian Global Funds Management Asia Ltd v Securities Commission*,[73] a much cited Privy Council decision which is accepted as setting out the domestic law on this matter.[74] For Lord Hoffmann, the answer to the question of whose act is to be attributed to the company lies, not in metaphysics, not in searching for some alter ego of the company, but in the construction of the particular substantive rule. It is for the court to ask whose act or knowledge or state of mind is for the purpose of that rule intended to count as the act, knowledge, or state of mind of the company, applying the usual canons of interpretation, taking into account the language of the rule (if it is a statute) and its content and policy.[75] The scope and application of the *Meridian* principle is the central issue in this area, but before exploring it, we must first consider the metaphysics to which Lord Hoffmann alluded.

## Directing mind and will

**4-34** Prior to *Meridian Global Funds Management Asia Ltd v Securities Commission*[76] the rule of attribution commonly relied on was that of 'the directing mind and will of the company' which requires the identification of the natural person or persons who are seen as the embodiment of the company such that their acts may be attributed to the company (the identification doctrine). This doctrine derives from *Lennard's Carrying Co Ltd v Asiatic Petroleum Co Ltd*[77] where Viscount Haldane famously noted:

> 'My Lords, a corporation is an abstraction. It has no mind of its own any more than it has a body of its own; its active and directing will must consequently be sought in the person of somebody who for some purposes may be called an agent, but who is really the directing mind and will of the corporation, the very ego and centre of the personality of the corporation.'

At issue in *Lennard's Carrying Co Ltd v Asiatic Petroleum Co Ltd* was whether a ship-owning company could escape liability for loss of cargo damaged by fire which, under s 502 of the Merchant Shipping Act 1894, it could only do if it could show that the loss occurred without its actual fault or privity. As the managing director of the company knew that the relevant ship's boilers were unsafe and that was the cause of the fire, his knowledge as the directing mind and will of the company was attributed to the company, and therefore the company could not show that the loss occurred without its actual fault. But as Lord Hoffmann subsequently explained in *Meridian*,[78] on closer analysis, Viscount Haldane was using 'directing mind and will' as merely descriptive of the person designated for the

---

[73] [1995] 2 BCLC 116, PC.

[74] *Meridian* has been relied on in numerous cases subsequently. It was cited with approval in the House of Lords in *Stone & Rolls Ltd v Moore Stephens* [2009] 2 BCLC 563, see at [39] (Lord Phillips); at [104] (Lord Scott); at [134] (Lord Walker). See Lord Walker in *Moulin Global Eyecare Trading Ltd v Commission of Inland Revenue* [2014] HKEC 419 at [77], HKCFA: 'Meridian is now rightly regarded as the leading case on the topic of attribution in company law.'　　　　　　　　　　　　[75] [1995] 2 BCLC 116 at 122.

[76] [1995] 2 BCLC 116, PC.

[77] [1915] AC 705 at 713, HL; see also Lord Denning in *HL Bolton (Engineering) Co Ltd v TJ Graham & Sons Ltd* [1957] 1 QB 159 at 172, CA.　　　　　　　　　　[78] [1995] 2 BCLC 116 at 124, 126.

purposes of the Merchant Shipping Act 1894, s 502, as the person whose acts were the acts of the company.[79]

**4-35** To identify the directing mind and will of the company, it is necessary to consult the company's constitution which typically vests all powers of management in the board and there is no doubt that the board collectively represents the directing mind and will of the company such that its acts are the acts of the company, as are the decisions of the shareholders in general meeting. Equally, at the other end of the spectrum, it is clear that not all acts of all employees can be attributed to the company, for not all will have the status and authority which in law makes their acts in the matter under consideration the acts of the company.[80]

**4-36** That 'the directing mind and will' does not encompass more junior management was confirmed by the House of Lords in *Tesco Supermarkets Ltd v Nattrass*.[81] In this case, Tesco was prosecuted under the Trade Descriptions Act 1968 for the failure of one of its shop managers to ensure that goods advertised for sale at a particular price were in fact being offered for sale at that price. It was a defence under the 1968 Act to show that the act was due to the default of some 'other person'. The company pleaded on appeal that the manager did not amount to the directing mind and will of the company and therefore the company could assert that the act was due to the default of some 'other person'. The House of Lords agreed and held that the shop manager, one of several hundred, could not be treated as the embodiment of the company and his acts and defaults could not be attributed to the company. The offence was indeed due to the act or default of 'another person' and not of the company itself.[82] As Lord Reid noted:[83]

> 'Normally the board of directors, the managing director and perhaps other superior officers of a company carry out the functions of management and speak and act as the company. Their subordinates do not … But the board of directors may delegate some part of the functions of management, giving to their delegate full discretion to act independently of instructions from them. I see no difficulty in holding that they have thereby put such a delegate in their place so that within the scope of the delegation he can act as the company … If the criminal act of an officer servant or agent including his state of mind, intention, knowledge or belief can be identified with the company then it is an act of the company.'

**4-37** There the law rested until Lord Hoffmann, initially in *El Ajou v Dollar Land Holdings plc*,[84] and then authoritatively in *Meridian Global Funds Management Asia Ltd v Securities Commission*,[85] set out a broader purposive approach which considers the issue of attribution not from the position in the corporate hierarchy of the defaulting agent or employee, but rather with a view to the purpose of the statutory (or other) provision and

---

[79] See Lord Walker's comments in *Moulin Global Eyecare Trading Ltd v Commission of Inland Revenue* [2014] HKEC 419 at [67], HKCFA, that 'this belated recognition (in *Meridian*) of this important qualification to the directing mind and will concept—that the statutory context in *Lennard's* required the identification of the directing mind and will of the company to see if those responsible for the loss of the cargo were the responsible officers for the company—'considerably reduces its apparent force'.

[80] *R v Andrews Weatherfoil Ltd* [1972] 1 All ER 65 at 70, per Eveleigh J. See too *HL Bolton (Engineering) Co Ltd v TJ Graham & Sons Ltd* [1957] 1 QB 159 at 172, CA. 'Some of the people in the company are mere servants and agents who are nothing more than hands to do the work and cannot be said to represent the mind or will. Others are directors and managers who represent the directing mind and will of the company and control what it does. The state of mind of those managers is the state of mind of the company and is treated by the law as such.'      [81] [1972] AC 153, HL.

[82] Cf *Tesco Supermarket Ltd v Brent LBC* [1993] 1 WLR 1037.    [83] [1972] AC 152 at 171.

[84] [1994] 1 BCLC 464.    [85] [1995] 2 BCLC 116, PC.

to furthering that purpose. The necessity for taking this broader approach arises from the situation where the acts in question have been carried out by, or the knowledge at issue lies with, individuals who cannot be identified as the directing mind and will of the company in circumstances where vicarious liability is not relevant. In those circumstances, unless another rule of attribution can be applied, the acts and knowledge of those individuals cannot be attributed to the company and the relevant rule cannot be applied to the company which would usually be an unsatisfactory outcome in the absence of evidence that the rule was not intended to apply to companies.

**4-38**   In *El Ajou v Dollar Land Holdings plc*[86] the Court of Appeal accepted that the fraudulent intent of the non-executive chairman of a company should be imputed to the company in a 'knowing receipt' case. He was the 'directing mind and will of the company' with respect to the particular transaction at issue—the company's receipt of investment funds which the chairman knew to be the proceeds of fraud—and his knowledge was the company's knowledge. Nourse and Rose LJJ agreed with Hoffmann LJ that depending on the context, the directing mind and will of the company might be found in different persons, not necessarily at board level. Nourse LJ noted that it '… is necessary to identify the natural person or persons having management and control in relation to the act or omission in point',[87] and concluded that the directing mind and will of the company was the chairman in relation to the relevant transaction, though not with respect to the rest of the business.[88] Rose LJ agreed that the directors are, *prima facie*, likely to be regarded as the company's directing mind and will, whereas particular circumstances may confer that status on non-directors. He went on to note that a company's directing mind and will may be found in different persons for different activities of the company.[89] In this instance, for the limited purposes here relevant to the receipt of the money, the chairman was the directing mind and will of the company.[90] Hoffmann LJ agreed that the non-executive chairman of the company should be treated, for the purpose of the transaction at issue, as the directing mind and will, a reflection of the point later made by him in *Meridian Global Funds Management Asia Ltd v Securities Commission*,[91] that the term 'directing mind and will' will often be the most appropriate description of the person whose acts, for the relevant purpose, do count as the acts of the company, but that not every attribution rule needs to be forced into that formula.

### Meridian Global Funds Asia Ltd v Securities Commission

**4-39**   Returning to *Meridian Global Funds Management Asia Ltd v Securities Commission*,[92] in this case two employees of a Hong Kong investment management company (Meridian), one of them the company's chief investment officer, used company funds to purchase a 49 per cent stake in a listed New Zealand company. The purchase was not disclosed by Meridian as required under the New Zealand Securities Amendment Act 1988 which essentially required the disclosure of significant shareholdings as soon as the person acquiring them 'knows or ought to know' that the person is a substantial security holder in the company. The question was whether the knowledge of the employees should be attributed to Meridian so that it was in breach of the statutory requirement. The company argued that, in the absence of knowledge by the directing mind and will (i.e. the board) of the acquisition of the shares, there was no breach.

---

[86] [1994] 1 BCLC 464.       [87] [1994] 1 BCLC 464 at 473.        [88] [1994] 1 BCLC 464 at 474.
[89] [1994] 1 BCLC 464 at 477.      [90] [1994] 1 BCLC 464 at 477.        [91] [1995] 2 BCLC 116 at 126, PC.
[92] [1995] 2 BCLC 116, PC.

**4-40**   The Privy Council found that, on a true construction of the relevant statute and in view of the policy of the legislation, it was appropriate to attribute the knowledge of a senior employee (the chief investment officer) to the company, since otherwise the policy of the Act would be defeated and there would be a premium on the board paying as little attention as possible to what its investment managers were doing. Accordingly, Meridian knew that it was a substantial shareholder in another company when that was known to the employee who had authority to acquire the shares. Meridian was therefore in breach of the disclosure requirement.

**4-41**   In a now much cited speech, Lord Hoffmann reviewed the whole question of attribution. The primary rules of attribution in company law are to be found in the company's constitution, typically the articles, which will determine how decisions of the company are to be reached, commonly by resolution of the board of directors or of the shareholders in general meeting, and additionally company law recognises the unanimous informal assent of the shareholders in a solvent company as an act of the company.[93] There are also general principles of attribution, such as agency and vicarious liability, as noted, which will determine whether the acts of others count as the acts of the company. Lord Hoffmann went on:[94]

> 'The company's primary rules of attribution together with the general principles of agency, vicarious liability and so forth are usually sufficient to enable one to determine its rights and obligations. In exceptional cases, however, they will not provide an answer. This will be the case when a rule of law, either expressly or by implication, excludes attribution on the basis of the general principles of agency or vicarious liability. For example, a rule may be stated in language primarily applicable to a natural person and require some act or state of mind on the part of that person "himself", as opposed to his servants or agents. This is generally true of rules of the criminal law, which ordinarily impose liability only for the actus reus and mens rea of the defendant himself. How is such a rule to be applied to a company?'

He noted that if the court decided that a substantive rule of law (whether a statutory or common law rule) was intended to apply to a company, it then had to decide how the rule was intended to apply and whose act or knowledge or state of mind was for that purpose intended to count as the act, knowledge, or state of mind of the company.[95] Although in some cases that could be determined by applying the 'directing mind and will' test, that test was not appropriate in all cases. Instead, Lord Hoffmann said, it was a question of construction in each case as to whether the particular rule requires that the knowledge that an act has been done, or the state of mind with which it was done, should be attributed to the company.[96] For example, in *Tesco Supermarkets Ltd v Nattrass*[97] discussed at **4-36**, the acts or defaults of the store manager were not attributed to the company, Lord Hoffmann explained, because the purpose of the statutory provision in that case, the protection of consumers, did not require that the offence be an absolute one.[98] In *Re Supply of Ready Mixed Concrete (No 2), Director General of Fair Trading v Pioneer Concrete (UK) Ltd*,[99] however, it was necessary to attribute the acts of the employees to the company.

---

[93] [1995] 2 BCLC 116 at 121, PC.     [94] [1995] 2 BCLC 116 at 122.     [95] [1995] 2 BCLC 116 at 122.
[96] [1995] 2 BCLC 116 at 122. Lord Hoffmann was quite clear that the principle he was laying down was applicable to any rule and was not limited to a statutory rule, see [1995] 2 BCLC 116 at 122; see also Nourse LJ in *Odyssey Re (London) Ltd v OIC Run-off Ltd* [2001] 1 Lloyd's Rep IR 1 at 11 but Buxton LJ, dissenting in *Odyssey*, makes the point (at 96) that *Meridian* was formulated, and is most easily understood, in the context of the application of statutory rules and it is much less easy to apply it to a rule of the common law.
[97] [1972] AC 153, HL.     [98] [1995] 2 BCLC 116 at 122.     [99] [1995] 1 BCLC 613, HL.

In this case, a company was liable in contempt when its employees, while acting in the course of their employment but contrary to instructions issued by the board, carried out a deliberate act contrary to a restrictive practices order imposed on the company. The restrictive practices legislation would otherwise be worth little, Lord Hoffmann noted, if the company could avoid liability for what its employees did on the basis that the board did not know about it.[100]

**4-42**   In other words, to ensure the effective application of a statutory provision or other rule to a company, it may be necessary to consider a different approach to attribution. Finally, Lord Hoffmann ended with a note of caution, pointing out that their Lordships:[101]

> 'would wish to guard themselves against being understood to mean that whenever a servant of a company has authority to do an act on its behalf, knowledge of that act will for all purposes be attributed to the company. It is a question of construction in each case as to whether the particular rule requires that the knowledge that an act has been done, or the state of mind with which it was done, should be attributed to the company.'

**4-43**   An illustration of the use of a special rule of attribution in this way arising from the need to apply a particular statutory provision to a company can be seen in *Re Bank of Credit and Commerce International SA (in liquidation) (No 15); Morris v Bank of India.*[102] The liquidators of BCCI alleged that the defendant bank, by entering into various transactions, knowingly participated in the fraudulent trading of BCCI giving rise to a civil liability under IA 1986, s 213. The key issue was whether those at the bank responsible for entering into the transactions at issue knew that they were thereby assisting BCCI to perpetrate a fraud on its creditors and whether their knowledge should be attributed to the bank. The various transactions had been assisted and facilitated by a bank official (S) who was the general manager of the London branch of the bank.

**4-44**   Applying *Meridian Global Funds Management Asia Ltd v Securities Commission*[103] the Court of Appeal looked to the construction and purpose of IA 1986, s 213 and concluded that the wording and policy behind the section indicated that it would be inappropriate to limit attribution for its purposes to the board or those specifically authorised by a resolution of the board.[104] The crucial question was whose knowledge counted, for the purposes of IA 1986, s 213, as corporate knowledge of the bank. Given that transactions of this nature would be dealt with at a level below that of the board, it would in practice defeat the effectiveness of the section, the court said, if liability was limited to those cases in which the board of directors was directly privy to the fraud.[105] Turning to the facts of the case, the court thought this was plainly an appropriate case for attribution. S had a senior position in the bank, he brought the transactions to the bank, the board relied on him in relation to them, he was given a free hand to negotiate them, and they were plainly suspicious.[106] His knowledge was more relevant than that of any member of the board or of anyone else in the bank and it was necessary, given the purpose of the provision, to attribute his knowledge to the bank which was therefore liable.[107] But the Court of Appeal was careful to emphasise (as their Lordships had done in *Meridian*) that it would be wrong to attribute to a company the knowledge of any agent irrespective of the particular facts.[108] It is necessary in each case to look at the purpose of the statutory provision and consider whether, in those particular circumstances, the statutory purpose will be defeated unless

[100]  [1995] 2 BCLC 116 at 123.        [101]  [1995] 2 BCLC 116 at 126.        [102]  [2005] 2 BCLC 328.
[103]  [1995] 2 BCLC 116, PC.        [104]  [2005] 2 BCLC 328 at [112].
[105]  [2005] 2 BCLC 328 at [112], [120].        [106]  [2005] 2 BCLC 328 at [126].
[107]  [2005] 2 BCLC 328 at [120].        [108]  [2005] 2 BCLC 328 at [129], [130].

a special rule of attribution (which may include attributing the acts of employees lower down the corporate hierarchy) is applied.[109]

**4-45**   Another Privy Council application of *Meridian Global Funds Management Asia Ltd v Securities Commission*[110] can be found in *Lebon v Aqua Salt Co Ltd*[111] where the issue was whether knowledge of a prior sale of land could be attributed to a company (the second purchaser) when that knowledge rested in one of its directors who was also the promoter and substantial shareholder in the company. Their Lordships considered that the substantive purpose of the relevant rule here was to prevent an inequitable trumping of the title of a first purchaser by a second purchaser with knowledge of the first transaction and the question for the court then is which rule of attribution would best serve the purpose of that rule.[112] They concluded that the substantive rule did require that the knowledge of the director, promoter, and substantial shareholder be attributed to the company. He knew of the earlier sale and it should not be possible for the company to have better rights against the first purchaser than he alone would have had. Information relevant to the company's affairs in the possession of one director, however that occurs, can properly be regarded as information in the possession of the company itself.[113]

**4-46**   Further civil law application of a 'special rule' of attribution can be found in *Odyssey Re (London) Ltd v OIC Run-off Ltd*[114] where the Court of Appeal by a majority held that the evidence of a witness who committed perjury was attributable to the company though, at the time of acting, he was no longer a director or employee or even an agent of the company (meaning that the primary or general rules of attribution did not apply to attribute his intent to perjure to the company). For the court, it was a question of applying a special rule of attribution and asking whose act was, for the purpose of giving evidence, the act of the company. On the facts, the court by a majority concluded the evidence of the individual was the act of the company. This individual was instrumental in the transaction which was the subject of the evidence and he took a lead in the preparation and presentation of the evidence. In those circumstances, his perjury was the perjury of the company and the judgment in favour of the company was set aside. In *Sudarshan Chemical Industries Ltd v Clariant Produkte (Deutschland) GmbH*[115] at issue was whose knowledge as to the potential invalidity of a patent was to be treated as knowledge of the company for the purposes of the Patent Act 1977, s 70(2A)(b). The Court of Appeal, applying *Meridian,* concluded that, for the purpose of this provision, the controlling mind of the company must include at least the mind of the properly informed patent attorney or, put another way, the minds of the patent attorney and the inventor.[116] In other words, the knowledge of the employees most closely connected to and knowledgeable about the patent should be treated as knowledge of the company for this statutory purpose.

### *Meridian* in the criminal context

**4-47**   While support for the purposive approach laid down in *Meridian Global Funds Management Asia Ltd v Securities Commission*[117] seems well established in the civil context now, the position is less clear where a criminal liability is involved where there seems to be judicial support for maintaining the orthodox attribution rule requiring intent to

---

[109] [2005] 2 BCLC 328 at [129]–[130].      [110] [1995] 2 BCLC 116, PC.      [111] [2009] 1 BCLC 549.
[112] [2009] 1 BCLC 549 at [25].
[113] [2009] 1 BCLC 549 at [24]–[26], applying Moore-Bick LJ in *Jafari-Fini v Skillglass Ltd* [2007] EWCA Civ 261 at [98].      [114] [2001] 1 Lloyd's Rep IR 1.
[115] [2014] RPC 6, CA.      [116] [2014] RPC 6 at [130]–[132].      [117] [1995] 2 BCLC 116, PC.

be found in the 'directing mind and will' of the company at board or 'superior officer' level. The point was addressed by the Court of Appeal in *A-G's Reference (No 2 of 1999)*[118] (liability for manslaughter) which noted that:

> 'Lord Hoffmann's speech in the *Meridian* case, in fashioning an additional special rule of attribution geared to *the purpose of the statute* [emphasis added], proceeded on the basis that the primary "directing mind and will" rule still applies although it is not determinative in all cases. In other words, he was not departing from the identification theory but re-affirming its existence.'

**4-48**   The starting point in the criminal law remains therefore the application of the directing mind and will theory, applying *Tesco Supermarkets Ltd v Nattrass*.[119] The question is whether it is possible to identify someone whose acts can be equated with the directing mind and will of the company such that his acts and knowledge, being the acts and knowledge which constitute the offence, are the acts and knowledge of the company. Even Lord Hoffmann in *Meridian* accepted that reference to the 'directing mind and will' is often the most appropriate description of the person designated for the purpose of the relevant attribution rule.[120] If, on the other hand, the 'guilty' party cannot be identified as the directing mind and will of the company so that route of attribution is not open, the issue is whether the purpose and policy of the rule under consideration (such as the statutory provision in *Meridian* itself involving a criminal liability) requires the application of a special rule of attribution in order to ensure that the particular prohibition/requirement can be applied to companies.

**4-49**   An example of this step approach to the application of *Tesco Supermarkets Ltd v Nattrass*[121] and *Meridian Global Funds Management Asia Ltd v Securities Commission*[122] can be seen in *R v St Regis Paper Company Ltd*.[123] A company operated a number of mills and it was convicted along with an employee (a technical manager) of offences under the Pollution Prevention and Control (England and Wales) Regulations.[124] The employee gave false environmental pollution readings to the Environmental Protection Agency and was convicted, as was the company, of the offence of intentionally making a false entry in the records. The company was convicted, not on the basis that the employee was the directing mind and will of the company, but on the basis of a special rule of attribution to give effect to the policy of the legislation, applying *Meridian*. The Court of Appeal quashed the conviction, finding that there was no basis in law for attributing the dishonest intent of the technical manager to the company. The general rule of attribution, the directing mind and will theory, as laid down in *Tesco Supermarkets Ltd v Nattrass*[125] should be applied, the court held, and it was not appropriate in the circumstances to seek a special rule of attribution to avoid emasculating the legislation, as the trial judge had put it.[126] The importance of

---

[118]   [2000] 2 BCLC 257 at 268.

[119]   As a matter of precedent, but see Brooke LJ in *Odyssey Re (London) Ltd v OIC Run-off Ltd* [2001] 1 Lloyd's Rep IR 1 at 66, who accepts that that might be the case but it should not impede the development of the *Meridian* approach in civil cases, while Buxton LJ, see at 94, dissenting in that case, emphasised the importance of *Tesco v Nattrass* as binding authority on attribution in criminal law, noting that the analysis in *Meridian* is 'at best an imperfect guide to the correct approach to the rule for attribution of a crime …'. See too Ferran, n 143, at 258–9 who notes that any retreat from *Meridian* on the criminal side is not necessarily a matter for regret if the alternative was unacceptable judicial activism in circumstances where often it is not possible to determine the policy and purpose behind the substantive rule.

[120]   See [1995] 2 BCLC 116 at 124b.      [121]   [1972] AC 153, HL.      [122]   [1995] 2 BCLC 116, PC.

[123]   [2012] 1 Cr App R 14.      [124]   SI 2000/1973.      [125]   [1972] AC 153, HL.

[126]   [2012] 1 Cr App R 14 at [7]–[11], [14].

avoiding environmental pollution could not be overstated, but the regulations had sought to meet that danger in a carefully graduated way imposing both offences of strict liability and those which required proof of intention.[127] As a matter of statutory construction of the regulations, there was no warrant for imposing liability on the company by virtue of the intentions of one who could not be said to be the directing mind and will of the company, i.e. the statutory purpose here did not require a special rule of attribution.[128]

**4-50**    Despite some expectation that *Meridian* would see the demise of the 'directing mind and will' approach, it survives then particularly in the criminal jurisdiction, not just as a descriptive term for the person whose conduct, applying a purposive approach, is for the specific purpose treated as the conduct of the company (which is how Lord Hoffmann explained it in *Meridian*), but as a distinct rule of attribution.[129]

**4-51**    The significance of this attribution issue in the criminal context may dwindle over time as Parliament seems to have taken on board these difficulties and in relation both to corporate manslaughter and bribery offences has preferred to legislate specifically for the manner in which corporate liability may arise[130] rather than to leave any room for further debate as to the relevant rule of attribution.[131] Future legislation imposing corporate liability may well commonly make clear the basis on which that liability can arise, but for the moment, particularly (and perhaps exclusively) in the context of criminal offences, the courts seem wedded to the directing mind and will approach, as laid down in *Tesco Supermarkets Ltd v Nattrass*,[132] with *Meridian* allowing an alternative approach if needed to ensure the application of the relevant rule to a company.[133]

### Non-attribution in cases of breach of duty

**4-52**    A further scenario to consider is the situation where a company director is involved in a breach of duty to the company. If, applying the rules of attribution discussed in the earlier part of this chapter, the knowledge of the director is to be attributed to the company, the question is whether, by virtue of that attribution, the company becomes complicit in the wrongdoing such that a defence of *ex turpi causa* (essentially precludes claims based on the claimants' own illegality) may become relevant.[134]

---

[127]  [2012] 1 Cr App R 14 at [14].

[128]  [2012] 1 Cr App R 14 at [12]. See Payne, n 133, who comments that this conclusion was an odd reading of the statutory provisions, given that there must be a clear purpose, on most people's reading, to those provisions, namely that environmental pollution records must be accurate, and given that purpose, it would be appropriate to attribute the knowledge of this employee to the company. Maintaining records will never be a task done by the 'directing mind and will'.                   [129]  See Ferran, n 143, at 250.

[130]  See the Corporate Manslaughter and Corporate Homicide Act 2007, s 1 and the Bribery Act 2010, ss 7 and 8.

[131]  The Law Commission has looked at the identification principle as part of a wider project, see Law Commission Consultation Paper No 195, *Criminal Liability in Regulatory Contexts* (2010), and hopes to return to a full-scale project on corporate liability in the future.                   [132]  [1972] AC 153, HL.

[133]  See Ferran, n 143, at 246–7, who notes that the unwillingness of the judiciary, for reasons which are unclear, to extend the more flexible approach in *Meridian* 'looks disappointing'. See also Payne, 'Corporate Attribution and the Lessons of Meridian' in P Davies and J Pila (eds), *The Jurisprudence of Lord Hoffmann: A Festschrift for Leonard H Hoffmann* (2015) who notes that the lessons of *Meridian* have not been wholly learned and that a return to the principle set out by Lord Hoffmann would bring clarity to what is a rather confused area of the law.

[134]  The proper approach to the defence of illegality is governed now by *Patel v Mirza* [2016] UKSC 42, [2017] 1 All ER 191. See Worthington, n 154, at 128–31, who considers that the illegality defence, in so far as it prevents claimants from recovering benefits from their own personal wrongdoing, will never apply to companies since the wrongdoing will necessarily always be the act of an individual rather than the company.

**4-53** There are three scenarios which need to be considered:[135] (i) where a third party sues the company as a result of the wrong committed by the director and attributed to the company; (ii) where the company sues a third party and the claim is linked to a wrong committed by the director; and (iii) where the company seeks to sue a director for breach of duty together with anyone implicated in the breach of duty.

**4-54** The first scenario is where a third party sues the company, for example, because of a tort or other wrongdoing committed by a director or an employee for which the company is liable, the company is a wrongdoer (because the wrong has been attributed to it) and liable to the third party accordingly.[136] In this case, as Patten LJ explained in *Bilta (UK) Ltd v Nazir*,[137] 'the interests of the third party who is the intended victim of the unlawful conduct takes priority over the loss which the company will suffer through the actions of its own directors'.[138]

**4-55** In the second scenario, where a company sues a third party, for example, the company auditor for negligence in failing to detect fraud by the company's controller, the question is whether the third party can raise the defence of *ex turpi causa* on the basis that the company is a wrongdoer. In *Stone & Rolls Ltd v Moore Stephens*,[139] the company had been used as a vehicle for fraud by S, its beneficial owner. The liquidator of the company tried to sue the company's auditors in negligence, but the auditors argued that the fraudster's conduct was to be attributed to the company such that the company itself was the fraudster and any claim by the company was therefore barred by the *ex turpi causa* principle.[140] The House of Lords divided 3–2 in favour of allowing the auditors' defence, but the judgments were 'a morass of complex reasoning'[141] offering no discernible ratio[142] and the decision is much criticised.[143] It is now relegated to the sidelines and, as Lords Toulson and Hodge said in *Jetivia SA v Bilta (UK) Ltd*,[144] it should only be considered 'as authority for the point which it decided, namely that on the facts of that case, no claim lay against the auditors'.[145]

**4-56** More recently, in *Singularis Holdings Ltd v Daiwa Capital Markets Europe Ltd*[146] a company wished to sue its bank for failing in its duty of care to the company when it allowed the company's managing director and sole shareholder to transfer very large sums of money to other companies belonging to the director. The court rejected the bank's argument that its duty of care to a customer did not apply in circumstances where the fraudster controlled the customer. The court did not think it would be right to attribute the

---

[135] Lim, 'Attribution in Company Law' (2014) 77 MLR 794. This approach was adopted in *Jetivia SA v Bilta (UK) Ltd* [2015] UKSC 23, [2015] 1 BCLC 443 at [87] by Lord Sumption; and at [204] by Lords Toulson and Hodge.

[136] See, for example, *El Ajou v Dollar Land plc* [1994] 1 BCLC 464 (company liable in knowing receipt).

[137] [2014] 1 BCLC 302, CA; aff'd sub nom *Jetivia SA v Bilta (UK) Ltd* [2015] UKSC 23, [2015] 1 BCLC 443.

[138] [2014] 1 BCLC 302 at [34]. As Lim, n 135, points out, at 802, no third party would be willing to do business with any company if the law were to deny them the basic right to sue the company for wrongdoing done to the third party by the company. [139] [2009] 2 BCLC 563.

[140] [2008] 2 BCLC 461 at 493, per Rimer LJ.

[141] Ferran, n 143, at 251; and see Watts, n 143, [2014] JBL 161 at 166 ('intractable reasoning').

[142] As Lord Walker, of the majority, acknowledged, see *Moulin Global Eyecare Trading Ltd v Commission of Inland Revenue* [2014] HKEC 419 at [100], HKCFA.

[143] See Davies, 'Auditors' Liability: No Need to Detect Fraud' (2010) 68 CLJ 505; Halpern, '*Stone & Rolls Ltd v Moore Stephens*: An Unnecessary Tangle' (2010) 73 MLR 487; Watts, '*Stone & Rolls Ltd v Moore Stephens*: Audit Contracts and Turpitude' (2010) 126 LQR 14; Ferran, 'Corporate Attribution and the Directing Mind and Will' (2011) 127 LQR 239. [144] [2015] UKSC 23, [2015] 1 BCLC 443.

[145] [2015] UKSC 23, [2015] 1 BCLC 443 at [154]; and see Lord Neuberger's equally dismissive comments at [30]. [146] [2017] 1 BCLC 625, aff'd [2018] EWCA Civ 84.

director's fraud to the company in order to defeat the company's claim in negligence against the bank, for to do so would denude the duty of care owed by the bank of any value in cases where it is most needed, namely to protect a company from the fraudulent conduct of a trusted signatory.[147]

## The wrongdoing director and assistants

**4-57**  The third scenario is where the company seeks to sue the wrongdoing directors and those who have assisted them; this situation falls within what is known as the rule in *Hampshire Land*,[148] which prevents the attribution to a principal of his agent's knowledge of the agent's own breach of duty.[149] In the company context, it means that a director of the company cannot rely on his own knowledge of his own breaches of duty imputed to the company to defeat a claim by the company against the director and those complicit with him for loss caused by his breach. As Lord Walker put it in *Moulin Global Eyecare Trading Ltd v Commissioner of Inland Revenue*[150] '… the injustice and absurdity of such a defence is obvious and for more than a century judges have had no hesitation in rejecting it.'

**4-58**  The key company authority is *Belmont Finance Corp Ltd v Williams Furniture Ltd*.[151] The facts are complicated but, for our purposes, it suffices to say that the company, through formal decisions of its board (and therefore applying the primary rules of attribution, by act of the company) entered into illegal transactions regarding the sale of shares in the company which resulted in significant financial loss to the company. Subsequently the company sought to sue its directors for breach of duty. Initially the claim was dismissed on the basis that the company was a co-conspirator with the wrongdoers. On appeal, Buckley LJ ruled that the directors' knowledge of the illegality of their transactions was not to be imputed to the company for the essence of the arrangement was to deprive the company improperly of a large part of its assets. He went on:[152]

> 'As I have said, the company was a victim of the conspiracy. I think it would be irrational to treat the directors, who were allegedly parties to the conspiracy, notionally as having transmitted this knowledge to the company; and indeed it is a well-recognised exception from the general rule that a principal is affected by notice received by his agent that, if the agent is acting in fraud of his principal and the matter of which he has notice is relevant to the fraud, that knowledge is not to be imputed to the principal. So in my opinion the plaintiff company should not be regarded as a party to the conspiracy, on the ground of *lack of the necessary guilty knowledge*' [emphasis added].

---

[147] [2017] 1 BCLC 625 at [184], aff'd [2018] EWCA Civ 84 at [57]. The failure of the company to supervise the fraudster (there was an inactive board of directors which failed to monitor the sole active director) justified a reduction in damages, however, on the basis of contributory negligence.

[148] *Re Hampshire Land Co* [1896] 2 Ch 743. See Worthington, n 154, at 131, who makes the valid point that we should cease to refer to the *Hampshire Land* principle which is merely a 'distracting and uninformative label'. All that is involved here is 'a careful application of the ordinary rules of attribution'.

[149] *Jetivia SA v Bilta (UK) Ltd* [2015] UKSC 23, [2015] 1 BCLC 443 at [9], [71], [181]. The rule is commonly known as the fraud exception, but it is not limited to fraud and this nomenclature should be abandoned, Lord Neuberger has suggested, at [9].

[150] [2014] HKEC 419, 13 March 2014, at [80]. Lord Walker agrees now, at [101], that the exception in *Hampshire Land* is relevant only to claims by a company against its directors and not more widely, as he wrongly suggested in *Stone & Rolls Ltd v Moore Stephens* [2009] 2 BCLC 563 at [143].

[151] [1979] Ch 250, described by Lord Walker in *Moulin Global Eyecare Trading Ltd v Commissioner of Inland Revenue* [2014] HKEC 419 at [85] as 'the first important case in the modern history of the fraud exception'. See also *JC Houghton & Co v Nothard Lowe & Wills* [1928] AC 1.

[152] [1979] Ch 250 at 261–2.

In the absence of the *Hampshire Land* principle, a company would never be able to enforce directors' duties for it would always be met with the allegation that it too was a wrongdoer.[153]

**4-59** The issue of attribution was addressed in detail by the Supreme Court in *Jetivia SA v Bilta (UK) Ltd*,[154] also reported as *Bilta (UK) Ltd v Nazir*. The company, Bilta (UK) Ltd, had been the vehicle for a VAT fraud on HMRC. The company through its liquidators wished to sue its former directors (one of whom was also the sole shareholder, hence there was a sole actor element here) and their accomplices for breach of fiduciary duty and dishonest assistance in breach of duty which deprived the company of assets which would have enabled it to meet its VAT liabilities to HMRC. The defence raised the argument that the criminal conduct of the directors had to be attributed to the company with the result that, applying *ex turpi causa*, the company was precluded from suing the directors. The Court of Appeal rejected this argument and ruled that the law will not allow the enforcement of directors' duties (as envisaged by the CA 2006 and the IA 1986) to be compromised by the director's reliance on his own wrong and the company is a victim for these purposes, even if the losses it suffers from the breach consist of the compensation that it has to pay to a third party damaged by the fraud,[155] in this case to the primary victim, HMRC.[156]

**4-60** The Supreme Court dismissed an appeal and held that, where a company has been the victim of wrongdoing by its directors, or of which its directors had notice, then the wrongdoing, or knowledge, of the directors cannot be attributed to the company as a defence to a claim brought against the directors by the company for the loss suffered by the company as a result of the wrongdoing, *even where the directors were the only directors and shareholders of the company* (emphasis added),[157] and even though the wrongdoing or knowledge of the directors may be attributed to the company in many other types of proceedings.[158] There is strong support in the Supreme Court for the *Meridian* approach that the question of attribution must depend on the nature and factual context of the claim in question and then it must be asked whether or not it is appropriate to attribute an action by, or a state of mind of, a company director or agent to the company or the agent's principal.[159] Accordingly, the appellants could not raise *ex turpi causa* as a defence to the claims against them.

**4-61** The position reached now is that it is settled law (as the court noted in *UBS AG v Kommunale Wasserwerke Leipzig*)[160] that, where a company claims against a third party in respect of

---

[153] See Lim, 'Attribution in Company Law' (2014) 77 MLR 794 at 802; Watts (2010) 126 LQR 14 at 18–19; *Bowstead on Agency* (20th edn, 2014), para 8-213.

[154] [2015] UKSC 23, [2015] 1 BCLC 443, aff'g [2014] 1 BCLC 302, CA, noted Lim, 'Attribution in Company Law' (2014) 77 MLR 794. On the Supreme Court decision, see Fletcher, 'Fraudulent Trading, ex turpi causa, and Directors' Duties: The Supreme Court Rulings in Bilta (UK) Ltd v Nazir' [2016] Insolv Int 12; Lim, 'Attribution and the Illegality Defence' (2016) 79(3) MLR 476; Worthington, 'Corporate Attribution and Agency: Back to Basics' (2017) 133 LQR 118. [155] [2014] 1 BCLC 302 at [42], [75].

[156] [2014] 1 BCLC 302 at [45], per Patten LJ. See Lim, n 153, at 806–7 who suggests that we need to move away from the language of 'victim' which is unnecessary to the analysis of why we have the rule in *Belmont Finance Corp Ltd v Williams Furniture Ltd*, which is based on the separate legal personality of the entity and the need to be able to enforce directors' duties; there is no need for the 'victim' metaphor as well.

[157] So refuting the erroneous suggestion by Lords Walker and Brown in *Stone & Rolls v Moore Stephens* that the *Hampshire Land/Belmont* principle does not apply in the situation where the director is a 'sole actor,' see [2009] 2 BCLC 563 at [167]–[168], [198]–[203].

[158] [2015] UKSC 23, [2015] 1 BCLC 443 at [7], [33], [64], [181].

[159] See [2015] UKSC 23, [2015] 1 BCLC 443 at [9], per Lord Neuberger; at [41]–[43] per Lord Mance; and at [181] per Lords Toulson and Hodge. Lord Sumption offers some support for this position at [92], but see at [86].

[160] [2017] EWCA Civ 1567, [2017] 2 Lloyd's Law Reports 621 at [147], citing Lords Toulson and Hodge in *Jetivia v Bilta (UK) Ltd* [2015] 1 BCLC 443 at [207].

that person's involvement as an accessory (whether as a co-conspirator, an accomplice, or a dishonest assistant) to a breach of fiduciary duty by one of company's directors, the state of mind of the director who was in breach of his fiduciary duty will not, as a matter of policy, be attributed to the company. It would be absurd and unjust to permit the third party in that situation to use the behaviour of the fraudulent director as a defence.[161] The principle that prevents attribution in these cases is equally applicable where the third party is not directly an accomplice of the fraudulent director, but the director and the third party are both accomplices of a further third party, all engaged in different aspects of a fraud upon the company.[162] In all these cases, the company is the victim of the fraud and it would be absurd to attribute to the company knowledge of any aspect of that fraud which is held by one of its directors, for the purpose of constructing an entirely artificial theory that the company is to be taken as having consented to it.[163]

---

[161] [2017] EWCA Civ 1567, [2017] 2 Lloyd's Law Reports 621 at [148].
[162] [2017] EWCA Civ 1567, [2017] 2 Lloyd's Law Reports 621 at [149]–[151].
[163] [2017] EWCA Civ 1567, [2017] 2 Lloyd's Law Reports 621 at [151].

# 5

# The company constitution

## A  Defining the constitution

**5-1**  The company's constitution is defined in CA 2006, s 17 in the following terms:

> 'Unless the context otherwise requires, references in the Companies Acts to a company's constitution include—
>
> (a)  the company's articles, and
>
> (b)  any resolutions and agreements to which Chapter 3 applies (see section 29).'

**5-2**  Every company must have articles of association contained in a single document divided into paragraphs numbered consecutively.[1] Model forms of articles are provided for public and private companies limited by shares and for companies limited by guarantee and any company may adopt all or any of the provisions of the relevant model articles for that type of company.[2] Model articles are not intended to be a strait-jacket and the draftsman is free to add, subtract, or vary, as the needs of the case suggest.[3]

**5-3**  Each company must register its articles (CA 2006, s 18(2)) and if, on formation of a limited company, articles are not registered or, if articles are registered, in so far as they do not exclude or modify the relevant model articles, the relevant model articles form part of the company's articles automatically (s 20(1)). Larger companies usually exclude all of the model articles and draw up an entire set of articles appropriate to their circumstances while drawing on the model articles in many respects. Even with smaller companies, the shareholders on formation may have matters of particular concern to them, such as issues concerning share transfers or the appointment of directors, and it is preferable for these matters to be the subject of provisions specifically drawn up to cover their individual circumstances.[4] These provisions can then be combined with the remainder of the model articles by stating that the model articles apply except to the extent that they are excluded (s 20(1)(b)).

**5-4**  While it is possible to include the model provisions by reference,[5] it is preferable to draw up a single document which includes the customised matters and the matters relied on

---

[1]  CA 2006, s 18(1), (3).

[2]  CA 2006, s 19(3). See The Companies (Model Articles) Regulations 2008, SI 2008/3229. It is the model articles in force at the date of the company's registration which apply: s 20(2); subsequent amendments of the model articles do not affect a company registered before the amendment: s 19(4). Many companies on the register of companies remain subject to the 1985 Table A and some are still governed by the 1948 Table A. Effectively, Table A was a previous version of model articles.

[3]  *Gaiman v National Association for Mental Health* [1971] Ch 317.

[4]  Many small companies are purchased 'off the shelf', i.e. already incorporated, with the result that the shareholders rarely consider or negotiate the articles, merely accepting whatever version is offered which will typically be the model articles.

[5]  See *Explanatory Notes to the Companies Act 2006*, para 76.

from the model articles. This approach avoids the inconsistencies which can arise from having to look for the articles in two places and prevents uncertainty as to the extent to which specific model provisions have been excluded or modified. At common law persons dealing with a company are deemed under the doctrine of constructive notice to have notice of the company's articles of association,[6] but the impact of this doctrine is much reduced by CA 2006, ss 39–40 (s 39 is discussed at **5-14**; s 40 is discussed at **9-28**).

**5-5**  The resolutions and agreements referred to in CA 2006, s 17(b) (i.e. those to which Chapter 3 applies) are resolutions and agreements listed in s 29 which must be registered with the registrar of companies (s 30). Basically there are two types of resolutions,[7] ordinary and special resolutions. An ordinary resolution is a resolution passed by a simple majority (s 282(1)) and a special resolution is a resolution passed by a majority of not less than 75 per cent (s 283(1)). Resolutions are considered at **17-16**.

**5-6**  The categories of resolutions which must be registered are:

- any special resolution (s 29(1)(a));
- any resolution or agreement which to be effective should have been passed by a special resolution, but was instead agreed to by all the members (or a resolution which to be effective should have been passed by some particular majority or otherwise in some particular manner by a class of shareholders but was agreed to by all the members of the class) which resolution or agreement is nevertheless effective (and therefore should be registered) because of the *Duomatic* principle[8] that informal unanimous assent is tantamount to a resolution (s 29(1)(b) and (c));
- any resolution varying class rights (see **16-38**) which is not a special resolution (s 29(1)(d));
- other resolutions (i.e. ordinary resolutions) which are required by any enactment to be registered (s 29(1)(e)). This ensures that ordinary resolutions of importance must also be registered. For example, a resolution granting authority for an allotment of shares by the directors, though an ordinary resolution, must be registered,[9] as must an ordinary resolution granting a company authority for market purchases of its own shares,[10] and an ordinary resolution of members of a private company incorporated before 1 October 2008 allowing the directors to authorise conflicts of interest.[11] A resolution for voluntary winding up under IA 1986, s 84(1)(a) must also be registered.[12]

**5-7**  There has always been some uncertainty as to whether the requirement for registration extends to shareholder agreements (s 29 and its predecessors refer to resolutions or agreements) and this matter is not clarified by the Companies Act 2006. In practice, shareholder

---

[6]  *Ernest v Nicholls* (1857) 6 HL Cas 401; *Mahony v East Holyford Mining Co* (1875) LR 7 HL 869; *Irvine v Union Bank of Australia* (1877) 2 App Cas 366, PC; *Wilson v Kelland* [1910] 2 Ch 306.

[7]  The CA 2006 abolished the category of extraordinary resolutions (essentially required 75 per cent majority of those voting, but differed from a special resolution in that only 14 rather than 21 days' notice was required) though transitional arrangements ensure that the requirements in a company's articles or a contract for an extraordinary resolution remain effective and CA 2006, s 29 applies to any such extraordinary resolution: see SI 2007/2194, art 9, Sch 3, para 23.

[8]  *Re Duomatic Ltd* [1969] 1 All ER 161, discussed at **17-73**; it was noted in the Parliamentary debates that the requirement to register resolutions based on informal unanimous assent is rarely observed.

[9]  CA 2006, s 551(8), (9).      [10]  CA 2006, s 701(1), (8).

[11]  The Companies Act 2006 (Commencement No 5, Transitional Provisions and Savings) Order 2007, SI 2007/3495, art 9, Sch 4, Pt 3, para 47.

[12]  IA 1986, s 84(3).

agreements are not registered and are regarded as purely private contractual documents. Anyone consulting the company's articles needs to bear in mind, therefore, the possibility (which they should enquire about) that there is a private shareholders' agreement behind the public constitution. Shareholder agreements are discussed at **5-67**.

**5-8**    The definition of the constitution in CA 2006, s 17 is not exhaustive ('include') and is subject to context. Beyond the articles and resolutions, the memorandum of association would also be considered to be a constitutional document. Its importance is limited by s 8 to signalling the wish of the subscribers to form a company and their agreement to become members of the company and, in the case of a company limited by shares, to take at least one share each. An indication of other documents which make up the company's constitution can be found in s 32 which, in the context of documents which must be provided to members on request, identifies the constitutional documents as including the company's articles, any resolutions and agreements that have been recorded by the registrar under s 29; a copy of the company's current certificate of incorporation, and a current statement of capital (which will give the total number of shares in the company, their aggregate nominal value, the aggregate amount, if any, unpaid on the shares and any class rights). For the purposes of Part 10 (directors' duties), an expanded definition of the constitution is provided in s 257 to include, in addition to the matters mentioned in s 17, (a) any resolution or other decision come to in accordance with the constitution[13] and (b) any decision by the members, or by a class of members, that is treated as equivalent to a decision by the company, a reference to decisions reached on the basis of the informal unanimous assent of the members which, applying *Re Duomatic Ltd*[14] (see **17-73**), is equivalent to a decision of the company. The expanded definition means that the directors must act in accordance with the articles (s 17(a)), any special (or other) resolution registrable with the registrar of companies (s 17(b)), any resolution or other decision reached under the constitution (s 257(1)), and any decision reached by virtue of the informal unanimous assent of the members (s 257(2)).

**5-9**    There are therefore potentially a number of elements to the constitution depending on the context, but for most purposes, the key document is the articles of association.

## B  Content of the articles

### Internal rules

**5-10**    The articles set out the internal rules and regulations which govern the relationship between the members and the company. The matters typically covered in the articles include the appointment and removal of directors, their powers, the conduct of directors' and shareholders' meetings, voting procedures, capital matters (including share transfer and transmission), and the declaration of dividends. If the company is a limited company, whether limited by shares or by guarantee, the liability of the members must be limited by the constitution (CA 2006, s 3(1)) so, for example, the model articles for private companies limited by shares provide that 'the liability of the members is limited to the amount, if any, unpaid on the shares held by them'.[15]

---

[13]  For example, the articles may require an ordinary resolution on some matter which resolution is not registrable, not being within CA 2006, s 29, and so not within the definition of the constitution in s 17.

[14]  [1969] 1 All ER 161.

[15]  See The Companies (Model Articles) Regulations 2008, SI 2008/3229, reg 2, Sch 1, para 2.

## Provisions previously contained in a company's memorandum

**5-11**  Prior to the reforms effected by the CA 2006, a company's memorandum of association was an important constitutional document. Under CA 2006, s 8 it merely serves to record the agreement of the members to form an association (see **1-23**). For companies formed under the CA 1985 and its predecessors, provisions that were contained in the memorandum (including provisions for entrenchment) are treated now as provisions of the company's articles (CA 2006, s 28(1), (2)) and as such may be altered by a special resolution under s 21 (other than provisions for entrenchment which remain entrenched (s 28(3))).[16] Entrenchment is discussed at **5-17**.

## Objects clauses

**5-12**  Prior to the CA 2006, companies were required to state their objects in the memorandum and the objects determined the company's capacity. Acts outside of the objects were ultra vires and void,[17] though the impact of that doctrine was reduced almost to obsolescence by a combination of drafting techniques, judicial interpretation, and statutory reform.[18] The position has been further affected by a significant change effected by the CA 2006.

**5-13**  Companies are no longer required to state their objects and, unless a company's articles specifically restrict the objects of the company, a company's objects are unrestricted (CA 2006, s 31(1)). Companies formed under the CA 2006 generally do not restrict their objects (though some businesses such as charitable companies may still find it useful to do so) and therefore most companies have unrestricted capacity and no issue of ultra vires can arise. For companies formed under the CA 1985 and its predecessors, as noted, the objects clauses previously set out in the memorandum now form part of their articles and are open to alteration and deletion by way of special resolution under CA 2006, s 21 (see **5-15**). For such companies, deleting their objects puts them in the same position as companies formed under the CA 2006, their capacity is unrestricted, and no issue of ultra vires can arise. It seems that many listed companies have taken the opportunity to delete their objects and so their capacity is unrestricted.

**5-14**  Alternatively, companies formed under the CA 1985 and its predecessors may choose to retain their objects clauses in their articles and, as mentioned, some companies formed under the CA 2006 may find it useful to restrict their objects as permitted by s 31. Strictly speaking, such companies may still enter into ultra vires transactions, i.e. acts beyond the restricted capacity limited by their objects clauses, but s 39 provides that the validity of an act done by a company cannot be called into question on the ground of a lack of capacity by reason of anything in the company's constitution.[19] The ultra vires point cannot be raised, therefore, but what can be raised within the company is the directors' failure to observe the limitation in the articles which is a failure by the directors to act in accordance with the constitution, as required by s 171. That duty is discussed in Chapter 9.

---

[16]  Care must be taken not to delete the limited liability clause, however, see text to n 15.

[17]  *Ashbury Railway Carriage and Iron Co Ltd v Riche* (1875) LR 7 HL 653.

[18]  Legislative intervention to protect third parties arose out of the need to implement the First Company Law Directive, Directive 68/151/EEC, 1968 OJ Spec Ed (1) 41, art 9, now Directive 2017/1132, OJ L 169/46, 30.6.2017, art 9.

[19]  The application of CA 2006, s 39 is modified for charitable companies, see s 42.

## C Amending the articles

### The statutory power to amend the articles

**5-15**    A company may amend its articles of association by special resolution[20] (CA 2006, s 21(1)) and any agreement or article purporting to deprive a company of the power to amend its articles is invalid on the ground that it is contrary to the statute.[21] The statute does allow for the entrenchment of provisions in the articles, however, such that they cannot be altered by a special resolution (s 22); entrenchment is discussed at **5-17**. In effect, therefore, the general power of amendment in s 21 is subject to any use of entrenched provisions as allowed by s 22. The articles may also be altered by order of a court or other authority so as to restrict or exclude the power of the company to amend its articles, in which case the company must give notice of that fact to the registrar (s 23(1)(c)).[22] An alteration cannot require a member to take more shares or in any way increase his liability to contribute to the company's share capital or otherwise to pay money to the company (i.e. payments in his capacity as a shareholder) without his consent (s 25). Furthermore, the variation of class rights set out in the articles is governed by s 630(2) and not by s 21 (class rights are discussed at **16-37**). Finally, at common law, the power to alter the articles must be exercised bona fide for the benefit of the company as a whole, see **5-21**. A member joins a company on the basis of the articles as they stand at the time he joins and on the understanding that the articles may be changed.[23] If a member wishes to protect himself against particular alterations, he will need to consider some of the protective devices which are available, mechanisms which in effect erode the principle that a company cannot be denied the power to alter the articles.

**5-16**    One possibility is weighted voting rights granted to a shareholder or group of shareholders to ensure that the other shareholders cannot muster the necessary votes to achieve a special resolution,[24] a result which can also be achieved by the shareholders or some of them reaching an agreement outside of the articles as to how they will exercise their voting

---

[20]    A special resolution means a resolution passed by a majority of not less than 75 per cent: CA 2006, s 283(1). A special resolution amending the articles must be forwarded to the registrar of companies within 15 days after it is passed or made: ss 29(1)(a), 30(1); and a copy of the articles as altered must be sent to the registrar not later than 15 days after the amendment takes effect: s 26, see *Gunewardena v Conran Holdings Ltd* [2017] 2 BCLC 14. As to penalties for non-compliance, see s 27. The position is modified for charitable companies, see s 21(2). See also *Cane v Jones* [1980] 1 WLR 1451 and **17-73**.

[21]    *Walker v London Tramways Co* (1879) 12 Ch D 705; *Malleson v National Insurance & Guarantee Corpn* [1894] 1 Ch 200; *Punt v Symons & Co Ltd* [1903] 2 Ch 506. See also *Russell v Northern Bank Development Corp Ltd* [1992] 3 All ER 161, HL. While a company cannot be precluded from altering its articles, to act on the altered articles may nevertheless be a breach of contract (giving rise to liability in damages) if the altered position is contrary to a stipulation in a contract validly made before the alteration: *Southern Foundries (1926) Ltd v Shirlaw* [1940] AC 701 at 740–1; *Cumbrian Newspapers Group Ltd v Cumberland and Westmorland Herald Newspaper and Printing Co Ltd* [1986] 2 All ER 816 at 831.

[22]    The company must also give notice to the registrar if the court or other authority by order subsequently alters the articles to remove any restriction on or exclusion of the power to amend the articles: CA 2006, s 23(2)(b)(ii). If a company is subject to an order of the court or other authority restricting its power to amend the articles, on any subsequent amendment of the articles, the company must provide the registrar with a statement of compliance, certifying that any alteration has been made in accordance with the order of the court or other authority: s 24(1)–(3).

[23]    *Allen v Gold Reefs of West Africa Ltd* [1900] 1 Ch 656 at 672–3, per Lindley MR; *Greenhalgh v Arderne Cinemas Ltd* [1950] 2 All ER 1120 at 1127, per Evershed MR; *Malleson v National Insurance & Guarantee Corp* [1894] 1 Ch 200 at 205, 206. See also *Peters' American Delicacy Co Ltd v Heath* (1939) 61 CLR 457 at 507, per Dixon J.

[24]    See *Bushell v Faith* [1969] 1 All ER 1002.

rights on any resolution to alter the articles.[25] Another possibility is for the shareholder to seek to secure class rights (see **16-26**) to herself which can only be varied in accordance with s 630(2).[26] A further possibility is for the shareholders to regulate their relationship *inter se* by way of a shareholders' agreement entirely distinct from the articles, an agreement which has the merits of being a private contract which cannot be altered without consent. Shareholder agreements are discussed at **5-67**.

## Provision for entrenchment

**5-17**  As noted, the power to amend the articles in CA 2006, s 21 is subject to any provision for entrenchment governed by s 22 which recognises that specified provisions may not be subject to alteration by special resolution. This entrenchment mechanism was provided for by s 22, in part, as a necessary consequence of the changes made to the memorandum of association demoting it from its previous role as an important constitutional document (see **1-23**). Previously, when shareholders wished to entrench provisions of the constitution, they could do so by including them in the memorandum and precluding their alteration. With the memorandum reduced to the status of a declaration of association (s 8), a new method of entrenchment is required and s 22(1) provides that:

> 'A company's articles may contain provision ("provision for entrenchment") to the effect that specified provisions of the articles may be amended or repealed only if conditions are met, or procedures are complied with, that are more restrictive than those applicable in the case of a special resolution.'[27]

**5-18**  The provision for entrenchment must relate to specified provisions of the articles and it is not possible to entrench all of the articles since to do so would deprive the company of the statutory power to alter the articles. A provision for entrenchment may be included in the articles from formation or it may be added by a subsequent amendment of the articles[28] and, in either case, the registrar must be informed (CA 2006, s 23(1)) so as to ensure that anyone searching the register appreciates that the articles contain such provision.[29] The requirement in CA 2006, s 22(2) that inclusion of a provision for entrenchment in the articles must be on formation or by an amendment of the articles agreed to by all the members of the company has not been brought into force[30] because of the uncertain relationship between s 22 and class rights (see CA 2006, ss 629–640 and **16-26**). The

---

[25]  This type of arrangement is not caught by the prohibition on the company restricting its power to alter its articles, see *Russell v Northern Bank Development Corp Ltd* [1992] 3 All ER 161, HL.

[26]  CA 2006, s 630(2) provides that rights attached to a class of a company's shares may only be varied: (a) in accordance with provision in the company's articles for the variation of those rights; or (b) where the company's articles contain no such provision, if the holders of shares of that class consent to the variation in accordance with this section; and s 630(3) provides that this is without prejudice to any other restrictions on the variation of rights (for example, from a court order).

[27]  A condition might be that a 90 per cent majority is required for alteration. The procedures to be complied with may be more restrictive than for a special resolution, for example, with regard to giving notice of the resolution. See the definition of special resolution in CA 2006, s 283 (see **17-20**), and note its application also to a special resolution of members of a class.

[28]  As noted at **5-11**, provisions previously included in the old-style memorandum including provisions entrenched in the memorandum are now treated as provisions of the articles and, where a provision was previously entrenched in the memorandum, it remains as an entrenched provision in the articles, see CA 2006, s 28(2).          [29]  See *Explanatory Notes to the Companies Act 2006*, para 84.

[30]  The decision not to commence CA 2006, s 22(2) is explained in the Explanatory Memorandum to The Companies Act 2006 and Limited Liability Partnerships (Transitional Provisions And Savings) (Amendment) Regulations 2009, SI 2009/2476, paras 7.5–7.7.

Department for Business, Innovation and Skills (BIS) received representations that, on one interpretation, s 22(2) could prevent the creation and variation of class rights. It is not uncommon for the articles to create class rights and to provide that they can only be varied with the consent of, say, 90 per cent of the class, in which case, as the rights cannot be altered by a special resolution, this is a provision for entrenchment within s 22(1). If s 22(2) were in force, such class rights could only be created either on formation or with the agreement of all the shareholders. Such a limitation would be unduly restrictive of the directors' ability to manage the company's share capital structure. Therefore, s 22(2) has not been commenced and class rights can continue to be created at any time and, if a variation of those class rights can only occur on terms which fall within s 22(1), the class right is entrenched. Entrenchment should be of no consequence in these circumstances since entrenchment merely means that a provision is not open to alteration by special resolution under s 21 and can be altered only in accordance with its own provisions for alteration which is the position in any event under s 630(2)(a), see **16-37**.[31]

**5-19**    An entrenched provision, once included in the articles, may be altered in accordance with the method indicated in the provision for entrenchment.[32] Also, for the avoidance of doubt, s 22(3) makes clear that the fact that a provision is entrenched does not prevent amendment of the articles by agreement of all the members of the company (so even a provision which is stated to be irrevocable can be overridden, but only if all agree) or by order of the court or other authority having power to alter the company's articles.

**5-20**    If a company's articles are amended by the members (or altered by court or other order) so as to remove a provision for entrenchment, the registrar must be informed of that fact (s 23(2)) and the company must also provide a statement of compliance certifying that any alteration has been made in accordance with the articles (s 24(2), (3)).[33]

## Common law limits to the power to amend the articles

**5-21**    The important common law limitation on the power to alter the articles was famously articulated by Lindley MR in *Allen v Gold Reefs of West Africa Ltd*[34] as follows:

> 'Wide, however, as the language of s 50 [CA 2006, s 21(1)] is, the power conferred by it must, like all other powers, be exercised subject to those general principles of law and equity which are applicable to all powers conferred on majorities and enabling them to bind minorities. It must be exercised, not only in the manner required by law, but also bona fide for the benefit of the company as a whole, and it must not be exceeded.'

**5-22**    In this case the court permitted an alteration which extended a company's lien (and powers of sale) on partly-paid shares to fully paid-up shares, despite the fact that the change

---

[31]   See n 26 for text of CA 2006, s 630(2). This lack of impact presumably explains why BIS was willing to commence the rest of s 22, but that is not to say that the relationship between s 22 and s 630 is easy to understand. There is a view that it would have been better if it had been made clear that s 22 has no application to class rights and also a view that BIS should not have commenced any of the provisions of s 22 until these issues as to the relationship between s 22 and s 630 were resolved.

[32]   Initially, it was intended that an entrenched provision could not be altered or repealed, but the Government was subsequently persuaded that rendering a provision unalterable would create problems.

[33]   In the Parliamentary debates, it was explained that the purpose of this requirement is to force the directors to pause and take stock and ensure that they have satisfied themselves that any necessary restrictions in the constitution have been observed; it also ensures that the public record is accurate; and if the company has overlooked any special requirements in altering the articles, the registrar of companies is able to ask the company as to the position: see 678 HL Debs GC19, 30 January 2006.

[34]   [1900] 1 Ch 656 at 671, CA.

impacted on only one shareholder holding fully-paid shares (or rather on his estate, as he was deceased at the time of the alteration). It was because the member had died owing arrears on partly-paid shares that the company wanted to extend the lien to fully-paid shares which formed part of his estate. The court agreed that it was bona fide for the benefit of the company as a whole that the company should have a lien to secure debts due to it.[35] An alteration applicable to all members and for the benefit of the company cannot be impeached on the grounds of bad faith merely because its practical impact is felt by only one member.[36] As Warrington LJ put it later in *Sidebottom v Kershaw, Leese & Co Ltd*,[37] it is commonly the case that the circumstance of an individual member may awake the directors to the problem which the alteration is designed to resolve, but the fact that it impacts on one shareholder of itself does not call into question the bona fides of the shareholders.[38]

**5-23**   Beyond this famous dictum of Lindley MR, the judgments in *Allen v Gold Reefs of West Africa Ltd*[39] offer little guidance as to the scope and substance of this 'bona fide for the benefit of the company as a whole' test (hereinafter the *Allen* test) and to some extent the courts ever since have been exercised by its meaning.

**5-24**   Some elaboration of the *Allen* test can be found in two subsequent Court of Appeal judgments: *Shuttleworth v Cox Bros & Co (Maidenhead) Ltd*[40] and *Greenhalgh v Arderne Cinemas Ltd*[41] of which *Shuttleworth* is the more illuminating.[42]

**5-25**   In *Shuttleworth v Cox Bros & Co (Maidenhead) Ltd*[43] a provision in the company's articles conferred life tenure on the directors unless disqualified on one of six grounds. One of the directors failed to account for company money and property and the articles were altered to add a further ground for disqualification, namely that any director should resign on being asked by all his co-directors to resign. Once the articles had been altered, the defaulting director was asked to resign. He unsuccessfully challenged the validity of the alteration.

**5-26**   The Court of Appeal started by criticising the view that had been expressed in the lower court in the earlier case of *Dafen Tinplate Co Ltd v Llanelly Steel Co Ltd*[44] that the *Allen* test had two distinct components, bona fides and the benefit of the company.[45] The Court of Appeal stressed that there is only one test and the proper approach was summed up by Scrutton LJ as follows:[46]

> '[W]hen persons, honestly endeavouring to decide what will be for the benefit of the company and to act accordingly, decide upon a particular course, then, *provided* [emphasis added] there are grounds on which reasonable men could come to the same decision, it does not matter whether the Court would or would not come to the same decision or a different decision. It is not the business of the Court to manage the affairs of the company. That is for the shareholders and directors.'

---

[35]   Vaughan Williams LJ dissented as he thought that the resolution was not passed in good faith, being really passed merely to defeat the existing rights of an individual shareholder, see [1900] 1 Ch 656 at 677.

[36]   [1900] 1 Ch 656 at 675. See also *Sidebottom v Kershaw, Leese & Co Ltd* [1920] 1 Ch 154; *Greenhalgh v Arderne Cinemas Ltd* [1950] 2 All ER 1120; *Shuttleworth v Cox Bros & Co (Maidenhead) Ltd* [1927] KB 9.

[37]   [1920] 1 Ch 154, CA.      [38]   [1920] 1 Ch 154 at 171–2; and see at 166–7, per Lord Sterndale MR.

[39]   [1900] 1 Ch 656 at 671, CA.      [40]   [1927] 2 KB 9, CA.      [41]   [1950] 2 All ER 1120, CA.

[42]   The difficulties with Evershed MR's judgment in *Greenhalgh* are such (see Hannigan, n 110 at 479–80) that it is probably best relegated to the sidelines.

[43]   [1927] 2 KB 9.      [44]   [1920] 2 Ch 124, Ch D.      [45]   [1927] 2 KB 9 at 19, 22.

[46]   [1927] 2 KB 9 at 23, cited with approval in *Citco Banking Corp NV v Pusser's Ltd* [2007] 2 BCLC 483 at 489, PC, per Lord Hoffmann.

**5-27**  The central question is whether the shareholders honestly believe the alteration to be for the benefit of the company as a whole but, in order that the test should not be wholly subjective, there is the proviso that, even if the shareholders' honesty is unchallenged, an alteration will not stand if it is such that 'no reasonable men could consider it for the benefit of the company'.[47] The requirement that the shareholders exercise their power to alter the articles in good faith is simply a reflection of the traditional equitable constraints on the ability of a majority to bind a minority, as Lindley MR said in *Allen v Gold Reefs of West Africa Ltd*.[48] It protects the minority by ensuring that alterations motivated by malice, fraud, and personal benefit cannot stand while respecting the commercial judgement of shareholders acting genuinely for the benefit of the company.[49] The proviso that an alteration will not stand if it is such that 'no reasonable men could consider it for the benefit of the company' simply confirms that there are some alterations that 'cannot be regarded as being for the benefit of the company, no matter how honestly the majority believe them to be'.[50] Subjective good faith cannot be allowed to prevail where a reasonable shareholder can see no benefit to the company and the absence of such benefit would in any event cast doubt on the assertions of bona fides by the shareholders.[51]

**5-28**  The core element to the test (and the proviso) is the requirement that the alteration be for the benefit of the company as a whole. That is the limit to the power which 'must not be exceeded', to use Lord Lindley's words,[52] otherwise the exercise is a fraud on a power and void.[53]

**5-29**  In *Greenhalgh v Arderne Cinemas Ltd*,[54] the company's articles contained restrictive provisions governing the transfer of shares. Anyone wishing to sell their shares in the company was required to offer them first to existing members. If no member wished to purchase the shares, the shares could then be sold to an outside purchaser, but only with

---

[47] [1927] 2 KB 9 at 18, per Bankes LJ: '[an alteration must not be] … so oppressive as to cast suspicion on the honesty of the persons responsible for it, or so extravagant that no reasonable men could really consider it for the benefit of the company'; at 24, per Scrutton LJ: '[an alteration will not stand if] … the decision of the shareholders, though honest, is such that no reasonable men could have come to it upon proper materials …'; qualifications endorsed by Atkin LJ, at 26. See Sealy, '"Bona Fides" and "Proper Purposes" in Corporate Decisions' [1989] 15 Monash U L Rev 265 at 277–8.

[48] [1900] 1 Ch 656 at 671.

[49] See *Rights & Issues Investment Trust Ltd v Stylo Shoes Ltd* [1964] 3 All ER 628 at 631; *Sidebottom v Kershaw, Leese & Co Ltd* [1927] 2 KB 9 at 23, 26, per Atkin LJ: 'It is not a matter of law for the Court whether or not a particular alteration is for the benefit of the company; nor is it the business of the judge to review the decision of every company in the country on these questions.'

[50] *Constable v Executive Connections Ltd* [2005] 2 BCLC 638 at 649–50; and see Sealy, n 47; *Hutton v West Cork Rly Co* (1993) 23 Ch D 654 at 671, per Bowen LJ: 'Bona fides cannot be the sole test, otherwise you might have a lunatic conducting the affairs of the company, and paying away its money with both hands in a manner perfectly bona fide yet perfectly irrational.'

[51] See *Shuttleworth v Cox Bros & Co (Maidenhead) Ltd* [1927] 2 KB 9 at 23.

[52] *Allen v Gold Reefs of West Africa Ltd* [1900] 1 Ch 656 at 671.

[53] See Worthington, 'Corporate Governance: Remedying and Ratifying Directors' Breaches' (2000) 116 LQR 638 at 646–50—majority shareholders are not allowed to use their powers for purposes outside the contemplation of the grant; *Vatcher v Paul* [1915] AC 372 at 378; *British Equitable Assurance Co Ltd v Bailey* [1906] AC 35 at 42, per Lord Lindley; *Re Halt Garage (1964) Ltd* [1982] 3 All ER 1016 at 1037, per Oliver J; *Peters' American Delicacy Co Ltd v Heath* (1939) 61 CLR 457 at 511–12, per Dixon J. Also note the very useful summation of the constraints on an exercise of a power as explained by Rimer J in *Redwood Master Fund Ltd v TD Bank Europe Ltd* [2006] 1 BCLC 149 at [105], though not involving an alteration of articles, rather the variation of the terms of a loan facility.

[54] [1950] 2 All ER 1120.

the consent of the board of directors. The articles were altered to allow for the direct sale of shares to an outsider without having to offer them first to the existing shareholders, provided the sale was approved by an ordinary resolution of the company in general meeting. A minority shareholder challenged the validity of this alteration. The court concluded that the alteration was merely a relaxation of the very stringent restrictions on transfer in the existing articles and as such was bona fide for the benefit of the company as a whole.[55]

**5-30**  As to the meaning of 'the company as a whole', while the balance of dicta in the cases can be read as interpreting the phrase as meaning the corporate entity,[56] Evershed MR in *Greenhalgh* had no doubt that the phrase 'the company as a whole' meant the shareholders as a body.[57] Regarding 'the company as a whole' as the corporators as a whole makes sense in the context of the power which is being exercised. It is a power to alter the contractual relationship between the members *inter se*[58] and between them and the company and as such should be governed by considerations as to what is in the best interests of the members as a whole, and their collective interests are reflected in the commercial interests of the entity. In many of the cases, it makes little difference to the outcome, therefore, whether the meaning of 'the company as a whole' is expressed as the entity rather than the corporators or vice versa, given that it can be difficult to distinguish the interests of the collective body of the shareholders from the entity. For example, it was in the interests of the corporators and the company in *Allen*[59] that the company obtained security with respect to debts owed to it; it was in the interests of the corporators and the company in *Greenhalgh*[60] that the company's strict pre-emption provisions on transfer were relaxed;[61] it was in the interests of the corporators and the company in *Sidebottom v Kershaw, Leese & Co Ltd*[62] that the articles allowed for the compulsory acquisition of the shares of members who were competitors of the company; it was in the interests of the corporators and the company in *Shuttleworth*[63] that the articles were amended to facilitate the removal of unsatisfactory directors. In fact, when the cases are considered in detail, there is evidence of considerable judicial wavering (even within a case) between viewing the company as an entity and viewing it as the corporators.[64] Overall, in the context of these types of alterations, the community of interest between the corporators and the entity is such that it matters little whether the benefit sought is expressed as the benefit of the company as a whole or the benefit of the collective body of members.

---

[55] [1950] 2 All ER 1120 at 1127.

[56] See Lindley MR in *Allen v Gold Reefs of West Africa Ltd* [1900] 1 Ch 656 at 671 who clearly meant the corporate entity, as did Romer LJ, at 682; as did Sterndale MR and Warrington LJ in *Sidebottom v Kershaw, Leese & Co Ltd* [1920] 1 Ch 154 at 165–6 and 171, respectively; as did Scrutton and Atkin LLJ in *Shuttleworth v Cox Bros & Co (Maidenhead) Ltd* [1927] KB 9 at 23 and 26, respectively.

[57] [1950] 2 All ER 1120 at 1126. See Flannigan, 'Shareholder Fiduciary Accountability' [2014] JBL 1 at 26 who comments that Evershed MR's assertion is 'baseless'.

[58] *Peters' American Delicacy Co Ltd v Heath* (1939) 61 CLR 457 at 506, per Dixon J.

[59] *Allen v Gold Reefs of West Africa Ltd* [1900] 1 Ch 656.

[60] *Greenhalgh v Arderne Cinemas Ltd* [1950] 2 All ER 1120.

[61] The company's interest would lie in the ability to raise capital by issuing shares as a result of their increased marketability following the relaxation of the pre-emption provisions.

[62] [1920] 1 Ch 154, CA.

[63] *Shuttleworth v Cox Bros & Co (Maidenhead) Ltd* [1927] 2 KB 9.

[64] See, for example, *Sidebottom v Kershaw, Leese & Co Ltd* [1920] 1 Ch 154 at 166, 169; see too Rixon, n 78, 454 who concluded: 'In short, "the company as a whole" is a Delphic term employed by different judges in different circumstances to signify different things …'; see also Sealy, n 47, 269–70.

**5-31**   Given the general approach of the courts to the *Allen* test, it is unsurprising that it is rare for a challenge to an alteration to succeed (and the onus of proof is on the person challenging the alteration).[65] This judicial reluctance to interfere was confirmed by the Privy Council in *Citco Banking Corp NV v Pusser's Ltd*.[66] In this case the company had two main shareholders, one of whom held 28 per cent of the shares and was the company chairman, the other held 13 per cent and was the appellant bank, and the rest of the shares were widely held. The alteration to the articles had the effect of giving the chairman voting control of the company. On the resolution to alter the articles, 1,123,665 votes were cast for the resolution and 183,000 votes against the resolution. All of the dissenting votes were cast by the appellant bank which argued that the alteration was passed in the interests of the chairman gaining control and not in the interests of the company. The Privy Council dismissed the challenge to the validity of the alteration, applied *Shuttleworth*, see **5-25**, and accepted that the test can be stated succinctly by asking whether reasonable shareholders could consider the amendment to be for the benefit of the company.[67] Stated like this, the test looks more objective than subjective,[68] but this is a condensed statement of the traditional test, i.e. could the shareholders genuinely have believed the alteration to be for the benefit of the company and was that belief one which a reasonable shareholder could have held? The authorities in any event make it difficult to determine whether the subjective or objective element is pre-eminent.[69] On the facts in *Citco*, the shareholders could have concluded in good faith that they accepted the arguments as to why the amendment would be in the interests of the company (the company needed further capital and potential investors wished the chairman to have control of the company). Just as an alteration may be for the benefit of the company though it is to the detriment of one member (as in *Allen*) so an alteration may be for the benefit of the company as a whole notwithstanding that it operates to the particular advantage of some or one shareholder.[70] In the absence of any attack on his bona fides, the Privy Council also confirmed that there is no reason why a member who benefits from an alteration (in this case, the chairman) should not vote, as a shareholder, in favour of that alteration.[71]

**5-32**   The Privy Council focus in *Citco* on *Shuttleworth v Cox Bros & Co (Maidenhead) Ltd*[72] suggests that their Lordships are content that the position now reached on the 'bona fides' test maintains a proper balance between the freedom necessary for the majority to make constitutional changes and the need to protect the minority against unfair alterations. The resolutely minimalist judgment in *Citco* indicates a preference certainly for the

---

[65] *Peters' American Delicacy Co Ltd v Heath* (1939) 61 CLR 457; *Citco Banking Corp NV v Pusser's Ltd* [2007] 2 BCLC 483, PC.

[66] [2007] 2 BCLC 483, PC. See Williams (2007) CLJ 500.

[67] [2007] 2 BCLC 483 at [24], [25], PC, per Lord Hoffmann.

[68] See Kershaw, *Company Law in Context* (2009), p 602, who comments that this way of putting the test is incorrect or at least potentially misleading. On the other hand, Chivers et al (eds), *The Law of Majority Shareholder Power* (2nd edn, 2017), para 1.21, question the subjective formulation in *Shuttleworth*, see **5-26**, and query whether it provides the minority with adequate protection.

[69] See *Sidebottom v Kershaw, Leese & Co Ltd* [1920] 1 Ch 154 at 165–6, 171–2 where the court appears to give almost equal weight to the requirement of subjective good faith and an objective benefit to the company in ridding itself of a competing shareholder.

[70] [2007] 2 BCLC 483 at [17]. See *Rights & Issues Investment Trust Ltd v Stylo Shoes Ltd* [1964] 3 All ER 628 at 631.

[71] [2007] 2 BCLC 483 at [26]–[27], citing the established principle that shareholders are free to exercise their votes in their own interests, see *Burland v Earle* [1902] AC 83 at 94.

[72] [1927] 2 KB 9, CA.

established approach.[73] In *Re Charterhouse Capital Ltd*,[74] Sir Terence Etherton distilled from the cases the following principles (citations omitted) governing alterations, and the Privy Council in *Staray Capital Ltd v Yang*[75] has acknowledged that these principles are a convenient summary of the relevant law in this area:

(1) The limitations on the exercise of the power to amend a company's articles arise because, as in the case of all powers, the manner of their exercise is constrained by the purpose of the power and because the framers of the power of a majority to bind a minority will not, in the absence of clear words, have intended the power to be completely without limitation. These principles may be characterised as principles of law and equity or as implied terms.

(2) A power to amend will be validly exercised if it is exercised in good faith in the interests of the company.

(3) It is for the shareholders, and not the court, to say whether an alteration of the articles is for the benefit of the company but it will not be for the benefit of the company if no reasonable person would consider it to be such.

(4) The view of shareholders acting in good faith that a proposed alteration of the articles is for the benefit of the company, and which cannot be said to be a view which no reasonable person could hold, is not impugned by the fact that one or more of the shareholders was actually acting under some mistake of fact or lack of knowledge or understanding. In other words, the court will not investigate the quality of the subjective views of such shareholders.

(5) The mere fact that the amendment adversely affects, and even if it is intended adversely to affect, one or more minority shareholders and benefit others does not, of itself, invalidate the amendment if the amendment is made in good faith in the interests of the company.

(6) A power to amend will also be validly exercised, even though the amendment is not for the benefit of the company because it relates to a matter in which the company as an entity has no interest but rather is only for the benefit of shareholders as such or some of them, provided that the amendment does not amount to oppression of the minority or is otherwise unjust or is outside the scope of the power.

(7) The burden is on the person impugning the validity of the amendment of the articles to satisfy the court that there are grounds for doing so.

**5-33** Their Lordships in *Citco* did accept that the 'bona fides for the benefit of the company as a whole' test is not appropriate in the context of an alteration adjusting the conflicting interests of the shareholders[76] and 'some other test of validity is required'.[77] This point refers to the issue raised most notably in the Australian case, *Peters' American Delicacy Co Ltd v Heath*,[78] as to the inappropriateness of the *Allen* test when the alteration at issue more directly pits one section of the members against another, where those in favour

---

[73] Their Lordships declined the opportunity to consider further the meaning of Evershed MR's judgment in *Greenhalgh v Arderne Cinemas Ltd* [1950] 2 All ER 1120 or to explore the controversial Australian decision in *Gambotto v WCP Ltd* (1995) 182 CLR 432, discussed at **5-40**.

[74] [2015] 2 BCLC 627 at [90].     [75] [2017] UKPC 43 at [34].

[76] See *Peters' American Delicacy Co Ltd v Heath* (1939) 61 CLR 457 at 512, per Dixon J; also Rixon, n 78.

[77] [2007] 2 BCLC 483 at [18].

[78] (1939) 61 CLR 457 at 507. See Rixon, 'Competing Interests and Conflicting Principles: An Examination of the Power of Alteration of Articles of Association' (1986) 49 MLR 446.

of the amendment have interests directly competing or conflicting with the interests of those opposed.[79] The issue was explained by Dixon J as follows:

> 'If the challenged alteration relates to an article which does or may affect an individual, as, for instance, a director appointed for life or a shareholder whom it is desired to expropriate, or to an article affecting the mutual rights and liabilities *inter se* of shareholders or different classes or descriptions of shareholders, the very subject matter involves a conflict of interests and advantages.[80] To say that the shareholders forming the majority must consider the advantage of the company as a whole in relation to such a question seems inappropriate, if not meaningless, and at all events starts an impossible inquiry. The "company as a whole" is a corporate entity consisting of all the shareholders. If the proposal put forward is for a revision of any of the articles regulating the rights *inter se* of shareholders or classes of shareholders, the primary question must be how conflicting interests are to be adjusted, and the adjustment is left by law to the determination of those whose interests conflict, subject, however, to the condition that the existing provision can be altered only by a three-fourths majority.'

**5-34** In the intervening decades since that case, it would seem that the courts have had neither the opportunity nor the inclination (even when an opportunity presented itself) to devise a new test.[81] There may be a variety of reasons for the lack of development. First, even when there are competing interests, it is possible for the court to apply the traditional test and still resolve how the competing interests should be balanced, as will be seen in the expropriation cases discussed at **5-35**. In *Citco Banking Corp NV v Pusser's Ltd*,[82] it could be argued that the alteration did give rise to competing interests since most shareholders lost power while the majority shareholder's power was consolidated, yet still their Lordships were content to apply the traditional test. Secondly, minorities are well protected now by the CA 2006, s 994 which allows a member to petition for relief on the ground, *inter alia*, that an actual or proposed act or omission of the company (including an act or omission on its behalf) is or would be unfairly prejudicial to the interests of the members generally or of some part of its members including at least himself.[83] This provision (discussed in

---

[79] On the facts in *Peters' American Delicacy*, the alteration dealt with the manner in which dividends and bonus shares were to be distributed and the change was to the advantage of those holding fully-paid shares and to the disadvantage of those holding partly-paid shares—the company had 511,000 fully-paid shares in issue and 169,000 partly-paid.

[80] Dixon J went on to give some examples of issues where amendments to the articles might give rise to these sorts of conflicts between shareholders, such as amendments to voting rights, the basis of distributing profits, the basis of dividing surplus assets on a winding up, preferential rights in relation to profits or to surplus assets, or any other question affecting the mutual interests of shareholders.

[81] A new test might lie along the lines of 'proper purpose' or oppression as suggested by Dixon J in *Peters' American Delicacy Co Ltd v Heath* (1939) 61 CLR 457 at 512, but the adoption of a proper purpose test in *Gambotto v WCP Ltd* (1995) 182 CLR 432, see **5-40**, attracted considerable criticism precisely on the ground that a proper purpose test is no more certain in application in this context than the 'bona fides' test, while an oppression test (also favoured in *Gambotto*) is unnecessary in the light of CA 2006, s 994 (unfairly prejudicial conduct). For a scathing rejection of the view that a new test is required in cases of shareholder conflicts, see Flannigan, 'Shareholder Fiduciary Accountability' [2014] JBL 1 at 27–9, who disputes the view that shareholder matters *inter se* involve no corporate interest and who argues that the only acceptable test here is to ask whether the shareholders voted with the intention to benefit the corporation or themselves selectively.

[82] [2007] 2 BCLC 483, PC.

[83] Using CA 2006, s 994, Mr Greenhalgh (see **5-29**) would surely have succeeded in obtaining redress, but not necessarily in getting the alteration set aside, since the remedy commonly awarded to successful petitioners under s 994 is a purchase order, see **19-85**. A shareholder who wishes to remain in the company and prevent an alteration taking place will still have to go down the *Allen* route, for while the court could make an order on a successful petition requiring the company not to make any, or any specified, alterations in its articles without the leave of the court (s 996(2)(e)), such an order is unlikely to be granted, see **19-80**.

detail in Chapter 19) allows the court considerable latitude in assessing whether conduct is unfairly prejudicial and provides a basis for challenging an alteration where there are competing interests between the majority and the minority without the need to devise a further 'alteration' test.[84] In *Re Charterhouse Capital Ltd, Arbuthnott v Bonnyman*,[85] the Court of Appeal considered, obiter, that the power to amend will be validly exercised in these circumstances provided the amendment does not amount to oppression of the minority or is otherwise unjust or is outside the scope of the power of amendment. Sir Terence Etherton (with whom Lewison and McCombe LJJ agreed) noted that, in a case where the company as an entity has no interest in the amendment, he would prefer to express the test in terms of vitiating factors, such as oppression and the scope of the power, rather than the language of benefit to hypothetical members.[86]

### Compulsory transfer provisions

5-35    The application of the *Allen* test in the context of compulsory transfer provisions is dominated by three decisions: *Sidebottom v Kershaw, Leese & Co Ltd*;[87] *Brown v British Abrasive Wheel Co Ltd*;[88] and *Dafen Tinplate Co Ltd v Llanelly Steel Co Ltd*.[89]

5-36    In *Sidebottom v Kershaw, Leese & Co Ltd*[90] the alteration allowed the directors to require any shareholder who competed with the company's business to transfer his shares at their full value to nominees of the directors. The plaintiffs (who held 711 out of 7,620 issued shares) sought a declaration that the alteration was invalid.[91] The court accepted that such a power could be included in the articles from incorporation[92] and could be included subsequently by way of alteration of the articles, provided the exercise of the power of alteration is beyond challenge, being done bona fide for the benefit of the company as a whole.[93] It had already been established that an alteration applicable to all is not open to impeachment solely on the basis of its impact on a particular shareholder.[94] Looking at the facts in *Sidebottom*, the Court of Appeal had no hesitation in finding that the resolution had been passed bona fide for the benefit of the company as a whole. The court accepted that it was clearly for the company's benefit 'that they should not be obliged to have amongst them as members persons who are competing with them in business, and who may get knowledge from their membership which would enable them to compete better'.[95]

5-37    In *Brown v British Abrasive Wheel Co Ltd*[96] the majority shareholders held 98 per cent of the shares and wished to alter the articles so as to permit them to acquire at fair value the shares of the remaining 2 per cent shareholders. The majority anticipated that further capital would be required for the development of the company and they were willing to provide it only if they could acquire the 2 per cent minority.[97] The plaintiff shareholders (who held 50 shares out of an issued share capital of 50,000) successfully sought an injunction preventing the company from altering the articles in this way. Astbury J held that the proposed alteration was merely for the benefit of the majority, enabling them

---

[84] See *Re Charterhouse Capital Ltd, Arbuthnott v Bonnyman* [2015] 2 BCLC 627 at [48] (even if an amendment of the articles is legally valid, it may still be unfairly prejudicial for the purposes of CA 2006, s 994).
  [85] [2015] 2 BCLC 627.     [86] [2015] 2 BCLC 627 at [96].     [87] [1920] 1 Ch 154, CA.
  [88] [1919] 1 Ch 290.     [89] [1920] 2 Ch 124.     [90] [1920] 1 Ch 154, CA.
  [91] [1920] 1 Ch 154 at 163–5.     [92] *Phillips v Manufacturers' Securities Ltd* (1917) 116 LT 290.
  [93] [1920] 1 Ch 154 at 164, per Lord Sterndale MR.
  [94] *Allen v Gold Reefs of West Africa Ltd* [1900] 1 Ch 656; see also *Greenhalgh v Arderne Cinemas Ltd* [1950] 2 All ER 1120; *Shuttleworth v Cox Bros & Co (Maidenhead) Ltd* [1927] 2 KB 9.
  [95] [1920] 1 Ch 154 at 166, per Lord Sterndale MR.     [96] [1919] 1 Ch 290.
  [97] Without further capital, the majority said the company might have to go into liquidation, see [1919] 1 Ch 290 at 295–6.

to do forcibly what they were unable to effect by agreement with the minority.[98] This judgment is unsound on the law for, as the Court of Appeal pointed out in *Sidebottom*,[99] Astbury J did not apply the *Allen* test.[100] Notwithstanding that clear error, Astbury J did expressly find that the shareholders had acted for their own benefit in approving the alteration rather than honestly endeavouring to act for the benefit of the company.[101] On that basis, the Court of Appeal agreed that the decision in the case was right.[102]

**5-38**   The final authority is *Dafen Tinplate Co Ltd v Llanelly Steel Co Ltd*.[103] The background was that the company had been formed on the basis of an expectation (though no legal obligation) that the shareholders would purchase supplies from the company. One shareholder who had an interest in a competing business began purchasing his supplies from that other company. Being unable to acquire his shares by agreement, the company altered the articles to provide that the majority of shareholders could determine that the shares of any member (other than one principal shareholder) should be offered for sale by the directors to anyone of their choice at a fair value to be fixed by the directors. The court refused to permit the alteration saying that it would have enabled the majority shareholder compulsorily to acquire the shares of any other member '… although there may be no complaint of any kind against his conduct and it cannot be suggested that he has done, or contemplates doing, anything to the detriment of the company'.[104] To say that such an unrestricted and unlimited power of expropriation was for the benefit of the company, Peterson J said, was to confuse the interests of the majority with the benefit of the company as a whole.[105] The approach taken by Peterson J[106] was criticised by the Court of Appeal in *Shuttleworth v Cox Bros (Maidenhead) Ltd*[107] without casting doubt, however, on the outcome of the case which was clearly correct, given the finding that the majority in supporting the alteration were not honestly endeavouring to act for the benefit of the company.

**5-39**   On the basis of these authorities, it might be thought that the law is clear. The difficulty is that the authorities are of limited value, being two first instance decisions which have been criticised by the Court of Appeal on a point of law, and a Court of Appeal decision which is of limited value since the facts were so clear-cut. Interestingly, when the court was asked in *Constable v Executive Connections Ltd*[108] to consider the position in the

---

[98]   [1919] 1 Ch 290 at 294.

[99]   See *Sidebottom v Kershaw, Leese & Co Ltd* [1920] 1 Ch 154 at 163, 170, and 173, per Lord Sterndale MR, Warrington LJ, and Eve J, respectively.

[100]   Astbury J took a broad approach and asked whether the enforcement of the proposed alteration against the minority was within the ordinary principles of justice and whether it was for the benefit of the company as a whole, see [1919] 1 Ch 290 at 295–6.

[101]   [1919] 1 Ch 290 at 298. There was some evidence in the case that the majority had an eye to personal profit in seeking to buy out the minority. The company's position had improved, bank funding was accessible, opportunities were anticipated, and the court seemed to find that there was an element of the majority seeking to ensure that the spoils of future prosperity went to them and were not shared with any minority shareholders.

[102]   See *Sidebottom v Kershaw, Leese & Co Ltd* [1920] 1 Ch 154 at 167, per Lord Sterndale MR; at 172, per Warrington LJ.        [103]   [1920] 2 Ch 124.

[104]   [1920] 2 Ch 124 at 138.        [105]   [1920] 2 Ch 124 at 141.        [106]   See [1920] 2 Ch 124 at 140.

[107]   [1927] 2 KB 9 at 19, 22. The court criticised the suggestion by Peterson J that where there was a conflict between the view of the shareholders and of the court as to the merits of the alteration, the court's view should prevail.

[108]   [2005] 2 BCLC 638 (application for a declaration that an alteration was invalid and of no effect and for an injunction preventing the company from acting on the alteration).

more modern setting of altering the articles to include a 'drag-along' clause,[109] the court indicated some uncertainty as to the boundaries of permissible alterations to allow for compulsory transfer.[110]

**5-40**  It is worth digressing at this point to consider the controversial decision of the Australian High Court, *Gambotto v WCP Ltd*,[111] where the court specifically rejected the 'bona fide for the benefit of the company' test as the appropriate test governing alterations and favoured a more objective consideration of the proper purpose for the exercise of the power of alteration.[112] More specifically, the court considered that the proper purpose for the expropriation of shares is if it could reasonably be apprehended that the continued shareholding is detrimental to the company and expropriation is a reasonable means of eliminating or mitigating that detriment.[113] The court went on to note that the majority cannot expropriate the minority merely to secure for themselves some commercial advantage to be derived from a new corporate structure.[114] The court further considered that the burden in expropriation cases is on the majority to prove that the alteration is for a proper purpose and is fair in all the circumstances.[115]

**5-41**  In this case, the alteration (approved without the majority shareholder voting) would have enabled the majority shareholder (99.7 per cent) to acquire the minority's shares (50,590 shares, 0.3 per cent) at full value which would have generated tax advantages of approximately A\$4m for the company.[116] The minority shareholders who objected held 15,898 shares, 0.1 per cent of the issued share capital. On the facts, the court found that there was no suggestion that the continued presence of the minority was harmful to the company's business activities or that they had acted in any way to the company's detriment. All that was suggested was that there were tax and administrative advantages for the company in expropriating the minority shareholders.[117] The court did not accept that such commercial advantages of themselves could constitute a proper purpose for an alteration of the articles allowing for expropriation and so the alteration was invalid.

---

[109] The essence of a drag-along provision is that, on an offer for shares in a company being accepted by the majority of shareholders, the majority may require the minority to transfer their shares to the offeror on the same terms. Usually the article will constitute someone, such as the company secretary if there is one, to act as agent for the reluctant shareholder and execute a share transfer to implement the drag-along. For an example, see *Re Charterhouse Capital Ltd, Arbuthnott v Bonnyman* [2015] 2 BCLC 627 at [36].

[110] For a detailed discussion of the issues surrounding alterations to allow for compulsory transfer provisions, see Hannigan, 'Altering the Articles to Allow for Compulsory Transfer—Dragging Minority Shareholders to a Reluctant Exit' [2007] JBL 471; Chivers et al (eds), *The Law of Majority Shareholder Power* (2nd edn, 2017), Ch 1.

[111] (1995) 182 CLR 432, noted Prentice (1996) 112 LQR 194. See generally Boros, 'Altering the Articles of Association to Acquire Minority Shareholdings' in Rider (ed), *The Realm of Company Law* (1998); and the very useful collection of essays on the case in Ramsay (ed), *Gambotto v WCP Ltd: Its Implications for Corporate Regulation* (1996), hereinafter Ramsay (ed).

[112] (1995) 182 CLR 432 at 444.

[113] (1995) 182 CLR 432 at 445–6; the examples given by the court were expropriation of a competitor or if necessary to ensure that the company could continue to comply with a regulatory regime governing the principal business of the company, for example regarding foreign ownership of shares in a regulated industry.

[114] (1995) 182 CLR 432 at 446.        [115] (1995) 182 CLR 432 at 447.

[116] The alteration would have enabled any member entitled to 90 per cent or more of the issued shares to acquire compulsorily the remaining shares at \$1.80 per share.

[117] The court noted that it was difficult to conceive of circumstances in which financial and administrative benefits would not be a consequence of the expropriation of minority holdings: (1995) 182 CLR 432 at 448.

**5-42**  This decision attracted considerable criticism on a variety of grounds[118] including, so far as compulsory transfer was concerned, that the result was economically inefficient and gave too much weight to proprietary interests and too much power to the minority shareholders.[119] In fact, the approach taken by the Australian High Court on the compulsory transfer point has much to commend it[120] and is compatible with the outcome of the English compulsory transfer cases, even if the legal basis is different. *Sidebottom v Kershaw, Leese & Co Ltd*[121] was a case where the continued presence of the minority shareholder (a competitor) was detrimental to the conduct of the company's business so the alteration was rightly allowed. In *Brown v British Abrasive Wheel Co Ltd*[122] and *Dafen Tinplate Co Ltd v Llanelly Steel Co Ltd*[123] the alterations provided for the inclusion of naked compulsory transfer provisions for the benefit and advantage of the majority shareholders and rightly were not allowed. The difference is that *Gambotto* contains a clearly articulated position on the issue of what is a permissible compulsory transfer provision whereas, as *Constable v Executive Connections Ltd*[124] makes clear, the position here is more uncertain.

**5-43**  The Company Law Review declined to embrace *Gambotto*, preferring to leave the matter to the courts to develop.[125] As noted, their Lordships in the Privy Council in *Citco Banking Corp NV v Pusser's Ltd*[126] also considered it unnecessary to consider *Gambotto* (*Citco* did not concern compulsory transfer) but they did note that, in their view, *Gambotto* has no support in the English authorities.[127]

**5-44**  The issue of compulsory transfer came before the Court of Appeal in *Re Charterhouse Capital Ltd, Arbuthnott v Bonnyman*.[128] In this case, A held 8.91 per cent of the shares in the defendant company which carried on a private equity business. In 2008 he retired from the business, but like other retirees retained his shares. Eventually, concerns arose that retirees held or would shortly hold a controlling interest in the company and it was considered that structure was unsustainable as a business model. A scheme was put in place whereby a company (WSL), which was a vehicle for the active members of the management team, made an offer to acquire all shares in the company for £15.15m (the WSL offer) and this offer was accepted by all of the members of the company including all the retirees except A. It was a condition of the WSL offer, among others, that those who accepted it should vote in favour of an amendment to the articles, as duly happened. WSL proposed to exercise drag-along provisions in the articles of association in their amended form in order to acquire A's shares. A brought a petition alleging conduct unfairly prejudicial to his interests, including in particular the amendment to the articles in order, he said, to expropriate his shares.

---

[118] See generally the commentaries on the case mentioned in n 111.

[119] See Hannigan, n 110, at 488 and the commentaries cited there.

[120] See generally Hannigan, n 110, and esp at 490–2. Essentially any alteration to add a compulsory transfer provision fundamentally alters the implicit basis of the bargain made between the shareholders on coming together in the company. The essence of the association is that the investment made by each shareholder is permanent and the relationship between the shareholders *inter se* is ongoing until such time as a shareholder chooses to exercise his right of voluntary exit by disposing of his shares. The bargain can be altered by agreement of the parties or by statute, but not by the exercise of majority power to alter the articles, save where the continued presence of the minority is detrimental to the conduct of the company's business.

[121] [1920] 1 Ch 154, CA.         [122] [1919] 1 Ch 290.

[123] [1920] 2 Ch 124.         [124] [2005] 2 BCLC 638.

[125] See Company Law Review, *Modern Company Law for a Competitive Economy: Completing the Structure* (2000), paras 5.94–5.99.

[126] [2007] 2 BCLC 483.         [127] [2007] 2 BCLC 483 at [20].         [128] [2015] 2 BCLC 627.

**5-45**    The court dismissed the petition, a position upheld by the Court of Appeal. The company's articles and a shareholders' agreement had always contained 'drag and tag' rights on a change of control so it was not a case of the articles being altered to add drag-along or expropriation clauses where none existed before. These provisions were part of the original commercial bargain between the founding members of which the petitioner had been one and the alteration to the articles merely allowed for amended provisions. The WSL offer and consequent change in the articles of association had not been targeted purely at the petitioner and intended as an expropriation. All of the other relevant shareholders had agreed to the purchase of their shares on exactly the same terms. There was no evidence of bad faith or improper motive on the part of those voting to approve the alteration nor that the price paid for the shares was outside the range which was considered reasonable and it was a price which all the other shareholders were happy to accept. The alteration was one which shareholders could reasonably have considered to be in the interests of the company.

**5-46**    The Privy Council in *Staray Capital Ltd v Yang*[129] also considered an amendment to allow for compulsory acquisition of shares. Their Lordships upheld the decision of the BVI courts that an alteration which allowed for the compulsory redemption of a member's shares was passed bona fide for the benefit of the company as a whole though it could only have affected the minority (20 per cent) shareholder whose shares the majority shareholder had already tried to acquire. The alteration provided that shareholders who acquired their holdings as a result of material misstatements, whether fraudulent or negligent, or who committed acts which may result in the company incurring or suffering disadvantage or negative publicity, should have their shares redeemed at fair market value as determined by a valuer.

**5-47**    The Court of Appeal of the BVI had concluded that it was reasonable for a company to take the view that 'members who had acquired their shares by misrepresentation or who had committed acts which may result in the company suffering detriment' should have their shares redeemed. On the authorities, the fact that the majority shareholder wanted the minority out of the company did not in itself mean that the resolution was passed mala fide. The lower court judge had been entitled to find that the resolution was 'not so oppressive as to cast suspicion on the honesty of those responsible for it or so extravagant that no reasonable men could really consider it for the benefit of the company'. On the facts, the Privy Council upheld the ruling of the BVI courts that the alteration was valid, but a notice served on the minority shareholder to redeem his shares in accordance with the altered articles was invalid since no material misrepresentations by him had been established on the facts.

## D  Interpreting the articles

### A contract with distinctive features

**5-48**    The articles form a contract, but it is a statutory contract with its own distinctive features, as the Court of Appeal explained in *Bratton Seymour Service Co Ltd v Oxborough*,[130] deriving its binding force not from a bargain struck between the parties, but from the terms of the statute (see CA 2006, s 33, at **5-53**).[131] The contract can be altered by a special resolution without the consent of all the contracting parties (s 21). Unlike an ordinary

---

[129] [2017] UKPC 43.    [130] [1992] BCLC 693, CA.    [131] [1992] BCLC 693 at 698, per Steyn LJ.

contract, it is not defeasible on the grounds of misrepresentation, common law mistake, mistake in equity, undue influence, or duress and it cannot be rectified by the court even if the articles do not accord with what is proved to have been the intention of the parties.[132] Once registered, the articles are one of the statutory documents of the company open to inspection by anyone minded to deal with the company or to take shares in it, hence it is not for the court to rectify the articles, even if they do not reflect the parties' intention, rather the members must alter the articles using the procedure provided by s 21.[133]

**5-49**　The articles are a commercial document, and, in the event of any ambiguity, the courts will construe them so as to give them reasonable business efficacy where a construction tending to that result is admissible on the language of the articles,[134] but terms cannot be implied from extrinsic circumstances. In *Bratton Seymour Service Co Ltd v Oxborough*[135] the court could not imply a term in the articles of association of a company set up to manage a block of flats that the shareholders should make a financial contribution to the upkeep of the amenity areas of the development. Such a term could not be derived from the language of the articles, but purely from extrinsic circumstances and was, the court said, a type of implication which, as a matter of law, can never succeed in the case of articles of association.[136] The court emphasised that potential shareholders are entitled to look to and rely on the articles as registered without being concerned that the courts might add terms by implication derived from extrinsic surrounding circumstances.[137]

### Interpreting the articles

**5-50**　The position on the implication of terms into contracts generally was dominated for some time by the Privy Council speech by Lord Hoffmann in *AG of Belize v Belize Telecom*[138] which concerned the implication of a term into articles of association. As to the proper approach to construction—and implication, Lord Hoffmann thought, is an exercise in construction of the document[139]—he emphasised that the court does not have power to improve the articles (or a contract or other instrument) to make them fairer or more

---

[132]　[1992] BCLC 693 at 698, CA.

[133]　[1992] BCLC 693 at 696, per Dillon LJ. See *Scott v Frank F Scott* [1940] 1 Ch 794 (articles should have included a provision on pre-emption on the death of a shareholder; the court could not rectify the articles to include such a provision).

[134]　*Holmes v Keyes* [1958] 2 All ER 129 at 138; also *BWE International Ltd v Jones* [2004] 1 BCLC 406, CA; *Dashfield v Davidson* [2009] 1 BCLC 220. In *Tett v Phoenix Property and Investment Co Ltd* [1986] BCLC 149, for example, the court was able as a matter of construction to resolve difficulties surrounding the operation of a badly drafted pre-emption clause in the articles. See also *Pennington v Crampton* [2004] BCC 611.

[135]　[1992] BCLC 693, CA. See also *Mutual Life Insurance Co of New York v The Rank Organisation Ltd* [1985] BCLC 11.

[136]　[1992] BCLC 693 at 698, per Steyn LJ. There can be a fine line between refusing to imply terms from extrinsic circumstances and a generous construction of a provision in the articles to give effect to the obvious intention of the parties: see *Folkes Group plc v Alexander* [2002] 2 BCLC 254 where, faced with an alteration of the articles which, as a result of the misplacing of an inserted provision, gave rise to an absurd result, the court supplied five words so that the articles assumed a meaning reflecting a true sense of what was intended. Rimer J acknowledged, at [22], that his approach to the interpretation of the amended article might be regarded as close to the limits of what is permissible as a pure exercise of construction.

[137]　[1992] BCLC 693 at 699, per Sir Christopher Slade; at 698–9, per Steyn LJ.

[138]　[2009] 2 BCLC 148; see also *Mediterranean Salvage and Towage Ltd v Seamar Trading and Commerce Inc; The Reborn* [2010] 1 All ER (Comm) 1. The approach of Lord Hoffmann was applauded for bringing clarity and certainty (see Peters (2009) 68 CLJ 513) and criticised for inappropriately affording the courts greater room to alter the bargain made (see Davies 'Recent Developments in the Law of Implied Terms' [2010] LMCLQ 140).

[139]　[2009] 2 BCLC 148 at [18].

reasonable. The court is concerned only to discover what the articles would mean to a reasonable person having all the background knowledge which would reasonably be available to the audience to whom the instrument is addressed.[140] Implication of a term is not an addition to an instrument, it only spells out what the instrument means.[141] In every case in which it is said that some provision ought to be implied, the question for the court, Lord Hoffmann said, is whether such a provision would spell out in express words what the instrument, read against the relevant background, would reasonably be understood to mean.[142]

**5-51** The Supreme Court reviewed the law on implication of terms in *Marks and Spencer plc v BNP Paribas Securities Services Trust Company (Jersey) Ltd*[143] (the facts are irrelevant and concerned the terms of a lease) and in so doing relegated the *Belize* approach of Lord Hoffmann to the sidelines.[144] On implying terms, the Supreme Court ruled that a term would be implied in a detailed commercial contract only if that was necessary to give the contract business efficacy (and necessity for business efficacy involves a value judgement) or it was so obvious that it went without saying (the officious bystander); and the implication of a term was not dependent on proof of the actual intention of the parties, but was concerned with what notional reasonable people, in the position of the parties at the time when they were contracting, would have agreed. Lord Neuberger went on to comment that the approach of Lord Hoffmann in *Belize* had been interpreted wrongly as having changed the law on implication of terms (being viewed as treating reasonableness as a sufficient ground for implying a term) whereas the law remains, as noted above, based on business efficacy and the officious bystander. As for Lord Hoffmann's suggestion that the process of implication was part of the exercise of interpretation, Lord Neuberger did not agree, for such an approach, he said, would obscure the fact that construing the words used and implying additional words are different processes governed by different rules.[145] Typically, it is only after the process of construing the express words is complete that the issue of an implied term falls to be considered.

**5-52** In *Re Coroin Ltd, McKillen v Misland (Cyprus) Investments Ltd*[146] the Court of Appeal refused to interpret a detailed pre-emption provision addressing the sale of members' shares as extending to the more indirect sale of shares in a corporate member. Rimer LJ noting that it is not part of the court's interpretative exercise to improve upon the instrument which it is called upon to construe.[147] No question of implication arises if the plain

---

[140] [2009] 2 BCLC 148 at [16]. And with respect to the articles, as noted earlier, extrinsic evidence is not admissible in the construction of the articles, *Bratton Seymour Services Ltd v Oxborough* [1992] BCLC 693, discussed at **5-49**. Evidence of background facts would be admissible in construing a shareholders' agreement, see David Richards J in *Re Coroin Ltd* [2011] EWHC 3466 at [69]–[76].

[141] [2009] 2 BCLC 148 at [18].     [142] [2009] 2 BCLC 148 at [21].     [143] [2016] AC 742.

[144] Lord Neuberger acknowledged that the decision in *Belize* was a unanimous decision of the Privy Council, but nevertheless considered that the right course now is to say that 'those observations should henceforth be treated as characteristically inspired discussion rather than authoritative guidance on the law of implied terms', at [31].

[145] [2016] AC 742 at [26].

[146] [2012] 2 BCLC 611, [2012] EWCA Civ 179, aff'g [2011] EWHC 3466—see the first instance judgment at [60]–[76] where David Richards J reviews the authorities on construing the articles of association.

[147] [2012] 2 BCLC 611 at [54]. The Court of Appeal subsequently also refused to imply a term in the articles requiring a shareholder to notify the company of events which triggered a pre-emption provision in the articles, since there was no need for such notification, given that other provisions of the articles prevented a shareholder from transferring his shares in breach of the pre-emption provisions in any event, see *Re Coroin Ltd (No 2)* [2013] 2 BCLC 583.

and ordinary meaning of the words used in the articles is clear and does not give rise to a commercial absurdity.[148] In those circumstances, there is no scope for implication.[149]

## E  Enforcing the articles

**5-53**  Generally, the courts have been reluctant to hold that an individual member has a right to have all of the articles observed, despite the wording of CA 2006, s 33(1) which provides that:

> 'The provisions of a company's constitution bind the company and its members to the same extent as if there were covenants on the part of the company and of each member to observe those provisions.'

**5-54**  The wording in CA 2006, s 33 is a clarification of the wording in CA 1985, s 14 ('… articles, when registered, bind the company and the members to the same extent as if they had been signed and sealed by each member …'). But, as was emphasised in the Parliamentary debates,[150] the only purpose of the amended wording is to state explicitly that the company is a party to the constitution as well as the members, as was established by *Hickman v Kent or Romney Marsh Sheepbreeders' Association*[151] which is discussed at **5-57**. The new wording does not extend a member's right to enforce the articles. Likewise, the existence now of a specific statutory duty on directors to act in accordance with the constitution (CA 2006, s 171) does not alter the position (the duty is owed to the company, s 170(1)) and does not confer on members a right to enforce every provision of the constitution.

**5-55**  The reason for imposing limits to the enforcement of the articles is linked to the rule in *Foss v Harbottle*[152] (see **20-1**) which has two elements: first, the proper plaintiff in respect of a wrong allegedly done to a company is *prima facie* the company; secondly, where the alleged wrong is a transaction which might be made binding on the company by a simple majority of the members, no individual member of the company is allowed to bring a claim in respect of it.[153] The rule is based on two fundamental principles of company law, namely respect for the separate legal personality of the company and the principle of majority rule. In addition to reflecting those fundamental principles, the rule has certain practical advantages. It prevents multiplicity of shareholder suits and eliminates wasteful and vexatious actions by shareholders trying to harass the company. If a breach of the constitution is seen therefore as a wrong done to the company, rather than to the rights of individual members, it will fall within the rule and the majority have the option of ratifying the breach. If a breach can be regarded as an infringement of a member's personal

---

[148]  See *Thompson v Goblin Hills Hotels* [2011] 1 BCLC 587, PC.

[149]  *Sugarman v CJS Investments LLP* [2015] 1 BCLC 1. See also *Jackson v Dear* [2014] 1 BCLC 186—there was no scope for adding an implied term to a shareholders' agreement limiting the ability of the shareholders who were party to the agreement from exercising powers in the articles to remove a director. The agreement expressly addressed the appointment and removal of directors by the parties to the agreement but was silent about the parties' powers under the articles. In those circumstances, the court said, the agreement had no effect on the power under the articles and to imply a term that it did would be to rewrite the parties' contract.

[150]  See 450 HC Debs, col 1087, 19 October 2006; 686 HL Debs, col 435, 2 November 2006.

[151]  [1915] 1 Ch 881.       [152]  (1843) 2 Hare 461.

[153]  *Prudential Assurance Co Ltd v Newman Industries Ltd (No 2)* [1982] 1 All ER 354 at 357, CA; and see *Edwards v Halliwell* [1950] 2 All ER 1064 at 1066, per Jenkins LJ. As Mellish LJ explained in *MacDougall v Gardiner* (1875) 1 Ch D 13 at 25 '… if the thing complained of is a thing which in substance the majority of the company are entitled to do … there can be no use in having litigation about it, the ultimate end of which is only that a meeting has to be called, and then ultimately the majority gets its wishes.'

rights, a wrong done to him personally rather than a wrong done to the company, he is untroubled by the rule in *Foss v Harbottle* and may proceed with a personal claim. It can be appreciated, therefore, that an expansive view of a member's personal rights under the articles might enable him to sidestep the rule entirely, something which the courts would regard as unacceptable, given the policies underlying the rule.

**5-56**   The courts have reconciled their desire to uphold the rule in *Foss v Harbottle*[154] and the fact that the statute creates a contract between the company and the members under CA 2006, s 33 by drawing a difficult distinction between: (1) provisions in the articles which do create enforceable personal rights conferred on a member qua member (not subject to the rule in *Foss v Harbottle*); and (2) provisions which relate to matters of internal management of the company. Breaches of the latter provisions amount only to internal irregularities and as such are open to ratification by the majority and are not actionable by individual shareholders.

### Company may enforce the articles against a member

**5-57**   As noted at **5-54**, the rewording of CA 2006, s 33 has clarified that the company and the members are parties to the contract laid down in the articles, a point established in *Hickman v Kent or Romney Marsh Sheepbreeders' Association*.[155] In this case, the articles provided that disputes between the company and a member should be referred to arbitration. A member in dispute with the company commenced legal proceedings and the company brought proceedings to stop his action and require him to go to arbitration. The court held that a company is entitled as against its own members to enforce and restrain breaches of the articles. On the facts, the member was bound and the dispute was referred to arbitration.

### A member may enforce the articles against a member

**5-58**   It is also the case, as was accepted in *Rayfield v Hands*,[156] that a member may enforce the articles directly against the other members. In that case, as a matter of construction of the articles, a member wishing to transfer his shares was able to require the other members to take the shares and the court allowed a member to enforce that provision against the other members. Such actions are unusual and, more generally, the expectation would be that the contract would be enforced through the company.[157]

### A member cannot always enforce the articles against the company

**5-59**   As noted at **5-55**, a shareholder's entitlement to enforce what he perceives to be his rights under the articles is problematic with the courts taking a restrictive approach to the issue in order not to undermine the rule in *Foss v Harbottle*.[158]

**5-60**   The many conflicting authorities on this issue were reviewed in *Hickman v Kent or Romney Marsh Sheepbreeders' Association*[159] and Astbury J concluded that the effect of the authorities is that rights purporting to be given by the articles in a capacity other than that of a member cannot be enforced against the company. Only membership rights which have been conferred on the member qua member can be enforced and so, when considering whether a provision can be enforced, it has to be asked whether it is intended

---

[154]  (1843) 2 Hare 461.        [155]  [1915] 1 Ch 881.        [156]  [1960] Ch 1.
[157]  See *Welton v Saffery* [1897] AC 299 at 315.        [158]  (1843) 2 Hare 461.
[159]  [1915] 1 Ch 881 at 900.

to confer rights on a member in that capacity. Provisions identified by the courts as conferring rights on the members qua members include the right of a member to have his vote recorded,[160] to have a dividend paid in cash if the articles so specify,[161] and to enforce a declared dividend as a legal debt.[162] For example, in *Pender v Lushington*[163] the chairman of a general meeting of shareholders improperly refused to record some of the votes cast. This refusal was an infringement of a member's right qua member and the shareholders were able to get an injunction restraining the company from acting on the resolutions passed. In *Wood v Odessa Waterworks Co*[164] a member was entitled to require the company to pay a dividend in cash when the articles so provided. Rights with respect to share transfer, for example to enforce compliance with a pre-emption provision on transfer, may also be enforced.[165] Members qua members may also insist on the proper conduct of meetings.[166] There are then instances in which the articles do create rights for individual shareholders which they can positively enforce. On other occasions, it is not a case that the shareholder wishes to enforce a particular right, rather he wishes to prevent the majority acting in disregard of a requirement in the articles where they have not sought first to amend the articles by a special resolution as required by CA 2006, s 21.

**5-61** Certainly examples can be found where the court was prepared to restrain the company in such circumstances. In *Edwards v Halliwell*,[167] for example, two members of a trade union (similar to a company for these purposes) successfully restrained an attempt by a delegate meeting to increase the members' contribution without obtaining the two-thirds majority required under their rules. In *Quin & Axtens Ltd v Salmon*[168] the articles of association provided that certain transactions could not be entered into without the consent of both managing directors who were significant shareholders in the company. In this instance, one of the directors dissented, but the company in general meeting nevertheless tried to authorise the transaction without that director's consent. The Court of Appeal rejected the purported authorisation, finding that this was an attempt to alter the terms of the contract between the parties by an ordinary rather than a special resolution, a view affirmed by the House of Lords.[169]

---

[160] See *Pender v Lushington* (1877) 6 Ch D 70.

[161] See *Wood v Odessa Waterworks Co* (1889) 42 Ch D 636.

[162] *Re Severn and Wye and Severn Bridge Railway Company* [1896] 1 Ch 559.

[163] (1877) 6 Ch D 70. Cf *McDougall v Gardiner* (1875) 1 Ch D 13 (a member was denied relief when a chairman refused to call a poll in circumstances prescribed by the articles, the court regarding the matter as one of internal management: this case has been much criticised and is best confined to its facts).

[164] (1889) 42 Ch D 636.

[165] *Hurst v Crampton Bros (Coopers) Ltd* [2003] 1 BCLC 304 (when a member purported to transfer shares in breach of the pre-emption requirements in the articles, that transfer was defeasible at the suit of a member). See also *Re a company (No 005136 of 1986)* [1987] BCLC 82 where Hoffmann J took the view that a complaint by a member about improper allotments of shares by the directors was in substance a complaint that his contractual rights as a shareholder under the articles had been infringed and so any claim would be a personal claim, but see Joffe et al, *Minority Shareholders* (5th edn, 2015), para 3.64, which notes that the decision should be treated with caution.

[166] See *Kaye v Croydon Tramways Co* [1898] 1 Ch 358; *Tiessen v Henderson* [1899] 1 Ch 861; and *Baillie v Oriental Telephone and Electric Co Ltd* [1915] 1 Ch 503 (shareholders can prevent the company acting on resolutions improperly passed because of inadequate notice of the resolution to the shareholders).

[167] [1950] 2 All ER 1064.     [168] [1909] 1 Ch 311, aff'd [1909] AC 442.

[169] [1909] 1 Ch 311 at 319, aff'd [1909] AC 442. The Court of Appeal based its reasoning on the division of power between the board and the general meeting, governed by *Automatic Self-Cleansing Filter Syndicate Co Ltd v Cuninghame* [1906] 2 Ch 34, CA, see **9-5**, which depends on the terms of the articles but which typically precludes the general meeting interfering with management powers conferred on the directors other than by special resolution; the other side of that coin is that the members have a right to expect the division of power laid down in the articles to be observed.

**5-62**   However, there is considerable inconsistency in the case law on these matters and in *Grant v United Kingdom Switchback Railways Co*[170] and *Irvine v Union Bank of Australia*[171] the courts permitted the majority in general meeting to ratify conduct by the directors in breach of the articles. In *Grant* the directors had entered into a particular contract with a third party although, under the terms of the articles, all of the directors bar one were prevented from voting on that contract because of a conflict of interest. The majority in general meeting passed a resolution approving and adopting the agreement and authorising the directors to carry it into effect. The court rejected an application by a shareholder for an injunction to restrain the company from proceeding with the contract. In *Irvine* the directors borrowed money in excess of a credit limit imposed by the articles and the court accepted that such an internal irregularity was ratifiable by a simple majority of shareholders. Ratification of an unauthorised act, the court said, is not the same as conferring a general power to do similar acts in the future. The shareholders' action is not so much approval of a breach of the articles, but rather the adoption or affirmation of an unauthorised act and, as such, it has no implications for the future.

**5-63**   These cases are supposedly distinguishable from the general principle that the majority cannot prevail where a special resolution is required on the basis that they involved only internal irregularities and were not attempts to alter for all time the terms of the contract between the members as embodied in the articles. Drawing the line between conduct which is an attempt by a simple majority to ignore the requirement for a special majority and conduct which is merely the ratification of an internal management irregularity is difficult, but it is clear that the scope for ratifying internal irregularities undermines the protection afforded to the minority by the need for a special resolution to amend the articles.

**5-64**   In practice, a shareholder aggrieved at difficulties in enforcing his rights under the articles of association, or at non-compliance by the majority with the terms of the articles, is likely to petition for relief under CA 2006, s 994, alleging that the affairs of the company are being conducted in a manner which is unfairly prejudicial to his interests or that an act or proposed act or omission of the company is or would be so prejudicial. This route is preferable to attempting to overcome the difficulties inherent in trying to enforce the contract established by CA 2006, s 33.

## The articles are not enforceable by outsiders

**5-65**   The articles are a statutory contract between the company and the members and do not constitute a contract between a company and an outsider (i.e. a non-member) or members claiming in a capacity other than as a member.[172] In *Eley v Positive Life Assurance Co*[173] a person named in the articles as a solicitor was unable to enforce that provision when the company employed someone else; the articles conferred no rights as between him and the company.

**5-66**   Any right claimed by an outsider must be conferred by a separate agreement outside the articles.[174] On occasion, that extrinsic contract may be made by the company with an

---

[170] (1888) 40 Ch D 135.       [171] (1877) 2 App Cas 366.

[172] *Pritchard's Case* (1873) LR 8 Ch 956; *Melhado v Porto Alegre Rly Co* (1874) LR 9 CP 503; *Eley v Positive Life Assurance Co* (1876) 1 Ex D 20, 88; *Browne v La Trinidad* (1887) 37 Ch D 1; *Hickman v Kent or Romney Marsh Sheepbreeders' Association* [1915] 1 Ch 881; *Beattie v E & F Beattie Ltd* [1938] Ch 708.

[173] (1876) 1 Ex D 20, 88.

[174] This point is confirmed by the Contracts (Rights of Third Parties) Act 1999, s 6(2), which provides that the 1999 Act does not confer any rights on a third party in the case of any contract binding on a company and its members under CA 2006, s 33.

outsider on the basis of the articles and such a contract may even be inferred from the conduct of the parties.[175] In *Re New British Iron Co, ex p Beckwith*[176] the articles provided for the annual remuneration of the directors. As such, of course, the articles did not constitute a contract to pay that amount of remuneration to the directors. But, the court said, where, on the footing of that article, the directors were employed by the company and accepted office, the terms of that article as to remuneration were embodied in and formed part of the contract between the company and the directors.[177] An extrinsic contract derived from the articles in this way suffers from the disadvantage that the articles can be unilaterally changed by the company by special resolution under CA 2006, s 21, so altering the implied contract.[178]

## F  Supplementing the constitution—shareholders' agreements

**5-67**  In addition to the articles of association, shareholders may enter into a shareholders' agreement which is a separate contractual agreement between shareholders (or some of them) dealing with various aspects of their relationship. Matters commonly dealt with in a shareholders' agreement include voting rules, the provision of capital, the transfer of shares, and the appointment of directors.[179]

**5-68**  A shareholders' agreement has a number of advantages over articles of association:

- the agreement is a contract and binding on the parties to it[180] and subject to all the usual contractual remedies in the event of breach. It does not involve the parties in discussions as to whether a right is conferred qua member or whether the rule in *Foss v Harbottle* applies, see **5-55**. Likewise, enforcement of outsider rights conferred by the agreement is not a problem. A disadvantage is that the agreement can only bind those party to it, of course, and so a new agreement is required where there is a change in the composition of the shareholders though the agreement itself may address the issue of future participants;[181]

- the agreement is drawn up to address the particular position of the shareholders whereas the standard articles operate without regard to individual circumstances;

---

[175]  *Swabey v Port Darwin Gold Mining Co* (1889) 1 Meg 385.

[176]  [1898] 1 Ch 324.        [177]  [1898] 1 Ch 324 at 326.

[178]  See *Swabey v Port Darwin Gold Mining Co* (1889) 1 Meg 385, where the terms as to the directors' remuneration were changed subsequently, but such alteration must not be retrospective.

[179]  See generally, Cheung, 'Shareholders' Agreements—Shareholders' Contractual Freedom in Company Law' [2012] JBL 504; also *Hollington on Shareholders' Rights* (8th edn, 2016), paras 3–53 et seq who notes at 3–59 that there is 'surprisingly little authority on the special characteristics of shareholders' agreements and the breach thereof'. The fact that a shareholders' agreement deals with some aspects of their relationship does not preclude the shareholders from also relying on additional provisions in the articles, so provisions dealing with the appointment and removal of directors by the parties to the agreement did not limit the ability of the parties to exercise other powers in the articles with respect to the removal of directors, see *Jackson v Dear* [2014] 1 BCLC 186.

[180]  Evidence of background facts is admissible in the construction of a shareholders' agreement, but not in the construction of articles of association, see *Re Coroin Ltd* [2011] EWHC 3466 at [70]–[76].

[181]  It is common to provide that new members of the company are required to become parties to the shareholders' agreement (and transferor members undertake to procure their adherence) by entering into a deed of adherence so that the agreement binds all present and future shareholders. For an example of such a clause, see *Re Coroin Ltd* [2011] EWHC 3466 at [42]. As to the consequences of breach of such a clause, see *Hollington*, n 179, para 3–56.

- the process of drawing up an agreement can be useful in getting the members to focus on issues of concern to them and identifying ways in which disputes might be resolved, were they to arise;

- the agreement cannot be altered by a majority of the parties (unless the agreement so provides) as the articles can, so a shareholder party to the agreement is assured that changes cannot occur without his consent; and often a term of agreement will be that the parties will not seek to alter certain provisions in the articles;[182]

- the agreement is a private contract whereas the articles are a public document registered with the registrar of companies.

**5-69**  These various advantages mean that a shareholders' agreement is particularly useful in certain circumstances, such as small family companies where it may help them address more fully the nature of their relationships *inter se* and with the company and, crucially, the manner of exiting from the business, given that a shareholder cannot simply demand back his capital. A shareholders' agreement is also commonly used in the quite different context of joint venture companies where commercially astute parties do not want their relationship to be governed by the vagaries of CA 2006, s 33.

---

[182] Such a provision is effective as it does not prevent the company from altering its articles, it merely prevents the shareholders from voting for an alteration: see *Russell v Northern Bank Development Corp Ltd* [1992] 3 All ER 161, HL.

# PART II

# Corporate Governance— Directors' Roles and Responsibilities

# 6

# Corporate governance–board structure and shareholder engagement

## A Introduction

**6-1** As the number of shareholders in a company increases, it is obviously impossible for all to be involved in the management and control of the company's affairs and so a separation commonly develops between those who collectively own the company through their combined shareholdings (the shareholders) and those who manage it (the directors).[1] Problems can arise from this separation of ownership and control as distance from the day-to-day running of the business makes it difficult for shareholders to restrain any managerial excesses, whether such excesses are the result of incompetence, self-dealing, or outright fraud. No single mechanism can provide an answer to this so-called agency problem between shareholders and directors[2] and a variety of responses is required. Much of the focus is on internal mechanisms (such as shareholders' rights and board structures) though external mechanisms too have a role to play. Disclosure requirements are important components of governance ensuring that business is conducted in an open and transparent way. The assumption is that the full glare of publicity makes directors more circumspect in their activities and that disclosure assists shareholders in monitoring those activities and allows shareholders and creditors to assess the risks involved. To this end, much effort has been expended since the financial crisis in 2008 on improving the content of the annual accounts and reports and, crucially, ensuring the quality of the external audit of those accounts. Disclosure issues are considered in Chapter 18. For underperforming management in the largest companies, the markets may operate as an additional constraining force with takeovers providing a means by which to displace an existing board. That threat of displacement, it is argued, provides an incentive for efficient management. For dishonest and fraudulent management, external mechanisms lie in the hands of various regulatory authorities. The maintenance of confidence in the proper conduct of business and the protection of investors and markets may require intervention and, possibly, an investigation of the company's affairs. The

---

[1] The theory of the separation of ownership and control originates in the famous work by Berle and Means, *The Modern Corporation and Private Property* (1932). For a modern study of the position in Europe where, unlike the UK and the US, shareholding is much more concentrated and dominant blockholders are common (giving rise to greater scope, perhaps, for conflicts between majority and minority shareholders) see Barca and Becht, *The Control of Corporate Europe* (2001).

[2] See Davies, *Introduction to Company Law* (2nd edn, 2010), pp 110–11 on the inappropriateness legally, but not factually, of this 'agency' characterisation while accepting that it is the widely adopted terminology.

exercise of investigation powers is primarily a matter for the Department for Business, Energy & Industrial Strategy acting through the Investigation and Enforcement Services of the Insolvency Service (which act in respect of 'live' companies despite being part of the Insolvency Service). Listed companies can expect scrutiny by the Financial Conduct Authority (FCA). Beyond these regulatory bodies lie the police and the Serious Fraud Office.

**6-2**   The starting point, however, is that good corporate governance primarily stems from internal structures. The classic definition of corporate governance, taken from the Cadbury Report and often cited, is that corporate governance is the system by which companies are directed and controlled with boards of directors responsible for the governance of the company while the role of the shareholders is to appoint the directors and the auditors and to satisfy themselves that an appropriate governance structure is in place.[3] In keeping with those parameters, much of the substantive corporate governance debate[4] has centred on:

   (1) the structure and role of the board of directors and, in particular, the role of independent non-executive directors. As a preliminary point, executive directors are those directors concerned with the day-to-day management of the company. They will have extensive management powers delegated to them by the articles and they typically have service contracts with the company which together with the articles delimit their powers and responsibilities.[5] Non-executive directors are directors without executive management responsibilities who provide constructive challenge and strategic guidance for the company and hold management to account[6]—their precise role is discussed in detail later. They commonly have letters of appointment setting out their role and responsibilities. The Companies Act 2006 does not refer to or distinguish between executive and non-executive directors, these are essentially business terms. All directors are subject to the general duties laid down in CA 2006, Pt 10, though, when considering the duty of care and skill, the different functions of the non-executive directors will be relevant, as discussed in Chapter 11.

   (2) shareholder engagement—here the emphasis is on enhancing the stewardship role of the institutional investors (addressed by the Stewardship Code, 2012) and on revitalising the general meeting as a shareholders' forum (addressed in part by the Shareholders' Rights Directive, reflected in the CA 2006 as amended) and on facilitating the engagement of the indirect investor with investee companies (addressed by CA 2006, Pt 9) in recognition of the fact that shareholdings in the largest companies are now commonly held by nominees through a chain of intermediaries, possibly a cross-border chain.

---

[3] See *The Committee on the Financial Aspects of Corporate Governance* (1992) (known as the Cadbury Committee) para 2.5; the UK Corporate Governance Code (2018), p 1, para 1. See also the Financial Services and Markets Act 2000, s 89O(2).

[4] There is an extensive literature on corporate governance but, as a starting point, see Watson and Vasudev (eds), *Innovations in Corporate Governance, Global Perspectives* (2017); Choudhury and Petrin, *Understanding the Company, Corporate Governance and Theory* (2017); Moore and Petrin, *Corporate Governance, Law, Regulation and Theory* (2017); Davies and Hopt et al, *Corporate Boards in Law and Practice, A Comparative Analysis in Europe* (2013).

[5] See *Harold Holdsworth & Co (Wakefield) Ltd v Caddies* [1955] 1 All ER 725.

[6] See, for example, Rimer J in *Re Kaytech International plc, Secretary of State for Trade and Industry v Kaczer* [1999] 2 BCLC 351 at 407; Park J in *Re Continental Assurance Co of London plc* [2007] 2 BCLC 287 at [399]. On non-executive directors generally, see Sweeney-Baird, 'The Role of the Non-executive Director in Modern Corporate Governance' (2006) 27 Co Law 67; Parkinson, 'Evolution and Policy in Company Law: The Non-executive Director' in Parkinson, Gamble, and Kelly (eds), *The Political Economy of the Company* (2000).

These issues are the focus of this chapter and the debate on them sharpened following the financial crisis of 2007–08 which moved corporate governance issues back to the top of the regulatory and reform agenda. Once the most acute problems in the financial sector had been addressed (stabilising the banks), attention turned to other aspects of the crisis, including the failures of corporate governance across many financial institutions which enabled the banks to engage in such reckless conduct. The debate on corporate governance in the financial institutions then evolved into a debate as to whether there were improvements in corporate governance that could and should be adopted more generally.

**6-3** The focus of the chapter is on publicly traded companies with widely dispersed shareholdings though corporate governance is an issue for all public companies and large private companies.

## The evolution of codes of corporate governance

**6-4** The role of non-executive directors in UK companies arguably can be traced to the part-time, idle, disengaged, non-executives of mid-nineteenth-century England, but their modern role came to the fore with the Cadbury Committee report[7] in 1992. The Committee drew up a Code of Corporate Governance for listed companies (now premium listed companies) based on a board structure composed of mainly independent non-executive directors involved especially on audit, remuneration, and nomination committees[8] and operating on a comply or explain basis, i.e. companies were expected to comply with the Code or explain their reasons for non-compliance (see **6-10**). Over the following years, various reviews ensured the continued evolution of the Cadbury Code[9] into a Combined Code of Corporate Governance within the remit (since 2003) of the Financial Reporting Council (FRC). In the wake of the financial crisis of 2007–08, the FRC reviewed the content and overall effectiveness of the Combined Code[10] taking into account the recommendations of the Walker Report on corporate governance issues in UK banks and other financial industry entities.[11] The FRC then reissued the Code as the UK Corporate Governance Code (the UK Code) in June 2010 and new editions are published every two years. In February 2017, the FRC decided on a comprehensive review of the Code for various reasons including that the Code is now 25 years old, but also as

---

[7] *The Committee on the Financial Aspects of Corporate Governance* (1992) chaired by Sir Adrian Cadbury.

[8] Financial institutions may decide also to have a separate risk committee, see FCA Handbook, SYSC 21.

[9] Notably as a result of the work of the Greenbury Committee, see *Study Group on Directors' Remuneration* (1995); the Hampel Committee, see *Report of Committee on Corporate Governance* (1998); the Higgs Review, see *Review of the Role and Effectiveness of Non-executive Directors* (2003); and the *Smith Report on Audit Committees, Report to the FRC* (2003).

[10] See FRC, *Review of the Effectiveness of the Combined Code, Call for Evidence* (March 2009); FRC, *Review of the Effectiveness of the Combined Code: Progress Report and Second Consultation* (July 2009); FRC, *Consultation on the Revised Corporate Governance Code* (December 2009).

[11] Walker, *A Review of Corporate Governance in UK Banks and other Financial Industry Entities, Final Recommendations* (November 2009) (hereafter Walker Report), a review and report by Sir David Walker carried out at the invitation of the Government and preceded by a consultation paper of the same name in July 2009. See generally Hannigan, 'Board Failures in the Financial Crisis—Tinkering with Codes and the Need for Wider Corporate Governance Reforms' Part 1 (2011) 32 Co Law 363, and Part 2 (2012) 33 Co Law 35.

a response to issues raised by a Government Green Paper (November 2016) on corporate governance reform.[12] The FRC concluded its review with a public consultation in December 2017 including a draft revised Code.[13] The revised Code focuses on the Code principles with much of the mundane detail which had built up over the years in the Code deleted or removed to the board guidance[14] which the FRC issues to support the Code. The revised 2018 Code will apply to financial years commencing on or after 1 January 2019. The text which follows reflects the proposed 2018 Code—its wording had not been finalised at the time of writing (note the new Code was issued in July 2018).

**6-5**   There are a number of other influential codes or guidance which have evolved alongside the UK Code. For smaller companies with a standard listing or traded companies which are not on a regulated market (i.e. companies on AIM, see **21-106**), the Quoted Companies Alliance has published a widely accepted Code which reflects the requirements of the UK Code in a way which is relevant to smaller companies.[15] The Association of Investment Companies has a code which is intended to help boards of investment companies meet the requirements of the UK Code[16] and the Institute of Directors developed corporate governance guidelines to assist unlisted companies.[17] Internationally significant instruments would include the G20/OECD Principles of Corporate Governance (2016) and the ICGN (International Corporate Governance Network) Global Corporate Governance Principles (2017).

**6-6**   Developments at the European level have been very much in step with the UK, given that the Cadbury Code was the pioneer in this field. A report commissioned by the European Commission in 2002 found that, ten years after Cadbury, most EU Member States had very similar 'comply or explain' codes to the UK.[18] In the light of that finding, the Commission concluded there was no need for a European Code as such.[19] Such interventions as the European Commission has made on corporate governance issues have been mainly by way of Recommendations, such as its 2005 Recommendation on the role of non-executive directors[20] or through various governance requirements included in relevant Directives. For example, Directive 2006/43 on audit, as amended by Directive 2014/56/EU,[21] requires (art 39) certain companies[22] to have an audit committee. The Accounts Directive 2013/34/EU requires large companies to include a corporate governance statement in their annual reports.[23] The Commission's 'Action Plan' on European

---

[12]   See BEIS, Corporate Governance Reform: Green Paper (November 2016) BEIS/16/56; and Government Response to the Green Paper Consultation (August 2017); see also the influential report of the House of Commons, *Business, Energy and Industrial Strategy Committee, Corporate Governance*, Third Report of Session 2016–17, HC 702 (March 2017).

[13]   FRC, Proposed Revisions to the UK Corporate Governance Code (December 2017).

[14]   FRC Guidance on Board Effectiveness (2018).

[15]   See QCA, *Corporate Governance Code for Small and Mid-Sized Quoted Companies* (2013).

[16]   See AIC, *Code of Corporate Governance and Guidance for Investment Companies* (July 2016) which is endorsed by the FRC as helpful to investment companies in meeting their obligations under the UK Code, see FRC, UK Corporate Governance Code (2018), p 2.

[17]   See IOD, *Corporate Governance, Guidance and Principles for Unlisted Companies in the UK* (2010).

[18]   See Weil, Gotshal, and Manges, *Comparative Study of Corporate Governance Codes Relevant to the European Union and its Member States* (2002).

[19]   See European Commission, *Modernising Company Law and Enhancing Corporate Governance in the EU—A Plan to Move Forward*, COM (2003) 284 final, 21.5.2003, para 3.1.

[20]   Commission Recommendation on the role of non-executive or supervisory directors of listed companies and on the committees of the (supervisory) board (2005/162/EC), OJ L 52, 25.2.2005, p 51.

[21]   OJ L 158/220, 27.5.2014, art 1, para 32.

[22]   Public interest entities which, for our purposes, is essentially (though the category is wider than this) companies admitted to trading on a regulated market.          [23]   OJ L 182/19, 29.6.2013, art 20.

company law and corporate governance (December 2012)[24] identified a number of areas where the Commission would concentrate its efforts including enhancing transparency by companies and engagement by shareholders.[25] These action points have been implemented by amendments to the Shareholders' Rights Directive[26] by Directive 2017/828. Shareholder engagement is discussed at **6-48**.

## B  Corporate governance and large, privately-held, companies

**6-7**   Recent years have seen the collapse of some high-profile privately-owned companies where, with hindsight, standards of corporate governance proved to be low. Subsequent reviews by Parliamentary committees drew attention to the fact that, while economically significant, these companies fell outside the remit of the UK Corporate Governance Code, not being listed, or even public companies.[27] This debate also raised the issue of whether a focus on public companies with regard to corporate governance is misplaced as the number of public companies has been declining for decades. In 2016, public companies in England and Wales made up only 0.2 per cent of the register, just 5,812 companies,[28] so, if governance is focused only on public or listed companies (an even smaller subset of public companies), quite a lot of large businesses escape the net.

**6-8**   In a Green Paper,[29] the Government noted that there are many reasons why large privately-held companies should meet minimum standards of corporate governance, not least because their economic size means that their collapse has repercussions across society. Also, businesses accorded the privilege of limited liability should act responsibly in return and higher standards of corporate governance improve company reputations, their ability to raise capital, and the sustainability of the enterprise.[30] It was also acknowledged in the Green Paper that many well-run private companies already adhere to some form of code, perhaps modifying the UK Code for their situation or relying on governance principles developed by the Institute of Directors.[31] Having considered the responses to the Green Paper, the Government invited the FRC to bring together a Coalition Group of business interests (Investment Association, Institute of Directors, etc) under the chairmanship of James Wates, to develop a voluntary code of corporate governance principles for large privately-held companies.[32] The principles will aim to promote:

- 'best practice in corporate governance and reporting arrangements,
- public trust and confidence through greater transparency in the manner in which large privately-owned companies conduct their business,

[24] Commission Communication, *Action Plan: European company law and corporate governance— a modern legal framework for more engaged shareholders and sustainable companies*, COM (2012) 740 final, 12.12.2012. The background to the Action Plan can be found in European Commission, *Corporate Governance in Financial Institutions and Remuneration Policies*, COM (2010) 284, 2 June 2010; and accompanying Commission Staff Working Document, SEC (2010) 669; and European Commission Green Paper, *The EU Corporate Governance Framework* (April 2011), COM (2011) 164.

[25] See European Commission, COM (2014) 213, pp 2–10.

[26] Directive 2007/36/EC, OJ L 184/17, 14.7.2007 as amended by Directive 2017/828, OJ L 132/1, 20.5.2017.

[27] See the House of Commons, Work and Pensions and Business, Innovation and Skills Committees, BHS, First Report of the Work and Pensions Committee and Fourth Report of the Business, Innovation and Skills Committee of Session 2016–17, HC 54 (July 2016).

[28] Companies House, *Companies Register Activity in the UK 2016–17*, Table A3.      [29] See n 12.

[30] See n 12, paras 3.1–3.3.      [31] See n 17.

[32] The HC BEIS Committee Report, n 12, also recommended the introduction of a Code for private companies (March 2017).

- strong corporate culture and integrity within large private businesses, encourage broader consideration of workforce and wider stakeholder representation and interests;
- investor, lender and creditor confidence to facilitate long-term value and improved productivity.'[33]

The principles will be voluntary so companies which have already adopted principles, such as those drawn up by the Institute of Directors, will be able to continue to do so. As explained at **6-10**, the effectiveness of the UK Code depends on the requirement in the UK Listing Rules for premium listed companies to report on how they have applied the principles and explain any areas of non-compliance with the Code provisions. Any principles for privately-held companies will also need a degree of underpinning which will act as the incentive towards adoption. Hence, the Government intends to require the largest privately-held companies and unlisted public companies with more than 2,000 employees (thought to be in the region of 1,400 companies) to report (assuming they do not already report under the UK Code or DTR 4) in the directors' report and on their website as to the details of any UK code with which they comply, and to provide an explanation of any non-compliance with any provisions of their adopted code, and if the company has not adopted a code, it will be required to explain its reasons.[34]

## C  The UK Corporate Governance Code

### Application and status

**6-9**    The UK Code previously consisted of main principles, supporting principles, and Code provisions which over time became a somewhat lengthy, over-prescriptive, and unwieldy structure. The 2018 Code resets the principles (Prin) as the heart of the Code with additional provisions (Prov). The focus for companies, boards, and shareholders should be on their application (including their spirit) in the context of the particular circumstances of the company.[35]

### Comply or explain—Premium listed companies

**6-10**    The Listing Rules require UK and overseas listed companies with a premium listing of equity shares (see **21-103**) to include in their annual report and accounts:[36]

(i) a statement of how the listed company has applied the Main Principles of the UK Corporate Governance Code in a manner that would enable shareholders to evaluate how the principles have been applied; and

(ii) a statement as to whether the listed company has: (a) complied throughout the accounting period with all relevant provisions set out in the UK Corporate Governance Code or (b) not complied throughout the accounting period with all relevant provisions set out in the Code and if so, setting out: (i) those provisions, if any, it has not complied with; (ii) in the case of provisions whose requirements are

---

[33] FRC, Press Release, 30 January 2018 announcing James Wates as chair of the Coalition Group.

[34] Government response to Green Paper, n 12, paras 3.28–3.33. Such a requirement was added to the AIM rules recently, see rule 26. See the Companies (Miscellaneous Reporting) Regulations 2018 (only in draft at time of writing).

[35] UK Corporate Governance Code (2018), p 1.          [36] See FCA Listing Rules, LR 9.8.6(6); 9.8.7.

of a continuing nature, the period within which, if any, it did not comply with some or all of those provisions; and (iii) the company's reasons for non-compliance.[37]

The Listing Rules further require (LR 9.8.10(2)) that the auditors review this statement of compliance by the company so far as the statement relates to:

(i) the directors' explanation in the annual report of their responsibility for preparing the company's accounts (required by Prov 27);

(ii) the directors' annual review of the effectiveness of the internal control systems (required by Prov 28); and

(iii) the company's practice as to the establishment, role, and responsibilities of the audit committee (required by Prov 26).

**6-11** A failure to include the required 'comply or explain' statement is a breach of the Listing Rules and punishable as such,[38] and the FRC has stressed that this formal requirement for transparency coupled with the shareholders' ability to remove boards (where the explanations are unsatisfactory) means that a 'comply or explain' code is not self-regulation.[39] True, it is not self-regulation in the sense of regulation of a trade or profession by members in their own self-interest, but a code which is not mandated by law and which attracts no legal sanctions for non-compliance with the code and which is dependent on market support for its effectiveness is still some steps removed from 'hard law'.

**6-12** The 'comply or explain' approach was pioneered by the Cadbury Committee (see **6-4**) and it is now a near universal feature of corporate governance codes around the world. Any reaction to explanation rather than compliance is left to market participants and, depending on the circumstances and the issue, reaction may range from indifference to a significant fall in share price. In the case of egregious failures of corporate governance, in theory shareholders may be provoked into exercising their right to remove directors under CA 2006, s 168, but that would be very unusual. More commonly, institutional shareholders would expect a dialogue with the board as to the reasons for any non-compliance. Commonly, there are complaints by shareholders that the explanations provided are inadequate and complaints by boards that shareholders pay insufficient attention to the reasons and have a mechanistic response to non-compliance.[40] The FRC stresses that explanations should be seen as a positive opportunity, not an onerous obligation.[41] In turn,

---

[37] See FRC, *Developments in Corporate Governance and Stewardship 2016* (January 2017), p 9 which reports that compliance is high with over 90 per cent of FTSE 350 companies reporting that they complied with all, or all but one or two, of its provisions.

[38] Listed companies must comply with the Listing Rules: Financial Services and Markets Act 2000, s 96(1); penalties may be imposed for non-compliance: s 91(1).

[39] FRC, *Response to the European Commission Green Paper on the EU Corporate Governance Framework* (2011), p 3.

[40] In its annual report, the FRC noted that too many explanations are of poor quality, and better explanations would include company-specific context and historical background and information on what mitigating actions have been taken to address any additional risk: see FRC, *Developments in Corporate Governance 2016* (January 2017), p 11. It is important that the company explains how its alternative approach is consistent with the spirit of the Code provision from which the company is deviating. The EU *Study on Monitoring and Enforcement Practices in Corporate Governance in the Member States* (2009) also found the overall quality of explanations to be 'unsatisfactory'. See Keay, 'Comply or Explain in Corporate Governance Codes: In Need of Greater Regulatory Oversight?' (2014) 34 Legal Studies 279.

[41] See FRC, UK Corporate Governance Code (2018), p 2; see also FRC, *What Constitutes an Explanation under Comply-or-Explain? Notes of Discussions* (February 2012).

the shareholders should pay due regard to the company's individual circumstances and not treat explanations in a mechanistic way.[42] The European Commission, acknowledging that inadequate explanations are often provided, issued a Recommendation in 2014 to provide guidance for listed companies on the nature of the explanations required where they depart from the relevant code, stressing the need for shareholders to be given clear, accurate, and comprehensive information to enable them to assess the consequences of the departure from the relevant requirement.[43]

**6-13**  Though there are concerns about the effectiveness of 'comply or explain', neither the Company Law Review (see **2-6**), nor the Walker Review (see **6-4**), nor the FRC found any support for putting the UK Code on a statutory basis.[44] On occasion, however, where a soft law approach has not worked, particular statutory measures have been introduced. For example, the original requirements as to the disclosure of directors' remuneration policy started as a Code provision and then evolved into a statutory requirement for a directors' remuneration report for quoted companies requiring formal shareholder approval of remuneration policy and its implementation, see **18-43**. Equally, as the FRC points out, sometimes the requirements of the UK Code can be stricter than the legal requirements, such as with respect to the annual election of directors (Prov 18) which is not a statutory requirement but which is now standard practice.

### Corporate governance statements

**6-14**  The 'comply or explain' obligation discussed at **6-10** applies to premium listed companies, but all companies admitted to trading on a regulated market (which encompasses companies with a premium or a standard listing) are required by the Disclosure and Transparency Rules (DTR)[45] to include a corporate governance statement[46] either in the directors' report (DTR 7.2.1), or as a separate report published with the annual report, or on the company's website (DTR 7.2.9) which must indicate which code the company is subject to (in the case of a premium listing, obviously this will be the UK Code) and explain any non-compliance with it (DTR 7.2.3R). The corporate governance statement must also describe the main features of the company's internal control and risk management systems in relation to the financial reporting process and include a description of the composition and operation of the company's board and its committees. For companies with a premium listing, there is a considerable degree of overlap between what is required under the DTR rules and the UK Code,[47] but the requirements are not identical. For example, DTR 7.2.5R requires a description of the main features of the company's internal control and risk management systems in relation to the financial reporting process. The UK Code requires the board to monitor the company's risk management and

---

[42]  See FRC, UK Corporate Governance Code (2018), p 2.

[43]  See Commission Recommendation of 9 April 2014 on the quality of corporate governance reporting ('comply or explain'), 2014/208/EU, OJ L 109/43, 12.4.2104.

[44]  See Company Law Review, *Final Report*, vol 1 (2001), para 3.49; *Completing the Structure* (2000), para 12.50. The Government agreed that the Combined Code should remain as a non-statutory document: see *Modernising Company Law* (Cmnd 5553-I, 2002), paras 5.7–5.16. See too, Walker Report, n 11, paras 1.15– 1.21, 2.4, 2.23, Annex 3; FRC, *Review of the Effectiveness of the Combined Code: Progress Report and Second Consultation* (July 2009), pp 3–4 (FRC shares the market's view that the flexible 'soft-law' approach remains the most appropriate way of raising standards of corporate governance in listed companies).

[45]  The DTR are drawn up by the UK Listing Authority (UKLA), part of the Financial Conduct Authority.

[46]  Implementing Directive 2013/34/EU (the Accounts Directive), OJ L 182/19, 29.6.2013, art 20.

[47]  Compliance with certain specified equivalent provisions of the UK Corporate Governance Code will satisfy certain requirements of the DTR, see DTR 7.2.4G, also 7.2.8G.

internal control systems and, at least annually, to review their effectiveness and report on that review (Prov 28). The DTR rules are mandatory, unlike the Code, so companies must ensure that they meet the requirements of the DTR even if they choose not to comply with elements of the Code. The European Commission 2014 Recommendation on the quality of corporate governance reporting raised concerns about the quality of these corporate governance statements, stressing the need for shareholders to be given clear, accurate, and comprehensive information specific to the company and its particular characteristics and situation to enable them to gain a good understanding of the manner in which the company is governed.[48]

## D Corporate governance requirements—the board of directors

### Composition of the board

**6-15**   The board should include an appropriate combination of executive and non-executive directors (including in particular independent non-executive directors) such that no individual or small group of individuals can dominate the board's decision making (Prin F). Independent non-executive directors, including the chair, should constitute a majority of the board (Prov 1). Interestingly, the FRC reports that this provision is the provision with the most frequent explanation of non-compliance, and often with poor explanations for non-compliance other than that the company considers its arrangements appropriate for the company.[49] Several of the reviews following the financial crisis highlighted the incompetence of many boards of financial institutions, with the European Commission noting that the failure of boards 'to identify, understand and ultimately control the risks to which their financial institutions were exposed' lay at the heart of the origins of the crisis.[50] Prin I provides that the board and its committees should have a balance of skills, experience, independence, and knowledge.

**6-16**   In keeping with the need to ensure competent, fit for purpose, boards, the UK Code says there should be a formal, rigorous, and transparent procedure for the appointment of new directors to the board (Prin J). All directors should be subject to annual re-election (Prov 18). The board should undertake a formal and rigorous annual evaluation of its own performance, the chair, and individual directors (Prov 21) and it should report on the process in the annual report on the work of the nomination committee (Prov 23). Companies should consider having an externally facilitated board evaluation three years (Prov 21).[51]

---

[48]  See Commission Recommendation 2014/208/EU, OJ L 109/43, 12.4.2014.

[49]  FRC, *Developments in Corporate Governance and Stewardship 2016* (January 2017), p 6.

[50]  European Commission, *Corporate Governance in Financial Institutions and Remuneration Policies*, COM (2010) 284, para 3.3. There were concerns that the companies had focused too much on independence in the boardroom and not enough on competence. See FRC, *2009 Review of the Combined Code: Final Report* (December 2009), paras 3.17–3.18; also Walker Report, n 11, para 3.10. see OECD, *Corporate Governance and the Financial Crisis, Conclusions and Emerging Good Practices to Enhance Implementation of the Principles* (February 2010), para 50. See Moore, 'The Evolving Contours of the Board's Risk Management Function in UK Corporate Governance' (2010) 10 JCLS 279 who notes, at 308, the 'significant normative influence of the directorial independence doctrine over recent years in providing companies' governance structures with an effective hallmark of legitimacy'.

[51]  This move to external evaluation was one of the measures recommended in the Walker Report and see also European Commission Green Paper, n 24, para 1.3.

**6-17**  Board appointments should be based on merit and objective criteria, and promote diversity of gender, social and ethnic backgrounds, cognitive and personal strengths (Prin J). Various issues surrounding board composition have attracted renewed debate recently. For decades, the question of worker directors or worker representation has arisen in various contexts and, more recently, questions about the gender balance and ethnic representation at board level also. The Government's preference on all of these matters is for a voluntary approach,[52] mainly driven by disclosure requirements, but the House of Commons, BEIS Committee, Report on Corporate Governance (hereafter HC BEIS Committee Report) noted that reporting requirements under the UK Code appear not to have the intended effect in tackling the homogeneity of board composition.[53] As the HC BEIS Committee noted, a company should reflect the makeup of the population which supplies its customers, creditors, and employees; further, diversity widens the company's talent pool and is market facing so enabling companies to combine social justice with competitive advantage.[54] Boardroom diversity will dilute the 'group-think' which contributes to the lack of constructive challenge within a board.[55] Reflecting the increased focus on these issues, the UK Code gives the nomination committee a more explicit obligation to develop a diverse pipeline in the company (Prov 17) and Principle J requires appointment and succession plans to promote diversity, as noted.

**6-18**  *Worker representation* Worker representation has been revisited in the context of discussion of the application of CA 2006, s 172 which requires directors to have regard to a variety of stakeholder interests, including the company's employees. An initiative which arose from that debate was a proposal for boards, via an obligation in the UK Code, to explore mechanisms for more effective engagement with the workforce; the issue is considered at **10-38**.

**6-19**  *Gender* In 2012, the European Commission put forward a proposal for a Directive setting a minimum objective of having women in 40 per cent of non-executive board positions in listed companies in Europe by 2020.[56] The proposal was supported by the Parliament but has remained deadlocked at the Council level, with a number of Member States supporting the objective but objecting to binding measures. The Commission remains committed to the adoption of the Directive in due course.[57] The issue of gender diversity gained prominence in the UK following the publication of the Davies Report on women on boards[58] which found that in 2011 women made up only 12.5 per cent of the boards of FTSE 100 companies. Lord Davies recommended that FTSE 100 boards should aim for a minimum of 25 per cent female representation by the end of 2015, a figure which

---

[52] See business-led initiatives to support diversity, such as the Future Board Scheme and the Women's Business Council. The Department for Business, Energy and Industrial Strategy has set up a Business Diversity and Inclusion Group (September 2017) to bring all the initiatives together.

[53] HC BEIS Committee Report, n 12, para 119.

[54] HC BEIS Committee Report, n 12, para 131. See also Government response to Green Paper, n 12, para 5.13.  [55] See European Commission Green Paper, n 24, para 1.1.3.

[56] European Commission Green Paper, n 24, para 1.1.3; followed by a Commission initiative involving a proposal for a Directive on gender balance among non-executive directors of listed companies (November 2012)—supported by the EU Parliament, see COM/2012/0614 final—2012/0299 (COD).

[57] See European Commission, 'EU Action Plan for 17–19, Tackling the gender pay gap' COM (2017) 678, 20.11.2017 (see Action 3).  [58] Lord Davies, *Women on Boards* (February 2011), URN 13/745.

was reached.[59] The figure is deceptive, however, as it combines executive and non-executive positions and, as the HC BEIS Committee pointed out, only 10 per cent of executive director positions in FTSE 100 companies are held by women compared with 33.7 per cent of non-executive posts.[60] A further independent business-led review (the Hampton-Alexander review),[61] following on from the work of Lord Davies, has raised the target to 33 per cent women on FTSE 350 boards and 33 per cent women in FTSE 100 leadership teams by 2020. The latter target is intended to ensure that women are represented within the leadership teams from which executive board appointments are commonly made. The latest report from the Hampton-Alexander Review (2017) suggests that relatively slow progress is now being made, particularly on women in leadership roles. The Equality and Human Rights Commission has suggested that the target for all new appointments to senior and executive management level positions should be 50 per cent women, and the HC BEIS Committee agreed.[62] The Government considers, however, that, for the moment, the Hampton-Alexander target is sufficiently demanding and appropriate and the Government will monitor the situation over the next three years to see how matters develop. [63] As already noted, Principle J of the 2018 UK Code provides that 'both appointments and succession plans should be based on merit and objective criteria and promote diversity of gender, social and ethnic backgrounds, cognitive and personal strengths', while the nomination committee should oversee the development of a diverse pipeline for succession (Prov 17).

**6-20** *Race* Attention has also focused on race following the Parker review (led by Sir John Parker) which found a dearth of people of colour in the boardrooms of the largest companies (51 of the FTSE 100 companies at July 2017 had no directors of colour) and a resulting failure to reflect the ethnic diversity of the UK.[64] The Parker Review recommended that each FTSE 100 Board should have at least one director of colour by 2021 and each FTSE 250 Board should have at least one director of colour by 2024. It also recommended additional transparency in annual reports with companies describing the steps they have taken to increase ethnic diversity. The Parker Review will report annually on progress. The HC BEIS Committee Report recommended that the FRC take up this issue and give ethnicity as much prominence as gender diversity[65] and, as noted above, the 2018 UK Code does now refer in Principle J to diversity of gender, social, and ethnic backgrounds.

**6-21** *Narrative reporting in support of diversity* The HC BEIS Committee Report in general recommended that the UK Code should require boards to provide greater information

---

[59] See 'Women on Boards', Davies Review Annual Report 2015, p 4. See also 'Improving the Gender Balance on British Boards', Davies Review, Five Year Summary (October 2015). HC BEIS Committee Report, n 12, notes that the figure now is 26.7 per cent of FTSE 100 positions held by women, see para 118. See also FRC, *Consultation Document: Gender Diversity on Boards* (May 2011).

[60] HC BEIS Committee Report, n 12, para 122.

[61] Hampton-Alexander Review, 'Improving Gender Balance in FTSE Leadership' (November 2016) and second report (November 2017).                [62] HC BEIS Committee Report, n 12, paras 123, 127.

[63] See Government response to Green Paper, 14, para 5.16.

[64] The Parker Review Committee, 'A Report into the Ethnic Diversity of UK Boards' (October 2017), following an earlier consultation in 2016. As the HC BEIS Committee Report, n 12, para 128 noted, 14 per cent of the UK population is from a non-white ethnic group, but only 8 per cent of board positions in FTSE 100 are held by directors of colour of which only 1.5 per cent are UK citizens.

[65] HC BEIS Committee Report, n 12, para 132.

in their annual reports on diversity on their boards and in the workforce, covering diversity of gender, ethnicity, social mobility, and of perspective, including with respect to the executive pipeline.[66]

**6-22**    A quoted company[67] is required to include in the strategic report (see **18-31**) a breakdown of the number of persons of each sex who are directors, senior managers,[68] and employees of the company (CA 2006, s 414C(8)). The UK Code requires listed companies when reporting on the work of the nomination committee to explain how diversity supports the company in meeting its strategic objectives (Prov 23).

**6-23**    The HC BEIS Committee Report recommended, in agreement with the McGregor Smith review on race in the workplace,[69] that all FTSE 100 companies should be required to publish their workforce data broken down by ethnicity and by pay band. The Government prefers a non-legislative response for the moment, leaving it to companies to see the value in providing this information and to institutional investors to see the value in seeking this information.[70] The Government noted the significant improvement in gender representation through voluntary measures and it intends to take a similar approach on ethnic representation.[71]

## Core responsibilities of the board

**6-24**    The UK Code starts with the principle that a successful company is led by an effective and entrepreneurial board whose function is to promote the long-term sustainable success of the company, generate value for shareholders, and contribute to wider society (Prin A). As for the directors, they are required to act with integrity and lead by example in the best interests of the company (Prin D). The board's role is to:

- establish the company's purpose, strategy and values,
- ensure the resources are in place for the company to meet its objectives and measure performance against them, and
- establish a framework of prudent and effective controls which enables risk to be assessed and managed (Prins A and B).

**6-25**    Section 4 of the UK Code focuses on some of the core responsibilities of the board and this part of the Code is supplemented by detailed guidance on risk management and internal control issued by the FRC.[72] The directors should explain in the annual report their responsibility for preparing the annual report and accounts, and state that they consider the annual report and accounts to be a fair, balanced, and understandable report which provides the information necessary for shareholders to assess the company's position, performance, business model,

---

[66]  HC BEIS Committee Report, n 12, para 139.    [67]  See CA 2006, s 385.

[68]  There are complexities as to how 'senior manager' is defined in different companies so, as the HC BEIS Committee Report, n 12, noted, it makes it hard to assess progress on gender equality when they report. The BEIS Committee Report supported the Hampton-Alexander recommendation that the Government in consultation with business should clarify or supplement the definition so as to be consistent, based on the executive committee or the nearest equivalent in each company. The FRC gives a steer in the 2018 UK Code, defining senior management in the Code as the executive committee or the first layer of management below board level, including the company secretary (see Code, p 7, fn 3).

[69]  Race in the Workplace: The McGregor-Smith Review, Independent review by Baroness McGregor-Smith considering the issues affecting black and minority ethnic (BME) groups in the workplace (February 2017).

[70]  Government response, n 12, p 4.

[71]  Government response to Green Paper on Corporate Governance (August 2017), para 5.17.

[72]  FRC, *Guidance on Risk Management, Internal Control and Related Financial and Business Reporting* (September 2014).

and strategy (Prov 27). The board should assess the basis on which the company generates and preserves value over the long term and should describe in the annual report how opportunities and risks to the future success of the business have been considered and addressed (Prov 1). A particular requirement is that, in annual and half-yearly financial statements, the board should state whether it considers it appropriate to adopt the going concern basis of accounting[73] in preparing the statements, and identify any material uncertainties regarding the company's ability to continue to do so over a period of at least 12 months from the date of approval of the financial statements (Prov 30). Further, under the Listing Rules, LR 9.8.6, the annual report must include a statement made by the directors that the business is a going concern, together with supporting assumptions or qualifications as necessary.[74] These matters are all reflective of the directors' legal duties to prepare annual accounts giving a true and fair view of the company's position (see **18-14**), drawn up in accordance with relevant accounting standards, with 'going concern' being a fundamental accounting concept underlying the preparation of those accounts.[75]

**6-26** Closely linked to this going concern statement are broader responsibilities[76] reflected in Principle N, that the board must determine the nature and extent of the principal risks it is willing to take in order to achieve its strategic objectives. The board should satisfy itself that the company's internal controls are robust and allow for prudent and effective risk assessment and management (Prin N). The provision in the Code on these issues reflects the recommendations of the Sharman Inquiry report *Going Concern and Liquidity Risk*,[77] which were developed further by the FRC.[78] Essentially, the Sharman Inquiry explored broader 'going concern' issues concerning risk, risk appetite, and strategy where the issues are not accounting issues of going concern, but broader issues of liquidity and solvency and long-term viability.[79] Sharman considered that it was important that stakeholders would have information about the economic and financial viability of the company which would help demonstrate the directors' stewardship and governance of the company in that respect. To reflect those broader issues, Sharman recommended that the directors' conclusions about the going concern status of the company should be set in the context of the company's business model, strategy, and principal risks. Their statements should address a longer time period than the one-year accounting framework and provide a more qualitative judgement of the company's position with the audit committee reporting on the robustness of the assessment processes behind the board's statements.[80] Provisions 29 and 31 of the 2018 Code now reflect these elements so, under Prov 29, the board must confirm in the annual report that they have carried out a robust assessment of the principal risks (financial and

---

[73] Guidance on how to approach this going concern issue is provided in FRC, *Guidance on Risk Management, Internal Control and Related Financial and Business Reporting* (September 2014), Appendix A.

[74] This statement must be prepared in accordance with FRC guidance, see FRC, *Guidance on Risk Management, Internal Control and Related Financial and Business Reporting* (September 2014), p 24.

[75] See CA 2006, ss 394, 396; SI 2008/409 Sch 1, paras 11–14; SI 2008/410, Sch 1, paras 11–14.

[76] See FRC, *Guidance on Risk Management, Internal Control and Related Financial and Business Reporting* (September 2014), para 25.

[77] See Sharman Inquiry, *Going Concern and Liquidity Risks: Lessons for Companies and Auditors* (June 2012).

[78] See FRC, *Implementing the Recommendations of the Sharman Panel* (January 2013) which built on earlier FRC consultations (which were also relied on by Sharman); see FRC *Effective Company Stewardship, Next Steps* (September 2011), Ch 4, following on from FRC consultation paper, *Effective Company Stewardship, Enhancing Company Reporting and Audit* (January 2011). A useful summary of the evolution of these requirements is included in FRC, *Guidance on Risk Management, Internal Control and Related Financial and Business Reporting* (September 2014), paras 9–18.

[79] See note 77, Recommendations 3 and 4, paras 109–137.

[80] Sharman final report, n 77, p 2, para 6 and Recommendations 3 and 4.

non-financial) facing the company[81] including those that would threaten its business model, future performance, solvency, or liquidity and they must describe the principal risks and explain how they are being managed or mitigated. A particularly important requirement is the longer term viability statement which is required by Provision 31 which requires an explanation of how the board has assessed the prospects of the company, over what period it has done so, and why it considers the period to be appropriate.[82] To date, most companies report on a three-year time frame.[83] The board must also monitor the company's risk management and internal control systems (covering all material controls including financial, operational, and compliance controls) and, at least annually, carry out a review of their effectiveness,[84] and report on that review in the annual report (Prov 28). In turn, an audit committee should be established (Prov 24) and, for listed companies, an audit committee is a legal requirement, see **6-36**. The role of the audit committee is discussed at **6-40**.

## The chair of the board

**6-27**  Considerable importance is attached under the UK Code to dividing the responsibilities at the head of the company between an independent chair of the board who is responsible for leadership of the board and the chief executive with responsibility for the running of the business. The UK Code position is that these roles should not be exercised by the same individual (Prov 9).[85] The responsibilities of the chair, the chief executive, senior independent director, board, committees, and management should be clear, set out in writing, agreed by the board, and made publicly available (Prov 9).[86]

**6-28**  Post the FRC/Walker reviews, it was decided to give greater emphasis to the role of the chair and the UK Code states as a principle that the chair is responsible for the overall effectiveness of the board in directing the company (Prin E), to which end he must ensure the effective contribution of all non-executive directors (Prin E).

**6-29**  In keeping with the chair's specific responsibility for ensuring the effectiveness of the board, the chair must act on the evaluation of the board, recognising strengths and addressing weaknesses (Prov 22). In turn, the non-executive directors, led by the senior independent director, should be responsible for appraising the chair (Prov 12). The chair should hold meetings with the non-executive directors without executive directors being present (Prov 11).

---

[81] See FRC, *Guidance on Risk Management, Internal Control and Related Financial and Business Reporting* (September 2014), Section 6.

[82] See FRC, *Guidance on Risk Management, Internal Control and Related Financial and Business Reporting* (September 2014), Appendix B, para 3; and see para 1 which notes that 'this statement is intended to express the directors' view about the longer term viability of the company over an appropriate period of time selected by them'.

[83] See FRC, *Developments in Corporate Governance and Stewardship 2016* (January 2017), p 13 which notes that the lack of variation between sectors (two-thirds of companies choosing three years) was surprising and that companies should provide clearer disclosure of why the period chosen is appropriate for the particular company.

[84] See FRC, *Guidance on Risk Management, Internal Control and Related Financial and Business Reporting* (September 2014), Section 5 as to what is required of this review.

[85] If the chief executive is to move up, the matter should be discussed in advance with the major shareholders and the reasons explained to the shareholders and posted on the company website, see UK Corporate Governance Code, Prov 19.

[86] On the evolving role of the chair, see Owen and Kirchmaier, 'The Changing Role of the Chair: Impact of Corporate Governance Reform in the UK 1995–2005' (2008) 9 EBOR 187.

**6-30** The company chair typically will work closely on governance matters with the company secretary[87] who is responsible for advising the board on all governance matters (Prov 16). The appointment and removal of the company secretary is a matter for the board as a whole (Prov 16).

## The non-executive directors

**6-31** Non-executive directors need not be independent but independent non-executive directors, including the chair, should constitute the majority of the board (Prov 11). Non-executive directors should be selected (as should all the directors) through a formal rigorous and transparent procedure (Prin J) and all directors should ensure that they have sufficient time for their board responsibilities (Prov 14). Concerns have frequently been express as to whether non-executive directors devote enough time to their position given that, typically, each will have a number of non-executive posts. The Code does not limit the number of other positions which a non-executive director may hold, it merely requires that external appointments should not be undertaken without prior approval of the board (Prov 14).[88]

### Independence

**6-32** The annual report must identify each non-executive director considered by the board to be independent (Prov 11).[89] In a strengthening of the provisions on independence,[90] the 2018 UK Code provides (Prov 15) that an individual should not be considered independent for the purposes of board or committee composition if the person

- is or has been an employee of the company or group within the last five years;
- has or has had within the last three years, a material business relationship with the company either directly or as a partner, shareholder, director, or senior employee of a body that has such a relationship with the company;
- has received or receives additional remuneration from the company apart from a director's fee, participates in the company's share option or a performance-related pay scheme, or is a member of the company's pension scheme;
- has close family ties with any of the company's advisers, directors, or senior employees;
- holds cross-directorships or has significant links with other directors through involvement in other companies or bodies;
- represents a significant shareholder; or
- has served on the board for more than nine years from the date of their first election.

The importance of independence is underscored by the Listing Rules which require a premium listed company with a controlling shareholder (essentially, controlling more

---

[87] A public company must have a company secretary: CA 2006, s 271.

[88] The FRC's *Guidance on Board Effectiveness* (2011), p 6 states that a non-executive director's letter of appointment should state the minimum time required of the director and should seek the individual's confirmation that he or she can devote that amount of time to their role.

[89] The Company Law Review noted that independence cannot be legislated for since 'the quality required is a state of mind and character and relevant experience, rather than some formal indication of independence', see Company Law Review, *Developing the Framework* (2000), para 3.148.

[90] The 2016 Code, provision B.1.1. gave the board greater leeway to determine whether someone was independent, despite having these degrees of connection with the business.

than 30 per cent of the votes) to have the election of independent directors approved by resolution of the shareholders and by resolution of the independent shareholders.[91] The board should appoint one of the independent non-executive directors to be the company's senior independent director whose role is to provide a sounding board for the chair and to serve as an intermediary for the other directors and shareholders (Prov 12). This senior director should meet with the non-executive directors without the chair being present at least annually to appraise the chair's performance and on other occasions as necessary (Prov 12).

### Qualities of a non-executive director

**6-33**    As part of a unitary board (a point specifically underlined by the Code), non-executive directors should provide constructive challenge, strategic guidance, offer specialist advice, and hold management to account (Prin G). This principle is a clearer articulation of the position as compared with previous versions of the Code which concentrated on constructive challenge and contribution to strategy. One of the key conclusions of the Walker Report (see **6-4**) was that non-executives in financial institutions had been particularly poor at providing this essential 'challenge' role.[92] Challenge is particularly difficult, of course, without a measure of understanding of the issue being discussed and Walker expressed further dismay at the lack of knowledge of the banking business displayed by the non-executive directors which made it difficult for them to make an effective contribution to governance. Without an in-depth knowledge of a company's affairs, Walker noted, it is often impossible even to articulate the issue, never mind probe the executives on the detail.[93] As noted at **6-15**, following the Walker/FRC reviews, the emphasis is on the board and its committees having a balance of skills, experience, independence, and knowledge (Prin I). In any event, directors are under a legal duty to have sufficient knowledge and understanding of a company's business so as to enable them properly to discharge their duties as directors,[94] see Chapter 11. As every review of the Code creates ever more functions to be undertaken by the non-executive directors, as well as imposing greater board responsibility generally for risk management, we can expect to see a continued emphasis on board competence rather than formal independence[95] and this will apply especially to the non-executive directors given the importance of their 'challenge' role.

### Role of the non-executive director

**6-34**    Turning to the specific responsibilities of non-executive directors, as mentioned, their core roles are to provide constructive challenge, strategic guidance, offer specialist advice, and hold management to account (Prin G). The UK Code further identifies, in Prov 13, the non-executive director's role as being to scrutinize and hold to account the performance of management and individual directors against agreed performance objectives.

---

[91]  LR 9.2.2E; and see LR 6.1.4B.

[92]  See Walker Report, n 11, p 12, which specifically found that challenge had been missing from the process of decision-making in the boards of financial institutions.

[93]  See Walker Report, n 11, para 4.3. See, for example, the *Penrose Report of the Equitable Life Enquiry* (March 2004).          [94]  See CA 2006, s 174; *Re Barings (No 5) plc* [1999] 1 BCLC 433.

[95]  See Moore, n 50, at 307; also Hannigan, 'Board Failures in the Financial Crisis—Tinkering with Codes and the Need for Wider Corporate Governance Reforms' Part 1 (2011) 32 Co Law 363, and Part 2 (2012) 33 Co Law 35.

They are responsible for appointing and, where necessary, removing executive directors (Prov 13). The Code goes on to spell out key roles for non-executive directors on the nomination, audit, and remuneration committees.

## E Board committees

### The nomination committee

**6-35**  A company should have a nomination committee and a majority of the committee's members should be independent non-executive directors with a minimum membership of three (Prov 17).[96] This committee plays a key role in ensuring that a board has the right balance of skills, experience, independence, and knowledge. The committee's role is to lead the process for board appointments and succession planning and overseeing the development of a diverse pipeline. The work of the nomination committee should be described in the annual report including details on board evaluations, appointments, diversity issues, and gender balance, including how diversity supports the company in meeting strategic objectives (Prov 23).

### The audit committee

**6-36**  The audit committee is the key corporate governance committee with Section 4 of the UK Code making extensive provision for audit committees and their role, supplemented by FRC *Guidance on Audit Committees*.[97] More importantly, it is a requirement of Directive 2006/43, as amended by Directive 2014/56/EU on audit, that public interest entities (essentially, but broader than companies admitted to trading on a regulated market), have an audit committee,[98] a requirement implemented by the FSA Disclosure and Transparency Rules (DTR) 7.1.1–7.1.5 which apply to companies with a premium or standard listing. To minimise the overlapping requirements, compliance with the provisions of the UK Code as to the composition and work of the audit committees also suffices for compliance with the DTR requirements (DTR 7.1.1).

**6-37**  The significance of the audit committee is stressed by the FRC guidance which notes that it has 'a particular role, acting independently from the executive, to ensure that the interests of shareholders are properly protected in relation to financial reporting and internal control'.[99] Details of the work of the committee must be set out in the company's annual report (Prov 26), a requirement intended, in part, to increase the visibility of the committee and help build confidence in financial reporting.[100]

---

[96]  For criticism of this approach and a preference for greater shareholder involvement in board appointments, see Tomorrow's Company Report, *Bridging the UK engagement gap through Swedish-style nomination committees* (March 2010); and report by Chris Philp MP, 'Restoring Responsible Ownership: Ending the Ownerless Corporation and Controlling Executive Pay' (September 2016) in conjunction with the High Pay Centre.

[97]  See FRC, *Guidance on Audit Committees* (2016). See generally, Hannigan, 'Empire-building: The Rise of the Audit Committee' in Watson and Vasudev (eds), *Innovations in Corporate Governance: Global Perspectives* (2017), pp 124–50.

[98]  Directive 2006/43/EC, OJ L 157/87, 9.6.2006, as amended by Directive 2014/56/EU, OJ L 158/196, 27.5.2014, art 39.    [99]  See FRC, *Guidance on Audit Committees* (2016), para 3.

[100]  See FRC, *Effective Company Stewardship, Next Steps* (September 2011), p 12. See also FRC Lab Project Report, *Reporting of Audit Committees* (October 2013).

**6-38**  This report must describe the work of the committee in discharging its responsibilities including (Prov 26):

(i) the significant issues that the committee considered in relation to the financial statements, and how these issues were addressed;

(ii) an explanation of how it has assessed the effectiveness of the external audit process and the approach taken to the appointment or reappointment of the external auditor, information on the length of tenure of the current audit firm and when a tender was last conducted, and advance notice of any retendering plans;[101]

(iii) if the board has not supported the committee's recommendation for appointment of the external auditor, an explanation of the recommendation and a statement of the board's reasons for a different position;

(iv) an explanation of the absence of internal audit function if there is none;

(v) if the external auditor provides non-audit services, an explanation of how auditor objectivity and independence are safeguarded.

### Composition

**6-39**  The audit committee should consist of independent non-executive directors, with a minimum membership of three, at least one of whom has 'recent and relevant financial experience' while the committee as a whole must have competence relevant to the sector (Prov 24). The chair of the board should not be a member (Prov 24). Directive 2006/43/EC,[102] as amended by Directive 2014/56/EU, requires the audit committee of a public-interest entity to be composed of non-executives, a majority of whom must be independent, and one of the committee must have competence in accounting and/or auditing while the committee as a whole must have competence relevant to the sector in which the company is operating. The FRC guidance stresses the importance of a frank, open, working relationship and a high level of mutual respect between the audit committee, the board, the executives, and the internal and external auditors.[103]

### Roles and responsibilities

**6-40**  The main roles and responsibilities of the audit committee should include (Prov 25):

- monitoring the integrity of the financial statements of the company, and any formal announcements relating to financial performance and reviewing significant financial reporting judgements contained in them;

- reviewing the company's internal financial controls[104] and, unless expressly addressed by a risk committee or by the board, reviewing the internal control and risk management systems;

- monitoring and reviewing the effectiveness of the company's internal audit function (and if there is none, annually to review the position, and to make a recommendation to the board);

---

[101]  Directive 2006/43 as amended by Directive 2014/56 requires all public interest entities to tender every ten years and to rotate auditors after 20 years, another example of soft law evolving into or being replaced by hard law, see CA 2006, s 494ZA.

[102]  Directive 2006/43/EC, OJ L 157/87, 9.6.2006, as amended by Directive 2014/56/EU, OJ L 158/196, 27.5.2014, art 39.          [103]  See FRC *Guidance on Audit Committees* (2016), para 4.

[104]  The FRC *Guidance on Audit Committees* (2016), para 40, defines internal financial controls as the systems established to identify, assess, manage, and monitor financial risks.

- making recommendations to the board in relation to the appointment, reappointment, and removal of the external auditor and approving their remuneration and terms of engagement;

- reviewing and monitoring the external auditor's independence and objectivity, and the effectiveness of the audit process; and

- developing and implementing policy on the engagement of the external auditor to supply non-audit services and reporting to the board; and

- reporting to the board on how the committee has discharged its responsibilities.

**6-41** This bare outline of the identified tasks under the Code does not capture the full extent of the audit committee's role.[105] The Sharman Inquiry report, *Going Concern and Liquidity Risk*, in June 2012,[106] envisaged a stronger relationship between auditors, the audit committee, and the board and these ideas were taken forward by the FRC.[107] What is envisaged is an extensive exchange of information and monitoring and reviewing between the auditors and the audit committee, coupled with comprehensive reporting to the board and to the shareholders on the roles played and tasks undertaken, all reflected in a revised auditing standard.[108] In particular, the auditors are required to communicate to the audit committee the information that the auditor believes relevant to the board in fulfilling its reporting obligations under what is now Section 4 of the Code (see **6-25**), for example as to going concern status and long-term viability of the company (Provs 30, 31).[109] To reinforce the directors' obligations with respect to risk management, the auditors are required to give a statement in their report as to whether the auditor has anything material to add or to draw attention to in relation to the directors' confirmation that they have carried out a robust assessment of the principal risks facing the entity and the description of those risks in the annual report; the directors' statement as to the adoption of the going concern basis of accounting;[110] and their explanation as to how they have assessed the prospects of the entity and the period which they have chosen for that assessment.[111] A similar approach is evident in EU Regulation 537/2014[112] which requires an additional report from the auditor to the audit committee covering every aspect of the work undertaken, processes utilised, and judgements reached by the auditors.[113]

---

[105] See Hannigan, 'Empire-building: The Rise of the Audit Committee' in Watson and Vasudev (eds), *Innovations in Corporate Governance: Global Perspectives* (2017), pp 124–150.

[106] See Sharman Inquiry, *Going Concern and Liquidity Risks: Lessons for Companies and Auditors* (June 2012), esp Recommendations 4 and 5.

[107] See FRC, *Implementing the Recommendations of the Sharman Panel* (January 2013) which built on earlier FRC consultations (which were also relied on by Sharman), and see FRC, *Effective Company Stewardship, Next Steps* (September 2011), Ch 4; FRC consultation paper, *Effective Company Stewardship, Enhancing Company Reporting and Audit* (January 2011).

[108] ISA (UK) 260, 'Communication with those charged with governance' (June 2016). Those charged with governance are defined as the persons with responsibility for overseeing the strategic direction of the entity and obligations relating to its accountability. In the UK these persons include the directors, executive and non-executive, and the members of an audit committee, where one exists (para 10).

[109] ISA 260, para 16–1. See also ISA 260, para A7, which states that good governance principles suggest that the auditor would be invited to regularly attend meetings of the audit committee and that the committee will meet with the auditor without management present at least annually.

[110] If the auditors consider that the use of the going concern assumption is inappropriate, the auditor must express an adverse opinion, see ISA (UK) 570, *Going Concern* (June 2016), para 21; and the auditor is obliged to communicate with those charged with governance events or conditions that may cast significant doubt on the entity's ability to continue as a going concern, see para 25.

[111] ISA (UK) 570, *Going Concern* (June 2016), para 18–2.   [112] OJ L 158/77, 27.5.2014.

[113] See art 11, OJ L 158/77, 27.5.2014, which identifies 16 headings of information which should be provided to the audit committee.

## The remuneration committee

### Background

**6-42**  The level of executive remuneration, especially in quoted companies, continues to be the subject of debate, reflecting concerns that the sums awarded are out of step with company performance and investor returns.[114] As the Government itself noted:[115]

> 'FTSE 100 CEO total pay has increased from an average of around £1m in 1998 to over £4m today, fuelling a widespread perception that boardroom remuneration is increasingly disconnected from the pay of ordinary working people. It is also questionable whether long-term company performance has consistently matched this rapid growth in pay.'

The House of Commons Committee on Business, Energy and Industrial Strategy found that the drivers of executive remuneration are: globalisation; scarcity of talent, performance-related pay; remuneration consultants ratchetting up pay; ineffective remuneration committees; a lack of shareholder engagement; weak boards; and executive greed.[116] It also concluded that 'overall pay levels have now been ratcheted up to levels so high that it is impossible to observe a credible link between pay and performance. At a time when average pay has remained relatively stable, these increases have served to undermine public trust in business.'[117] The problem is easy to state but harder to solve.[118] After a lengthy period relying on well-intentioned exhortations in the UK Code, and a purely advisory vote by shareholders on directors' remuneration packages, it was decided that, for quoted companies,[119] legislative intervention was required. The CA 2006 requires a detailed directors' remuneration report (see **18-43**) and shareholder approval of remuneration policy (binding) and practice (advisory) and prohibits payments not in accordance with an approved policy (see **13-20**). The Shareholder Rights Directive 2007/36/EC, as amended by Directive 2017/828,[120] includes similar measures on remuneration of directors of traded companies (effective from 10 June 2019), namely a binding vote on remuneration policy at least every four years (though Member States have the option of making this vote advisory[121]) and an advisory vote on a detailed remuneration report

---

[114]  See HC BEIS Committee Report, n 12, Ch 5; Government response to the Green Paper, n 12, Ch 1; Green Paper on Corporate Governance Reform (November 2016), pp 16–33. For earlier reports painting a very similar picture, see BIS, *Executive Remuneration, Discussion Paper* (September 2011), paras 13–22; BIS, *A Long-term Focus for Corporate Britain—a call for evidence* (October 2010).

[115]  Government response to the Green Paper, n 12, para 1.1.

[116]  See HC BEIS Committee Report, n 12, para 77.

[117]  HC BEIS Committee Report, n 12, para 99.

[118]  See the Investment Association, Report of the Executive Pay Working Group (July 2016)—many of the ideas there on the remuneration committee are reflected in the 2018 Code; see also report by Chris Philp MP, 'Restoring Responsible Ownership, Ending the Ownerless Corporation and Controlling Executive Pay' (September 2016) in conjunction with the High Pay Centre.

[119]  Defined CA 2006, ss 226A, 385; see generally CA 2006, Ch 4A (ss 226A–226F) on control of directors' remuneration payments.

[120]  Directive 2017/828, OJ L 132/1, 20.5.2017, art 1 inserting art 9a (right to vote on remuneration policy) and art 9b (remuneration report) into Directive 2007/36. Previous initiatives at EU level had included a non-binding Recommendation 2009/385/EC on remuneration of directors in listed companies in 2009, complementing an earlier Recommendation in 2004; a follow-up report a year later found variable implementation by the Member States: *Report on the Application by Member States of the 2009 Recommendation on Directors' Remuneration,* COM (2010) 285 final, 2.5.2010. See Ferrarini, Moloney, and Ungureanu, 'Executive Remuneration in Crisis: A Critical Assessment of Reforms in Europe' (2010) 10 JCLS 73 who criticise the Commission for moving from supporting effective incentive alignment into the muddier waters of 'fairness'.

[121]  If the advisory vote rejects the remuneration policy, the company must bring forward a revised policy the following year, see Directive 2007/36, art 9a(3), as inserted by Directive 2017/828, art 1, OJ L 132/1, 20.5.2017.

(though Member States have the option of replacing this vote, in the case of small and medium-sized companies, with a discussion in the general meeting[122]). A central role in the control and management of remuneration issues is accorded under the UK Code to the remuneration committee.

### Composition and role of the remuneration committee

**6-43**  The UK Code provides that companies should have a remuneration committee of independent non-executive directors with a minimum membership of three, and the company chair should not chair the remuneration committee and may be a member of the committee only if independent (Prov 32). Before appointment as chair of the committee, the appointee should have served on a remuneration committee for a minimum of at least 12 months (Prov 32).

**6-44**  The committee has delegated responsibility for determining the company's policy on director remuneration (all directors, including non-executive directors) and setting the remuneration for the board and senior management (Prov 33) and senior management would normally be the first tier below board level. Specifically, the remuneration committee should oversee remuneration and workforce policies and practices and take these into account when setting the policy for director remuneration (Prov 33). This provision is new in the 2018 UK Code and is a nod in the direction of workforce remuneration when setting executive remuneration. In future, the directors' remuneration report (see **18-43**) will include information on the pay ratio between the CEO's pay and the average pay of a company's UK workforce. In the Green Paper on Corporate Governance Report, it was noted that:[123]

> 'In 1998 the ratio of average FTSE 100 CEO pay to the average pay of full-time employees in the UK was 47:1. This ratio increased to 132:1 in 2010 and stood at 128:1 in 2015.'

The inclusion of this ratio had been resisted by business on the basis, *inter alia*, that it is a meaningless and potentially misleading piece of information and that comparisons across sectors are difficult. The Government's view is that the information provides a valuable and dynamic reference point to demonstrate how executive pay relates to the employees as a whole. Details of this new requirement were awaited at the time of writing.

### Criticisms of the remuneration committee

**6-45**  As noted, these Code provisions are reinforced now by legislative intervention which in part was a reaction to the apparent inability or unwillingness of the remuneration committee to act in the shareholders' interests in addressing the absolute levels of remuneration of executive directors, especially in quoted companies. There have also been concerns that non-executive directors have been insensitive to wider factors such as pay and employment conditions elsewhere in the company or the group,[124] something which the 2018 Code specifically requires the committee to take into account, as noted at **6-44**, when setting the policy for director remuneration (Prov 33). A particular issue is whether non-executive directors are sufficiently independent so as to be able to align remuneration with the long-term interests of the shareholders. Given that non-executive directors will frequently hold or have held executive posts elsewhere, they themselves may be part

---

[122]  Directive 2007/36, art 9b(4), as inserted by Directive 2017/828, art 1, OJ L 132/1, 20.5.2017.

[123]  Green Paper on Corporate Governance Reform (November 2016), para 1.2; see also HC BEIS Committee Report, n 12, paras 113–115. See the Companies (Miscellaneous Reporting) Regulations 2018, in draft at time of writing.

[124]  See BIS, *A Long-term Focus for Corporate Britain—a call for evidence* (October 2010), para 5.11.

of a culture of high pay with the result that they are unlikely to challenge generous executive remuneration.[125] At the Government's instigation, the FRC consulted as to whether to recommend that non-executive directors who are executive directors in other companies should not serve on remuneration committees. The FRC concluded that there was no data which would support a correlation between executive presence on the remuneration committee and levels of shareholder dissatisfaction with remuneration; it found no support for a proposed ban of this nature and the matter was not taken further.[126] Likewise, there has been no market support for suggestions that the composition of the remuneration committee might be reconsidered (for example, to include shareholder or employee representatives).[127] The Government did float some other ideas for increased scrutiny of remuneration by shareholder committees, mandatory disclosure of voting records by institutional investors, and ways of having greater individual shareholder say on pay.[128] None of these proposals found much support and the Government's preferred solution was for the FRC to strengthen the remuneration committee, for example, by requiring that the chair of the committee serve on a remuneration committee for at least 12 months before becoming chair (Prov 32).[129]

**6-46** As executive remuneration arrangements have become more complex, remuneration committees have found the process of setting remuneration extremely challenging[130] and there may be competence issues which require addressing. Just as the audit committee requires at least one member with recent and relevant financial experience, there is an issue as to the level of expertise required on a remuneration committee.[131] A lack of expertise may mean that remuneration committees are too dependent on remuneration consultants who in turn may have conflicting interests as they often have close relationships with the company management.[132] If remuneration consultants are appointed, this is the responsibility of the committee and the consultants must be identified in the annual report and a statement made as to whether they have any other connection with the company or individual directors (Prov 35). For quoted companies, full details of any persons used to materially assist the remuneration committee on remuneration issues, including details of how the committee satisfied itself as to their objectivity and independence, and the fees paid to the consultants, must be disclosed in the directors' remuneration report.[133]

**6-47** Non-executive directors on the remuneration committee need to be mindful of their duty to negotiate strongly in the shareholders' interests, in fulfilment of their obligations under CA 2006, s 172, to promote the success of the company for the benefit of the members as a whole, having regard to a wide range of factors including the interests

---

[125] See BIS, *Executive Remuneration, Discussion Paper* (September 2011), paras 81–82.

[126] See FRC, *Proposed Revisions to the UK Corporate Governance Code, Consultation Document* (April 2014), p 7; FRC, *Directors Remuneration, Consultation Document* (October 2013).

[127] See Treasury Committee, 9th Report, Session 2008–09, 'Banking Crisis: reforming corporate governance and pay in the City' (HC 519), para 77; BIS, *Executive Remuneration, Discussion Paper* (September 2011), paras 84–90.  [128] See Green Paper on Corporate Governance Reform (November 2016).

[129] See HC BEIS Committee Report, n 12, paras 107–109, which recommended that the chair of a remuneration committee be expected to resign if their proposals do not receive the backing of 75 per cent of voting shareholders.

[130] See BIS, *Executive Remuneration, Discussion Paper* (September 2011), para 79.

[131] The EU Commission's 2009 Recommendation, see n 120, suggests that at least one member should have knowledge of and experience in the field of remuneration, see para 7.1.

[132] See BIS, *A Long-term Focus for Corporate Britain—a call for evidence* (October 2010), para 5.11.

[133] SI 2008/410, Sch 8, para 22.

of the company's employees.[134] Shareholders should also consider laying and passing a motion of censure of the remuneration committee when appropriate. The reputational consequences of such a motion might exert sufficient pressure on the committee to focus minds on the need to negotiate remuneration packages which are more balanced in the company's interests. While the requirements for shareholder approval of remuneration policy have increased the degree of engagement between boards and shareholders on this issue and, increasingly, shareholders do vote against excessive packages, it is too early to say whether the changes have had any real impact on the overall level of remuneration being awarded, or whether remuneration is being aligned more closely to company performance, or whether the bargaining dynamic between the executive directors and the company has been altered.[135] If no changes occur, the fault lies, surely, with the shareholders for failing to hold the remuneration committees to account, though they are under considerable pressure now to do so as issues surrounding executive pay continue to dominate corporate governance debates. In 2017, the Government noted that:[136]

'While many companies have responded positively to the reforms introduced in 2013, a persistent small minority of businesses continue to disregard the views of shareholders on pay each year. There are also few signs that many remuneration committees take seriously enough their existing obligations to take account of wider workforce pay and conditions in setting executive remuneration. The Government also recognises concerns expressed by many respondents about the unnecessary complexity and uncertainty of executive pay, particularly around the potential outcomes of long-term incentive plans.'

In an attempt to impose some controls, many important investor bodies draw up, annually, their own principles on remuneration for the guidance of boards, such as the Investment Association's Principles of Remuneration (2017), setting out their expectations as to executive remuneration packages. The influential Pensions and Lifetime Savings Association (PLSA) in its Corporate Governance Policy and Voting Guidelines (2017) recommended that, if shareholders vote against a company's remuneration policy, they should also oppose the re-election of the remuneration committee chair as a company director. In response to the Government's expressed concerns,[137] the FRC has strengthened the 2018 UK Code, as noted at **6-50**, in terms of what is required by boards when they encounter significant shareholder (20 per cent) dissent on a resolution (which there frequently is on remuneration resolutions). Also, in response to the Government, the Investment Association has set up a public register of shareholder opposition to resolutions[138] so this information on shareholder dissent is now publicly available in one place.

---

[134] See Villiers, 'Executive Pay: A Socially-Oriented Distributive Justice Framework' (2016) 37(5) Co. Law 139; Villiers, 'Controlling Executive Pay: Institutional Investors or Distributive Justice?' (2010) 10 JCLS 309. Villiers notes that repeated attempts to solve the executive pay dilemma by seeking pay for performance and by increasing shareholder power have failed and she argues for an alternative fairness approach based on distributive justice, which would take greater account of the wider social issues here. For a contrary position, that the issue is merely one of improving the alignment of shareholder and management interests, and not one of reflecting societal expectations, even if 'fairness' could somehow be captured, see Ferrarini et al, n 120.

[135] See Ndzi, 'UK Shareholder Voting on Directors' Remuneration: Has Binding Vote Made any Difference?' (2017) Co Law 139 for a comprehensive review of the position and the conclusion that shareholders are 'rather uninterested' in remuneration issues. Continuing to focus on a response from them is therefore unlikely to make much of an impact on controlling executive pay.

[136] Government response to the Green Paper, n 12, pp 2–3.

[137] Government response to the Green Paper, n 12, paras 1.45–1.59.

[138] Government response to the Green Paper, n 12, pp 2–3; para 1.45—the Investment Association offered to set up this register in their response to the Green Paper.

## F  Shareholder engagement

### Introduction

**6-48**   As well as an effective board, good corporate governance depends on effective shareholder control of the board, but as the European Commission has noted, while we tend
to presume effective control by shareholders, each governance crisis shows cracks in that
presumption.[139] Hence a great deal of discussion now focuses on the importance of securing, not just better shareholder participation in the annual general meeting (the orthodox forum for the exercise of shareholder power), but better shareholder engagement in
the broadest sense in the interests of good corporate governance. A useful description of
'shareholder engagement' is that it involves 'actively monitoring companies, engaging
in a dialogue with the company's board, and using shareholder rights, including voting
and cooperation with other shareholders, if need be, to improve the governance of the
investee company in the interests of long-term value creation'.[140] The UK Code no longer
addresses engagement in detail, it being a matter which is governed by the Stewardship
Code, discussed at **6-56**.

### The board and the shareholders

**6-49**   Under the UK Code, in addition to formal general meetings, the board should seek regular engagement with major shareholders in order to understand their views on governance and performance against the strategy and committee chairs likewise with regard to
significant matters within their areas of responsibility (Prov 5). The chair must ensure
that the board has a clear understanding of the views of shareholders (Prov 5).

### Effective general meetings

**6-50**   Additionally, the 2018 Code provides that when more than 20 per cent of votes have been
cast against a resolution, the company should explain when announcing the result of voting what actions it intends to take to consult shareholders in order to understand the reasons behind the vote result, with an update being published no more than 6 months after
the vote (Prov 6).[141] The board should then follow up on the matter in the annual report
or at the next annual general meeting explaining the impact which the feedback from
shareholders has had on the decisions taken by the board (Prov 6). To bring extra visibility
to these issues, the Investment Association has set up, at the request of the Government[142]
a Public Register which is an aggregated list of publicly available information regarding

---

[139] See European Commission Green Paper, *The EU Corporate Governance Framework* (COM (2011)
164), para 3.5. Many of the reviews of the causes of the financial crisis criticised shareholders, not just
for being passive and inactive and failing to control the boards of financial institutions, but for implicitly
supporting excessive risk-taking by boards in favour of short-term profits: see Walker Report, n 11, paras
5.10–5.11; OECD, *Corporate Governance and the Financial Crisis: Key Findings and Main Messages* (June
2009), Ch 5 (shareholders in the financial crisis were ineffective, reactive, passive, there was evidence of
reluctant and mechanical voting and an unwillingness to express dissent).

[140] European Commission Green Paper, see n 139, para 2.1. The UK Stewardship Code, see **6-56**, states
that engagement is purposeful dialogue with companies on matters such as strategy, performance, risk,
capital structure, and corporate governance, including culture and remuneration, as well as on issues that
are the immediate subject of votes at general meetings, see FRC, *UK Stewardship Code* (2012), p 1, para 4.

[141] The FRC had previously noted a poor level of disclosure by companies with regard to how they
responded or intended to respond to shareholder votes, see FRC, *Developments in Corporate Governance
and Stewardship 2016* (January 2017), p 18.

[142] The Investment Association offered to develop this register in its response to the Government Green
Paper on Corporate Governance.

meetings of companies in the FTSE All-Share who have received significant shareholder opposition to proposed resolutions or have withdrawn a resolution prior to a shareholder vote. The aim is to highlight companies that receive a high vote against or withdraw a resolution, and to understand the process used by those companies to identify and address the concerns of their shareholders. The Register is already providing a rich trove of detail in an easily accessible form showing the level of dissent across a whole range of issues.

**6-51**  Another way of enhancing the importance of the general meeting is to return specific powers to the shareholders, by statute if necessary. Shareholders have been given an advisory vote on the directors' remuneration report and a binding vote on the company's remuneration policy (CA 2006, ss 439 and 439A), see **18-45**. It might be possible to identify other issues which could be the subject of specific approval, such as the report of the audit committee (see **6-37**). The CA 2006 already requires shareholder approval of various actions (such as a purchase of the company's own shares)[143] or transactions (such as substantial property transactions where directors have a conflict of interest[144]) and, for premium listed companies, the Listing Rules impose additional shareholder approval requirements.[145] The Takeover Code also places power firmly in the hands of the shareholders of the offeree company who must not be denied the opportunity to decide on the merits of a bid.[146] The result is a certain level of transparency and accountability and, in cases where shareholder authorisation is required, some control over these matters by the shareholders. But there is a balance to be struck between requiring shareholder approval of matters and unduly restricting management powers. Calling general meetings in public companies with large numbers of shareholders is a time-consuming and expensive business. Probably, the current range of matters which require shareholder approval is appropriately balanced and the issue is not so much that the general meeting's jurisdiction is too limited, but rather that procedures need to be fine-tuned to ensure effective shareholder participation at the general meeting. The rules in this regard were comprehensively overhauled by the CA 2006 and further modified to reflect the requirements of the Shareholders' Rights Directive 2007/36; they are discussed in Chapter 17. It suffices to highlight a few key issues here, bearing in mind that these issues are of greatest significance in the publicly traded company.

**6-52**  There is a greater focus on electronic means of communication which offer low cost and timely disclosure to all shareholders equally: see **17-6**. The largest companies with widely dispersed shareholdings make extensive use of their websites for instant communication with all shareholders. It is common to have live streaming of analyst and other meetings so that all shareholders, rather than just the largest, can be part of the process. Documentation can be made available to all shareholders via a website quickly and at very low cost.

**6-53**  Voting, attendance, and participation rights at meetings have been reviewed, modified, and extended so that mechanisms are available which allow shareholders flexibility as to how they engage with the company. For example, the CA 2006 confers enhanced rights on proxies to attend, speak, and vote at general meetings (see **17-10**). Members representing at least 5 per cent of the total voting rights of the members are able to require the

---

[143] CA 2006, ss 694, 701.     [144] See CA 2006, s 190.

[145] Shareholder approval is required for class 1 (i.e. large) transactions: Listing Rules (LR) 10.5.1(2); for related party transactions: LR 11.1.7; for certain employees' share schemes or long-term incentive schemes: LR 9.4.1R; and for certain discounted option arrangements: LR 9.4.4.

[146] See Takeover Code, General Principle 3.

circulation of statements concerning a matter referred to in a proposed resolution to be dealt with at a meeting or other business to be dealt with at that meeting (s 314: see **17-45**). Provided they meet the 5 per cent voting rights threshold, members can require the circulation of a written resolution in the case of a private company (s 292: see **17-29**), or the circulation of a proposed resolution to be moved at an annual general meeting of a public company (s 338: see **17-41**), and they can requisition a general meeting (s 303: see **17-46**). The costs issue (which in the past has been a deterrent to the use of such powers) has been addressed with the company required to carry the costs of circulation in some instances. Members of a quoted company can demand an independent assessment of the outcome of a poll (s 342: see **17-15**) and can raise audit concerns on the company's website (s 527: see **18-23**). The result should be that shareholders are able to influence the agenda of the meeting rather than being dictated to by the board, though it has to be acknowledged that some of these powers have always been available and shareholders have shown little interest in exercising them and that remains the position.

### Activist institutional investors

**6-54** If there is to be meaningful shareholder engagement with companies, in effect it means there must be engagement between institutional investors and boards as institutions are the most influential shareholders in listed UK companies. The latest ONS (Office of National Statistics) Share Ownership Survey (as at 31 December 2016) found that insurance companies held 4.9 per cent in value of shares in UK listed companies (down from 14.7 per cent at the end of 2006) and pension funds held 3 per cent in value (down from 12.7 per cent); in each case, these are the lowest recorded percentages of holdings by insurance companies and pension funds respectively. At the end of 2016, then, together they held 7.9 per cent which, when coupled with unit trust holdings of 9.1 per cent, gives an aggregate institutional holding in the region of 17 per cent with banks and other financial institutions holding a further 9.9 per cent and individuals with 12.3 per cent. Holdings by rest-of-the-world investors have reached a record 53.9 per cent in terms of value.[147] This survey also notes that shares are increasingly held in multiple-ownership pooled accounts, where the beneficial owner is unknown to the company and these holdings accounted for an estimated 62.5 per cent of the total holdings by value at the end of 2016.[148]

**6-55** The theory is that well-informed, well-financed, and influential institutional investors can and must make a significant contribution to higher standards of corporate governance.[149] Some would see institutional investors as effectively policing large companies for the benefit of all, adopting an almost regulatory-like role, but they are concerned

---

[147] ONS, *Share Ownership—Share Register Survey Report 2016* (November 2017); also Kay Review of UK Equity Markets and Long-Term Decision Making (July 2012), Chs 2 and 3; also BIS, *A Long-Term Focus for Corporate Britain, a call for evidence* (October 2010), Ch 4 which reviews the state of equity ownership in the UK. See generally Cheffins, *Corporate Ownership and Control: British Business Transformed* (2008); also Dignam and Galanis, 'Corporate Governance and the Importance of the Macroeconomic Context' (2008) 28 Ox JLS 201.

[148] ONS, *Share Ownership—Share Register Survey Report 2016* (November 2017). See BIS, *Building a Culture of Long-term Equity Investment, Implementation of the Kay Review: Progress Report* (October 2014), BIS/14/1157, para 2.124.

[149] See, for example, Chiu and Katelouzou, 'Making a Case for Regulating Institutional Shareholders' Corporate Governance Roles' (2018) JBL 67; Noguera, 'Institutional Investors and the Stewardship Code: An Analysis of why Institutional Investors do not Monitor or Engage' (2017) ICCLR 107; Garrido and Rojo, 'Institutional Investors and Corporate Governance: Solution or Problem?' in Hopt and Wymeersch, *Capital Markets and Company Law* (2003).

not to undertake a wider role, conscious that their obligations lie to their end-investors whose concern is improved shareholder returns. Over the years, engagement typically has occurred behind the scenes,[150] but increasingly institutional investors are willing (or obliged) to take a more public stance, fuelled in part by the need to correct what they see as erroneous comment about their apparent lack of engagement. It is still exceptional, however, for an institutional shareholder to put resolutions to the annual general meeting or to vote against the reappointment of incumbent management, though increasingly they are willing to withhold their votes on an issue. This tactic allows them to avoid a positive vote against a board while still expressing their disquiet about a particular matter. In so far as institutional shareholders have intervened, certainly in the past decade, the focus of their engagement (at least publicly) has been mainly on narrow issues of executive pay and board composition rather than corporate performance as such. Often, intervention attracts headlines (notably concerning the rejection of remuneration packages) but does not deter other companies from subsequently offering equally unacceptable pay packages to their executives, see **6-47**. Companies now express some frustration that engagement is so narrowly focused on this issue of pay rather than more central issues of company strategy and performance.[151] Often, because intervention tends to be reactive rather than proactive, it only comes after there has been significant destruction of shareholder value. Sometimes, intervention itself is criticised, as in the case of hedge-fund activism.[152]

## The Stewardship Code

**6-56**  In 2002 the Institutional Shareholders Committee (ISC) issued an influential 'Statement of Principles on the Responsibilities of Institutional Investors'[153] which in 2009 was re-designated as the ISC Code on the Responsibilities of Institutional Investors and which aimed to set out best practice guidance for investors. This ISC code on responsibilities became, in effect, the UK Stewardship Code which was adopted by the FRC in July 2010,[154] giving effect to recommendations to that effect in the Walker Report.[155] Walker commented, in particular, that 'those who have significant rights of ownership and enjoy

---

[150] An interesting paper by Becht et al, 'Returns to Shareholder Activism, Evidence from a Clinical Study of the Hermes UK Focus Fund', ECGI Finance Working Paper, No 138 (2008) showed that practically all of the engagement of this fund with investee companies took place privately and without resort to mechanisms such as resolutions. This study also concluded that there were substantial effects and benefits associated with shareholder activism in the form of private engagements by an activist fund. See also Goergen et al, 'Do UK Institutional Shareholders Monitor their Investee Firms?' (2008) JCLS 39.

[151] See the Report of the Collective Engagement Working Group, December 2013, p 12. For that reason, it is not intended that the Investor Forum, see **6-65**, would have routine remuneration issues as a core focus, only if questionable remuneration policies were a symptom of broader issues such that they become more of a strategic question. See also FRC, *Developments in Corporate Governance and Stewardship 2016* (January 2017), p 27, noting the frustration of companies and investors that the focus on remuneration can overshadow other important issues.

[152] The activism of hedge funds is often criticised and there can be a sense that more 'traditional' institutional shareholders sometimes resent the sudden appearance of hedge funds on the scene. Often hedge funds are accused of acting in a way which is little more than a form of market manipulation where a fund conducts a very public campaign against a company to try to force a re-structuring or sale.

[153] The ISC was composed of the ABI and NAPF together with the Association of Investment Companies (AIC) and the Investment Management Association (IMA).

[154] See FRC, *Implementation of the Stewardship Code* (July 2010), paras 7, 19 which acknowledged that the Code is little more than the ISC Statement of Principles with minor amendments. For criticism of this approach, see Roach, 'The UK Stewardship Code' (2011) 11 JCLS 463.

[155] See Walker Report, n 11, Ch 5, esp Recommendations 16–20.

the very material advantage of limited liability should see these as complemented by a duty of stewardship'.[156] The latest version of the Stewardship Code was issued in October 2012. At the time of writing, the FRC has announced a review of the Stewardship Code with a public consultation to follow in mid-2018.

**6-57** In addition to the Stewardship Code, some prominent investors also publish their own guidelines on engagement, voting, and corporate governance standards in companies in which they invest.[157] For example, the PLSA Stewardship Disclosure Framework, which the Pensions and Lifetime Savings Association promotes, nudges signatories to the Stewardship Code to make a more explicit statement of their stewardship policies and activities. Further, while originally pioneered by the UK, there are now many versions of stewardship codes around the world, in jurisdictions as diverse as Canada, South Africa, Switzerland, and Japan,[158] as well as multi-national efforts such as the ICGN Global Stewardship Code (2016). The European Commission has adopted a similar approach with amendments to the Shareholders' Rights Directive which will apply from June 2019.[159] The institutional investors will be required to disclose how they take the long-term interests of their beneficiaries into account in their investment strategies and to disclose their engagement policy, including its implementation, on their website.[160] The description of the engagement policy must include how they monitor and conduct dialogue with investee companies, how they exercise voting rights, cooperate with other shareholders, and communicate with relevant stakeholders. Asset managers will be under similar obligations.[161] In each case, the obligations are on a comply or explain basis. As institutional investors and asset managers rely heavily on proxy advisors (businesses which provide advice and voting services to investors), the Directive also requires proxy advisors to disclose on their websites information about any code of conduct which they apply, and how they prepare their research, advice, and voting recommendations.[162]

**6-58** The UK Stewardship Code is addressed to institutional investors, by which is meant asset managers and asset owners with equity holdings in UK listed companies.[163] Like the UK Corporate Governance Code, the Stewardship Code operates on a comply or explain basis.[164] A statement of compliance or explanation must be put on the institutional

---

[156] See Walker Report, n 11, para 5.7 where Walker commented that 'the potentially highly influential position of significant holders of stock in listed companies is a major ingredient in the market-based capitalist system which needs to earn and to be accorded an at least implicit social legitimacy' which it can so do at least by larger fund managers assuming obligations to attend to the performance of investee companies over the long as well as the short term.

[157] Typically issued annually, see, for example, the PLSA, *Corporate Governance Policy and Voting Guidelines* (the Pensions and Life Savings Association).

[158] See generally Hannigan, 'The Rise of Stewardship—"Smoke and Mirrors" or Governance Realignment?' in Siekmann et al (eds), *Festschrift für Theodor Baums* (2017), pp 561–78. Examples of similar approaches would include the EFAMA (European Fund and Asset Management Association) Code for External Governance Principles for the exercise of ownership rights in investee companies (April 2011) and the UN-backed Principles for Responsible Investment launched in 2006.

[159] Directive 2007/36, as amended by Directive 2017/828, OJ L 132/1, 20.5.2017, art 3g.

[160] Directive 2007/36, as amended by Directive 2017/828, OJ L 132/1, 20.5.2017, art 3g.

[161] Directive 2007/36, art 3i.

[162] Directive 2007/36, art 3j. They are also required to inform their clients without delay of any actual or potential conflict of interest that might influence their research, advice, or voting recommendations. These obligations apply to any proxy advisor, though they are neither registered nor have their head office in the EU, if they carry out their activities through an establishment in the EU (reflecting the reality that the main advisors are US businesses). See ESMA, Report on Proxy Advisors' Best Practice Principles (December 2015), ESMA/2015/1887.

[163] Stewardship Code (2012), p 2, para 2.

[164] Stewardship Code (2012), p 4.

investor's website explaining how the principles of the Stewardship Code have been applied and disclosing the specific information required by the Principles or explaining any non-compliance.[165] Adherence to the Stewardship Code is reinforced by an FCA requirement that all UK-authorised asset managers disclose on their websites a statement of commitment to the Stewardship Code or explain why it is not appropriate to their business model.[166] The FRC also encourages service providers (i.e. proxy voting and other advisory services) to disclose how they carry out the wishes of their clients with respect to each of the principles of the Code relevant to their activities.[167] The FRC continues to promote the value of the Stewardship Code, noting encouraging signs of more engagement on a wider range of issues, but it also accepts that a large majority of Code signatories are not following through on their commitment to the Code, that there are concerns about the quality of reporting against the Code principles, both in terms of coverage and the depth of statements, and about the quality of explanations when provisions of the Code have not been followed. The picture then is one of limited progress and the FRC concedes that it is 'concerned about the state of commitment to the Code'.[168]

### Purpose of the Stewardship Code

**6-59** The Stewardship Code 'sets out the principles of effective stewardship by investors. In so doing, the Code assists institutional investors better to exercise their stewardship responsibilities, which in turn gives force to the "comply or explain" system.'[169]

### Content of the Stewardship Code

**6-60** The Stewardship Code consists of Principles and Guidance on each principle. The principles of the Stewardship Code are straightforward—institutional investors should:[170]

- publicly disclose their policy on how they will discharge their stewardship responsibilities;
- have a robust policy on managing conflicts of interest in relation to stewardship which should be publicly disclosed;
- monitor their investee companies;
- establish clear guidelines on when and how they will escalate their stewardship activities;
- be willing to act collectively with other investors where appropriate;[171]
- have a clear policy on voting and disclosure of voting activity;
- report periodically on their stewardship and voting activities.[172]

---

[165] Stewardship Code (2012), p 2, para 3. The institution then notifies the FRC that a statement has been posted on the institution's website and the name of the institution is published on a list maintained on the FRC's website: Code, p 3, para 14.

[166] See FCA Handbook, COBS 2.2.3R: a firm, other than a venture capital firm, which is managing investments for a professional client that is not a natural person must disclose clearly on its website, or if it does not have a website in another accessible form: (1) the nature of its commitment to the Financial Reporting Council's Stewardship Code; or (2) where it does not commit to the Code, its alternative investment strategy. [167] Stewardship Code (2012), p 3, para 11.

[168] FRC, *Developments in Corporate Governance and Stewardship 2014* (January 2015), pp 17, 20, 22.

[169] Stewardship Code (2012), p 1, para 3.

[170] Stewardship Code (2012), p 5. Compliance with the Code does not constitute an invitation to manage the affairs of a company or preclude a decision to sell a holding, where this is considered in the best interest of clients or beneficiaries: Stewardship Code (2012), p 1, para 7.

[171] See discussion at **6-65** of the Investor Forum which has been set up to assist with collective engagement.

[172] The Stewardship Code, Guidance to Principle 7, states that those signing up to the Code should consider obtaining an independent opinion on their engagement and voting processes.

**6-61**　　There is little about these principles which is particularly challenging for asset managers, little that is mandatory, other than a certain level of disclosure and, probably, little of value.[173] A lot of attention in the context of engagement is focused on the exercise of voting power and one of the difficult issues is whether institutional shareholders should be required to vote at general meetings, given the significant blocks of shares which they hold. The Government has threatened from time to time that it will consider introducing a legal requirement to vote if institutions do not exercise their voting rights,[174] but it would prefer that institutional investors voluntarily engage in the manner suggested by the Stewardship Code which does not impose any mandatory voting requirement. There is some evidence that the public debate on the issue of voting has resulted in a greater number of institutional votes being cast, though it is not clear to what extent this is considered voting as opposed to 'box-ticking' compliance outsourced to proxy advisory services.[175] The relevant guidance in the Stewardship Code[176] states that institutional investors should seek to vote all shares held; should not automatically support the board; should inform the company in advance with reasons if they intend to vote against a resolution or abstain. It also suggests that institutional shareholders should disclose the use, if any, of proxy voting or other voting advisory services, and describe the scope of such services. They should identify the providers and disclose the extent to which they follow, rely upon, or use recommendations made by such services. This issue of the use of proxy voting or advisory services is also one which concerns the European Commission and the amendments to the Shareholder Rights Directive require greater transparency from proxy advisers both with respect to how they reach their recommendations, but also about any conflicts of interest which may influence those recommendations, see earlier at **6-57**.

## Challenges to shareholder engagement

**6-62**　　The way forward appears to rest quite firmly on greater shareholder engagement, but this enthusiasm for shareholder engagement may be misplaced or at least based on unrealistic expectations.[177] As noted, shareholder engagement is not new, though it has a raised profile now, and there is little sense to date of anything particularly different emerging when compared with past practice. There is some level of ongoing intervention, typically on the issue of executive pay and board composition, these being the two issues which are easiest for shareholders to address, but without any significant change in the role played by shareholders in the largest companies. One reason for the lack of change may be that the environment in which the debate about shareholder engagement is taking place is possibly less conducive to engagement than previously. When serious discussion first started (probably about 20 years ago) of greater institutional shareholder engagement, insurance companies and pension funds did form a (relatively) homogeneous grouping

---

[173]　See generally, Hannigan, n 158; also Reisberg, 'The UK Stewardship Code: On the Road to Nowhere?' (2015) JCLS 217; Cheffins, 'The Stewardship Code's Achilles Heel' (2010) 73 MLR 1004; Roach, n 154.

[174]　The Government has a power under CA 2006, s 1277 to bring in regulations to require institutions to provide information as to the exercise of their voting rights, but it has not used this power to date. See generally Schmolke, 'Institutional Investors' Mandatory Voting Disclosure' (2006) 7 EBOR 767.

[175]　An Investment Management Association survey found that, where the activity is managed in-house 99 per cent of respondents voted 100 per cent of their UK shares; 73 per cent of respondents publicly disclosed their voting records, see joint report of the Investment Association and Pensions and Life Savings Association, *Stewardship in Practice* Sept 2016 (September 2017), Sections 5–7.

[176]　Stewardship Code (2012) Guidance to Principle 6.

[177]　See generally Cheffins, 'The Stewardship Code's Achilles Heel' (2010) 73 MLR 1004.

of 'institutional investors', but there is no such homogeneity now.[178] Insurance companies' and pension funds' holdings have been declining for many years now and overseas investors' holdings now amount to more than 53 per cent of listed shares by value.[179] Encouraging engagement by those investors is more challenging,[180] not because of geographical remoteness (an irrelevance in the digital age) but because they are less susceptible to domestic political pressure to engage. All involved have different investment time scales and strategies. Greater engagement is being sought in an environment when it is probably unrealistic to expect much by way of common interest between these many types of investors, so limiting the scope for common action.

**6-63**    There are also many practical issues relating to shareholder engagement which need to be considered. Improved meeting procedures and rules in the CA 2006, Pt 13, are helpful, but long-standing institutional concerns about matters such as the priority they must give to their obligations to their end-investors, the resources required for engagement, the difficulties of building a coalition of support,[181] free-rider issues, and the need to retain freedom to pursue their own investment strategies have not evaporated with the adoption of the Stewardship Code. These difficulties mean that it is important to have realistic expectations of what shareholder engagement can contribute to corporate governance. That is not to deny that engagement is important for governance generally as it provides another point of intervention and scrutiny of boards, but its real value is when it is used by individual investors as a tool for limiting their risk. Selfish focused engagement could increase the possibility for some alert investors of exiting from disastrous investments before all value is destroyed[182] and their exit may alert others as to the approaching calamity so bringing matters to a head rather sooner and reducing the ultimate losses. This selfish engagement does little to contribute to the long-term sustainability of the enterprise, however, and is essentially a response based on exit rather than addressing under-performance.

### Long-term investment and engagement

**6-64**    A much broader debate is the contribution which the institutional investors can make to the long-term success of the company. In the wake of the financial crisis, one of the issues raised for consideration was whether there is a problem of short-termism in equity markets (i.e. a focus by investors and asset managers on short-term returns at the expense of a longer term perspective) and, if so, how it might be addressed.[183] The concern is that there

---

[178] Millstein, 'Directors and Boards amidst Shareholders with Conflicting Values', Charkham Memorial Lecture, 9 July 2008.

[179] See the statistics at **6-54**, and the ONS *Share Ownership—Share Register Survey Report 2016* (November 2017).

[180] These difficulties explain why, despite their declining holdings, local institutions are expected to take the lead on engagement though the FRC hopes that investors based outside the UK will commit to the Stewardship Code as their support where they have significant holdings can make a real difference, see FRC, *Implementation of the Stewardship Code* (July 2010), para 25. The OECD would also encourage greater engagement by foreign investors, see OECD, *Corporate Governance and the Financial Crisis: Conclusions and emerging good practices* (February 2010), para 7.6.

[181] See Keay, 'Company Directors Behaving Poorly: Disciplinary Options for Shareholders' [2007] JBL 656 at 659–62.

[182] The importance of this self-interested engagement is another reason why direct shareholding by individual investors will become a thing of the past. Few individuals have the resources for the level of monitoring of their small portfolios which is necessary if they are to avoid the sort of cataclysmic losses borne by small investors in recent decades (ranging from Railtrack, to Equitable Life, to Halifax Bank of Scotland).

[183] BIS, *A Long-Term Focus for Corporate Britain, a call for evidence* (October 2010); also *Report of the Reflection Group on the Future of European Company Law* (2011), Ch 3.

is evidence of too great an obsession with the short term (holding periods for shares had shrunk to eight months by 2007 compared to in excess of five years in the 1960s)[184] with shareholders looking for instant returns and directors looking to satisfy that demand rather than focus on longer term strategies which would possibly be more beneficial to the company and its investors, employees etc. If engagement could be shifted to a focus on long-term investment, that might be more beneficial to the economy as a whole. To address these issues, the Government set up an independent review (the Kay Review) of investment in UK equity with a brief to examine the whole investor chain and the role of all the players, from company boards, through pension funds, advisers and fund managers, to ultimate beneficiaries, including, in particular, the time scales considered by companies and investment managers and whether the markets and Government policy give sufficient encouragement to boards to focus on long-term development of their businesses. The Kay Review's final report ranges widely from the structure of shareholdings and the nature of the investment chain to the regulation of the markets and the importance of fiduciary duties.[185] Amongst the recommendations most relevant to corporate governance were recommendations for a continued development of the Stewardship Code; for greater shareholder control of directors' remuneration (discussed at **18-45**); for a greater role for fiduciary duties in the investment chain (discussed later in the chapter); and for an investors' forum to be established to facilitate collective engagement by investors in UK companies.[186]

### Investor Forum

**6-65**   An investors' forum was set up in October 2014 by the investment industry 'to foster better relations between UK corporate and their owners', to build partnerships across the investment chain.[187] It describes itself as seeking 'to contribute to long-term investment performance by promoting cultural change and enhancing shareholder stewardship'. It is hoped that the Investor Forum will facilitate the inclusion of international investors, a reflection of the market realities previously mentioned. The intention is that 'where appropriate and requested by the participants, the Investor Forum will facilitate the formation of investor groups to engage collectively'.[188] The Forum does seem to be developing some activities and it has brought a measure of transparency to some of its engagements which are reported on its website, so this is potentially an important body which will develop further in the coming years.[189]

---

[184]  See BIS, n 183, para 4.19; also European Commission Green Paper, see n 139, para 2.2.

[185]  *Kay Review of UK Equity Markets and Long-Term Decision Making* (July 2012).

[186]  See BIS, *Building a Culture of Long-term Equity Investment, Implementation of the Kay Review: Progress Report* (October 2014), BIS/14/1157, which summarises developments on the many matters covered by the Kay Review since it reported in 2012.

[187]  Undated document from the Investor Forum. The background to its foundation is set out in *Report of the Collective Engagement Working Group* (December 2013). The Investor Forum has been constituted as a Community Interest Company with a board of directors representing the interests of the investment chain—asset owners, asset managers, and company representatives. See also BIS, *Building a Culture of Long-term Equity Investment, Implementation of the Kay Review: Progress Report* (October 2014), BIS/14/1157, para 1.9; see also paras 2.19–2.26 on the background to the setting up and role of the Investor Forum.

[188]  Page 10, undated and untitled document from the Investor Forum available on its website, www. investorforum.org.uk (2015). Previously assurance has been obtained from the Takeover Panel that collective engagement would not of itself constitute those involved as a concert party: see Takeover Panel, Practice Statement 2009/26, *Shareholder Activism*; also ESMA Statement 2014/677, 20 June 2014, setting out a list of activities ('White List') that shareholders can cooperate on without the presumption of acting in concert for the purposes of the Takeover Directive.

[189]  See The Investor Forum Annual Review for 2017.

## The investment chain—enfranchising the indirect investor

**6-66**  In keeping with the general theme of shareholder engagement, especially in larger companies, the CA 2006, Pt 9 introduces some innovative provisions with respect to the enfranchisement of indirect holders. The modern practice is that most individual investors hold shares through an intermediary and have no direct relationship with the company in which they have invested. For its part, the company looks solely to the legal owner as reflected in the register of members and does not have regard to beneficial interests (CA 2006, s 126). Often the result is that the person with the voting rights (the investment manager) is uninterested in exercising them whereas the ultimate beneficial owner of the shares might be interested but does not have the legal right to exert any direct influence over the company in which his money is invested. The classic example is the pension fund investment where sums are passed from the contributor through the hands of trustees and managers in an ever-lengthening chain to the company raising capital. Even identifying shareholders, or at least those with the true economic interest, along the investment chain can be difficult as a result of stock lending practices and long chains, possibly across borders (see further at **6-73**).[190] It is often argued that shareholder engagement demands some mechanism whereby the indirect investor, the actual provider of the capital, can engage with and be recognised by the company.[191]

**6-67**  These enfranchisement provisions were the subject of intense debate in Parliament with various permutations being considered before agreement was finally reached on what is now CA 2006, Pt 9. The idea of enfranchising or involving the indirect investor seems attractive, but in practice it is difficult to devise a workable, cost-effective, mechanism, particularly once cross-border investors are involved. Traded companies with large numbers of registered shareholders and unquantifiable numbers of beneficial interests behind them are concerned that a liberal approach to enfranchising those beneficial interests could lead to administrative chaos and dramatically increase the costs of maintaining and operating their share registers. The CA 2006, Pt 9 is a modest step forward, reflecting the numerous compromises necessary to gain Parliamentary approval, rather than a radical departure from the general rule that the company looks to the registered shareholder.

**6-68**  Part 9 allows for the recognition of indirect investors in two ways: (1) any company can choose to permit the registered member to nominate another person to enjoy or exercise all or any specified rights of the member in relation to the company (CA 2006, s 145); and (2) traded companies can allow a member to nominate another person to enjoy 'information rights' so that the company must communicate with that other person directly (s 146).[192]

## Nominating another to exercise rights of a member

**6-69**  Any company may provide in its articles that a member can nominate another person to enjoy or exercise all or any specified rights of that member in relation to the company

---

[190]  See European Commission Green Paper, see n 139, paras 2.4–2.6. See also Walker, Final Report, n 11, Ch 5.

[191]  The Company Law Review noted the growing separation between the legal ownership and beneficial ownership and considered the grant of at least some 'control rights' to the beneficial owners while envisaging that market solutions will emerge as electronic communications make it easier for companies, intermediaries, and ultimate beneficial owners to exercise these control rights: see Company Law Review, *Final Report*, vol 1 (2001), paras 3.51, 7.1; *Completing the Structure* (2000), paras 5.2–5.12; *Developing the Framework* (2000), paras 4.7–4.18.

[192]  For detailed guidance on Pt 9, see ICSA *Guidance on Part 9, Companies Act 2006, Indirect Investors—Information Rights and Voting* (2007).

(CA 2006, s 145). Anything which can be done by the member can then be done by the nominated person, in particular the nominated person can exercise the rights to circulate resolutions and statements (ss 292, 314, 338), to require the directors to call a meeting (s 303), to appoint a proxy (s 324), and to receive written resolutions, notice of meetings, and annual accounts and reports (ss 291, 310, 423). To date, few companies, if any, appear to have chosen to alter their articles to allow for nomination in this way.

### Information rights

**6-70**  A member in a traded company can nominate a person on whose behalf he holds shares to enjoy 'information rights' by which is meant that the nominee has the right to receive all shareholder communications and the right to receive the annual accounts and reports (CA 2006, s 146). The rights of the nominee are in addition to the rights of the registered member (s 150(5)). A registered member is not required to nominate another person for information rights and, even if nominated, the registered member can terminate the nomination at any time (s 148(2)).[193] The documents or information which the nominee is entitled to are provided by a website, unless the nominee requests the registered member to notify the company that the nominee wishes to receive hard copies and the nominee provides a postal address for that purpose (s 147(2), (5)).

**6-71**  Where a notice of a meeting is sent to a nominated person, the notice must state that the nominated person may have the right to be appointed as a proxy or to appoint someone else as a proxy and may be able to give his voting instructions directly to the registered shareholder, depending on the agreement between the nominee and the person by whom he was nominated (s 149). A failure by the company to recognise information rights is actionable (as a breach of the articles) only by the registered shareholder and not by the nominated person (s 150(2)).

**6-72**  After all the Parliamentary discussion, once enacted the provisions appear to have attracted little interest.[194] In so far as the provisions require companies to facilitate the changes by choosing to alter their articles (to allow for nomination of another), they have shown no inclination to do so, not least because there is no pressure from shareholders for the articles to be changed. In so far as nominee shareholders may nominate the beneficial owners to enjoy information rights, it would appear they have not done so, perhaps out of inertia or a concern about the administrative burden of altering existing arrangements. In so far as the whole process depends on the indirect investors showing some interest in exercising these rights, they have not done so, probably because the rights mainly amount to a right to receive information via a website (a compromise based on the need to limit the costs involved). As much of the information on websites is anyway on open access and so in the public domain, shareholders have no particular reason to exercise these rights. The provisions are then on the statute book but they have had little impact to date.

### The investment chain and the Kay Review

**6-73**  The Kay Review (at **6-64**) considered in detail the structure of shareholding in large companies and found what had been evident for some time, namely that there has been what

---

[193]  Furthermore, CA 2006, s 148(7) provides that a nomination can be terminated where no response is received within 28 days to a query from the company as to whether the indirect investor wishes to retain his information rights (only one such enquiry may be made per annum).

[194]  Part 9 was alluded to in *Eckerle v Wickeder Westfalenstahl GmbH* [2013] 3 WLR 1316, see **16-4**.

Kay called 'an explosion of intermediation' with associated costs and with a lack of trust between the various elements of the chain. The report noted that 'between the company and the saver are now interposed registrars, nominees, custodians, asset managers, managers who allocate funds to specialist asset managers, trustees, investment consultants, agents who "wrap" products, retail platforms, distributors and independent financial advisers'.[195] Part of the solution (in addition to trying to shorten the chain), Kay thought, lay in applying fiduciary standards to all relationships in the investment chain which involve discretion over the investments of others or advice on investment decisions.[196] Kay also recommended that the Law Commission review the legal concept of fiduciary duty as applied to investment to address uncertainties and misunderstandings on the part of trustees and their advisers.[197] The Law Commission consulted and reported on these matters in 2014 focusing on pensions and pension fund trustees.[198] As was acknowledged, it was a somewhat unusual response by the Law Commission in that it did not focus on recommendations for legislative reform, but rather sought to explain the nature of fiduciary and other duties to act in the best interests of investors and to describe how these duties apply to investment intermediaries.[199] The Law Commission also drew up some brief guidance for pension fund trustees as to their duties when setting an investment strategy. The Government hopes that this report and guidance from the Law Commission will serve to reassure trustees that they can take into account a variety of factors when reaching investment decisions beyond merely maximising short-term returns and so in that way they can be encouraged to take a long-term view.[200]

**6-74** Quite apart from these issues as to the length and cost of the chain, and the standards of conduct governing the intermediaries, the European Commission is also concerned about the difficulty for companies of identifying their beneficial owners, so amendments to the Shareholder Rights Directive 2007/36/EC (affecting traded companies only) give companies additional rights to demand information from intermediaries as to the identity of the beneficial owners and also to require companies to pass information down the chain to the shareholder and to require intermediaries to pass voting instructions from the shareholder back up the chain to the investee company.[201] The aim is to facilitate, in particular, the participation of and voting by the shareholders in general meetings. The latter elements reflect the type of Part 9 provisions introduced here, but in the more complex context of lengthy, cross-border chains. The ability to identify beneficial owners is not a significant issue here, given the introduction of the register of people with significant influence (see discussion at **16-91**) and powers in the companies legislation which allow public companies (and many companies replicate these powers in their articles) to ask registered shareholders to divulge on whose behalf they hold the shares (see s 793).

---

[195] Kay Review, n 147, para 3.7.

[196] Kay Review, n 147, para 6.13. A Shareholder Voting Working Group was set up to look at difficulties in the chain and released a paper for consultation in 2015 but there seems to have been no follow-up to that initiative.   [197] Kay Review, n 147, Ch 10 and Recommendation 9.

[198] Law Commission, *Fiduciary Duties of Investment Intermediaries* (July 2014), Law Com No 350; and earlier consultation paper of the same name, Consultation Paper No 215 (October 2013).

[199] Law Com No 350; n 198, paras 1.36–1.38. In so far as the report made recommendations, they were for action by the Pension Regulator, the Financial Conduct Authority, and the Government; the Government has indicated that the relevant departments are following up on the Law Commission's work: see BIS, *Building a Culture of Long-term Equity Investment, Implementation of the Kay Review: Progress Report* (October 2014), BIS/14/1157, paras 2.57–2.66 and Table 1 which sets out the Government's response to the Law Commission's report.   [200] See BIS, *Progress Report*, n 199, paras 2.63–2.64.

[201] See Directive 2007/36, as amended by Directive 2017/828, OJ L 132/1, 20.5.2017, arts 3a–3e.

# 7

# Board composition–appointment and removal of directors

## A  Appointment of directors

**7-1**  The directors are responsible for the management of the company's business for which purpose they may exercise all the powers of the company.[1] The expectation is that the directors act collectively as a board but the articles invariably provide that any of the powers conferred on the directors by the articles can in turn be delegated by them to smaller committees or individual directors or other persons.[2] The proceedings of the board are regulated by the articles of association which will contain detailed rules covering matters such as the manner of decision-making by the directors,[3] the calling of directors' meetings,[4] and quorum requirements.[5] Minutes must be kept of all board meetings.[6]

**7-2**  'Director' as such is not defined in the Companies Act 2006 (CA 2006) which provides simply that 'director' includes any person occupying the position of director, by whatever name called,[7] so making it clear that the title used is not the determining factor in deciding whether someone is a director. It is possible for someone to be a director though described as a manager or governor and, equally, companies may describe employees as,

---

[1] See The Companies (Model Articles) Regulations 2008, SI 2008/3229, reg 2, Sch 1, art 3 (Ltd); reg 4, Sch 3, art 3 (Plc).

[2] See The Companies (Model Articles) Regulations 2008, SI 2008/3229, reg 2, Sch 1, art 5 (Ltd); reg 4, Sch 3, art 5 (Plc).

[3] The general rule about decision-making by the directors of a private company is that any decision must be either a majority decision of the directors at a meeting or a unanimous decision (of those eligible to vote on the matter) by written resolution: see The Companies (Model Articles) Regulations 2008, SI 2008/3229, reg 2, Sch 1, art 7 (Ltd), but see also art 16 'subject to the articles, the directors may make any rule which they think fit about how they take decisions …'. In the case of a public company, decisions may (not 'must' as in the case of the private company articles) be taken at a directors' meeting or in the form of a directors' written resolution: see arts 7, 13, 18 (Plc) and they too, subject to the articles, may make any rule which they think fit about how they take decisions: art 19 (Plc). The articles may provide that the voting rights of the director at board meetings reflect the voting rights of their appointing shareholders, see *Re Coroin Ltd, McKillen v Misland (Cyprus) Investments Ltd* [2011] EWHC 3466 at [9].

[4] See The Companies (Model Articles) Regulations 2008, SI 2008/3229, reg 2, Sch1, art 9 (Ltd); reg 4, Sch 3, art 8 (Plc).

[5] See The Companies (Model Articles) Regulations 2008, SI 2008/3229, reg 2, Sch 1, art 11(2) (Ltd); reg 4, Sch 3, art 10(2) (Plc).

[6] CA 2006, s 248. There is no provision for inspection of such minutes by the members unlike the minutes of any general meeting which are available for inspection by any member: s 358.

[7] CA 2006, s 250. See Browne-Wilkinson V-C in *Re Lo-Line Electric Motors Ltd* [1988] 2 All ER 692 at 699: 'In my judgment the words "by whatever name called" show that the subsection is dealing with nomenclature; for example where the company's articles provide that the conduct of the company is committed to "governors" or "managers".'

say, marketing or personnel directors without their occupying the position of director in law. Legally, there are three classes of director which concern us, the de jure director, the de facto director, and the shadow director.

## B **De jure directors**

**7-3**	A de jure director is someone formally and validly appointed to the board. The application for registration of a company which is submitted to the registrar of companies must contain the names of the proposed first directors (first directors and company secretary if the company is a public company or is a private company which has chosen to have a company secretary)[8] and include a statement by the subscribers to the memorandum of association that each of the persons named as a director has consented to act in the relevant capacity (CA 2006, s 12). On the certificate of incorporation being issued by the registrar, those persons named as directors in the application for registration are deemed to have been appointed to office (s 16(6)). Thereafter the manner of appointment is a matter for the articles which typically provide that appointments may be made by the shareholders by ordinary resolution or by a decision of the directors.[9] It is possible, but unusual, for the articles to provide for the appointment of directors by persons who are not shareholders, such as a major creditor.[10] The UK Corporate Governance Code provides that all directors of companies subject to the Code (premium listed companies) should be subject to annual election, see **6-16**.[11]

**7-4**	A private company need have only one director whereas a public company must have at least two (CA 2006, s 154). For the first time, the CA 2006 sets a minimum age for a director which is 16 years and an appointment in breach of this requirement is void.[12]

**7-5**	Consideration was given in the course of the Company Law Review to prohibiting the use of corporate directors, but the decision was taken to continue to permit them[13] but subject to a requirement for at least one natural person on the board.[14] Corporate directors can make it difficult to determine who controls a company and the investigation and

---

[8]	CA 2006, s 9(4)(c).

[9]	See The Companies (Model Articles) Regulations 2008, SI 2008/3229, reg 2, Sch 1, art 17 (Ltd); reg 4, Sch 3, art 20 (Plc). In the case of a public company, such an appointment is held only until the next following annual general meeting when the appointee can be re-elected: art 20(2)(a). Usefully, the model articles for private companies provide that where, as a result of death, a private company is left with no shareholders and no directors (as where the company is a sole member company and the sole member is also the sole director) the personal representative of the last shareholder to die has the right to appoint a director: see art 17(2) (Ltd).

[10]	*Kuwait Asia Bank v National Mutual Life* [1990] BCLC 868 at 891.

[11]	UK Corporate Governance Code (2018) Provision 18.

[12]	CA 2006, s 157(1), (4), though such 'directors' remain liable for their acts: see s 157(5). Regulations may allow for exceptional cases (none have been made): s 158. Under-age directors in office on 1 October 2008 automatically ceased to be directors (s 159(2)). A previous restriction (CA 1985, s 293) on persons aged 70 or more acting as a director of a public company has been repealed.

[13]	The register of directors must include the corporate name and registered office of any company holding the office of director as well as other details: CA 2006, s 164.

[14]	CA 2006, s 155 (to be repealed from a date to be appointed, see Small Business, Enterprise and Employment Act 2015, s 87(2) and see n 15); *Re Bulawayo Market and Offices Co Ltd* [1907] 2 Ch 458. The Secretary of State has power to direct a company to appoint the right number of directors or to ensure that at least one director is a natural person: CA 2006, s 156. See also Company Law Review, *Modernising Company Law* (Cmnd 5553-I, 2002), paras 3.32–3.34.

prosecution of corporate frauds can be impeded when it is possible to have corporate shareholders and directors, often based on further layers of corporate entities, some of which may be registered in other jurisdictions. It can also be difficult to apply meaningful sanctions to corporate directors.

**7-6**    The Government returned to the issue in 2013 and, as an element of the commitment to bring greater transparency to bear on company ownership and controllers, it decided to prohibit the use of corporate directors, subject to exceptions.[15] Hence, with effect from a date to be appointed, directors must be natural persons save where a corporate director is permitted by regulations to be made under CA 2006, s 156B.[16] The exceptions are likely to be for group structures involving large listed companies and large private companies which are subject to a high degree of transparency and regulation in any event and where there are practical reasons of commercial convenience which may warrant the continued use of corporate directors in those cases.[17] But the provision has not been commenced and, so for the moment, corporate directors are permissible generally.

**7-7**    In the case of a public company, each proposed director must be voted on individually, otherwise the resolution is void, unless those voting consent unanimously to a block resolution (CA 2006, s 160).[18] This requirement ensures that shareholders can express their disapproval of a particular director without having to reject the entire board. The acts of a director are valid notwithstanding any defect which may afterwards be discovered in his appointment or qualification (CA 2006, s 161). This section covers the situation where there has been a breach of the requirements regarding appointment with the result that the appointment is defective, but it does not validate the acts of someone who has never been appointed at all but who simply purports to fill the office of director,[19] nor can it assist a party having knowledge of the facts giving rise to the defect or a party who is put on inquiry but does not inquire.[20]

**7-8**    The model articles for public companies (see **5-2**) provide for the appointment of alternate directors. Such a director is appointed by a director to exercise that director's powers and carry out that director's responsibilities in relation to the taking of decisions by the directors.[21] Except as otherwise provided, alternate directors are deemed for all purposes to

---

[15] For the background to these changes, see BIS, *Transparency & Trust: Enhancing the Transparency of UK Company Ownership and Increasing Trust in UK Business*, Consultation Paper (July 2013), BIS 13/959, pp 50–2; and Government Response to that Consultation (April 2014), BIS/14/672, pp 44–6.

[16] CA 2006, s 156A(1), (5), as substituted by the Small Business, Enterprise and Employment Act 2015, s 87(4). Existing corporate directors will have a transitional period of one year, by which time they will either need to be replaced by individuals or they must fall within whatever exceptions are prescribed by regulations. See Ellis, 'The Continued Appointment of Corporate Directors' (2016) Co Law 203.

[17] See BIS, *Corporate Directors, Scope of exceptions to the prohibition of corporate directors* (November 2014), BIS/14/1017; BIS, *Small Business, Enterprise and Employment Act 2015, Companies transparency*, Fact Sheets, BIS/15/266, p 4.

[18] For premium listed companies with a controlling shareholder (essentially 30 per cent or more of the votes), there are additional requirements to ensure the election of independent directors which must be approved by resolution of the shareholders and by resolution of the independent shareholders of the company: Listing Rules 9.2.2ER; and see LR 6.1.4B.

[19] *Morris v Kanssen* [1946] AC 459; *British Asbestos Co Ltd v Boyd* [1903] 2 Ch 439; *Dawson v African Consolidated Land and Travel Co* [1898] 1 Ch 6.

[20] See *Re New Cedos Engineering Co Ltd* [1994] 1 BCLC 797 at 812; *British Asbestos Co Ltd v Boyd* [1903] 2 Ch 439.

[21] See The Companies (Model Articles) Regulations 2008, SI 2008/3229, reg 4, Sch 3, arts 25–27 (Plc). As an alternate is deemed for all purposes to be a director (art 26(2)(a)), his appointment must be notified to the registrar of companies as required by CA 2006, s 167.

be directors, are liable for their own acts and omissions and are not agents of or for their appointors.[22]

**7-9** Every company must keep a register of its directors giving the following details for an individual director: name, a service address, the country or state (or part of the UK) in which the director is usually resident, his or her nationality, business occupation (if any), and date of birth.[23] This register must be open to inspection at the registered office or other specified place by members of the company free of charge and by the public for such fee as may be prescribed.[24] Private companies may elect to maintain this register on the public register, to be known in this context as the central register, in which case the obligations as to entry of information on the register become an obligation to deliver the information to the registrar of companies.[25]

**7-10** Since the CA 2006, there is no requirement for a director's usual residential address to be given in the register of directors and a service address may be given instead which may be the company's registered office (s 163(5)). The residential address is available to a wide range of public authorities and other parties, such as liquidators and creditors, who may seek a court order requiring disclosure of a residential address.[26] This change was introduced in order to provide additional protection for directors from harassment and threats by persons such as animal rights extremists.[27] The company is required to maintain a register of directors' residential addresses (s 165) and private companies may elect to maintain this information on the central register (s 167A(1)). This register is not open to inspection.[28] Appointments (and resignations) of directors must be notified within 14 days to the registrar of companies (s 167) and any such notification is then publicised by the registrar in the *London Gazette*.[29]

---

[22] See The Companies (Model Articles) Regulations 2008, SI 2008/3229, reg 4, Sch 3, art 26(2) (Plc).

[23] CA 2006, s 162(1), (2). There is no longer any requirement to give details of other directorships held by that director. The day element of a date of birth is protected information, not for public disclosure, in order to reduce the potential for identity fraud, see CA 2006, ss 1087(1)(da), 1087A.

[24] CA 2006, s 162(3), (5); SI 2008/3006.

[25] The election may be made by the subscribers at the time of incorporation or subsequently by the company itself: CA 2006, s 167A(2). An election can be withdrawn and then the company's obligation to maintain the register revives, see s 167E.

[26] See CA 2006, ss 243, 244, 1088; The Companies (Disclosure of Address) Regulations 2009, SI 2009/214, as amended.

[27] Initially, directors (and others, including the company secretary) at serious risk of violence or intimidation were able to apply to the registrar of companies for a confidentiality order: see CA 1985, ss 723B–723F; Companies (Particulars of Usual Residential Address) (Confidentiality Orders) Regulations 2002, SI 2002/912; and that remains the case for addresses on the register prior to the reforms effected by the CA 2006, see s 1088 and SI 2009/214.

[28] The details contained on the company's register of residential addresses are notified to the registrar of companies on the appointment of a director (CA 2006, s 167). This information is classified as 'protected information' which cannot be disclosed by the company or by the registrar of companies save to the extent permitted by the Act, for example disclosure on the order of a court: CA 2006, ss 240–246; s 1087(1)(b); also The Companies (Disclosure of Address) Regulations 2009, SI 2009/214, as amended.

[29] CA 2006, ss 1077, 1078. A company cannot rely against other persons on any change among the company's directors if that change has not been officially notified in the *Gazette* at the material time unless the other person was aware of it; and it cannot rely on any change within 15 days of the notice in the *Gazette* if the other party was unavoidably prevented from knowing of the change at that time: s 1079(1)–(3). However, the effect of s 1079 is purely negative and it does not entitle the company to treat the gazetting of an event as giving notice to all the world: *Official Custodian for Charities v Parway Estates Developments Ltd* [1984] 3 All ER 679.

## C **De facto directors**

**7-11**    Essentially, a de facto director is someone who is part of the corporate governing structure of the company and who has assumed the status and functions of a company director so as to make himself liable as if he were a de jure director.[30] It is possible, for example, for a shareholder or a consultant to the company to act in a way which makes him a de facto director.[31] But he must have assumed the office of director and it is necessary to distinguish between a person acting in another capacity, for example as a mere agent, employee, or adviser of the company or solely as a shareholder protecting his investment.[32] If it is unclear whether the acts of the person in question are referable to an assumed directorship or to some other capacity, the person in question is entitled to the benefit of the doubt.[33]

**7-12**    The question whether someone is a de facto director is likely to arise where a penalty or liability may be imposed[34] on a 'director', such as disqualification[35] or liability for wrongful trading,[36] or misfeasance[37] and the individual attempts to evade the penalty or liability by relying on the fact that he is not a de jure director, i.e. not a formally and properly appointed director. The case is usually being brought by a liquidator who needs to establish that the individual is a de facto director.

---

[30] *Re Paycheck Services 3 Ltd, Revenue and Customs Commissioners v Holland* [2011] 1 BCLC 141 at [93]; *Smithton Ltd v Naggar* [2014] BCC 482; *Re Kaytech International plc, Secretary of State for Trade and Industry v Kaczer* [1999] 2 BCLC 351 at 402–3, CA; also *Secretary of State for Trade and Industry v Tjolle* [1998] 1 BCLC 333 at 343–4; *Re Hydrodam (Corby) Ltd* [1994] 2 BCLC 180 at 183. See generally Noonan and Watson, 'Examining Company Directors through the Lens of De Facto Directorship' [2008] JBL 587.

[31] See *Secretary of State for Trade and Industry v Becker* [2003] 1 BCLC 555 at [45]; *Secretary of State for Trade and Industry v Hollier* [2007] BCC 11 at [80]; also *Secretary of State for Trade and Industry v Jones* [1999] BCC 336 at 349 where Jonathan Parker J noted that a substantial shareholder in a quasi-partnership who takes an active role in running the affairs of the company may constitute himself a de facto director; likewise, Hildyard J in *Secretary of State for Business, Innovation and Skills v Chohan* [2015] BCC 755 at [137]: a 100 per cent owner of a company is not insulated from potential liability as a de facto or shadow director by the expedient of purporting to rely on his influence as a shareholder if he is exercising powers usually reserved to a director or influencing and controlling those acting as directors.

[32] See *Secretary of State for Trade and Industry v Hollier* [2007] BCC 11 at [81] where Etherton J noted that this distinction is between someone who participates, or has the right to participate, in collective decision-making on corporate policy and strategy and its implementation, on the one hand, and others who may advise or act on behalf of, or otherwise for the benefit of, the company, but do not participate in decision-making as part of the corporate governance of the company. In that case, a son was not a de facto director when he acted out of a wish to assist his father in the family company, but without participating in strategic or policy decisions on a par with any other directors of the company, whereas another son was a de facto director for he did exercise real control and gave instructions over a wide range of the company's activities, even though equally motivated to help his father. See also *Re Hydrodam (Corby) Ltd* [1994] 2 BCLC 180 at 183.

[33] *Re Richborough Furniture Ltd* [1996] 1 BCLC 507 at 524; also *Re Mumtaz Properties Ltd, Wetton v Ahmedi* [2012] 2 BCLC 109 at [30]; and *Re UKLI Ltd, Secretary of State for Business, Innovation and Skills v Chohan* [2015] BCC 755 at [38].

[34] See *Re Paycheck Services 3 Ltd, Revenue and Customs Commissioners v Holland* [2011] 1 BCLC 141 at [82], where Lord Collins explores the history of the de facto classification and concludes that the concept was significantly expanded in the 1980s to impose some particular liability on persons never appointed when previously it had been used mainly in the context of defective appointments or purported appointments.

[35] See, for example, *Re Lo-Line Electric Motors Ltd* [1988] BCLC 698.

[36] See, for example, *Re Hydrodam (Corby) Ltd* [1994] 2 BCLC 180.

[37] See *Re Paycheck Services 3 Ltd, Revenue and Customs Commissioners v Holland* [2011] 1 BCLC 141; *Re Idessa Ltd, Burke v Morrison* [2012] 1 BCLC 80; *Primlake Ltd v Matthews Associates* [2007] 1 BCLC 666.

## Definitional issues

**7-13**  The Supreme Court confirmed in *Re Paycheck Services 3 Ltd, Revenue and Customs Commissioners v Holland*[38] that there is no single decisive test for determining whether someone is a de facto director, and indeed it is not necessary that the term 'de facto director' be given the same meaning in all of the different contexts in which a director may be liable.[39] In the context of the fiduciary duty of a director not to dispose wrongfully of the company's assets, the crucial question is whether the person assumed the office of director and with it the duties of a director.[40] All the relevant factors must be taken into account, including the purpose of the rule being applied.[41] The court may look, for example, at whether the director is the sole person directing the affairs of the company (or acting with others equally lacking in a valid appointment) or acting on an equal footing with other true directors in directing its affairs;[42] and whether there is a holding out by the company of the individual as a director and whether he used the title,[43] considering whether, taking all the circumstances into account, the individual is part of the corporate governing structure of the company.[44] Of course, most small companies do not have formal corporate governing structures and so there the court will look at the nature of the particular company and how its affairs are run and the individual's conduct in that regard and whether it amounts to assuming the office of director.[45]

**7-14**  In *Re Kaytech International plc, Secretary of State for Trade and Industry v Kaczer*,[46] for example, the Court of Appeal concluded that a person who was deeply and openly

---

[38] [2011] 1 BCLC 141. See Yap, 'De Facto Directors and Corporate Directorships' [2012] JBL 579.

[39] [2011] 1 BCLC 141 at [93], per Lord Collins, with whom Lords Hope and Saville agreed, at [43] and [100] respectively. See also *Re Mumtaz Properties Ltd, Wetton v Ahmed* [2012] 2 BCLC 109 at [32]; *Re Idessa Ltd, Burke v Morrison* [2012] 1 BCLC 80 at [37]; also *Secretary of State for Trade and Industry v Tjolle* [1998] 1 BCLC 333 at 343–4; *Re Kaytech International plc, Secretary of State for Trade and Industry v Kaczer* [1999] 2 BCLC 351 at 423.

[40] *Re Paycheck Services 3 Ltd, Revenue and Customs Commissioners v Holland* [2011] 1 BCLC 141 at [93] and Lord Hope at [39]; *Re Idessa Ltd, Burke v Morrison* [2012] 1 BCLC 80 at [37]; *Smithton Ltd v Naggar* [2014] BCC 482 at [28], [33]. See Millett J in *Re Hydrodam (Corby) Ltd* [1994] 2 BCLC 180 at 182: those who assume to act as directors and who thereby exercise the powers and discharge the functions of a director, whether validly appointed or not, must accept the responsibilities which are attached to the office.

[41] See *Re Paycheck Services 3 Ltd, Revenue and Customs Commissioners v Holland* [2011] 1 BCLC 141 at [39], [93]. See also Morse, 'Shadow and De Facto Directors in the Context of Proceedings for Disqualification on the Grounds of Unfitness and Wrongful Trading' in Rider (ed), *The Corporate Dimension* (1998).

[42] See *Re Richborough Furniture Ltd* [1996] 1 BCLC 507. An 'equality of footing' is not a requirement, it is merely one of the factors to be considered, as Hildyard J noted in *Secretary of State for Business, Innovation and Skills v Chohan* [2015] BCC 755, at [41], expressing a preference for a looser formulation as to whether the person has undertaken acts or functions such as to suggest that his remit to act in the management of the company is the same as if he were a de jure director. The suggestion in *Elsworth Ethanol Co Ltd v Hartley* [2015] 1 BCLC 221 that 'equal footing' is especially important, at [54], should be treated with caution.

[43] *Secretary of State for Trade and Industry v Tjolle* [1998] 1 BCLC 333, per Jacob J. Other factors considered by Jacob J, at 344, included whether the individual had proper information (e.g. management accounts) on which to base decisions; and whether the individual had to make major decisions. Initially, applying *Re Hydrodam (Corby) Ltd* [1994] 2 BCLC 180, 'holding out' was seen as an essential requirement, now it is merely one of the factors which the court will consider, see *Smithton Ltd v Naggar* [2014] BCC 482 at [53]; Noonan and Watson, n 30, at 605–8.

[44] *Re Paycheck Services 3 Ltd, Revenue and Customs Commissioners v Holland* [2011] 1 BCLC 141 at [90], [91], per Lord Collins, citing *Secretary of State for Trade and Industry v Tjolle* [1998] 1 BCLC 333 at 343–4; *Re Kaytech International plc, Secretary of State for Trade and Industry v Kaczer* [1999] 2 BCLC 351 at 423. See also *Re Mea Corporation Ltd, Secretary of State for Trade and Industry v Aviss* [2007] 1 BCLC 618 at [83]–[84]; *Secretary of State for Trade and Industry v Hollier* [2007] BCC 11 at [68].

[45] See *Mumtaz Properties Ltd, Wetton v Ahmed* [2012] 2 BCLC 109 at [46]–[47].

[46] [1999] 2 BCLC 351, CA.

involved in the company's affairs, who devoted himself to the company's financial and property interests, and who dealt with creditors, suppliers and the company's professional advisers, was not merely a consultant or company secretary but a de facto director. In *IRC v McEntaggart*[47] an undischarged bankrupt (and therefore someone automatically disqualified from being a director) who was described as the moving spirit within a construction company and whose role extended to matters such as negotiating and signing contracts, and who was involved in nearly all aspects of the management of the company's affairs, was a de facto director. In *Re Idessa Ltd, Burke v Morrison*[48] an individual who exercised real influence over the company's affairs and acted on an equal footing with the de jure director, and who had the same salary and access to the company's bank account, financial records, and payroll functions as the de jure director, and who was held out as a director in the company's business plan, could fairly be regarded as part of the company's corporate governance, however much he downplayed his role when giving evidence, and he was liable as a de facto director. In *Re Mumtaz Properties Ltd, Wetton v Ahmed*[49] a person who, within an informally run family business, dealt with suppliers and local authorities, who had a director's loan account on which he could make drawings for his personal benefit, and who the court found to be one of the nerve centres from which the company's activities radiated, was a de facto director. He was part of the corporate governance structure of the company and was jointly and severally liable with the other directors for the misapplication of the company's funds.

**7-15**    On the other hand, in *Secretary of State for Trade and Industry v Tjolle*,[50] the court concluded that a manager employed by a holiday company who had a variety of titles including 'sales and marketing director' and even, for a period, 'deputy managing director', who sometimes attended board meetings, but who was never involved in any financial matters and who had no access to the company accounts, was not a de facto director. Likewise, in *Gemma Ltd v Davies*[51] a wife with purely clerical functions who was not involved in decision-making and who had no real influence in the governance of the company was not a de facto director.

### Directors of corporate directors

**7-16**    As noted, the Supreme Court had the opportunity in *Re Paycheck Services 3 Ltd, Revenue and Customs Commissioners v Holland*[52] to consider some of the issues surrounding de facto directors. The central issue in the case was a narrow one of whether a director of a corporate director of a subject company could himself be a de facto director of the subject company.[53] The case was decided on a 3–2 ruling; Lords Hope and Collins, with whom Lord Saville agreed, delivered the majority ruling, but there is trenchant dissent from Lords Walker and Clarke.

---

[47] [2006] 1 BCLC 476. See also *Re Moorgate Metals Ltd* [1995] 1 BCLC 503.

[48] [2012] 1 BCLC 80, see at [35]–[40].    [49] [2012] 2 BCLC 109.

[50] [1998] 1 BCLC 333. See also *Re Red Label Fashions Ltd* [1999] BCC 308.

[51] [2008] 2 BCLC 281. See too *Re Neath Rugby Ltd, Hawkes v Cuddy* [2008] 1 BCLC 527 where a wife was the de jure director, but the court found she was a mere cipher for her husband such that all of her acts and omissions were his acts and omissions so, in those circumstances, he was a de facto director.

[52] [2011] 1 BCLC 141. See Watts, 'De Facto Directors' (2011) 127 LQR 162.

[53] See also *Secretary of State for Trade and Industry v Hall* [2009] BCC 190 (an individual may through his control of a corporate director constitute himself a de facto director of a subject company but whether or not he does so depends on what the individual procures the corporate director to do); also *Re Hydrodam (Corby) Ltd* [1994] 2 BCLC 180.

**7-17**  The facts were that a number of companies (the subject companies, 42 in total) had been set up to secure certain tax advantages. The subject companies declared dividends on a regular basis at the behest of their sole corporate director, Paycheck Directors Ltd, which in turn could only act through its director, Mr Holland.[54] The Revenue Commissioners wished to establish that Mr Holland was a de facto director of the subject companies (alongside the de jure corporate director) in order to sue him (under IA 1986, s 212, misfeasance procedure) for breach of fiduciary duty in misapplying subject company funds. The companies had paid dividends which turned out to be improper because inadequate provision had been made for corporation tax. The subject companies had gone into insolvent liquidation leaving the Revenue, as their sole creditor, owed in the region of £3.5m for unpaid corporation tax.

**7-18**  Agreeing with the Court of Appeal in refusing the Revenue's claim, Lord Hope based his judgment primarily on the need to respect the status of the corporate director as a separate legal entity. Decisions of the corporate director must be treated as such and not as decisions of the person or persons who individually or collectively are the directors of the corporate director. 'So long as the relevant acts are done by the individual entirely within the ambit of the discharge of his duties and responsibilities as a director of the corporate director, it is to that capacity that his acts must be attributed.'[55] Lord Collins considered that to impose fiduciary duties on Mr Holland as a de facto director of the subject companies when all his acts could be attributed in law to the corporate director would be an unjustifiable judicial extension of the concept of de facto director.[56] If he was to be a de facto director of the subject companies simply because he was the guiding mind behind their sole corporate director, then this would be so in the case of every company with a sole corporate director and would go beyond the law as it stands and, Lord Collins said, beyond the function of the court.[57] In the context of the fiduciary duty of a director not to dispose wrongfully of the company's assets, Lord Collins agreed that the crucial question is whether the person assumed the duties of a director.[58] That person must be part of the corporate governing structure and must have assumed a role in the company sufficient to impose on him a fiduciary duty to the company and to make him responsible for the misuse of its assets.[59] That was not the situation here. For the dissenters, Lords Walker and Clarke, the fact that Mr Holland was the only individual involved, that he took all the decisions as to the payment of the dividends that the corporate director purported to take and that he was the single guiding mind behind the corporate director meant that he was a de facto director of the subject companies as well as a de jure director of Paycheck Directors Ltd.[60] In their view, it was 'artificial and wrong' and 'arid formalism' to say that Holland was merely discharging his duties as a director of Paycheck Directors.[61] Lord

---

[54]  Strictly speaking the corporate director had two directors, Mr and Mrs Holland, but the case proceeded on the basis that Mr Holland was the sole director of the corporate director.

[55]  [2011] 1 BCLC 141 at [42] (Lord Hope), at [96] (Lord Collins), at [98] (Lord Saville), a view also taken by the Court of Appeal, see [2009] 2 BCLC 309.

[56]  [2011] 1 BCLC 141 at [54], the origins of which lie in defective appointments of directors.

[57]  [2011] 1 BCLC 141 at [96].

[58]  [2011] 1 BCLC 141 at [93], citing *Re Hydrodam (Corby) Ltd* [1994] 2 BCLC 180 at 183 and *Re Lo-Line Electric Motors Ltd* [1988] BCLC 698 at 707. See also *Re Idessa Ltd, Burke v Morrison* [2012] 1 BCLC 80 at [37]. See Watts, 'De facto Directorships' (2011) 127 LQR 162.          [59]  [2011] 1 BCLC 141 at [93]–[94].

[60]  [2011] 1 BCLC 141 at [115], per Lord Walker; at [129], per Lord Clarke.

[61]  [2011] 1 BCLC 141 at [115], per Lord Walker; at [142], per Lord Clarke. See Watts (2011) 127 LQR 162 at 163, 168 who criticises the minority for their willingness to apply a broad and undiscriminating fact-centred concept of de facto director which would have as a consequence that the individuals so classified would then be subject to the strict liability of directors with respect to the misapplication of company assets.

Collins rejected their approach noting that the use of corporate directors had been considered by Parliament which allows for their appointment and so, in his view, it is not for the courts to expand the category of de facto director and classify the individual directors (whether sole or multiple) of a corporate director as de facto directors of the subject companies.[62] As discussed earlier at **7-6**, the position from a date to be appointed is that corporate directors will be prohibited unless permitted by regulations to be made under CA 2006, s 156C.

**7-19**   In *Smithton Ltd v Naggar*[63] the Court of Appeal had an opportunity to revisit these issues. The company was a joint venture in financial services and N was the chairman of the majority shareholder, its parent company. He had significant business dealings with the company through connected parties and so was also a client of the company. The court at first instance rejected the claim that N was a de facto director concluding that the alleged conduct on his part was that to be expected from someone who was the chairman of the majority shareholder of the company and also a major client of the company and that he had in fact acted in that capacity. Dismissing an appeal, Arden LJ considered the nature of a de facto directorship and built upon the approach of Lord Collins in *Re Paycheck Services Ltd*[64] that the key issue is the assumption of office. She concluded that:[65]

- the question of whether someone is a de facto director is not to be approached by asking whether the individual performed acts which a director would normally do;
- it is not enough that the act in question could have been done by a director; the burden is on the claimant to establish that the individual did indeed do that act in that capacity—it is a question of the capacity in which that person was acting;
- the assessment of the capacity in which a person acts is one of fact and degree and context and is to be determined objectively, taking all the circumstances into account.

Arden LJ noted that the majority in *Re Paycheck Services 3 Ltd, Revenue and Customs Commissioners v Holland*[66] placed no weight on the fact that Mr Holland was involved in all the directorial decisions made on behalf of the subject companies, so that the volume of decisions which a person is said to have made as a de facto director will not have significance if those decisions were made in some other capacity.[67] In *Smithton Ltd v Naggar*[68] the individual in question had engaged in various discussions and decisions affecting the company, but that involvement was readily explicable on the basis of, and did not go beyond, his role as a client of the company or as chairman of the company's largest shareholder. He was not a de facto director.

## Liabilities of de facto directors

**7-20**   Whether a particular statutory provision which applies to a 'director' applies to a de facto director is a question of construction of the provision.[69] With respect to the general duties of directors in CA 2006, Pt 10, Ch 2, given that a de facto director is a person who has

---

[62] [2011] 1 BCLC 141 at [96].      [63] [2014] BCC 482, aff'g [2014] 1 BCLC 602.
[64] Especially [2011] 1 BCLC 141 at [93]–[96].      [65] [2014] BCC 482 at [34]–[45], also [66], [70].
[66] [2011] 1 BCLC 141.      [67] [2014] BCC 482 at [26].      [68] [2014] BCC 482 at [121], [125].
[69] See *Re Lo-Line Electric Motors Ltd* [1988] BCLC 698 at 706; *Dean v Hiesler* [1942] 2 All ER 340. De facto directors do fall within the disqualification provisions in the Company Directors Disqualification Act 1986 (*Re Lo-Line*); the IA 1986, s 214, wrongful trading (*Re Hydrodam (Corby) Ltd* [1994] 2 BCLC 180) and IA 1986, s 212, misfeasance (*Re Paycheck Services 3 Ltd, Revenue and Customs Commissioners v Holland* [2011] 1 BCLC 141).

assumed a role in the corporate governing structure of the company, it follows that a de facto director in addition to assuming the powers of the office has assumed the duties of the office.[70] In *Primlake Ltd v Matthews Associates*[71] a company had sold land with significant development potential and much of the purchase money found its way into the hands of an architect involved in the sale. On the company going into liquidation, the liquidators alleged that the architect was actually a de facto director of the company who had received the money (£800,000 approx) in breach of his duties to the company. The defendant argued that he was merely a consultant to the company assisting it in finding a purchaser for the land and that the sums received had been professional fees due for his services. The court found that the individual controlled the company and ran its entire business. He negotiated the crucial contracts and made all decisions, both tactical and strategic.[72] It was only for tax reasons, the court found, that he had not actually been appointed as a director. He was a de facto director and, the court held, in breach of duty by enriching himself at the expense of the company and liable accordingly.

## D  Shadow directors

**7-21**  A number of provisions in the Companies Act 2006, the Insolvency Act 1986 (IA 1986), and the Company Directors Disqualification Act 1986 (CDDA 1986), apply to a shadow director.[73] This category is used to extend the reach of those statutory provisions[74] to include individuals who are influential in the running of the company but who do not take up a formal position on the board, typically, in order to avoid potential liabilities, or because they are already disqualified from being a director,[75] or because they prefer the anonymity of remaining off the board. Despite the nomenclature, though the shadow director may indeed be 'lurking in the shadows', it is not an essential ingredient of the definition. In *Secretary of State for Trade and Industry v Deverell*,[76] Morritt LJ gives the example of the person resident abroad who owns all the shares but operates the company through a local board of directors. If such a person gives directions to the local board as to what to do, then though the person takes no steps to hide his part in the affairs of

---

[70] *Re Paycheck Services 3 Ltd, Revenue and Customs Commissioners v Holland* [2011] 1 BCLC 141 at [93]. See also *Statek Corp v Alford* [2008] BCC 266 at [107] (de facto director owed fiduciary duties in respect of company assets within his control); *Shepherds Investment Ltd v Walters* [2007] 2 BCLC 207 at [73]–[81] (de facto director in breach of the no-conflict duty in developing a competing business and exploiting and diverting business opportunities of the company for his own benefit). See also *Secretary of State for Trade and Industry v Elms* (16 January 1997, unreported) approved in *Secretary of State for Trade and Industry v Tjolle* [1998] 1 BCLC 333 at 343–4.     [71] [2007] 1 BCLC 666.

[72] [2007] 1 BCLC 666 at [311].

[73] See, for example, CA 2006, s 223; IA 1986, ss 6A, 206(3), 208, 210, 211, 214(7), 216, 249, Sch A1, paras 41(5), 42(3); CDDA 1986, ss 4(2), 6(3C), 8(1), 9E(5). The appointment of shadow directors must be notified to the registrar of companies under CA 2006, ss 162, 167; unsurprisingly, this rarely happens.

[74] See generally Noonan and Watson, 'The Nature of Shadow Directorship: Ad Hoc Statutory Intervention or Core Company Law Principle' [2006] JBL 763 esp at 781–2, who argue that the legislative intent is more far-reaching than merely extending the reach of certain statutory provisions as an anti-avoidance measure. Rather, in their view, the imposition of liabilities on shadow directors is a legislative reinforcement of the division of power within a company whereby shareholders should exercise control through the constitutional organs of the company and not by non-constitutional means, by usurping the powers of the board. The latest discussions by BIS, noted at **7-36**, on extending the definition of shadow directors and on imposing duties on shadow directors would support this view of the role played by the concept of 'shadow director'.

[75] A person may already be the subject of a disqualification order or undertaking under the CDDA 1986 and an undischarged bankrupt is automatically disqualified from acting as a company director save with the leave of the court: CDDA 1986, s 11.     [76] [2000] 2 BCLC 133 at [36].

the company, he may be a shadow director. In *Re Paycheck Services 3 Ltd, Revenue and Customs Commissioners v Holland*,[77] Lord Walker gives the example of the CEO of a holding company who openly gives instructions to the board of a subsidiary. In *Vivendi SA v Richard*[78] the person found to be a shadow director quite openly instructed the sole de jure director as to business matters and the de jure director relied on him, acted on his instructions, and gave effect to his decisions. The allegation that someone is a shadow director commonly arises in disqualification proceedings under the CDDA 1986 or wrongful trading claims under IA 1986, s 214, see Chapter 15.

### Definitional issues

**7-22**    A shadow director is defined in CA 2006, s 251(1) as a person in accordance with whose directions or instructions the directors of a company are accustomed to act,[79] but a person is not regarded as a shadow director by reason only that the directors act (a) on advice given by that person in a professional capacity; (b) in accordance with instructions, a direction, guidance, or advice given by that person in the exercise of a function conferred by or under an enactment; (c) in accordance with guidance or advice given by that person in that person's capacity as a Minister of the Crown (within the meaning of the Ministers of the Crown Act 1975).

**7-23**    A body corporate is not to be regarded as a shadow director of any of its subsidiary companies for certain purposes of the CA 2006[80] (including the general duties of directors) by reason only that the directors of the subsidiary are accustomed to act in accordance with its directions or instructions (s 215(3)). This exemption ensures that the parent company is not treated as a (shadow) director of its own subsidiary, owing duties to it under CA 2006, Ch 10, Parts 2, 4, and 6. Also, this exemption for the parent company does not extend to individual directors of the parent company who, depending on their conduct, may be shadow directors of a subsidiary company.[81]

**7-24**    The instructions given by a shadow director must be given to the de jure directors so as to affect their decisions as directors and not their decisions in some other capacity.[82] It is

---

[77] [2011] 1 BCLC 141 at [109].    [78] [2013] BCC 771 at [128]–[131].

[79] A one-off instruction or involvement is not sufficient and it is necessary to show a pattern of conduct in which the de jure director or directors are accustomed to act on the instructions of the alleged shadow director: *Secretary of State for Trade and Industry v Becker* [2003] 1 BCLC 555; *Ultraframe (UK) Ltd v Fielding* [2005] EWHC 1638 at [1270]–[1278]. See also *Re Unisoft Group Ltd (No 3)* [1994] 1 BCLC 609 at 620 where Harman J considered that 'accustomed to act' must refer to acts not on one individual occasion, but over a period of time and as a regular course of conduct.

[80] i.e. CA 2006, Pt 10, Ch 2 (general duties of directors); Ch 4 (transactions requiring members' approval); or Ch 6 (contract with sole member who is also a director) so a limited, but significant, range of provisions.

[81] This exemption for parent companies in CA 2006, s 251 is not contained in the equivalent definition of shadow director in IA 1986, s 251 and so for the purposes of those provisions of the IA 1986 which apply to shadow directors (such as wrongful trading liability under s 214, see *Re Hydrodam (Corby) Ltd* [1994] 2 BCLC 180 at 184), a parent company may be a shadow director if the requisite level of influence is present. For a misfeasance claim under IA 1986, s 212, the definition in CA 2006, s 251 will apply, presumably, as the Insolvency Act provision is merely procedural, if the cause of action is a breach of the substantive duties in the CA 2006. Likewise, this parent company exemption is not included in the CDDA 1986 definition of shadow director, see s 22(5); nor is there any parent company exemption in the definition of director in the Financial Services and Markets Act 2000, s 417(1), see text to n 122.

[82] See *Re Coroin Ltd (No 2)* [2012] EWHC 2343, [2013] 2 BCLC 583 at [594], [600]. In this case, it was alleged that a nominee director acted on instructions from his appointor when negotiating with other shareholders for the sale of their shares. David Richards J pointed out that, even if true, these allegations would be irrelevant to the question whether the appointor was a shadow director for the director's acts in the context of the sale negotiations were not acts in his capacity as a director.

sufficient if the majority of the board is accustomed to act on the directions of the shadow director and it is not necessary that all the directors should so act.[83]

**7-25** The statutory definition of a 'shadow director' was considered in detail by the Court of Appeal in *Secretary of State for Trade and Industry v Deverell*[84] where Morritt LJ set out a number of now much cited propositions elaborating on the statutory definition:[85]

'(1) The definition of a shadow director is to be construed in the normal way to give effect to the parliamentary intention ascertainable from the mischief to be dealt with and the words used …

(2) The purpose of the legislation is to identify those, other than professional advisers, with real influence in the corporate affairs of the company. But it is not necessary that such influence should be exercised over the whole field of its corporate activities …

(3) Whether any particular communication from the alleged shadow director, whether by words or conduct, is to be classified as a direction or instruction must be objectively ascertained by the court in the light of all the evidence. In that connection I do not accept that it is necessary to prove the understanding or expectation of either giver or receiver. In many, if not most, cases it will suffice to prove the communication and its consequence … Certainly the label attached by either or both parties then or thereafter cannot be more than a factor in considering whether the communication came within the statutory description of direction or instruction.

(4) Non-professional advice may come within that statutory description. The proviso excepting advice given in a professional capacity appears to assume that advice generally is or may be included. Moreover the concepts of "direction" and "instruction" do not exclude the concept of "advice" for all three share the common feature of "guidance".

(5) It will, no doubt, be sufficient to show that in the face of "directions or instructions" from the alleged shadow director the properly appointed directors or some of them cast themselves in a subservient role or surrendered their respective discretions. But I do not consider that it is necessary to do so in all cases. Such a requirement would be to put a gloss on the statutory requirement that the board are "accustomed to act in accordance with" such directions or instructions.'

**7-26** These criteria show the court moving away from a strict interpretation of the statutory definition to a more flexible one: the influence exerted need not be over all of the company's affairs; the 'directions and instructions' may blend into advice and guidance; and the de jure directors need not have surrendered their roles as long as they are accustomed to act etc.

**7-27** In *Deverell* the proceedings were disqualification proceedings against two individuals who claimed that they were consultants to the insolvent company and were not therefore directors or shadow directors in respect of whom disqualification proceedings could be brought. The court found that one was concerned at the most senior level and with most aspects of the direction of the company's affairs[86] while the other's involvement went far

---

[83] *Re Coroin Ltd (No 2)* [2012] EWHC 2343, [2013] 2 BCLC 583 at [594]; *Lord v Sinai Securities* Ltd [2005] 1 BCLC 295 at [27], *Ultraframe (UK) Ltd v Fielding* [2005] EWHC 1638 at [1272]; *Re Hydrodam Ltd* [1994] BCLC 180 at 183.  [84] [2000] 2 BCLC 133.

[85] [2000] 2 133 at 144–5. See Noonan and Watson, n 74, at 775–8 for critical commentary on these propositions.  [86] [2000] 2 BCLC 133 at 150.

beyond that of a consultant on matters directly affecting the company's financial affairs.[87] The court concluded that both individuals were shadow directors.[88]

**7-28**    In *Re Mea Corporation, Secretary of State for Trade and Industry v Aviss*[89] the evidence was that the two individuals in question (one of whom was the owner of the businesses) decided matters with regard to the recruitment of employees and the payments of creditors, they handled funding negotiations with the banks and tax matters with the Inland Revenue. The key allegation, as far as the court was concerned, was that they decided on the application within a group of companies of a group treasury policy which resulted in all companies remitting funds to the parent company which then determined how those funds were used and which creditors got paid. In particular, funds were paid to companies outside of the group in which one of the directors had a personal interest. Despite the protestations of the boards of companies in the group, this policy persisted which, the court said, showed the level of control exercised by these individuals. The court had no hesitation in finding that this ability to dictate policy in an area of corporate affairs as critical as the application of trading income and the payment of trade creditors made them shadow directors.[90] In *Vivendi SA v Richards*[91] the individual in question prepared the company's business plan, devised strategy, engaged with key advisers, looked for investments for the company (so looked somewhat like a de facto director) but primarily he was the person to whom the sole de jure director turned to, deferred to, and in accordance with whose directions and instructions the de jure director was accustomed to act, hence he was a shadow director.

**7-29**    Clearly, a controlling shareholder is potentially at risk of being classified as a shadow director, if they act vis-à-vis the de jure directors (by directions or instructions) in a way which brings them within the criteria outlined earlier, including that the board or a majority of the board must be accustomed to act on those directions or instructions.[92] The mere fact of nomination, even of a majority of the board, does not result in the appointor becoming a shadow director, however, unless they direct or instruct as required by the statutory definition.[93] Likewise with regard to the company's creditors, their demands of the company may look like 'directions or instructions' and the board may appear to be accustomed to act on those demands, but it may equally merely be a case of enforcement by the creditors of their contractual rights.[94]

---

[87] [2000] 2 BCLC 133 at 153.

[88] Arguably, one of the defendants, given his level of involvement with the actual conduct of the company's affairs, should more accurately have been classified as a de facto director rather than a shadow director, see **7-11**. See Noonan and Watson, n 74 at 773, who make the point that this reasoning might have been a result of a desire on the court's part to ensure that these individuals were disqualified—the Secretary of State had not claimed they were de facto directors. Equally, it might be the type of case which now would be said to involve a person acting sometimes as a de facto director and sometimes as a shadow director, see *Secretary of State for Business, Innovation and Skills v Chohan* [2015] BCC 755.

[89] [2007] 1 BCLC 618.    [90] [2007] 1 BCLC 618 at [106].    [91] [2013] BCC 771 at [127]–[131].

[92] Subject to the limited parent company exception in CA 2006, s 215(3). *Vivendi SA v Richards* [2013] BCC 771; *Re Mea Corporation, Secretary of State for Trade and Industry v Aviss* [2007] 1 BCLC 618 are examples of controlling shareholders being found to be shadow directors. See also *Secretary of State for Trade and Industry v Jones* [1999] BCC 336 at 349. As already discussed, shareholders are at risk also of being a de facto director if their conduct brings them within the definition of a de facto director. The point well made by Noonan and Watson, n 74, is that the liability is deserved, since the shareholders in these instances have chosen to ignore the constitutional division of power between board and shareholders.

[93] See *Re Coroin Ltd (No 2)* [2012] EWHC 2343, [2013] 2 BCLC 583 at [600].

[94] See also *Re PFTZM Ltd, Jourdain v Paul* [1995] 2 BCLC 354 at 367, the mere exercise of rights as a secured creditor is insufficient; also *Re a Company No 005009 of 1987, ex p Copp* [1989] BCLC 13 at 21, a claim against the company's bankers later 'rightly' abandoned ([1990] BCLC 324 at 326). See Morse, 'Shadow and De Facto Directors in the Context of Proceedings for Disqualification on the Grounds of Unfitness and Wrongful Trading' in Rider (ed), *The Corporate Dimension* (1998).

In *Ultraframe (UK) Ltd v Fielding*[95] Lewison J noted that a creditor is entitled to protect his own interests as creditor without necessarily becoming a shadow director, and even if the board feel they have little practical choice other than to accede to the requests of a creditor, that means the creditor has influence, but it does not necessarily mean that he has become a shadow director. If creditors were to find that their enforcement of their contractual rights (which may be extensive) gives rise to a shadow directorship, that could have a chilling effect on lending which would be unsatisfactory and something which the courts are likely to have in mind when faced with an allegation that a creditor is a shadow director. An Australian authority of interest on this point is *Buzzle Operations v Apple Computer*[96] where at first instance and on appeal the court declined to find a creditor to be a shadow director, though closely involved in dealings with the company and its management. Hodgson JA made the point that, while the directors in such a case may on many occasions act in accordance with the instructions or wishes of the creditor, they do so because they have reached their own decision that it is in the interests of the company.[97]

**7-30**   While the categories of de facto and shadow director might have been seen initially as mutually exclusive,[98] the distinction between the categories has been eroded with the common element being that the courts are looking to identify those with real influence in the corporate affairs of the company.[99] Usually both categories will not be relevant,[100] but it is conceptually possible for a person to be both a de facto and a shadow director, certainly consecutively, and even simultaneously, as where a person assumes 'the functions of a director as regards one part of the company's activities (say, marketing) and gives directions to the board as regards another (say, manufacturing and finance) so constituting him a de facto and a shadow director at the same time'.[101] For example, in *Secretary of State for Business, Innovation and Skills v Chohan*[102] the court considered that the defendant, C, had been both a de facto and a shadow director. As Hildyard J put it, 'his involvement and influence were consistent, but the manner of its exercise was changeable' so when C was directly involved in the company making certain financial decisions (loans to third parties, paying dividends), he was acting as a de facto director; in other instances where he was exercising real influence in the management of the company (sending instructions by email from abroad), he was a shadow director.[103]

---

[95]   [2005] EWHC 1638 at [1267] and [1268].

[96]   (2011) 82 ACSR 703, CA, NSW, aff'g (2010) 77 ACSR 410.      [97]   (2011) 82 ACSR 703 at [9].

[98]   See Millett J in *Re Hydrodam (Corby) Ltd* [1994] 2 BCLC 180 at 183.

[99]   *Re Paycheck Services 3 Ltd, Revenue and Customs Commissioners v Holland* [2011] 1 BCLC 141 at [91], per Lord Collins, who makes the point that the distinction is impossible to maintain with the extension of the concept of de facto director from the 1980s onwards as a mechanism for imposing liability on those assuming the office, and see at [110], per Lord Walker ('… not the case that the concepts of de facto and shadow director are fundamentally different …'); also at [127], per Lord Clarke. See *Re Kaytech International plc, Secretary of State for Trade and Industry v Kaczer* [1999] 2 BCLC 351 at 424, CA; *Secretary of State for Trade and Industry v Hollier* [2007] BCC 11 at 27. See Noonan and Watson, n 74, who are critical of this approach which they argue does not sufficiently acknowledge the differing characteristics and purposes of the differing concepts of de facto and shadow directors, de facto directors having assumed the position whereas shadow directors usurp the decision-making functions of the board.

[100]   See, for example, *Secretary of State for Trade and Industry v Becker* [2003] 1 BCLC 555 at 564–5; *Re Kaytech International plc* [1999] 2 BCLC 351 at 424.

[101]   See *Re Mea Corporation Ltd, Secretary of State for Trade and Industry v Aviss* [2007] 1 BCLC 618 at [89], per Lewison J; *Re Paycheck Services 3 Ltd, Revenue and Customs Commissioners v Holland* [2011] 1 BCLC 141 at [127], per Lord Clarke.      [102]   [2015] BCC 755.

[103]   [2015] BCC 755 at [49].

Nevertheless, as David Richards J pointed out in *Re Coroin Ltd, McKillen v Misland (Cyprus) Investments Ltd:*[104]

> 'None of these authorities suggests that there is not a real distinction between de facto and shadow directors, nor would it be proper to do so given the distinction drawn by the Companies Act. The fact, as Lord Collins observed in [*Re Paycheck Services Ltd*], that the distinction has been eroded does not mean that it has disappeared. For the most part, it remains. The fact that persons in both categories will have a real influence in the corporate governance of the company does not mean that it need only be shown that a person has such influence for him to be both a de facto and a shadow director.'

**7-31**   At a functional level, a de facto director situation typically involves the exercise of powers usually reserved to a director as they assume the office and a shadow director situation typically involves the exercise of influence and control over those acting as directors.[105]

### Liabilities of shadow directors

**7-32**   A real distinction between de facto and shadow directors exists with respect to statutory liability, given that shadow directors are liable only if a statutory provision is specifically extended to them, as is often the case. More particularly, this raises an issue as to whether shadow directors are subject to common law fiduciary duties and, now, whether they are subject to the general duties applicable to directors under CA 2006, Pt 10, Ch 2 (ss 171–180).

### Fiduciary duties of shadow directors

**7-33**   The position at common law is the subject of a number of somewhat ambiguous first instance authorities. In *Yukong Line of Korea Ltd v Rendsburg Corp Investment*[106] Toulson J held that the defendant was a shadow director and in clear breach of fiduciary duty to the company when he arranged for the transfer of the contents of the company's bank account to a third party (owned by the director) immediately following the company's wrongful repudiation of a charterparty, so putting the funds out of reach of the company's creditors. Toulson J found specifically that the defendant controlled the company's activities, he was the only person involved in running the company,[107] and he was its sole beneficial owner, so it is not surprising that he should have been found to be a fiduciary. Arguably, a modern analysis would be that he was a de facto director rather than a shadow director, having assumed the office and exercised the powers of a director, rather than someone instructing the directors as to how to act. Having assumed the office and dealt with the company's assets, the fiduciary duty would follow, see 7-20. In *Ultraframe (UK) Ltd v Fielding*[108] Lewison J did not think that it did necessarily follow from the fact that someone fell within the statutory definition of shadow director that it would be right to impose on him the same fiduciary duties as are owed by a de jure or de facto director. In his view, the indirect influence exerted by a paradigm shadow director who did not

---

[104]   [2012] EWHC 521 at [34].
[105]   See Hildyard J in *Secretary of State for Business, Innovation and Skills v Chohan* [2015] BCC 755 at [137].
[106]   [1998] 2 BCLC 485 at 502.
[107]   There were two de jure directors, but they appear to have been complete figureheads living in another country and with limited contact with the shadow director who negotiated and signed and repudiated the charterparty and transferred the bank funds.           [108]   [2005] EWHC 1638.

directly deal with, or claim the right to deal directly with, the company's assets would not usually be sufficient to impose fiduciary duties upon him.[109] But he went on to say that someone with access to the company's assets, for example, a signatory to the company's bank account, is subject to a fiduciary duty to use it only for the benefit of the person to whom the account belongs, while noting that this did not mean that wider fiduciary duties are imposed. Having said that, in *Re Mea Corporation Ltd, Secretary of State for Trade and Industry v Aviss*[110] Lewison J seems to have assumed that a shadow director owed a duty to act in the company's interests, though on the facts the persons identified as shadow directors there might as easily have been classed as de facto directors. Most recently, the matter came before Newey J in *Vivendi SA v Richards*[111] where he considered that Lewison J in *Ultraframe* had understated the extent to which shadow directors owe fiduciary duties. The allegations in this case centred on the withdrawal of company funds (£10m) by the de jure director and a shadow director at a time when the company was in significant financial difficulties. As assuming to act in relation to the property or affairs of another can attract fiduciary duties, Newey J considered that a shadow director would normally owe a fiduciary duty of good faith (or loyalty) and could reasonably be expected to act in the company's interests rather than his own interests when giving directions and instructions.[112] He reached this conclusion for a number of reasons including that a shadow director will have assumed to act in relation to the company's affairs and to ask the de jure directors to exercise powers that exist exclusively for the benefit of the company so he must accept responsibility at least as regards the directions or instructions which he gives. He also considered that a shadow director's role in a company's affairs may be every bit as important as that of a de facto director and de facto directors are considered to owe fiduciary duties, see **7-20**, and that public policy, so far as it may matter, points towards fiduciary duties being imposed on shadow directors.[113]

**7-34**    On the facts in *Vivendi SA v Richards*, as the de jure director and the shadow director were trying dishonestly to extract the company's remaining cash before it collapsed and, thus, to thwart the company's creditors, the court found each to be in breach of the fiduciary duty to have regard to creditors' interests at a time when the company was doubtfully solvent (CA 2006, s 172(3)).[114] Support for the 'penetrating and convincing analysis' of Newey J followed in *R v R*[115] where the President of the Family Division, Munby LJ, endorsed his approach, albeit only in interlocutory proceedings. As a result, in *R v R*, the court restrained a divorcing husband (a shadow director of the family business which he had run with his wife) from competing with that business as, on Newey J's analysis, a shadow director owed a fiduciary duty to avoid a conflict between his personal interests and the company's interests. On this basis, the fiduciary obligations have been extended beyond duties owed when giving directions or instructions. The Court of Appeal has been more cautious, pointing out, also in interlocutory proceedings, that the law is not entirely settled as to the circumstances in which a shadow director owes fiduciary duties.[116]

---

[109] [2005] EWHC 1638 at [1289]. Noonan and Watson, n 74, argue that shadow directors should be liable to the same extent as the directors they instruct so, if the instruction makes the director liable for breach of duty, the shadow director should have a secondary liability in respect of that breach. See also **7-37**.

[110] [2007] 1 BCLC 618 at [109]–[110]. See also Toulson J in *Yukong Line of Korea Ltd v Rendsburg Corp Investment* [1998] 2 BCLC 485 at 502.                                    [111] [2013] BCC 771 at [143].

[112] [2013] BCC 771 at [141], [142].

[113] [2013] BCC 771 at [142]. Newey J also considered that there was a compelling analogy with company promoters who owe fiduciary duties as a result of their acceptance and use of powers 'which so greatly affect the interests of the corporation'.                                    [114] [2013] BCC 771 at [157], [165], [178].

[115] [2013] EWHC 4244 (Fam).             [116] See *Sukhoruchkin v Van Bekestein* [2014] EWCA Civ 399 at [41].

**7-35**   It is not surprising that there is movement in favour of extending fiduciary duties in this way, given that, post-*Deverill*, the distinction between de facto and shadow directors has been eroded, as discussed at **7-30**, so that it is difficult to sustain an argument that only de facto directors should be subject to fiduciary duties.

### Application of statutory duties

**7-36**   With regard to the general duties of directors, CA 2006, s 170(5) provides, with effect from 26 May 2015, that the general duties imposed on directors by CA 2006, Pt 10, Ch 2, apply to shadow directors where and to the extent that they are capable of so applying.[117] The Secretary of State may also by regulations make provision about the application of the general duties of directors to shadow directors.[118] BIS has not yet indicated what approach it intends to take, whether all of the duties will apply or only some, and whether they will apply in all circumstances or only with respect to the directions or instructions given by them. Statutory support for imposing fiduciary duties can be found in s 260 which allows for derivative claims against directors and in s 260(5)(b) provides that, for the purposes of those provisions, 'a shadow director is treated as a director'. A shadow director is therefore someone against whom a derivative claim for negligence, default, breach of duty or breach of trust can be brought so it would be odd if a shadow director is not subject to any duties in the first place.[119] There are other statutory inconsistencies. For example, the IA 1986, s 212 (misfeasance) does not extend to shadow directors,[120] but ss 214 and 246ZB (wrongful trading)[121] do, as does s 216 (prohibited names). The Financial Services and Markets Act 2000 does not use the term 'shadow director', but defines 'director' in relation to a body corporate as including a person in accordance with whose directions or instructions (not being advice given in a professional capacity) the directors of a body corporate are accustomed to act (s 417).[122] In this way, shadow directors are swept into, and subject to, all of the provisions of that Act which apply to a director, a technique which could have been used in the CA 2006.[123]

**7-37**   Finally, it is possible to disqualify a person who exercises influence over an individual director and so does not fall within the definition of a shadow director. If the individual

---

[117] As substituted by the Small Business, Enterprise and Employment Act 2015, s 89(1). BIS considered that there are advantages to an explicit application of the general duties to shadow directors, not least to remove any potential lack of accountability, see BIS, *Transparency & Trust: Enhancing the Transparency of UK Company Ownership and Increasing Trust in UK Business, Government Response* (April 2014), BIS/14/672, para 198. See also Witney, 'Duties Owed by Shadow Directors' [2016] JBL 311.

[118] Small Business, Enterprise and Employment Act 2015, s 89(2).

[119] If a shadow director is to be subject to these duties, they should also have the protection, such as it is, of CA 2006, s 1157 (discussed at **14-79**), but that section, as currently drafted, does not extend to shadow directors.

[120] Though it does apply to those who, not being an officer of the company, have been concerned in or have taken part in the promotion, formation, or management of the company: IA 1986, s 212(1)(c).

[121] Yet there is a considerable overlap between wrongful trading and breaches of CA 2006, s 172(3) and s 174 and hence misfeasance claims, see for example, *Roberts v Frohlich* [2011] 2 BCLC 625. IA 1986, s 213 (fraudulent trading) applies to 'any person'.

[122] There is no exemption for parent companies, unlike in CA 2006, s 251.

[123] See De Lacy, 'The Concept of a Company Director: Time for a New, Expanded And Unified Statutory Concept' [2006] JBL 267 who argued for this approach in the 2006 Act; and more recently, Griffin, 'Confusion Surrounding the Characteristics, Identification and Liability of a Shadow Director' [2011] Insolv Intel 44. See also the Australian Corporations Act 2001, s 9 which defines director as including de facto and shadow directors so all the provisions applicable to directors apply across all the categories, unless the context indicates otherwise; likewise the New Zealand Companies Act 1993, s 126 applies all of the duties of directors to shadow directors.

director, called the main transgressor, is disqualified as unfit under CDDA 1986, s 6, and this other person has exercised the requisite amount of influence over the main transgressor, then that person too may be disqualified (CDDA 1986, s 8ZA(1)).[124] The requisite amount of influence exists if any of the conduct for which the main transgressor is disqualified is the result of the main transgressor acting in accordance with the person's directions or instructions (CDDA 1986, s 8ZA(2)), subject to an exclusion where the main transgressor acts on advice given by the person in a professional capacity.

## E Remuneration of directors

**7-38** Executive directors, at least in public companies and larger private companies, typically have a service contract with the company covering such matters as their remuneration, the duration of the appointment, and the amount of compensation payable in the event of dismissal. In public listed companies, controversy over such contracts and, in particular, over the remuneration and compensation packages contained within them, has been a central issue in the corporate governance debate, as discussed at **6-42** et seq. In smaller private companies, the directors may not have express service contracts, relying instead on more informal arrangements, but this practice should be avoided as it can be a source of subsequent disputes.[125] Non-executive directors are typically appointed on the basis of a formal letter of appointment, especially in larger companies, and this too is a formal contractual document.

**7-39** In the absence of a contract, a director cannot rely on the articles as constituting a contract between himself and the company,[126] although it may be possible for a director to pursue a claim to recover payment on the basis of an implied extrinsic contract.[127] Exceptionally, a director may attempt to claim on a *quantum meruit* basis for services rendered and accepted by the company,[128] or on the basis of an equitable allowance,[129] but the courts are reluctant to allow such claims by directors.[130]

**7-40** The mere holding of office by itself does not entitle a director to remuneration,[131] but the articles invariably provide, as the model articles do, that the directors are entitled to such remuneration as the directors determine both for their services as directors (i.e. for

---

[124] With effect from 1 October 2015; equivalent provision is made where the main transgressor is disqualified under CDDA 1986, s 8 (unfitness following investigation): see s 8ZE.

[125] See, for example, *Lloyd v Casey* [2002] 1 BCLC 454.

[126] *Hickman v Kent or Romney Marsh Sheepbreeders Association* [1915] 1 Ch 881: see discussion at **5-57**.

[127] See *Re New British Iron Co, ex p Beckwick* [1898] 1 Ch 234.

[128] *Currencies Direct Ltd v Ellis* [2002] 2 BCLC 482, CA; *Craven-Ellis v Canons Ltd* [1936] 2 KB 403; but there is no scope for a *quantum meruit* claim by a director when the articles have already made express provision for special remuneration for a director: *Guinness plc v Saunders* [1990] 1 All ER 652, HL; see also *Re PV Solar Solutions Ltd* [2018] 1 BCLC 58 at [255]–[259] where the court notes that neither *Craven-Ellis v Canons* nor *Currencies Direct v Ellis* are strong foundations for a *quantum meruit* award and that *Guinness v Saunders* makes it clear that a *quantum meruit* should not be allowed in the case of a de jure director.

[129] See *Boardman v Phipps* [1967] 2 AC 46.

[130] The position on *quantum meruit* and equitable allowance claims was restrictively stated in *Guinness plc v Saunders* [1990] 1 All ER 652, HL. Directors are precluded from contracting with their companies for their services except in the circumstances authorised by the articles of association; likewise there should be no remuneration for their services except as provided by the articles of association. To allow otherwise might encourage fiduciaries to put themselves in a position where there is a conflict between their personal interest and their duties as fiduciaries; and see *Cobbetts LLP v Hodge* [2010] 1 BCLC 30 at [118].

[131] *Hutton v West Cork Rly Co Ltd* (1883) 23 Ch D 654.

holding the office) and for any other services (i.e. as executive or non-executive directors) which they undertake.[132] Allowing the directors to determine their own remuneration gives rise to an obvious conflict of interest.[133] In larger public companies, the matter is managed by delegating the issue to a remuneration committee composed exclusively of non-executive directors, as is recommended by the UK Corporate Governance Code (see discussion at **6-42**). Quoted companies must draw up a detailed directors' remuneration report and shareholder approval is required of the company's remuneration policy and of the implementation of that policy in any given financial year (CA 2006, s 439 and 439A), see **18-45**. Payments to directors (including payments for loss of office) must be consistent with the approved remuneration policy or be approved by a resolution of the members (CA 2006, s 226B), see **13-20**.

**7-41**   Where remuneration is paid, the court does not concern itself with the quantum of that remuneration and does not attempt to compare the market value of the services rendered with the amount of remuneration actually paid.[134] The court must be satisfied that the payment is genuinely remuneration, however, and not a sham transaction masking an improper return of capital to the shareholders.[135] Equally, as the Court of Appeal noted in *Currencies Direct Ltd v Ellis*,[136] there is no requirement that there is a specific agreement fixing the level or rate of remuneration or defining a formula for ascertaining a definite amount to be paid. Remuneration is consideration for work done or to be done and it may be paid in an infinite variety of ways and not necessarily to the person providing the consideration.[137] Excessive payments at a time when the company is in financial difficulties may be challenged by a liquidator[138] and such payments are often relied on as evidence of unfitness in disqualification proceedings (see **15-93**).

**7-42**   Long-term service contracts (essentially where the period of notice is longer than two years) require shareholder approval, subject to certain exceptions (see **13-8**), as do payments for loss of office in certain circumstances (see **13-11**).

---

[132]   See The Companies (Model Articles) Regulations 2008, SI 2008/3229, reg 2, Sch 1, art 19 (Ltd); reg 4, Sch 3, art 23 (Plc). Equally the general meeting may resolve to pay a director for the mere holding of office, even if he undertakes no specific duties: *Re Halt Garage (1964) Ltd* [1982] 3 All ER 1016. If the articles require a specific body to determine the remuneration and the correct body has not done so, the director has no claim for payment under the articles: *Guinness plc v Saunders* [1990] 1 All ER 652, HL.

[133]   See, for example, *Re Blue Index Ltd* [2014] EWHC 2680 at [42] et seq where the court considered a quasi-partnership where two of the directors determined their own remuneration which was drawn by them without formality and then ratified when they approved the accounts at the end of the year. Given their obvious conflict of interests, their failure to consult the minority shareholder, or to take professional advice as to the appropriate level of remuneration, the directors were in breach of their fiduciary duty in failing to consider the company's interests when determining the remuneration.

[134]   See *Re Halt Garage (1964) Ltd* [1982] 3 All ER 1016 at 1039, per Dillon J: '... assuming that the sum is bona fide voted to be paid as remuneration, it seems to me that the amount ... must be a matter of management for the company to determine in accordance with its constitution which expressly authorises payment for directors' services'. But, where in the context of an unfairly prejudicial claim an allegation is made of excessive remuneration, the court must determine whether the amount drawn was appropriate, applying 'objective commercial criteria', and within the bracket that executives with those responsibilities and duties would expect to receive: *Irvine v Irvine (No 1)* [2007] 1 BCLC 349 at [268], [270]; and see Arden LJ in *Re Tobian Properties Ltd, Maidment v Attwood* [2013] 2 BCLC 567 at [36].

[135]   *Re Halt Garage (1964) Ltd* [1982] 3 All ER 1016.        [136]   [2002] 2 BCLC 482.

[137]   [2002] 2 BCLC 482 at [20].

[138]   For example, under IA 1986, s 212 (misfeasance); see *Re Halt Garage (1964) Ltd* [1982] 3 All ER 1016.

# F Termination of appointment

## Removal from office

**7-43**   A company may by ordinary resolution at a meeting remove a director before the expiration of his period of office, notwithstanding anything in any agreement between him and the company (CA 2006, s 168(1)).[139] It is also common for the articles to allow for all of the directors acting together to give notice to a director to vacate office.[140] There are a number of practical considerations which the company must bear in mind, however, before exercising this power of removal.

**7-44**   A particular issue is the amount of damages which may be payable to a dismissed director as the statutory power to remove a director does not deprive a person removed under it of compensation or damages payable in respect of the termination of his appointment as director or of any appointment terminating with that as director (CA 2006, s 168(5)). Compensation for loss of office is discussed at **13-11**.

**7-45**   In smaller private companies, exercise of the power of removal may trigger a petition by the sacked director who is also a shareholder, under CA 2006, s 994, alleging that his removal from the board amounts to unfairly prejudicial conduct (see **19-60**). A director in this type of company can protect himself to some extent against the possibility of removal by the inclusion of a provision in the articles entitling the director, as a shareholder, to weighted votes on any resolution to remove him from the board, a practice permitted by the House of Lords in *Bushell v Faith*.[141] In that case, the articles of the company provided that on a resolution to remove a particular director, his shares would carry three times the number of votes they normally carried. As a consequence, it was impossible for the other shareholders to pass the required ordinary resolution to remove him. Ungoed-Thomas J at first instance refused to permit the practice saying that it made a mockery of the Act, but the Court of Appeal and the House of Lords approved it[142] and it remains a valid method of entrenchment for directors.

## Retirement

**7-46**   The model articles for public companies provide for the retirement of all the directors at the first annual general meeting and for the rotation of directors thereafter with a selected number retiring each year, although they remain eligible for re-election.[143]

---

[139]   A written resolution may not be used: CA 2006, s 288(2)(a). At least 28 days' notice of the resolution must be given and the director concerned is entitled to be heard at the meeting where it is proposed to remove him and to have representations circulated to the shareholders, subject to certain constraints: s 169. The power to remove a director under this provision does not derogate from any power to do so by any other method: s 168(5)(b), such as a provision in the articles allowing for the removal of a director by resolution of the board.

[140]   See *Jackson v Dear* [2014] 1 BCLC 186; directors when exercising such a power must do so in good faith in the interests of the company; and see n 146.          [141]   [1970] 1 All ER 53, HL.

[142]   See [1970] 1 All ER 53 at 57, per Upjohn LJ: 'Parliament has never sought to fetter the right of a company to issue shares with such rights or restrictions as it thinks fit.'

[143]   See The Companies (Model Articles) Regulations 2008, SI 2008/3229, reg 4, Sch 3, art 21 (Plc). Private companies commonly dispense with rotation hence there is no provision for rotation in the model articles for private companies.

### Resignation

**7-47**  A director may resign at any time by notice to the company and he will cease to be a director in accordance with the terms of that notice.[144]

### Vacating office

**7-48**  A person ceases to be a director in the event of the occurrence of various events specified in the articles including, for example, on being prohibited by law from being a director or a bankruptcy order being made.[145] It is common to include a provision that a person ceases to be a director if he is requested in writing to resign by all his co-directors.[146]

### Disqualification from office

**7-49**  The Company Directors Disqualification Act 1986 provides for a variety of grounds on which a person may be disqualified from being a director of a company. In practice almost all disqualification orders or undertakings are made under CDDA 1986, s 6 (unfit directors of insolvent companies).[147] A disqualification order or undertaking means that, for a specified period, a person may not be a director of a company, act as receiver of a company's property, or in any way, whether directly or indirectly, be concerned or take part in the promotion, formation, or management of a company unless (in each case) he has the leave of the court (CDDA 1986, s 1).[148] Disqualification is considered in Chapter 15.

---

[144] See The Companies (Model Articles) Regulations 2008, SI 2008/3229, reg 2, Sch 1, art 18(f) (Ltd); reg 4, Sch 3, art 22(f) (Plc).

[145] See The Companies (Model Articles) Regulations 2008, SI 2008/3229, reg 2, Sch 1, art 18(a), (b) (Ltd); reg 4, Sch 3, art 22(a), (b) (Plc).

[146] Such a provision is effective and the office is vacated on the service of the notice even if the directors making the request act for an ulterior motive: *Lee v Chou Wen Hsien* [1985] BCLC 45 where the PC declined to reinstate the ousted director.

[147] In 16–17, 1366 disqualification orders or undertakings were secured overall, of which 1105 were under CDDA 1986, s 6 (unfit directors): *Companies House Management Information 2016–17*, Table 6.

[148] See also The Companies (Model Articles) Regulations 2008, SI 2008/3229, reg 2, Sch 1, art 18(a) (Ltd), reg 4, Sch 3, art 22 (Plc) which provide that a director ceases to be a director as soon as he is prohibited from being a director by law.

# 8

# A statutory statement of directors' duties

## A Introduction

**8-1** One of the most important changes implemented by the CA 2006 is the inclusion for the first time of a statutory statement of directors' general duties in Pt 10, Ch 2. The background to this change was a recommendation in 1996 from the Law Commission, following a review of directors' duties, that there should be a statement of the principal duties, but without any alteration to them.[1] From the outset, the Company Law Review (CLR) indicated that it regarded the case for a legislative statement of the general duties of directors as clearly made out.[2] It set aside concerns from the legal profession that such a statement would restrict the development of the law; would create uncertainty while the 'new' duties are interpreted by the courts; would encourage the courts to second-guess business decisions; and would be of little assistance to the lay director who would still need advice as to the nature of the obligations imposed.[3]

**8-2** The CLR considered that a legislative statement was important for three main reasons:[4] on grounds of clarity and accessibility; to enable the law to be updated to reflect modern business practices, especially on conflicts of interest; and to address what the CLR called the 'scope' issue, i.e. in whose interests companies should be run. The CLR's clear intention was to modernise and alter the law and not merely to replicate the current position in a statutory statement. Accordingly, it recommended a full codification of directors' duties replacing the corresponding equitable and common law rules.[5]

## B The statutory statement

**8-3** The statutory statement of the general duties is set out in CA 2006, Pt 10, Ch 2 which provides for the following duties of directors:

---

[1] See Law Commission, *Company Directors: Regulating Conflicts of Interests and Formulating a Statement of Duties* (Law Comm No 261), (Cm 4436, 1999), para 4.36 and the draft statement of principles set out in Appendix A to that Report; preceded by a consultation paper of the same name, Consultation Paper No 153 (1998), Pt 13 of which surveys previous proposals for a statutory statement of directors' duties.

[2] See Company Law Review, *Developing the Framework* (2000), paras 3.14–3.19; also *Completing the Structure* (2000), paras 3.6, 3.11–3.31; *Final Report*, vol 1 (2001), paras 3.5–3.11.

[3] See Law Society Company Law Committee, *Company Law Review—Developing the Framework* Memorandum No 401 (August 2000), pp 1–22; also Memorandum No 412 (February 2001); Company Law Review, *Completing the Structure* (2000), para 3.6 (the Review noted 'we do not find these objections convincing').

[4] Company Law Review, *Final Report*, vol 1 (2001), para 3.7.

[5] See Company Law Review, *Final Report*, vol 1 (2001), paras 3.9–3.10.

- duty to act within their powers (s 171);
- duty to promote the success of the company (s 172);
- duty to exercise independent judgement (s 173);
- duty to exercise reasonable care, skill, and diligence (s 174);
- duty to avoid conflicts of interest (s 175);
- duty not to accept benefits from third parties (s 176);
- duty to declare interest in proposed transactions with the company (s 177).

**8-4**    The general duties are owed by a director which includes a de jure director (i.e. one formally appointed to the office) and a de facto director where a person has assumed a role in the corporate governing structure sufficient to impose those obligations on him[6] (see **7-20**). For shadow directors, s 170(5), as substituted, provides that the general duties apply to a shadow director of a company where and to the extent that they are capable of so applying[7] and the Secretary of State may by regulations make provision about the application of the general duties in ss 171–177 to shadow directors, see **7-36**. For the avoidance of doubt, s 170(2) ensures that, in certain circumstances, former directors remain subject to ss 175 and 176 as to the post-resignation exploitation of property, information, or opportunity (see **12-33**) and the receipt of benefits from third parties (see **12-68**).

**8-5**    The duties are cumulative so, except as otherwise provided, more than one of the general duties may apply in any given case (s 179). For example, while directors might be able and willing to authorise a conflict of interest under s 175(4)(b), they also have to bear in mind their duty under s 172 to promote the success of the company. An exercise of the duty of care, skill, and diligence (s 174) will often overlap with the need to exercise independent judgement (s 173). The duty to exercise powers for the purposes for which they are conferred (s 171(b)) will overlap with the duty to promote the success of the company (s 172) and the need to act in accordance with the constitution (s 171(a)). There is quite a degree of overlap between the provisions in ss 175, 176, and 177 dealing with conflicts of interest and regard must be had also to s 182 which is not part of the general duties at all. The precise inter-relationship of the statutory duties is something which will emerge in the case law over time. The relationship with other provisions must also be taken into account such as s 232(4) (provisions in articles dealing with conflicts of interest), s 239 (ratification of acts of directors), and Pt 10, Ch 4, ss 188–226 which deal with specific conflicts of interests. The statement of duties in CA 2006, Pt 10, Ch 2 may contain only 12 sections, but they are complex statements of the law far removed from the type of accessible statement of duties which the Law Commission originally envisaged[8] and which the CLR had asserted would be one of the main advantages of a statutory statement.[9]

**8-6**    The statement of duties in CA 2006, Pt 10, Ch 2 is also not exhaustive. It merely sets out the general duties and directors are subject to various other duties including statutory duties under the CA 2006 itself (such as the duty to maintain accounting records and prepare accounts, ss 386, 394), duties under the IA 1986, and duties under the general law

---

[6] See *Re Paycheck Services 3 Ltd, Revenue and Customs Commissioners v Holland* [2011] 1 BCLC 141 at [93]; and see **7-20**, n 70, and the authorities cited there.

[7] Substituted by the Small Business, Enterprise and Employment Act 2015, s 89(1), with effect from 26 May 2015.

[8] See Law Commission Report, n 1, Appendix A.

[9] See generally Aherne, 'Directors' Duties, Dry Ink and the Accessibility Agenda' (2012) 128 LQR 114.

such as employment law or health and safety legislation. In *Goldtrail Travel Ltd v Aydin*[10] the court accepted that the long-recognised claim to recover trust assets—directors are trustees from the outset of the company's assets and liable to make good assets which they have misapplied upon the same footing as if they were trustees, applying *Re Lands Allotment Co*[11]—need not be pleaded as a distinct breach of a particular duty within CA 2006, ss 171–177, though clearly any misapplication of corporate assets in breach of duty is capable of being brought within ss 171(b), 172, and 175.

**8-7**  The statement does not set out the remedies for breach of duty. The Government was unable to draft a satisfactory statutory codification of the myriad remedies available for breach of fiduciary duty (and note the statutory statement does not describe the duties as fiduciary duties, see **14-11**, so even that point is unclear) and so limited itself to stating in CA 2006, s 178 that breach of the statutory duties attracts the same remedies as breach of the corresponding common law or equitable rules.

**8-8**  The relationship between the statutory statement and the pre-existing law on directors' duties is addressed in CA 2006, s 170(3) and (4) which state:

'(3)  The general duties are based on certain common law rules and equitable principles as they apply in relation to directors and have effect in place of those rules and principles as regards the duties owed to a company by a director.

(4)  The general duties shall be interpreted and applied in the same way as common law rules or equitable principles, and regard shall be had to the corresponding common law rules and equitable principles in interpreting and applying the general duties.'

**8-9**  On the one hand, CA 2006, s 170(3) states that these provisions apply 'in place of' the old rules so, applying the usual rules of statutory interpretation, existing case law on the 'old' law should no longer be relevant and the starting point should be to interpret the language of the statute.[12] On the other hand, section 170(4) states that the general duties are to be interpreted and applied in the same way as common law or equitable principles and regard is to be had to the corresponding common law rules and equitable principles in interpreting and applying the general duties.[13]

**8-10**  Some of the provisions clearly do state the corresponding common law or equitable principle or at least something quite close to it. For example, the director's duty to exercise his powers for the purposes for which they are conferred (CA 2006, s 171) is a positive statement of the common law prohibition on exercising powers for a collateral purpose. The duty to exercise care, skill, and diligence in s 174 is identical to what was the existing common law duty of care and skill. Some of the provisions are modified versions of the common law and equitable principles. For example, the duty to act bona fide in the interests of the company has been restated in s 172 as a duty to promote the success of the company. Other duties have been modified in application, most notably the no-conflict duty which now allows independent directors to authorise profit-making by directors in a situation of a conflict of interest (s 175(4)(b)).

---

[10] [2015] 1 BCLC 89 at [65].      [11] [1894] 1 Ch 616 at 631, 638.

[12]  See *Bank of England v Vagliano Brothers* [1891] AC 107 at 144–5, per Lord Herschell.

[13]  For example in *Premier Waste Management Ltd v Towers* [2012] 1 BCLC 67, though the case predated the coming into force of the Companies Act 2006, Mummery LJ noted, at [3]–[6], that the statutory provisions extract and express the essence of the equitable principles which they replace and, in a case such as this one, a director profiting from his position, the relevant statutory provisions would be ss 172, 175, and 176.

**8-11**  The issue of the relationship between CA 2006, s 170(3) and (4) was considered at length in the Parliamentary debates before the Solicitor General was moved to comment as follows:[14]

> '[T]he courts should continue to refer to existing case law on the corresponding common law rules and equitable principles, *except where it is obviously irreconcilable with the statutory statement* [emphasis added]. The rich body of case law on and wisdom about the general duties may continue to be used—no one would benefit from abandoning the wisdom accumulated over several centuries—we do not propose to lose that.'

**8-12**  In practice, there has been an entirely pragmatic judicial response to the position. As the Solicitor General had noted, no one wants to lose the accumulated wisdom of the common law and the courts are anxious not to create unnecessary uncertainty in an area as commercially important as directors' duties. The development of directors' duties in an incremental fashion has continued as before, save that development is now based on a statutory framework.

## C  Duties owed to the company

**8-13**  Directors owe their general duties to the company and not to the shareholders, individually or collectively,[15] nor do they owe any duties directly to the company's creditors, individually or collectively.[16] This common law principle[17] is expressed in CA 2006, s 170(1). It follows that enforcement of the general duties is a matter for the company, a point which the Government was keen to emphasise in the Parliamentary debates whenever concerns were expressed that the inclusion of a statutory statement exposed directors to a greater risk of being sued, particularly in the light of the introduction of the statutory derivative claim in CA 2006, Pt 11 (see Chapter 20).

**8-14**  An application of the principle can be seen in *Peskin v Anderson*.[18] A dispute arose out of the sale by the Royal Automobile Club Ltd (RACL) of its motoring services business which essentially resulted in the shareholders in RACL receiving £34,000 each in respect of the sale. The claimants were all former shareholders whose membership had ceased before the sale and so they did not receive any part of the benefits flowing from the sale. They brought an action against the directors of RACL claiming damages for breach of fiduciary duty by the directors in failing to disclose to the shareholders the proposals relating to the sale of the business. The Court of Appeal dismissed the claim for directors do not, solely by virtue of the office of director, owe fiduciary duties to the shareholders, collectively or individually.

---

[14] HC Debs, Session 2005–06, Standing Committee D, column 536 (6 July 2006). See also *Burns v Financial Conduct Authority* [2017] EWCA Civ 2140 at [65].

[15] Not even if appointed as the nominee of a particular shareholder or class of shareholders: *Scottish Co-operative Wholesale Society Ltd v Meyer* [1958] 3 All ER 66, HL; *Boulting v ACTT* [1963] 1 All ER 716, CA; *Re Neath Rugby Ltd (No 2), Hawkes v Cuddy* [2009] 2 BCLC 427. As to nominee directors, see **10-17**.

[16] *Multinational Gas and Petrochemical Co v Multinational Gas and Petrochemical Services Ltd* [1983] 2 All ER 563; *Yukong Line Ltd of Korea v Rendsburg Investments Corp of Liberia* [1998] 2 BCLC 485. Where a company owes fiduciary obligations to a client or joint venturer, it is possible for a director of the company also personally to owe fiduciary obligations to that client or joint venturer: see *Satnam Investment Ltd v Dunlop Heywood & Co Ltd* [1999] 1 BCLC 385, CA; *JD Wetherspoon plc v Van de Berg & Co Ltd* [2007] PNLR 28, Ch D; *Ross River Ltd v Waveley Commercial Ltd* [2014] 1 BCLC 545, CA.

[17] See *Percival v Wright* [1902] 2 Ch 421.          [18] [2001] 1 BCLC 372.

**8-15** The shareholders may specifically appoint the directors as their agents in any matter, of course, in which case the directors will owe them the fiduciary duties arising from that agency relationship.[19] Directors may also find themselves liable to shareholders under ordinary legal principles, for example in misrepresentation, if they give misleading advice or abuse their position.[20] Liability issues under this heading may be an issue in the context of takeovers where shareholders rely on the advice of the directors as to the merits of any bid before them. Where a takeover bid has been made, the directors must give sufficient information to the shareholders and refrain from misleading them.[21] In the case of competing bids, the directors must do nothing to prevent the shareholders from choosing to take the best price,[22] but the courts do not accept that the board must inevitably be under a positive duty to recommend and take all steps within its power to facilitate whichever is the highest offer.[23] If directors take it on themselves to give advice to current shareholders, they have a duty to advise in good faith and not fraudulently and not to mislead, whether deliberately or carelessly.[24] If a director misrepresents the financial position of the company so as to induce the shareholders to transfer their shares to him for a nominal consideration, he is liable in damages for negligent misrepresentation in the usual way.[25]

**8-16** Exceptionally the courts may consider that the relationships within the company do give rise to fiduciary duties as between the directors and their shareholders. The leading authority is *Coleman v Myers*,[26] a decision of the New Zealand Court of Appeal which has been cited with approval by the English courts. In this case, the court held that the directors did owe fiduciary duties to the shareholders including a duty not to mislead them on the sale of their shares. The court thought the fiduciary obligation arose from the nature of the relationships within this family company where the minority shareholders habitually looked to the directors for guidance on matters affecting their interests.[27]

**8-17** The approach in *Coleman v Myers* was endorsed in *Re Chez Nico (Restaurants) Ltd*[28] by Browne-Wilkinson V-C who agreed that fiduciary duties can arise between the directors and the shareholders which might include a duty of disclosure where directors are purchasing shares in the company from shareholders.

**8-18** In *Peskin v Anderson*,[29] noted at **8-14**, the claimants failed to establish that the directors owed duties to the shareholders so the claimants attempted to argue in the alternative that their circumstances brought them within the *Coleman v Myers* qualification, i.e. that special circumstances existed which brought the directors into a fiduciary relationship with the shareholders. The Court of Appeal agreed that a fiduciary duty may be owed by a director to a shareholder personally where a special factual relationship exists between the parties in the particular case. As Mummery LJ noted, events may take place which

---

[19] *Allen v Hyatt* (1914) 30 TLR 444; *Briess v Woolley* [1954] 1 All ER 909. See for example *Parks of Hamilton Holdings Ltd v Campbell* [2014] CSIH 36, [2014] SC 726, where a managing director and shareholder in a company agreed to act as agent for all the shareholders in selling their shares to a purchaser so placing himself in a fiduciary relationship with them and thus in breach of his fiduciary duties when he negotiated additional profits for himself on the sale of the shares.

[20] *Gething v Kilner* [1972] 1 All ER 1166; *Dawson International plc v Coats Paton plc* [1989] BCLC 233, CS (OH); *Platt v Platt* [2001] 1 BCLC 698.

[21] *Re a Company* [1986] BCLC 382; *Gething v Kilner* [1972] 1 All ER 1166.

[22] *Heron International Ltd v Lord Grade* [1983] BCLC 244.      [23] *Re a Company* [1986] BCLC 382.

[24] *Dawson International plc v Coats Paton plc* [1989] BCLC 233, CS (OH).

[25] See *Platt v Platt* [2001] 1 BCLC 698, CA.      [26] [1977] 2 NZLR 225.

[27] See also the interesting decision of the New South Wales Court of Appeal in *Brunninghausen v Glavanics* (1999) 46 NSWLR 538, noted Goddard (2000) 116 LQR 197.

[28] [1992] BCLC 192 at 208.      [29] [2001] 1 BCLC 372.

bring a director into direct and close contact with the shareholders in a manner capable of generating fiduciary obligations.[30] On the facts in *Peskin*, however, the court found that there were no relevant dealings, negotiations, communications, or other contact directly between the directors and the shareholders. The actions of the directors had not caused the shareholders to leave the company when they did. Most important of all, prior to being approached by a bidder for the business, there was nothing sufficiently concrete and specific, either in existence or in contemplation, for the directors to disclose to the shareholders.[31] The court concluded that there was nothing special in the factual relationship between the directors and the shareholders to give rise to a fiduciary duty of disclosure.[32]

**8-19** The issue of directors' duties to shareholders arose recently in *Sharp v Blank*[33] where Nugee J usefully reviewed all of the authorities before concluding:

> 'I take it therefore to be established law, binding on me, that although a director of a company can owe fiduciary duties to the company's shareholders, he does not do so by the mere fact of being a director, but only where there is on the facts of the particular case a "special relationship" between the director and the shareholders. It seems to me to follow that this special relationship must be something over and above the usual relationship that any director of a company has with its shareholders. It is not enough that the director, as a director, has more knowledge of the company's affairs than the shareholders have: since they direct and control the company's affairs this will almost inevitably be the case. Nor is it enough that the actions of the directors will have the potential to affect the shareholders—again this will always, or almost always, be the case. On the decided cases the sort of relationship that has given rise to a fiduciary duty has been where there has been some personal relationship or particular dealing or transaction between them.'

The case concerned the ill-fated acquisition by Lloyds Bank of HBOS and the pleadings included an allegation that the directors of Lloyds owed fiduciary duties to the Lloyds shareholders and acted in breach of those duties when they recommended the acquisition to the shareholders as being in their best interests. On an application to strike out this part of the pleadings, the court found a plea of breach of fiduciary duty to be unsustainable. There was no special relationship with the shareholders and the directors had not accepted to act for or on their behalf in any extended sense.

---

[30] [2001] 1 BCLC 372 at 379.    [31] [2001] 1 BCLC 372 at 384.

[32] [2001] 1 BCLC 372 at 384. See also *Platt v Platt* [1999] 2 BCLC 745 where, at first instance, the court was prepared to find that a fiduciary relationship had arisen between a director and two shareholders (his brothers). The director had acquired their shareholdings on the basis of a misrepresentation and, the court found, in breach of a fiduciary duty owed to them. The Court of Appeal confirmed the finding as to a liability in misrepresentation, but expressly declined to comment on the correctness of the finding of a breach of a fiduciary duty: see [2001] 1 BCLC 698.

[33] [2017] BCC 187 at [12].

# 9

# Duty to act within constitution and powers

## A Introduction

'A director of a company must—

(a)  act in accordance with the company's constitution, and

(b)  only exercise powers for the purposes for which they are conferred.' (CA 2006, s 171)

**9-1**  At common law the equivalent obligation was stated in terms of a duty to act bona fide in the interests of the company and a requirement for directors to exercise their powers for a proper purpose and not for any collateral (i.e. personal or sectional) purpose. The CA 2006 splits that duty into distinct obligations: to act in accordance with the constitution (defined s 257 and see **5-8**) and to exercise powers for the purposes for which they are conferred in s 171 and to act to promote the success of the company in s 172. This demarcation clarifies the elements of these obligations, but there remains a degree of overlap between them, as we shall see. This chapter concentrates on s 171 while s 172 is discussed in Chapter 10.

**9-2**  Turning to the distinct components of CA 2006, s 171. First, s 171(a) is concerned with ensuring that the directors respect the division of power agreed within the company as between the shareholders and the directors. As we shall see, the typical division of power is that, subject to the articles and any directions given by the shareholders by special resolution,[1] the directors are 'responsible for the management of the company's business for which purpose they may exercise all the powers of the company'.[2] The issues under s 171(a) are the scope of the authority given to the directors by the constitution (see **5-8** as to the definition) and the implications, internally and externally, when they ignore or breach the terms of that mandate, whether collectively or individually.

**9-3**  Secondly, CA 2006, s 171(b) sets out the duty to exercise powers for the purposes for which they are conferred, i.e. to promote the success of the company and not, say, to advance the personal interests of a director or directors. In the past it was considered that the issue of an abuse of authority by the exercise of a power for an improper purpose was distinct from the agency issue presented by an absence of authority,[3] but it is now clear, as is

---

[1]  See The Companies (Model Articles) Regulations 2008, SI 2008/3229, reg 2, Sch 1, art 4 (Ltd); reg 4, Sch 3, art 4 (Plc).

[2]  See The Companies (Model Articles) Regulations 2008, SI 2008/3229, reg 2, Sch 1, art 3 (Ltd); reg 4, Sch 3, art 3 (Plc).

[3]  See Millett J in *Macmillan Inc v Bishopsgate Investment Trust plc (No 3)* [1995] 3 All ER 747 at 753, relying on *Bowstead on Agency*, but the *Bowstead* position on this has changed, see *Bowstead and Reynolds on Agency* (21st edn, 2017), para 3-011: 'It is implicit in conferral of authority that the principal intends the agent to exercise the relevant powers in the interests of the principal. An agent who deliberately or recklessly exercises powers against the interests of the principal must know that he acts without his principal's consent, and therefore acts without authority.'

discussed in detail later, and as s 171 implicitly acknowledges, that the two issues are more directly intertwined.[4] The issues under s 171(b) include determining whether a power has been exercised for an improper purpose and the implications, internally and externally, of such an abuse of power.

**9-4**    The overall picture is complex but progress is being made to a more coherent framework based solidly on agency law.[5] A lack of authority and the exercise of authority for an improper purpose are distinct issues as CA 2006, s 171 makes clear, but there is considerable overlap between them with each problem being addressed in much the same way (as a matter of agency law), bringing much needed coherence to this important aspect of directors' duties. Unfortunately, the opportunity was not taken in the CA 2006 to expressly state that framework nor indeed to address some of the recognised uncertainties with regard to the scope of CA 2006, s 40 which, as we shall see at **9-28**, has an important role to play in terms of protecting third parties against any want of authority on the part of the directors.

## B  The constitutional division of power within a company

### Authority conferred

**9-5**    Before considering problems of a want of authority, it is necessary to consider the authority normally conferred by the constitution (as defined in CA 2006, s 257). As determined by the Court of Appeal in *Automatic Self-Cleansing Filter Syndicate Co Ltd v Cuninghame*,[6] the relationship between a board and the shareholders is a contractual relationship based on the articles which determine the extent of the management powers conferred on the board. The model articles provide (and this provision is common to practically all companies) that 'subject to the articles, the directors are responsible for the management of the company's business for which purpose they may exercise all the powers of the company',[7] but the shareholders may by special resolution direct the directors to take, or refrain from taking, specified action.[8] Also, as the division of power is 'subject to the articles',

---

[4] See *Criterion Properties plc v Stratford UK Properties LLC* [2006] 1 BCLC 729, HL; also the valuable analysis of these issues in Payne and Prentice, 'Company Contracts and Vitiating Factors: Developments in the Law on Directors' Authority' [2005] LMCLQ 447. Payne and Prentice go on to comment (at 455) that 'the distinction between an act being an abuse of authority and one being in excess of authority is wafer thin, but nevertheless they are conceptually distinct and explicit in [CA 1985] s 35A (now CA 2006, s 40). That provision addresses a want of authority, not an abuse of power, but as an abuse of power gives rise to a want of authority, the overlap is clear': see **9-19**.

[5] See *Criterion Properties plc v Stratford UK Properties LLC* [2006] 1 BCLC 729, HL; and Payne and Prentice, n 4.

[6] [1906] 2 Ch 34, CA; *Gramophone and Typewriter Ltd v Stanley* [1908] 2 KB 89 at 98, CA; *Salmon v Quin & Axtens Ltd* [1909] 1 Ch 311, CA; aff'd sub nom *Quin & Axtens Ltd v Salmon* [1909] AC 442, HL; *Howard Smith Ltd v Ampol Petroleum Ltd* [1974] AC 821 at 837, PC; see also *Breckland Group Holdings Ltd v London & Suffolk Properties Ltd* [1989] BCLC 100.

[7] See The Companies (Model Articles) Regulations 2008, SI 2008/3229, reg 2, Sch 1, art 3 (Ltd); reg 4, Sch 3, art 3 (Plc). In turn the directors may delegate any of the powers conferred on them to any committee or any director or any other person, as they think fit: art 5 (Ltd); art 5 (Plc). The extent of the delegated powers will depend on the terms of the delegation, but also on the implied authority arising from the office held, see *Smith v Butler* [2012] BCC 645 at [36]; also *Mitchell & Hobbs (UK) Ltd v Mill* [1996] 2 BCLC 102; externally, a third party may be able to rely on the appearance of authority, see discussion at **9-16**.

[8] See The Companies (Model Articles) Regulations 2008, SI 2008/3229, reg 2, Sch 1, art 4 (Ltd); reg 4, Sch 3, art 4 (Plc).

the articles may allow for matters to be determined by the shareholders by an ordinary resolution. Shareholders do have a common law residual power of management, but this exceptional power only arises if the board is unable to act,[9] or is deadlocked, or for all practical purposes has ceased to exist.[10] The shareholders may resolve the situation by appointing another director and, once a functioning board is in operation, the powers of management revert to it. In addition to the powers granted to the board by the articles, the statute in many cases confers powers on the directors.

**9-6**   The division of power is predominantly in favour of the board then at the expense of the shareholders and the CA 2006 has shifted the balance further in favour of the board. The CA 1985 permitted certain corporate actions when authorised by the shareholders by resolution or by the articles (such as an allotment of shares (CA 1985, s 80), or purchase of the company's own shares (CA 1985, s 162)), but the position regarding these matters under the CA 2006 is that the company (and therefore the directors in the exercise of their management powers) has the particular power unless prohibited by the articles. In other words, now there must be a positive decision via the articles to subject a power to shareholder control, otherwise the power vests in the directors. For example, a company has power to purchase its own shares unless restricted by the articles (CA 2006, s 690) and the directors of a private company with one class of shares (which is almost invariably the case) have the power to allot shares unless prohibited by the articles (s 550).

**9-7**   Some matters are reserved for the shareholders by statute, such as the right to amend the articles (CA 2006, s 21), to reduce the share capital[11] (s 641), and to petition for a voluntary winding up (IA 1986, s 84(1)(b)). As noted at **9-5**, the delegation of power to the directors is also subject to the articles and to any directions given, on an ad hoc basis, by way of a special resolution.[12] Constraints which might be imposed via the articles might include monetary limits on powers to borrow, or a requirement for the consent of named directors to the exercise of a particular power,[13] or constraints in the form of procedural requirements, for example with respect to the calling of meetings, quorum requirements, or procedures for the execution of documents. If the directors ignore a requirement of the articles, a shareholder cannot force compliance unless the article in question confers a right on the shareholder qua member, see discussion at **5-60**, though if the shareholder knew of the matter in advance, the shareholder may seek injunctive relief. On the other hand, any director who fails to act in accordance with the constitution is in breach of s 171(a) so potentially at risk of a claim by the company or a derivative claim by a shareholder (subject to the permission of the court) for breach of duty. In this way, a balance is achieved, the business of the company is not disrupted by numerous personal claims by individual shareholders, but in an egregious case the possibility exists of a claim for breach of duty and that possibility deters directors from casually ignoring requirements of the constitution. In smaller companies, the preference will be for redress via a petition alleging unfairly prejudicial conduct under CA 2006, 994.

**9-8**   There are other constraints too. As discussed in Chapter 5, companies may restrict their objects under the CA 2006, s 31 and companies formed under previous legislation may

---

   [9] *Foster v Foster* [1916] 1 Ch 532.       [10] *Barron v Potter* [1914] 1 Ch 895.

   [11] A reduction must be confirmed, however, by the court or supported by a solvency statement by the directors, see CA 2006, s 641(1).

   [12] See The Companies (Model Articles) Regulations 2008, SI 2008/3229, reg 2, Sch 1, art 4 (Ltd); reg 4, Sch 3, art 4 (Plc). Giving directions on an ad hoc basis tends to be difficult because shareholders lack the necessary information to intervene at an early stage and typically only find out about events after they have occurred.

   [13] See *Quin & Axtens Ltd v Salmon* [1909] 1 Ch 311, CA, aff'd [1909] AC 442, HL.

choose to retain their objects clauses in the articles. In either case, the objects act as a constraint on directors' authority (third parties are protected against issues of lack of capacity by s 39). The articles also normally confer on the shareholders a power to appoint directors though the directors usually also have a power to appoint.[14] If the company is a listed company, the Listing Rules require shareholder approval of certain transactions,[15] as do CA 2006, Pt 10, Ch 4 (discussed in Chapter 13) and Ch 4A, with shareholders in quoted companies having a binding vote on the directors' remuneration policy (s 439A) and an advisory vote on its implementation (s 439). Most crucially, the shareholders have power to remove a director (s 168) and the shareholders retain ultimate control of the company through their ability to sell their shares to new owners.[16]

**9-9**    The division of power is not entirely one-sided, then, but even so, the practical position is that all the powers of the company are vested in the directors, though with considerable variation in practices within companies and as between the largest public companies and the small private company.

**9-10**    In a small private company, a formal division of power between the directors and the shareholders is often meaningless as they are frequently the same individuals acting as shareholders and as directors without differentiating particularly between those capacities. This reality is recognised by the CA 2006 which dispenses with many of the formal decision-making mechanisms which otherwise operate. For example, private companies need not hold an annual general meeting (AGM) of shareholders, unless they want to, while public companies must hold an AGM (CA 2006, s 336). The expectation is that, in a private company, many if not all decisions will be taken by written resolution rather than through formal meetings (see s 281). To that end, the procedures for written resolutions have been modified and, in particular, the requirement for unanimity dropped (ss 282(2), 283(2)). In their day-to-day activities, these companies are untroubled by any formal division of responsibilities between the directors and the shareholders. Nevertheless, even in such companies, it is important for the persons involved to appreciate their respective roles as directors and as shareholders because of the consequences which may attach to failing to act in the way required by the relevant capacity. For example, directors are subject to fiduciary duties which do not apply to shareholders. Equally, on occasion a decision may need to be taken or a transaction authorised by the shareholders rather than the directors, for example on an alteration of the articles (s 21) or approval of a substantial property transaction in which a director has an interest (s 190).

**9-11**    In large private and public companies, on the other hand, there is a distinct division of power and responsibility between the board of directors and the shareholders with all powers of management firmly vested in the board. The board's role in practice is supervisory rather than managerial with extensive powers delegated to individual directors and to professional executive managers operating just below board level, a group largely ignored by the legal structure.[17] The issue in these companies is trying to ensure shareholder engagement so that the shareholders act as an effective counterbalance to

---

[14]  See The Companies (Model Articles) Regulations 2008, SI 2008/3229, reg 2, Sch 1, art 17 (Ltd); reg 4, Sch 3, art 20 (Plc). In the case of a public company, a director appointed by the directors must retire at the next annual general meeting, though he may be reappointed: art 21(2)(a) (Plc).

[15]  See FCA, *Listing Rules*, LR 10 Significant transactions.

[16]  See *Howard Smith Ltd v Ampol Petroleum Ltd* [1974] AC 821 at 837–8.

[17]  See Berle and Means, *The Modern Corporation and Private Property* (1932); Eisenberg, *The Structure of the Corporation* (1976); Parkinson, *Corporate Power and Responsibility* (1993), Ch 2.

all powerful directors. As discussed in Chapter 6, shareholders have increased rights in terms of controlling and influencing the conduct of business at general meetings and listed companies, in particular, are expected to engage fully with their major shareholders, whatever the strict legal division of powers.

## C **Types of authority**

### **Actual authority**

**9-12**   Actual authority may be express or implied actual authority. As noted at **9-5**, the directors collectively have extensive actual authority. For an individual director, express actual authority arises from an explicit conferring of authority on a director which would typically be recorded in the board minutes. Implied actual authority arises from the position which the individual holds. For example, if an individual is appointed as a managing director, implied authority authorises him to do all such things as fall within the usual scope of that office.[18] In *Hely-Hutchinson v Brayhead Ltd*[19] the chairman of the company also acted as its de facto managing director.[20] He entered into contracts on the company's behalf on his own initiative and subsequently reported them to the board which acquiesced in this practice. Later the board refused to honour certain undertakings which the director had given. He had agreed that the company would indemnify the plaintiff in respect of loans which the plaintiff made to a business in which the company was interested. The Court of Appeal found that the director lacked express actual authority and he had no implied actual authority as the office of chairman did not carry authority to enter into contracts without the sanction of the board. As de facto managing director, however, he did have implied actual authority. This authority would be implied from the circumstance that the board by its conduct over many months had acquiesced in his acting as managing director and committing the company to contracts without the necessity of sanction from the board.[21] It followed that the company was bound by the indemnities which he had given to the plaintiff.[22]

**9-13**   It is clear that a managing director or, in modern terminology, a chief executive officer (CEO), by virtue of his position has actual or apparent authority co-extensive with the power of the board to manage the business. It is likely that the courts would also consider a finance director, or chief financial officer (CFO), certainly in a large company, to have extensive authority, actual and apparent, with respect to matters within the usual scope of the office of a finance director.[23] These individual directors by virtue of their management positions are seen as having extensive authority to bind the company. The position

---

[18]   *Hely-Hutchinson v Brayhead Ltd* [1967] 3 All ER 98, CA; *Hopkins v TL Dallas Group Ltd* [2005] 1 BCLC 543. *Smith v Butler* [2012] BCC 645 at [28] (implied authority is subject to the articles and any express agreements—on the facts, the managing director did not have implied authority to dismiss the executive chairman of the board).          [19]   [1967] 3 All ER 98, CA.

[20]   As to de facto directors, see **7-11**.          [21]   [1967] 3 All ER 98 at 103, CA.

[22]   The plaintiff was also one of the directors of Brayhead so there was a further issue in the case that the plaintiff had not disclosed his interest in the (indemnity) transaction with the company in breach of what is now CA 2006, s 177, see **12-75**. As discussed, the indemnity transaction turned out to be authorised and therefore binding on Brayhead whereas the non-disclosure rendered the transaction voidable. However, all the parties conceded that too much time had elapsed to allow for rescission and therefore Brayhead had lost the right to avoid the transaction.

[23]   See *Harold Holdsworth & Co v Caddies* [1955] 1 All ER 725.

is different with respect to the company chairman, for his main responsibility is running the board, not running the business of the company,[24] so his actual authority to bind the company is limited, likewise his apparent authority. Beyond the CEO and CFO offices, individual directors will have such actual authority as is delegated to them expressly and such implied actual authority as arises from any position they hold as an executive director, i.e. they are impliedly authorised to do such things as fall within the usual scope of that executive office.[25] They may have considerable apparent authority also, as is discussed later.

**9-14**    There is then a hierarchy of authority where the board has the greatest actual and apparent authority to manage the business, with CEOs and CFOs having extensive authority in respect of matters within the usual scope of their offices. Individual directors as such may have the least express actual authority to bind the company, though they have implied actual authority consistent with the scope of their office and, possibly, apparent authority.

**9-15**    The limits to actual authority were succinctly expressed by the court in *Re Capitol Films Ltd, Rubin v Cobalt Pictures Ltd*:[26]

> '[I]t is implicit that a director of a company only has actual authority to act in a manner which is in the interests of his company. If he acts in a manner which is contrary to the interests of his company, his actions will be without authority, and the agreement which he purports to make will not bind the company unless the third party can rely upon the doctrine of apparent authority.'

### Apparent authority

**9-16**    Apparent (or ostensible) authority is the authority of an agent as it appears to others[27] and it can operate to enlarge actual authority or to create authority where no actual authority exists.[28] Its use in the company context is primarily to provide authorisation for the individual director who does not hold one of the executive posts (such as CEO or CFO) which the law recognises as conferring considerable actual authority, as discussed earlier, and so has no or limited actual authority to bind the company on the basis of the position which he holds.[29] The leading authority is *Freeman and Lockyer v Buckhurst Park Properties (Mangal) Ltd*[30] where the director in question managed the company's property and acted on its behalf. The board had been aware of his conduct and had acquiesced in it. In that role the director employed the plaintiff architects to draw up plans for the development of land held by the company. The development ultimately collapsed and the plaintiffs sued the company for their fees. The company denied that the director had any authority to employ the architects. The court found that, while he had never been appointed managing director (and therefore had no actual authority, express or implied), the company

---

[24] See the UK Corporate Governance Code (2014), A.2, and **6-27**.
[25] *Hely-Hutchinson v Brayhead Ltd* [1967] 3 All ER 98.
[26] [2011] 2 BCLC 359 at [53], per Richard Snowden QC, sitting as a Deputy Judge of the High Court.
[27] *Hely-Hutchinson v Brayhead Ltd* [1967] 3 All ER 98 at 102, CA, per Lord Denning.
[28] See *First Energy (UK) Ltd v Hungarian International Bank Ltd* [1993] BCLC 1409 at 1422–3.
[29] See *Bowstead & Reynolds on Agency* (21st edn, 2017), para 3-01 et seq: the distinction essentially is between actual authority arising from the consensual relationship between the principal and agent and authority as it appears to third parties. '… the authority which the third party is entitled to assume the agent has is in most situations the authority which would normally be implied between principal and agent in the circumstances. The actual and apparent authority will therefore normally coincide' (para 3-004); also '… the essence of apparent authority is an appearance emanating from the principal', at para 8-020; see *Smith v Butler* [2012] BCC 645 at [29].      [30] [1964] 1 All ER 630, CA.

had held him out as being the managing director which conferred on him an ostensible authority which would bind the company.[31] The architects were entitled to rely on that ostensible or apparent authority and the company was liable for the fees. Lord Diplock identified the key conditions which must be met for apparent authority to arise, namely a representation of the authority of the agent made to the third party by a person or persons with actual authority to manage the business and the third party must have been induced by the representation to enter into the contract, i.e. the third party must in fact have relied on the representation.[32]

**9-17**    For apparent authority to arise, the agent must have been held out by someone with actual authority[33] to carry out the transaction and an agent cannot hold himself out as having authority.[34] The acts of the principal must constitute a representation that the agent has a particular authority and must be reasonably so understood and relied upon by the other party who deals with the agent on the faith of the representation. In determining whether a principal has represented his agent as having authority to enter into the particular transaction, the court has to consider the totality of the principal's conduct.[35] The commonest form of holding out is permitting the agent to act in the conduct of the principal's business[36] and in many cases the holding out consists solely of the fact that the company has invested the agent with a particular office, e.g. 'managing director' or 'secretary'.[37] The

---

[31] This case must be distinguished from *Hely-Hutchinson* (see **9-12**). In *Hely-Hutchinson*, the director was found to have been a de facto managing director and it was from that position that the court found that the director did have implied actual authority. The director in *Freeman & Lockyer* did not hold such a position and therefore there was less scope for finding implied actual authority as opposed to looking for some apparent authority. See also n 29 as to the relationship between implied actual and apparent authority.

[32] [1964] 1 All ER 630 at 646. A further requirement, that under its memorandum or articles of association the company must not have been deprived of the capacity either to enter into a contract of the kind sought to be enforced or to delegate authority to enter into a contract of that kind to the agent, is irrelevant now, as following the abolition of the ultra vires doctrine, companies generally have unlimited capacity.

[33] Although the courts have also accepted the following principle set out in *Bowstead and Reynolds on Agency* (21st edn, 2017), para 8-019: 'It seems correct in principle to say that an agent can have apparent authority to make representations as to the authority of other agents, provided that his own authority can finally be traced back to a representation by the principal or to a person with actual authority from the principal to make it', but see further para 8-021, and *Kelly v Fraser* [2013] 1 AC 450, PC that an agent may have usual authority to communicate that those with actual authority have exercised that authority; also *Re Ing (UK) Ltd v Versicherung* [2007] 1 BCLC 108 at [100]. But see Yap, 'Apparent Authority: Doctrinal Underpinnings and Competing Policy Goals' [2014] JBL 72 as to the risks involved in allowing an agent who does not have authority to enter into a transaction to have apparent authority to inform third parties that the transaction has been approved and who notes that the approach in *Kelly v Fraser* may swing the balance too far in favour of the third party. In *Kelly v Fraser* Lord Sumption gives the example of the role of the company secretary as an example of an agent in this type of situation, see at [13].

[34] *Freeman and Lockyer v Buckhurst Park Properties (Mangal) Ltd* [1964] 1 All ER 630, CA; *British Bank of the Middle East v Sun Life Assurance Co of Canada (UK) Ltd* [1983] BCLC 78, HL; *Armagas Ltd v Mundogas SA (The Ocean Frost)* [1986] 2 All ER 385, HL. See too *Hudson Bay Apparel Brands LLC v Umbro International Ltd* [2011] 1 BCLC 259 at [53]; *Thanakharn v Akai Holdings Ltd (No 2)* [2011] 1 HKLC 357, HKCFA, at [70]–[71], per Lord Neuberger.

[35] *Egyptian International Foreign Trade Co v Soplex Wholesale Supplies Ltd, The Raffaella* [1985] BCLC 404 at 411, CA, per Browne-Wilkinson V-C.

[36] *Freeman and Lockyer v Buckhurst Park Properties (Mangal) Ltd* [1964] 1 All ER 630 at 645, per Diplock LJ.

[37] *Egyptian International Foreign Trade Co v Soplex Wholesale Supplies Ltd, The Raffaella* [1985] BCLC 404 at 411, CA, per Browne-Wilkinson V-C. As Toulson J commented in *Re Ing (UK) Ltd v Versicherung* [2007] 1 BCLC 108 at [104]: '... many instances of ostensible authority arise by implication from acts of a quite general nature, typically putting an agent in a position which may normally be expected to carry a certain level of authority', see also at [125].

very act of appointing someone as a director is a representation that they have the usual authority of someone in that position. The holding out may also come from a course of conduct where the agent has a course of dealing with a particular contractor and the principal acquiesces in the practice and honours transactions arising out of it.[38] For these reasons, an individual director may acquire considerable apparent authority.

**9-18**   The problem with apparent authority is that it cannot be relied upon if the other party knows or is put on inquiry as to some limitation which prevents the authority arising.[39] This may be knowledge, including constructive notice,[40] of the company's articles which might clearly indicate a lack of authority, for example, where the articles state that no individual director may enter into a transaction in excess of £1m. A third party is deemed (by the doctrine of constructive notice) to be aware of that limitation even if the third party has not actually read the articles, though if he can rely on CA 2006, s 40, discussed in detail at **9-28**, the third party is unaffected even by actual knowledge of such a limitation.

**9-19**   It is more likely that the scenario will be one where it is alleged the third party cannot rely on the apparent authority for the very nature of the proposed transaction may indicate that a director is acting contrary to the interests of the company (and necessarily for an improper purpose) which would negate actual authority. In other words, that the reliance by the third party on the representation is unreasonable.[41] As Lord Scott commented in *Criterion Properties plc v Stratford UK Properties LLC*[42] (see **9-72**):

> '[I]f a person dealing with an agent knows or has reason to believe that the contract or transaction is contrary to the commercial interests of the agent's principal, it is likely to be very difficult for the person to assert with any credibility that he believed the agent did have actual authority. Lack of such a belief would be fatal to a claim that the agent had apparent authority.'

**9-20**   In *A L Underwood Ltd v Bank of Liverpool*[43] a bank was put on inquiry when a director paid cheques drawn in favour of the company into his personal bank account. If put on inquiry by the circumstances, the third party should make such inquiries as ought reasonably to be made to ensure the agent's authority is sufficient to bind the principal.[44] In *Hopkins v TL Dallas Group Ltd*[45] a third party was unable to hold a company to undertakings given

---

[38]   See *Armagas Ltd v Mundogas SA* [1986] 2 All ER 385 at 389–90, HL, per Lord Keith.

[39]   *A L Underwood Ltd v Bank of Liverpool* [1924] 1 KB 775, CA; *B Liggett (Liverpool) Ltd v Barclays Bank Ltd* [1928] 1 KB 48; *Morris v Kanssen* [1946] 1 All ER 586, HL; *Rolled Steel Products (Holdings) Ltd v British Steel Corpn* [1985] 3 All ER 52, CA; *Criterion Properties plc v Stratford UK Properties LLC* [2006] 1 BCLC 729, HL. See, for example, *Hudson Bay Apparel Brands LLC v Umbro International Ltd* [2011] 1 BCLC 259 at [54], where there could not be apparent authority when the third party dealing with the company knew (from previous negotiations) that the company representative in the US did not have authority to execute agreements on behalf of the company which could only be executed by a senior employee in the UK.

[40]   Constructive notice does not affect anyone able to rely on CA 2006, s 40, since that section permits parties within it to ignore constitutional limitations on the power of the directors, but the doctrine has not been abolished otherwise. CA 1985, s 711 A which would have done so was never brought into force and was repealed by CA 2006, s 1295, Sch 16.

[41]   See *Bowstead & Reynolds on Agency* (21st edn, 2017): 'It seems that the proper approach in commercial cases is to apply the objective interpretation which one person is entitled to put on another's words and conduct in the light of the facts known to the former', para 8-048.

[42]   [2006] 1 BCLC 729 at 741, HL.

[43]   [1924] 1 KB 775, CA. A third party can only rely on apparent authority provided he does not know that the director has no actual authority; *Re Capitol Films Ltd, Rubin v Cobalt Pictures Ltd* [2011] 2 BCLC 359 at [55], applying Lord Scott in *Criterion*; also *Hopkins v TL Dallas Group Ltd* [2005] 1 BCLC 543 at [88].

[44]   *Hopkins v TL Dallas Group Ltd* [2005] 1 BCLC 543.          [45]   [2005] 1 BCLC 543.

by a deputy managing director (who had subsequently been dismissed for dishonesty) when the recipient of the undertakings had been on the clearest notice that the transactions were abnormal and suspicious. In those circumstances, the court said, the recipient should have sought confirmation of the propriety and regularity of the transaction from the managing director of the company. The director had no actual authority to execute the undertakings[46] and the recipient could not rely on any apparent authority on the director's part in the light of his failure to inquire. Accordingly, the undertakings were not binding on the defendant company and could not be enforced against it.

**9-21** In *Wrexham AFC Ltd v Crucialmove Ltd*[47] the company was a football club. A director and the company secretary executed a declaration on behalf of the company that the freehold of the football ground (which had been purchased with funding provided by a third party) was held on trust for the third party. However, what was not disclosed was that the director and the third party had entered into a joint venture agreement for the redevelopment of the ground to their personal advantage. Clearly, in those circumstances, the third party knew that the director had a conflict of interest between his personal interests and his duty to the company. The ownership of the freehold was subsequently challenged by the club which disputed the authority of the director (who was company chairman and an executive director) to execute the declaration of trust.

**9-22** The court found that this was a highly unusual case where the third party was not dealing with company officers of whom he knew nothing. Because of the joint venture agreement, the third party knew of all the circumstances that meant that the director had a conflict of interest in securing the freehold of the land and in making the declaration of trust. The third party was on notice that the director was entering into the transaction for an improper purpose and in breach of his fiduciary duty to the company and he was bound to inquire whether the transaction had been authorised or approved by the company or its board. Given that the third party was on notice and had failed to inquire, the Court of Appeal held that he could not rely on any apparent authority of the director as a matter of agency law nor on the statutory protection provided for third parties by CA 2006, s 40[48] (this latter point is discussed further at **9-35**). The court upheld a declaration by the lower court that the freehold of the land was held on trust for the company, subject to a charge in favour of the third party in respect of the purchase price.

**9-23** Another example of the third party being on notice can be found in *Re Capitol Films Ltd, Rubin v Cobalt Pictures Ltd*.[49] In this case, the company was in severe financial difficulties and the director assigned most of the company's main assets (distribution rights in films) to the third party for an undefined consideration (the provision by the third party of 'certain services' and a 'certain amount' of financing to the company). In those circumstances, the court held, the third party knew that the director was acting contrary to the commercial interests of his company and could have no actual authority which meant, applying the dictum of Lord Scott in *Criterion Properties*, cited at **9-19**, that the third party equally could not rely on the doctrine of apparent authority. A clinching consideration

---

[46] The director had no express actual authority for this transaction. Equally, despite the title of deputy managing director, he had no implied actual authority because the giving of undertakings of this nature did not fall within the usual scope of the office of deputy managing director. He was subordinate to an executive chairman and to an executive managing director and had no responsibility in relation to these types of undertakings.

[47] [2008] 1 BCLC 508, CA. See too *Rolled Steel Products (Holdings) Ltd v British Steel Corpn* [1984] BCLC 466 at 497, 507–8, 517–18, CA.     [48] [2008] 1 BCLC 508 at [45], [47].

[49] [2011] 2 BCLC 359.

here was that the director who acted for the company was also the director of the third party and he signed the assignment documents on behalf of the company (without regard for the company's commercial interests) and for the third party. As the court noted, if the same person purports to act as a director on behalf of both parties to a transaction, it is self-evident that the other contracting party must be taken to know of the lack of authority of that person to act for the company.[50]

**9-24**    The issues of reliance and inquiry are closely linked and the position was considered by Lord Neuberger sitting in the Hong Kong Court of Final Appeal in a decision which is now often cited, *Thanakharn v Akai Holdings Ltd (No 2)*,[51] where he concluded that apparent authority cannot be relied on if the third party's belief in it is dishonest or irrational, which includes turning a blind eye and being reckless. Lord Neuberger did not think that inquiry was the right test,[52] preferring to set a threshold of dishonesty or irrationality before disentitling the third party from relying on apparent authority. The result is to make it more difficult for the company to disavow the authority of the agent. Lord Neuberger noted that '[i]n a commercial context, absent dishonesty or irrationality, a person should be entitled to rely on what he is told; this may occasionally cause harsh results, but it enables people engaged in business to know where they stand.'[53] It is not a question of constructive notice or whether a reasonable person would have been put on inquiry, for that reduces the threshold too far in favour of the principal and denies third parties the protection they deserve in commercial dealing. Hence Lord Neuberger's preference for the higher threshold of dishonesty or irrationality.

**9-25**    In *Thanakharn v Akai Holdings Ltd (No 2)*[54] a bank entered into a highly unusual transaction with a company from which the company gained no benefit, but the bank gained significantly, and which was carried out in disregard of normal bank procedures. The bank was found to have behaved irrationally (the court did not find any dishonesty) and could not rely, therefore, on the apparent authority of the company's chief executive officer who committed the company to the transaction. This approach of Lord Neuberger was endorsed by Gross LJ in *Quinn v CC Automotive Group Ltd*[55] who reminded us that the question is of an honest belief by the third party, not whether the belief is reasonable, before concluding that '... an analysis founded on reliance and belief leaves little room for any consideration of whether the third party was "put on inquiry"'.[56] There is an issue therefore as to whether the circumstances in which a third party cannot rely on

---

[50] [2011] 2 BCLC 359 at [53]–[55].

[51] [2011] 1 HKLC 357. See Yap, 'Knowing Receipt and Apparent Authority' (2011) 127 LQR 350; also Wan, 'Lack of Authority and its Effect on Corporate Transactions with Third Parties, *Thanakharn v Akai Holdings*' [2011] JBL 385. But *Bowstead & Reynolds on Agency* (21st edn, 2017), paras 8-49, 8-50.

[52] See [2011] 1 HKLC 357 at [56]–[61]; he concludes that the authorities cited at n 39 can be explained on other grounds and not as laying the test for when apparent authority is negated.

[53] [2011] 1 HKLC 357 at [52]. The need to have regard to the way in which business is actually conducted is also evident in the Privy Council judgment in *Kelly v Fraser* [2013] 1 AC 450.

[54] [2011] 1 HKLC 357.

[55] [2011] 2 All ER (Comm) 584 at [23]. There is also some first instance support, see *Gaydamak v Leviev* [2012] EWHC 1740 at [249], per Vos J; *Newcastle International Airport Ltd v Eversheds* [2013] PNLR 5 at [108]–[109], per Proudman J; *LNOC Ltd v Watford AFC Ltd* [2013] EWHC 3615 at [90]–[92]; *Acute Property Developments Ltd v Apostolou* [2013] EWHC 200 at [39]; *PEC Ltd v Asia Golden Rice Co Ltd* [2014] EWHC 1583 at [73], per Andrew Smith J.

[56] [2011] 2 All ER (Comm) 584 at [23], though he considered that whether the third party has been put on inquiry might be relevant to the 'blind eye' aspect of 'dishonest or irrational' or if the agent was acting outside of the usual authority of a person holding the position he holds, citing *Bowstead and Reynolds* (19th edn), paras 9-054–9-055.

apparent authority should be described in terms of the third party (in addition to cases of actual knowledge, of course) being put on inquiry or in terms of whether they have acted dishonestly or irrationally. At one level, it may not matter. Lord Neuberger indicated in *Thanakharn v Akai Holdings Ltd (No 2)*[57] that he had some doubts as to the extent to which, in practice, there would be much difference in outcome between these two approaches, and it is not clear that any of the English authorities would have been decided any differently if a threshold of dishonesty and irrationality was used.[58] The significance of the change would lie in the reassertion of the importance of commercial certainty and this articulation in terms of dishonesty and irrationality can be seen as subtly tilting the law towards the protection of third parties. This articulation also gives greater clarity than a test based on 'being put on inquiry' which merely then begs the question of what circumstances put the third party on inquiry, but its adoption awaits a decision of the higher English courts. The approach of Lord Neuberger has been criticised as 'based on a misunderstanding of prior authorities and of general principle' by the editors of *Bowstead and Reynolds on Agency*,[59] noting that 'it would be remarkable, therefore, if the law were to treat a representation founded solely on the principal's conduct—there being no verbal communication directly between the principal and third party—as virtually conclusive even though a reasonable person would have spotted counter-signals and inquired about them'. The crucial point made by *Bowstead and Reynolds on Agency* is that 'the process of determining whether apparent authority is made out is ultimately a single process rather than a rigid two-step process of finding a holding out and then inquiring as to the third party's state of knowledge'.[60] The point is made at **9-19** that there must be a representation which it is reasonable for the third party to rely upon—there is no apparent authority in the face of unreasonable reliance on the holding out.

## D  Statutory protection for third parties

**9-26**  As discussed at **9-5**, the directors' mandate to manage the business, their authority to act on the company's behalf, is derived from the constitutional division of power within the particular company set out primarily (but not exclusively) in the articles[61] as well as the authority conferred on them by agency law. A failure to act within the scope of their authority is a breach by the directors of CA 2006, s 171(a) and leaves persons dealing with the company through them as parties to an unauthorised transaction. This risk of being party to an unauthorised transaction would seem to require third parties to scrutinise carefully the company's constitution and the limits to the directors' authority, collectively and individually. But that type of scrutiny is time-consuming and expensive in the context of commercial operations and, therefore, both domestically and as a result of EU requirements, the policy balance here favours, externally, commercial certainty and the

---

[57]  [2011] 1 HKLC 357 at [50].

[58]  See Lee and Ho, 'Reluctant Bedfellows: Want of Authority and Knowing Receipt' (2012) 75 MLR 91 at 93 who make the point that 'the language of irrationality should be understood only as emphasising a fluid and variable standard of reasonable reliance that accommodates commercial needs', citing counsel in the case, Mr Sumption QC.     [59]  (21st edn, 2017), para 8-050.

[60]  (21st edn, 2017), para 8-050.

[61]  The constitution is defined more broadly than the articles, see CA 2006, s 17; and see **5-8**. It is also possible that the directors' powers may be limited by directions given by the shareholders by special resolution: see The Companies (Model Articles) Regulations 2008, SI 2008/3229, reg 2, Sch 1, art 4 (Ltd); reg 4, Sch 3, art 4 (Plc).

protection of the third party over any need, internally, to protect shareholders by upholding constitutional constraints on the authority of the directors. That policy is reflected in CA 2006, s 40 and, at common law, by agency law, as discussed at **9-16**, and the rule in *Turquand's* case, discussed at **9-46**.

**9-27**   As far as third parties are concerned, the practical context in which a problem is likely to arise is where a company wishes to disown a transaction (usually as a result of a change in circumstances which makes the transaction disadvantageous) by alleging that the director (or directors) responsible had no authority to enter into it or has exceeded some constitutional limitation on his authority. A third party may have an action for damages for breach of an implied warranty of authority against a director in such circumstances,[62] but he is usually more concerned with holding the company to the transaction. The answer to a problem of a want of authority lies, as discussed, in agency law and, as to constitutional limitations on authority, in statute.

### Companies Act 2006, s 40

**9-28**   Statutory protection for third parties dealing with the company is provided by CA 2006, s 40 which implements the requirements of the First EC Company Law Directive in this regard.[63] Section 40(1) states:

> 'In favour of a person dealing with a company in good faith, the power of the directors to bind the company, or authorise others to do so, is deemed to be free of any limitation under the company's constitution.'

The statutory provision operates only 'in favour of' a person dealing with a company in good faith so the company needs to authorise the transaction if it wants to hold the other party to it.

**9-29**   Before looking in detail at the application of s 40, note in particular that s 40 has effect subject to CA 2006, s 41 where the parties to the transaction include a director of the company or of its holding company or a person connected (as defined in s 252) with such a director.[64] In that situation, the transaction is voidable at the instance of the company subject to the possibility that the right to avoid may be lost in the usual ways (*restitutio impossible*, rights of bona fide third parties for value intervene, etc: see s 41(4)). Further, the director and connected person and any director who authorised the transaction (subject to the defence in s 41(5)) may be civilly liable under s 41(3) and under any other rule

---

[62]   *Hely-Hutchinson v Brayhead Ltd* [1967] 3 All ER 98, CA.

[63]   The relevant provision is art 9 of the First Council Directive on Company Law, 68/151/EEC, OJ Spec Edn 1968, p 41 (now consolidated as Directive 2009/101/EC, OJ L 258/11, 1.10.2009) which provides as follows: '(1) Acts done by the organs of the company shall be binding upon it even if those acts are not within the objects of the company, unless such acts exceed the powers that the law confers or allows to be conferred on those organs. However, Member States may provide that the company shall not be bound where such acts are outside the objects of the company, if it proves that the third party knew that the act was outside those objects or could not in view of the circumstances have been unaware of it; disclosure of the statutes shall not of itself be sufficient proof thereof. (2) The limits on the powers of the organs of the company, arising under the statutes or from a decision of the competent organs, may never be relied on as against third parties, even if they have been disclosed.' See the detailed account of art 9 by Edwards, *EC Company Law* (1999), Ch 1, pp 33–45, though some of the difficulties in implementation identified there (see pp 42–4) appear to have been addressed by subtle changes in the drafting of CA 2006, s 40, see discussion in text.

[64]   CA 2006, ss 40(6), 41(2). Section 40 also has effect subject to s 42 where the company is a charity: s 40(6).

of law such as for breach of duty (s 41(1)). The application of s 41 may give rise to the situation where a transaction is valid with respect to one party under s 40(1), because they are unaffected by the application of s 41 (see s 41(6)), and voidable with respect to another party to the same transaction if they are a director or connected person under s 41(2). In that situation, the court has wide powers to affirm, sever, or set aside the transaction on such terms as appear to be just (s 41(6)).

## A person dealing in good faith

**9-30**  An issue which has arisen is whether a director can be a 'person' for these purposes so as to rely on the protection of CA 2006, s 40. In *Smith v Henniker-Major & Co*,[65] while agreed that, as a matter of ordinary language, 'person' may include a director, the majority in the Court of Appeal did not accept that a director could rely on the statutory provision with respect to an error as to authority when he was the author of his own mistake.[66] The judicial reluctance to accept that a director (where he is the author of and hopes to be the beneficiary of the lack of authority) can rely on the protection of the statutory provision is understandable. As Schiemann LJ commented, there should be no difficulty in excluding from 'person' the very directors who overstepped the limitations in the company's constitution. But the case is not a very useful authority for the facts were exceptional,[67] as the court stressed, and there are three difficult judgments agreeing and conflicting with one another in almost equal measure.[68] There is no need to consider it further for the position has been clarified by the rewording of CA 2006, s 40(6) which now states expressly that s 40 has effect subject to s 41.[69] In other words, when a director is a party (or one of the parties) to the transaction, his position is governed by s 41, not s 40. The starting point as regards a director is that the transaction is voidable under s 41 (s 41(2)), see **9-29**.

**9-31**  In *EIC Services Ltd v Phipps*,[70] the Court of Appeal was also robust in rejecting, obiter, a first instance finding that a shareholder could rely on CA 2006, s 40 as a 'person' dealing in good faith. The case concerned an unauthorised bonus issue to shareholders in breach of the articles and the question was whether the shareholders could rely on s 40 so as to hold on to the shares which had been erroneously allocated and which had increased in value significantly. As discussed at **9-32**, the court held in any event that a bonus issue does not amount to a 'dealing' with the company, but had there been a dealing, the court did not accept that a shareholder could be a 'person' for these purposes. Peter

---

[65]  [2002] 2 BCLC 655, CA.

[66]  See [2002] 2 BCLC 655 at [110], per Carnwath LJ, who stressed that the director here was also the chairman and the person entrusted with ensuring that the constitution was observed; also at [123], per Schiemann LJ. Robert Walker LJ dissented on the basis of the relationship between what is now CA 2006, s 40 and s 41, but the basis of his dissent has been eroded by the fact that s 40(6) now states expressly that s 40 has effect subject to s 41.

[67]  The facts were that a 30 per cent shareholder and director, Smith, at an inquorate board meeting (attended only by himself) had the company assign to him what was in effect its sole asset, namely a claim against a firm of solicitors for damages in respect of a sale of land. The validity of the assignment was challenged by the solicitors. Mr Smith claimed that, as he was a person dealing with the company in good faith, he could rely on the statutory protection and was unaffected by any (quorum) limitation on the powers of the board. He lost.

[68]  See Walters, 'Section 35 A and Quorum Requirements: Confusion Reigns' (2002) 23 Co Law 325.

[69]  The previous wording was that CA 1985, s 322 A (now CA 2006, s 41) had effect notwithstanding CA 1985, s 35 A (now CA 2006, s 40): CA 1985, s 35A(6).          [70]  [2004] 2 BCLC 589, CA.

Gibson LJ, with whom Sedley LJ and Newman J agreed, thought the answer lay in the First Company Law Directive, art 9, which is implemented by CA 2006, s 40 and which is intended to protect 'third parties'.[71] While noting that the Directive does not define 'third parties', Peter Gibson LJ thought it tolerably clear from the Directive itself that the term 'third parties' does not include the company or its members and there was no reason to think that a provision intended to implement the Directive had gone further than the Directive in the absence of any other known mischief which the section was intended to counteract.[72]

**9-32**  For the purpose of CA 2006, s 40, a person 'deals with' a company if he is a party to any transaction or other act to which the company is a party.[73] In *EIC Services Ltd v Phipps*,[74] noted at **9-31**, the Court of Appeal did not accept that an issue of bonus shares by a company to its shareholders, an internal arrangement involving no change in proportionate shareholdings and a consequence of a single resolution applicable to all shareholders, could amount to a 'dealing' with the company for these purposes.[75] Peter Gibson LJ noted that, as a matter of ordinary language, the section contemplates a bilateral transaction between the company and the person dealing with the company or an act to which both are parties.[76]

**9-33**  As to the good faith requirement in s 40(1), the statute goes to great lengths to ensure that it is difficult for a person dealing with a company to be in bad faith, in particular, by imposing a presumption of good faith and absolving the third party from an obligation to inquire to a certain extent. The key provision is CA 2006, s 40(2)(b) which provides as follows:

'(2)  For this purpose—…

(b)  a person dealing with a company—

(i)  is not bound to enquire as to any limitation on the powers of the directors to bind the company or authorise others to do so,

(ii)  is presumed to have acted in good faith unless the contrary is proved, and

(iii)  is not to be regarded as acting in bad faith by reason only of his knowing that an act is beyond the powers of the directors under the company's constitution.'

**9-34**  As is clear from (iii), the statutory protection extends even to providing that a person cannot be regarded as acting in bad faith by reason *only* of his knowing that an act is beyond the powers of the directors under the company's constitution (i.e. beyond their authority). At common law, persons dealing with a company are deemed under the doctrine of constructive notice to have notice of the company's articles of association and various

[71]  The full text of art 9 is set out at n 63.

[72]  [2004] 2 BCLC 589 at [37]. Nor did he think that any inference as to the application of CA 2006, s 40 to shareholders could be drawn from the fact that the legislature dealt specifically with transactions with directors in s 41.

[73]  CA 2006, s 40(2)(a). This wording ensures that the provision applies to gratuitous as well as commercial transactions.                                                                                [74]  [2004] 2 BCLC 589, CA.

[75]  See Payne and Prentice, n 4, 463, who cogently criticise this finding and point out that at the very least a bonus issue amounts to an act to which the company is a party, see CA 2006, s 40(2)(a). See also *Cottrell v King* [2004] 2 BCLC 413 at [29] where it was doubted, obiter, whether the operation of pre-emption provisions in the articles requiring notice to be given by a member to the other members who might then purchase the member's shares could be said to be 'dealing with the company' for these purposes.

[76]  [2004] 2 BCLC 589 at [35].

public documents (and this doctrine has not been repealed)[77] but this deemed knowledge is irrelevant under CA 2006, s 40 since even actual knowledge of a constitutional limitation does not establish bad faith. To establish bad faith, it is necessary to show something additional such as knowledge of, or being put on inquiry as to, an improper purpose on the part of the directors, or some collusion by the third party in a breach by the directors of their duties.[78]

**9-35** The circumstances needed to rebut the presumption of good faith were considered in *Wrexham AFC Ltd v Crucialmove Ltd*,[79] discussed at **9-21**, where the third party knew that the director executing a particular agreement on behalf of the company had a conflict of interest. As discussed, the Court of Appeal held that the third party who knows of, or is on inquiry as to, an improper purpose and who fails to inquire cannot rely on apparent authority and, as a matter of agency law, cannot hold the company to the transaction.[80] The Court of Appeal also held that CA 2006, s 40 was of no assistance to the third party as the statutory provision does not absolve a person dealing with the company from any duty to inquire when the circumstances are such as to put that person on inquiry.[81] This case provides important clarification of the limits to the good faith presumption in s 40(2)(b)(ii). The section operates to negate any knowledge (actual or constructive) of *constitutional* limitations on the powers of the directors to bind the company and to relieve the third party from the obligation to inquire as to such limitations. But if a third party is put on inquiry by the circumstances of the transaction (which must be by something other than knowing of a lack of authority) and fails to inquire, then he cannot rely on s 40. The policy objectives of securing commercial certainty and the protection of the third party against constitutional limitations do not extend to protecting a third party with notice of a wider problem.

**9-36** To sum up, if the problem facing the third party is merely a want of authority on the part of the directors because of some constitutional limitation, CA 2006, s 40 offers full protection to the third party acting in good faith assuming the various statutory requirements

---

[77] See *Ernest v Nicholls* (1857) 6 HL Cas 401; *Mahony v East Holyford Mining Co* (1875) LR 7 HL 869; *Irvine v Union Bank of Australia* (1877) 2 App Cas 366, PC. The doctrine of constructive notice was to have been abolished by CA 1985, s 711 A but that provision was never brought into force and it was repealed by CA 2006, s 1295, Sch 16. This deemed notice can prevent apparent authority arising at common law; see **9-18**.

[78] See *Barclays Bank Ltd v TOSG Trust Fund Ltd* [1984] BCLC 1 (on the earlier but similarly worded provision, European Communities Act 1972, s 9). Driving a hard bargain does not point to bad faith, but if it was established that a third party, with a director's assistance, was secretly working to rob the company of its assets, that would point to a lack of good faith, see *Ford v Polymer Vision Ltd* [2009] 2 BCLC 160 at [92]–[93].

[79] [2008] 1 BCLC 508, CA.      [80] [2008] 1 BCLC 508 at 523.

[81] [2008] 1 BCLC 508 at 523. This approach is consistent with *International Sales and Agencies Ltd v Marcus* [1982] 3 All ER 551, at 559–60, where Lawson J (addressing the European Communities Act 1972, s 9, an earlier version of CA 2006, s 40) decided that a third party who received from a director sums of money which the recipient knew came improperly from the company's funds was liable applying constructive trust principles as a recipient of company money knowingly paid in breach of trust. The statutory purpose, he said, was to protect innocent parties who entered into transactions which the companies might otherwise seek to avoid but the statute did not affect the operation of a constructive trust if the facts gave rise to such a trust. This position also means that the complication of a person being within the statutory protection with respect to a lack of authority, but beyond the section with respect to an improper purpose cannot arise. A third party who is put on inquiry as to a proper purpose is not in good faith; a position reinforced by *Cooperatieve Rabobank 'Vecht en Plassengebied' BA v Minderhoud* [1998] 2 BCLC 507, ECJ where the court agreed that the provisions of the First Company Law Directive (which are reflected in CA 2006, s 40) are intended to protect innocent parties dealing with the company but they do not prevent the application of national laws on matters such as conflicts of interests to any agreement purportedly entered into by a company. See also Edwards, *EC Company Law* (1999), Ch 1, pp 38–9.

('dealing', etc) are met. But where the third party is put on inquiry by something other than merely knowing of a lack of authority (such as knowledge, actual or constructive, of an improper purpose) and fails to inquire, the statutory presumption of good faith in CA 2006, s 40(2)(b)(ii) is rebutted and the protection of the section is not available.[82]

**9-37**   If for some reason (for example, no 'dealing' for these purposes) a third party cannot bring himself within CA 2006, s 40 in the first place, then he must rely on agency law if he is to bind the company when faced with a want of authority on the part of a director or directors. The difficulty is that, as a matter of agency law, even constructive notice of a want of authority puts him on inquiry and a failure to inquire means that he cannot rely on any apparent authority. In that regard, the statute offers greater protection since, under the statute, a third party is not put on inquiry merely by knowing of a lack of authority (CA 2006, s 40(2)(b)(iii)). Equally, if a person dealing with a company is on notice that the directors are exercising the relevant power for purposes other than the purposes of the company, he cannot rely on the ostensible authority of the directors and, on ordinary principles of agency, cannot hold the company to the transaction.[83] Being put on inquiry as to the directors' purposes removes any credible belief in the directors' actual authority which, as Lord Scott commented in *Criterion Properties plc v Stratford UK Properties LLC*,[84] is fatal to any claim that the agent had apparent authority, see **9-19**.

### Constitutional limitations may be disregarded

**9-38**   Assuming these thresholds in terms of 'a person' 'dealing' and 'good faith' can be met, limitations imposed by the company's constitution on the powers of the directors to bind the company or their powers to delegate to others may be disregarded. For example, if the articles limit the power of the directors to borrow up to £5m, a bank which lends in excess of that amount to the company is unaffected by the limitation, assuming the bank deals in good faith. Constitutional limitations are found primarily in the company's articles (CA 2006, s 17) but s 40(3) broadens the application of the section to include limitations deriving from a resolution of the company or any class of shareholders, or from any agreement between the members of the company or of any class of shareholders.[85] Such limitations on the powers of the directors do not affect a person dealing with the company in good faith.

**9-39**   The wording of CA 2006, s 40(1) (see at **9-28**), 'the power of the directors', differs slightly but significantly from its predecessor, CA 1985, s 35A. The 1985 wording referred to constitutional limitations on 'the power of the board of directors' which led to debate as to whether requirements such as quorum requirements for a valid board meeting were limitations on the power of the board (and so within the section) or addressed the logically prior question of what constitutes a board of directors (and so were not within the section). A majority in the Court of Appeal in *Smith v Henniker-Major & Co*,[86] obiter,

---

[82] Of course there is an element of linkage here as to how a person is put on inquiry as to an improper purpose. While knowledge of a constitutional limitation (i.e. of a lack of authority) does not affect a person dealing in good faith with the company (CA 2006, s 40(2)(b)(iii)), that knowledge might put the third party on inquiry as to an exercise of a power for an improper purpose. A failure then to inquire will negate this presumption of good faith: see *Wrexham AFC Ltd v Crucialmove Ltd* [2008] 1 BCLC 508; Payne and Prentice, n 4, 455.

[83] *Rolled Steel Products (Holdings) Ltd v British Steel Corpn* [1984] BCLC 466 at 508, per Slade LJ.

[84] [2006] 1 BCLC 729 at [31], HL.

[85] Resolutions of the company would include either resolutions of the board or the shareholders which addresses a concern raised by Edwards, n 63, 43–4, as to the improper implementation of the First Directive, art 9.     [86] [2002] 2 BCLC 655 at [41], [126]. See **9-30** and n 67.

favoured the former view, though the latter view had been favoured at first instance.[87] By removing the reference to 'the board', the wording expands the scope of the section and eliminates, it would seem, any scope for further debate as to whether procedural limitations are included. The section applies to any constitutional limitations on the powers of the directors to bind the company which must include quorum or other procedural requirements as these are matters that limit the powers of the directors to act.[88] In *Ford v Polymer Vision Ltd*[89] the court accepted that specific provisions concerning the holding of board meetings (a requirement for notice to certain directors and a requirement that meetings be held outside the UK, neither of which were observed in this instance) were limitations under the constitution for the purposes of s 40(1). The alternative interpretation leaves us with the sort of contorted categorisation of provisions in the articles evident in the judgments in *Smith v Henniker-Major & Co*[90] ('constitutional limitations', 'procedural requirements', and 'nullities'). Rather than indulge in such debate, it is preferable to adopt a generous approach to the section and the protection of third parties in line with the purpose of the First Directive.[91]

**9-40** The wording of CA 2006, s 40(1) (see **9-28**) also raises a question which had arisen under a previous version of the provision,[92] namely as to the meaning of 'the directors' in this context. Having changed the wording from the 'board of directors' to 'the directors', it is clear that the section covers acts of the board and of any director authorised (in the sense of having actual authority to bind the company) to represent the company (i.e. the act need not be the act of the board collectively).[93] Support for interpreting 'directors' in accordance with that approach can be found in *Criterion Properties plc v Stratford UK Properties LLC*[94] which concerned the authority of two only of the directors and the court accepted that CA 1985, s 35 A (now CA 2006, s 40) might be relevant, and in *Wrexham AFC Ltd v Crucialmove Ltd*[95] which likewise concerned two only of the directors (the company chairman and the managing director) and where again the court considered s 35 A to be relevant. In *International Sales & Agencies Ltd v Marcus*[96] too the court was content that the statutory protection might apply to acts of someone who was only one of a number of directors, in that case the sole effective director to whom all actual authority to act for the company had been delegated.

**9-41** The result is a statutory provision which increases significantly the security of third parties dealing in good faith with the company. The downside for the shareholders is that the company does not have the option of disowning unauthorised transactions. But the shareholders are not entirely powerless, see **9-42**, and, as noted, a third party on inquiry as to an improper purpose is not protected by the section, nor can directors or connected

---

[87] See [2002] BCC 544 where Rimer J had concluded that, as the board was inquorate, there was no act of the board of directors to which CA 1985, s 35 A might apply.

[88] See *TCB Ltd v Gray* [1986] 1 All ER 587 at 597 where Browne-Wilkinson V-C thought that any provision in the articles as to the manner in which the directors can act as agents of the company (such as rules governing the affixing of the company seal) is a limitation on their power to bind the company.

[89] [2009] 2 BCLC 160 at [74], [78], Blackburne J noting that there is every good reason why such defects should be within the purview of s 40.          [90] [2002] 2 BCLC 655 at [41], [126].

[91] See Payne and Prentice, n 4, 457–8; and see *Ford v Polymer Vision Ltd* [2009] 2 BCLC 160 at [78].

[92] i.e. under s 9 of the European Communities Act 1972 which referred to transactions decided on by the directors: see Farrar and Powles (1973) 36 MLR 270; Collier and Sealy (1973) 32 CLJ 1.

[93] To be within the section, the directors must have actual (express or implied) authority to bind the company since the purpose of the provision is to prevent limits imposed on an existing authority from affecting a third party. See Edwards, *EC Company Law* (1999), pp 43–4.

[94] [2006] 1 BCLC 729 at [28]–[29], HL.          [95] [2008] 1 BCLC 508 at [47].

[96] [1982] 3 All ER 551 at 560.

persons rely on the statutory scheme (CA 2006, s 40(6)), so a balance is struck between commercial certainty and shareholder protection.

### Possible redress for shareholders

**9-42**  A member may obtain an injunction to restrain 'the doing of an act which is beyond the powers of the directors although no such proceeding may lie in respect of an act to be done in fulfilment of a legal obligation arising from a previous act of the company' (CA 2006, s 40(4)). An injunction cannot be obtained, therefore, to restrain the execution of an executory contract. Given that s 40 prevents shareholders from disowning an unauthorised transaction, it might be thought that shareholders have an incentive to monitor the conduct of the directors in order to prevent such transactions by injunctive relief. The practical difficulties of doing this, and the natural inertia of many shareholders, mean that this is unlikely to occur. In practice the members simply never find out about transactions in time to seek injunctive relief so making this provision somewhat irrelevant.

**9-43**  Shareholders are not without redress, however, for while a third party dealing with the company in good faith is able to hold a company to a transaction entered into in disregard of constitutional limitations on the powers of the directors, the directors responsible are in breach of the duty imposed by CA 2006, s 171(a) to act in accordance with the constitution and liable to indemnify the company for any loss suffered as a consequence. That the director is liable for breach of duty is confirmed by CA 2006, s 40(5) which provides that the protection afforded by s 40(1) does not affect any liability incurred by the directors, or any other person, by reason of the directors exceeding their powers. Note that this provision applies not just to directors, but to 'any other person' who may also be liable to the company on the basis of involvement in the breach of duty by the director.[97]

**9-44**  If the person dealing with the company cannot bring himself within the statutory protection in s 40, the unauthorised transaction is void[98] and not binding on the company though it is always open to the board or the shareholders, as appropriate, subsequently to decide not to treat the unauthorised transaction as a nullity but to affirm or adopt it,[99] if they so choose. If the company does not adopt or affirm the transaction, it remains a void transaction and the third party is liable, on the basis of a total failure of consideration, to account for any benefits obtained.[100] Where the company's assets have been transferred to a third party in circumstances where the transaction is void, it may also be possible

---

[97]  See *International Sales and Agencies Ltd v Marcus* [1982] 3 All ER 551 and n 81.

[98]  For example, in *EIC Services Ltd v Phipps* [2004] 2 BCLC 589 the board's failure to observe the requirements of the articles governing the issue of bonus shares meant that the share issue was void and the shareholders could not claim title to the allocated shares. See also *Guinness plc v Saunders* [1990] BCLC 402, HL, where a committee of the board purported to award remuneration to an individual director when it had no power to do so under the articles. The contract in question was void for want of authority. See also *Clark v Cutland* [2003] 2 BCLC 393, CA.

[99]  An act in excess of the board's authority can be affirmed or adopted by an ordinary resolution even though an alteration to the board's powers for all time would require a special resolution: *Irvine v Union Bank of Australia* (1877) 2 App Cas 366, PC; *Grant v United Kingdom Switchback Railways Co* (1888) 40 Ch D 135, CA.

[100]  *Guinness plc v Saunders* [1990] BCLC 402. See *Thanakharn v Akai Holdings* [2011] HKLC 357—void contract provided for the transfer of share certificates to the third party who then sold them—the contract being void, the third party had no right to retain the share certificates or sell them and the company had a claim for conversion of the shares.

to bring a claim for knowing receipt, if the other elements of that claim can be met,[101] see **14-63**.

**9-45**   Regardless of affirmation or adoption of the transaction, the directors responsible remain liable for breach of their duties under s 171. Whether the shareholders would wish to relieve a director from liability for breach of duty in these circumstances is a separate matter. The limits to the shareholders' powers to ratify breaches of duty are discussed at **19-43**.

## The indoor management rule

**9-46**   In addition to the protection afforded by apparent authority and the CA 2006, s 40, a third party may look to the common law rule in *Royal British Bank v Turquand*[102] which provides that persons dealing with a company are not obliged to inquire into the internal proceedings of a company but can assume that all acts of internal management have been properly carried out, save where an outsider knows or is put on inquiry as to the failure to adhere to procedures.[103] Insiders, i.e. persons holding positions within the company, are prevented from relying on the rule as they are in a position to know whether there has been compliance with the internal requirements.[104]

**9-47**   In *Royal British Bank v Turquand*[105] the board of directors had borrowed money without having the transaction authorised by a resolution of the company in general meeting as required by the deed of settlement (i.e. their articles). The court held that the company was bound by the borrowing as the resolution was a matter of internal management which the third party could assume had been correctly carried out.[106] In *Mahony v East Holyford Mining Co*[107] a bank was entitled to accept cheques drawn and signed by the directors in the manner authorised by the articles and was not obliged to query whether the individuals signing the cheques were validly appointed as directors.

---

[101]   See *Thanakharn v Akai Holdings* [2011] HKLC 357; Conaglen and Nolan, 'Contracts and Knowing Receipt: Principles and Application' (2013) 129 LQR 359; Lee and Ho, 'Reluctant Bedfellows: Want of Authority and Knowing Receipt' (2012) 75 MLR 78; Yap, 'Knowing Receipt and Apparent Authority' (2011) 127 LQR 350.                                                            [102]   (1856) 6 E & B 327.

[103]   *B Liggett (Liverpool) Ltd v Barclays Bank Ltd* [1928] 1 KB 48; *Morris v Kanssen* [1946] 1 All ER 586, HL; *Rolled Steel Products (Holdings) Ltd v British Steel Corpn* [1985] 3 All ER 52, CA; *Wrexham AFC Ltd v Crucialmove Ltd* [2008] 1 BCLC 508 at [46], CA. A further refinement to the rule is that it does not apply if the document which the outsider seeks to rely on is a forgery: see *Ruben v Great Fingall Consolidated* [1906] AC 439, HL; also *Kreditbank Cassel GmbH v Schenkers Ltd* [1927] 1 KB 826, CA; but this limitation has been criticised, see *Lovett v Carson Country Homes* [2009] 2 BCLC 196 at [92]–[95]. (*Ruben's* case does not mean that a forged document can in no circumstances have any effect whatsoever, for a party may be estopped from disputing the validity of a forged document. The principle of apparent authority is a broad reflection of the principles of estoppel, the court said, and it is accepted that, in appropriate circumstances, a principal may be bound by the fraudulent acts of an agent (and forgeries are no different to other fraudulent acts) in circumstances where there is ostensible authority.)

[104]   *Morris v Kanssen* [1946] 1 All ER 586, HL; *Howard v Patent Ivory Manufacturing Co* (1888) 38 Ch D 156; cf *Hely-Hutchinson v Brayhead Ltd* [1967] 3 All ER 98.

[105]   (1856) 6 E & B 327.

[106]   The court noted that the party here, on reading the deed of settlement, would find not a prohibition from borrowing but a permission to do so on certain conditions. Finding that the authority might be made complete by a resolution, he would have a right to infer the fact of a resolution authorising that which on the face of the document appeared to be legitimately done.

[107]   (1875) LR 7 HL 869.

**9-48**  The question is whether any role remains for the rule in *Turquand's* case in the light of CA 2006, s 40 and provisions such as s 161 precluding challenges to the acts of a director on the basis of a defect in his appointment (see **7-7**). For example, the situation in *Royal British Bank v Turquand*[108] would now be within s 40 as it involved a limitation on the board's authority to act. The scope of CA 2006, s 40 is broader in that it applies to any constitutional limitation on the powers of the directors whereas the rule in *Turquand* is limited to internal procedural irregularities. The circumstances in which the protection of the section and of the rule are lost are similar (party is put on inquiry and fails to inquire) but it may be possible to resort to the rule where a third party cannot bring themselves within the thresholds set by CA 2006, s 40 (for example, as to 'dealing with the company') though insiders are precluded from relying on the rule (as they are from relying on s 40, see **9-30**). All of which makes it difficult to envisage circumstances in which it would still be necessary to have recourse to the rule. It might conceivably be of some assistance with respect to reliance on the apparent authority of an individual director (where apparent authority can be established, but there is then some additional internal management requirement which has not been complied with), but it does not enable a party to hold the company to an unauthorised transaction entered into by a director. It allows a third party to assume that a transaction within the authority of the directors has been properly carried out, but it requires the third party to establish the fact of authority, actual or apparent, in the first place.[109]

## E Exercise of a power for an improper purpose

**9-49**  The duty to exercise a power for the purposes for which it is conferred, set out in CA 2006, s 171(b) (see **9-1**), applies to the exercise by the directors of any of their powers, be it the power to make allotments of shares;[110] to make calls on shares;[111] to refuse to register share transfers;[112] to order the forfeiture of shares;[113] to alienate the property of the company;[114] to expel a member;[115] or to enter into agreements with third parties.[116] The wider the power conferred, the more difficult it may be to restrain the directors,[117] but the duty brings an objective measure of control to the exercise of a power in contrast to s 172 which is primarily subjective (a director must act in the way he considers, in good faith, is most likely to promote the success of the company for the benefit of the members as a whole, see Chapter 10). The onus of proving an improper purpose lies on the claimant.[118]

---

[108]  (1856) 6 E & B 327.

[109]  See *Northside Developments Pty Ltd v Registrar-General* (1989–90) 170 CLR 146 at 198.

[110]  See *Punt v Symons & Co Ltd* [1903] 2 Ch 506; *Piercy v S Mills & Co Ltd* [1920] 1 Ch 77; *Hogg v Cramphorn Ltd* [1966] 3 All ER 420; *Bamford v Bamford* [1969] 1 All ER 969; *Howard Smith Ltd v Ampol Petroleum Ltd* [1974] 1 All ER 1126.

[111]  *Galloway v Halle Concerts Society* [1915] 2 Ch 233; *Alexander v Automatic Telegraph Co* [1900] 2 Ch 56.

[112]  *Re Smith & Fawcett Ltd* [1942] 1 All ER 542; *Re Bede Steam Shipping Co Ltd* [1917] 1 Ch 123.

[113]  *Re Agriculturalist Cattle Insurance Co, Stanhope's Case* (1866) 1 Ch App 161.

[114]  See *Bishopsgate Investment Management Ltd v Maxwell* [1993] BCLC 1282; *Ford v Polymer Vision Ltd* [2009] 2 BCLC 160.

[115]  See *Gaiman v National Association for Mental Health* [1970] 2 All ER 362; noted Prentice (1970) 33 MLR 700.

[116]  See *Lee Panavision Ltd v Lee Lighting Ltd* [1992] BCLC 22, CA.

[117]  See *Re Smith & Fawcett Ltd* [1942] 1 All ER 542; *Gaiman v National Association for Mental Health* [1970] 2 All ER 362, noted Prentice (1970) 33 MLR 700.

[118]  *Re Coalport China Co* [1895] 2 Ch 404; *Charles Forte Investments Ltd v Amanda* [1964] 1 Ch 240 at 255, 260–1.

## The substantial purpose for exercise

**9-50**   The leading authority on the proper purpose duty is the Privy Council decision in *Howard Smith Ltd v Ampol Petroleum Ltd*.[119] The leading speech was given by Lord Wilberforce who explained that the proper approach to an exercise of a power is:[120]

> 'to start with a consideration of the power whose exercise is in question … Having ascertained, on a fair view, the nature of this power, and having defined as can best be done in the light of modern conditions the, or some, limits within which it may be exercised, it is then necessary for the court, if a particular exercise of it is challenged, to examine the substantial purpose for which it was exercised, and to reach a conclusion whether that purpose was proper or not.'

**9-51**   The first step is to construe the article conferring the power in order to ascertain the nature of the power and the limits within which it may be exercised. In theory, the article could be limitless, permitting the exercise of the power in question for any purpose,[121] but even an apparently limitless power is inherently limited by a need to exercise it in order to promote the success of the company in accordance with s 172(1).[122] Of course, in many cases, there may not be a specific power as such, rather the directors will be exercising their powers of general management conferred on them by the articles (see **9-5**).[123]

**9-52**   Having established the limits, if any, to the power, the second step is to determine the substantial purpose or purposes for which it was exercised. This is not always easy to decide and may involve a detailed examination of the facts. Here Lord Wilberforce noted that:[124]

> 'the court … is entitled to look at the situation objectively in order to estimate how critical or pressing, or substantial or, per contra, insubstantial an alleged requirement may have been. If it finds that a particular requirement, though real, was not urgent, or critical, at the relevant time, it may have reason to doubt, or discount, the assertions of individuals that they acted solely in order to deal with it, particularly when the action they took was unusual or even extreme.'

**9-53**   In keeping with the reluctance of the judiciary to review the business decisions of directors, Lord Wilberforce accepted that there are difficulties of proof here which will require crediting the bona fide opinion of the directors, if such is found to exist, and respecting their judgement as to matters of management.[125] Having done so, he went on, the ultimate conclusion must be as to the side of a fairly broad line on which the case falls.[126]

---

[119]   [1974] AC 821, PC, noted Birds (1974) 37 MLR 580.        [120]   [1974] AC 821 at 835.

[121]   See *Re Smith & Fawcett Ltd* [1942] 1 All ER 542 at 545, per Lord Greene; also Prentice (1970) 33 MLR 700. See Nolan, 'Controlling Fiduciary Power' (2009) 68 CLJ 293 at 299 who reminds us that the proper purpose doctrine looks 'to the particular ends intended to be achieved through certain particular acts and determines whether such ends are contemplated (and therefore authorised) by the power in question'.

[122]   *Re Smith & Fawcett Ltd* [1942] 1 Ch 304; *Re Coalport China Co* [1895] 2 Ch 404 at 409–10. Where the directors' duty under s 172(3) is engaged, rather than s 172(1), such that the interests of the company's creditors are paramount, then the proper purposes for which powers may be exercised must necessarily include advancing the interests of the company's creditors: *Re HLC Environmental Projects Ltd, Hellard v Carvalho* [2014] BCC 337 at [99]. The scope and application of s 172(3) is considered at **10-41**.

[123]   See, for example, *CAS (Nominees) Ltd v Nottingham Forest FC plc* [2002] 1 BCLC 613; also The Companies (Model Articles) Regulations 2008, SI 2008/3229, reg 2, Sch 1, art 3 (Ltd); reg 4, Sch 3, art 3 (Plc).

[124]   *Howard Smith Ltd v Ampol Petroleum Ltd* [1974] AC 821 at 832.

[125]   [1974] AC 821 at 832.        [126]   [1974] AC 821 at 835.

**9-54**   Having carried out this exercise and identified the actual purpose for which the power was exercised, that actual purpose then has to be measured against the range of permissible purposes for the exercise of that power, as indicated by the articles or ascertained by the court, in order to decide whether that actual exercise was proper. Provided that the substantial purpose for which the power was exercised is a proper purpose, the exercise of the power is not invalidated by the presence of some other improper, but insubstantial, purpose. For example, some incidental benefit obtained by a director does not invalidate the exercise of the power unless his self-interest was the substantial purpose for the exercise of the power.[127] Equally, if the substantial purpose was improper, a director's honest belief that he was acting in the interests of the company is insufficient to validate the exercise of the power.[128]

**9-55**   Turning to the facts in *Howard Smith Ltd v Ampol Petroleum Ltd*,[129] the case concerned a takeover battle for a company where the directors favoured a particular bidder and made an allotment of shares to that bidder with a view to diluting the holdings of the potential rival bidders (who were the existing majority shareholders) for the company.[130] It was accepted that the directors were not motivated by any purpose of personal gain or advantage or desire to retain their posts. The Privy Council agreed with the trial judge that, although the directors had acted honestly, it was unconstitutional for the directors to use their fiduciary powers over the shares in the company for the purpose of destroying an existing majority or creating a new majority. As the directors' primary purpose was to alter the majority shareholding, the directors had improperly exercised their powers and the allotment was invalid.

**9-56**   The Privy Council did accept in *Howard Smith Ltd v Ampol Petroleum Ltd*[131] that, as far as a power to allot shares is concerned, that power is not restricted to cases where the company requires additional capital. Such a power may be used (unless the articles otherwise provide), for example, to foster business connections,[132] to ensure that the company has the requisite number of shareholders to exercise its statutory functions[133] and to reach the best commercial agreement for the company, even if this has the effect of defeating a takeover bid.[134]

---

[127]   *Ngurli v McCann* (1954) 90 CLR 425 at 440; *Mills v Mills* (1938) 60 CLR 150 at 164–5; *Hirsche v Sims* [1894] AC 654 at 660–1. See also *Whitehouse v Carlton Hotel Pty Ltd* (1987) 5 ACLC 421 at 427, cited with approval by Lord Sumption (with whom Lord Hodge agreed) in *Eclairs Group plc v JKX Oil & Gas plc* [2016] 1 BCLC 1 at [22] where the Australian High Court added the refinement that where there are competing permissible and impermissible purposes, the preferable view is that, regardless of whether the impermissible purpose was the dominant one or but one of a number of significant contributing causes, an allotment will be invalidated if the impermissible purpose was causative in the sense that but for its presence the power would not have been exercised (citing Dixon J in *Mills v Mills* (1938) 60 CLR 150). See too *Redwood Master Fund Ltd v TD Bank Europe Ltd* [2006] 1 BCLC 149 at [105].

[128]   *Howard Smith Ltd v Ampol Petroleum Ltd* [1974] AC 821; *Re a company, ex p Glossop* [1988] BCLC 570 at 577; *Lee Panavision Ltd v Lee Lighting Ltd* [1992] BCLC 22 at 31; *Extrasure Travel Insurances Ltd v Scattergood* [2003] 1 BCLC 598 at 619. See too Briggs LJ in *JKX Oil & Gas plc v Eclairs Group Ltd* [2014] 2 BCLC 164 at [118].                                                   [129]   [1974] AC 821.

[130]   Briefly, the company had majority shareholders A+B who together held 55 per cent of the shares and they were interested in acquiring total control of the business. The company did need additional capital and the directors made an allotment of 4.5m shares to H which was also interested in acquiring control of the business. The allotment to H had the effect of reducing A+B's control to 36.6 per cent and put H in a position to take over the company.                                                   [131]   [1974] AC 821 at 835.

[132]   See *Harlowe's Nominees Pty Ltd v Woodside Oil Co* (1968) 121 CLR 483, H Ct Aust.

[133]   See *Punt v Symons & Co Ltd* [1903] 2 Ch 506.

[134]   See *Teck Corpn Ltd v Millar* (1972) 33 DLR (3d) 288, S Ct BC; noted Ziegel [1974] JBL 85.

**9-57** As is clear from *Howard Smith Ltd v Ampol Petroleum Ltd*[135] the courts are alert to attempts by the directors to manipulate control of the company by the improper exercise of the power to allot shares and this case is but one of a long line of authorities on this issue. In *Punt v Symons & Co Ltd*[136] an injunction was granted to prevent the company from holding a meeting when an improper allotment had been made for the purpose of securing the passing of a resolution at that meeting; in *Piercy v S Mills & Co Ltd*[137] an allotment made for the purpose of destroying the voting control of the existing majority shareholders was held to be invalid; in *Hogg v Cramphorn Ltd*[138] an allotment was invalid where its primary purpose was to ensure control of the company by the directors and their supporters; likewise in *Bamford v Bamford*[139] an allotment was invalid when made with an eye primarily on the exigencies of a takeover and not with a single eye to the benefit of the company.

**9-58** It should be noted that, in addition to the constraints imposed by CA 2006, s 171, improper allotments of shares to manipulate the control position within a company are constrained now by a variety of statutory requirements (see **21-29** et seq). Directors must have authority to allot either via the articles or by resolution (s 551) and generally allotments must be on a rights basis subject to certain exceptions, exclusions, and disapplications.[140] The CA 2006 does allow directors of a private company with only one class of shares to allot shares without shareholder approval (s 550), a power which is potentially open to abuse as the cases discussed at **9-57** illustrate, but the requirement for a rights issue remains, subject to the statutory exceptions. Further, shareholders can challenge allotments, even an allotment on a rights basis, as being unfairly prejudicial conduct[141] (see Chapter 19). In larger public companies, the directors' ability to manipulate control in takeover situations is subject also to the constraints imposed on defensive actions by incumbent management by the Takeover Code.

**9-59** As noted, the duty to exercise a power for the purposes for which it is conferred applies to all the powers which directors possess and is not limited to the exercise of the power to allot shares.[142] In *Extrasure Travel Insurances Ltd v Scattergood*,[143] for example, two directors transferred funds from the company to another company in the group in order to meet the demands of a pressing creditor of that other company. Applying *Howard Smith v Ampol*, the court concluded that:[144]

---

[135] [1974] AC 821.    [136] [1903] 2 Ch 506.    [137] [1920] 1 Ch 77.    [138] [1966] 3 All ER 420.
[139] [1970] Ch 212.

[140] A rights issue requires that shares are offered to existing shareholders in proportion to their existing holdings; rights issues are discussed at **21-34**.

[141] CA 2006, s 994. See *Re Sunrise Radio Ltd, Kohli v Lit* [2010] 1 BCLC 367 (rights issue at par unfairly prejudicial, for even if the substantial purpose of the rights issue was to raise capital, a failure to give proper consideration to the price of the issue (so benefiting those who took up the offer and disadvantaging those who did not) would ordinarily be a breach of the duty to act fairly as between the shareholders as required by CA 2006, s 172(1)(f)); *Dalby v Bodilly* [2005] BCC 627 (allotment made by the company's sole director and 50 per cent shareholder which had the effect of diluting the other 50 per cent shareholder to a 5 per cent shareholder was the plainest possible breach by the director of his fiduciary duty); see **19-53**.

[142] See for example *Madoff Securities International Ltd v Raven* [2013] EWHC 3147 at [440]—the issue was whether borrowing by the directors which left the company highly capitalised was improper. The court found that the power exercised was the power to borrow money. The purposes for which it was conferred included raising capital for potential use by the company in its business. The purpose for which it was exercised was to raise capital for potential use by the company in its business. The power was not exercised for a purpose other than that for which it was conferred.

[143] [2003] 1 BCLC 598.    [144] [2003] 1 BCLC 598 at 633.

- the power in question was the directors' ability to deal with the assets of the company in the course of trading;

- the purpose for which that power was conferred on the directors was broadly to protect the company's survival and to promote its commercial interests in accordance with its objects;

- the substantial purpose for which the power was actually exercised was to enable the recipient company to meet its liabilities and not to preserve the transferor company;

- it followed that the purpose for which the transfer was made was plainly improper.[145]

**9-60**   In *Bishopsgate Investment Ltd v Maxwell (No 2)*[146] the court found a director in breach of his fiduciary duty when he gave away the company's assets for no consideration to a private family company of which he was a director. This was an exercise of the power to alienate property of the company for an improper purpose and the director was liable to indemnify the company for the loss of those assets.[147] In *Criterion Properties plc v Stratford UK Properties LLC*[148] the court questioned whether it could be a proper exercise of the directors' powers to commit the company in effect to a poison pill arrangement which deterred takeover bidders and protected the interests of certain directors,[149] see **9-72**. In *Re McCarthy Surfacing Ltd*[150] it was an improper exercise of power by the directors to allocate profits under a bonus scheme for the purpose of advancing the interests of the majority shareholders and to ensure that none of the proceeds went to the (estranged) minority shareholders in the form of dividends. In *HLC Environmental Projects Ltd, Hellard v Carvalho*,[151] during a period when the company was insolvent, the sole director caused the company to make payments to its parent company, to himself, to a third party bank whose debt was guaranteed by the parent company, and to a group employee. The court noted that the power in question is a power to deal with the company's assets, the proper purpose for the exercise of that power is to advance the company's business and commercial interests, and, in a case where s 172(3) is engaged because the company is insolvent or doubtfully solvent (see **10-41**), that means advancing the interests of the company's creditors. The court found that, in respect of each payment, the substantial purpose for the exercise of the power was to assist the payees (and in the case of the payment to the bank to assist the parent company indirectly) without any consideration as to the best interests of the company's creditors as a whole, despite the company having and the director knowing it to have substantial creditors and liabilities and no projects or revenue stream and no reasonable prospect of gaining any projects or revenue. The court held that all of the payments were made in breach of s 171(b).

**9-61**   The criticism levied at these authorities is that the courts are imposing limits on powers which have not been so limited, either expressly or impliedly, by the shareholders (the

---

[145] See also *Lee Panavision Ltd v Lee Lighting Ltd* [1992] BCLC 22 at 30 where the court found that it was unconstitutional and beyond the powers of outgoing directors, however much they thought it in the company's interests, to commit the company to a management agreement with a third party (with whom the outgoing directors were closely associated) which would have deprived the incoming directors of all management powers. The court refused to assist the third party to enforce the agreement.

[146] [1993] BCLC 1282.          [147] [1993] BCLC 1282 at 1286.          [148] [2006] 1 BCLC 729, HL.

[149] See too *Ford v Polymer Vision Ltd* [2009] 2 BCLC 160 where the court had concerns about an option agreement entered into by two directors to sell the business to F. The court looked at the one-sided nature of the agreement and thought that the terms agreed, especially as to the price and the time frame (a 10-year option), seemed much more favourable to F than to the company. It was at least arguable, the court said, that committing the company to the disposal of all its assets and undertaking on such terms was an improper exercise of power, see at [89].          [150] [2009] 1 BCLC 622.

[151] [2014] BCC 337 at [106], [116], [124], [131].

articles commonly grant all powers to the directors without limit, see **9-5**) and that the courts are using this doctrine to do what they consistently say they do not do, namely review business decisions reached by the directors. Of course, there is an element of the courts reviewing business decisions according to their perception of the standards expected of a fiduciary office-holder,[152] reflecting in essence objective judgements as to the conduct expected of directors.[153] If the powers are limitless, as they commonly are, the courts necessarily construct limits to the powers by reference to corporate practice and a judicial view of proper standards of conduct,[154] but the approach is not unduly interventionist[155] and it has to be set against the more subjective test in CA 2006, s 172.

**9-62**  It is useful to contrast the approach in *Extrasure Travel Insurances Ltd v Scattergood*,[156] and in *CAS (Nominees) Ltd v Nottingham Forest FC plc*.[157] In *Extrasure*, see **9-59**, the directors allowed company funds to be transferred away to assist companies with which the directors were connected and which were in financial difficulty. The directors had no regard to the company's interests (or its creditors) in so acting and they were held liable. In *CAS (Nominees) Ltd v Nottingham Forest FC plc*[158] the directors of a parent company had a choice as to whether to sell shares in a subsidiary directly to an outsider in order to raise much needed funds for the subsidiary or to raise funds via the parent company shareholders. This was not a case where there was an issue as to diluting the existing shareholders' interests, as was the scenario in the cases discussed at **9-57**. Instead a good faith business decision was taken to sell shares directly to an outsider and bypass the shareholders in the parent company. The shareholders of the parent company argued that the board of the parent company had exercised its powers for an improper purpose. The court dismissed the shareholders' petition finding that the directors were exercising their powers of management of the business (in this case managing an asset, the investment in the subsidiary) and, given a genuine desire to raise capital, they had not exercised their powers to manage for a purpose foreign to their proper ambit. At issue ultimately was a business choice as to how to solve a funding problem in a subsidiary. In the absence of a breach of any statutory requirements or bad faith on the part of the directors, the court was content to let their business judgement stand.

### Proper purpose after *Eclairs*

**9-63**  The Supreme Court had an opportunity to revisit some of the issues surrounding the proper purpose doctrine in *Eclairs Group Ltd v JKX Oil and Gas plc*.[159] The context was

---

[152] See Nolan, 'The Proper Purpose Doctrine and Company Directors' in Rider (ed), *The Realm of Company Law* (1998), pp 20–2.

[153] See Sealy, '"Bona Fides" and "Proper Purposes" in Corporate Decisions' (1989) 15 Mon ULR 265 at 276: 'the courts are in truth making naked value judgments'; and see Sealy, 'Directors' Duties Revisited' (2001) 22 Co Law 79 at 82.

[154] See Nolan, 'Controlling Fiduciary Power' (2009) 68 CLJ 293 at 303: '... the courts will be driven to stipulate the purpose of powers by means of their own default implications, generated by reference to common corporate practice and widely-held expectations of those involved in companies.'

[155] See Lord Wilberforce in *Howard Smith Ltd v Ampol Petroleum Ltd* [1974] AC 821 at 832 cautioning against second-guessing the business judgement of directors.

[156] [2003] 1 BCLC 598.       [157] [2002] 1 BCLC 613.       [158] [2002] 1 BCLC 613.

[159] [2016] 1 BCLC 1, rev'g [2014] 2 BCLC 164, CA, and restoring the decision of Mann J at [2014] 1 BCLC 202. See Nolan, 'Proper Purposes in the Supreme Court' [2016] 132 LQR 369; Worthington, 'Directors' Duties and Improper Purposes' (2016) 75(2) CLJ 213; Shaw-Mellors, 'Directors' Duties and the Proper Purpose Rule' [2016] JBL 241; Tjio, 'The Proper Purpose Rule' [2016] LMCLQ 176; Teele Langford, and Ramsay, 'The Proper Purpose Rule as a Constraint on Directors' Autonomy—*Eclairs v JKX plc*' (2017) 80(1) MLR 110.

the exercise by directors of powers contained in a company's articles (similar to the powers of the court in CA 2006, Pt 22) to impose restrictions on voting and other rights of shareholders following non-compliance by shareholders with a request for information regarding the beneficial ownership of their shares.

**9-64**    In this case, having received responses to the relevant requests which the directors had reasonable cause to believe were false or materially incorrect, restrictions were imposed on shareholders holding 39 per cent of the shares. The effect was to disenfranchise persons whom the board considered were potential takeover bidders for the company. As a consequence of the restrictions, the board was able to secure the passing of special resolutions at a general meeting authorising, *inter alia*, the directors to make market purchases of its shares, disapplying the statutory pre-emption rights on the allotment of shares and reappointing certain directors, resolutions which were opposed by the 39 per cent shareholders.[160] At first instance, Mann J had ruled that the restrictions were ineffective because the directors had been motivated by an improper purpose, namely, to thwart shareholders perceived to be corporate raiders rather than to secure the disclosure of information as to beneficial ownership of the shares.[161] Mann J found that four of the six directors were concerned only with the effect of the restriction notices on the outcome of the general meeting, while accepting that their bona fides and the genuineness of their desire to benefit the company as a whole could not be challenged.[162] The Court of Appeal by a majority allowed an appeal and held that the proper purpose doctrine, laid down in *Howard Smith Ltd v Ampol Petroleum Ltd*,[163] had no significant application to the operation of CA 2006, Pt 22 or equivalent provisions in the articles.[164] The restrictions had been properly imposed. The whole point of these unlimited powers vested in the directors was to restrict the voting rights of a shareholder at a general meeting and it was a very likely scenario, therefore, that the most probable timing for a disclosure notice would be when some controversial resolutions were pending and the board's predominant motive for acting would be to disenfranchise these shareholders.[165] The majority accepted 'of course' that directors are not permitted to use their powers to stage a constitutional coup or to subvert the company's constitution, but the power to impose restrictions was itself part of the constitution.[166] Furthermore, for the majority, the significant point was that recipients of a restriction notice could readily prevent the restrictions by providing full and correct answers and so they were victims of their own choices, not a victim of any improper use of a power by a board of directors.[167] The highlight of the Court of Appeal judgment is a dissenting judgment by Briggs LJ, described later by Lord Sumption in the Supreme Court hearing as 'a formidable dissent'.[168] Briggs LJ rejected any suggestion that non-compliance by the defaulting shareholders was a principled reason for treating the exercise of a fiduciary power to be free from the proper purpose doctrine.[169] The proper purpose doctrine derives, he pointed out, from the fact that a power is fiduciary and its exercise can have a draconian effect upon shareholders' rights and upon the constitutional balance between the powers of the shareholders and the powers of the board. Included within that constitutional balance is the ability of the minority to block special resolutions, an ability which

---

[160]  In fact, as an interim measure the shareholders were allowed to vote at the general meeting on the basis that the effectiveness of their voting would be resolved at the later trial, see [2014] 2 BCLC 169 at [7], [31].

[161]  [2014] 1 BCLC 202.      [162]  [2014] 1 BCLC 202 at [200].      [163]  [1974] AC 821.

[164]  [2014] 2 BCLC 164, CA (per Longmore LJ and Sir Robin Jacob; Briggs LJ dissenting).

[165]  [2014] 2 BCLC 164, CA, at [139, [142].      [166]  [2014] 2 BCLC 164 at [137].

[167]  [2014] 2 BCLC 164 at [135]–[136], a point emphatically rejected by the Supreme Court, see [2016] 1 BCLC 1 at [39]; also Nolan, n 159, 370.

[168]  [2016] 1 BCLC 1 at [29].      [169]  [2014] 2 BCLC 164 at [127].

was defeated here by the exercise of these powers which trespassed on the shareholders' rights.[170] Briggs LJ considered that it did no service to the maintenance of constitutional corporate governance for the Court of Appeal to water down the healthy principle that directors' fiduciary powers must only be exercised for a proper purpose.[171]

**9-65**   The Supreme Court agreed with Briggs LJ, overruled the majority in the Court of Appeal, and re-imposed the orthodoxy that the exercise of all directors' powers is subject to the proper purpose doctrine and it is an abuse of power to exercise powers for a purpose other than that for which they were conferred. As Lord Sumption explained:

> '[T]he proper purpose rule is not concerned with excess of power by doing an act which is beyond the scope of the instrument creating it … It is concerned with abuse of power, by doing acts which are within its scope but done for an improper reason.'[172]

The doctrine has its origin in the equitable doctrine of 'fraud on a power' and company directors, as fiduciaries, have always been subject to the doctrine which is 'one of the main means by which equity enforces the proper conduct of directors'.[173] Crucially, and rejecting the approach of the Court of Appeal, the proper purpose rule is not dependent on any limitation on the scope of a power as a matter of construction, it is a principle by which equity controls the exercise of a fiduciary's powers in respects which are not, or not necessarily, determined by the instrument.[174] Lord Sumption further noted that, not only is the use of directors' powers to influence the outcome of a general meeting an abuse of power, it also 'offends the constitutional distribution of powers between the different organs of the company, because it involves the use of the board's powers to control or influence a decision which the company's constitution assigns to the general body of shareholders'.[175]

**9-66**   In terms of identifying the purpose of a power, the court agreed that the purpose of a power will rarely be expressed in the articles and it will usually depend on an inference from the mischief of the provision conferring it, which is itself deduced from its express terms, from an analysis of their effect, and from the court's understanding of the business context.[176] Looking at this particular power to impose restrictions on shareholders, Lord Sumption found that it had three closely related purposes: (i) to induce a shareholder to comply with a disclosure notice; (ii) to protect the company and its shareholders against making decisions about their respective interests in ignorance of relevant information; and (iii) as a punitive sanction for the failure to comply with the information request.[177] All were directly related to the non-provision of information requisitioned by a disclosure notice.[178] The trial judge had found that the majority of the directors when deciding to impose the restrictions were interested only in the effect on the outcome of the forthcoming general meeting.[179] Therefore, the power had been exercised for an improper purpose and the original decision of Mann J was restored.[180]

---

[170]  [2014] 2 BCLC 164 at [101]–[102].

[171]  [2014] 2 BCLC 164 at [123]. He went on: 'To do so on the ground that the disenfranchised shareholders were controlled by raiders from whom the directors were understandably, and commendably, concerned to protect the company would be to make bad law out of a hard case.'

[172]  [2016] 1 BCLC 1 at [15].      [173]  [2016] 1 BCLC 1 at [15]–[16], [37].

[174]  [2016] 1 BCLC 1 at [30].      [175]  [2016] 1 BCLC 1 at [16].      [176]  [2016] 1 BCLC 1 at [30]–[31].

[177]  [2016] 1 BCLC 1 at [32]–[33]. Worthington, n 159, at 214 makes the point that really there is one purpose here, the second point (ii) above, done by means of incentives and punishments.

[178]  [2016] 1 BCLC 1 at [32].      [179]  [2016] 1 BCLC 1 at [41].      [180]  [2016] 1 BCLC 1 at [44].

**9-67**  It is possible to fit this analysis squarely into the *Howard Smith v Ampol* approach. Having identified the scope of the power, the substantial purpose for which the power was exercised in *Eclairs* was undoubtedly improper. However, while the decision reached could have been reached in that orthodox way (and all members of the court were agreed on the outcome), Lord Sumption (with whom Lord Hodge agreed) favoured a different approach explicitly based on causation.[181] Lord Mance (with whom Lord Neuberger agreed) had some doubts, however, about the views expressed by Lord Sumption,[182] and Lord Clarke (with whom Lord Neuberger also agreed) preferred to defer a conclusion on the broader issues raised by Lord Sumption until they are the subject of full argument before the court.[183]

**9-68**  Essentially, the issue revolves around the proper approach when there are multiple concurrent purposes for the decisions reached by directors, as will commonly be the case. Lord Sumption favoured a move from the orthodox *Howard Smith v Ampol* approach, discussed above, to a 'but for' approach.[184] He suggested that, if the position is that, but for the improper purpose, the power would not have been exercised, the decision cannot stand, even if the directors also had some proper purposes in mind, to which, perhaps, they attached greater importance.[185] Lord Sumption would see *Howard Smith Ltd v Ampol* in those terms—but for the improper purpose (to dilute the majority), the power (to allot shares) would not have been exercised, and therefore it was invalid.[186] He regarded the language of Lord Wilberforce in *Howard Smith v Ampol* ('substantial' or 'primary' purpose, see **9-50**) as referring to the causative purpose which accounted for the board's decision.[187] Vice versa, Lord Sumption considered that '... if there were proper reasons for exercising the power and it would still have been exercised for those reasons even in the absence of improper ones, it is difficult to see why justice would require the decision to be set aside'.[188] Later, he concedes that this argument was not before the court in this case.[189]

**9-69**  There are a number of points which can be made regarding Lord Sumption's suggestions. First, his suggested approach is not necessarily that far removed from the orthodoxy of *Howard Smith Ltd v Ampol* in that, if the improper purpose is causative, it could be argued that the substantial purpose for which the power is exercised is improper, hence it would be improper under *Howard Smith* in any event.[190] Secondly, it is not clear that this approach brings any additional clarity or certainty to the application of the doctrine, as Lord Mance pointed out,[191] since the difficulties in determining substantial purpose are merely replaced by difficulties in determining what is causative. A further point raised by Lord Mance is whether the wording of s 171(b) (a director must 'only' exercise powers for the purposes for which they are conferred) has changed the law such that the presence of

---

[181] [2016] 1 BCLC 1 at [21].          [182] [2016] 1 BCLC 1 at [50]–[55].          [183] [2016] 1 BCLC 1 at [44].
[184] [2016] 1 BCLC 1 at [17]–[24].          [185] [2016] 1 BCLC 1 at [21].          [186] [2016] 1 BCLC 1 at [24].
[187] [2016] 1 BCLC 1 at [24] and see his endorsement of the Australian decision, *Whitehouse v Carlton Hotel Pty*, n 127. Others have doubted whether Lord Wilberforce did have causation in mind, see Shaw-Mellors, n 159, 247;
[188] [2016] 1 BCLC 1 at [21]; and see Mann J [2014] 1 BCLC 202 at [228], [235]–[237]. As Worthington, n 159, notes at 214, maybe if the directors in *Eclairs* had worded their motives more appropriately, all might have been well.          [189] [2016] 1 BCLC 1 at [43].
[190] See Teele, Langford, and Ramsay, n 159, at 119 who note that the difference between the 'but for' test and the substantial purpose test is 'more pronounced than real' given that even under the 'but for' test the improper purpose must be a significantly contributing cause.
[191] [2016] 1 BCLC 1 at [54]. On the other hand, Worthington, n 159, at 215, thinks that Lord Sumption's analysis is 'compelling and likely to prove enormously influential' while conceding at 216 that the case 'teases those seeking certainty'.

any improper purpose is a breach of s 171.[192] It is difficult to support that interpretation, especially as no change is flagged by the Explanatory Notes to the section which state that the section is merely a codification of the common law position (which was not premised on 'only' proper purposes). Further, s 170(4) retains the common law interpretation of the law. Interpreting the statutory provision as having surreptitiously brought about a significant change in directors' duties is unwarranted and, as Nolan points out, would put 'an intolerable burden' on directors.[193]

## Consequences of acts in excess of power or abuse of power

**9-70**  There are a number of different scenarios which can arise. The wrongdoing may be a breach of authority by the board or an individual director. The directors may have exercised their powers for an improper purpose. In each case, there may or may not be a breach of s 172(1), a failure to act to promote the success of the company. Not all breaches will be breaches of s 172 as where, despite exercising their powers for an improper purpose, directors act in what they honestly believe to be the interests of the company, as was the case, for example, with the directors in *Howard Smith Ltd v Ampol Petroleum Ltd*[194] and in *Eclairs plc v JKX Oil and Gas plc*.[195] When looking at the consequences, there are also a variety of parties to consider. For the directors, the question is whether they are in breach of duty. For third parties, the question usually is whether the transaction is valid and binding on the company. For the shareholders, there may be a question of whether to ratify the wrongdoing so as to relieve the directors from liability and, less frequently, there may be a question of whether to affirm the transaction but the rules of agency and the application of CA 2006, s 40, discussed earlier, usually ensure that the company is bound in any event. An act may be a breach of duty (as where a power is exercised for an improper purpose), but there may be no personal gain by the directors. There is little legal clarity on the outcome in these multi-dimensional situations.[196]

**9-71**  An act by a director in breach of his authority can be ratified as any principal can ratify the acts of an agent in excess of his powers. An act in excess of the board's authority can be affirmed or adopted by an ordinary resolution even though an alteration to the board's powers for all time would require a special resolution.[197] As discussed earlier, acts in excess of a director's authority or the board's authority can be binding on the company in any event without the need for any ratification or affirmation, either as a matter of agency law or because of the application of CA 2006, s 40. A third party put on inquiry by circumstances suggesting the director or the board are not acting in the company's interests, but in bad faith or for an improper purpose, will not be able to rely on agency or s 40 to validate the transaction for the 'authority to act as agent includes only authority to act honestly in pursuit of the interests of the principal',[198] see **9-24**. A failure so to act negates

---

[192] [2016] 1 BCLC 1 at [51]; see also Lord Sumption at [21] '... the [statutory] duty is broken if the directors allow themselves to be influenced by *any* improper purpose.'  [193] Nolan, n 159, 372.

[194] [1974] AC 821.    [195] [2016] 1 BCLC 1.

[196] See Worthington, 'Corporate Attribution and Agency: Back to Basics' (2017) 133 LQR 118 who argues that these matters should be treated as cases of an abuse of authority so that the remedies lie primarily internally against the wrongdoing agent and the company is bound vis-à-vis third parties unless the third party knew of the breach of duty.

[197] *Irvine v Union Bank of Australia* (1877) 2 App Cas 366, PC; *Grant v United Kingdom Switchback Railways Co* (1888) 40 Ch D 135, CA.

[198] *Bowstead and Reynolds on Agency* (21st edn, 2017), para 3-010; *Hopkins v TL Dallas Group Ltd* [2005] 1 BCLC 543 at [88]; see *Criterion Properties plc v Stratford UK Properties LLC* [2006] 1 BCLC 729 at [31].

any actual authority and the transaction is void as regards the principal.[199] As Slade LJ explained in *Rolled Steel Products (Holdings) Ltd v British Steel Corpn*,[200] '... a party dealing with the company cannot rely on the ostensible authority of its directors to enter into a particular transaction if he knows they in fact have no such authority because it is being entered into for improper purposes. Neither the rule in Turquand's case nor more general principles of the law of agency will avail him in such circumstances ...'

**9-72**    These issues were considered by the House of Lords in *Criterion Properties plc v Stratford UK Properties LLC*.[201] The question was whether a managing director of a company and another director could commit the company to an arrangement known as a poison pill (which has the effect of warding off takeover bidders and deterring them from making a bid to shareholders) which in this case was drafted in extremely wide and onerous terms but which was beneficial to the directors concerned. There had been considerable confusion in the lower courts as to the proper approach to this issue,[202] but their Lordships were resolutely clear that the matter is one of agency law.[203] The issue which needed to be resolved was whether the directors had actual or apparent authority to enter into such an arrangement, a factual matter which was remitted to trial. Lord Scott explained the position succinctly:

> '[I]f a person dealing with an agent knows or has reason to believe that the contract or transaction is contrary to the commercial interests of the agent's principal, it is likely to be very difficult for the person to assert with any credibility that he believed the agent did have actual authority. Lack of such belief would be fatal to a claim that the agent had apparent authority.'

**9-73**    Further, as *Wrexham AFC Ltd v Crucialmove Ltd*[204] makes clear, the third party in this situation is equally unable to rely on CA 2006, s 40 because the section imposes the same duty to inquire as agency law. In this case (the facts are given at **9-21**), the third party knew that the director executing a particular agreement was in breach of his fiduciary duties to the company. In those circumstances, the third party was bound to inquire whether the transaction had been authorised or approved by the company or its board. Given he was on notice and had failed to inquire, the Court of Appeal held that the third party could not rely as a matter of agency law on any apparent authority of the director, nor could he rely on CA 2006, s 40, for the statutory provision, the court said, does not absolve a person dealing with the company from any duty to inquire when the circumstances are such as to put that person on inquiry.[205] Where the third party knows of a lack of authority or the belief in authority is irrational or dishonest, the outcome is the same then under agency law or the Companies Act. A third party put on inquiry with respect to the exercise of a power in a manner contrary to the company's interests and who fails to inquire cannot rely on either apparent authority or the statute for protection. The third party is

---

[199] See *Bowstead and Reynolds on Agency* (21st edn, 2017), para 3-011; *Hopkins v TL Dallas Group Ltd* [2005] 1 BCLC 543 at [88]; *Criterion Properties plc v Stratford UK Properties LLC* [2006] 1 BCLC 729 at [31]; *Re Capitol Films Ltd, Rubin v Cobalt Pictures Ltd* [2011] 2 BCLC 359 at [53]–[55]; *GHLM Trading Ltd v Maroo* [2012] 2 BCLC 369 at [171]. See also Mitchell, 'Stewardship of Property and Liability of Account' [2014] Conv 215 at 218–19.

[200] [1985] 3 All ER 52 at [83].        [201] [2006] 1 BCLC 729, HL.

[202] See [2003] 2 BCLC 129, CA, [2002] 2 BCLC 151, Ch D. In error, the lower courts had approached the matter essentially on the basis of the unconscionability of the conduct of the third party and issues of 'knowing receipt', see [2006] 1 BCLC 729 at [2], [27], HL, a 'faulty elision of the issues' as Lord Nicholls commented, at [2].                                        [203] [2006] 1 BCLC 729 at [2], [28].

[204] [2008] 1 BCLC 508, CA.        [205] [2008] 1 BCLC 508 at 523–4.

not protected and if in receipt of assets/benefits under the contract, he must account for them,[206] for the transaction is void and the company is not bound.[207] A third party who is able to rely on the apparent authority of the agent, or on the protection of s 40, because he is in good faith and not aware of any improper purpose is able to hold the company to the transaction (assuming there are no other problems with the transaction) and, for the avoidance of doubt, the shareholders may choose to affirm the transaction though entered into in breach of authority.[208] Likewise, where a director acts for an improper purpose, they may be acting within the scope of their authority—for example, the directors in *Eclairs v JKX Oil & Gas Ltd*[209] were authorised to impose restrictions on shareholders in certain circumstances, they then acted for an improper purpose in imposing restrictions to influence voting at a general meeting, but they did act in what they honestly considered to be the interests of the company. A bona fide exercise of a power for an improper purpose is voidable and so the company can choose to affirm the transaction or decision.[210] But where directors exercise a power improperly in a transaction to benefit themselves, then the agreement between them and the company is unenforceable.[211]

**9-74**  Where ratification of the director's breach of duty is required, whether breach of s 171 or s 172, that is a separate matter governed by s 239 and requiring ratification by disinterested shareholders, see **20-46**. Where the shareholders choose not to ratify the director's breach of duty,[212] the director is liable to account for any gain or to indemnify the company for any loss caused by the exercise of the power for an improper purpose.[213] In an appropriate case, the exercise of powers for an improper purpose is evidence of unfitness justifying disqualification.[214]

---

[206] See *Guinness v Saunders* [1990] BCLC 402, HL; and see *Criterion Properties plc v Stratford UK Properties LLC* [2006] 1 BCLC 729 at 732, HL; *Rolled Steel Products (Holdings) Ltd v British Steel Corpn* [1985] 3 All ER 52, CA. See Conaglen and Nolan, 'Contracts and Knowing Receipt: Principles and Application' (2013) 129 LQR 359; Yap, 'Knowing Receipt and Apparent Authority' (2011) 127 LQR 350.

[207] *Rolled Steel Products (Holdings) Ltd v British Steel Corpn* [1985] 3 All ER 52 at 83, CA. See *Snell's Equity* (33rd edn, 2014), para 10-030, which suggests nullity only in so far as that is possible given the context and this will not be the case if the power is conferred by statute where the exercise of the power will be rendered voidable by equity, see n 208.

[208] *Bamford v Bamford* [1969] 1 All ER 969, CA; *Hogg v Cramphorn* [1967] Ch 254. See Nolan, 'The Proper Purpose Doctrine and Company Directors' in Rider (ed), *The Realm of Company Law* (1998), p 32 who comments that there is no good reason why a majority of shareholders should be able to ratify a colourable allotment of shares, while also noting that *Hogg* and *Bamford* are out of line with earlier authorities that an exercise of a power for an improper purpose is void: see *Punt v Symons & Co Ltd* [1903] 2 Ch 506; *Piercy v S Mills & Co Ltd* [1920] 1 Ch 77; see also Nolan (2009) 68 CLJ 293. Nolan writing in *Snell's Equity* (33nd edn, 2014), para 10-030 offers the alternative explanation for *Bamford* and for *Hogg* that these are cases of allotments in exercise of a statutory power which is not subject to the doctrine of fraud on a power and the most that equity can do in those circumstances is render the transaction voidable.

[209] [2016] 1 BCLC 1.

[210] *Bamford v Bamford* [1969] 1 All ER 969, CA; *Hogg v Cramphorn* [1967] Ch 254.

[211] See *Re McCarthy Surfacing Ltd* [2009] 1 BCLC 622 at [82].

[212] See *Bishopsgate Investment Ltd v Maxwell (No 2)* [1993] BCLC 1282; also *Extrasure Travel Insurances Ltd v Scattergood* [2003] 1 BCLC 598 at [153].

[213] See, for example, *Extrasure Travel Insurances Ltd v Scattergood* [2003] 1 BCLC 598 at [158]—loss would be the amount by which the company's assets were diminished by a transfer of assets for an improper purpose to a parent company, but subject to taking into account the extent to which the transfer extinguished a genuine debt.

[214] See, for example, *Re Looe Fish Ltd* [1993] BCLC 1160.

# 10

# Duty to promote the success of the company

## A Introduction

**10-1**  At common law, directors were under a duty to act bona fide in what they considered to be the interests of the company, interpreted as meaning in the interests of the shareholders as a general body, balancing the short-term interests of present members against the long-term interests of future members.[1] There was also a statutory obligation on directors to 'have regard in the performance of their functions to the interests of the company's employees in general as well as the interests of its members' (CA 1985, s 309). Additionally, the courts developed the duty to include within it a requirement for directors to have regard to the interests of creditors where the company is insolvent or of doubtful solvency and it is the creditors' money which is at risk.[2] Further control over the directors was imposed by the obligation to exercise their powers for a proper purpose and this proper purpose doctrine is retained by CA 2006, s 171 (discussed in Chapter 9) and continues to constrain directors in the exercise of their powers.

**10-2**  The duty to act bona fide in the interests of the company is restated in s 172(1) as a duty to act[3] to promote the success of the company,[4] as follows:

'(1)  A director of a company must act in the way he considers, in good faith, would be most likely to promote the success of the company for the benefit of its members as a whole, and in doing so have regard (amongst other matters) to—

(a)  the likely consequences of any decision in the long term,

(b)  the interests of the company's employees,

(c)  the need to foster the company's business relationships with suppliers, customers and others,

(d)  the impact of the company's operations on the community and the environment,

---

[1]  *Re Smith & Fawcett Ltd* [1942] Ch 304 at 306; Second Savoy Hotel Investigation, Report of the Inspector (1954) HMSO; *Gaiman v National Association for Mental Health* [1971] Ch 317 at 330.

[2]  *West Mercia Safetywear Ltd v Dodd* [1988] BCLC 250, CA. See further at **10-41**.

[3]  The provision applies to 'acts' and is not limited to decision-making, formal or informal, nor to business conducted at board meetings.

[4]  In *Re Southern Counties Fresh Foods Ltd* [2008] EWHC 2810 at [52], Warren J noted that the old and the new formulations 'come to the same thing' with the modern formulation giving 'a more readily understood definition of the scope of the duty'. The obligation in CA 2006, s 172 is qualified by s 247 (restating CA 1985, s 719) which permits the directors to make provision for the benefit of the employees or former employees on the cessation or transfer of the business, even though such acts are not to promote the success of the company.

    (e)  the desirability of the company maintaining a reputation for high standards of business conduct, and

    (f)  the need to act fairly as between members of the company.'

This duty has effect 'subject to any enactment or rule of law requiring directors, in certain circumstances, to consider or act in the interests of creditors of the company' (s 172(3)), see **10-41**. The duty is also modified in application where the purposes of the company include purposes other than for the benefit of the members (s 712(2)), as discussed at **10-14**. As a result, those wishing to form companies with objectives other than or in addition to increasing shareholder value, such as charitable ventures, may find it useful to include objects clauses in their articles to ensure that the constitution reflects the company's priorities and guides the directors as to what constitutes 'success' in their context.

**10-3**    In the Parliamentary debates on the CA 2006, the Government stressed that there are not two duties in s 172—a duty to act in good faith and to have regard to the factors listed—there is only one duty: it is for directors to decide as a matter of business judgement what would be most likely to promote the success of the company for the benefit of its members as a whole and the factors are subordinate to that overriding duty.[5] In this way, it was hoped also to curb the scope for allegations of breach of duty arising from a supposed failure to have regard to one or more of the factors. For the purposes of discussion, the duty is separated in this chapter into its component elements, but this general point, that there is only one duty in s 172(1), must not be overlooked.

## B  Duty to act in good faith

**10-4**    The first point about the duty in CA 2006, s 172(1) is that it is a subjective test. A director must act in the way he considers (not what a court may consider), in good faith, would be most likely to promote the success of the company[6] for the benefit of its members as a whole, and the duty applies to all acts of a director. The position was explained by Jonathan Parker J in *Regentcrest plc v Cohen*[7] as follows:

> 'The question is not whether, viewed objectively by the court, the particular act or omission which is challenged was in fact in the interests of the company; still less is the question whether the court, had it been in the position of the director at the relevant time, might have acted differently. Rather, the question is whether the director honestly believed that his act or omission was in the interests of the company. The issue is as to the director's state of mind.'

**10-5**    In *Regentcrest plc v Cohen*[8] the directors of a property development company waived a clawback claim (valued at £1.5m) which the company had under an agreement with the vendors of certain property to it. The vendors (S and F) were members of the board of the company and the clawback payment was waived at a meeting which took place 12 days before a petition for winding up the company was presented by a creditor. In return for

---

[5] Originally, the drafting of this provision required that the directors 'must' have regard to these factors, but the Bill was amended to remove the second 'must', as it was suggested that using 'must' twice might have implied a separate duty: see HL Deb, vol 681, cols 845, 883–4 (9 May 2006).

[6] *Re Smith & Fawcett Ltd* [1942] Ch 304 at 306.

[7] [2001] 2 BCLC 80 at 105. See too *Extrasure Travel Insurances Ltd v Scattergood* [2003] 1 BCLC 598 at [90]. As to whether a director's duty of good faith requires a director to disclose misconduct on his part, see **12-6**.

[8] [2001] 2 BCLC 80. See also *Re Welfab Engineers Ltd* [1990] BCLC 833.

waiving the claim, S and F undertook to work for the company for no remuneration for a period of years. The interested directors declared their interest and took no part in the proceedings nor did they vote in respect of the resolution to waive the clawback.

**10-6**     On winding up, the liquidators claimed that the directors who waived the clawback claim had acted in breach of their duty to the company and were liable to make good the loss to the company. It was alleged that the directors did not honestly believe that the waiver was in the interests of the company and that the sole reason for agreeing to it was to protect the vendors (their fellow directors) from liability.

**10-7**     Applying the subjective approach, the court found that the board had acted bona fide. The decisive consideration in the minds of the directors in agreeing to waive the clawback claim had been the need to maintain a united board and not to create a situation in which two of the directors were being sued by the company and were contesting the claim. The company was in difficult negotiations with its creditors at that time and suing two of its directors would have given rise to the gravest misgivings on the part of anyone concerned in trying to save the company. In voting in favour of the waiver, the court concluded that the directors honestly believed that they were acting in the best interests of the company. Accordingly, the claim for breach of duty failed.

**10-8**     Deferring to the honest belief of the directors, if that is found to exist, reflects the traditional view that the courts must not get involved in reviewing the exercise of business judgement by the directors and, in particular, must avoid reviewing a situation with the benefit of hindsight.[9] That approach has long been summed up by the famous dictum of Lord Eldon LC in *Carlen v Drury*[10] to the effect that the court is not to be required 'to take the management of every playhouse and brewhouse in the kingdom'. As Lord Wilberforce put it in *Howard Smith Ltd v Ampol Petroleum Ltd*:[11]

> 'There is no appeal on merits from management decisions to courts of law: nor will courts of law assume to act as a kind of supervisory board over decisions within the powers of management honestly arrived at.'

Equally, there may be disagreements between the directors as to the commercial wisdom of a particular decision and a dissenting director is not in breach of his duty to act in what he considers in good faith to be the interests of the company (nor is he obliged to resign or to refuse to be party to the implementation of the decision) simply because if left to himself he would do things differently.[12]

**10-9**     For a director to rely on his honest belief, there must be some evidence that he has actually considered the matter. If a director has not considered the interests of the company at all, the test cannot be one of honest belief. For example, in *Extrasure Travel Insurances Ltd v Scattergood*[13] the court did not believe that the defendant directors had ever formed any opinion at all,[14] never mind an honest belief, that a transfer of moneys from one company to another company in a group to enable that second company to pay a pressing

---

[9] See *Regentcrest plc v Cohen* [2001] 2 BCLC 80 at 106–7; also *Facia Footwear Ltd v Hinchcliffe* [1998] 1 BCLC 218 at 228.     [10] (1812) 1 Ves & B 154 at 158.

[11] [1974] 1 All ER 1126 at 1131; see also *Burland v Earle* [1902] AC 83 at 93, per Lord Davey.

[12] *Madoff Securities International Ltd v Raven* [2013] EWHC 3147 at [193], [236], per Popplewell J.

[13] [2003] 1 BCLC 598 at 619.

[14] [2003] 1 BCLC 598 at 632–3. See also *Re McCarthy Surfacing Ltd, Hequet v McCarthy* [2009] 1 BCLC 622 (board had not reached a bona fide decision not to pay dividends in the interests of the company, rather the board consistently failed, in breach of their duties, to consider whether to declare dividends).

creditor was in the interests of the transferor company. The court found that the directors made the transfer simply because the second company needed the money, the transferor company had the money, and the creditor of the second company was pressing. In those circumstances where a director has not considered the interests of the company at all, has not turned his mind to this issue, the question for the court is, not the honest belief of the directors (since none exists), but whether an intelligent and honest director of the company concerned could in the whole of the circumstances reasonably have believed the transaction to be for the benefit of the company, often referred to as the *Charterbridge* test.[15] Further, a failure to consider whether the matter is in the interests of the company will amount to a failure to exercise care and skill.[16]

**10-10**    Where the directors have considered the matter, as noted above, the test of their bona fides is essentially subjective, but even then there must be some limits to it,[17] including at least the other duties, especially the duty in CA 2006, s 171 to act for a proper purpose and mere honesty will not trump an improper purpose.[18] The court will not accept in an unquestioning way a director's assertion that he acted bona fide when the facts might appear to suggest otherwise, bearing in mind Bowen LJ's comments in *Hutton v West Cork Rly Co*[19] to the effect that bona fides cannot be the sole test, for a lunatic may act perfectly bona fide yet perfectly irrationally.

**10-11**    The limits to the subjective test lie then along the boundaries of unreasonableness and detriment to the company.[20] As Jonathan Parker J noted in *Regentcrest plc v Cohen*,[21] where it is clear that the act or omission under challenge resulted in substantial detriment to the company, the director will have difficulty in persuading the court that he honestly believed it to be in the company's interest. For example, in *Re Genosyis Technology Management Ltd, Wallach v Secretary of State for Trade and Industry*[22] two directors were disqualified for entering, on behalf of the company, into a settlement agreement with a customer under which the company gave up a claim for £1.25m (which was instead paid to

---

[15]    [2003] 1 BCLC 598 at [91], applying *Charterbridge Corp Ltd v Lloyds Bank Ltd* [1969] 2 All ER 1185 at 119; also *Re Southern Counties Fresh Foods Ltd* [2008] EWHC 2810 at [53], per Warren J; *Madoff Securities International Ltd v Raven* [2013] EWHC 3147 at [194], [244]–[245], [252]–[253], [437]–[438]; *Re PV Solar Solutions Ltd* [2018] 1 BCLC 58 at [77]. The test is of general application: *Colin Gwyer & Associates Ltd v London Wharf* [2003] 2 BCLC 153 at [87]. See Teele, Langford, and Ramsay, 'Directors' Duties to Act in the Interests of the Company—Subjective or Objective' [2015] JBL 173 who note the English preference for this approach while the Australian courts have given it a mixed reception. The difficulty, as the authors see it, is that it is indefensible in policy terms, having found that directors have not considered the interests of the company in respect of a particular matter, not then to find them in breach of duty, see at 180–1. This approach, they assert, undermines the importance of consideration of the company's interests which is a key facet of s 172(1).

[16]    See *Madoff Securities International Ltd v Raven* [2013] EWHC 3147 at [265].

[17]    See *Re a Company, ex p Glossop* [1988] BCLC 570 at 577, per Harman J ('It is vital … to remember that actions of boards of directors cannot simply be justified by invoking the incantation 'a decision taken bona fide in the interests of the company').

[18]    *Howard Smith Ltd v Ampol Petroleum Ltd* [1974] 1 All ER 1126.        [19]    (1993) 23 Ch D 654 at 671.

[20]    See Teele, Langford, and Ramsay, 'Directors' Duties to Act in the Interests of the Company', who argue for a test which is primarily subjective, coupled with the court looking to objective factors to assess whether the director's belief is honestly held, and then for the court to consider whether the decision is one that no reasonable director would consider to be in the interests of the company even if the director honestly holds the belief in question. It is not clear that this approach would actually be much of a change or improvement on what is the current position in any event.

[21]    [2001] 2 BCLC 80 at [120]. See also *Roberts v Frohlich* [2011] 2 BCLC 625 at [91]–[97]; honest belief turned into irrational optimism and wilful blindness and a failure to act bona fide in the interests of the company.        [22]    [2007] 1 BCLC 208.

its parent company) and gained a maximum of £166,000. Even if it was accepted that the directors honestly believed this settlement to be in the interests of the company (because the subsidiary would continue to benefit from the support of the parent), the court said they had no reasonable grounds for that belief and were in breach of their duties.[23]

**10-12**    Often the bad faith of the director is relatively evident. In *Neptune (Vehicle Washing Equipment) Ltd v Fitzgerald (No 2)*[24] the court had little difficulty in concluding that a sole director was not acting in the interests of the company, but was acting exclusively to further his own personal interests, when he procured an ex gratia payment to him by the company of £100,000 on termination of his service contract with the company.[25] Likewise, a director who pays away significant sums of the company's money either knowing that the recipient is not entitled to it, or at the very least, without regard to the entitlement of the recipient, cannot be said to have an honest belief that payment was in the interests of the company.[26] Similarly, a director who releases, without prepayment, a significant quantity of stock to a customer (who already owes the company money in circumstances where there is no real prospect of recouping it) cannot reasonably believe the transaction to be in the interests of the company.[27] In *Dickinson v NAL Realisations Ltd*,[28] a director and controlling shareholder attempted to drain the company of assets so as to defeat any potential award against the company in pending environmental litigation. He had the company enter into a sale and leaseback arrangement with him regarding the company's main factory. There was no evidence the company needed to raise cash, nor any indication of the benefit of the transaction to the company, nor was there any professional valuation to support the (questionable) price paid. He also acquired the company's shareholding in a subsidiary for £1, an asset the court found to be worth at least £214,000. The court found that in this transaction, as with the factory sale, that the director was acting to promote his own interests rather than the interests of the company.

## C  The success of the company for the benefit of the members as a whole

**10-13**    The duty in CA 2006, s 172 is expressed in terms of promoting the success of the company and 'success' is a matter for the members to determine; they define the objectives of the company and then it is for the directors to promote the success of the company in those terms.[29] The directors will be guided by their business judgement and their knowledge of the nature and purpose of the company, reinforced by anything in the company's

---

[23]  [2007] 1 BCLC 208 at [21].

[24]  [1995] BCC 1000. Cf *Runciman v Walter Runciman plc* [1992] BCLC 1084 where the court accepted that the directors had acted bona fide and in the interests of the company in extending a director's service contract for five years.

[25]  See [1995] BCC 1000 at 1017 for a discussion of the evidence which showed a lack of bona fides on the part of the director which included, for example, the furtive and secretive manner in which he acted and the fact that he knew the shareholders would not have approved the payment.

[26]  See *Primlake v Matthews Associates* [2007] 1 BCLC 666 at [313] (de jure director paid out in excess of £800,000 from the company's funds to a de facto director when neither director had an honest belief that the de facto director was entitled to payment).

[27]  See *Simtel Communications Ltd v Rebak* [2006] 2 BCLC 571 at [104] (an intelligent and honest man in the position of the director could not in all the circumstances have reasonably believed that the transaction was for the benefit of the company).

[28]  [2017] EWHC 28, [2018] 1 BCLC 623.        [29]  See HL Deb, vol 678, GC 258 (6 February 2006).

constitution.[30] In practice, directors will probably prefer not to have anything specific on this issue in the articles so as to give themselves maximum flexibility to determine the direction of the company's business, safe in the knowledge that the courts will not second-guess their business judgement (see **10-8**). In some circumstances, such as where there are different classes of shareholders so decisions of the directors may adversely affect the interests of one class and benefit another, it is accepted that the question is not so much one of the interests of the company as one of what is fair as between different classes of shareholders.[31] Indeed, regardless of whether there are different classes as such, directors must be mindful of the need to act fairly as between members of the company (s 172(1)(f)), see **10-29**.[32]

**10-14** For most companies, 'success' is usually defined in economic terms, looking to a long-term increase in shareholder value,[33] but success may be measured in other ways. For example, where the company is formed to acquire a business or carry out a joint venture, success is measured against those objectives. Some companies also exist for purposes other than the benefit of the members and CA 2006, s 172(2) envisages that companies may have a combination of purposes, not all of which are commercial or profit-orientated.[34] The application of s 172(1) in such circumstances is modified by s 172(2) in the manner explained in *Stimpson v Southern Private Landlords Association*.[35] In this case, concerning permission to continue a derivative claim (see **20-35**), the respondent company was not a trading company, but a not-for-profit organisation formed as a company limited by guarantee rather than a company limited by shares. It operated essentially as a trade association where the members did not have any interest in its assets and remained members only for so long as they paid their subscriptions. The court noted that CA 2006, s 172(2) contemplates two different situations: where the objects of the company consist of purposes other than the benefit of its members (in which case the director's duty is to achieve those purposes) and where the purposes of the company include purposes other than the benefit of its members. In the latter case, a director must act in a way that he considers in good faith would be most likely to promote the success of the company for the benefit of its members as a whole whilst at the same time achieving these other purposes and, if there is a conflict between those dual purposes, a balancing exercise is required of the director in the exercise of his honest business judgement.[36]

**10-15** The duty is to promote the success of the company for the benefit of the members as a whole and, for most purposes, this means promoting the interests of the entity which

---

[30] CA 2006, s 171(a) requires a director to act in accordance with the constitution and the constitution is broadly defined for the purposes of directors' general duties as including the articles and all binding decisions of the members, whether formal or informal (ss 17, 257), so the directors may have to take into account any guidance in ordinary resolutions of the shareholders in determining what can be regarded as 'success' in a particular company: see HL Deb, vol 678, GC 255–8 (6 February 2006).

[31] *Mills v Mills* (1938) 60 CLR 150 at 164, per Latham CJ; *Howard Smith Ltd v Ampol Petroleum Ltd* [1974] 1 All ER 1126 at 1134.

[32] *Mutual Life Insurance Co of New York v Rank Organisation Ltd* [1985] BCLC 11; *Re BSB Holdings Ltd (No 2)* [1996] 1 BCLC 155.

[33] See HL Deb, vol 678, GC 258 (6 February 2006).

[34] CA 2006, s 172(2) provides that where or to the extent that the purposes of the company consist of or include purposes other than the benefit of its members, sub-s (1) has effect as if the reference to promoting the success of the company for the benefit of its members were to achieving those purposes.

[35] [2010] BCC 387.

[36] [2010] BCC 387 at [26]; *Explanatory Notes to the Companies Act 2006*, para 330.

typically calls for a balancing of the short and long-term interests of the shareholders.[37] This is so even in the context of a takeover bid when it might be thought that the only relevant interest is the interests of the current shareholders.[38] Where the company is solvent, the predominant interest to which the directors are likely to have regard will be the members' interests, while having due regard to the factors listed in s 172, and generally what is in the interests of the predominant shareholder is likely to be in the interests of the long-term success of the company.[39] For decades, there has been a debate about the failure of boards to focus on the long term, often linked it is thought to the fact that directors' remuneration depends on short-term success, when the economic needs of the country would prefer a focus on the long-term sustainability of the entity.[40] The Kay Review (see **6-64**) reported in 2012 on the issues to little discernible effect.[41] The 2018 UK Corporate Governance Code (in draft at the time of writing) does identify the board's function as being to promote the long-term sustainable success of the company and it suggests that the board should assess the basis on which the company generates and preserves value over the long term.[42]

**10-16**  Where the company is one of a group, the requirement remains that the directors must act to promote the success of the separate legal entity, the individual company, and not look solely to the overall interests of the group, indeed to disregard the interests of the particular company is grounds for possible disqualification, see **3-75**. It may be, of course, that the most effective way to promote the success of the company is to promote the success of the group. For example, it may be appropriate for a subsidiary to provide financial support for the rest of a group, though the group is in financial difficulty, when the continued prosperity and the very existence of the subsidiary may depend on the group remaining in business, as is commonly the case.[43] A decision of the directors of a subsidiary company to continue lending to the group could still be a decision taken bona fide in the interests of the company, see **3-72**.

---

[37] This was very much the position at common law, see n 1.

[38] This point is reinforced by the Takeover Code in 2011 which notes that the offer price is not the determining factor for the board of the offeree company when giving its opinion on any takeover offer (Takeover Code, note 1 to rule 25.2) and the board is not precluded from taking into account any other factors which it considers relevant and these would certainly include the interests of the employees.

[39] See *Madoff Securities International Ltd v Raven* [2013] EWHC 3147 at [220], where Popplewell J concluded that, provided the company was solvent, a director could honestly believe that payments in accordance with the wishes of the shareholder who held all the voting shares bar one was in the interests of the company—admittedly this was a commercial payment, could the shareholder ask the company to make gift payments to a charity?

[40] See generally Keay who has explored the difficulties in adopting either a shareholder or stakeholder model and who argues cogently for greater consideration of the sustainability of the entity, see Keay, *The Corporate Objective: Corporations, Globalisation and the Law* (2011); Keay, 'The Ultimate Objective of the Company and the Enforcement of the Entity Maximisation and Sustainability Model' (2010) 6 JCLS 351; Keay 'Ascertaining the Corporate Objective: An Entity Maximisation and Sustainability Model' (2008) 71 MLR 663.

[41] See *Kay Review of Equity Markets and Long-term Decision Making, Final Report* (July 2012). For the background to the review, see BIS, 'A Long-term Focus for Corporate Britain, A call for evidence' (October 2010), URN 10/1225 and BIS, 'A Long Term Focus for Corporate Britain', Summary of responses (March 2011), URN 11/797.

[42] FRC, Proposed Revisions to the UK Corporate Governance Code (December 2017), Code Principle 1 and Provision 1.

[43] See *Facia Footwear Ltd v Hinchcliffe* [1998] 1 BCLC 218 at 225–6, 228–9; also *Nicholas v Soundcraft Electronics Ltd* [1993] BCLC 360.

## The nominee director and the interests of his appointor

**10-17**   The obligation to promote the interests of the company also raises issues about the role of nominee directors appointed to represent particular interests.[44] It is common commercial practice for directors to be appointed to represent, for example, the interests of the venture capitalist who may be a significant but not majority shareholder and who wants some protection for his investment, or the joint venture partner who wants to ensure the company properly pursues that joint venture, or the lender who wants to keep the company's activities under close scrutiny. The issue also arises with respect to group companies where the holding company appoints nominee directors to the boards of subsidiary entities. As noted earlier, the director must act in the interests of the subsidiary, not the group, though their interests may coincide and if the subsidiary is wholly owned (and does not become insolvent) then little of consequence arises from the blurring of lines between the entities. The position is different if there are minority interests, in which case nominee directors appointed by the parent company must not conduct the affairs of the company in the interests of the parent company and in a manner unfairly prejudicial to the interests of the minority.[45]

**10-18**   The position under the CA 2006 (which makes no specific mention of nominee directors) is that all directors owe their general duties to the company (s 170(1)) and, as discussed, s 172 requires a director to act in a way most likely to promote the success of the company. The theoretical position then is clear: once appointed the nominee director's obligations lie to the company and its interests, not to the appointor and his interests. In practice the position is more complicated with the appointor expecting that his interests will be safeguarded, his voting intentions carried out, and even, perhaps, that he will have access to information from the company's boardroom. But these commercial expectations raise several legal difficulties. For example, a nominee director (or any director) must respect the company's confidential information and is not entitled to convey such information to his appointor without the consent of the company. A director is required to exercise independent judgement under s 173 and so a nominee director cannot vote automatically in accordance with the wishes of his appointor, though the position may be modified by the company's constitution, a point discussed at **11-58**. Another duty likely to cause difficulties for the nominee director is the no-conflict duty (s 175(1)), though that duty can be managed in that s 175(4)(b) allows for the authorisation of conflicts of interest by disinterested directors and s 177 merely requires conflicts between a director and his company in respect of proposed transactions to be disclosed to the other directors. At the practical level, what matters most for nominee directors is this ability to be released from the no-conflict duty and they are probably less concerned about any general release (and, possibly, have no expectation that they could or should be released) from their core obligations under s 172. The problems of a nominee director with respect to conflicts are no different from any director with a conflict of interest, the main difference being that the nominee's conflict will usually be evident from the outset. As conflicts of interest are discussed in detail in Chapter 12, that discussion is not repeated here.

**10-19**   The main issue to be considered here is the extent to which the nominee director is required by s 172 to promote the success of the company when his appointor may expect,

---

[44] See Ahern, 'Nominee Directors' Duty to Promote the Success of the Company: Commercial Pragmatism and Legal Orthodoxy' (2011) 127 LQR 118.

[45] *Scottish Co-operative Wholesale Society Ltd v Meyer* [1959] AC 324, HL (inaction of nominee directors in face of decision by majority shareholder to terminate the business of the company amounted to conduct of the company's affairs in an oppressive manner and a breach by the directors of their duties), see **3-76**.

wish, even demand, that the nominee act to promote the interests of the appointor. The issue came before the Court of Appeal in *Re Neath Rugby Ltd (No 2), Hawkes v Cuddy*[46] where the court confirmed that:[47]

- the fact that a director has been nominated by someone does not, of itself, impose a duty on the director owed to his nominator;

- though the nominated director may owe duties to his nominator arising from some other relationship (such as being an officer or employee of the nominator) or by reason of a formal or informal agreement, that cannot detract from the director's duty to the company when he is acting as director;[48]

- the director may take the interests of his appointor into account, provided that his decisions as a director are in what he genuinely believes to be the best interests of the company.

To a large extent this ruling confirms the pre-existing position, noted earlier in the context of groups, that the director's duty is to the company but that a nominee director may have regard to the interests of the appointor so long as those interests are consistent with promoting the success of the company.[49] As the duty to promote the success of the company is a (predominantly) subjective duty, that combination of obligation to the company with the subjective belief of the director may offer some leeway for the nominee director to accommodate his duty to the company and the commercial expectations of his appointor. In *Central Bank of Ecuador v Conticorp*[50] the Privy Council considered the position of a nominee director of an investment company which had raised significant funds from investors and then paid them away in irrecoverable loans to companies associated with the controlling shareholder of the investment company. The director's defence was that he was paid only a very small amount per annum for acting as director and that he was merely acting on instructions from the shareholders who had nominated him. The Privy Council found that, in breach of his fiduciary duty, the director had blindly and ignorantly following the shareholders' instructions without further thought when his duty was to understand the company's interests and apply his own mind to the company's interests. As Lord Mance noted, 'a nominee director is not entitled to forego, or surrender to another, any exercise of his discretion, however paltry the amount he may be paid'.[51] Further, it is irrelevant to the question of breach of duty, whether any loss was caused thereby to the company, but that will have a bearing on whether any relief is possible.[52]

---

[46] [2009] 2 BCLC 427, CA at [32]–[33], affirming on this point Lewison J's ruling in [2007] EWHC 2999, [2008] BCC 390.

[47] Cuddy had been appointed a director of O Ltd by N, a 50 per cent shareholder in O Ltd. Cuddy was also a de facto director of N. At issue was the extent of the obligations owed by Cuddy to N when acting as a director of O Ltd.

[48] See *Scottish Cooperative Wholesale Society v Meyer* [1959] AC 324 at 366–7; *Kuwait Asia Bank EC v National Mutual Life Nominees Ltd* [1990] BCLC 868 at 892; *Boulting v Association of Cinematograph Television and Allied Technicians* [1963] 1 All ER 716 at 723.

[49] Ahern, n 44, sees this positive statement of the position as evincing some pragmatism in mediating between strict legal principle and commercial reality (p 131) while acknowledging that there is no great distance between the old absolutist approach and this stance which Ahern labels as a 'corporate primacy approach'. It is possible to find some evidence of this approach in earlier cases too, see, for example, *Nicholas v Soundcraft Electronics Ltd* [1993] BCCLC 360 at 366–7. The board of a subsidiary company which included nominees appointed by the parent company was not in breach of duty in failing to sue the parent company for sums due to the subsidiary, a decision which the court considered to be a sensible business judgement on the board's part in the interests of both companies, given that the subsidiary's continued existence depended on the group remaining afloat and the parent company could not afford to pay the subsidiary the amount due.

[50] [2016] 1 BCLC 26, PC.          [51] [2016] 1 BCLC 26 at [45].          [52] [2016] 1 BCLC 26 at [46].

**10-20**  Turning to CA 2006, s 173(2) and the permitted modification of the duty to exercise independent judgement, and bearing in mind the cumulative nature of a director's duties (s 179), the constitution could make provision for the nominee director to consult his appointor and to suspend his independent judgement in favour of his appointor's views and to vote in accordance with the appointor's view, but only to the extent that this is consistent with his duty under s 172 to promote the success of the company.[53] Section 172 is a statement of the fundamental obligation of loyalty of the fiduciary to the company and a modification of s 173(1) cannot negate the obligation to comply with s 172, a point reinforced by *Re Southern Counties Fresh Foods Ltd, Cobden Investments Ltd v RWM Langport Ltd*.[54] In this case counsel unsuccessfully argued that a nominee director may advance the interests of his appointor rather than the company if the shareholders unanimously so agree.[55] While accepting that certain directors' duties can be qualified by the unanimous assent of the shareholders, Warren J thought, rightly it is suggested, that it was doubtful whether, as a matter of English law, it is possible to release a director from his general duty to act in the best interests of the company.[56]

## D  Having regard to various factors

**10-21**  One of the initially controversial elements of CA 2006, s 172 is the list of factors in s 172(1)(a)–(f), set out at **10-2**, to which a director must have regard (amongst other matters) when acting in the way he considers, in good faith, would be most likely to promote the success of the company for the benefit of the members as a whole.

### Background—the pluralist debate

**10-22**  The issue for the Company Law Review (CLR) was whether directors should be required to adopt a more inclusive approach and consider the interests not just of the company's shareholders, employees, and creditors, as was the position at common law, but broader constituencies such as its suppliers, customers, and the community at large.[57] The CLR defined the issue as one of the scope of company law, meaning for what purposes and in whose interests should companies be run, which for the CLR essentially involved a choice between enlightened shareholder value and a pluralist approach.[58]

---

[53]  To the extent that his conduct is inconsistent with the interests of the company, i.e. where a director favours the interests of his appointor, it may be grounds for an unfairly prejudicial petition under CA 2006, s 994, see *Scottish Cooperative Wholesale Society v Meyer* [1959] AC 324 at 366–7.

[54]  [2008] EWHC 2810.

[55]  See *Re Neath Rugby Ltd (No 2), Hawkes v Cuddy* [2009] 2 BCLC 427 at [43].

[56]  [2008] EWHC 2810 at [67]. Warren J did think it might be possible, where the nominee is acting as negotiator for his appointor in agreeing a deal with the company, that the shareholders by unanimous agreement might relieve the nominee in those negotiations from an obligation to act to promote the success of the company, assuming that the nominee is excluded from board discussions or votes on the matter. But it is not clear that such a scenario should be regarded as a relief from the application of s 172, rather the duty engaged in that situation is primarily the no-conflict duty and the application of that duty can be tempered by shareholder authorisation under s 180(4)(a) or by independent directors under s 175(4)(b).

[57]  See Goldenberg, 'Shareholders v Stakeholders: The Bogus Argument' (1998) 19 Co Law 34; Plender, *A Stake in the Future: The Stakeholding Solution* (1997); RSA Inquiry, *Tomorrow's Company* (1995); Parkinson, *Corporate Power and Responsibility* (1993), Ch 9.

[58]  Company Law Review, *Completing the Structure* (2000), para 3.1; also *Strategic Framework* (1999), Ch 5; *Developing the Framework* (2000), Chs 2 and 3; *Completing the Structure* (2000), Ch 3.

**10-23**   The enlightened shareholder value approach is based on the idea that maximising share-holder value is in principle the best means of securing overall prosperity.[59] The pluralist approach is based on the idea that a company should serve a wider range of interests not subordinate to, or as a means of achieving, shareholder value, but as valid in their own right, i.e. the interests of a number of constituencies should be advanced without the interests of a single constituency (shareholders) prevailing.[60] This approach would enable, and indeed require, the directors to override shareholders' interests in circumstances where this would be in the interests of the company as widely defined by those stakeholders.

**10-24**   As the enlightened shareholder value approach is essentially the status quo, the argument for the CLR centred on whether the pluralist approach should be adopted. Following consultation, the CLR found that there were strong philosophical arguments against such an approach on the grounds that:

- it would not necessarily achieve its objective and would have the effect of leaving the directors with a broad (and largely unpoliced) managerial discretion;

- it was unnecessary since broader interests such as employees and creditors are included within the range of interests to which directors had to have regard at common law and it would suffice simply to clarify the legal position;

- the pluralist approach would achieve external benefits through company law which are better served by specific legislation applicable to all businesses (and not just registered companies) on planning, environmental, and competition law, etc;

- there was a risk that the pluralist approach (by diluting the obligation owed to shareholders) would enable directors to frustrate takeovers against the wishes of the shareholders and so distort the operation of the market for corporate control which is an important mechanism in holding directors to account.[61]

**10-25**   More generally, there were concerns that any alteration to a pluralist approach would turn directors away from being business decision-makers and into moral, political, and economic arbiters.[62]

**10-26**   A number of technical difficulties with the pluralist approach were also identified including:[63]

- the need to decide which interest should prevail if there was a conflict;

- the need to frame directors' duties differently to take account of the shift in approach;

- the need to alter board composition to reflect the differing interests;

- the need to rethink the division of power between the board and the general meeting as well as the ability of one interest group (the shareholders) to appoint and remove the board; and

- the proper approach to the enforcement of such a duty (a key objection as far as the CLR was concerned).[64]

**10-27**   Following consultation, the CLR found support for and duly recommended retaining the existing common law duty on directors to operate companies for the benefit of their

---

[59]   Company Law Review, *Strategic Framework* (1999), para 5.1.11.
[60]   Company Law Review, *Strategic Framework* (1999), paras 5.1.12–5.1.13.
[61]   Company Law Review, *Developing the Framework* (2000), para 3.24; see also *Strategic Framework* (1999), paras 5.1.25–5.1.29; also HL Deb, vol 678, GC 273 (6 February 2006).
[62]   See Company Law Review, *Developing the Framework* (2000), para 2.21.
[63]   Company Law Review, *Developing the Framework* (2000), paras 3.26–3.31; and Ch 2.
[64]   See Company Law Review, *Completing the Structure* (2000), para 3.5.

shareholders,[65] but that the duty should be framed in an inclusive way which would give due recognition to the importance of considering the long-term implications of decisions and of fostering effective relationships over time with employees, customers, and suppliers and in the community more widely.[66] The CLR rejected the pluralist approach as neither workable nor desirable[67] and it considered that a more inclusive statement, while it would make little difference to the common law position, would have a major influence on changing behaviour and the climate of decision-making.[68] The Government was in favour of this type of approach which it considered would also make the law clearer to directors than any duty defined in terms of acting bona fide in the interests of the company.[69] The result is a broad, aspirational, statement of the core obligation of loyalty owed by a company director.[70] While there continues to be debate about the drafting of s 172(1), the Government has indicated that it has no plans to amend the wording, but it hopes that guidance which it has asked the GC100 to produce (see **10-34**) will 'stimulate wider debate and understanding of the flexibilities inherent in the existing wording of section 172'.[71]

## The inclusive statement of relevant factors

**10-28**   As part of their duty to promote the success of the company, the directors are required by CA 2006, s 172(1) to have regard to all of the factors on the list (set out at **10-2**),[72] but they are not precluded from considering other matters ('amongst other matters'). For example, the list makes no reference to short-term considerations, only long-term consequences, but this does not preclude directors considering short-term matters. Likewise, there is no mention of pension matters, but this issue would fall within the requirement to have regard to the interests of the employees. Some of the factors merely reflect the pre-existing position—for example, the directors' obligation to have regard to the likely consequences of any decision in the long term (s 172(1)(a));[73] to have regard to employees' interests (s 172(1)(b));[74] and the need to act fairly as between members of the company (s 172(1)(f)).[75]

---

[65]   Company Law Review, *Developing the Framework* (2000), para 2.11.

[66]   Company Law Review, *Developing the Framework* (2000), para 2.11, Ch 2, paras 3.17–3.31; *Completing the Structure* (2000), paras 3.1–3.24; *Final Report*, vol 1 (2001), paras 3.5–3.10.

[67]   Company Law Review, *Completing the Structure* (2000), para 3.5.

[68]   See Company Law Review, *Developing the Framework* (2000), para 3.58, but see Worthington, 'Reforming Directors' Duties' (2001) 64 MLR 439 at 445–8.

[69]   The White Paper *Modernising Company Law* (Cm 5553-I, 2002), paras 3.3–3.5.

[70]   See the discussion in Hannigan, 'Reconfiguring the No Conflict Rule, Judicial Strictures, a Statutory Restatement and the Opportunistic Director' (2011) 23 SAcLJ 714 at 723–6 as to whether this duty is a fiduciary duty, as it is commonly described.

[71]   Government response to the Green Paper on Corporate Governance (August 2017), para 2.46.

[72]   See comments by Minister Margaret Hodge, HC Official Report, SC D (Company Law Reform Bill), 13 July 2006, col 591—the duty is not a pluralist duty: directors are required to have regard to the factors laid out when promoting the success of the company for the benefit of its members but a director who puts one of those factors ahead of his overarching duty to promote the success of the company acts in breach of that duty to the company.

[73]   Second Savoy Hotel Investigation, Report of the Inspector (1954) HMSO; *Gaiman v National Association for Mental Health* [1971] Ch 317 at 330, per Megarry J.

[74]   Previously CA 1985, s 309. In the context of a takeover bid for a company, the obligation to have regard to employee interests is underscored by the Takeover Code which requires the board of the offeree company when giving its opinion to the shareholders of the offeree company on the takeover offer to include its views on the effect of implementation of the offer on all the company's interests, including, specifically, employment and its views on the offeror's strategic plans for the offeree company and their likely repercussions on employment: Takeover Code, rule 25.2.

[75]   *Mutual Life Insurance Co of New York v Rank Organisation Ltd* [1985] BCLC 11.

**10-29**    This duty to act fairly between members is a significant protection for minority share-holders. The leading authority is *Mutual Life Insurance Co of New York v Rank Organisation Ltd*[76] where the company decided to make an issue of shares to its exist-ing ordinary shareholders excluding any ordinary shareholders from the United States and Canada. The exclusion was imposed in order to avoid the onerous regula-tory requirements of those jurisdictions. The excluded shareholders' objections were rejected by the court. Goulding J ruled that the directors' powers were subject to two limitations, that their powers must be exercised in good faith in the interests of the company *and* that they must be exercised fairly as between different shareholders. Both elements were satisfied on the facts. The directors honestly believed that raising capital in this way was advantageous to the company and gave a prospect of continu-ing benefit to all the shareholders. The exclusion of the North American shareholders did not affect their shares nor the rights attached to them and was due to a difficulty resulting only from their own personal situation. The law does not require the inter-ests of the company to be sacrificed to the particular interests of a group of sharehold-ers, as *Mutual Life Insurance v Rank* makes clear, but it does require the director to consider the particular position within the company. In *Re BSB Holdings Ltd (No 2)*[77] this duty required the directors (when undertaking a complex financing agreement) to have considered the effect of the proposals on the different groups of shareholders within the company and a failure to do so was a breach of duty, though on the facts, the failure did not amount to unfairly prejudicial conduct[78] for the purposes of (now) CA 2006, s 994.

**10-30**    The significance of this obligation to act fairly as between the shareholders was high-lighted in *Re Sunrise Radio Ltd, Kohli v Lit*[79] where a rights issue was made by a com-pany for the genuine purpose of raising capital, though it was made at a time when it was likely that the minority shareholder would not take up the shares and therefore faced dilution (from a 15 per cent holding to 8.33 per cent). Furthermore, the rights issue was priced at par when the evidence was that the shares, which were taken up by the majority shareholder, could have been issued for a significantly higher price so the minority shareholder suffered a dilution in the value as well as in the size of her holding. The court held that, even if the directors had acted in accordance with the duty to exer-cise their powers for a proper purpose (s 171), they were in breach of their duty to act fairly between shareholders (s 172(1)(f)). The court noted that what is the proper price for shares will necessarily fall within a range of possibilities, but the board is required to consider all these matters fairly in the interests of all groups of shareholders and having regard to the foreseeable range of responses from the shareholders to the rights issue. Where it is known or foreseen that the minority may not be able or wish to subscribe, the directors in the interests of even-handedness and fairness must consider the price which can be extracted from those who are willing to subscribe or be in breach of their duties to the company.[80] On the facts, issuing the shares at par without considering any alternative, particularly when the directors (as the majority shareholders) benefited appreciably from the issue at par, was a breach of duty and unfairly prejudicial to the petitioner.[81]

---

[76]  [1985] BCLC 11; see also *Re BSB Holdings Ltd (No 2)* [1996] 1 BCLC 155 at 249.

[77]  [1996] 1 BCLC 155.     [78]  See [1996] 1 BCLC 155 at 251.

[79]  [2010] 1 BCLC 367.     [80]  [2010] 1 BCLC 367 at [95].

[81]  See also *Re McCarthy Surfacing Ltd, Hequet v McCarthy* [2009] 1 BCLC 622 (distribution of profits via a bonus scheme for management so denying the minority shareholders any opportunity to participate was a breach of the duty to act fairly between the shareholders).

**10-31**  The remaining factors: the need to foster business relationships, (s 172(1)(c)); the impact of operations on the community and the environment (s 172(1)(d)); and the desirability of maintaining a reputation for high standards of business conduct (s 172(1)(f)) are new in the sense that they have not previously been explicitly articulated in this way and, as noted at **10-27**, they are intended to give effect to the desire for a more inclusive definition of this duty. On the other hand, as was pointed out in the Parliamentary debates, these factors are matters which any well-informed and conscientious director would have regard to in any event.[82] The difference now is that there is a duty on directors to have regard to each of these factors when acting on behalf of the company.

**10-32**  There is the possibility, even a probability, that in any given scenario there will be a conflict between two or more of the factors. An example would be where there is a possible takeover bid for the company which will give the shareholders a significant financial return, but which will result in job losses, or where a decision to continue with opencast mining might be to the advantage of the shareholders and the employees, but to the detriment of the environment, and so on. The resolution of such conflicts is a matter for the business judgement of the directors, acting in good faith and exercising appropriate care and skill[83] as was made clear in *Shepherd v Williamson*.[84] In this case, a whistle-blowing director had to balance, the court said, the deleterious consequences of his conduct as far as relations with the company's major customer were concerned (disclosing anti-competitive behaviour to them) and the potential for damage to the company's employees if a contract with that customer was not gained (s 172(1)(a), (b), and (c)), against the company's reputation as a whole (s 172(1)(e)) in the light of the fact that the company had given the then Office of Fair Trading (OFT) undertakings about its conduct which it was at risk of breaching. Balancing those considerations was a matter for the director's subjective judgement in compliance with his duty to promote the success of the company.[85] The court concluded that the director could not be criticised for wanting to ensure that a contract was not obtained by the use of collusive activities (so avoiding a problem with the OFT), irrespective of whether it meant that the company might lose the contract altogether (and so cause a loss of business).

### Honest and careful regard to the factors

**10-33**  There was some criticism in the Parliamentary debates as to the limited nature of the requirement 'to have regard' to the factors and the Government was careful to emphasise that that standard must be measured against the overall requirements for directors to act in good faith and with care and skill which means that directors cannot pay mere lip service to the statutory requirements.[86] There were also initial concerns that directors, in

---

[82]  See DTI, *CA 2006, Duties of Company Directors, Ministerial Statements* (June 2007), p 2: '... pursuing the interests of shareholders and embracing wider responsibilities are complementary purposes, not contradictory ones' (Minister Margaret Hodge).

[83]  Lowry suggests that an effect of the requirement to have regard to constituencies outside the narrow realm of members' interests is that it will allow directors to defend almost any bona fide decision aimed at promoting the success of the company, see Lowry, 'The Duty of Loyalty of Company Directors: Bridging the Accountability Gap through Efficient Disclosure' (2009) 68 CLJ 607 at 621. Far from restricting directors' decision-making, the effect of CA 2006, s 172 may be to free up their discretion.

[84]  [2010] EWHC 2375 at [103]–[104].

[85]  The court was considering the director's conduct in the context of an unfairly prejudicial petition brought by him based in part on his exclusion from the company following his whistle-blowing to the customer.

[86]  What is required is a 'proper consideration' of the issues, that the directors think about them rather than merely tick boxes, according to Minister Margaret Hodge: see HC Deb, vol 450, col 789, (17 October 2006). See also *Explanatory Notes to the Companies Act 2006*, para 328; HL Deb, vol 681, GC 846 (9 May 2006).

their anxiety to demonstrate that they had complied with s 172(1), would look to document every step in the decision-making process, something which would be particularly problematic, given that not every decision is taken at a board meeting and given that the section is not limited in application to formal decision-making. Indeed the converse is the position, with relatively few matters decided formally by the board compared to the large variety of matters decided upon every day by the directors.

**10-34**    The Government's position was that nothing new or additional is required, just the normal documentation which would accompany any decision of the directors, since CA 2006, s 172(1) merely identifies the factors which a reasonable director exercising care and skill in the carrying out of his functions would consider anyway.[87] This position is reinforced by advice from the influential GC100 group which advised companies not to adopt the practice of referring to CA 2006, s 172 in board minutes.[88] The GC100 advice noted that, prior to the CA 2006, board minutes did not record that the directors, in reaching decisions, had complied with their duties and nothing in the CA 2006 requires a change to that practice. That advice appears to have been heeded and there is little evidence of companies compiling copious documentation to ensure compliance with s 172(1). In 2017, the Government asked the GC100 Group to prepare and publish new advice and guidance on the practical boardroom interpretation of s 172.[89] No doubt, on occasion, in the largest companies and for the most complex or contentious matters, directors may want to make sure that formal board decisions are challenge-proof so board minutes may refer to the s 172 factors. In that type of context, directors may want to bolster those decisions with references to internal papers, perhaps even consultants' reports and advice from outside experts, so as to show, not only that they had regard to the factors, but that they exercised appropriate care and skill in considering them. That practice would be the exception rather than the norm,[90] however, and, post-implementation, decision-making by directors appears to have continued much as before. As discussed later, the duty set out in s 172 is not enforceable by any of the stakeholder groups, only by the company or shareholders bringing a derivative claim on behalf of the company, so litigation is likely to be rare and that too reinforces the status quo. Honest decision-making based on reasonable grounds is what is required. Assuming the directors reach that standard, they are at no greater risk of liability under s 172 than they were under their previous obligation to act bona fide in the interests of the company.[91] It also has to be borne in mind that the courts will not second-guess business decisions of directors, see **10-8**, and that remains the position under s 172.

---

[87] See HL Deb, vol 681, GC 841 (9 May 2006) where Lord Goldsmith, speaking for the Government, refused to accept that anything about CA 2006, s 172 makes it necessary to have some particular form of paper trail. See also HC Official Report, SCD (Company Law Reform Bill), cols 591–2.

[88] The GC100 group essentially represents general counsel and company secretaries of the FTSE 100 companies.

[89] Government response to the Green Paper on Corporate Governance Reform (August 2017), para 2.46. It is expected that the new guidance will be available in late 2018.

[90] For an interesting consideration of whether lawyers' advice to corporate clients on the scope and implementation of CA 2006, s 172 may change boardroom practice in this way, see Loughrey, Keay, and Cerioni, 'Legal Practitioners, Enlightened Shareholder Value and the Shaping of Corporate Governance' (2008) 8 JCLS 79.

[91] See Keay, 'The Duty to Promote the Success of the Company: Is it Fit for Purpose in a Post-financial Crisis World?' in Loughrey (ed), *Directors' Duties and Shareholder Litigation in the Wake of the Financial Crisis* (2012) who comments that, while the duty in s 172 might be educational (as far as directors are concerned), it is vague and provides little direction or even guidance and amounts to little more than a continuation of the modus operandi employed in the past by directors which is that they will consider wider interests to the extent that that action will enhance shareholder interests. Certainly, the hype surrounding the introduction of s 172(1) has been long overtaken by a sense of its prosaicness.

**10-35**  Some of the early concerns surrounding the possible impact of CA 2006, s 172 related to the fact that CA 2006, Pt 11 provides, for the first time, for a statutory derivative claim (see Chapter 20). Part 11 allows for claims by any member against any director for a breach of any duty owed by a director to the company (s 260(3)).[92] Recovery is solely for the benefit of the company and not for the individual claimant. The concern was that shareholder activists would look to use the combination of the new derivative procedure and s 172 to challenge business decisions of directors on the basis of an alleged failure to have regard to the factors set out in the section. A derivative claim could be used to seek judicial review, in effect, of a commercial decision of management. As discussed in Chapter 20, in practice there has not been any significant use of the derivative claim and these concerns about the combined effect of s 172 and a statutory derivative claim have proved unfounded to date.

**10-36**  Of course, even if shareholders brought a derivative claim and could establish a failure to consider a particular factor or factors, it is not clear what an appropriate remedy might be or how any loss might be quantified. For example, if it was established that the directors failed to take into account the interests of the employees in a particular matter and 50 employees had lost their jobs, there would be a breach of duty on the part of the directors but no loss suffered by the company to which the duty is owed.

**10-37**  More recently, the debate has moved on from concerns about litigation to concerns about whether the directors merely pay lip service to the section and the stakeholder interests reflected in it. The extent to which workforce concerns are acknowledged or addressed at board level is something which arises in numerous contexts (shareholder dividends versus employee pay rises, boardroom remuneration versus workforce pay levels, pension plan deficits, etc). For large companies, there is an increasing consumer/customer focus on issues surrounding the supply chain, child labour, human rights issues, sustainability, as well as environmental matters generally. Section 172 makes room for all of these matters in boardroom deliberations, but it is difficult to assess the degree to which the interests of the stakeholders actually are taken into account. Of course, some companies are exemplars of detailed reporting on these issues and it was always intended that the impact and effectiveness of s 172 would be assessed through disclosures to be made in the strategic report (discussed at **10-39**). The Government has acknowledged, however, that the reporting elements need to be improved as to require directors to explain in greater detail how they have had regard to all of these interests.[93]

**10-38**  More explicitly, the Government invited the FRC to develop a new principle in the UK Corporate Governance Code (see **6-9**) to strengthen the voice of employees.[94] The FRC was asked to consult on a specific Code provision requiring premium listed companies to adopt on a 'comply or explain' basis (see **6-10**) one of three employment engagement

---

[92]  A member needs the permission of the court to bring the claim and various thresholds are set in CA 2006, Pt 11. In particular, when considering applications for permission the court has to consider whether a person acting in accordance with his duty under CA 2006, s 172 would seek to continue the claim and the importance which he would attach to continuing the claim (see ss 263(2)(a), 263(3)(b)). In applying those provisions, the courts have been clear that directors, when weighing up the factors in s 172, are essentially reaching a commercial decision which the courts are ill-equipped to take and that some directors could legitimately conclude one way on an issue whereas others, equally legitimately, could take the opposite view: see *Iesini v Westrip Holdings Ltd* [2011] 1 BCLC 498 at [85]–[86], and the discussion at **20-44**.

[93]  Government response to the Green Paper on Corporate Governance (August 2017), paras 2.34–2.38; and see the Green Paper on Corporate Governance Reform (November 2016). See the Companies (Miscellaneous Reporting) Regulations 2018 (in draft at time of writing).

[94]  Government response to the Green Paper on Corporate Governance (August 2017), paras 2.39–2.44.

mechanisms as a method of gathering the views of the workforce, namely, use of a desig-nated non-executive director, a formal employee advisory council, or a director appointed from the workplace.[95] These three options now appear in the proposed 2018 Code as Provision 3 while Principle C of the 2018 Code states that 'in order for the company to meet its responsibilities to shareholders and stakeholders, the board should ensure effec-tive engagement with, and encourage participation, from these parties'. These proposals are only in draft, at the time of writing, so it remains to be seen whether they will survive through to the final version of the 2018 Code. The proposals raise the question as to why the workforce has been given greater prominence than other stakeholders, though prag-matic reasons can be advanced for that preference. As to which of the proposed mecha-nisms companies might adopt, the designated non-executive director might appeal in some companies where an existing non-executive director could be tasked with work-force engagement and reporting to the board on workforce concerns. Appointing a direc-tor from the workforce raises issues as to the nomination process and the width of the electorate (trade union/non-union etc) and the duties of nominee directors (discussed earlier) may not be well understood by the workforce, and also the power of removal would need to be considered. These legal issues might mean that companies would prefer an employee advisory council which as a structure would not disrupt the existing legal framework governing the unitary board.

## The link to the strategic report

**10-39**   The proper place to refer to the CA 2006, s 172 factors is in the strategic report which is required of all companies other than small companies,[96] see **18-31**. The purpose of the strategic report is expressly stated to be 'to inform members of the company and help them assess how the directors have performed their duty under section 172' (s 414C(1)).[97] The strategic report must contain a fair review of the company's business and a description of the principal risks and uncertainties facing the company. It must provide a balanced and comprehensive analysis of the development and performance of the company's business during, and the company's position, at the end of the financial year, consistent with the size and complexity of the business, with additional information required of quoted companies. The detailed content of the strategic report is considered at **18-33**.

**10-40**   The role assigned to the strategic report by CA 2006, s 414C(1) reflects the Government's intention that the restated duty in s 172 should bring about a cultural change in how companies perceive their responsibilities,[98] rather than generate pointless bureaucratic

---

[95] FRC, Proposed Revisions to the UK Corporate Governance Code (December 2017).

[96] CA 2006, s 414A, 4141B, 414C. The CLR was keen to require large public and private companies to report widely on the business and its affairs as part of their annual reporting requirements. See Company Law Review, *Final Report,* vol 1 (2001), paras 3.28–3.45; *Completing the Structure* (2000), paras 3.7–3.10; 3.32–3.42; *Developing the Framework* (2000), paras 2.19–2.26, 3.85, 5.74–5.100; *Strategic Framework* (1999), paras 5.1.44–5.1.47.

[97] That disclosure is an integral element in reinforcing s 172, while also helping shareholders fulfil their stewardship role, is highlighted by the suggestion from the Sharman Inquiry that the directors' assessment of whether the entity is a going concern should be addressed also in the Strategic Report as part of the discussion of the business strategy and the principal risks facing the entity. Sharman saw addressing these issues of risk and the solvency of the entity as integral to the directors' duty under s 172, see The Sharman Inquiry, *Going Concern and Liquidity Risks: Lessons for Companies and Auditors, Preliminary report and recommendations of the Panel of Inquiry* (November 2011), paras 7, 13 and discussion at **6-26**.

[98] See Minister Margaret Hodge, n 82, '… s 172 is a "radical departure" from the previous law which catches a cultural change …': see Introduction to Ministerial Statements.

procedures restricting decision-making. The focus on disclosure of the company's performance and position in the strategic report is intended to require companies to acknowledge and respond to the interests of the stakeholders affected by their activities. Large businesses do look to a much wider agenda and broader constituencies than merely the company's own shareholders, in any event, and extensive narrative reporting by them is commonplace, driven by domestic and EU requirements which require stakeholders to be acknowledged and which have evolved quite independently of any obligations arising by virtue of s 172. Nevertheless, respondents to the Government's Green Paper on Corporate Governance Reform published in November 2016[99] thought there is room for further improvements to reporting under s 172, as did the House of Commons Business, Energy and Industrial Strategy Committee in its report on corporate governance in March 2017.[100] The Government has agreed and reporting requirements are to be strengthened by requiring all large companies, private as well as public, to explain how their directors comply with the requirement under s 172 to have regard to employee interests and to fostering relationships with suppliers, customers, and others. Companies will have to show how the directors have had regard to the need to foster the company's business relationships with suppliers, customers and others, and the effect of that regard, including on the principal decisions taken by the company during the financial year.[101]

## E  Considering the creditors' interests

**10-41**  A director's duty to act in the way he considers, in good faith, would be most likely to promote the success of the company for the benefit of its members as a whole has effect 'subject to any enactment or rule of law requiring directors, in certain circumstances, to consider or act in the interests of creditors of the company' (CA 2006, s 172(3)).[102] This provision preserves the common law obligation to have regard to creditors' interests which had its origins in influential Australian and New Zealand decisions to this effect.[103] This approach was endorsed by the Court of Appeal in *West Mercia Safetywear Ltd v Dodd*[104] where Dillon LJ approved the following statement by the New South Wales Court of Appeal in *Kinsela v Russell Kinsela Pty Ltd*:[105]

---

[99]  Government Response to the Corporate Governance Green Paper (August 2017), paras 2.22–2.24.

[100]  HC BEIS Committee, Third Report of Session 2016–17, *Corporate Governance*, HC 702, April 2017, paras 31–35.

[101]  Government Response to the Corporate Governance Green Paper (August 2017), paras 2.35–2.38; see the Companies (Miscellaneous Reporting) Regulations 2018, in draft at time of writing. The Government also asked the Institute of Chartered Secretaries and Administrators (ICSA) and the Investment Association (IA) to complete their joint guidance on how boards could engage with stakeholders and this has now been published, see ICSA, IA, 'The Stakeholder Voice in Board Decision Making' (September 2017).

[102]  See Keay, 'Directors' Duties and Creditors' Interests' (2014) 130 LQR 443 and more generally Keay, *Company Directors' Responsibilities to Creditors* (2007); Morgan, 'Directors' Duties in the Insolvency Context' (2015) Insolv Intell 1; Davies, 'Directors' Creditor—Regarding Duties in Respect of Trading Decisions in the Vicinity of Insolvency' (2006) 7 EBOR 301; Milman, 'Strategies for Regulating Managerial Performance in the Twilight Zone: Familiar Dilemmas, New Considerations' [2004] JBL 493.

[103]  Especially *Walker v Wimborne* (1976) 50 ALJR 446 and *Nicholson v Permakraft (NZ) Ltd* [1985] 1 NZLR 242. See Dawson, 'Acting in the Best Interests of the Company—For Whom are Directors "Trustees"?' (1984) 11 NZULR 68.

[104]  [1988] BCLC 250. See also *Brady v Brady* [1988] 2 All ER 617, HL; *Re Horsley & Weight Ltd* [1982] 3 All ER 1045 at 1055–6.

[105]  (1986) 4 ACLC 215 at 223, per Street CJ.

'In a solvent company the proprietary interests of the shareholders entitle them as a general body to be regarded as the company when questions of the duty of directors arise . . . But where a company is insolvent the interests of the creditors intrude. They become prospectively entitled, through the mechanism of liquidation, to displace the power of the shareholders and directors to deal with the company's assets. It is in a practical sense their assets and not the shareholders' assets that, through the medium of the company, are under the management of the directors pending either liquidation, return to solvency, or the imposition of some alternative administration.'[106]

**10-42**  In the *West Mercia* case, a director had arranged for his company to partially repay a debt due from the company to its parent company at a time when he knew the company to be insolvent. The sole reason he had organised the payment of £4,000 was that he had personally guaranteed the debts of the parent company and he wanted to reduce his personal liabilities under that guarantee. The court found that the director in causing the company to make this payment at that time had acted in disregard of the interests of the general creditors of the company and in breach of his duty to the company. The fact that the payment was of a debt owed by the company did not alter the fact it was a breach of his duty to act in the interest of the creditors generally. He was ordered to repay £4,000 with interest.[107]

**10-43**  This common law obligation to have regard to the interests of creditors in this way, though the subject of some criticism,[108] is now an accepted component of a director's duties.[109] It might have been expected that this obligation would have been developed and reflected in the statutory statement of directors' duties in CA 2006, Pt 10, Ch 2, but this turned out to be a matter on which, surprisingly, the Company Law Review had little of substance to say[110] and the matter has been left to develop at common law,[111] as CA 2006, s 172(3) provides. As with all directors' duties, this duty is owed to the company (CA 2006, s 170(1), see **8-13**) and it is not owed directly to the creditors.[112]

**10-44**  Section 172(3) refers to any enactments which require directors to consider or act in the interests of creditors and relevant enactments in that regard are the Company Directors Disqualification Act (CDDA) 1986 and the Insolvency Act (IA) 1986. As a practical matter, the issue of whether the directors did consider the creditors' interests is always an exercise in hindsight and the duty in CA 2006, s 172(3) only has an impact if the company

---

[106] [1988] BCLC 250 at 252.

[107] See the discussion at **10-58** on the appropriate remedy in these cases.

[108] See Watts [2014] JBL 161 at 162–3 who comments that the notion of a duty to creditors is both too broad and too narrow and who queries why, outside of capital maintenance principles, directors should owe a generalised duty to creditors; see also Sealy, 'Directors' Duties—An Unnecessary Gloss' (1988) 47 CLJ 175 at 177.

[109] For example, see *Yukong Line Ltd of Korea v Rendsburg Investments Corp of Liberia* [1998] 2 BCLC 485 (transfer of funds by a director from insolvent company's bank account to a company he controlled with a view to putting those funds beyond the reach of the company's sole creditor was a clear breach of the director's fiduciary duties); also *Re Capitol Films Ltd, Rubin v Cobalt Pictures Ltd* [2011] 2 BCLC 359 at [49].

[110] Initially the CLR was not inclined to include any specific obligation to creditors though there was concern that, without some reference to creditors, the statutory statement of directors' duties would not be exhaustive. Some limited proposals were included belatedly in the *Final Report*, but rejected in any event by the Government which preferred to proceed as set out in CA 2006, s 172(3). See Company Law Review, *Developing the Framework* (2000), paras 3.72–3.73; also the draft statutory statement of directors' duties in Company Law Review, *Final Report*, vol 1 (2001), Annex C, paras 8 and 9; and, *Final Report*, vol 1 (2001), paras 3.12–3.20.

[111] See *Modernising Company Law* (Cm 5553-I, 2002), paras 3.8–3.14.

[112] *Multinational Gas and Petrochemical Co v Multinational Gas and Petrochemical Services Ltd* [1983] 2 All ER 563 at 585; *Yukong Line Ltd of Korea v Rendsburg Investments Corp of Liberia* [1998] 2 BCLC 485. See also *Kuwait Asia Bank EC v National Mutual Life Nominees Ltd* [1990] 3 All ER 404, PC.

actually becomes insolvent and goes into either liquidation or administration. Only then will the question of whether the directors gave sufficient consideration to creditors' interests come to the fore as a liquidator or administrator looks to see if she can establish a liability on the directors' part in respect of the dissipation of company assets in breach of that duty. Imposing a personal liability may be helpful to the creditors collectively, especially if the directors have liability insurance. Trading to the detriment of creditors' interests may warrant a finding of unfitness and disqualification under the CDDA 1986, s 6 (see **15-88**) and, possibly, liability for wrongful trading under IA 1986, ss 214 and 246ZB, i.e. continuing to trade after a point in time when a director knew or ought to have known that there was no reasonable prospect that the company would avoid entering insolvent administration or insolvent liquidation, see **15-18**.[113] The IA 1986 also addresses transactions which adversely affect creditors' interests such as transactions defrauding creditors (IA 1986, s 423), transactions at an undervalue (IA 1986, s 238, see **15-46**), and preferences (IA 1986, s 239, see **15-60**). The precise overlap and relationship between the directors' common law duty to creditors preserved by CA 2006, s 172(3) and the statutory provisions is still evolving, as is discussed later in the chapter.

## Triggering the duty to consider or act in the creditors' interests

**10-45**  The main issue for directors is the point in time at which this obligation to consider or act in the interests of the creditors displaces the duty to act for the benefit of the members as a whole. Clearly, where the company is solvent, there is no need for directors to consider or act in the interests of the creditors who will get paid in the usual way or who can otherwise enforce their contractual rights to payment. Clearly, where the company is insolvent, the interests of the creditors should be the focus of the directors' decisions and conduct. The difficult area is when the company is under financial pressure so it may weave in and out of 'doubtful solvency' or 'near insolvency' or be on the verge of insolvency.[114] For example, a company may lose a major customer and endure a difficult period before subsequently gaining a new order when its finances improve. In some sectors, such as the airline industry, companies may flirt with insolvency because of extraneous circumstances such as soaring oil prices. Depending on the duration of the problem, companies may survive or may collapse. Yet the imposition of an obligation to have regard to creditors' interests in precisely that 'zone of insolvency' or in the 'vicinity of insolvency', to use the American terminology, is essential to curb the incentives for directors at that stage to take on excessive risks, basically because as far as they are concerned all is probably lost.[115]

---

[113]  It is a defence for a director to show that he took every step with a view to minimising the potential losses to the company's creditors that he ought to have taken: IA 1986, s 214(3).

[114]  In determining whether the company was insolvent, the court will approach the question by applying IA 1986, s 123(1)(e) and s 123(2) which establish cashflow and balance sheet tests to determine whether a company is able to meet its debts as they fall due; the application of these provisions was addressed by the Supreme Court in *BNY Corporate Trustee Services Ltd v Eurosail-UK plc* [2013] 1 BCLC 613; see **24-35**; and see also Lewison LJ's useful summary of *Eurosail* in *Re Casa Estates Ltd, Bucci v Carman* [2014] BCC 269 at [27]; see **24-37**. Likewise, the cashflow and balance sheet position will be relevant to whether the company is doubtfully solvent or in a parlous financial state or on the verge of insolvency, etc. It should also be noted that the threshold under s 172(3) is more fluid than that required with respect to wrongful trading (IA 1986, ss 214, 246ZB) which only comes into play where the directors knew or ought to have concluded that there was no reasonable prospect that the company would avoid entering insolvent administration or liquidation.

[115]  See generally Davies, 'Directors' Creditor—Regarding Duties in Respect of Trading Decisions in the Vicinity of Insolvency' (2006) 7 EBOR 301. Also Milman, 'Strategies for Regulating Managerial Performance in the Twilight Zone: Familiar Dilemmas, New Considerations' [2004] JBL 493.

**10-46**　In one of the influential New Zealand decisions, *Nicholson v Permakraft (NZ) Ltd*,[116] Cooke J thought creditors were entitled to consideration if the company was insolvent, or near-insolvent, or of doubtful solvency, or if a contemplated payment or other course of action would jeopardise its solvency. In *Re MDA Investment Management Ltd, Whalley v Doney*,[117] the court thought the obligation to have regard to creditors' interests arose where the company was in 'a dangerous financial position' or the company was 'in financial difficulties to the extent that its creditors are at risk'. In *Colin Gwyer & Associates Ltd v London Wharf (Limehouse) Ltd*[118] the court held that where the company is insolvent or of doubtful solvency or on the verge of insolvency and it is the creditors' money which is at risk, the directors must consider the interests of the creditors as paramount. In *Facia Footwear v Hinchcliffe*,[119] Sir Richard Scott thought that, given 'the parlous financial state of the company', the directors had to have regard to the interests of the creditors when paying out company's funds (at a time when it was hopelessly insolvent) to support the continued trading of other companies in the group.[120] In *Re Capitol Films Ltd, Rubin v Cobalt Pictures Ltd*[121] the company was at the very least in dire financial difficulties if not patently insolvent, so the duty was engaged. In *E-Clear (UK) plc v Elia*[122] (where the company repaid debts due to a director) the court looked to see whether the company had been insolvent or on the brink of insolvency at the relevant time, noting that 'absent actual or imminent insolvency, the repayment of debts owed by the company would be unobjectionable'. In *Vivendi SA v Richards*[123] payments of £10m were extracted from a company between March 2004 and February 2005 before the company went into insolvent liquidation. The court found that the company was insolvent from January 2004 and the directors were well aware of the company's 'fragility' and 'vulnerability'. The payments were not in the company's interests and were made to extract the remaining cash in the company before liquidation and to thwart the creditors' interests rather than to benefit them.

**10-47**　In *Re HLC Environmental Projects Ltd, Hellard v Carvalho*,[124] it was said that directors are not free to take action which puts at real (as opposed to remote) risk the creditors' prospects of being paid,[125] but, in *BTI 2014 LLC v Sequana SA*,[126] Rose J rejected that approach. She considered that the 'real risk' approach would be a significant lowering of the threshold which was not consistent with the authorities and for which there was no justification.[127] Having given detailed consideration to the cases, Rose J concluded that the cases show that the question is whether the company is on the verge of insolvency or of doubtful solvency,

---

[116] [1985] 1 NZLR 242 at 249, 250.　　[117] [2004] 1 BCLC 217 at [75].

[118] [2003] 2 BCLC 153 at [74]. The same formulation was adopted by Newey J in *GHLM Trading Ltd v Maroo* [2012] 2 BCLC 369 at [173].

[119] [1998] 1 BCLC 218.

[120] [1998] 1 BCLC 218 at 228; and note the comments by Sir Richard Scott on the importance of not applying hindsight in judging the directors' conduct and of recognising that the interests of the creditors sometimes lie in conduct which ensures a continuation of trading, see also **3-74** et seq.

[121] [2011] 2 BCLC 359.　　[122] [2013] 2 BCLC 455 at [24], CA.

[123] [2013] BCC 771 at [152], [157].　　[124] [2014] BCC 337 at [89].

[125] [2014] BCC 437 at [88]–[89], per Deputy Judge John Randall QC, citing Giles JA in *Kalls Enterprises Pty Ltd v Baloglow* [2007] NSWCA 191, [2007] 25 ACLC 1094 at [162]; and see support for this approach in *Re PV Solar Solutions Ltd* [2018] 1 BCLC 58.

[126] [2017] 1 BCLC 453.

[127] The authorities are reviewed by Rose J at [464]–[484]. As was noted in *Dickinson v NAL Realisations Ltd* [2017] EWHC 28 [2018] 1 BCLC 623, at [119], if the threshold is set too low, so treating the duty to the creditors as arising earlier than currently required, it has a potentially inhibiting effect on the freedom of the directors to act.

or is in a precarious or parlous financial state.[128] There is no justification for engaging the duty at an earlier point. On the facts in *BTI 2014 LLC v Sequana*, the directors had taken into account a potential liability of the company, had provided for it in the accounts, and then distributed the remaining assets to the members (a parent company) via dividend payments. There was a real risk that the provision in the accounts would turn out to be inadequate so the question was whether the obligation to take creditors' interests into account was triggered from that point, given the risk. Rose J rejected that approach which, she said, would be a significant inroad into the normal application of directors' duties. 'It cannot be right that whenever a company has on its balance sheet a provision in respect of a long term liability which might turn out to be larger than the provision made, the creditors' interests duty applies for the whole period during which there is a risk that there will be insufficient assets to meet the liability.'[129] She considered that, on a proper analysis, the cases where the duty was triggered could be described as cases where the company was actually insolvent or on the verge of insolvency or in a precarious or parlous financial state.

**10-48**    Support for the approach of Rose J can be found in *Dickinson v NAL Realisations Ltd*.[130] In that case, the director carried out a series of transactions in 2010 (including a share buyback) designed to diminish the company's assets so that they would be unavailable to claimants in pending environmental litigation against the company, should they be successful. The prospect of litigation had become apparent in 2008–09. Judgment in the environmental proceedings was eventually given in late September 2012 with damages of £1.2m plus costs awarded against the company which went into administration earlier that month. The buyback was challenged as being a breach of the duty in s 172(3). The court noted that, at the time of the buyback, the company was trading successfully and had ample capital and liquidity to continue to do so in the ordinary course. There was 'a real risk of insolvency if the claim was lost and resulted in a large liability, but also a real prospect that it would never become insolvent' and the claim might well have been defeated.[131] The court preferred the approach of Rose J and agreed that the cases do not justify a finding that directors are required to give priority to creditors just because there is a recognised risk of adverse events that would lead to insolvency.[132] To do otherwise, and treat the duty to creditors as arising at that earlier point of 'real risk' would have 'potentially inhibitory effects'.[133] In *Singularis Holdings Ltd v Daiwa Capital Markets Europea Ltd*[134] there was overwhelming evidence that the company was, at the least, in a highly precarious state, so that the duty to have regard to the creditors' interests was engaged. Once engaged in that case, the duty precluded the making of gratuitous payments to other companies in a group controlled by the company's sole shareholder to the detriment of the company's creditors.

**10-49**    Overall, it would seem the test is settling on where the company is on the verge of insolvency or of doubtful solvency or is in a precarious or parlous financial state which brings the trigger point quite close to the time where IA 1986, s 214 (wrongful trading) will be engaged in any event. Keeping the trigger at this level rather than a real (and not remote) risk removes, as was said in *Dickinson v NAL*, an inhibiting factor from the directors' decision-making.[135] It will not necessarily insulate their conduct from challenge subsequently

---

[128]   [2017] 1 BCLC 453 at [477], [483]. See too *Singularis Holdings Ltd v Daiwa Capital Markets Europe Ltd* [2017] 1 BCLC 625 at [130]; *Dickinson v NAL Realisations Ltd* [2017] EWHC 28 at [118], [120]; *Secretary of State for Business, Innovation and Skills v Akbar* [2017] EWHC 2856 at [85].

[129]   [2017] 1 BCLC 453 at [479].          [130]   [2017] EWHC 28, [2018] 1 BCLC 623.

[131]   [2017] EWHC 28, [2018] 1 BCLC 623, at [120].

[132]   [2017] EWHC 28, [2018] 1 BCLC 623, at [118].          [133]   [2017] EWHC 28, [2018] 1 BCLC 623, at [119].

[134]   [2017] 1 BCLC 625 at [132], [137].          [135]   [2017] EWHC 28, [2018] 1 BCLC 623, at [119].

by creditors, but challenge would have to be through the IA transaction provisions, if the s 172(3) duty is not engaged. This may not be the optimal outcome as far as creditors are concerned for the transaction provisions can be difficult to apply successfully, though reliance on IA 1986, s 423, in *BTI 2014 LLC v Sequana SA*,[136] may suggest otherwise. It may be that stepping back from a test of 'real but not remote' risk to a test of being on the verge or brink of insolvency will dampen the significance and effectiveness of s 172(3).

**10-50**    Faced with an allegation that, as directors, they failed to have regard to the interests of the creditors, directors may be tempted to argue that they did not know or could not have been aware that the company had passed the threshold, but this is unlikely to succeed. Given that the claim will only be brought if company has gone into insolvent liquidation, it should not be difficult to show, at the very least, that the directors knew the facts which rendered the company insolvent or on the brink of insolvency and their ignorance of the legal consequences will be no defence.[137] Furthermore, every company must keep adequate accounting records sufficient to disclose, with reasonable accuracy, at any time, the financial position of the company at that time (CA 2006, s 386(1), (2)(b)). Directors must prepare annual accounts and large and medium-sized companies must have those accounts audited and, in any event, they would normally have monthly or quarterly management accounts which should ensure an appreciation of the company's position.[138] Directors are obliged under s 174 to exercise care, skill, and diligence in the performance of their functions as directors which requires, *inter alia*, an appropriate level of knowledge of the company's affairs and its financial position at any time (see **11-31**).[139] Also, it is implicit in many of the factors to which directors must have regard under s 172(1) that the directors need to be aware of the company's financial position. In considering any matter and in order to have proper regard to the interests of the employees, or to the need to foster business relationships with suppliers, or to the impact of the company's operations on the community, a director needs to know the company's financial position. Indeed, more broadly, it is difficult to see how any director could honestly fulfil his duty to promote the success of the company if he is unaware of the company's financial position, at least in general terms.

**10-51**    This duty to have regard to creditors' interests in certain circumstances does not mean that the company must cease trading when the company is in financial difficulties or indeed insolvent. The directors are entitled to continue to trade if they honestly believe it is possible that the company can trade its way out of the financial difficulties[140] (an

---

[136]  [2017] 1 BCLC 453.

[137]  See *HLC Environmental Projects Ltd, Hellard v Carvalho* [2014] BCC 337 at [95].

[138]  Small companies are exempt from an audit (CA 2006, s 477, see **18-55** et seq) unless they choose to have one and the downside to the exemption may be that the directors do not have outside accounting/audit advice which would draw their attention to the company's financial position. The risk of directors breaching the obligation to have regard to creditors' interests may be greater potentially then in an audit exempt company, but the reality in these companies is that the directors will be faced with pressing creditors including their bank, unpaid tax bills, and recurrent cashflow difficulties which mean that they could not be unaware of the company's financial problems.

[139]  See *Re Westmid Packing Services Ltd, Secretary of State for Trade and Industry v Griffiths* [1999] 2 BCLC 704; *Re Galeforce Pleating Co Ltd* [1999] 2 BCLC 704; *Re Landhurst Leasing plc, Secretary of State for Trade and Industry v Ball* [1999] 1 BCLC 286; *Re Park House Properties Ltd* [1997] 2 BCLC 530.

[140]  For example, in *E-Clear (UK) plc v Elia* [2013] 2 BCLC 455 while the company was balance sheet insolvent, the court thought it had not been established that it was on the brink of insolvency given that it still had sufficient financial support to continue to run its business and the director may then be entitled to take an optimistic view of the future; likewise in *Roberts v Frohlich* [2011] 2 BCLC 625, while the company was balance sheet insolvent, the directors were entitled to be optimistic for a period that the company could trade out of its difficulties.

outcome that would most protect creditors), though if the company continues to trade past a point in time when the directors knew or ought to have concluded that there was no reasonable prospect of avoiding insolvent liquidation,[141] the directors may be personally liable for wrongful trading under IA 1986, s 214.[142]

## Assessing the directors' conduct in the light of s 172(3)

**10-52**  Where the duty is engaged, because the company is on the verge or brink of insolvency or in a precarious or parlous financial state, or a contemplated payment or other course of action would jeopardise its solvency and put its creditors at risk,[143] s 172(3) requires the directors to consider the interests of the creditors as paramount for, in this context, as Nourse LJ explained in *Brady v Brady*,[144] the interests of the company are the interests of the existing creditors only.[145] The directors must consider or act in the creditors' interests as a class and a director who acts to advance the interests of a particular creditor, without believing the action to be in the interests of creditors as a class, commits a breach of duty.[146]

**10-53**  Given the obligation to consider or act in the creditors' interests, the question under s 172(3), as under s 172(1), is as to the director's honest belief that his act or omission was in the interests of the creditors as a class,[147] with the court approaching the issue of honest belief in the manner described above at **10-4** et seq. As noted, it is a subjective test of honest belief bordered to some extent by issues of reasonableness and detriment to the company, see **10-11**. Evidence that the director had unreasonably overlooked a material fact would cast doubt on an honest belief.[148] Where the director never actually considered

---

[141]  See *Secretary of State v Gill* [2006] BCC 725 at [143]–[144]; *Secretary of State for Trade and Industry v Gash* [1997] 1 BCLC 341 at 348–9.

[142]  See, for example, *Singla v Hedman* [2012] 2 BCLC 61; *Re Kudos Business Solutions Ltd, Earp v Stevenson* [2012] 2 BCLC 65; in each case the company had committed itself to contracts which it had no reasonable prospects of fulfilling, meaning the directors ought to have known that there was no reasonable prospect of avoiding insolvent liquidation.

[143]  See *Nicholson v Permakraft (NZ) Ltd* [1985] 1 NZLR 242 at 249, 250, per Cooke J.

[144]  [1988] BCLC 20 at 40–1.

[145]  *Colin Gwyer & Associates Ltd v London Wharf (Limehouse) Ltd* [2003] 2 BCLC 153 at [74]; *Roberts v Frolich* [2011] 2 BCLC 625 at [85], [94]; *Re HLC Environmental Projects Ltd, Hellard v Carvalho* [2014] BCC 337 at [92]; *Re PV Solar Solutions Ltd* [2018] 1 BCLC 58 at [64]; *Secretary of State for Business, Innovation and Skills v Khan* [2017] EWHC 288 at [16]. On the question of paramountcy, see statements to the contrary by Park J in *Re MDA Investment Management, Whalley v Doney* [2004] 1 BCLC 217 at [70], [75] (the directors must have regard to the interests of the creditors as well as the interests of the shareholders); and by Lewison J in *Ultraframe (UK) Ltd v Fielding* [2005] EWHC 1638 at [1304] '... when a company, whether technically insolvent or not, is in financial difficulties to the extent that its creditors are at risk, the duties which the directors owe to the company are extended so as to encompass the interests of the company's creditors as a whole, as well as those of the shareholders'. But the weight of dicta is in favour of paramountcy. Keay (2014), n 102, supports the alternative balanced approach when the company is not actually insolvent, see at 452–3. But this would require having a different test depending on the company's financial position at the relevant time and would add to the uncertainty surrounding the application of s 172(3).

[146]  *GHLM Trading Ltd v Maroo* [2012] 2 BCLC 369. It is possible for payments to particular creditors to still be payments in the interests of the general body of creditors, for example in *Re Continental Assurance plc* [2007] 2 BCLC 287, payments made by directors of an insolvent company to two creditors (IATA and ABTA) were likely to be in the interests of the general body of creditors since any chance of selling the business would be written off if the company defaulted on paying those particular creditors, see at [422].

[147]  Jonathan Parker J in *Regentcrest plc v Cohen* [2001] 2 BCLC 80 at [120].

[148]  See *Re HLC Environmental Projects Ltd, Hellard v Carvalho* [2014] BCC 337 at [92], [96]. In this case the director had unreasonably overlooked a very material, though contingent, interest of a large creditor which cast doubt on the validity of the director's decision-making process. See also *Re PV Solar Solutions Ltd* [2018] 1 BCLC 58 at [78].

the position of the company's creditors, for example, where he was unaware or indifferent to the company's financial position, the question is whether an intelligent and honest man in the position of a director of the company concerned could in the circumstances have reasonably believed the transaction to be for the benefit of the company.[149] Furthermore, the hypothetical director would be expected to take into account all the relevant factors known to him or which ought to have been known to him at that time.[150]

**10-54**     In *Roberts v Frohlich*,[151] for example, the directors were in breach of duty where the court found that their wilful blindness to the company's mounting financial problems meant that they could not have had an honest belief that continued work on a development site (the company's business was property development) was in the company's interests which, given the parlous state of its finances, meant the paramount interests of the company's creditors. In *Re HLC Environmental Projects Ltd, Hellard v Carvalho*[152] liquidators brought misfeasance proceedings against a sole director who, during a period when the company was insolvent, caused the company to make payments to its parent company, to himself, to a third party bank whose debt was guaranteed by the parent company, and to a group employee. The court found that, in respect of each payment, the substantial purpose for the exercise of the power was to assist the payees and, in the case of the payment to the bank, to assist the parent company indirectly. No consideration was given to the best interests of the company's creditors as a whole, despite the company having (and the director knowing it to have) substantial creditors and liabilities and no projects or revenue stream and no reasonable prospect of gaining any projects or revenue. An intelligent and honest man in the director's position could not, in the circumstances, have considered the payments for the benefit of the company's creditors as a whole. The court held that all the payments were made in breach of CA 2006, s 171(b) and s 172(3). In *GHLM Trading Ltd v Maroo*,[153] the directors sold the company's stock at a time when it was of doubtful solvency or on the verge of insolvency, if not insolvent, and they sold it to a company connected with them in part to extinguish an unsecured claim which they had against the company. The court found that they did not consider the interests of the creditors, but acted to advance their own interests in breach of their duty to have regard to the interests of the creditors as a class. In *Re PV Solar Solutions Ltd*,[154] the directors were found to have preferred their own interests to those of the company and its creditors (they had the company make substantial payments to their pension plans), and unreasonably failed to take into account the very material interests of a large creditor (a supplier), such that they could not be considered to have had regard to the creditors' interests. Given their breach of duty to act in the interests of the creditors, the court ordered that they were jointly and severally liable to repay £750,000 to the company.

---

[149] *Charterbridge Corp Ltd v Lloyds Bank Ltd* [1969] 2 All ER 1185 at 119; *Colin Gwyer & Associates Ltd v London Wharf (Limehouse) Ltd* [2003] 2 BCLC 153 at [73], [80], [88]; *Re HLC Environmental Projects Ltd, Hellard v Carvalho* [2014] BCC 337 at [92]; *Re PV Solar Solutions Ltd* [2018] 1 BCLC 58 at [77].

[150] See *Re HLC Environmental Projects Ltd, Hellard v Carvalho* [2014] BCC 337 at [92], [96]. See also *Vivendi SA v Richards* [2013] BCC 771 at [152], [157], [165], [178]—directors gave no consideration to the company's creditors, being merely anxious to extract the company's remaining cash before the company failed.

[151] [2011] 2 BCLC 625 at [94]. See also *Re Oxford Pharmaceuticals Ltd* [2009] 2 BCLC 485.

[152] [2014] BCC 337 at [106], [116], [124], [131].

[153] [2012] 2 BCLC 369 at [176]. See also *Re MDA Investment Management Ltd, Whalley v Doney* [2004] 1 BCLC 217 at [74]–[76], [105], [108], a sale of a business with half the consideration paid not to the company, but without justification to a partnership 80 per cent controlled by a director of the company was a breach of the duties he owed to the general body of creditors of the company.

[154] [2018] 1 BCLC 58.

**10-55**  On the other hand, in *Re Pro4Sport Ltd*,[155] the court accepted that the sale of the business (at a time when the company was insolvent so the duty was engaged) to another company under the same ownership for a deferred purchase price (which later proved irrecoverable when the purchaser became insolvent) was a decision made in good faith. The director did consider the interests of creditors and honestly believed that his actions were in the interests of creditors. He consulted professional advisers, he had the assets valued, he was entitled to believe that the purchasing company would be able to honour the payment schedule. He accepted a deferred consideration because there was no offer from anyone of an immediate consideration.

### Relationship with provisions of the IA 1986

**10-56**  A cause of action in respect of a breach of duty under s 172(3) exists regardless of whether any of the specific provisions of the Insolvency Act 1986, such as s 239 (preferences), are in point. Often the facts which support a breach of s 172(3) could equally be used as the basis for a statutory claim under IA 1986, s 239, see **15-60**, but a claim for breach of s 172(3) exists independently of any claim available under s 239, as Newey J noted in *GHLM Trading Ltd v Maroo*.[156] Vice versa, conduct may amount to a statutory preference (assisted by the presumption in s 239(6)) without being a breach of duty at common law which has to be proved without the assistance of presumptions.[157] Equally, there may be a claim under the statute and for a preference[158] or a claim can be brought on the basis of a breach of duty under s 172(3) and as a transaction at an undervalue (s 238) and it is possible that the liquidator may fail on the statutory element while succeeding on the common law duty.[159] Of course, the facts will dictate whether a common law misfeasance or a breach of IA 1986, or both, should be pursued. The advantages of relying on the general duty in s 172(3) rather than a statutory liability can be seen in *Re HLC Environmental Projects Ltd, Hellard v Carvalho*;[160] the facts are discussed at **10-54**. Though the payments in that case, for example, the payments to the bank, may have been to reduce genuine liabilities, the court said that the director was choosing which creditors to pay and which to leave exposed to a real risk of being left unpaid. The payments had all the hallmarks of preferences, but the advantage to using CA 2006, s 172(3) rather than IA 1986, s 239 (preferences) is that the preference provisions only apply essentially to a two-year period prior to the company going into liquidation whereas, using CA 2006, s 172(3), the liquidator was able to challenge transactions which took place almost four years previously. The general duty effectively extends the reach of the liquidator beyond the periods prescribed by the Insolvency Act 1986. In *Re Continental Assurance Co*,[161] Park J said that he considered it to be 'entirely wrong to use a misfeasance action to get around [a] liquidator's inability to use s 239' (in that case because there was no desire to prefer), citing Hart J in

---

[155]  [2016] 1 BCLC 257.

[156]  [2012] 2 BCLC 369 at [168]. But see *Knight v Frost* [1999] 1 BCLC 364 at 382, per Hart J, that a director who in breach of duty caused the company to discharge the debt in favour of a particular creditor is not liable to make good the money so paid away unless the requirements of the statutory preference are met (a view endorsed in *Re Continental Assurance Co* [2007] 2 BCLC 287 at [442] by Park J). Newey J distinguishes between questions of breach and remedy and these comments by Hart J address the question of remedy. Newey J agrees (at [169]) that the applicability of IA 1986, s 239 (preference) may have a bearing on what, if any, remedy is available in respect of a breach of duty. It may be difficult with respect to a preference not within s 239 to show loss to the company. Loss is not essential to the statutory liability under s 239.

[157]  See *Re Brian D Pierson* [2001] 1 BCLC 275 at 299.

[158]  See, for example, *Re Oxford Pharmaceuticals Ltd* [2009] 2 BCLC 485.

[159]  For an example, see *Re MDA Investment Management Ltd, Whalley v Doney* [2004] 1 BCLC 217.

[160]  [2014] BCC 337.        [161]  [2007] 2 BCLC 287 at [420].

*Knight v Frost*[162] to similar effect. But, Newey J in *GHLM Trading Ltd v Maroo*[163] disagreed with that approach noting that whether or not the conditions of s 239 are met is not determinative of whether there is a breach of duty.

**10-57**   As noted, the jurisprudence under CA 2006, s 172(3) is only at the embryonic stage so the precise content and relationship with the statutory provisions remain to be resolved. In *Roberts v Frohlich*,[164] see **10-54**, the court found that liability for wrongful trading and breach of duty may arise in respect of the same period of time,[165] a conclusion which is doubtful since it would seem that s 172(3) must come into play at an earlier stage than s 214, indeed that is one of the strengths of s 172(3).[166] On the facts in *Roberts v Frohlich*, the point mattered little since the directors were liable on multiple grounds so perhaps the court did not look very carefully at the precise relationship between each of the grounds of liability, other than to remain alert to the risk of double recovery. But if the obligations under CA 2006, s 172(3) co-exist with those under IA 1986, s 214 (and now s 246ZB), then one or other of the provisions is redundant and, given the difficulties in applying s 214 (see **15-22**), the development of an open-textured obligation under s 172(3) seems more attractive and effective.[167] As discussed at **10-47**, the decision in *BTI 2014 LLC v Sequana*[168] does bring the trigger point (verge, brink of insolvency) much closer to s 214 and so in that way erodes some of the value of s 172(3).

## Appropriate remedy

**10-58**   Typically, a breach of the duty to consider or act in the creditors' interests will involve the company making payments to some creditors (often connected with the director) and not to others. The appropriate remedy, *prima facie*, is an order against the director, having misapplied company funds, to restore the trust fund,[169] but as the payment has gone to a creditor of the company in discharge, wholly or partially, of a debt of the company, the court may add a proviso to the order for repayment that any dividend payable to creditors of the company on winding up, in so far as attributable to the debt which has been discharged by the director, is payable to the director and not to that creditor so as to avoid a windfall for that creditor.[170] In other words, the director will be reimbursed to the extent that a genuine debt was discharged.

**10-59**   In *GHLM Trading Ltd v Maroo*[171] Newey J said that a company claiming for redress in respect of a failure to have regard to creditors' interests as required by s 172(3) is 'likely to need to show (a) that the company had suffered a loss, (b) that the director has profited (so that the no profit rule operates), or (c) that the transaction is not binding on the company'.

---

[162] [1999] 1 BCLC 364 at 381–2.     [163] [2012] 2 BCLC 369 and see n 156.
[164] [2011] 2 BCLC 625.     [165] [2011] 2 BCLC 625 at [94], [112]–[113].
[166] See Werdnik, 'Wrongful Trading Provision—Is it Efficient?' (2012) 25 Insolv Int 81 at 82.
[167] Ironically then, just as some amendments are made to wrongful trading by the Small Business, Enterprise and Employment Act 2015, ss 117 and 118, see **15-20**, it may be overtaken in practical value by the development of claims for breach of s 172(3).
[168] [2017] 1 BCLC 453.
[169] *West Mercia Safetywear Ltd v Dodd* [1988] BCLC 250 at 253. A claim for equitable compensation will not lie, for if the payment has extinguished a debt, the company will have suffered no loss, see *Re Continental Assurance Co of London plc* [2007] 2 BCLC 287 at [419].
[170] See *West Mercia Safetywear Ltd v Dodd* [1988] BCLC 250 at 255; also *Re HLC Environmental Projects Ltd, Hellard v Carvalho* [2014] BCC 337 at [142]–[151]—this proviso is not called for where the (creditor) recipient of the payment is the director himself; having restored the trust fund, he can claim in the liquidation of the company for any sums which he claims are owed to him by the company.
[171] [2012] 2 BCLC 369 at [169].

In this case, as discussed at **10-54**, the directors sold the company's stock to a company connected with them in part to extinguish an unsecured claim which they had against the company. The court considered the most straightforward remedy was to render the sale void and, as the recipient company was on notice of the breach of duty, the company was entitled to recover the stock or proceeds of sale of the stock, leaving the recipient company to substantiate its claims in the company's liquidation.

**10-60**  Disqualification proceedings under the CDDA 1986 may also be based on this failure to consider or act in the creditors' interests, usually wrapped up with other evidence (for example of preferences and undervalue transactions) to make a case of trading to the detriment of creditors (see **15-100**). For example, in *Re Mea Corporation Ltd, Secretary of State for Trade and Industry v Aviss*[172] directors were disqualified in essence for causing or allowing each of three companies to trade to the detriment of creditors. At a time when those companies were under increasing pressure from creditors and were each unable to pay their debts as they fell due (i.e. were insolvent), the directors allowed such cash as was available to be paid out to other companies in which one of the directors had a substantial personal interest. In *Re Genosyis Technology Management Ltd, Wallach v Secretary of State for Trade and Industry*[173] two directors were disqualified for entering, on behalf of the company, into a settlement agreement with a customer under which the company gave up a claim for €1.25m (which was instead paid to its parent company) and gained a maximum of £166,000. Given the company was insolvent at the time of the settlement, the court found the directors in breach of their duty to have regard to the creditors' interests.

---

[172]  [2007] 1 BCLC 618 at [76], [109].     [173]  [2007] 1 BCLC 208.

# 11

# Duty of care, skill, and independent judgement

## A Introduction

**11-1**  It is important that, in addition to their fiduciary obligations, directors should be subject to duties of care and skill appropriate to the modern commercial world, bearing in mind the increased emphasis on higher standards of corporate governance. The duty of care, skill, and diligence is not a fiduciary duty, as CA 2006, s 178(2) makes clear.[1] The most often cited explanation of the distinction between fiduciary and other duties is that given by Millett LJ in *Bristol & West Building Society v Mothew*[2] where he emphasised that fiduciary duties are duties peculiar to fiduciaries, breach of which attracts legal consequences different from those consequent upon the breach of other duties. Breach of fiduciary duties attracts equitable remedies which are primarily restitutionary or restorative rather than compensatory, as would be the case on a breach of a duty of care. Millett LJ went on to make the point that the core of fiduciary duties is loyalty and a breach of fiduciary duty is primarily about disloyalty, so mere incompetence is not enough.[3] The duty of care and skill in CA 2006, s 174 is therefore a reflection of the common law duty of care and liability for breach may lie in tort or, additionally, in contract where a director has a contract of employment as it is an implied contractual term that an employee will exercise reasonable care and skill in the performance of his duties.[4] It may be that there is more debate to be had about the nature of the duty,[5] notwithstanding the wording of s 178(2), which is ambiguous in any event and refers to enforcement of a duty rather than the nature of the duty. The distinction is important because damages awarded in tort are awarded on a narrower basis than equitable compensation, see *AIB Group (UK) plc v Redler*,[6] discussed in detail at **14-13**. There is an interesting discussion of the issue in

---

[1] See the Explanatory Notes to the CA 2006, para 322 ('… care, skill and diligence … is not considered to be a fiduciary duty').    [2] [1996] 4 All ER 698 at 711–12.

[3] [1996] 4 All ER 698 at 711–12. See also *Extrasure Travel Insurances Ltd v Scattergood* [2003] 1 BCLC 598 at [89]: 'Fiduciary duties are concerned with concepts of honesty and loyalty, not with competence' (Deputy Judge Jonathan Crow). See Teele Langford, 'The Distinction between the Duty of Care and the Duties to Act Bona Fide in the Interests of the Company and for Proper Purposes' (2013) 41 Australian Business Law Review 337. But see the robust criticism (highly readable) of 'the extreme narrowness of Millett LJ's approach to fiduciary duty' by retired Australian High Court judge, Dyson Heydon, 'Modern Fiduciary Liability: The Sick Man of Equity?' (2014) 20 Trusts & Trustees 1006.

[4] *Lister v Romford Ice & Cold Storage Ltd* [1957] 1 All ER 125.

[5] See Heydon, n 3, who considers that the position has been altered by the decision in *Pitt v Holt* [2013] 2 AC 108 such that there are aspects of the obligation to exercise care and skill which, depending on context, may be fiduciary, see Heydon at 1018–20 as to whether care and skill is in fact an aspect of the duty of loyalty and the duty of good faith. See Ho and Lee (2014) 130 LQR 542; *Youyang v Minter Ellison* (2003) 212 CLR 484 at [39], H Ct of Aust.    [6] [2014] 3 WLR 1367, UKSC.

*Re Level One Residential (Jersey) Ltd*,[7] where the issue mattered for limitation purposes under Jersey law (it was acknowledged that the Jersey law of fiduciary duty is the same as English law).[8] The court found that:

> 'The common-law duty of care will doubtless generally arise by virtue of the assumption of responsibility. However, the duty inherent in the office of director and arising by virtue of the office is an equitable rather than a common-law duty. The substantive content of the duties of care owed in equity and at common law (tort) is likely to be identical or practically so [citing *Base Metal Trading Ltd v Shamurin*[9]] … It does not follow that the remedies awarded for breaches of the two duties—equitable compensation in the one case, damages in the other—are necessarily awarded on identical principles.'[10]

The court noted that the distinction between the general common law duty of care and the specific equitable duty of care, though a fine one, is identified by Tuckey LJ as follows in *Base Metal v Shamurin*:[11] '… the duty of care in tort is not company specific, whereas the equitable duty is. The company provides the context in which the director assumes responsibility but is not crucial to the existence of the common law duty.'[12] The court in *Re Level One Residential (Jersey) Ltd*,[13] having acknowledged that the law of negligence in Jersey is the same as English law, concluded that the director's duty of care and skill is best seen as an equitable duty or, if one prefers, as a sui generis duty arising out of the relationship of a director to his company.[14]

**11-2** Prior to the CA 2006, the courts had looked to IA 1986, s 214(4) as an accurate statement of the general standard of care and skill expected of directors,[15] applying it beyond the confines of that section (which concerns wrongful trading).[16] Section 214(4) requires the conduct of a director to be measured against the standard of a reasonably diligent person having both the general knowledge, skill, and experience that may reasonably be expected of a person carrying out the same functions as are carried out by that director in relation to the company, and the general knowledge, skill, and experience that that director has. That approach was endorsed by the Law Commission,[17] the Company Law Review,[18] and the Government[19] and is reflected in CA 2006, s 174 which, with minimal changes,[20] reproduces the wording of IA 1986, s 214(4). The standard of care, skill, and

---

[7] [2017] EWHC 1105 (Ch), esp at [89]–[96].     [8] [2017] EWHC 1105 at [55].

[9] [2005] 1 WLR 1157.

[10] [2017] EWHC 1105 at [93]–[94]; and see Lord Reid in *AIB Group (UK) plc v Redler* [2014] 3 WLR 1367, UKSC, at [136]–[138].     [11] [2005] 1 WLR 1157 at [57].

[12] [2017] EWHC 1105 at [103].     [13] [2017] EWHC 1105.     [14] [2017] EWHC 1105 at [98], [113].

[15] See *Re D'Jan of London Ltd, Copp v D'Jan* [1994] 1 BCLC 561; *Norman v Theodore Goddard* [1991] BCLC 1028; *Re Landhurst Leasing plc, Secretary of State for Trade and Industry v Ball* [1999] 1 BCLC 286 at 344; *Cohen v Selby* [2001] 1 BCLC 176 at [21].

[16] Liability for wrongful trading arises where a director is found to have continued trading after a point in time when he knew or ought to have concluded that there was no reasonable prospect of the company avoiding entering insolvent administration or going into insolvent liquidation, see **15-22**.

[17] Law Commission, *Company Directors: Regulating Conflicts of Interests and Formulating a Statement of Duties* (Law Comm No 261), 1999, Ch 5.

[18] Company Law Review, *Final Report*, vol 1 (2001), p 346 and Annex C; and see *Developing the Framework* (2000), pp 40–3.

[19] See *Modernising Company Law* (Cm 5553-I, 2002), paras 3.2–3.7.

[20] 'Diligence' is expressly included in the section, but the case law had already established the need for a director to exert and apply himself in the conduct of the company's affairs and the courts do penalise those found to be inattentive to their duties: see, for example, *Re Park House Properties Ltd* [1997] 2 BCLC 530, discussed at **11-21**.

diligence therefore remains as previously established and the existing case law remains relevant (CA 2006, s 170(4)).

**11-3**   Though the standard expected is now clearly identified, the content of this duty is a work in progress for the courts. For a period, much valuable guidance on the duty of care and skill was found in the large number of reported cases on disqualification proceedings brought against a director of an insolvent company on the ground that his conduct had shown him to have fallen below the standards of probity and competence (i.e. care and skill) expected of a director.[21] Disqualification is mainly dealt with now by administrative undertakings (see **15-77**) with the result that this source of authorities on care and skill has largely dried up.

**11-4**   The importance of the disqualification authorities reflects the fact that, in practice, directors are rarely sued for negligence in the management of a company's affairs.[22] As with the other duties of directors, enforcement of the duty of care and skill takes place, if at all, when the company goes into insolvent liquidation where a liquidator may consider it worthwhile to pursue a director for misfeasance (see **15-3**) or wrongful trading under IA 1986, s 214 (see **15-18**). Disqualification proceedings may be brought on the grounds of unfitness, though here the relevant standard is more frequently described as a standard of 'probity and competence', rather than stated in the traditional terms of care and skill,[23] but if the allegation is incompetence without dishonesty, it must be incompetence to a high degree[24] (see **15-96**). It remains to be seen whether changes to allow for greater assignment of claims by insolvency practitioners[25] and the provision of more widely drawn criteria for determining unfitness[26] will increase the number of claims and proceedings brought against directors based on incompetence.

**11-5**   Of course, for many small companies, family ties are usually stronger than concerns about standards of care and skill. For solvent private companies, in so far as allegations of negligence arise, they tend to do so in the context of unfairly prejudicial petitions under CA 2006, s 994 and with limited success (see **19-56**). In part, there is a judicial view that, if the shareholders choose to appoint directors who are poor managers, then, short of insolvency, that is a matter for them. Of course, in many small companies, the directors and the shareholders are the same people. Another constraint on judicial enthusiasm for negligence claims against directors is their long-held view that the courts should not interfere or second-guess directors on matters of business judgement (see **10-8**), especially with hindsight, and frequently what is presented as a claim in negligence is merely a disagreement on business strategy or decisions. Furthermore, as the courts point out,

---

[21]   CDDA 1986, s 6.

[22]   A phenomenon which is not unique to the UK, the position is similar across the Member States, see Gerner-Beuerle and Schuster, 'The Evolving Structure of Directors' Duties in Europe' (2014) 15 EBOR 192 at 199.

[23]   See *Re Landhurst Leasing plc, Secretary of State for Trade and Industry v Ball* [1999] 1 BCLC 286 at 344; *Secretary of State for Trade and Industry v Gray* [1995] 1 BCLC 276 at 286.

[24]   *Re Sevenoaks Stationers (Retail) Ltd* [1991] 1 BCLC 325 at 337; *Re Barings plc (No 5)* [1999] 1 BCLC 433 at 483–4, aff'd [2000] 1 BCLC 523, CA.

[25]   IA 1986, s 246ZD, inserted by Small Business, Enterprise and Employment Act 2015, s 118, giving liquidators and administrators powers to assign claims with respect to fraudulent and wrongful trading, transactions at an undervalue, preferences, and extortionate credit transactions.

[26]   See CDDA 1986, Sch 1, see **15-99**, inserted by Small Business, Enterprise and Employment Act 2015, s 106(6), covering, for example, the extent to which the person was responsible for the causes of any material contravention by a company of any applicable legislative or other requirement; or for the causes of a company becoming insolvent; as well as the nature and extent of any loss or harm caused, or any potential loss or harm which could have been caused, by the person's conduct in relation to a company (paras 1, 2, and 4).

directors are not trustees and they are appointed precisely in order to take risks in an environment of risk which is, after all, the purpose of the limited company. The point can be illustrated by *Roberts v Frohlich*.[27] This case involved a construction business, building and selling units on an industrial estate. There was an initial three-month period when the project was just starting, when there were financial pressures and yet the directors continued on with the project. When considering whether they had been negligent in so doing, the court said that they had made poor business decisions and misjudged the level of risk, in part out of optimism. However, it was important not to judge them with hind-sight and the question to be asked was whether no reasonable director could have made the judgement about the future which was made by them.[28] Their project was speculative and risky, but risk is inherent in economic activity. Therefore, Norris J concluded, their continued trading in this three-month period had been a misjudgement, but it was not negligent.[29] By the end of that initial period, however, there was mounting evidence of significant financial difficulties, the company had no cash resources, and the costs of the project were escalating. In those circumstances, the court said, no reasonably competent director would have continued with the development and the directors were in breach of their duties of care and skill in continuing past that point.[30]

**11-6**  Issues of competence are central to corporate governance concerns in public companies, especially in the wake of the financial crisis which highlighted a dearth of competence in the boards of financial institutions.[31] The UK Corporate Governance Code emphasises the need for the board and its committees to have a balance of skills, experience, inde-pendence, and knowledge (see **6-15**).[32] The board is expected to undertake an annual evaluation of its own performance and that of its committees and individual directors.[33] It is for the shareholders to remove directors if they are dissatisfied with their perfor-mance and the UK Code recommends (and it is now accepted practice) that all direc-tors be subject to annual election,[34] so shareholders annually have the chance to remove incompetent directors.

## Litigation risks

**11-7**  Occasionally and exceptionally, a public company with a new board in place may sue the company's former directors for negligence and such litigation can have an impact on directors,[35] even if the litigation is rarely prosecuted to fruition. Non-executive directors in particular are exercised by the reputational damage done even by threatened litigation. There were some concerns that the statutory derivative claim under CA 2006, Pt 11, which for the first time allows derivative claims to be brought on the basis of negligence,[36] would encourage litigation but, as discussed at **20-72**, this has not occurred.

---

[27] [2011] 2 BCLC 625.     [28] [2011] 2 BCLC 625 at [108].     [29] [2011] 2 BCLC 625 at [108].
[30] [2011] 2 BCLC 625 at [94], [102].
[31] See Loughrey, The Director's Duty of Care and Skill and the Financial Crisis' in Loughrey (ed), *Directors' Duties and Shareholder Litigation in the Wake of the Financial Crisis* (2013); Hannigan, 'Board Failures in the Financial Crisis—Tinkering with Codes and the Need for Wider Corporate Governance Reforms' Part 1 (2011) 32 Co Law 363; Part 2 (2012) 33 Co Law 35.
[32] FRC, UK Corporate Governance Code (2018), Prin I.
[33] FRC, UK Corporate Governance Code (2018), Prov 21, see **6-16**.
[34] FRC, UK Corporate Governance Code (2018), Prov 18.
[35] See, for example, the *Equitable Life* case. For the story of this litigation which was ultimately dropped, see *Equitable Life Assurance Society v Bowley* [2004] 1 BCLC 180; Reed (2006) 27 Co Law 170.
[36] At common law, a derivative claim did not lie for negligence, see *Pavlides v Jensen* [1956] 2 All ER 518.

**11-8**  Any attempt to pursue a claim in negligence faces the difficulty of establishing that a duty of care was owed to the company in respect to the kind of loss which has occurred,[37] and that the loss claimed is attributable to the breach of duty relied on.[38] Recently, the courts appear to be taking a robust line on causation with respect to negligent directors. In *Weavering Capital (UK) Ltd v Peterson*,[39] a case involving the collapse of a hedge fund management company with $500m losses from swaps trading,[40] the issue was the liability of an executive director. She was the wife of the managing director who was primarily responsible for the losses and who had been found liable in deceit in other proceedings.[41] The allegation was that she had failed to exercise care and skill in that she should have discovered what was happening with the business and challenged her husband as to the swaps trading. Her defence was that, had she asked him to explain the transactions in issue, she would have believed whatever explanation he offered and therefore she would have behaved no differently. Hence, her failure to act did not cause any loss. This defence was rejected by the court, properly so, as the Court of Appeal affirmed. At first instance, the court found that the question is not what the director would have done, but what a reasonable director would have done and the court had found that no explanation could have been given by the husband which would have satisfied a reasonable director. The absence of a satisfactory explanation would have led to further enquiries and the cessation of trading. In negligently allowing the business to continue, she and the other negligent directors caused the loss claimed and were liable accordingly.[42] Likewise, another director in the case could not have been satisfied by any explanations given by the managing director and he too should have brought the company's business to a halt and was liable for his failure to do so.[43] The case is a salutary lesson to directors who are disinclined to rock the boat. It will often be the case that the claim for negligence will be on this basis, where the claim is with respect to omissions which allowed the damage to occur or continue. If directors were to be exempted from the consequences of their omissions on the basis of a lack of causation, then there would be little scope for claims in negligence to be brought. The approach in *Weavering Capital (UK) Ltd v Peterson* is also consistent with the earlier Court of Appeal decision in *Lexi Holdings Ltd v Luqman*[44] where the claim in negligence

---

[37] See *South Australian Asset Management Corp v York Montague Ltd* [1996] 3 All ER 365 at 370; also *Re Continental Assurance Co of London plc* [2007] 2 BCLC 287 at [378]–[380], [405]; see also *Bishopsgate Investment Management Ltd v Maxwell (No 2)* [1993] BCLC 814 at 829–30; *Caparo Industries plc v Dickman* [1990] 2 AC 605 at 627. Generally, see *Customs and Excise Commissioners v Barclays Bank* [2006] 4 All ER 256; *MAN Nutzfahrzeuge AG v Freightliner Ltd* [2008] 2 BCLC 22 at [44]–[51] where there is a useful summary of the authorities by Chadwick LJ, CA; also Arden LJ in *Johnson v Gore Wood & Co* [2003] EWCA Civ 1728 at [91].

[38] In *Madoff Securities International Ltd v Raven* [2013] EWHC 3147 at [294], the court found some of the directors in breach of their duty of care and skill in failing to consider whether certain payments made by the company were in the interests of the company. But the court concluded that the breach of care and skill was not causative of any loss for, had they considered the interests of the company, they would still have thought the payments were in the interests of the company and the payments would still have been made. Therefore the breach of duty caused no loss.

[39] [2012] EWHC 1480, [2012] Lloyd's Rep FC 561, overruled on an insignificant point by the Court of Appeal, [2015] BCC 741, [2013] EWCA Civ 71, where the case is reported as *Weavering Capital (UK) Ltd v Dabhia*, but otherwise the Court of Appeal generally endorsed the approach taken at first instance to the duty of care owed by directors.

[40] There is a useful summary of the manner in which the losses were incurred at [2015] BCC 741, [2013] EWCA Civ 71 at [4]–[15].

[41] Faced with huge trading losses, the managing director tried to hide the situation and made false representations to investors to ensure they would not try to withdraw their funds and discover the losses.

[42] [2012] EWHC 1480, [2012] Lloyd's Rep FC 561 at [176]–[178], [2013] EWCA Civ 71, [2015] BCC 741 at [49]–[55].

[43] [2013] EWCA Civ 71, [2015] BCC 741 at [52]–[55].    [44] [2009] 2 BCLC 1, CA.

was made against two non-executive directors in respect of their failure to act with regard to wrongdoing by their fraudster brother, an executive director. Again, their defence was that, even if they had carried out their duties, the losses would still have occurred, for the losses were caused by the fraud of their brother, not by their failure to alert others to the fact that he was a fraudster. Briggs J had accepted their defence at first instance, but was overruled by the Court of Appeal. Had the directors acted as they should have, they would have questioned their brother about his conduct, as to which he could not have provided a satisfactory explanation, which would have required them to inform the board and the auditors. Steps would then have been taken to prevent the subsequent misapplication of company funds by their brother. Loss to the extent of those misapplications was caused, the Court of Appeal held, by their failure to perform their duties.[45]

**11-9** The issue of causation was also significant in *Newcastle International Airport Ltd v Eversheds LLP*[46] which involved negligence claims arising from the renegotiation of the executive directors' service contracts which were unduly favourable to the directors. In this case, the Court of Appeal found that the company's solicitors had been in breach of their duties of care to their client in not providing a brief memorandum explaining the extent and nature of the changes to the directors' bonuses which had been made in the redrafted contracts, but that negligence was not causative of any substantial loss (£2 damages were awarded).[47] The evidence showed that the non-executive director who chaired the remuneration committee (who would have received the memo, had it been provided) would not have read the document (or if she had, would have misunderstood it) and therefore the contracts would still have been signed, and the company would have suffered the same consequences because of the chair of the remuneration committee's breach of duty.[48]

**11-10** A director who knowingly allows a practice of improper loans to directors to continue is to be treated as having authorised the payments, even though he does not have actual knowledge of each individual payment at the time when it is made, and so is jointly and severally liable therefore for their repayment.[49] Further, the director is not merely in breach of the duty of care and skill and liable on that basis for allowing the misapplication to occur and continue, but is treated as party to the misapplication by having authorised or permitted it.[50] In such circumstances, it is the duty of a director aware of the improper payments, not merely to ensure that a stop is put to the practice, but that steps are taken to recover the indebtedness outstanding to the company.[51] This level of liability

---

[45] [2009] 2 BCLC 1 at [50], [53]. Cf *Dickinson v NAL Realisations Ltd* [2017] EWHC 28, [2018] 1 BCLC 623, at [160] where the court found two negligent directors did not cause any loss—the company suffered loss from transactions carried out by the sole effective director where he had a conflict of interest. The negligent directors had abdicated all their responsibilities and allowed him to run the business as he saw fit. The court concluded that their inactivity did not enable the loss, since if they had challenged him, he would have engineered their removal. This outcome seems somewhat generous compared to the authorities above, but it was a company with no independent shareholders to turn to, which perhaps underlies the court's conclusion. It is not clear why they should not have been expected to raise their concerns with the auditors.

[46] [2014] 2 All ER 728, rev'g in part [2013] PNLR 5.    [47] [2014] 2 All ER 728 at [85], [102].

[48] [2014] 2 All ER 728 at [88], [89], [98]–[100].

[49] *Queensway Systems Ltd v Walker* [2007] 2 BCLC 577; *Neville v Krikorian* [2007] 1 BCLC 1, CA; see also *Lexi Holdings v Luqman* [2007] EWHC 2652 at [201]–[205], [215].

[50] *Madoff Securities International Ltd v Raven* [2013] EWHC 3147 at [192], per Popplewell J; *Queensway Systems Ltd v Walker* [2007] 2 BCLC 577; *Neville v Krikorian* [2007] 1 BCLC 1, CA.

[51] *Neville v Krikorian* [2007] 1 BCLC 1, CA. The director's liability on this basis is for the difference between the amount which the company could have recovered at the date when the director became aware of the improper loans and the amount recoverable at the time of the claim. See also *Lexi Holdings v Luqman* [2007] EWHC 2652 at [201]–[205], [215]; *Madoff Securities International Ltd v Raven* [2013] EWHC 3147 at [295].

for the careless director should act as a considerable deterrent to turning a blind eye to the wrongdoing of others, to failing to act when action is required.

**11-11**    Notwithstanding these cases, it is rare for directors to be sued directly for breach of the duty of care and skill. However, the general duties imposed on directors under CA 2006, Pt 10, Ch 2, are cumulative (s 179) and conduct which is in breach of care and skill may equally be open to challenge on other grounds such as that the director has acted for an improper purpose in breach of s 171, or has failed to promote the success of the company in breach of s 172, or failed to exercise independent judgement as required by s 173. In *Re Bradcrown Ltd, Official Receiver v Ireland*,[52] for example, a finance director was in breach of his duty of care in abdicating all responsibility for a complex transaction whereby the company transferred away its assets valued at £3.7m for no consideration. In so acting the director also failed to act bona fide in the interests of the company and he used his powers for an improper purpose in divesting the company of its assets for no consideration. In many cases therefore where liability is established in respect of a breach of fiduciary duty, it would also have been possible to have brought a claim for breach of care and skill. As noted at **11-1**, there are certain practical advantages in pursuing a breach of fiduciary duty rather than a claim in negligence.

# B  The statutory standard of care, skill, and diligence

## Collective and individual responsibilities

**11-12**    The starting point is the collective responsibility of the board for the management of the company's affairs, but equally directors' duties are 'personal and inescapable' duties[53] and, within that collective responsibility, each director must meet the appropriate standard of care, skill, and diligence. Much cited on this point is the statement of Lord Woolf MR in *Re Westmid Packing Services Ltd, Secretary of State for Trade and Industry v Griffiths* as follows:[54]

> '[T]he collegiate or collective responsibility of the board of directors of a company is of fundamental importance to corporate governance under English company law. That collegiate or collective responsibility must however be based on individual responsibility. Each individual director owes duties to the company to inform himself about its affairs and to join with his co-directors in supervising and controlling them.'

**11-13**    The standard expected is laid down in CA 2006, s 174:

> '(1) A director of a company must exercise reasonable care, skill and diligence.
>
> (2) This means the care, skill and diligence that would be exercised by a reasonably diligent person with—

---

[52] [2001] 1 BCLC 547 at 561. See too *Roberts v Frohlich* [2011] 2 BCLC 625 at [4]–[6] where overlapping claims were made as to a failure to act in the interests of the company, including a failure to have regard to creditors' interests; a failure to exercise reasonable care and skill; and wrongful trading.

[53]  See *Secretary of State for Trade and Industry v Goldberg* [2004] 1 BCLC 597 at [29], per Lewison J, relying on *Re Westmid Packing Services Ltd, Secretary of State for Trade and Industry v Griffiths* [1998] 2 BCLC 646 at 654.

[54]  [1998] 2 BCLC 646 at 653, a view endorsed by the courts on many subsequent occasions: see, for example, *Re Kaytech International plc, Secretary of State for Trade and Industry v Kaczer* [1999] 2 BCLC 351 at 425, CA; *Re Landhurst Leasing plc* [1999] 1 BCLC 286 at 346; *Re Barings plc (No 5)* [1999] 1 BCLC 433 at 486.

(a)  the general knowledge, skill and experience that may reasonably be expected of a person carrying out the functions carried out by the director in relation to the company, and

(b)  the general knowledge, skill and experience that the director has.'

**11-14**   The standard set is an objective minimum standard, that of a reasonably diligent person who has taken on the office of director, set in the context of the functions undertaken, with that objective minimum standard capable of being raised (but not lowered) in the light of the particular attributes of the director in question.[55] The personal attributes of the director cannot lower the standard set in s 174(2)(a) for that would mean that a subjective standard would always apply, determined by those personal attributes.

**11-15**   If a director is a professional person, such as a chartered accountant, s 174(2) requires him to meet the standard to be expected of a reasonably diligent director carrying out the functions carried out by him in that company and having that personal attribute. In *Weavering Capital (UK) Ltd v Peterson*[56] one of directors of a hedge fund management company was a very experienced trader with significant knowledge of trading in derivatives. Therefore, the test was whether, given her experience, knowledge, and intelligence, she had acted as a reasonable director of a hedge fund management company would have acted. In *Roberts v Frohlich*,[57] the court took into account that the two directors of a construction company were, respectively, professionally qualified accountants and engineers with substantial experience of property development and so the standard is what can reasonably be expected of persons with those attributes carrying out those functions.[58]

**11-16**   The standard is that of the reasonably competent director carrying out those functions in that company and the court does not look to impose unrealistically high levels of skill. For example, in *Re Continental Assurance Co of London plc*[59] non-executive directors of an insurance company could be expected to appreciate the general accounting requirements applicable to insurance companies, but could not be required to be specialists in sophisticated accounting issues pertaining to insurance companies, even if they possessed accounting qualifications.[60]

## Functions undertaken

**11-17**   Flexibility in the application of the statutory standard is maintained by the obligation to have regard to the functions carried out by the director in relation to the company in question. This point was emphasised by Jonathan Parker J in *Re Barings plc (No 5), Secretary of State for Trade and Industry v Baker (No 5)*[61] where he stressed that the competence of the director must be assessed in the context of and by reference to the role in

[55]  See *Re Brian D Pierson (Contractors) Ltd* [2001] 1 BCLC 275 at 302.
[56]  [2012] EWHC 1480, see n 39.        [57]  [2011] 2 BCLC 625.
[58]  [2011] 2 BCLC 615 at [100], [111]. As the company's financial position evolved and deteriorated, given the directors' actual skill and experience (accounting qualifications and knowledge of construction industry) and the abilities to be expected of directors participating in financial oversight and project management of a new-build development, they ought to have concluded that there was no reasonable prospect of avoiding insolvent liquidation.
[59]  [2007] 2 BCLC 287.        [60]  [2007] 2 BCLC 287 at [254]–[258].
[61]  [1999] 1 BCLC 433, aff'd [2000] 1 BCLC 523, CA.

the management of the company which was in fact assigned to him or which he in fact assumed and by reference to his duties and responsibilities in that role.[62] He went on:[63]

'Thus the existence and extent of any particular duty will depend upon how the particular business is organised and upon what part in the management of that business the respondent could reasonably be expected to play (see *Bishopsgate Investment Management Ltd (in liq) v Maxwell (No 2)* [1993] BCLC 1282 at 1285 per Hoffmann LJ). For example, where the respondent was an executive director the court will assess his conduct by reference to his duties and responsibilities in that capacity. Thus, while the requisite standard of competence does not vary according to the nature of the company's business or to the respondent's role in the management of that business—and in that sense it may be said that there is a 'universal' standard—that standard must be applied to the facts of each particular case.'

**11-18**   By focusing on the functions which an individual undertakes or which are entrusted to him, the court is able to calibrate the content of the duty in the light of the size and complexity of the business and the position of the individual director.[64] In this way, it is possible to accommodate within the same legal standard the managing director of a multi-million pound banking company, the non-executive director of an insurance company and a teenage director of a family company carrying on business in a limited way. It is clear that there are certain minimum functions expected of any director who takes on the office of director which include compliance with the statutory requirements with regard to the maintenance of proper accounting records and the preparation of accounts.[65] The relevant functions beyond the minimum will depend on the post held, the tasks assigned, and how the company organises its affairs. It is also necessary to consider the exercise of the functions in the context of the company's financial position and the care and skill required; the acts which might justifiably be undertaken in a solvent company might be quite different from what would be appropriate in relation to a company of doubtful solvency.[66]

**11-19**   As to the extent of a director's functions, of course, it is not the case that all directors must be involved in all of the company's affairs. A director is not under any obligation to undertake a definitive part in the conduct of the company's business and roles vary according to the size and business of the particular company.[67] Equally, a director cannot reduce his role to such an extent that he is in effect making no or only the most minimal contribution to the collective responsibility of the directors to supervise and control the company's business,[68] not even if it is a family company.

---

[62] [1999] 1 BCLC 433 at 484, aff'd [2000] 1 BCLC 523 at 535, CA. See also *Re Continental Assurance Co of London plc, Secretary of State for Trade and Industry v Burrows* [1997] 1 BCLC 48 at 57–8; *Re Produce Marketing Consortium Ltd (No 2)* [1989] BCLC 520 at 550; *Re Vintage Hallmark Ltd, Secretary of State for Trade & Industry v Grove* [2007] 1 BCLC 788 at [9].     [63] [1999] 1 BCLC 433 at 484.

[64] See *Re Produce Marketing Consortium Ltd (No 2)* [1989] BCLC 520 at 550.

[65] See *Re Produce Marketing Consortium Ltd (No 2)* [1989] BCLC 520 at 550; *Re Queens Moat Houses plc, Secretary of State for Trade and Industry v Bairstow (No 2)* [2005] 1 BCLC 136.

[66] See *Roberts v Frohlich* [2011] 2 BCLC 625 at [98].

[67] See *Re Barings plc (No 5), Secretary of State for Trade and Industry v Baker (No 5)* [1999] 1 BCLC 433 at 436.

[68] See *Re Westmid Packing Services Ltd, Secretary of State for Trade and Industry v Griffiths* [1998] 2 BCLC 646 at 653. An incentive to act may be found in the many provisions of the CA 2006 which impose criminal sanctions on the company and on any 'officer in default'. An officer is in default if he authorises or permits, participates in, *or fails to take all reasonable steps* to prevent the contravention: s 1121(3). On this basis (the definition is different from that which previously applied, CA 1985, s 730(5), which was limited to officers who knowingly and wilfully authorised or permitted the contravention), the inactive, ill-informed, director may find it difficult to escape liability for contraventions by others.

**11-20**    In such businesses, there is a tendency for a spouse or offspring to take on a directorship without ever playing any role (or indeed intending to play any role) in the management of the company's affairs. Typically such individuals regard themselves as simply having a nominal or honorific title. The courts do not accept that a director may have such a role. As was noted in *Re Brian D Pierson (Contractors) Ltd*:[69]

> 'The office of director has certain minimum responsibilities and functions, which are not simply discharged by leaving all management functions, and consideration of the company's affairs to another director without question, even in the case of a family company … One cannot be a "sleeping" director; the function of "directing" on its own requires some consideration of the company's affairs to be exercised.'

**11-21**    In *Re Park House Properties Ltd*[70] the directors of a company were a husband, his wife, and his two teenage children. The husband was responsible for the conduct of the affairs of the company and he was disqualified as unfit on the grounds of continuing to trade in disregard of creditors' interests, non-filing of company accounts, and allowing the company to expend £173,000 on an extension to a property, the benefit of which would go to the director personally rather than the company. His wife played no part whatever in the affairs of the company and his son and daughter played only very marginal roles in its affairs. None of them received any remuneration as directors. Nevertheless, all three were disqualified. The court held that each of them, by virtue of sheer inactivity over the period of their respective directorships, had been guilty of conduct which made him or her unfit. Neuberger J emphasised that:[71]

> 'The law imposes statutory and fiduciary duties on directors of companies and even where, as here, the respondents received no payment, and any advice given to [the husband] would have been unlikely to have been acted on, they cannot escape from those duties. [Their] complete inactivity in relation to, and complete uninvolvement with, the running of the company, the financial problems of the company, the preparation and filing of the accounts, and the decision to spend a substantial sum on the construction of the extension … lead to the conclusion that, in the absence of special circumstances, they are unfit.'

**11-22**    In *Re Galeforce Pleating Co Ltd*[72] a textile company collapsed with losses of approximately £438,000. The directors of the company included a husband and wife and one other. In the disqualification proceedings brought against the wife, she pleaded that she had 'a most negligible actual involvement in the running of the company'.[73] Disqualifying her for a period of five years, the court emphasised that it was not a sufficient discharge of a director's responsibilities to maintain 'a negligible actual involvement' in the affairs of the company. So long as an individual continues to hold office as a director and, in particular to receive remuneration from it, it is incumbent upon that person, the court said, to inform herself as to the financial affairs of the company and to play an appropriate role in the management of its business. If a director is not prepared to discharge her responsibilities properly, the appropriate course is to resign. Furthermore, the court stressed that

---

[69] [2001] 1 BCLC 275 at 309–10. The case concerned a director's wife who though also a director and drawing remuneration as such had only a very limited clerical role in the company. The court found that Mrs Pierson, in ignoring the signals of financial difficulties and failing to appreciate even the questions that ought to have been asked about the company's affairs, was instrumental in the company continuing to trade and therefore was liable for wrongful trading under IA 1986, s 214. See also *Re Finch (UK) plc* [2016] 1 BCLC 394 at [29].

[70] [1997] 2 BCLC 530. See also *Re Westminster Property Management Ltd (No 2), Official Receiver v Stern (No 2)* [2001] BCC 305 at [197].

[71] [1997] 2 BCLC 530 at 555–6.        [72] [1999] 2 BCLC 704.        [73] [1999] 2 BCLC 704 at 716.

it is not an excuse for a director to say that the running of a company is left to his or her spouse.[74]

**11-23**    For the same reasons, the courts are unwilling to accept that someone can be a professional nominee director acting for hundreds, if not thousands, of companies in return for an annual fee.[75] Such a person cannot realistically be carrying out any functions with regard to those companies.

### The functions of an executive director

**11-24**    If a director is an executive director, his conduct must be considered against what could be expected of a reasonably diligent person carrying out his duties and responsibilities as an executive director in that company. A managing director, for example, would have general responsibility to oversee the activities of the company.[76] An executive director would normally have responsibility (subject to any appropriate delegation) for common management tasks such as signing cheques. A reasonably diligent director in that position would not sign blank cheques,[77] nor cheques of such a large amount in the context of the company's business as would put him on inquiry without first seeking a full explanation as to their purpose,[78] nor sign a simple insurance proposal form without checking the accuracy of its contents.[79] If the director performs a special function, such as a 'finance director', the special skills expected of a person in that capacity are to be expected of him[80] and a failure to meet those standards will be a breach of his individual responsibilities. In *Re AG (Manchester) Ltd, Official Receiver v Watson*[81] the court was particularly critical of a finance director who allowed an inner group of directors to take key decisions on dividends and other financial matters without reference to the board as a whole. Such conduct fell below the standard expected of a finance director who, in a private company, is often an essential brake, the court said, on the financial ambitions of the shareholders. It was the finance director's duty, whatever the conduct of the other directors, the court said, to ensure that the company was run in accordance with the articles and the Companies Act.[82] In *Weavering Capital v Peterson*[83] an executive director of a hedge fund company with extensive trading expertise tried to defend her position in the face of multi-million dollar losses caused by unauthorised swaps dealing by the managing director (her husband), by suggesting that she had a confined area of responsibility and limited functions, but the court found that suggestion both factually and legally unsustainable.

---

[74] [1999] 2 BCLC 704 at 716.

[75] See *Official Receiver v Vass* [1999] BCC 516. See also *Re Kaytech International plc, Secretary of State for Trade and Industry v Kaczer* [1999] 2 BCLC 351 (director claimed to be a director of 1,000 Isle of Man companies, see at 414). The court noted in *Kaytech* that the law should give no encouragement to the notion that if a man takes on so many directorships that he cannot remember them, he is thereby released from the heavy responsibilities which he has undertaken: [1999] 2 BCLC 351 at 426, per Robert Walker LJ.

[76] See *Re Continental Assurance Co of London plc* [2007] 2 BCLC 287 at [399].

[77] *Dorchester Finance Co Ltd v Stebbing* [1989] BCLC 498. When signing cheques, a director is only required to satisfy himself that the cheque has been authorised by the board. He need not verify that the money is in fact required for the particular purpose specified or is indeed expended on that purpose, assuming that the cheque comes before him for signature in the regular way having regard to the usual practice of that company: *Re City Equitable Fire Insurance Co Ltd* [1925] Ch 407 at 452.

[78] *Secretary of State for Trade and Industry v Swan* [2005] BCC 596 at [177]–[179], see **11-26**.

[79] *D'Jan of London Ltd, Copp v D'Jan* [1994] 1 BCLC 561 (the effect of the lack of care in this instance was to deprive the company of insurance cover when the policy was invalidated because of inaccuracies in the proposal form).

[80] *Re Brian D Pierson (Contractors) Ltd* [2001] 1 BCLC 275 at 310.        [81] [2008] 1 BCLC 321.

[82] [2008] 1 BCLC 321 at [181].        [83] [2012] EWHC 1480.

The test, Proudman J said, is whether what the director did was that which a reasonable director of a hedge fund management company in her position, with her experience, actual knowledge, and intelligence should have done, and whether she acquired a sufficient knowledge of the company's business to discharge her duties.[84] On this score, she had failed. Her knowledge, experience, and duties were such that she could and should have brought to an end the unauthorised swaps dealing.[85] The court also noted that she was highly paid and her level of reward was a relevant factor in resolving the issue of the extent of her duties and responsibilities. It was not that her fitness depended on how much she was paid, Proudman J said, but rather that the higher the level of reward, the greater the responsibilities reasonably to be expected (*prima facie* at least) to go with it.[86]

### The functions of a non-executive director

**11-25** Much of the interest in this area concerns the standards expected of non-executive directors in public companies where the courts must balance the need to promote higher standards of corporate governance against concerns that too high a standard will deter able people from accepting directorships. The functions of non-executive directors in public companies are considered in detail in Chapter 6. They play particularly important roles on matters such as risk management, financial reporting, and internal financial controls (see at **6-34**), and have significant responsibilities on the nomination, audit, and remuneration committees, all of which will permeate judicial perceptions of the standards expected of them.[87]

**11-26** For example, a non-executive director of a listed company approached by senior executives about possible financial wrongdoing within the company was not acting as a reasonably careful and diligent director when he merely discussed the concerns with the chief executive and the finance director and took no further steps in the matter, as happened in *Secretary of State for Trade and Industry v Swan*,[88] a disqualification case. In this case, the non-executive director was also the deputy chairman of the company and a member of the company's audit committee, the company was a listed company, and the matter concerned financial impropriety involving significant sums of money. The allegations were serious, the sources reliable, and merely consulting the finance director was an inadequate response, the court thought, in a situation where 'decisive, courageous and independent action' (including consulting his fellow non-executives and the auditors) was required of a non-executive director. The director's want of competence, the court said, related to a failure to pursue an enquiry with sufficient vigour.[89] Given that his conduct fell below that expected of someone in his position and with his experience, the director was disqualified.

---

[84] [2012] EWHC 1480, [2012] Lloyd's Rep FC 561 at [174], see n 39.

[85] [2012] EWHC 1480, [2012] Lloyd's Rep FC 561 at [178], see n 39.

[86] [2012] EWHC 1480, [2012] Lloyd's Rep FC 561 at [164], see n 39. See *Re Barings plc (No 5)* [1999] 1BCLC 433 at 488.

[87] See *Re Continental Assurance Co of London plc* [2007] 2 BCLC 287 at [399], where Park J accepted that one of the duties of non-executive directors is to monitor the performance of the executive directors; also *Re Kaytech International plc, Secretary of State for Trade and Industry v Kaczer* [1999] 2 BCLC 351 at 407 (Rimer J): 'The functions of a non-executive lie in the monitoring of the manner in which the executives are conducting the affairs of the company'; also Langley J in *Equitable Life Assurance Society v Bowley* [2004] 1 BCLC 180 at 189 '... plainly arguable that a company may reasonably at least look to non-executive directors for independence of judgment and supervision of executive management'. The UK Corporate Governance Code (2018) states that they should 'provide constructive challenge, strategic guidance, offer specialist advice and hold management to account' (Prin G).

[88] [2005] BCC 596.     [89] [2005] BCC 596 at [247].

**11-27**    As noted at **11-9**, in *Newcastle International Airport Ltd v Eversheds LLP*,[90] while the claim in the case was by the company against its legal advisers, much of the case revolved around the conduct of the non-executive chair of the remuneration committee whose breaches of the duty of care the court found to be causative of the loss suffered by the company. As discussed in Chapter 6, remuneration committees have a significant role in larger companies and the level of care and skill expected of the chair of such a committee will reflect those responsibilities. On the facts, the court found, and the Court of Appeal saw nothing to doubt this finding, that this non-executive chair consistently misread or misunderstood the contents of documents, disliked reading long documents, and was inclined to make unjustified assumptions as to what they said.[91] The net result was that the remuneration committee which she chaired agreed new service contracts for two executive directors which conferred on them substantial non-discretionary bonuses which ultimately cost the company a lot more than it had expected to pay.[92] Indeed, the trial judge found that there were comprehensive shortcomings in the performance of all the members of the remuneration committee, all non-executive directors, who variously did not read or understand or challenge issues surrounding these contracts and who did not properly understand the nature and extent of the commitments being made to the executive directors through these bonus arrangements.[93]

## C  The content of the duty

**11-28**    While the statute identifies the standard of care, skill, and diligence required, it remains for the courts to add content to the duty. Unfortunately most of the authorities to date are first instance decisions and there has been little opportunity for the higher courts to explore these issues. A leading authority is the decision of Jonathan Parker J in *Re Barings plc (No 5) Secretary of State for Trade and Industry v Baker (No 5)*[94] where he identified certain propositions, now widely cited, with which the Court of Appeal subsequently agreed without further elaboration.

**11-29**    In the *Barings* case a number of senior directors of an investment bank were found to be unfit (though there was no question as to their honesty and integrity) and disqualified as a result of their failure to supervise a 'rogue trader' within the bank whose unauthorised trading resulted in losses of £827m and the collapse of the bank. Jonathan Parker J summarised the duties of directors as follows:[95]

(1)    Directors have, both collectively and individually, a continuing duty to acquire and maintain a sufficient knowledge and understanding of the company's business to enable them properly to discharge their duties as directors.

(2)    Whilst directors are entitled (subject to the articles of association of the company) to delegate particular functions to those below them in the management chain, and to trust their competence and integrity to a reasonable extent, the exercise of

---

[90] [2014] 2 All ER 728, rev'g in part [2013] PNLR 5.    [91] [2014] 2 All ER 728 at [99]–[100].

[92] The trial judge found that the chair never did the simple arithmetic to arrive at actual figures for the bonuses and did not even realise that they were likely to be substantial in amount: see [2012] EWHC 2648 at [80].

[93] [2012] EWHC 2648 at [118], [119], [129], [131]. As to potential conflict of interests within the non-executive directors, see at [52], [81]–[82].

[94] [1999] 1 BCLC 433, aff'd [2000] 1 BCLC 523, CA.

[95] [1999] 1 BCLC 433 at 489, aff'd [2000] 1 BCLC 523 at 535, CA.

the power of delegation does not absolve a director from the duty to supervise the discharge of the delegated functions.

(3) No rule of universal application can be formulated as to the duty referred to in (2) above. The extent of the duty, and the question whether it has been discharged, must depend on the facts of each particular case, including the director's role in the management of the company.

**11-30**  For ease of discussion, we will consider each of these elements separately, though in practice they overlap and cannot be regarded as discrete elements. Most complaints will involve all of them: a lack of understanding of the business, a failure to participate and supervise, an absence of knowledge which prevents a director from exercising independent judgement, all of which make it difficult for a director to assert that he is acting in a way likely to promote the success of the company. It is a cumulative picture of incompetence and breach of other duties which typically emerges.

## Knowledge of the company's affairs

**11-31**  The importance of sufficient knowledge and understanding of the company's business, both collectively and individually, in order to supervise and control the conduct of the company's affairs, is highlighted by the *Barings* case itself. As noted at **11-29**, the Barings group of companies collapsed in 1995 with losses of £827m following the unauthorised trading activities of a single 'rogue trader' in Singapore. The disqualification proceedings reported in *Re Barings plc (No 5), Secretary of State for Trade and Industry v Baker (No 5)*[96] concerned three of the directors, all of whom were found to be unfit and they were disqualified for periods ranging from four to six years. In essence, the court concluded that the directors had little understanding of the nature of the rogue trader's activities and were not therefore in a position to exercise the requisite level of supervision.[97] The court noted with respect to the most senior director that his failures in this regard amounted 'not so much to bad management but non-management'. Jonathan Parker J commented that 'it is a truism that if a manager does not properly understand the business which he is seeking to manage, he will be unable to take informed management decisions in relation to it'.[98]

**11-32**  As noted at **11-20**, in a family business, it is not uncommon for family members to be directors without having anything to do with the running of the business and so they have no knowledge of the company's affairs. The courts have consistently found such directors to be unfit.[99] This is not to say that each director must have detailed knowledge

---

[96]  [1999] 1 BCLC 433, aff'd [2000] 1 BCLC 523.

[97]  See [1999] 1 BCLC 433 at 528–9, 574–5, 600. See also *Weavering Capital UK Ltd v Peterson* [2012] EWHC 1480, see n 39, where an over-promoted director who was out of his depth on the board of a hedge fund management company was found to have failed to acquire a sufficient knowledge and understanding of the business.

[98]  See [1999] 1 BCLC 433 at 528. This problem was common to the boards of the banks which collapsed in the financial crisis in 2007–08; the Walker Review found there was a lack of banking knowledge within the boards which made it difficult, if not impossible, for there to be any challenge to the executives' business strategy, see *A Review of Corporate Governance in UK banks and other financial industry entities*, Final recommendations, November 2009, also see **6-4**; Hannigan, n 31.

[99]  See, for example, *Re Brian D Pierson (Contractors) Ltd* [2001] 1 BCLC 275; *Re Park House Properties Ltd* [1997] 2 BCLC 530; *Re Galeforce Pleating Co Ltd* [1999] 2 BCLC 704, discussed at **11-20** et seq. Likewise, courts do not accept that someone can be a professional nominee director of hundreds of companies for it is impossible for the nominee to have a sufficient knowledge of the companies to discharge his duties as a director of them, see **11-23**.

of the day-to-day conduct of a company's affairs, for their role depends on the way in which the company's business is organised. The question is whether they have knowledge sufficient to exercise their collective and individual responsibility to supervise and monitor the conduct of the company's affairs.[100]

**11-33**    The court assesses a director's level of knowledge against the standard set in CA 2006, s 174 (see **11-13**). In *Re Queens Moat Houses plc, Secretary of State for Trade and Industry v Bairstow (No 2)*[101] dividends had been declared improperly on the strength of accounts which were misleading and did not give a true and fair view of the company's affairs. In disqualification proceedings, the court assessed the defendant director's knowledge on the basis, first, of objectively considering (as required by CA 2006, s 174(2)(a)) what could be expected of a reasonably diligent person who was the chairman and senior executive director of the company. Secondly, the court subjectively considered (as required by s 174(2)(b)) what could be expected of that director, given his wide business experience and knowledge of the company's affairs (he had been a director for 20 years) while also acknowledging that he had no formal accountancy qualifications. The court accepted that, given that the preparation of the accounts had been properly delegated to the finance director, the director was not in breach of his duty in failing to appreciate that the accounting treatment of certain items in the accounts (i.e. technical specialist information beyond his competence) was misleading. Because of his business experience and knowledge of the company's affairs, he ought to have been aware, however, that the accounts showed inflated turnover and profits (i.e. business information within his comprehension) and were therefore misleading. He was in breach of duty and disqualified for six years.

**11-34**    In *Re Westmid Packing Services Ltd, Secretary of State for Trade and Industry v Griffiths*,[102] also disqualification proceedings, the court found that the directors did not know that the dominant director had used company assets to support other businesses of his own and did not know that he had the company cross-guarantee the borrowings of those businesses. This failure to keep themselves properly informed about the company's financial position was sufficient to justify their disqualification though it was the sole allegation of unfitness established against them. In *Re Kaytech International plc, Secretary of State for Trade and Industry v Kaczer*,[103] Rimer J thought that a non-executive director has to ensure that he is informed about the company's constitution, its board membership, the nature and course of its business, and its financial position from time to time so that he is in a position to monitor the manner in which the executives are conducting the company's affairs. In *Raithatha v Baig*[104] the directors of a not-for-profit company took office and assumed the company's affairs were in order when in fact the company needed to register for VAT which was not done. The court held that they had failed to acquire sufficient knowledge of the business to enable them to discharge their duties. They were

---

[100] See *Re Vintage Hallmark, plc, Secretary of State for Trade & Industry v Grove* [2007] 1 BCLC 788 at [56]—what is required is a good general knowledge of the business.

[101] [2005] 1 BCLC 136.      [102] [1998] 2 BCLC 646 at 652.

[103] [1999] 2 BCLC 351 at 407. In *Lexi Holdings plc v Luqman* [2008] 2 BCLC 725, reversed on other grounds, see [2009] 2 BCLC 1, the court did not accept that non-executive directors of a company engaged in the business of making loans secured on real property had a duty to appraise themselves of the detailed provisions of the loan facility agreement which the company had with Barclays Bank (that task could properly be delegated to one of the executive directors with banking experience), but they did have a duty to have made some study of the company's loan book since that lay at the heart of understanding the company's business.

[104] [2017] EWHC 2059.

not required to have the specialist knowledge of an accountant, but they needed to ask about the company's VAT position, rather than assume the position was in order. The company had accountants, but the directors did not seek their advice as to whether VAT registration was required. Hence, the directors had failed to discharge their duties of care and skill.

**11-35**  The law does not require an unreasonable level of knowledge, however, as was made clear in *Re Continental Assurance Co of London plc*.[105] This case concerned the collapse of a small insurance company in 1992. Large and unexpected losses had arisen which came to the board's attention in June 1991. In this litigation the liquidators sought contributions to the company's assets from the directors on the grounds of wrongful trading and/or misfeasance (see **15-18**). A particular issue was an allegation that the company applied inappropriate accounting policies which showed the company to be solvent in July 1991 when, had an appropriate accounting policy been adopted by the company, the directors would and should have appreciated that the company was insolvent and they should have taken steps to stop trading. The court found that for the directors to have reached that conclusion would have required knowledge of accounting concepts of a particularly sophisticated nature. Declining to hold the directors liable, Park J rejected any idea that the law imposes such an unrealistically high standard of skill. He noted:[106]

> 'In my view, [the directors] would have been expected to be intelligent laymen. They would need to have a knowledge of what the basic accounting principles for an insurance company were ... They would be expected to be able to look at the company's accounts and, with the guidance which they could reasonably expect to be available from the finance director and the auditors, to understand them. They would be expected to be able to participate in a discussion of the accounts, and to ask intelligent questions of the finance director and the auditors. What I do not accept is that they could have been expected to show the sort of intricate appreciation of recondite accounting details possessed by a specialist in the field ...'

**11-36**  On the facts, Park J found that the directors took a wholly responsible and conscientious attitude both to the company's position and to their own responsibilities as directors at all times from and after the first crisis board meeting in 1991 when the unexpected losses were reported to them. The directors did not ignore the question of whether the company could properly continue to trade; on the contrary, the court found that they considered it directly, closely and frequently.[107] The case against them was dismissed.

## Delegation and the residual duty of supervision

**11-37**  It has long been accepted that an intelligent devolution of labour must be possible[108] and a company could not hope to run its business in an efficient manner if the directors were required to do everything themselves and were not permitted to delegate on a wide scale, though the extent to which they can do so depends on the provisions of the company's articles.[109] At the same time, some matters must remain the collective responsibility of

---

[105] [2007] 2 BCLC 287.     [106] [2007] 2 BCLC 287 at [258].     [107] [2007] 2 BCLC 287 at [107].
[108] *Dovey v Cory* [1901] AC 477 at 485; also *Huckerby v Elliott* [1970] 1 All ER 189.
[109] The model articles provide that, subject to the articles, the directors are responsible for the management of the company's business, for which purpose they may exercise all the powers of the company and they may delegate any of the powers conferred on them under the articles. See The Companies (Model Articles) Regulations 2008, SI 2008/3229, reg 2, Sch 1, arts 3, 5 (Ltd); reg 4, Sch 3, arts 3, 5 (Plc).

the board of directors, such as the responsibility of the board to approve the company's annual accounts.[110]

**11-38**    Having permitted delegation, and in the absence of grounds for suspicion, the law does not require that the directors should distrust and constantly supervise those to whom tasks have been delegated for this would defeat the whole purpose. Directors do retain a residual duty of supervision, however, as was made clear by Jonathan Parker J in *Re Barings plc (No 5), Secretary of State for Trade and Industry v Baker (No 5)*,[111] see **11-29**. The key point is that it is delegation, not abdication, which is permissible.[112] A number of common scenarios emerge from the authorities.

**11-39**    First, there is the dominant member syndrome, where directors defer to a particular individual on the board such that in effect they delegate all power to him, abdicate their own responsibilities, and exercise no residual supervision. The dominant director(s) may be someone on whom the other directors are unduly reliant and therefore they are reluctant to challenge or question him. They may owe him their positions on the board, particularly if they are former employees promoted by him to the board.[113] The courts are clear, however, that a board must not permit one individual to dominate and use the other directors in this way. As Popplewell J said in *Madoff Securities International Ltd v Raven*,[114] it is a breach of duty for a director 'to allow himself to be dominated, bamboozled or manipulated by a dominant fellow director' where such involves a total abrogation of responsibility. In *Dickinson v NAL Realisations Ltd*[115] two directors (one the spouse of the sole effective director, the other an employee in practice) were found to have allowed themselves to be wholly dominated by the sole effective director. They were content to go along with whatever he decided, without knowing of the substance of the matter and without challenge. The court said it was a complete failure to engage in any responsibility and a breach of their inescapable personal responsibilities and of duty by them.

**11-40**    In *Re Westmid Packing Services Ltd, Secretary of State for Trade and Industry v Griffiths*,[116] for example, the court disqualified two of the executive directors for breach of their inescapable personal responsibilities by allowing themselves to be manipulated and deceived by another member of the board who was the dominant and controlling influence in the business. Their failure to act allowed the dominant director to use the company's assets to fund his other businesses by way of interest-free unsecured loans which ultimately proved irrecoverable and brought the company to ruin.[117]

---

[110] CA 2006, s 414. See *Re Landhurst Leasing plc, Secretary of State for Trade and Industry v Ball* [1999] 1 BCLC 286 at 346, relying on *Re City Equitable Fire Insurance Co Ltd* [1925] Ch 407.

[111] [1999] 1 BCLC 433, aff'd [2000] 1 BCLC 523, CA.

[112] There can be other consequences to abdication so a sole director who, in breach of his duties of care and skill to the company, abrogates entirely his duties with regard to health and safety as regards the company's operations and who is then injured may find that the company has a defence to its otherwise absolute liability to him in respect of that injury: *Brumder v Motornet Service and Repairs Ltd* [2013] 2 BCLC 58 at [45]–[49].

[113] See, for example, *Weavering Capital (UK) Ltd v Peterson* [2012] EWHC 1480 at [59]–[63], see n 39, where the court considered the position of a marketing director in a hedge fund company—the court found and the Court of Appeal accepted these findings, that the director took his lead from the managing director, that his grasp of what was going on was 'foggy', and that he was over-promoted and out of his depth.

[114] [2013] EWHC 3147 at [191].    [115] [2017] EWHC 28, [2018] 1 BCLC 623, at [159].

[116] [1998] 2 BCLC 646.    [117] [1998] 2 BCLC 646 at 653.

**11-41**    In *Re Landhurst Leasing plc, Secretary of State for Trade and Industry v Ball*[118] the court disqualified two executive directors who had taken a relatively subordinate role (reflecting the fact that they had been promoted to the board from the ranks of the employees) vis-à-vis the conduct of the affairs of the company by two forceful joint managing directors who were convicted of criminal offences in respect of their management of the company. The disqualified directors had failed to draw the board's attention to sham transactions of which they were aware and to ensure that the accounts made adequate provision for bad debts and credit risks.[119] As to the boundaries of delegation, Hart J concluded that a director might rely on his co-directors to the extent that (1) the matter in question lay within their sphere of responsibility given the way in which the particular business was organised, and (2) that there existed no grounds for suspicion that that reliance might be misplaced.[120] However, Hart J continued, even where there were no reasons to think the reliance was misplaced, a director might still be in breach of duty if he left to others matters for which the board as a whole had to take responsibility, for example the responsibilities of the board to approve the company's annual accounts.[121]

**11-42**    Sometimes the dominant element is not an individual but an inner group of directors, as in *Re AG (Manchester) Ltd, Official Receiver v Watson*.[122] In this case, the court disqualified for six years a finance director and subsequent chief executive who acquiesced in a system under which members of an inner group of directors took all the key decisions without reference to the board as a whole with the result that the other directors were effectively reduced to the role of departmental managers with no serious input at board meetings on issues affecting the running of the company.[123]

**11-43**    A second scenario is the abdication of responsibility to other directors without exercising any residual supervision by an inactive director of a family business.[124] In *Re Westminster Property Management Ltd, Official Receiver v Stern (No 2)*[125] a property development company had collapsed with multi-million pound losses and the two directors before the court in disqualification proceedings were a father and son. With respect to the son, the court considered that 'he was not conscious of his position or duties as a director, that he never undertook those duties except as dictated by his father (for example, to sign cheques or accounts) and that he applied his mind barely, if at all, to the consequences of his position as a director'. He was disqualified for four years for this abrogation of his duties as a director.[126] As well as disqualification, inactivity on the part of a director can lead to a personal liability, as is discussed at **11-8**.

---

[118] [1999] 1 BCLC 286. See also *Re Bradcrown, Official Receiver v Ireland* [2001] 1 BCLC 547 where a finance director (who had been promoted from being an employee) was found to have exercised no independent judgement and to have deferred in all matters to the managing director. The court noted that this was the clearest case of accepting office as a director but intending from the outset to act as a loyal employee.

[119] See [1999] 1 BCLC 286 at 349 and 353.

[120] [1999] 1 BCLC 286 at 346; see also *Cohen v Selby* [2001] 1 BCLC 176 at [28]–[29].

[121] [1999] 1 BCLC 286 at 346, relying on *Re City Equitable Fire Insurance Co Ltd* [1925] Ch 407.

[122] [2008] 1 BCLC 321.    [123] See [2008] 1 BCLC 321 at [178].

[124] See *Re Brian D Pierson (Contractors) Ltd* [2001] 1 BCLC 275; *Re Galeforce Pleating Co Ltd* [1999] 2 BCLC 704; *Re Park House Properties Ltd* [1997] 2 BCLC 530, discussed at **11-20** et seq.

[125] [2001] BCC 305 at [197].

[126] See also *Re AG (Manchester) Ltd, Official Receiver v Watson* [2008] 1 BCLC 321 where a director who was the wife of the controlling shareholder was disqualified. Though a director, she left all financial and strategic decisions to an inner group of directors (including her husband) and was content to take substantial dividends from the company regardless of how and whether they could be paid. The court found her conduct in failing to act independently and in the interests of the company amounted to an abdication of responsibility and justified her disqualification for four years (see at [187]).

**11-44**  A third scenario is where financial and accounting matters are delegated to a finance director. When a problem subsequently emerges, the other directors tend to claim that they had no responsibility in the matter, given that it was properly delegated to another. Again, the issue is their failure to exercise any residual supervision.

**11-45**  The situation can be illustrated by *Re Queens Moat Houses plc, Secretary of State for Trade and Industry v Bairstow (No 2)*,[127] the facts of which are at **11-33**. In this case the court agreed that, with regard to the preparation and content of the financial statements, the chief executive was entitled to delegate those matters to the finance director. Such matters were properly within the finance director's area of responsibility and competence and the chief executive had no reason to doubt that the functions properly delegated had been properly performed. But many of the matters in the accounts were matters that it should have been apparent to the chief executive, given his business experience and knowledge of the company, were of doubtful accuracy and propriety. He was in breach of his duties, not for having improperly delegated the task of preparing the financial statements, but for failing to exercise his residual duty of supervision when those financial statements came to the board for approval.[128] The position can be contrasted with that in *Re Continental Assurance Co of London plc*,[129] the facts of which are at **11-35**. Park J there concluded that the board of an insurance company was entitled to rely on the advice of the finance director and the company's auditors as to whether the company was solvent and the appropriateness of the company's accounting policies and systems. The directors did not blindly accept what was put before them, but engaged in detailed and critical consideration of the company's accounts,[130] while looking for detailed guidance on technical matters to the finance director and the auditors as they were perfectly entitled to do.[131]

**11-46**  Another example of a failure to supervise can be found in *Secretary of State for Trade and Industry v Swan*[132] where a chief executive of a listed company was disqualified for signing large cheques (two for £1m each, two for £4m each) without enquiring what they were for, though the court considered that (because of their size in the context of the company's business) they called out for comment and enquiry.[133] His defence (that he relied on his finance director and finance department to verify the cheques) was rejected as an abdication of his responsibilities. His duty of supervision should have been triggered by the size of the cheques and the unusual nature of the transactions.[134] His unfitness in this case lay, the court said, in an absence of vigilance.[135]

**11-47**  Clearly, the extent of the residual duty to supervise depends on a variety of factors including the nature of the business; the nature and extent of the delegation; the standing and status of the person to whom the matter is delegated; the remuneration of the director;[136]

---

[127] [2005] 1 BCLC 136.     [128] See [2005] 1 BCLC 136 at [89].     [129] [2007] 2 BCLC 287.

[130] [2007] 2 BCLC 287 at [402]–[403].

[131] [2007] 2 BCLC 287 at [287], [403]. See also *Secretary of State for Trade and Industry v Gill* [2006] BCC 725.     [132] [2005] BCC 596.

[133] [2005] BCC 596 at [217].

[134] [2005] BCC 596 at [129], [177], [217]. There was no supporting documentation with the cheques which were matching cheques of equal and extraordinary amounts related to the company's practice of cheque-kiting, a practice which generates brief false balances in bank accounts and which the court described as, at the very least, commercially improper and unacceptable (at [212]). On the other hand, it was not unreasonable for the chief executive to delegate and rely on the finance director and other accounting personnel to deal with and confirm details in a circular to shareholders in the absence of anything to alert him to some discrepancy.     [135] [2005] BCC 596 at [221].

[136] On this, see *Re Barings plc (No 5)* [1999] 1 BCLC 433 at 488. Even an unpaid director has obligations which they accept when they become director: see *Re Park House Properties Ltd* [1997] 2 BCLC 530 at 555–6.

the nature of the transaction; and the potential risk/losses involved.[137] In larger companies with complex businesses, whether a director has discharged his individual role involves an examination of the systems for which he personally has responsibility while, at board level, the collective responsibility of the directors is to satisfy themselves that the task delegated and the system instituted is appropriate to the level of risk involved—hence the emphasis in the UK Corporate Governance Code on the collective responsibility of the board for the long-term success of the company.[138]

**11-48**   The final variation on the delegation/abdication point comes with reliance on professional advisers. Of course, there are many circumstances in which reliance on professional advisers, such as auditors, is perfectly proper, as was noted in *Re Continental Assurance Co of London plc*.[139] Similarly in *Re Stephenson Cobbold Ltd, Secretary of State for Trade and Industry v Stephenson*[140] where it was alleged that a non-executive director (who was a cheque signatory) should be disqualified as unfit on the grounds, *inter alia*, that he had allowed an executive director to use company funds for personal expenditure. The court found that the non-executive director had queried the transactions at issue with the company's auditors and, in those circumstances, he was entitled to rely on the explanations given by the auditors (that the payments were part of the director's usual remuneration arrangements) as reassurance that the financial side of the company was being run properly.

**11-49**   On the other hand, excessive reliance amounting to a total abrogation of responsibility can be seen in *Re Bradcrown Ltd, Official Receiver v Ireland*[141] where a finance director relied entirely on professional advisers in respect of a complex transaction, the net effect of which was that the company transferred away its main assets for no consideration. In terms of reliance on professional advisers, the court noted that the issue is essentially one of degree. In the instant case, although the director was entitled to rely on professional advice, he had asked no questions and simply did what he was told, abdicating all responsibility. In those circumstances, the court held that he could not seek refuge in the fact that professional advisers were involved in the transactions and he was disqualified for two years.

**11-50**   There is a risk that if too great a reliance on professional advisers is permitted then, in larger companies especially, directors will expend the shareholders' money in having professional advisers approve their every move in order to reduce the individual risk to themselves. A line needs to be drawn therefore between justified reliance and abrogation

---

[137] The more critical the risk or the more extensive the potential losses (for example, from unauthorised derivatives trading where the losses can run out of control very quickly), the greater the duty of residual supervision.

[138] FRC, The UK Corporate Governance Code (2018), Prin A. See further discussion in Chapter 6.

[139] [2007] 2 BCLC 287. See too *Green v Walkling* [2008] 2 BCLC 332; also *Re Pro4Sport Ltd, Hedger v Adams* [2016] 1 BCLC 257—director of company in financial difficulties had sought advice from a firm of business advisers and had entered into a transaction to sell the company's stock on their advice. Subsequently, it was suggested that the terms of the transaction might have been more favourable to the vendor, but the court thought the fact that the director was relying on professional advice was an important factor when assessing whether he was in breach of his duty of care. On the facts, he was not at fault.

[140] [2000] 2 BCLC 614. See also *Norman v Theodore Goddard* [1991] BCLC 1028 where it was reasonable for a director to rely on information regarding the company's investments supplied to him by a solicitor who was a partner in an eminent firm of City solicitors. It turned out that the solicitor had misappropriated the company's money. Looked at in the light of how standards have developed since this decision, the case seems close to the borderline with the director almost abrogating his responsibilities to the company.

[141] [2000] 1 BCLC 547.

of responsibility and those lines depend on the nature of the company and its business and the position of the director. Essentially, the issue is whether it is reasonable in all the circumstances for the director to rely on the professional adviser. A director of a small family company may be entitled to put greater reliance on professional advisers than a highly paid and qualified finance director at an international bank; conversely, the complexity of transactions in the latter situation may justify greater reliance on advisers in certain circumstances.

## D  Duty to exercise independent judgement

**11-51**  The CA 2006, s 173 provides as follows:

'(1)  A director of a company must exercise independent judgment.

(2)  This duty is not infringed by his acting—

(a)  in accordance with an agreement duly entered into by the company that restricts the future exercise of discretion by its directors, or

(b)  in a way authorised by the company's constitution.'

**11-52**  As was explained in the Parliamentary debates, this obligation in s 173(1) to exercise independent judgement does not restrict a director's ability to take advice or to rely on advice (to the extent permissible under the duty of care and skill, as discussed) nor does it require the director himself to be independent.[142] A requirement to exercise independent judgement does not mean that directors may not honestly and reasonably defer to one of their number with greater experience or expertise (in the absence of grounds of suspicion and provided their conduct does not amount to a total abrogation of responsibility) and trust his views as to the interests of the company.[143]

**11-53**  In *Central Bank of Ecuador v Conticorp*[144] the Privy Council considered the position of a nominee director of an investment company which had raised significant funds from investors and then paid them away in irrecoverable loans to companies associated with the controlling shareholder of the investment company. The director's defence was that he was paid only a very small amount per annum for acting as director and that he was merely acting on instructions from the shareholders who had nominated him. The Privy Council found that, in breach of his fiduciary duty, the director had blindly and ignorantly following the shareholders' instructions without further thought when his duty was to understand the company's interests and apply his own mind to the company's interests.[145]

**11-54**  Section 173(2)(a) reflects long-standing common law authorities on the directors' obligation not to fetter their discretion. An important authority on this issue is *Thorby v Goldberg*[146] where the directors of a company agreed as part of a broader restructuring transaction to allot shares in a particular manner at a later date. They then failed to do as they had promised. In an action to force them to make the allotment of the shares, they pleaded that the undertaking was an invalid fettering of their discretion on their part. The

---

[142]  HC Official Report, SC D (Company Law Reform Bill), 11 July 2006, col 598.

[143]  See *Madoff Securities International Ltd v Raven* [2013] EWHC 3147 at [220], [235], [237], per Popplewell J.

[144]  [2016] 1 BCLC 26, PC.  [145]  [2016] 1 BCLC 26 at [45].

[146]  (1964) 112 CLR 597, H Ct of Australia. See Prentice (1977) 89 LQR 107 at 111–13.

court rejected this argument, holding that the time for exercising their discretion was at the time of entering into the agreement. Provided they had considered the interests of the company at that time, the agreement was valid. It was not the case that the directors had wrongly fettered their discretion, rather that they had already exercised it.[147]

**11-55** In *Fulham Football Club Ltd v Cabra Estates plc*[148] the Court of Appeal emphatically endorsed the approach taken in *Thorby v Goldberg*.[149] In this case, the directors of a company had entered into undertakings to support, and to refrain from opposing, planning applications by another party for the development of certain land in return for the receipt by the company of large sums of money. The directors subsequently wanted to give evidence to a planning inquiry opposing the development and sought a declaration that they were not bound by the undertakings and were entitled to give such evidence to the inquiry as they considered to be in the interests of the company.

**11-56** The Court of Appeal held that they were bound by the undertakings. As the undertakings given by the directors were part of contractual arrangements which conferred substantial benefits on the company, the directors had not improperly fettered the future exercise of their discretion by giving those undertakings. Nor was there any scope for the implication of a term into those undertakings that the directors would not be required to do anything that would be inconsistent with their fiduciary duties to the company.[150] The distinction which must be drawn, the court said, is between directors fettering their discretion (which is prohibited) and directors exercising their discretion in a way which restricts their future conduct (which is permissible). The directors had exercised their independent judgement at the time when they gave the undertakings not to oppose the planning application and therefore it was not a case of fettering their discretion, but rather a case that they had already exercised it. Certainly there will be many transactions where the proper time for the exercise of the directors' judgement is the time of the negotiation of the contract rather than the time when the contract is to be performed.[151]

**11-57** The duty to exercise independent judgement is not infringed by a director acting in a way authorised by the company's constitution: CA 2006, s 173(2)(b) (and 'constitution' is as defined in s 257). The model articles for public and private companies provide that, subject to the articles, the directors may delegate any of the powers conferred on them under the articles.[152] To the extent that the articles allow for delegation, and subject to the need to exercise a residual duty of supervision, as already discussed, directors can be relieved of the obligation to exercise independent judgement with respect to the delegated task.

**11-58** One possibility raised in the Parliamentary debates is that this provision makes it possible for the status of the nominee director to be enshrined in the constitution.[153] It has always been the position that a nominee once appointed owes his duty to the company, as is the

---

[147] (1964) 112 CLR 597 at 618, per Owen J.     [148] [1994] 1 BCLC 363; noted Griffiths [1993] JBL 576.
[149] (1964) 112 CLR 597.
[150] To the extent that earlier authorities (*John Crowther Group plc v Carpets International plc* [1990] BCLC 460 and *Rackham v Peek Foods Ltd* [1990] BCLC 895—directors' undertakings to use best endeavours to secure shareholder consent to transactions were subject to directors' duties to act in interests of the company) could be read as laying down a general proposition that directors can never bind themselves as to the future exercise of their fiduciary powers, the Court of Appeal considered they were wrong and the decisions should be limited to the particular facts: [1994] 1 BCLC 363 at 393.
[151] See *Thorby v Goldberg* (1964) 112 CLR 597 at 605–6.
[152] See The Companies (Model Articles) Regulations 2008, SI 2008/3229, reg 2, Sch 1, arts 3, 5 (Ltd); reg 4, Sch 3, arts 3, 5 (Plc).
[153] HC Official Report, SC D (Company Law Reform Bill), 11 July 2006, col 601.

case with any director (CA 2006, s 170(1)), and the nominee is not able to, nor required to, follow the instructions of the person nominating him, though in practice the legal position is no doubt often ignored, see the discussion at **10-17**. Section 173(2)(b), set out at **11-51**, allows the position to be regularised in that the articles may relieve a nominee director from this obligation to exercise independent judgement, but it applies only to that duty and the nominee director remains subject to all the other general duties, in particular his duty under s 172 to act in the way he considers, in good faith, would be most likely to promote the success of the company, see the discussion at **10-19**. A nominee director continues therefore to have a somewhat uncomfortable role in terms of managing the conflicting demands of duties to the company and the expectations of his nominating shareholder.

# 12

# Duty to avoid a conflict of interest

## A Introduction

**12-1** Central to a director's duties is the long-established equitable rule precluding a fiduciary from entering, without consent, into engagements in which he has, or can have, a personal interest[1] conflicting, or which possibly may conflict, with the interests of those whom he is bound to protect (the no-conflict rule),[2] and the equally inflexible rule that, without consent, a person in a fiduciary position is not entitled to profit from that position[3] (the no-profit rule or, more accurately no secret profit rule[4]). Together the no-conflict and no (secret) profit rules reflect the duty of undivided loyalty owed by a fiduciary to his principal.[5] The rationale for the two strands is that the no-conflict rule is designed to prevent the judgement of the fiduciary being swayed by self-interest and the no-profit rule is designed to strip the disloyal fiduciary of gains made in breach of duty.[6] In most instances, both rules will be relevant, as where a director profits personally in a situation where his personal interests conflict with the company's interests.

**12-2** These long-standing principles are reflected now in CA 2006, s 175 which provides that:[7]

'(1) A director of a company must avoid a situation in which he has, or can have, a direct or indirect interest that conflicts, or possibly may conflict, with the interests of the company.

---

[1] See David Richards J in *Newgate Stud Co v Penfold* [2008] 1 BCLC 46 at [231] who comments that, leaving aside the cases of a competing fiduciary duty, none of the authorities define a director's 'interest' in terms other than a personal financial interest, direct or indirect, of the director.

[2] *Aberdeen Rly Co v Blaikie Bros* (1854) 1 Macq 461 at 471–2, per Lord Cranworth; *Imperial Mercantile Credit Association v Coleman* (1873) LR 6 HL 189; '… human nature being what it is, there is danger, in such circumstances, of the person holding a fiduciary position being swayed by interest rather than by duty, and thus prejudicing those whom he was bound to protect': *Bray v Ford* [1896] AC 44 at 51, per Lord Herschell. See Farrar and Watson, 'Self-dealing, Fair Dealing' (2011) 11 JCLS 495 on the history of this rule.

[3] *Regal (Hastings) Ltd v Gulliver* [1942] 1 All ER 378, HL; also *Parker v McKenna* (1874) 10 Ch App 96; *Boardman v Phipps* [1967] 2 AC 46, HL.

[4] See Millett, 'Equity's Place in the Law of Commerce' (1998) 114 LQR 214 at 216 who comments: 'We ought to stop repeating the inaccurate incantation that equity does not permit a trustee to profit from his trust. Of course it does. What it forbids is his making a secret or uncovenanted profit from his trust.'

[5] *Bristol and West BS v Mothew* [1996] 4 All ER 698 at 712. CA 2006, s 172 is a declaratory statement of the fiduciary nature of the relationship between a company and a director who must act to promote the interests of his beneficiary, in this case, the success of the company. A conflict of interest undermines that relationship and so is prohibited by s 175.

[6] See *Chan v Zacharia* (1984) 154 CLR 178 at 198; and see *King Productions Ltd v Warren* [2000] 1 BCLC 607. See *Ultraframe (UK) Ltd v Fielding* [2005] EWHC 1638 at [1306]–[1322]; *Quarter Master UK v Pyke* [2005] 1 BCLC 245 at [53]–[56] for useful overviews of the rules; also Smith, 'Fiduciary Relationships: Ensuring the Loyal Exercise of Judgment on Behalf of Another' (2014) 130 LQR 608.

[7] The application of CA 2006, s 175 to charitable companies is modified in accordance with s 181.

(2) This applies in particular to the exploitation of any property, information or opportunity (and it is immaterial whether the company could take advantage of the property, information or opportunity).'

The courts will interpret and apply this duty in the light of the corresponding common law rules and equitable principles (s 170(4), see **8-8**) so the existing case law and principles 'continue to apply with undiminished authority',[8] but read in the light of the statute. The statutory scheme clearly adopts the no-conflict rule, set out in s 175(1), as the core obligation with the no-profit rule, reflected in s 175(2), as a subset of that broader obligation.[9] This approach ends the debate as to whether there is one rule or two and is a valuable clarification of the law.[10] There is one rule, a no-conflict rule, and a prohibition on profiting when in a position of conflict. The no-conflict duty generally ceases to apply once a director resigns since the duty is intended to prevent a director in the exercise of his powers from being swayed by his self-interest,[11] but a former director continues to be subject to the no-conflict rule as regards the exploitation of property, information, or opportunity of which he became aware at a time when he was a director (CA 2006, s 170(2)(a)).

**12-3**   The strictness of the duty imposed by CA 2006, s 175(1) and (2) (note the application to indirect interests) is tempered by:

   (i)   the exclusion of situations that cannot reasonably be regarded as likely to give rise to a conflict of interest (s 175(4)(a));

  (ii)   the possibility of authorisation under s 175(4)(b) or s 180(4);

 (iii)   the disapplications—section 175 does not apply to a conflict of interest arising in relation to a transaction or arrangement with the company (s 175(3)) which is governed by a separate duty of disclosure under s 177 and s 182; and a director is not required to comply with s 175 if the conflicted transaction is approved or is exempt from approval under CA 2006, Pt 10, Ch 4, or Ch 4A (see Chapter 13), which requires shareholder approval of specific transactions with or payments to directors (s 180(2)).

**12-4**   Traditionally the courts have applied the no-conflict, no-profit, rules with unyielding strictness, regarding it as of fundamental importance that a company is entitled to the

---

[8]  *Burns v Financial Conduct Authority* [2017] EWCA Civ 2140 at [65].

[9]  See *Boardman v Phipps* [1966] 3 All ER 721 at 756, per Lord Upjohn; *New Zealand Netherlands Society 'Oranje' Inc v Kuys* [1973] 2 All ER 1222. See generally Conaglen, 'The Nature and Function of Fiduciary Loyalty' (2005) 121 LQR 452. The distinguished Australian judge and author, PD Finn, described the no-profit rule as a 'loose end' to the general no-conflict rule: see Finn, *Fiduciary Obligations* (1977), p 246.

[10]  On the one or two rule debate, for example, see *Chan v Zacharia* (1984) 154 CLR 178 at 198; *Ultraframe (UK) Ltd v Fielding* [2005] EWHC 1638 at [1305]–[1306]; *Don King Productions Inc v Warren* [2000] 1 BCLC 607 at 629–30, CA; *Gencor ACP Ltd v Dalby* [2000] 2 BCLC 734 at 741. See Smith, 'Fiduciary Relationships: Ensuring the Loyal Exercise of Judgment on Behalf of Another' (2014) 130 LQR 608 who argues strongly for two rules as they fulfil different functions, one setting aside potentially tainted exercises of judgment (no conflict), the other reflecting the beneficiary's primary entitlement to the profit, see 625–31. See also Hannigan, 'Reconfiguring the No Conflict Rule—Judicial Strictures, a Statutory Restatement and the Opportunistic Director' (2011) 23 SAcLJ 714.

[11]  See *Ultraframe (UK) Ltd v Fielding* [2005] EWHC 1638 at [1309]–[1310], per Lewison J; also *Wilkinson v West Coast Capital* [2007] BCC 717 at [251]; *Quarter Master UK Ltd v Pyke* [2005] 1 BCLC 245 at 264; *CMS Dolphin Ltd v Simonet* [2001] 2 BCLC 704 at [96]; *A-G v Blake* [1998] 1 All ER 833 at 841.

undivided loyalty of its directors.[12] As Rix LJ noted in *Foster Bryant Surveying Ltd v Bryant*,[13] these duties are 'exacting requirements, exactingly enforced'. Two main justifications are put forward for such a strict approach. First, the deterrent argument, i.e. the duties must be rigorously applied so as not to offer any encouragement to fiduciaries (in this context, directors) to pursue their own interests at the expense of their beneficiaries (in this context, the shareholders).[14] Secondly, a strict approach is an efficient way of addressing the agency problem within companies, by which is meant the difficulty which shareholders have in monitoring the conduct of their directors.[15] Holding fiduciaries to exacting obligations reduces the need for such monitoring. As Mummery LJ stated in *Premier Waste Management Ltd v Towers*:[16] 'The rationale and the justice of the [no-conflict] principle lie in its strict regard for the protection of those interests potentially at risk from a director who does not give his undivided loyalty to the company.' There may even be a windfall element to the recoveries as a director can be liable to account regardless of whether the company could exploit the property, information, or opportunity from which the director has profited (see further at **12-26**),[17] and that too is consistent with the underlying policy of deterrence.

**12-5** Notwithstanding that starting point, the position is not one of unremitting severity for the emphasis on the fact-specific nature of these fiduciary obligations has always allowed a certain amount of judicial flexibility in the application of the duties[18] and, as

---

[12] See *Parker v McKenna* (1874) 10 Ch App 96 at 124, per James LJ; *New Zealand Netherlands Society 'Oranje' Inc v Kuys* [1973] 2 All ER 1222 at 1225, per Lord Wilberforce; *Industrial Development Consultants Ltd v Cooley* [1972] 2 All ER 162 at 173–4, per Roskill J; *Premier Waste Management Ltd v Towers* [2012] 1 BCLC 67 at [9]; *Burns v Financial Conduct Authority* [2017] EWCA Civ 2140 at [73]–[74]. As Getzler notes, '[t]he law of fiduciaries is based on the simple moral and practical insight that strong powers must be allied to strong duties', see Getzler, 'Financial Crisis and the Decline of Fiduciary Law' in Morris and Vines (eds), *Capital Failure, Rebuilding Trust in Financial Services* (2014), p 198.

[13] [2007] 2 BCLC 239 at [76].

[14] See *Murad v Al-Saraj* [2005] EWCA 959 at [74]; *Quarter Master UK v Pyke* [2005] 1 BCLC 245 at [70]; *Lindsley v Woodfull* [2004] 2 BCLC 131 at [30]; *Guinness plc v Saunders* [1990] BCLC 402; also generally Conaglen, n 9. See too Grantham, 'Can Directors Compete with the Company?' (2003) 66 MLR 109 who comments (at 112) that equity imposes such rigorous obligations because of the beneficiary's vulnerability to the fiduciary, the need to maintain the sanctity of relationships of trust and confidence, and the difficulty of actually proving breach of duty; Getzler, n 12, notes that fiduciary duties tend to be applied where there are steep information asymmetries in favour of the manager and inhibitions on the beneficiary's ability to monitor the discretionary power of that manager, at p 198. Smith, 'Fiduciary Relationships: Ensuring the Loyal Exercise of Judgment on Behalf of Another' (2014) 130 LQR 608 at 627 finds the deterrence arguments unpersuasive.

[15] See *Item Software (UK) Ltd v Fassihi* [2005] 2 BCLC 91 at [66]. See too *Parks of Hamilton Holdings Ltd v Campbell* [2014] CSIH 36, [2014] SC 726, where the court explained that the severity of the fiduciary duty not to profit reflects the relative lack of supervision by the beneficiary which coupled with the high degree of discretion typically afforded to fiduciaries means that fiduciaries' activities are less amenable to control by their principals, so justifying very strict rules which should not be relaxed, at [39], per Lord Drummond Young.

[16] [2012] 1 BCLC 67 at [9].

[17] See *Regal (Hastings) Ltd v Gulliver* [1942] 1 All ER 378. Many of the cases have a windfall element to them, see *Industrial Development Consultants Ltd v Cooley* [1972] 2 All ER 162; *Crown Dilmun v Sutton* [2004] 1 BCLC 468; *Quarter Master UK v Pyke* [2005] 1 BCLC 245, all discussed later in the chapter.

[18] See *Foster Bryant Surveying Ltd v Bryant* [2007] 2 BCLC 239 at [76], per Rix LJ; *Wilkinson v West Coast Capital* [2007] BCC 717 at [245]; *In Plus Group Ltd v Pyke* [2002] 2 BCLC 201 at [80], per Sedley LJ; *Henderson v Merrett Syndicates* [1995] AC 145 at 206, per Lord Browne-Wilkinson; *Boardman v Phipps* [1966] 3 All ER 721 at 756–7, per Lord Upjohn. But see *Premier Waste Management Ltd v Towers* [2012] 1 BCLC 67 at [9]: '… flexibility in the application of the no conflict rule does not undermine the strict nature of the liability enshrined in the principle where it applies', per Mummery LJ.

Arden LJ has noted, 'equity has been able skilfully to adapt remedies against defaulting fiduciaries to meet the justice of the case'.[19] Also, a fiduciary who wants relief from the strict application of the law always has the option of seeking the informed consent of the shareholders by ordinary resolution after full and frank disclosure of all relevant matters,[20] an option retained by CA 2006, s 180(4)(a) (see **12-58**). Directors also have the option of seeking the approval of disinterested directors without the need for disclosure to the shareholders, a measure introduced by the CA 2006 in order to address concerns that the no-profit rule, in particular, might be unduly harsh[21] and unduly restrictive of entrepreneurial freedom to compete with companies.[22] In fact, as noted earlier, it has always been possible for directors to exploit conflicts with the consent of the company and the 'harsh' application of the no-conflict rule necessarily arises only where consent has not been sought, probably because the director was aware that approval would not have been forthcoming.[23] It is difficult for a fiduciary who has profited secretly in breach of duty, who has not sought the consent of the company to that profit, to argue when caught that the law is too strict.

## A duty of disclosure

**12-6**    As Sedley LJ explained in *In Plus Group Ltd v Pyke*,[24] the no-conflict cases show that not only must the fiduciary not place himself in a position of conflict or possible conflict, 'if, even accidentally, he finds himself in such a position, he must regularise or abandon it', i.e. he must disclose the conflict of interest and seek authorisation or abandon the opportunity. The director has the option of resigning his position, of course, but resignation will not allow him to exploit property, information, or opportunity of which he became aware as a director in circumstances in which he had a conflict or possible conflict of interest (CA 2006, s 170(2)(a)), discussed at **12-33**. A difficult issue is whether there is any general duty of disclosure by directors to the company. In *Bhullar v Bhullar*[25] Jonathan Parker LJ (with whom Brooke and Schiemann LJJ agreed) concluded that 'the existence of the opportunity [to acquire an adjacent property] was information which it was relevant for the company to know', and, he went on, 'it follows that the appellants [directors] were under

---

[19]   *Murad v Al-Saraj* [2005] EWCA 959 at [81].

[20]   As Conaglen notes, getting consent is an easy route for fiduciaries to avoid the constraining effect of the fiduciary principle, but it requires the fiduciary to negotiate with his principal, once the principal is fully informed by disclosure of all material facts: see Conaglen, n 9, 561–2. See further at **12-38**.

[21]   See *Warman International Ltd v Dwyer* (1995) 182 CLR 544 at 561, Aust HC ('the liability of the fiduciary should not be transformed into a vehicle for the unjust enrichment of the plaintiff'); a point taken on board by Lewison J in *Ultraframe (UK) Ltd v Fielding* [2005] EWHC 1638 at [1588]; also *Fyffes Group Ltd v Templeman* [2000] 2 Lloyd's Rep 643 at 672; *Crown Dilmun v Sutton* [2004] 1 BCLC 468 at [211]–[212].

[22]   See, for example, *Murad v Al-Saraj* [2005] EWCA 959 at [82]–[83], per Arden LJ; at [121]–[122], per Jonathan Parker LJ, but see criticism by Conaglen, n 9, who robustly and rightly argues that 'it would subvert the incentive structure of fiduciary doctrine if fiduciaries were encouraged to think that they can make a profit in breach of fiduciary duty and then proceed to court (if caught) to argue about how much of it they ought to be able to keep', at 577. For academic comment in favour of modernising the no-conflict, no-profit rules, see Lowry and Edmunds, 'The No Conflict-No Profit Rules and the Corporate Fiduciary: Challenging the Orthodoxy of Absolutism' [2000] JBL 122, and criticism by Kershaw, 'Lost in Translation: Corporate Opportunities in Comparative Perspective' (2005) 25 Ox JLS 603.

[23]   As Jacob LJ put it in *Imageview Management Ltd v Jack* [2009] 1 BCLC 724 at [7], any agent doubtful of his position should make full disclosure to his principal, '... the mere fact that he has doubts will generally be a message from his conscience'.

[24]   [2002] 2 BCLC 201 at [86].      [25]   [2003] 2 BCLC 241.

a duty to communicate it to the company',[26] applying Roskill J in *Industrial Development Consultants Ltd v Cooley*.[27] This approach was developed, controversially, in *Item Software (UK) Ltd v Fassihi*[28] by Arden LJ (with whom Holman and Mummery LJJ agreed) into a prescriptive obligation on a director to disclose his own misconduct to his company,[29] not as a result of some free-standing duty of disclosure,[30] but, as Arden LJ saw it, as part of the fundamental duty of loyalty to which a director is subject, that is, the director's duty to act in what he in good faith considers to be the best interests of his company.[31]

**12-7** This approach seems unnecessarily wide. There are three entangled issues here: the duty of a director to disclose his or her own misconduct (a difficult issue),[32] the duty to act in the interests of the company under s 172, and the no-conflict duty under s 175. As discussed below, the no-conflict rule is widely drawn and precludes a director from exploiting opportunities, information, and property without the informed consent of the company and so the duty to disclose arises if a director wishes to exploit a conflict of interest.[33] The whole point of the no-conflict duty is that personal interests must not conflict with the interests of the company reflected by s 172, so any breach of no-conflict duty is necessarily a breach of the duty to act in the interests of the company. Framed in these terms, rather than a duty to disclose misconduct, the approach in *Fassihi* is uncontroversial. In *Shepherds Investments Ltd v Walters*,[34] which purported to apply *Item Software*, a director who remained in post while developing and selling his own directly competing products was in a position of conflict so that he was required to disclose his activities and get the company's informed consent to what he was doing. In *Item Software (UK) Ltd v Fassihi*[35] the defendant director should have disclosed that, while the company was negotiating with a client (and the director was part of the negotiating team) for the renewal of an important distribution contract, he was negotiating to secure the contract for his personal benefit. He could only

---

[26] [2003] 2 BCLC 241 at [41]. As Millett explains in 'Bribes and Secret Commissions Again' (2012) 71 CLJ 583 at 602, the liability is not about the appropriation of information, it is that '… being trusted to act in the interests of his principal to the exclusion of his own, a fiduciary is bound either to use the information for the benefit of his principal or not to make use of it at all'. [27] [1972] 2 All ER 162 at 173–4.

[28] [2005] 2 BCLC 91, especially at [40]–[41], [63]–[68]. See generally Moore, 'Revisiting the "Duty to Confess": A Director's Duty to Disclose his own Misconduct' (2016) Company Law Newsletter 1.

[29] See also *Crown Dilmun v Sutton* [2004] 1 BCLC 468 at [181]; *British Midland Tool Ltd v Midland International Tooling Ltd* [2003] 2 BCLC 523 at [89]. It is not entirely clear whether Arden LJ was limiting the duty to disclosure of misconduct rather than the wider category of 'information which it is relevant for the company to know', but, as she bases the disclosure obligation on the duty to act in the best interests of the company, it must also extend to the wider category where such disclosure is in the best interests of the company, see [2005] 2 BCLC 91 at [44]; Etherton J in *Shepherds Investments Ltd v Walters* [2007] 2 BCLC 202 at [132] clearly sees it as extending to the wider category; see also *GHCM Trading Ltd v Maroo* [2012] 2 BCLC 369 at [195] (no reason to restrict the disclosure that can be necessary to misconduct).

[30] Arden LJ expressly stated that she did not consider it correct to infer from *Bhullar v Bhullar* or *IDC v Cooley* that a fiduciary owes a *separate* and independent duty to disclose his own misconduct or more generally information of relevance and concern to his principal: see [2005] 2 BCLC 91 at [41]. See Smith, 'Fiduciary Relationships: Ensuring the Loyal Exercise of Judgment on Behalf of Another' (2014) 130 LQR 608 at 631–2 who strongly supports Arden LJ's position on the basis that a beneficiary is entitled to everything arising from the sphere of fiduciary management, including profits, but also all information acquired by the fiduciary including information as to his own misconduct.

[31] [2005] 2 BCLC 91 at [41]. For a fuller discussion of the issue, see Hannigan, 'Reconfiguring the No Conflict Rule—Judicial Strictures, a Statutory Restatement and the Opportunistic Director' (2011) 23 SAcLJ 714.

[32] See Berg (2005) 121 LQR 213 who is critical of the imposition of a duty to disclose misconduct; also Ho and Lee, 'A Director's Duty to Confess: A Matter of Good Faith' (2007) 66 CLJ 348.

[33] Assuming he is not under a contractual obligation to disclose information. See Hannigan, n 31, 718–27. See too *Boardman v Phipps* [1967] 2 AC 46; *New Zealand Netherlands Society v Kuys* [1973] 1 WLR 1126.

[34] [2007] 2 BCLC 202.    [35] [2005] 2 BCLC 91.

have regularised that conflict by disclosing his plan to acquire the distribution contract for himself and seeking consent.[36] In that sense, he had a duty to communicate information to the company which it was relevant for it to know. Disclosure is a required step if the director wishes to exploit the situation of conflict in which he finds himself and non-disclosure necessarily is a failure to act in the interests of the company. In *Cullen Investments Ltd v Brown*,[37] for example, a director failed to disclose that he was exploiting a business opportunity in Germany with respect to which he had a clear conflict of interest. The court found that his failure to disclose his conflict of interest put him in breach of s 172 and s 175.[38] In *Haysport Properties Ltd v Ackerman*,[39] the defendant, who was the sole effective director of the two claimant companies, had the companies provide loans and security to another company in which he had a personal interest. Peter Smith J held that the director was hopelessly conflicted and in breach of his duties to the claimant companies. He considered that 'it was well established that a director has a duty to disclose his own wrongdoing',[40] but as the case concerns an undisclosed conflict of interest, it fits into the jurisprudence above, that disclosure is required to avoid being in breach of the no-conflict duty.

## B Scope of the duty to avoid conflicts of interest

### S 175(1)—Avoiding a conflict or possible conflict of interest

**12-8** Section 175(1) provides that a director of a company must avoid a situation in which he has, or can have, a direct or indirect interest that conflicts, or possibly may conflict, with the interests of the company. This requirement largely mirrors the equitable no-conflict rule famously laid down by Lord Cranworth in *Aberdeen Railway Co v Blaikie Bros*[41] where he noted that:

> 'it is a rule of universal application, that no one, having [fiduciary] duties to discharge shall be allowed to enter into engagements in which he has or can have a personal interest conflicting or which possibly may conflict with the interests of those whom he is bound to protect.'

**12-9** The no-conflict duty applies (CA 2006, s 175(7)) whether the conflict is between 'interest' and 'duty' (between the direct or indirect interests[42] of a director and his duty to promote the interests of the company) and also where there is a conflict or possible conflict between 'duties' (for example, where a director is a director of two or more companies and has a separate duty to advance the interests of each company). In theory, there is no rule that a director cannot be a director of another company, even a company which is wholly or partly engaged competitively in the same trade.[43] In practice, there is significant potential

---

[36] [2005] 2 BCLC 91 at [44].    [37] [2017] EWHC 1586.

[38] [2017] EWHC 1586 at [244]–[245].    [39] [2016] 2 BCLC 522.

[40] [2016] 2 BCLC 522 at [56], citing *Item Software (UK) Ltd v Fassihi* [2004] BCC 994; *Tesco Stores Ltd v Pook* [2003] EWHC 823 (Ch); [2004] IRLR 618 (an employee case where Peter Smith J presided).

[41] (1854) 1 Macq 461 at 471. For an illuminating analysis of this case and its underlying principles, see Farrar and Watson, 'Self-dealing, Fair Dealing and Related Party Transactions—History, Policy and Reform' (2011) 11 JCLS 495.

[42] See *Transvaal Lands Company v New Belgium (Transvaal) Land and Development Company* [1914] 2 Ch 488 at 503—the extent of the interest or the fact that it is indirect is irrelevant, as long as there is a conflict of interest.

[43] *London and Mashonaland Exploration Co Ltd v New Mashonaland Exploration Co Ltd* [1891] WN 165, approved in *Bell v Lever Bros* [1932] AC 161, HL by Lord Blanesburgh, but see n 46. See Christie, 'The Director's Fiduciary Duty not to Compete' (1992) 55 MLR 506.

for conflicts of interest, for example, where a director of Company A is also a director of Company B which is a customer or supplier of Company A or where a director is a director of Company A and of Company B and each company is seeking business from Company C. Disclosure and consent is the key to these conflicts and the director who holds two directorships in situations of potentially conflicting interests is in breach of the obligation of undivided loyalty which he owes to each company unless he secures the informed consent of each company.[44] As Millett LJ commented in *Bristol and West BS v Mothew*:[45]

> 'Even if a fiduciary is properly acting for two principals with potentially conflicting interests he must act in good faith in the interests of each and must not act with the intention of furthering the interests of one principal to the prejudice of those of the other … He must not allow the performance of his obligations to one principal to be influenced by his relationship with the other. He must serve each as faithfully and loyally as if he were his only principal.'

**12-10** This issue of multiple, possibly competing, directorships is important in practice and large companies commonly adopt articles which allow for the exclusion of the conflicted director from receipt of information and participation in discussions and exempt him from any obligation to disclose confidential information belonging to the other company, etc. Practical difficulties persist, however, in managing day-to-day issues which give rise to possible conflicts and resignation may prove to be the only possible course. Any director will find it difficult to serve two masters without being in breach of his obligation to one or the other.[46]

**12-11** Liability under CA 2006, s 175(1) arises from a situation of conflict or of possible conflict and there need not be an actual conflict of interest, just a real sensible possibility of conflict.[47] The 'real sensible possibility' threshold (much cited)[48] is derived from Lord Upjohn in *Boardman v Phipps* where he said:[49]

---

[44] See *Bristol and West BS v Mothew* [1996] 4 All ER 698 at 712, per Millett LJ.

[45] [1996] 4 All ER 698 at 713.

[46] See *In Plus Group Ltd v Pyke* [2002] 2 BCLC 201 at [81], [84], CA, where Sedley LJ made clear that he thought the position of a competing director is almost unsustainable and it was clear that all three judges in the case believed the *Mashonaland* principle, see n 43, to be of very limited application, as where in effect the position of the director in one company is purely nominal to such an extent that the director attracts no fiduciary obligations from that position; see Grantham (2003) 66 MLR 109. See also *Scottish Co-operative Wholesale Society Ltd v Meyer* [1959] AC 324 at 367–8, HL.

[47] For example, in *Fiona Trust & Holding Corp v Privalov* [2010] EWHC 3199 at [73], Andrew Smith J, discussing gifts and bribes, noted that it is a question of fact depending on the circumstances of each case where the line is to be drawn 'between "a little present" and a bribe', the question being whether the 'gift' is sufficient to create a 'real possibility' of a conflict between interest and duty. 'It is not whether such a conflict is actually created.' See also *Burns v Financial Conduct Authority* [2017] EWCA Civ 2140 at [75], per Kitchin L: 'It is clearly not necessary that the possibility should have already matured into an actual and existing conflict of interest.'

[48] For an unusual case where the court accepted there was no possible conflict, see *Wilkinson v West Coast Capital* [2007] BCC 717. A shareholders' agreement to which all (including the company) were party provided that the consent of 65 per cent of the shareholders was required for any further acquisitions by the company. As two of the directors owned 50 per cent of the shares, they were able to block any further acquisitions by the company, so there was no possibility of the company having an interest in an acquisition secured by them personally.

[49] [1966] 3 All ER 721 at 756; and see his earlier comments to similar effect in *Boulting v ACTAT* [1963] 2 QB 606 at 637–8: '… a broad rule like this must be applied with common sense and with an appreciation of the sort of circumstances in which over the last 200 years and more it has been applied and thrived. It must be applied realistically to a state of affairs which discloses a real conflict of duty and interest and not to some theoretical or rhetorical conflict.' See *Aberdeen Railway Co v Blaikie Bros* (1854) 1 Macq 461 at 471–2, per Lord Cranworth; *Transvaal Lands Company v New Belgium (Transvaal) Land and Development Company* [1914] 2 Ch 488; also *Cowan de Groot Properties Ltd v Eagle Trust plc* [1991] BCLC 1045 at 1116; *Re Dominion International Group plc (No 2)* [1996] 1 BCLC 572 at 597.

'The phrase "possibly may conflict" requires consideration. In my view it means that the reasonable man looking at the relevant facts and circumstances of the particular case would think that there was a real sensible possibility of conflict; not that you could imagine some situation arising which might, in some conceivable possibility in events not contemplated as real sensible possibilities by any reasonable person, result in a conflict.'

In statutory form, the limitation is negatively expressed in s 175(4)(a) so as to exclude from the ambit of the no-conflict duty situations that cannot reasonably be regarded as likely to give rise to a conflict of interest,[50] with 'likely' continuing to be defined, it can be expected, as 'a real sensible possibility', so there is no change in the law. References hereinafter to 'possibly may conflict' or 'not reasonably likely' should be read, respectively, in the light of and by reference to s 175(4)(a). Obviously, much of the case law discussed in this chapter, given its vintage, refers only to a 'real sensible possibility of conflict' and not to the statute.[51]

## Applying the 'simple', strict, no-conflict rule

**12-12**    Jonathan Parker LJ noted in *Bhullar v Bhullar*[52] that the no-conflict rule (now s 175(1)) is essentially a simple rule 'albeit it may in some cases be difficult to apply'. The problem lies in identifying that a conflict exists and directors are poor at realising when they are in a position of conflict or, perhaps, they recognise the conflict but choose to ignore it or, perhaps, the courts surprise them with the breadth of the rule.

**12-13**    In *Bhullar v Bhullar*[53] two directors of a family company were found to be in breach of the no-conflict rule when they acquired property adjacent to the company without telling the company that the property was available for purchase. They had come across the information that the property was for sale quite by chance and in circumstances which had nothing to do with their directorships. The company was a family business which was deadlocked and it had been agreed by the shareholders that the company would not acquire further properties. The intention was that the parties would go their separate ways but they had not actually taken any formal steps to bring the business to an end.[54] The court found that the directors' personal interest in acquiring the property was in conflict with their duty to promote the company's interests which required them to communicate the existence of the opportunity to the company[55] which could then have considered whether to acquire it. Having noted that the no-conflict rule is

---

[50] See generally Lim, 'Directors' Fiduciary Duties: A New Analytical Framework' (2013) 129 LQR 242 on the operation of the exclusion in s 175(4)(a). He argues that if the board considers and rejects an opportunity, the opportunity would then fall within s 175(4)(a) and be open to a director to exploit. But the board's consideration of the matter shows that this opportunity does indeed give rise to a conflict of interest and the only method to authorise a conflict is by the disinterested directors or by the company. A mere decision by the board not to proceed will not resolve the conflict for the director—to do that, he needs actual authorisation. This situation is not within s 175(4)(a) which addresses the situation where a conflict never arose in the first place.

[51] The Government considered that CA 2006, s 175(4)(a) introduces a requirement of reasonableness, see HL Deb, vol 678, GC 293 (6 February 2006), but it is not clear that the provision does much other than reflect the limitation already identified by Lord Upjohn.

[52] [2003] 2 BCLC 241 at [30]. See *Wilkinson v West Coast Capital* [2007] BCC 717 at [252]–[253] on the difficulty in identifying in any given situation whether the relevant element of conflict is present.

[53] [2003] 2 BCLC 241, noted Armour (2004) 63 CLJ 33; Prentice and Payne (2004) 120 LQR 198.

[54] See [2003] 2 BCLC 241 at [10], [22].

[55] As to the duty to communicate information to the company, see **12-6**.

as stated by Lord Cranworth in *Aberdeen Rly C v Blaikie Bros*[56] (see at **12-8**), Jonathan Parker LJ went on:[57]

'In a case such as the present, where a fiduciary has exploited a commercial opportunity for his own benefit, the relevant question, in my judgment, is not whether the party to whom the duty is owed (the company, in the instant case) had some kind of beneficial interest in the opportunity: in my judgment that would be too formalistic and restrictive an approach. Rather, the question is simply whether the fiduciary's exploitation of the opportunity is such as to attract the application of the [no-conflict] rule.'

In the court's view, the directors in this case had, at the material time, 'one capacity and one capacity only in which they were carrying on business, namely as directors of the company. In that capacity, they were in a fiduciary relationship with the company.'[58] There was a real sensible possibility of conflict, the court said, and they were in breach of their duty when they acquired the property for themselves.

**12-14**   The case highlights the breadth of the no-conflict duty. A director can be in breach of the no-conflict rule though he does not exploit his fiduciary position in the sense of using information or opportunity acquired in that capacity although, of course, that feature may be and often is present. The application of the no-conflict rule is not dependent on the information being obtained by a director in the exercise of his functions as a director, it depends on whether the information places the director in a situation of conflict or possible conflict. There is no need to show the exploitation of property 'belonging' to the company—there is no proprietary element to it[59]—merely a need for a real sensible possibility of conflict and the fiduciary's exploitation of the situation.[60] This is an important point with respect to so-called corporate opportunities, opportunities which arise in the course of the business and which directors may be tempted to take for themselves. As Lewison LJ explained in *FHR European Ventures v Mankarious*[61] 'an opportunity' cannot realistically be said to 'belong' to anyone. After all, he said, 'you cannot assign it or transfer it; you cannot charge it; you cannot leave it by will', and he went on to note that in *Bhullar* the court decisively rejected the notion that it was necessary to identify some form of beneficial ownership of the opportunity itself. As the company is entitled to the undivided loyalty of its directors, the very act of a director putting himself in a position of conflict or possible conflict is a breach of duty, without more, as was explained in *Quarter Master (UK) Ltd v Pyke*:[62]

'It is not because he has made a profit from trust property or a profit from his fiduciary position that the director is liable under the conflict rule. Rather, it is because, being in a fiduciary position, he has entered into a transaction, inconsistent with his fiduciary duty of loyalty to the company, which has yielded the profit and he has thereby misused his

---

[56]  (1854) 1 Macq 461.

[57]  [2003] 2 BCLC 241 at [28], cited with approval in the Supreme Court in *FHR European Ventures LLP v Cedar Capital Partners LLC* [2014] 2 BCLC 145 at [14], per Lord Neuberger.

[58]  [2003] 2 BCLC 241 at [41].

[59]  A point reflected in the absence of any reference to property, information, or opportunity *of the company* in CA 2006, s 175(2) (set out at **12-2**). This wording was deliberately chosen as it is for the courts to determine whether the exploitation of the property, information, or opportunity has given rise to a conflict of interest, see HL Deb, vol 681, GC 864 (9 May 2006). *Bhullar v Bhullar* [2003] 2 BCLC 241 at [28]. See also Lewison J in *Ultraframe (UK) Ltd v Fielding* [2005] EWHC 1638 at [1355]: 'The application of the no-conflict rule does not depend on establishing that the company has a proprietary interest in the business opportunity that has been diverted'; and Kershaw, 'Does it Matter how the Law Thinks about Corporate Opportunities?' (2005) 25 Legal Studies 533.

[60]  [2003] 2 BCLC 241 at [27]–[28].     [61]  [2013] 2 BCLC 1 at [57].

[62]  [2005] 1 BCLC 245 at [54]–[55], per Paul Morgan QC, sitting as a Deputy Judge.

position. The opportunity to make the profit may not arise from the director's fiduciary position; he might just as well have had the opportunity if he had not been in that position but even so, his liability in respect of the profit arises because of the conflict of interest. In many cases, where the conflict rule applies, the director will also have taken advantage of the property of the company or of his fiduciary position but this will not always be so.'

**12-15** Another significant authority is *Cook v Deeks*[63] where two of the three directors of a Canadian railway company diverted a contract in which the company was interested to another company which they had formed. The Privy Council found that, while they were directors and with their duties to the company entirely unchanged, they had proceeded to negotiate in reality on their own behalf.[64] There was a clear conflict between their personal interests in securing the contract and their duty to secure it for the company. Having exploited their positions to obtain it for themselves, the court held that the benefit of the contract belonged in equity to the company and the directors were bound to hold it on behalf of the company.[65]

**12-16** In *Industrial Development Consultants Ltd v Cooley*[66] Cooley had been employed as managing director by the company (IDC) and was actively involved in negotiations with the Eastern Gas Board to secure certain construction contracts for IDC.[67] It became clear that the Gas Board was not prepared to contract with IDC. A year later, the Gas Board approached Cooley and indicated a willingness for him personally to take on the management of these construction projects. He promptly resigned from IDC (giving the company the misleading impression that he was ill) and took the contracts offered by the Gas Board which were in substance the work that the company had unsuccessfully attempted to obtain the previous year. Roskill J held that, as a director, Cooley occupied a fiduciary position which subjected him to an obligation to avoid possible conflicts between his personal interests and his fiduciary duty. Information which came to him while he was managing director (i.e. the knowledge that the Gas Board was back in the market and looking to place these construction contracts) and which was of concern to the company and was relevant to the company to know was information which it was his duty, because of his fiduciary position, to pass on to the company.[68] Instead he embarked upon what was, the court found, a deliberate policy and course of conduct which put his personal interest in direct conflict with his pre-existing and continuing duty as managing director of the company.[69] As such, the defendant was liable to account to the plaintiffs for all the benefit he received under the contract with the Gas Board.

**12-17** The statute in s 175(1) reflects this line of authority from *Aberdeen Railway v Blaikie Bros*[70] through to *Bhullar v Bhullar*[71] which focuses on the 'simple' question of whether the director has exploited a conflict of interest in breach of his duty of undivided loyalty and it is not suggested that the outcome under the statute would have been any different in these cases. This line of authority was endorsed by the Supreme Court in *FHR European Ventures LLP v Cedar Capital Partners LLC*,[72] which is discussed in Chapter 14.

**12-18** One of the advantages of the 'bright line' approach, favoured in *Bhullar* and reflected in the statute, of asking the simple question of whether there is or may be a conflict or possible conflict of interest, is that it avoids any need for a corporate opportunities doctrine

---

[63] [1916] 1 AC 554, PC.  [64] [1916] 1 AC 554 at 559–60.
[65] [1916] 1 AC 554 at 564.  [66] [1972] 2 All ER 162.
[67] It is also important that it was Cooley who was conducting the negotiations: see *Furs Ltd v Tomkies* (1936) 54 CLR 583; *Framlington Group plc v Anderson* [1995] 1 BCLC 475.
[68] [1972] 2 All ER 162 at 173–4. See **12-6** as to this 'duty' to pass on information.
[69] [1972] 2 All ER 162 at 173–4.  [70] (1854) 1 Macq 461.
[71] [2003] 2 BCLC 541.  [72] [2014] 2 BCLC 145.

which looks to whether the director has appropriated an opportunity or a maturing business opportunity *of* the company.[73] It is still appropriate to have some regard to the nature of the opportunity etc vis-à-vis the scope of the company's business, however, since the scope of the business determines the extent of the company's interests and therefore whether there is a real sensible possibility of a conflict for the director.[74] Usually, there is little difficulty in deciding whether a situation/opportunity has attracted the application of the no-conflict rule for in many of the cases, such as *Cook v Deeks*[75] and *IDC v Cooley*,[76] the company has been actively pursuing the contract which the director has secured for himself. In *Bhullar v Bhullar*,[77] however, we find that a company had an interest in acquiring an adjacent property though the company was deadlocked and had effectively decided not to pursue any further acquisitions.

**12-19**    The strictness with which the English courts approach the no-conflict rule can be seen in *Re Allied Business and Financial Consultants Ltd, O'Donnell v Shanahan*,[78] hereinafter *O'Donnell v Shanahan*. In this case, the trial judge favoured, though the Court of Appeal did not, a more pragmatic assessment of what is a 'possible' conflict looking in detail at what the company is actually doing rather than what might conceivably be possible. The central allegation of breach of duty in this case concerned the involvement by two (of the three) directors of a company[79] with a client of the company in the acquisition of an investment property. The directors had been approached by a third party to find a purchaser for the property and, after an initial deal fell through, the directors found a client who was willing to proceed, but only on the basis, which they agreed to, that he would share the deal 50/50 with the two directors and that he would not pay a commission to the company (a commission to the company had been integral to the initial failed deal).[80] The court also found, as a fact, that had the opportunity to acquire the property been presented to the company, the company would not have been willing or able to accept the opportunity.[81] At first instance, the court found no breach of the no-conflict rule or of the no-profit rule, but, on appeal, the decision was reversed on both grounds.

---

[73] A corporate opportunities approach typically involved a consideration of the factors identified by Laskin J in *Canadian Aero Service Ltd v O'Malley* (1973) 40 DLR (3d) 371 at 391 such as 'the position or office held, the nature of the corporate opportunity, its ripeness, its specificness and the director's relation to it, the amount of knowledge possessed, the circumstances in which it was obtained, etc'. But see Lim, n 50, who disagrees with this interpretation of *Bhullar* and argues, at 261–2, that a maturing business opportunity test is relevant to the application of s 170(2)(a) to former directors, but that is an unnecessary complication, given that the simple question under s 170(2)(a) is as stated in the text at **12-34**.

[74] See Lim, n 50, who argues for a greater focus on whether an opportunity falls within the scope of the business, but that would be a backward step for the courts away from the 'simple' rule identified by *Bhullar v Bhullar* and reflected in s 175(1), namely whether the director's exploitation of the opportunity presents a real sensible possibility of conflict, see **12-12**.

[75] [1916] AC 554, PC.    [76] [1972] 2 All ER 162.    [77] [2003] 2 BCLC 541.

[78] [2009] 2 BCLC 666, rev'g [2009] 1 BCLC 328. For a detailed discussion of this case, see Hannigan, 'Reconfiguring the No Conflict Rule—Judicial Strictures, a Statutory Restatement and the Opportunistic Director' (2011) 23 SAcLJ 714; also Ahern, 'Guiding Principles for Directorial Conflicts of Interest: *Re Allied Business*' (2011) 74 MLR 596.

[79] [2009] 2 BCLC 666 at [32]. The company was a quasi-partnership formed originally between four individuals, but subsequently involving only these three shareholder/directors, each holding 2,525 shares; the fourth shareholder retained 25 shares but had left the business many years earlier.

[80] [2009] 2 BCLC 666 at [23]–[24]. Had the company received a £30,000 commission, it would have been divided equally between the three director/shareholders as was their custom. In fact there was no loss to the shareholders here for the two defendant directors paid the third director the amount of commission which she would otherwise have received.

[81] [2009] 2 BCLC 666 at [35].

**12-20**　At first instance, the court thought there could not be a real sensible possibility of conflict in the circumstances because the company's business was the provision of financial advice and assistance, and though property investment could have fallen within its open-ended objects, actually it was not within the scope of the company's business, even taking an extended view of the scope of that business (i.e. considering the likelihood of the company extending its business into other areas).[82] The Court of Appeal rejected that conclusion finding that, while the company's business initially was the provision of financial advice and assistance, it had diversified into a variety of property and investment roles.[83] In the acquisition at issue, it acted essentially as an estate agent, something which it had not done previously and which, the court thought, indicated that its categories of activities were not closed.[84] By failing to secure a commission for the company on the second deal, a deal in which they participated, the directors had preferred their own interests to the company's interests in breach of the no-conflict rule. The core of the judgment by Rimer LJ (with whom Waller and Aikens LJJ agreed) is a strong affirmation of the underlying rationale of the no-conflict and no-profit rules which is to underpin the fiduciary's duty of undivided loyalty to his beneficiary. 'If the opportunity comes to him in his capacity as a fiduciary, his principal is entitled to know about it. The director cannot be left to make the decision as to whether he is allowed to help himself to its benefit.'[85] Once the opportunity came to the directors' attention in their capacity as directors, the only proper course, Rimer LJ said, was to obtain the company's informed consent to their private venture which they did not do.[86] He noted that the rigorous application of the no-profit rule does not allow for any discussion of the possibility or impossibility of the company making the profit, relying on Lord Russell's famous dictum (set out at **12-23**) in *Regal (Hastings) Ltd v Gulliver*[87] that liability arises from the mere fact of a profit being made while standing in a fiduciary relationship.[88] This uncompromising approach to the no-conflict duty (and the no-profit rule subsumed within it) offers the greatest protection to the company against the opportunistic and disloyal director, an approach confirmed by the Supreme Court in *FHR European Ventures LLP v Cedar Capital Partners*,[89] discussed in Chapter 14.

### S 175(2) Exploiting property, information, or opportunity

**12-21**　In addition to avoiding a situation of conflict as required by CA 2006, s 175(1), the no-profit rule in s 175(2), set out at **12-2**, particularly prohibits the exploitation of any property, information, or opportunity in circumstances where there is a conflict, or possible conflict, of interest. As already noted, the prohibition is not limited to the exploitation of property, etc, of or belonging to the company ('any property'), see **12-14**.

---

[82] [2009] 1 BCLC 328 at [208], [212]. Deputy Judge Sheldon QC did take into account that the company had branched (in the very transaction under scrutiny) into estate agency, but that was some way removed, he said, from contemplating property investment by the company itself.

[83] [2009] 2 BCLC 666 at [5]–[7] (its activities included arranging the purchase and sale of properties, acting as agents for banks and building societies, placing investments for clients, and providing advice on financial and business restructuring).

[84] [2009] 2 BCLC 666 at [53]; 'there was no bright line marking off what it did and did not do', at [71].

[85] [2009] 2 BCLC 666 at [55].　　[86] [2009] 2 BCLC 666 at [60].　　[87] [1942] 1 All ER 378 at 386.

[88] Hence it was irrelevant that the company would not have taken the opportunity, if it had been offered; that the third director had been paid her share of that missed commission; that she knew all along that the defendants had their own property investment company and she knew almost immediately of their involvement in the property transaction which they conducted largely in front of her. None of these factors altered the fact that the directors were in breach of duty.

[89] [2014] 2 BCLC 145.

**12-22**   At common law, the no-profit duty has its origins in the leading trust case of *Keech v Sandford*,[90] but the most famous application of the rule in company law is *Regal (Hastings) Ltd v Gulliver*.[91] In this case a company could not finance the acquisition of additional cinemas which it wished to acquire. It was unable to put up sufficient share capital for the acquiring subsidiary and instead that capital was put up by the directors who then profited personally on the sale of the shares in the subsidiary. The new controllers of the company successfully sued the former directors to recover those profits.

**12-23**   The House of Lords found that the directors had obtained their profits by reason of and in the course of the execution of their office as directors of Regal.[92] They had entered into the transaction in the course of their management and in utilisation of their opportunities and special knowledge as directors.[93] They were thus liable to account, notwithstanding that they had acted bona fide throughout.[94] As directors, they were in a situation of conflict between their personal interests and their duty to the company and they exploited the conflict to their own advantage. In such circumstances, Lord Russell said:[95]

> '[t]he rule of equity which insists on those, who by use of a fiduciary position make a profit, being liable to account for that profit, in no way depends on fraud, or absence of bona fides; or upon such questions or considerations as whether the profit would or should otherwise have gone to the plaintiff, or whether the profiteer was under a duty to obtain the source of the profit for the plaintiff, or whether he took a risk or acted as he did for the benefit of the plaintiff, or whether the plaintiff has in fact been damaged or benefited by his action. The liability arises from the mere fact of a profit having, in the stated circumstances, been made. The profiteer, however honest and well-intentioned, cannot escape the risk of being called upon to account.'

**12-24**   Examples of undisclosed profiting in a situation of conflict abound. In *Gencor ACP Ltd v Dalby*[96] a director had in effect been running a parallel competing business for many years, diverting contracts for the company's products to companies which he controlled in breach of the no-conflict and no-profit duties. In *Crown Dilmun v Sutton*[97] the director of a property development company was liable when he took for himself a development opportunity despite the clear conflict of interest between him and the company. In *Quarter Master UK Ltd v Pyke*[98] the directors, at a time when the company was in significant financial difficulties, engaged in a strategy to salvage for themselves a major ongoing contract with a customer. There was a conflict of interest between their seeking to obtain the contract for themselves, to which end they exploited the company's customer database and goodwill for their own benefit, and their duty to the company to seek ways to maximise the value of the contract for the company and its creditors (even if the company was no longer in a position to continue the contract itself). The court held that they acted in breach of the no-conflict and the no-profit rule and were liable to account for the profits which they made as a result of their breach of fiduciary duty.

---

[90] (1726) Sel Cas Ch 61.       [91] [1942] 1 All ER 378, HL.
[92] [1942] 1 All ER 378 at 389, per Lord Russell.       [93] [1942] 1 All ER 378 at 392, per Lord Macmillan.
[94] The actual decision in *Regal* has been criticised: see Davies and Worthington, *Gower and Davies' Principles of Modern Company Law* (9th edn, 2012), para 16–150: '... the case can be seen as one in which equitable principles were taken to inequitable conclusions'; also Jones (1968) 84 LQR 472 at 497. But see Sullivan (1979) 42 MLR 711 who points out that the directors had a would-be purchaser in mind throughout and that there were other shareholders in *Regal* who could have put up some of the money required but who were not invited to do so. See also *Boardman v Phipps* [1966] 3 All ER 721, HL.
[95] [1942] 1 All ER 378 at 386.       [96] [2000] 2 BCLC 734.
[97] [2004] 1 BCLC 468.       [98] [2005] 1 BCLC 245.

**12-25**     These cases would still be decided the same way under the statute, but they would be decided on the basis of the application of CA 2006, s 175(1) and (2). The defendant directors in these cases, while still in post, had allowed a clear conflict to arise between their personal interests and their duty to their companies and they had sought to exploit the conflict for their personal advantage.

### Liability regardless of the company's position

**12-26**     This strict liability to account applies regardless of whether the company could take advantage of the property, opportunity, or information (CA 2006, s 175(2)). It suffices that the director has profited from a situation of conflict and it is better to apply a strict rule than to attempt to investigate whether, in fact, the company could or would have exploited the opportunity.[99] That is a particularly difficult matter to investigate given that many of the factors relevant to it may lie within the director's control (such as the company's ability to borrow money) which the director may have manipulated precisely in order to show that the company could not or would not have exploited the opportunity. There is also no room for a discussion of whether the fiduciary did indeed advance the interests of his principal or whether there was an actual conflict of interest.[100] All of these considerations were dismissed by Lord Russell in *Regal (Hastings) Ltd v Gulliver*,[101] set out at **12-23**, and that strict approach is reflected in s 175(2).

**12-27**     In *Regal*, discussed at **12-22**, the inability of the company to fund the acquisition of additional cinemas was irrelevant to the directors' liability for breach of the no-profit rule. There are numerous cases where, when determining the liability of the director who has exploited a conflict of interest, the court has disregarded the fact that the company might not have wished or been able, typically for financial reasons, to have taken the opportunity, or where the third party might not have been willing to deal with the company. In *Industrial Development Consultants Ltd v Cooley*,[102] see **12-16**, the fact that the company only had a 10 per cent chance of securing the construction contracts at issue was irrelevant to the liability of the director.[103] In *Crown Dilmun v Sutton*,[104] see **12-24**, it was irrelevant whether the company would/could have taken the major contract which the director diverted to a company that he had formed. In *Quarter Master UK Ltd v Pyke*,[105] see **12-24**, the fact that a key client had indicated that it was not likely to renew a contract with the company (which was in significant financial difficulties) was irrelevant to the directors' liability to account when they took the contract on their own behalf. In *O'Donnell v Shanahan*,[106] see **12-19**, it was irrelevant that the company would not have taken the opportunity to acquire the investment property had it been offered to the company. Likewise, in *Bhullar v Bhullar*,[107] see **12-13**, where Jonathan Parker LJ noted that

---

[99]  See *Regal (Hastings) Ltd v Gulliver* [1942] 1 All ER 378 at 392; also *Furs Ltd v Tomkies* (1936) 54 CLR 583 at 592, and see *Gwembe Valley Development Co v Koshy* [2004] 1 BCLC 131 at [44]–[45]; and *Wilkinson v West Coast Capital* [2007] BCC 717 at [255]. But for criticism of the view that investigation of these matters is too difficult, see *Murad v Al-Saraj* [2005] EWCA 959 at [82], [155].

[100]  See Conaglen, 'The Extent of Fiduciary Accounting and the importance of Authorisation Mechanisms' (2011) 70 CLJ 548 at 599–60, a fiduciary should not be allowed to claim an honest belief that he acted in the company's interests, for that approach would just incentivise fiduciaries to engineer situations in which they could make such an argument. See also *Fiona Trust v Privalov* [2010] EWHC 3199 at [72] (if a bribe is paid to an agent, it does not assist the briber or the agent to show that in fact the agent acted in his principal's best interests); *Airbus Operations Ltd v Withey* [2014] EWHC 1126 at [123]–[124] (no answer to say undisclosed benefit made no difference to the principal or that the principal suffered no loss).

[101]  [1942] 1 All ER 378 at 386.        [102]  [1972] 2 All ER 162, CA.        [103]  [1972] 2 All ER 162 at 176.
[104]  [2004] 1 BCLC 468.        [105]  [2005] 1 BCLC 245.        [106]  [2009] 2 BCLC 666.
[107]  [2003] 2 BCLC 241, CA. See too *Wrexham AFC Ltd v Crucialmove Ltd* [2008] 1 BCLC 508 at [40].

'whether the company could or would have taken that opportunity, had it been made aware of it, is not to the point'.[108]

### The no-conflict rule and the departing director

**12-28**  A director may resign at any time even though such resignation may damage or harm the company.[109] Equally, there is nothing to stop a person forming the intention, while a director, to set up in competition with his company after his directorship ceases (subject to any contractual constraints) for the no-profit rule is not intended to hinder directors in the exploitation of the general fund of knowledge and expertise acquired while a director.[110] A director is also able to take preliminary steps to investigate or forward that intention to compete, provided he does not engage in any actual competitive activity[111] and so does not reach the situation where there is a conflict or possible conflict between his interests and his duty to the company.

**12-29**  The problem is that it is difficult to identify the point in time when the mere intention to compete turns into a conflict of interest[112] and, by and large, the case law shows that directors in that situation commonly overstep the mark.

**12-30**  The discussion here is limited to liability for breach of fiduciary duty but many directors will have service agreements with express provisions governing the solicitation of customers and use of confidential information post-resignation.[113] In many cases, therefore, the director may also face claims based on a breach of contract or common law obligations of confidence. It has also become common, where several former directors of a company are sued for involvement in a new business competing with the old company, to allege that not only did the directors act in breach of fiduciary duty, but that they combined together (and possibly with others) to injure the company by unlawful means, the unlawful means being the breach of fiduciary duty. Hence a claim is made that they are liable for damages in conspiracy as well as for breach of fiduciary duty and also for breach of contract.

### Intending to resign

**12-31**  In *Colman Taymar Ltd v Oakes*[114] a director was liable when he failed to disclose his intention to compete with the company and, while still a director, used confidential information and the company's staff to assist him in securing leases and hiring equipment for his new business. In *Shepherds Investments Ltd v Walters*[115] the defendant directors were liable when, while still directors and without disclosing their plans, they took very

---

[108] [2003] 2 BCLC 241 at [41]. See too *Goldtrail Travel Ltd v Aydin* [2016] 1 BCLC 635, CA given that, when considering whether a director is in breach of duty, it is irrelevant to consider whether the company could in fact have benefited or taken advantage of the opportunity, that fact is also irrelevant when considering the compensation that the company is entitled to recover from the director.

[109] See *CMS Dolphin Ltd v Simonet* [2001] 2 BCLC 704 at [87].

[110] See *Island Export Finance Ltd v Umunna* [1986] BCLC 460 at 482–3; *Balston Ltd v Headline Filters Ltd* [1990] FSR 385 at 412. As noted in *Berryland Book Ltd v BK Books Ltd* [2009] 2 BCLC 709 at [25] (reversed in part for reasons which are irrelevant here, [2010] EWCA Civ 1440), the court has to be astute to ensure that litigation is not used as an illegitimate trade protection exercise so as to stifle legitimate competition.

[111] See *Balston Ltd v Headline Filters Ltd* [1990] FSR 385 at 412, per Falconer J; also *Framlington Group plc v Anderson* [1995] 1 BCLC 475 at 495–6, 498.

[112] See *Shepherds Investments Ltd v Walters* [2007] 2 BCLC 202 at [108]; *Balston Ltd v Headline Filters Ltd* [1990] FSR 385 at 412, per Falconer J; also Watts, 'The Transition from Director to Competitor' (2007) 123 LQR 21.

[113] See, for example, *Kingsley IT Consulting Ltd v McIntosh* [2006] BCC 875.

[114] [2001] 2 BCLC 749.          [115] [2007] 2 BCLC 202.

active steps to promote a competing business to be carried on by them in the future. They drew up business plans and financial projections, contacted advisers, sought backers, and drafted complicated documentation relating to the new company's financial products. In *Simtel Communications Ltd v Rebak*[116] the defendant director was liable when, while still a director and employee of the company and without disclosing his plans, he set up a competing company, diverted contracts to that company, solicited the company's customers, removed information, and destroyed computer files, all to the advantage of his new business.

**12-32**    As these cases show, many preparatory steps to form a competing business will give rise to a possible conflict of interest[117] with the result, given the obligation to disclose and seek authorisation for that conflict,[118] that the director is propelled towards resignation at the earliest possible moment.[119] This approach provides maximum protection for the company by ensuring, in effect, that a disloyal director cannot remain in post without disclosing his intention to resign and to compete. This forced early disclosure allows a company to manage the process, for example by requiring that the director leaves immediately or, where a period of notice is enforced, ensuring that the departing director no longer has access to customer data or commercially valuable information.

### Resignation

**12-33**    By resigning, as Hart J noted in *British Midland Tool Ltd v Midland International Tooling Ltd*,[120] a director 'puts an end to his fiduciary obligations to the company so far as concerns any future activity by himself, provided it does not involve any exploitation of confidential information or business opportunities available to him by virtue of his directorship'. As noted at **12-2**, the no-conflict duty generally falls away on resignation,[121] but a former director remains subject to the no-conflict rule (CA 2006, s 175) as regards the exploitation of property, information, or opportunity of which he became aware at a time when he was a director (s 170(2)(a)).

**12-34**    This duty obviously comes with a built-in expiry date in the sense that the longer the period post-resignation, the less likely it is that it can be established that the former director is exploiting property etc of which he became aware when he was a director. This prohibition does not extend to *any* property, information, or opportunity of which the director became aware during that period for such a restriction would be contrary to

---

[116] [2006] 2 BCLC 571. See *Berryland Books Ltd v BK Books Ltd* [2009] 2 BCLC 709, rev'd on other grounds [2010] EWCA Civ 1440.

[117] See *British Midland Tool Ltd v Midland International Tooling Ltd* [2003] 2 BCLC 523 at [90] and *Shepherds Investments Ltd v Walters* [2007] 2 BCLC 202 at [108] as to what may be permissible/impermissible, but the courts are reluctant to give precise guidance as the circumstances vary so much from case to case. In *First Subsea Ltd v Balltec Ltd* [2014] EWHC 866, the court was prepared to accept that discussions about setting up a competing business and obtaining legal advice did not take the director into a breach of duty, but once he went ahead and (while still in post) submitted a bid on behalf of his new company for a project which he knew or ought to have known his company would be bidding for, then he was in breach of fiduciary duty, at [207]–[211].

[118] *Industrial Development Consultants Ltd v Cooley* [1972] All ER 162; *Bhullar v Bhullar* [2003] 2 BCLC 241; *Item Software (UK) Ltd v Fassihi* [2005] 2 BCLC 91; see also *Crown Dilmun v Sutton* [2004] 1 BCLC 468 at [179]; *Shepherds Investments Ltd v Walters* [2007] 2 BCLC 202 at [128]; and Watts (2007) 123 LQR 21.

[119] See *British Midland Tool Ltd v Midland International Tooling Ltd* [2003] 2 BCLC 523; *Coleman Taymar Ltd v Oakes* [2001] 2 BCLC 749.

[120] [2003] 2 BCLC 523.

[121] See *Ultraframe (UK) Ltd v Fielding* [2005] EWHC 1638 at [1310], per Lewison J; also *Wilkinson v West Coast Capital* [2007] BCC 717 at 768, per Warren J.

public policy.[122] There must be some link between the exploitation of the property, information, or opportunity and the fiduciary position which the director held (as s 170(2)(a) indicates). The link is to the exploitation of property, information, or opportunity acquired in circumstances where the director had a conflict, or possible conflict, of interest. As the no-profit duty in s 175(2) is an element of the broader no-conflict duty in s 175(1), there can be no liability under the no-profit rule in the absence of an exploitation of a conflict of interest. The intention in s 170(2)(a) is to prevent the easy evasion of the no-conflict rule by resignation rather than to inhibit unduly the entrepreneurial activities of individuals merely because they once held a directorship.

**12-35**   For example, in *CMS Dolphin Ltd v Simonet*[123] a director of the claimant company, an advertising agency, left the company and set up a new business. All the staff of the company subsequently joined him as did the principal clients of the company. The company successfully brought an action against him claiming breach of fiduciary duty and seeking an account of profits made by him. The court found that the former director took away from the company the benefit of contracts with existing clients and the business opportunities it had with those clients.[124] Another example of exploitation by a former director of property, information, or opportunities in a situation of conflict can be found in *Industrial Development Consultants Ltd v Cooley*,[125] see **12-16**, where the director resigned in order to take a contract with the Gas Board which the company was anxious to secure for itself. In *Kingsley IT Consulting Ltd v McIntosh*[126] a company had secured two contracts from a client and had just signed a third contract when the director resigned. The client then terminated the third contract with the company and awarded it to a company set up by the director prior to his resignation.[127] The court found that the former director had acquired the third contract in circumstances where he was bound to carry it out for the benefit of the company, if he was to carry it out at all. In all these cases, the directors are liable for exploiting, post-resignation, an opportunity of which they became aware when they were directors and in respect of which they had a conflict of interest.

**12-36**   The circumstances of resignation can vary greatly, however, as Rix LJ noted in *Foster Bryant Surveying Ltd v Bryant*,[128] and, while the cases discussed earlier are clear examples of directors resigning in order to exploit property, information, or opportunity in a situation of a conflict of interest, other cases are less clear-cut and require careful consideration by the courts. Sometimes resignation is as a result of a breakdown in relations within a company rather than an intention to exploit a conflict of interest. In that scenario, when the defendant does resign and subsequently secures a contract with the company's main customer, the courts have been content (in the absence of use of actual company property, such as customer data or technical drawings) to find there is no liability to account.[129]

---

[122]  See *Island Export Finance Ltd v Umunna* [1986] BCLC 460 at 482–3; *Murad v Al-Saraj* [2005] EWCA Civ 959 at [62].

[123]  [2001] 2 BCLC 704.

[124]  See also *Berryland Books Ltd v BK Books Ltd* [2009] 2 BCLC 709 at [32] (reversed in part for reasons which are irrelevant here, see [2010] EWCA Civ 1440).

[125]  [1972] 2 All ER 162.       [126]  [2006] BCC 875.

[127]  No explanation was given as to why the client terminated the contract, but the court concluded that it happened because the director asked the client to transfer the contract to his new company.

[128]  [2007] 2 BCLC 239, CA.

[129]  See Rix LJ in *Foster Bryant Surveying Ltd v Bryant* [2007] 2 BCLC 239 at [93]: 'As for the innocence of [the director's] resignation, although the matter may not be free of doubt, it seems well arguable on the authorities that it is critically opposed to liability to account [in the case of a retiring director] where there is no active competition or exploitation of company property while the defendant remains a director.'

Examples can be found in *Island Export Finance Ltd v Umunna*,[130] *In Plus Group Ltd v Pyke*,[131] and *Foster Bryant Surveying Ltd v Bryant*,[132] but it must be noted that the facts of these cases are exceptional (essentially the fiduciary relationship has been all but extinguished).[133]

**12-37**  In *Island Export Finance Ltd v Umunna*,[134] following a breakdown in relations within the company, a director (whom the court considered to be the managing director only in name)[135] resigned and within a few months obtained orders from the Cameroon postal authorities for his new company (this was business which previously the company had secured). At the time of his resignation, the court found the company was not actively pursuing further business with the Cameroon authorities. The court rejected a claim for breach of duty finding that there was no conflict of interest at the time he resigned (given the company had moved on to new activities) and, even if there was, the director did not resign in order to exploit it, hence there was no liability to account.[136] In *In Plus Group Ltd v Pyke*[137] the director in question had been excluded from all aspects of running the company for almost 15 months before his resignation which he had delayed to protect his interests as a shareholder in the company. In the absence of a fiduciary relationship (as a result of his exclusion) and any misuse of company property, he was not liable to account on contracts which he subsequently obtained from the company's main customer. In *Foster Bryant Surveying Ltd v Bryant*[138] the period was shorter, the director had ceased to act in any role as a director three months before his formal resignation, but the scenario was the same. Personal relations within the company had broken down and after a period effectively of isolation the director resigned and subsequently secured contracts from the company's main customer.[139] The Court of Appeal upheld the trial judge's finding that there was no breach of fiduciary duty by the director. His resignation had been innocent of any disloyalty or conflict of interest, i.e. he had not resigned to exploit a conflict of interest, there was no finding that any property or opportunity of the company has been taken or exploited by him, and he was not liable.[140]

### Disclosure and authorisation by independent directors

**12-38**  Prior to the CA 2006, a fiduciary who wanted relief from the strict application of the no-conflict duty had to seek the informed consent of the shareholders after full and frank

---

[130] [1986] BCLC 460.     [131] [2002] 2 BCLC 201, CA.     [132] [2007] 2 BCLC 239, CA.

[133] See Lowry and Sloszar, 'Judicial Pragmatism: Directors' Duties and Post-resignation Conflict of Duty' [2008] JBL 83.

[134] [1986] BCLC 460; see Grantham (2003) 66 MLR 109.

[135] [1986] BCLC 460 at 468.     [136] [1986] BCLC 460 at 482.

[137] [2002] 2 BCLC 201, CA. See also *First Subsea Ltd v Balltec Ltd* [2014] EWHC 866 where a director deliberately chose not to resign for some time because he did not want to trigger a compulsory transfer of his shares as required by the articles. He had been suspended and ordered not to communicate with staff or conduct business on behalf of the company, but the court held that he chose to remain as a director for his own purposes and therefore his fiduciary duties had not been reduced to vanishing point, but fell to be discharged in the context of the limited position in which he found himself, at [201], [203]. A difference here was that the evidence showed he could attend and call board meetings, he still had access to company financial information, and could still assert his authority internally in the company as a director, see at [200].

[138] [2007] 2 BCLC 239, see Lowry and Sloszar, n 133, [2008] JBL 83.

[139] The contracts came as a result of an initiative by the customer, not by the resigning director. A feature of this case was that the company's major client was willing to continue to use the company for as much work as it could handle but wished also to continue to work with the departing director and to that end offered to (and did) set him up in business following his departure from the company.

[140] [2007] 2 BCLC 239 at [89].

disclosure of all relevant matters,[141] although the articles typically allowed for certain conflicts (essentially interests in transactions with the company and related companies) to be dealt with by disclosure to the board.[142] These matters are discussed further later.

### Reform in the CA 2006—authorisation by directors

**12-39**  The major change in the CA 2006 is that the directors (other than interested directors) may authorise a conflict of interest and profiting therefrom (s 175(4)(b)). Authorisation by the directors overrides any common law requirement for shareholder approval *unless* (and this is an important qualification in terms of shareholder protection) an enactment[143] or the company's constitution imposes a requirement for shareholder approval (see s 180(1)). The power to authorise must be exercised by the disinterested directors acting in accordance with their duties, such as the duty to act in a way most likely to promote the success of the company (s 172)[144] and exercising care and skill (s 174). The director seeking authorisation remains subject to all his other duties which are cumulative (s 179) including the duty to act to promote the success of the company. An interesting puzzle raised by Farrar and Watson is whether even disclosure and fairness, or in this context disclosure and approval, can immunise a director if there is evidence that the director has not acted bona fide in the best interests of the company, for our purposes in accordance with his statutory duty under s 172.[145] Of course, whether anyone would subsequently be in a position to challenge an authorisation once granted is another matter, so these constraints may be more theoretical than real.

**12-40**  As Lord Wedderburn, the distinguished company lawyer, commented in the House of Lords, to alter from a position of shareholder approval to a point where only the authorisation of the board is required is to enter uncharted territory[146] and the Government accepted in the Parliamentary debates that this is a significant change to the law.[147]

**12-41**  The change originates from a recommendation of the Company Law Review (CLR) that 'the statute should (subject to any stricter rule in the company's constitution, or adopted by agreement) allow the company's rights to be waived by the board, acting independently of any conflicted director'.[148] The justifications suggested by the CLR for such a change (while acknowledging the possibility of board collusion) included that requiring shareholder approval is impractical and onerous; it is inconsistent with the principle that it is

---

[141]  *New Zealand Netherlands Society 'Oranje' Inc v Kuys* [1973] 2 All ER 1222; *Gwembe Valley Development Co Ltd v Koshy* [2004] 1 BCLC 131 at [65]; *Murad v Al-Saraj* [2005] EWCA Civ 959 at [71].

[142]  See, for example, The Companies (Tables A to F) Regulations 1985, SI 1985/805, Table A, art 85, set out at n 187; also arts 94 and 95.

[143]  For example, CA 2006, Pt 10, Ch 4 and 4A require shareholder approval in certain instances.

[144]  See Farrar and Watson, 'Self-dealing, Fair Dealing and Related Party Transactions—History, Policy and Reform' (2011) 11 JCLS 495, at 520–1, as to whether sufficient attention is paid by those approving conflicts as to whether or not it is a good idea for the company to enter into the transaction at all.

[145]  See Farrar and Watson, n 144, esp at 505, 520–3. They also make the point that, for larger (not just listed) companies, a useful reform might be to combine approval with an adequate explanatory statement to members, possibly approved by a regulator.

[146]  HL Deb, vol 678, GC 321–322, and 324 (9 February 2006). See generally De Mott, 'The Figure in the Landscape: A Comparative Study of Directors' Self-interested Transactions' (1999) 3 CfiLR 190.

[147]  See HL Deb, vol 678, GC 337 (9 February 2006): 'This is an area where the statutory statement of the general duties of directors will have made changes—I do not shrink from saying that they are significant changes—to the common law rules and equitable principles concerning conflicts of interest' (Lord Goldsmith for the Government). It is because of the significance of the change that companies formed under the CA 1985 are only able to take advantage of the new provisions if they pass a resolution allowing for independent authorisation in accordance with s 175(5), see n 158 and **12-44**.

[148]  Company Law Review, *Final Report*, vol 1 (2001), para 3.24.

for the board to make business assessments; and it stifles entrepreneurial activity.[149] The CLR concluded that allowing disinterested board approval would 'strike the right balance between … encouraging efficient business operations and the take-up of new business opportunities … and providing effective protection against abuse'.[150] The Government agreed that it was important that the no-conflict duty did not 'impose impractical and onerous requirements which stifle entrepreneurial activity'.[151]

**12-42** The argument that the no-conflict duty stifles entrepreneurial activity ignores the fact that the duty merely prevents a director in a situation of a conflict of interest from exploiting that situation. It does not mean that an economic opportunity is discarded. The opportunity will be exploited instead by someone other than a fiduciary with a conflict of interest. The central concern of the CLR and the Government initially seems to have been the narrow issue of liability in circumstances where the company could not or would not have taken the opportunity (a matter which, as discussed at **12-26**, is irrelevant to the application of the duty). The initial question was whether that element of the duty might be relaxed. The final broader change to the law arose because the CLR concluded, as the courts have done, that requiring a director to prove that the company could not have exploited the opportunity would raise major factual uncertainties. The solution, as far as the CLR and the Government were concerned, was to provide for board authorisation excluding the interested directors.[152]

**12-43** It is difficult to justify this change in the law even if it is accepted, as is sometimes argued, that the application of the no-conflict duty can be somewhat harsh. In fact, it is difficult to identify cases where the outcome could be so described.[153] In any event, the harshness of the application of fiduciary duties has always been an integral element of their deterrent effect, see **12-4**, and the harshness can be mitigated in terms of the remedies which the court is prepared to grant.[154] Far from 'encouraging efficient business operations' as the Company Law Review envisaged,[155] this shift to board authorisation may encourage the type of conduct which was criticised in earlier times. Instead of directors avoiding situations of possible conflict, they have the option of considering situations with a view to exploiting them personally, assuming they can get authorisation. They will be tempted to consider opportunities with half an eye to the personal exploitation of the opportunity rather than looking at it solely in terms of their duty to promote the success of the company for the benefit of the members as a whole.

### Requirements for authorisation—public and private companies

**12-44** For a public company to take advantage of this authorising power, the company's constitution must include an enabling provision allowing directors to exercise this power: CA 2006, s 175(5)(b).[156] The model articles do not make any provision for authorisation

---

[149] Company Law Review, *Final Report*, vol 1 (2001), para 3.23.

[150] Company Law Review, *Final Report*, vol 1 (2001), para 3.27.

[151] DTI, *Company Law Reform* (Cm 6456, 2005), para 3.3.

[152] Company Law Review, *Final Report*, vol 1 (2001), para 3.24.

[153] *Regal (Hastings) Ltd v Gulliver* [1942] 1 All ER 378, is commonly cited as an example, but see n 94. The outcome in *O'Donnell v Shanahan* [2009] 2 BCLC 666 seems harsh, see n 88, but the court did not have evidence before it as to the extent of any profit made by the defaulting fiduciaries which might alter the perception of the case.

[154] See *Murad v Al-Saraj* [2005] EWCA Civ 959 at [81], per Arden LJ ('… equity has been able skilfully to adapt remedies against defaulting fiduciaries to meet the justice of the case').

[155] See Company Law Review, *Final Report*, vol 1 (2001), para 3.27.

[156] Public companies formed under the CA 1985 must change their articles to allow for authorisation and many have done so to take advantage of this relaxation in the law. Public companies formed under the CA 2006 routinely include an authorisation provision in their articles.

so it cannot arise by default.[157] Vice versa, in the case of private companies formed under the CA 2006, the directors have the power to authorise conflicts in accordance with s 175(4) so long as there is nothing in the constitution which invalidates authorisation by the directors: s 175(5)(a). In the case of a private company incorporated before 1 October 2008, the members must pass an ordinary resolution permitting authorisation to be given by the directors.[158]

*Public companies*

**12-45**  With regard to public companies, it is difficult to see why directors in such companies would ever authorise private profit-making by a director in a situation of possible conflict between his personal interests and his duty to the company, especially in the light of the remuneration arrangements commonly available to directors of such companies, a fortiori where the company is a publicly traded company. The shareholders in these companies rightly demand and expect single-minded loyalty of their highly paid directors.[159] It might be argued that shareholders in public companies have a choice on this matter, given that they need to agree to the inclusion of an authorisation provision in the articles (CA 2006, s 175(5)(b)). In practice, the widely dispersed nature of shareholdings in public companies means that shareholders exercise little influence over the content of the constitution. Here, as on other matters, it is for institutional shareholders to take the lead, but they are not opposed to the adoption of authorisation provisions by public companies.[160] Presumably they take the view that their presence and influence ensure that most boards of public companies will be circumspect in their use of this power. Hence, it is commonplace for public companies to adopt the necessary authorising provision in their articles. Authorising directors in public companies may be wary, however, of granting authorisation as they remain bound by their own general duties[161] and they will also have an eye to protecting their own reputations.

*Private companies*

**12-46**  The greatest concern about the change from shareholder approval to board authorisation must lie with regard to the private company with a small number of shareholder/directors. In such companies, the exclusion of the interested director(s) from the board for the

---

[157]  See The Companies (Model Articles) Regulations 2008, SI 2008/3229, art 14 (Ltd); art 16 (Plc).

[158]  The Companies Act 2006 (Commencement No 5, Transitional Provisions and Savings) Order 2007, SI 2007/3495, art 9, Sch 4, Pt 3, para 47. Note that this requirement for shareholders to pass a resolution permitting the directors to authorise in accordance with CA 2006, s 175(5)(a) is not a transitional arrangement—it applies indefinitely to private companies formed before 1 October 2008. Each such private company must obtain a resolution of its shareholders before its directors are in a position to exercise these authorisation powers.

[159]  See *Bristol & West BS v Mothew* [1996] 4 All ER 698 at 712, per Millett LJ.

[160]  The GC100 Guidance, para 1.8 notes that shareholders (i.e. institutional shareholders) are unlikely to raise objections to the exercise of these authorisation powers provided the company has a sound governance structure, effective procedures for exercising the powers, and confirms compliance with such procedures. The GC100 group essentially represents general counsel and company secretaries of the FTSE 100 companies and it has issued guidance on conflicts: GC100: *Companies Act 2006—Directors' Conflicts of Interest*, 18 January 2008 (hereinafter the GC100 Guidance).

[161]  See HL Deb, vol 678, GC 326 (9 February 2006). The authorising directors will need to consider how allowing the conflict would promote the success of the company. The GC100 Guidance (n 160) suggests, for example, that allowing directors to accept other directorships could be seen as gaining access to industry or sector expertise which could be valuable to the company, but leaving aside other directorships, there is some difficulty in seeing the benefit to the company where a director seeks authorisation to pursue and profit from an opportunity in circumstances where he has a conflict of interest.

purposes of authorisation will do little to turn the board into an independent arbiter of this issue. In all probability the remainder of the board will be family members or close business colleagues who are likely to be incapable of exercising any independence on the issue of a director personally exploiting an opportunity in circumstances where he has a conflict between his personal interests and his duty to promote the success of the company. It will be difficult to assess the motives of the authorising directors in such small companies and the courts have always been sceptical (or realistic) about their ability to determine directors' motives in the face of an assertion that the directors honestly considered the interests of the company.[162]

**12-47**    The diversion and exploitation of corporate opportunities, information etc is central to the many disputes in these companies[163] which end up in court as petitions alleging unfairly prejudicial conduct under CA 2006, s 994 (see Chapter 19). Following the change in the law, the diversion of contracts and the exploitation of information and opportunities etc becomes approved profit-making by a director and, while a petitioner might be able to show prejudicial conduct, it is not unfair. A petitioner would need to show that the exercise of the power to authorise (or possibly even seeking authorisation) was contrary to understandings between the shareholders such that it amounted to conduct of the company's affairs in an unfairly prejudicial manner.[164] That argument may be difficult to make given that, in the case of a private company, if there was an understanding as to the exclusion of the power to authorise, it would be expected that specific provision would have been made to that effect in the articles, as is required by CA 2006, s 175(5)(a). Also, as noted at **12-44**, private companies formed before 1 October 2008 must pass a resolution allowing their directors to exercise these authorisation powers, in which case that resolution, arguably, would negate any suggestion that there was an understanding that the powers would not be exercised. Evidence of such a resolution will point the other way, to a taking of a power, not a resiling from it. It may not be possible therefore to challenge an authorisation using CA 2006, s 994.

**12-48**    It is also possible to envisage situations where the risk is to the company's creditors as where the directors (in a mutually beneficial way) divert business away from the company, as part of authorised conflicts, until eventually the company is left with insufficient assets to meet the claims of creditors. Again, theoretically, a claim for misfeasance under IA 1986, s 212 could lie against the conflicted director (not for breach of CA 2006, s 175, but possibly for breach of s 172(3) or against the authorising directors (again, possibly for breach of s 171 or s 172(3))), but whether a claim would be brought is problematic, given the costs issues involved in funding litigation by a liquidator, even before considering the difficulties of establishing the substantive case of breach of duty.

### Obtaining authorisation

**12-49**    Authorisation by disinterested directors is required. The section does not make clear whether authorisation can be by a committee of the board—it merely requires authorisation 'by the directors', a formula adopted in many company articles, though some articles specify that authorisation is a matter for the board. Arguably, the thrust of the

---

[162]  See *Regal (Hastings) Ltd v Gulliver* [1942] 1 All ER 378 at 392, HL, per Lord Wright; *Ex p James* (1803) 8 Ves 337 at 345: 'no court is equal to the examination and ascertainment of the truth in these cases'.

[163]  See for example, *Re Little Olympian Each-Ways Ltd (No 3)* [1995] 1 BCLC 454; *Re Full Cup International Trading Ltd* [1995] 1 BCLC 636; *Lloyd v Casey* [2002] 1 BCLC 454; *Allmark v Burnham* [2006] 2 BCLC 437; *Re Baumler (UK) Ltd, Gerrard v Koby* [2005] 1 BCLC 92.

[164]  See **19-59**; *O'Neill v Phillips* [1999] 2 BCLC 1, HL.

provision is consideration of 'the matter' by the directors as a board. But, as boards have considerable flexibility under the articles as to how any matter is addressed and since articles commonly provide that directors may delegate to any committee or person, it would seem that authorisation may be dealt with outside of a formal board meeting.[165]

**12-50**    Authorisation may be unconditional or subject to any restrictions which the disinterested directors choose to impose and, usually, the articles provide that authorisation may be varied or revoked at any time which gives the company flexibility to reconsider its position as circumstances may change. In terms of conditions attached to authorisation, the articles commonly provide for the exclusion of the conflicted directors from meetings and from the receipt of information on matters related to the conflict (and may specifically provide, for the avoidance of doubt, that such non-attendance and non-participation does not amount to a breach of duty by the conflicted directors). The articles also commonly provide that the conflicted director is not obliged to disclose to the company information that is confidential to a third party.

**12-51**    Authorisation is required with regard to specific transactions ('the matter') and it is not possible for a director to give a general notice of matters[166] giving rise to a conflict of interest in contrast with the position under CA 2006, s 177(2) (see **12-88**). The explanation given in the Parliamentary debates for the difference in approach was that s 177 deals with transactions where the company is a party to the transaction and will know the matters surrounding it, but the type of conflict of interest governed by s 175 will necessarily relate to things of which the company knows nothing and in respect of which a general notice would not suffice.[167]

**12-52**    There is no prescribed level of disclosure by a director (indeed s 175 makes no explicit reference to disclosure merely requiring that the matter be proposed to the directors for authorisation). In deciding whether there has been adequate disclosure, the court will be guided, no doubt, by the common law requirement of full and frank disclosure as to the nature of the opportunity so that the other (authorising) directors can see what the director's interest is and how far it extends, see the discussion at **12-86**. A director will have every incentive to make maximum disclosure for the consequence of inadequate disclosure is that authorisation is not validly obtained and the director would be in breach of the no-conflict duty (subject to the ability of independent shareholders subsequently to ratify the breach, see s 239).

**12-53**    Authorisation is only effective if the director in question and any other 'interested directors' are excluded from the quorum[168] (they do not have to be excluded from participation

---

[165] The GC100 Guidance, see n 160, envisages companies using a reviewing committee to review annually the exercise of the power, but the power should be exercised by the board (see Guidance para 4.10). It would seem that informal unanimous assent of the disinterested directors would also suffice, see *Runciman v Walter Runciman plc* [1992] BCLC 1084 at 1092.

[166] See *Moxon v Litchfield* [2013] EWHC 3957 (no authorisation when the strict requirements of the section were not met and in any event a purported general authorisation is not within the scope of the provision, see at [193]).

[167] See HL Deb, vol 678, GC 328 (9 February 2006) where Lord Goldsmith noted that a general notice in this context would leave the company too much in the dark.

[168] CA 2006, s 176(6)(a). The Government emphasised that compliance with the requirements of CA 2006, s 175(6) (quorum and voting position) does not of itself guarantee that it is a valid authorisation, but non-compliance with these elements renders it automatically invalid and the constitution may impose additional requirements: see HL Deb, vol 678, GC 326 (9 February 2006).

in the discussion, though the articles may so provide)[169] and the matter must be agreed without their voting or the matter would have been agreed to even if their votes had not been counted (CA 2006, s 175(6)(b)). There is no definition of who is an 'interested' director for these purposes and so is excluded. Many family companies have husbands and wives as directors and the question is whether a husband (as a disinterested director for the purpose of s 175(4)) could authorise an interested director, his wife, to exploit a situation on her own account.[170] The CA 2006 does not expressly address this point,[171] but if it is possible for a spouse to be treated as a disinterested director for these purposes, the risk of board collusion is significantly increased.

**12-54**    The answer lies not in definitions of family relationships for there is always a risk that the exercise of fiduciary duty may be influenced by any personal relationship.[172] The proper approach is to focus on the granting of authorisation and ask whether the authorising director, though not having a personal interest in the transaction, has a conflict of interest with regard to the granting of authorisation (i.e. a conflict between a personal interest in facilitating the other director by granting authorisation and his duty to promote the success of the company). If so, that (different) conflict would mean that the director would have to step aside by virtue of his obligations under CA 2006, s 175(1), unless the shareholders consent to his acting despite that conflict or, possibly, the articles so provide, relying on s 180(4)(a) and (b). Whether the authorising director would recognise the conflict of interest in this situation is another matter.

**12-55**    This same approach would apply to business associates on the board who may be close personal friends of the director seeking authorisation, though not related by family connection. As discussed at **12-48**, there is a risk of mutually supportive collusion between the interested director and such associates who may divide up opportunities between themselves and the company on a basis which favours their personal interests rather than the interests of the company as a whole. The risk from such collusion lies on the minority shareholders and the creditors. As appropriate, such directors too should be treated as having a conflict of interest and unable to grant authorisation, unless the shareholders otherwise resolve.

**12-56**    In small private companies, these exclusions may mean that there are no disinterested directors capable of forming a quorum or voting and so authorisation by the directors may not be possible,[173] which solves the problems identified at **12-46**. Of course, in any type of company, there may be occasions when all the directors are conflicted.[174] In these situations, the common law option, retained by CA 2006, s 180(4)(a), of seeking the informed consent of the shareholders would then be useful, see **12-58**.

---

[169] See Clark, 'UK Company Law Reform and Directors' Exploitation of "Corporate Opportunities"' (2006) ICCLR 231 at 239 who notes that, given the degree of influence that directors may exert on fellow directors, the interested directors should have been excluded from participation.

[170] See Prentice and Payne, 'The Corporate Opportunity Doctrine' (2004) 120 LQR 198 at 201.

[171] Many provisions of CA 2006, Pt 10, Ch 4 (for example, s 190) extend the application of various provisions to directors and connected persons (defined in s 252) but this categorisation is not used for the purposes of s 175(5).

[172] See David Richards J on this issue in *Newgate Stud Co v Penfold* [2008] 1 BCLC 46 at [240]–[242].

[173] In more dubious cases, we can expect to see people appointed to the board for short time periods precisely to provide a quorum of 'disinterested' directors who can authorise the matter and the courts will need to be alert to this possibility, as they were in a different context in *Re In a Flap Envelope Ltd* [2004] 1 BCLC 64.

[174] See, for example, *Lee Panavision Ltd v Lee Lighting Ltd* [1992] BCLC 22.

**12-57**  Finally, it is curious that there is no provision for shareholders to be notified of any authorisations granted under CA 2006, s 175(4)(b), whether in a public or in a private company (bearing in mind that shareholders do not have access to board minutes and also that authorisation may have been granted other than at a board meeting). The CLR had indicated that disclosure of the transaction in the annual accounts and reports would be an important safeguard,[175] but the Government was not persuaded that any additional protection was required other than the measures in s 175(6) re quorum and voting etc and the duties imposed on authorising directors.[176] It is impossible therefore for shareholders to gauge the extent to which these powers are being exercised and in what circumstances. Given the absence of any transparency, shareholders should consider imposing a disclosure requirement via the articles and larger companies may want to find a disclosure mechanism which is appropriate in their context.[177] The conflicted directors will also wish to ensure that there is an accurate record internally so that there is no ambiguity about the authorisation granted, its date, terms, and any restrictions, etc. Likewise, it is in the company's interests to maintain a detailed record in case of future disputes and possible litigation.

## Authorisation/ratification by the company

**12-58**  Where there are difficulties in securing authorisation by disinterested directors, it may be possible to look for shareholder authorisation[178] and s 180(4)(a) provides that all the general duties imposed on directors, including CA 2006, s 175, are subject to any rule of law enabling the company to give authority for anything to be done or omitted by the directors, or any of them, that would otherwise be a breach of duty. Another possibility is to seek to ratify a breach after it has occurred and ratification is governed by s 239 which requires a resolution of members other than the interested director (and connected members). While shareholders may appear to have a freer hand on authorisation which is not governed by the statute, there are common law limits which must be borne in mind. The general position is that a shareholder has a right to vote on any matter though he has a personal interest opposed to or different from the interests of the company, but that right is subject to some ill-defined constraints which preclude its use in what can be described as an oppressive, unfair, and improper manner.[179] Depending on the nature of the conflict for which authorisation is sought, those common law constraints may prevent persons voting as shareholders to give themselves authorisation as directors to exploit for their personal benefit a situation where, as directors, they have a conflict of interest. The common law position may therefore be closer to s 239 than might initially appear. For a fuller discussion of authorisation and ratification, see **20-46**.

---

[175] Company Law Review, *Final Report*, vol 1 (2001), para 3.24.

[176] See HL Deb, vol 678, GC 325–6 (9 February 2006).

[177] See GC100 Guidance, n 160, which suggests including information in the annual corporate governance element of the directors' report and, perhaps, a register of authorisations, see para 4.7.

[178] In the case of wholly-owned subsidiaries, a parent company may prefer to authorise conflicts in this way rather than give the boards of the subsidiaries the power to authorise conflicts of interest.

[179] See *North-West Transportation Co Ltd v Beatty* (1887) 12 App Cas 589, at 593–4, 600, per Sir Richard Baggallay, PC (director was able to vote as a shareholder to ratify his own undisclosed conflict of interest in a transaction with the company, but the transaction in that case was fair, the price market based, and the company benefited from the transaction, see at 596); also *Burland v Earle* [1902] AC 83 at 94, PC; *Menier v Hooper's Telegraph Works* (1874) 9 Ch App 350; *Cook v Deeks* [1916] AC 554 at 564, PC (majority shareholders cannot make a present to themselves of an asset belonging in equity to the company). See also *Citco Banking Corp NV v Pusser's Ltd* [2007] 2 BCLC 483 at [27]. See generally Hannigan, 'Limitations on a Shareholder's Right to Vote—Effective Ratification Revisited' [2000] JBL 493.

**12-59**  Authorisation must be on the basis of actual disclosure and consent and what the beneficiaries might have done, if there had been disclosure, is irrelevant[180] and the disclosure must be of all material facts[181] including disclosure of the source and scale of any profit to be made by the director,[182] so that the shareholders know what the director's interest is and how far it extends.[183]

**12-60**  Authorisation is typically by way of an ordinary resolution, but the *Duomatic* principle (informal unanimous assent, see **17-73**) can be called upon to authorise a conflict of interest as the Court of Appeal affirmed in *Sharma v Sharma*.[184] In this case, the informal unanimous assent of three shareholders (consisting of express consent by one and silence on the part of two, see **17-75**) sufficed to authorise a clear conflict of interest when the sole director of a family business (formed to acquire dental practices) also acquired dental practices in her own name. The director was found to have made full disclosure of the material facts and so, the shareholders, with full knowledge of the material facts, had acquiesced in an arrangement whereby the director could acquire some dental practices for herself and some for the company.[185] In those circumstances, the court said, there was no breach of duty by her.

### Authorisation via the articles

**12-61**  A company may make provision in its articles for conflicts of interest and the general duties owed by a director are not infringed by anything done or omitted to be done in accordance with those provisions (CA 2006, s 180(4)(b)). The extent to which such provision may be made is limited by s 232 which prohibits provisions exempting directors from liability for breach of duty, save such provision in the articles 'as has previously been lawful for dealing with conflicts of interest' (s 232(4)). There is uncertainty as to how much leeway this gives with respect to modifying the application of s 175 via provisions in the articles. It is unlikely that the courts will accept anything in the nature of a universal authorisation via the articles, for example with regard to conflicts arising from a particular class of transactions. Indeed when it is considered that Parliament has already significantly modified the no-conflict duty via s 175(4)(b), it seems unlikely that the courts will see much scope for further dilution of the duty in s 175 by provisions in the articles,[186]

---

[180] *Murad v Al-Saraj* [2005] EWCA 959 at [70]–[71].

[181] Informed consent is only effective if it is given after 'full disclosure': *FHR European Ventures LLP v Cedar Capital Partners LLC* [2014] 2 BCLC 145 at [5], per Lord Neuberger. *New Zealand Netherlands Society 'Oranje' Inc v Kuys* [1973] 2 All ER 1222. See Getzler who notes that the 'demanding requirement' of informed consent entrenches the obligation of loyalty, Getzler, 'Financial Crisis and the Decline of Fiduciary Law' in Morris and Vines (eds), *Capital Failure, Rebuilding Trust in Financial Services* (2014), pp 205–6.

[182] *Gwembe Valley Development Co Ltd v Koshy* [2004] 1 BCLC 131 at [66]; *Newgate Stud Co v Penfold* [2008] 1 BCLC 46 at [226]–[227]. See *FHR European Ventures LLP v Mankarious* [2012] 2 BCLC 39 at [104]–[107], disclosure of receipt of a commission without disclosing the amount, especially where the amount was significantly larger than customary, is insufficient, and see at [77]–[83] where Simon J usefully summarises the authorities on disclosure. See too *Parks of Hamilton Holdings Ltd v Campbell* [2014] CSIH 36, [2014] SC 726, an interesting Scottish case where a shareholder negotiating the sale of all the shares in the company as agent for all the shareholders failed to disclose additional profits which he secured in respect of his own position; the court emphasised that disclosure must be direct to the beneficiary and not via a third party (such as solicitors) and must be full disclosure of all material facts.

[183] *Movitex Ltd v Bulfield* [1988] BCLC 104 at 121; *Imperial Mercantile Credit Association v Coleman* (1873) LR 6 HL 189 at 205.

[184] [2014] BCC 73, [2013] EWCA Civ 1287. See also *Lee v Futurist Developments Ltd* [2011] 1 BCLC 653 at [46].

[185] [2014] BCC 73 at [59], [69], [72].

[186] The Government emphasised in the debates that it did not want a return to the old practice of widely drafted exemption clauses: see HL Deb, vol 682, cols 721–2 (23 May 2006).

a point confirmed by the wording of s 232(4) ('such provision as has previously been law-ful'). Generally therefore companies restrict their articles to repeating the wording of s 175(1) and making provision for authorisation, as discussed at **12-50**.

**12-62**   Measures 'previously lawful' included relatively modest pragmatic provisions reflect-ing the reality of business relationships, such as 1985 Table A, art 85[187] allowing a direc-tor, subject to disclosure, to be a party to, or otherwise interested in, any transaction or arrangement with the company or in which the company is otherwise interested (now reflected in CA 2006, s 177, discussed at **12-75**). Additionally, provision was commonly made (see 1985 Table A, arts 94, 95) to deal with quorum and voting requirements for board meetings where a conflicted transaction with the company was being considered. That background would further support the view that there is little scope for provisions in the articles with respect to the broader conflicts governed by s 175.

**12-63**   Of course, it is possible to use the articles to tighten, not to loosen, the requirements of CA 2006, s 175 by requiring shareholder approval in addition to authorisation by the direc-tors (see s 180(1)). In some companies shareholders may be more comfortable with the protection of shareholder approval rather than director approval, however disinterested.

### Disapplication of s 175

**12-64**   Finally, it should be noted that section 175 does not apply to a conflict of interest arising in relation to a transaction or arrangement with the company (s 175(3))[188] which is governed by a separate duty of disclosure under s 177 and s 182, discussed at **12-75**; and a director is not required to comply with s 175 if the conflicted transaction is approved or is exempt from approval under CA 2006, Pt 10, Ch 4, or Ch 4A, which require shareholder approval of specific transactions with or payments to directors (s 180(2)), see Chapter 13.

## C  Benefits from third parties

### Introduction

**12-65**   The CA 2006, s 176 makes provision for a distinct aspect of the no-conflict duty, namely the acceptance by directors[189] of benefits from third parties which would include the

---

[187]  The Companies (Tables A to F) Regulations 1985, SI 1985/805, Table A, art 85 provided as follows: 'Subject to the provisions of the Act, and provided that he has disclosed to the directors the nature and extent of any material interest of his, a director notwithstanding his office—(a) may be a party to, or other-wise interested in, any transaction or arrangement with the company or in which the company is otherwise interested; (b) may be a director or other officer of, or employed by, or a party to any transaction or arrange-ment with, or otherwise interested in, any body corporate promoted by the company or in which the com-pany is otherwise interested; and (c) shall not, by reason of his office, be accountable to the company for any benefit which he derives from any such office or employment or from any such transaction or arrangement or from any interest in any such body corporate and no such transaction or arrangement shall be liable to be avoided on the ground of any such interest or benefit.'

[188]  See *Burns v Financial Conduct Authority* [2017] EWCA Civ 2140 at [67]–[68] as to some uncertainty as to the scope of s 175(3).

[189]  The provision is limited to benefits accepted by the director, leaving some apparent scope for evasion by way of benefits conferred on persons connected with the director. For example, a third party might pay the university fees of the director's children in return for the director's support in ensuring that the company awards a contract to that third party. Leaving aside the difficulty in discovering such arrangements, the direc-tor would be in a position of conflict and CA 2006, s 175(1) would apply so such arrangements would be caught.

acceptance of bribes, the law looking broadly to any benefit or commission or bribe which puts the recipient in a position of conflict in breach of his duty of loyalty. The civil liability of a director is the same with respect to bribes, benefits, and secret profits (see Chapter 14), but additionally bribery is a criminal offence under the Bribery Act 2010.[190]

**12-66**    The relationship between CA 2006, s 176 and s 175 is unclear, in particular as to whether it is possible for directors to authorise (under s 175(4)(b)) the acceptance of benefits from third parties (obviously there is no question of authorising the acceptance of bribes). On the one hand, there seems no reason why benefits cannot be authorised since, as the Explanatory Notes make clear,[191] a situation where a director benefits from his position will fall into both sections, as a conflict and exploitation of a conflict within s 175 (there must be a conflict for s 176 to apply, see s 176(4)) and an acceptance of a benefit under s 176, and the duties are cumulative in any event, s 179. If s 175 also applies, then s 175(4)(b) must apply in the absence of any provision excluding its particular application in the context of s 176. It would also appear inconsistent that, under s 175, a director could be authorised by disinterested directors to exploit an opportunity for his personal benefit (which might yield significant profit) while his acceptance of a benefit conferred by reason of his position (which while generating a conflict may be quite a modest benefit) cannot be so authorised. Further support for the view that s 175 does apply is that s 180 deals with specific overlaps and exclusions between ss 175, 176, 177, and Pt 10, Ch 4 and 4A. It would have been easy for Parliament to have added a clause excluding the application of s 175 in circumstances which fall within s 176, but it did not do so.

**12-67**    On the other hand, it may be argued that the reason why benefits are singled out in CA 2006, s 176 is precisely to ensure that they cannot be so authorised, supported by the fact that the Explanatory Notes appear to rule out the possibility of board authorisation.[192] Section 176 is distinguishable from the broad brush of s 175 as it focuses on benefits conferred by reason of being a director or doing or not doing anything as a director, i.e. the focus is on the office of director *and* on payments by third parties that undermine the integrity of that office. In *FHR European Ventures LLP v Cedar Capital Partners LLC*[193] (see **14-28**) Lord Neuberger noted that bribes, and also secret commissions, undermine trust in the commercial world. Looked at in that light, as a matter of policy, it is right that payments by third parties conferred on directors by reason of their office should not be capable of authorisation by the board.

### The scope of the duty

**12-68**    As with s 175, liability is not dependent on establishing that the director acted to advantage the giver of the benefit or that the company suffered loss as a consequence, it suffices that a possible conflict has arisen for the principal is entitled to the undivided loyalty of

---

[190] Both the giver and the recipient of a bribe would be guilty of an offence under the Bribery Act 2010, ss 1 and 2. On bribes, see *Fiona Trust & Holding Corp v Privalov* [2010] EWHC 3199 at [70]–[73]; *Daraydan Holdings Ltd v Solland International Ltd* [2005] Ch 119 at [52]–[53]. 'Bribery is an evil practice which threatens the foundations of any civilised society': *Attorney General for Hong Kong v Reid* [1994] 1 All ER 1 at 4, per Lord Templeman. See too *Fyffes Group Ltd v Templeman* [2000] 2 Lloyd's Rep 643.

[191] See *Explanatory Notes to the Companies Act 2006*, para 344.

[192] See *Explanatory Notes to the Companies Act 2006*, para 344, though the statement in that paragraph is not entirely free from ambiguity, stating first that the acceptance of a benefit giving rise to an actual or potential conflict of interest will fall within s 175 as well as s 176 before then stating that s 176 is not subject to any provision for board authorisation. Of course, if s 175 applies, then s 175(4)(b) applies.

[193] [2014] 2 BCLC 145 at [42].

his agent.[194] The prohibition extends to a former director who may not accept benefits from third parties conferred by reason of things done or omitted by the director before he ceased to be a director (s 170(2)(b)). 'Benefit' for these purposes is to be given its ordinary dictionary meaning, of 'a favourable or helpful factor, circumstance, advantage or profit' and, in particular, 'benefit' is not limited to a tangible corporeal advantage.[195] All benefits, whether in cash or kind, such as appointing the director to another position, are included.[196]

**12-69** In *Premier Waste Management Ltd v Towers*[197] a director borrowed machinery for personal use from one of the company's customers (total benefit to the director in the region of £5,000).[198] The parties did not know one another, it seems, but a company employee asked the customer whether he could assist. Arguably, the benefit was conferred on the director by reason of his being a director with the customer assuming, presumably, that there would be some advantage to him in doing the favour, even if he did not know the director personally. The director did not disclose the arrangement (which he considered to be an entirely private matter) to the company which subsequently sued him for breach of the no-conflict rule. Having lost at first instance, the director appealed unsuccessfully. The matter predated the CA 2006 but, applying the statute, the situation may be interpreted as a benefit from a third party conferred on the director by reason of his being a director in breach of s 176.

**12-70** On appeal, Mummery LJ emphasised the simple, strict, and salutary duties of loyalty and no conflict to which directors are subject which he said are intended to recognise the primacy of the interests of the company which the director is trusted not to betray. Thus the fact that the company would not have been interested in this transaction with the customer, the absence of any finding of bad faith on the part of the director, the absence of quantifiable loss suffered by the company, the fact that the benefit to the director was small, and that the customer received no benefit from it, were all irrelevant[199] and, in Mummery LJ's view, missed the point.[200] A director's liability for disloyalty in office does not depend on proof of fault or proof that a conflict of interest has in fact caused the company loss. The simple position was that the director owed fiduciary duties and acted in breach of them by depriving the company of the ability to consider whether it objected to the opportunity offered by the customer being diverted away from the company to the director personally.[201]

## Limits to the duty

### Benefits from related companies or service agreements

**12-71** There are exemptions for benefits received from the company or associate companies or from persons acting on their behalf or from companies which provide services to the company via the director (CA 2006, s 176(2)). These exemptions are designed to ensure that directors' remuneration and service contract agreements, especially the common arrangement for the provision of a director's services via a management company, are not within the prohibition (see s 176(3)).

---

[194] *Fiona Trust & Holding Corp v Privalov* [2010] EWHC 3199 at [73]; *Daraydan Holdings Ltd v Solland International Ltd* [2005] Ch 119 at [52]–[53] with regard to bribes, but equally applicable to benefits obtained in a situation of conflict.

[195] See HC Official Report, SC D (Company Law Reform Bill) 11 July 2006, col 622 (Solicitor General).

[196] See HL Deb, vol 678, GC 330 (9 February 2006).

[197] [2012] 1 BCLC 67.      [198] See [2012] 1 BCLC 67 at [20].

[199] See Lord Russell in *Regal (Hastings) Ltd v Gulliver* [1942] 1 All ER 378, cited earlier in the text at **12-23**.

[200] [2012] 1 BCLC 67 at [48], [51].      [201] [2012] 1 BCLC 67 at [48].

### Acceptance not likely to give rise to conflict

**12-72**    There is no de minimis financial threshold with the Government choosing instead to limit the scope of the provision by reference to the risk of a conflict of interest[202] and so the duty is not infringed if the acceptance of the benefit cannot reasonably be regarded as likely to give rise to a conflict of interest[203] (CA 2006, s 176(4)). This limitation means that 'ordinary' commercial hospitality (meals, gifts, tickets for entertainment or sporting events) is not caught.[204] Guidance as to benefits which 'cannot reasonably be regarded as likely to give rise to a conflict of interest' may be provided in the articles (see **12-74**).

### Benefits approved or exempt under Part 10, Ch 4 or 4A

**12-73**    A director is not required to comply with CA 2006, s 176 if the transaction in respect of which the benefit arises is approved by the shareholders or is exempt from approval in accordance with CA 2006, Pt 10, Ch 4 or 4A (s 180(2)), see Chapter 13.

## Authorised by the company or via the articles

**12-74**    The shareholders may authorise the acceptance of benefits from third parties (CA 2006, s 180(4)(a)) and may ratify a breach of s 176 in accordance with s 239. The limits to authorisation and ratification are discussed at **20-46**. Acceptance of a bribe would be a breach of s 172 and s 176 and a criminal offence under the Bribery Act 2010 and cannot be authorised or ratified by the shareholders, not even unanimously. As noted, the articles may make provision for the acceptance of benefits from third parties (s 180(4)(b)), subject to s 232(4), see **12-61**, but for the reasons given there, which would be equally applicable to s 176, the scope for use of the articles is limited.

# D  Proposed transactions with the company

### Scope of the duty under s 177

**12-75**    The distinct situation where a director is in any way directly or indirectly interested[205] in a proposed transaction or arrangement *with the company* is governed by CA 2006, s 177, not by s 175,[206] and see **12-92**. A director's conflict of interest in a proposed transaction

---

[202]  See HC Official Report, SC D (Company Law Reform Bill) 11 July 2006, cols 622–4 (Solicitor General). The Government considered that any financial thresholds would be purely arbitrary.

[203]  See *Fiona Trust & Holding Corp v Privalov* [2010] EWHC 3199 at [73], quoted at n 47, as to bribes and 'little presents'; in *Premier Waste Management Ltd v Towers* [2012] 1 BCLC 67, discussed at **12-69**, the benefit was £5,000 but still placed the director in a position of possible conflict.

[204]  The 'value' of some of these benefits, such as tickets to prestigious events, may be greater than their financial value and hospitality over a long period of time may be cumulatively valuable so it may be difficult to determine at what point 'hospitality' crosses over into a conflict of interest prohibited by s 176.

[205]  See *Transvaal Lands Co v New Belgium (Transvaal) Land and Development Co* [1914] 2 Ch 488 at 503.

[206]  Of course, a situation under CA 2006, s 175 of potential conflict may evolve into a situation which then is governed by s 177 when that conflict gives rise to an actual transaction or arrangement with the company, for example, the director who is a potential supplier to the company (so within s 175) and who then secures a supply contract with the company for his business (and so is within s 177): see the GC100 Guidance, n 160. Vice versa, where a director acquires an interest in Company X and then a proposed transaction arises between his company and Company X, that is governed by s 177, but the circumstances of the director's interest in Company X (apart from the transaction) may fall within s 175. So the realities of business life may not lend themselves to the neatness of an application of s 175 or of s 177.

*with the company* may arise in all sorts of direct and indirect ways and it is not necessary for the director to be a party to the transaction with the company.[207]

**12-76** The leading authority is *Aberdeen Rly Co v Blaikie Bros*[208] where a company was entitled to set aside a contract for the purchase of railway equipment entered into between it and a partnership when it transpired that the chairman of its board of directors was also a partner in the partnership. The conflict of interest is obvious: the director is obliged to act in the interests of the company, in this case, to purchase goods on behalf of the company at the lowest possible price while, as a member of the partnership, he wishes to sell the goods at the highest price.[209] Where such a conflict exists, the law recognises that the director, despite his best intentions, may be swayed by his own self-interest.[210] The fact that the director is only one member of the partnership which is contracting with the company does not affect the application of the no-conflict rule nor does the fact that the transaction is fair nor is the extent of the director's interest relevant.[211] All that is relevant is the existence of a possible conflict of interest and duty. In *Movitext Ltd v Bulfield*[212] the directors leased property which they owned to the company and took security from the company with respect to its obligations under the lease. As the owners of the property, the directors were the lessors while, as directors of the company, they were acting for the tenant. In *Gwembe Valley Development Co Ltd v Koshy*[213] the company purchased foreign currency from another business controlled by the company's managing director. In these transactions, the director is on both sides of the relationship, acting on behalf of the company and acting on his own behalf and so in a position of conflict between his personal interest and his duty to promote the interests of the company. In *Burns v Financial Conduct Authority*[214] a non-executive director of company A sent various emails to Company B seeking a non-executive post with Company B at a time when Company B was in discussions with Company A as to how to develop their business relationship. Her unsuccessful defence was that, as no agreement had yet been concluded by the two companies and it was only a 'speculative prospect' at the time of the emails, she had no conflict of interest for the purposes of s 177. Only a brief survey of the authorities was necessary for the Court of Appeal to conclude that the director had placed herself in a position of conflict of interest when she sent the relevant emails.

> 'She was actively soliciting a remunerative relationship with [Company B], for her own personal benefit, at the very same time as she owed an undivided duty of loyalty to [Company A] to consider B's possible future business relationship with A dispassionately and with her mind unclouded by any potential conflict of interest. In our view, there was clearly a sufficient likelihood of a conflict of interest, viewed objectively, to engage the duty of disclosure under section 177(1), and to render the exception in sub-section (6) inapplicable.'[215]

---

[207] See, for example, *Burns v Financial Conduct Authority* [2017] EWCA Civ 2140.

[208] (1854) 1 Macq 461; and see Farrar and Watson (2011) 11 JCLS 495 on its significance and in particular on the relationship between *Aberdeen Railway v Blaikie* and the duty in s 172 to promote the success of the company suggesting that, while compliance with s 177 may ensure no breach of the self-dealing rule, it may not discharge the fundamental obligation of a director to promote the success of the company, to use the language of s 172.

[209] (1854) 1 Macq 461 at 471–2.

[210] (1854) 1 Macq 461 at 471–2; *Transvaal Lands Co v New Belgium (Transvaal) Land and Development Co* [1914] 2 Ch 488.

[211] (1854) 1 Macq 461 at 471–2; *Transvaal Lands Co v New Belgium (Transvaal) Land and Development Co* [1914] 2 Ch 488 at 503.

[212] [1988] BCLC 104.     [213] [2004] 1 BCLC 131.

[214] [2017] EWCA Civ 2140.     [215] [2017] EWCA Civ 2140 at [76].

As to her argument that she had not sought to influence the decisions of Company A in favour of Company B, the court noted that 'the point was not whether she actively favoured [B] in the competitive process, but whether [A] could count on her undivided loyalty at a time when she was making undisclosed overtures to [B] for her own benefit'.[216] The court upheld the finding that she had an undisclosed conflict of interest which had formed the basis for a justified conclusion by the Financial Conduct Authority that she was not a fit and proper person to be authorized by them for certain investment roles.

**12-77**   Of course, the mere existence of a conflict of interest is not necessarily to the company's disadvantage and the application of a strict no-conflict duty with regard to transactions with the company can be commercially inconvenient. The director may be willing to give the company a favourable deal and the prohibition of dealings between a director and his company may force a company to incur costs in contracting with an outsider when an insider is the sole or most favourable source of the goods or services which the company requires.[217] The director may have been appointed to the board precisely in order to foster certain business relationships and so possible conflicts may exist from the outset. Prohibiting all conflicts might simply drive these matters underground with directors going to some lengths to hide their involvement in particular transactions.

**12-78**   At common law, the commercial inconvenience typically was overcome by a provision in the articles requiring disclosure of the conflict and that disclosure regime was adopted in the CA 2006 as the statutory regime.[218] Hence s 177 requires a director who is in any way, directly or indirectly, interested in a proposed transaction or arrangement with the company to declare the nature and extent of that interest to the other directors,[219] before the company enters into the transaction or arrangement (s 177(1), (4)). Disclosure of the conflict of interest is required, not approval.[220] As the disclosure is before the company enters into the transaction, the board has the choice whether or not to proceed in the light of this information.[221] If not, that ends the matter. If, following compliance with s 177, the company does proceed, that decision to proceed in the light of the conflict can be seen as a consent by the company to the conflict (and to the director benefiting from the conflict[222]) and the transaction is not voidable at the option of the shareholders, unless an enactment[223] or the articles require shareholder approval (s 180(1)).

**12-79**   The statutory provision is limited to proposed transactions or arrangements with the company though the equivalent provision in Table A, art 85, extended to the director being a party to, or otherwise interested in, any transaction or arrangement with the company or in which the company was otherwise interested. It is customary therefore for companies to adopt this wider formulation in their articles (see **12-91**).

---

[216]   [2017] EWCA Civ 2140 at [78].

[217]   See *Boulting v Association of Cinematograph, Television and Allied Technicians* [1963] 2 QB 606 at 637.

[218]   The Company Law Review took the view that if, in practice, all companies opted out of the rule in *Aberdeen Rly Co v Blaikie Bros* (1854) 1 Macq 461 and substituted disclosure requirements instead, the law should reflect that practice and the rule should be disclosure.

[219]   This provision does not apply to shadow directors unlike CA 2006, s 182 which is specifically applied to shadow directors by s 187.

[220]   Note Lewison J in *Secretary of State for Trade and Industry v Goldberg* [2004] 1 BCLC 597 at [35]: 'This [required declaration of interest] is no mere formal requirement. It is a fundamental safeguard of the general obligation of a fiduciary not to place himself in a position where his interests conflict with those of the person to whom he owes fiduciary duties.'

[221]   The company can consider whether to enter into the transaction, on what terms, and with what safeguards, see HL Deb, vol 678, GC 334 (9 February 2006).

[222]   Assuming he has disclosed the benefit, see **12-86**.

[223]   For example, CA 2006, Pt 10, Ch 4 and 4A require shareholder approval in many instances.

**12-80**  Though not required to comply with s 175, a director subject to the disclosure obligations of s 177 remains subject to all the other general duties (s 179). Disclosure under s 177 does not obviate the need for compliance with Pt 10, Ch 4 or 4A which may require shareholder approval and it is also possible for the company's constitution to require shareholder approval in addition to disclosure under s 177 (see s 180(1)).[224]

**12-81**  In the event of a failure to disclose as required, any resulting contract with the company is voidable (because of the undisclosed conflict of interest in breach of duty) and may be set aside at the instance of the company without any enquiry as to the fairness or otherwise of the transaction.[225] The company has a choice whether to affirm or avoid the contract.[226] The right to avoid the contract is lost if: (1) the company delays unduly before rescinding; or (2) *restitutio in integrum* becomes impossible; or (3) the rights of bona fide third parties intervene.[227] If the company wishes to rescind the contract, the decision to rescind must be communicated clearly and promptly and until then the contract is valid and binding and continues in existence.[228] The contract cannot be rescinded if it has been fully performed.[229]

**12-82**  The company may hold the director to account for any profit which he has made from the transaction or require him to indemnify the company against any loss incurred and liability is not dependent on the company being able as a matter of law to rescind the contract.[230] Typically, a considerable period of time will have elapsed and the contract will have been performed before the director's breach of duty comes to light. It is an obligation to make good losses that would not have been suffered but for the breach of duty.[231]

---

[224] A premium listed company must comply with the Listing Rules (LR) requirements with respect to related party transactions ('related party' is defined in LR 11.1.4R and includes directors and substantial shareholders) which, subject to certain exceptions, require the transaction (other than transactions in the ordinary course of business) to be notified to the market, a circular sent to the shareholders (including a statement by the board that the transaction or arrangement is fair and reasonable as far as the shareholders are concerned and that the directors have been so advised by an independent adviser), and prior approval of the shareholders obtained (with the related party and associates required to abstain from voting)—there are modifications for smaller transactions, see LR 11.

[225] CA 2006, s 178(1); *Hely-Hutchinson v Brayhead Ltd* [1967] 3 All ER 98 at 103–4, 106–7, CA; *Guinness plc v Saunders* [1990] BCLC 402 at 417; also *Transvaal Lands Co v New Belgium (Transvaal) Land and Development Co* [1914] 2 Ch 488.

[226] A contract can be affirmed even if the company is in liquidation: *Ultraframe (UK) Ltd v Fielding* [2005] EWHC 1638 at [1441]. An unqualified demand for payment of sums due under a voidable contract amounts to an election to affirm the contract: *Ultraframe (UK) Ltd v Fielding* [2005] EWHC 1638 at [1449].

[227] *Hely-Hutchinson v Brayhead Ltd* [1967] 3 All ER 98.

[228] See *Re Marini Ltd* [2004] BCC 172 at 196.

[229] See, for example, *Re Marini Ltd* [2004] BCC 172; *MacPherson v European Strategic Bureau Ltd* [1999] 2 BCLC 203 at 219–20.

[230] See *Gwembe Valley Development Co Ltd v Koshy* [2004] 1 BCLC 131 at [144]–[145] (director liable to account for profit made on undisclosed conflict of interest in transaction with the company despite the contract having long been performed and therefore incapable of being set aside); also *Re MDA Investment Management Ltd, Whalley v Doney* [2004] 1 BCLC 217 at [111] where likewise the conflicted transaction could no longer be set aside but the director was liable to account for profit gained by him personally on the transaction; also dissenting judgment of Bowen LJ in *Re Cape Breton* (1885) 29 Ch D 795. In *Cape Breton* the majority held that the company could not affirm the contract *and* hold the director to account: *Re Cape Breton Co* (1885) 29 Ch D 795, but the distinguishing feature there was that the company deliberately adopted the contract with full knowledge of the conflict, see at 801. In the other cases, the company has lost the right to avoid the contract rather than positively affirmed it. A liability regardless of rescission is consistent with the statutory remedies in CA 2006, ss 195(3) and 213(3).

[231] *AIB Group (UK) Ltd v Redler* [2014] 3 WLR 1367.

## Interests which must be disclosed

**12-83**    The disclosure obligation applies to any interest, direct or indirect, of the director so a disclosure obligation may arise even though the director is not actually a party to the transaction with the company.[232] The duty of disclosure is not expressly extended to transactions or arrangements between the company and a connected person (as defined in CA 2006, s 252), but it is implicit in the statutory scheme that disclosure of such indirect interests is required with s 185(2)(b) providing that a general notice (permissible under s 177(2)(b)(ii)) may indicate that the director is to be regarded as interested in any transactions between the company and a specified connected person.[233]

**12-84**    The disclosure requirement extends to any transaction within CA 2006, Pt 10, Ch 4[234] so that transaction still requires formal disclosure to the directors[235] in accordance with s 177. Of course, given that Pt 10, Ch 4 requires shareholder approval (unless the transaction is exempt under that Part), it may be possible to establish that the directors 'knew or ought to have been aware' of the transaction and so disclosure is not required (s 177(6)(b)), but rather than rely on that provision, it is preferable, and easy, to make a formal declaration under s 177.

## Interests excluded from disclosure

**12-85**    The expansive scope of CA 2006, s 177(1) is modified by certain exclusions in s 177(5) and (6). Disclosure is not required of the following interests:

- an interest of which the director is not aware or where the director is not aware of the transaction or arrangement in question, which might be the case in respect of indirect interests (the director is treated, however, as being aware of matters of which he ought reasonably to be aware)[236] (s 177(5));

- an interest that cannot reasonably be regarded as likely to give rise to a conflict of interest (s 177(6)(a)). The company may use the articles to identify de minimis transactions which fall within this category and do not require disclosure under s 177. In a case of doubt, of course, it is preferable to make a declaration;

- an interest if and to the extent that the other directors are already aware of it (for these purposes, the other directors are treated as aware of anything of which they

---

[232] See *Burns v Financial Conduct Authority* [2017] EWCA Civ 2140.

[233] This interpretation is supported by the *Explanatory Notes to the Companies Act 2006* which state (para 347): 'An interest of another person in a contract with the company may require the director to make a disclosure under this duty, if that other person's interest amounts to a direct or indirect interest on the part of the director.'

[234] Matters within Pt 10, Ch 4A (directors' remuneration and loss of office payments, quoted companies only) will fall within the exemption from disclosure in s 177(6)(c) as concerning the terms of the director's service contract.

[235] The exemption in CA 2006, s 180(2) for transactions approved or exempt under Pt 10, Ch 4 applies only to ss 175 and 176 and not to s 177.

[236] Although this issue as to what the director ought reasonably to be aware of was the subject of some debate in Parliament, the Government's view was that the requirement reflected the current law. On the equivalent wording in CA 2006, s 182, the Solicitor General commented that 'this is an objective test so that it will take into account any relevant circumstances relating to that director; it will focus on the individual director. This is the question that will be asked: what is it reasonable to expect a director in those circumstances to have been aware of? For example, a non-executive director might be expected generally to be less aware of the individual transactions or arrangements entered into by a company': see HC Official Report, SC D (Company Law Reform Bill) 11 July 2006, col 628.

ought reasonably to be aware)[237] (s 177(6)(b)). The problem with this exemption is that, given that the consequence of non-disclosure is a breach of duty, few directors will want to rely on this exclusion and the safest course of action is to make a formal declaration;

- an interest in the terms of a director's service contract which terms have been or are to be considered by a meeting of the directors or a committee of the directors appointed for the purpose under the company's constitution,[238] an exclusion which addresses an issue which had arisen in the case law (s 177(6)(c)).[239]

### Manner and timing of disclosure

**12-86** The courts require strict compliance with the requirements of CA 2006, s 177 as it is the means by which a conflict of interest is addressed and the burden of proof is on the director to show that he made full disclosure before the company entered into the transaction or arrangement (s 177(3)). The disclosure required is full and frank disclosure of the nature and extent of the director's interest so that the other directors can see what the director's interest is and how far it extends.[240] Once made, further disclosure may be needed where a declaration proves to be, or becomes, inaccurate or incomplete (s 177(3)), but there is no need to update the original disclosure unless the transaction is still a 'proposed transaction' for these purposes. If it is not, s 182 would then apply.

**12-87** Disclosure must be to the other directors[241] and it would seem that disclosure to a committee of directors is insufficient[242] other than where the committee is merely the mechanism by which information is conveyed to all the directors. As disclosure has to be made to the other directors, there is no requirement of disclosure in the case of a private company with a sole director, but the director in that case must have regard to his obligations under CA 2006, s 171 (to act in accordance with the constitution) and s 172 (to promote the success of the company).[243]

---

[237] For a situation where the directors were aware or ought reasonably to have been aware of the nature and extent of a conflict, see *Re Marini Ltd* [2004] BCC 172. Previously, there were conflicting views as to whether formal disclosure was required even though all of the directors were aware informally of the conflict of interest: see *Lee Panavision Ltd v Lee Lighting Ltd* [1992] BCLC 22 at 33.

[238] The requirement that the committee be appointed 'for the purpose' suggests that it must be a formal appointments/remuneration committee rather than an ad hoc management committee.

[239] See *Runciman v Walter Runciman plc* [1992] BCLC 1084.

[240] *Movitex Ltd v Bulfield* [1988] BCLC 104 at 121; *New Zealand Netherlands Society 'Oranje' Inc v Kuys* [1973] 2 All ER 1222; *Imperial Mercantile Credit Association v Coleman* (1873) LR 6 HL 189 at 205. See also *Ultraframe (UK) Ltd v Fielding* [2005] EWHC 1638 at [1432]. See *FHR European Ventures LLP v Mankarious* [2012] 2 BCLC 39 at [104]–[107], disclosure of receipt of a commission without disclosing the amount, especially where the amount was significantly larger than customary, is insufficient, and see at [77]–[83] where Simon J usefully summarises the authorities on disclosure; also *Wrexham AFC Ltd v Crucialmove Ltd* [2008] 1 BCLC 508 at [31], [39]–[41].

[241] There is no mechanism for shareholders to be notified of disclosures made under CA 2006, s 177. Large companies must disclose, in notes to their accounts, particulars of transactions which the company has entered into with related parties if such transactions are material and have not been concluded under normal market conditions: see SI 2008/410, Sch 1, Pt 3, para 72. The Listing Rules (LR) require disclosure to and prior shareholder approval of certain related party transactions, see LR 11 and n 224.

[242] See *Guinness plc v Saunders* [1988] BCLC 607 at 611. For the same reasons, disclosure to the company secretary is insufficient unless the secretary is the mechanism by which information is relayed to all the directors: see comments by Solicitor General, HC Official Report, SC D (Company Law Reform Bill) 11 July 2006, col 630.

[243] To require a sole director to make disclosure to himself is a nonsense, see HL Deb, vol 678, GC 343 (6 February 2006). Where a sole director enters into a contract with his own company, the company must ensure there is a written record of the terms: CA 2006, s 231.

**12-88**    The declaration may (but need not) be made at a meeting of the directors[244] or it can be by notice to the directors in writing[245] or by way of a general notice.[246] There are detailed requirements in ss 184 and 185 as to what is a notice in writing or a general notice for these purposes.

**12-89**    A further issue is whether a director, having made a declaration of a conflict of interest, is able to participate in the meeting which considers the transaction. This matter is left to the company's articles and it is common for the articles to provide that the director shall not count in the quorum and his vote shall not count when the board considers the conflicted transaction or matter.[247] The model articles provide that the director is not to be counted for quorum or voting purposes, subject to: (1) a decision of the company by ordinary resolution to allow him to be counted, or (2) where the director's interest cannot reasonably give rise to a conflict (which is somewhat pointless since the section does not apply when the interest cannot reasonably give rise to a conflict, see s 177(6)(a)), or (3) where the director's conflict of interest arises from a 'permitted cause' which in the model articles (reflecting the position as it was under 1985 Table A, art 94) include guarantees given by or to a director in respect of an obligation incurred by or on behalf of the company or any of its subsidiaries; or subscription, or agreements to subscribe, for any shares or securities of the company or any of its subsidiaries or to underwrite or guarantee any subscription for any such shares; and arrangements with respect to pensions schemes and employee benefit schemes.[248] Other common permitted causes where the conflicted director may vote and count towards the quorum are resolutions regarding the purchase of directors' liability insurance (CA 2006, s 233) or the granting of directors' qualifying indemnities (s 234) or resolutions approving defence funding expenditure (s 205) and, in the case of public companies, resolutions about contracts with another company where the director has an interest of below 1 per cent in the equity share capital or voting rights of that other company. The list of permitted causes when the director can vote and can count towards the quorum, notwithstanding a conflict of interest, is often quite widely drawn in the articles.

### Authorisation by the shareholders or articles

**12-90**    As discussed at **12-58**, all the general duties imposed on directors, including CA 2006, s 177, are subject to any rule of law enabling the company to give authority, for anything to be done or omitted by the directors, or any of them, that would otherwise be a breach

---

[244] There are merits in a formal declaration at a board meeting, see Lightman J in *Neptune (Vehicle Washing Equipment) Ltd v Fitzgerald* [1995] 1 BCLC 352 at 359: all the directors are reminded of the interest; it is an occasion for a statutory pause for thought about the existence of the conflict of interest and the duty to prefer the interests of the company; and the disclosure should be a distinct happening at a meeting and be recorded in the minutes.

[245] In accordance with CA 2006, s 184: s 177(2)(b)(i). A notice in writing under CA 2006, s 184 is deemed to form part of the proceedings of a meeting of directors and therefore must be formally recorded in the minutes (applying s 248): see s 184(5).

[246] In accordance with CA 2006, s 185: s 177(2)(b)(ii). A general notice must be given at a meeting or it must be brought up and read at the next board meeting after it is given, to ensure that it forms part of the minutes of the meeting: ss 185(4), 248. A general notice may be to the effect that the director is a member of a specified company or firm and is to be regarded as interested in any contract which may, after the date of the notice, be made with that company or firm; or that the director is connected with a specified person and is to be regarded as interested in any contract which may, after the date of the notice, be made with that person: s 185(2).

[247] The articles may also provide that the director should not participate in the discussion of the matter.

[248] See The Companies (Model Articles) Regulations 2008, SI 2008/3229, art 14 (Ltd); art 16 (Plc).

of duty (s 180(4)(a)). It is also possible for the shareholders to ratify a breach of duty in accordance with s 239. The limits to authorisation and ratification are discussed at **20-46**.

**12-91**  As noted at **12-61**, it is possible for a company to include provisions in its articles to deal with conflicts of interest, and the general duties owed by a director are not infringed by anything done or omitted to be done in accordance with those provisions (s 180(4)(b)). The potential breadth of any provision in the articles is limited by CA 2006, s 232(4) to such provision in the articles 'as has previously been lawful for dealing with conflicts of interest'. Despite its partial reflection in s 177, many companies repeat the content of 1985, Table A, art 85 in their articles[249] and also Table A, arts 94 and 95 which dealt with quorum and voting requirements for board meetings where conflicts are considered, all measures which would be classified as provisions 'previously considered lawful'. The CA 2006 model articles also include certain provisions on conflicts within s 177 which companies may choose to adopt.[250] Hence it is common to find in the articles provisions allowing directors, subject to disclosure as required by s 177, to have an interest:

- by virtue of being a party to a transaction with the company or in which the company is otherwise interested,
- by virtue of being a director or officer or employee, or otherwise interested in (for example as a shareholder) any holding company or subsidiary company of the company or any other company in which the company has an interest,
- by virtue of the provision of paid professional services to the company or another company in the group by the director or his firm,
- by holding other directorships where there was no conflict of interest at the time of that appointment.

Finally, the articles can require shareholder approval of a conflict in addition to compliance with s 177 (see s 180(1)).

## E  Existing transactions with the company

**12-92**  Section 182 provides that a director (and a shadow director)[251] who is in any way, directly or indirectly, interested in a transaction or arrangement that has been entered into by the company, must declare the nature and extent of the interest to the other directors[252] as soon as is reasonably practicable.[253] As was explained in the Parliamentary debates, the reason for the distinction between s 177 and s 182 is that where it is a proposed transaction (s 177), the company is still in a position to decide whether it wishes to proceed with the transaction in the light of the conflict of interest whereas, if the conflict has arisen subsequently in respect of an existing transaction (s 182), the company has limited options in terms of responding to the conflict.[254] In the latter case, it is still important for disclosure to be made so that the company is aware of the director's conflict of interest which may be relevant to future decisions concerning the transaction.

---

[249]  The text of art 85 is set out at n 187.

[250]  See The Companies (Model Articles) Regulations 2008, SI 2008/3229, art 14 (Ltd); art 16 (Plc).

[251]  CA 2006, s 187: in this case notice in writing is required in accordance with s 184: s 187(4).

[252]  As to the required disclosure where there is only one director though there should be more, see s 186.

[253]  CA 2006, s 182(1), (4). Failure to make a declaration as soon as is reasonably practicable does not affect the underlying duty to make the declaration.

[254]  See HL Deb, vol 678, GC 334 (9 February 2006).

**12-93**    A number of possible scenarios will attract the application of CA 2006, s 182. One possibility is that the director had an interest in a proposed transaction with the company
which he neglected to disclose under s 177, in which case he is in breach of s 177 and also
in breach of s 182, assuming that the transaction has been entered into and he has not disclosed his interest. Another possibility is that the director had no interest in the transaction
for the purpose of s 177 at the time it was entered into, but subsequently becomes interested,
directly or indirectly, in the transaction or becomes aware of an interest in the transaction
(assuming it was not one which he ought reasonably to have been aware of, see s 177(5)).
On this basis, he need comply only with s 182. A third scenario is where he becomes interested in a transaction after it has been entered into (for example, he becomes a shareholder
in a company which has already secured a supply contract from the company) and so
must disclose his interest under s 182. Time passes and the renegotiation of the contract
arises, in which case it is arguable that the contract becomes a proposed transaction again
and he now comes under a duty to disclose his interest under s 177, unless he chooses to
rely on the defence in s 177(6)(b) that the other directors are aware or ought reasonably
to be aware of his interest. Section 175 does not apply to the conflict of interest arising
in relation to the proposed transaction (see s 175(3)), but there is potential here for the
application of s 175 more broadly in that the director now has an interest in a company
which may compete with his company in respect of some transaction, for example both
look to win a contract from the same customer. In that case, the director has a conflict of
interest generally that now falls within s 175. It is important therefore in every scenario to
remember that more than one duty may apply and the various duties may apply in different ways at different stages of a transaction or transactions.

**12-94**    The wording of s 182 reflects that of CA 1985, s 317 and the nature of that section was
considered by the Court of Appeal in *Hely-Hutchinson v Brayhead Ltd*[255] which concluded
that s 317, now CA 2006, s 182, merely created a statutory duty of disclosure.[256] The only
sanction for non-compliance with s 182 is that a director is liable to a fine and a breach of
s 182, or indeed compliance with it, has no effect on the validity of any contract entered
into by the company. Likewise, non-compliance with s 182 does not give a company a separate right of action for damages against a director; any right of action must arise from a
breach of fiduciary obligation by a director and not from a contravention of this section.[257]

**12-95**    The disclosure requirements under CA 2006, s 182 are identical to those outlined at **12-86**
et seq with respect to s 177. Disclosure may be at a meeting or by notice in writing or a general notice (s 182(2)). If the declaration proves to be or becomes inaccurate or incomplete, a
further declaration must be made (s 182(3)). A declaration is not required if the interest has
already been declared under s 177 (i.e. when it was merely a proposed transaction); or if the
interest cannot reasonably be regarded as likely to give rise to a conflict of interest; or is an
interest that the other directors are already aware of or ought reasonably to be aware of; or
the interest concerns the director's service contract which has been or is to be considered
by a meeting or committee of directors appointed for that purpose (s 182(1), (6)).

---

[255]  [1967] 3 All ER 98; endorsed by Lord Goff in *Guinness plc v Saunders*[1990] 1 All ER 652 at 665.
[256]  See [1967] 3 All ER 98 at 109, per Lord Pearson.
[257]  *Coleman Taymar Ltd v Oakes* [2001] 2 BCLC 749; *Movitex Ltd v Bulfield* [1988] BCLC 104 at 125.

# 13

# Specific conflicts—CA 2006, Part 10, Ch 4, and Ch 4A

## A Introduction

**13-1**  Following the discussion in Chapter 12 of the general duties governing conflict of interests, we turn in this chapter to consider CA 2006, Pt 10, Ch 4, and Ch 4A, which regulate transactions with directors where the conflict of interest between the director's personal interests and his duty to the company is thought to be particularly acute such that it is appropriate to seek shareholder approval for the following transactions, namely:

- directors' service contracts;
- payments for loss of office;
- quoted companies—remuneration payment and payments for loss of office (Ch 4A);
- substantial property transactions; and
- loans and similar financial transactions.

**13-2**  To a large extent, the provisions of CA 2006, Pt 10, Ch 4 reflect the long-established position on these transactions previously set out in CA 1985, Pt X. Such changes as were made[1] in 2006 were as a result, primarily, of a Law Commission review of CA 1985, Pt X.[2] The outcome was a number of mainly technical changes to the provisions and a closer alignment of their requirements so as to give greater consistency of approach. The overall effect is that CA 2006, Pt 10, Ch 4 generally relaxes the constraints previously imposed on these particular transactions and the criminal penalties imposed by CA 1985, Pt X have been removed on the basis that the civil consequences of breach provide sufficient deterrence.[3] Given the change in approach, it is important that directors, whether beneficiaries of these arrangements or instrumental in authorising them, remember their general duties under ss 171–177. Minority shareholders and creditors may have to rely on those general duties for protection against abuse of the more permissive provisions of Pt 10, Ch 4. Concerns over shareholders' ability to control directors' remuneration in quoted companies are reflected in measures introduced by Pt 10, Ch 4A.

---

[1]  See *Modernising Company Law* (2002) Cm 5553-I, paras 3.19–3.20; *Company Law Reform* (2005) Cm 6456, para 3.3; also the Company Law Review, *Developing the Framework* (2000), paras 3.86–3.89 and Annex C; *Completing the Structure* (2000) paras 4.8–4.21; and the *Final Report* (2001), paras 6.8–6.14.

[2]  See Law Commission, *Company Directors: Regulating Conflicts of Interests and Formulating a Statement of Duties* (Law Comm No 261), 1999, esp Section B (hereinafter Law Commission Report); preceded by a consultation paper of the same title, see Law Comm No 153, 1998.

[3]  See 678 HL Official Report (5th Series) GC 359 (9 February 2006).

**13-3** In respect of these transactions, therefore, directors must comply with their general duties under CA 2006, Pt 10, Ch 2 *and* seek shareholder approval under Pt 10, Ch 4 or 4A (s 180(3)), but if a transaction is approved by the shareholders under Ch 4 or 4A, or is exempt from approval under Ch 4 or 4A, it is not necessary for the director also to comply with s 175 (duty to avoid conflicts of interest) or s 176 (duty not to accept benefits from third parties): s 180(2). These are the only duties disapplied in these circumstances and compliance with the rest of the general duties remains a requirement.

## Overview of the general scheme of Part 10, Ch 4

**13-4** The provisions apply to directors including shadow directors (CA 2006, s 223(1)).[4] In many instances, the provisions extend also to transactions with connected persons, a category defined at length in ss 252–256. Essentially, the key categories of persons connected with a director are:

- members of his family;[5]
- a body corporate with which he is connected;[6]
- trustees of a trust the beneficiaries of which are the director or members of his family or companies with which he is connected (with an exemption for trustees of an employees' share scheme or a pension scheme);
- any partner of the director or a partner of any person who by virtue of any of the other categories is connected with that director; and
- certain firms with which the director is connected (s 252(2)).

**13-5** The overall scheme adopted in CA 2006, Pt 10, Ch 4 is that, for each class of conflicted transaction, prior shareholder approval is required by an ordinary resolution unless the articles specify a higher majority.[7] Where approval in a private company is by way of the written resolution, a memorandum setting out particulars of the proposed transaction/payments etc[8] must be circulated to the members eligible to vote on the resolution at or before the time at which the proposed resolution is sent to the members.[9] Where approval

---

[4] Shadow director is defined in CA 2006, s 251 and note s 251(3) which contains an exemption for parent companies in respect of Pt 10, Ch 4 transactions.

[5] Defined in CA 2006, s 253 and includes a director's spouse or civil partner, parents, his children or step-children of whatever age (previously, the category was limited to minor children), any cohabiting partner, and minor children of the cohabitant if they live with the director.

[6] Defined in CA 2006, s 254. Essentially, a director is connected with a body corporate if the director and persons connected with him together are interested in at least 20 per cent of the equity share capital of that company or are entitled to exercise or control the exercise of more than 20 per cent of the voting power at any general meeting of that company: s 254(2); and references to voting power, the exercise of which is controlled by a director, include voting power whose exercise is controlled by a body corporate controlled by him: s 254(4). See also s 255(2), (4), as to when a director controls a body corporate. See also CA 2006, Sch 1 (connected persons, interests in shares or debentures).

[7] References in the provisions to a resolution are to an ordinary resolution: CA 2006, s 281(3). Informal unanimous consent also suffices, at least under s 188 (shareholder approval of a director's service contract): *Wright v Atlas Wright (Europe) Ltd* [1999] 2 BCLC 301; and s 190 (shareholder approval of certain substantial property transactions): *NBH Ltd v Hoare* [2006] 2 BCLC 649 at [43]; the position with respect to improper loans may be more problematic, given the risk they could pose to creditors, see **17-81**.

[8] Other than in the case of a substantial property transaction within CA 2006, s 190 where there is no requirement of a memorandum, but the company still needs to ensure that the shareholders have sufficient information if they are to pass a resolution approving the transaction.

[9] CA 2006, ss 188(5), 197(3), 198(4), 200(4), 203(3), 217(3), 218(3), 219(3).

is by way of a resolution at a meeting, a like memorandum must be made available for inspection by the members for not less than 25 days before the meeting and at the meeting itself.[10] An accidental failure to send a memorandum to one or more members is disregarded for the purposes of determining whether this requirement has been met, subject to any contrary provision in the articles (CA 2006, s 224).[11] Approval is not required where the company is a wholly-owned subsidiary.[12]

**13-6**    A transaction which falls within more than one provision (for example a director may obtain a loan from the company and enter into a substantial property transaction at the same time) requires approval under each applicable provision (which should not prove a problem in practice since they are relatively uniform in approach) but it is not necessary to pass a separate resolution for the purposes of each provision.[13]

## B  Directors' long-term service contracts: CA 2006, ss 188–189

**13-7**    The length of directors' service contracts, particularly in public companies, has been controversial because of the level of compensation payable in the event of early termination of the contract.

**13-8**    CA 2006, s 188 requires prior shareholder approval[14] of any provision under which the guaranteed term of a director's employment with the company or, where he is a director of a holding company, within the group consisting of that company and its subsidiaries is, or may be, longer than two years.[15] Approval is not required where the company is a wholly-owned subsidiary (s 188(6)). The 'guaranteed term of a director's employment' has a distinct statutory meaning. It is a period longer than two years during which the director is employed if that employment cannot be determined by the company by notice or it can be so terminated only in specified circumstances (CA 2006, s 188(3)(a)) or, in the case of a contract which is terminable by the company by notice, the period of notice required is or may be longer than two years (s 188(3)(b)).[16] A provision included in contravention of s 188 and without the approval of the members is void, to the extent of the contravention, and the contract is deemed to contain

---

[10]  CA 2006, ss 188(5)(b), 197(3)(b), 198(4)(b), 200(4)(b) 203(3)(b), 217(3)(b), 218(3)(b), 219(3)(b).

[11]  This provision was added for the avoidance of doubt, but it does seem generously drafted, see 681 HL Official Report (5th Series), col 872 (9 May 2006). In small private companies, it may be difficult to prove that an opportune omission was not accidental. When coupled with the ability to pass a written resolution by a majority (CA 2006, s 282) rather than unanimity, as was previously the case, minority shareholders may find themselves ill-informed and unable to prevent approval being given.

[12]  CA 2006, ss 197(5)(b), 198(6)(b), 200(6)(b), 210(6)(b), 203(5)(b), 217(4)(b), 218(4)(b), 219(6)(b).

[13]  CA 2006, s 225. See 678 HL Official Report (5th Series) GC 360 (9 February 2006).

[14]  The approval required is of the company entering into the arrangement. If the arrangement is with a director of the company's holding company, the approval of the shareholders of the holding company is also required: CA 2006, s 188(2), but not if the company is a wholly-owned subsidiary.

[15]  CA 2006, s 188(1); the period was reduced from five years under the CA 1985. As before, rolling contracts, where the contract is novated daily, so that on any day there is always a two-year period of notice to run, remain an option. The Law Commission was critical of the use of such devices to circumvent the statutory policy (see Law Commission Report, n 2, paras 9.31–9.33) but the Company Law Review took the position that such rolling contracts are consistent with the policy objective of limiting the maximum period of notice in respect of which the director can receive compensation on termination: see Company Law Review, *Developing the Framework* (2000), paras 3.86–3.89 and Annex C. A 'company' means a UK registered company, see s 188(6).

[16]  Where the guaranteed term falls partly within CA 2006, s 188(3)(a) and (3)(b), the periods are aggregated: s 188(3).

a term entitling the company to terminate the contract at any time by the giving of reasonable notice (s 189). For premium listed companies, see **21-103**, the position is stricter in effect as the UK Corporate Governance Code (2018) states that notice or contract periods should be set at one year or less (Prov 39)[17] and that is accepted as the norm for listed companies.[18]

**13-9**  Directors' service contracts are defined in CA 2006, s 227 in such a way as to include contracts of service, contracts for services, and letters of appointment as directors (commonly used for non-executive appointments).[19]

> **'Directors' service contracts**
>
> (1)  For the purposes of this Part a director's "service contract", in relation to a company, means a contract under which—
>
> > (a)  a director of the company undertakes personally to perform services (as director or otherwise) for the company, or for a subsidiary of the company, or
> >
> > (b)  services (as director or otherwise) that a director of the company undertakes personally to perform are made available by a third party to the company, or to a subsidiary of the company.
>
> (2)  The provisions of this Part relating to directors' service contracts apply to the terms of a person's appointment as a director of a company. They are not restricted to contracts for the performance of services outside the scope of the ordinary duties of a director (CA 2006, s 227).'

**13-10**  The scope of CA 2006, s 227 was explained by Lord Sainsbury in the Parliamentary debates in the following terms:[20]

> 'Subsection (1)(a) covers contracts of service such as any employment contract that the director may hold with a company or a subsidiary of the company of which he is director, for example, as executive director, or any contract for services that he personally undertakes to perform as such.
>
> Subsection (1)(b) covers the case where those services are made available to the company through a third party such as a personal services company. In either case, the contract must require the director personally to perform the service or services in question.
>
> Subsection (2) brings within the definition of a service contract letters of appointment to the office of director. Many directors will have no contract of service or for services with the company. The second sentence of subsection (2) ensures that the definition of "service contracts" includes arrangements under which the director performs duties within the scope of the ordinary duties of the director, as well as contracts to perform duties outside the scope of the ordinary duties of the director. Without that, the term "service contract" might be interpreted as applying only to the latter type of contract.'

---

[17]  The Joint Statement on Executive Contracts and Severance by the Association of British Insurers (ABI) and the National Association of Pension Funds (NAPF), February 2008, para 3.5, stresses that a one-year notice period should not be seen as a floor. The statement strongly encourages boards to consider shorter periods since compensation for risks run by senior executives is already implicit in the absolute level of remuneration which they receive which mitigates the need for substantial contractual protection.

[18]  For premium listed companies, see **21-103**, the directors' annual report must include details of the unexpired term of any director's service contract of a director proposed for election or re-election at the next annual general meeting, and, if any director proposed for election or re-election does not have a service contract, a statement to that effect: Listing Rules, LR 9.8.8R.

[19]  See 678 HL Official Report (5th Series) GC 361–2 (9 February 2006); and Law Commission Report, n 2, paras 9.9–9.11.          [20]  8 HL Official Report (5th Series) GC 361–2 (9 February 2006).

Details of directors' service contracts must be available for inspection by any member at the company's registered office or other specified place.[21]

## C  Payments for loss of office: CA 2006, ss 215–221 (non-quoted companies)

**13-11**  Directors' remuneration arrangements typically make provision for payments to the director as compensation for the loss of office or on retirement from office. Problems most commonly arise when the company attempts to dismiss an executive director with a service contract. If the finance director is appointed by contract for a fixed term and the company exercises its power to remove him as a director before that term expires, the company will be liable in damages as the courts will imply a term that the company undertakes to do nothing of its own accord (for example, by terminating his post as a director) to bring to an end the circumstances necessary to enable a person to act as finance director.[22] As discussed at **13-8**, measures are in place to require shareholder approval of lengthy periods of notice. Further, the statutory controls on payments for loss of office (ss 215–221) were tightened in the CA 2006 (when compared with CA 1985, ss 313–316) with an emphasis on anti-avoidance provisions.

**13-12**  Compensation payments (sometimes dubbed 'rewards for failure') are often controversial, particularly in listed public companies where the size of such payments has attracted media attention and investor anger, especially as resignations or retirements may arise as a result of poor performance. For quoted companies, loss of office payments are governed by s 226C, discussed at **13-19**, which allows for such payments only to the extent that they are consistent with an approved directors' remuneration policy or if they are approved by a shareholders' resolution.

### Payments requiring approval

**13-13**  The basic scheme is that a company may not make a payment for loss of office (or on retirement) to a director of the company or to a director of its holding company unless the proposed payment is approved by a resolution of the members of the company and, if necessary, the members of the holding company (CA 2006, s 217(1)–(3)). Similar provisions apply: (1) where a payment for loss of office is made in connection with the transfer of the whole or any part of the undertaking or property of the company (s 218); and (2) where a payment for loss of office is in connection with a transfer of shares in the company, or

---

[21] CA 2006, s 228. The 'specified place' is a single alternative location situated in the same part of the UK as the company's registered office: s 1136; The Companies (Company Records) Regulations 2008, SI 2008/3006, reg 3. Members have rights to inspect and to take copies of any service contract: CA 2006, s 229; SI 2008/3006, Pt 3. These disclosure requirements extend to shadow directors (s 230) but they are unlikely to have service contracts.

[22] *Shindler v Northern Raincoat Co Ltd* [1960] 2 All ER 239; *Southern Foundries (1926) Ltd v Shirlaw* [1940] 2 All ER 445, HL. Where a director does not have a separate service contract and has simply been appointed under the articles, his position can be terminated at any time and he cannot recover any damages: *Read v Astoria Garage (Streatham) Ltd* [1952] 2 All ER 292. Indeed the company may specifically alter its articles to facilitate the removal of such a director and he will not be entitled to any relief: *Shuttleworth v Cox Bros & Co (Maidenhead) Ltd* [1927] 2 KB 9. It would be unusual now for a director, certainly in larger companies, not to have a service contract.

in a subsidiary of the company, resulting from a takeover bid[23] (s 219). Approval is not required if the company is a wholly-owned subsidiary.[24] If a payment is made in contravention of the requirement for member approval, the payment is held by the recipient on trust for the company making the payment and any director who authorised the payment is jointly and severally liable to indemnify the company that made the payment for any loss resulting from it.[25]

**13-14** The key to the statutory scheme is the expanded definition of 'payment for loss of office' in CA 2006, s 215 which includes payments for loss of office or on retirement as a director but also for loss of or in connection with retirement from any other office or employment in connection with the management of the company's affairs or the affairs of a subsidiary. The Law Commission had recommended this change in order to address a gap in the protection afforded to shareholders arising from the decision of the Privy Council in *Taupo Totara Timber Co Ltd v Rowe*[26] (interpreting the equivalent New Zealand section). The Privy Council had concluded that the then statutory disclosure requirement did not apply to any payment made to a director in respect of his executive position with the company. That loophole is closed by CA 2006, s 215(1).

**13-15** The definition extends to payments to directors or past directors (CA 2006, s 215(1)); payments in cash and in kind (s 215(2)); payments by other persons at the direction of the company (s 215(4)); payments to connected persons and to other persons at the direction or for the benefit of the director or connected person (s 215(3));[27] and payments to directors of holding companies.[28] All these payments need shareholder approval unless they fall within the exempt categories.

### Payments not requiring approval

**13-16** Approval is not required for a payment made in good faith:

(1) in discharge of an existing legal obligation,[29]

(2) by way of damages for breach of such an obligation,

---

[23] The purpose of the provision is to avoid the risk that directors may obtain advantageous payments from persons launching a takeover bid which should in fact go to the members in return for their shares, see comments by Lord Sainsbury, 678 HL Official Report (5th Series) GC 358 (9 February 2006).

[24] CA 2005, ss 217(4)(b), 218(4)(b), 219(6)(b).

[25] CA 2006, s 222(1); s 222(2)–(5) set out the permutations where more than one requirement is breached. In particular, the claims of the offeree shareholders under s 219 have priority over those of the company under s 217; see *Explanatory Notes to the Companies Act 2006*, para 413.

[26] [1978] AC 537, [1977] 3 All ER 123. See Law Commission Report, n 2, paras 7.38–7.48.

[27] The Law Commission considered that the provision should not be extended to connected persons, but the Company Law Review disagreed on the basis that other provisions of this Part apply to connected persons and therefore this loophole should also be closed: see the Company Law Review, *Developing the Framework* (2000), Annex C, para 5.

[28] CA 2006, ss 217(2), 218(2). The Law Commission had recommended this change to reflect the reality that many companies are today organised in groups and to prevent avoidance: see the Law Commission Report, n 2, paras 7.68–7.71.

[29] The 'existing legal obligation' must arise independently (for example, from a contract of employment) of the event giving rise to the payment for loss of office. It will not suffice if, as part of the event giving rise to the loss of office, a legal obligation is entered into to pay compensation: CA 2006, s 220(2), (3). The exemption allows payments to be made by associated companies (see s 220(2)) so a subsidiary may make a payment to a director in respect of a legal obligation of its holding company: see 678 HL Debs, GC 350 (9 February 2006).

(3)  by way of settlement or compromise of any claim arising in connection with the termination of a person's office or employment, or

(4)  by way of pension in respect of past services[30] (CA 2006, s 220(1)).

**13-17**  The exemption for payments in discharge of existing legal obligations—most 'golden parachutes' are a contractual obligation—gives statutory effect to the interpretation of the previous provision adopted by the Privy Council in *Taupo Totara Timber Co Ltd v Rowe*[31] and so merely states what was considered to be the law in any event. Overall, the exceptions are wide enough (especially the exemption for payments in discharge of existing legal obligations and that for pension payments) to ensure that few payments need the approval of the general meeting hence the significant level of shareholder dissatisfaction in listed public companies with these payments and the need for additional controls, see **13-19**.

**13-18**  Large and medium-sized companies must include details of the total amount of the directors' remuneration including the value of company contributions to the directors' pension scheme, the aggregate amount of any compensation paid for loss of office and payments to third parties for directors' services in the notes to the company's annual accounts.[32]

## D  Quoted companies–remuneration payments and payments for loss of office–ss 226A–226F

**13-19**  The general provisions on payments for loss of office (CA 2006, ss 215–221) do not apply to quoted companies (as defined in s 385[33]) which are governed instead by ss 226A–226F which apply to remuneration payments generally and to payments for loss of office.[34]

**13-20**  A quoted company may not make a remuneration payment or a payment for loss of office (defined in s 215, discussed at **13-14**)[35] to a person who is or has been a director of the company unless:

(a)  the payment is consistent with the approved directors' remuneration policy (which is set out in the directors' remuneration report, see **18-43**),[36] or

(b)  the payment is approved by resolution of the members of the company (s 226B and s 226C).[37]

Nothing in these provisions, however, authorises the making of a remuneration payment or a payment for loss of office in contravention of the articles (s 226D(5)). An obligation,

---

[30]  A further (and it would seem pointless) exception is provided for small payments which do not exceed £200: CA 2006, s 221.

[31]  [1977] 3 All ER 123 (interpreting the equivalent New Zealand provision). The Law Commission had recommended that, as that decision was likely to be followed, the statutory provision should be amended to make the position clear: Law Commission Report, n 2, paras 7.6–7.16.

[32]  CA 2006, s 412; The Large and Medium-sized Companies and Groups (Accounts and Reports) Regulations 2008, SI 2008/410, reg 8, Sch 5.

[33]  See CA 2006, s 385(2); a quoted company means a company whose equity share capital is listed in the UK or in an EEA State, or is admitted to dealing on either the New York Stock Exchange or Nasdaq.

[34]  CA 2006, s 215(5), subject to transitional provisions with respect to certain payments within s 226D(6).

[35]  See also CA 2006, s 226A(2)–(4) which deems certain payments to be payments for loss of office.

[36]  Meaning the most recently approved remuneration policy, approved in accordance with CA 2006, s 439.

[37]  Similar measures have been introduced via amendments to the Shareholder Rights Directive 2007/36, arts 9a and 9b, with effect from June 2019, OJL 132/1, 20.5.2017, but Member States have the option to make the vote on remuneration policy only an advisory vote.

however arising, to make a payment which would be in contravention of ss 226B and 226C has no effect (s 226E(1)), so protecting a company against contractual claims by directors.

**13-21**     Shareholders have a binding vote by ordinary resolution on the remuneration policy (CA 2006, s 439A), see **18-45**, and an advisory vote by ordinary resolution on the implementation of that policy (s 439), allowing them to react to how the company actually implemented the approved policy. In order to help shareholders monitor exit payments, where a person ceases to be a director of a quoted company, the company must post on its website as soon as reasonably practicable, (a) the name of the person concerned, (b) particulars of any remuneration payment and any payment for loss of office made or to be made to the person after ceasing to be a director, including the amount of the payment and how it was calculated (s 430(2B), (4A)).

**13-22**     The level of executive remuneration in quoted companies has been a controversial issue for some time[38] and the detailed disclosures required by the directors' remuneration report (see **18-43**) are intended to ensure that the shareholders are fully informed when asked to approve the company's remuneration policy and the remuneration packages for executive directors. For quoted companies applying the UK Corporate Governance Code (2018), the remuneration committee (see **6-42**) has delegated responsibility for determining the policy for director remuneration and setting remuneration for the board and senior management (Provision 33). The Code (2018) states (Principle O) that the board should satisfy itself that company remuneration and workforce policies and practices promote its long-term success and are aligned with its strategy and values. The reference to the workforce is a nod towards one of the main criticisms, that directors' remuneration is set in disregard of workforce remuneration policies, with restraint applied to the latter but not the former. The Code also provides that remuneration schemes and policies should include (clawback) provisions that would enable the company to recover and/or withhold sums or share awards, and specify the circumstances in which it would be appropriate to do so (Provision 37). These provisions enable a company to withhold payment or recover payments already made where, for example, the company has suffered a failure in risk management which only comes to light at a later date, or there is a downturn in performance which was previously unreported, such that the payments can no longer be justified. As noted at **13-8**, notice or contract periods should be set at one year or less (Prov 39). The Code also states that, in normal circumstances, shares granted or other forms of long-term incentives should be subject to a vesting and holding period of at least five years and that longer periods, including post-employment periods, may be appropriate (Prov 36). The focus in the remuneration report on the disclosure of the terms of remuneration and the focus in the Code on terms which remuneration committees should bear in mind or consider means that, for the largest companies, the law is dictating to some extent the terms, though not the levels, of executive remuneration. Market practice and the demands of institutional investors, many of whom have very detailed remuneration principles which they expect companies to adhere to, also dictate to some degree the terms of these contracts, see **6-47**. Meanwhile, the Government has commissioned

---

[38] See Geiler and Renneboog, 'Managerial Compensation: Agency Solution or Problem?' (2011) 11 JCLS 99, which discusses the component elements of the typical package. The authors conclude that many compensation contracts 'promote managerial self-dealing and the skimming of profits' (at 138), which may not be quite what shareholders had in mind. They noted that the use of stock options raises particular difficulties involving costs, manipulation, and incentive effects, while pay for performance is problematic given the difficulty of determining valid benchmarks. See also BIS, *Executive Remuneration, Discussion Paper* (September 2011), Ch 5.

research into how share buyback schemes are used and the review will examine whether the schemes are being used to inflate executive pay.[39]

**13-23** In the event that a remuneration payment or a payment for loss of office is made without approval, that payment is held by the recipient on trust for the company or other person making the payment.[40] Further, in the case of a payment by a company, any director who authorised the payment is jointly and severally liable to indemnify the company that made the payment for any loss resulting from it (s 226E(2)(b)), unless the authorising director can show that he or she has acted honestly and reasonably and the court considers that, having regard to all the circumstances of the case, the director ought to be relieved of liability[41] to the extent that the court thinks fit (s 226E(5)).

## E Substantial property transactions: CA 2006, ss 190–196

**13-24** Substantial property transactions are governed by CA 2006, s 190 (previously CA 1985, ss 320–322) which provides in subsection (1) that, subject to certain exceptions, a company may not enter into an arrangement under which:

  (a) a director of the company or its holding company, or a person connected with such a director,[42] acquires or is to acquire[43] from the company (directly or indirectly) a substantial non-cash asset (see **13-27**); or

  (b) the company acquires or is to acquire a substantial non-cash asset (directly or indirectly) from such a director or a person so connected;

  unless the arrangement has been approved by a resolution of the members of the company or is conditional[44] on such approval being obtained.'[45]

---

[39]  BEIS, Press Release, 28 January 2018.

[40]  CA 2006, s 226E(2)(a). Specific provision is made with respect to payments for loss of office on the transfer of the whole or any part of the undertaking of the company, or on a transfer of shares in the company resulting from a takeover bid, see s 226E(3) and (4).

[41]  Cf the wording of CA 2006, s 1157, discussed at **14-79**.

[42]  Defined in CA 2006, s 252 and see **13-4**. A trustee of an employee pension scheme, even if the beneficiaries include the directors of the company, is not a connected person for these purposes: see s 252(c); *Granada Group Ltd v Law Debenture Pension Trust Corp Plc* [2017] 2 BCLC 1, CA. The court will not expand on the statutory definition, see Lewison LJ in *Granada Group Ltd*, at [35], 'Parliament has chosen a specific class of person who falls within the definition of "connected person", and that must be taken to be the limit of relevant third parties, particularly since the definition of a connected person emphasises that a person is connected with a director "if but only if" that person falls within the class.'

[43]  There is no basis for interpreting 'is to acquire' as 'may acquire' so if there is only a possibility that a person may acquire an asset which would bring them within the section, the section is not engaged: *Smithton Ltd v Naggar* [2014] 1 BCLC 602 at [110], per Arden LJ.

[44]  Allowing a company to enter into a conditional arrangement was new in the CA 2006 and follows a Law Commission recommendation that companies should have that commercial freedom and flexibility: see the Law Commission Report, n 2, paras 10.8–10.10. If the transaction is conditional on approval which is not secured, the company is not subject to any liability by reason of the failure to obtain the required approval: CA 2006, s 190(3).

[45]  Previously, the transaction would have had to be disclosed in the notes to the company's accounts, see CA 1985, s 232, Sch 6, Pt II, para 15(c), but this is no longer a requirement. A substantial property transaction might in some circumstances have to be recorded in the notes to the accounts as a material related party transaction, see The Large and Medium-sized Companies and Groups (Accounts and Reports) Regulations 2008, SI 2008/410, Sch 1, para 72. Disclosure to the directors is required under CA 2006, s 177 so the item will be recorded in the board minutes (s 248(1)). For premium listed companies (see **21-103**), there are extensive disclosure and approval requirements for related party transactions in Listing Rules, LR 11.

**13-25**   No approval of the members is required if the company is a wholly-owned subsidiary (s 190(4)(b)); in those circumstances, the expectation would be that the parent company's control suffices to prevent abusive transactions. If the arrangement is between a company and a director of the company's holding company or a person connected with such a director, the arrangement must also be approved by a resolution of the members of the holding company.[46] If approval is required, but not obtained, the transaction is voidable (s 195(2)) but it is possible for the members (and, if necessary, the members of the holding company) to affirm the arrangement within a reasonable period (s 196) in which case it can no longer be avoided under the statute.

**13-26**   The purpose of requiring prior shareholder approval is to provide the members of a company with an opportunity to check on any potential abuse of position by directors and it allows a matter to be more widely considered and a more objective decision reached.[47] The section does not prohibit the interested director from voting as a shareholder in favour of the arrangement at the general meeting,[48] though the articles may do so, and there are common law limitations on voting which may need to the considered, see **20-46**.

**13-27**   Approval is required only if the value of the non-cash asset, at the time the arrangement is entered into, exceeds 10 per cent of the company's asset value and is more than £5,000 or exceeds £100,000 (s 191); and the onus is on the person alleging the contravention of the statutory provision to prove that the value of the non-cash asset exceeds the requisite value.[49] The question whether an arrangement falls within s 190(1) must be asked on the basis of the arrangement as at its inception.[50] 'Non-cash asset' is defined in CA 2006, s 1163(1) as meaning 'any property or interest in property, other than cash',[51] and, in that context, means a proprietary interest.[52] The definition is extended in s 1163(2) which provides that the reference to the transfer or acquisition of a non-cash asset includes the creation or extinction of an estate or interest in, or a right over, any property,[53] and the discharge of a liability of any person, other than a liability for a liquidated sum. In *Granada Group Ltd v Law Debenture Pension Trust Corp Plc*,[54] the issue before the Court of Appeal was whether the directors of a company had acquired a non-cash asset from the company when the company granted an equitable charge over assets (£40m worth of gilts) to secure the company's pension obligations under the pension scheme. The directors

---

[46]   CA 2006, s 190(2). For an example of the importance of securing the approval of the holding company (where necessary), see *British Racing Drivers' Club Ltd v Hextall Erskine & Co* [1997] 1 BCLC 182.

[47]   See *British Racing Drivers' Club Ltd v Hextall Erskine & Co* [1997] 1 BCLC 182 at 198. Informal unanimous assent suffices: see *NBH Ltd v Hoare* [2006] 2 BCLC 649, but see **17-80**.

[48]   The limitations on voting in CA 2006, s 239(4) apply only to voting to ratify a breach of duty.

[49]   *Niltan Carson Ltd v Hawthorne* [1988] BCLC 298. See also the Scottish case *Micro Leisure Ltd v County Properties and Developments Ltd* [2000] BCC 872 where the court concluded that the value should be determined in the context of the particular transaction which might include taking into account the value of the property to the director which may be different from the market value.

[50]   *Smithton Ltd v Naggar* [2014] 1 BCLC 602 at [95]; *Ultraframe (UK) Ltd v Fielding* [2005] EWHC 1638 at [1392].

[51]   This interest too must be enforceable: see *Granada Group Ltd v Law Debenture Pension Trust Corp Plc* [2017] 2 BCLC 1, CA, at [33]. See *Ultraframe (UK) Ltd v Fielding* [2005] EWHC 1638 at [1367]–[1410], esp at [1387]. A new anti-avoidance provision requires a series of arrangements or transactions to be aggregated: see s 190(5). A company's 'asset value' means the value of the company's net assets determined by reference to its most recent statutory accounts or, if no such accounts have been so prepared, the amount of the company's called-up share capital: s 191(3).

[52]   *Granada Group Ltd v Law Debenture Pension Trust Corp Plc* [2017] 2 BCLC 1, CA

[53]   CA 2006, s 1163(2) extends to rights that are not proprietary rights, provided that they can still be properly described as rights in or over property, see *Granada Group Ltd v Law Debenture Pension Trust Corp Plc* [2017] 2 BCLC 1, at [26]–[28], CA.           [54]   [2017] 2 BCLC 1, CA.

were beneficiaries of the scheme and the grant of the security had not been approved by the shareholders. The company tried to argue that what is now s 190 was engaged and that 'interest' in s 1163(1) went further than a legal or equitable proprietary interest, encompassing any economic or financial interest or advantage, and that the charging of the gilts was intended to confer an advantage on the directors which therefore constituted an interest. The Court of Appeal rejected the argument. The directors' rights to compel adherence to the pension scheme were personal rights against the trustee, not enforceable rights or interests in or over company assets which is what is required by s 1163(2).[55] These were personal rights that a director had by virtue of his status as a beneficiary under a trust, they were not rights which a beneficiary acquired from the company for the purposes of s 190(1). The Court of Appeal concluded there was no acquisition by the directors or connected persons (employee scheme trustees are not connected persons) of a non-cash asset and no approval was required.

**13-28**   The application of the statutory provision can be illustrated by *Re Duckwari plc (No 1)*,[56] where a company (Offerventure) entered into a contract to purchase a property for £495,000. Having paid the deposit, Offerventure agreed to pass the property on to Duckwari in return for Duckwari repaying the deposit to Offerventure and undertaking to pay the remaining purchase price. The shareholders in Offerventure were C and his wife and C was a director of Duckwari. The transaction was an agreement, therefore, by a company (Duckwari) to acquire a non-cash asset[57] from a person (Offerventure) connected with one of its (Duckwari's) directors. The acquisition was of a non-cash asset within the statutory threshold[58] and the approval of the shareholders of Duckwari was required under what is now CA 2006, s 190. Given that such approval had not been obtained, the transaction was in contravention of the statutory requirements. The liabilities arising from this contravention are discussed at **13-49**.

**13-29**   Approval is not required for a transaction between a company and a person in his character as a member of the company whether the acquisition is by a member from the company, or by the company from a member (s 192(a)).[59]

**13-30**   Approval is not required in the case of a transaction between a holding company and its wholly-owned subsidiary, or between two wholly-owned subsidiaries of the same holding company (CA 2006, s 192(b)). This exemption is designed to facilitate intra-group activities which might otherwise be affected because the acquiring company is a connected person of a director of the transferring company[60] and so the transaction would be within the general provision.

---

[55] [2017] 2 BCLC 1 at [39]–[40].      [56] [1997] 2 BCLC 713.

[57] Millett LJ noted that the asset acquired could be described either as the benefit of the purchase contract (i.e. the right of Offerventure to call for completion of the contract and conveyance of the property on the payment of the purchase price) or as Offerventure's beneficial interest in the property which was subject to an unpaid vendor's lien for the balance of the purchase money: see [1997] 2 BCLC 713 at 724–5.

[58] Millett LJ noted that, on whatever view was taken of the nature of the non-cash asset, see n 57, the asset was worth at least £49,500, see [1997] 2 BCLC 713 at 725. The trial judge had established that 10 per cent of the company's asset value in this case was £44,399 and therefore the case fell within the relevant financial thresholds: see [1997] 2 BCLC 713 at 715, 721.

[59] Lord Sainsbury noted that the intention in providing an exemption for members is to ensure that transactions such as a dividend *in specie*, the distribution of assets to a member on a winding up in satisfaction of his rights qua member, a duly sanctioned return of capital other than in cash, and issues of shares are clearly within the exemption and do not require shareholder approval: see 678 HL Debs, GC 347 (9 February 2006).      [60] See CA 2006, s 252 and **13-4**.

**13-31**   Approval is not required (either of the members of the company or of the holding company) for an arrangement entered into by a company which is being wound up (unless it is a members' voluntary winding up[61]) or is in administration (CA 2006, s 193).[62] The purpose is to ensure that a liquidator or administrator is not hampered in the execution of his duties when the directors may be the only possible purchasers of the assets of the company in liquidation or administration.

**13-32**   For the avoidance of doubt, CA 2006, s 190(6) makes clear that approval is not required in respect of a transaction so far as it relates to anything to which a director of the company is entitled under his service contract (as defined in s 227, see **13-9**) or to payments for loss of office (as defined in s 215, see **13-14**).[63]

**13-33**   As the consequences of contravention of the substantial property provisions (CA 2006, s 195) and the consequences of contravention of loan, quasi-loan, etc provisions (s 213) are essentially identical, the matter is discussed at **13-49**.

## F  Loans, quasi-loans, and credit transactions: CA 2006, ss 197–214

**13-34**   The CA 2006 significantly alters the position on loans from that which applied under the CA 1985. That Act prohibited (on pain of criminal sanctions) loans to directors and to connected persons and further prohibited quasi-loans and credit transactions in the case of relevant companies (essentially public companies or companies part of a group which contained a public company).

### Shareholder approval required

**13-35**   For private companies (other than private companies associated with public companies) loans[64] to directors[65] and directors of the holding company are permissible with the approval of the members and, if necessary, the members of the holding company. Shareholder approval is also required if the company is to give guarantees or provide security in connection with a loan made by any person to a director of the company or of its holding company. Approval is not required if the company is a wholly-owned subsidiary[66] and there are also various exemptions when approval is not needed. There are no restrictions on loans to connected persons (other than the need for the directors to adhere to their general duties when entering into such arrangements) nor on loans to directors of subsidiary companies provided that the director is not also a director of the holding company.

---

[61] In that case, the members retain an interest in the disposal of the company's assets.

[62] See 681 HL Official Report (5th Series), col 870 (9 May 2006). The exemption was not extended to receivers or administrative receivers apparently for fear of abuse of the provision, see HC Official Report, SC D (Company Law Reform Bill) (11 July 2006), col 632; also *Demite Ltd v Protech Health Ltd* [1998] BCC 638.         [63] See the Law Commission Report, n 2, paras 10.11–10.13.

[64] 'Loan' is not defined by the statute but the essence of a loan is a requirement for repayment: see *Champagne Perrier-Jouet SA v HH Finch Ltd* [1982] 3 All ER 713 at 717; *First Global Media Group Ltd v Larkin* [2003] EWCA Civ 1765 at [41]. Frequently, there is a dispute as to whether the sum paid has been paid as a loan (subject to repayment) or as an advance on remuneration (not subject to repayment): see, for example, *Currencies Direct Ltd v Ellis* [2002] 2 BCLC 482, CA.

[65] 'Director' includes shadow directors: CA 2006, s 223(1)(c).         [66] CA 2006, s 197(5)(b).

**13-36**   Public companies and companies associated with a public company[67] require shareholder approval, unless the company is a wholly-owned subsidiary,[68] for loans and also for quasi-loans,[69] credit transactions[70] and for the giving of guarantees and the provision of security, in this case whether the arrangement is for a director of the company or a director of its holding company or a person connected with such a director, but subject to certain exemptions discussed at **13-41**.

**13-37**   If prior approval is not obtained, the arrangement is voidable, but it is possible for the members (and, if necessary, the members of the holding company) to affirm the arrangement within a reasonable period (CA 2006, s 214).

**13-38**   In addition to shareholder approval, details of advances and credits granted by the company to its directors and of guarantees of any kind entered into by the company on behalf of its directors, must be included in the notes to the company's accounts (CA 2006, s 413).

**13-39**   The ability of companies, especially small private companies, to enter into these types of financial arrangements for their directors is potentially damaging to creditors' interests, especially in small private companies where shareholder approval would be easy to secure, though shareholders are constrained by common law limits to voting power, see **20-46**. Directors remain subject to their general duties in CA 2006, ss 171–177 and s 172(3) may be particularly relevant (need to consider or act in the interests of creditors in certain circumstances, see **10-41**).

**13-40**   As before, in order to reduce the possibility of transactions being constructed in a way which circumvents the requirements for approval, arrangements such as back-to-back transactions (whereby another person enters into a transaction which, if it had been entered into by the company, would have required approval) and the assignment and assumption by the company of rights and obligations which, if entered into directly by the company, would require shareholder approval, also require shareholder approval (CA 2006, s 203(1)), unless the company is a wholly-owned subsidiary (s 203(5)(b)).

## Shareholder approval not required

**13-41**   There are a variety of exemptions when approval by the members is not required. Generally the CA 2006 increased the scope of the exemptions and, in some cases, modified their application, for example to extend them to directors of holding companies and connected persons. Exemptions under more than one heading may apply.

### Expenditure incurred on company business

**13-42**   This generous exemption, being the most general in application, is important in practice for directors. Approval is not required for anything done by a company to provide

---

[67] 'Associated company' is defined in CA 2006, s 256 which replaces a more complex definition of a relevant company in CA 1985, s 331. A holding company is associated with all its subsidiaries and a subsidiary is associated with its holding company and all the other subsidiary companies of its holding company: see *Explanatory Notes to the Companies Act 2006*, para 406.         [68] CA 2006, ss 198(6)(b), s 200(6)(b), s 201(6)(b).

[69] CA 2006, s 199(1): a quasi-loan is a transaction whereby payments are made by a creditor (the company) on behalf of the borrower (the director), or the company reimburses expenditure incurred by another party for the director, on terms that the director or a person on his behalf will reimburse the company or in circumstances giving rise to a liability on the part of the director to reimburse the company.

[70] CA 2006, s 202(1): a credit transaction is a transaction under which one party (the creditor) supplies any goods or sells any land under a hire-purchase agreement or a conditional sale agreement, leases or hires any land or goods in return for periodical payments, or otherwise disposes of land or supplies goods or services on the understanding that payment, in whatever form, is to be deferred.

a director of the company, or of its holding company, or a person connected with any such director with funds to meet expenditure incurred or to be incurred by him for the purposes of the company or for the purpose of enabling him properly to perform his duties as an officer of the company, or to enable any such person to avoid incurring such expenditure (CA 2006, s 204). In this case, the aggregate value of the transactions must not exceed £50,000.

### Expenditure on defending proceedings or in connection with regulatory action or investigation

**13-43**    Approval is not required for anything done by a company to provide a director of the company, or of its holding company, with funds to meet expenditure incurred or to be incurred by him in defending any criminal or civil proceedings in connection with any negligence, default, breach of duty or breach of trust by him[71] in relation to the company or an associated company or in connection with an application for relief[72] or to enable any director to avoid incurring such expenditure (CA 2006, s 205), see **14-67**. The terms of the loan must provide for the loan to be repaid, or any liability of the company incurred in connection with any such loan to be discharged, in the event that the director is convicted in the proceedings or judgment is given against him (s 205(2)) though the company could decide to extend this requirement of repayment in the interests of the company, for example, to cover the settlement of any claim without a conviction or judgment.

**13-44**    For the avoidance of doubt,[73] it is specifically provide that shareholder approval is not required for anything done by the company to provide a director of the company or of its holding company with funds to meet expenditure incurred or to be incurred by him in defending himself in an investigation by a regulatory authority or against action proposed to be taken by a regulatory authority in connection with any alleged negligence, default, breach of duty or breach of trust by him in relation to the company or an associated company or to enable any such director to avoid incurring such expenditure (CA 2006, s 206), see **14-68**. In this instance, notably, there is no requirement that the funds be repaid but the directors authorising the provision of funds may wish to impose requirements as to repayment in the interests of the company.

### Small amounts

**13-45**    A company may make a loan or quasi-loan or give a guarantee or provide security (whether to or for a director of the company or of a holding company or even to a connected person) provided the aggregate of the relevant amounts does not exceed £10,000 (CA 2006, s 207(1)). Approval is not required for credit transactions where the aggregate value does not exceed £15,000 (s 207(2)). There is also an exemption for credit transactions if the company enters into the transaction in the ordinary course of its business and the value of the transaction is not greater and the terms are not more favourable than those which it is reasonable to expect the company to have offered to a person of the same financial standing but unconnected with the company (s 207(3)).

---

[71]  This exemption was narrowed from that in CA 1985, s 337A which applied to expenditure incurred in defending 'any criminal or civil proceedings'.

[72]  i.e. an application under CA 2006, s 661 (acquisition of shares by innocent nominee) or, more commonly, an application under s 1157 (general power of court to grant relief).

[73]  In the Government's opinion such expenditure is already included within the exemption for defence expenditure: see 678 HL Official Report (5th Series) GC 351–2 (9 February 2006); 681 HL Official Report (5th Series), col 871 (9 May 2006).

### Loans to associated companies

**13-46**    Approval is not required for loans or quasi-loans to, or credit transactions for, an associated body corporate or the giving of a guarantee or provision of security in connection with a loan or quasi-loan to an associated body corporate (CA 2006, s 208). The definition of associated bodies corporate in s 256 covers bodies which are subsidiaries of the other company or bodies which are both subsidiaries of the same body corporate, so this exemption allows for intra-group transactions.

### Money-lending companies

**13-47**    A company which is a money-lending company (defined in CA 2006, s 209(2)) may make a loan or quasi-loan to any person provided the loan is made in the ordinary course of the company's business and the amount of the loan is not greater, and the terms are not more favourable, than that or those which it is reasonable to expect the company to have offered to a person of the same financial standing but unconnected with the company (s 209). There is no monetary limit.

**13-48**    A money-lending company may also make a loan to a director or a director of its holding company or one of its employees to enable such a person to purchase their only or main residence, to improve their dwelling house, or in substitution for a loan provided by a third party for any of those purposes, provided that loans of that type are ordinarily made by the company to its employees on terms no less favourable (s 209(3), (4)).

### Consequences of contravention of loan or substantial property provisions

**13-49**    One of the aims of the restatement of these provisions in CA 2006, Pt 10, Ch 4, was to align the remedies more closely so the consequences of breach are practically identical[74] in s 195 (consequence of contravention of substantial property provisions) and s 213 (consequence of contravention of loan, quasi-loan, etc, provisions). The abolition of the criminal sanctions attached to improper loans further clarifies the position regarding remedies since there is no longer any issue of recovery on an illegal contract.[75]

**13-50**    Any arrangement or any transaction entered into in pursuance of the arrangement (and in the case of a substantial property transaction, whether by the company or by any other person) without members' approval in contravention of the relevant statutory requirement is voidable at the instance of the company unless:

(1)    restitution of any money or other asset that was the subject matter of the arrangement or transaction is no longer possible; or

(2)    the company has been indemnified for the loss or damage suffered by it; or

(3)    rights acquired in good faith, for value and without actual notice of the contravention by a person who is not a party to the arrangement or transaction would be affected by its avoidance (CA 2006, ss 195(2), 213(2)).

**13-51**    Regardless of whether the arrangement has been avoided, and without prejudice to any liability which might otherwise arise,[76] any director with whom the company entered

---

[74] There is a slight difference in the wording as between CA 2006, s 195(2)(b) and s 213(2)(b) but it is difficult to see that it makes any practical difference.

[75] See *Currencies Direct Ltd v Ellis* [2002] 1 BCLC 193, appealed on other grounds; *Tait Consibee (Oxford) Ltd v Tait* [1997] 2 BCLC 349.                                     [76] CA 2006, ss 195(8), 213(8).

into the arrangement; any connected person who entered into the arrangement with the company; the director with whom any such person is connected; and any other director who authorised[77] the transaction or arrangement[78] is liable as follows (CA 2006, ss 195(4), 213(4)), subject to certain defences:[79]

(1)  to account to the company for any gain that he has made directly or indirectly by the arrangement or transaction; and

(2)  jointly and severally with any other person so liable to indemnify the company[80] for any loss or damage resulting from the arrangement or transaction (ss 195(3)(a) and (b), 213(3)(a) and (b)).[81]

**13-52**  The scope of the obligation to indemnify the company was considered in *Re Duckwari plc (No 2)*,[82] the facts of which are discussed at **13-28**. The company, Duckwari, acquired a non-cash asset (a property) from a person connected with one of its directors in 1989 for £495,000. There was no evidence that the property had been under or over-valued at the time of purchase. By May 1993, however, when the property was valued for the purposes of the proceedings, and following the collapse of the property market, it was valued at £90,000. As it was no longer possible to avoid the transaction, the company sought an indemnity for the loss suffered by it. This hearing revolved around the point in time at which the loss or damage caused by the transaction should be measured.

**13-53**  The Court of Appeal held that the loss recoverable is the difference between the cost of the unauthorised acquisition and the amount realised on the sale of the asset and not the difference between the cost of the acquisition and the market value of the acquisition at that date. In other words, the full risk of the depreciation in value of the asset (which in fact occurred here) falls on the director or connected person who are treated as trustees liable

---

[77]  The burden of proof is on the company to show that the transaction was authorised by the director, but it is for the authorising director to prove the absence of knowledge which founds the statutory defence: *Lexi Holdings plc v Luqman* [2008] 2 BCLC 725 at [171], rev'd on other grounds [2009] 2 BCLC 1.

[78]  A director who knowingly allows a practice of improper loans to directors to continue is to be treated as having authorised the payments, even though he does not have actual knowledge of each individual payment at the time when it is made, and is jointly and severally liable therefore for their repayment: *Queensway Systems Ltd v Walker* [2007] 2 BCLC 577; *Neville v Krikorian* [2007] 1 BCLC 1, CA. It is the duty of a director not merely to ensure that a stop is put to the practice, but that steps are taken to recover the indebtedness outstanding to the company: *Neville v Krikorian* [2007] 1 BCLC 1, CA.

[79]  If the arrangement is between a company and a connected person, the director to whom he is connected is not liable if he shows that he took all reasonable steps to secure the company's compliance with the statutory requirements: CA 2006, ss 195(6), 213(6). A person so connected and any director who authorised the transaction are not liable if he can show that, at the time the arrangement was entered into, he did not know the relevant circumstances constituting the contravention: ss 195(7), 213(7). See *Lexi Holdings plc v Luqman* [2008] 2 BCLC 725 at [177], rev'd on other grounds [2009] 2 BCLC 1.

[80]  See *Re Broadside Colours and Chemicals Ltd, Brown v Button* [2011] 2 BCLC 597 (improper loans made to three directors—their liability is personal with respect to individual loans received by them and a claim in respect of the recovery of those loans is for the recovery of trust property and therefore no limitation period applies, but their joint liability to indemnify the company with respect to improper loans arises when the loan is made and is statute barred after six years).

[81]  In the case of a substantial property transaction in contravention of CA 2006, s 190(1)(a) (acquisition from the company at an undervalue), the liability of the director etc is to account under s 195(3)(a) and, in the case of a contravention of s 190(1)(b) (acquisition by the company at an overvalue), the liability of the director etc is to indemnify the company against loss under s 195(3)(b): see *Re Duckwari plc (No 2)*, *Duckwari plc v Offerventure Ltd* [1998] 2 BCLC 315 at 320; *NBH Ltd v Hoare* [2006] 2 BCLC 649 at [48]; CA 2006, s 190(1) is set out at **13-24**. In either case, it must be a gain made *by* or loss resulting *from* the arrangement or transaction.   [82]  [1998] 2 BCLC 315, CA.

to make good the misapplication of the company's money.[83] Such liability to account for the amount of the company's loss is strict and no question of foreseeability or remoteness, in particular, the foreseeability of a depreciation in value, arises.[84]

**13-54**   Finally, it should be noted that the common law is specifically preserved by s 195(8) (substantial property transactions) and s 213(8) (loans etc) which state that 'nothing in this section (i.e. s 195 and s 213 dealing with the civil consequences of contravention of the provisions governing substantial property transactions or loans etc) shall be read as excluding the operation of any other enactment or rule of law by virtue of which the transaction or arrangement may be called into question or any liability to the company may arise'. It is therefore open to a liquidator using IA 1986, s 212 (misfeasance) to pursue improper loans as misapplications of company money and a breach of duty by the directors rather than rely on a breach of the statute.[85] Where a director has received company money, as in a loan from the company, the burden is on him to show that the payment was proper and, likewise, where there are credit entries on the director's loan account, the burden is on the director to justify those credit entries and, if he cannot, the entries must be disregarded.[86]

---

[83]   See [1998] 2 BCLC 315 at 322.

[84]   *Re Duckwari plc (No 3)* [1999] 1 BCLC 168 at 171. At this subsequent hearing, the Court of Appeal clarified that the indemnity extends only to the loss resulting from the acquisition and does not extend to the means by which the acquisition was brought about. Duckwari could not recover, therefore, for costs incurred when it borrowed to fund the acquisition. But see *Murray v Leisureplay plc* [2005] EWCA Civ 963, [2005] IRLR 946 at [98], [117] where doubts are expressed as to this ruling in *Duckwari (No 3)*.

[85]   For examples, see *Queensway Systems Ltd v Walker* [2007] 2 BCLC 577; *Re Mumtaz Properties Ltd, Wetton v Ahmeed* [2012] 2 BCLC 109.

[86]   *GHLM Trading Ltd v Maroo* [2012] 2 BCLC 369.

# 14

# Directors' liabilities for breach of duty

## A Introduction

**14-1** Having reviewed the nature and extent of directors' duties to the company in Chapters 9 to 13, we turn in this chapter to consider the extent of the potential liabilities of directors for breach of those duties.

**14-2** As the duties of directors are owed to the company (CA 2006, s 170(1), see **8-13**), it is for the company to sue, though in limited circumstances a shareholder may sue derivatively on behalf of the company under CA 2006, Pt 11 (see Chapter 20). While it is for the company to sue, a claim may not be brought, despite an apparent breach of duty, for a number of reasons. The decision to litigate is a management matter for the board which must weigh up the time, costs, and adverse publicity involved and the likelihood of success and of recovery from the defaulting director. All things considered, the board may legitimately decide that it is not in the company's interests to sue.[1] Of course, in reaching that decision, the directors have to bear in mind their own duties, especially under s 171 to exercise their powers for the purposes for which they are conferred, under s 172 to promote the success of the company, and under s 174 to exercise care and skill. Frequently, a quiet resignation and possibly some agreement as to the repayment of sums to the company are preferable and justifiable. Litigation may arise on a change of control following a takeover when an incoming board may consider it has grounds for complaint against the former directors, or on liquidation where a liquidator may consider pursuing misfeasance (breach of duty) claims against the former directors in the hope of recovering some funds for the company's creditors.

**14-3** As far as the shareholders collectively are concerned, they too may choose to settle or waive or compromise a claim against a director for breach of duty[2] and they may choose to ratify a breach of duty (subject to certain limits to ratification, discussed at **20-46**). Individual shareholders may bring a derivative claim in some circumstances (see Chapter 20), but such claims are still unusual. Typically, a shareholder litigant will prefer to seek individual redress using CA 2006, s 994, the broad unfairly prejudicial jurisdiction (see Chapter 19), though on occasion (and exceptionally) recovery for the company may be the outcome of such proceedings, see **19-83**.

**14-4** Possible claims would be for breach of fiduciary duty or for breach of s 174, the duty of care and skill. Another possibility is a claim for breach of the director's contract of

---

[1] See CA 2006, s 239(6)(b) which confirms that the directors have the power to agree not to sue or to settle or release a claim made by them on behalf of the company.

[2] See, for example, *Smith v Croft* [1986] BCLC 207.

employment, if he has one.[3] It may be that the breaches of duty and of contract complained of (especially where business is diverted to another company set up by a director) amount to the tort of conspiracy to injure the company's business by unlawful means enabling a claim in tort to be brought against the fiduciary and those who are accessories to the breach.[4] Claims may be on multiple grounds,[5] subject to the court being alert to attempts at double recovery. For example, a company cannot claim for an account of profits for breach of duty and for damages for breach of contract arising out of the same actions but must elect as to which remedy to pursue.[6]

**14-5** In addition to civil claims, there is a possibility (admittedly slight) of criminal prosecution, for example, for fraud under the Fraud Act 2006, or receipt of a bribe under the Bribery Act 2010, and a dishonest agreement by directors to impede a company in the exercise of its right to recover secret profits made by them may constitute a conspiracy to defraud.[7] Disqualification proceedings post-insolvency are also a possibility, essentially on the basis that the breaches of duty establish that a person is unfit to be involved in the management of a company (disqualification is discussed in Chapter 15).

**14-6** There are then a variety of possible consequences where directors are found to have acted in breach of duty. The focus of this chapter is the extent of a director's civil liability for breach of fiduciary duty and the liability of third parties involved in some way in that breach of duty.[8] The ability to mitigate potential liabilities through reliance on indemnity provisions, insurance, and by application to the court for relief is also considered.

## B  Claim for breach of fiduciary duty

### Introduction

**14-7** The original intention was to complement the statutory statement of directors' duties in the CA 2006 with a statement of remedies for breach of duty, see **8-7**, but it proved impossible to devise a coherent and comprehensive statement of the multiple options available. Instead, CA 2006, s 178 preserves the existing law and allows for its continued development in the normal way. Section 178 provides:

'(1) The consequences of breach (or threatened breach) of sections 171 to 177 are the same as would apply if the corresponding common law rule or equitable principle applied.

(2) The duties in those sections (with the exception of section 174 (duty to exercise reasonable care, skill and diligence)) are, accordingly, enforceable in the same way as any other fiduciary duty owed to a company by its directors.'

---

[3] See, for example, *Simtel Communications Ltd v Rebak* [2006] 2 BCLC 571; *Shepherds Investments Ltd v Walters* [2007] 2 BCLC 202. As to whether a third party who engages with the defaulting fiduciaries in a new venture is liable in damages in tort for having induced or procured a breach of contract on their part, see *Mainstream Properties Ltd v Young*, one of the appeals in *OBG v Allan* [2007] 4 All ER 545, HL.

[4] *OBG Ltd v Allan* [2007] 4 All ER 545, HL. See *Simtel Communications Ltd v Rebak* [2006] 2 BCLC 571; *British Midland Tool Ltd v Midland International Tooling Ltd* [2003] 2 BCLC 523; *First Subsea Ltd v Balltec Ltd* [2018] 1 BCLC 20, CA.

[5] For an example of the multiple claims which may be made, see *First Subsea Ltd v Balltec Ltd* [2018] 1 BCLC 20, CA.

[6] See *Coleman Taymar Ltd v Oakes* [2001] 2 BCLC 749 at [79]–[80].

[7] *Adams v* The Queen [1995] 2 BCLC 17, PC.

[8] See, generally, the valuable analysis of the remedies awarded against defaulting fiduciaries by Elliott and Mitchell, 'Remedies for Dishonest Assistance' (2004) 67 MLR 16, esp at 23–36.

### Terminology—fiduciaries—trustee-like responsibilities

**14-8**    A fiduciary was defined by Millett LJ in *Bristol & West BS v Mothew*[9] as someone who has undertaken to act for or on behalf of another in a particular matter in circumstances which give rise to a relationship of trust and confidence. Those circumstances commonly are control of the person's assets or part of their assets and autonomy to act in their respect.[10] Given that, typically, directors have all powers of management over the company and its assets, directors are indisputably fiduciaries.[11] As directors are fiduciaries and as the most common class of fiduciaries are trustees, it is common to describe directors as trustees[12] and to describe breaches of duty by them as breaches of trust or of fiduciary duty and, in particular, to equate directors with trustees for the purpose of their liability to make good any misapplication of the company's assets. The classic statement of their position comes from Lindley LJ in *Re Lands Allotment Co*:[13]

> 'Although directors are not properly speaking trustees, yet they have always been considered and treated as trustees of money which comes to their hands or which is actually under their control; and ever since joint stock companies were invented directors have been liable to make good moneys which they have misapplied upon the same footing as if they were trustees.'

The point was also made in the same case by Kay LJ noting that: '[a]s directors they are not trustees at all. They are only trustees *qua* the particular property which is put into their hands or under their control, and which they have applied in a manner which is beyond the powers of the company.'[14] Given his position, a director's possession of a company asset, in the language of Millett LJ, '... is coloured from the first by the trust and confidence by means of which he obtained it, and his subsequent appropriation of the property to his own use is a breach of that trust'.[15]

**14-9**    It is common in this context of claims and remedies to talk of directors being liable as constructive trustees, but this use should be avoided as it is misleading. As Millett LJ explained in the much cited *Paragon Finance plc v D B Thakerar & Co*,[16] the term 'constructive trustee' is used in two entirely different ways, first, in the sense of someone who is really a trustee (class 1 *Paragon*) and, secondly, where a constructive trust is imposed as a remedy consequent to some unlawful transaction (class 2 *Paragon*) when a person sufficiently implicated in a fraud is rendered accountable in equity.[17] Describing the latter as a constructive trustee is unfortunate, Millett LJ said, since such a person is not

---

[9] [1996] 4 All ER 698 at 711, and see *FHR European Ventures LLP v Cedar Capital Partners LLC* [2014] 2 BCLC 145 at [5]. See generally Millett, 'Equity's Place in the Law of Commerce' (1998) 114 LQR 214; also Eder J in *Saltri III Ltd v MD Mezzanine SA SICAR* [2013] 2 BCLC 217 at [123] for a valuable summation of the essence of a fiduciary relationship.

[10] See Conaglen, 'The Nature and Function of Fiduciary Loyalty' (2005) 121 LQR 452.

[11] See Finn, *Fiduciary Obligations* (1977), Ch 1; Finn, 'The Fiduciary Principle' in Youdan (ed), *Equity, Fiduciaries and Trusts* (1989), Ch 1; *Regal (Hastings) Ltd v Gulliver* (1942) 1 All ER 378 at 395; *Williams v Central Bank of Nigeria* [2014] 2 All ER 489 at [9].

[12] The analogy is not entirely accurate as directors, unlike trustees, are risk-takers and appointed as such.

[13] [1894] 1 Ch 616 at 631; *Belmont Finance Corp v Williams Furniture Ltd* [1980] 1 All ER 393 at 405; *Re Duckwari plc (No 2)* [1998] 2 BCLC 315 at 321–2; *JJ Harrison (Properties) Ltd v Harrison* [2002] 1 BCLC 162 at [29]. See also *Great Eastern Railway Co v Turner* (1872) LR 8 Ch App 149.

[14] [1894] 1 Ch 616 at 639.

[15] *Paragon Finance plc v DB Thakerar & Co* [1999] 1 All ER 400 at 409, per Millett LJ.

[16] [1999] 1 All ER 400. See generally Smith, 'Constructive Trusts and Constructive Trustees' (1999) 58 CLJ 294.

[17] [1999] 1 All ER 400 at 409.

in fact a trustee at all and the phrase 'constructive trust' is being used as nothing more than 'a formula for equitable relief'.[18] He went on: 'They are in reality neither trustees nor fiduciaries, but merely wrongdoers.'[19] The terminology for this class of case, Millett LJ subsequently said, should be 'accountable in equity',[20] and equitable accounting can encompass both proprietary and non-proprietary claims.[21] The distinction drawn by Millett LJ is widely accepted with, for example, Lord Sumption in *Williams v Central Bank of Nigeria*,[22] agreeing that these persons within the second category are not trustees, rather they are persons 'who have exposed themselves to equitable remedies by virtue of their participation in the unlawful misapplication of trust assets', either as dishonest assistants or knowing recipients. In these cases, he noted, the intervention of equity is purely remedial.

**14-10**  That directors who misappropriate the company's property for themselves in breach of duty are class 1 *Paragon* trustees is beyond dispute, as Chadwick LJ noted in *JJ Harrison (Properties) Ltd v Harrison*.[23] In that case a director acquired land at an undervalue from his company in circumstances which amounted to a breach of his duty to act in the interests of the company (now CA 2006, s 172). The director subsequently sold that land for a substantial gain. The Court of Appeal concluded that his possession of the land was subject to his pre-existing obligations as a trustee of that land (a class 1 *Paragon*), a status derived not from the transaction by which he came to possess the property, but from his appointment as a director.[24] Therefore he held the property on trust, i.e. as a trustee, for the company and when he sold it, he sold it for the company, see further at **14-19**. As Patten LJ explained in *First Subsea Ltd v Balltec Ltd*,[25] the defining characteristic of the class 1 *Paragon* is that the trustee should be in lawful possession of trust property, citing *JJ Harrison (Properties) Ltd v Harrison*[26] as an example of the category.

---

[18] [1999] 1 All ER 400 at 409, citing Ungoed-Thomas J in *Selangor United Rubber Estates Ltd v Cradock and Others (No 3)* [1968] 1 WLR 1555 at 1582, that the defendant shall be liable as though he were a trustee, though he is not a trustee; *Williams v Central Bank of Nigeria* [2014] 2 All ER 489 at [62]. See Swadling, 'The Fiction of the Constructive Trust' (2011) 64 Current Legal Problems 399 who rails against the use of the language of 'constructive trusts' when what is involved is merely court orders for the payment of money or the transfer of particular rights to claimants.

[19] [1999] 1 All ER 400 at 412.

[20] *Dubai Aluminium Co Ltd v Salaam* [2003] 1 All ER 97 at [142]. As Lord Sumption noted in *Williams v Central Bank of Nigeria* [2014] 2 All ER 489 at [7], 'there are few areas in which the law has been so completely obscured by confused categorisation and terminology as the law relating to constructive trustees'. See Swadling, n 18, p 415 fn 77 who doubts that matters are improved by the use of 'accountable' which he says is as much a part of the fiction as constructive trusteeship.

[21] *FHR European Ventures LLP v Cedar Capital Partners LLC* [2014] UKSC 45, [2014] 2 BCLC 145 at [36], per Lord Neuberger.

[22] [2014] 2 All ER 489 at [9], citing Millett LJ in *Paragon*, and at [13].

[23] [2002] 1 BCLC 162 at [29], citing Millett LJ in *Paragon*. See too *Williams v Central Bank of Nigeria* [2014] 2 All ER 489 at [9], per Lord Sumption.

[24] [2002] 1 BCLC 162 at 175. For examples of directors being held to be trustees of the company's assets, see *Belmont Finance Corp Ltd v Williams Furniture Ltd (No 2)* [1980] 1 All ER 393 at 405 (improper financial assistance); *Bishopsgate Investment Management Ltd v Maxwell (No 2)* [1993] BCLC 1282 (director gave away the company's assets for no consideration to a private family company of which he was a director); *Bairstow v Queens Moat Houses plc* [2001] 2 BCLC 531 (unlawful distributions by directors); also *Rolled Steel Products v British Steel* [1985] 3 All ER 52 at 88. This trustee-like status has limitation consequences for claims against directors for breach of duty, see **14-40**: *Williams v Central Bank of Nigeria* [2014] UKSC 10, [2014] 2 All ER 489.

[25] [2018] 1 BCLC 20 at [45], CA.

[26] [2002] 1 BCLC 162 at [29], citing Millett LJ in *Paragon*. See too *Williams v Central Bank of Nigeria* [2014] 2 All ER 489 at [9], per Lord Sumption.

### Fiduciary duties

**14-11**    Whether the general duties owed by directors are fiduciary duties is a moot point.[27] Some of the duties certainly are, such as the no-conflict provisions in ss 175 and 176 and the complementary provision in s 177 while the duty in s 171 prohibiting the exercise of powers for an improper purpose can be seen as a manifestation of the broader equitable doctrine of fraud on a power.[28] Section 174 is thought not to be a fiduciary duty, rather it reflects the common law on negligence, but as discussed at **11-2**, that analysis might be up for debate. Other provisions arguably are not fiduciary duties, such as s 172 which merely states the obligation of loyalty which is the distinguishing overarching characteristic of a fiduciary. It states 'the essence of a fiduciary relationship ... that the fiduciary subordinates his own interests to his principal's'.[29] That section is a statement, a signalling, of the obligation of loyalty that a fiduciary acts, if at all, to promote the interests of his beneficiary so a director must act, if at all, to promote the success of the company.[30] 'The essence of a fiduciary relationship ... is that one party pledges itself to act in the best interest of the other. The fiduciary relationship has trust, not self-interest, at its core...'[31] The proscriptive fiduciary duties which support that obligation of loyalty are the no-conflict, no-profit rules which, in the context of company directors, are expressed in CA 2006, s 175(1) and (2), as a no-conflict duty within which is subsumed a proscription on profiting in a position of conflict.[32]

---

[27] See generally Conaglen, *Fiduciary Loyalty* (2010), esp Ch 3. In the much cited words of Millett LJ: 'The expression "fiduciary duty" is properly confined to those duties which are peculiar to fiduciaries and the breach of which attracts legal consequences differing from those consequent upon the breach of other duties. Unless the expression is so limited it is lacking in practical utility. In this sense it is obvious that not every breach of duty by a fiduciary is a breach of fiduciary duty': *Bristol & West BS v Mothew* [1996] 4 All ER 698 at 710. But see the robust criticism (highly readable) of 'the extreme narrowness of Millett LJ's approach to fiduciary duty' by retired Australian High Court judge, Dyson Heydon, 'Modern Fiduciary Liability: The Sick Man of Equity?' (2014) 20 Trusts & Trustees 1006—and note also his criticism of '... plague bacillus hatched in academic laboratories' at 1011. See too Heydon, 'Threats to Judicial Independence: The Enemy Within' (2013) 129 LQR 205.

[28] See Conaglen, *Fiduciary Loyalty* (2010), pp 44–50; Worthington, 'Corporate Governance: Remedying and Ratifying Directors' Breaches' (2000) 116 LQR 638. The proper purpose issue is linked closely to issues of authority, see *Criterion Properties v Stafford*, at **9-19**; Mitchell, 'Stewardship of Property and Liability to Account' [2014] Conv 215 at 218–19. The linkage exists, but, as the Supreme Court confirmed in *Eclairs Group Ltd v JKX Oil and Gas plc* [2016] 1 BCLC 1, the proper purpose principle is a reflection of the equitable doctrine of fraud on a power and is not merely a question of contractual interpretation and authority. For a view that these obligations of acting bona fide and of proper purposes are fiduciary duties, see Teele Langford, 'Solving the Fiduciary Puzzle—the Bona Fide and Proper Purpose Duties of Company Directors' (2013) 41 ABLR 127 and earlier at (2009) 31 ABLR 326. See *Grimaldi v Chameleon Mining NL* (2012) 200 FCR 296 at [174] which notes that Australian fiduciary law is concerned with standard setting via the no-conflict, no-profit rules, but is also concerned with judicial review of the exercise of powers, duties, and discretion given to a fiduciary to be exercised in the interests of another.

[29] *Saltri III Ltd v MD Mezzanine SA SICAR* [2013] 2 BCLC 217 at [123], per Eder J. See further Hannigan, 'Reconfiguring the No Conflict Rule, Judicial Strictures, a Statutory Restatement and the Opportunistic Director' (2011) 23 SAcLJ 714 at 723–6; Conaglen, *Fiduciary Loyalty* (2010), pp 54–8; Finn, 'The Fiduciary Principle' in Youdan (ed), *Equity, Fiduciaries and Trusts* (1989), pp 27–8.

[30] See Edelman, 'When do Fiduciary Duties Arise?' (2010) 126 LQR 302 at 322–3 noting the problems with this 'extremely vague' duty. For example, see *Pilmer v Duke Group Ltd* [2001] 2 BCLC 773 at [136], Aust H Ct, where Kirby J comments that the essence of the fiduciary principle is undivided loyalty which requires the fiduciary to advance the interests of his beneficiary and not to have a conflict with the interests of the beneficiary: s 172 can be said to represent a high level statement of that obligation of loyalty.

[31] *Canson Enterprises Ltd v Boughton* (1991) 85 DLR (4th) 129 at [61], per McLachlin J.

[32] See Mitchell, 'Equitable Compensation for Breach of Fiduciary Duty' (2013) 66 Current Legal Problems 307 at 310–16 who discusses the nature of fiduciary duties and whether they are disabilities or duties, especially now that compensation for loss can be claimed.

**14-12** There are advantages in obligations being categorised as fiduciary obligations, primarily with respect to the availability of what have been described as 'more elastic' remedies in the event of breach.[33] For example, claims for breach of fiduciary duty may be subject to more generous limitation periods (discussed at **14-40**) than if the claim was for breach of a common law obligation. A claim can be made for profits made by the fiduciary though the company itself could not have made the profits and has suffered no loss.[34] In the much cited words of Lord Russell in *Regal (Hastings) Ltd v Gulliver*:[35]

> '[t]he rule of equity which insists on those, who by use of a fiduciary position make a profit, being liable to account for that profit, in no way depends on fraud, or absence of bona fides; or upon such questions or considerations as whether the profit would or should otherwise have gone to the plaintiff, or whether the profiteer was under a duty to obtain the source of the profit for the plaintiff, or whether he took a risk or acted as he did for the benefit of the plaintiff, or whether the plaintiff has in fact been damaged or benefited by his action. The liability arises from the mere fact of a profit having, in the stated circumstances, been made. The profiteer, however honest and well-intentioned, cannot escape the risk of being called upon to account.'

**14-13** The obligation to make good losses suffered by the company (equitable compensation[36]) applies on a more generous basis, designed to deter,[37] than a common law obligation to pay damages (issues of foreseeability and remoteness are, in general, irrelevant), though the loss must still be shown to have been caused by the breach of fiduciary duty.[38] The nature and extent of equitable compensation was addressed by the Supreme Court in *AIB Group (UK) plc v Redler*.[39] A bank lent £3.3m to a couple and released the money to the solicitor acting for the bank and the couple on the basis that a prior charge to Barclays would be redeemed in full and the bank would obtain a first charge over the couple's home for £3.3m. In error, the solicitors redeemed only part of the debt owed to Barclays

---

[33] See *Swindle v Harrison* [1997] 4 All ER 705 at 732, per Mummery LJ. See the interesting dissenting judgment of Kirby J (Aust H Ct) in *Pilmer v Duke Group Ltd* [2001] 2 BCLC 773 at [149]–[154] where he considers the benefits of claiming remedies for breach of fiduciary duty.

[34] See, for example, *Regal (Hastings) Ltd v Gulliver* [1942] 1 All ER 378, HL; *Industrial Development Consultants Ltd v Cooley* [1972] 2 All ER 162; *Quarter Master UK v Pyke* [2005] 1 BCLC 245, see **12-26**. Cf damages in contract and tort which generally require damage or loss as a consequence of the breach of contract or tortious conduct.

[35] [1942] 1 All ER 378 at 386.

[36] The term 'equitable compensation' is another term which is used indiscriminately. In this context, the term means the sum payable as compensation to make good a loss caused by a breach of fiduciary duty, rather than to describe the equitable obligation to account for a benefit obtained by a fiduciary in breach of duty, as it was used by Lord Neuberger in *FHR European Ventures LLP v Cedar Capital Partners LLC* [2014] 2 BCLC 145 at [1], a use criticised by Davies (2015) 78 MLR 672 at 690.

[37] See comments by Kirby J (Aust H Ct) dissenting in *Pilmer v Duke Group Ltd* [2001] 2 BCLC 773 at [153] explaining that 'it is because equitable relief has large objectives (which he describes elsewhere as compensatory *and* prophylactic) that the measure of equitable compensation will often differ from the measure of common law damages. Often, it will be greater.' See too comments of Arden LJ in *Lindsley v Woodful* [2004] 2 BCLC 131 at [30] on the deterrence element.

[38] Loss is assessed at the date of the trial and with the benefit of hindsight: *AIB Group (UK) plc v Redler* [2014] 3 WLR 1367 at [135].

[39] *AIB Group (UK) plc v Redler* [2014] 3 WLR 1367. See Watts, 'Agents' Disbursal of Funds in Breach of Instructions' (2015) LMCLQ 118; Paul S. Davies, 'Remedies for Breach of Trust' (2015) 78(4) MLR 672; Ho, 'Equitable Compensation on the Road to Damascus?' (2015) 131 LQR 213; Shaw-Mellors, 'Equitable Compensation for Breach of Trust: Still Missing the Target?' [2015] JBL 165; Cam, 'Clarifying the Law for Breach of Commercial Trusts: *AIB Group (UK) plc v Mark Redler & Co*' (2014) 28 Trust LI 226.

leaving Barclays with a prior charge for £273,777 with the bank having a second charge for its loan. The couple defaulted and the property was sold for £1.2m, of which the bank received £867,697. The bank sued the solicitors and argued that they were entitled to compensation in the full amount of £3.3m less the amount recovered by it on the basis that, when the solicitors failed to carry out the bank's instructions, they acted in breach of trust and the bank was entitled to the reconstitution of the trust fund as it was at the time of the breach, i.e. £3.3m. The Court of Appeal and first instance judge, though reaching the result by different routes,[40] limited the compensation to £273,777 being the loss caused by the breach, applying *Target Holdings Ltd v Redferns*[41] and the broad principle identified there by Lord Browne-Wilkinson, namely that '[e]quitable compensation for breach of trust is designed to achieve exactly what the word compensation suggests: to make good a loss in fact suffered by the beneficiaries and which, using hindsight and common sense, can be seen to have been caused by the breach'.[42]

**14-14**  The Supreme Court unanimously endorsed the approach in *Target Holdings* as correct with Lord Toulson noting that it would be 'a backward step' for the court to depart from Lord Browne-Wilkinson's fundamental analysis in that case or to re-interpret it.[43] He also said that, absent fraud (which was not present in this case and which might give rise to other public policy considerations), it would not be right to impose or maintain a rule that gives redress to a beneficiary for loss that would have been suffered if the trustee had properly performed its duties.[44] Lord Reed pointed out that interpreting what Lord Browne-Wilkinson said as meaning that equitable compensation should be assessed in the same way as common law damages was to misunderstand what he had said.[45] Lord Browne-Wilkinson had not intended to depart from the orthodox view that the equitable obligation arising from a breach of trust is to restore the trust fund to the position it would have been in but for the breach and the measure of compensation should be assessed on that basis at the date of the judgment.[46] That measure of compensation, to make good a loss resulting from the breach of duty, is the same whether the claim is classified as 'substitutive' or 'reparative',[47] so rejecting the criticism that in *Target Holdings Ltd v Redferns*

---

[40]  See [2013] EWCA Civ 45, rev'g in part [2012] EWHC 35.

[41]  [1995] 3 All ER 785, see at 793–4, per Lord Browne-Wilkinson who drew heavily upon the dissenting judgment of McLachlin J in the Canadian Supreme Court in *Canson Enterprises Ltd v Boughton & Co* (1991) 85 DLR (4th) 129, which provides a detailed discussion of the rationale and approach to equitable compensation. McLachlin J's judgment was considered in detail and with approval by the UK Supreme Court in *AIB Group (UK) plc v Redler* [2014] 3 WLR 1367, see at [79]–[89]; also *Swindle v Harrison* [1997] 4 All ER 705 at 732–3, per Mummery LJ, noted (1998) 114 LQR 181; *Nocton v Lord Ashburton* [1914] AC 932. See generally Mitchell, 'Equitable Compensation for Breach of Fiduciary Duty' (2013) 66 Current Legal Problems 307; Elliott and Mitchell, n 8, 28–30; Lowry and Edmunds, 'The Corporate Opportunity Doctrine: The Shifting Basis of the Duty and its Remedies' (1998) 61 MLR 515 at 527–32; Capper, 'Compensation for Breach of Trust' [1997] Conv 14.

[42]  [1995] 3 All ER 785 at 798.

[43]  [2014] 3 WLR 1367 at [63]. Lord Toulson considered Lord Browne-Wilkinson's judgment in depth at [25]–[36], as Lord Reed did at [98]–[116]. See Shaw-Mellors, 'Equitable Compensation for Breach of Trust: Still Missing the Target?' [2015] JBL 165 who criticises the decision for entrenching *Target Holdings v Redferns*. Watts, n 39, stresses that the correct approach would have been to require the reconstitution of the trust fund but the decision can be justified on the basis that the bank did not act promptly to demand restoration. Ho, 'Equitable Compensation on the Road to Damascus?' (2015) 131 LQR 213 is more positive and sees value in the bold stepping away from the artificial steps of falsification of account to a more transparent inquiry into all subsequent events and receipts that are relevant in assessing the loss that would not have occurred but for the breach.

[44]  [2014] 3 WLR 1367 at [62].    [45]  [2014] 3 WLR 1367 at [116].    [46]  [2014] 3 WLR 1367 at [116].

[47]  [2014] 3 WLR 1367 at [66], [73], per Lord Toulson, at [134] per Lord Reed.

Lord Browne-Wilkinson had confused the two types of claim.[48] That terminology was adopted by some commentators and judges to distinguish between claims to restore a trust fund (substitutive relief) or claims for a breach of fiduciary duty (a reparative claim) though, as Lord Toulson noted, in a practical sense, both claims are reparative.[49] Lords Toulson and Reed also were agreed that where the trust arises in a commercial setting where the parties' relationship is primarily and extensively covered by contractual terms, the 'but for' measure of compensation applying *Target Holdings* may well be very similar to what would be recovered if damages were sought at common law for breach of contract.[50] Nevertheless, while there are some similarities between equitable compensation and the assessment of common law damages, the rules are not the same, a trust imposing different obligations in a different kind of relationship from contractual or tortious relationships.[51] In the trust context, the appropriate measure is to compensate for the loss which would not have been suffered but for the breach.[52]

**14-15**    On that analysis, in *AIB Group (UK) plc v Redler*, had the solicitors performed their trust, the bank would have had a first charge for £3.3m; as it was they had a second charge worth £273,777 less because of Barclay's prior interest. The measure of loss then was £273,777. To hold otherwise would be to make the solicitors liable for the wholly inadequate security which the bank had accepted for the loan.[53] As Lord Toulson noted, '[t]o say that there has been a loss to the trust fund in the present case of £2.5m by reason of the solicitors' conduct, when most of that sum would have been lost if the solicitors had applied the trust fund in the way that AIB had instructed them to do, is to adopt an artificial and unrealistic view of the facts.'[54] On the other hand, critics of the decision see it as downgrading the fundamental obligation of a trustee to reconstitute a trust fund where it has been misapplied in favour of a focus on the loss caused by the breach.[55] The starting point should be the duty of the trustee to act in accordance with his mandate, rather than merely seeking to compensate the beneficiary for loss caused by improper conduct. As Davies has commented,[56] the result may undermine the confidence of beneficiaries that the trustee will act in accordance with the trust, may lessen any deterrence felt by the fiduciary by reducing the likelihood that he will be required to reconstitute the fund, and may be indicative that the courts are now more tolerant of breach of trust—the latter would certainly be unfortunate were it to be true and applied to company directors.

---

[48] [2014] 3 WLR 1367 at [56], per Lord Toulson; see Mitchell, 'Stewardship of Property and Liability to Account' [2014] Conv 215 at 224–6 (arguing that causation is irrelevant to a substitutive claim so the court in *Target Holdings* erred, first, in treating the claim as reparative when it was substitutive and, secondly, in applying a causation test to what was a substitutive claim); see also Mitchell, 'Equitable Compensation for Breach of Fiduciary Duty' (2013) 66 Current Legal Problems 307 at 323–5. See also Elliott, 'Remoteness Criteria in Equity' (2002) 65 MLR 588.

[49] [2014] 3 WLR 1367 at [54].

[50] [2014] 3 WLR 1367 at [70], [71], per Lord Toulson, at [137], per Lord Reed. This is not to say that there are different rules for traditional (ongoing) trusts and trusts in a commercial setting (which may be completed quickly), rather just an acknowledgement that the contractual basis of the relationship may have a bearing on the question of fact as to whether there has been a loss applying the 'but for' test.

[51] [2014] 3 WLR 1367 at [76], per Lord Toulson, at [136]–[137], per Lord Reed.

[52] [2014] 3 WLR 1367 at [73], per Lord Toulson, at [116], [134], per Lord Reed.

[53] [2014] 3 WLR 1367 at [140].      [54] [2014] 3 WLR 1367 at [65].      [55] See Watts, Davies, n 39.

[56] See Davies, n 39, 693–4. See also Davies (2018) 134 LQR 165 at 167: 'That decision [in *AIB v Redler*] departed from previous orthodoxy in rather brusque fashion based upon somewhat unsatisfactory reasoning that should perhaps be revisited by the Supreme Court …'

**14-16**   Liability for breach of duty is an individual liability and, as between defaulting directors, liability is joint and several.[57] A director who is aware of a fellow director's breach of fiduciary duty and takes no steps to prevent it, will not only be in breach of his own duty of care and skill, he will be treated as party to and in breach of duty in the manner of his fellow wrongdoing director.[58] Having said that, the court will not order a contribution[59] by the non-participating director where sums have been misappropriated for the wrongdoer's exclusive benefit.[60]

## Misapplication of company assets

**14-17**   As already noted at **14-8**, directors are trustees from the outset of the company's assets and liable to make good assets which they have misapplied upon the same footing as if they were trustees, applying *Re Lands Allotment Co*[61] and it is for the fiduciary to justify any payment out of trust funds in any case where there is doubt as to whether it is properly made.[62] In *Goldtrail Travel Ltd v Aydin*[63] the court accepted that the long-recognised claim to recover trust assets need not be pleaded as a distinct breach of a particular duty within CA 2006, ss 171–177, though in any event any misapplication of corporate assets in breach of duty must be capable of being brought within ss 172 and 175.

**14-18**   Where the breach of duty involves a misappropriation of company assets by the director, the company may pursue a proprietary claim where it can trace the asset or an identifiable substitute[64] so, if the director still has the asset, the court can order the director to transfer

---

[57]  See *Re Lands Allotment Co* [1894] 1 Ch 616; *Re Carriage Co-operative Supply Association* (1884) 27 Ch D 322.

[58]  *Neville v Krikorian* [2007] 1 BCLC 1 at [49]–[51], CA; *Lexi Holdings v Luqman (No. 1)* [2007] EWHC 2652 (Ch) at [201]–[205]; *Madoff Securities International Ltd v Raven* [2013] EWHC 3147, [2014] LL Rep FC 95 at [192]. While the cases commonly involve a misappropriation of company assets, Briggs J in *Lexi Holdings*, above, was clear that the position is equally applicable to 'any improper practice' by a director, including misappropriation of company money and transactions in breach of [CA 2006, s 190], at [202]–[205]. Where the directors do not know of the transactions, they cannot be made liable as parties to the misapplication, though their lack of knowledge may be a result of a failure to exercise care and skill: see *Dickinson v NAL Realisations Ltd* [2017] EWHC 28, [2018] 1 BCLC 623 at [160].

[59]  i.e. a contribution under the Civil Liability (Contribution) Act 1978, s 1. Under s 2(1) of that Act, the amount of the contribution is such as may be found by the court to be just and equitable having regard to the extent of that person's responsibility for the damage in question.

[60]  *Dawson v Bell* [2016] EWCA Civ 96; [2016] 2 BCLC 59 at [52]. See *Clegg v Pache* [2017] EWCA Civ 256—a 50 per cent shareholder and one of only two directors had protested to the other director about the latter's misconduct in diverting funds and business opportunities of the company to another company which was the alter ego of the wrongdoing director. The Court of Appeal, overruling the lower court, said there was no basis for identifying any significant share of the liability for the company's losses as falling on the non-wrongdoing director rather than falling entirely upon the wrongdoer, at [69].

[61]  [1894] 1 Ch 616 at 631, 638.

[62]  *Ross River Ltd v Waveley Commercial Ltd* [2014] 1 BCLC 545 at [64], [94], [96], [120], [126]. Hence where a company director receives company money or assets, the burden of proof is on the director to explain the relevant transactions and to show that a payment or receipt was a proper one: *GHLM Trading Ltd v Maroo* [2012] 2 BCLC 369 at [148]–[149] (directors must explain debit and credit entries to a directors' loan account); also *Re HLC Environmental Projects Ltd, Hellard v Carvalho* [2014] BCC 337 at [115]; *Re Idessa (UK) Ltd, Burke v Morrison* [2012] 1 BCLC 80 at [28]. See also n 67.

[63]  [2015] 1 BCLC 89 at [65].

[64]  *JJ Harrison (Properties) Ltd v Harrison* [2002] 1 BCLC 162 at 175; *Re Lands Allotment Co* [1894] 1 Ch 616 at 631, 638, 657; *Cook v Deeks* [1916] AC 554 at 564; *Keech v Sandford* (1726) Sel Cas Ch 61. See generally Goode, 'The Recovery of a Director's Improper Gains: Proprietary Gains for Infringement of Non-Proprietary Rights' in McKendrick (ed), *Commercial Aspects of Trusts and Fiduciary Obligations* (1992).

it *in specie* to the company.[65] A proprietary claim, assuming the asset or its traceable proceeds can be identified, prevails against all the world other than a bona fide purchaser for value without notice of the breach of duty, even where there have been numerous successive transactions, so long as the tracing exercise is successful and no bona fide purchaser for value without notice has intervened.[66] Where a proprietary claim exists and the moneys beneficially owned by the company can be traced to, but have been inextricably mixed with, funds of the defaulting fiduciary, the proprietary claim is not lost, rather the onus is on the defaulting fiduciary to establish, on the balance of probabilities, which part of the mixed fund is his property.[67] Further, on a proprietary claim, the company can require that the director make good the trust property *and* any benefit derived therefrom.[68] Crucially, on the bankruptcy of the defaulting fiduciary, the proprietary claim prevails over the claims of the fiduciary's creditors. Clearly then a proprietary claim is advantageous, but if the possibility has been extinguished, for example, because the asset or its identifiable substitutes cannot be traced or a bona fide third party purchaser has intervened, the company may still pursue a personal claim that the director compensate the company for the loss.[69] A personal claim will often produce the same result in value as a proprietary claim, but the disadvantage of a personal claim is that it does not give rise to any equitable tracing or following and it ranks *pari passu* with the claims of the other unsecured creditors of the defaulting fiduciary so the bankruptcy of the fiduciary may affect the ability of the claimant company to recover.[70]

**14-19**   In *JJ Harrison (Properties) Ltd v Harrison*[71] a director acquired land at an undervalue from his company in circumstances which amounted to a breach of duty.[72] The director

---

[65] See *Foskett v McKeown* [2000] 3 All ER 97 at 120. As Lord Millett emphasised in *Boscawen v Bajwa* [1995] 4 All ER 769 at 777, this is only one of the proprietary remedies which is available to a court of equity. If the plaintiff's money has been applied by the defendant, for example, not in the acquisition of property but in its improvement, then the court may treat the land as charged with the payment to the plaintiff of a sum representing the amount by which the value of the defendant's land has been enhanced by the use of the plaintiff's money. If the plaintiff's money has been used to discharge a mortgage on the defendant's land, the court may achieve a similar result by treating the land as subject to a charge by way of subrogation in favour of the plaintiff, see, for example, *Primlake Ltd v Matthews Associates* [2007] 1 BCLC 666.

[66] *Foskett v McKeown* [2000] 3 All ER 97 at 122, per Lord Millett; also *Re Lehman Brothers International (Europe) (No 2)* [2010] 2 BCLC 301 at [331]. Moneys held on trust may be traced into other assets even if those other assets are passed on before the trust moneys are paid to the person transferring them, provided that that person acted on the basis that he would be reimbursed. In order to trace money into substitutes, it was not necessary that the payments should occur in chronological order, or any particular order: *Relfo Ltd v Varsani* [2015] 1 BCLC 14, CA.

[67] *Sinclair Investments (UK) Ltd v Versailles Trade Finance Ltd* [2011] 2 BCLC 501 at [138]–[141], per Lord Neuberger, (overruled on other grounds) who explained that the burden should not be other than the normal civil standard of proof out of principle and out of fairness to the other creditors of the defaulting fiduciary. If, after considering the evidence, the court concludes that it is more probable than not that a particular sum of money held by the defaulting fiduciary is not attributable to the funds (or the identifiable substitute of the funds) of the beneficiary, the court should refuse a tracing remedy.

[68] *JJ Harrison (Properties) Ltd v Harrison* [2002] 1 BCLC 162 at [52]; *CMS Dolphin Ltd v Simonet* [2001] 2 BCLC 704 at [96]–[97].

[69] *AIB Group (UK) plc v Redler* [2014] 3 WLR 1367; *Target Holdings Ltd v Redferns* [1995] 3 All ER 785 at 793–4; *Foskett v McKeown* [2000] 3 All ER 97 at 122.

[70] See *FHR European Ventures LLP v Cedar Capital Partners LLC* [2014] 2 BCLC 145, at [1]; see Nolan, 'Bribes: A Reprise' (2011) 127 LQR 19 at 22 for a useful summation of the advantages of proprietary claims over personal claims.   [71] [2002] 1 BCLC 162.

[72] He failed to ensure that the company receive up-to-date information on the planning position and the development potential of the site and sought personally to exploit the commercial opportunities relating to the land of which he, but not the company, was aware.

subsequently sold that land for a substantial gain. The Court of Appeal held that his possession of the land was subject to his pre-existing obligations as a trustee of that land, derived not from the transaction by which he came to possess the property, but from his appointment as a director.[73] Therefore he held the property on trust for the company and the company was entitled to the entire proceeds of sale, subject only to an allowance to the director limited to the purchase price paid by him and any expenditure incurred by him for the preservation or enhancement of the value of the land.[74] In *Clark v Cutland*[75] misappropriated company funds were diverted to a director's pension fund with the result that the trustees of the pension fund, though no personal claim lay against them as volunteers, held the property on behalf of the company. The company was entitled to trace the asset (the payments made into the pension fund) and to seek proprietary relief in the form of a charge over the pension fund assets to secure the sum due to the company.[76]

**14-20**    In *Primlake Ltd v Matthews Associates*[77] a de facto director extracted £836,500 from company funds in breach of duty. The company had a proprietary claim to the company's funds or their traceable proceeds which allowed the company to recover funds from the director's wife, a volunteer with no knowledge of the circumstances, to the extent that she still had control of funds which were identifiable as the property or the substitute for the property of the company.[78] In the absence of any participation by her in some way in the breach of duty,[79] no personal claim lay against her with respect to funds which had passed through their joint account.[80]

**14-21**    Where an asset has been misapplied and there has been a subsequent loss in value of the asset, that loss must be made good by the director/trustee as part of the process of reinstating that trust asset.[81] In *Re Duckwari plc (No 2), Duckwari plc v Offerventure Ltd (No 2)*[82] a director had the company expend funds on acquiring an asset which had subsequently fallen in value, in part due to the collapse of the property market. The transaction by which the company acquired the asset was in contravention of the statutory provisions (now CA 2006, s 190) governing substantial property transactions between a company and a director or person connected with a director, see **13-28**. The court held the director was liable to make good the full amount of the misapplication of the company's funds so the loss arising from the acquisition (including the loss as a result of the fall in the property market) fell on the director/trustee, see **13-52**. Imposing liability, Nourse LJ noted: 'it is well recognised that the basis on which a trustee is liable to make good a misapplication of trust moneys is strict and sometimes harsh, especially where, as here, there has been a huge depreciation in the value of the asset acquired.'[83] He also noted that, given the failure to obtain shareholder approval as required, it was not unfair for the loss to fall on the director.

---

[73] [2002] 1 BCLC 162 at 175.     [74] See [2002] 1 BCLC 162 at 182–3.

[75] [2003] 2 BCLC 393, CA.     [76] [2003] 2 BCLC 393 at 404.     [77] [2007] 1 BCLC 666.

[78] [2007] 1 BCLC 666 at [334]. The couple also used some of the company's money to repay the mortgage on their home and release it from a bank charge. The court held that the company was entitled to be subrogated to the bank's position to the extent that the company's money had been used to discharge the debt and redeem the charge, see at [340]. See *Boscawen v Bajwa* [1995] 4 All ER 769. Also *Clegg v Pache* [2017] EWCA Civ 256 at [87]–[91], where a wife who received £50,500 from her husband, a director acting in breach of his duties to his company, was bound, as a volunteer, by the company's interest in the sums paid and was ordered to repay the money.

[79] See *Foskett v McKeown* [2000] 3 All ER 97 at 120.     [80] [2007] 1 BCLC 666 at [336].

[81] See Millett, 'Equity's Place in the Law of Commerce' (1998) 114 LQR 214 at 227.

[82] [1998] 2 BCLC 315.     [83] [1998] 2 BCLC 315 at 324.

## Bribes, secret commissions, and secret profits

**14-22**  It is possible for directors to profit in breach of their duties to the company without any misapplication or misappropriation of company assets. A typical scenario is where a director profits by diverting to himself business opportunities which present themselves and which he takes in conflict with the company's interests. A director may accept bribes or secret commissions from a third party. The essence of a bribe or secret commission was summed up by HH Judge Havelock-Allan QC in *Airbus Operations Ltd v Withey*[84] as follows: (1) receipt of money or a valuable benefit, (2) by a person who owes a fiduciary duty of loyalty to a principal with whom the donor of the money or benefit wishes to transact business,[85] (3) which is kept secret from the principal, and (4) which places the recipient in a position where his interest may potentially conflict with the fiduciary duty owed to his principal. A bribe is given with an overt intention to corrupt the recipient (and is a criminal matter under the Bribery Act 2010 in addition to any civil liability) whereas a secret commission is given, perhaps, with a more implicit expectation that the interests of the donor will be advanced by the fiduciary,[86] so there are fine nuances between whether something is a bribe or a secret commission, but civilly they are treated the same, as we shall see.

**14-23**  The question of whether a bribe or secret commission received by a fiduciary should be the subject of a personal or of a proprietary claim by a beneficiary was problematic until recently because of the divergence of opinion which existed as to whether the courts should follow *Lister v Stubbs*[87] (long-standing Court of Appeal decision that there was only a personal liability to account for a bribe and there was no scope for proprietary remedies) or *Attorney General for Hong Kong v Reid*[88] (persuasive, more recent, Privy Council decision that *Lister v Stubbs* was wrongly decided and a proprietary remedy is entirely appropriate to ensure that the fiduciary cannot benefit from his breach of duty and to deter wrongdoing).[89] A voluminous debate on the issue raged for 20 years[90] until, in *Sinclair Investments (UK) Ltd v Versailles Trade Finance Ltd*,[91] the Court of Appeal held that, as a matter of precedent, it was not open to the court to follow the decision in *AGHK*

---

[84]  [2014] EWHC 1126 at [88].

[85]  There need not be a contractual nexus between the person paying the bribe or secret commission and the principal, see *Airbus Operations Ltd v Withey* [2014] EWHC 1126 at [433]–[434].

[86]  See *Bowstead on Agency* (21st edn, 2017), para 6-085.

[87]  (1890) 45 Ch D 1, CA. For example, in *Daraydan Holdings Ltd v Solland International Ltd* [2005] 4 All ER 73 at 92–3, Lawrence Collins J indicated that, if necessary, he would have followed *AGHK v Reid* and not *Lister v Stubbs*. On the facts in *Daraydan*, he considered it possible to distinguish *Lister v Stubbs* as the price paid by the company for the services obtained had been increased by the suppliers by the amount of the bribes which the suppliers had had to pay to secure the contract. The bribes were derived directly from the claimants' property therefore and the claimants were entitled to proprietary relief. See also Toulson J in *Fyffes Group Ltd v Templeman* [2000] 2 Lloyd's Rep 643 at 668–72.

[88]  [1994] 1 All ER 1, PC.

[89]  See [1994] 1 All ER 1 at 9, per Lord Templeman. In *Reid*, the bribes had been invested in a number of properties which had increased in value substantially. The fiduciary had to account not just for the bribe but for the increased value of the property representing the bribe since otherwise he would receive a benefit from his breach of duty.

[90]  See in particular Millett, 'Bribes and Secret Commissions' [1993] RLR 7; Hayton, 'Proprietary Liability for Secret Profits' [2011] 127 LQR 487; Nolan, 'Bribes: A Reprise' (2011) 127 LQR 19. Goode, 'Proprietary Liability for Secret Profits—a Reply' (2011) 127 LQR 493, Goode, 'Ownership and Obligation in Commercial Transactions' (1987) 103 LQR 433. The extensive academic literature on the matter is gathered by Worthington (2013) 72 CLJ 720, n 103.

[91]  [2011] 2 BCLC 501, aff'g [2011] 1 BCLC 202. See the literature on this case cited in n 103.

*v Reid*. In any event, on the specific issue, Lord Neuberger MR (with whom Richards and Hughes LJJ agreed) considered that the decision in *AGHK v Reid* was unsound for a bribe could not possibly be said to be an asset which the fiduciary is under a duty to take for the beneficiary though he acknowledged that limiting the claim to a personal claim meant that the faithless fiduciary would not be accountable for further gains derived from the benefit or bribe.[92]

**14-24**    In *Sinclair Investments (UK) Ltd v Versailles Trade Finance Ltd*[93] a company (TPL) raised funds from investors for a trade finance business to be carried on, on TPL's behalf, by another company (VTFL). In fact, VTFL was just a vehicle for an enormous fraud by its two directors (including C) who were also the directors of TPL. A consequence of the fraud was the artificial inflating of the value of another company (VGP) and its shares. VGP was the parent company of VTFL. C sold his shareholding in VGP for £28.6m before the fraud was discovered and the companies collapsed into insolvency. The essence of the case is a claim by TPL for breach of duty[94] by its director C who had allowed the company's funds to be misused in this fraudulent way, creating the bubble around VTFL and VGP which allowed C ultimately to sell the shares and realise a large sum of money. TPL asserted that it had a proprietary claim to the proceeds of sale of the shares as an unauthorised gain made by C in breach of duty.[95] As other parties, specifically a number of creditor banks, had received varying amounts of the sale proceeds, whether the claim was a proprietary claim was a crucial question, since a proprietary claim prevails against all the world save bona fide purchasers for value without notice. The issue then would have been whether the recipient banks had notice. On the other hand, if the claim was merely a personal claim against C for profiting in breach of his fiduciary duties, then TPL's claim would rank *pari passu* with the rest of C's unsecured creditors.[96]

**14-25**    The Court of Appeal agreed with Lewison J in the lower court that the claim was a personal claim.[97] The money received by C from the proceeds of sale of the shares was derived from his fiduciary position and in plain breach of his fiduciary duties, but it was not money which was part of the assets of TPL, or derived from such assets.[98] Lord Neuberger noted that a fundamental distinction exists between a fiduciary (the director) enriching himself by depriving a claimant beneficiary (the company) of an asset and a fiduciary enriching himself by doing a wrong to the beneficiary.[99] The receipt of a bribe is the same as unauthorised profit-making by a director; in each case, there is a breach of duty which entitles the company to bring a personal claim for the amount of the bribe or the unauthorised profit. Lord Neuberger concluded that a beneficiary has a proprietary claim in respect of any money or asset acquired by a fiduciary in breach of his duties to the beneficiary where

---

[92] [2011] 2 BCLC 501 at [89]. The Australian Federal Court rejected the approach in *Sinclair Investments* in favour of *AGHK v Reid*, see *Grimaldi v Chameleon Mining NL (No 2)* [2012] 287 ALR 22 at [569]–[584], esp [582].                              [93] [2011] 2 BCLC 501, CA, aff'g [2011] 1 BCLC 202.

[94] The claims of TPL had been assigned to the claimant, Sinclair, see [2011] 2 BCLC 501 at [23].

[95] See [2011] 2 BCLC 501 at [25], where the claim is summarised and see [32]. TPL also had a more straightforward claim in respect of TPL funds held by VTFL—it was accepted that VTFL owed TPL fiduciary duties with respect to those funds. In those circumstances, the misappropriation of those funds by VTFL gave rise to a clear proprietary claim which could only be defeated by a bona fide purchaser for value without notice. These funds had been distributed to creditor banks of VTFL at a time when the banks were bona fide purchasers for value without notice so defeating the proprietary claim, though TPL did have a proprietary claim with respect to funds held by VTFL after the point when the banks had notice of that proprietary claim, see at [142]–[148].                              [96] See [2011] 2 BCLC 501 at [48].

[97] See the interesting commentary by Hicks, 'Constructive Trusts of Fiduciary Gain: Lister Revived?' [2011] 1 Conv 62; and by Nolan, 'Bribes: A Reprise' (2011) 127 LQR 19 on the first instance decision.

[98] [2011] 2 BCLC 501 at [55].                    [99] [2011] 2 BCLC 501 at [80].

(i) the asset or money is or has been beneficially the property of the beneficiary or (ii) the trustee acquired the asset or money by taking advantage of an opportunity or right which was properly that of the beneficiary, otherwise (iii) a beneficiary could not claim a proprietary interest, but was entitled to an equitable account of profits made or compensation for losses incurred.[100] He concluded that a claimant could not claim proprietary ownership of an asset purchased by the defaulting fiduciary with funds which, although they could not have been obtained if he had not enjoyed his fiduciary status, were not beneficially owned by the claimant or derived from opportunities beneficially owned by the claimant.[101] TPL did not have a proprietary claim to the proceeds of sale, therefore, and consequently the issue of whether the banks were bona fide purchasers for value without notice did not arise.[102]

**14-26**  There were many uncertainties about, and objections to, the approach taken in *Sinclair Investments (UK) Ltd v Versailles Finance Ltd*[103] including, in particular, uncertainty as to the circumstances (of Lord Neuberger's second category, see **14-25**) in which a proprietary claim would arise because the trustee took '*advantage of an opportunity or right which was properly that of the beneficiary*' [emphasis added].[104] As Sir Terence Etherton commented, extra-judicially, '[t]hose expressions represented his [Lord Neuberger's] gloss on the case law and are not to be found in the cases themselves'.[105] Determining whether a trustee had so acted, it was suggested, would involve complex factual analysis[106] which would lengthen and increase the cost of litigation. More broadly, the concern was that limiting proprietary claims to misuse of property and allowing only personal relief in respect of abuse of position[107] gave undue weight to

---

[100]  [2011] 2 BCLC 501 at [88], per Lord Neuberger.   [101]  [2011] 2 BCLC 501 at [89], see also at [50].

[102]  Nevertheless, the court considered, obiter, that once a person knows certain facts, he should only be treated as appreciating the legal consequences if he actually knew of the consequences or if in all the circumstances he ought reasonably to have appreciated those consequences. The Court of Appeal took a rather generous approach in this case, being reluctant to hold that the banks were on notice for many months (though eventually they were on notice of the proprietary claim of the claimants, see n 95) even when the transactions at issue were entered into 'in the shadow of insolvency and fraud', the court noting the importance of not interpreting or developing the law of notice in such a way as to interfere unacceptably with ordinary and honest commerce. See [2011] 2 BCLC 501 at [98]–[112], esp [109], endorsed by PC in *Papadimitriou v Credit Agricole Corpn* [2015] 1 WLR 4265, see Pearce [2015] Conv 522; Watts (2015) 131 LQR 511.

[103]  The decision in the Court of Appeal attracted a voluminous commentary, see Hayton, 'Proprietary Liability for Secret Profits' (2011) 127 LQR 487; Hayton, 'No Proprietary Liability for Bribes and Other Secret Profits' (2011) 25 Trust LI 3; Goode, 'Proprietary Liability for Secret Profits—A Reply' (2011) 127 LQR 493; Virgo, 'Profits Obtained in Breach of Fiduciary Duty: Personal or Proprietary Claim?' (2011) 70 CLJ 502; Nolan, 'Bribes: A Reprise' (2011) 127 LQR 19; Millett, 'Bribes and Secret Commissions Again' (2012) 71 CLJ 583; Hayton, 'The Extent of Equitable Remedies: Privy Council versus Court of Appeal' (2012) 33 Co Law 161; Hayton, 'The Development of Equity and the "Good Person" Philosophy in Common Law Systems' [2012] Conv 263; McGrath, 'Constructive Trusts: an Analysis of Sinclair v Versailles' [2012] LMCLQ 517; Hedlun, 'Secret Commissions and Constructive Trusts: Yet again!' [2013] JBL 747; Chambers, 'Constructive Trusts and Breach of Fiduciary Duty' [2013] Conv 241; Smith, 'Constructive Trusts and the No-Profit Rule' (2013) 72 CLJ 260; Worthington, 'Fiduciary Duties and Proprietary Remedies: Addressing the Failure of Equitable Formulae' (2013) 72 CLJ 720. All of the above literature must be read now in the light of *FHR European Ventures LLC v Cedar Capital Partners LLP* [2014] 2 BCLC 145, discussed at **14-28**.

[104]  *Sinclair Investments (UK) Ltd v Versailles Trade Finance Ltd* [2011] 2 BCLC 501 at [88], per Lord Neuberger. See the robust criticism by Millett, 'Bribes and Secret Commissions, Again' (2012) 71 CLJ 583 at 600.

[105]  Etherton, 'The Legitimacy of Proprietary Relief' (2014) 2 Birkbeck Law Review 59 at 76.

[106]  See McGrath, n 103, 535 on the 'evidential nightmare' which would ensue; also Sir Terence Etherton in *FHR European Ventures LLP v Mankarious* [2013] 2 BCLC 1 at [116], CA.

[107]  Which, as Worthington points out, turns out to mean 'use of position', see Worthington, n 103, 731.

the claims of the fiduciary's creditors.[108] This approach, it was said, undervalued the fiduciary relationship at the heart of the claim[109] in a manner inconsistent with the principles evident from *Keech v Sandford*,[110] *Boardman v Phipps*,[111] and *Regal Hastings v Gulliver*[112] which clearly held that all profits obtained by a fiduciary by reason of his fiduciary position are held for his principal.[113] Further, by shrinking the availability of proprietary relief, it was argued, the court was undermining the deterrent effect of fiduciary obligations in an area (bribes and secret commissions) where deterrence was particularly important.[114]

**14-27**   An opportunity to revisit these issues arose almost immediately in *FHR European Ventures LLC v Mankarious*[115] where the respondent agent, while acting for the buyers in negotiating the purchase of a hotel, received a €10m secret commission from the sellers of the hotel. The buyers paid €211.5m for the hotel and sought to claim the €10m. At first instance, the court held that the claim was a personal claim, applying *Sinclair Investments (UK) Ltd v Versailles Finance Ltd*.[116] The Court of Appeal overruled that decision, concluding that the agent had denied his clients the opportunity to acquire the hotel for €201.5m rather than €211.5m.[117] It was possible to bring the claim within *Sinclair Investments* as the benefit obtained by the agent had been obtained by 'taking advantage of an opportunity which was properly that of the principal' so he must be taken to hold the benefit for his principals who were entitled to proprietary relief.[118] Sir Andrew Morritt concluded his judgment by noting that the decision in *Sinclair Investments* had made the law more complex and uncertain and that it was difficult to draw a borderline between personal and proprietary relief in the manner laid down by Lord Neuberger (see **14-25**).[119] He commented, pointedly, that the Supreme Court would want to address the policy issues raised by *Sinclair Investments* ranging from the need to deter fraud and corruption, to stripping fiduciaries of all benefits obtained, to the position of the fiduciary's creditors, while

---

[108] See Nolan, 'Bribes: A Reprise' (2011) 127 LQR 19 at 22–3, who cautions against taking concerns about injustice to the unsecured creditors of the fiduciary too far; Worthington, n 103, at 750 notes that creditors must take their fiduciary as they find him with all pre-insolvency proprietary interests respected on insolvency; McGrath, n 103, at 521–2 argues that the debate as to the rights of the fiduciary's creditors versus the claims of the principal is misconceived for the first issue is to determine whether the principal has a proprietary claim and that must be answered without regard at this stage to the consequences for others if that is indeed the case. Cf Rotherham, 'Policy and Proprietary Remedies: Are we all Formalists Now' (2012) 65 Current Legal Problems 529; Chambers, 'Constructive Trusts and Breach of Fiduciary Duty' [2013] Conv 241 who raises concerns for the innocent creditors of the fiduciary who are affected by a proprietary claim against the fiduciary, even in circumstances where the principal has suffered no loss.

[109] See Etherton, 'The Legitimacy of Proprietary Relief' (2014) 2(1) Birbeck Law Review 59 who discusses, *inter alia*, the core policy of equity to accord special value to fiduciary relationships, giving the fullest possible protection, recouping to the most perfect extent benefits obtained in breach of duty, and acting as a deterrent (see at 74 and 76); also Millett, 'Bribes and Secret Commissions Again' (2012) 71 CLJ 583 at 599–600; Hedlun, 'Secret Commissions and Constructive Trusts: Yet again!' [2013] JBL 747.

[110] (1726) Sel Cas Ch 61.     [111] [1966] 3 All ER 721.

[112] [1942] 1 All ER 378.     [113] See McGrath, n 103.

[114] See *Grimaldi v Chameleon Mining NL (No 2)* [2012] 287 ALR 22 at [569]–[584], esp [582]; see also Watts (2013) 129 LQR 527 at 532–3 who suggests that the deterrence argument can be overdone.

[115] The substantive first instance hearing is reported at [2012] 2 BCLC 39, Ch D; with the court's order being drawn up later and reported at [2013] 2 BCLC 1.

[116] [2013] 2 BCLC 1.

[117] [2014] Ch 1. Interestingly, Worthington, n 103, at 746, suggests that *Lister v Stubbs* could be analysed in those terms also—the dishonest agent there prevented his principal from obtaining a better price and so, having taken on his own account an opportunity which it was his duty to pursue for his principal, he held the benefit for the principal.

[118] [2013] 2 BCLC 1 at [35], [72], [110].     [119] [2013] 2 BCLC 1 at [116].

having an eye to the international perspective where the approach in *Sinclair Investments* was out of line with that in many other comparator jurisdictions such as Australia, New Zealand, Singapore, and Canada.[120] The matter went to the Supreme Court, therefore, with a clear invitation from the Court of Appeal to resolve some of these issues.

**14-28**  The Supreme Court decision is reported as *FHR European Ventures LLP v Cedar Capital Partners LLC*.[121] The question for the Supreme Court was whether a bribe or secret commission should be treated as the property of the principal given that these payments differ in quality from other benefits obtained by an agent in that they are not derived from assets which are or should be the property of the principal and they could not have been intended to be property of the principal.[122] The Supreme Court (in a single judgment given by Lord Neuberger), having reviewed the academic debate and the case law, concluded that there was no plainly right or plainly wrong answer to the nature of the liability as a matter of pure legal authority, but considerations of practicality and principle supported the case that a bribe or secret commission accepted by an agent is held on trust for his principal.[123] *Lister v Stubbs*[124] was overruled as was *Sinclair Investments (UK) Ltd v Versailles Finance Ltd*,[125] at least in so far as it relied on or followed *Lister*.[126] That the claim for a bribe or secret commission should be proprietary could be justified on the basis that:[127]

- bribes and secret commissions undermine civilised society and trust in the commercial world and one would expect the law to be particularly stringent in relation to a claim against an agent who has received a bribe or secret commission and it could not be less stringent compared to other benefits obtained by an agent in breach of fiduciary duty where the law does give the principal a proprietary interest, citing *Boardman v Phipps*;[128]
- arguments that a proprietary remedy would be unfair to the fiduciary's creditors by reducing his estate were overstated since the bribe should not be in the fiduciary's estate in the first place;[129]
- the bribe or commission will have reduced the benefit to the principal of the transaction and so can fairly be said to be his property (Lord Neuberger noted that it must be quite likely that, in the absence of the commission, the vendor here would have been prepared to sell for less than €211.5m);[130]
- it should be possible for the principal to be able in equity to trace the proceeds of a bribe into other assets and to follow them into the hands of knowing recipients and, to enable tracing, the claimant must have a proprietary interest;

---

[120] [2013] 2 BCLC 1 at [116].    [121] [2014] 2 BCLC 145.

[122] [2014] 2 BCLC 145 at [7], [9], [30]–[31].

[123] [2014] 2 BCLC 145 at [32], [35], [46]–[50]. For commentary on the Supreme Court decision, see Gummow, 'Bribes and Constructive Trusts' (2015) 131 LQR 21; Banerjee, 'European Ventures Gone Wrong' (2014) 27 Insolv Int 123; Whayman, 'Proprietary Remedy Confirmed for Bribes and Secret Commissions' [2014] Conv 518.

[124] (1890) 45 Ch D 1.    [125] [2011] 2 BCLC 501.    [126] [2014] 2 BCLC 145 at [50].

[127] [2014] 2 BCLC 145 at [41]–[45].    [128] [2014] 2 BCLC 145 at [41]–[42].

[129] [2014] 2 BCLC 145 at [43], relying on *Daraydan Holdings Ltd v Solland International Ltd* [2005] 4 All ER 73 at [86], per Lawrence Collins J.

[130] [2014] 2 BCLC 145 at [37]. It is not always the case that the bribe or secret commission will have had an effect on the price paid by the principal. In *Airbus Operations Ltd v Withey* [2014] EWHC 1126 it was accepted (at [73], [124], [431]) that the secret commission paid by a sub-contractor to an agent of the principal had had no impact on the pricing of the services received by the principal or their quality—nevertheless, the principal was entitled to recovery the commission; see also *Reading v Attorney –General* [1951] AC 507 at 515.

- a proprietary claim is accepted in other common law jurisdictions such as Australia, New Zealand, Canada, and Singapore for all benefits obtained in breach of fiduciary duty and it is highly desirable at least to lean in favour of harmonising the development of the common law around the world.

The Supreme Court concluded, therefore, that 'where an agent acquires a benefit which came to his notice as a result of his fiduciary position, or pursuant to an opportunity which results from his fiduciary position, the equitable rule (the rule) is that he is to be treated as having acquired the benefit on behalf of his principal, so that it is beneficially owned by the principal. In such cases, the principal has a proprietary remedy in addition to his personal remedy against the agent ...'[131]

**14-29**  The debate is then settled, at last, and in a way which probably most of the protagonists wanted, namely a proprietary remedy reinforcing the fiduciary obligation of loyalty and stripping the disloyal fiduciary of all of his gains, though there are some issues surrounding *FHR European Ventures v Cedar Capital Partners* which require further consideration. As noted, the conclusion in *FHR European Ventures* is that proprietary relief arises where the agent acquires a benefit which came to his notice 'as a result of his fiduciary position or pursuant to an opportunity which results from his fiduciary position',[132] which means all profits secured by way of misuse of corporate assets, bribes, secret commissions, and all benefits from exploiting property, information, or opportunity (to use the language of CA 2006, s 175(2)) are subject to proprietary claims. The Supreme Court's approval of *Bhullar v Bhullar*[133] reinforces that there is no element of proprietary link with respect to profiting from an opportunity, no limitation to 'properly belonging to the company', Lord Neuberger citing[134] Jonathan Parker LJ's dictum in *Bhullar v Bhullar*[135] that:

'where a fiduciary has exploited a commercial opportunity for his own benefit, the relevant question, in my judgment, is not whether the party to whom the duty is owed (the company, in the instant case) had some kind of beneficial interest in the opportunity: in my judgment that would be too formalistic and restrictive an approach. Rather, the question is simply whether the fiduciary's exploitation of the opportunity is such as to attract the application of the [no-conflict] rule.'

**14-30**  The position adopted in *FHR European Ventures* is a return to the orthodoxy of Lord Russell in *Regal (Hastings) Ltd v Gulliver*[136] where he said:

'The rule of equity which insists on those, who by use of a fiduciary position make a profit, being liable to account for that profit, in no way depends on fraud, or absence of bona fides; or upon such questions or considerations as whether the profit would or should otherwise have gone to the plaintiff, or whether the profiteer was under a duty to obtain the source of the profit for the plaintiff, or whether he took a risk or acted as he did for the benefit of the plaintiff, or whether the plaintiff has in fact been damaged or benefited by his action. The liability arises from the mere fact of a profit having, in the stated circumstances, been made. The profiteer, however honest and well-intentioned, cannot escape the risk of being called upon to account.'

Lord Russell went on: '... the directors standing in a fiduciary relationship to Regal in regard to the exercise of their powers as directors, and having obtained these shares by reason and only by reason of the fact that they were directors of Regal and in the course of the execution

[131] [2014] 2 BCLC 145 at [7], see also [9], [33], [35], [45].    [132] [2014] 2 BCLC 145 at [7].
[133] [2003] 2 BCLC 241.    [134] [2014] 2 BCLC 145 at [14], [30], [36].
[135] [2003] 2 BCLC 241 at [28].    [136] [1967] 2 AC 134 at 144–5.

of that office, are accountable for the profits which they have made out of them'.[137] As stated in *Bhullar v Bhullar*,[138] the defendant directors 'had, at the material time, one capacity and one capacity only in which they were carrying on business, namely as directors of the company'. The consequence of their position as directors means, as Smith puts it,[139] '... that whatever may be extracted from that sphere of activity is attributed as between the fiduciary and the beneficiary, as a matter of primary right, to the beneficiary ... It is not necessary to say that opportunities or information "belong" to the beneficiary in a legal sense; the rule is activated when opportunities or information are used to acquire rights, if they can be said to have been acquired from acting in the fiduciary role.'[140] It is the point made by Millett J, writing extra-judicially, and emphasised by Lord Templeman in *AGHK v Reid*[141] that, when a fiduciary makes a profit, equity assumes he has acted in accordance with his duty to further the interests of his beneficiary, or in the context of company directors, to act to promote the success of the company and so the profit gained is treated as gained on behalf of and held for the principal. Any profit made is indeed as a result of his position.

**14-31**  The position is summed up by Patten LJ in *First Subsea Ltd v Balltec Ltd*[142] where, having considered *FHR European Ventures v Cedar Capital*, he concludes:

> '... a constructive trust will be imposed on fiduciaries ... regardless of whether it is possible to treat the benefit or payment received by the agent as derived from property in which the principal had a pre-existing interest. This is consistent with cases like *Phipps v Boardman* [1967] 2 AC 46 and the decision in *Bhullar v Bhullar* [2003] 2 BCLC 24.'

The decision in *FHR European Ventures v Cedar Capital Partners* is a ringing endorsement of the proprietary claim as the enforcement of the fiduciary obligation arising from the nature of the fiduciary relationship—the fiduciary's duty is to make a profit, if he makes it at all, for his principal, the nexus being that he makes it, receives it, by reason of his relationship.[143] As Longmore LJ explains in *Novoship (UK) Ltd v Nikitin*,[144] equity's response to profiting in breach of the duty of loyalty is to enforce the duty so that the benefit cannot be kept by the fiduciary for himself. Hence in *FHR European Ventures v Cedar Capital Partners* there are numerous references to the proposition that all unauthorised benefits which an agent receives in breach of fiduciary duty are caught by proprietary

---

[137]  [1967] 2 AC 134 at 149.

[138]  [2003] 2 BCLC 241 at [41], per Jonathan Parker LJ. See also *Re Allied Business and Financial Consultants Ltd* [2009] 2 BCLC 666 at [54], [58]–[59], [69], per Rimer LJ.

[139]  Smith, 'Constructive Trusts and the No-profit Rule' (2013) 72 CLJ 260 at 261–2. There is, therefore, in his view no question as to whether some profits attract a proprietary remedy and others do not, there are simply profits extracted from the sphere of fiduciary management. See also Smith, 'Fiduciary Relationships: Ensuring the Loyal Exercise of Judgment on Behalf of Another' (2014) 130 LQR 608 at 628–9: '... when the fiduciary, through the use of the levers of control that he holds over the beneficiary's autonomy, is able to extract some wealth or value, the law ascribes it to the beneficiary as a matter of primary right'. He goes on to explain that the rule is not that if a fiduciary profits from their position, they must disgorge it, rather it is that a fiduciary cannot profit from their position because any profit made will not belong to the fiduciary. See too Etherton, 'The Legitimacy of Proprietary Relief' (2014) 2 Birkbeck Law Review 59 at 82.

[140]  In the context of company directors, to use the language of CA 2006, s 175(1) and (2), profits are extracted in circumstances where the director has a conflict of interest; and see Conaglen 'The Extent of Fiduciary Accounting and the Importance of Authorisation Mechanisms' (2011) 70 CLJ 548 at 551, n 8.

[141]  [1994] 1 All ER 1 at 10, citing Millett, 'Bribes and Secret Commissions' (1993) 1 RLR 7 at 20.

[142]  [2018] 1 BCLC 20 at [37], CA.

[143]  The judgment in *FHR European Ventures LLP v Cedar Capital Partners LLC* is essentially an endorsement of Millett's extra-judicial writing, see Millett, 'Bribes and Secrets Commissions Again' (2012) 71 CLJ 583. As Getzler explains: 'By treating the fiduciary as if he were honest, fiduciary law helps to make him honest', see Getzler, 'Financial Crisis and the Decline of Fiduciary Law' in Morris and Vines (eds), *Capital Failure, Rebuilding Trust in Financial Services* (2014), p 205.       [144]  [2015] 2 WLR 526.

relief,[145] that any benefit acquired by an agent as a result of his agency and in breach of his fiduciary duty is held on trust for his principal.[146] Further, the Supreme Court endorsed a proprietary remedy even in the case of an honest fiduciary, as in *Boardman v Phipps*,[147] and did not suggest that the proprietary remedy be limited to cases of dishonest fiduciaries.[148]

**14-32**   The question is whether any situation remains where there could only be personal relief with respect to a benefit obtained by a director in breach of duty. Applying *FHR European Ventures*, it would be possible now to claim proprietary relief, for example, in a situation such as that in *Gwembe Valley Development Co Ltd v Koshy*[149] where a director profited from an undisclosed conflict of interest in a currency transaction to which the company was party. The facts in *Sinclair Investments (UK) Ltd v Versailles Trade Finance Ltd*[150] too would give rise to a proprietary claim now. The Court of Appeal concluded in *Sinclair Investments* that the benefit which C obtained was derived from his fiduciary position and in plain breach of his fiduciary duties.[151] The profit on the shares was a benefit which the agent acquired through an opportunity resulting from his fiduciary position; it was his fiduciary position with TPL which gave him control of TPL's assets which were used to inflate the value of VTFL and hence inflate the value of the shares in its parent company. On that basis, the claim is a proprietary claim.[152] If there is a class of benefit made by a fiduciary which gives rise only to a personal claim, it would seem to be small, undefined, possibly non-existent.[153] The 'simple answer' may indeed be the broadest

---

[145] [2014] 2 BCLC 145 at [19], [20], [30], [33].

[146] [2014] 2 BCLC 145 at [35], [36], [45]. By not explicitly stating the principle as encompassing all unauthorised benefits, Whayman says the Supreme Court has 'left the door open for cases where a proprietary remedy is denied in circumstances which are not clear', see Whayman, 'Proprietary Remedy Confirmed for Bribes and Secret Commissions' [2014] Conv 518 at 521.        [147] [1967] 2 AC 46.

[148] See Watts, 'Tyrrell v Bank of London—an Inside Look at an Inside Job' (2013) 129 LQR 527 at 532 who suggested that proprietary remedies (to which he is opposed) might be limited to the dishonest fiduciary, but the Supreme Court went the other way, endorsing the grant of proprietary relief in the case of an honest fiduciary (and incidentally ending any debate as to whether the relief granted in *Boardman v Phipps* [1967] 2 AC 46 was proprietary, see [2014] 2 BCLC 145 at [14]); likewise Sir Terence Etherton in the Court of Appeal, see [2013] 2 BCLC 1 at [91]–[93]. See Whayman, 'Proprietary Remedy Confirmed for Bribes and Secret Commissions' [2014] Conv 518 at 524 who wonders if, even the honest fiduciary is subject to a proprietary claim, whether the consequence of *FHR European Ventures Ltd*, even if not expressly spelt out by the Supreme Court, is to make proprietary relief available in almost every case.

[149] [2004] 1 BCLC 131. At the time only a personal claim was brought, see [2004] 1 BCLC 131 at 165, per Mummery LJ: '… it is clear in our view that any trust imposed on [the director] is a class 2 trust within Millett LJ's classification', a view criticised by Elliott and Mitchell, 'Remedies for Dishonest Assistance' (2004) 67 MLR 16 at 32; also Hayton, 'Proprietary Liability for Secret Profits' (2011) 127 LQR 487 at 490; also McGrath, n 103, 542–5.

[150] [2011] 2 BCLC 501, CA, aff'g [2011] 1 BCLC 202.        [151] [2011] 2 BCLC 501 at [55], [92].

[152] As Conaglen seems to support, see Conaglen, 'Proprietary Remedies for Breach of Fiduciary Duty' (2014) 73 CLJ 490 at 492; and Worthington, n 103, at 744 ('It is hard to describe this gain in any way other than a gain derived from the "use" of the principal's assets'); but see Etherton, n 105, at 85 who thinks that analysis of *Sinclair* somewhat controversial—admittedly writing ahead of *FHR European Ventures*; see also *Foskett v McKeown* [2000] 3 All ER 102.

[153] See Worthington, n 103, writing ahead of the Supreme Court decision in *FHR European Ventures*, who while attempting to come up with an alternative analysis of *Sinclair* concluded that practically all profiting will give rise to a proprietary claim with there being very few cases of benefits which would merit only a personal claim (at 748). She would have limited proprietary claims essentially to misuse of a principal's property, and gains from a conflict of interest if the opportunity etc ought to have been obtained for the principal, with gains from a misuse of position not falling within the above two categories being personal, while recognising that many cases of misuse of position will involve a conflict and so will fall into her second proprietary category. Illustrating the difficulties here in identifying a personal claim only, Worthington considers *Attorney General v Reid* to fall into that category, though it did involve a conflict of interest, it was not a benefit which ought to have been obtained for the principal. *FHR European Ventures v Cedar Capital* now supports a proprietary remedy in *AGHK v Reid* so even the small category which Worthington thought would justify a personal claim only has been extinguished by the decision in *FHR European Ventures v Cedar Capital*.

formulation, that all benefits obtained by a fiduciary in breach of duty are held on trust for her principal,[154] but a further complication then is that those jurisdictions which favour proprietary relief with respect to all benefits obtained by the fiduciary do so on the basis of a remedial constructive trust where the court has a discretion as to whether to grant proprietary relief.[155] The English courts favour an institutional constructive trust (where the court's role is to declare its existence[156]) and have declined to endorse the remedial constructive trust,[157] but the 'simple answer' above may now force a reconsideration of that position.[158]

### The extent of the liability to account

**14-33** The purpose of a liability to account for secret profits is to strip the defaulting fiduciary of his profit[159] and the burden of proof is on the defaulting fiduciary to show that the profit is not one for which he should account.[160]

**14-34** In many instances, the breach of duty by a director will involve the exploitation by the director of some property, information, or opportunity in a situation of conflict of interest in breach of s 175(1) and (2) (see **12-21** et seq). As the Supreme Court confirms in *FHR European Ventures v Cedar Capital Partners LLC*,[161] a director who exploits such a situation on his own behalf holds the fruits of that breach of duty as a trustee on behalf of the company. Hence, in *Cook v Deeks*[162] (see **12-15**) the benefit of a contract (which the company had been pursuing but which the directors secured on their own behalf) belonged in equity to the company and the directors were bound to hold it on behalf of the company. In *Bhullar v Bhullar*[163] (see **12-13**) the opportunity to acquire a neighbouring property

---

[154] See Watts, 'Tyrrell v Bank of London—an Inside Look at an Inside Job' (2013) 129 LQR 527 at 532–3 who argues that the grant of proprietary remedies is overkill and that simplicity is only a good thing if the benefits (of a proprietary remedy) outweigh the costs, which he disputes, and he would argue that, as a starting point, a proposition that all remedies for wrongs are personal is arguably even simpler.

[155] See *Grimaldi v Chameleon Mining NL (No 2)* [2012] 287 ALR 22 at [582]–[583], a flexibility which allows the court to take into account matters such as the insolvency of the defendant fiduciary.

[156] See Millett, 'Bribes and Secret Commissions, Again' (2012) 71 CLJ 583 at 589.

[157] See *FHR European Ventures LLP v Cedar Capital Partners LLC* [2014] 2 BCLC 145 at [47] where Lord Neuberger noted that the concept of a remedial constructive trust was authoritatively said not to be part of English law, citing Lord Browne-Wilkinson in *Westdeutsche Landesbank Girozentrale v Islington LBC* [1996] 2 All ER 961 at 996–8. Gummow (2015) 131 LQR 21 at 26 notes that what Lord Browne-Wilkinson actually said was that whether English law should adopt a remedial constructive trust would have to be decided in some future case where the point was directly in issue, [1996] 2 All ER 961 at 998. See also *Re Polly Peck plc (No 2)* [1998] 3 All ER 812; and see Swadling, 'The Fiction of the Constructive Trust' (2011) 64 Current Legal Problems 399 at 431–2 who makes the point that all 'constructive trusts' are remedial since in truth they are nothing more than court orders and so he considers this distinction between remedial and institutional trusts is just a further fiction.

[158] See Conaglen, 'Proprietary Remedies for Breach of Fiduciary Duty' (2014) 73 CLJ 490 at 492–3.

[159] See *Murad v Al-Saraj* [2005] EWCA Civ 959 at [56], per Arden LJ; at [108], per Jonathan Parker LJ; *United Pan-Europe Communications NV v Deutsche Bank AG* [2000] 2 BCLC 461 at 484, CA. *Airbus Operations Ltd v Withey* [2014] EWHC 1126 at [126], [127], [438], [461].

[160] See *Murad v Al-Saraj* [2005] EWCA Civ 959 at [77]; also *Clegg v Pache* [2017] EWCA Civ 256 at [59]; just as it is for the fiduciary to justify any payment out of trust funds in any case where there is doubt as to whether it is properly made: *Ross River Ltd v Waveley Commercial Ltd* [2014] 1 BCLC 545 at [64], [94], [96], [120], [126].

[161] [2014] 2 BCLC 145.

[162] [1916] 1 AC 554.    [163] [2003] 2 BCLC 241.

was exploited by the directors on their own behalf so they held the property on trust for the company.

**14-35**   If a director diverts contracts, opportunities, etc to a partnership where he is only one of the number of partners, he is liable to account to the full extent of the profit made on the contract, even if his partners are entitled to a share of those profits and are ignorant of his breach of duty, but to the extent that a number of the partners are implicated in the breach of duty, they are jointly and severally liable.[164]

**14-36**   Often the opportunity taken also leads to other opportunities, for which the dishonest fiduciary must also account. In *CMS Dolphin Ltd v Simonet*[165] a director of the claimant company, an advertising agency, left the company and set up a new business. All the staff of the company subsequently joined him as did the principal clients of the company. The court found that the director took away from the company the benefit of contracts with existing clients and the business opportunities the company had with those clients. The director was held liable to account for the profits derived from those contracts/opportunities which he had diverted from the company to his new business, together with a sum to take account of other benefits derived from those contracts, for example, other contracts might not have been won, or profits made on them, without the opportunity or cash-flow benefit which flowed from the contracts unlawfully obtained.[166] In *Lindsley v Woodfull*[167] (the case concerned a partnership but the same principles apply) a partner who diverted to his own business a contract which the partnership had been pursuing had to account for the profits from the contract *and* the profits from its subsequent renewal[168] as those profits are consequent upon the breach of duty. In *Kingsley IT Consulting Ltd v McIntosh*[169] (see **12-35**) the director's liability to account extended from the profit derived from the contract which he had diverted from his company to the profit derived from two subsequent extensions of that contract.

**14-37**   If a director in breach of duty diverts away an opportunity to a company which he owns or controls or has an interest in, it is not necessary to consider piercing or lifting the corporate veil. The position is more straightforward with the director liable for his breach of duty for which he must account and the company liable as a third party on the basis of dishonest assistance or of knowing receipt.[170] For example, in *Quarter Master UK v Pyke*[171]

---

[164] *Imperial Mercantile Credit Association v Coleman* (1873) LR 6 HL 189 at 208–9. The 'innocent' partner in this case turned out to be acquainted with the whole (conflicted) transaction from first to last and as such was implicated in the breach of duty—he too was a wrongdoer, hence they were jointly and severally liable for the same breach.                                                              [165] [2001] 2 BCLC 704.

[166] [2001] 2 BCLC 704 at [97], subject to taking into account the expenses connected with those profits and a reasonable allowance for overheads.

[167] [2004] 2 BCLC 131.

[168] See [2004] 2 BCLC 131; indeed the partner had to account for profits made on those contracts even after he had left the partnership as profit arising from his breach of duty, see at [28]. There will come a point, of course, as Jonathan Parker LJ noted in *Murad v Al-Saraj* [2005] EWCA Civ 959 at [115], when it can safely be said that profits of a business are not attributable to the opportunity taken from the original company and are not tainted by the conflict in which the defaulting directors had placed themselves.

[169] [2006] BCC 875. See too *Quarter Master UK Ltd v Pyke* [2005] 1 BCLC 245.

[170] For example, in *Crown Dilmun v Sutton* [2004] 1 BCLC 468 the defaulting director held 49 per cent of the company which secured the contract diverted by the director from his own company. The recipient company was liable on the basis of knowing receipt because the director's knowledge of his breach of duty was attributed to the company with serious consequences for the majority shareholder of the recipient company who had no knowledge of the breach of fiduciary duty (see at [200]–[201]).

[171] [2005] 1 BCLC 245.

(see **12-24**) the directors obtained a contract for themselves in breach of the no-conflict rule when the contract should have been obtained for their company and they were liable to account for the profits made by them. The company to which they diverted the contract was also liable to account for the profits derived by it from the arrangements on the basis of knowing receipt.[172] The director's liability is to account for all of *his* gain and where his gain is indirect through, for example, an increase in value of his shareholding in a company which exploited the opportunity etc, he must still account for that gain as part of his personal liability to account for all of his profits.[173] Where there is an overlap between the recipient company's liability and the director's liability to account, the court is careful to prevent double recovery.

**14-38**    In limited circumstances, the court may lift the corporate veil, applying *Prest v Petrodel Resources Ltd*[174] (see Chapter 3), to see if the company is merely the director's alter ego. An essential distinction is drawn in *Prest* between piercing the corporate veil (to be done only in very exceptional and limited circumstances where a person is under an existing legal obligation or liability or subject to an existing legal restriction which he deliberately evades or whose enforcement he deliberately frustrates by interposing a company under his control)[175] and lifting the veil (to identify the real actors behind the company).[176] In *Airbus Operations Ltd v Withey*,[177] applying *Prest v Petrodel*, the court lifted the veil of two companies to establish that they were mere alter egos for two fiduciaries who had obtained secret commissions and the companies were liable accordingly with the fiduciaries.[178]

**14-39**    Finally, in keeping with the strict approach taken to breaches of fiduciary duty (and bearing in mind the fiduciary could have sought the consent of the beneficiaries by full disclosure), the courts are reluctant to exercise their discretion to grant an equitable allowance to the fiduciary for his work and skill[179] in generating the profits for which he is being held accountable. The aim is to ensure that fiduciaries are denied any incentive to act in breach of fiduciary duty, though an allowance will be made for costs incurred in securing the profit.[180] An allowance will only be granted if it can be given without undermining the fiduciary obligation to avoid conflicts of interest and doubts were expressed in *Guinness plc v Saunders*[181] as to whether such an allowance could ever be permitted in the case of company directors acting in breach of their fiduciary obligations. In *Quarter Master UK Ltd v Pyke*,[182] see **12-24**, applying *Guinness plc v Saunders*, the court refused

---

[172]  See [2005] 1 BCLC 245 at [79].

[173]  *Gwembe Valley Development Co Ltd v Koshy* [2004] 1 BCLC 131 at [137].

[174]  [2014] 1 BCLC 30.        [175]  [2014] 1 BCLC 30 at [35].

[176]  [2014] 1 BCLC 30 at [28].        [177]  [2014] EWHC 1126 at [453]–[463].

[178]  The court applying *Gencor v Dalby* [2000] 2 BCLC 734 at [25]–[26]—the company in *Gencor* was little more than a cover for the director's bank account.

[179]  *Phipps v Boardman* [1966] 3 All ER 721.

[180]  In *Clegg v Pache* [2017] EWCA Civ 256 at [60]–[61], an allowance for overheads was made; also *CMS Dolphin Ltd v Simonet* [2001] 2 BCLC 704 at [97] where an allowance was possible for overheads and expenses connected with exploiting the corporate opportunities which the wrongdoer had diverted to his own business, but not for a salary for the wrongdoer. In *Cobbetts v Hodge* [2010] 1 BCLC 30 an allowance was made for the costs of acquiring shares from which the fiduciary profited personally, but no allowance was made for his work and skill to enhance their value. In *Lee v Futurist Developments Ltd* [2011] 1 BCLC 654, a director had to account for a secret commission which he obtained subject to an allowance limited to legitimate expenses incurred in securing the commission.

[181]  [1990] 1 All ER 652; see *Re PV Solar Solutions Ltd, Bell v Hughes* [2018] 1 BCLC 58.

[182]  [2005] 1 BCLC 245 at 271–2.

any allowance for the directors who diverted a contract away from the company to themselves. There was no evidence that they had exercised any special skills or taken unusual risks and the fact that the company could not have obtained the contract (it was in severe financial difficulties) did not make the facts sufficiently special to persuade the court to exercise its discretion.

### A limitation defence

**14-40**   Faced with the extensive liabilities which can arise from a breach of duty, a director will often plead a limitation defence which may well be available given that it can take a long time for breaches of duty to come to light. Often a change of ownership of the company is necessary before anyone considers pursuing a wrongdoing director. The Limitation Act 1980, s 21(3) provides for a six-year limitation period for an action by a beneficiary to recover trust property or in respect of any breach of trust, subject to s 21(1) which provides that no period of limitation prescribed by this Act shall apply to an action by a beneficiary under a trust, being an action:

    (a)  in respect of any fraud or fraudulent breach of trust to which the trustee was a party or privy; or

    (b)  to recover from the trustee trust property or the proceeds of trust property in the possession of the trustee, or previously received by the trustee and converted to his use.[183]

**14-41**   In *Williams v Central Bank of Nigeria*[184] the Supreme Court by a majority limited the application of s 21 in two ways holding that:[185]

    (i)  'trustee' in s 21(1) means a trustee as such (i.e. a class 1 *Paragon*) and not a person described as a 'constructive trustee' (class 2 *Paragon)* as a shorthand for someone subject to equitable remedies by virtue of being a wrongdoer, whether as a dishonest assistant or knowing recipient[186] (majority was 4-1 on this point, Lord Mance dissenting). This analysis is consistent with the approach of Millett LJ in *Paragon* which categorises as true trustees those with the pre-existing obligations of trustees (including company directors, as we have seen) which is not the case with accessory liability where the wrongdoers' role and possession is adverse to the beneficiaries from the beginning.[187] Knowing recipients and dishonest assistants will be subject to the general six-year limitation period in the Limitation Act 1980, s 21(3).[188]

---

[183] The running of a limitation period can also be delayed where there has been deliberate concealment, etc, see Limitation Act 1980, s 32 (postponement of limitation period in case of fraud, concealment, or mistake).

[184] [2014] 2 All ER 489. See Davies, 'Limitation in Equity' [2014] LMCLQ 313; Watterson, 'Limitation of Actions, Dishonest Assistance and Knowing Receipt' (2014) 73 CLJ 253; Lee, 'Constructing and Limiting Liability in Equity' (2015) 131 LQR 39.

[185] The facts are irrelevant for our purposes. Essentially, a Nigerian businessman paid $6.5m to a solicitor in 1986 who, in alleged breach of trust, paid most of it over to the Nigerian Central Bank in what the businessman alleged was a scam perpetrated by the Nigerian Security Services. The claim was an attempt to recover the money from the Central Bank as a dishonest assistant or knowing recipient of the money. The Bank raised a limitation defence.

[186] This majority was made up of Lord Sumption (with whom Lord Hughes agreed), Lord Neuberger, and Lord Clarke. See [2014] 2 All ER 489 at [26], [28]–[29], [31], per Lord Sumption; at [57], [64], [66], [90], per Lord Neuberger; at [165], per Lord Clarke. See also *Cattley v Pollard* [2007] Ch 353; *Halton International Inc (Holdings) Sarl v Guernroy Ltd* [2006] EWCA Civ 801.

[187] *Paragon Finance plc v D B Thakerar & Co* [1999] 1 All ER 400 at 408–9.

[188] Subject to the possible application of the Limitation Act 1980, s 32 (postponement of limitation period in case of fraud, concealment, or mistake).

(ii) that s 21(1)(a) should be interpreted narrowly so as to apply only to a trustee who is a party or privy to a fraud or fraudulent breach of trust; it does not extend to anyone involved in a fraud or fraudulent breach to which the trustee is party or privy (the majority was 3-2 on this point, Lords Mance and Clarke dissenting). For Lords Sumption (with whom Lord Hughes agreed) and Neuberger, this provision (s 21(1)(a)) is limited to true trustees, a view consistent with their reading of the section overall; the wording 'to which the trustee was party or privy' is there to distinguish between honest and dishonest trustees. The liability of an accessory is independent of any fraud on the part of the trustee and there is no reason therefore why the limitation period vis-à-vis a non-trustee should depend on and differ depending on the honesty or dishonesty of the trustee.[189]

**14-42**   Lord Mance dissented on both rulings, considering it to be a perfectly principled analysis of the section, consistent with its wording, history, and the Parliamentary intention, for s 21(1)(a), see **14-40**, to capture both the fraudulent trustee and his dishonest assistant, noting that the oddity of the majority view on this point is that one of the conspirators has a limitation defence, but the other does not.[190] In his opinion, those guilty of knowing receipt should likewise be unable to avail of a limitation defence and should be treated as trustees within the scope of s 21(1)(b).[191] Lord Clarke (while agreeing with the majority that 'trustee' in the section means a true trustee and accessories are not true trustees) agreed with Lord Mance on this second point regarding the meaning of s 21(1)(a). Given the wording ('to which the trustee was a party or privy') Lord Clarke thought it was intended to encompass both the trustee and any other person liable in respect of a fraud or fraudulent breach of trust and therefore a dishonest assistant or knowing recipient in the case of a fraud or fraudulent breach of trust to which the trustee was party should be treated in the same way as the trustee for limitation purposes.[192]

**14-43**   The judgment in *Williams v Central Bank of Nigeria* has its difficulties, especially on the second issue where the minority's reading of s 21(1)(a) is attractive.[193] On the other hand, the majority position on the first issue,[194] that trustees means true trustees and not accessories in respect of whom the formula 'constructive trustee' is merely a shorthand for equitable relief is consistent with the common acceptance of the much cited analysis of this matter offered by Millett J in *Paragon*. It has the merit of clarity, it helps in the development of a coherent position and removes uncertainty on this important matter,[195] so reducing litigation costs.

---

[189] [2014] 2 All ER 489 at [34]–[35], per Lord Sumption; at [96]–[99] per Lord Neuberger; and see Davies, n 184, 315.

[190] [2014] 2 All ER 489 at [124], [129], [157], [161]. But, as Lord Hoffmann pointed out in *Peconic Industrial Developments Ltd v Lan Kwok Fai* [2009] 5 HKC 135 at [24] there is a key distinction here: one party is a fiduciary, the dishonest assistant is not. From a policy perspective, the more egregious behaviour is by the fiduciary and the harsher treatment of the fiduciary reinforces the deterrence effect. On the other hand, without the dishonest assistance, some of these breaches by a fiduciary might not occur.

[191] [2014] 2 All ER 489 at [160]–[161].          [192] [2014] 2 All ER 489 at [176].

[193] See [2014] 2 All ER 489 at [129], [157], [161], per Lord Mance; at [171], [175]–[176], per Lord Clarke. See Lee, n 184, 41; and Davies, n 184, 316, who note that, while the minority view may represent the more faithful interpretation of the provision, to read it in that way does not sit comfortably with the fact that the focus of accessory liability is on the culpability of the defendant, not the trustee.

[194] Though open to criticism in terms of textual analysis, see Lee, n 184, 42; and in terms of their conclusion that a knowing recipient is not a trustee, see Watterson, n 184, 255–6.

[195] See at [116]–[117], per Lord Neuberger; also Davies, n 184.

**14-44**   The position then is that LA 1980, s 21(3) sets the primary limitation period for a claim against directors for a breach of duty at six years.[196] No limitation defence is available, however, where the claim is within s 21(1)(a) or s 21(1)(b) which are considered below.

### (i) Claim for any fraud or fraudulent breach of duty–LA 1980, s 21(1)(a)

**14-45**   As to what makes a breach of duty fraudulent, in *Armitage v Nurse*[197] Millett LJ considered that it 'connotes at the minimum an intention on the part of the trustee to pursue a particular course of action, either knowing that it is contrary to the interests of the beneficiaries or being recklessly indifferent as to whether it is contrary to their interests or not'. He went on:

> 'It is the duty of a trustee to manage the trust property and deal with it in the interests of the beneficiaries. If he acts in a way which he does not honestly believe is in their interests then he is acting dishonestly. It does not matter whether he stands, or thinks he stands, to gain personally from his actions. A trustee who acts with the intention of benefiting persons who are not the objects of the trust is not the less dishonest because he does not intend to benefit himself.'[198]

There must be an absence of honesty or good faith and this can include being reckless as to the consequences of the action complained of.[199] In *Gwembe Valley Development Co Ltd v Koshy*[200] a director gained a profit of £5m from an undisclosed conflict of interest in a currency transaction between the company and a business in which he had an interest. The Court of Appeal upheld the first instance conclusion that he was dishonest in pursuing a particular cause of action in his own interests, either knowing that it was contrary to the interests of the company or recklessly indifferent as to whether it was so contrary. No limitation period applied. In *First Subsea Ltd v Balltec Ltd*[201] a director who resigned, set up his own company, and competed for business opportunities against his former company was held to have done so knowing his acts would injure his former company and intending that they should. His breach of duty was fraudulent, i.e. dishonest, and no limitation period applied.

### (ii) Claim to recover company (trust) property or proceeds etc–LA 1980, s 21(1)(b)

**14-46**   As already noted, it is common for a claim against a director to be a claim to recover company property so this ground is frequently relied upon to counter a limitation defence by a director. In *Haysport Properties Ltd v Ackerman*,[202] the defendant, who was the sole effective director of the two claimant companies, had the companies provide loans and security in 2005 to another company in which he had a personal interest. There was no benefit to the claimant companies in these arrangements which were on uncommercial terms. Eventually, the director was removed from office in 2011 and a new board issued a claim form in June 2014, well outside the six-year limitation period. Peter Smith J held

---

[196] There is no longer any need to argue for six years by way of analogy with contract and tort claims, applying LA 1980, s 36. As Patten LJ pointed out in *First Subsea Ltd v Balltec Ltd* [2018] 1 BCLC 20 at [50], the effect of the decisions in *Williams v Central Bank of Nigeria* [2014] 2 All ER 489 and *Paragon Finance plc v DB Thakerar & Co* [1999] 1 All ER 400 is that a director is a 'trustee' for the purposes of LA 1980, s 21 which is directly applicable to claims which are made against a director for breach of duty.

[197] [1997] 2 All ER 705 at 711.       [198] [1997] 2 All ER 705 at 711.

[199] Per Patten LJ, *First Subsea Ltd v Balltec Ltd* [2018] 1 BCLC 20 at [64], CA.

[200] [2004] 1 BCLC 131 at [135], aff'g on this point [2002] 1 BCLC 478 at [273].

[201] [2014] EWHC 866 at [474], aff'd [2018] 1 BCLC 20 at [64]–[69].

[202] [2016] EWHC 393 (Ch), [2016] 2 BCLC 522.

that the director was hopelessly conflicted and in breach of his duties to the claimant companies, but he was not dishonest. As a claim to recover trust property, it fell within LA 1980, s 21(1)(b) and no limitation period applied. In *Bhullar v Bhullar*,[203] the claim was for losses suffered by certain family companies when unauthorised loans and payments were made by the companies to a company owned by one of the directors of the family companies. It was a claim to recover trust property and fell within s 21(1)(b) such that no limitation period applied.

**14-47**  Section 21(1)(b) requires that the property or its proceeds be received by the director and in *Burnden Holdings (UK) Ltd v Fielding*[204] the question was whether receipt by a company controlled by a director is receipt by the director for these purposes. In this case, the property in question (the company's shareholding in a subsidiary company) had been transferred from the claimant company to X Co and hence to Y Co by way of a distribution *in specie*. For the purposes of the case, it was assumed that the distribution was unlawful. A limitation defence was raised by the defendants (directors of the claimant who allegedly acted in breach of duty in making the transfer) who argued that, as they were merely shareholders in X Co and then in Y Co, they had never received the property for the purposes of LA 1980, s 21(1)(b) and, so, a six-year period applied and defeated the claim.

**14-48**  The Court of Appeal agreed that, on a literal reading of s 21(1)(b), it requires the defendant trustee to have received the property and therefore this scenario where the property is received by a company controlled by the defendant would not fall within s 21(1)(b).[205] David Richards LJ said, however, that it would be surprising if the section only applied where literally the defendant received the property, given the prevalence of the use of companies to hold assets. If the section were to be construed in that way, to apply only to those cases where the trustee (the director in our context) directly and personally acquires the trust property, its evident purpose would be much constrained and easily avoided.[206] The Court of Appeal concluded, therefore, endorsing the approach in *Re Pantone 485 Ltd*,[207] that a construction of the provision which includes within its terms a transfer of property to a company directly or indirectly controlled by the trustee is within the meaning of the provision.[208] It followed, on the facts, that the transfers from the claimant company to Company X and hence to Company Y were transfers of company property to a company directly or indirectly controlled by the directors and a claim to recover that property was within s 21(1)(b) such that no limitation period applied.

**14-49**  The directors appealed unsuccessfully to the Supreme Court[209] which adopted a more straightforward analysis. In the case of company directors, the court noted, s 21(1)(b) did not become inapplicable merely because the misappropriated property had remained legally and beneficially owned by corporate vehicles, rather than having become vested in law or in equity in the defaulting directors.[210] Lord Briggs, giving the judgment of the court, considered that if directors have misappropriated trust property before action is brought by the company to recover it, they may or may not by that time still be in possession of it.[211] But if their misappropriation of the company's property amounts to a conversion of it to their own use, they will still necessarily have previously received it, by virtue of being the fiduciary

---

[203] [2017] EWHC 407.
[204] [2018] UKSC 14, [2018] 2 WLR 885, aff'g on different grounds [2017] EWCA Civ 557, [2017] 1 WLR 39.
[205] [2017] EWCA Civ 557, [2017] 1 WLR 39, aff'd on different grounds, [2018] UKSC 14, [2018] 2 WLR 885.
[206] [2017] EWCA Civ 557, [2017] 1 WLR 39 at [37].       [207] [2002] 1 BCLC 266.
[208] [2017] EWCA Civ 557, [2017] 1 WLR 39 at [37].       [209] [2018] UKSC 14, [2018] 2 WLR 885.
[210] [2018] UKSC 14, [2018] 2 WLR 885 at [16].       [211] [2018] UKSC 14, [2018] 2 WLR 885 at [19].

stewards of it as directors.[212] Individual directors are regarded as being in possession, or in previous receipt, of company property by virtue of their office. On the assumed facts, the defendant directors converted the company's shareholding in the subsidiary company when they procured or participated in the unlawful distribution of it. That was a taking of the company's property in defiance of the company's rights of ownership and the defendants had previously received the property because, as directors of the claimant company, they had been its fiduciary stewards from the outset.[213] It may well be, he said, that in relation to trustees who are company directors, the requirement in LA 1980, s 21(1)(b) that the property be 'previously received' by the trustee adds little to or nothing to the conditions for the dis-application of a limitation period.[214] The court also considered that there is no need to have regard to anti-avoidance in construing section 21(1)(b). The deliberate use of a corporate vehicle to distance a defaulting trustee from the receipt or possession of misappropriated trust property might justify lifting the corporate veil and, in any event, it would in most cases justify a finding of fraud within the meaning of section 21(1)(a) of the 1980 Act. [215]

### Claim for an account of profits made in breach of duty

**14-50**  There remains the issue of whether a claim for an account of profits as a result of a breach of duty, as opposed to equitable compensation for the loss of company property, falls within s 21(1)(b). In the Court of Appeal in *Burnden Holdings (UK) Ltd v Fielding*,[216] David Richards LJ indicated, obiter, that he was inclined to think a claim for an account of profits would not be within s 21(1)(b).[217] As discussed earlier, where there is a breach of duty in circumstances which generate a profit for the wrongdoing director, but there is no misappropriation or use of company property to generate the profit, the company's claim is not a claim to recover company property, but to have an accounting in equity of the profit made in breach of duty. As explained by Norris J at first instance in *First Subsea Ltd v Balltec Ltd*,[218] the distinction is between wrongful dealing with pre-existing assets that have been entrusted to the fiduci-ary, as where a director abuses the power of disposition which he has over company prop-erty, and a claim to an account of profits which comes into existence by reason of the breach of fiduciary duty itself and in respect of which the director is to be treated as if he were a trustee. The point is addressed in *Gwembe Development Ltd v Koshy*[219] where the Court of Appeal agreed that the claim (for profit made from an undisclosed conflict of interest) was not to recover property, but merely an accounting for a profit. Now, given *FHR European Ventures LLP v Cedar Capital LLC*,[220] it is possible to seek personal and proprietary relief, but the claim remains one for the profit made, not a claim to recover property, hence it is not within s 21(1)(b). In *First Subsea Ltd v Balltec Ltd*,[221] a director resigned from this company and formed another company which immediately tendered for certain contracts in competition with his former company. His new company secured one contract which was therefore lost to the company and it was accepted that the new company's presence in the market forced his former company to lower their tender price on another contract by approximately £300,000 in order to secure it. On a claim being brought against the director for breach of duty, he raised a limitation defence. On appeal, the Court of Appeal applied *Gwembe Valley v Koshy*[222] and held that the claim is for an accounting of profits made in breach of duty, but not involving a misappropriation of company assets.[223] The director's disloyalty is a breach of duty for which he is accountable in equity but it is not a claim

---

[212] [2018] UKSC 14, [2018] 2 WLR 885 at [19], [22].          [213] [2018] UKSC 14, [2018] 2 WLR 885 at [22].
[214] [2018] UKSC 14, [2018] 2 WLR 885 at [19]–[20].          [215] [2018] 2 WLR 885 at [16].
[216] [2016] EWCA Civ 557, [2017] 1 WLR 39.          [217] [2016] EWCA Civ 557, [2017] 1 WLR 39 at [38].
[218] [2014] EWHC 866 at [472].          [219] [2004] 1 BCLC 131.          [220] [2014] 2 BCLC 145.
[221] [2008] 1 BCLC 20.          [222] [2014] EWHC 866 at [472].          [223] [2018] 1 BCLC 20 at [59]–[63].

within s 21(1)(b) to recover possession of or the proceeds of company property. The claim will fall within s 21(1)(a), however, if the claimant can establish that it was a fraudulent breach of duty.[224] On the facts in *First Subsea Ltd v Balltec*, the court at first instance had concluded that the director had acted dishonestly, knowing or being recklessly indifferent to whether his actions would injure those to whom he owed his fiduciary duties, and the Court of Appeal concluded that that finding was open to the trial judge.[225] Therefore, no limitation period applied to the claim by virtue of LA 1980, s 21(1)(a).

**14-51** In practice, since all secret profit making by directors will be contrary to the interests of the company, it will be straightforward to allege that the case falls within s 21(1)(a) as a fraud or fraudulent breach of duty, but the claim must be pleaded as such and not as a claim to recover trust property. Indeed, fraud was also the solution in *Gwembe Valley Development Co Ltd v Koshy*[226] where the court concluded that the director had deliberately and dishonestly concealed his conflict of interest from his fellow directors and so it was a fraud or fraudulent breach of trust on his part and no limitation period applied.

## C Liability of third parties

**14-52** Third party liability may arise on one of two main grounds (and in many cases on both):[227]

(1) on the basis of 'dishonest assistance' where the third party has participated or assisted in the breach by the director of his duties;[228]

(2) on the basis of 'knowing receipt' of company funds.

Another possibility is to seek to hold the third party liable in damages as party to a conspiracy to injure by unlawful means,[229] the unlawful means being the breach of fiduciary duty, or, perhaps, on the basis of procuring or inducing a breach of contract by the director.[230] Liability under the respective headings is not cumulative[231] and a payment, for example, under a personal liability to account in equity will discharge *pro tanto* damages awarded in respect of the same conduct on the grounds of unlawful means conspiracy and

---

[224] The approach of the Court of Appeal seemed to find favour with the Supreme Court, see obiter comment in *Burden v Fielding* [2018] 2 WLR 885 at [11].

[225] [2018] 1 BCLC 20 at [472]; see also *Taylor v Davies* [1920] AC 636.     [226] [2004] 1 BCLC 131.

[227] See, for example, *Williams v Central Bank of Nigeria* [2014] 2 All ER 489; *Novoship (UK) Ltd v Nikitin* [2015] 2 WLR 526.

[228] *Royal Brunei Airlines v Tan* [1995] 3 All ER 97, PC; *Barnes v Addy* (1874) LR 9 Ch App 244.

[229] *OBG Ltd v Allan* [2007] 4 All ER 545, HL. See *Simtel Communications Ltd v Rebak* [2006] 2 BCLC 571; *British Midland Tool Ltd v Midland International Tooling Ltd* [2003] 2 BCLC 523; *Aerostar Maintenance International Ltd v Wilson* [2010] EWHC 2032 at [172]–[177], [189]–[191]. See too the cautionary words of Morgan J in *Aerostar*, at [170], as to the undesirability, where accessory liability is being determined both on the basis of equitable liability (dishonest assistance and knowing receipt) and on the basis of the tort of conspiracy to injure by unlawful means, of differing principles governing accessory liability.

[230] See *Mainstream Properties Ltd v Young* [2007] 4 All ER 545, HL; *Aerostar Maintenance International Ltd v Wilson* [2010] EWHC 2032 at [163]–[166]. There is no independent tort of procuring a breach of fiduciary duty, rather accessory liability is imposed via dishonest assistance and knowing receipt, see *First Subsea Ltd v Balltec Ltd* [2014] EWHC 866 at [351]–[353].

[231] In *Law Society of England & Wales v Isaac* [2010] EWHC 1670 at [99], Norris J cautioned against the temptation to advance multiple analyses of the same facts in terms of differing causes of action unless it is anticipated to produce a significantly different outcome in terms of ultimate recovery, having regard to a defendant's means. His words appear to have fallen on deaf ears, see *Airbus Operations Ltd v Withey* [2014] EWHC 1126 at [75]; *Madoff Securities International Ltd v Raven* [2013] EWHC 3147 at [15], [19].

liability under dishonest assistance and knowing receipt in respect of the same breach of duty will simply provide a different basis for recovery for the sums in question.[232]

**14-53**   As discussed earlier, following *Williams v Central Bank of Nigeria*[233] a knowing recipient or dishonest assistant can rely on the six-year limitation period prescribed by the Limitation Act 1980, see **14-40** et seq.[234] Liability is fault-based, for participation in wrongdoing[235] and proprietary relief can be ordered if the facts warrant it (i.e. the company's assets or their identifiable substitutes are in the hands of the accessory).[236]

**14-54**   In an appropriate case, a dishonest assistant or a knowing recipient can be liable to account for profits made by them as well as to make good a loss,[237] but, as an accessory is not a fiduciary and is not being sued for breach of fiduciary duty, the court has a discretion and may decline to make an order for an account of profits if it would be disproportionate.[238]

## Dishonest assistance

**14-55**   It is not a requirement for a claim for dishonest assistance that the breach of duty by the fiduciary should have been dishonest. It is '... clear that knowing assisters are liable on account of their own dishonesty, irrespective of the dishonesty of the trustees',[239] nor is there a requirement that the breach of duty should involve property held on trust or its misapplication or appropriation.[240]

### Meaning of dishonesty

**14-56**   The nature of 'dishonesty' was considered by the Privy Council in *Royal Brunei Airlines v Tan*[241] which established that, in this context, acting dishonestly means simply not acting as an honest person would in the circumstances and, for the most part, dishonesty is to be equated with conscious impropriety.[242] It is an objective standard and an individual is expected to attain the standard which would be observed by an honest person placed in those circumstances.[243] Ultimately, Lord Nicholls thought that, 'in most cases, an honest person should have little difficulty in knowing whether a proposed transaction, or his participation in it, would offend the normally accepted standards of honest conduct'.[244]

---

[232]   See *Law Society of England & Wales v Isaac* [2010] EWHC 1670 at [100].

[233]   *Williams v Central Bank of Nigeria* [2014] UKSC 10, [2014] 2 All ER 489 at [9], [57], [66].

[234]   [2014] UKSC 10, [2014] 2 All ER 489.

[235]   *Novoship (UK) Ltd v Nikitin* [2015] 2 WLR 526 at [80], [86], [107].

[236]   See *Ultraframe (UK) Ltd v Fielding* [2005] EWHC 1638 at [1486]: 'If [the recipient] has retained it, or if he has retained property which is an identifiable substitute for the original trust property, then the claimant is entitled simply to assert his proprietary rights in that property ... If the recipient has not retained the trust property, and its proceeds are no longer identifiable, then the claimant has a personal remedy against the recipient'; *Twinsectra Ltd v Yardley* [2002] 2 All ER 377 at 403, per Lord Millett.

[237]   *Novoship (UK) Ltd v Nikitin* [2015] 2 WLR 526 at [75], [82], [86], [91]–[93]. See also *Fiona Trust & Holding Corp v Privalov* [2010] EWHC 3199 at [63]–[66] and the authorities cited there; *Ultraframe (UK) Ltd v Fielding* [2005] EWHC 1638 at [1589]–[1594], per Lewison J. See generally Elliott and Mitchell, 'Remedies for Dishonest Assistance' (2004) 67 MLR 16; Ridge, 'Justifying the Remedies for Dishonest Assistance' (2008) 124 LQR 445.   [238]   *Novoship (UK) Ltd v Nikitin* [2015] 2 WLR 526 at [116]–[120].

[239]   *Williams v Central Bank of Nigeria* [2014] 2 WLR 355 at [35], per Lord Sumption; *Royal Brunei Airlines v Tan* [1995] 3 All ER 97 at 102, PC, per Lord Nicholls: '... dishonesty on the part of the third party would seem to be a sufficient basis for his liability, irrespective of the state of mind of the trustee who is in breach of trust'.

[240]   *Novoship v Nikitin* [2015] 2 WLR 526 at [91]–[92], approving *Fiona Trust & Holding Corp v Privalov* [2010] EWHC 3199 at [61]; *JD Weatherspoon plc v Van den Berg* [2009] EWHC 639 at [518]–[520], per Peter Smith J.

[241]   [1995] 3 All ER 97, PC.   [242]   [1995] 3 All ER 97 at 105–6, per Lord Nicholls.

[243]   [1995] 3 All ER 97 at 107, per Lord Nicholls.   [244]   [1995] 3 All ER 97 at 107.

Subsequently some ambiguity as to the nature of the test was generated by the House of Lords' decision in *Twinsectra Ltd v Yardley*[245] which was (mis)read as introducing a subjective requirement that the defendant must appreciate that his conduct is dishonest.[246] Lord Hoffmann clarified the position in *Barlow Clowes International Ltd v Eurotrust International Ltd*[247] noting that:

> '[a]lthough a dishonest state of mind is a subjective mental state, the standard by which the law determines whether it is dishonest is objective. If by ordinary standards a defendant's mental state would be characterised as dishonest, it is irrelevant that the defendant judges by different standards.'[248]

**14-57**  In *Abou-Rahmah v Abacha*[249] the Court of Appeal accepted the statement of the law in *Barlow Clowes* as a statement of the law of England and Wales,[250] and the courts now look to *Twinsectra* as interpreted in *Barlow Clowes*.[251] The effect, as Sir Andrew Morritt summarised it in *Starglade Properties Ltd v Nash*,[252] is that the relevant standard is 'the ordinary standard of honest behaviour'. In *Ivey v Genting Casinos (UK) Ltd*[253] (the facts are irrelevant for our purposes) the Supreme Court confirmed that the approach to dishonesty, whether in civil or criminal proceedings, is as identified in *Barlow Clowes*. The first step is to determine the actual state of an individual's knowledge or belief as to the facts and whether it is a genuinely held belief, but there is no requirement that his belief must be reasonable; the question is whether it is genuinely held:

> 'When once his actual state of mind as to knowledge or belief as to facts is established, the question whether his conduct was honest or dishonest is to be determined ... by applying the (objective) standards of ordinary decent people. There is no requirement that the defendant must appreciate that what he has done is, by those standards, dishonest.'[254]

In *Starglade Properties Ltd v Nash*,[255] a director did not consider it dishonest to prefer some creditors of the company over another—he paid off all the creditors out of money which he was required to hold on trust for the one creditor who was not paid.[256] The court held that the deliberate removal of the assets of an insolvent company so as to entirely defeat the just claim of a creditor was not in accordance with the ordinary standards of honest commercial behaviour, nor could a man in the position of the defendant have thought otherwise, notwithstanding a lack of understanding as to the legal position.[257]

---

[245] [2002] 2 All ER 377.

[246] See [2002] 2 All ER 377 at 382–3, 'a consciousness that one is transgressing ordinary standards of honest behaviour', per Lord Hoffmann; and at 387, '... whether the defendant knows that his conduct is dishonest by the ordinary standards of honest and reasonable men', per Lord Hutton.

[247] [2006] 1 All ER 333, PC; see Conaglen and Gaymour (2006) 65 CLJ 18; Yeo (2006) 122 LQR 171.

[248] [2006] 1 All ER 333 at [10], see also at [15]–[16].

[249] [2007] 1 Lloyd's Rep 115; see Ryan [2007] Conv 168; Lee [2007] JBL 209.

[250] See [2007] 1 Lloyd's Rep 115 at 129–30. At least Arden LJ did; Rix LJ (at 119, 120) still seemed to suggest there is some element of subjectivity to it while Pill LJ (at 133) thought it unnecessary to enter the debate.

[251] *Starglade Properties Ltd v Nash* [2010] EWCA Civ 1314, [2011] 1 Lloyd's Rep 102.

[252] [2010] EWCA Civ 1314, [2011] 1 Lloyd's Rep 102 at [32].

[253] [2017] 3 WLR 1212, [2017] UKSC 67.      [254] [2017] 3 WLR 1212, [2017] UKSC 67 at [74]–[75].

[255] [2010] EWCA Civ 1314, [2011] 1 Lloyd's Rep 102.

[256] The claimant company had a negligence claim against a surveyor which it assigned to L Ltd. The defendant, the sole director and member of L, undertook in writing on behalf of L to pay to the claimant half of the net money received from the claim and to hold all money so received on trust. L having become insolvent, the defendant director used the money received to pay off numerous creditors of L, but did not pay the claimant the amount due under the agreement. The director was sued as a dishonest assistant in the breach of trust by L Ltd.

[257] [2010] EWCA Civ 1314, [2011] 1 Lloyd's Rep 102 at [39]. See also *Vivendi SA v Richards* [2013] BCC 771 at [192].

**14-58**    The court, when deciding whether a person is acting honestly, looks at all the circumstances known to the person at the time and has regard to his attributes such as his experience and intelligence and the reason why he acted as he did and assesses that conduct against an objective standard of honest behaviour.[258]

**14-59**    It is not necessary for the accessory to know every element of the breach of duty by the fiduciary, but he must know that the fiduciary is doing something which he is not entitled to do[259] and it is sufficient if he knows or suspects that the transaction is such as to render his participation dishonest.[260] For example, in *Goldtrail Travel Ltd v Aydin*[261] commercial contracts were entered into between the defendant companies and the claimant travel company under which commission (£1.4m) was payable to the claimant travel company for agreeing to source (plane) seats from a third party, but the defendant companies paid the commission to a company wholly owned and controlled by the dishonest director of the claimant travel company who negotiated the contracts. The court held the defendants' conduct was dishonest as they knew that money due to the travel company was being paid to a director of the travel company; they also knew that some of the documents surrounding the transactions were sham documents; that the structure of the deal was 'unorthodox', and that possibly the tax authorities and travel regulators were being deceived.[262] The court had little difficulty in finding their conduct dishonest. They had to compensate the travel company for the loss of commission of £1.4m.

**14-60**    In *Novoship (UK) Limited v Nikitin*[263] the dishonest assistance consisted of a defendant negotiating (charterparties) with an agent in circumstances where the defendant knew the agent had not disclosed to his principal that the agent had taken bribes in other transactions. The defendant knew this because he too was a recipient of bribes together with the agent in those other transactions. The Court of Appeal held that the dishonesty of the defendant consisted of continuing to negotiate charterparties with the agent, given his knowledge of the agent's breach of duty. By doing so, he dishonestly assisted that agent in his continuing breach of duty to his principal.[264]

### Extent of the liability

**14-61**    The liability in a dishonest assistance case is for the loss caused by the breach of duty in which the defendant has assisted[265] and it is not necessary to show that the assistance itself is causative of any loss.[266] In an appropriate case and as a matter for the court's discretion, a dishonest assistant may be held to account also for any profit which he makes from

---

[258]    *Royal Brunei Airlines v Tan* [1995] 3 All ER 97 at 107, PC.

[259]    *Ultraframe (UK) Ltd v Fielding* [2005] EWHC 1638 at [1505]–[1506]. For examples of dishonest assistance, see *Simtel Communications Ltd v Rebak* [2006] 2 BCLC 571 (former employee dishonestly assisted in director's breach of duty as contracts diverted from the company to a new business set up by the director and former employee); *Statek Corpn v Alford* [2008] BCC 266 (individual dishonestly assisted two directors misappropriate $19.8m from a company by passing company money from its accounts through his bank accounts and on to the two directors).

[260]    *Madoff Securities International Ltd v Raven* [2013] EWHC 3147 at [351], per Popplewell J, citing *Agip (Africa) Ltd v Jackson* [1990] Ch 265 at 294; *Barlow Clowes International Ltd v Eurotrust International Ltd* [2006] 1 WLR 1477 at [28]; *Abou-Rahmah v Abacha* [2007] 1 All ER 827 at [39].

[261]    [2016] 1 BCLC 635.        [262]    [2015] 1 BCLC 89 at [146]–[154], see also [131].

[263]    [2015] 2 WLR 526.        [264]    [2015] 2 WLR 526 at [55]–[59].

[265]    As Mance J said in *Grupo Torras SA v Al Sabah* [1999] CLC 1469 at 1666 (rev'd on other grounds [2001] CLC 221): 'The relevant enquiry is … what loss or damage resulted from the breach of trust or fiduciary duty which has been dishonestly assisted … it is necessary to identify what breach of trust or duty was assisted and what loss may be said to have resulted from that breach of trust or duty.'

[266]    *Madoff Securities International Ltd v Raven* [2013] EWHC 3147 at [340], per Popplewell J.

his dishonest assistance,[267] even if the claimant has suffered no loss.[268] As noted earlier, a dishonest assistant is not a trustee and liability is imposed, not for breach of fiduciary duty, but for an equitable wrong and, as such, common law rules of causation, remoteness, and measure of damages do apply, as the Court of Appeal held in *Novoship (UK) Ltd v Nikitin*.[269] This requires, for example, that a distinction be drawn between wrongdoing which is the effective cause of a loss or profit and one which is merely the occasion for the loss or profit.[270] In *Novoship (UK) Ltd v Nikitin*[271] a dishonest assistant (N) had entered into ship charters at market rates with a dishonest agent of the ship owner (P). These transactions were at market rates and in the interests of the ship owner, but the court held that they were tainted by N's knowledge that the agent was dishonest and had not disclosed his dishonesty to P. N knew of the agent's dishonesty because he and the agent had each received bribes with respect to other charters entered into contemporaneously between P and third parties. The court found, however, that while the agent was in continuing breach of his fiduciary duty and N was a dishonest assistant in those breaches, what N acquired as a result of his dishonest assistance was the use of the vessels at the market rate (the charters).[272] That was merely the occasion for him to make a profit. The real or effective cause of the profits he made (more than $100m) was an unexpected change in the market rates of hire which made the charters very valuable.[273] The court held that there was an insufficient direct causal connection between entry into the charters at market rates and the resulting profits to justify an accounting by N for those profits.[274] Further, the Court of Appeal concluded that the grant of an account of profits against a non-fiduciary is at the court's discretion and it may be withheld, for example, where it would be disproportionate in relation to the particular form and extent of wrongdoing.[275]

---

[267] *Novoship (UK) Ltd v Nikitin* [2015] 2 WLR 526, at [75]–[84], approving *Fiona Trust & Holding Corp v Privalov* [2010] EWHC 3199 at [63]–[66] and the authorities cited there and agreeing with the policy justifications put forward in *Consul Development Pty Ltd v DPC Estates Pty Ltd* (1975) 132 CLR 373 at 397, namely recovery of profits deters persons from assisting the disloyal fiduciary and out of equity with the fiduciary—if the fiduciary has to account for profit made, those who assist him should account also; also *Fyffes Group Ltd v Templeman* [2000] 2 Lloyd's Rep 643; *Ultraframe (UK) Ltd v Fielding* [2005] EWHC 1638 at [1594], per Lewison J; and see *Goldtrail Travel Ltd v Aydin* [2016] 1 BCLC 635 at [44], it is not relevant whether the company would have taken the opportunity (which is equally irrelevant to whether there is a breach of fiduciary duty, CA 2006, s 175(2)), the issue is the dishonest assistance of the fiduciary's breach of duty and whether the breach caused the loss.

[268] See *Airbus Operations Ltd v Withey* [2014] EWHC 1126 at [504]. In this case, involving secret commissions paid to fiduciaries by a sub-contractor, it was accepted that the claimant had received services of a good standard and that the price of the services had not been inflated by the commissions, so the claimant could not point to any loss. Nevertheless, the dishonest assistants were liable to account for the secret commissions which they received by reason of assisting an agent of the claimant to breach his fiduciary duty to the claimant: at [73], [506].

[269] [2015] 2 WLR 526 at [107]–[108], [114]–[115]. For criticism of the approach taken in *Novoship*, see Gummow, 'Dishonest Assistance and Account of Profits' [2015] CLJ 405 who queries whether equity is so bereft of available principle as to necessitate recourse to a restrictive common law analogy. Vice versa, see Devonshire, 'Account of Profits for Dishonest Assistance' (2015) 74 CLJ 222 who argues that the anomalous resort to common law causation and remoteness can be resolved by treating dishonest assistance as a common law wrong for which damages are available.

[270] [2015] 2 WLR 526 at [108]. The court noted, at [103], that in the case of a dishonest assistant sued for loss, a causal connection is required, citing *Grupo Torras SA v Al-Sabah* [2001] CLC 221 at [119] and *Casio Computer Co Ltd v Sayo* [2001] EWCA Civ 661 at [15], that 'it is not necessary to show a precise causal link between the assistance and the loss. Loss caused by the breach of fiduciary duty is recoverable from the accessory. This is the relevant causal connection for this purpose.'

[271] [2015] 2 WLR 526. See valuable discussion by Davies, 'Gain-based Remedies for Dishonest Assistance' (2015) 131 LQR 173.                                      [272] [2015] 2 WLR 526 at [114].

[273] [2015] 2 WLR 526 at [114].      [274] [2015] 2 WLR 526 at [115].      [275] [2015] 2 WLR 526 at [116]–[119].

On the facts in *Novoship (UK) Ltd v Nikitin,* the Court of Appeal considered recovery of the profits would be disproportionate.[276] Hence P's claim for an account of profits by the dishonest assistant failed.

**14-62**    In *Goldtrail Travel Ltd v Aydin*[277] (see **14-59**) the causation issues were more straightforward. There were two aspects to the dishonest assistance. The defendant companies should have paid commission to the claimant travel company but paid the money instead to a Seychelles company owned by a dishonest director of the travel company. The director in a misapplication of company money paid certain sums to the defendant companies to assist them in making those commission payments to his Seychelles company. The court held that the dishonest assistants were liable for the amount of misapplied sums which they had received from the travel company as losses caused to the travel company by the misapplication of the company's funds in which the defendants had assisted. In the alternative, they were liable for the amount of the commissions paid by them to the Seychelles company which the travel company should have received, as those commissions were obtained by the director in breach of his duty (CA 2006, s 175) to the company in which the defendants had assisted. A further issue which arose in *Goldtrail Travel Ltd v Aydin*[278] was whether the dishonest assistants were able to set off against their accountability for being accessories, legitimate commercial debts due by them to the (now insolvent) travel company arising from their ordinary business transactions. The court refused to allow such a set-off.[279]

## Knowing receipt

**14-63**    Liability in knowing receipt depends on the prior existence of an asset which is the subject of a trust in favour of a beneficiary,[280] but it does not require proof of any dishonesty on anyone's part.[281] As Lord Hoffmann stated in *El Ajou v Dollar Land Holdings plc*[282] for a claim in knowing receipt, it is necessary for the claimant to show:

> 'first, a disposal of his assets in breach of fiduciary duty;[283] secondly, the beneficial receipt by the defendant of assets which are traceable as representing the assets of the plaintiff; and thirdly, knowledge on the part of the defendant that the assets he received are traceable to a breach of fiduciary duty.'

---

[276] [2015] 2 WLR 526 at [120].

[277] [2015] 1 BCLC 89, aff'd save on one minor point [2016] 1 BCLC 635.

[278] [2015] 1 BCLC 89, aff'd save on one minor point [2016] 1 BCLC 635.

[279] See [2015] 1 BCLC 89 at [160]–[171], applying *Manson v Smith* [1997] 2 BCLC 161, aff'd save on one minor point [2016] 1 BCLC 635. Rose J at first instance noted that if the defendants were seriously disadvantaged by that refusal of set-off, it was a risk they took, having dishonestly assisted the director of the travel company in breach of his fiduciary duty, [2015] 1 BCLC 89 at [167].

[280] *Novoship v Nikitin* [2015] 2 WLR 526 at [89]; *Barnes v Addy* (1874) LR 9 Ch App 244 at 251–2; *El Ajou v Dollar Land Holdings plc* [1994] 1 BCLC 464 at 478.

[281] *Williams v Central Bank of Nigeria* [2014] 2 All ER 489 at [35]; *BCCI v Akindele* [2000] 4 All ER 221.

[282] [1994] 1 BCLC 464 at 478. See *Belmont Finance Corp v Williams Furniture Ltd (No 2)* [1980] 1 All ER 393 at 405, CA. See also *JJ Harrison (Properties) Ltd v Harrison* [2002] 1 BCLC 162; *Bairstow v Queens Moat Houses plc* [2001] 2 BCLC 531; *Re Duckwari plc (No 2), Duckwari plc v Offerventure Ltd (No 2)* [1998] 2 BCLC 315 at 321, per Nourse LJ. See Sealy, 'The Director as Trustee' (1967) 25 CLJ 83.

[283] See Conaglen and Nolan, 'Contracts and Knowing Receipt: Principles and Application' (2013) 129 LQR 359 making the point that where a contract (under which an asset is transferred) is binding on the company by virtue of the apparent authority of an agent (say, a director), no claim in knowing receipt will lie, though the agent is in breach of his duty to the company. A valid contract having resulted, that insulates the recipient against any claim for knowing receipt. The position would be different if the contract was void, for example, as illegal.

The claim in the case of knowing receipt is receipt-based and primarily restitutionary, there must be a receipt by one person of trust property or its traceable proceeds from another, and receipt must be by the defendant for his own benefit or in his own right rather than as a nominee or agent for the benefit of someone else.[284] The claim against the knowing recipient is to recover any benefit which he has received or acquired as a result of the knowing receipt.[285] Whether the trust property can be recovered depends on whether it or its traceable proceeds can be identified and, if it has been disposed of or dissipated, there is no longer a proprietary claim but monetary restitution must be made.[286] A knowing recipient is not a trustee since, as has been said frequently, most recently by Lord Sumption in *Williams v Central Bank of Nigeria*,[287] the accessory's possession is 'at all times wrongful and adverse to the rights of both the true trustees and the beneficiaries. No trust has been reposed in him.'

**14-64**  The nature of 'knowing receipt' liability was comprehensively reviewed and the current state of the law is as stated by the Court of Appeal in *Bank of Credit and Commerce International (Overseas) Ltd v Akindele*[288] which adopted a markedly different approach to the basis of liability than the earlier authorities which had focused on liability arising from (increasingly convoluted) degrees of knowledge. The Court of Appeal held that dishonesty is not an essential ingredient of a claim for knowing receipt, and the test for knowledge in such a claim is simply whether the defendant's knowledge makes it unconscionable for him to retain the benefit of the receipt.[289] Although such a test cannot avoid difficulties of application, the court thought it preferable to the complexity of the previous categorisations of knowledge for these purposes.[290] Moreover, Nourse LJ thought, this approach should better enable the courts to give common-sense decisions in the commercial context in which claims in knowing receipt are now frequently made, paying equal regard, on the one hand, to the need to avoid the mischief of paralysing trade and, on the other hand, to the realisation that there are cases in which a commercial man should not be allowed to shelter behind the exigencies of

---

[284]  *Trustor v Smallbone* [2001] 2 BCLC 436 at [19]; *Agip (Africa) Ltd v Jackson* [1990] Ch 265 at 291–2.

[285]  See *Ultraframe (UK) Ltd v Fielding* [2005] EWHC 1638 at [1577], per Lewison J and see at [1520]: 'But the proprietary remedy does not depend on profit. It is not a claim for unjust enrichment. As Lord Millett explained [in *Foskett v McKeown* [2000] 3 All ER 97 at 121–122] ...: "Conversely, a plaintiff who brings an action like the present must show that the defendant is in receipt of property which belongs beneficially to him or its traceable proceeds, but he need not show that the defendant has been enriched by its receipt. He may, for example, have paid full value for the property, but he is still required to disgorge it if he received it with notice of the plaintiff's interest."'

[286]  See *Twinsectra Ltd v Yardley* [2002] 2 All ER 377 at 403, per Lord Millett; *Ultraframe (UK) Ltd v Fielding* [2005] EWHC 1638 at [1486].

[287]  [2014] 2 All ER 489 at [31], and see Lord Neuberger at [57]–[64] and the authorities there cited who concluded: 'Nobody involved ... has ever placed any relevant trust and confidence in the recipient', at [64].

[288]  [2000] 4 All ER 221, applying *Belmont Finance Corporation Ltd v Williams Furniture Ltd (No 2)* [1980] 1 All ER 393; see also *Charter plc v City Index Ltd* [2008] 3 All ER 126 at [7]; also *El Ajou v Dollar Land Holdings plc* [1994] 1 BCLC 464 at 478.

[289]  [2000] 4 All ER 221 at 235.

[290]  The older authorities had established that a third party who received company funds might be liable to the company if he received the funds with *knowledge* of the directors' breach of duty, whether it be actual knowledge, or knowledge in the sense that he wilfully shut his eyes to the obvious, or wilfully and recklessly failed to make the type of inquiries which an honest and reasonable man would have made: see *Selangor United Rubber Estates Ltd v Cradock (No 3)* [1968] 2 All ER 1073; *Eagle Trust plc v SBC Securities Ltd* [1992] 4 All ER 488; *Re Montagu's Settlement Trusts* [1992] 4 All ER 308; *Polly Peck International plc v Nadir (No 2)* [1992] 4 All ER 769; *Cowan de Groot Properties Ltd v Eagle Trust plc* [1992] 4 All ER 700.

commercial life.[291] In cases where a fiduciary has set up a company to receive secret profits made by the fiduciary in breach of duty, the knowledge of the fiduciary can be attributed to the recipient company, applying the usual rules of attribution, so as to establish that the recipient company is a 'knowing recipient', assuming that the knowledge attributed is sufficient so as to make it unconscionable for the company to retain the benefit obtained by it.[292]

## D  Claims for negligence

**14-65**     The duty of care and skill and liabilities arising from breach of such duty are discussed in Chapter 11.

## E  Managing potential liabilities

**14-66**     Given that a director is potentially liable on the various grounds, the next issue is the extent to which it is possible for directors to manage those potential liabilities through mechanisms such as contractual clauses excluding or limiting liability or through insurance cover. An option is to seek authorisation or ratification from the shareholders, as discussed at **20-46**. Liability is also reduced in some contexts by the provision of 'safe harbours', for example in the context of misleading statements in the strategic or directors' report (see **18-47**). Another possibility is that the amount of the liability might be reduced or waived where the director successfully applies for relief under CA 2006, s 1157, which requires the director to satisfy the court that he has acted honestly and reasonably and ought fairly to be excused, see **14-79**.

**14-67**     Quite apart from any potential liability for breach of duty, a major concern for any director is the potential litigation costs involved if he is sued whether by the company or in a derivative claim brought on behalf of the company by a shareholder. Commercial litigation tends to be lengthy and directors are concerned that funding an expensive and lengthy defence may exhaust their personal resources so that by the time they win (if they do) and the case is dismissed, they are personally bankrupt, although able to recover their costs. This particular issue is addressed by CA 2006, s 205, whereby companies are permitted (but not required) to provide a director of the company or of a holding company with funds to meet expenditure incurred or to be incurred by a director in defending any criminal or civil proceedings in connection with any alleged negligence, default, breach of duty, or breach of trust by him in relation to the company (which would include any derivative claim) or in connection with any application by him to the court for relief under s 1157. Of course, the decision to grant such funding must be taken by the other directors in accordance with their fiduciary duties, in particular the duty to exercise their powers for a proper purpose (s 171). If funding is provided, it must be repaid if the director is convicted in criminal proceedings, or judgment is given against him in any civil proceedings, or the court refuses him relief on an application under s 1157 (s 205(2)).

---

[291] [2000] 4 All ER 221 at 236. See Hayton, 'Suing Third Parties Involved in Fraud: Some Key Issues' (2012) Trust LI 197 at 202–3 who suggests 'dishonest dealing' would be a less opaque identifier than 'unconscionable'; and Lord Nicholls in *Royal Brunei Airlines v Tan* [1995] 2 AC 378 at 392 discussing the meaning of the word 'unconscionable' where he said: 'If unconscionable means no more than dishonesty, then dishonesty is the preferable label.'

[292] See *Crown Dilmun Ltd v Sutton* [2004] 1 BCLC 468 at [198]–[203].

**14-68** Directors of larger companies are almost equally concerned about becoming embroiled in a regulatory investigation or disciplinary proceeding which can also be a lengthy process requiring legal representation. To address such concerns, a company may provide a director or a director of its holding company with funds on a similar basis, as discussed, to meet expenditure incurred in defending himself in an investigation by a regulatory authority, or against action proposed to be taken by a regulatory authority, such as the Financial Conduct Authority, in connection with any alleged negligence, default, breach of duty, or breach of trust by the director in relation to the company or an associated company (CA 2006, s 206). In this instance, strangely, there is no express requirement for the funding to be repaid in the way provided by s 205(2), noted earlier. In neither case is shareholder approval required for the provision of this funding.

## Exemption provisions

**14-69** Historically, companies included in their articles widely drafted exemption clauses relieving their officers from liability arising from breaches of their duties save in the case of wilful negligence or default,[293] but the Greene Committee on Company Law recommended that the practice be prohibited.[294] The current prohibition is set out in CA 2006, s 232(1) which provides that any provision, whether contained in the articles or in any contract with the company or otherwise,[295] that purports to exempt a director of a company (to any extent) from any liability that would otherwise attach to him in connection with any negligence, default, breach of duty, or breach of trust in relation to the company is void.[296]

**14-70** An important (and obscure) qualification to the prohibition is that it does not prevent the company from including in its articles 'such provision as has previously been lawful for dealing with conflicts of interest' (s 232(4)). The extent to which companies can lawfully include provisions in their articles in respect of conflicts is discussed at **12-61**.

## Indemnity provisions

**14-71** As is the case with exemption provisions, any direct or indirect provision by a company of an indemnity (to any extent) for a director of the company, or of an associate company,[297] against any liability in connection with any negligence or breach of duty etc in relation to the company of which he is a director, is void, other than permitted insurance cover or qualifying indemnities (CA 2006, s 232(2)).

---

[293] See *Re Brazilian Rubber Plantations and Estates Ltd* [1911] 1 Ch 425; *Re City Equitable Fire Insurance Co Ltd* [1925] Ch 407.

[294] The Greene Committee on Company Law (Cmnd 2657, 1929), paras 46–47. The prohibition was introduced by CA 1929, s 152.

[295] CA 2006, s 232(3). The words 'or otherwise' are to be construed *eiusdem generis* with the preceding words 'whether contained in the company's articles or in any contract with the company', the genus being any arrangement between the company and its officers: *Burgoine v London Borough of Waltham Forest* [1997] 2 BCLC 612.

[296] CA 2006, s 232(2): see generally *Burgoine v London Borough of Waltham Forest* [1997] 2 BCLC 612. The equivalent provision with respect to the liability of auditors is CA 2006, s 532(1), but it is subject to s 532(2) which allows certain indemnity provisions and liability limitations agreements, see **18-89**. As to 'default', see *Customs & Excise Commissioners v Hedon Alpha Ltd* [1981] 2 All ER 697; and n 305.

[297] A parent company cannot indemnify the directors of its subsidiary and the subsidiary cannot indemnify the directors of its parent company. It used to be the practice in some groups that one group company would indemnify the director of another group company and so circumvent the rule that a company could not indemnify its own directors. This loophole was closed by the CAICE Act 2004.

**14-72**   The background to the introduction of indemnities (by the Companies (Audit, Investigations and Community Enterprise) Act 2004) was that there had been several high-profile cases, including in particular litigation involving the non-executive directors of Equitable Life,[298] which generated a sense that directors are subject to significant litigation risks which may deter able people from accepting posts unless they are protected against that risk. Domestically, there were concerns about the length of possible proceedings; the difficulty of funding legal representation (which of course is a general problem, not particular to company directors); and the enormous sums being claimed which are likely to outstrip any available insurance. For larger companies with operations in the US, there were concerns that their directors were exposed to even greater litigation risks because of shareholder class actions and, possibly, more aggressive regulators. There was also a sense of more activist shareholders with some, such as aggressive hedge funds, perhaps more attuned to using litigation than had previously been the case. It was also argued that the availability of a statutory derivative action, now CA 2006, Pt 11, coupled with the statutory statement of directors' duties, would encourage and facilitate litigation though this has not proved to be the case, to date at least, see **20-72**.

**14-73**   There is no doubt an element of truth in these concerns, but no doubt too that they were exaggerated in order to extract the maximum possible concessions from the Government. The result is that, despite the initial impression given by CA 2006, s 232(2) prohibiting indemnities (see **14-72**), companies may provide extensive indemnities protecting their directors against personal liability in a wide range of circumstances, though not where the liability is to the company itself. There, Parliament did draw the line.

### Qualifying third party indemnity provisions

**14-74**   In essence, a company may indemnify a director against liability incurred (including costs) by the director to a third party (i.e. someone other than the company or an associated company, defined in CA 2006, s 256), such as a shareholder or regulator provided certain conditions are met (s 234).[299] These indemnities are known as qualifying third party indemnity provisions (QTPIPs).

**14-75**   A company (likewise an associated company) cannot provide an indemnity in respect of:

- any liability of a director to the company or to an associated company;
- any criminal penalties;
- any regulatory penalties;
- any liability incurred by the director in defending criminal proceedings in which he is convicted, or civil proceedings brought by the company or associated company in which judgment is given against him, or in respect of an unsuccessful application for relief[300] (CA 2006, s 234(2)).

---

[298]   For the story of this litigation, see *Equitable Life Assurance Society v Bowley* [2004] 1 BCLC 180; also Reed (2006) 27 Co Law 170. In a nutshell, the new owners of Equitable Life sued the previous board essentially alleging that the company's acute financial difficulties arose as a result of incompetence on the part of the directors—the claim was ultimately dropped.

[299]   A failure to meet the conditions means that the indemnity is void since it then falls back within the prohibition in CA 2006, s 232(2), see **14-70**. Equivalent indemnity provision is available for directors of corporate trustees of occupational pension schemes: see s 235.

[300]   i.e. under CA 2006, s 1157.

**14-76** The existence of any QTPIP must be disclosed in the directors' report (s 236) and copies of the qualifying indemnity provision must be available for inspection by any member (s 237), but shareholder approval of the QTPIP is not required.

**14-77** As with decisions on defence costs funding (see **14-67**), the decision to grant indemnities to directors must be taken by the other directors in accordance with their fiduciary duties, in particular the duty to exercise their powers for a proper purpose (s 171). In practice, for large companies, the granting of indemnities has become routine with annual reports commonly recording that the company has provided indemnities to their directors to the extent permitted by law.[301]

### Insurance provision

**14-78** A company is not prevented from purchasing and maintaining for a director of the company, or of an associate company, insurance against any liability attaching to a director in connection with any negligence, default, breach of duty, or breach of trust in relation to the company of which he is a director (CA 2006, 233). Public companies commonly purchase directors' and officers' (D & O) liability insurance[302] and, as costs have decreased in recent years, it is increasingly common in large private companies also.

### Application to court for relief

**14-79** The court has power under CA 2006, s 1157 to relieve an officer[303] of the company from liability[304] where the officer is or may be liable in respect of negligence, default,[305] breach of duty, or breach of trust, if the court is satisfied that he has acted honestly and reasonably and that, having regard to all the circumstances of the case, he ought fairly to be

---

[301] See also The Companies (Model Articles) Regulations 2008, SI 2008/3229, reg 2, Sch 1, art 52 (Ltd); reg 4, Sch 3, art 85 (Plc) and note the width of the drafting.

[302] See Mukwiri, 'Directors' and Officers' Insurance in the UK' (2017) 28(4) EBL Rev 547; also Deane, 'D & O Insurance' [2008] PLC 23; also Paolini, 'Lending Sub-prime and Advising on Financial Instruments from a D & O Insurance Perspective' [2012] JBL 432. See also The Companies (Model Articles) Regulations 2008, SI 2008/3229, reg 2, Sch 1, art 53 (Ltd); reg 4, Sch 3, art 86 (Plc).

[303] Defined in CA 2006, s 1173 as including a director, manager, or secretary. It does not extend to shadow directors in the absence of an express provision to that effect: see *Ultraframe (UK) Ltd v Fielding* [2005] EWHC 1638 at [1452]; it does include liquidators: *Re Powertrain Ltd* [2017] 1 BCLC 95; and administrators: *Re Home Treat Ltd* [1991] BCLC 705.

[304] Including a liability to account for profits, see *Coleman Taymar Ltd v Oakes* [2001] 2 BCLC 749; but not a liability to repay sums paid to a director under a void contract: *Guinness plc v Saunders* [1990] 2 AC 663 at 695, 702; or, it seems, a liability to make a contribution for wrongful trading under IA 1986, s 214: *Re Produce Marketing Consortium Ltd* [1989] 3 All ER 1; nor a liability arising under IA 1986, s 423, see *Dickinson v NAL Realisations Ltd* [2017] EWHC 28, [2018] 1 BCLC 623, at [154], or CA 2006, s 994, because in those cases, the liability does not arise from a breach of duty. 'May be liable' allows the court to make an order for prospective relief, see *Re Powertrain Ltd* [2017] 1 BCLC 95.

[305] By 'default' is meant some fault or misconduct by a director or officer in their capacity as such in the discharge of their obligations under the companies legislation, see *Customs & Excise Commissioners v Hedon Alpha Ltd* [1981] 2 All ER 697. It was accepted, obiter, in *Re Duckwari plc (No 2)* [1998] 2 BCLC 315 at 325 that 'default' includes the personal liability of directors to indemnify the company under the statutory provisions governing conflicts of interest, now set out in CA 2006, Pt 10, Ch 4 (specific conflicts); and see *Queensway Systems Ltd v Walker* [2007] 2 BCLC 577 at [67].

excused.[306] The scope of the provision is limited to relief in cases where the company or someone on its behalf (such as a liquidator) is seeking to enforce the personal duties that directors owe to the company.[307] The provision does not apply to proceedings by a third party (i.e. a creditor) to recover a debt owed by the director.[308]

**14-80**    It is an absolute precondition to the grant of relief that the director has acted honestly and reasonably and the burden of proving honesty and reasonableness is on those who ask for relief.[309] Whether the director has acted honestly and reasonably is essentially an objective test.[310] In applications under this section, the court tends to take a broad look at all the circumstances of the case[311] in order to determine whether the director ought fairly to be excused, rather than seek for these purposes to impose discrete thresholds as to 'honesty' and 'reasonableness',[312] and conduct may be reasonable for this purpose despite amounting to a lack of reasonable care at common law. In *Re D'Jan of London Ltd*[313] a director in breach of his duty of care had signed an insurance form without reading it. Had he done so, he would have discovered the inaccurate information which subsequently caused the insurance company to repudiate liability under the policy. Although he was careless, the court granted him partial relief, finding that he had acted honestly and reasonably and Hoffmann LJ thought that what had happened could have happened to any busy man.[314]

---

[306] The CA 2006, s 1157 restates CA 1985, s 727 without substantive amendment. The CLR proposed, but the Government rejected, that the 'reasonableness' requirement be dropped. For a valuable analysis of the provision and the CLR proposals, see Edmunds and Lowry, 'The Continuing Value of Relief for Directors' Breach of Duty' (2003) 66 MLR 195 who note, *inter alia*, the importance of the section for directors of small family companies where directors' liability insurance is not feasible.

[307] *Customs & Excise Commissioners v Hedon Alpha Ltd* [1981] 2 All ER 697; *IRC v McEntaggart* [2006] 1 BCLC 476.

[308] For that reason, relief is not available with respect to liability incurred under the 'phoenix' name prohibition in IA 1986, ss 216, 217: *First Independent Factors & Finance Ltd v Mountford* [2008] 2 BCLC 297; or in proceedings under CDDA 1986, s 15 (liability of disqualified person for debts incurred when acting though disqualified): *IRC v McEntaggart* [2006] 1 BCLC 476; or in proceedings to recover taxes: *Customs & Excise Commissioners v Hedon Alpha Ltd* [1981] 2 All ER 697 (no relief in respect of liability for unpaid betting and gaming tax).

[309] *Bairstow v Queens Moat Houses plc* [2001] 2 BCLC 531, CA; and see *Re In a Flap Envelope Ltd* [2004] 1 BCLC 64. It is not reasonable for directors to fail to make provision in the accounts for the possibility that tax relief might not be forthcoming on a particular scheme with the result that improper dividends are paid: *Re Loquitur Ltd* [2003] 2 BCLC 442.

[310] See *Bairstow v Queens Moat Houses plc* [2001] 2 BCLC 531 at [58] (criticising the first instance judge for suggesting it was subjective, see [2000] BCC 1025 at 1034).

[311] See *Ultraframe (UK) Ltd v Fielding* [2005] EWHC 1638 at [1451]: 'the expression "the circumstances of the case" does not mean the litigation, it primarily means the circumstances in which the breach took place but it may include a review of the director's stewardship of the company, but not a more wide ranging inquiry into the director's character and behaviour.'

[312] Sometimes the court finds that the director has acted honestly but not reasonably and sometimes that he has acted honestly and reasonably, but in the circumstances ought not to be excused, though the section envisages that 'honesty' and 'reasonableness' are threshold requirements which trigger the court's discretion to look at the fairness of the situation: see Edmunds and Lowry, n 306, on the mingling of these elements by the courts.

[313] [1994] 1 BCLC 561. See also *Inn Spirit Ltd v Burns* [2002] 2 BCLC 780 at [29]–[30].

[314] [1994] 1 BCLC 561 at 564; see Edmunds and Lowry, n 306, 207–10, as to the approach adopted by Hoffmann LJ in this instance. See *Madoff Securities International Ltd v Raven* [2013] EWHC 3147 at [335]–[336] where Popplewell J said he would, had it been necessary, have applied the section to relieve directors of liability where they had failed to consider whether certain payments made were in the interests of the company. He would have done so, he said, as the directors had acted honestly and reasonably, the payments caused no loss to the company, the directors did not benefit from the payments, the payments were approved by all the voting shareholders, the degree of fault, if any, was venial, and the consequences of personal liability would have been unduly harsh and disproportionate to any degree of fault.

In *Dickinson v NAL Realisations Ltd*[315] the court refused relief in respect of breaches of duty by two directors who deferred to a dominant third director in complete abrogation of their individual responsibilities as directors. No dishonesty was alleged but they acted unreasonably in abandoning any effective role in the management of the company. In *Raithatha v Baing*[316] the directors of a company, in breach of their duties of care and skill, had failed to have the company register for VAT when it needed to register. The company was later wound up by HMRC. The court agreed there was no dishonesty by the directors who had assumed that the company did not need to register, but their conduct was not reasonable so as to be excused liability. The failure to explore the tax position and to take professional advice as to that position was unreasonable.

**14-81** Ultimately, the court has considerable discretion under this provision for, once a director establishes that he has acted honestly and reasonably, the court must still be satisfied that the director 'ought fairly to be excused'. The court is very unlikely to exercise its discretion to relieve a director from liability if the director has obtained a material personal benefit through a breach of duty,[317] or if the director gains at the expense of the creditors, as where he seeks to be relieved of a liability to repay money to the company which would be available to meet the creditors' claims.[318]

**14-82** There is some potential for a director to obtain relief under IA 1986, s 212(3), even in circumstances where relief has been refused under CA 2006, s 1157. Section 212 is discussed at **15-3** and it suffices for present purposes to note that it provides a summary mechanism whereby an order of the court can be obtained for repayment, contribution, accounting, etc by a director who has been guilty of any misfeasance or breach of any fiduciary or other duty in relation to the company. Crucially, IA 1986, s 212(3) provides that the court may make such an order for restoration, accounting, contribution etc 'as the court thinks just'. The extent to which that discretionary power can be used to relieve the director of liability was discussed, obiter, in *Re Paycheck Services 3 Ltd, Revenue and Customs Commissioners v Holland*,[319] see **15-5**, by both the Court of Appeal and Supreme Court

---

[315] [2017] EWHC 28, [2018] 1 BCLC 623, at [162].

[316] [2017] EWHC 2059.

[317] See *Dickinson v NAL Realisations Ltd* [2017] EWHC 28 [2018] 1 BCLC 623 (director acted in his own interests rather than the interests of the company when he had the company enter into a sale and leaseback of its factory (with him) without obtaining a professional valuation to support the price being paid by him); *Premier Waste Management Ltd v Towers* [2012] 1 BCLC 67 at [54]-[55] (director personally benefited from conflict of interest, relief refused); *Re In a Flap Envelope Co Ltd* [2004] 1 BCLC 64 (director as a shareholder was a beneficiary of improper financial assistance given by the company in breach of CA 1985, s 151); *Re Marini Ltd* [2004] BCC 172 (receipt of improper dividends—it would not be fair if the director benefited and the creditors suffered). See also *Cullen Investments Ltd v Brown* [2017] EWHC 2793 (no relief for a director who was a solicitor and well versed in company law when he failed to disclose a conflict of interest from which he benefited; he did not act reasonably).

[318] See *Inn Spirit Ltd v Burns* [2002] 2 BCLC 780 at [30]: '... I cannot see that the court could or should excuse [the directors] from liability at the expense of the creditors of the company ...' (Rimer J) (improper dividend paid to directors/shareholders which amounted to an improper misapplication of almost the entire assets of the company); also *First Global Media Group Ltd v Larkin* [2003] EWCA Civ 1765 (improper drawings by directors ... out of the question, the Court of Appeal said, that the directors could be fairly excused from repaying the money when the people out of the money were the creditors of the company); also *Queensway Systems Ltd v Walker* [2007] 2 BCLC 577 at [70]; *Re HLC Environmental Projects Ltd, Hellard v Carvalho* [2014] BCC 337 at [116]-[117], [124]-[125], [133]; *Re Cosy Insulation Ltd* [2016] 2 BCLC 319 at [166]; *Re Bowes Watts Clargo Ltd* [2017] EWHC 7879 at [128], director benefited and acted in disregard of creditors' interests, relief refused.

[319] [2011] 1 BCLC 141, SC, aff'g [2009] 2 BCLC 309.

which were agreed that, whatever the scope of the discretion under IA 1986, s 212(3), it is as to the order that should be made once liability has been established, i.e. as to how much the director must pay. The section is not intended to replicate or extend the court's power to grant relief against liability under CA 2006, s 1157 and therefore it is not permissible in the exercise of that discretion under IA 1986, s 212(3) to order that the director need make no payment at all.[320]

---

[320] [2011] 1 BCLC 141 at [51], per Lord Hope, agreeing with Rimer LJ [2009] 2 BCLC 309 at [108]–[110], with whom Lords Walker and Clarke also agreed, see [2011] 1 BCLC 141 at [124] and [146], respectively.

# 15

# Directors' liabilities and vulnerable transactions on insolvency

## A Introduction

**15-1**   In addition to the formal processes of dealing with an insolvent company by liquidation, administration etc, the collapse of the company is also the time when the conduct of the directors of the company is reviewed.[1] Generally, the emphasis is on civil remedies and recoveries for creditors. There are a small number of provisions (essentially IA 1986, ss 206–211) which create criminal offences[2] as does CA 2006, s 993 (fraudulent trading) although the number of prosecutions under these provisions is low. On the civil side, redress for breach of duty by directors is available through the summary action for misfeasance (IA 1986, s 212) while particular types of trading are targeted for civil recoveries, namely fraudulent trading (ss 213, 246ZA) and wrongful trading (ss 214, 246ZB). A liquidator or administrator may also seek to challenge certain transactions which took place in the run-up to liquidation or administration, for example, on the basis that they were transactions at an undervalue (s 238) or intended to prefer a particular creditor (s 239). The phoenix syndrome, i.e. continuing to trade using the name by which the insolvent company was known or a name which is so similar as to suggest an association with that company, attracts criminal and civil liabilities (ss 216, 217). More broadly, the overall conduct of the directors is reviewed in order to determine whether disqualification is an appropriate response.

**15-2**   With the exception of disqualification proceedings (and even there the numbers are modest), limited use is made of these provisions, in part, because of the investigative difficulties which liquidators and administrators face in trying to bring cases against directors and of a lack of funding to pursue these matters. To facilitate use of these provisions, liquidators and administrators now have greater powers to assign claims to third parties,[3] and a liquidator no longer requires the sanction of the court or liquidation committee or creditors (depending on the circumstance) to bring proceedings under IA 1986, ss 213, 214, 238, 239.[4] The costs of litigation are liquidation expenses within IR 2016, rr 6.42,

---

[1]  A number of the provisions, e.g. IA 1986, ss 206–211, apply to 'officers' which includes a director, manager, or secretary (see CA 2006, s 1173, applied by IA 1986, s 251), but our discussion focuses primarily on directors. See generally Goode, *Principles of Corporate Insolvency* Law (4th edn, 2011), Chs 13, 14; Finch, *Corporate Insolvency Law* (2nd edn, 2009), Ch 16.

[2]  The offences under the IA 1986 relate mainly to offences committed by officers of the company in the course of or just prior to winding up and they range from fraudulently removing the company's property, to destroying or falsifying entries in the company's books, to failing to co-operate and assist the liquidator in a winding up.

[3]  The power to assign claims is expanded by IA 1986, s 246ZD, inserted by the Small Business, Enterprise and Employment Act 2015, s 118, and applies to IA 1986, s 213 (and s 246ZA), s 214 (and s 246ZB), ss 238, 239, 244.

[4]  IA 1986, ss 165(2), 167(1), as substituted by the Small Business, Enterprise and Employment Act 2015, s 120. The background to this change can be found in Insolvency Service, *Red Tape Challenge—changes to insolvency law to reduce unnecessary regulation and simplify procedures,* July 2013, paras 39–46.

7.108 and administration expenses within IR 2016, r 3.51 and payable in priority from the assets of the company, but subject to a requirement that the secured or preferential creditors must consent to litigation expenses in excess of £5,000 (IR 2016, rr 6.44, 7.111). Though claims are limited by these funding difficulties, the provisions are thought to have some deterrent value and provide liquidators and administrators with some nego-tiating weapons when dealing with directors of insolvent companies.[5] When claims are brought, they are often brought on multiple grounds so it is not uncommon to find allega-tions of misfeasance, wrongful trading, transactions at an undervalue, and preferences all in the one case.[6]

## B  Misfeasance procedure—IA 1986, s 212

**15-3**  The misfeasance provision is a procedural mechanism whereby actions may be brought, typically by liquidators (though the section is wider than that and it is possible for a claim to be brought by a creditor) typically against directors (again the section is wider than that) with a view to holding them liable for a breach of duty to the company.[7] The section provides 'a summary procedure in a liquidation for obtaining a remedy against delin-quent directors without the need for an action in the name of the company. It does not create new rights and obligations.'[8]

**15-4**  The section enables the court, on the application of the official receiver, the liquidator, or any creditor, or a contributory with the leave of the court,[9] to examine the conduct of any officer[10] of the company to see if they have misapplied or retained or become accountable for money or other property of the company or been guilty of any misfeasance or breach of fiduciary or other breach of duty to the company (so negligence is included).[11] The court may order the person to repay, restore, or account for the money or property or to make such contribution to the assets of the company (payment is to the company and not to the applicant) as the court thinks just (IA 1986, s 212(3)).[12]

---

[5]  But see Williams, 'What Can We Expect to Gain from Reforming the Insolvent Trading Remedy?' (2015) 78 MLR 55, and n 60.

[6]  There is a difference between misfeasance claims (where sums recovered form part of the general assets of the company and so are capable of being caught by a prior floating charge) and sums recovered pursu-ant to IA 1986, ss 213 or 214, 238, 239 which are held by the office-holder on behalf of the creditors of the company and do not form part of the assets subject to the floating charge, see **15-37**; where there are concur-rent claims, the court will be careful to prevent double recovery, see *Re Idessa Ltd, Burke v Morrison* [2012] 1 BCLC 80 at [128]. See also *Re Kudos Business Solutions Ltd, Earp v Stevenson* [2012] 2 BCLC 65.

[7]  See generally Doyle, 'Misfeasance Proceedings: Chasing the Delinquents' (1994) 7 Insolv Int 25, 35; Oditah, 'Misfeasance Proceedings against Company Directors' [1992] LMCLQ 207.

[8]  *Cohen v Selby* [2001] 1 BCLC 176 at [20], per Chadwick LJ; see also *Re DKG Contractors Ltd* [1990] BCC 903.

[9]  IA 1986, s 212(5).

[10]  'Officer' includes director: IA 1986, s 251; and includes de facto directors: see *Re Paycheck Services 3 Ltd, Revenue and Customs Commissioners v Holland* [2011] 1 BCLC 141 at [55]; *Re Idessa Ltd, Burke v Morrison* [2012] 1 BCLC 80.

[11]  See *Re Barton Manufacturing Co Ltd* [1998] 1 BCLC 740; *Re D'Jan of London Ltd, Copp v D'Jan* [1994] 1 BCLC 561; also *Re Welfab Engineers Ltd* [1990] BCLC 833.

[12]  See Park J in *Re Continental Assurance Co of London plc* [2007] 2 BCLC 287 at [393]; the section (s 212) might give the court a measure of discretion as to the remedy for misfeasance, being a discretion which would not exist, or at least would not be so extensive, at common law.

**15-5**  The court's power under IA 1986, s 212(3) is discretionary, but the extent of this discretion is unclear and was the subject of conflicting views, obiter, in *Re Paycheck Services 3 Ltd, Revenue and Customs Commissioners v Holland*[13] in the Court of Appeal and the Supreme Court though there was, at least, a degree of unanimity that the discretion cannot be used to reduce a director's liability to nothing.[14] It is a discretion as to the order that should be made once liability has been established and the section is not intended to replicate or extend the court's power to grant relief against liability under CA 2006, s 1157,[15] see **14-79**. It enables the court to adjust the remedy to the circumstances of the particular case[16] and allows 'the delinquent director to submit that the wind should be tempered' on the particular facts.[17]

**15-6**  On the facts in *Re Paycheck Services 3 Ltd*,[18] the company had paid unlawful dividends. At first instance, the court found the director liable, declined to award relief under what is now CA 2006, s 1157, see **14-79**, and ordered under IA 1986, s 213(3) that the director's liability to make restitution should be limited to the amount of tax outstanding on the unlawful payments. The Revenue Commissioners were the applicants under s 212. The discussion of liability became moot when the higher courts agreed that the individual was not a de facto director after all (see **7-16**) and therefore could not be liable to repay the unlawful dividends. However, the majority in the Court of Appeal (Ward and Elias LJJ) agreed that the order made (limiting the director's obligation to repay) would have been appropriate. Rimer LJ disagreed saying that the correct approach is to decide whether the director is liable, then whether he is entitled to relief under what is now CA 2006, s 1157 and then to make a fair order under IA 1986, s 212 reflecting the wrong committed—paying unlawful dividends—and the refusal of relief under s 1157.[19] In Rimer LJ's view, the appropriate order would have required the repayment of the full amount of the unlawful dividends. Having refused relief under CA 2006, s 1157, there was no basis, Rimer LJ said, for reintroducing relief and giving effect to it by using IA 1986, s 212. In the Supreme Court, Lords Clarke and Walker agreed with Rimer LJ.[20] But Lord Hope in the Supreme Court preferred the view of the majority in the Court of Appeal and agreed that, in the exercise of its discretion under IA 1986, s 212(3), it was open to the court to limit the award to what was required to make up the deficiency of a particular creditor where the misfeasance claim was made by a party other than the liquidator.[21] The approach of Rimer LJ is to be preferred. A director who is liable to reinstate the company's assets and who is refused relief under CA 2006, s 1157 (which relief requires him to have acted honestly and reasonably) should not be able, by the back door of IA 1986, s 212, to obtain what he

---

[13]  [2011] 1 BCLC 141, SC, aff'g [2009] 2 BCLC 309.

[14]  [2011] 1 BCLC 141 at [49], per Lord Hope; [2009] 2 BCLC 309 at [108]–[110], per Rimer LJ with whom Lords Walker and Clarke agreed, see [2011] 1 BCLC 141 at [124], [146].

[15]  [2009] 2 BCLC 309 at [103], per Rimer LJ, with whom Lords Walker and Clarke agreed at [2011] 1 BCLC 141 at [124] and [146], respectively.

[16]  [2011] 1 BCLC 141 at [124] and [146], per Lords Walker and Clarke, agreeing with Rimer LJ at [2009] 2 BCLC 209 at [110]; *Re Loquitar Ltd* [2003] 2 BCLC 442 at [245].

[17]  *West Mercia Safetywear Ltd v Dodd* [1988] 2 BCLC 250 at 253, per Dillon LJ; *Re Paycheck Services 3 Ltd* [2011] 1 BCLC 141 at [51], [124], [146]; [2009] 2 BCLC 309 at [110].

[18]  [2011] 1 BCLC 141, SC, aff'g [2009] 2 BCLC 309.

[19]  [2009] 2 BCLC 309 at [103], [110]–[112].

[20]  [2011] 1 BCLC 141 at [124] and [146].

[21]  [2011] 1 BCLC 141 at [49], [51], approving [2009] 2 BCLC 309 at [133]–[134], [143]. There was a degree of agreement that recovery of the full amount would have been appropriate had the claim been brought by a liquidator or the official receiver, see [2009] 2 BCLC 309 at [143], per Ward LJ and, in the Supreme Court, at [2011] 1 BCLC 141 at [49], per Lord Hope.

could not obtain under CA 2006, s 1157. The purpose of IA 1986, s 212(3) is to temper the relief where that is required by the circumstances, such as where otherwise there might be a windfall to an undeserving party (for example, the repayment to the company of the amount paid in unlawful dividends by a director might result in a windfall to the very shareholders who had received the dividends), but should not otherwise be used to relieve a director of liability.

**15-7**  Any recoveries on the grounds of misfeasance are in respect of pre-existing rights of the company and are therefore capable of being charged or assigned by the liquidator.[22] Such recoveries (as an asset of the company) are subject to the claims of a floating chargeholder (i.e. where the charge is over the whole of the undertaking, as is commonly the case, the recoveries fall within the grasp of the charge)[23] and subject to the prior payment of the expenses of administration or winding up[24] and the preferential debts.[25]

## C  Fraudulent and wrongful trading

### Fraudulent trading

**15-8**  Liability for fraudulent trading is imposed on persons knowingly a party to the carrying on of any business of a company with intent to defraud creditors of the company, or creditors of any other person, or for any fraudulent purpose.[26]

**15-9**  There are two aspects to fraudulent trading:[27]

- a civil liability in IA 1986, s 213 which applies when the company is in the course of winding up when a liquidator may apply for a declaration that any persons[28] knowingly parties to the carrying on of the business in the manner stated are to be liable to make such contribution to the company's assets as the court thinks proper;[29]

- a criminal offence contained in CA 2006, s 993 which applies regardless of whether the company is in winding up.

The IA 1986, s 246ZA, inserted by the Small Business, Enterprise and Employment Act 2015, s 117(1), allows for fraudulent trading applications by an administrator where the company has gone into administration and it appears that any business of the company has been carried on with intent to defraud creditors of the company or creditors of

---

[22]  *Re Oasis Merchandising Services Ltd* [1997] 1 BCLC 689.

[23]  This is not the case with recoveries, for example, for wrongful trading, see **15-37**, and so the court will take into account the differing positions in cases where a liquidator claims, as is common, on a number of grounds, see, for example, *Re Idessa Ltd, Burke v Morrison* [2012] 1 BCLC 80 at [128] as to the adjustment of amounts recoverable where there were successful claims in misfeasance and for wrongful trading.

[24]  IA 1986, s 115.     [25]  IA 1986, s 175(2).

[26]  'The word "creditor" ... in its ordinary meaning, denotes one to whom money is owed; whether that debt can presently be sued for is immaterial': *R v Smith (Wallace Duncan)* [1996] 2 BCLC 109, CA.

[27]  See generally Keay, *Company Directors' Responsibilities to Creditors* (2007), Chs 3–6.

[28]  The provision has extra-territorial effect ('any persons') in the same manner and for the same reasons as IA 1986, s 236, has extra-territorial effect, as to which see n 138 and *Bilta (UK) Ltd v Nazir* [2015] UKSC 23, [2015] 2 WLR 1168; *Re Paramount Airways Ltd* [1992] BCLC 710.

[29]  In a creditors' voluntary liquidation or a compulsory winding up, a liquidator can only bring a claim under this section with sanction of the court or the creditors: IA 1986, Sch 4, Pt I, para 3.

any other person, or for any fraudulent purpose.[30] As the provision mirrors s 213 in all respects with the substitution of administration for liquidation, for ease of exposition the discussion is limited to liquidation and the reader should read the discussion with an eye to IA 1986, s 246ZA. A liquidator or administrator may also assign any rights of action under ss 213 or 246ZA (s 246ZD(2)).

### Civil liability

**15-10**  This civil liability is less important now in the light of the provision on wrongful trading in IA 1986, ss 214 and 246ZB (based on negligence), see **15-18**, and any liquidator or administrator interested in seeking civil recoveries is likely to look to those provisions, so avoiding the difficult task of establishing an intent to defraud. On occasion, recourse to fraudulent trading is useful, however, because it applies to a wider category of respondents ('any persons')[31] whereas wrongful trading applies only to directors or shadow directors.

**15-11**  A distinction must be drawn between an individual creditor who is defrauded in the course of the carrying on of the business of the company—he has his individual remedy under the general law—and fraudulent trading.[32] Fraudulent trading requires that the business of the company has been carried on with intent to defraud creditors of the company. If that is the position, liability arises, even if then only one creditor is shown to have been defrauded.[33] The power to order a contribution is compensatory and not penal[34] as the penal position is preserved in CA 2006, s 993 and Parliament could not have intended that the civil power would be used to punish a wrongdoer.[35] The principle on which the contribution power should be exercised is that the contribution to the assets in which the company's creditors will share in the liquidation or administration should reflect (and compensate for) the loss which has been caused to those creditors by the carrying on of the business with an intent to defraud.[36] Where there are several respondents, the court may order that they be jointly and severally liable, but equally may make a separate assessment of the contribution to be made by each.[37]

**15-12**  Any sums recovered by the liquidator or administrator are impressed with a statutory trust in favour of the unsecured creditors rather than for the creditor(s) defrauded.[38] Recoveries do not form part of the assets of the company so as to fall within the grasp of any floating charge[39] for they arise post the commencement of the winding up or administration as a result of the exercise of a statutory power by a liquidator or administrator, but they are subject to the prior claims of the expenses of the winding up or administration[40] and any preferential debts.[41]

---

[30] For the background to the extension of these provisions to administrators: see BIS, *Transparency & Trust: Enhancing the Transparency of UK Company Ownership and Increasing Trust in UK Business*, Government Response (April 2014), BIS/14/672, pp 64–6; and consultation paper of same name (July 2013), BIS 13/959, pp 71–2.     [31] See *Re BCCI (No 15), Morris v Bank of India* [2005] 2 BCLC 328.

[32] *Morphitis v Bernasconi* [2003] 2 BCLC 53, CA.

[33] *Re Gerald Cooper Chemicals Ltd* [1978] 2 All ER 49; *Morphitis v Bernasconi* [2003] 2 BCLC 53, CA.

[34] *Re BCCI (No 15), Morris v Bank of India* [2005] 2 BCLC 328 at 356, CA; *Re Overnight Ltd, Goldfarb v Higgins* [2010] 2 BCLC 186.     [35] *Morphitis v Bernasconi* [2003] 2 BCLC 53, CA.

[36] *Morphitis v Bernasconi* [2003] 2 BCLC 53, CA; *Re Overnight Ltd, Goldfarb v Higgins* [2010] 2 BCLC 186.

[37] *Re Overnight Ltd, Goldfarb v Higgins* [2010] 2 BCLC 186 (that is the position under IA 1986, s 214, see **15-33**, and given the similar wording in immediately adjacent statutory provisions, the court said no distinction in approach should be drawn between ss 213 and 214).

[38] *Re Esal (Commodities) Ltd* [1997] 1 BCLC 705, CA.

[39] IA 1986, s 176ZB. See *Re Oasis Merchandising Services Ltd, Ward v Aitken* [1997] 1 BCLC 689 at 698–700, CA.

[40] IA 1986, s 115.     [41] IA 1986, s 175(2).

## Criminal offence

**15-13** Fraudulent trading is also a criminal offence under CA 2006, s 993 and prosecutors find it useful because of the wide variety of company frauds which may fall within its scope, assuming that it is possible to establish an intent to defraud to the criminal burden of proof. On the other hand, it may prove of diminishing importance as the Fraud Act 2006 offers prosecutors a range of open-ended fraud provisions which may be more suitable in a given case.

**15-14** The section applies not just to the carrying on of the business of the company with an intent to defraud creditors, but to the carrying on of business for any fraudulent purpose.[42] Provided the business has been carried on with an intent to defraud creditors, it suffices even though only one creditor has been defrauded,[43] although most cases would involve a pattern of fraudulent trading by the defendant. The second limb of the fraudulent trading provision (any fraudulent purpose) does not necessarily incorporate an intent to deceive or actual deception of creditors. Concealment of ownership to obtain a business advantage that would otherwise be denied is sufficient if there is a dishonest intent and the second limb requires that the purpose be dishonest.[44]

**15-15** The type of conduct commonly involved includes the obtaining of credit from suppliers with no intention of paying for those goods; persuading customers to place large deposits with no intention of supplying the goods; obtaining credit from banks and factors by false invoices or accounts; falsifying accounts to show inflated profits; and trading to defraud HM Revenue & Customs. But the mere granting of a preference to a creditor is not, without more, fraudulent trading.[45]

**15-16** The essence of fraudulent trading is dishonesty[46] and it is not enough to show that the company has continued to trade while insolvent (although such conduct may give rise to liability for wrongful trading, discussed later). Instead the conduct must '... involve actual dishonesty, involving, according to current notions of fair trading among commercial men, real moral blame'.[47] Although this is a strict standard, it will clearly be satisfied where directors allow a company to incur credit when they have no reason to think the creditors will ever be paid.[48] It will also be established, as the Court of Appeal made clear in *R v Grantham*,[49] where credit is incurred at a time when the directors have no good reason to think funds will become available to pay the creditors when their debts become due or shortly thereafter.

**15-17** Liability extends beyond directors to any persons 'knowingly parties to the carrying on of the business' with intent to defraud which will include those exercising at least some

---

[42] See *Re Overnight Ltd, Goldfarb v Higgins* [2010] 2 BCLC 186 (as the company's business could only have been carried on at a loss had it not been for a VAT fraud, it could be readily concluded that the company's business was carried on with intent to defraud a creditor or for a fraudulent purpose); *R v Kemp* [1988] QB 645, CA (victims here were not creditors but customers of the company who were induced to accept worthless goods which they were duped into buying); *Re Sarflax Ltd* [1979] 1 All ER 529 (distributing the proceeds of the realisation of assets could constitute carrying on business); also *Re Augustus Barnett & Son Ltd* [1986] BCLC 170.

[43] *Morphitis v Bernasconi* [2003] 2 BCLC 53, CA; *Re Gerald Cooper Chemicals Ltd* [1978] 2 All ER 49.

[44] *R v Hollier, R v Booth* [2013] EWCA Crim 2041.      [45] *R v Sarflax* [1979] 1 All ER 529.

[46] The ordinary criminal law test of dishonesty as laid down in *R v Ghosh* [1982] 2 All ER 689 applies.

[47] *Re Patrick and Lyon Ltd* [1933] Ch 786 at 790, per Maugham J. See *R v Cox, R v Hedges* [1983] BCLC 169.

[48] *Re William C Leitch Bros Ltd* [1932] 2 Ch 71.      [49] [1984] 3 All ER 166, CA.

positive role in the management of the business.[50] Creditors can be party to fraudulent trading if they accept money knowing it has been procured by carrying on business with intent to defraud creditors and for the very purpose of paying their debts.[51] Third parties who are involved in and who assist and benefit from the offending business, or the business carried on in an offending way, and do so knowingly and therefore dishonestly do fall, or at least can fall, within the provision.[52] A company secretary who merely carries out the administrative functions of such an office, however, is not concerned in the management of the company or in carrying on its business.[53]

## Wrongful trading

**15-18**  The difficulties in establishing the intent to defraud necessary to give rise to liability for fraudulent trading led the Cork Committee to recommend the introduction of a provision for wrongful trading under which civil liability could arise without proof of fraud or dishonesty and without requiring the criminal standard of proof.[54]

**15-19**  Only a liquidator or an administrator can bring wrongful trading proceedings. IA 1986, s 214 allows a liquidator of a company in the course of winding up to apply where certain conditions are met for an order that a director (including a shadow director) make such contribution[55] to the company's assets as the court thinks proper.[56] The conditions are that:

- the company has gone into insolvent liquidation;[57] and
- at some time before the commencement of the winding up, the director (who was a director at that time) knew or ought to have concluded that there was no reasonable

---

[50] See *Re BCCI (No 15), Morris v Bank of India* [2005] 2 BCLC 328, CA (bank knowingly party to the carrying on of business with intent to defraud when general manager of London branch of the bank was party to that fraudulent trading, see **4-43**). Someone who orchestrates, organises, or can seize control of the business concerned is within the provision: *Re BCCI, Banque Arabe v Morris* [2001] 1 BCLC 263; see also *Re Overnight Ltd, Goldfarb v Higgins* [2010] 2 BCLC 186 (company secretary had the requisite knowledge when he deliberately chose not to make enquiries about what he must have realised appeared to be dishonest transactions).    [51] *Re Gerald Cooper Chemicals Ltd* [1978] 2 All ER 49.

[52] *Re BCCI, Banque Arabe v Morris* [2001] 1 BCLC 263.

[53] *Re Maidstone Building Provisions Ltd* [1971] 3 All ER 363. Cf the role of the company secretary in *Re Overnight Ltd, Goldfarb v Higgins* [2010] 2 BCLC 186.

[54] See the Cork Committee Report (Cmnd 8558, 1982), Ch 44. As to wrongful trading generally, see Keay, n 27, Chs 7–10; also Keay, 'Wrongful Trading: Problems and Proposals' (2014) 65 NILQ 63. On the difficulty in balancing directors' duties to shareholders and to creditors in the vicinity of insolvency, see Davies, 'Directors' Creditor—Regarding Duties in Respect of Wrongful Trading Decisions in the Vicinity of Insolvency' (2006) 7 EBOR 301.

[55] The declaration by the court is for the recovery of a sum of money although there is nothing to preclude the liquidator from accepting property to satisfy that liability: see *Re Farmizer Products Ltd* [1997] BCC 655, CA, aff'g [1995] 2 BCLC 462. The limitation period is six years from the date when the company went into insolvent liquidation, applying Limitation Act 1980, s 9: *Re Farmizer Products Ltd*.

[56] IA 1986, s 214(1), (7). Relief is not available under CA 2006, s 1157, see **14-79**; *Re Produce Marketing Consortium Ltd* [1989] 3 All ER 1. Once found liable for wrongful trading, the court can also make a disqualification order under CDDA 1986, s 10: see, for example, *Re Idessa Ltd, Burke v Morrison* [2012] 1 BCLC 80 at [137]; *Re Brian D Pierson (Contractors) Ltd* [2001] 1 BCLC 275 at 312.

[57] A company goes into insolvent liquidation for these purposes if it goes into liquidation at a time when its assets are insufficient for the payment of its debts and other liabilities and the expenses of the winding up: IA 1986, s 214(6); and a company enters insolvent administration if it enters administration at a time when its assets are insufficient for the payment of its debts and other liabilities and the expenses of the administration: s 214(6A). In each case, the test is a balance sheet test of insolvency, rather than cash-flow, test of insolvency.

prospect that the company would avoid[58] going into insolvent liquidation or entering insolvent administration (s 214(2)).

Section 214(4) provides that the facts which a director of a company ought to know or ascertain, the conclusions which he ought to reach, and the steps which he ought to take are those which would be known or ascertained, or reached or taken, by a reasonably diligent person having both:

(1) the general knowledge, skill, and experience that may reasonably be expected of a person carrying out the same functions as are carried out by that director in relation to the company, and

(2) the general knowledge, skill, and experience that that director has.

**15-20**   More recently, provision was made for wrongful trading applications by an administrator, IA 1986, s 246ZB, inserted by the SBEE Act 2015, s 117(2) with effect from 1 October 2015. Applications may be made by an administrator where the company has gone into insolvent administration and at some prior time the director knew or ought to have concluded that there was no reasonable prospect that the company would avoid entering insolvent administration or going into insolvent liquidation.[59] As IA 1986, s 246ZB mirrors s 214 in all respects with the substitution of insolvent administration for insolvent liquidation, for ease of exposition the discussion is limited to liquidation and the reader should read the discussion with an eye to IA 1986, s 246ZB.[60] A liquidator or administrator may also assign any rights of action (including the proceeds of an action) under ss 214 or 246ZB (s 246ZD(2)(b)).

**15-21**   As discussed in Chapter 11, IA 1986, s 214(4) was taken to set the standard of care and skill for directors in all contexts and not just in relation to wrongful trading, hence it is replicated now in CA 2006, s 174 as one of the general duties of directors. As noted at **11-14**, the standard imposed by IA 1986, s 214(4) is an objective minimum standard, that of a reasonably diligent person who has accepted the office of director, set in the context of the functions undertaken, with that objective minimum standard capable of being raised in the light of the particular attributes of the director in question.[61] There is something of an overlap between s 214 and a director's duty to have regard to creditors' interests in cases of insolvency or doubtful solvency as required by CA 2006, s 172(3), discussed at

---

[58] See Keay, 'Wrongful Trading: Problems and Proposals' (2014) 65 NILQ 63 who notes that the provision has been ineffective and argues, *inter alia*, that to be effective, it should be reconfigured to prohibit the incurring of further debt by the company when the director knows or ought to have known that the company was unable to pay its debts. See also Moss, 'No Compensation for Wrongful Trading—Where Did it All Go Wrong?' (2017) Insolv Intell 49 (and addendum at 88); Rajak, 'The Complex Story of Wrongful Trading' (2017) Company Law Newsletter 392; Williams, n 60; also Werdnik, 'Wrongful Trading Provision—Is it Efficient?' (2012) 25 Insolv Int 81. Wrongful trading proceedings can also be brought against a member of an LLP: IA 1986, s 214A.

[59] For the background to the extension of this provision to administrators: see BIS, *Transparency & Trust: Enhancing the Transparency of UK Company Ownership and Increasing Trust in UK Business,* Consultation Paper (July 2013), BIS 13/959, pp 71–2; and Government Response (April 2014), BIS/14/672, pp 64–6.

[60] Note the detailed critique of s 214 by Williams, 'What Can We Expect to Gain from Reforming the Insolvent Trading Remedy?' (2015) 78 MLR 55, who considers that there is no evidence to support that there is a significant problem of wrongful trading and therefore these amendments are unlikely to result in any great increase in the use of s 214. Its limited use is not due, in his view, to defects in the section which can be remedied by legislative changes of this nature. Williams also notes that other provisions such as IA 1986, s 212 and 238 may be more relevant in terms of pursuing directors and equally that the personal resources of directors of insolvent companies may be depleted such that pursuing them is pointless. His conclusion is that the gains to be made from reforming s 214 are limited.

[61] See *Re Brian D Pierson (Contractors) Ltd* [2001] 1 BCLC 275 at 302.

**10-41**, and the courts are still developing the precise overlap and boundaries, see **10-57**. As discussed in the context of CA 2006, s 172(3), directors are subject to a variety of obligations in terms of maintaining financial records and preparing accounts which should help them appreciate at any given time the company's financial position. Proper regard to their duties of care and skill should also ensure that they are well informed about the company's financial position (see **10-50**). The purpose of IA 1986, s 214 in effect is to force them to act on that knowledge or risk a personal liability under this provision, but often, whether out of optimism or 'head in the sand' blindness, directors fail to act until too late with disastrous consequences for the company's creditors.[62] At the same time, the courts do not want to take such a strict approach that cautious directors, for fear of wrongful trading, rush too soon to put their companies into administration or liquidation. The courts are conscious of the stultifying effect 'if the law were to require company directors to put their companies into liquidation at the first sign of trouble'.[63]

### Identifying the relevant time

**15-22**  The first step in applying IA 1986, s 214 is identifying the point in time when the directors, acting to the standard required by s 214(4), knew or ought to have concluded there was no reasonable prospect that the company would avoid going into insolvent administration or entering insolvent liquidation.[64]

**15-23**  As Lewison J explained in *Re Hawkes Hill Publishing Co Ltd*:[65]

'It is important at the outset to be clear about the relevant question. The question is not whether the directors knew or ought to have known that the company was insolvent. The question is whether they knew or ought to have concluded that there was no reasonable prospect of avoiding insolvent liquidation. As Chadwick J. pointed out in *Re C S Holidays Ltd; Secretary of State for Trade and Industry v Gash* [1997] B.C.C. 172; [1997] 1 W.L.R. 407 (at p.178; 414): "The companies legislation does not impose on directors a statutory duty to ensure that their company does not trade while insolvent; nor does that legislation impose an obligation to ensure that the company does not trade at a loss. Those propositions need only be stated to be recognised as self-evident. Directors may properly take the view that it is in the interests of the company and of its creditors that, although insolvent, the company should continue to trade out of its difficulties. They may properly take the view that it is in the interests of the company and its creditors that some loss-making trade should be accepted in anticipation of future profitability. They are not to be criticised if they give effect to such view."'

He went on to note that, when asking whether the directors ought to have known there was no reasonable prospect of avoiding insolvent liquidation, the answer 'depends on rational expectations of what the future might hold. But directors are not clairvoyant and the fact that they fail to see what eventually comes to pass does not mean that they are guilty of wrongful trading.'[66] The court does not approach the question of what they ought to have known or concluded with hindsight.[67]

---

[62]  See, for example, *Roberts v Frohlich* [2011] 2 BCLC 625 at [112], discussed at **15-25**.

[63]  *Re Hawkes Hill Publishing Ltd* [2007] BCC 937 at [47].

[64]  It is not a requirement that the company be insolvent at the time of that knowledge: *Nicholson v Fielding* EWHC, unreported, 15 September 2017, at [37].      [65]  [2007] BCC 937 at [28].

[66]  [2007] BCC 937 at [41]; *Re Ralls Builders Ltd* [2016] BCC 293 at [171]–[173].

[67]  *Re Ralls Builders Ltd* [2016] BCC 293 at [173]; *Re Hawkes Hill Partnership Ltd* [2007] BCC 937 at [47]; *Re Idessa Ltd, Burke v Morrison* [2012] 1 BCLC 80 at [112]–[114], [119]–[121] (proper regard must be had to the difficult choices which often confront directors when deciding whether to continue to trade and on what basis).

**15-24**  In *Official Receiver v Doshi*,[68] a director who knew that his company could only continue to trade as a result of fraudulent invoicing ought to have concluded that there was no reasonable prospect that the company would avoid going into insolvent liquidation. In *Re Cubelock Ltd*[69] the question was whether the directors were liable for wrongful trading from the beginning of trading as the company was balance sheet insolvent (assets insufficient to meet its liabilities) from the outset. The court rejected the claim, noting that it is common for companies to trade in this manner in the initial months of business.[70] In *Re The Rod Gunner Organisation Ltd, Rubin v Gunner*[71] the court agreed that the directors were entitled for a period of approximately six months (March to September 1998) to accept assurances from a new chief executive that he would be able to raise funds to deal with the company's pressing financial needs but, as he repeatedly failed to make good on his promises, the court said, no reasonably diligent director would have continued to give him the benefit of the doubt. By October 1998, the court held, they ought to have known that there was no reasonable prospect that the company would avoid going into insolvent liquidation. Similarly, in *Re Ralls Builders Ltd*[72] at a time when the directors knew that the company was insolvent, they were entitled for a few weeks to pursue a potential investor who promised to inject significant sums into the business. But, the lack of any progress with him and his repeated failures to produce the money which he indicated would be available ought to have led the directors to conclude that there was no longer any rational basis for expecting him to provide the funding needed to save the company. A realistic assessment of the situation should have led them to conclude that they could not rely on him and there was no reasonable prospect of the company avoiding insolvent liquidation.[73]

**15-25**  In *Roberts v Frohlich*[74] the directors of a property development company continued the business for a year after a point where the court said the most rudimentary accounts would have shown the company to be balance sheet and cash-flow insolvent with immediate liabilities mounting and restricted access to bank finance and with attempts at attracting new investment having collapsed. The directors were driven by this stage by 'wilfully blind optimism' and a 'reckless belief' that 'something might turn up'. Given the developing financial position, given their actual skills and experience,[75] and the abilities to be expected of directors participating in financial oversight and project management of a new-build development, they ought to have concluded that there was no reasonable prospect of avoiding insolvent liquidation.[76] In *Re Idessa Ltd, Burke v Morrison*[77] the company continued to trade for more than two years after the date when (a) the contract which was its main source of income came to an end, and (b) external investors ceased

---

[68]  [2001] 2 BCLC 235.       [69]  [2001] BCC 523. See also *Re Hawkes Hill Partnership Ltd* [2007] BCC 937.

[70]  Cf *Singla v Hedman* [2010] 2 BCLC 61 at [96]–[100], [107] (a sole director who committed his company to onerous contractual obligations at a time when it had £2 of share capital and no funding in place ought to have known at the date of the contract that there was no reasonable prospect of the company avoiding insolvent liquidation, given it had no means of honouring its obligations—the director had nothing more than a speculative hope that things would work out); also *Re Kudos Business Solutions Ltd, Earp v Stevenson* [2012] 2 BCLC 65 (company had contracted to supply DX services which contracts the directors had no reason to believe could be fulfilled; on that basis, the rational expectation would be that there was no reasonable prospect of avoiding insolvent liquidation).

[71]  [2004] 2 BCLC 110. Cf *Hawkes Hill Partnership Ltd* [2007] BCC 937.       [72]  [2016] BCC 293.

[73]  [2016] BCC 293 at [216].       [74]  [2011] 2 BCLC 625 at [111].

[75]  [2011] 2 BCLC 625 at [101]–[102]; the two directors were respectively a professionally qualified accountant and an engineer with substantial experience of property development.

[76]  [2011] 2 BCLC 623 at [112]–[113].

[77]  [2012] 1 BCLC 80; see also *Re Kudos Business Solutions Ltd, Earp v Stevenson* [2012] 2 BCLC 65.

to contribute significant sums to support the continued trading of the company which had always been balance sheet insolvent. The court concluded that the combined loss of income from the external investors and from the key contract meant that the directors ought to have concluded that, as of the date of those events, there was no reasonable prospect that the company would avoid insolvent liquidation.[78]

**15-26** What is missing in these cases is a realistic assessment of the company's situation and a rational basis for the decision to continue to trade.[79] The factors which swing the pendulum in the other direction are matters such as grounds for believing that new orders can be secured or time is needed to collect payments from existing customers, or the existence of a strategy for continued trading, and reliance on professional advice.

**15-27** In *Re Continental Assurance Co of London plc*[80] a small insurance company collapsed in 1992. Large and unexpected losses had arisen which came to the board's attention in June 1991. The liquidators alleged that the company applied inappropriate accounting policies which showed the company to be solvent when, had an appropriate accounting policy been adopted by the company, the directors would and should have appreciated that the company was insolvent and they should have taken steps to stop trading.[81] The court found that for the directors to have reached these conclusions would have required of them knowledge of accounting concepts of a particularly sophisticated nature. Park J rejected any idea that IA 1986, s 214(4) imposes such an unrealistically high standard of skill. On the facts, he found that the directors had taken a wholly responsible and conscientious attitude both to the company's position and to their own responsibilities as directors at all times from and after the first crisis board meeting in 1991 when major and unexpected losses were reported to them. The directors did not ignore the question of whether the company could properly continue to trade; on the contrary, the court found that they considered it directly, closely, and frequently.[82] They were entitled, the court said, to have regard to the accounts before them and to the opinion of the finance director and the auditors that the company was solvent. They did not just accept in an unquestioning way the figures which were put before them, but questioned the executive directors closely and at length on them and were satisfied with the explanations given.[83] Overall, the court considered that the way in which the directors reacted to the financial crisis which developed was entirely appropriate. They were not liable for wrongful trading.[84]

**15-28** In *Re Hawkes Hill Publishing Co Ltd*[85] the directors had started up a small publishing company which was still insolvent after ten months of trading. The court noted that, while the directors ought to have known that the company was insolvent, that did not lead to the conclusion that there was no prospect of avoiding insolvent liquidation.[86] At the time of the alleged wrongful trading, there was a real prospect that an outside investor

---

[78] [2012] 1 BCLC 80 at [119].   [79] See *Re Ralls Builders Ltd* [2016] BCC 293 at [174] et seq, [216].

[80] [2007] 2 BCLC 287.

[81] In fact, the court concluded that, even if an alternative accounting approach had been taken, the company was solvent in June 1991: see [2007] 2 BCLC 287 at [247].

[82] *Re Continental Assurance Co of London plc* [2007] 2 BCLC 287 at [107].

[83] *Re Continental Assurance Co of London plc* [2007] 2 BCLC 287 at [261].

[84] See Keay, n 27, at 98 who criticises the emphasis placed by Park J on the need for some blameworthy behaviour by the directors when the section does not require the establishment of any wrongdoing. The issue, Keay says, is merely whether the directors should have concluded that there was no reasonable prospect of avoiding insolvent liquidation. It can be argued that the court is not so much looking to establish blameworthiness but merely using that measure as a device to determine whether the directors should have concluded there was no reasonable prospect of avoiding insolvent liquidation.

[85] [2007] BCC 937. See too *Re Ralls Builders Ltd* [2016] BCC 293 at [206].   [86] [2007] BCC 937 at [41], [44].

might be prepared to invest, the directors had engaged an accountant who advised them that the business had a promising future, and there was no pressure from creditors until much later.[87] The liquidators' application was dismissed.

**15-29**   In *Nicolson v Fielding*,[88] which concerned the collapse of a car transport business in 2009, the court found that, throughout 2008 and 2009, the directors were constantly monitoring the company's situation. They were in detailed discussions with HMRC, they were acting on exemplary management accounts, they were taking tough decisions, laying off staff and mothballing lorries, all against a backdrop of the financial crisis of 2007–08, oscillating fuel prices, and a car industry entering a significant downturn of uncertain duration.[89] The court found the directors recognised the seriousness of the company's position throughout, had a strategy to ensure its ongoing viability, and acted reasonably.[90] They had no knowledge that the company had no reasonable prospect of avoiding insolvent liquidation at the dates alleged by the liquidator (June or October 2008), nor would an objective director have concluded by those dates that the company was doomed.[91] Even as the position deteriorated, the directors continued to revise their strategy, HMRC was willing even in early 2009 to give the company further time to pay, and the company actually made a profit before tax in the year 2009 down to July.[92] They were not liable.

### The 'every step' defence

**15-30**   Even if it is established that a director knew or ought to have concluded that entering insolvent administration or going into insolvent liquidation could not be avoided (and the onus is on the administrator or liquidator to establish that), the director has a defence if he can satisfy the court (and the onus is on the director in this regard) that, after that point in time was reached, he took every step with a view to minimising the potential loss to the company's creditors as he ought to have taken[93] (IA 1986, s 214(3), s 246ZB(3)). Having said that, the threshold set is high ('every step').[94] In *Re Brian D Pierson Ltd*[95] the court noted that it is not sufficient for these purposes for a director to claim that he continued to trade with the intention of trying to make a profit. The provision is intended to apply, the court said, to cases 'where, for example, directors take specific steps with a view to preserving or realising assets or claims for the benefit of creditors, even if they fail to achieve that result, and it does not cover the very act of wrongful trading itself'.[96] Attempting to secure additional financing, reaching agreements with creditors, taking professional advice, and working closely with the company's bank would all be steps which, normally, the court would accept as steps designed to protect the creditors' interests. Cautious and risk-averse directors may consider that the only appropriate step is

---

[87]   [2007] BCC 937 at [45].       [88]   EWHC, unreported, 15 September 2017.

[89]   EWHC unreported, 15 September 2017, at [97]–[98].

[90]   EWHC unreported, 15 September 2017, at [103].

[91]   EWHC unreported, 15 September 2017, at [102].

[92]   EWHC unreported, 15 September 2017, at [104].

[93]   See *Re Idessa Ltd, Burke v Morrison* [2012] 1 BCLC 80 (directors who during the relevant period had continued to pay themselves the same salaries and incur the same type of expenses, who had not made any costs savings, or put in place any strategy to repay creditors, or who had not given any thought at all to the creditors and the impact on them of continuing to trade, could not be said to have taken every step to minimise potential loss to the company's creditors), at [120].

[94]   As Goode points out, this may mean no more than 'every reasonable step' when read with 'reasonably diligent person', see Goode, *Principles of Corporate Insolvency Law* (4th edn, 2011), para 14–44.

[95]   [2001] 1 BCLC 275.       [96]   [2001] 1 BCLC 275 at 308.

to put the company into administration, liquidation etc, but that is not what the legislation necessarily demands though, obviously, it may be the only practical step in many instances.

**15-31**   The scope of this defence was considered in *Re Ralls Builders Ltd*.[97] The company was a construction company and continuing to trade allowed it to complete contracts and collect payments from customers which were used to reduce the company's overdraft (as required by the terms of the bank's debenture securing the overdraft by fixed and floating charges). The liquidators applied for a wrongful trading contribution and the directors relied upon the defence. Snowden J explained the position as follows:[98]

> 'The function and wording of the two subsections of s.214 are different. Section 214(1) provides for a financial remedy in effect to restore the financial position of the company to what it would have been had the wrongful trading not occurred. Section 214(1) is thus a provision that focuses on the consequences of wrongful trading for unsecured creditors as a whole. In contrast, s.214(3) focuses on the regime which the director puts in place to protect creditors *after the relevant time* (emphasis added), rather than the result. If a director can show that he took "every step … as he ought to have taken" after the relevant time "with a view" to minimising the potential loss to creditors, he avoids liability under s.214(1), even if he does not actually succeed in his objective.'

He went on:[99]

> 'Given the express wording of s 214(3) ("every step"), I think that it is plain that s.214(3) is intended to be a high hurdle for directors to surmount. I therefore think that it is right to construe s.214(3) strictly and to require a director who wishes to take advantage of the defence offered by that subsection to demonstrate not only that continued trading was intended to reduce the net deficiency of the company, but also that it was designed appropriately so as to minimise the risk of loss to individual creditors. Otherwise a director could make out the defence under s.214(3) by claiming that he traded on with a view to reducing the overall deficiency for creditors as a general body, irrespective of how he achieved that result as between creditors.'

**15-32**   Snowden J considered that, on the facts in *Re Ralls Builders Ltd*, the manner in which the directors continued trading after the relevant point in time meant that the company's bank and some of its existing unsecured creditors were paid at the expense of new creditors who ended up not being paid. Snowden J considered that the failure by directors to have taken steps that they 'ought to have taken' to protect the interests of the new creditors prevented them from being able to rely upon the defence.[100] Therefore, while determining the existence of a net deficiency looks to the position of the creditors as a group, rather than whether individual creditors were impacted, when it comes to the defence available to the directors, it will be relevant to consider whether the directors did in fact discriminate as between creditors.

### Extent of any liability

**15-33**   Once liability is established, the extent of any contribution to the company's assets is a matter for the court's discretion and the aim here is primarily compensatory rather than

---

[97] [2016] EWHC 243, [2016] BCC 293.     [98] [2016] BCC 293 at [244].     [99] [2016] BCC 293 at [245].
[100] [2016] BCC 293 at [246].

penal to ensure that any depletion of the assets attributable to the period of wrongful trading is made good.[101] It may be that no contribution will be ordered, as discussed at **15-34**.

**15-34**   On the issue of the quantum of liability for wrongful trading, as a starting point the court looks to determine the increase in net deficiency of the company as regards unsecured creditors between the date when the directors ought to have concluded that there was no reasonable prospect of avoiding insolvent liquidation and the date when the company actually went into insolvent liquidation or administration.[102] This approach is based largely on obiter comments by Park J in *Re Continental Assurance Co of London plc*[103] which are widely cited. Although Park J concluded that the directors had acted properly in that case (see **15-27**), he addressed the issue of quantum in some detail and summed up the issue as one of an increase in net deficiency reflecting the loss to the company of the continued trading between the date when the company should have been put into liquidation and the date of actual liquidation.[104] There must be a connection between that increase and the conduct of the directors which resulted in the wrongful trading. Park J was anxious not to describe this as an issue of causation;[105] nevertheless he thought that there must be some nexus between the wrongfulness of the directors' conduct and the losses which the liquidator seeks to recover. For example, the company might incur losses during the period of wrongful trading as a result of bad weather which had nothing to do with the directors' conduct.[106] He considered that the proper principle would be that liability should be limited to those consequences which are attributable to that which made the act wrongful. As Snowden J said in *Re Ralls Builders Ltd*,[107] 'losses that would have occurred in any event as a consequence of a company going into a formal insolvency process should not be laid at the door of directors under s 214'. In that case, the deficiency increased because of the particular difficulties in dealing with customers of an insolvent construction company. The appropriate test is not whether new debt is incurred after the first date, or whether cash was paid out after that date; the only proper question is whether, on a net basis, the company is worse off as a result of the continuation of trading.[108] If, on the balance of probabilities, there is no increase in net deficiency attributable

---

[101] *Re Produce Marketing Consortium Ltd (No 2)* [1989] BCLC 520 at 553–4; see also *Re Purpoint Ltd* [1991] BCLC 49. The court has the power to defer debts owing from the company to any person found liable for wrongful trading: IA 1986, s 215(4), which is applied in administration by s 246ZC.

[102] *Re Ralls Builders Ltd* [2016] BCC 293 at [241]–[242]. But see Moss, n 58, who argues that this approach is disgraceful and the appropriate remedy should be the new liabilities incurred after the relevant time which should not have been taken on once the directors realised there was no reasonable prospect of avoiding insolvent liquidation.

[103] [2007] 2 BCLC 287; and see *Re Marini Ltd* [2004] BCC 172 at [68]; noted Spence (2004) 17 Insolv Int 11; *Re Ralls Builders Ltd* [2016] BCC 293 at [241].

[104] [2007] 2 BCLC 287 at 294, 296 (interim judgment) and at [296]–[297]. See *Re Idessa Ltd, Burke v Morrison* [2012] 1 BCLC 80 at [127]; also *Re Bangla Television Ltd, Valentine v Bangla Television Ltd* [2010] BCC 143 (at a time when the company was hopelessly insolvent and the directors knew or ought to have known that the company could not avoid insolvent liquidation, directors committed the company to a transfer of its assets for no consideration so giving rise to a straightforward increase in the net deficiency of the company (by £250,000) for which amount the directors were jointly and severally liable).

[105] Park J noted that Chadwick LJ had been content in *Cohen v Selby* [2001] 1 BCLC 176 at [21] to assume that it may not be necessary to establish a causal link between the wrongful trading and any particular loss. But see Moss, n 58, who points out that the causal link is impossible or very difficult to establish in many cases.

[106] Citing *Re Brian D Pierson (Contractors) Ltd* [2001] 1 BCLC 275 at 310.

[107] [2016] EWHC 243, [2016] BCC 293 at [242].

[108] *Re Marini Ltd* [2004] BCC 172 at [68]. But see Moss, n 58, who considers the law to be a disgrace on this point, and given all the decisions are first instance, he considers that a court should not consider itself bound to follow this wrong path, as he would see it.

to the wrongful trading,[109] then section 214(1) is not engaged and no contribution order can be made, even if some creditors are treated unfairly during the period of wrongful trading,[110] as where existing creditors are repaid, leaving new creditors unpaid. In *Re Ralls Builders Ltd*[111] this was what had occurred and, while the court said the directors should not have permitted this conduct, as there was no increase in net deficiency, there was no basis for a contribution order.

**15-35**    It can be difficult to determine the net deficiency, as companies in financial difficulties often fail to maintain accounting records. In cases where that situation has arisen due to the failure of the directors to keep proper records, on occasion the court has decided, on a rough and ready basis, that the net increase in deficiency is the increase in debts due to creditors after the relevant date.[112]

**15-36**    In *Re Continental Assurance Co of London plc*[113] Park J also considered the issue of individual director liability. The starting point, he concluded, is that liability under IA 1986, s 214 is a several liability (i.e. a personal liability of the director) and not a joint and several liability, for it is plain that 'the focus is on the individual director and his conduct, not on the joint conduct of a board of directors as a whole ... it is not a case of a single claim against the board collectively'.[114] Of course, he said, the court in the exercise of its discretion may order that the liability be joint and several, but the initial duty of the court is to determine how much individually each director ought to contribute.[115] Essentially, there are three steps, the court must determine the net deficiency, then identify how much of the increase in net deficiency is attributable to the wrongful trading, and then consider the fair order to be made between the various respondents.[116]

**15-37**    Any recoveries obtained under this provision, being property which arises only after the administration or liquidation of the company and which is recoverable only by the administrator or liquidator pursuant to his statutory powers, is held by him on a statutory trust for distribution to the company's unsecured creditors.[117] These sums are not subject therefore to the claims of the holder of a floating charge over all the undertaking

---

[109] As in *Re Ralls Builders Ltd* where the court thought that the continued trading, to allow for the completion of projects and the collection of customer debts, produced a better result for the creditors than an earlier cessation of trading, [2016] BCC 293 at [270]. See Moss, n 58, for scathing criticism of this decision.

[110] *Brooks v Armstrong* [2017] BCC 99 at [120]; *Re Ralls Builders Ltd* [2016] BCC 293 at [270].

[111] [2016] BCC 293.

[112] *Re Purpoint Ltd* [1991] BCC 121; *Re Kudos Business Solutions Ltd* [2012] 2 BCLC 65; *Re Idessa (UK Ltd)* [2012] BCC 315; and see discussion in *Brooks v Armstrong* [2017] BCC 99 at [67]–[86].

[113] [2007] 2 BCLC 287.

[114] *Re Continental Assurance plc* [2007] 2 BCLC 287 at [385]. But see Prentice, 'Corporate Personality, Limited Liability and the Protection of Creditors' in Grantham and Rickett (eds), *Corporate Personality in the 20th Century* (1998), pp 122–3.

[115] See *Re Continental Assurance* [2007] 2 BCLC 287 at [387]; *Re Brian D Pierson (Contractors) Ltd* [2001] 1 BCLC 275 at 311; *Re Bangla Television Ltd, Valentine v Bangla Television Ltd* [2010] BCC 143 at [57]; *Re Idessa Ltd, Burke v Morrison* [2012] 1 BCLC 80 at [129] (given equal degrees of involvement in the management of the company and therefore the wrongful trading, the court ordered that the directors' liability be joint and several). See *Nicholson v Fielding*, 15 September 2017, EWHC, at [118] (where one of the directors was 'no more than a numbers man' and had 'no real say' compared to the other two executive directors, the court thought it would have been appropriate, had they been found liable, to make all three directors jointly and severally liable for half the amount and make the two executives jointly and severally liable for the other half.

[116] *Nicholson v Fielding*, 15 September 2017, EWHC, at [27]–[29].

[117] IA 1986, s 176ZB. See *Re Oasis Merchanding Services Ltd, Ward v Aitken* [1997] 1 BCLC 689 at 698–700, CA; see Keay, n 27, 104–6.

of the company (IA 1986, s 176ZB). The contribution recovered goes to meet the claims of all the unsecured creditors rather than specifically the claims of creditors whose debt arose in the period of wrongful trading.[118] The recoveries are subject, however, to the prior claim of the expenses of winding up which include litigation costs and preferential debts. Though the floating chargeholder does not benefit directly from the recoveries, the chargeholder benefits indirectly in that the floating charge realisations are subject to the prior claims of the expenses of winding up and preferential debts to the extent that the general assets of the company are insufficient (IA 1986, s 176ZA). If the recoveries from wrongful trading swell the general assets, there is less need to have resort to the floating charge realisations so, to that extent, the floating chargeholder benefits.

**15-38**   To judge by the level of reported cases,[119] there has been limited use of IA 1986, s 214. There is anecdotal evidence of advisers in large companies advising frequently on the potential liability for wrongful trading despite the fact that claims for wrongful trading are rare and unlikely to succeed where the directors have behaved responsibly, as is made clear in *Re Continental Assurance*,[120] discussed at **15-27**.[121] While directors would be concerned about the potential (unquantifiable) civil liability, though they have insurance cover, directors of such companies are concerned particularly about the reputational damage involved if they were to be sued for wrongful trading following the collapse of their company. For smaller companies,[122] the issues are different but equally pressing in that a personal liability would wipe out the advantages of having incorporated in the first place. Given that in these companies the directors are likely also to be shareholders and employees, a significant personal liability as directors on top of the loss of whatever capital they have contributed (which admittedly may be small) and the loss of their employment is a matter of some concern to them and they are unlikely to have insurance cover. For that reason, directors of small companies also show some awareness of this potential liability.

**15-39**   In 2013, the then Department for Business, Innovation and Skills, as part of a wider consultation on transparency and trust in UK business, consulted on issues surrounding civil recoveries in cases of directors' misconduct.[123] Respondents suggested that the limited use of measures such as IA 1986, s 214 can be explained in terms of the high evidential threshold, concerns that directors would not have the ability to pay claims even if successful (as already noted, few will have insurance), and that liquidators are not usually in a position to fund litigation. The Insolvency Act 1986, s 246ZD, now allows liquidators and administrators to assign claims for, *inter alia*, fraudulent and wrongful trading

---

[118] As Snowden J explained in *Re Ralls Builders Ltd* [2016] BCC 293 at [236] '… the purpose of s 214 is not to provide differential redress for individual creditors depending on an assessment of the extent of their loss caused by the period of wrongful trading'; see also *Re Purpoint Ltd* [1991] BCC 121 at 128–9.

[119] See BIS, *Transparency & Trust: Enhancing the Transparency of UK Company Ownership and Increasing Trust in UK Business,* Government Response (April 2014), BIS/14/672, para 260, which notes that, since 1986, there have only been around 30 reported wrongful trading cases, about 50 preference claims, and about 80 reported cases arising from undervalue transactions.

[120] [2007] 2 BCLC 287.

[121] See Keay, n 27, Ch 10 who summarises the many defects of the provision and points out that it needs to be redrafted and refocused if it is to prove useful.

[122] Keay, n 27, makes the point that the reported cases where liability has been imposed have been, exclusively, small closely held companies.

[123] See BIS, *Transparency & Trust: Enhancing the Transparency of UK Company Ownership and Increasing Trust in UK Business,* Government Response (July 2013), BIS 13/959, pp 71–2; and Government Response (April 2014), BIS/14/672, pp 64–6.

to creditors and third parties which may make it more likely that these claims will be pursued.

## D  Prohibition on the re-use of company names

**15-40**   When a company has gone into insolvent liquidation, its directors may be tempted to set up another company immediately under the same or a similar name or may already have several other companies incorporated, all with similar names. The business then continues much as before, a practice often referred to as the phoenix syndrome. The second company frequently operates from the same premises, commonly using the same assets acquired in a fire sale from the liquidator and exploiting what remains of the former company's goodwill. Not surprisingly, existing creditors are aggrieved by these practices and the public concerned about the ability of such 'rogue' directors to operate in this fashion.[124]

**15-41**   The phoenix syndrome is governed by IA 1986, s 216 which renders the re-use of the name of a company which has been wound up insolvent a criminal offence in certain circumstances.[125] Any directors concerned (and others) may incur personal liability under s 217 for debts incurred during the period of the offence,[126] though little use appears to be made of this provision.

### The prohibition

**15-42**   Where a company has gone into insolvent liquidation,[127] it is an offence (except with the leave of the court or in such exceptional circumstances as laid down in the Insolvency Rules 2016, Pt 22) for a director or shadow director of the company who was in post any time in the 12 months preceding the liquidation:

(1)  to be a director of, or in any way directly or indirectly be concerned or take part in the promotion, formation or management of, any other company known under a prohibited name; or

(2)  in any way, directly or indirectly, be concerned or take part in the carrying on of a business carried on (otherwise than by a company) under a prohibited name (IA 1986, s 216(1), (3)).

---

[124]  The problem has been reduced since the IA 1986 required liquidators to be licensed insolvency practitioners so collusive deals to pass over assets are much less likely, though the Company Law Review took the view that the phoenix problem remains significant. See Company Law Review, *Final Report* (July 2001), paras 15.55–15.77; also Milman, 'The Phoenix Syndrome' [2001] Insol L 199. See generally Carter, 'The Phoenix Syndrome—The Personal Liability of Directors' (2006) 19 Insolv Int 38.

[125]  It is an offence of strict liability: *R v Cole, Lees, Birch* [1998] 2 BCLC 235. Any misuse of the name is a factor to be taken into account in disqualification proceedings: *Re Migration Services International Ltd* [2000] 1 BCLC 666. The provision does not apply to partners of a wound up partnership: *Re Newton's Coaches Ltd* [2017] BCC 34.

[126]  See *First Independent Factors Ltd v Mountford* [2008] 2 BCLC 297; *First Independent Factors Ltd v Churchill* [2007] 1 BCLC 293; *Ricketts v Ad Valorem Factors Ltd* [2004] 1 BCLC 1, CA.

[127]  For these purposes, a company goes into insolvent liquidation if it goes into liquidation at a time when its assets are insufficient for the payment of its debts and other liabilities and the expenses of the winding up: IA 1986, s 216(7).

**15-43**  A prohibited name is a name by which the company was known[128] in the 12 months pre-ceding liquidation or a name which is so similar to it as to suggest an association with that company (IA 1986, s 216(1), (3)).[129] The prohibition on the use of the name lasts for five years (s 216(3)). The penalty for contravention is imprisonment or a fine (s 216(4)) and s 217 imposes a personal liability for all the debts and other liabilities incurred by a company when a person, in contravention of s 216, is involved in the manage-ment of the company or when a person acts or is willing to act on the instructions of a person whom he knows to be acting in contravention of s 216.[130] Liability therefore extends beyond the director or shadow director acting in breach of s 216 to persons who act on their instructions. Liability is joint and several with the company for the relevant debts (s 217(4), (5)). A claim may be brought by any creditor for a declaration that the directors are personally liable for the relevant debt or debts and recovery is by the applicant for the debt owed to him. An assignee of a debt may bring proceedings and it makes no difference to the legitimacy of the debt which is the basis of a s 217 claim whether the debt was acquired before or after the defunct company went into liquidation.[131]

**15-44**  The emphasis in the provision is on the use of the company name. The prohibition is on the re-use of the name or a similar name by a director or shadow director. It does not prevent those directors from being directors of another company as long as that company does not use a prohibited name nor does it stop another company from using the name as long as the directors and shadow directors have no connection with that company. The intention is to prevent any exploitation by the directors of any remaining goodwill in the insolvent company, but these sections do not address concerns about the ability of individuals to set up again in business following an earlier insolvency. That problem is addressed through disqualification which is discussed at **15-80**.

### The exceptions

**15-45**  As noted, the prohibitions apply save where re-use of the name is permitted with the leave of the court or in three exceptional cases prescribed in the IR 2016. The first case essen-tially allows directors to continue to act when a successor company acquires the whole or substantially the whole of the business from the liquidator and notice is given to the

---

[128]  i.e. including business names as well as the company's registered name.

[129]  As to whether a name suggests an association with another company, the question is whether the similarity between the two names is such as to give rise to a probability that members of the public, com-paring the names in the relevant context, would associate the two companies with each other, whether as successor companies or as part of the same group: see *First Independent Factors Ltd v Mountford* [2008] 2 BCLC 297.

[130]  Liability is limited to the debts and liabilities incurred in carrying on business or part of the business under a prohibited name: *Glasgow City Council v Craig* [2009] 1 BCLC 742 (prohibited name related to restaurant business, company using prohibited name ran a restaurant and separate wine bar and used the prohibited name only in the restaurant business; the directors who were personally liable under IA 1986, s 217 for involvement in a company using a prohibited name were liable only for debts incurred in running the restaurant business and not the wine bar). See also *R v Weintroub* [2011] EWCA Crim 2167 where confis-cation orders were made under the Proceeds of Crime Act 2002, s 76 (confiscation of benefits received from criminal conduct) in respect of directors convicted of breach of IA 1986, s 216—the Court of Appeal ruled that the amount of the benefit which could be recovered was the benefit which the directors received from acting as directors when prohibited from doing so, i.e. the full amount of salary and dividend received by them—and not some proportion attributable to the misuse of the name.

[131]  *First Independent Factors Ltd v Mountford* [2008] 2 BCLC 297; *Ricketts v Ad Valorem Factors Ltd* [2004] 1 BCLC 1, CA.

creditors that the director will be acting in that capacity in the successor company (IR 2016, r 22.4). The second case is where the court which winds up the insolvent company gives a director leave to use a prohibited name (IR 2016, r 22.6).[132] The third excepted case is set out in IR 2016, r 22.7. A former director can continue to act in the affairs of an established company even though it is known by a prohibited name provided that that company has been using that name for at least a year before the insolvent company went into liquidation and the company was not a dormant company (i.e. inactive) during that time.[133] This exception addresses the situation where a director may have numerous companies all with quite similar names and, when one becomes insolvent, he wishes to continue his business activities as a director of or be involved in the management of the others. As the other companies are known by prohibited names, were it not for this exemption, he would be caught by the prohibition.

## E  Avoidance of transactions prior to winding up

### Transactions at an undervalue—IA 1986, s 238

**15-46**  Section 238 essentially allows a liquidator or administrator to challenge a transaction previously entered into by the company as being at an undervalue and the court is able to make such order as it thinks fit for restoring the position to what it would have been if the company had not entered into the transaction. A liquidator or administrator may also assign any rights of action under s 238 (s 246ZD(2)). There is considerable similarity between IA 1986, s 238 and IA 1986, s 423 (transactions defrauding creditors) and therefore a certain cross-over between the authorities on these provisions. There are a number of differences to note, however, between the provisions.[134] Essentially, s 423 is applicable in a broader range of circumstances; it is not dependent on the company being insolvent or in liquidation or administration and there is no time period limiting the review of the transaction, unlike the two-year limit in s 238. Secondly, applications under s 423 can be by the liquidator or the administrator but also, with the leave of the court, by any victim of the transaction.[135] Thirdly, it must be shown under s 423(3) that the purpose of the transaction was to put assets beyond the reach of the claimant or otherwise prejudice a claimant. Fourthly, despite the heading, fraud is not a requirement of s 423 claim. The significance of s 423 was highlighted by *BTI 2014 LLC v Sequana SA*.[136] In this case, a company declared two dividends to its parent company which then sold its shareholding in the company to new owners. The dividends were legal under CA 2006, Part 23, but the court concluded that the purpose of the second dividend was to put assets beyond the reach of potential claimants against the company with respect to known environmental liabilities. Rose J concluded that the discretionary payment of a dividend to shareholders is a transaction for no consideration within s 423 and to preclude challenge to dividends

---

[132]  See *Penrose v Official Receiver* [1996] 1 BCLC 389; followed in *Re Lightning Electrical Contractors Ltd* [1996] 2 BCLC 302.

[133]  It is sufficient for the purpose of IR 2016, r 22.7 that either the registered name or a trading name of the established company is a prohibited name. In either circumstance, if the company is 'known by' a prohibited name during the relevant period, a director is entitled to rely on r 22.7: *ESS Production Ltd v Sully* [2005] 2 BCLC 547, CA.

[134]  See generally Stubbs, 'Section 423 of the Insolvency Act in Practice' (2008) 21 Insolv Int 17.

[135]  IA 1986, s 424(1)(a); see *National Bank of Kuwait v Menzies* [1994] 2 BCLC 306, CA.

[136]  [2017] 1 BCLC 453. See Graham (2017) Co Law 116.

under the provision would reduce its efficacy given the many instances where directors and shareholders are the same or linked individuals.[137]

**15-47**  The key questions under IA 1986, s 238 are:

- has the company gone into administration or liquidation?
- did the company enter into a transaction at an undervalue with any person [138] within the period of two years ending with the onset of insolvency?[139] and
- was this transaction at a time when the company was unable to pay its debts[140] or did it become unable to pay its debts in consequence of the transaction?[141] This requirement is presumed when the transaction is entered into by the company with a connected person.[142]

An undervalue arises if:

(a) the company makes a gift to that person or otherwise enters into a transaction with that person on terms that provide for the company to receive no consideration; or

(b) the company enters into a transaction with that person for a consideration the value of which, in money or money's worth, is significantly less than the value, in money or money's worth, of the consideration provided by the company.[143]

**15-48**  It is essential to establish that there is a transaction and that the transaction is something which the company has 'entered into' which connotes the taking of some step or act of participation by the company.[144] In determining whether there is a transaction at an

---

[137] [2017] 1 BCLC 453 at [497]–[502]. With regard to the appropriate remedy, Rose J concluded that the court had to try to achieve a result that met the statutory objective of restoring the claimants to the position they would have been in had the second dividend not been paid. The company was ordered to pay the sum of $138.4 million: [2017] EWHC 211—that decision is under appeal.

[138] The provision applies to any person wherever resident and an application may be made against a person resident abroad with no place of business in the UK and who does not carry on business within the jurisdiction: *Re Paramount Airways Ltd* [1992] BCLC 710, CA, but the width of such a provision is subject to the safeguard that the court has a discretion to make such order as it thinks fit and the court will need to be satisfied that the defendant has a sufficient connection with England for it to be just and proper to make an order against him despite the foreign element: *Re Paramount Airways Ltd*, at 721; and as to the factors which the court will consider in determining whether there is a sufficient connection, see at 722. See also n 28.

[139] The expression 'the onset of insolvency' is defined in detail in IA 1986, s 240(3).

[140] Within the meaning of IA 1986, s 123, see discussion at **24-31**. The court will look to make sure it is not just a period of temporary illiquidity, see *Re Cosy Insulation Ltd* [2016] 2 BCLC 319 (picture was not temporary illiquidity, there was an endemic shortage of funds).

[141] IA 1986, s 240(2); see *Evans v Jones* [2017] 1 BCLC 184, CA.

[142] IA 1986, s 240(2). The precise definition of persons connected with the company is complex: see IA 1986, ss 249 and 435, but broadly it includes any directors or shadow directors of the company: ss 249(a), 251; and their families, partners, and associated companies: s 435(2), (3), (6), (8).

[143] IA 1986, s 238(4). See *Re Taylor Sinclair (Capital) Ltd* [2001] 2 BCLC 176 where the court considered that, with the exception of gifts which are expressly included, a transaction must have an element of dealing between the parties.

[144] *Re Ovenden Colbert Printers Ltd, Hunt v Hosking* [2014] 1 BCLC 291 (a transaction whereby trust funds held by an accountant on trust for a company were paid away by the accountant to a third party did not constitute a transaction 'entered into' by the company so as to bring the case within IA 1986, s 238). See *Re Hampton Capital Ltd, Murphy v Elite Performance Cars Ltd* [2016] 1 BCLC 374; the mere transmission of money, without any dealing between the parties, could not constitute the entering into of a transaction. The language of s 238(4) requires some engagement, or at least communication, between the parties. The onus is on the liquidator to show that there had been a 'transaction', and that a payment was either a gift or a transaction in which the value of the consideration received by the company was significantly less than that provided by the company: *Re Kiss Cards Ltd* [2017] BCC 489.

undervalue, the court starts by identifying the relevant transaction and the consideration for that transaction.[145] The issue is whether the consideration provided by the transferee is 'significantly less' than the value provided by the transferor company. On this point, a comparison must be made between the value obtained by the company and the value of the consideration provided by the company,[146] though it may be difficult to assess the relative weight of the consideration provided when the transaction may already be several years old by the time the liquidator has an opportunity to review it. Both the consideration provided and received must be measurable in money or money's worth; both must be considered from the company's point of view and a comparison must be made between two figures representing the actual value of the consideration.[147]

**15-49**   The issue of the transaction and the nature of the consideration to be valued were considered by the House of Lords in *Phillips v Brewin Dolphin Bell Lawrie Ltd*.[148] The company carried on business as stockbrokers and its assets included computer equipment which it held on lease. A purchaser wished to acquire part of the company's business for £1.25m. For commercial and tax reasons, the transaction was structured into two elements, one the sale of the business via a wholly-owned subsidiary of the company with the purchaser buying the shares in the subsidiary for a nominal £1 and taking on the costs of certain redundancy payments. Another company associated with the purchaser leased the computer equipment from the company at an annual rent. The company was wound up and the liquidator contended, as against the purchaser and the associated company, that the share sale agreement was a transaction at an undervalue within the meaning of IA 1986, s 238.

**15-50**   The trial judge held that the equipment lease was not part of the consideration which was limited to the £1 and the redundancy payments (worth approximately £325,000) and, since the *prima facie* value of the business sold was £1.05m, the transaction was at an undervalue, a decision affirmed by the Court of Appeal.[149] An appeal was dismissed, but the House of Lords disagreed with the lower courts as to the nature of the transaction. In the view of Lord Scott, the transaction was clear—the sale of shares in return for agreements by the purchaser and the associated company. It was plain that, apart from the consideration under the share sale agreement, the sub-lease agreement also formed part of the consideration. The key issue was the value of that consideration. On the facts, the sub-lease provided no value since the company was not entitled to sub-lease the equipment in this way and it had been repossessed shortly after the agreement had been entered into. Therefore, while the lease was part of the consideration, it added nothing of value to the agreement. It followed that the company had entered into a transaction, namely the share sale agreement, at an undervalue and that the amount of the undervalue was £725,000, i.e. £1,050,000 (the value of the asset sold) less £325,000 (the value received and which had been paid in respect of redundancies).[150]

---

[145]   *National Westminster Bank plc v Jones* [2002] 1 BCLC 55, CA (a s 423 case).

[146]   *Re MC Bacon Ltd* [1990] BCLC 324.

[147]   *Re MC Bacon Ltd* [1990] BCLC 324. See the difficulties in valuing the consideration received by the company in *Lord v Sinai Securities Ltd* [2005] 1 BCLC 295. Sometimes the undervalue is evident, as in *Re Cosy Insulation Ltd* [2016] 2 BCLC 319, where a company sold its carbon credits to a company owned by the same shareholder and director for £100,000, that company sold 45 per cent of the carbon credits 17 days later for £684,442.

[148]   [2001] 1 BCLC 145; noted by Parry [2001] Insolv Law 58; Moss [2001] 14 Insolv Int 29; see also Mokal and Ho, 'Consideration, Characterisation, Evaluation: Transactions at an Undervalue after *Phillips v Brewin Dolphin*' [2001] JCLS 359.

[149]   See [1999] 1 BCLC 714, CA.          [150]   [2001] 1 BCLC 145 at [32].

**15-51**    The value of the asset sold by the company (in this case, the value of the shares in the sub-sidiary), Lord Scott noted, is *prima facie* not less than what a reasonably well-informed purchaser is prepared to pay in an arm's length negotiation.[151] As for the value of the con-sideration received, where the value of any consideration is speculative (as in the case of the lease agreement here), it is for the party who relies on that consideration to establish its value.[152]

**15-52**    This willingness of the House of Lords to treat the lease agreement and the share sale agreement as one transaction is of practical importance since there may be, as here, good business and taxation reasons for dividing the consideration into a number of separate, though linked, transactions, not all of them necessarily with the company. By treating the combined elements as the transaction, this approach maximises the consideration provided and lessens the possibility of there being an undervalue unless, as here, some element of the consideration is of doubtful value. At the same time, the policy of the leg-islation is upheld by the finding that those who provide speculative consideration must establish its value and, where they cannot, the result will be recovery by the liquidator.

**15-53**    A debatable point is whether the creation by a company of a charge over its assets in favour of a creditor is a transaction at an undervalue. In *Re MC Bacon Ltd*[153] Millett J ruled against such a conclusion. In his view the creation of a charge could not amount to an undervalue as it does not deplete the company's assets and neither the granting of the debenture nor the consideration received by the company in granting the charge can be measured in money or money's worth.[154] Arden LJ makes the point in *Hill v Spread Trustee Co Ltd*[155] that the grant of a charge could be for no consideration (and therefore would be within IA 1986, s 238(4)(a) even if the application of s 238(4)(b) is ruled out, see **15-47**) as where a charge is granted to a creditor who is not in fact pressing for repayment so there is no forbearance as consideration (as there was in *Re MC Bacon Ltd*).[156] Equally, Arden LJ queried why the value of the creditor's right to have recourse to the security and to take priority over the other creditors should be left out of account.[157] Professor Goode makes the point that a charge in these circumstances should be challenged as a preference and not as an undervalue since the creditor benefits from being able to look to the assets secured rather than being left to claim as an unsecured creditor.[158] As Millett J noted, the creation of the security adversely affects the rights of other creditors in the event of insolvency.[159]

**15-54**    As noted at **15-50**, there are two important time thresholds for the application of s 238. First, that the transaction at an undervalue was entered into within the period of two years ending with the onset of insolvency (s 240(1)) which is defined in some detail in s 240(3). Secondly, that the transaction was at a time when the company was unable to pay its debts within the meaning of s 123[160] or becomes unable to pay its debts within the

---

[151] [2001] 1 BCLC 145 at [30].       [152] [2011] 1 BCLC 145 at [27].       [153] [1990] BCLC 324.

[154] [1990] BCLC 324 at 341; *Re Mistral Finance Ltd* [2001] BCC 27.       [155] [2007] 1 BCLC 450 at [93], [138].

[156] The bank exercised forbearance in that case by not calling in its overdraft and honouring cheques and it provided fresh advances to the company: see [1990] BCLC 324 at 340.

[157] See [2007] 1 BCLC 450 at [138].

[158] See Goode, *Principles of Corporate Insolvency* Law (4th edn, 2011), para 13–38.

[159] [1990] BCLC 324 at 340.

[160] The section contains a cash-flow test in s 123(1)(e) and a balance sheet test in s 123(2), the meaning of which was explored in detail by the Supreme Court in *BNY Corporate Trustee Services Ltd v Eurosail-UK 2007–3BL plc* [2013] 1 BCLC 613; and see Lewison LJ in *Re Casa Estates Ltd* [2014] 2 BCLC 49 at [27]–[32] who summarises the ruling in *Eurosail*.

meaning of that section in consequence of the transaction (s 240(2)), with a presumption in relation to the requirements of s 240(2), unless the contrary is shown, when the transaction is entered into by a company with a connected person.[161] In *Re Casa Estates (UK) Ltd, Carman v Bucci*[162] payments had been made by a company to a connected person which were potentially recoverable as transactions at an undervalue and a question arose as to whether the company was unable to pay its debts at the time of the transaction. It was established that, at the time, the company was solvent on a cash-flow basis, but insolvent on a balance sheet basis, and so the court held that the presumption in s 240(2) had not been rebutted. The appellant argued in the Court of Appeal that, once the company was solvent on a cash-flow basis, the court should not have gone on to consider the balance sheet test. The Court of Appeal dismissed the appeal. The tests of cash-flow insolvency and balance sheet insolvency feature as part of a single exercise, namely to determine whether a company is unable to pay its debts as they fall due. In addition, when applying the cash-flow test, it is not enough merely to ask whether the company is, for the time being, paying its debts as they fall due, the court must go on to inquire, how it is managing to do so. On the facts in this case, the company was only cash-flow solvent as it was using money being deposited with it by customers to pay its debts instead of investing it in property on the customers' behalf. It was therefore insolvent, the presumption in s 240(2) had not been rebutted, and the various payments made to the connected person had been made at a time when the company was unable to pay its debts.

### The order of the court

**15-55**  Section 241 lists a wide variety of orders which the court may make in the context of restoring the company to the position it would have been in had the company not entered into the transaction at an undervalue, including orders requiring property to be vested back in the company and requiring any person to make payments to the administrator or liquidator in respect of benefits received by him from the company.[163] The power is very wide and extends to recovery from any person who has received a benefit from the company unless that person can show (and the onus is on him) that he acted in good faith and for value.[164] In *Phillips v Brewin Dolphin Bell Lawrie Ltd*,[165] discussed at **15-49**, as the transaction could not be reversed, the court ordered the purchaser of the shares to pay the amount of the undervalue to the liquidator. In *National Westminster Bank plc v Jones*[166] the court ordered that a suspect transfer of assets be reversed so as to place assets back in the ownership of an individual who was subject to various outstanding mortgages.

**15-56**  The court's discretion extends to not making any order, as happened in *Re MDA Investment Management Ltd*,[167] even though there was a clear transaction at an undervalue. The company's business had been sold for £2.41m, but the company had only received £1m since the rest of the consideration had been diverted by a director, in breach of duty, to a partnership of which he was a partner. The company was in insolvent liquidation and therefore an order to restore the company to the position prior to the transactions would have been positively detrimental to the company since the company would have been in an even worse position if it had not entered into the transaction at all (at least it had received £1m).

---

[161]  See **24-31** et seq.      [162]  [2014] 2 BCLC 49.

[163]  There is a presumption of the interest being acquired or the benefit received other than in good faith in the circumstances outlined in s 241(2A), (3)–(3C); but sub-transferees acquiring interests or benefits in good faith and for value are protected: IA 1986, s 241(2).

[164]  See IA 1986, s 241(2), (3); also *Re Sonatacus Ltd* [2007] 2 BCLC 627.      [165]  [2001] 1 All ER 673, HL.

[166]  [2002] 1 BCLC 55, CA.      [167]  [2004] 1 BCLC 217.

**15-57**   The court's concern is with the company and it is less concerned with protecting the position of the other party to the transaction. In *Lord v Sinai Securities*[168] Hart J noted that it is arguable that the court's primary and possibly only concern is the restoration of the company's position. The position of the counterparty needs to be considered by the court as a general matter of discretion, but the court is not obliged to ensure that his position is restored in every particular to the status quo before the transaction. There will be many cases where that is simply impossible.

**15-58**   The court will not make an order if it is satisfied that the company entered into the transaction in good faith and for the purpose of carrying on its business and at the time it did so there were reasonable grounds for believing that the transaction would benefit the company (IA 1986, s 238(5)). For example, a sale of an asset at what appears, with hindsight, to be an undervalue may be explicable as having been the best option available to the company at that time when it was undergoing serious cash-flow difficulties which could only be solved by an expeditious sale. The onus of proof in this regard is on those asserting that the transaction is in good faith and beneficial to the company.[169]

**15-59**   Any recoveries obtained under this provision, not being property of the company, but property which arises only after the liquidation or administration of the company, and which is recoverable only by the liquidator or administrator pursuant to his statutory powers is held by him on a statutory trust for distribution to the company's unsecured creditors,[170] but subject to the expenses of administration or winding up and any preferential debts.

### Preferences—IA 1986, s 239

**15-60**   One of the main objectives in the winding up of an insolvent company (see **24-58**) is to ensure the equal treatment of creditors. To help achieve this the court is given a power to set aside, on the application of a liquidator or administrator, transactions or arrangements entered into by the company which have the effect of preferring a creditor or creditors ahead of other creditors. A liquidator or administrator may also assign any rights of action under s 239 (s 246ZD(2)).

**15-61**   A preference can arise, for example, where an unsecured creditor is paid by the company in circumstances where this is done to ensure that on insolvency the creditor is not left to claim against the pooled assets with the risk of non-payment which that entails; or where the company at the eleventh hour gives security to an unsecured creditor for the same reason; or where the directors ensure that the company pays those creditors whose debts are personally guaranteed by the directors.[171] The rules on preferences do not stop companies from paying their creditors as insolvency looms, but the company has to show that the transaction was as a result of ordinary commercial considerations. Bear in mind also that there is something of an overlap between s 239 and a director's duty to have regard to

---

[168] [2005] 1 BCLC 295.

[169] *Re Barton Manufacturing Co Ltd* [1999] 1 BCLC 740 at 743 (a considerable volume of evidence will be needed to convince the court of the bona fides of a gift made by the company in these circumstances).

[170] IA 1986, s 176ZB. See *Re Oasis Merchandising Services Ltd, Ward v Aitken* [1997] 1 BCLC 689 at 698–700, CA.

[171] Such conduct may also merit disqualification on the grounds of unfitness, see *Re Sykes (Butchers) Ltd, Secretary of State for Trade and Industry v Richardson* [1998] 1 BCLC 110 (director caused the company to reduce its bank overdraft which he had personally guaranteed instead of settling the claims of the company's trade creditors).

creditors' interests in cases of insolvency or doubtful solvency as required by CA 2006, s 172(3), discussed at **10-55**, and that the courts are still developing the precise overlap and boundaries.[172]

**15-62**  Section 239 sets out in some detail what constitutes a preference and there are a variety of conditions which must be satisfied:

- the company has gone into administration or liquidation;[173]
- the company has given a preference to any person;
- the preference was given within the period of six months ending with the onset of insolvency[174] or, in the case of a connected person, within the period of two years ending with the onset of insolvency;[175]
- at the time of giving the preference, the company must have been unable to pay its debts[176] or it must have become unable to pay its debts in consequence of the preference;
- there must have been a desire on the company's part to prefer that person; and there is a presumption of a desire to prefer in the case of a connected person.[177]

**15-63**  A company gives a preference to a person if:

- that person is one of the company's creditors or a surety or guarantor for any of the company's debts or other liabilities (s 239(4)(a)); and
- the company does anything or suffers anything to be done which (in either case) has the effect of putting that person into a position which, in the event of the company going into insolvent liquidation, will be better than the position he would have been in if that thing had not been done (IA 1986, s 239(4) (b)).[178]

**15-64**  A key element in establishing the existence of a preference is that:

- the company which gave the preference to any person must have been influenced in deciding to give it by a desire to produce in relation to that person the effect mentioned in s 239(4)(b);[179] and

---

[172]  See *GHLM Trading v Maroo* [2012] 2 BCLC 368 and discussion at **10-55**.

[173]  IA 1986, ss 239(1), 238(1).

[174]  The expression 'the onset of insolvency' is defined in detail in IA 1986, s 240(3).

[175]  IA 1986, s 240(1). 'Connected person' is defined expansively in IA 1986, s 249; and see also s 435 and n 142. See *Re Thirty-Eight Building Ltd* [1999] 1 BCLC 416 as to connected persons—trustees of a pension scheme which was the recipient of large sums of company money in circumstances which would otherwise amount to a preference but which had been received more than six months prior to the insolvency were not connected persons due to the exception in IA 1986, s 435(5)(b), despite the fact that four of the five trustees were beneficiaries of the trust and were connected persons—the presence of a fifth independent trustee and the fact that they acted collectively meant they were not connected persons; see also [2000] 1 BCLC 201.

[176]  Within the meaning of IA 1986, s 123, see n 160. There is no presumption with respect to this element of this provision, unlike under IA 1986, s 238, see s 240(2); and the burden of proof on this issue is on the liquidator.

[177]  IA 1986, s 239(6); save where the person is connected by reason only of being an employee of the company.

[178]  The effect of the preference must be to benefit the recipient in one of those capacities, as a creditor, surety, or guarantor, and if his position in those capacities has not been improved, then there is no preference: see *Re Oxford Pharmaceuticals Ltd, Wilson v Masters International Ltd* [2009] 2 BCLC 485; also see *Lewis v Hyde* [1997] BCC 976, PC (on the equivalent New Zealand provision). If the position of the person allegedly preferred is no different from what it would have been if the company had gone into liquidation, then there is no preference: *Re Hawkes Hill Publishing Ltd* [2007] BCC 937 at [31].     [179]  IA 1986, s 239(5).

- where the company has given the preference to a connected person, there is a presumption, unless the contrary is shown, that the company was influenced in deciding to give the preference by such a desire to prefer (i.e. to produce the effect mentioned in s 239(4)(b)).[180]

It is the decision of the company to give the preference which must be influenced by a desire to produce the effect set out in s 239(4)(b), and the question of when the decision to give the preference is made is a question of fact to be determined in the particular circumstances of each case.[181] For example, where a preference stems from the grant of security to a creditor who would otherwise be unsecured, the relevant time is the time when the decision to grant security was made;[182] when a preference arises from the payment of a creditor who would otherwise receive only a dividend as a creditor in a liquidation, the relevant time is when the company decided to make the payment, and, as David Richards J noted, the existence of a contractual obligation to grant the security or repay a debt is neither necessary nor of itself sufficient to determine when the decision to give the preference is made.[183] Even if there is a contractual obligation to do something, such as repay a debt, it is still for the directors to decide to make the payment and it is by reference to that decision that the desire to prefer must be sought.[184]

**15-65** The requirement of a desire to prefer was considered in *Re MC Bacon Ltd*[185] where a liquidator applied to the court to set aside, as a preference, a debenture granted by the company to its bank. The company had gone into insolvent liquidation in August 1987 (the onset of insolvency) with an estimated deficiency as regards unsecured creditors of £329,435. At that date, the company's overdraft at the bank stood at £235,530. This overdraft was secured by a debenture granted by the company in May 1987, i.e. within the six months prior to the onset of insolvency at a time when the company was unable to pay its debts. The court emphasised that a key element in the test of what is a preference is that the company acted out of a positive wish to improve the creditor's position in the event of its own insolvent liquidation. There is no need for direct evidence of the requisite desire; its existence may be inferred from the circumstances of the case. The mere presence of the requisite desire is not sufficient by itself, it must have influenced the decision of the company to enter into the transaction. But it is sufficient if it is one of the factors which operated on the minds of those who made the decision and it need not have been the only factor or even the decisive one.[186] Here the company did not positively wish to improve the bank's position, its only concern was that the bank should not call in the overdraft and force the company to stop trading. When the company gave the security to the bank, it did so out of a desire to continue trading. The debenture was not therefore void as a preference.

**15-66** Given the need to establish a desire to prefer in this way, it is not surprising that the preference provisions operate most effectively with respect to connected persons where the

---

[180] IA 1986, s 239(6).  [181] *Re Stealth Construction Ltd* [2012] 1 BCLC 297 at [37], [56], [63].
[182] *Re MC Bacon Ltd* [1990] BCLC 324.  [183] *Re Stealth Construction Ltd* [2012] 1 BCLC 297 at [63].
[184] *Wills v Corfe Joinery Ltd* [1998] 2 BCLC 75 at 78, per Lloyd J; see at **15-68**.
[185] [1990] BCLC 324, Ch D; *Re Hawkes Hill Publishing Ltd* [2007] BCC 937. See Fletcher [1991] JBL 71.
[186] [1990] BCLC 324 at 335–6, Ch D; see *Re Living Images Ltd* [1996] 1 BCLC 348; and *Re Oxford Pharmaceuticals Ltd, Wilson v Masters International Ltd* [2009] 2 BCLC 485 at [82]; there was a preference when a desire to prefer was in some way an influencing factor in certain payments from a subsidiary to a parent company.

liquidator is assisted by the statutory presumption of a desire to prefer.[187] In that situation, the alleged beneficiary must satisfy the court that, on the balance of probabilities, the alleged preferor was acting solely by reference to proper commercial considerations in having made the payment.[188]

**15-67**  Certainly, preferences given to connected persons just prior to the collapse of the company are the precise types of transaction which the Cork Committee thought should be challenged.[189] A typical example can be seen in *Re Exchange Travel (Holdings) Ltd*[190] where in July 1990 the company repaid loans made by the directors to the company of £200,000 (approximately) before going into administration in September 1990 with a deficiency running into millions of pounds. Such payments are patently preferences and the directors were ordered to pay the amounts received by them back to the liquidator leaving them to claim as unsecured creditors in the liquidation.

**15-68**  Similarly, in *Wills v Corfe Joinery Ltd*[191] repayment of directors' loans by the company (on 2 February 1995) just prior to ceasing to trade (on 6 February 1995) constituted a preference. The payments were made at a time when other creditors were pressing, employees were being made redundant and so, the court asked, why did the directors choose to pay these creditors? 'In the absence of evidence to show that it was purely for commercial reasons, there is nothing to rebut the statutory presumption [of a desire to prefer] and, indeed, everything to support that statutory presumption.'[192] In *Re Finch (UK) plc*[193] the presumption was not rebutted when a director devised a scheme to redeem his shares and have the company convey certain properties to him in respect of the redemption price. Once he became a creditor for the amount due on the redemption of his shares, meeting this liability to him by conveying the properties to him was something which, in the event of the company going into insolvent liquidation, put him in a better position than if that step had not been taken.[194] The properties would be part of his assets rather than those of the company. The court found that the scheme was an attempt to extract the properties from the company because the director appreciated the company was at serious risk of insolvency.[195] In *Re Cosy Seal Insulation Ltd*[196] the court found that the director had the company make a variety of payments to him by way of salary and reduction of his loan account and repaid significant sums to another company also owned by the director at a time when the company was insolvent. The court found that the only motivation for the payments must have been a desire to prefer himself over other creditors who at this point were either paid late or not at all.

**15-69**  Another common scenario is where a director ensures that a particular creditor gets paid because the director has personally guaranteed that debt. In *Re Agriplant Services Ltd*,[197]

---

[187] IA 1986, s 239(6). 'Connected person' is defined in IA 1986, s 249 and s 435 and see n 142. The statutory presumption may be rebutted, see for example *Re Brian D Pierson* [2001] 1 BCLC 275 at 298; *Re Fairway Magazines Ltd, Fairbairn v Hartigan* [1993] 1 BCLC 643 at 649–50. The fact that there is a statutory preference is not sufficient to compel the conclusion that there is also a misfeasance on the part of the director, for misfeasance must be proved positively, and a statutory presumption provided by s 239 cannot be relied on to reverse the burden of proof in a misfeasance claim: *Re Brian D Pierson (Contractors) Ltd* [2001] 1 BCLC 275 at 299f.          [188] *Re Oxford Pharmaceuticals Ltd, Wilson v Masters International Ltd* [2009] 2 BCLC 485.
[189] See the Cork Committee Report (Cmnd 8558, 1982), paras 1257–1258.          [190] [1996] 2 BCLC 524.
[191] [1998] 2 BCLC 75. See *Re Hawkes Hill Publishing Ltd* [2007] BCC 937—payment to a bank which reduced the director's personal guarantee was not influenced by a desire to prefer, but was motivated by a desire to salvage which could be salvaged for the company.
[192] [1998] 2 BCLC 75 at 82, per Lloyd J. See also *Re DKG Contractors Ltd* [1990] BCC 903 (payments of £417,763 to one of the directors in the 10 months before liquidation).          [193] [2016] 1 BCLC 394.
[194] [2016] 1 BCLC 394 at [22[.          [195] [2016] 1 BCLC 394 at [24].          [196] [2016] 2 BCLC 319.
[197] [1997] 2 BCLC 598.

S was a director of A Ltd which hired equipment from C Ltd and S personally guaranteed any indebtedness arising from that equipment hire. S ensured that A Ltd paid £20,000 to C Ltd two weeks before A Ltd was placed in voluntary liquidation. The court held that the £20,000 payment constituted a preference given to the creditor and to the director since it had the effect of improving the position of the creditor and the director (as a contingent creditor under his guarantee)[198] in the event of the insolvent liquidation of the company. The director tried to persuade the court that the payment was motivated by the commercial needs of A Ltd, namely the need to keep machinery on site so that A Ltd could continue in operation. The court found, however, that his main motivation was his own personal guarantee of that indebtedness. The director clearly had a desire to prefer himself, Jonathan Parker J noted, but it was only by improving the position of the creditor on an insolvent liquidation of the company that his own position under the guarantee could be improved. The payment was therefore a preference in relation to the creditor and the director. The court ordered the creditor to repay the £20,000 to the company with interest and ordered the director to pay the creditor £20,000 pursuant to his guarantee so that the position was restored to what it would have been on insolvency—i.e. the director would have had to meet the creditor's claim under his guarantee.

**15-70**    In *Re Sonatacus Ltd*[199] a company made a payment of £50,000 to C Ltd at a time when the company was insolvent or it became insolvent as a consequence of the payment. The payment arose because C Ltd had lent £65,000 to a director of the company who had then lent the money on to the company. The company therefore owed its director £65,000 and he owed C Ltd. The Court of Appeal held that the payment to C Ltd constituted a preference to the director (the director was the creditor) since the company was in effect repaying a loan by him to the company. C Ltd in turn had received a benefit from the preference given by the company to the director and an order could be made against it for recovery of the benefit under IA 1986, s 241(1)(d). It could only retain the benefit if the benefit had been received in good faith (s 214(2)). In the instant case, the evidence fell short of establishing that C Ltd had received the money in good faith and the onus was on C Ltd to establish its good faith. The controller of C Ltd knew of the financial difficulties of the company which is why he had been reluctant to lend directly to the company. He must have known, the court found, that it was likely that the repayment had been made by the company at a time when it was insolvent or at the least he must have shut his eyes to that possibility. Accordingly, C Ltd was liable to repay £50,000 to the liquidator.

**15-71**    Where the court is satisfied that a preference has been given, the court may make such order as it thinks fit for restoring the position to what it would have been if the company had not given that preference.[200] Typically the court orders the repayment by the creditor of the amount received, as can be seen in the cases already discussed. In *Re Finch (UK) plc*, discussed at **15-68**, the preference involved redeeming the director's shares and conveying certain properties to him, so the order made reversed these transactions, the properties remained in the ownership of the company, and the shares were not redeemed, but deemed still to be held by the director (of course, they were worthless at this stage). Where the preference amounts to the payment of a sum of money to a creditor, the obvious starting point to any relief is that the recipient creditor should be ordered to repay the money

---

[198]  See IA 1986, s 239(4); see **15-63**.      [199]  [2007] 2 BCLC 627.
[200]  IA 1986, s 239(3). The range of orders the court can make is the same as in relation to a transaction at an undervalue: s 241(1), discussed at **15-55**. The court may make an order against only some of the parties involved: see *Re Agriplant Services Ltd* [1997] 2 BCLC 598 at 610. See also *Hawkes Hill Publishing Ltd* [2007] BCC 937.

but orders against a third party should only be made as part of the process of restoration of the company's position where the third party is in possession of assets applied in making the preference or has otherwise benefited in monetary terms from the payment in some direct and tangible way.[201] If an order would put the company in a worse position, the court will not make an order.[202]

**15-72**  Any recoveries obtained under this provision, being property which arises only after the liquidation or administration of the company and which is recoverable only by the liquidator or administrator pursuant to his statutory powers, are held by him on a statutory trust for distribution to the company's unsecured creditors[203] and are not available to a holder of a floating charge, but they are subject to the expenses of administration or winding up and any preferential debts.

## Extortionate credit transactions—IA 1986, s 244

**15-73**  Liquidators and administrators may challenge an extortionate credit transaction (i.e. where the company is a party to a transaction for, or involving, the provision of credit to the company) entered into by the company in the three years before the company went into administration or liquidation (IA 1986, s 244(1), (2)). A liquidator or administrator may also assign any rights of action under s 244 (s 246ZD(2)). The test of whether a transaction is extortionate is whether, having regard to the risk accepted by the person providing the credit, the terms of it require grossly exorbitant payments in respect of the provision of the credit or it otherwise grossly contravenes ordinary principles of fair dealing (s 244(3)).[204] It is presumed, unless the contrary is proved, that a transaction with respect to which an application is made under this provision is or was extortionate (s 244(4)). It is for those who seek to uphold the transaction to show that it is or was not an extortionate credit transaction. If the office-holder's challenge is successful, the court's powers extend to setting aside the whole or part of any obligations created by the transaction, varying any of its terms or requiring the creditor to repay any sums to the liquidator.[205]

## Avoidance of floating charges—IA 1986, s 245

**15-74**  Section 245 is designed to invalidate floating charges given close to insolvency which simply secure past indebtedness and provide no new benefits to the company.[206] The effect of the invalidity is to deprive the creditor of the security which he thought he had obtained

---

[201]  *Re Oxford Pharmaceuticals Ltd, Wilson v Masters International Ltd* [2009] 2 BCLC 485.

[202]  See *Re Hawkes Hill Publishing Ltd* [2007] BCC 937 at [35].

[203]  IA 1986, s 176ZB. See *Re Oasis Merchandising Services Ltd, Ward v Aitken* [1997] 1 BCLC 689 at 698–700, CA.

[204]  The test for 'extortionate' in a commercial transaction where the interest rates are spelled out at the outset is a very stringent one: *White v Davenham Trust Ltd* [2011] BCC 77, at [47]–[50] (case involved a high risk commercial transaction with interest rates of 3 per cent per month in the event of default; arguable, however, that a substantial increase in the interest rate on default is a penalty clause—here the rate effectively doubled on default—and unenforceable at common law).

[205]  IA 1986, s 244(4). One of the functions of this section is to prevent companies in effect preferring a creditor by agreeing artificially high rates of interest on the creditor's debt. If arrears of interest are allowed to build up, the creditor's proof of debt is artificially increased. See the Cork Committee Report (Cmnd 8558, 1982), 1379–81.

[206]  For the background to this provision, see the Cork Committee Report (Cmnd 8558, 1982), paras 1551–1556.

and to prevent the substitution of a secured debt for an unsecured debt. Only the charge is rendered void, the underlying debt remains valid and, if the debt is repaid before winding up, the fact that the charge would have been void in the winding up does not affect the repayment.[207] In appropriate circumstances, it may be possible to challenge the repayment as a preference.

**15-75**   A floating charge is invalid and open to challenge by a liquidator or administrator under IA 1986, s 245 if the charge was created within the 12 months ending with the onset of insolvency[208] and at the time, or as a result of the transaction, the company was unable to pay its debts.[209] Where the charge was created in favour of a person connected with the company, the relevant period is extended to two years before the onset of insolvency and it is irrelevant whether or not the company was unable to pay its debts at the time.[210] Even if these conditions are satisfied, the floating charge is nevertheless valid to the extent that money is paid or goods or services are supplied to the company or any debt of the company is reduced or discharged at the same time as, or after, the creation of the charge (s 245(2)).

**15-76**   In *Power v Sharp Investments Ltd*[211] the board of a company (Shoe Lace Ltd) resolved in March 1990 to grant a debenture to its parent company, Sharp. The debenture granting a fixed and floating charge was duly executed on 24 July 1990 in respect of sums of money which had been advanced by Sharp in April, May, June, and finally on 16 July 1990. A petition for winding up was presented on 4 September and the company was compulsorily wound up on 20 November. The liquidator challenged the validity of the charge in the light of IA 1986, s 245.

**15-77**   The Court of Appeal found that there was insufficient contemporaneity between the prior payments made by the debenture holder and the execution of the charge so as to bring it within IA 1986, s 245(2) which requires the consideration to be paid at the same time as, or after, the creation of the charge. The words were clearly included by the legislature, the court said, for the purpose of excluding from the exemption the amount of moneys paid to the company before the creation of the charge even though they were paid in consideration for the charge. On any other construction, these words would be mere surplusage.[212] Sir Christopher Slade concluded that:[213]

> 'no moneys paid before the execution of a debenture will qualify for the exemption under the subsection [i.e. under s 245(2)] unless the interval between payment and execution is so short that it can be regarded as minimal and payment and execution can be regarded as contemporaneous.'

As the court noted, 'it is always open to the lender not to lend until the charge has actually been executed; that must be the prudent course'.[214] This situation is distinguishable, the court said, from the case where the promise to execute a debenture creates a present equitable security and moneys are advanced in reliance upon it. In that case, the delay between the advances and the execution of the formal instrument of charge are immaterial as the charge has already been created and is immediately registrable so that other creditors have the opportunity of learning of its existence.[215]

---

[207]   *Mace Builders (Glasgow) Ltd v Lunn* [1987] Ch 191, CA.
[208]   The 'onset of insolvency' is defined in detail in IA 1986, s 245(5).        [209]   IA 1986, s 245(2), (3)(b), (4).
[210]   IA 1986, s 245(2), (3)(a).        [211]   [1994] 1 BCLC 111, CA.        [212]   [1994] 1 BCLC 111 at 122, CA.
[213]   [1994] 1 BCLC 111 at 123, CA.
[214]   [1994] 1 BCLC 111 at 123, CA, quoting Hoffmann J at first instance, see [1992] BCLC 636, Ch D; see also *Rehman v Chamberlain* [2012] BCC 770.        [215]   [1994] 1 BCLC 111 at 122, CA.

**15-78**    The fresh sums received must be received by the company and it is insufficient if sums are advanced by the third party to the company's bank to reduce the company's overdraft which the third party has guaranteed. The money paid direct to the bank never becomes freely available to the company and thus is not paid 'to it' within the meaning of the section.[216]

## F  Disqualification of directors

### Legislative framework and purpose

**15-79**    Disqualification is governed by the Company Directors Disqualification Act 1986,[217] as amended, and the purpose of the CDDA 1986 was stated succinctly by Lord Woolf MR in *Re Blackspur Group plc, Secretary of State for Trade and Industry v Davies*[218] as follows:

> 'The purpose of the 1986 Act is the protection of the public, by means of prohibitory reme-dial action, by anticipated deterrent effect on further misconduct and by encouragement of higher standards of honesty and diligence in corporate management, from those who are unfit to be concerned in the management of a company.'

That the protection of the public (broadly defined to include all relevant interest groups, such as shareholders, employees, lenders, customers, and other creditors)[219] is the key consideration is evident from the wording of the statute itself which authorises an appli-cation for disqualification (and the acceptance of a disqualification undertaking) where it appears that it is expedient in the public interest for the director to be disqualified (CDDA 1986, s 7).[220] Disqualification is not a criminal matter, but a civil proceeding and disquali-fication is not intended as a punitive measure,[221] though there is a punitive element to the proceedings. Removing the privilege of trading through a limited liability company does involve a substantial interference with the freedom of the individual[222] and car-ries a degree of stigma for anyone who is disqualified.[223] On the other hand, there are approximately 3.4 million companies on the register, each of which must have at least one

---

[216] *Re Fairway Magazines Ltd, Fairbairn v Hartigan* [1993] 1 BCLC 643; see Prentice (1993) 109 LQR 371; also *Re Orleans Motor Co Ltd* [1911] 2 Ch 41.

[217] On disqualification, see generally Walters and Davis-White, *Directors' Disqualification and Insolvency Restrictions* (3rd edn, 2009); Finch, *Corporate Insolvency Law: Perspectives and Principles* (2nd edn, 2009), pp 716–40; Williams, 'Disqualifying Directors: A Remedy Worse than the Disease?' [2007] 7 JCLS 213; Hicks, 'Director Disqualification: Can it Deliver?' [2001] JBL 433.

[218] [1998] 1 BCLC 676 at 680.

[219] See *Re Tech Textiles Ltd, Secretary of State for Trade and Industry v Vane* [1998] 1 BCLC 259 at 268; also *Hill v Secretary of State for the Environment, Food and Rural Affairs* [2006] 1 BCLC 601 at [11] (the 'public' consists of, or at least includes as a primary class, those who might extend credit to the company).

[220] See *Secretary of State for Trade and Industry v Gray* [1995] 1 BCLC 276 at 288; see also *Re Lo-Line Electric Motors Ltd* [1988] 2 All ER 692 at 696; and *Re Sevenoaks Stationers (Retail) Ltd* [1991] 1 BCLC 325 at 329; *Re Westmid Packing Services Ltd, Secretary of State for Trade and Industry v Griffiths* [1998] 2 BCLC 646 at 654–5; *Re Barings plc (No 5)* [1999] 1 BCLC 433 at 482.

[221] *Re Liberty Holdings Unlimited, Owen v Secretary of State for Business, Innovation and Skills* [2017] BCC 298 at [28]—it is important that the civil consequences of disqualification are not used as further punishment where someone is disqualified following conviction for a criminal offence.

[222] See *Re Lo-Line Electric Motors Ltd* [1988] 2 All ER 692 at 696, per Browne-Wilkinson V-C; also *Re Crestjoy Products Ltd* [1990] BCLC 677 at 681.

[223] *Re Westminster Property Management Ltd, Official Receiver v Stern* [2000] 2 BCLC 396 at 423, per Henry LJ.

director, so the numbers actually being disqualified (approximately 1,400 per annum) are very small and likely to remain so.[224]

**15-80**   Nevertheless, as there is limited enforcement of directors' duties through actions by the company or derivative claims by shareholders, disqualification proceedings do provide a measure of indirect enforcement. Its importance must not be overstated, however, for, until recently, this was enforcement without any personal liability on the part of the director to account for any personal gains or make good any losses arising from any breach of his duties. Following reforms effected by the Small Business, Enterprise and Employment Act 2015, it is possible for the court, on the application of the Secretary of State,[225] to make a compensation order against a disqualified person in favour of one or more creditors of an insolvent company.[226] An application may be made if the following conditions are met:[227] (a) the person is subject to a disqualification order or disqualification undertaking, and (b) conduct for which the person is subject to the order or undertaking has caused loss to one or more creditors of an insolvent company of which the person has at any time been a director. A compensation order, if made, is an order requiring the person against whom it is made to pay an amount specified in the order: (a) to the Secretary of State for the benefit of (i) a creditor or creditors specified in the order; (ii) a class or classes of creditor so specified; (b) as a contribution to the assets of a company so specified (CDDA 1986, s 15B(1)). When specifying an amount, the court must in particular have regard to: (a) the amount of the loss caused; (b) the nature of the conduct which caused the loss;[228] (c) whether the person has made any other financial contribution in recompense for the conduct, whether under a statutory provision or otherwise (CDDA 1986, s 15B(3)). While it is not expected that this power will be used frequently, it is a step towards recognising that what matters to creditors is recoveries and that, for disqualified directors, liability is a much greater concern than any 'stigma' attached to disqualification.

## Grounds for disqualification

**15-81**   While the CDDA 1986 provides for a wide variety of grounds on which disqualification orders may be made,[229] in practice almost all disqualification orders or undertakings are

---

[224]  The latest statistics (see Companies House, Management Information, 2016–2017, Table 6) show 1,366 disqualifications in 2016–17, 1,327 the previous year. Fluctuations in numbers tend to reflect resource issues at the Insolvency Service rather than anything else, and the numbers tend to range relatively consistently between 1,200 and 1,400 a year.

[225]  The application must be made before the end of two years from the date of the disqualification order or undertaking: CDDA 1986, s 15A(5); a compensation undertaking may be accepted in place of an order: s 15A(2).

[226]  'Insolvent' is defined in CDDA 1986, s 15A(4). For the background to the introduction of this power, see BIS, *Transparency and Trust: Enhancing the Transparency of UK Company Ownership and Increasing Trust in UK Business,* Government Response (April 2014), BIS/14/672, paras 259–262; 267–269; 273–275; and discussion paper of same title (July 2013), BIS/13/959, paras 11.13 to 11.17.

[227]  CDDA 1986, s 15A(3). The conduct in question must have occurred after 1 October 2015 when this provision came into force; see SI 2016/890.    [228]  i.e. conduct which falls within CDDA 1986, s 15A(3)(b).

[229]  Other possible grounds include where a person is convicted of an indictable offence in relation to a company (CDDA 1986, s 2); persistent default in respect of filing documents with registrar of companies (s 3); fraudulent trading or other fraud (s 4); where disqualification is expedient in the public interest (ss 1A, 8); infringement of competition law (ss 9A–9E); where civilly liable under s 213 (fraudulent trading) or s 214 (wrongful trading) (s 10). See *R v Chandler* [2016] BCC 212, CA (disqualification order under s 2 quashed, it had been something of an afterthought to the sentencing for the offences when the individual must have proper notice of the allegations of misconduct which rendered him unfit to be a director and an opportunity to address them). To date there appears to have been only one disqualification order for competition infringements, see Competition and Markets Authority, Press Release, 1 December 2016.

made under CDDA 1986, s 6 (duty of court to disqualify unfit directors of insolvent companies)[230] and unfitness is discussed at **15-93**. It is possible to seek disqualification orders and undertakings with respect to a person who has been convicted outside Great Britain of a relevant foreign offence in relation to a company including an overseas company (CDDA 1986, s 5A).[231] A relevant foreign offence for these purposes is an offence in connection with the promotion, formation, or management of a company or liquidation or receivership of a company or similar and which corresponds to an indictable offence in England and Wales (CDDA 1986, s 5A(3)).

## The disqualification order or undertaking

**15-82**  A disqualification order is an order made against a person that for a period specified in the order, he shall not be a director of a company, act as receiver of a company's property, or in any way, whether directly or indirectly, be concerned or take part in the promotion, formation, or management of a company unless (in each case) he has the leave of the court, and he shall not act as an insolvency practitioner (CDDA 1986, s 1).[232] The courts take a broad approach to the prohibition on being 'concerned in the management of a company' which is widely cast in order to make it impossible for a disqualified person to be part of the management and central direction of a company's affairs.[233] The court cannot pick and choose elements of the prohibitions in CDDA 1986, s 1 to apply in a particular case, but must order that the person be disqualified from any of these activities for the set period.[234]

**15-83**  A disqualification undertaking has an identical effect to a disqualification order and undertakings are agreed between a director and the Disqualification Unit of the Insolvency Service without the need to involve the courts.[235] Undertakings are possible in cases of disqualification on the grounds of certain convictions abroad, of unfitness on insolvency, and where disqualification is expedient in the public interest in the case of persons disqualified for instructing unfit directors (CDDA 1986, s 1A(1)). The use of undertakings enables non-contentious cases to be dealt with expeditiously so hastening the commencement of the disqualification period (to the advantage both of the public and the disqualified director) and reducing the burden of costs on the disqualified director, but there is no obligation on a director to offer an undertaking nor on the Secretary of

---

[230]  Companies House, Companies House, Management Information, 2016–2017, Table 6, shows 1,366 disqualifications in 2016–17, of which 1,105 were under CDDA 1986, s 6 (unfit directors of insolvent companies).

[231]  For the background to the extension to offences committed overseas, see BIS, *Transparency & Trust: Enhancing the Transparency of UK Company Ownership and Increasing Trust in UK Business,* Government Response (April 2014), BIS/14/672, paras 226–236; and consultation paper of same name (July 2013), BIS 13/959, paras 64–68; 14.7–14.8.

[232]  See also The Companies (Model Articles) Regulations 2008, SI 2008/3229, reg 2, Sch 1, art 18 (Ltd), reg 4, Sch 3, art 22 (Plc) which provide that a director ceases to be a director as soon as he is prohibited from being a director by law.

[233]  *R v Campbell* [1984] BCLC 83. See *Hill v Secretary of State for the Environment, Food and Rural Affairs* [2006] 1 BCLC 601 (undischarged bankrupt who was the effective manager running a company and who made two important contracts on its behalf affecting its future activities was a person concerned in the management of a company).

[234]  *R v Cole* [1998] 2 BCLC 234, CA; *Re Gower Enterprises Ltd (No 2)* [1995] 2 BCLC 201.

[235]  The background and purpose of the changes to allow for undertakings is described by Chadwick LJ in *Re Blackspur Group plc (No 3), Secretary of State for Trade and Industry v Davies (No 2)* [2002] 2 BCLC 263 at [10]–[20]; see also *Re INS Realisations Ltd, Secretary of State for Trade and Industry v Jonkler* [2006] 2 BCLC 239 at [18]–[20].

State to accept it and disputed cases are still a matter for the courts. Nevertheless, most disqualifications now are the subject of undertakings rather than court orders.[236] Once made or given, the order or undertaking is notified to the registrar of companies for entry on the register of disqualified directors which is open to inspection by the public (CDDA 1986, s 18).

15-84    Undischarged bankrupts are automatically disqualified from acting as directors or in the promotion, formation, or management of a company without the leave of the court (CDDA 1986, s 11) and, even after the discharge of their bankruptcy, unfit bankrupts may be subject to bankruptcy restriction orders (BROs) or bankruptcy restriction undertakings (BRUs) which are very similar in effect to disqualification orders or undertakings. It is an offence for a person to act as a director of a company, or directly or indirectly to take part in or be concerned in the promotion, formation, or management of a company, without the leave of the court, at a time when (1) he is an undischarged bankrupt or (2) a BRO or BRU is in force in respect of him (CDDA 1986, s 11). An undischarged bankrupt or a bankrupt subject to a BRO so acting is also civilly liable for the debts of the company incurred when so acting (CDDA 1986, s 15) (see **15-105**).

## The period of disqualification

15-85    The period of disqualification varies depending on the grounds for disqualification. In most cases, the maximum period is 15 years[237] and, where the court makes a disqualification order on the grounds of unfitness in the case of insolvency, there is a minimum period of disqualification of two years.[238] In *Re Sevenoaks Stationers (Retail) Ltd*[239] the Court of Appeal identified three brackets of periods of disqualification for the purposes of CDDA 1986, s 6, essentially two to five years where the case is not very serious, six to 10 years for serious cases which do not merit the top bracket, and over 10 years for particularly serious cases. Reference to these brackets is standard practice when determining the period of disqualification. In *Re Westmid Packing Services Ltd, Secretary of State for Trade and Industry v Griffiths*[240] Lord Woolf MR noted that in truth the fixing of the period of disqualification is little different from any sentencing exercise. The period of disqualification should be fixed, he said, by starting with an assessment of the correct period to reflect the gravity of the offence and then allowing for any mitigating factors.[241] A director may appeal against his disqualification and the Secretary of State may (and does)

---

[236] Companies House, Management Information, 2016–2017, Table 6, shows 1,366 disqualifications in 2016–17, of which 1,105 were under CDDA 1986, s 6 (unfit directors of insolvent companies), of which 989 were by undertakings, so 90 per cent approximately by undertaking. A consequence is far fewer reported disqualification cases and so fewer opportunities for the court to consider and comment on directors' conduct and fitness for office.

[237] CDDA 1986, ss 2(3)(b), 4(3), 6(4), 8, 10. Where a person is disqualified for persistent default, or on conviction of an indictable offence by a court of summary jurisdiction, or on conviction of summary offences in relation to returns to the registrar of companies, the maximum period of disqualification is five years: ss 3(5), 2(3)(a), 5(5).                                    [238] CDDA 1986, s 6(4).

[239] [1991] BCLC 325 at 328. Additional guidance as to the appropriate period of disqualification in cases of VAT missing trader fraud is given in *Secretary of State for Business, Innovation and Skills v Warry* [2014] 1 BCLC 447 (minimum of 11 years if knowingly involved, minimum of seven and a half years if did not know but ought to have known).                                    [240] [1998] 2 BCLC 646.

[241] [1998] 2 BCLC 646 at 655; also *Re Bradcrown Ltd, Official Receiver v Ireland* [2001] 1 BCLC 547 at [14]. See *Re Normanton Wells Properties Ltd, Official Receiver v Jupe* [2011] 1 BCLC 191 at [21], a substantial or significant return to creditors might be a mitigating factor.

appeal against the length of disqualification imposed by the court.[242] A person subject to a disqualification undertaking may apply to the court to reduce the period for which the undertaking is in force or to provide for it to cease to be in force, but this jurisdiction does not extend to annulling or rescinding the undertaking from the start.[243]

### Leave to act despite being disqualified

**15-86** The statute expressly provides that a disqualified person (whether disqualified by order or by undertaking) may apply for leave to act and it need not be leave to act as a director, it can be leave to act in the management, other than to act as an insolvency practitioner.[244] The court's discretion to grant leave is unfettered by any statutory condition or criterion.[245] On an application for leave, it was common to consider that the court had to balance the protection of the public and any practical need that the applicant should be able to act as a director of a particular company.[246] But need is not a threshold requirement for leave and the better approach is for the court to exercise its discretion, having regard to all the relevant factors including need.[247] In carrying out this balancing task, the court must pay attention in particular to the nature of the defects in company management which led to the disqualification and ask itself whether, if leave were granted, a situation might arise in which there would be a risk of recurrence of those defects.[248] The court must also bear in mind the legislative policy of disqualifying unfit directors to minimise the risk of harm to the public, the deterrent function of disqualification, and that objective must not be undermined by the approach of the court to the issue of leave.[249] The ultimate question is the risk of repetition of the conduct that gave rise to the disqualification.[250]

**15-87** The court may grant leave subject to certain conditions,[251] typically restricting the director to acting in a named company or companies, limiting the roles which the individual

---

[242] See, for example, *Secretary of State for Trade and Industry v McTighe (No 2)* [1996] 2 BCLC 477 (eight and four-year periods increased to 12 and six years respectively).

[243] CDDA 1986, s 8A; *Re Blackspur Group plc (No 4), Eastaway v Secretary of State for Trade and Industry* [2006] 2 BCLC 489 at [51]. See also *Re INS Realisations Ltd, Secretary of State for Trade and Industry v Jonkler* [2006] 2 BCLC 239 at [40]–[41] (jurisdiction to reduce period of undertaking to be used sparingly and only where there are special circumstances) *Taylor v Secretary of State for Business, Innovation and Skills* [2016] 2 BCLC 350 (special circumstances must have arisen since the undertaking was given which, by reason of their type or gravity, were not intended to be covered by the undertaking or which could not have been foreseen at the time the undertaking was given).

[244] CDDA ss 1(1), 17. As to an application for leave, see *Secretary of State for Trade and Industry v Collins* [2000] 2 BCLC 223, CA. It is possible to apply even if the disqualification is under CDDA 1986, s 2 (convicted of a criminal offence) though such an applicant faces an uphill struggle to persuade the court: see *Re Liberty Holdings Unlimited, Owen v Secretary of State for Business, Innovation and Skills* [2017] BCC 298 at [33].

[245] *Re Dawes & Henderson (Agencies) Ltd (No 2)* [1999] 2 BCLC 317. The cases are intensely factual therefore, but see Bristoll, 'Permission to Act While Disqualified—a Balancing Act' [2014] Insolv Int 49 for a very useful review of the courts' approach.

[246] *Re Barings plc (No 4), Secretary of State for Trade and Industry v Baker* [1999] 1 BCLC 262 at 269. See *Re Tech Textiles Ltd, Secretary of State for Trade and Industry v Vane* [1998] 1 BCLC 259 at 269; see also *Secretary of State for Trade and Industry v Barnett* [1998] 2 BCLC 64 at 72; *Re Dawes & Henderson (Agencies) Ltd (No 2)* [1999] 2 BCLC 317 at 326.

[247] *Re Liberty Holdings Unlimited, Owen v Secretary of State for Business, Innovation and Skills* [2017] BCC 298 at [29].

[248] *Re Barings (No 4), Secretary of State for Trade and Industry v Baker* [1999] 1 BCLC 262 at 269; *Re Dawes & Henderson (Agencies) Ltd (No 2)* [1999] 2 BCLC 317 at 325.

[249] See *Re Tech Textiles Ltd, Secretary of State for Trade and Industry v Vane* [1998] 1 BCLC 259 at 267; *Re Barings plc (No 4), Secretary of State for Trade and Industry v Baker* [1999] 1 BCLC 262 at 269.

[250] *Re Liberty Holdings Unlimited, Owen v Secretary of State for Business, Innovation and Skills* [2017 BCC 298, at [23].

[251] See *Secretary of State for Trade and Industry v Collins* [2000] 2 BCLC 223 at 235; *Re Tech Textiles Ltd, Secretary of State for Trade and Industry v Vane* [1998] 1 BCLC 259.

may undertake, and imposing conditions as to the composition of the board in the company in question.[252] Particularly unusual conditions were imposed in *Harris v Secretary of State for Business, Innovation and Skills*[253] including that an investor in the company convert his loans into preference shares, that stock valuations and an annual review of the company's assets and liabilities be undertaken by experienced, independent, auditors, and that no dividends be paid which would have the effect of reducing the company's distributable profits to less than £50,000. A failure to observe the conditions of leave means that the director is acting without leave and in breach of his disqualification order[254] which is a criminal offence and leaves him open to potential personal liability (see discussion at **15-105**).

## Grounds for disqualification—Unfit directors of insolvent companies

**15-88** As noted, most disqualification orders or undertakings are made under CDDA 1986, s 6 (duty of court to disqualify unfit directors of insolvent companies). The office-holder (an official receiver, liquidator, administrator, or administrative receiver, collectively referred to as the office-holder) in respect of a company which is insolvent must prepare a conduct report about each person who was a director[255] or shadow director[256] of the company (a) on the insolvency date, or (b) at any time during the period of three years ending with that date.[257] A conduct report must, in relation to each person, describe any conduct of the person which may assist the Secretary of State in deciding whether it is expedient in the public interest to seek a disqualification order or undertaking under s 6 on the grounds of unfitness (s 7A(3)). Section 6 provides for the disqualification of a person who is or has been a director of a company which has become insolvent (whether while he was a director or subsequently) where the court finds that his conduct as a director of that company (either taken alone or taken together with his conduct as a director of one or more other companies or overseas companies) makes him unfit to be concerned in the management of a company.[258] In practice, this means the office-holder must report to the Insolvency Service which is an executive agency of the Department for Business, Energy and Industrial Strategy.

**15-89** For these purposes, a company is insolvent if (a) the company is in liquidation[259] and at the time it went into liquidation its assets were insufficient for the payment of its debts and other liabilities and the expenses of the winding up, (b) the company has entered administration, or (c) an administrative receiver of the company has been appointed (CDDA 1986, s 7A(2)).

---

[252] See, for example, *Re Dawes & Henderson Ltd* [1999] 2 BCLC 317 at 328; *Re Gibson Davies Ltd* [1995] BCC 11.   [253] [2014] EWHC 1381.

[254] *Re Brian Sheridan Cars Ltd, Official Receiver v Sheridan* [1996] 1 BCLC 327.

[255] The word 'director' in this context includes a de facto director: *Re Lo-Line Electric Motors Ltd* [1988] 2 All ER 692; *Re Kaytech International plc, Secretary of State for Trade and Industry v Kaczer* [1999] 2 BCLC 351. A corporate director may be disqualified: see *Official Receiver v Brady* [1999] BCC 847.

[256] CDDA 1986, s 7A(12). As to shadow directors, see **7-21**.

[257] CDDA 1986, s 7A. This requirement for a report in every insolvency on every director is a change and a simplification from the previous position which required the office-holder to form a view as to whether it was expedient in the public interest to make a report.

[258] CDDA 1986, s 7A.

[259] Defined by IA 1986, s 247, incorporated by CDDA 1986, s 22(3), as the time when the company passes a resolution for voluntary winding up or the time of the court order in the case of a compulsory winding up.

**15-90**  Having considered the report, if it appears to the Secretary of State (i.e. the Insolvency Service) that it is expedient in the public interest[260] that a disqualification order under CDDA 1986, s 6 should be made against any person, an application may be made by the Secretary of State to the court for a disqualification order.[261] Before this occurs, notice is given to the director (under CDDA 1986, s 16) of the intention to proceed under s 6 and this notice will draw his attention to the possibility of his offering a disqualification undertaking rather than having the matter determined by the court.[262]

**15-91**  Following the application by the Secretary of State or official receiver, the court must make a disqualification order for a minimum period of two years and a maximum of 15 years if it is satisfied that the conduct of that person as a director of that company makes him unfit to be concerned in the management of a company.[263]

**15-92**  Finally, it is possible to disqualify a person who has exercised influence over an individual director who has been found to be unfit and disqualified. If the individual director, called the main transgressor, is disqualified as unfit under CDDA 1986, s 6, and this other person has exercised the requisite amount of influence over the main transgressor, then that person too may be disqualified (CDDA 1986, s 8ZA(1) and s 8ZC).[264] The requisite amount of influence exists if any of the conduct for which the main transgressor is disqualified is the result of the main transgressor acting in accordance with the person's directions or instructions (CDDA 1986, s 8ZA(2)), subject to an exclusion where the main transgressor acts on advice given by the person in a professional capacity. In addition to being disqualified following on from the disqualification of the main transgressor, that person may also be the subject of a compensation order,[265] see **15-80**.

### The court's approach to the issue of unfitness

**15-93**  A review of reported cases where disqualification proceedings have been brought under CDDA 1986, s 6 (unfitness in cases of insolvency) reveals a very similar fact scenario in each case.[266] Often the director has been associated with a number of companies which have gone into insolvent liquidation over a relatively short period of time. The allegations of unfitness typically include that the director caused or permitted the company to trade to the detriment of its creditors; that the company continued trading while insolvent,

---

[260] The question whether it is expedient in the public interest to commence and thereafter to pursue applications for disqualification is a matter for the Secretary of State and not for the court: *Re Blackspur Group plc, Secretary of State for Trade and Industry v Davies* [1998] 1 BCLC 676 at 680; *Re Barings plc (No 3), Secretary of State for Trade and Industry v Baker* [1999] 1 BCLC 226 at 252; and see *Re Blackspur Group plc (No 3), Secretary of State for Trade and Industry v Davies (No 2)* [2002] 2 BCLC 263 at [10], per Chadwick LJ.

[261] CDDA 1986, s 7(1). Except with the leave of the court, an application for a disqualification order under CDDA 1986, s 6 must not be made after the end of three years beginning with the day on which the company became insolvent: CDDA 1986, s 7(2), increased to three years from the previous two-year limit by the Small Business, Enterprise and Employment Act 2015, s 108(1), from 1 October 2015. The time period runs from the happening of the first of the events specified (going into liquidation, administration etc) in CDDA 1986, s 6(2): *Re Tasbian (No 1) Ltd* [1991] BCLC 56, CA. See *Secretary of State v Gifford* [2012] 1 BCLC 710 on the court's approach to giving leave to proceed after the expiry of the specified period.

[262] As to the content of this s 16 notice, see *Re Surrey Leisure Ltd, Official Receiver v Keam* [1999] 1 BCLC 731.

[263] CDDA 1986, s 6(1), (4).

[264] For equivalent provision where the main transgressor is disqualified under CDDA 1986, s 8 (disqualification expedient in the public interest): see ss 8ZD and 8ZE.    [265] CDDA 1986, s 15A(3), (6).

[266] See, for example, *Re Amaron Ltd, Secretary of State for Trade and Industry v Lubrani* [2001] 1 BCLC 562, aff'g [1997] 2 BCLC 115; *Re Galeforce Pleating Co Ltd* [1999] 2 BCLC 704; *Re Landhurst Leasing plc, Secretary of State for Trade and Industry v Ball* [1999] 1 BCLC 286.

usually by means of pursuing a policy of paying only those creditors who pressed; and that Crown debts were retained to finance continued trading (these grounds are discussed in more detail later). Despite the financial difficulties, the directors continue throughout the period to obtain significant personal benefits by way of remuneration and frequently by misappropriating corporate assets and opportunities. Examples of the type of misconduct commonly featured in the cases include the granting of preferences to themselves and to family and friends,[267] the transfer or use of the company's assets for inadequate consideration or without security for the sale price,[268] and undisclosed conflicts of interest resulting in personal gain.[269]

**15-94** It is clear that many of the allegations suggest breaches of a director's duties, though in this context the conduct is usually described in terms of a failure to meet the required standards of competence and probity.[270] For example, trading in disregard of creditors' interests is a failure to act as required by CA 2006, s 172(3), while managerial incompetence and inertia is a failure to exercise care and skill as required by s 174, and the continued receipt of excessive personal benefits and the misappropriation of corporate assets involves breaches of the no-conflict rule set out in s 175.

**15-95** A finding of breach of duty is neither necessary (had it been so, the section would not be defined in terms of 'unfitness') nor of itself sufficient for a finding of unfitness, however, as was explained by Jonathan Parker J in *Re Barings plc (No 5), Secretary of State for Trade and Industry v Baker (No 5)*,[271] a point specifically endorsed by the Court of Appeal.[272] Clearly, a director may be guilty of misfeasance or breach of duty without that breach necessarily meaning that he is unfit and should be disqualified.[273] Equally, a director may be unfit, though no breach of duty is established, but his conduct fails to reach an acceptable level of commercial probity.[274] In particular, unfitness by reason of incompetence may be established without proof of a breach of duty, as where a respondent shows himself so completely lacking in judgement as to justify a finding of unfitness, notwithstanding that he has not been guilty of misfeasance or breach of duty.[275] Lewison J agreed on this point in *Secretary of State for Trade and Industry v Goldberg*[276] while acknowledging that the court must be very careful before holding that a director is unfit because of conduct that does not amount to a breach of any duty, whether contractual, tortious, statutory, or equitable.

---

[267] See *Secretary of State for Trade and Industry v Gray* [1995] 1 BCLC 276; *Re Living Images Ltd* [1996] 1 BCLC 348; *Re Sykes (Butchers) Ltd, Secretary of State for Trade and Industry v Richardson* [1998] 1 BCLC 110.

[268] *Secretary of State for Trade and Industry v McTighe (No 2)* [1996] 2 BCLC 477; *Re Keypak Homecare Ltd* [1990] BCLC 440; *Re Normanton Wells Properties Ltd, Official Receiver v Jupe* [2011] 1 BCLC 191.

[269] *Re Dominion International Group plc (No 2)* [1996] 1 BCLC 572; *Re Godwin Warren Control Systems plc* [1993] BCLC 80. See *Secretary of State for Business, Enterprise and Regulatory Reform v Sullman* [2009] 1 BCLC 397 at [100]–[106], [116] (extraction of personal gains by directors must be subject to the most rigorous application of the standards of fit conduct).

[270] See *Re Landhurst Leasing plc* [1999] 1 BCLC 286 at 344; *Secretary of State for Trade and Industry v Gray* [1995] 1 BCLC 276 at 286.    [271] [1999] 1 BCLC 433 at 486.

[272] See [2000] 1 BCLC 523 at 535. See too *Secretary of State for Business, Enterprise and Regulatory Reform v Sullman* [2009] 1 BCLC 397 at [30].

[273] See, for example, *Re Deaduck Ltd, Baker v Secretary of State for Trade and Industry* [2000] 1 BCLC 148.

[274] See *Secretary of State for Business, Enterprise and Regulatory Reform v Sullman* [2009] 1 BCLC 397 at [30], [43], [103]–[106]; as Norris J noted, at [82], 'fit conduct entails as much an assessment of the commercial realities of managing a business as an appreciation of legal nicety'.

[275] *Re Barings plc (No 5)* [1999] 1 BCLC 433 at 486.    [276] [2004] 1 BCLC 597.

**15-96**  Just as it is not necessary to show a breach of duty (though there commonly is a breach), it is not necessary to show dishonesty,[277] though often that element is present,[278] and unfitness may be shown by conduct which is merely incompetent. Where there is no dishonesty of any kind, however, because of the serious nature of a disqualification order, the burden on the Secretary of State is to satisfy the court that the conduct complained of demonstrates incompetence of a high degree.[279]

**15-97**  The burden of proof is on the applicant for the disqualification order and to the civil standard of the balance of probabilities and it is for the Secretary of State to establish the matters on which the allegations of unfitness are based and for the court to be satisfied that the conduct alleged is sufficiently serious to warrant disqualification.[280]

**15-98**  Overall, the question for the court to decide, taking a broad brush approach,[281] is whether the conduct complained of,[282] viewed cumulatively and taking into account any extenuating circumstances accompanying the conduct in question, has fallen below the standards of probity and competence appropriate for persons fit to be directors of companies trading with the privilege of limited liability.[283]

**15-99**  In considering whether to disqualify someone or to accept a disqualification undertaking, the court or the Secretary of State, as the case may be, must: (a) in every case, have regard in particular to the matters set out in paras 1 to 4 of CDDA 1986, Sch 1 (set out below); (b) in a case where the person concerned is or has been a director of a company or overseas company, also have regard in particular to the matters set out in paras 5 to 7 of that Schedule.[284] The Schedule is not exhaustive,[285] however, and the court is entitled to

---

[277]  See *Secretary of State for Trade and Industry v Goldberg* [2004] 1 BCLC 597 at [40].

[278]  See, for example, *Re Bunting Electric Manufacturing Co Ltd, Secretary of State for Trade and Industry v Golby* [2006] 1 BCLC 550 (finance director dishonestly acting in his personal interests in breach of duty to the company).

[279]  *Re Barings plc (No 5), Secretary of State for Trade and Industry v Baker (No 5)* [1999] 1 BCLC 433 at 483–6; endorsed on appeal, [2000] 1 BCLC 523 at 535, CA, but the degree of incompetence required should not be exaggerated. See also *Re Sevenoaks Stationers (Retail) Ltd* [1991] 1 BCLC 325 at 337: incompetence or negligence 'in a very marked degree' is enough to render a director unfit, but it need not be 'total' incompetence.

[280]  *Secretary of State for Trade and Industry v Swan* [2005] BCC 596 at [77], per Etherton J. Care must be taken in formulating the allegations which suggest unfitness: *Official Receiver v Key* [2009] 1 BCLC 22 (a lengthy disqualification might have been imposed if the charges had been properly formulated—the public are entitled to expect that all charges which the claimant has a reasonable prospect of establishing against a defendant will be included in order that the period of disqualification will be commensurate with the conduct alleged).

[281]  See *Secretary of State for Trade and Industry v Goldberg* [2004] 1 BCLC 597 at [41]; *Re Westmid Packing Services Ltd, Secretary of State for Trade and Industry v Griffiths* [1998] 2 BCLC 646 at 658; *Secretary of State for Business, Enterprise and Regulatory Reform v Sullman* [2009] 1 BCLC 397 at [114], [118], also at [71] where Norris J noted that 'the essential simplicity of the question', whether the director's conduct renders him unfit, must remain at the forefront of the court's consideration.

[282]  'The reason for disqualification can only be a person's "conduct as a director." "Conduct" encompasses both acts and omissions. The phrase "as a director" means "in his capacity as a director" ... Even if the case is based on allegations of dishonesty, the dishonesty in question must be dishonesty "as a director"': *Secretary of State for Trade and Industry v Goldberg* [2004] 1 BCLC 597 at [46], per Lewison J.

[283]  *Secretary of State for Trade and Industry v Gray* [1995] 1 BCLC 276 at 284; *Re Barings plc (No 5), Secretary of State for Trade and Industry v Baker (No 5)* [1999] 1 BCLC 433 at 483; endorsed on appeal, [2000] 1 BCLC 523 at 535, CA; also *Secretary of State for Business, Enterprise and Regulatory Reform v Sullman* [2009] 1 BCLC 397 at [118] (inviting the public to deal with the company on a false basis in a material particular falls below the standard of commercial probity which the law is entitled to expect of a limited liability company).

[284]  CDDA 1986, s 12C(1), (4).

[285]  *Re Barings plc (No 5), Secretary of State for Trade and Industry v Baker (No 5)* [1999] 1 BCLC 433; *Re Migration Services International Ltd, Official Receiver v Webster* [2000] 1 BCLC 666 (breach of IA 1986, s 216—misuse of company name—may be taken into account even though not mentioned in the Schedule).

take into account any misconduct that shows unfitness.[286] Schedule 1 was substituted by the Small Business, Enterprise and Employment Act 2015, s 106(6), and now provides that the matters to be taken into account in determining unfitness are as follows:

*Matters to be taken into account in all cases*

1   The extent to which the person was responsible for the causes of any material contravention by a company or overseas company of any applicable legislative or other requirement.

2   Where applicable, the extent to which the person was responsible for the causes of a company or overseas company becoming insolvent.

3   The frequency of conduct of the person which falls within paragraph 1 or 2.

4   The nature and extent of any loss or harm caused, or any potential loss or harm which could have been caused, by the person's conduct in relation to a company or overseas company.

*Additional matters to be taken into account where person is or has been a director*

5   Any misfeasance or breach of any fiduciary duty by the director in relation to a company or overseas company.

6   Any material breach of any legislative or other obligation of the director which applies as a result of being a director of a company or overseas company.

7   The frequency of conduct of the director which falls within paragraph 5 or 6.

The intention behind the introduction of a new Schedule is to allow the court and the Insolvency Service greater flexibility to consider the materiality of a director's conduct, culpability, and track record and the nature and extent of the losses caused,[287] which is useful but it is not likely to alter dramatically the approach of the court in assessing unfitness.[288]

### Failure to have regard to creditors' interests

**15-100**   As discussed in Chapter 10, the duty of directors to act to promote the success of the company is subject to an obligation to have regard to the interests of the company's creditors in situations of insolvency or doubtful solvency, see CA 2006, s 172(3) and the discussion at **10-41**. Breaches of that obligation, often described in disqualification proceedings as trading while insolvent to the detriment of the creditors, are central usually to the allegations of unfitness in most disqualification proceedings brought under CDDA 1986, s 6, given that it is a pre-condition of that section that the company must have become insolvent (see **15-88**).

**15-101**   A common problem in these cases is that the directors continue to trade after a point in time when the company's financial position is hopeless instead of putting the company into insolvent liquidation and so the continued trading is unwarranted and at the creditors' risk. Merely trading while the company is insolvent is insufficient, as the Court of

---

[286] *Re Amaron Ltd, Secretary of State for Trade and Industry v Lubrani* [2001] 1 BCLC 562, aff'g [1997] 2 BCLC 115.

[287] See BIS, *Transparency and Trust: Enhancing the Transparency of UK Company Ownership and Increasing Trust in UK Business*, Government Response (April 2014), BIS/14/672, paras 220–225; and discussion paper of same title (July 2013), BIS/13/959, paras 10.1–10.21.

[288] See *Secretary of State v Akbar* [2017] EWHC 2856 at [98] '... makes little real difference'.

Appeal stressed in *Secretary of State v Creggan*;[289] it must be established that, in addition to causing the company to trade while insolvent, the director knew or ought to have known that there was no reasonable prospect of meeting creditors' claims.

**15-102** The courts are alert to and very critical of such trading without a reasonable prospect of meeting creditors' claims. In *Secretary of State for Trade and Industry v Collins*[290] the directors (who were disqualified for periods of seven to nine years) caused the company to continue to trade to September 1994 when they knew by November 1993 that there was no reasonable prospect of avoiding insolvent liquidation. The company was eventually compulsorily wound up with a deficiency of £11.3m. In *Re Amaron Ltd, Secretary of State for Trade and Industry v Lubrani*[291] the directors (who were disqualified for three years) unreasonably continued to trade for 21 months after the time when they knew the company was making losses on an increasingly large scale.[292] On the other hand, in *Secretary of State for Trade and Industry v Gill*[293] the court rejected any suggestion of unfitness where directors continued to accept customer deposits to facilitate ongoing trading while they searched for a commercial solution to the company's difficulties. The key difference was that, while the company did subsequently go into liquidation, the court accepted that at all material times there was a reasonable prospect of avoiding insolvency.

**15-103** A common scenario is that in a group situation, or where there are related businesses, the directors disregard the interests of the creditors of an individual company in the interests of the overall business in clear breach of their duty to promote the success of that individual company. For example, in *Re Mea Corporation Ltd, Secretary of State for Trade and Industry v Aviss*[294] directors were disqualified for periods ranging from seven to 11 years, in essence, for causing or allowing each of three companies to trade to the detriment of creditors. At a time when those companies were under increasing pressure from creditors and were each insolvent, the directors allowed such cash as was available to be paid out to other companies in which one of the directors had a substantial personal interest in disregard of the interests of the creditors of the individual companies. In *Secretary of State for Business, Innovation and Skills v Doffman*[295] the court was particularly critical of two directors who disregarded the separate interests of individual companies within a group of companies in which they were the sole shareholders and transferred assets between the companies without regard to the interests of the transferor.

**15-104** Another common scenario is that, as the company's financial position worsens, the directors adopt a deliberate policy involving some decision, conscious or unconscious on their part, of paying only those creditors who press for payment or those who are essential to the continued operation of the company.[296] In effect, they operate a policy of unfair discrimination

[289] [2002] 1 BCLC 99 at [3], CA; and see Chadwick J in *Secretary of State for Trade and Industry v Gash* [1997] 1 BCLC 341 at 348–9.

[290] [2000] 2 BCLC 223. See also *Secretary of State for Trade and Industry v McTighe (No 2)* [1996] 2 BCLC 477; *Re Living Images Ltd* [1996] 1 BCLC 348; *Official Receiver v Stern (No 2)* [2002] 1 BCLC 119, CA; *Secretary of State for Trade and Industry v Hollier* [2007] BCC 11.

[291] [2001] 1 BCLC 562, aff'g [1997] 2 BCLC 115.     [292] See [2001] 1 BCLC 562 at 566.

[293] [2006] BCC 725.

[294] [2007] 1 BCLC 618 at [107]–[111]. See too *Re Genosyis Technology Management Ltd, Wallach v Secretary of State for Trade and Industry* [2007] 1 BCLC 208; *Secretary of State for Trade and Industry v Goldberg* [2004] 1 BCLC 597 (director disqualified for, *inter alia*, allowing company moneys to be used for the purpose of other businesses connected with the controller of the company in disregard of the corporate personalities and interests of the companies involved).     [295] [2011] 2 BCLC 541.

[296] *Re Verby Print for Advertising Ltd, Fine v Secretary of State for Trade and Industry* [1998] 2 BCLC 23 at 39; *Official Receiver v Key* [2009] 1 BCLC 22.

between creditors.[297] In *Re Sevenoaks Stationers (Retail) Ltd*[298] the Court of Appeal held that the adoption of such a policy, of itself, merits a finding of unfitness and disqualification.[299] The directors are taking unfair advantage of the forbearance on the part of the creditors not pressing for payment and are trading at those creditors' expense while the company is in financial difficulty. If the evidence does not suggest a deliberate policy, but rather a general uncaring and dismissive attitude to the company's creditors, then an allegation of unfair discrimination will not be made out, though it may be possible to establish that trading has been at the risk of or to the detriment of the creditors.[300] Where the period during which the non-pressing debts have accrued is short, or where the amount outstanding is not a substantial proportion of the company's total deficiency, the court may be reluctant to conclude that there was a policy of non-payment.[301] A related issue is the non-payment of Crown debts (i.e. sums sue to HM Revenue and Customs in respect of PAYE, National Insurance, and VAT receipts) which often account for a significant proportion of the deficiency on liquidation. Initially the courts regarded the non-payment of Crown debts as particularly culpable,[302] but in *Re Sevenoaks Stationers (Retail) Ltd*[303] the Court of Appeal rejected this approach. The issue is the significance of that non-payment and whether it is part of a deliberate decision by the directors only to pay those creditors who press for payment and to retain sums which should have been paid to creditors (be they the Crown or otherwise) to fund the company's continued trading.[304] As noted, that discrimination in itself is evidence which justifies a finding of unfitness. In *Secretary of State for Business v Khan*[305] the court disqualified a director who kept the business going by adopting a discriminatory policy of choosing not to pay HMRC, in effect using HMRC's money (almost £1m) as working capital and without informing HMRC of the true position for a period of seven months. The court thought this a serious case which merited a five-year disqualification.

### Consequences of acting while disqualified

**15-105**   It is a criminal offence punishable by imprisonment or a fine or both for a person to act in breach of a disqualification order or undertaking or while an undischarged bankrupt or subject to a bankruptcy restriction order or undertaking (CDDA 1986, ss 11 and 13).[306] Civil liability is governed by CDDA 1986, s 15 which provides that a disqualified

---

[297] See *Re Verby Print for Advertising Ltd, Fine v Secretary of State for Trade and Industry* [1998] 2 BCLC 23; *Official Receiver v Dhaliwall* [2006] 1 BCLC 285.　　　　　　　　　[298] [1991] 3 All ER 578.

[299] [1991] BCLC 325 at 337. See *Re Hopes (Heathrow) Ltd, Secretary of State for Trade and Industry v Dyer* [2001] 1 BCLC 575; *Re Structural Concrete Ltd, Official Receiver v Barnes* [2001] BCC 578; *Secretary of State for Trade and Industry v McTighe (No 2)* [1996] 2 BCLC 477 at 486–7f.

[300] See *Official Receiver v Key* [2009] 1 BCLC 22 at [75], where the court was critical of the failure of the OR to bring charges other than a charge of a policy of unfair discrimination (which policy could not be found on the facts) where there was evidence of trading in disregard of creditor interests and the payment of preferences to connected persons which, had they been alleged, might have resulted in a lengthy period of disqualification.

[301] See *Official Receiver v Key* [2009] 1 BCLC 22 at [64]; *Re Verby Print for Advertising Ltd, Fine v Secretary of State for Trade and Industry* [1998] 2 BCLC 23 at 39.

[302] See *Re Lo-Line Electric Motors Ltd* [1988] 2 All ER 692 at 698, per Browne-Wilkinson V-C.

[303] [1991] BCLC 325.

[304] [1991] BCLC 325 at 337. See also *Re GSAR Realisations Ltd* [1993] BCLC 409 at 412, per Ferris J; *Re Verby Print for Advertising Ltd, Fine v Secretary of State for Trade and Industry* [1998] 2 BCLC 23.

[305] [2017] EWHC 288.

[306] It is also possible that the Insolvency Service might seek a Serious Crime Prevention Order under the Serious Crime Act 2007 against an individual acting in breach of a disqualification order, as they did in the case identified in their Press Release, 7 April 2017—the first time they have secured a SCPO; in this case, the SCPO provided for additional restrictions on the disqualified director for a period of five years.

person involved in the management of a company, in contravention of a disqualification order or undertaking, is personally liable, jointly and severally with the company, for the debts of the company contracted at that time. The liability also applies to any person who is involved in the management of the company and who acts or is willing to act on instructions given without leave of the court by a person whom he knows at that time to be disqualified.[307] This liability has a significant deterrent effect by making it risky for a co-director to act with a disqualified person in the management of a company.

**15-106** The effect of CDDA 1986, s 15 was considered in *Re Prestige Grindings Ltd, Sharma v Yardley*[308] where the court held that it confers on each creditor a direct statutory right of action against the disqualified director in respect of the debt owed to the creditor by the company, but the right must be exercised by individual creditors and it is not open to a liquidator to use the section acting as a representative of all the creditors. On the facts here, Inland Revenue and Customs as an individual creditor was able to claim the debt due to it by the company from the two directors on the grounds of one of them acting while disqualified and the other acting on the instructions of someone whom he knew to be disqualified. Likewise in *Inland Revenue Commissioners v McEntaggart*[309] where an undischarged bankrupt who acted as a director was liable for the company's debts due to the Revenue. The court noted that, in effect, CDDA 1986, s 15 imposes a collateral liability on the part of the disqualified directors for the debts of the company. Furthermore, as liability is in respect of recovery of a debt by a third party, it is not open to the director to seek relief under CA 2006, s 1157 which allows the court to grant relief where a director has been held liable to the company for negligence, default, breach of duty, or breach of trust (see **14-79**). To have a direct claim in this way is valuable, but there is little evidence of many creditors being in a position to take advantage of this direct liability. Apart from this (occasional) civil liability, in practice, there is little policing of disqualification orders and undertakings once they have been put in place. Such enforcement action as occurs is likely to arise only when the conduct of the disqualified director has been brought to the attention of the Secretary of State in some way, such as where a further venture collapses or a member of the public complains.

---

[307] As to whether they are willing so to act, note the presumption in CDDA 1986, s 15(5).
[308] [2006] 1 BCLC 440.     [309] [2006] 1 BCLC 476.

# PART III

# Corporate Governance– Shareholders' Rights and Remedies

# 16

# Membership and the incidents of membership

## A  Becoming a member

**16-1**  Membership of a company is governed by CA 2006, s 112 which provides: (1) that the subscribers of a company's memorandum of association (discussed at **1-23**) are deemed to have agreed to become members of the company and on its registration become members and must be entered as such in its register of members; and (2) that every other person who agrees[1] to become a member of a company, and whose name is entered in its register of members, is a member of the company.[2] A private company may elect (with unanimous shareholder approval) not to maintain its own register of members, but to maintain this information on the public register kept by the registrar of companies (s 128A(1)). Given that the average number of members in a company is two,[3] for most companies, maintaining a register is not a significant issue. The discussion in this chapter is predicated on there being a company register of members, but it should be read in the light of this alternative method of record-keeping, as s 112A describes it. Additionally, all companies are required to maintain a register of persons of significant control (PSC) which requires the disclosure of beneficial owners, essentially where they own or control more than 25 per cent of the shares or voting rights of the company etc, see at **16-91**.

**16-2**  The fundamental importance of entry on the register of members is highlighted by the Supreme Court decision in *Enviroco Ltd v Farstad Supply A/S*[4] where the dispute related to claims under a charterparty. For the purpose of that dispute, the issue was whether a company (B) was a subsidiary of another company (A) within the definition in what is now CA 2006, s 1159(1)(c), which requires that A be *a member* of B and have control in the way outlined in that provision (see **1-56**). In this case, A did own shares in B, but A had charged those shares in B as security to a bank and, in accordance with Scots law, A had had to register those shares in the name of the bank's nominee with the result that the register of members showed the bank's nominee as the member of Company B, not

---

[1]  This requirement of agreement is satisfied when a person assents to become a member and it does not require that there should be a binding contract between the person and the company: *Re Nuneaton Borough Association Football Club Ltd* [1989] BCLC 454, CA.

[2]  See *Re Florence Land and Public Works Co, Nicol's Case, Tufnell and Ponsonby's Case* (1885) 29 Ch D 421, CA.

[3]  Companies House Statistical Release, Companies Register Activities 2016–17, Table A7.

[4]  [2011] 2 BCLC 165; and see Lan, 'The Curious Case of a Subsidiary' (2012) 128 LQR 351 who notes at 353 that the very strict position taken by the Supreme Court was probably because it felt that the decision would have little application in practice, since it is unusual under English law to assign shares by way of security. Lan also notes that the case highlights the dangers surrounding the common practice of incorporating statutory definitions into commercial contracts.

Company A. As Lord Collins put it, essentially the question was whether the putative holding company remained a 'member' notwithstanding that the shares were registered in the name of the nominee.

**16-3** The Supreme Court ruled that it is a fundamental principle of English law, reflected in what is now CA 2006, s 112, that, except where express provision is made to the contrary, the person on the register of members is the member to the exclusion of any other person, unless and until the register is rectified.[5] This has been the position since the Companies Act 1862 and the companies legislation would be unworkable, the court said, if that were not so.[6] On this basis, A was no longer a member of B and could not claim that B was its subsidiary on the basis of the application of what is now CA 2006, s 1159(1)(c).[7] While there has been criticism of the outcome,[8] there is no dispute that the law required this conclusion, given the role assigned to entry on the register of members.

**16-4** Another illustration of the importance of the entry on the register of members can be found in *Eckerle v Wickeder Westfalenstahl GmbH*[9] where beneficial owners of shares were unable to object to the passing of a special resolution that the company re-register as a private company. Shareholders may object to the court in these circumstances provided they are the 'holders of not less in the aggregate than 5 per cent in nominal value of the company's issued capital' (CA 2006, s 98). The company successfully objected to the applicants' standing on the basis that the shares were registered in the name of a nominee shareholder and were not directly held by the minority beneficial interests who were objecting. The court agreed that, on the wording of CA 2006, s 98(1), only the registered shareholder may object, not the indirect investors. A further complication was that the registered holder, as a nominee for many investors, had voted some shares for the re-registration resolution as well as voting against the resolution. Section 98(1) rules out an objection 'by a person who has consented to or voted in favour of the resolution'. The net result was that the indirect investors were not 'holders' entitled to object under CA 2006, s 98(1) and the registered holder, having voted some shares in favour of the resolution, could not object under s 98(1). Norris J indicated some concern that this reading of the CA 2006, s 98(1) deprives indirect investors of the protection provided by the section, but the wording of the section offered no other conclusion unless he was to embark upon what would be 'an impermissible form of judicial legislation'.[10] The court gave judgment for the company.

---

[5] [2011] 2 BCLC 165 at [37], per Lord Collins with whom the rest of the court agreed.

[6] [2011] 2 BCLC 165 at [38].

[7] Also, while the statute does make provision (CA 1985, s 736A(6) and (7), now CA 2006, Sch 6, paras 6 and 7) attributing rights held by a nominee to another person and attributing rights attached to shares held by way of security to the person providing the security, those provisions are concerned with rights, not membership, and refer to voting rights and the right to appoint the board for the purposes of the definitions (of holding company and subsidiary) in CA 1985, 736, now CA 2006, s 1159, see [2011] 2 BCLC 165 at [41]–[43], [64].

[8] Even their Lordships seemed doubtful of the outcome, Lord Clarke commenting that 'on any sensible view of the facts', B was throughout a subsidiary of A, see [2011] 2 BCLC 165 at [72], and see Lord Collins at [5]. See also an interesting piece by Anderson, 'Scottish Share Pledges in the Supreme Court' [2012] 16 Edin L Rev 99 at 101–2 who notes the Supreme Court's preference for form over substance and for a legalistic interpretation of the relevant provisions with little heed to the practical implications, but he also notes, at 103, that it is difficult to fault the Supreme Court's impeccable legal reasoning and that the somewhat convoluted statutory provisions are the source of the problem; and see n 4.         [9] [2013] 3 WLR 1316.

[10] [2013] 3 WLR 1316 at [31].

**16-5**  Typically, entry on the register is a matter for the directors and routine entries are dealt with by the company secretary (where there is a company secretary). Listed public companies use the services of professional registrars to maintain their share registers. Inspection of the register and its rectification is discussed at **16-79** et seq. For the most part, entry on the register of members happens without any difficulty and so, having acquired some shares, the shareholder becomes a member of the company. In general, the shareholders are the members of the company and the terms 'shareholders' and 'members' may be used interchangeably.[11]

**16-6**  As practically all the companies on the register of companies are companies limited by shares, the initial stage in the process of becoming a member of a company involves becoming a shareholder and there are four methods of becoming a shareholder:

(1)  by subscribing to the memorandum of association;

(2)  by taking up an allotment of shares by the company;

(3)  by a transfer of shares from an existing member;

(4)  by a transmission of shares on the death or bankruptcy of a member.

**16-7**  As noted at **16-1**, the subscribers to the company's memorandum are deemed to have agreed to become members and on registration of the memorandum they must be entered as such in the company's register of members (CA 2006, s 112(1)). The memorandum states that each subscriber agrees to become a member and undertakes, in the case of a company having a share capital, to take at least one share (s 8(1)). It is unusual for any problems to arise with regard to subscribers.

**16-8**  The allotment of shares by the company to existing or new investors is a matter for the directors, subject to certain statutory constraints. The duties of directors in this regard (to exercise their powers for a proper purpose) are discussed in Chapter 9 while the statutory constraints and mechanics of allotment are discussed in Chapter 21. Following an allotment, the company issues share certificates to the shareholders, unless the shares are being held in uncertificated form, discussed at **16-10**, and the shareholders' names are entered on the register of members. Few problems with entry on the register of members occur in these cases since, obviously, the company has decided to allot more shares and is willing to accept new members.

**16-9**  Problems are most likely to arise on the transfer and transmission of shares. Here the company is a bystander to transactions (in the case of transfers) and dispositions (in the case of transmission) which alter the membership of the company. On occasion, particularly in private companies, the directors may be unhappy at a change in the membership and this can give rise to problems for the transferees with respect to securing the entry of their names on the register of members.

**16-10**  In terms of the process of transfer, for most companies the process involves a proper instrument of transfer (i.e. a paper form) and a (paper) share certificate. The company gives effect to the transfer or transmission by removing the name of the transferor from the register of members and inserting the name of the transferee. The company cancels the share certificate in the name of the transferor and issues a new certificate in the name of the transferee. Larger publicly traded companies have uncertificated shares which are

---

[11]  An example of an exception would be where the company is a company limited by guarantee without a share capital, in which case the company has members but no shareholders.

transferred electronically[12] and in this case there is no requirement for a proper instrument of transfer or for paper share certificates with a member's shareholding recorded electronically. However, private companies and the majority of private investors continue to hold their shareholdings in certificated form while institutional and professional investors hold their shareholdings in uncertificated form. For many years, there have been discussions, if not much progress, on full dematerialisation, the process of moving entirely from paper share certificates to electronic shareholding,[13] the main difference being that the share certificate would cease to be *prima facie* evidence of title. On the horizon is the Central Securities Depositories Regulation (EU) 909/2014 on settlement and central securities depositories,[14] known as CSDR, art 3(1) of which requires transferrable securities admitted to trading which are issued after 1 January 2023 to be in dematerialised form and for all transferable securities admitted to trading to be dematerialised with effect from 1 January 2025. It was expected that the Department for Business would lay a statutory instrument giving effect to these requirements in 2017,[15] but it has yet to appear at the time of writing.[16] It should be borne in mind that 99.8 per cent of companies in the UK are private limited companies which are not affected by these measures; for them paper share certificates seem likely to continue for some time yet.

## Share certificates

**16-11**  Unless the conditions of issue of the shares otherwise provide, within two months after the allotment of any shares, or within two months after a transfer of any shares being lodged with a company, the company must complete and have ready for delivery the relevant share certificates.[17] This requirement to issue a share certificate does not apply where the shares are in uncertificated form.[18]

---

[12] For such companies, the company's register of members means the company's issuer register of members and the Operator register of members: SI 2001/3755, as amended, reg 20(4). The 'Operator' is the electronic settlement platform for shares and other securities known as CREST which is operated by Euroclear UK and Ireland, the central securities depositary for both the UK and Irish markets. The legal underpinning of electronic settlement is provided by CA 2006, Pt 21, Ch 2 and the Uncertificated Securities Regulations 2001, SI 2001/3755, as amended. The CA 2006, s 786(1)(b) makes provision for regulations requiring companies to adopt electronic holdings, but no such regulations have been made.

[13] At various times, there have been informal working groups of interested parties under the auspices of the Institute of Chartered Secretaries and Administrators attempting to move matters forward, but with little apparent public support or political will.                    [14] OJ L 257/1, 28.8.2014.

[15] The Treasury consulted on implementation of the CSDR Regulation in December 2015 and said BEIS would issue its own consultation on art 3(i) which did not happen. The Treasury responded to its consultation in September 2017 indicating that BEIS would lay amendments in 2017 to the Uncertificated Securities Regulations 2001, SI 2001/3755 but no amendments have been laid at the time of writing.

[16] An industry body in the UK representing interested parties such as issuers, broker organisations, company registrars, and Euroclear, the UK central securities depository, did issue an initial working paper suggesting a way forward which attempts to mimic the current legal framework so far as possible while allowing for dematerialisation, see 'An industry proposed model for dematerialisation', 9 December 2014—a somewhat anonymous document, but the membership of the working group behind it is given in Appendix 3 to the document. The Kay Review had also recommended the Government should explore the most cost-effective means for individual investors to hold shares directly on an electronic register: see *Kay Review of UK Equity Markets and Long-Term Decision Making* (July 2012), Recommendation 17, paras 12.14 to 12.17; also BIS Report, *Building a Culture of Long-Term Equity Investment, Implementation of The Kay Review: Progress Report* (October 2014), paras 1.9 and 2.119–2.123.

[17] CA 2006, ss 769(1), 776(1), subject to the exemptions in ss 769(2), 776(3).

[18] See The Uncertificated Securities Regulations 2001, SI 2001/3755, as amended, reg 38(2).

**16-12**  The certificate is *prima facie* (not conclusive) evidence of title (CA 2006, s 768(1)) and the presumption arising from it can be rebutted, but the company may be estopped from denying the facts stated in the certificate. In *Re Bahia and San Francisco Rly Co*[19] the court noted:

> 'The power of giving certificates is . . . for the benefit of the company in general; and it is a declaration by the company to all the world that the person in whose name the certificate is made out, and to whom it is given, is a shareholder in the company, and it is given by the company with the intention that it shall be so used by the person to whom it is given, and acted upon in the sale and transfer of shares.'

**16-13**  For example, if the company issues certificates which describe shares as fully paid-up when they are not and a third party relies on the certificate, the company is estopped from denying that they are fully-paid.[20] In *Bloomenthal v Ford*[21] a lender lent money to a company on the basis that he would have as security fully-paid shares in the company. The company gave him certificates for 10,000 shares of £1. The certificates stated that he was the registered holder of the shares, and that on each of them the full amount had been paid. No money had in fact been paid upon the shares. The company subsequently collapsed and the lender was placed on the list of contributories. It was held by the House of Lords that the company and its liquidator were estopped from denying the certificate and that the shares were fully-paid. The lender could have found out the true position by enquiry but there was no actual notice and he had acted in good faith. In recognition of the reality of modern trading systems, where a company applies to have its shares listed on an exchange or traded through a settlement system such as CREST, which in either case require the shares to be fully-paid, the company is to be taken as having represented to potential acquirers of its shares that they are fully-paid, and acquirers are taken to have relied on that representation, unless the company proves the contrary.[22] Hence, in *Blomqvist v Zavarco plc*,[23] a traded company was estopped from denying that a shareholder's holding was fully-paid unless the company could prove (which on the facts it could not) that the shares were not fully-paid in fact and that the holder was aware of that position when he acquired them.

**16-14**  If a share certificate is issued following the presentation of a forged transfer, the company is not estopped from denying its validity. This is because the person presenting the transfer impliedly warrants the authenticity of the transfer.[24] A purchaser from such a person is in a better position and can claim compensation from the company if he is displaced by the true owner since the purchaser relies not on the forged transfer but on the certificate issued by the company.[25] A forged share certificate is said to be a nullity and does not bind

---

[19] (1868) LR 3 QB 584 at 595. See also *Cadbury Schweppes plc v Halifax Share Dealing Ltd* [2007] 1 BCLC 497 where the company was estopped from denying the validity of share certificates issued to fraudsters (and subsequently sold by them) who had stolen the identities of genuine shareholders.

[20] See *Burkinshaw v Nicolls* (1878) 3 App Cas 1004. Where there is a subsequent transfer and the transferor had acquired a good title by estoppel, the transferee acquires a good title even if he had actual notice that the shares were only partly-paid: *Re Stapleford Colliery Co, Barrow's Case* (1880) 14 Ch D 432, CA. Cf *Re London Celluloid Co* (1888) 39 Ch D 190 at 197, CA.          [21] [1897] AC 156, HL.

[22] *Blomqvist v Zavarco plc* [2017] 1 BCLC 373.          [23] [2017] 1 BCLC 373.

[24] The presentor of the improper transfer must indemnify the company against liability arising from the company acting on the invalid transfer: *Sheffield Corporation v Barclay* [1905] AC 392; *Yeung Kai Yung v Hong Kong & Shanghai Banking* [1980] 2 All ER 599.

[25] *Re Bahia and San Francisco Railway Co* (1868) LR 3 QB 584; *Balkis Consolidated Co v Tomkinson* [1893] AC 396; *Dixon v Kennaway & Co* [1900] 1 Ch 833. See also *Cadbury Schweppes plc v Halifax Share Dealing Ltd* [2007] 1 BCLC 497.

the company,[26] but, arguably, the extent to which a third party can rely on a forged share certificate might be better approached as a question of the apparent authority of the agent to bind his principal.[27]

## Restrictions on membership

**16-15**  As a general rule, anyone may be a member but there are restrictions imposed on some classes of persons.

### Minors

**16-16**  There is no prohibition on minors[28] being shareholders although the company may refuse to accept a minor as a shareholder.[29] Applying ordinary contract law rules, a contract to purchase shares is voidable by a minor before or within a reasonable time of attaining his majority. If the minor repudiates the contract, he is not liable for future calls but he cannot recover the purchase price unless there has been a total failure of consideration,[30] which is unlikely to be the case. Given that shares are normally issued as fully-paid, there is little reason now for repudiation. Until the minor repudiates, he has full rights of membership.

### Subsidiary companies

**16-17**  A company cannot be a member of itself, a point originally established in *Trevor v Whitworth*[31] and stated in CA 2006, s 658 which provides that any purported acquisition by a company of its own shares, other than in accordance with the provisions of the Act, is void (see **22-9**) and an offence by the company and any officer in default. The Act further provides that, subject to certain exceptions, a body corporate cannot be a member of its holding company and any allotment or transfer of shares in a company to its subsidiary is void (s 136).[32] The policy behind this prohibition is to reinforce the rule in *Trevor v Whitworth*[33] and prevent any reduction of capital whereby capital provided by a parent company to a subsidiary is returned by the subsidiary to the parent company. The prohibition cannot be avoided by using a nominee for the prohibition applies to a nominee acting on behalf of a subsidiary as to the subsidiary itself (s 144).

**16-18**  There are a number of exceptions, however, when a subsidiary may hold shares in its holding company, for example where the subsidiary holds the shares only as a personal representative or trustee (CA 2006, s 138)[34] or in the ordinary course of its business as

---

[26]  *Ruben v Great Fingall Consolidated* [1906] AC 439.

[27]  See *Lovett v Carson Country Homes* [2009] 2 BCLC 196 at [92]–[95] (*Ruben's* case does not mean that a forged document can in no circumstances have any effect whatsoever, for a party may be estopped from disputing the validity of a forged document. The principle of apparent authority is a broad reflection of the principles of estoppel, the court said, and it is accepted that, in appropriate circumstances, a principal may be bound by the fraudulent acts of an agent (and forgeries are no different to other fraudulent acts) in circumstances where there is ostensible authority).

[28]  That is anyone under 18 years of age in England and Wales: Family Law Reform Act 1969, s 1; anyone under 16 in Scotland.

[29]  *Re Asiatic Banking Corpn, Symon's Case* (1870) Ch App 298. For companies with uncertificated shares, the power to refuse to register a transfer to a minor is retained, see The Uncertificated Securities Regulations 2001, SI 2001/3755, as amended, regs 27(4)(b), 28(4)(b).

[30]  *Steinberg v Scala (Leeds) Ltd* [1923] 2 Ch 452, CA.       [31]  (1887) 12 App Cas 409, HL.

[32]  'Holding company' and 'subsidiary' are defined in CA 2006, s 1159 and Sch 6.

[33]  (1887) 12 App Cas 409, HL.

[34]  Unless the holding company or a subsidiary of it is beneficially interested under the trust, see CA 2006, s 138(1).

an authorised dealer in shares (s 141). Equally, where a company acquired shares in circumstances where it would not have been within the prohibition on a subsidiary being a member of its holding company, but would now fall within the prohibition, the company may remain as a member of the holding company (and receive bonus issues in respect of its holding) but it has no right to vote those shares on a written resolution or in general or class meetings (s 137).

## B Classes of shares

**16-19**    It is common for the articles of association to give a company complete freedom to issue shares with such rights and restrictions as the company may by ordinary resolution determine[35] although most companies (public and private) limit their structures to ordinary shares. Where a more sophisticated share structure is required (for example, to facilitate a division of control in a joint venture company), the company may have more classes of shares, typically ordinary and preference shares, and possibly several forms of each. The particular rights in any given company depend on the terms of issue.

### Ordinary shares

**16-20**    Ordinary shares (often loosely described as equities) carry the residual rights of participation in the income and capital of the company which have not been granted to other classes. Ordinary shareholders have no right to any fixed dividend (i.e. a return on their investment usually expressed as so many pence per share) on their shares, but after the payment of any dividends to preference shareholders, the ordinary shareholders enjoy the remainder of the surplus profits actually distributed as dividend by the directors. Distributions are considered in detail at **22-88** et seq.

**16-21**    In difficult times, the ordinary shareholders run the risk that the profits available for distribution will be inadequate and will not extend beyond (or indeed to) the payment of the dividend due on the preference shares. In prosperous times, however, the preference shareholders are restricted to their fixed dividend and the ordinary shareholders enjoy all of the surplus distributable profits. For example, if the company has distributable profits of £30,000 and the fixed dividend payable to preference shareholders costs £20,000, then the ordinary shareholders share a fund of £10,000. On the other hand, if the company has distributable profits of £300,000, the preference shareholders remain entitled as before to their dividend of £20,000 and the ordinary shareholders share the remaining £280,000. The ordinary shareholders run the risk of no dividend or a small dividend, as we can see, but they also stand to scoop the pool in the event that the company makes significant profits. Preference shareholders take less risk and so are entitled to less return.

**16-22**    Ordinary shareholders have a right to a return of capital ranking after the preference shares but, as with dividends, ordinary shares claim the pool of surplus assets in a solvent winding up after the return of capital to all other shareholders.

**16-23**    Ordinary shares usually carry one vote per share although companies may attach such voting rights as they choose. For example, a company may provide that ordinary shares

---

[35]  See The Companies (Model Articles) Regulations 2008, SI 2008/3229, reg 2, Sch 1; art 22 (Ltd), reg 4, Sch 3, art 43 (Plc).

carry 10 votes per share or it may divide its ordinary shares into two classes of ordinary shares, one voting and one non-voting class. Non-voting ordinary shares are not common in the UK. Preference shareholders generally have limited voting rights so it is the ordinary shareholders who have voting control in general meetings. For premium listed companies, see **21-103**, Listing Principles 3 and 4 provide, respectively, that all equity shares in a class that has been admitted to premium listing must carry an equal number of votes on any shareholder vote and, where a listed company has more than one class of equity shares admitted to premium listing, the aggregate voting rights of the shares in each class should be broadly proportionate to the relative interests of those classes in the equity of the listed company.

### Preference shares

**16-24**    Typically, a preference share has a fixed preferential cumulative dividend[36] and a priority as to a return of capital on a winding up which ensures that the preference shareholders get their capital back ahead of the ordinary shareholders although, as shareholders, the preference shareholders rank after secured and unsecured creditors. Preference shareholders are non-participating as to surplus both while the company is a going concern (i.e. with respect to any further distributions of profits) and on a winding up (i.e. with respect to any surplus assets remaining after the creditors have been paid and capital has been returned to the shareholders). To ensure participation in any such surpluses, preference shares may be issued as participating preference shares, i.e. participating as to dividend and/or capital which means that the shares carry additional rights to participate in profits or assets. Preference shares usually have restricted voting rights limited to matters which affect their rights such as when their dividends are in arrears.

**16-25**    In some ways, the position of preference shareholders is akin to that of creditors and preference shares are often regarded as a hybrid category of investment between equity or share capital and loan capital. The fixed dividend payable to preference shareholders resembles the fixed interest payable on loan capital and the priority to a return of capital in a winding up resembles a creditor's right to a return of the capital sum. Equally, preference shares can carry rights quite similar to ordinary shares and the company may issue preference shares which are convertible into ordinary shares either on a set date or at the option of the shareholders or, in some circumstances, at the option of the company. As with all shares, the precise nature of a preference share depends on the terms of issue.

## C  Class rights

### Identifying a class right

**16-26**    Class rights may be set out in the articles or in the resolution creating them. In practice, they are usually set out in the articles.[37] If all the shares fall within one class, there are

---

[36] The payment of dividends is still dependent on the company having distributable profits as required by CA 2006, Pt 23, but if there are such profits then the terms of issue of preference shares usually require the payment of a dividend on fixed dates.

[37] The statement of capital which accompanies a return of allotment of the shares must give, for each class, the prescribed particulars of the rights attached to the shares, and the total number of shares of that class: CA 2006, s 555(3), (4). The registrar must also be notified of the assignment of a new name or designation to any class of members and of variations of class rights: ss 636, 637.

no class rights, only shareholder rights.[38] Where particular rights (such as the right to a dividend or to a return of capital on a winding up) are attached to certain shares, these are described as class rights.

**16-27** In *Cumbrian Newspapers Group Ltd v Cumberland and Westmorland Herald Co Ltd*,[39] Scott J broadened the classification of class rights to include rights conferred on a member of a company in his capacity as a member which rights are not attached to any particular class of shares. The member in this case had acquired 10 per cent of the shares in the company in 1968 and, at the same time and as part of the arrangement under which the shares were issued, the company adopted articles which gave this member, by name, certain rights of pre-emption, the right to appoint a director, and rights to transfer shares (the purpose being to enable the member to obstruct an attempted takeover). In 1985, the directors made clear that they proposed to call a general meeting to cancel the articles conferring these special rights on this member. The value of a right being classified as a class right is that a variation of rights attached to a class of shares is subject to statutory constraints, now CA 2006, s 630, which essentially provides that such rights cannot be varied or abrogated other than in accordance with a variation provision in the articles or, if the articles make no provision for variation, with the consent of the class in accordance with s 630(4). Scott J concluded that the shares for the time being held by this member did constitute a class for the purposes of the statutory procedure for variation of class rights, saying:[40]

'In my judgment, a company which, by its articles, confers special rights on one or more of its members in the capacity of member or shareholder thereby constitutes the shares for the time being held by that member or members a class of shares for the purposes of s 125 [now CA 2006, s 630, variation of class rights]. The rights are class rights.'

As the rights conferred in *Cumbrian* were class rights, the company could only alter them in accordance with the statutory procedure and the court made a declaration to that effect. Provisions which are classified as class rights therefore confer greater security on the beneficiary than rights conferred merely by the articles which are open to the risk of alteration by a special resolution under CA 2006, s 21(1). Class rights can therefore form a valuable element in the protection of minority shareholders[41] or any other special interests.[42] It is for this reason that the broad approach taken in *Cumbrian* is important and

---

[38] See *Union Music Ltd v Watson* [2003] 1 BCLC 453 at [39]; where there are no rights conferred on one shareholder which have not also been conferred on the other shareholder(s), there are no classes of shares.

[39] [1986] 2 All ER 816.

[40] [1986] 2 All ER 816 at 830. Cf *Re Blue Arrow plc* [1987] BCLC 585 at 590 (a right conferred on an individual by the articles (to remain president of the company) unrelated to any shareholding in any way cannot be described as a class right—a class right, Vinelott J said, is a right attaching, in some way, to a category of shares in the company).

[41] For example, the courts will not exercise their discretion under CA 2006, s 306 to call a general meeting if to do so would override a class right with respect to the calling of meetings: see *Harman v BML Group Ltd* [1994] 2 BCLC 674, see **17-53**.

[42] In the past the Government has used class rights to retain a measure of control of privatised companies by way of a so-called 'golden share', typically nothing more elaborate than a single £1 special preference share. The extent to which the use of golden shares to retain control in this way is permissible under European law has been addressed by the European Court of Justice which essentially concluded that such measures are contrary to the free movement of capital, but may in some circumstances be permissible in the protection of the public interest, provided the measures adopted are proportionate, objective, and non-discriminatory. See *Commission v Portugal* (Case C-367/98), *Commission v France* (Case C-483/99), *Commission v Belgium* (Case C-503/99) [2003] QB 233.

the decision can be justified on its facts, though not everyone agrees with it.[43] It is possible to protect minority or other interests also through the use of entrenched provisions in the articles and, as discussed at **5-17**, where a variation of class rights can only occur on terms which fall within CA 2006, s 22(1), the class right is an entrenched provision. Entrenchment should be of no consequence in these circumstances since entrenchment merely means that a provision is not open to alteration by special resolution under s 21 and can be altered only in accordance with its own provisions for alteration which is the position in any event under s 630(2)(a) on the variation of class rights, see **16-37**.

**16-28**   The application of CA 2006, s 630(1) must not be confused by reference to s 629 which addresses a quite distinct issue. Section 629 provides that 'for the purposes of the CA 2006, shares are of one class if the rights attached to them are in all respects uniform'.[44] This section defines when 'shares are of one class' rather than what is a class of shares— the heading to the section is misleading in this regard.[45] This definition is needed for the application of various provisions such as s 550 (directors' power to allot when private company has only one class of shares) and s 569 (disapplication of pre-emption rights when private company has only one class of shares).[46]

## Rules of construction

**16-29**   Certain rules of construction have been developed by the courts to assist them in identifying the rights attaching to each class of shares, given that they vary from company to company, but each case ultimately turns on the particular terms of issue.

### A presumption of equality

**16-30**   There is a presumption of equality as between shareholders with all shareholders being deemed to be entitled to the same proportionate part in the capital of the company.[47] This presumption is easily rebutted by an issue of shares on terms which give special rights with respect to matters such as dividends, the return of capital, or to voting at meetings of the company. As noted earlier, preference shareholders typically have a preferential right to a dividend and to a return of capital on a winding up.

### Rights granted are deemed to be exhaustive

**16-31**   There is a presumption that any rights attached to a share are deemed to be exhaustive.[48] The position was clearly expressed by Sargant J in *Re National Telephone Co*[49] as follows:

> '[T]he weight of authority is in favour of the view that, either with regard to dividend or with regard to the rights in a winding up, the express gift or attachment of preferential rights to preference shares, on their creation, is, prima facie, a definition of the whole of their rights in that respect, and negatives any further or other right to which, but for the specified rights, they would have been entitled.'

---

[43]  See Polack (1986) 45 CLJ 399; Morse [2008] JBL 96 at 98 who, respectively, describe it as an unwise and an unfortunate decision.

[44]  For these purposes, the rights attached to shares are not regarded as different from those attached to other shares by reason only that they do not carry the same rights to dividends in the 12 months immediately following their allotment: CA 2006, s 629(2).

[45]  A point confirmed by the *Explanatory Notes to the Companies Act 2006*, para 934 which points out that the statute does not define what amounts to a class which remains a matter for the common law.

[46]  See also CA 2006, s 725(1) (Treasury shares: maximum holding); s 974(2)(b) (Meaning of 'takeover offer').

[47]  *Birch v Cropper, Re Bridgewater Navigation Co Ltd* (1889) 14 App Cas 525 at 543, per Lord Macnaghten, HL.             [48]  *Re National Telephone Co* [1914] 1 Ch 755.

[49]  [1914] 1 Ch 755 at 774.

**16-32**   In *Will v United Lankat Plantations Co*[50] the attachment of preferential dividend rights to preference shares was presumed to be exhaustive as to their dividend rights. This had the effect of negating any right to further participation in any surplus profits of the company. This presumption of exhaustive rights can be rebutted by expressly declaring the shares to be participating preference shares with a right of participation in surplus profits after a certain percentage of dividend has been paid to the ordinary shareholders.[51]

**16-33**   Likewise where preference shares are given an express priority to a return of capital on a winding up, this negates any right to participate in surplus assets in a winding up.[52] Again, the terms of issue may enable preference shareholders to share in surplus assets with the other shareholders after their capital had been repaid, but it is for preference shareholders to show that they are entitled to participate further in this way.[53]

### A cumulative dividend

**16-34**   *Prima facie*, preference shares are entitled to a cumulative dividend, even in the absence of any such provision in the terms of issue.[54] This means that the preference shareholders are entitled to have any deficiencies in a given year made up from the profits of subsequent years before anything is distributed to other shareholders. Alternatively, preference shares may be issued as non-cumulative, but this must be clearly stated to ensure that the presumption does not apply.[55]

**16-35**   On a winding up, if the company is solvent, a question concerning the payment of arrears of dividend may arise. There is a *prima facie* presumption that dividends and arrears thereof are only payable while the company is a going concern and are no longer payable once winding up has begun.[56] That inference is rebuttable where there are express words in the terms of issue to the contrary or a definition in the right to dividend which is inconsistent with it.[57]

**16-36**   The net effect of these rules of construction is that class rights are usually spelt out in great detail in the terms of issue to avoid falling foul of one or other presumption.

## Variation or abrogation of class rights

**16-37**   The statutory scheme for variation of class rights was simplified on the recommendation of the Company Law Review and it is intended to provide a comprehensive code setting out the manner in which rights attached to a class of shares can be varied.[58]

**16-38**   A variation or abrogation[59] must be carried out in accordance with a variation provision in the articles or, if no provision is made in the articles, in accordance with the scheme in

---

[50] [1914] AC 11.        [51] See *Re Isle of Thanet Electric Supply Co Ltd* [1950] Ch 161.

[52] *Scottish Insurance Corpn Ltd v Wilsons and Clyde Coal Co Ltd* [1949] 1 All ER 1068; *Prudential Assurance Co Ltd v Chatterley-Whitfield Collieries Ltd* [1949] 1 All ER 1094, HL.

[53] *Re Isle of Thanet Electric Supply Co Ltd* [1950] Ch 161, CA; *Scottish Insurance Corpn Ltd v Wilsons and Clyde Coal Co Ltd* [1949] 1 All ER 1068, HL.        [54] *Webb v Earle* (1875) LR 20 Eq 556.

[55] *Staples v Eastman Photographic Materials Co* [1896] 2 Ch 303, CA (the terms of issue referred specifically to dividends paid out of the profits of each year).        [56] *Re Crichton's Oil Co* [1902] 2 Ch 86.

[57] *Re E W Savory Ltd* [1951] 2 All ER 1036 (reference to the ranking of the preference shares must have been a reference to what would happen on winding up); *Re Walter Symons Ltd* [1934] Ch 308.

[58] See Company Law Review, *Final Report,* vol 1 (2001), URN 01/942, para 7.28; *Completing the Structure* (2000), URN 00/1335, paras 5.42–5.44; *Developing the Framework* (2000), URN 00/656, paras 4.147–4.151. The statutory provisions on variation of class rights are extended to companies without a share capital, see s 631.

[59] References to variation include reference to abrogation: CA 2006, s 630(6). An alteration of an existing variation provision or the insertion of a variation procedure is itself a variation of class rights: s 630(5). See *Re House of Fraser plc* [1987] BCLC 293 at 301, 'variation' presupposes the continuance of rights in a varied state while 'abrogation' presupposes the termination of rights without satisfaction or fulfilment.

CA 2006, s 630(4)[60] which requires the consent in writing of the holders of not less than three-quarters in nominal value of the issued shares of that class or a special resolution of the class passed at a class meeting sanctioning the variation.[61] Note that the quorum requirement for a variation of class rights meeting is two persons present holding at least one-third in nominal value of the issued shares of the class in question[62] and this provision appears to override any provision in the company's articles as it is not expressed to be subject to those articles (s 334(4)(a)). In practice, provisions in the articles are generally drafted in broadly similar terms to the statutory scheme, but it is possible for the articles either to impose a stricter scheme or a less onerous one (for example, requiring an ordinary resolution). In either case, the provision in the articles must be obeyed and the statutory scheme in s 630(4) only applies in the absence of provision in the articles.[63]

**16-39**  At a class meeting so held, the shareholders must have regard to what is in the interests of the class.[64] In *Re Dee Valley Group plc*,[65] a case which concerned a class meeting ordered by the court to approve a scheme of arrangement, the court noted that, while court-ordered meetings are *sui generis*, the position is comparable with class meetings generally.[66] The court there concluded that the key is that the members of the class must vote in the interests of the class as whole and not in their own specific interests if they are different from the interests of the class.[67]

**16-40**  In the context of a company restructuring where the consent of a class of holders of loan securities (notes) was required, the Court of Appeal ruled, in *Azevedo v Imcopa Importação*,[68] that it is not inconsistent with English law for the issuer, the company, to offer a 'consent payment'[69] to noteholders who voted in favour of the resolution proposed to the class, where the payment and the basis on which it was payable were disclosed and

---

[60] Note CA 2006, s 630(3) which provides that the mechanisms for variation provided by s 630(2) (variation in accordance with a provision for variation in the company's articles or, in the absence of any such provision, in accordance with the statutory scheme in s 630(4)) are without prejudice to other restrictions on variation. Paragraph 937 of the *Explanatory Notes to the Companies Act 2006* states that s 630(3) has two consequences: (a) the company must comply with any more onerous regime in its articles for the variation of class rights (but s 630(2)(a) says that in any event); and (b) if the rights are entrenched, that protection cannot be circumvented by varying the rights using this (s 630) provision. But if the rights are entrenched, it is because there is a provision dealing with their amendment which is more restrictive than a special resolution (s 22(1)) and, if there is a provision dealing with their amendment, then s 630(2)(a) requires that procedure to be followed in any event. It is not clear then what purpose is served by CA 2006, s 630(3).

[61] The test is different under s 630(4)(a) and (b), (a) being of the total issued shares of that class while (b) is of the votes cast at the meeting by those entitled to vote and the difference may dictate which route is used in a particular case. As to the application of CA 2006, Pt 13, Ch 3 (meetings) to class meetings, see s 334.

[62] Excluding any shares held as treasury shares, as to which see **22-41**.

[63] See *Explanatory Notes to the Companies Act 2006*, paras 936, 937.

[64] *British America Nickel Corpn Ltd v O'Brien* [1927] AC 369; *Re Holders Investment Trust Ltd* [1971] 2 All ER 289 (certain preference shareholders voting at a class meeting to approve a reduction of capital were not entitled to take into account their interests as the holders of the majority of the ordinary shares in the company).          [65] [2017] 3 WLR 767.

[66] [2017] 3 WLR 767 at [44].

[67] [2017] 3 WLR 767 at [47], citing with approval, *British America Nickel* and *Re Holders Investments*, see n 64.          [68] [2014] 1 BCLC 72.

[69] Note the comments at [2014] 1 BCLC 72 at [36]–[37] concerning the incomplete litigation surrounding an exit consent clause in *Assenagon Asset Management SA v Irish Bank Resolution Corpn Ltd* [2013] 1 All ER 495 where Briggs J disallowed a provision which incentivised bondholders to vote in favour of a proposal requiring them to exchange their bonds for new bonds by providing that those who did not so vote would have their bonds cancelled for nominal consideration. The decision was to have been appealed but the insolvency of the issuer resulted in the litigation being abandoned and so the issue did not progress to the appellate level.

the payment was available to all members of the class, conditional only on their doing that which was within their power, namely exercising their right to vote in a particular way. In so concluding, the court cited with approval[70] from Viscount Haldane in *British America Nickel Corpn Ltd v O'Brien*[71] that the position is that 'while usually a holder of shares or debentures may vote as his interest directs, he is subject to the further principle that where his vote is conferred on him as a member of a class he must conform to the interest of the class itself when seeking to exercise the power conferred on him in his capacity of being a member. The second principle is a negative one, one which puts a restriction on the completeness of freedom under the first, without excluding such freedom wholly.' The only issue beyond those principles, the court said in *Azevedo*, is whether the company is able to strengthen its encouragement in favour of a vote by offering an incentive and the Court of Appeal could find no objection to that in principle under English law, so long as all is open and above board.[72] On this basis, similar incentives can presumably be offered with respect to securing a variation or abrogation of class rights more generally, provided all is disclosed and the incentive is available to all. But it remains the position that the dicta of Viscount Haldane, noted above and cited approvingly in the Court of Appeal, must be observed so that the test remains the interests of the class, which would rule out, it would seem, an unfair or oppressive resolution, even if supported by incentives openly available to all who voted for it.

**16-41** Where a class has consented to a variation, the holders of not less in total than 15 per cent of the issued shares of that class, provided that they did not consent to or vote for the variation, may apply to the court within 21 days to have the variation cancelled,[73] in which case the variation does not take effect until it has been confirmed by the court (CA 2006, s 633(2)–(4)). If the court is satisfied that the variation would unfairly prejudice the shareholders of the class represented by the applicant, it may disallow the variation; otherwise, it must confirm it and the court's decision is final (s 633(5)). In practice, this provision is rarely used, not least because it is unlikely that a court will overturn a variation which has been agreed to by three-quarters of the class.

### Judicial interpretation of 'variation or abrogation'

**16-42** The restrictions on variation or abrogation in CA 2006, s 630 only apply if what has occurred amounts to a variation or abrogation of the rights attached to a class (CA 2006, s 630(1), (6)) and the courts have restricted the protection afforded by the statute by interpreting 'variation' and 'abrogation' restrictively.

**16-43** In approaching the question of whether a variation or abrogation has occurred, the courts have drawn a distinction between matters affecting the rights attached to each share and matters affecting the enjoyment of those rights. Only variations or abrogations affecting the rights attached to a class of shares attract the protection of CA 2006, s 630(2). Where only the enjoyment of the right is affected, the shares may be commercially less valuable but their rights remain what they always were and the shareholders cannot demand the protection of the section.[74]

---

[70] [2014] 1 BCLC 72 at [59].     [71] [1927] AC 369 at 373–4.     [72] [2014] 1 BCLC 72 at [69].

[73] See discussion at **16-4** with respect to *Eckerle v Wickeder* [2013] 3 WLR 1316 which would be equally relevant here.

[74] The Company Law Review considered the provision of a specific remedy for shareholders in this situation but concluded that if shareholders in a class wish protection for their broader economic interests (as well as their rights) then they should contract for that protection: Company Law Review, *Completing the Structure* (2000), URN 00/1335, para 5.81, and see discussion at **16-54** of contractual protection for class interests.

**16-44**  A typical case is *White v Bristol Aeroplane Co Ltd*[75] where an issue of preference shares which would dilute the control of the existing preference shareholders was held not to be a variation. The new shares were to be issued to the existing ordinary shareholders and paid for out of the company's reserves. The company's articles provided that all or any of the rights or privileges attached to any class of shares might be affected, modified, varied, dealt with, or abrogated in any manner with the sanction of an extraordinary resolution passed at a separate meeting of the members of that class. It was argued by the plaintiff preference shareholder that the word 'affect' was wide and must be taken to cover a transaction which, though not necessarily modifying or varying rights, would in some way otherwise affect them. On this basis, it was argued, the proposed allotment was a variation requiring the consent of the existing preference shareholders.

**16-45**  The Court of Appeal disagreed. Evershed MR concluded that the new issue did not affect the rights or privileges of the existing preference shareholders which remained exactly as they were before. The preference shareholders might be affected as a matter of business by reason of the new preference shares which would be in the possession of the ordinary shareholders and which would have a majority over the existing preference shares. This outcome would only affect the enjoyment of the rights, however, and not the rights themselves and so the consent of the existing preference shareholders was not required. Romer LJ drew a distinction between rights on the one hand and the result of exercising the rights on the other hand. He noted:[76]

> 'The rights, as such, are conferred by resolution or by the articles, and they cannot be affected except with the sanction of the members on whom those rights are conferred; but the results of exercising those rights are not the subject of any assurance or guarantee under the constitution of the company, and are not protected in any way.'

**16-46**  Similarly, in *Greenhalgh v Arderne Cinemas Ltd*[77] a sub-division of a class of 10 shilling ordinary shares into two shilling shares was held not to vary the rights of Mr Greenhalgh, a holder of the existing two shilling ordinary shares, although the result of the sub-division was to alter control of the company. The court accepted that the effect was to alter his position as a matter of business but, as a matter of law, his rights were quite unaltered.[78]

### Reduction of capital and variation of class rights

**16-47**  Schemes for the reduction of capital (see **22-60** et seq) may involve paying off preference shareholders who are often reluctant to be 'expelled' from the company in this way, particularly when it means an end to high dividend returns which are no longer available in the market. The issue for the court is whether such a reduction of capital amounts to a variation or abrogation of the class rights of the preference shareholder so requiring the consent of the class.

**16-48**  The approach of the courts is to look at what the class rights would be in a winding up and to compare that position with the position which would arise under the proposed reduction. If what is proposed on reduction is in accordance with the class rights on a winding up, there is no variation requiring the consent of the class.[79]

**16-49**  For example, if the reduction is because capital has been lost or is unrepresented by available assets and the classes rank *pari passu* (equally), then *prima facie* the loss should be

---

[75] [1953] Ch 65, CA. See also *Re John Smith's Tadcaster Brewery Co Ltd* [1953] 1 All ER 518.
[76] [1953] Ch 65 at 82, CA.     [77] [1946] 1 All ER 512, CA.     [78] [1946] 1 All ER 512 at 518, CA.
[79] *Re Saltdean Estate Co Ltd* [1968] 3 All ER 829; *House of Fraser v ACGE Investments Ltd* [1987] AC 387, HL.

borne equally;[80] but if there are preference shares which have priority as to a return of capital on a winding up, the ordinary shares must bear the loss as they would do if the company was being wound up.[81] Alternatively, if the reduction of capital involves the return of surplus capital, that return will normally be to the preference shareholders who will usually have priority as to repayment of capital in a winding up.[82]

**16-50**  These issues were considered in *House of Fraser plc v ACGE Investments Ltd*[83] where the ordinary shareholders passed a special resolution approving the paying off of the whole of the preference share capital of the company as being in excess of the wants of the company. No class meeting of the preference shareholders was held to approve the reduction. The company's articles provided that the special rights attached to any class of shares could only be modified, commuted, affected, or dealt with, with the consent of the holders of the class of shares. The preference shareholders argued that the failure to obtain their consent meant that the court could not confirm the reduction of capital.

**16-51**  The House of Lords accepted that this issue was definitively addressed by Buckley J in *Re Saltdean Estate Co Ltd*,[84] a case on almost identical facts. In a much cited judgment Buckley J confirmed the long-established position that, where capital is to be repaid, that class of capital should first be repaid which would be returned first in a winding up of the company.[85] If the preference shareholders are entitled to prior repayment of capital in a winding up, the first class of capital to be repaid should *prima facie* be the preferred shares. Such a proposed cancellation is not an abrogation of the rights attached to those shares when it is in accordance with the right and liability to prior repayment of capital attached to their shares. The liability to prior repayment on a reduction of capital, corresponding to their right to prior return of capital in a winding up, forms an integral part of the definition or delimitation of the bundle of rights which make up the preferred share. Giving effect to it does not involve the variation or abrogation of any rights attached to such shares. Buckley J concluded that this vulnerability to prior repayment in this way is, and has always been, a characteristic of preferred shares.[86]

**16-52**  Applying that approach in *House of Fraser plc v ACGE Investments Ltd*,[87] the House of Lords found that the proposed reduction of capital involved the extinction of the preference shares in strict accordance with the contract embodied in the articles of association to which the preference shareholders were party. The preference shareholders had a right to a return of capital in priority to other shareholders and that right was not affected, modified, dealt with, or abrogated, but was given effect to by the proposed reduction with the result that the consent of the preference shareholders was not required.[88]

**16-53**  This is the position in any instance where the preference shareholders have priority as to a return of capital, even if they also have further rights of participation as regards

---

[80] See *Bannatyne v Direct Spanish Telegraph Co* (1886) 34 Ch D 287, CA where the preference shareholders had no preference as to capital, but only as to dividend.

[81] *Re Floating Dock Company of St Thomas Ltd* [1895] 1 Ch 691.

[82] *Re Chatterley-Whitfield Collieries Ltd* [1948] 2 All ER 593, aff'd sub nom *Prudential Assurance Co Ltd v Chatterley-Whitfield Collieries Ltd* [1949] 1 All ER 1094, HL; *Scottish Insurance Co Ltd v Wilsons & Clyde Coal Co Ltd* 1948 SC 360, aff'd [1949] 1 All ER 1068, HL; *Re Fowlers Vacola Manufacturing Co Ltd* [1966] VR 97; *Re Saltdean Estate Co Ltd* [1968] 3 All ER 829; *House of Fraser v ACGE Investments Ltd* [1987] AC 387, HL.

[83] [1987] AC 387, HL.     [84] [1968] 3 All ER 829.     [85] See esp [1968] 3 All ER 829 at 831–2.

[86] [1968] 3 All ER 829 at 833–4. See also *Bannatyne v Direct Spanish Telegraph Co* (1886) 34 Ch D 287, CA; *Scottish Insurance Co Ltd v Wilsons & Clyde Coal Co Ltd* 1948 SC 360, aff'd [1949] 1 All ER 1068 at 1077–8, per Lord Simonds, HL.     [87] [1987] AC 387, HL.

[88] [1987] AC 387 at 393.

dividend.[89] It is not clear whether preference shares which are participating as to surplus on a winding up could be dealt with in this way although *Re William Jones & Sons Ltd*[90] suggests that they can.

### Deemed variations or abrogations—a contractual solution

**16-54**  The decisions in cases such as *White v Bristol Aeroplane Co Ltd*,[91] *Greenhalgh v Arderne Cinemas Ltd*,[92] and *House of Fraser plc v ACGE Investments Ltd*[93] highlight the limits to the protection which can be conferred by class rights when it is left to the courts to determine whether a variation or abrogation has occurred.

**16-55**  A class of shareholders can avoid the risk of a restrictive interpretation by the courts of what constitutes a variation of their class rights by identifying in the terms of issue matters (such as a reduction or an increase in capital) which are deemed to be a variation or abrogation of the rights attached to that class and so will require the consent of the class. In that way, the scope for judicial determination of whether a variation or abrogation has occurred is reduced.

**16-56**  The courts will give effect to such provisions and will interpret them in the light of their protective purpose. In *Re Northern Engineering Industries plc*[94] the articles stated that the rights of any class were to be deemed to be varied by the reduction of the capital paid up on those shares. The company proposed to reduce its capital by paying off its preference shares and cancelling them without obtaining the consent of the class. The company argued that the provision in the articles only applied to a 'reduction', i.e. something which involved a diminution or lessening from one number to a smaller number. It did not apply to a reduction to zero.

**16-57**  The Court of Appeal rejected this argument finding that the provision in the articles must be construed in the light of its purpose, namely the protection of the shareholders of the class affected. It applied both where there was a piecemeal reduction of capital and where there was complete repayment of their investment. A reduction of capital without the consent of the class affected could not be confirmed.

**16-58**  Given that reductions of capital by private companies need not require court confirmation where the directors are willing to make a solvency statement (see CA 2006, s 641(1) and discussion at **22-69**), those investing in a class of shares should take care to: (a) specify the rights attached to the class, (b) provide a mechanism for the variation of those rights in the articles, and (c) identify matters of concern which are to be deemed to be variations so triggering that variation mechanism.

## D  Share transfer and transmission

### Introduction

**16-59**  Shares are personal property (CA 2006, s 541) and are transferable in the manner provided by the company's articles (s 544(1)), subject to the Stock Transfer Act 1963 which overrides any requirements in the articles to allow fully-paid shares to be transferred by

---

[89]  *Re Saltdean Estate Co Ltd* [1968] 3 All ER 829.

[90]  [1969] 1 All ER 913. In that instance, however, the preference shareholders raised no objection to being paid off, probably because they were to be paid off in full although the shares stood at less than par. Moreover, there was no present prospect of the company being wound up so the enjoyment of any surplus on a winding up would not occur for many years.  [91]  [1953] Ch 65, CA.

[92]  [1946] 1 All ER 512, CA.  [93]  [1987] AC 387, HL.  [94]  [1994] 2 BCLC 704.

a simplified process and to regulations[95] which allow for the electronic transfer of shares (CA 2006, s 544(2)).

**16-60**	A company may not register a transfer of shares unless a proper instrument of transfer has been delivered to the company (s 770(1)). A proper instrument of transfer for these purposes is an instrument appropriate or suitable for stamp duty purposes[96] and this restriction is imposed to facilitate the raising of taxation. The requirement as to a proper instrument of transfer is subject to exceptions where the transfer is an exempt transfer within the Stock Transfer Act 1982 or is in accordance with regulations dealing with uncertificated securities (CA 2006, s 770(1)).

## A *prima facie* right to transfer shares

**16-61**	A shareholder has a *prima facie* right to transfer his shares and directors have no discretionary powers, independent of any powers given to them by the articles, to refuse to register a transfer.[97] Any restriction of this right to transfer must be clearly stated in the articles and the right to transfer is not to be cut down by uncertain language or doubtful implications.[98] If restrictions on transfer are laid down by the articles, they must be complied with. The directors have no power to authorise registration in circumstances where there has been a breach of the articles and any purported transfer in breach of the articles is defeasible at the suit of a member.[99] Following a breach of pre-emption provisions in the articles which provided that no share or any interest in a share could be transferred, sold, or otherwise disposed of other than as provided by the pre-emption provisions, the transaction as between the transferor and transferee is null and void and wholly ineffective, but if entry on the register of members is secured, the transferee enjoys all of the rights of a member unless and until the register is rectified by the removal of his name.[100]

### Restrictions on the transfer of shares

**16-62**	In practice, it is customary for the articles of a private company (and private companies make up 99.8 per cent of the register of companies) to impose restrictions on the transfer of shares.[101] These restrictions are usually justified on the basis that many such companies are small family concerns or quasi-partnership-type ventures where it is important to the existing members to retain control over the membership of the company. It is unusual for

[95] See The Uncertificated Securities Regulations 2001, SI 2001/3755, as amended by Companies Act 2006 (Consequential Amendments) (Uncertificated Securities) Order 2009, SI 2009/1889; also *Mills v Sportsdirect.com* [2010] 2 BCLC 143 at 147.		[96] *Nisbet v Shepherd* [1994] 1 BCLC 300.
[97] *Re Smith, Knight & Co, Weston's Case* (1868) 4 Ch App 20.
[98] *Re Smith & Fawcett Ltd* [1942] 1 All ER 542; *Stothers v William Steward (Holdings) Ltd* [1994] 2 BCLC 266, CA. See also *BWE International Ltd v Jones* [2004] 1 BCLC 406 at [24]. See *Re Coroin Ltd, McKillen v Misland (Cyprus) Investments Ltd* [2011] EWHC 3466 at [73] where David Richards J would distinguish between provisions in the articles and in shareholder agreements with the language of the former being more strictly construed than the latter.
[99] *Hurst v Crampton Bros* [2003] 1 BCLC 304; *Tett v Phoenix Property and Investment Co Ltd* [1986] BCLC 149, CA. See also *Curtis v J J Curtis & Co* [1986] BCLC 86, NZCA.
[100] *Re Coroin Ltd (No 2), McKillen v Misland (Cyprus) Investments Ltd* [2013] 2 BCLC 583, Ch D, 744, CA, at [89]–[91], per Arden LJ; at [142]–[143], per Moore-Bick LJ and at [163]–[165], per Rimer LJ, each citing *Hunter (Emily) v T H V Hunter*, CA, unreported 19 April 1934. Arden LJ makes the point, at [88], that it was an incident of any interest in a share in the company that it could not be transferred except in accordance with the provisions on transfer in the articles.
[101] Until 1980 it was mandatory for private companies to include a restriction on the transfer of their shares in the articles: see CA 1948, s 28 repealed by CA 1980, Sch 4.

public companies to impose any restrictions on transfer and shares in listed public companies must be freely transferable.[102] A provision commonly included in the articles is one to the effect that the directors may, in their absolute discretion and without assigning any reason therefore, decline to register any transfer of any share, whether or not it is a fully-paid share.[103] The CA 2006 modified that type of provision by requiring the company to give reasons for a refusal to register a transfer (s 771(1)), though this does not affect the right to refuse.

**16-63**   In addition to a discretion conferred on directors to refuse to register transfers, pre-emption provisions are commonly included to ensure that existing members have the opportunity to buy any shares that may be for sale before they are offered outside the company. For example, a member wishing to sell is often permitted to transfer his shares to an existing member without restriction, but where he seeks to transfer to an outsider, a pre-emption provision comes into effect. This provision normally requires the intending transferor[104] to give notice to the company secretary or other nominated person who must notify the other members that there are shares available for purchase.[105] If the other members make an offer for the shares, the transferor may accept or reject their offer but, if he rejects it, he is precluded normally from proceeding with the transfer of the shares to an outsider. If the shares are not taken up by the other shareholders, the transferor is usually entitled at that stage to offer his shares to an outside purchaser, subject to the proviso that the directors may refuse to register a transfer in such circumstances.[106] Disputes as to whether these types of provisions have been triggered are common and much litigation is devoted to construing what are often quite intricate clauses.[107] For example, where a company had drawn up a detailed, lengthy, complex, pre-emption provision addressing

---

[102]  See Listing Rules LR 2.2.4R, subject to limited exceptions which are irrelevant for our purposes.

[103]  This provision was contained in the 1948 Table A, see CA 1948, Sch 1, Table A, Pt II, reg 3.

[104]  Disputes as to whether these types of provisions have been triggered are common and arise in a variety of situations depending on the wording of the articles, see *Lyle & Scott Ltd v Scott's Trustees* [1959] 2 All ER 661; *Safeguard Industrial Investments Ltd v National Westminster Bank Ltd* [1982] 1 All ER 449; *Theakston v London Trust plc* [1984] BCLC 390; *Re Sedgefield Steeplechase Co (1927) Ltd, Scotto v Petch* [2000] 2 BCLC 211, Ch D, aff'd [2001] BCC 889, CA; *Hurst v Crampton* [2003] 1 BCLC 304; *Re Coroin Ltd, McKillen v Misland (Cyprus) Investments Ltd* [2012] EWCA Civ 179, [2013] 2 BCLC 611.

[105]  Notice to the members of a pre-emption right having been triggered amounts to an option conferred on the other members to purchase the shares at the price determined by the articles—that option creates an equitable interest which prevails over the interest of a donee of the shares incorrectly registered as the holder of the shares: *Cottrell v King* [2004] 2 BCLC 413; *Tett v Phoenix Property and Investment Co Ltd* [1984] BCLC 599 at 619, rev'd on other grounds [1986] BCLC 149.

[106]  These pre-emption provisions tend to be lengthy and complex and the courts sometimes have to interpret them purposefully to give them business efficacy: see *Pennington v Crampton* [2004] BCC 611; *Tett v Phoenix Property and Investment Co Ltd* [1986] BCLC 149, CA. See also *Blindley Heath Investments Ltd v Bass* [2017] 3 WLR 166—all concerned had forgotten that the shareholders had entered into a prior shareholders' agreement containing pre-emption rights requiring first offers to existing shareholders. The shareholders purported to sell their shares to an outsider in breach of the pre-emption requirement and the directors then refused to register the transfers. The Court of Appeal upheld the first instance ruling that an estoppel by convention applied and the parties had conducted themselves on the basis of a common assumption that there were no valid rights of pre-emption. It would be unconscionable to allow the directors to go back on that assumption.

[107]  See *Lyle & Scott Ltd v Scott's Trustees* [1959] 2 All ER 661; *Safeguard Industrial Investments Ltd v National Westminster Bank Ltd* [1982] 1 All ER 449; *Theakston v London Trust plc* [1984] BCLC 390; *Re Sedgefield Steeplechase Co (1927) Ltd, Scotto v Petch* [2000] 2 BCLC 211, Ch D, aff'd [2001] BCC 889, CA; *Hurst v Crampton* [2003] 1 BCLC 304; *Re Coroin Ltd, McKillen v Misland (Cyprus) Investments Ltd* [2012] EWCA Civ 179, [2013] 2 BCLC 611.

a wide variety of circumstances in which pre-emption rights were triggered, the absence of an express term applying the pre-emption provisions to a disposal of the shares in a corporate shareholder told against a construction of the provision as extending to such a disposal.[108] Where a provision is aimed at preventing transfers of legal title to shares, it does not extend to arrangements which change the control of those shares without any transfer of legal title.[109]

### Absolute discretion to refuse registration

**16-64** With regard to an absolute discretion, as noted, a common provision is one which states that the directors may, in their absolute discretion, decline to register any transfer of any share. The leading authority is *Re Smith & Fawcett Ltd*[110] where the Court of Appeal accepted that where the articles contain a provision such as this, drafted in the widest possible terms, there is no limitation on the exercise by directors of that power other than the standard requirement that, as a fiduciary power, it must be exercised bona fide in what the directors consider—and not what a court may consider—to be in the interests of the company, and not for any collateral purpose.[111] In reaching their decision, the directors are *prima facie* presumed to have acted in good faith and the onus of proof is on those challenging their decision.[112] Now the limitation on their powers would be expressed in terms of the directors' duty in CA 2006, s 171 to exercise their powers for the purpose for which they are conferred which, given it is an absolute power, means (applying s 172) it must be exercised in the way the directors consider most likely to promote the success of the company having regard, in this instance, to the need to act fairly as between members of the company (s 172(1)(f)). Given the judicial acknowledgement of the importance of these provisions in private companies, as exemplified by the Court of Appeal in *Re Smith & Fawcett*,[113] the courts are likely to be still quite generous in the amount of leeway which they give directors exercising an absolute power of this nature, in the absence of evidence of bad faith.

**16-65** Some constraint is imposed on the directors now by the obligation to give reasons for a refusal to register a transfer (CA 2006, s 771(1)),[114] which offers some scope for discovering the basis for the directors' decision and therefore, potentially, some basis for challenging a refusal. The transferee can ask for further information as to the reasons for the refusal though the company is not required to hand over board minutes (s 772(1)(b)).

### A limited power to refuse registration

**16-66** The directors' power to refuse to register may be a more limited power and such provisions vary greatly from company to company. For example, the articles may provide that the directors may refuse to register any transfer: (1) where the company has a lien on the

---

[108] *Re Coroin No 1 Ltd* [2011] EWHC 3466 at [102], per David Richards J. The absence of such a provision was striking, the court thought, because change of control provisions are a familiar feature of a joint venture or other commercial agreement, at [104], aff'd [2012] 2 BCLC 611, CA.

[109] *Re Coroin Ltd (No 2), McKillen v Misland (Cyprus) Investments Ltd* [2013] 2 BCLC 583, Ch D, 744, CA.

[110] [1942] 1 All ER 542.

[111] [1942] 1 All ER 542 at 543. See *Re Bell Brothers, ex p Hodgson* (1891) 7 TLR 689; *Re Coalport China Co* [1895] 2 Ch 404; also *Popely v Planarrive Ltd* [1997] 1 BCLC 8.

[112] See *Village Cay Marina Ltd v Acland* [1998] 2 BCLC 327 at 335–6, PC, per Lord Hoffmann, citing *Charles Forte Investments Ltd v Amanda* [1963] 2 All ER 940; see also *Re Coalport China Co* [1895] 2 Ch 404; *Popely v Planarrive Ltd* [1997] 1 BCLC 8 at 16.    [113] [1942] 1 All ER 542.

[114] Reversing the long-standing common law position that the directors could not be required to give reasons: *Re Gresham Life Assurance Society, ex p Penney* (1872) 8 Ch App 446.

shares; (2) where it is not proved to their satisfaction that the proposed transferee is a responsible person; (3) where the directors are of the opinion that the proposed transferee is not a desirable person to admit to membership.[115]

**16-67**  In *Re Bede Steam Shipping Co*[116] the articles provided that the directors might decline to register a transfer of any shares if, in their opinion, it was contrary to the interests of the company that the proposed transferee should be a member thereof. The directors admitted that no inquiry had been made as to the fitness of the transferees. The transfers in question had been rejected because a majority of the board objected to the transferor disposing of single shares or small lots of shares to individuals with a view to increasing the number of shareholders who would support him. The Court of Appeal found that the articles required the directors to focus on the qualities of the transferee and identify reasons why he was unsuitable.[117] The particular objections which the directors had focused on were more concerned with the motives and attitudes of the transferor. These were not grounds provided for by the articles and so the transferees were entitled to be registered.

### Time-limits

**16-68**  Registration may be secured as a result of the failure of the directors to exercise their discretion to refuse registration within the requisite time period. The directors must register the transfer or decide to refuse and notify the transferee of the refusal and give reasons for the refusal as soon as practicable and, in any event, within two months of the transfer being lodged with the company (CA 2006, s 771(1)). Once the two-month period has elapsed, the directors are no longer able to exercise their discretion[118] and an application may be made under s 125 (or s 128G, as the case may be) to have the register rectified by the inclusion of the name of the transferee.

### Position as between the vendor and purchaser when registration refused

**16-69**  Where the directors have correctly exercised their discretion so making the decision to refuse registration unimpeachable, the vendor and the purchaser of the shares are left in the position that they cannot now complete the transaction by having the purchaser registered. The position on a valid sale of shares is that the equitable title to the shares passes to the purchaser once the contract is made (assuming the contract is specifically enforceable— if not, no equitable title passes), and the legal title passes on completion and registration by

---

[115]  See *Re Coalport China Co* [1895] 2 Ch 404. Other examples can be found in *Re Gresham Life Assurance Society, ex p Penney* (1872) 8 Ch App 446; *Berry and Stewart v Tottenham Hotspur Football & Athletic Co* [1935] Ch 718.

[116]  [1917] 1 Ch 123. See also *Re Bell Brothers, ex p Hodgson* (1891) 7 TLR 689; *Re The Ceylon Land & Produce Co, ex p Anderson* (1891) 7 TLR 692.

[117]  See also *Holman v Adams Securities Ltd* [2010] EWHC 2421, where the court refused to strike out a petition alleging unfairly prejudicial conduct (see CA 2006, s 994) where central to the dispute was the operation of a provision in the articles allowing the directors to refuse to register any transfer of any shares to any person whom they considered to be undesirable. The court noted that it was at least arguable that the blanket operation of such a policy without consideration by the directors of the merits of each individual application for transfer could be unfairly prejudicial, particularly against the background of use of the provision to persuade minority shareholders to sell their shares to the company and the non-exercise of the policy when it came to the transfer of the majority shareholders' shares to a new holding company.

[118]  This outcome is not required by CA 2006, s 771 which simply imposes a fine for default (s 771(3)) but it was accepted in *Re Swaledale Cleaners Ltd* [1968] 3 All ER 619 that this can be the only consequence of requiring the power to be exercised within two months; also *Re Inverdeck Ltd* [1998] 2 BCLC 242. Where the directors decide to refuse to register a transfer within the time-frame, but fail to notify the transferee of the refusal, the failure to notify (while it attracts a fine) does not nullify the decision: *Popely v Planarrive Ltd* [1997] 1 BCLC 8.

the company.[119] The vendor provides the purchaser with a duly signed transfer form and the share certificates for submission to the company for registration. Unless the contract so provides, the vendor does not promise to secure registration and, if the directors do refuse to register the transfer, the vendor is not liable in damages for breach although he will hold the shares as bare trustee for the purchaser.[120] Where the parties are agreeable to such an outcome, they can negate the effect of the directors' refusal to register.

**16-70**  An imperfect gift of shares will take effect in equity if the donor has done everything necessary to enable the donee to enforce a beneficial claim to the shares without further assistance from the donor[121] (typically the donor will have delivered the share transfer form and the relevant certificates to the donee, but no registration has taken place). In those circumstances, the donor remains the legal owner, but having done all in his own power to transfer the shares, beneficial ownership will pass to the donee pending registration as the legal owner. In *Curtis v Pulbrook*[122] an attempt by a donor to gift part of his shareholding in a family company to his wife and daughter failed when he merely delivered new share certificates to them (he was one of the directors of the company) without executing any share transfer forms and without delivering his own share certificates from which their interest was to be carved.[123] A gift also failed in *Kaye v Zeital*[124] where the donor merely gave a blank transfer form (undated and unsigned) to the donee without any share certificate. In neither case had the donor done all in his power to procure the transfer of the shares to the donee so the gifts failed as imperfect gifts. Sometimes, in these cases, it is possible to construe the situation as giving rise to a trust because of some detrimental reliance by the donee upon the imperfect gift in such a way as to bind the conscience of the donor[125] or to find that a shareholder has made an effective declaration of trust in favour of another. For example, where a shareholder signed a letter indicating that he was holding certain shares for another and delivered the letter together with a signed blank share transfer form to that other, though no share certificates were delivered, the court held it was an effective declaration of trust in favour of that other.[126]

## Transmission of shares

**16-71**  Transmission arises by operation of law on the death or bankruptcy of a member. On the death of a shareholder, the shares are transmitted to his personal representative and the

---

[119]  *Sociéé Générale de Paris v Walker* (1885) LR 11 App Cas 20; see also *Roots v Williamson* (1888) 38 Ch D 485; *Ireland v Hart* [1902] 1 Ch 522. See Lewison J in *Mills v Sportsdirect.com Retail Ltd* [2010] 2 BCLC 143 at [74]–[76], [86]–[89]. Likewise, where a shareholder mortgages their shares and a power of sale arises which is exercised by the mortgagee, the purchaser acquires only the beneficial interest in the shares and the registered shareholder retains the legal title until the register of members is rectified, see *Archer v Fabian Investments Ltd* [2017] UKPC 9, [2017] BCC 367 at [22].

[120]  *Re Rose, Rose v IRC* [1952] 1 All ER 1217. As to the position of the vendor under an uncompleted contract for the sale of shares, see *Musselwhite v Musselwhite & Son Ltd* [1962] 1 All ER 201; *JRRT (Investments) Ltd v Haycraft* [1993] BCLC 401; *Michaels v Harley House (Marylebone) Ltd* [1999] 1 BCLC 670, CA.

[121]  *Re Rose* [1949] Ch 78; *Re Rose, Rose v IRC* [1952] 1 All ER 1217. See Luxton [2012] Conv 70 at 75: intention, even a fervent desire, is not sufficient, the donor must have done everything necessary.

[122]  [2011] 1 BCLC 638, see Luxton [2012] Conv 70.

[123]  See [2011] 1 BCLC 638 at [45]; and see the critical comments by Briggs J about the lack of any identifiable or rational policy objective in the rules governing the circumstances when equity will and will not perfect an imperfect gift of shares, at [47].                    [124]  See [2010] 2 BCLC 1 at [43].

[125]  See *Pennington v Waine* [2002] 2 BCLC 448 (gift effective, though no delivery of a stock transfer form, nor of the share certificates, the court thought nothing turned on the absence of share certificates since throughout they had been held by the company and therefore could not be delivered by the donor).

[126]  See *Shah v Shah* [2010] EWCA Civ 1408.

production of the grant of probate of the will, or letters of administration of the estate, or confirmation as executor of a deceased person must be accepted by the company as sufficient evidence of the grant (CA 2006, s 774).

**16-72** The position on transmission is generally governed by the articles and the model articles provide that a person becoming entitled to a share in consequence of death or bankruptcy may choose either to become a holder of the share or to have someone else registered as the transferee.[127] Usually, the election by the personal representative or trustee in bankruptcy to be registered or to have someone else registered has the effect of triggering any pre-emption provisions which may exist and will be subject to any discretion vested in the directors to refuse to register any transfer.[128]

## E The register of members

### Status and contents of the register of members

**16-73** Every company must maintain a register of members (CA 2006, s 113) unless it is a private company which elects to keep the relevant information on the register kept by the registrar instead of entering it in the company register of members (s 128A), in which case it is described as the central register.[129] Entry on the register (whether maintained by the company or by the registrar) is essential to membership in all cases save that of subscribers to the memorandum (ss 112, 112A), as noted at **16-1**.[130]

**16-74** A company registered in England and Wales is not concerned with trusts over its shares and no notice of any trust, expressed, implied, or constructive, is to be entered on the register or be receivable by the registrar.[131] However, while the company is entitled and obliged to deal only with the registered owner, in the context of CA 2006, Pt 22 provisions (and equivalent provisions in the company's articles) which are specifically designed to enable public companies to discover the identity of the beneficial owners of their shares, the courts will recognise the standing of those beneficial owners to challenge the exercise of directors' powers under these provisions, as the Court of Appeal ruled in *JKX Oil & Gas plc v Eclairs Group Ltd*[132] The court considered this wider standing was appropriate given that the exercise of these powers (which can disenfranchise the registered shareholder)

---

[127] See The Companies (Model Articles) Regulations 2008, SI 2008/3229, reg 2, Sch 1, art 27(2) (Ltd), reg 4, Sch 3, art 66(2) (Plc). An instrument of transfer of a share of a deceased member may be made by his personal representative (though not himself a member) and is as effective as if he had been a member at the time of execution of the instrument: CA 2006, s 773. See also *Scott v Frank F Scott (London) Ltd* [1940] Ch 794.

[128] See, for example, the provisions at issue in *Re Benfield Greig Group plc, Nugent v Benfield Greig Group plc* [2000] 2 BCLC 488 at 497 and *Dashfield v Davidson* [2009] 1 BCLC 220 at [8]; and see comments of Lewison J at [53] as to the mandatory nature of the obligations in that case and at [54] on the benefits of having these provisions in a private company.

[129] CA 2006, s 128A(2) inserted by s 94 and Sch 5, para 3, Small Business, Enterprise and Employment Act 2015.

[130] If the company holds shares as treasury shares (see **22-41**), the company must be entered in the register as the member holding those shares: CA 2006, s 124(2).

[131] CA 2006, s 126; *Société Générale de Paris v Walker* (1885) 11 App Cas 20. Nothing in CA 2006, s 126 affects what may be entered in a company's PSC register, see **16-92**, or receivable by the registrar in relation to people with significant control over a company (even if they are members of the company): s 790M(11)(b). The difficulties which can arise from a failure to recognise beneficial owners, given the prevalence of shareholding via intermediaries, can be seen in *Eckerle v Wickeder Westfalenstahl GmbH* [2013] 3 WLR 1316, see **16-4**.                                                                   [132] [2014] 2 BCLC 164.

by the company's directors (without having to go to court) has important economic consequences for the wide class of those with interests in the shares. In those circumstances, where a genuine dispute arises as to the validity or regularity of steps taken under the CA 2006, Pt 22 regime, or the regime under the articles, the law ought to afford the widest scope for persons economically affected by the taking of those steps to challenge them in court.[133]

**16-75** The register of members maintained by the company is *prima facie*, but not conclusive,[134] evidence of any matters directed or authorised by the Companies Act to be inserted in it (s 127); and where the register is maintained by the registrar, the central register is *prima facie* evidence of any matters about which a company is required to deliver information to the registrar under Part 8, Ch 2A.[135]

**16-76** The register must include details of the names and addresses (which need not be residential addresses) of the members of the company (s 113(2)). The register of members must disclose the date of entry on the register as a member and the date of ceasing to be a member (s 113(2)), dates which affect voting and dividend rights and the right to participate in corporate actions such as a rights issue. If the number of members of a limited company falls to one or increases from one to two or more members, the register of members must include a statement that the company has only one member, or has ceased to have only one member, as the case may be, and must give the dates of these occurrences (s 123).

**16-77** Where the company has elected to provide information to the registrar for a central register, it must deliver a statement of the information contained in its current register (s 128B(5)(b)) and thereafter it must retain its historic register, though it need not update it (s 128D(3)). No doubt there will be plenty of scope for the register retained and the central register not to match, but as already noted, once the company elects for a central register, it is the central register which is *prima facie* evidence as noted at **16-75**. During the period when the election is in force, the company is obliged to deliver to the registrar any relevant information that the company would during that period have been obliged to enter in its register of members (were it not for the election) and it must do so as soon as reasonably practicable after the company becomes aware of the information and, in any event, no later than the time by which the company would have been required to enter the information (see **16-68**) in its register of members (s 128D(2), (4)). There is a criminal sanction for non-compliance (s 128D(6)), but as with so many other criminal sanctions in the Act, it is difficult to envisage many or even any prosecutions for non-compliance.

**16-78** The register of members if maintained by the company must be available for inspection at the registered office or other place specified by the regulations[136] and the registrar of companies must be notified of that place (s 114). Larger public companies do not maintain their own registers, but use professional registrar services instead, hence the need to permit the register to be inspected other than at the registered office. In an age of computerised records, the physical location of the register becomes less important, provided it is not outside the country of registration.

---

[133] [2014] 2 BCLC 164 at [37].

[134] See *Reese River Silver Mining Co v Smith* (1869) LR 4 HL 64 at 80, per Lord Cairns; also *Re Briton Medical and General Life Association* (1888) 39 Ch D 61 at 72, per Stirling J.

[135] CA 2006, s 128H(1), other than with respect to information to be included in a statement under s 128B(5)(b) (which is the statement of the current register which is delivered to the registrar when the company elects to use the public register) and any necessary updating of that statement under s 128B(6): s 128H(2).        [136] See CA 2006, s 1136 and see SI 2008/3006.

## Inspection of the register

**16-79** The register of members is open to inspection and any person seeking to exercise the right either to inspect the register or to obtain a copy thereof or a copy of any part of the register must make a request to the company to that effect (CA 2006, s 116(3)). There are detailed requirements, discussed below, with respect to the request which the company can refuse only if it obtains a court order (a no-access order). Where a private company chooses to maintain its register with the registrar, as it is a public register,[137] the company gives up the ability to block requests in this way, which for some companies would be a reason not to elect for a central register. Where the company maintains its own register, a request for access must:

(1) identify the name and address of the individual making the request or the name and address of the individual responsible for making a request on behalf of an organisation (s 116(4)(a) and (b));

(2) specify the purpose for which the information is to be used (s 116(4)(c));

(3) indicate whether the information is to be disclosed to any other person; if so, full details must be given of that other person and the purpose for which the information is to be used by that person (s 116(4)(d)).[138]

In *Fox-Davies v Burberry plc*,[139] see at **16-82**, the Court of Appeal held that these requirements in s 116(4) are mandatory such that a company is not obliged to comply with a request that does not contain the necessary information while allowing that substantial compliance with s 116(4)(d) might suffice in an appropriate case. On the facts in this case, there was a wholesale non-compliance with sub-section (4)(d) which justified the company in not complying with the request.

**16-80** It is an offence for a person knowingly or recklessly in making a request to include a statement which is misleading, false, or deceptive in a material particular (s 119(1)). It is also an offence for a person in possession of information following a request to inspect the register to disclose the information obtained to another person knowing or having reason to suspect that that person may use the information for a purpose which is not a proper purpose (s 119(2)).

**16-81** The company has five working days either to comply with the request or to apply to the court for an order that the company need not comply with the request. If the court is satisfied that the inspection is not for a proper purpose, it can direct the company not to comply with the request (s 117(3)) and it can extend the order to preclude compliance with similar requests (s 117(4)) so ensuring that a company cannot be bombarded with like requests and forced to go to court every time to get an order justifying non-compliance. In addition, where the court concludes that the purpose is not a proper purpose, the court can order that the company's costs of the application be paid in whole or in part by the person who made the inspection request, even if he is not party to the application to the court (s 117(3)(b)). If following an application the court does not so order, the company

---

[137] Note that a person inspecting the central register may ask the company to confirm that all information that the company is required to deliver to the registrar with respect to the central register has been delivered: CA 2006, s 128F(1) and it is an offence not to respond to this request: s 128F(2).

[138] The background to this provision which was new in the CA 2006 is that there were concerns that access to the register was being abused, for example by commercial organisations using it to cold call shareholders, and by individuals such as animal rights protesters who used the information not merely to campaign, but to harass shareholders which in some cases ended in criminal assaults and damage.

[139] [2017] EWCA Civ 1129, [2017] BCC 387.

must immediately comply with the request to inspect the register (s 117(5)). It is an offence for the company to fail to do so in the absence of a court order allowing it to refuse and the court can compel disclosure if need be (s 118(3)).

**16-82** The Court of Appeal had the opportunity in *Burry & Knight Ltd v Knight*[140] to consider for the first time the making of no-access orders under CA 2006, s 117. The appellant was a shareholder in the respondent companies. His request for access to the register of members of the companies was refused on the basis of improper purpose, as the court held and the Court of Appeal confirmed. It was found that his purpose in circulating shareholders with details of long past irregularities was not a proper one because that communication could not confer anything of value on fellow shareholders. A further investigation of those stale allegations could be of no benefit to the companies or their shareholders. The court did order that a letter be circulated to shareholders on a particular matter, but access to the register was refused. In dismissing his appeal, the Court of Appeal took the opportunity to provide detailed guidance as to the application of the statutory provisions, as follows:[141]

(1) The words 'proper purpose' in CA 2006, s 117(3) should be given their ordinary, natural meaning. A proper purpose ought generally, in the case of a member, to relate to the member's interest in that capacity and/or to the exercise of shareholder rights.

(2) The court must find what the purpose of the request is, which will normally be found in the request itself, but the court is not restricted to the purpose as stated in that document.

(3) On a s 117(3) application, the onus is on the company to demonstrate to the court that the court should be satisfied that the request is for an improper purpose.[142] 'Satisfied' means satisfied on a balance of probabilities. It follows that it is not enough that the purpose is capable of being, or might possibly be, an improper one if the court is not satisfied that it is in fact improper.

(4) The way the statutory provisions are framed (the company must comply with a request for access unless it gets a court order) signals the importance that Parliament attaches to the exercise of the right of access to the share register and reflects a strong presumption in favour of shareholder democracy and a policy of upholding principles of corporate transparency and good corporate governance. Those factors point in favour of the court exercising its discretion sparingly and with circumspection where requests are made by shareholders to communicate with fellow shareholders. If a shareholder cannot communicate with fellow shareholders, it puts the board into a very strong position, and the corporate governance of the company is weakened. A strong case would be required to prevent access. It is in principle for shareholders to assess whether a communication is of value to them and what action they should take.

(5) It is not for the court to rule out access on discretionary grounds. The policy behind s 117(3) is that access be refused where a person is disqualified by his purpose. Where there are a mixture of purposes, some proper and some improper, the court must still make a no-access order if any of the purposes are improper, because the contrary conclusion would undermine the protection which the no-access provision

---

[140] [2015] 1 BCLC 61; see also *Burberry Group plc v Fox-Davies* [2015] EWHC 222.
[141] [2015] 1 BCLC 61 at [18]–[30], [82]–[87].
[142] See also *Burberry Group plc v Fox-Davies* [2017] EWCA Civ 1129, [2017] BCC 387.

was intended to give. A request for access for a proper purpose can still be accommodated, for example, by the court ordering the company to facilitate communication with the members by acting as a post-box for mail between the applicant and the members, as was ordered by the Court of Appeal in *Pelling v Families Need Fathers Ltd*[143] (applying a somewhat similar provision in the CA 1985). A *Pelling* type order can also be made under CA 2006, s 117, where there is a mix of proper and improper purposes.[144]

(6) An application for a no-access order should, where possible, be heard summarily rather than after the delay and expense of a trial, not least because a long delay in obtaining a copy of the register of members might itself be destructive of the alleged proper purpose of the person seeking it.

In *Burberry Group plc v Fox-Davies*[145] an application for access to the Burberry register of members was brought by a businessman who hoped to make money by tracking down 'lost members' of the company and reuniting them with their shareholdings for a fee. He was not forthcoming as to the scale of the fees that might be applied. In fact, the company already engaged agents to track such shareholders including on a possible no fee basis. The question was whether the company was entitled to refuse this application as being for an improper purpose.

**16-83**    The starting point, the Court of Appeal said, is that the onus is on the company to establish that a purpose is not proper. In looking at 'purpose', the court would start with the purpose stated in the request, but the court is not confined to that statement and could look at the evidence before it on the balance of probabilities and then make an evaluative judgment as to whether the identified purpose is a proper purpose. It is not necessary that the purpose be in the interests of the shareholders, there is no such qualification in the legislation, and it is not necessary to imply it. A purpose could be commercially motivated without being improper, it would depend on the means of achieving the purpose. The applicant intended to obtain personal information about the shareholders by using the statutory machinery and then to use that information for his financial advantage. Without information about the charges to be applied by him, the court could not properly determine whether or not his purpose was proper. He choose not to provide the information and the court was justified therefore in directing the company that it did not have to comply with his request to access the register.

### Confirmation statement—the demise of the annual return

**16-84**    Until June 2016, all companies (with some exemptions) were required to deliver an annual return to the registrar of companies giving details about the company's registered office, the directors and the company secretary, the company's business activities, share capital, and membership.[146] In the case of traded companies, disclosure in the annual return was only required of a limited category of traded companies[147] and only in respect of members who held 5 per cent or more of the issued shares of any class of the company who were required to give their names, addresses, and details of their shareholdings.[148] The Small Business, Enterprise and Employment Act 2015 brought to an end the submission of a formal 'annual return' and substituted for it a requirement to file a 'confirmation statement'.

---

[143] [2002] BCLC 645.      [144] [2015] 1 BCLC 61 at [87]–[88].

[145] [2017] EWCA Civ 1129, [2017] BCC 387.

[146] In the case of non-traded companies, only the shareholders' names (not addresses) and details of shareholdings were required: CA 2006, s 856A.      [147] See CA 2006, s 856B(1).

[148] CA 2006, s 856B(3).

**16-85**   With effect from 30 June 2016, a new CA 2006, Pt 24, as substituted, requires companies to provide a confirmation statement no later than the last day of the review period, that period being within 12 months of the day of incorporation or 12 months beginning with the day after the end of the previous review period, confirming that their information on the public record is up to date (s 853A(1), (3)). If the company has had an opportunity to provide an earlier confirmation statement, for example because it needed to notify the registrar of a change of directors, the next confirmation statement is required within 12 months of that confirmation statement. Essentially, the change is from a fixed annual return to a requirement to check and confirm the information on the public record at least once in a 12-month period which gives the company greater flexibility as to when it updates its information. At least once in a 12-month period, however, it has to confirm that the information on the public record is correct. The information which must be reported or updated or confirmed is similar: particulars of the registered office, the directors and secretary, the share capital and membership,[149] the company's business activities, and the trading status of the shares. On occasion, the confirmation statement will have to be accompanied by other information such as a statement of capital or shareholder information or information concerning the PSC register (see ss 853D, 853F, 853I). Small companies may welcome the abolition of the annual return but whether they find the requirements for confirmation statements any easier to comply with is a moot point.

### Rectification of the register of members

**16-86**   The details in the register of members can be challenged, for instance, on the grounds of mistake, but any shareholder wishing to challenge an entry must act promptly.[150] Rectification of the register maintained by the company is governed by CA 2006, s 125 (and where the company has elected to maintain the information on the register maintained by the registrar, the equivalent provision is s 128G) which provides that if:[151]

'(a)  the name of any person is, without sufficient cause, entered in or omitted from the company's register of members; or

(b)  default is made, or unnecessary delay takes place in entering on the register the fact of any person having ceased to be a member;

the person aggrieved, or any member of the company, or the company may apply to the court for rectification of the register.'

**16-87**   The court has a discretion to refuse the application or to order rectification and the payment by the company of any damages sustained by any party aggrieved (s 125(2)). There is no necessity to show any wrongdoing by the company and any question of omission by error or entry by error can be raised.

---

[149]  As before, disclosure of membership of traded companies is limited to non DTR5 issuers; a DTR5 issuer is a company subject to Chapter 5 of the FCA, Disclosure and Transparency Rules which requires disclosure of major shareholders to the market in any event, see CA 2006, s 853G.

[150]  *Re Scottish Petroleum Co* (1883) 23 Ch D 413 at 434, CA.

[151]  The directors of a company may rectify the register of members without any application to the court if there is no dispute about the matter and the circumstances are such that the court would order rectification: *Reese River Silver Mining Co v Smith* (1869) LR 4 HL 64 at 74; *Hartley's Case* (1875) 10 Ch App 157; *First National Reinsurance Co Ltd v Greenfield* [1921] 2 KB 260 at 279; but ordinarily the protection of the court's order is essential to any rectification by the removal of the name of a registered holder of shares: *Re Derham and Allen Ltd* [1946] Ch 31 at 36.

**16-88**    The power to rectify has been exercised where there was no valid allotment of shares;[152] or the allotment was irregular;[153] or where a transfer of shares was improperly registered or registration was refused.[154]

**16-89**    The nature of the jurisdiction to rectify the register was considered in *Re Piccadilly Radio plc*.[155] In this instance, shares in a radio company were transferred without obtaining the consent of the Independent Broadcasting Authority (IBA) as required by the articles of association. Other shareholders in the company, with a view to preventing certain proposals being agreed to at a general meeting, sought rectification of the share register by deleting the names of the transferees and restoring the name of the original transferor. Millett J, despite finding that there had been a breach of the articles, refused rectification. In his opinion, the statutory procedure provided a discretionary remedy and the court must consider the circumstances in which and the purpose for which the relief was sought. The circumstances here did not warrant rectification for a number of reasons. The applicants had no interest in the shares and were not seeking to have their own names restored to the register. They were seeking to disenfranchise opposition to certain proposals to be put to the general meeting and had seized on a breach of an article of which the IBA itself did not complain. Moreover, the transferor did not seek rectification and the company itself did not support the application.

**16-90**    The Privy Council considered the scope of the jurisdiction when considering the identical provision in the BVI (British Virgin Islands) Companies Act 2004 in *Nilon Ltd v Royal Westminster Investments SA*.[156] The case concerned a dispute as to whether a shareholder in a BVI company had agreed to allot or procure the allotment of shares to the claimants who sought rectification of the register of members of the company to reflect their alleged ownership of an agreed proportion of the shares of the company. The defendant alleged that the claimants were creditors of the company, not shareholders. The issue for the court was an application to serve out of the jurisdiction with respect to that dispute. The Privy Council rejected the application and ruled that the rectification claim should be struck out. Lord Collins noted that two points arise from the long-standing authorities on rectification of the register. First, that the summary nature of this jurisdiction makes it an unsuitable vehicle if there is a substantial factual question in dispute.[157] Secondly, that proceedings for rectification can only be brought where the applicant has a right to registration by virtue of a valid transfer of legal title and not merely a prospective claim against the company dependent on the conversion of an equitable right to a legal title by an order for specific performance of a contract.[158] As the claimants had not established a

---

[152] See *Re Homer District Consolidated Gold Mines, ex p Smith* (1888) 39 Ch D 546 at 551; *Re Portuguese Consolidated Copper Mines Ltd* (1889) 42 Ch D 160, CA.

[153] See *Re Homer District Consolidated Gold Mines, ex p Smith* (1888) 39 Ch D 546; *Re Cleveland Trust plc* [1991] BCLC 424 (register rectified by deletion of bonus shares after bonus issue mistakenly made); *Re Thundercrest Ltd* [1995] 1 BCLC 117 (register rectified by cancellation of improper allotment to two members).

[154] See *Re Copal Varnish Co Ltd* [1917] 2 Ch 349; *Welch v Bank of England* [1955] 1 All ER 811 (restoration of status quo after forged transfers); *International Credit and Investment Co (Overseas) Ltd v Adham* [1994] 1 BCLC 66 (restoration of status quo: no proper share transfers were executed, merely entries made in the share register purporting to deprive the true owner of his entire holding); *Re New Cedos Engineering Co Ltd* [1994] 1 BCLC 797 (on their true construction, a right to be registered existed under the articles); *Stothers v William Steward (Holdings) Ltd* [1994] 2 BCLC 266 (directors purported to exercise discretion to refuse registration which power, on the true construction of the articles, they did not possess).          [155] [1989] BCLC 683.

[156] [2015] UKPC 2, [2015] 3 All ER 372.          [157] [2015] UKPC 2, [2015] 3 All ER 372 at [37].

[158] [2015] UKPC 2, [2015] 3 All ER 372 at [51]. In so far as *Re Hoicrest Ltd* [2000] 1 BCLC 194, CA, suggested otherwise, it was wrongly decided.

present right to the shares, they had no arguable case for a present right to rectification of the register and the claim for rectification was struck out.

### The register of people with significant control (PSC register)

**16-91**  Following commitments made at a G28 summit in 2013, the UK Government introduced a public register of beneficial ownership with respect to people who have significant control of companies. The governing provisions are CA 2006, Pt 21A and Sch 1A, inserted by the Small Business, Enterprise and Employment Act 2015, with effect from 6 April 2016.

**16-92**  All UK registered companies, subject to limited exceptions,[159] are required to maintain a register of people with significant control over the company, known as a PSC register (ss 790B(1), 790M(1)).[160] In the absence of an election to keep a central register, the company must deliver details of its PSC register to the registrar at least once every 12 months (s 853I) together with a confirmation statement, see **16-84**. There is a duty on the company to take reasonable steps to find out if anyone is a registrable person or entity and if so to identify them (s 790D(1)) and such persons must notify the company of their status if the company has not served a notice on them (s 790G). References to a person with or having significant control over a company are to an individual who meets one or more of the specified conditions set out in CA 2006, Sch 1A (s 790C(2), (3)). The obligations are extended to legal entities if the legal entity would have come within the definition of a person with significant control if it had been an individual (s 790C(6), (7)). There are five conditions set out in Sch 1A, Pt 1:

(1) that X holds, directly or indirectly, more than 25 per cent of the shares in company Y;

(2) that X holds, directly or indirectly, more than 25 per cent of the voting rights in company Y;

(3) that X holds the right, directly or indirectly, to appoint or remove a majority of the board of directors of company Y;

(4) that X has the right to exercise, or actually exercises, significant influence or control over company Y;

(5) that (a) the trustees of a trust or the members of a firm that, under the law by which it is governed, is not a legal person meet any of the other specified conditions (in their capacity as such) in relation to company Y, or would do so if they were individuals, and (b) X has the right to exercise, or actually exercises, significant influence or control over the activities of that trust or firm.

**16-93**  CA 2006, Sch 1A, Pts 2–4 provide extensive guidance on the scope of those categories. Statutory guidance is also provided by BEIS as to the meaning of 'significant influence or control' for the purposes of the Schedule (Sch 1A, Pt 3, para 24(1)) and non-statutory guidance is also available on the BEIS website.[161] Particulars of the identity of the PSC are required (name, service address, nationality, date of birth, date on which became a PSC, etc)

---

[159] CA 2006, s 790B(1), other than DTR5 issuers—companies to which the FCA, Disclosure and Transparency Rules, Ch 5 apply and companies excluded by regulations.

[160] A private company may elect to keep this information on the register (known as the central register) kept by the registrar rather than maintain it itself (CA 2006, s 790W(1), (2)), but the election is of no effect if any person who is a registrable person or entity and whose particulars are stated in the PSC register objects to a central register (s 790X(1)–(3)).

[161] See at www.gov.uk. The length of the non-statutory guidance reflects the complexity of the statutory scheme.

as well as information as to the nature of the control (i.e. as to which of the criteria bring this person within the definition of a PSC), see s 790K. For many small companies, of course, the register will be of little concern (given they only have two members and the identity of the PSC will be self-evident), but for companies with any number of share-holders including perhaps chains of corporate shareholders, including entities registered overseas, maintaining an accurate register is challenging and costly. The register must be available for inspection by any person without charge (s 790O) subject to a right to refuse access if the court so orders (s 790P), in the same manner as with access to the register of members, see **16-79**. The court has a power to rectify the PSC register (s 790V) in the same manner as the register of members, see **16-86**.

# 17

# Decision-making and company meetings

## A Introduction

**17-1**  As discussed in Chapter 9, the typical division of power within a company is that the power to manage the company is vested in the board of directors with very limited powers retained by the shareholders (see **9-5**). Those powers include statutory rights, such as the right to alter the articles (CA 2006, s 21), or to increase or reduce the share capital,[1] and other powers, such as the power to appoint the directors, customarily given to the general meeting by the articles.[2] In some instances, the statute requires shareholder approval of various transactions, such as any purchase of the company's own shares[3] or particular transactions where directors have a conflict of interest.[4] Previously, the forum for the shareholders to exercise such powers as they possess was the general meeting of the company and the mechanism was by resolutions of the shareholders passed at such meetings. The Companies Act 1985 therefore provided a basic framework for meetings while allowing matters of detail to be determined by the company's articles.

**17-2**  For private companies, given the small numbers of shareholders commonly involved, a formal general meeting is not a significant or appropriate forum for most decision-making. In keeping with the 'think small first' philosophy (see **2-7**), the CA 2006 therefore provides that a resolution of the members of a private company may be passed as a written resolution or at a meeting (s 281(1)) and the expectation is that the members will act through written resolutions and meetings will be the exception.[5] It is also possible for the shareholders unanimously to agree on any matter informally (see **17-73**).

**17-3**  For public companies, the scheme is quite different. In a public company, decisions must be made at a meeting of the members or a class of members,[6] as the case may be (CA 2006, s 281(2)) and the CA 2006 precludes public companies from using written resolutions.[7]

---

[1]  See CA 2006, ss 617–619 (increasing share capital) and s 641 (reduction of share capital).

[2]  The Companies (Model Articles) Regulations 2008, SI 2008/3229, reg 2, Sch 1, arts 17–18 (Ltd); reg 4, Sch 3, arts 20–22 (Plc).                                              [3]  CA 2006, ss 690–701.

[4]  For example, substantial property transactions governed by CA 2006, s 190.

[5]  For single member companies, details of decisions which have effect as if agreed to by the company in general meeting (for example, where the statute requires a shareholder resolution on some matter, such as a reduction of capital: CA 2006, s 641) must be provided to the company (unless the decision is reached by a written resolution) so as to ensure there is a record of the decision and it can be seen that there is compliance with the statutory requirements: CA 2006, s 357.

[6]  See generally Kosmin and Roberts, *Company Meetings and Resolutions: Law, Practice and Procedure* (2nd edn, 2013).

[7]  There is some debate as to whether the prohibition applies only to resolutions required by the Companies Act 2006 as opposed to resolutions required by the company's articles, see **17-26**.

Moreover, public companies must hold an annual general meeting within six months of the financial year end (s 336(1)). For these companies, the annual general meeting of shareholders is intended to provide an opportunity for the shareholders not only to take decisions but to hold the directors to account for their stewardship of the company. Too often, the reality is that the shareholders are a remote dispersed group with individually little influence and collectively lacking a unified voice on matters of substance. The emphasis in recent years therefore has been on trying to ensure that the general meeting does act as an effective counterbalance to the board and considerable attention is now paid to this issue in the interests of good corporate governance, see **6-50**.

**17-4**   As discussed at **6-54**, shareholders in traded companies range from individual shareholders with a few hundred shares to institutional shareholders with millions of shares and it is not unusual to find that 80 per cent of the company's shareholders are individuals but they hold only 20 per cent of the shares (and the votes attached) while 20 per cent of the shareholders are institutions holding 80 per cent of the shares and the votes. The effectiveness of shareholder control through the general meeting to a large extent will be determined therefore by the willingness of the institutional investors to exercise their voting power (see the discussion of these corporate governance issues at **6-54**). In this chapter, we look at the mechanisms for meetings. If the general meeting is to assume its intended role as an important component of our corporate governance structures, the legal requirements set out in the CA 2006 must enhance its effectiveness and ensure that shareholders are heard and the rules must facilitate all shareholders, whether individual or institutional, in the exercise of their voting power.[8]

**17-5**   The Shareholder Rights Directive (reflected in the CA 2006, as amended) also focuses on improving the mechanisms of participation, especially cross-border participation, so as to facilitate and encourage shareholder engagement in traded companies,[9] see **2-24**. In keeping with the general theme of shareholder engagement, the CA 2006 Pt 9 introduced measures aimed at engaging with indirect shareholders and that aspect is considered at **6-66**. Before proceeding, it should be noted that, while the CA 2006 provisions on decision-making concentrated on private, public, and quoted companies,[10] implementation of the Shareholder Rights Directive required provision for traded companies[11] which is a slightly narrower category than quoted companies (though the essence of both is that the companies are admitted to trading on a regulated market) so the statute now contains a sometimes confusing mix of provisions applicable to these distinct categories of companies. Traded companies for the purposes of the Shareholder Rights Directive (SRD) are companies incorporated in a Member State and whose shares are admitted to trading on a regulated market situated or operating within a Member State (art 1).

---

[8] Many of these issues were addressed in detail by the Company Law Review which favoured incremental reform of meeting procedures rather than wholesale changes: see Company Law Review, *Modern Company Law for a Competitive Economy, Final Report*, vol 1 (2001), URN 01/942, paras 7.5–7.16; *Completing the Structure* (2000), URN 00/1335, paras 5.18–5.40; *Developing the Framework* (2000), URN 00/656, paras 4.24–4.64; *Company General Meetings and Shareholder Communication* (1999), URN 99/1144.

[9] Directive 2007/36/EC, OJ L 184/17, 14.7.2007, implemented by The Companies (Shareholders' Rights) Regulations 2009, SI 2009/1632.

[10] Defined CA 2006, ss 361, 385 as a company whose equity share capital: (a) has been included in the official list in accordance with the provisions of FSMA 2000, Pt VI; or (b) is officially listed in an EEA State (i.e. EU with Norway, Iceland, and Liechtenstein); or (c) is admitted to dealing on either the New York Stock Exchange or Nasdaq (an American stock exchange).

[11] Defined in CA 2006, s 360C, as a company any shares of which carry rights to vote at general meetings and are admitted to trading on a regulated market in an EEA State (see n 10) by or with the consent of the company.

**17-6**   The CA 2006 also allows for the use of electronic communications.[12] The overall communications scheme (CA 2006, ss 1143–1148 and Schs 4 and 5) is somewhat complex, but essentially the Act allows companies to communicate with shareholders by hard copy, electronically, or via a website or any other mechanism agreed with the recipient.[13] Hard copy documents may be handed to the shareholder or posted and hard copies are always available to shareholders free of charge even if they opt for other methods of communication.[14] Electronic communications such as email may be used if the shareholder opts in to such use and provides an email address.[15] Websites can be used to communicate with shareholders if the company's articles or a shareholder resolution allow for such use.[16] Where a company has that power, it must ask the shareholder individually whether he consents to website communication, but crucially if the shareholder declines to answer, he is deemed to have assented to website use.[17] In this way, shareholder inertia is turned into assent to website communication though any shareholder, at any time, can require communications in hard copy. Where shareholders have assented or have been deemed to have assented, the company must still send them a notification, either by letter or email, alerting them to the fact that information has been posted on the website.[18] Companies may be deemed also to have accepted electronic communications from shareholders. For example, if a company gives an electronic address in a notice calling a meeting, or in an instrument of proxy sent out by the company, or in an invitation to appoint a proxy issued by the company, it is deemed to have agreed that any document or information relating to the meeting may be sent by electronic means to that address (s 333) and the largest companies use this method to deal, for example, with proxy appointments.

**17-7**   The largest companies also make extensive use of their websites as a means of communicating with their investors and this is both facilitated (as noted in **17-6**) and required by the legislation. The CA 2006 requires quoted companies to use their website to publish their annual accounts and reports (s 430); to report the results of polls taken at a general meeting and any independent assessor's report on such polls (ss 341, 351); and members of the company holding a certain percentage of the shares can require a statement to be put on the website setting out any audit concerns which they may have (s 527). A traded company must publish on a website a wide variety of information in advance of a meeting including the contents of the notice of the meeting, details of the share capital and voting rights, as well as of members' statements, resolutions, and matters of business received by the company (where not already included in the notice of the meeting) and that information mainly must be available on or before the date on which notice of the meeting is given and kept available for a period of two years after that date (s 311A).

## B  Voting entitlement

### Voting in person

**17-8**   Subject to any provision in the company's articles,[19] on a vote on a resolution on a show of hands at a meeting, each member present in person has one vote and, on a poll taken at a

---

[12] The use of electronic communication had been endorsed by the Companies Act 1985 (Electronic Communications) Order 2000, SI 2000/3373, but only to a limited extent and effect.

[13] CA 2006, Sch 5, paras 2, 5, 8, 15.       [14] CA 2006, s 1145(1), (3), also Sch 5, para 3.

[15] CA 2006, Sch 5, paras 6, 7.       [16] CA 2006, Sch 5, para 10(2).       [17] CA 2006, Sch 5, para 10(3).

[18] CA 2006, Sch 5, para 13.

[19] See *Sugarman v CJS Investments LLP* [2015] 1 BCLC 1, CA, discussed at **5-52**, considering an exclusion provision in articles which gave rise to a potentially uncommercial outcome, but not one so absurd as to require the implication by the court of additional correcting provisions.

meeting (where the actual votes cast by each member are counted), every member has one vote for each share held by him (CA 2006, s 284(2), (3)). In practice, voting rights are spelt out expressly in the articles. The CA 2006 recognises that a member may hold shares on behalf of a number of beneficial owners and s 152 provides that a member holding shares in a company on behalf of more than one person is not required to exercise all the rights attached to the shares (which would include voting rights) in the same way.[20] A member is able therefore to cast votes for and against a resolution in accordance with the instructions of the beneficial owners.

**17-9**     Certain classes of shares may carry restricted voting rights; for example, it is commonly the case that preference shareholders may only vote on matters of direct concern to them, see **16-24**. Equally, the articles may confer enhanced rights; for example, a shareholder may be given three times the number of votes on a particular matter than is otherwise the case.[21]

## Voting by proxy

**17-10**     Proxies are instruments executed by voting members of a company in favour of another person enabling that person to exercise the member's voting rights at a meeting. The position with respect to proxy rights was clarified and improved by the Companies Act 2006 and the company's articles can confer even more extensive rights (s 331). Any member of a company who is entitled to attend and vote at meetings (including class meetings) of the company may appoint another person, whether a member or not, as his proxy to exercise all or any of his rights to attend and to speak and vote at a meeting of the company (s 324). A proxy must vote in accordance with any instructions given by the member who appointed him (s 324A). A proxy is entitled to vote on a show of hands and on a poll (s 285) and a proxy can demand a poll and his demand is the same as a demand by a member (s 329). It is common to appoint the company chairman as a proxy, but given the right of a proxy to speak at a meeting, that may not be entirely appropriate since it could result in the chairman having to speak against a resolution. In the case of a company having a share capital, a member may appoint more than one proxy in relation to a meeting provided that each proxy is appointed with respect to different shares (s 324(2)). This flexibility is particularly important in larger companies where the registered shareholder is frequently a nominee for a number of beneficial owners and the ability to appoint multiple proxies allows their differing interests to be individually represented at the meeting.

**17-11**     The instrument appointing a proxy may be in writing or contained in an electronic communication.[22] The proxy must be lodged with the company ahead of the meeting and the company's articles may not contain any requirement that it be received by the company

---

[20]  Nothing in CA 2006, s 284 is to be read as restricting the effect of s 152 (exercise of rights by nominees) or s 285 (voting by proxy) or s 323 (voting by corporate representatives): s 284(5).

[21]  See *Bushell v Faith* [1969] 1 All ER 1002 (shareholder had three times the number of votes he usually had on any resolution calling for his removal from the board, so giving him an effective veto on his own removal).

[22]  Notice of the appointment of a proxy may be by electronic communication where the company is agreeable to appointments being made in this way and has provided an address for this purpose: CA 2006, s 333. As to the content and form of a proxy, see The Companies (Model Articles) Regulations 2008, SI 2008/3229, reg 2, Sch 1, art 45 (Ltd); reg 4, Sch 3, art 38 (Plc); and see the specific requirements re notice of appointment of a proxy in the case of a traded company: CA 2006, s 327(A1). The Listing Rules, LR 9.3.6R, require a proxy to be a three-way (for, against, withheld) in keeping with the requirements of the UK Corporate Governance Code (2014), E.2.1.

more than 48 hours before a meeting in order that the appointment be effective.[23] This is to ensure that the shareholders have flexibility and are not forced at an early date to decide whether they will attend or appoint a proxy. At the same time, the 48-hour window allows the company enough time to determine who is to attend and in what capacity. The notice of the meeting must draw attention to the rights to appoint a proxy (CA 2006, s 325). Termination of the appointment is governed by s 330.

## Voting by corporate representatives

**17-12** Companies may hold shares in other companies and such corporate shareholders may attend meetings through corporate representatives and a corporate representative is entitled to exercise the same powers as if the corporation were an individual member of the company (CA 2006, s 323 (1), (2)). It is also possible for a corporation to appoint multiple corporate representatives though the voting position can become difficult in that situation and they must be careful to vote on a poll in respect of different shareholdings. If, on a poll, they purport to exercise voting powers in respect of the same shares and they exercise that power in different ways, the power is treated as not having been exercised at all (s 323(4)). A better solution is not to appoint corporate representatives, given the uncertainties and ambiguities in s 323, but to appoint multiple proxies.[24] The problem with using proxies is that notice of the appointment must be given to the company not later than a clear 48 hours before the meeting (s 327(2)) which in some circumstances may be impractical.

## Polls

**17-13** Resolutions at meetings can be, and in smaller companies normally are, passed on a show of hands but a poll (where the votes cast are counted) may be demanded in a meeting to obtain a more accurate picture reflecting the members' shareholdings.[25] Increasingly larger companies vote only on a poll so as to avoid complexities in counting votes on a show of hands where multiple proxies or corporate representatives are present.

**17-14** The company's articles cannot exclude the right to demand a poll at a general meeting, save in respect of the election of the chairman and the adjournment of the meeting.[26] Furthermore, the articles cannot make ineffective a demand for a poll which is made either by not less than five voting members, or by a member or members representing not less than 10 per cent of the total voting rights of all members having the right to vote on the resolution, or by a member or members holding shares conferring a right to vote on the resolution, being shares on which an aggregate sum has been paid up equal to not less than 10 per cent of the total sum paid up on all the shares conferring that right (CA 2006,

---

[23] CA 2006, s 327(2)(a). Non-working days are excluded when calculating the earliest deadline that can be specified in the articles: s 327(3).

[24] That solution is suggested by the *Explanatory Notes to the Companies Act 2006* which state: 'If a corporation wishes to appoint people with different voting intentions or with authority to vote different blocks of shares, they should appoint proxies' (para 569).

[25] The model articles provide that a resolution put to a vote at a general meeting must be decided on a show of hands unless a poll is duly demanded: see The Companies (Model Articles) Regulations 2008, SI 2008/3229, reg 2, Sch 1, art 43 (Ltd), reg 4, Sch 3, art 34 (Plc).

[26] CA 2006, s 321(1)(a) and (b). The Companies (Model Articles) Regulations 2008, SI 2008/3229, reg 2, Sch 1, art 45(2) (Ltd), reg 4, Sch 3, art 36(2) (Plc) allow a poll to be demanded by the chairman, the directors, two or more persons having the right to vote on the resolution, or a person or persons representing not less than one-tenth of the total voting rights of all shareholders.

s 321(2)). On a poll taken at a general meeting of the company, a member entitled to more than one vote need not, if he votes, use all his votes or cast all the votes he uses in the same way (s 322).

**17-15**   Where a poll is taken at a general meeting of a quoted company or a traded company the company must ensure that information on the outcome of the poll is made available on a website (CA 2006, s 341). In particular, the number of votes cast in favour and the number of votes cast against the resolution must be set out and, in the case of a traded company, more detailed voting information is required (s 341(1A)). Further provision is made for the proper scrutiny of polls of quoted companies in the light of concerns expressed as to the accuracy of polls.[27] Members of a quoted company representing not less than 5 per cent of the total voting rights of all the members who have the right to vote on the matter, or not less than 100 members having the right to vote on the matter and holding shares paid up on average per member of not less than £100,[28] may require the directors to obtain an independent report on any poll taken or to be taken at a general meeting of the company (s 342). Any report made by the independent assessor on a poll must be made available on the company's website (s 351). This mechanism may prove valuable (though it appears unused to date) to companies where the resolution is controversial or the margin of victory, or defeat, narrow. It is also now possible for the company's articles to make provision that voting on a resolution on a poll in a meeting may include votes cast in advance[29] and, in the case of a traded company, such provision can be subject only to such requirements and restrictions as are necessary to verify the identity of the person voting (s 322A).

## C  Resolutions

**17-16**   Resolutions fall into two categories, ordinary and special,[30] and, in the case of a private company, may be passed either in writing or at a meeting (CA 2006, s 281(1)). A public company may not use written resolutions and must pass resolutions (including resolutions of a class of members) at a meeting (s 281(2)), but see **17-26**. A resolution at a meeting is validly passed if notice of the meeting and of the resolution is given and the meeting is held and conducted in accordance with the provisions of the CA 2006 governing the conduct of meetings and annual general meetings (i.e. Pt 13, Chs 3 and 4) and the company's articles (s 301).

---

[27]   There has been concern about 'lost' votes, i.e. that the chain of intermediaries is now so long from beneficial owner through to the registered shareholder that voting instructions and/or votes get lost along the way so that either votes are not cast in accordance with instructions, or votes are not counted because of a confusion of instructions, or agents are not acting on instructions. The matter was the subject of a series of reports by Paul Myners, see Myners, *Review of Impediments to Voting UK Shares* (2004) with follow-up reports in 2005 (twice) and in 2007.

[28]   Indirect investors, subject to the requirements of CA 2006, s 153 being met, may count towards the 100 figure: CA 2006, s 342(2).

[29]   As to the time constraints, see CA 2006, s 322A(3)—essentially the company cannot impose a cut-off point for casting a vote in advance any earlier than 48 hours before the meeting or if the poll is not taken for 48 hours after it is demanded, 24 hours before the time for taking the poll.

[30]   Previously, there were also extraordinary and elective resolutions. Elective resolutions were used by private companies to elect to opt out of certain provisions of the companies legislation: CA 1985, s 379A. Extraordinary resolutions required a 75 per cent majority and 14 days' notice—they remain effective where a company's articles or a contract make provision for them: see the Companies Act 2006 (Commencement No 3, Consequential Amendments, Transitional Provisions and Savings) Order 2007, SI 2007/2194, art 9, Sch 3, para 23.

## Ordinary resolutions

**17-17**    If the Companies Act requires 'a resolution' and does not specify what type of resolution, this means an ordinary resolution which requires a simple majority unless the articles require a higher majority or unanimity (CA 2006, s 281(3)), but if the statute specifies an ordinary resolution or a special resolution (not less than 75 per cent), that requirement is mandatory so the mandatory limits, respectively, are a simple majority and not less than 75 per cent, as explained later, and the articles cannot impose a different majority requirement than that specified in the Act,[31] though anything that may be done by an ordinary resolution may equally be done by a special resolution (s 282(5)).

**17-18**    An ordinary resolution is a resolution passed by a simple majority of the members or a class of members (s 282(1)). A written resolution is passed by a simple majority if it is passed by members representing a simple majority of the total voting rights of eligible members (s 282(2)).[32] A resolution passed at a meeting on a show of hands is passed by a simple majority if it is passed by a simple majority of the votes cast by those entitled to vote (s 282(3)). A resolution passed on a poll is passed by a simple majority if it is passed by members representing a simple majority of the total voting rights of members who being entitled to do so vote in person, by proxy, or in advance (see **17-15**) on the resolution (s 282(4)).

**17-19**    There are no specific notice requirements for a resolution and the company will give notice of the resolution to the shareholders at the same time as it gives notice of the meeting (see **17-56**). In a few instances, the statute requires that special notice is given *to* the company of an ordinary resolution, for example on any resolution to remove a director[33] or an auditor.[34] A company's articles may also make provision for special notice. Special notice, for the purposes of the CA 2006, requires that notice of the intention to move the resolution is given to the company at least 28 days before the meeting (s 312(1)).

## Special resolutions

**17-20**    A special resolution means a resolution passed by a majority of *not less than* 75 per cent (CA 2006, s 283(1)) and it is required by the legislation on a number of occasions typically involving a matter of some significance, such as constitutional changes,[35] changes to the capital structure of the company,[36] or where the company resolves to go into winding up.[37]

**17-21**    A special resolution which is passed as a written resolution must be passed by a majority of not less than 75 per cent of the total voting rights of eligible members (s 283(2)).[38]

---

[31] See *Explanatory Notes to the Companies Act 2006*, para 523.

[32] 'Eligible members' in relation to a written resolution of a private company is defined by CA 2006, s 289 as the members who would have been entitled to vote on the resolution on the circulation date (defined in s 290 as the date on which the written resolution is sent to the members).

[33] CA 2006, s 168(2), or to appoint someone in his stead at the meeting at which he is removed.

[34] CA 2006, s 511(1). Special notice is also required of a resolution to appoint as auditor a person other than the retiring auditor: s 515(2).

[35] For example, a special resolution is required on an alteration of the articles of association: CA 2006, s 21(1); on a change of name: s 77(1); on the re-registration of a public company as a private company: s 97(1).

[36] For example, a special resolution is required on disapplying the statutory pre-emption rights: CA 2006, s 570; on a reduction of share capital: s 641.

[37] For example, a special resolution is required where a company resolves that it be wound up voluntarily: IA 1986, s 84(1)(b); and where a company resolves that the company be wound up by the court: s 122(1)(a).

[38] As to the definition of 'eligible members' see n 32.

Where a resolution of a private company is passed as a written resolution, the resolution is not a special resolution unless it is stated that it was proposed as a special resolution and, if the resolution so states, it may only be passed as a special resolution (s 283(3)).

**17-22**   A resolution passed at a meeting on a show of hands must be passed by a majority of not less than 75 per cent of the votes cast by those entitled to vote (s 283(4)). A resolution passed on a poll is passed by a majority of not less than 75 per cent if it is passed by members representing not less than 75 per cent of the total voting rights of members who being entitled to do so vote in person, by proxy, or in advance on the resolution (s 283(5)).

**17-23**   A resolution passed at a meeting is not a special resolution unless the notice of the meeting includes the text of the resolution and specifies the intention to propose the resolution as a special resolution and, if the notice of the meeting so states, the resolution may only be passed as a special resolution (s 283(6)). If the resolution is to be validly passed, it must be the same resolution as that identified in the notice of the meeting.[39]

## Written resolutions

**17-24**   As noted at **17-2**, the emphasis in the CA 2006 is on the use of written resolutions by private companies which is intended to expedite decision-making in such companies and to enable them to avoid the formalities involved in calling a meeting. The key advantages are speed (no notice of a meeting is required) and costs (likely to be minimal). Subject to two exceptions, any resolution may be passed as a written resolution (CA 2006, s 281(1)) and any provision in the company's articles precluding the use of written resolutions is void (s 300). The exceptions are that written resolutions may not be used (s 288(2)): (1) to remove a director under s 168; and (2) to remove an auditor from office under s 510 since, in these instances, the directors and auditors have the right to make representations at, or to, a general meeting.[40]

**17-25**   Written resolutions need no longer be unanimous, as was the case under the CA 1985. A written resolution requires the same majority (simple or not less than 75 per cent) as is required for an ordinary or special resolution passed at a meeting. The change means that in many private companies (depending on shareholder composition, of course) the resolution will effectively be passed before it is even circulated since minority shareholders by definition cannot block an ordinary resolution and may not (depending on their percentage holding) be in a position to block a special resolution. Of course, the same would be true of a resolution proposed at a meeting, but at least a meeting requires the majority to put forward some case for the action being undertaken and to hear opposing views. The minority may find it doubly frustrating to be outvoted and not heard. Some balance is restored, however, as members representing at least a 5 per cent holding can require a written resolution of their own to be circulated (see CA 2006, s 292 and **17-29**) and can require a meeting to be held (see s 303 and **17-46**).

**17-26**   The statutory scheme for written resolutions for private companies is mandatory with CA 2006, s 288(1) stating that a written resolution is a resolution proposed and passed in accordance with Pt 13, Ch 2 which means that companies must follow the statutory scheme rather than any written resolution provisions which companies may have in their articles. The CA 2006 no longer permits public companies to use written resolutions (s 281(2)), at least for resolutions required by the Act. This is a change to the previous law

---

[39] *Re Moorgate Mercantile Holdings Ltd* [1980] 1 All ER 40.     [40] See CA 2006, ss 169, 511(3), (5).

which permitted public companies to include provisions for written resolutions in their articles though their practical use was limited by the requirement that such resolutions had to be passed unanimously. Nevertheless in some circumstances they were of use to public companies. There seems no reason why public companies cannot use written resolutions for matters other than statutory requirements, if their articles so provide. In so far as it is permissible and practicable, public companies can rely also on informal unanimous shareholder assent (see **17-73**).

**17-27** Given the obligation to follow the statutory scheme on written resolutions, the key points to note are:

- A copy of the resolution must be sent to every eligible member (i.e. every member entitled to vote on the resolution, CA 2006, s 289);[41] accompanied by a statement as to how the member may signify agreement and a date by which the resolution must be passed otherwise it lapses under s 297 (s 291(4)).[42] If the resolution is to be a special resolution, it must so state (s 283(3)).

- The resolution may be circulated in hard copy or electronically or by way of a website, subject to compliance with the rules on electronic communications noted at **17-6**, and it must be sent at the same time (so far as reasonably practical) to all members.[43]

- Certain statutory schemes, such as those relating to a purchase by a company of its own shares (see **22-9**), require documents to be available for inspection by shareholders at the general meeting. Where a written resolution is used, copies of such documents as would otherwise be available at a general meeting must be circulated to the members at or before the time when the resolution is supplied for signature.[44]

- A written resolution lapses if the time-limit imposed by the articles elapses or, if there is no such limit, within 28 days of the circulation date (i.e. the date when the resolution is first sent to any member: s 290): s 297.

**17-28** A written resolution of a private company is passed when the required majority of eligible members signify their agreement to it (CA 2006, s 296(4)) and they do so when the company receives an authenticated document,[45] whether in hard copy or electronic form, identifying the resolution and indicating agreement to it (s 296(1), (2)).[46] Once a member has signified his agreement to a written resolution, he may not revoke his agreement (s 296(3)). A written resolution of a private company has effect as if passed by the company in general meeting or by a meeting of a class of members (s 288(5)). The company must keep a copy of all written resolutions for at least 10 years (s 355(1), (2)).

---

[41] A copy of the proposed resolution must be sent to the company's auditors: CA 2006, s 502, but merely for information. The auditor cannot delay the process and is not required to assent in any way to it so a failure to provide a copy has no consequence. The limitation to those entitled to vote means that non-voting members may be unaware of the resolution until it is passed and, if need be, registered at Companies House.

[42] But note that the validity of the resolution, if passed, is not affected by a failure to comply with these requirements, see CA 2006, s 291(7).

[43] If the resolution is sent via a website, it is not validly sent unless it is available on the website throughout the period from the circulation date (defined CA 2006, s 290) to the date on which the resolution lapses under s 297: s 299.

[44] For examples, see disapplication of pre-emption rights (CA 2006, 571(7)); off-market purchases of own shares (s 696(2)); redemption or purchase of own shares out of capital (s 718(2)); approval of directors' long-term service contracts (s 188(5)).

[45] If the company gives an electronic address in the document containing or accompanying the written resolution, it is deemed to have agreed to a response being made to that address: see CA 2006, s 298.

[46] There is no requirement for a signature, merely that agreement is signified which could be by email or even a text message, where electronic communications are permitted.

### Circulation of members' written resolutions

**17-29**   Directors may circulate a written resolution at any time (s 291). An innovation in the CA 2006 is that members holding 5 per cent of the total voting rights of members entitled to vote on the resolution (or such lesser figure as specified in the articles) may require the company to circulate a proposed written resolution and with it a statement of not more than 1,000 words on the subject matter of the resolution (s 292). Such matter is to be circulated at the members' expense, however, unless the company otherwise resolves (s 294(1)). If the company has not so resolved, it need not circulate the resolution and statement until the members deposit or tender a sum reasonably sufficient to meet the company's expenses in circulating it (s 294(2)). The costs may be modest if the shareholders have agreed to electronic or website communications and non-existent if the company has few members.

**17-30**   The company, or any person aggrieved, may apply to the court for an order that the company is not bound to circulate any statement on the ground that the right to have a resolution and statement circulated is being abused (s 295(1)) and there is potential for the members concerned to be penalised in costs (s 295(2)), a possibility that should prevent vexatious use of these provisions.

**17-31**   If the company fails to comply with the requirement to circulate the resolution and statement when otherwise required to do so, every officer in default is liable to a fine (s 293(1), (5)).

### Registering resolutions

**17-32**   The resolutions and agreements listed in CA 2006, s 29 must be registered with the registrar of companies under s 30, see discussion at **5-6**. Essentially this applies to any special resolution; any resolution or agreement whether of the company or of a class of shareholders which is effective because of the *Duomatic* principle[47] that informal unanimous assent is tantamount to a resolution, see **17-73**; any resolution varying class rights, see **16-37**, which is not a special resolution; and other resolutions (i.e. ordinary resolutions) which are required by statute to be registered (s 29).

**17-33**   A copy of the resolution (or, if not in writing, a memorandum setting out its terms) must be registered with the registrar of companies within 15 days after it is passed. A failure to comply with the registration requirement is an offence (CA 2006, s 30(2)).

## D  General meetings

### Meeting convened by the directors

**17-34**   The directors may at any time convene a meeting of the company (CA 2006, s 302) and, in the case of a public company, the directors must call an annual general meeting and they must also call a general meeting when a public company suffers a serious loss of capital (s 656) though this latter requirement is sometimes ignored in practice. Under the CA 1985 and the 1985 Table A, all general meetings other than the annual general meeting were called extraordinary general meetings,[48] but that terminology is not carried forward to the CA 2006 which describes company meetings as general meetings or the annual general meeting, as the case may be.

---

[47]  *Re Duomatic Ltd* [1969] 1 All ER 161.      [48]  See, for example, CA 1985, s 368; Table A, reg 36.

## Annual general meeting

**17-35** A public company must hold an annual general meeting within six months of its account-ing reference date, i.e. the financial year end (CA 2006, s 336(1)). Non-compliance is an offence.[49] Private companies (unless they are a traded company[50]) are not required to hold an annual general meeting, but may do so if they choose or if their articles require.

**17-36** Convening a general meeting is a matter for the directors (s 302) and, in the appropriate case, the notice calling the meeting must specify that it is the annual general meeting (s 337(1)). The notice requirements for general meetings are discussed at **17-56**.

**17-37** The statute does not dictate the business to be conducted at an annual general meeting but the typical business of such a meeting includes:

- laying the annual accounts, the strategic report (if any), the directors' report, the auditors' report (unless exempt) and, if the company is a quoted company, the direc-tors' remuneration report and policy, before the meeting;[51]
- re-electing retiring directors and electing new directors;[52]
- appointing an auditor, if required to do so,[53] and setting the auditor's remunera-tion[54] although in practice that matter is often delegated to the board; and
- declaring a dividend.[55]

**17-38** Any other matter may be included in the business of a general meeting provided proper notice of the matter is given. Public companies typically include resolutions relating to the allotment of shares, disapplying to a certain extent the statutory pre-emption rights and allowing a company to purchase its own shares.[56] It is common to include a resolution authorising the calling of general meetings, other than an annual general meeting, on not less than 14 clear days' notice, a consequence of changes effected by the Shareholders' Rights Directive, see **17-56**. Institutional shareholders, while willing to grant authority for meetings on 14 days' notice, caution against routine use of the power which can pre-vent shareholders having sufficient time to consider the issues before them. Quoted com-panies must submit the directors' remuneration report and the remuneration policy for shareholder approval as required by CA 2006, ss 439 and 439A, see **18-45**.

**17-39** Notice of the meeting must state the intention to propose any special resolution and must set out the text of any special resolution to be considered at the meeting. For other mat-ters, a difficult issue is the degree of detail which must be given with respect to matters other than the standard matters of business for, if the notice given is misleading, the court can restrain the holding of the meeting[57] and resolutions incorrectly notified are invalid

---

[49] CA 2006, s 336(4). Repeated failures to hold annual general meetings may amount to unfairly prejudicial conduct under what is now CA 2006, s 994: see *Re a company (No 00789 of 1987), ex p Shooter* [1990] BCLC 384.

[50] A private company which is a traded company must hold an annual general meeting within nine months of the year-end: CA 2006, 336. This provision derives from the implementation of the Shareholders' Rights Directive, see n 11, but it would be exceptional here for a private company to be a traded company.

[51] CA 2006, ss 437(1), 471(2).

[52] CA 2006, s 160. See The Companies (Model Articles) Regulations 2008, SI 2008/3229, reg 2, Sch 1, art 17 (Ltd); reg 4, Sch 3, arts 20–22 (Plc).

[53] See CA 2006, ss 485(1), 489(1).    [54] CA 2006, s 492(1).

[55] See The Companies (Model Articles) Regulations 2008, SI 2008/3229, reg 2, Sch 1, art 30 (Ltd); reg 4, Sch 3, art 70 (Plc).    [56] See CA 2006, ss 551, 571, 701 respectively.

[57] *Jackson v Munster Bank* (1884) 13 LR IR 118.

and not binding on the company.[58] The key requirement is that the notice must disclose all relevant facts so that a member can exercise an informed business judgement as to whether he ought to attend the meeting[59] and this requires a fair, candid, and reasonable explanation of the purpose or purposes for which the meeting is summoned.[60] Particular attention must be given to full and frank notice of any resolution involving a personal advantage to a director.[61] For example, a notice to the shareholders of an agreement to sell the business which failed to disclose the substantial payments which would be made to the directors personally as part of the agreement was invalid.[62]

**17-40**   Members holding a certain size of shareholdings have various rights as to the circulation of resolutions and statements and the inclusion of matters on the agenda for a meeting.

### Circulation of resolutions, inclusion of agenda matters at an annual general meeting

**17-41**   Members of a public company representing not less than 5 per cent of the total voting rights of all the members entitled to vote on the resolution or not less than 100 members[63] having the right to vote on the resolution holding shares paid up to the sum, per member, of at least £100 (CA 2006, s 338(3)), may require the company to give notice of a resolution to be moved at the next annual general meeting. It must be a resolution that may properly be moved and is intended to be moved at the annual general meeting so excluding resolutions which would be ineffective (because inconsistent with an enactment, the company's constitution, or otherwise), defamatory, frivolous, or vexatious (s 338(1), (2)). The request to give notice of the resolution may be in hard copy or electronic form, must identify the resolution of which notice is to be given, and it must be authenticated by the persons making it (CA 2006, s 338(4)). The request must be received by the company not later than six weeks before the annual general meeting to which it relates or, if later, the time at which notice is given of that meeting (s 338(4)).

**17-42**   In addition to this right to require the circulation of a resolution, in the case of a traded company, there is a right to request the inclusion of any matter in the business to be dealt with at an annual general meeting which may properly be included in the business, again excluding the defamatory, frivolous, and vexatious, and subject to the same membership thresholds as outlined in **17-41** (s 338A). The request in this case must be accompanied by a statement setting out the grounds for the request.

**17-43**   The company must carry the costs of circulation if the notice of the resolution, or the request to add to the agenda, is received before the end of the financial year preceding the annual general meeting (CA 2006, ss 340(1), 340B(1)) and, if not, the members must bear the costs of circulation unless the company otherwise resolves. If the company has not so resolved, it need not circulate the resolution or request until the members deposit or tender a sum reasonably sufficient to meet the company's expenses of circulation (ss 340(2), 340B(2)) and that potential expense may be an inhibiting factor, depending on the size of

---

[58]  *Baillie v Oriental Telephone and Electric Co Ltd* [1915] 1 Ch 503.
[59]  *Tiessen v Henderson* [1899] 1 Ch 861.
[60]  *Kaye v Croydon Tramways Company* [1898] 1 Ch 358 at 373, per Rigby LJ.
[61]  *Baillie v Oriental Telephone and Electric Co Ltd* [1915] 1 Ch 503; *Tiessen v Henderson* [1899] 1 Ch 861; *Kaye v Croydon Tramways Company* [1898] 1 Ch 358.
[62]  *Kaye v Croydon Tramways Company* [1898] 1 Ch 358.
[63]  Indirect investors, subject to the requirements of CA 2006, s 153 being met, may count towards the 100 figure.

the company. Of course, if the company is using electronic or website communication, the costs may be modest, being limited in effect to circulating hard copies to those who have opted for that mode of delivery.

**17-44**  If the company fails to comply with the requirement to circulate the resolution or request when otherwise required to do so, every officer in default is liable to a fine (s 339(4), (5) and s 340A(3), (4)).

## Circulation of statements, right to answers, at any general meeting

**17-45**  Subject to certain thresholds being met, members have a right under CA 2006, s 314 to circulate a statement of not more than 1,000 words to any general meeting of any company, public or private. This statement may be in addition to a resolution which the members (or other members) wish to circulate, it may be in respect of a resolution which the directors have given notice of or it may be in respect of any other business to be conducted at the meeting. The same requirements are imposed, as discussed at **17-41** et seq, with regard to the percentage of members required to trigger the right (s 314(2)), the restrictions on statements which are defamatory, vexatious etc (s 317), the position on costs so far as they apply to a public company (s 316), and that it is an offence by each officer in default if the company fails to circulate a statement when otherwise required to do so (s 315(3)). Further, at any general meeting of a traded company, the company must answer any question relating to the business being dealt with at the meeting put by a member subject to certain exceptions, as where to answer would be prejudicial to the good order of the meeting, would involve the disclosure of confidential information, or would be undesirable in the interests of the company, etc (s 319A).

## Meeting requisitioned by the members

**17-46**  The directors are required to call a general meeting once requested to do so by members representing at least 5 per cent of the paid-up capital of the company as carries the right to vote in general meetings (CA 2006, s 303(2)). The obligation to convene the meeting can only arise if the request is valid and where it is ineffective because of a defect in its form then, despite the threshold requirements being met, the directors are not obliged to call a meeting.[64]

**17-47**  A request must state the general nature of the business to be dealt with at the meeting and must be authenticated by the persons making it.[65] It may include the text of a resolution that may properly be moved and is intended to be moved at the meeting (CA 2006, s 303(4)) excluding resolutions which would be ineffective (because inconsistent with an enactment, the company's constitution, or otherwise), defamatory, frivolous, or vexatious (s 303(5)). If the resolution is a special resolution, the notice of the meeting must so state (s 283(5)). Notice of any resolution included in the request must be included in the notice of the meeting.[66]

---

[64] *Rose v McGivern* [1998] 2 BCLC 593; *Isle of Wight Railway Co v Tahourdin* (1883) 25 Ch D 320; see also *PNC Telecom plc v Thomas* [2003] BCC 202.

[65] CA 2006, s 303(4) and (6). A meeting convened on requisition cannot transact any business other than that covered by the terms of the requisition: *Ball v Metal Industries Ltd* 1957 SC 315, together with any resolutions which the directors might put forward and of which due notice has been given, see *Rose v McGivern* [1998] 2 BCLC 593.                              [66] CA 2006, ss 303(4)(b), 304(2), (3).

**17-48**   If within 21 days of becoming required to do so the directors do not call a meeting, to be held on a date not more than 28 days after the date of the notice convening the meeting, the members may themselves call a meeting (CA 2006, s 305(1)).

## Meeting convened by the court

**17-49**   The court has a discretionary power under CA 2006, s 306 (previously CA 1985, s 371) to order a general meeting to be held in such manner as it thinks fit if it is impracticable to call a meeting in the normal way or to conduct the meeting in the manner prescribed by the company's articles or the CA 2006. The court may exercise this power either of its own motion, or on the application of any director, or on the application of any member of the company who would be entitled to vote at the meeting.[67] The court may direct, in particular, that one member of the company present be deemed to constitute a meeting (s 306(4)).

**17-50**   The intention behind the power is to allow a company 'to get on with managing its affairs without being frustrated by the impracticability of calling or conducting a general meeting in the manner prescribed by the articles and the Act'.[68] This power may be invoked, for example, where a company finds itself without directors able to convene a meeting, or there is uncertainty as to who are the members, or the members are overseas and the company is unable to serve notice on them.[69] Occasionally, the power of the court is invoked because of the potential for violence. In *Re British Union for the Abolition of Vivisection*,[70] for example, it was impractical to call a general meeting of all 9,000 members of the BUAV when a previous meeting had degenerated into near riot and had been stopped by the police.

**17-51**   This power of the court to convene a meeting is often used to resolve cases where shareholders have refused to attend meetings so rendering them inquorate. By absenting themselves, the shareholders hope to prevent the majority shareholders from exercising their voting powers on a particular issue, typically the removal of the absent shareholders from office as directors.[71] The courts have generally refused to allow absent shareholders to gain an effective veto over company business in this way and so will order a meeting to be held which is quorate despite the absence of those shareholders.[72]

**17-52**   In *Re Opera Photographic Ltd*,[73] for example, the company had an issued share capital of 100 shares, divided 51/49 between the two parties who were also the directors. The articles provided that the quorum for a meeting of the directors or the shareholders was two. The parties fell out and the 51 per cent shareholder wanted to hold a general meeting in order

---

[67] CA 2006, s 306(2). The mere fact that a petition alleging unfairly prejudicial conduct has been presented under s 994 does not automatically oust the court's jurisdiction, but it may be a relevant factor in determining whether the court should exercise its discretion to call a meeting: *Harman v BML Group Ltd* [1994] 2 BCLC 674, CA; *Re Whitchurch Insurance Consultants Ltd* [1993] BCLC 1359; cf *Re Sticky Fingers Restaurant Ltd* [1992] BCLC 84.

[68] *Vectone Entertainment Holding Ltd v South Entertainment Ltd* [2004] 2 BCLC 224 at [32]; and see *Wheeler v Ross* [2011] EWHC 2527.

[69] See *Harman v BML Group Ltd* [1994] 2 BCLC 674 at 677. It is not sufficient that the meeting is to be chaired by a director whom some of the shareholders wish to remove from office—this does not render it 'impracticable' to call a meeting: *Might SA v Redbus Interhouse plc* [2004] 2 BCLC 449; see also *Monnington v Easier plc* [2006] 2 BCLC 283.      [70] [1995] 2 BCLC 1.

[71] See *Re El Sombrero Ltd* [1958] Ch 900; also *Re HR Paul & Son* (1973) 118 Sol Jo 166.

[72] See, for example, *Smith v Butler* [2012] BCC 645 at [54]; *Vectone Entertainment Holding Ltd v South Entertainment Ltd* [2004] 2 BCLC 224.      [73] [1989] BCLC 763.

to remove the 49 per cent shareholder from office as a director, but no meeting could be held because of the lack of a quorum. The court granted an application to convene a meeting of the company, taking the view that the quorum requirements in the articles of association could not be treated as conferring on the 49 per cent shareholder a form of veto to prevent the holding of a meeting to consider removing him from office as a director. Likewise in *Re Whitchurch Insurance Consultants Ltd*,[74] where a husband and wife were the only directors of the company and held 666 and 334 of the 1,000 issued shares of the company respectively: the personal and business relationship between them broke down and the husband wanted to hold a general meeting to pass a resolution removing his wife as a director. The quorum requirement was set at two members so no meeting could be held. The court agreed that an order convening a meeting should be made to allow a board of directors to be appointed.

**17-53**  There are limits to the discretion of the court under CA 2006, s 306, however, and there are two clear categories of cases where the discretion will not be exercised. In *Harman v BML Group Ltd*[75] the company's capital was divided into A and B shares and no shareholders' meeting was quorate without a B shareholder or proxy being present. The parties fell out and the other shareholders applied for an order under what is now CA 2006, s 306, allowing them to hold meetings without B. The Court of Appeal refused the application as the effect of ordering meetings without B would be to override a quorum requirement which, the court found, constituted a class right conferred on B so as to protect him from removal from office as a director. In *Ross v Telford*[76] a husband and wife were the directors of two companies and they were also equal shareholders of one of the companies. The quorum for board and general meetings of both companies was two with the result that both companies were potentially deadlocked at board and general meeting levels. The Court of Appeal refused an application by the husband for a court order convening a meeting with the view to appointing an additional director. It concluded that what is now CA 2006, s 306 is not an appropriate vehicle for resolving deadlock between two equal shareholders. It is a procedural section and is not designed to affect substantive voting rights or to shift the balance of power between shareholders by permitting a 50 per cent shareholder to override the wishes of the other 50 per cent shareholder. The shareholders had agreed that power would be shared equally and potential deadlock was a matter which they must be taken to have been agreed on with the consent and for the protection of each of them.

**17-54**  The limits to the court's discretion therefore are that the court will not order a meeting under CA 2006, s 306 where to order a meeting would negate a class right conferred on a shareholder[77] or where it would shift the balance of power in a company which is deadlocked 50/50 by virtue of the parties' agreement. The Court of Appeal confirmed these limitations in *Union Music Ltd v Watson*[78] where the shareholdings were split 51 per cent and 49 per cent and the two shareholders were the only directors. A shareholders' agreement provided that the consent of both shareholders was required for any meeting of the shareholders and the quorum for board meetings was set by the articles at two. Once the parties fell out, this meant that the company was deadlocked at board and general meeting level.

---

[74] [1993] BCLC 1359.  [75] [1994] 2 BCLC 674.  [76] [1998] 1 BCLC 82.

[77] See also *Alvona Developments Ltd v The Manhattan Loft Corporation (AC) Ltd* [2006] BCC 119 where, although there was no class right as such, the court did not think it would be appropriate to make an order (for a meeting to appoint further directors) when it would override an agreement between the parties that there would be one jointly appointed director. Cf *Smith v Butler* [2012] BCC 645.

[78] [2003] 1 BCLC 453, CA.

**17-55**  Overruling the first instance decision, the Court of Appeal ordered that a general meeting be held for the sole purpose of appointing another director which meeting was to be attended by the 51 per cent shareholder only. The court considered that the case was distinguishable from *Harman v BML Group Ltd*[79] and *Ross v Telford*.[80] Outside of the circumstances in those cases, the court said, a provision as to the consent of the shareholders to a meeting could be overridden by a court order so as to enable a company to have an effective board in a position to manage its affairs properly. One side or other has to prevail and Peter Gibson LJ could not see that the contractual provisions in the shareholders' agreement provided a sufficient reason why the power to order a meeting should not be exercised given that, on the facts in *Union Music*, neither of the exceptional circumstances limiting the court's discretion was applicable.

## E  Meeting procedures

### Notice of meetings

#### Minimum periods of notice

**17-56**  In the case of an annual general meeting of a public company (or a traded company, defined in CA 2006, s 360C), the minimum notice period is at least 21 clear days (s 307(2)(a), s 307A(1)(b)).[81] In the case of a general meeting, whether of a private or public company, at least 14 clear days' notice must be given (s 307(1), (2)(b)). A traded company may only call general meetings on at least 14 days' notice if (a) the meeting is not an annual general meeting, (b) the company offers the facility for shareholders to vote by electronic means accessible to all shareholders,[82] and (c) shareholders have passed, at the preceding annual general meeting or a general meeting held since that meeting, a special resolution approving the calling of meetings on at least 14 days' notice (s 307A).[83] All these periods of notice are minimum periods and the articles may provide for longer periods (ss 307(3), 307A(6)). Failure to give timely notice invalidates the meeting and nullifies the proceedings.[84]

**17-57**  It is possible for general meetings (other than for traded companies) to be called at shorter notice (s 307(4)) with the consent of a majority in number of the members having the right to attend and vote at the meeting and holding at least 95 per cent in nominal value of the shares carrying voting rights in public companies and 90 per cent in private companies,[85] but an annual general meeting of a public company which is not a traded company can only be called on short notice if the shareholders are unanimous (s 337(2)). There is no statutory provision for traded companies to hold general meetings on shorter notice

---

[79]  [1994] 2 BCLC 674.      [80]  [1998] 1 BCLC 82.

[81]  The periods of notice prescribed must be calculated excluding both the day on which notice is given and the day of the meeting: CA 2006, s 360.

[82]  It suffices for these purposes if members can appoint a proxy by means of a website: CA 2006, s 307A(3).

[83]  This position is a consequence of the implementation of the Shareholders' Rights Directive, art 3, n 9, which requires at least 21 days' notice for all general meetings of traded companies but gives Member States the option to allow traded companies to call meetings on 14 days' notice subject to these conditions. Hence a resolution of this nature has become a standard part of the business of an annual general meeting of traded companies so ensuring that they always have an existing authority to call general meetings on at least 14 days' notice, but there is some evidence of institutional shareholder opposition to these short notice resolutions on the basis that the time period is too short for shareholders to engage fully with the business of the meeting.      [84]  *Smyth v Darley* (1849) 2 HLC 789. See too CA 2006, s 301.

[85]  Private companies can increase that 90 per cent threshold to 95 per cent by their articles: CA 2006, s 307(6).

than the minimum prescribed (s 307A). Once there is agreement to short notice, there is no minimum period of notice which is required and it can be as brief as the members choose. Short notice can be particularly useful if the company needs to remove a director, approve a major transaction, or authorise changes to the capital structure, but some institutional shareholders and some overseas investors, as a matter of policy, oppose attempts to shorten notice periods.

### Manner of notice

**17-58**  Notice of a general meeting must be given in hard copy form, electronically, or by means of a website, or partly by one such means and partly by another (CA 2006, s 308).

### Persons entitled to notice

**17-59**  Subject to any provision of the company's articles and any enactment, notice of a general meeting must be given to every member (including any person entitled to a share in consequence of the death or bankruptcy of a member, if the company has been notified of their entitlement) and every director (CA 2006, s 310). Notice of a general meeting must be given to the company's auditor who is entitled to attend and to be heard on any part of the business which concerns him as auditor, a potentially very wide category (s 502).

**17-60**  An omission (other than an accidental omission within CA 2006, s 313) to give notice to any person entitled to it invalidates the meeting and nullifies the proceedings.[86] Failure to give notice because of an error on the part of directors, for example where they were under the erroneous impression that someone had ceased to be a member of the company, is not an accidental omission for these purposes.[87]

### Contents of notice

**17-61**  The notice must specify the time and date and place of the meeting and, subject to the company's articles (other than a traded company), must state the general nature of the business to be dealt with at the meeting (CA 2006, s 311(2)).[88] Every notice calling a meeting of a company (or of any class of the members) must contain a reasonably prominent statement that the member is entitled to appoint a proxy or proxies (see **17-10**) to attend and vote instead of him and that a proxy need not be a member (s 325). Where the meeting is the annual general meeting of a public company, the notice calling the meeting must so state (s 337). A quoted company, when giving notice of an accounts meeting, must draw attention to the right of the members to use the company website to draw attention to audit concerns.[89] A traded company which is required under s 388 to include any matter in the business to be conducted at the annual general meeting at the request of shareholders must give notice of the matter in the same manner and at the same time, or as soon as reasonably practicable thereafter, as it gives notice of the meeting (s 340A(1)). It must also publish the matter on the website which the company uses to publish information (as required by s 311A) in advance of the general meeting (s 340A(1)). There are very detailed

---

[86]  CA 2006, s 301; *Smyth v Darley* (1849) 2 HLC 789.

[87]  *Musselwhite v C H Musselwhite & Son Ltd* [1962] Ch 964.

[88]  A company whose shares are admitted to trading on a regulated market must provide information to holders on: (1) the place, time, and agenda of meetings; (2) the total number of shares and voting rights; and (3) the rights of holders to participate in meetings: DTR 6.1.12R.

[89]  See CA 2006, s 529; for the definition of 'quoted company,' see n 10; and for the 'accounts meeting' see CA 2006, s 437(3), essentially the general meeting of a public company at which the company's accounts are laid.

requirements as to the content of the notice to be given by a traded company with respect to matters such as setting out the website address used by the company to communicate with the shareholders, the manner of attending and voting (including voting in advance), the formalities for appointing proxies and the right to ask questions at the meeting (see s 311(3)).

## Location of meetings

**17-62**    In order for a meeting of members to be validly constituted, it is not necessary for all the members to be physically present in the same room. A valid meeting can be held using overflow rooms provided that all due steps are taken to direct those unable to get into the main meeting into the overflow room, and that there are adequate audio-visual links to enable those in all the rooms to see and hear what is going on in the other rooms and that there is appropriate opportunity to participate in the debate.[90]

## Chairman of meetings

**17-63**    Subject to any provision in the articles stating who may or may not be chairman, any member may be elected to be chairman by a resolution passed at the meeting (CA 2006, s 319).[91] The articles commonly provide that the chairman of the board of directors or, in his absence, some other director nominated by the directors, is to act as the chairman of the meeting.[92] It is the chairman's duty to preserve order, to conduct proceedings regularly, to deal with the business of the meeting, and to take care that the sense of the meeting is properly ascertained with regard to any question before it.[93] In the case of a vote on a resolution by show of hands, a declaration by the chairman that the resolution has/has not passed or passed with a particular majority is conclusive evidence of that fact without proof of the number or proportion of the votes in favour of or against the resolution (s 320(1)).[94] In the event of a dispute, the solution is to demand a poll[95] (see **17-13**).

## Adjournment of meetings

**17-64**    The chairman must adjourn if directed to do so by the meeting or if, within half an hour before the start, a quorum is not present, or if at any time during the meeting a quorum ceases to be present.[96]

---

[90] *Byng v London Life Association Ltd* [1989] BCLC 400, CA.

[91] See The Companies (Model Articles) Regulations 2008, SI 2008/3229, reg 2, Sch 1, art 40 (Ltd); reg 4, Sch 3, art 31 (Plc).

[92] There is no requirement that the chairman be 'neutral' and he may occupy the chair even though the matter for discussion is the removal of all of the directors including himself and the appointment of a new board: *Might SA v Redbus Interhouse plc* [2004] 2 BCLC 449.

[93] *National Dwelling Society v Sykes* [1894] 3 Ch 159. It appears (the wording is unclear) that the chairman has a casting vote at a general meeting on a resolution on a show of hands, see CA 2006, s 282(3) and s 283(4), but not on a poll, whereas under the 1985 Table A, reg 50, the chairman had a casting vote on a show of hands or on a poll. A saving provision in the Companies Act 2006 (Commencement No 3, etc) Order 2007, SI 2007/2194, art 9, Sch 3, para 23A allows companies (other than traded companies) which, immediately before 1 October 2007, had such a provision with respect to ordinary resolutions in their articles to retain it or reinsert it, if they have removed it from their articles.

[94] See The Companies (Model Articles) Regulations 2008, SI 2008/3229, reg 2, Sch 1, art 45(2) (Ltd); reg 4, Sch 3, arts 35 and 36(2)(Plc).

[95] A chairman may call a poll: see The Companies (Model Articles) Regulations 2008, SI 2008/3229, reg 2, Sch 1, art 42 (Ltd); reg 4, Sch 3, art 33 (Plc).

[96] See The Companies (Model Articles) Regulations 2008, SI 2008/3229, reg 2, Sch 1, art 42 (Ltd), reg 4, Sch 3, art 33 (Plc); *Salisbury Gold Mining Co Ltd v Hathorn* [1897] AC 268, PC.

**17-65**  The chairman may adjourn a meeting if the meeting consents to the adjournment or if it appears necessary to do so to protect the safety of any person attending the meeting or to ensure that the business of the meeting is conducted in an orderly manner.[97]

**17-66**  A chairman's decision to adjourn is invalid not only if it is taken in bad faith but also if he fails to take into account relevant factors, or takes into account irrelevant factors, or reaches a conclusion which no reasonable chairman could have reached, having regard to the purpose of his power to adjourn which is to ensure that the members have a proper opportunity to debate and vote on resolutions.[98]

**17-67**  In *Byng v London Life Association Ltd*[99] the Court of Appeal found that, in deciding to adjourn an overcrowded general meeting from the morning to the afternoon, the chairman had failed to take into account relevant factors. The court thought that there must be very special circumstances to justify a decision to adjourn the meeting to a time and place where, to the knowledge of the chairman, it could not be attended by a number of the members who had taken the trouble to attend the original meeting and who could not even lodge a proxy vote because it was too late to do so.[100]

**17-68**  No business is to be transacted at an adjourned meeting other than business which might properly have been transacted at the meeting from which the adjourned meeting took place. Resolutions passed at an adjourned meeting take effect from the date on which they are in fact passed and are not deemed passed on any earlier date (CA 2006, s 332).

## Quorum for meetings

**17-69**  Subject to the articles, two qualifying persons present at a meeting are a quorum,[101] but not if the two persons present are corporate representatives or proxies for the same member.[102] In other words, the requirement is that two separate members are represented. Any resolution passed at a meeting which is inquorate is void.[103]

**17-70**  One shareholder cannot form a meeting,[104] except:

- if there is only one shareholder in a class of shareholders, the assent of that shareholder is the equivalent of a meeting of the class;[105]

- if the company is a single member company (whether public or private, limited by shares or by guarantee), one qualifying person present is a quorum (CA 2006, s 318(1)); and

---

[97] See The Companies (Model Articles) Regulations 2008, SI 2008/3229, reg 2, Sch 1, art 42 (Ltd), reg 4, Sch 3, art 33 (Plc).                    [98] *Byng v London Life Association Ltd* [1989] BCLC 400, CA.
[99] [1989] BCLC 400.        [100] As to when a proxy must be lodged, see CA 2006, s 327 and **17-11**.
[101] See The Companies (Model Articles) Regulations 2008, SI 2008/3229, reg 2, Sch 1, art 39 (Ltd); reg 4, Sch 3, art 30 (Plc). As to the quorum for a variation of class rights meetings, see CA 2006, s 334(4).
[102] CA 2006, s 318(2). The wording is unclear because it appears to provide that neither of the two representatives or proxies can count towards the quorum (neither being a qualifying person), as opposed to allowing them to count as one member personally present.
[103] *Re Cambrian Peat, Fuel and Charcoal Ltd, De La Mott's Case and Turner's Case* (1875) 31 LT 773; *Re Romford Canal Co, Pocock's Claims* (1883) 24 Ch D 85.
[104] *Sharpe v Dawes* (1876) 2 QBD 25; *Re London Flats Ltd* [1969] 2 All ER 744.
[105] *East v Bennett Bros* [1911] 1 Ch 163; *Re RMCA Reinsurance Ltd* [1994] BCC 378. The case of a single member of a class is exceptional. Otherwise the ordinary meaning of the word 'meeting' is the coming together of two or more persons: *Re Altitude Scaffolding Ltd, Re T & N Ltd* [2007] 1 BCLC 199 (the court refused to sanction a scheme of arrangement under what is now CA 2006, s 899 which provided for class meetings requiring the attendance in person or by proxy of one member of a class only).

- where the court convenes a meeting under s 306 (see **17-49**), a direction may be given that one member present may constitute a quorum (s 306(4)).

## Minutes of meetings

**17-71**    Every company is required to keep minutes of general meetings (CA 2006, s 355(1)(b)) and of directors' meetings (s 248). Any minute purporting to be signed by the chairman of the meeting at which such proceedings took place or by the chairman of the next succeeding meeting is evidence of those proceedings (s 356(4)). Where a sole member takes any decision which has effect as if agreed by the company in general meeting, he must provide the company with details of the decision (s 357(2)).

**17-72**    The minutes of general meetings are open to inspection by any member without charge, and a member is entitled, on payment of a small fee, to copies (s 358(3), (4)). Where inspection is refused, the court may by order compel inspection (s 358(7)).

## F  The *Duomatic* principle—informal unanimous assent

**17-73**    Recognising that shareholders do not always observe all of the formalities of meetings and resolutions as envisaged by the legislation, the courts accept that the informal unanimous assent of all shareholders who have a right to attend and vote at a general meeting of the company and with full knowledge of the relevant facts is as binding as a resolution of the company in general meeting provided the persons assenting are competent to effect the act to which they have assented.[106]

**17-74**    This principle, that unanimous assent is tantamount to a resolution of a properly convened general meeting,[107] is known as the *Duomatic* principle[108] and companies and shareholders often need to resort to it to validate actions which are otherwise not in conformity with the requirements of the articles,[109] or the Companies Act[110] (discussed at **17-80**), or a shareholders' agreement.[111]

---

[106] *Re Express Engineering Works Ltd* [1920] 1 Ch 466; *Re Oxted Motor Co Ltd* [1921] 3 KB 32; *Parker & Cooper v Reading* [1926] Ch 975; *Re Duomatic Ltd* [1969] 1 All ER 161 at 168, per Buckley J; *Re New Cedos Engineering Co Ltd* [1994] 1 BCLC 797. Strictly speaking, registration of such assent is required in certain cases, see CA 2006, s 29(1)(b) and s 30, but this registration requirement is rarely, if ever, observed.

[107] Or of a class of shareholders: *Re Torvale Group Ltd* [1999] 2 BCLC 605. The principle also applies to informal decisions of directors, see *Runciman v Walter Runciman plc* [1992] BCLC 1084 at 1092.

[108] Though, as is frequently pointed out, the origins of the principle are much earlier than the *Duomatic* decision, see n 106.

[109] See *Re Duomatic Ltd* [1969] 1 All ER 161.

[110] See *Wright v Atlas Wright (Europe) Ltd* [1999] 2 BCLC 301, CA. It can be used to effect an amendment of the articles, see *Re Sherlock Holmes International Society Ltd (No 2)* [2017] 2 BCLC 14 at [72], provided the assent was unambiguous—where conduct alone is relied on, that conduct must lead to the conclusion that on the balance of probabilities the members intended to amend the articles and further intended to make the particular amendment contended for.

[111] See *Re Euro Brokers Holdings Ltd v Monecor (London) Ltd* [2003] 1 BCLC 506, CA (shareholders had accepted as valid and were bound by a call for capital made by email though a shareholders' agreement provided for capital calls to be made by formal notice from the board).

**17-75** Assent by the shareholders[112] for these purposes may be given formally or informally (i.e. without any meeting at all) and it need not be given simultaneously but at different times.[113] Assent need not be in writing, it may be oral, or tacit, in the form of acquiescence by the shareholders with knowledge of the matter,[114] but a mere internal decision by a shareholder cannot constitute assent, there must be material from which assent can be objectively ascertained or (in the case of acquiescence) inferred.[115] An example of tacit assent can be seen in *Sharma v Sharma*[116] where the shareholders of a family company were held to have unanimously assented to a conflict of interest on the part of the sole director (also a shareholder). The business was formed to acquire dental practices and the director had also acquired practices in her own name. An issue subsequently arose as to whether she had acted in breach of the no-conflict duty. The Court of Appeal held that the informal unanimous assent of the shareholders with full knowledge of the facts meant that the director was not in breach of her no-conflict obligations under CA 2006, s 175. She had disclosed her plans fully at a family gathering with the other shareholders who were her mother-in-law, brother-in-law, and husband—each was a shareholder together with the director, each holding 25 per cent of the shares. Her mother-in-law was found to have expressly consented[117] and the two brothers, while remaining silent, were held by the Court of Appeal to have tacitly assented. Jackson LJ explained that consent cannot be inferred from silence unless the shareholders know their consent is required, or the circumstances are such that it would be unconscionable for the shareholders to remain silent at the time and object after the event.[118] In the circumstances of this case, including the fact that the two brothers invariably deferred to their mother, the silence of the two men did amount to consent. If they were minded to object, they should have spoken up and done so promptly, and it would be unconscionable for them to keep quiet initially and

---

[112] It is debatable whether the assent of beneficial (as opposed to registered) owners will suffice. Lindsay J thought (probably) not in *Domoney v Godinho* [2004] 2 BCLC 15 at [44]–[45], but Mann J, obiter, in *Shakar v Tsitsekkos* [2004] EWHC 2659 at [67] thought there was no reason why the assent of the beneficial shareholders might not suffice, for example, where the nominee shareholder leaves all decisions to his beneficiary. Newey J, obiter, in *Re Tulsesense Ltd, Rolfe v Rolfe* [2010] 2 BCLC 525 at [42]–[43] was willing to assume, without deciding, that the assent of all the beneficial owners meets the *Duomatic* requirement. See *Jalmoon Pty Ltd v Bow* (1997) 15 ACLC 230 at 237–8. Vice versa, the assent of a nominee shareholder will bind the beneficial owner: *Re Bateson Hotels (1958) Ltd, Bateson v Bateson* [2014] 1 BCLC 507 at [46], [48], [53]–[55] (beneficial owner when he became registered owner could not bring a petition alleging unfairly prejudicial conduct when the conduct he complained of had been approved by the shareholders unanimously including by the trustee previously registered as the nominee shareholder in respect of the petitioner's shares).

[113] *Parker & Cooper Ltd v Reading* [1926] Ch 975. It must be assent of all the shareholders so a controlling shareholder who transfers some shares to the trustees of his personal pension scheme needs to appreciate that by doing so, he cannot rely on *Duomatic* without evidence of the trustees' support. It is not enough for him to assert that he can speak for the trustees because he established the pension scheme and was a beneficiary of it, see *Dickinson v NAL Realisations* [2017] EWHC 28, [2018] 1 BCLC 623, at [71]–[73].

[114] See *EIC Services Ltd v Phipps* [2004] 2 BCLC 589; *Re Ravenhart Service (Holdings) Ltd* [2004] 2 BCLC 376 at [89], [93]; *Re Torvale Group Ltd* [1999] 2 BCLC 605; *Re Bailey Hay & Co Ltd* [1971] 3 All ER 693.

[115] *Schofield v Schofield* [2011] 2 BCLC 319 at [32] approving Newey J in *Re Tulsesense Ltd, Rolfe v Rolfe* [2010] 2 BCLC 525 at [41]. See *Blindley Heath Investments Ltd v Bass* (CA) [2017] Ch 389 at [108] where, obiter, the Court of Appeal queried whether the *Duomatic* principle could extend to a decision taken at a meeting attended by only some shareholders in circumstances where the interests of those absent were represented by those present. The trial judge had indicated that such assents would be effective to amount to the assent of absent members, given their interests were represented—the Court of Appeal was clearly doubtful that such deemed proxy or representative assents sufficed.

[116] [2014] BCC 73.    [117] [2014] BCC 73 at [65].    [118] [2014] BCC 73 at [52].

raise objections only after a number of practices had been purchased, some for the director, some for the company.

**17-76**  On the other hand, in *Re BW Estates Ltd*[119] there were only two shareholders, one of whom was a corporate shareholder which had been dissolved. An issue for the court was whether the assent of the sole remaining shareholder (an individual) was sufficient for *Duomatic* purposes so as to validate a purported appointment of administrators to the company. The Court of Appeal held that, while the corporate shareholder had been dissolved, as long as its name remained on the register, it remained a shareholder, and therefore its assent was necessary if *Duomatic* was to apply. Its assent was impossible so *Duomatic* did not apply. The court noted that the requirement of *Duomatic* is the assent of all the shareholders 'who have a right to attend and vote at a general meeting of the company, not those of the shareholders that may be available at the time'.[120]

**17-77**  Sir Geoffrey Vos, C, noted:[121]

> 'Whatever, therefore, the precise status of such a [dissolved] member might be, it seems to me that the *Duomatic* principle simply cannot apply in a situation where one of the registered shareholders is a corporation which does not exist, because it requires the consent of all the registered shareholders and one of them is incapable of consenting. *Duomatic* is a valuable principle, but it would be wrong to assume that it must always be capable of applying.'

**17-78**  The principle cannot apply where the assent of the shareholders has never been sought[122] or where there is no evidence of any discussion or knowledge of the facts to enable them to assent.[123] It is not enough for *Duomatic* purposes to show that assent would probably have been given if asked, there has to be an actual assent,[124] an unqualified agreement, objectively established.[125]

**17-79**  Also, the persons assenting must be competent to effect the act to which they have assented,[126] i.e. it must be an act which the general meeting could have carried into effect so, for example, it must not be illegal. As shareholders cannot approve, even unanimously, an ultra vires distribution,[127] or an illegal act, or an act in fraud of the creditors,[128] the

---

[119] [2018] 2 WLR 1175, CA.    [120] [2018] 2 WLR 1175 at [81], CA.

[121] [2018] 2 WLR 1175 at [83], CA

[122] *EIC Services Ltd v Phipps* [2004] 2 BCLC 589 at [134]–[135], Ch D, per Neuberger J (appealed on unrelated grounds). Shareholder authorisation was required for the capitalisation of reserves and an allotment of bonus shares and, while the shareholders knew of the proposed bonus issue, their consent to the issue was neither sought nor given so, the court concluded, there could be no reliance on *Duomatic* to cure the omission of the necessary shareholder resolutions.

[123] *Queensway Systems Ltd v Walker* [2007] 2 BCLC 577.

[124] *EIC Services Ltd v Phipps* [2004] 2 BCLC 589 at [146]; and see *Re D'Jan of London Ltd* [1994] 1 BCLC 561 at 564; see *Secretary of State for Business, Innovation and Skills v Doffman (No 2)* [2011] 2 BCLC 541 at [40]: there cannot be reliance on *Duomatic* if the shareholders have never addressed their minds to the matter; also *Re PV Solar Solutions Ltd, Ball v Hughes* [2018] 1 BCLC 58 at [143].

[125] *Schofield v Schofield* [2011] 2 BCLC 319.

[126] *Re New Cedos Engineering Co Ltd* [1994] 1 BCLC 797; and see *Wright v Atlas Wright (Europe) Ltd* [1999] 2 BCLC 301 at 314–15, CA.

[127] *Re Exchange Banking Company, Flitcroft's Case* (1882) 21 Ch D 519; *Aveling Barford Ltd v Perion Ltd* [1989] BCLC 626 at 630–1; *Bairstow v Queens Moat Houses* [2001] 2 BCLC 531 at [36]; *Secretary of State for Business, Innovation and Skills v Doffman (No 2)* [2011] 2 BCLC 541 at [41].

[128] *Rolled Steel Products (Holdings) Ltd v British Steel Corp* [1985] 3 All ER 52 at 86; *Secretary of State for Business, Innovation and Skills v Doffman (No 2)* [2011] 2 BCLC 541 at [44]; *Re Bateson Hotels (1958) Ltd, Bateson v Bateson* [2014] 1 BCLC 507 at [51].

principle can have no application in such circumstances. Hence, where the company is insolvent or doubtfully solvent or the impugned transaction would jeopardise its solvency so the directors' duties under s 172(3) (see discussion at **10-41**) are engaged, then the *Duomatic* principle cannot be relied upon.[129]

**17-80**  A particular issue is the extent to which statutory requirements as to how a transaction or scheme might be carried out can be overridden by informal consent in this way. The principle cannot apply where the statutory requirement is clearly strict and mandatory.[130] In cases where the position is less clear, the court will consider the purpose and underlying rationale of the statutory formality in question and will refuse to allow reliance on the *Duomatic* principle to override statutory provisions where that rationale extends beyond the protection of the class which has purported to waive the provision.[131]

**17-81**  Hence the court has accepted that unanimous informal assent may suffice in place of the statutory requirement, now in CA 2006, s 188, for shareholder approval of a director's service contract, for the purpose of that provision does not extend beyond the benefit and protection of the shareholders of the company;[132] likewise CA 2006, s 190 which requires shareholder approval of certain substantial property transactions between a director and his company.[133] In those cases the statutory formality of a resolution in general meeting is open to waiver by the class for whose protection it is designed. With respect to the statutory scheme for the purchase of a company's own shares, the courts have allowed informal unanimous shareholder assent to override some of the procedural requirements surrounding such purchases, but not where the relevant procedural requirement was intended to protect a wider class of persons, in particular the company's creditors, rather than merely the shareholders.[134] In *Re Finch (UK) plc*[135] breaches of duties with respect to property transactions and the issue of redeemable shares in a company were cured by the application of *Duomatic* as both shareholders (husband and wife) approved these matters at a time when the company was neither insolvent nor on the verge of insolvency. But, breaches with respect to redemption of those shares other than out of distributable profits and in accordance with the company's accounts were not capable of being validated by *Duomatic* (being ultra vires and also because those statutory requirements were intended to protect creditors' interests).[136] The *Duomatic* principle was inapplicable, in any event, since by this time the company was insolvent or in financial difficulties such that its creditors were at risk.

---

[129] *West Mercia Safetywear Ltd v Dodds* [1988] BCLC 250; *Lexi Holdings plc v Luqman No 1* [2007] EWHC 2652 at [191]; and it is for the party who seeks to invoke the *Duomatic* principle in answer to a claim against them to prove, if it is disputed, that the company was solvent at the material time, at [193], per Briggs J; *Re PV Solar Solutions Ltd, Ball v Hughes* [2018] 1 BCLC 58.

[130] For example, in *Re Oceanrose Investments Ltd* [2008] EWHC 3475, [2009] Bus LR 947, Richards J considered a requirement in the Companies (Cross-Border Mergers) Regulations 2007, SI 2007/2974, reg 13, for a meeting of the members to approve the terms of a proposed merger to be a mandatory requirement, given that the regulations expressly provided for certain limited exceptions, none of which applied on the facts, and so left no room for the operation of the *Duomatic* principle. A meeting was required, therefore, even in the case of a company with only one (informed) shareholder who could not rely on *Duomatic*.

[131] *Wright v Atlas Wright (Europe) Ltd* [1999] 2 BCLC 301.

[132] *Wright v Atlas Wright (Europe) Ltd* [1999] 2 BCLC 301.

[133] *NBH Ltd v Hoare* [2006] 2 BCLC 649 at [43].

[134] *Kinlan v Crimmin* [2007] 2 BCLC 67 at [44]; *Dashfield v Davidson* [2008] BCC 222; *BDG Roof-Bond Ltd v Douglas* [2000] 1 BCLC 401 at 417; *Re Torvale Group Ltd* [1999] 2 BCLC 605. Cf *Re R W Peak (Kings Lynn) Ltd* [1998] 1 BCLC 193.

[135] [2016] 1 BCLC 394 at [19].          [136] [2016] 1 BCLC 394 at [28].

**17-82** The Company Law Review concluded that the *Duomatic* principle should be codified,[137] but the Government rejected that recommendation on the grounds that the common law position is very flexible (as can be seen from the case law) and codification would lead to rigidity and restrictions on the operation of this very beneficial principle.[138] Hence the Companies Act 2006 confirms that nothing in the provisions governing resolutions and meetings affects any enactment or rule of law as to things done otherwise than by passing a resolution (CA 2006, s 281(4)(a)).[139]

[137] Company Law Review, *Modern Company Law for a Competitive Economy, Final Report*, vol 1 (2001), URN 01/942, paras 7.17–7.26; also *Completing the Structure* (2000), URN 00/1335, paras 5.13–5.17; *Developing the Framework* (2000), URN 00/656, paras 4.21–4.23.

[138] See *Modernising Company Law* (Cm 5553-I, 2002), paras 2.31–2.35.

[139] See also CA 2006, s 239(6)(a) (ratification of acts of directors—nothing in the section affects the validity of a decision taken by unanimous consent of the members of the company).

# 18

# Informed shareholders and stakeholders—disclosure and the limited company

## A Introduction

### The role of disclosure

**18-1** Disclosure has always been seen, in part, as a price to be paid by those forming a company in return for the conferring of limited liability which insulates shareholders' personal wealth from the reach of the company's creditors unless the shareholders have been persuaded to give personal guarantees.[1] Against that general backdrop, the key purposes of disclosure would include:[2]

(1) to assist creditors to assess risk. Historically, disclosure requirements have been seen as a mechanism to assist creditors in assessing the risks of dealing with a limited company. The company puts forward information about itself and the creditor decides in the light of that information whether to deal with the company and on what terms (for example, as to price, interest and security required). In that context, financial information in the form of timely, independently audited, publicly available, annual accounts is particularly important, at least for the largest companies and their creditors, together with narrative reporting by directors on the activities and performance of the business.[3] These requirements are the focus of this chapter. Smaller companies are often heavily dependent on bank finance and will have a direct relationship with their bank (which will usually demand regular management accounts) and, probably, a small number of trade creditors who form a view as to the company's creditworthiness from their dealings with it rather than as a consequence of any mandated disclosure.

---

[1] Given that disclosure is designed primarily to protect creditors and others dealing with a limited liability company, an unlimited company (subject to certain exceptions) need not deliver accounts to the registrar of companies: CA 2006, s 448, though unlimited companies must prepare accounts for their shareholders: s 394.

[2] On the possible overuse of disclosure as a regulatory technique, see Sorensen, 'Disclosure in EU Corporate Governance—A Remedy in Need of Adjustment?' (2009) 10 EBOR 255; also generally Villiers, *Corporate Reporting and Company Law* (2006).

[3] See BIS, *Consultation on Audit Exemptions and Change of Accounting Framework*, (October 2011), URN11/1193, which noted that accessing company accounts and checking financial information were among the top reasons given by customers for obtaining company information held by Companies House and that they used that information to make business decisions, undertake credit assessments, due diligence, and to assess customers/suppliers, see para 52(c).

(2) to assist shareholders and others to make appropriate resource allocations and to hold management to account. The establishment of high standards of corporate governance requires quality financial and non-financial disclosure to enable shareholders and future investors to assess the company's management and profitability. Disclosure promotes efficient management and accountability as directors appreciate that their actions are subject to scrutiny. That transparency linked to concerns for their own business reputations can help to maintain appropriate standards of conduct. In Chapter 6, we discussed the importance of shareholders actively engaging in the governance of their companies. To do this effectively, shareholders require detailed accessible information, detailed enough for the sophisticated investor to appreciate the company's position without having to expend disproportionate time and resource in identifying key information and accessible enough so that all investors have the opportunity to understand the state of the company's affairs.

(3) to facilitate the operation of the capital markets. Investors need appropriate information to facilitate informed investment choice and the efficient allocation of capital by them and disclosure ensures investor protection and increases confidence in the proper functioning of the securities market.[4] The role of disclosure in the capital markets is beyond the scope of this book, but an example of its importance can be seen in the context of capital raising where, subject to exceptions, the Prospectus Regulation[5] requires a detailed prospectus to be prepared and published when a company wishes to offer its shares to the public and/or seeks admission to a regulated market (see **21-109**). Other Directives of note would include the Transparency Directive[6] (implemented mainly via the Disclosure and Transparency Rules (DTR) of the UKLA) which requires periodic disclosures by traded companies together with disclosure of major shareholdings and the Takeover Directive[7] (implemented mainly by the Takeover Code) which requires disclosure of control structures within a publicly traded company.

Disclosure may occur in a variety of ways, for example, through filing information such as the annual accounts at a public registry (the role of Companies House, the public registry, is discussed in Chapter 1), or by making certain company documents available for inspection at the company's registered office, or by discussing matters at annual general meetings (if a public company), or by making announcements to the markets (if a traded company). Increasingly, companies make extensive use of their websites to maintain ongoing disclosure with their shareholders and quoted companies are obliged to post information on their websites in certain circumstances.[8] Finally, the media also play an important role in bringing corporate information to the attention of the public.

---

[4] See Recital 7 to the Prospectus Regulation, n 5.

[5] Prospectus Regulation 2017/1129, OJ L 168/12, 30.6.2017, coming into force generally 21 July 2019, replacing Prospectus Directive 2003/71/EC.

[6] Directive 2004/109/EC, OJ L 390/38, 31.12.2004, as amended by Directive 2013/50/EU, OJ L 294/13, 6.11.2013. [7] Directive 2004/25/EC, OJ L 142/12, 30.4.2004, see art 10.

[8] For examples, see CA 2006, s 341 (obligation to post poll results on website); s 430 (obligation to publish annual accounts and reports on website); s 527 (ability of members to post audit concerns on the website). 'Quoted company' is defined in CA 2006, s 385 as a company whose equity share capital—(a) has been included in the official list in accordance with the provisions of Part 6 of the Financial Services and Markets Act 2000; (b) is officially listed in an EEA State (EU with Norway, Iceland, and Liechtenstein); or (c) is admitted to dealing on either the New York Stock Exchange or Nasdaq.

**18-2**  Most disclosure comes in the form of accounts and reports focusing on the financial position and the activities of the company, but mandated disclosure can extend in all directions so as to include, for example, health and safety issues, political donations, environmental concerns, and general corporate social responsibility. Most disclosure is addressed to shareholders or potential investors and/or creditors, present and future, but increasingly it is addressed to a wide variety of stakeholders who may have an interest in the company's affairs, such as employees and customers, local communities and the wider public, as well as local and national authorities.[9]

**18-3**  Many of the obligations are modified for the smallest companies with public companies subject to more onerous obligations than private companies and with the greatest transparency required of traded companies.

## The regulatory framework on accounting requirements

**18-4**  The statutory framework on accounts is laid down in CA 2006, Pt 15 augmented by a number of statutory instruments as a result of the decision to remove much of the accounting detail from the CA 2006 in the interests of clarity and to allow for ease of amendment in future. The key instruments which need to be read together with Part 15 are the Small Companies and Groups (Accounts and Directors' Report) Regulations 2008, SI 2008/409 and the Large and Medium-sized Companies and Groups (Accounts and Directors' Report) Regulations 2008, SI 2008/410, as amended which, respectively, set out the detailed requirements.[10]

**18-5**  The legislative framework reflects the requirements of the Accounting Directive 2013/34/EU[11] which replaced the Fourth and Seventh Company Law Directives which dealt with the presentation and content of a company's individual accounts[12] and consolidated or group accounts, respectively.[13] The Accounting Directive looks to reduce overall the regulatory burden on small companies, for example, by allowing them to prepare a simpler profit and loss account and balance sheet, by limiting disclosures in the notes to the accounts, and by removing any EU requirement for an audit leaving it to national law (UK small companies are already exempt from any audit requirement, see **18-55**). The Accounting Directive also harmonises the thresholds which define small and medium-sized companies so as to ensure that all companies across the EU are able to take advantage of the EU exemptions for that class of company which also has the additional benefit of improving the comparability of accounts.[14] Another significant measure is Directive 2014/95/EU,[15] the Non-Financial Reporting (NFR) Directive, amending the Accounting Directive and which applies to large companies with more than 500 employees. The NFR Directive requires additional disclosure of non-financial information (for example with

---

[9] See Company Law Review, *Developing the Framework* (2000), para 5.4; also *The Strategic Framework* (1999), paras 5.144–5.147.

[10] See also The Small Companies (Micro-Entities' Accounts) Regulations 2013, SI 2013/3309.

[11] OJ L 182/19, 29.6.2013. Implemented by The Companies, Partnerships and Groups (Accounts and Reports) Regulations 2015, SI 2015/980. The background is set out in BIS, *UK Implementation of the EU Accounting Directive* (August 2014), BIS/14/1025 and Government Response (January 2015), BIS/15/36.

[12] Fourth Council Directive (EEC) 78/660, OJ L 222/11, 14.8.1978.

[13] Seventh Council Directive (EEC) 83/349, OJ L 193/1, 18.7.1983.

[14] For the background to the Accounting Directive, see EU Commission Memorandum 13/540, 12.6.2013.

[15] OJ L 330/1, 15.11.2014. Implemented by The Companies, Partnerships and Groups (Accounts and Non-financial Reporting) Regulations 2016, SI 2016/1245.

regard to environmental, social, human rights, anti-corruption, and bribery measures), with effect for financial years commencing on or after 1 January 2017.

**18-6** The accounting measures are designed to ensure the highest standards of transparency (compatible with the economic size of the company) and comparability for the accounts of companies formed in the Member States. For larger companies, the key development was the adoption, not just within the EU, but globally, of international accounting standards drawn up by the IASB[16] rather than standards derived from national accounting practice, again a move designed to enhance the transparency and comparability of accounts.[17]

**18-7** The move within the EU to international accounting standards started with the adoption in 2002 of a Regulation on the application of International Accounting Standards (IAS)[18] which, since 1 January 2005, requires listed companies (see **21-103**) to draw up their consolidated accounts in accordance with IAS, now known as IFRS (International Financial Reporting Standards).[19] Directors must state in the notes to the accounts that the consolidated accounts have been prepared in accordance with IAS (CA 2006, s 406).[20] A company (other than a charity) has the option of preparing its individual accounts either in accordance with IAS or the CA 2006.[21] A parent company must ensure that its individual accounts and the individual accounts of its undertakings are prepared using the same framework, whether that is IAS or CA 2006, except to the extent that in the directors' opinion there are good reasons for not doing so (CA 2006, s 407). If a company prepares either its consolidated or individual accounts according to IAS for a financial year, it can switch back to the CA 2006 requirements in subsequent years, if there is a relevant change of circumstances as defined in s 395(4), or the directors may change regardless of a change of circumstance provided that they have not changed to Companies Act accounts in the preceding five years (s 395(4A)).

### Towards a new disclosure framework

**18-8** Clearly, both domestically and at the EU level, disclosure requirements are the regulatory tool of choice. But the financial crisis (from 2007–08 onwards) revealed that even extensive disclosure did not alert shareholders or regulators or Governments, to the impending crisis. Consequently, there has been much public debate between providers, users, and regulators as to the value, relevance, and effectiveness of much of the required disclosure with a consensus emerging of the need for more focused, targeted, effective disclosure. In the UK, the Financial Reporting Council (FRC) has responsibility for setting and promoting high standards of corporate reporting and corporate governance in the interests of investors. The FRC concentrates on publicly traded companies and the largest private companies and it acts through two FRC Board Committees (a Codes

---

[16] See n 19.

[17] The requirement to use IAS was intended to end what the then European Commissioner Bolkestein described as 'the current Tower of Babel' in financial reporting. See Commission Press Release, IP/02/827, 7 June 2002.

[18] Regulation (EC) No 1606/2002, OJ L 243/1, 11.9.2002; and European Commission Press Release, IP/02/827, 7 June 2002.

[19] International Accounting Standards were issued by the International Accounting Standards Committee which has since been replaced by the International Accounting Standards Board (IASB), an independent standard-setting body which issues IFRS.

[20] The AIM Rules also require AIM parent companies to prepare their accounts in accordance with IFRS, see r 19.

[21] Accounts prepared under the CA 2006 (called Companies Act accounts) either apply full UK GAAP or a modified version of UK GAAP for smaller entities. See n 45 on developments to the accounting standards.

and Standards Committee and a Conduct Committee). Key areas of activity for the FRC include issuing accounting standards[22] and proactively monitoring the annual accounts of public companies and large private companies to verify that they are complying with the requirements of the Companies Act 2006 and applicable accounting standards.[23] The FRC's overriding objective in setting accounting standards is stated to be 'to enable users of accounts to receive high-quality understandable financial reporting proportionate to the size and complexity of the entity and the users' information needs'.[24] The FRC also has responsibility for the UK Corporate Governance Code and the Stewardship Code and so plays a major role in corporate governance as well as with respect to accounting and audit matters. The Government has announced an independent review of the FRC's governance, impact, and powers which is due to be completed by the end of 2018.

### The audience and manner of disclosure

**18-9**  An important issue in any disclosure policy is to whom disclosure should be addressed, given concerns that accounts and reports are aimed at too many types of users. The FRC considers that it is appropriate for providers to refocus on the primary purpose of narrative disclosures which is 'providing investors with information that is useful for making their resource allocation decisions and assessing management's stewardship',[25] i.e. those who provide capital whether it be equity or loan capital. That approach works for large and for small companies, for even in the smaller companies, shareholders have to look to the effective use of their capital and have a legitimate interest in monitoring and reviewing the management of the company. Having identified the target audience, the FRC has adopted four regulatory principles governing disclosure, namely that the disclosures required should be targeted (a focus on the mischief to be addressed), proportionate (the requirements should be appropriate in extent and impact to the mischief and the type of company involved), coordinated (so as to avoid overlaps, for example, between UK and EU requirements and between differing bodies such as UKLA and the FRC), and clear (language should be more accessible, more useful for the user).[26] Other principles which guide the FRC's approach include that all material issues must be reported in a manner that is complete, neutral, free from error, fair, and balanced.[27] Finally, the FRC has adopted four communication principles which require that the information disclosed be communicated in a focused, open and honest, clear and understandable, interesting and engaging way.[28]

---

[22] Previously, the issuing of accounting standards was a matter for the Accounting Standards Board which was an operating body of the FRC. Now they are the work of the Accounting Council which reports to the Codes and Standards Committee of the FRC and the FRC is formally the prescribed body for setting accounting standards. See generally FRC, *Roles and Responsibilities* (June 2017).

[23] This work is still a matter for the Financial Reporting Review Panel which, ultimately, reports to the Conduct Committee of the FRC.

[24] See FRS 102, *Financial Reporting Standard for UK and Republic of Ireland*, (September 2015), Summary, para (ii).

[25] FRC, *Louder than Words: Principles and actions for making corporate reports less complex and more relevant* (FRC Discussion Paper, June 2009), hereinafter FRC *Louder than Words* (2009), p 5. See FRC, *Guidance on the Strategic Report* (June 2014), para 3.2.

[26] The FRC conducted extensive consultations on the nature and extent of disclosure, see FRC, *Louder than Words* (2009), n 25; also FRC, 'Cutting Clutter: Combating Clutter in Annual Reports' (FRC Discussion Paper, April 2011). This work is now carried forward under a general initiative called 'Clear and Concise Reporting' which focuses on communication, placement of information, and materiality in reporting, see the FRC Lab Report, *Towards Clear and Concise Reporting* (August 2014); FRC, *Clear and Concise Reporting: Developments in Narrative Reporting* (December 2015).

[27] FRC, *Effective Company Stewardship, Next Steps* (September 2011), p 3.

[28] See Feedback Statement—*Louder than Words*, October 2010, paras 3.6, 3.14; also FRC, *Louder than Words* (2009), n 25, 16–17, 40–1.

### The content of disclosure

**18-10**    As to content, for financial statements, the content of the disclosure is dictated in large part by the need to prepare the statements in accordance with either domestic (UK GAAP) or international accounting standards (IFRS) with the latter being mandatory only in respect of listed companies preparing consolidated accounts. Essentially, there are three possibilities: as noted at **18-7**, listed companies are required to prepare their consolidated accounts using IFRS, as adopted by the EU (the EU having indicated that it will not pursue initiatives for IFRS for SMEs). Companies not within that category may elect to apply IFRS. Companies which are not required to and do not elect to apply IFRS apply UK GAAP. Much of the discussion of accounting standards and their content is primarily technical accounting material which is not considered further here.

**18-11**    Since the financial crisis of 2007–08, there has been a much greater emphasis on narrative reporting as a crucial counterpart to the financial statements,[29] designed in part to facilitate stronger and more effective shareholder engagement.[30] Companies other than small companies are required to provide a strategic report in addition to the directors' report, see **18-31**.[31] Lengthy detailed directors' remuneration reports are required in quoted companies, see **18-43**. Changes have been made also to the auditors' reports, see **18-58**.

## B    The statutory scheme

**18-12**    The statutory provisions governing company accounts are lengthy and complex and it is not intended to provide a detailed accounting treatment in this chapter, but rather an overview of the requirements so as to appreciate the obligations on directors and the level and type of disclosure which is available to shareholders and stakeholders.

### Accounting records

**18-13**    Every company must keep adequate accounting records sufficient to show and explain the company's transactions and to disclose with reasonable accuracy, at any time, the financial position of the company at that time and to enable the directors to ensure that any accounts required to be prepared comply with the CA 2006 and, where applicable, IAS requirements.[32] A failure to maintain records is an offence by every officer in default[33] and prosecutions for breach of this requirement are (relatively) common. Also,

---

[29] See BIS, *The Future of Narrative Reporting: A Consultation* (August 2010); BIS, *The Future of Narrative Reporting: Consulting on a New Reporting Framework* (September 2011), URN 11/945; Government Response (March 2012), URN 12/588; FRRP Statement, February 2011, *Better reporting of risk*; also FRC, *Effective Company Stewardship, Next Steps* (September 2011), pp 4, 10.

[30] BIS, *The Future of Narrative Reporting: A Consultation* (August 2010); and see FRC, *Effective Company Stewardship, Next Steps* (September 2011), p 3.

[31] BIS, *The Future of Narrative Reporting: A Consultation* (August 2010).

[32] CA 2006, s 386; and see ICAEW Tech 01/11, *Guidance for Directors on Accounting Records under the CA 2006* (February 2011). Records must be maintained (for three years in the case of a private company and six years, if a public company (s 388(4))) at the company's registered office or such other place as the directors think fit and must at all times be open to inspection by the officers of the company (s 388(1)) and by the auditors (s 499(1)(a)). Inspection of company records is governed by The Companies (Company Records) Regulations 2008, SI 2008/3006. A shareholders' agreement may make provision for inspection of records by shareholders.

[33] CA 2006, s 387(1); unless the officer can show that he acted honestly and that in the circumstances the default was excusable: s 387(2).

non-compliance with this requirement will often be one of the grounds (evidencing unfitness) relied on against a director in disqualification proceedings,[34] see **15-99**.

## Prepare accounts

**18-14** Having maintained the required accounting records, the directors must prepare for the shareholders:

(1) individual accounts for each financial year[35] (CA 2006, s 394) unless exempt[36] and, in the case of companies admitted to trading on a regulated market, half-yearly financial reports are required;[37]

(2) a strategic report reviewing the company's activities (s 414A(1)), subject to a small companies' exemption (s 414A(2)), see **18-31**;

(3) a directors' report setting out core information regarding the company (s 415), subject to a small companies exemption from filing with the registrar (s 415A(1)); and an exemption from preparation for micro-entities (s 415(1A)), see **18-37**;

(4) a directors' remuneration report (s 420), but only if the company is a quoted company,[38] see **18-43**;

(5) an auditors' report (ss 475, 495), but many companies are audit exempt, see **18-55**;

(6) UK listed companies are required to provide an annual financial report which must include audited financial statements, a management report, and responsibility statements,[39] see DTR 4.1.5. The management report essentially combines the information contained in the directors' report and the strategic report, and will also contain a corporate governance statement and a non-financial reporting statement, as required by the Accounting Directive, as amended.

**18-15** A company's individual accounts under the CA 2006 consist of a balance sheet as at the last day of the financial period and a profit and loss account for the financial period and notes thereto.[40] The format of the accounts is determined by whether the company is a small or other company and is dictated by the regulations noted at **18-4**. In all cases, the applicable accounting principles are that the company is presumed to be carrying on business as a going concern,[41] the accounting policies adopted must be applied consistently, the amount of any item in the accounts must be determined on a prudent basis, and the accounts must be prepared on an accruals basis, reflecting transactions in the year to which they relate without regard to the date of receipt or payment.[42]

---

[34] For example, see *Re Galeforce Pleating Co Ltd* [1999] 2 BCLC 704; *Secretary of State for Trade and Industry v Arif* [1997] 1 BCLC 34.

[35] A company's financial year is determined in accordance with CA 2006, s 390.

[36] There is an exemption in respect of the preparation and delivery of individual accounts for dormant subsidiaries provided certain conditions are met (s 394A(1), (2), ss 448A–448C) and so long as the subsidiary does not fall within an excluded category as identified in s 394B. The key condition is a parent undertaking guarantee of the liabilities of the subsidiary to the effect specified in s 394C(3). Such subsidiaries, whether or not dormant, are also exempt from audit, see **18-55**. The conditions and the guarantee are discussed at **18-55**.

[37] UKLA Disclosure and Transparency Rules, DTR 4.2.2, as required by the Transparency Directive 2004/109/EC, OJ L 390/38, 31.12.2004, art 5(1).          [38] Defined CA 2006, s 385 and see n 8.

[39] See DTR 4.1.5; the content of the management report is set out in DTR 4.1.8–DTR 4.1.11; and the requirements with respect to responsibility statements are in DTR 4.1.12.          [40] CA 2006, s 396(1), (3).

[41] The UK Corporate Governance Code, Prov 30 (see **6-25**) and the Listing Rules LR 9.8.6(3) require directors to state in the annual financial statements that it is appropriate to adopt the going concern basis of accounting.

[42] SI 2008/409, Sch 1, paras 11–14 (small companies); SI 2008/410, Sch 1, paras 11–14 (large and medium-sized companies).

**18-16**    If a company's individual accounts are prepared as IAS individual accounts, the directors must state in a note to the accounts that the accounts have been prepared in accordance with international accounting standards (CA 2006, s 397). If the individual accounts have been prepared in accordance with the CA 2006, the accounts must, in the case of the balance sheet, give a true and fair view of the state of the affairs of the company as at the end of the financial year and, in the case of the profit and loss account, of the profit or loss for the financial year (s 396(2)). The significance of the 'true and fair view' is reinforced by s 393(1) which states that directors must not approve accounts unless they are satisfied that they give a true and fair view of the assets, liabilities, financial position, and profit or loss of the company and this requirement applies to all accounts, individual or group, and whether prepared in accordance with the CA 2006 or IAS requirements.[43]

### Accounts must give a true and fair view

**18-17**    The FRC is the prescribed body[44] with responsibility for determining domestic accounting standards, known as Financial Reporting Standards (FRS).[45] Accounting standards are authoritative statements of how particular types of transactions and other events should be reflected in financial statements and, accordingly, compliance with the appropriate accounting standards is normally necessary if the accounts are to give a true and fair view.[46]

**18-18**    As the FRC Guidance makes clear, while compliance with the appropriate accounting standards will normally result in a true and fair view,[47] where directors and auditors do not believe that following a particular accounting policy will give a true and fair view, they are legally required to adopt a more appropriate policy, even if this requires a departure from an accounting standard (known as the true and fair override). Where a proper explanation is given of the reason for the departure and its effects, the Conduct Committee of the FRC (the body with oversight) (see **18-8**) will be reluctant to substitute its own judgement for the board unless it is not satisfied that the board has acted reasonably.[48] On other occasions, while not utilising the true and fair override, directors may need to include additional information in the accounts or in the notes to the accounts to ensure that the accounts give a true and fair view and, of course, they can choose to

---

[43] Note also CA 2006, s 393(2) which requires the auditor to have regard to this duty of the directors when carrying out his functions as auditor.

[44] Prescribed under CA 2006, s 464; see SI 2012/1741, Pt 5, prescribing the FRC and revoking the previous prescription of the Accounting Standards Board; see also **18-8**.

[45] The core FRS are FRS 100 'Application of Financial Reporting Requirements' (March 2018); FRS 101 'Reduced Disclosure Framework' (March 2018); FRS 102 'The Financial Standard applicable in the UK and Republic of Ireland' (March 2018). FRSSE (Financial Reporting Standard for Smaller Entities) was withdrawn, following the implementation of the Accounting Directive, and a small companies regime is provided now within Section 1A of FRS 102; FRS 105, *The Financial Reporting Standard Applicable to Micro-entities* (March 2018).

[46] Accounting Standards Board, *Foreword to Accounting Standards* (June 1993), para 16.

[47] FRC, *True and Fair* (June 2014), p 3.

[48] FRC, *True and Fair* (June 2014), p 3. To allay stakeholder concerns, both the FRC and the Department for Business, Innovation and Skills (BIS) issued a public statement to this effect, see FRC Statement, *Accounting Standards are part of legally binding corporate reporting framework*, 3 October 2013; Statement by BIS, same title, 3 October 2013.

include additional information, even if not strictly needed, in order to provide a more complete picture of the company's position.[49]

**18-19** Given the importance of the 'true and fair view' principle underpinning the accounting requirements and that financial statements prepared to IAS requirements must present fairly the financial position of the company[50] rather than give a 'true and fair view', the FRC sought counsel's opinion on two occasions (2008 and 2013) as to the 'true and fair' requirement.[51] These opinions are reflected in the FRC, 'True and Fair' Guidance (2014) which confirms that 'the true and fair requirement remains of fundamental importance in IFRS and UK GAAP',[52] noting that fair presentation under IFRS is equivalent to a true and fair view. As counsel had indicated, the requirement set out in international accounting standards that the accounts present fairly the position of the company is not a different requirement to that of showing a true and fair view but is a different articulation of the same concept.[53] Further, the preparation of financial accounts is not a mechanical process where compliance with the accounting standards automatically ensures that the accounts give a true and fair view or a fair presentation; while highly likely to have that outcome, it does not guarantee it.[54] Hence, as the FRC Guidance states, objective professional judgement must be applied by the directors and the auditors to ensure that the financial statements do give a true and fair view or achieve a fair presentation.[55] The Guidance also reminds directors that the concept of prudence continues to underlie the preparation of accounts under both UK GAAP and IFRS.[56]

**18-20** Ultimately, the question whether the accounts do give a true and fair view is a matter of law for the courts to decide.[57] As Andrew Smith J explained in *Macquarie Internationale Investments Ltd v Glencore UK Ltd*,[58] while it might be that the quality of being 'true' is

---

[49] CA 2006, s 396(4). See FRC, *True and Fair* (June 2014), p 3. See BIS, *UK Implementation of the EU Accounting Directive* (August 2014), BIS/14/1025, para 8.16—if the limited notes which a small company is required to provide (see **18-25**) are insufficient to provide a true and fair view, the company will need to provide additional information. See too FRC, *Accounting Standards for Small Entities, Implementation of the EU Accounting Directive* (Consultation Document, September 2014), para 3 which indicates that the FRC anticipates directors will have to include additional information.           [50] See IAS 1, para 13.

[51] The Opinions of Martin Moore QC in 2008 and 2013 are posted on the FRC website: www.frc.org. uk. Previous legal opinions on this issue, written by Hoffmann and Arden in 1983 and 1984 and by Arden in 1993 and commissioned by the ASB are also available on the website. Martin Moore refers in his 2008 Opinion to the 'almost iconic status' achieved by those Opinions (see para 7).

[52] FRC, *True and Fair* (June 2014), p 1. The Guidance stresses that all involved in preparing the accounts, the directors and the auditors, must stand back at the end of the process of preparation and ensure that the accounts as a whole do give a true and fair view and, crucially, ensure that the consideration that they give to these matters is evident in their deliberations and documentation, see at p 4.

[53] Opinion of Martin Moore (2008), paras 23–29.

[54] Opinion of Martin Moore (2008), paras 41–45. See ISA (UK) 700, *Forming an Opinion and Reporting on Financial Statements* (June 2016), para A15–2 which repeats the point—it is not sufficient for either directors or auditors to conclude that financial statements give a true and fair view *solely* because they were prepared in accordance with applicable accounting standards.

[55] FRC, *True and Fair* (June 2014), p 1.           [56] FRC, *True and Fair* (June 2014), p 2.

[57] See Accounting Standards Board, *Foreword to Accounting Standards* (June 1993), esp paras 16–19, and Counsel's Opinion annexed thereto; see also Evans, '"True and fair" Revisited' [1990] LMCLQ 255; McGee, 'The True and Fair View Debate: A Study in the Legal Regulation of Accounting' (1991) 54 MLR 874. It is possible that there may be more than one 'true and fair view', hence the reference to 'a true and fair view', see Lord Neuberger in *BNY Corporate Trustee Ltd v Eurosail* [2011] 3 All ER 470 at [61]: 'Clearly, the fact that the figures have been audited and are said to convey a "true and fair" view of the company's position in the opinion of its directors should normally have real force. However, the figures will inevitably be historic, they will normally be conservative, they will be based on accounting conventions, and they will rarely represent the only true and fair view.'           [58] [2010] 1 BCLC 238 at [166], aff'd [2011] 1 BCLC 561.

directed to the accuracy of statements of fact and the quality of being 'fair' reflects that accounts involve matters of assessment and judgment, it would be arid and unhelpful to approach these issues as if they were separate questions. He said: 'The sensible and generally accepted approach is to recognise that "true and fair" is a composite phrase, and the requirement that financial statements be "true and fair" is a single, indivisible requirement.'[59]

**18-21**   The dispute in *Macquarie* was between the parties to the sale and purchase of a business. M had purchased the entire share capital of a number of subsidiaries of G on terms which included, *inter alia*, a warranty by the seller that the statutory accounts were prepared in accordance with relevant accounting standards and gave a true and fair view of assets and liabilities. M was subsequently liable for £3.1m in unexpected charges (as a result of an error by a supplier to one of the subsidiaries which had gone undetected by the supplier until after the sale). The question was whether G was in breach of the warranty when the existence of that liability had remained unknown and not reasonably discoverable by G at the time of the sale. Affirming the decision at first instance, the Court of Appeal agreed that, where statutory accounts are properly prepared in accordance with published professional standards, that is strong evidence that the accounts in question do present a true and fair view.[60] This was so here, despite the absence of any provision for the missing charges. The court agreed with the trial judge that it was difficult to see how the absence of provision for something which the seller did not know about, and could not reasonably have discovered, could mean that the accounts failed to give a true and fair view.[61]

## Approving accounts

**18-22**   The accounts must be approved by the board and signed on the balance sheet on behalf of the board by a director (CA 2006, s 414), likewise, the strategic report (s 414D), the directors' report (s 419) and the directors' remuneration report (s 422). The directors must not approve the accounts unless they are satisfied that the accounts give a true and fair view of the company's assets, liabilities, financial position, and profit or loss (s 393(1)). Provision is made for the revision of defective accounts or reports, either voluntarily by the directors (s 454),[62] or on the intervention of the Secretary of State (s 455), whose powers in this respect with regard to public and large private companies are exercised by the Conduct Committee of the Financial Reporting Council (see **18-8**).[63]

---

[59]   [2010] 1 BCLC 238 at [166].

[60]   See also *Revenue Commissioners v William Grant & Sons Distillers Ltd* [2007] 2 All ER 440 at [2], per Lord Hoffmann: 'Although the requirement that the initial computation shall give a true and fair view involves the application of a legal standard, the courts are guided as to its content by the expert opinions of accountants as to what the best current accounting practice requires. The experts will in turn be guided by authoritative statements of accounting practice issued or adopted by [the FRC], which are given statutory recognition by [s 464 of the CA 2006].'

[61]   On the same basis, the court rejected a claim for breach of equivalent warranties with respect to management accounts that had been provided to the purchaser and which had been prepared in accordance with relevant accounting standards while noting that a lesser degree of accuracy may be expected from management accounts than from statutory accounts subject to audit, see [2011] 1 BCLC 561 at [67], [86].

[62]   See also The Companies (Revision of Defective Accounts and Reports) Regulations 2008, SI 2008/373.

[63]   See Supervision of Accounts and Reports (Prescribed Body) and Companies (Defective Accounts and Directors' Reports) (Authorised Person) Order 2012, SI 2012/1439, art 7(4), (5). See the Conduct Committee Operating Procedures for reviewing corporate reporting (1 April 2017).

### Circulating, laying, and filing accounts

**18-23**  A copy of the accounts and reports must be sent to each member[64] and, if the company is a public company, laid by the directors before a general meeting known as the 'accounts meeting' (CA 2006, s 437(1), (3)). The accounts may be sent to the members in hard copy or electronic form, subject to the rules governing electronic communications (see **17-6**). A copy of the accounts and reports must be delivered (subject to exceptions) by the directors to the registrar of companies.[65] A quoted company must publish its accounts and reports on its website as soon as reasonably practicable (s 430) and is required to publish its financial statements within four months of the end of the financial year.[66] Members of a quoted company holding a certain percentage of the shares may require a company to put a statement on the company's website setting out any audit concerns which they may have (s 527) and the company when giving notice of the accounts meeting must draw attention to the right of the members to use the company website in this way (s 529).

**18-24**  In the case of a private company, a copy of the accounts must be sent to the members not later than nine months from the end of the financial year or, if earlier, the date on which the company actually delivers its accounts to the registrar (CA 2006, s 424(2)(a), s 444(2)). Nine months is a lengthy period which means that the accounts are of limited value when they finally appear on the public record. Public companies must send the accounts to the members at least 21 days before the accounts meeting (s 424(3)), and must deliver the accounts to the registrar of companies within six months from the end of the financial year (s 442(2)(b)). The effect of these long lead-in times for delivery to the registrar of companies means that, even with respect to compliant companies, the information provided to the public registry is quite dated. Despite these generous time scales, there are significant levels of non-compliance by companies, though a failure to deliver accounts to the registrar of companies is a criminal offence by the directors (s 451(1)) and late filing penalties apply (s 453).[67]

## C  Accounting requirements by class of entity

### Small companies

**18-25**  Exemptions are available as to the detail of the accounts to be prepared and delivered by small companies which meet certain statutory eligibility criteria. To qualify as a small company, a company must satisfy two or more of the following criteria in relation to the relevant year: the company's turnover must not exceed £10.2m; the balance sheet total[68]

---

[64]  CA 2006, s 423(1)(a); and also to the holders of the company's debentures and to every person entitled to receive notice of the company's meetings: s 423(1)(b), (c).

[65]  CA 2006, s 441 subject to small company and micro-entities exemptions, see **18-25** and **18-27**. Unlimited companies are exempt: see s 448.

[66]  FSA, Disclosure and Transparency Rules, DTR 4.1.3; for 'quoted company', see n 8.

[67]  See Companies (Late Filing Penalties) and Limited Liability Partnerships (Filing Periods and Late Filing Penalties) Regulations 2008, SI 2008/497. The penalty imposed varies in amount depending on the type of company and the period of the delay. Fines run from £150 for a private company which is not more than one month late filing up to £1,500 if more than six months late; equivalent figures for public companies are £750 and £7,500; penalties double if the offence is repeated in two consecutive years. See *R (on the application of Pow Trust) v Chief Executive and Registrar of Companies* [2003] 2 BCLC 295 where the court rejected a claim that such penalties infringe the European Convention on Human Rights.

[68]  Defined as the aggregate of the amounts shown as assets in the company's balance sheet: CA 2006, s 382(5).

must not exceed £5.1m; the number of employees must not exceed 50 (CA 2006, s 382);[69] and the company must not be excluded by s 384 from the small companies regime (i.e. must not be a public company, certain financial services companies, or a member of an ineligible group, for example, because the group contains a traded company[70]).

**18-26**  The accounts (i.e. balance sheet, profit and loss accounts, and accompanying notes) prepared for the members of a small company must comply with the required form and content and information to be provided in the notes as prescribed (CA 2006, s 396(3)).[71] The directors of a company subject to the small companies regime are only required to deliver the balance sheet to the registrar of companies (s 444(1)) and, if they choose not to deliver a profit and loss account, the copy of the balance sheet delivered must disclose that fact (s 444(5A)).[72] Small companies can prepare and deliver an abridged balance sheet and/or profit and loss account if all the shareholders consent to the abridgement (s 444(2A)).[73]

## Micro-entities

**18-27**  For a company to qualify as a micro-entity, it must meet two of the following three criteria: net turnover of not more than £632,000; a balance sheet total of not more than £316,000; and average number of employees during the year of not more than 10 (s 384A).[74] Certain companies are excluded from the micro-entities regime, even if they meet the size criteria, for example, financial services companies and companies excluded from the small companies regime (s 384B). Companies which do qualify for the micro-entity regime are permitted (but not required) to prepare an abridged balance sheet with a limited number of prescribed footnotes which must appear at the bottom of the balance sheet[75] and an abridged profit and loss account.[76] Accounts prepared in

---

[69] A parent company qualifies as a small company in relation to a financial year only if the group headed by it qualifies as a small group (see s 383(4)): s 383(1).

[70] For these purposes, 'traded company' means a company any of whose transferable securities are admitted to trading on a regulated market: CA 2006, s 474(1). One of the criteria for ineligibility used to be that a member of the group was a public company; that was narrowed as part of the implementation of the Accounting Directive to where a member of the group is a traded company, see s 384(2).

[71] See The Small Companies and Groups (Accounts and Directors' Report) Regulations 2008, SI 2008/409, Sch 1. See also CA 2006, ss 410A and 411: small companies need not give information on off-balance sheet arrangements or employee numbers and costs. The Accounting Directive prescribes and limits the information to be provided by small companies in the notes to their accounts. See BIS, *UK Implementation of the EU Accounting Directive* (August 2014), BIS/14/1025, paras 8.16 to 8.18.

[72] Provision was previously made for the delivery by small companies of 'abbreviated' accounts to the registrar of companies, but that provision for abbreviated accounts was abolished by SI 2015/980, reg 8(3)(d), (e); reg 21.

[73] See The Small Companies and Groups (Accounts and Directors' Report) Regulations 2008, SI 2008/409, Sch 1, para 1A. For the background, see BIS, *UK Implementation of the EU Accounting Directive* (August 2014), BIS/14/1025, para 8.21. In many small companies, the shareholders are the directors and also probably the employees, so they need little formal accounting information.

[74] This category was introduced for financial years ending on or after 30 September 2013. The background to these changes, an EU initiative, is set out in BIS, *Simpler Reporting for the Smallest Businesses, Discussion Paper* (August 2011), URN 11/1100. See also the Small Companies (Micro-Entities' Accounts) Regulations 2013, SI 2013/3008. In 2016/17, 8.2 per cent of UK companies (236,528 companies) filed accounts as micro-entities, so the category is proving useful, after an initially slow start: see *Companies House Management Information 2016/17*, Table 8.

[75] CA 2006, s 472(1A). The notes must cover the matters specified by SI 2008/409, Sch 1, para 57 and include details of guarantees and other financial commitments and information on directors' advances, credits, and guarantees required to be disclosed by CA 2006, s 413.

[76] SI 2008/409, Sch 1, para 1(1A).

accordance with the micro-entity provisions must include a prominent statement to that effect on the balance sheet, immediately above the director's signature (s 414(3)(a)). A micro-entity that prepares abridged accounts must also deliver a copy of those accounts, without the profit and loss account, to the registrar. The directors must still certify that the accounts give a true and fair view and s 393(1A) identifies specific considerations for directors of micro-entities as to how they determine whether the accounts give a true and fair view.

## Medium-sized companies

**18-28**  To qualify as a medium-sized company, a company must satisfy two or more of the following criteria in relation to the relevant year: the company's turnover must not exceed £36m; the balance sheet total must not exceed £18m; the number of employees must not exceed 250 (CA 2006, s 465); and the company must not be excluded by s 467 from the medium-sized companies regime (i.e. must not be a public company, certain financial services companies or a member of an ineligible group). For medium-sized companies, the accounting exemptions available are modest, and a balance sheet, profit and loss account, and a strategic report and directors' report must be prepared and delivered to the registrar in the usual way.[77]

## Large companies/public interest entities

**18-29**  Large companies are essentially those which on the balance sheet date exceed at least two of the three criteria noted in **18-28** for being a medium-sized undertaking. Large companies, whether private or public companies, must prepare and file full audited accounts,[78] i.e. they do not qualify for any of the de-regulatory measures available to micro, small, and medium-sized enterprises. A further classification at EU level is that of a public-interest entity (PIE), which is used in the Accounting Directive 2013/34,[79] the Audit Regulation 537/2014,[80] and the Non-Financial Reporting Directive 2014/95.[81] Essentially, a PIE is a traded company (admitted to trading on a regulated market in any Member State), any banking or insurance company, and any undertaking of significant public relevance designated as a PIE by a Member State because of the nature of their business, their size, or the number of their employees (the UK has not designated any entities as PIEs[82]). A PIE, whatever its economic size in terms of the usual thresholds of balance sheet/turnover/number of employees, must report generally as a large company.

---

[77] CA 2006, s 445, see The Large and Medium-sized Companies and Groups (Accounts and Directors' Report) Regulations 2008, SI 2008/410, para 4. It follows that very few companies, less than 0.1 per cent of the UK register (just 3,086 companies) take advantage of this category: see *Companies House Management Information 2016/17*, Table 8.

[78] In 2016/17, just 4.3 per cent of UK companies (123,649 companies) filed full accounts so most companies are able to bring themselves within a modified disclosure regime: *Companies House Management Information 2016/17*, Table 8.   [79] OJ L 182/19, 29.6.2013, art 2(1).

[80] OJ L 158/77, 27.5.2014, art 3, referring to art 2(13) in Directive 2006/43, OJ L 157/87, 9.6.2006.

[81] OJ L 330, 15.11.2014.

[82] See BIS, *Auditor Regulation, Discussion Document on the implication of the EU and wider reforms* (December 2014), BIS/14/1285, p 11.

### Group accounts

**18-30**   A parent company (other than a small parent company[83] or a company otherwise exempt from the requirement to prepare group accounts[84]) must prepare its own individual accounts *and* prepare group accounts (s 399(2)), namely, a consolidated balance sheet and consolidated profit and loss account for the whole group (s 404), subject to the possible exclusion of certain subsidiaries (s 405(2),(3)).[85] In some cases (essentially listed companies) consolidated accounts must be prepared in accordance with IAS (s 403(1)), see **18-7**, otherwise group accounts may be prepared in accordance with IAS or CA 2006 requirements (s 403(2)). The content and format are as prescribed by regulations.[86] Companies Act group accounts must give a true and fair view of the state of affairs of the group and the profit or loss of the group.[87] If the group accounts are prepared as IAS group accounts, the directors must state in a note to the accounts that the accounts have been prepared in accordance with international accounting standards (s 406).

## D  Narrative reporting requirements

### The strategic report

**18-31**   Save for companies entitled to the small companies exemption,[88] all companies must prepare a strategic report (s 414A). The strategic report is a separate stand-alone report reviewing the company's business. It evolved out of extensive consultations by the then Department for Business, Innovation and Skills (BIS) which addressed the need to improve the overall quality of narrative reporting.[89] At the same time, the FRC was considering initiatives to ensure that narrative reporting provided the context for and complemented the financial statements and gave a frank and honest assessment of the company's strategy, prospects, and risks.[90]

---

[83]   A parent company is not required to prepare and deliver group accounts if it heads a group which qualifies as a small group and it is not an ineligible group: CA 2006, ss 399, 383, 384(2). A group qualifies as a small group if it meets two of the following criteria in the relevant year: turnover must not exceed £10.2m net; the balance sheet total must not exceed £12.2m net; and the number of employees must not exceed 50: ss 381, 383 and see s 384(2) as to an ineligible group.

[84]   i.e. a company within the exemptions in CA 2006, ss 400–402, typically because it is itself a subsidiary of another parent company which prepares group accounts.

[85]   If all of the subsidiaries could be excluded, then the parent company is exempt from the requirement to prepare group accounts: CA 2006, s 406. In 2016/17, just 0.7 per cent of UK companies (21,133 companies) filed group accounts: see *Companies House Management Information 2016/17*, Table 8.

[86]   See The Large and Medium-sized Companies and Groups (Accounts and Reports) Regulations 2008, SI 2008/410, reg 9, Sch 6, Pt 1.

[87]   CA 2006, s 404(2); there is provision for the exclusion of some subsidiary undertakings from the group accounts: see s 405; and a parent company need not provide its individual profit and loss account to the registrar though it must still be approved by the directors: s 408(3).

[88]   See CA 2006, s 414B, i.e. a company which is entitled to prepare accounts in accordance with the small companies regime or would be so entitled were it not for being a member of an ineligible group.

[89]   The evolution of the changes to narrative reporting can be found in BIS, *The Future of Narrative Reporting—a Consultation* (August 2010), URN 10/1057; BIS, *The Future of Narrative Reporting—Consulting on a new reporting framework* (September 2011), URN 11/945 which proposed a strategic report and an annual directors' statement; followed by BIS, *The Future of Narrative Reporting—A New Structure for Narrative Reporting in the UK* (October 2012), URN 12/979, which put forward the structure which is now in the CA 2006, and dropped the proposal for the annual directors' statement. BIS will review the effectiveness of these changes to narrative reporting in 2018, see SI 2013/1970, Explanatory Memorandum, para 12.2.

[90]   See FRC, *Effective Company Stewardship* (January 2011); followed by FRC, *Effective Company Stewardship, Next Steps* (September 2011).

**18-32**  The purpose of the strategic report is specifically stated as 'to inform members of the company and help them assess how the directors have performed their duty under s 172 (duty to promote the success of the company)'.[91] As discussed in Chapter 10, the relationship between s 172 and the strategic report is particularly important and the Government is to legislate again to require directors to report explicitly with regard to the factors listed in s 172 in the strategic report. However, as discussed below, the strategic report is already the repository of a great deal of information about the company's business so it is not clear how additional reporting within it will be accommodated.

**18-33**  The strategic report must set out a fair review of the company's business and a description of the principal risks and uncertainties facing the company. It must also provide a balanced and comprehensive analysis of the development and performance of the company's business during the financial year, and the position of the company's business at the end of that year, consistent with the size and complexity of the business, using appropriate key performance indicators (s 414C(3)). The FRC *Guidance on the Strategic Report* (which is an important non-statutory guide in this context[92]) states that the information should be material to the shareholders and it is for the directors to apply judgement based on their assessment of the relevant importance of the matter to the company.[93] The FRC considers information is material if its omission or misrepresentation could reasonably be expected to influence the economic decisions shareholders take on the basis of the annual report as a whole.[94]

**18-34**  More extensive disclosure is required of quoted companies including a description of the company's strategy and of the company's business model and information on gender diversity of the board, senior management, and workforce (s 414C(8)). Further, to the extent necessary for an understanding of the development, performance or position of the company's business, the strategic report must include information on: the main trends and factors likely to affect the future development, performance and position of the company's business; and information about (a) environmental matters, (b) the company's employees, and (c) social, (d) community, and (e) human rights issues, together with any company policies on these matters and their effectiveness, including an obligation to explain the absence of such material if that is the case (s 414C(7)). Companies are not required to disclose information about impending developments or matters in the course of negotiation, however, if the disclosure would, in the opinion of the directors, be seriously prejudicial to the interests of the company (s 414C(14)).

**18-35**  As noted at **18-58**, further disclosures of non-financial information are required by the Non-Financial Reporting Directive 2014/95/EU[95] which applies to public interest entities (essentially traded companies, banking and insurance companies) with more than 500 employees.[96] Such large companies (there is an exemption for small and medium-sized entities, s 414CA(3)) must provide a non-financial information statement as part of their strategic report (s 414CA(1)). That non-financial information statement (s 414CB)

---

[91]  CA 2006, s 414C(1) and see **10-37**.

[92]  See also FRC, *Guidance on Risk Management, Internal Control and Related Financial and Business Reporting* (September 2014); the Companies (Miscellaneous Reporting) Regulations 2018, only available in draft at the time of writing.          [93]  FRC, *Guidance on Strategic Report* (2018), paras 5.5.

[94]  FRC, *Guidance on Strategic Report* (2018), para 5.2.

[95]  Accounting Directive 2013/34/EU, OJ L 182/19, 29.6.2013, art 19a, as amended by Directive 2014/95/EU, art 1(1), OJ L 330, 15.11.2014.

[96]  Directive 2014/95/EU, OJ L 330/1, 15.11.2014, amending Accounting Directive 2013/34/EU, arts 19a and 20; implemented by SI 2016/1245.

must contain information, to the extent necessary for an understanding of the company's development, performance, and position and the impact of its activity, relating to, as a minimum—environmental matters (including the impact of the company's business on the environment), the company's employees, social matters, respect for human rights, and anti-corruption and anti-bribery matters (s 414CB(1)). If the company does not pursue policies in relation to those matters, the information statement must provide a clear and reasoned explanation for not doing so (s 414CB(4)).

**18-36**   The information must include a brief description of the company's business model, a description of the policies pursued by the company in relation to these matters (environment, employees, social, human rights etc); any due diligence processes implemented by the company in pursuance of those policies; and a description of the outcome of those policies. The information must include a description of the principal risks relating to these environmental, employee, etc., matters arising in connection with the company's operations, and, where relevant and proportionate, a description of its business relationships, products, and services which are likely to cause adverse impacts in those areas of risk, a description of how the company manages the principal risks, and a description of the non-financial key performance indicators relevant to the company's business. Information seriously prejudicial to the company's interests does not need to be disclosed provided non-disclosure does not prevent a fair and balanced understanding of the company's position, etc (s 414CB(9)).

### The directors' report

**18-37**   Each company must prepare a directors' report for each financial year (CA 2006, s 415), unless it is a micro-entity.[97] A small company may prepare a modified directors' report (s 415A), however, and it need not deliver the report to the registrar (s 444(1)).

**18-38**   The content of the directors' report is prescribed by regulations,[98] and for small companies, very little information is required, merely the directors' names (s 416(1)(a)), information on political donations which small companies are unlikely to give in any event,[99] and information on any provision of qualifying third party indemnity provisions (s 236). Companies which are not small companies must give particulars[100] of any important events affecting the company which have occurred since the end of the financial year, and an indication of likely future developments in the business, as well as information on research and development activities, on overseas branches, on purchases of its own shares (only if a public company), on arrangements to inform and consult UK employees (only if number of employees exceed 250), and on the amount recommended for a dividend payment (s 416(3)).

**18-39**   In the case of companies with securities carrying voting rights admitted to trading on a regulated market, the directors' report must include information on the company's

---

[97]  For delivery requirements, see CA 2006, ss 445–447.

[98]  See The Small Companies and Groups (Accounts and Directors' Report) Regulations 2008, SI 2008/409, reg 7, Sch 5; The Large and Medium-sized Companies and Groups (Accounts and Reports) Regulations 2008, SI 2008/410, reg 10, Sch 7.

[99]  See The Small Companies and Groups (Accounts and Directors' Report) Regulations 2008, SI 2008/409, reg 7, Sch 5, para 2.

[100]  The Large and Medium-sized Companies and Groups (Accounts and Reports) Regulations 2008, SI 2008/410, reg 10, Sch 7.

voting and control structures[101] (as required by the Takeover Directive) and a corporate governance statement (as required by the Accounting Directive, art 20, see **6-14**).[102] In the case of quoted companies, disclosures must be made in the directors' report with respect to greenhouse gas emissions.[103] A premium listed company which has entered into an agreement with a controlling shareholder, as required by LR 9.2.2A, must make a statement to that effect in the annual report (LR 9.8.4(14)(a)).

**18-40** Not all narrative reporting by companies is contained in the annual reporting requirements and there is a move away to other methods of reporting, not least because annual reports are in danger of becoming an unfocused catch-all repository of information. An example of a different approach involving country by country reporting can be found in the extractive industry reporting, as required by the Accounting Directive, art 42. In the case of an undertaking which is a large undertaking or a public interest entity (essentially traded company) and a mining or quarrying undertaking or a logging undertaking[104] the directors must complete reports on payments (including taxes, licence fees, and royalties, whether in money or kind, subject to a de minimis of £86,000 (€100,000)) to governments (covering national, regional, or local authorities), on a country-by-country basis.[105] This report is not included in the annual financial statements but is a separate electronic report which is filed (on pain of criminal sanctions) with Companies House within 11 months of the end of the financial year.[106] In 2016, the European Commission also brought forward a proposal for a Directive requiring large multinational companies (global revenues in excess of €750m per annum) to publish on their websites key information on where they make their profits and where they pay their tax in the EU on a country-by-country basis.[107] The matter is still under discussion with the Parliament and the Council of Ministers.

**18-41** As can be seen, there is an inevitable creep towards including more and more information in the directors' report which does not necessarily add to the clarity or coherence of that document. But, it is also clear with the extractive industries disclosure and the proposal for tax information, neither of which is based on disclosure in the annual reports, that technology allows information to be made available and accessible in different ways.

---

[101] The Large and Medium-sized Companies and Groups (Accounts and Reports) Regulations 2008, SI 2008/410, reg 10, Sch 7, Pt 6.

[102] The requirements for listed companies are set out in the UKLA Disclosure and Transparency Rules (DTRs), see DTR 7.2. There is an option to provide a separate corporate governance statement or to provide the information via the company's website.

[103] The Large and Medium-sized Companies and Groups (Accounts and Reports) Regulations 2008, SI 2008/410, reg 10, Sch 7, Pt 7. See BEIS consultation, *Streamlined Energy and Carbon Reporting* (October 2017) on enhanced energy and carbon reporting, considering whether to broaden the disclosures required (for example, to include energy efficiencies) and the companies within the requirement (for example, all large public and private companies) and possibly requiring disclosure through websites rather than in the annual reports.

[104] A large undertaking for these purposes means an undertaking (including companies and LLPs) that meets at least two of the three following criteria—(a) its balance sheet total on its balance sheet date exceeds £18 million; (b) its net turnover on its balance sheet date exceeds £36 million; (c) the average number of employees during the financial year to which the balance sheet relates exceeds 250.

[105] See the Reports on Payments to Governments Regulations 2014, SI 2014/3209, with effect for financial years beginning on or after 1 January 2015.

[106] The proposal was flagged in Directive 2014/95/EU, art 1(6), OJ L 330/1, 15.11.2014, amending the Accounting Directive, 2013/34/EU, art 48.

[107] See Proposal for a Directive amending Directive 2013/34/EU: COM (2016) 198 final, 12.4.2016.

**18-42**  Where the company's accounts are subject to audit (see **18-49**), the directors' report must also contain a statement by the directors that there is no relevant audit information (i.e. information needed by the auditor in connection with the preparation of his report) of which the auditor is unaware and there are criminal sanctions for false statements to this effect (CA 2006, s 418). A director exercising care and skill needs to make such necessary enquiries of his fellow directors and otherwise as to enable him to meet his obligations under this provision (s 418(4)).

## The directors' remuneration report

**18-43**  Quoted companies have been required, since 2002, to draw up a detailed directors' remuneration report and submit it for shareholder approval by way, initially, of an advisory vote.[108] Now, two shareholder votes are required, one advisory vote on the remuneration paid to the directors and one binding vote on the adoption of the company's remuneration policy,[109] as discussed at **18-45**. Regulations prescribe in exhaustive detail the contents and layout of the report. Only an overview is given here, for the detail the reader is referred to the regulations.[110] To encourage frank disclosure in the remuneration report, the safe harbour in s 463, discussed at **18-47**, applies also to untrue or misleading statements in the directors' remuneration report.

**18-44**  There are three distinct elements to the remuneration report:

*The chairman's statement* The chair of the remuneration committee must draw up a statement summarising, for the relevant financial year, the major decisions on directors' remuneration, any substantial changes relating to directors' remuneration made during the year and the context in which those changes occurred and decisions were taken (Sch 8, para 3).

*The annual report on remuneration.* This part of the report addresses the manner in which remuneration has been paid in the financial year in question. An important element here is a requirement for a table showing the single total figure of remuneration for each director for the reported year and (for comparative purposes) the preceding financial year.[111] The table must disclose figures for each of the distinct components of remuneration including, *inter alia*, total salary and fees; taxable benefits; short-term incentives; long-term incentives vested in the year; and pension related benefits. This

---

[108]  All companies (other than micro-entities) must include details of the total amount of the directors' remuneration, any compensation paid for loss of office, and payments to third parties for directors' services in the notes to the company's annual accounts, though small companies need not include this information in the accounts delivered to the registrar: CA 2006, s 412; The Small Companies and Groups (Accounts and Directors' Report) Regulations 2008, SI 2008/409, regs 5, 6, and 9, Sch 3; The Large and Medium-sized Companies and Groups (Accounts and Reports) Regulations 2008, SI 2008/410, reg 8, Sch 5.

[109]  The background to the changes can be found in BIS, *Executive Remuneration, Discussion Paper* (September 2011); BIS, *Executive Pay, Shareholder Voting Rights Consultation* (March 2012), URN 12/639.

[110]  See The Large and Medium-sized Companies and Groups (Accounts and Reports) Regulations 2008, SI 2008/410, para 11, Sch 8. Best practice guidance is provided by the highly influential GC100 and Investor Group, *Directors' Remuneration Reporting Guidance* (2016). As to the application of the regulations and guidance, see BIS Research Paper Number 208, 'How companies and shareholders have responded to the new requirements on the reporting and governance of directors' remuneration' (March 2015), BIS/15/168. Unsurprisingly, given these are legal requirements, the research finds that most companies comply with most requirements, though many companies omitted to disclose the maximum future salary that may be paid under their remuneration policy. The report also found that shareholder dissent peaked in 2012 with 11 per cent dissent, now more commonly in the region of 9 per cent dissent.

[111]  SI 2008/410, Sch 8, paras 4 and 9.

part of the report must also include details of payments to past directors and payments for loss of office. These elements of the report must be reviewed by the company's auditor who must report to the members as to whether this information has been properly prepared (s 497(1)).

*Directors' remuneration policy*: This element of the report must contain in tabular form a description of each of the components of the remuneration package for the directors of the company (salary, benefits, pension and short-term and long-term incentive awards). With respect to each component, additional information must be provided as to: how that component supports the short and long-term strategic objectives of the company; how that component of the remuneration package operates; the maximum that may be paid in respect of that component; and the framework used to assess performance. The report must set out, in bar chart form, an indication of the level of remuneration that would be received by each director under the policy. Additionally, this part of the report must set out, *inter alia*, the company's policy on remuneration of non-executive directors and on payments for loss of office.

**18-45** Companies must put their remuneration policy to the shareholders for approval, by ordinary resolution, at least every three years (s 439A). In the event that shareholders refuse to approve the policy, the previously approved policy applies until such time as a new policy is approved. Companies may only make remuneration payments or payments for loss of office to directors in accordance with an approved policy or where the payment is approved by resolution of the shareholders (ss 226B and 226C), see detailed discussion at **13-19** et seq. The annual report on remuneration is put to the shareholders for approval by ordinary resolution (s 439). In this case, the shareholders' vote is advisory and so, if the annual report on remuneration is voted down, the vote does not affect the director's entitlement to his remuneration (s 439(5)), but at the next accounts meeting,[112] the company must bring forward its remuneration policy for shareholder approval (s 439A(2)).

**18-46** The FRC, in its annual review of corporate reporting for 2016/17, noted that stakeholders continue to find remuneration reports opaque, too long (on average more than 20 pages), complex, and unfocused.[113] It noted the need for companies to improve the discussion around remuneration and the link to the company's strategy, and to justify the remuneration of the company's executives. The FRC also found that very few companies address the impact on executive pay of broader societal issues such as fairness or explained how executive pay links to pay and conditions across the wider workforce. None of these findings are surprising and, as discussed in Chapter 6, executive remuneration remains a controversial matter. The Government has identified further measures to be taken to address the continuing concerns, including greater transparency.[114] Hence, quoted companies will be required to disclose in the remuneration report the ratio of CEO pay to the average pay of the company's UK workforce along with a narrative explaining changes to the ratio and how the ratio relates to pay and conditions across the wider workforce.[115] Quoted companies will also be required to provide a clearer explanation in their remuneration policies of a range of potential outcomes from complex, share-based incentive schemes. These schemes offer directors the greatest potential rewards and shareholders

---

[112] CA 2006, s 439A(8)(a), defined as the general meeting at which the company's annual accounts for a financial year are laid.      [113] FRC, *Annual Review of Corporate Reporting 2016/17* (October 2017), p 31.

[114] See BEIS, Government Response to the Green Paper, Corporate Governance Reform (August 2017), paras 1.50–1.53.

[115] BEIS, Government Response to the Green Paper, Corporate Governance Reform (August 2017), paras 1.50–1.53; The Companies (Miscellaneous Reporting) Regulations 2018—only available in draft at time of writing.

have great difficulty in appreciating the scale of potential awards under a particular set of circumstances. These additional disclosure requirements, the details of which were not available at the time of writing, are intended to address these inadequacies in the current reporting requirements.

### Directors' liabilities for disclosures

**18-47**   Given the level of narrative disclosures now required, directors have concerns about potential liabilities arising from erroneous statements, especially in the context of the strategic report requirements which, for quoted companies, require the inclusion of forward-looking statements. To address those concerns, a safe-harbour provision is included in CA 2006, s 463 which imposes liability on directors to compensate the company (only) for loss suffered by it as a result of any untrue or misleading statement in the strategic report, the directors' report, and, in the case of quoted companies, the directors' remuneration report.[116] A director can only be liable, however, if he knew the statement was untrue or misleading or was reckless as to whether it was untrue or misleading. In other words, liability can only arise in deceit (which is quite unlikely) and not in negligence, and liability can only be to the company (which is quite unlikely to sue) and only for loss suffered as a result of the statement (which it would be difficult to identify). A further indirect safe harbour is provided by FSMA 2000, s 90A and Sch 10A in respect of damage or loss suffered as a consequence of misleading statements or dishonest omissions in information disclosed by issuers of securities (so it will cover the annual accounts and reports) that are, with the consent of the issuer, admitted to trading on a securities market where the market is situated or operating in the UK or the UK is the issuer's home State.[117] FSMA 2000, Sch 10A sets out the circumstances in which an issuer (only) is liable to pay compensation[118] to a person who has acquired, continues to hold, or has disposed of securities in reliance on published information to which the Schedule applies[119] and who has suffered loss as a result of an untrue or misleading statement or omitted information in that published information.[120]

---

[116] The FRC, *Guidance on the Strategic Report* (June 2014) comments on the inclusion in the strategic report of material which is not required by the statute and notes that the legal position as to whether the protection in CA 2006, s 463 extends to such statements remains uncertain, see at para 3.17.

[117] These provisions were the result of the Davies Review instigated by the Treasury, see HM Treasury, *Extension of the Statutory Regime for Issuer Liability* (July 2008); *Davies Review of Issuer Liability: Final Report* (June 2007).

[118] See *Davies Review of Issuer Liability: Final Report* (June 2007), paras 54–59 as to why liability should not be extended to the directors individually—essentially because there are other sanctions etc which deter directors from making fraudulent or negligent statements such as the threat of FSA censure and the possibility that the company will sue the director where a director's conduct/statements have caused loss to the company and that liability of the director to the company is retained by FSMA 2000, Sch 10A, para 7(2) (a person other than the issuer is not subject to any liability, other than to the issuer, in respect of any loss).

[119] The category of information which is within the provision is very broadly defined as all information published by, or the availability of which is announced by, a regulatory information service, see FSMA 2000, Sch 10A, para 2, so it is much wider than merely periodic financial information.

[120] The statutory liability of the issuer is deceit based and an issuer within this provision is exempt from other forms of liability in respect of loss suffered as a result of misstatements, omissions etc, Sch 10A, para 3(2) and 3(3), but the exemption does not affect certain other specified liabilities, such as liability under FSMA s 90 (misleading statements in prospectus or listing particulars, see **21-119**) or liability for breach of contract or liability under the Misrepresentation Act 1967 or liability to a civil penalty or criminal liability: FSMA 2000, Sch 10A, para 7(3)—the width of these liabilities is such as to cast doubt on the value of this 'safe harbour'.

# E The regulatory framework for audit

## Assurance requirements

**18-48**   Disclosure of accounting information alone is insufficient without assurance as to the quality of that information which comes from the requirement that the accounts be audited. The regulatory framework for company audits and auditors is provided by CA 2006, Pt 16 (Audits) and Pt 42 (Statutory Auditors). Part 16 is our main concern,[121] the requirements as to audit; Part 42 concentrates on the regulation of the audit profession and public oversight issues. The requirements regarding audit are also the subject of significant EU measures in the form of the Eighth Company Law Directive 2006/43 which was initially adopted in 1984 and has been much amended, most recently by Directive 2014/56.[122] Additionally, there is Regulation 537/2014 on the statutory audit of public interest entities,[123] essentially listed companies, banks, insurance companies, and companies designated by Member States as public-interest entities (the UK has not designated any such entities). The FRC is the designated competent authority with responsibility for auditor regulation.[124] The amendments to the Eighth Company Law Directive and the adoption of a Regulation with respect to the audit of public interest entities is a consequence of the reviews of audit initiated in the light of the financial crisis.[125] Elements to note in respect of the Directive are that (a) Member States must ensure that statutory auditors carry out audits in accordance with international auditing standards and (b) audit requirements imposed at Member State level must reflect the size of the audited entity and auditing standards should be modified to ensure proportionate and simplified audits for SMEs. Elements to note in the Regulation are the additional restrictions on the provision of certain non-audit services, in some cases outright prohibition, in others dependent on the consent of the audit committee or the competent authority responsible for the supervision of auditors. There is also an emphasis on the need for professional scepticism in performing an audit, and a requirement for mandatory rotation of audit firms and key audit partners. There are also requirements for an expanded audit report and for a longer and more detailed report by the auditors to the audit committee.

## Appointment of auditors

**18-49**   Every company must appoint an auditor or auditors unless, for each financial year, the directors reasonably resolve otherwise on the ground that audited accounts are unlikely to be required (CA 2006, ss 485(1), 489(1)).[126] In the case of public companies, where an

---

[121] Part 16 reflects many provisions which originated in domestic reforms enacted post-Enron: see the Companies (Audit, Investigations and Community Enterprise) Act 2004.

[122] Directive 2006/43/EC OJ L 157/87, 9.6.2006, as amended by Directive 2014/56/EU, OJ L 158/196, 27.5.2014.         [123] OJ L 158/77, 27.5.2014.

[124] BIS, *Auditor Regulation, Discussion Document on the implication of the EU and wider reforms* (December 2014), BIS/14/1285, p 20. At the moment, there is a rather unclear division between the FRC and the Recognised Supervisory Bodies, essentially the professional accountancy bodies.

[125] See EU Commission, *Audit Policy: Lessons from the Crisis*, COM (2010) 561, 13.10.2010; and the UK Government Response (December 2010), URN 10/1346; European Commission, 'Reforming the Audit Market', Memo 11/856, 30.11.2011.

[126] Auditors appointed as such are officers of the company for the periods for which they are appointed: *Mutual Reinsurance Co Ltd v Peat Marwick Mitchell & Co* [1997] 1 BCLC 1; *Re London and General Bank* [1895] 2 Ch 166; *Re Kingston Cotton Mill Co* [1896] 1 Ch 6. The CA 2006 gives the Secretary of State power by regulations to make provision for the disclosure of the terms on which a company's auditor is appointed, remunerated, or performs his duties (s 493). This power has not been exercised to date.

auditor is to be appointed (which will be in all cases other than where the company qualifies as dormant, see **18-55**), the appointment must be made at the accounts meeting (s 489(2) and see **18-23**). Where the company is a public interest entity with an audit committee, the audit committee must make a recommendation on the appointment of the auditor to the board and must submit two names. If the board proposes someone other than one of the two names put forward by the audit committee, the board must give reasons for deviating from the choice of the committee (s 489A). Auditors may be individuals or firms and they must be appropriately qualified (s 1219). They must be members of recognised supervisory bodies (s 1212)[127] and meet independence requirements (s 1214).

**18-50**  In addition to their role as the company auditor, auditors frequently provide the company (especially larger companies) with additional non-audit services, such as advice on taxation matters, on corporate restructuring, information technology, and on human resources. Large companies must give details of any remuneration received by the auditor or an associate of an auditor in respect of non-audit services in a note to the company's accounts[128] while small and medium-sized companies must disclose the audit fee paid to their auditors.[129] The concern about the provision of non-audit services, which are typically much more lucrative than the statutory audit, is that the value of the services may compromise the independence of the auditor. To counter that threat, EU Regulation 537/2014 imposes significant restrictions on the provision of certain non-audit services to public-interest entities (PIEs) and members of the same group as the PIE incorporated in the EU. In some cases, there is an outright prohibition on the provision of non-audit services (such as certain tax, payroll, and accounting and internal audit services), in other cases provision is dependent on the consent of the audit committee or the competent authority responsible for the supervision of auditors, i.e. the FRC.[130] Even when non-audit services are permitted, the fee income from the permitted non-audit services is capped at 70 per cent of the average audit fee over the three preceding financial years.[131] The prohibitions extend to the auditors and firms which are members of the auditors' network.[132]

**18-51**  Since January 2015, FTSE 350 companies have been required to put their statutory audit out to tender at least once every 10 years, a measure introduced by a Competition and Markets Authority Order,[133] but required now in any event under the EU Regulation 537/2014 with respect to PIEs, though the EU Regulation allows for the audit to be retained for a further 10-year period if there has been a tendering process, see CA 2006, s 494ZA.[134] The same Order also requires the company's audit committee to negotiate and

---

[127] For example, they may be members of the Institute of Chartered Accountants of England and Wales (ICAEW) or the Institute of Chartered Accountants of Scotland (ICAS) or the Association of Chartered Certified Accountants (ACCA).

[128] CA 2006, s 494 and The Companies (Disclosure of Auditor Remuneration and Liability Limitation Agreements) Regulations 2008, SI 2008/489, as amended by SI 2011/2198, reg 5(1). The audit fee and all other fees receivable by the auditors for services supplied by them and their associates to the company, its subsidiaries, and associated pension schemes must be disclosed, subject to certain exceptions. This level of disclosure was part of the quid pro quo for the introduction of liability limitation agreements, see **18-90**.

[129] SI 2008/489, reg 4(1).          [130] EU Regulation 537/2014, OJ L 158/77, 27.5.2014, arts 4 and 5.

[131] EU Regulation 537/2014, OJ L 158/77, 27.5.2014, art 4.

[132] The UK implemented these requirements by a Revised Ethical Standard 2016 (June 2016), see I22. For the background, see BIS, *Auditor Regulation, Discussion Document on the implication of the EU and wider reforms* (December 2014), BIS/14/1285, pp 22–7.

[133] The Statutory Audit Services for Large Companies (Mandatory Use of Competitive Tender Processes and Audit Committee Responsibilities) Order 2014.

[134] EU Regulation 537/2014, OJ L 158/77, 27.5.2014, art 17. See BIS, *Auditor Regulation, Discussion Document on the implication of the EU and wider reforms* (December 2014), BIS/14/1285, pp 28–37.

agree the terms of the statutory audit services agreement, so ensuring the matter is in the hands of the independent non-executive directors rather than the executive directors.

## Exemption from obligation to appoint auditors

**18-52**   It might be expected that all companies' accounts should be audited, but small companies are audit-exempt. The argument against the need for a statutory audit for these companies is essentially one of the costs involved particularly when, it is argued, it is difficult to identify a real need for, or benefit from, the statutory audit. In many small companies, the shareholders typically are also the directors and often all concerned are members of one family so there is no shareholder need for an audit. Equally, the company's creditors in many cases consist of the company's bank (which would have its own picture of the company's finances) and a small number of trade creditors providing limited amounts of credit on short time scales. Hence, it is argued, neither is there an identifiable creditor need for an audit.

**18-53**   The arguments in favour of retaining the audit centre on the value to these small companies of obtaining professional assistance with their accounts at least once a year. Many of these companies are woefully unaware of their obligations with respect to a variety of accounting and taxation matters and the annual audit offers an opportunity for some professional advice. It also means that the auditors are in a position to draw the directors' attention to matters such as a drift towards insolvency (and their corresponding duties to creditors, see **10-41**) and the risk of possible liability for wrongful trading (see **15-18**) and disqualification (see **15-88**). Filing unaudited accounts with the registrar reduces the value of the public registry as searchers are unable to assess the reliability of the (minimal) information being presented by the company (remember small companies need only deliver a balance sheet to the registrar). Finally, given that not all small companies are wholly owned by the directors or their families, minority shareholders who are not directors and who do not have access to the company's records may need the reassurance of an annual independent review of the accounts, though this point is met, at least in part, by a provision whereby shareholders representing more than 10 per cent in nominal value of the issued share capital may require the company to have an audit (CA 2006, s 476).

**18-54**   The requirement for an audit was abolished in 1994, initially for companies with a turnover below £90,000;[135] now the threshold stands at £10.2m (s 477(1)). In 2016/17, 68 per cent of the companies on the UK register (1.96m companies) filed audit-exempt accounts.[136]

**18-55**   There are three main ways in which companies may be exempt from the audit requirement:[137]

(1) Under s 477, where the company qualifies as a small company in relation to that year under s 382 (see **18-25**) and it is not an excluded company within s 478.[138]

(2) Where the company is a dormant company within s 480. A company is a dormant company if it has no significant accounting transaction during the period in

---

[135] See The Companies Act 1985 (Audit Exemption) Regulations 1994, SI 1994/1935. For background to the change, see generally, Freedman and Godwin, 'The Statutory Audit and the Micro Company—An Empirical Investigation' [1993] JBL 105.

[136] See *Companies House Management Information 2016/17*, Table 8.

[137] There is also a limited exemption in respect of non-profit-making companies subject to public sector audit, see CA 2006, s 482.

[138] Excluded categories essentially are public companies or certain financial services or special register companies, see CA 2006, s 478; special rules apply to small companies which are part of a group, see s 479.

question, i.e. no transaction that requires to be entered in the company's accounting records (s 1169). A dormant company may be either a public or a private company, provided it is not otherwise ineligible (ss 480, 481). A company may be dormant for a variety of reasons. For example, it may have been incorporated to protect a company name; or it may be part of a group of companies where activities have been transferred to other parts of the group; or it may have been incorporated to carry out a venture which never got off the ground.

(3) Subsidiary companies audit exemption—qualifying subsidiaries are also exempt from the audit requirement (whether or not dormant).[139] A qualifying subsidiary is one which meets the criteria set out in s 479A and is not within the excluded categories in s 479B and subject to the giving of a guarantee as required by s 479C. The company's parent undertaking must be subject to the laws of an EEA member state and the subsidiary must be included in the audited consolidated accounts prepared by the parent company and the notes to those accounts must disclose that the company is exempt from audit; the shareholders of the subsidiary must unanimously agree to the audit exemption and a statement to that effect must be delivered to the registrar of companies (s 479A). The subsidiary must file the parent company's accounts with the registrar together with a declaration from the parent that it guarantees (s 479C) all liabilities of the subsidiary that are outstanding at the end of the financial year to which the exemption relates, until they are satisfied in full, and the guarantee is enforceable against the parent company by any person to whom the subsidiary company is liable in respect of those liabilities (s 479C(3)).[140]

**18-56** In any case, a company is not entitled to the audit exemption unless the balance sheet contains a statement by the directors to the effect that:

(1) the company is entitled to the exemption (CA 2006, s 475(2));

(2) shareholders holding 10 per cent of the shares have not sought an audit (s 475(3)(a));

(3) the directors acknowledge their responsibility for keeping accounting records and the preparation of the accounts (s 475(3)(b)).

If that statement is false, criminal penalties may arise for approving accounts which do not comply with the statutory requirements (s 414(4), (5)).

## Removal and resignation of auditors

**18-57** A company may by ordinary resolution at any time remove an auditor from office (CA 2006, s 510), but removal of the company's auditor from office on grounds of divergence of opinions on accounting treatments or audit procedures, or on any other improper grounds, is treated as being unfairly prejudicial to the interests of some part of the company's members so as to enable a member (not the auditor) to petition for relief in those circumstances (CA 2006, s 994(1A)).[141] An auditor may resign his office at any time by sending a notice to that effect to the company (s 516). An auditor of a public interest

---

[139] The background to these changes can be found in BIS, *Consultation on Audit Exemptions and Change of Accounting Framework* (October 2011), paras 38–53, 57–59.

[140] See ICAEW, Tech 07/13BL, *Exemption for audit by parent guarantee*.

[141] As noted in *Re Sunrise Radio Ltd, Kohli v Lit* [2010] 1 BCLC 367 at [9], the board may genuinely and correctly disagree with accounting treatments, but removal of the auditors on those grounds is unfairly prejudicial conduct, even though the conduct complained of may have no necessary impact on the value of the complaining shareholder's investment.

company must always send to the company a statement of his reasons for leaving[142] and an auditor of a non-public interest company must send to the company a statement of his reasons for leaving unless his term of office has come to an end or his reasons for leaving are exempt reasons[143] as defined in s 519A(3) and there is no information that the auditor thinks should be brought to the attention of the company's shareholders or creditors (s 519).[144] Where an auditor of a company sends a statement under s 519, the auditor must at the same time send a copy of the statement to the appropriate audit authority (s 522(1)) and the audit authority may forward the statement to the accounting authorities (s 524(1)). These elaborate notification requirements are designed to eliminate practices which may have existed in the past whereby disagreements between management and auditors were resolved by timely resignations or failures to re-appoint which left the shareholders (and the regulators) unaware of any audit concerns or tensions at the root of the departures.[145]

## F  The auditor's report

**18-58**   An auditor's primary task is to make a report to the company's members on the annual accounts of the company (CA 2006, s 495(1)). As Lord Oliver commented in *Caparo Industries plc v Dickman*:[146]

> '[T]he primary purpose of the statutory requirement that a company's accounts shall be audited annually is almost self-evident. The structure of the corporate trading entity, at least in the case of public companies whose shares are dealt with on an authorised stock exchange, involves the concept of a more or less widely distributed holding of shares rendering the personal involvement of each individual shareholder in the day to day management of the enterprise impracticable, with the result that management is necessarily separated from ownership. The management is confided to a board of directors which operates in a fiduciary capacity and is answerable to and removable by the shareholders who can act, if they act at all, only collectively and only through the medium of the general meeting. Hence the legislative provisions requiring the board annually to give an account of its stewardship to a general meeting of shareholders.'

### The content of the report

**18-59**   The auditors' report must identify the accounts subject to audit and the financial reporting framework that has been applied (CA 2006, s 495(2)) and it must describe the scope of the audit. The report must state whether in the auditor's opinion the accounts give a true and fair view:

(1)  in the case of an individual balance sheet, of the state of affairs of the company as at the end of the financial year;

---

[142]  If he does so send, he can require the directors to call a meeting to discuss the circumstances of his resignation: CA 2006, s 518.

[143]  Essentially, the exempt reasons are that the auditor is ceasing to act as an auditor, the company is becoming exempt from the audit, or the company is being wound up.

[144]  The auditor must make up his own mind as to whether there are circumstances which need to be brought to the attention of the mentioned parties and the court will presume that the auditors are acting in faithful discharge of their duty and not in pursuit of any private or collateral interest, unless the contrary is shown: *Jarvis plc v PricewaterhouseCoopers* [2000] 2 BCLC 368.

[145]  The procedures for notification were simplified from those originally contained in CA 2006, Pt 16 by amendments effected by the Deregulation Act 2015, s 18, and Sch 15.

[146]  [1990] 1 All ER 568 at 583.

(2)  in the case of an individual profit and loss account, of the profit or loss of the company for the financial year;

(3)  in the case of group accounts, of the state of affairs as at the end of the financial year, and the profit or loss for the financial year, of the undertakings included in the consolidation as a whole, so far as concerns members of the company (s 495(3)(a)).

The report must also state whether the annual accounts have been properly prepared in accordance with the relevant financial reporting framework and the requirements of the CA 2006 and, where applicable, IAS (s 495(3)(b), (c)). The report can be qualified or unqualified and the auditor may draw attention to matters by way of emphasis without qualifying the report (s 495(4)).[147]

**18-60**  The auditors' report must (a) state whether, in his opinion, based on the work undertaken in the course of the audit, (i) the information given in the strategic report (if any) and the directors' report for the financial year for which the accounts are prepared is consistent with those accounts, and (ii) any such strategic report and the directors' report have been prepared in accordance with applicable legal requirements; (b) state whether, in the light of the knowledge and understanding of the company and its environment obtained in the course of the audit, he has identified material misstatements in the strategic report (if any) and the directors' report; and (c) if applicable, give an indication of the nature of each of the misstatements (s 496). If the company is a quoted company, the auditors' report must state whether that part of the directors' remuneration report which is subject to review by the auditors has been properly prepared (s 497). Where the company prepares a separate corporate governance statement in respect of a financial year, the auditor must, in his report of the company's annual accounts for that year—(a) state whether, in his opinion, based on the work undertaken in the course of the audit, the information given in the statement in compliance with DTR 7.2.5 and 7.2.6 (information about internal control and risk management systems in relation to financial reporting processes and about share capital structures)—(i) is consistent with those accounts, and (ii) has been prepared in accordance with applicable legal requirements; (b) state whether, in the light of the knowledge and understanding of the company and its environment obtained in the course of the audit, he has identified material misstatements in the information in the statement referred to in paragraph (a); (c) if applicable, give an indication of the nature of each of the misstatements referred to in paragraph (b); and (d) state whether, in his opinion, based on the work undertaken in the course of the audit, DTR 7.2.2, 7.2.3, and 7.2.7 (information about the company's corporate governance code and practices and about its administrative, management, and supervisory bodies and their committees) have been complied with, if applicable (s 497A). If the auditor is of the opinion that adequate accounting records have not been kept; or the accounts are not in agreement with the accounting records; or the auditable part of the directors' remuneration report is not in agreement with the accounting records, he must so state in the audit report (s 498(2)). If an auditor fails to obtain all the information and explanations necessary for the purposes of the audit, he must so state in the audit report (s 498(3)); if the directors have claimed to be entitled to use the small companies regime and, in the auditor's opinion, they are not so entitled, he must so state in the audit report (s 498(5)). If certain information is not disclosed as to directors' benefits and remuneration when it is required to be disclosed,

---

[147] An auditors' report may be modified by adding an emphasis of matter paragraph to highlight a matter affecting the financial statements, see ISA 706 (UK), *Emphasis of matter paragraphs and other matter paragraphs in the independent auditor's report* (Revised June 2016).

the auditor must include the particulars in his report, so far as he is reasonably able to do so (s 498(4)).

**18-61**  Clearly, the statute now dictates much of the content of the auditors' report, but its form and content is also the subject of extensive professional guidance in an auditing standard, ISA 700.[148] Under ISA 700, the emphasis is placed on the auditor providing a clear written expression of opinion on the financial statements taken as a whole which includes evaluating whether sufficient appropriate audit evidence as to whether the financial statements as a whole are free from material misstatement, whether due to fraud or error, has been obtained and whether the financial statements give a true and fair view (para 8). The standard also requires that the report include a range of statements clarifying the distinct responsibilities of those charged with governance, the directors for our purposes, for the preparation of the financial statements (paras 33–36). The responsibilities of the auditor must also be set out in detail, including to audit and express an opinion on the financial statements (paras 37–42).[149] The intention is that drawing attention to this interrelationship between the responsibilities of those who prepare financial statements and those who audit them facilitates an understanding of the nature and context of the opinion expressed by the auditor.[150]

**18-62**  The significance of the audit report is enhanced by a requirement that the senior statutory auditor sign the report (ss 503, 504). In other words, the audit engagement partner must sign in his or her own name for and on behalf of the firm, a requirement which does not increase the personal liability of an auditor in any way (s 504(3)), but is designed to reinforce their appreciation of their personal professional responsibilities with regard to the audit. It is also a criminal offence to knowingly or recklessly cause an auditors' report on the annual accounts to include any matter that is misleading, false, or deceptive in a material particular or to omit statements otherwise required to be included (CA 2006, s 507).[151]

### The auditor's reporting obligations with respect to corporate governance requirements

**18-63**  For premium listed companies applying the UK Corporate Governance Code, there are additional matters on which the auditor must report with regard to the audit strategy, and the risks of material misstatement identified by the auditor, and the threshold of materiality which the auditor used for the financial statements as a whole, and the auditor is required to describe these matters in a manner that complements the description of the work of the audit committee (ISA 700, paras 19A and 19B). Further the auditor must indicate whether, when reading the other financial and non-financial information included in the annual report, the auditor has identified information that is materially inconsistent with the information in the audited financial statements or is apparently materially incorrect based on, or materially inconsistent with, the knowledge acquired by the auditor in the course of performing the audit or that is otherwise misleading (para 22A). For example, the auditor must so report by exception if the section describing the

---

[148]  ISA (UK) 700, *Forming an Opinion and Reporting on Financial Statements* (Revised June 2016).
[149]  ISA 700, para 15. The report must also include a description of the generic scope of the audit, para 16.
[150]  ISA 700, para A6.
[151]  i.e. a failure to include a statement that the accounts do not agree with accounting records, or that necessary information has not been included, or that the directors are wrongly using the small companies exemption: see CA 2006, s 507(2).

work of the audit committee does not appropriately address matters communicated by the auditor to the audit committee. As discussed at **6-41**, these additional requirements reflect the recommendations of the Sharman Inquiry and subsequent consultations by the FRC as to their implementation and are intended to strengthen the triangular relationship between the auditors, the audit committee, and the board. The obligations are reflected in a further auditing standard, ISA 260, on communication with those charged with governance which, in our context, means the directors, whether executive or non-executive.[152] ISA 260 requires the auditors to communicate, typically with the audit committee, about their responsibilities in relation to the audit, their independence, the scope of the audit, and significant findings from the audit and, where the company is subject to the UK Corporate Governance Code, to communicate information relevant to the fulfilment by the board and the audit committee of their responsibilities under Section 4 of the Code, which are discussed at 6-25.[153]

## G  Auditors' liability and limitation of liability

### The conduct of the audit

**18-64**  Many corporate collapses in the past have revealed significant fraudulent activity by the directors and/or other employees, indeed often long-running wrongdoing on a massive scale. The financial crisis revealed huge losses by banks built up over periods when they continued to secure 'clean' audit reports. That loss-making on the scale which afflicted UK and European banks as well as losses from corporate frauds has gone undetected by the companies' auditors raises issues as to: (1) the manner in which the auditors conduct an audit, and (2) their liabilities in the event that the audit fails to detect wrongdoing or significant poor performance by the company such that the accounts give an erroneous picture of the company's business.

**18-65**  As noted at **18-59**, an audit involves obtaining evidence about the amounts and disclosures in the financial statements sufficient to give reasonable assurance that the financial statements are free from material misstatement, whether caused by fraud or error.[154] There are a number of older authorities which establish that an auditor is not an insurer,[155] nor is he required to approach his work with suspicion or with a foregone conclusion that something is wrong, and he is justified, in the absence of suspicion, in believing employees in whom confidence is placed by the company.[156] An auditor should approach his work with an inquiring mind,[157] however, and once put on inquiry, he is under a duty to get to the bottom of the matter in question.[158] These older authorities must be treated with some caution for the courts are likely to expect higher standards from today's highly paid, professional auditors but they do provide some basic pointers as to what is expected of auditors.

**18-66**  In *Sasea Finance Ltd v KPMG*[159] the Court of Appeal concluded that where a company's auditors discover that a senior employee is defrauding the company on a massive scale,

---

[152]  ISA 260 (UK) *Communication with those charged with governance* (Revised June 2016).
[153]  ISA 260, paras 14–17.
[154]  ISA 700 (June 2016), n 148, para 11; and see *Barings plc v Coopers & Lybrand* [1997] 1 BCLC 427.
[155]  See *Re London and General Bank Ltd (No 2)* [1895] 2 Ch 673.
[156]  *Re Kingston Cotton Mill Co (No 2)* [1896] 2 Ch 279.
[157]  See Lord Denning in *Fomento (Sterling Area) Ltd v Selsdon Fountain Pen Co Ltd* [1958] 1 WLR 45 at 61.
[158]  *Re Thomas Gerrard & Son Ltd* [1967] 2 All ER 525.
[159]  [2000] 1 BCLC 236.

and that employee is in a position to continue doing so, the auditors would normally have a duty to report the discovery to the management immediately, not merely when rendering their report and, if the management are implicated in the wrongdoing, the auditors would have to report directly to a third party without the management's knowledge or consent.

**18-67**  To assist the auditors in their task, they have a right of access at all times to the company's books and accounts and they are entitled to require a wide range of persons, in particular the company's officers and employees, to provide them with such information and explanations as they think necessary for the performance of their duties (CA 2006, s 499). Criminal sanctions apply where the information or explanation is misleading, false, or deceptive in a material particular (s 501).[160] Auditors of a parent company with overseas subsidiaries can require the parent company to obtain from the subsidiary, its officers etc, such information or explanations as the auditor reasonably requires for the purposes of his duties as auditor and the parent company must take all such steps as are reasonably open to it to obtain that information etc (s 500). An auditor is entitled to receive all communications relating to a proposed written resolution of a private company and also has the right to be notified of and to attend any general meeting and to speak on any part of the business of the meeting which concerns him as auditor (s 502(2)). In practice, auditors rarely need to rely on their statutory rights in this regard since an auditor who is dissatisfied with his access to information or to the shareholders has other mechanisms at his disposal, most notably the ability to qualify his report (s 495(4)(a)), to add statements short of qualification (s 495(4)(b)), or to resign (s 516).

## Duty of care of auditors

**18-68**  A practical concern is the extent of any duty of care owed by the company's auditors to the company, the shareholders, and others who read and rely on the audited accounts. While there is much case law on the matter involving auditors (and other professionals), the courts are reluctant to find that a professional adviser owes a common law duty of care to a non-client.[161]

**18-69**  There are two possible types of claims:

(1)  claims by clients against their auditors which are straightforward claims in contract (since the auditors owe the company appointing them a duty to exercise reasonable care and skill in performing their contractual obligations) and in tort;[162] and

(2)  claims in tort by third parties who are not in any direct relationship with the auditors but who claim damages for losses arising from reliance on negligently audited accounts. The extent of any duty of care in tort to such users of the company's

---

[160]  There is a right against self-incrimination: see CA 2006, s 499(3). See *R v Gyrus Group Ltd* [2014] EWCA Crim 2945.

[161]  See *Bank of Credit and Commerce International (Overseas) Ltd v Price Waterhouse* [1998] BCC 617 at 636, per Sir Brian Neill; *BDG Roof-Bond v Douglas* [2000] 1 BCLC 401 at 420, per Park J. The Company Law Review made no recommendation for any statutory extension of auditors' duties of care, preferring to leave the issue to the development of the law of negligence in the normal way: see *Final Report* (2001), paras 8.134–8.135.

[162]  As the payment of improper dividends or bonuses is the natural and probable result of the false picture which the auditors have allowed the accounts to present, the auditors are liable for those amounts: *Re Thomas Gerrard & Son Ltd* [1967] 2 All ER 525 (auditors aware of discrepancies but failed to investigate further); *Re London and General Bank (No 2)* [1895] 2 Ch 673 (auditors omitted information from report to shareholders); and see *Barings plc v Coopers & Lybrand (No 1)* [2002] 2 BCLC 364; *Equitable Life Assurance Society v Ernst & Young* [2003] 2 BCLC 603.

accounts is problematic. A duty of care may arise between an auditor and another under two different but interrelated approaches:[163] because of an assumption of responsibility for the task/advice in question or because of meeting the three-fold test (foreseeability, proximity, and fairness) established in *Caparo Industries plc v Dickman*.[164] In practice the courts apply one or other or both approaches depending on the circumstances. The House of Lords in *Customs and Excise Commissioners v Barclays Bank*[165] made it clear that it is not possible to force the law into a single test.

As Hamblen J commented in *Standard Chartered Bank v Ceylon Petroleum*:[166]

'[R]ecent case law has emphasised the importance of a pragmatic approach which concentrates on the exchanges and dealings between the parties considered in their context rather than the application of high level statements of principle. Attention should be concentrated on "the detailed circumstances of the particular case and the particular relationship between the parties in the context of their legal and factual situation as a whole,"—per Lord Bingham in *Commissioners of Customs & Excise v Barclays Bank ...*'[167]

### An assumption of responsibility for the task/advice in question

**18-70**   Where the parties have a contractual or 'almost contractual'[168] relationship (for example, a client relationship or a relationship between an auditor and a regulatory authority[169]) and so fall clearly within the *Hedley Byrne & Co Ltd v Heller & Partners Ltd*[170] principle, the matter is relatively straightforward. This assumption of responsibility rests upon a relationship between the parties, which may be general or specific to the particular transaction, and which may or may not be contractual in nature.[171] Whether there is such an assumption of responsibility is a matter to be considered objectively.[172] Accountants who carry out specific reporting obligations under a statutory requirement to do so owe a duty of care to the regulatory authority to whom they report;[173] likewise, auditors may assume a duty of care to a regulatory authority.[174]

---

[163] There is possibly a third approach—the incremental approach approved by Lord Bridge in *Caparo Industries plc v Dickman* [1990] 1 All ER 568 at 576 where he stated that it is preferable that 'the law should develop novel categories of negligence incrementally and by analogy with established categories, rather than by a massive extension of a *prima facie* duty of care restrained only by indefinable "considerations which ought to negative, or to reduce or limit the scope of the duty or the class of person to whom it is owed"'. But the value of this approach has been doubted, see *Customs and Excise Commissioners v Barclays Bank* [2006] 4 All ER 256 at [7] ('little value as a test in itself'), per Lord Bingham; also Mitchell and Mitchell, 'Negligence Liability for Pure Economic Loss' (2005) 121 LQR 194.    [164] [1990] 1 All ER 568.
[165] [2006] 4 All ER 256, HL.    [166] [2011] EWHC 1785 at [478].    [167] [2006] 4 All ER 256 at [8].
[168] As Lord Bingham said, the paradigm situation being a relationship having all the indicia of contract save consideration, see *Commissioners of Customs & Excise v Barclays Bank* [2006] 4 All ER 256 at [4].
[169] See *Andrew v Kounnis Freeman* [1999] 2 BCLC 641.    [170] [1963] 2 All ER 575.
[171] *Henderson v Merrett Syndicates Ltd* [1994] 3 All ER 506 at 520, HL, per Lord Goff.
[172] *Commissioners of Customs & Excise v Barclays Bank* [2006] 4 All ER 256 at [5]; *Electra Private Equity Partners v KPMG Peat Marwick* [2001] 1 BCLC 589; *Henderson v Merrett Syndicates Ltd* [1994] 3 All ER 506 at 518–21; *Spring v Guardian Assurance plc* [1994] 3 All ER 129; *Williams v Natural Life Health Foods Ltd* [1998] 1 BCLC 689; *Peach Publishing Ltd v Slater & Co* [1998] BCC 139. See Jackson LJ's comments that, in his view, the conceptual basis upon which the concurrent (as in contract and tort) liability of professional persons in tort to their clients now rests is assumption of responsibility, noting that it is perhaps understandable that professional persons are taken to assume responsibility for economic loss to their clients. They expect their clients and possibly others to act in reliance upon their work product, often with financial or economic consequences, see *Robinson v PE Jones (Contractors)* [2011] 3 WLR 815 at [74]–[75].
[173] See *Law Society v KPMG Peat Marwick* [2000] 4 All ER 540.
[174] See *Andrew v Kounnis Freeman* [1999] 2 BCLC 641.

### Meeting the three-fold test established in *Caparo*

**18-71** Most disputes arise where there is no relationship between the auditor and the claimant and therefore the assumption of responsibility approach will not yield an answer and it is necessary to allege that the parties are sufficiently proximate to give rise to a duty of care on the part of the auditor on the basis of *Caparo Industries plc v Dickman*,[175] the leading authority on auditors' liability. In this case, having reviewed the authorities, the House of Lords concluded that in order for a duty of care to arise, there must be:[176]

    (1) a reasonable foreseeability of damage;

    (2) a relationship of sufficient 'proximity' between the party owing the duty and the party to whom it is owed; and

    (3) the imposition of the duty of care contended for should be just and reasonable in all the circumstances.

**18-72** It is relatively easy to establish the first element, a foreseeability of damage if accounts are negligently audited, but that is not sufficient of itself. The third element, the 'just and reasonable' consideration, was imposed by the court in order to prevent foreseeability alone giving rise, in the famous words of Cardozo CJ in *Ultramares Corpn v Touche*,[177] to 'liability in an indeterminate amount for an indeterminate time to an indeterminate class'.

**18-73** Most discussion has focused on the second element as to whether, on a particular set of facts, there is a relationship of sufficient proximity for a duty of care to arise. In *Caparo*, Lord Oliver identified the circumstances which should exist in order to establish the necessary relationship of proximity between the person claiming to be owed the duty (the advisee) and the adviser:[178]

    (1) the advice is required for a purpose, whether particularly specified or generally described, which is made known, either actually or inferentially, to the adviser at the time the advice is given;

    (2) the adviser knows, either actually or inferentially, that his advice will be communicated to the advisee, either specifically or as a member of an ascertainable class, in order that it should be used by the advisee for that purpose;

    (3) it is known, either actually or inferentially, that the advice so communicated is likely to be acted upon by the advisee for that purpose without independent inquiry; and

    (4) it is so acted upon by the advisee to his detriment.

**18-74** The key elements then are that the auditor knows (whether actually or inferentially) that his report will be communicated to a person (whether individually or as a member of a class) specifically for a particular purpose and that there would be reliance on it. It is because these are the key elements which may give rise to a duty of care with respect to third parties that professional guidance to auditors encourages the use of disclaimers in an attempt to minimise the potential for these elements being present.[179] Hence the

---

[175] [1990] 1 All ER 568; noted (1990) 106 LQR 349, [1990] MLR 824.

[176] [1990] 1 All ER 568 at 573–4, per Lord Bridge, though as Lord Bingham acknowledged in *Commissioners of Customs & Excise v Barclays Bank* [2006] 4 All ER 256 at [6], this three-fold test itself provides no straightforward answer to the question whether or not a party owes a duty of care.

[177] (1931) 255 NY 170 at 179.      [178] [1990] 1 All ER 568 at 589.

[179] The practice arises from the decision of the Scottish courts in *RBS plc v Bannerman* [2006] BCC 148 where the court considered that the absence of a disclaimer of liability to a third party could be a relevant circumstance pointing to an assumption of liability in respect of that third party's use of information provided by the auditor.

auditors' report commonly includes a paragraph to the effect that the report is made solely to the company's members in accordance with the CA 2006 and solely for the purposes of the CA 2006 and 'to the fullest extent permitted by law, we [the auditors] do not accept or assume responsibility to anyone other than the company and the company's members as a body for our audit work, for this report, or for the opinions we have formed'.[180]

**18-75**  In *Caparo*, as noted at **18-58**, the House of Lords concluded that the purpose of the audit is to enable the shareholders as a body to exercise informed control of the company.[181] It follows that auditors do not owe a duty of care to members of the public at large who rely on the audited accounts to buy shares; nor to an individual shareholder in the company who wishes to buy more shares in the company since an individual share-holder is in no better position than a member of the public at large;[182] nor to possible takeover bidders,[183] nor do they owe a duty of care to existing or future creditors who extend credit on the strength of the audited accounts.[184] In none of these cases is the relationship proximate enough, without more, to give rise to a duty of care. Returning to the facts in *Caparo*, the House of Lords found the auditors owed no duty of care to an existing shareholder in the company who purchased additional shares and took over the company in reliance on the audited accounts only to discover that the accounts were inaccurate. The auditors owed their duty to the shareholders as a body and not to an individual investor.

**18-76**  These issues can be illustrated by considering *Barings plc v Coopers & Lybrand (No 1)*.[185] This case arose out of the collapse of the Barings Bank group of companies as a result of the unauthorised activities of a rogue trader in the Far East who accumulated losses of about £800m. The parent company (P1) had a subsidiary (S1) which had a subsidiary (S2) and the rogue trader was an employee of S2. Following the collapse of the group, an action in contract and tort was brought by S2 against its auditors (D&T) in respect of their allegedly negligent audits of the company. An action in tort was also commenced against the auditors by P1 and S1. Essentially, these companies argued that, had the audit been conducted properly, the wrongdoing would have been uncovered, these companies would not have continued to advance funding to S2, and the group would not have collapsed. The court granted an application for the claim to be struck out.

**18-77**  Turning to the criteria established by *Caparo*, Evans-Lombe J pointed out that, in the case of a claim in tort against an auditor, it is necessary to plead and prove that at the time the auditor undertook his services, he must have had in contemplation that they would be relied on by the claimant for the purpose of a particular transaction or class of transactions. That reliance then must have resulted in the loss for which compensa-tion was claimed. Evans-Lombe J noted that these limitations (reliance on the audit for

---

[180] See ICAEW, *The Audit Report and Auditors' Duty of Care to Third Parties*, Technical release, Audit 01/03, as updated.     [181] See [1990] 1 All ER 568 at 583–4, 606–7.

[182] [1990] 1 All ER 568 at 581, 601, 607.

[183] *Caparo Industries plc v Dickman* [1990] 1 All ER 568; see also *James McNaughton Papers Group Ltd v Hicks Anderson & Co* [1991] BCLC 163; though the position may be different where representations are made after an identified bidder has emerged; see *Morgan Crucible Co plc v Hill Samuel Bank Ltd* [1991] BCLC 18; *Galoo Ltd v Bright Grahame Murray* [1994] 2 BCLC 492; where it may be possible, on the facts, to establish that a duty of care has been assumed: see *ADT v BDO Binder Hamlyn* [1996] BCC 808; also *Electra Private Equity Partners v KPMG Peat Marwick* [2001] 1 BCLC 589.

[184] *Al Saudi Banque v Clark Pixley* [1989] 3 All ER 361; *Berg Sons & Co Ltd v Mervyn Hampton Adams* [1993] BCLC 1045.     [185] [2002] 2 BCLC 364, Ch D.

a contemplated purpose) were necessary to control the scope of claims in this area of the law. He went on:[186]

'To the outsider it would seem far-fetched that the negligence of a subsidiary auditor of one of the minor subsidiary companies of a complex and substantial banking group should expose that auditor to liability for massive damages flowing from the collapse of the entire group, notwithstanding that it can be said that but for his negligence that collapse would not have taken place.'

**18-78**  As the auditors of S2, the auditors never had it in contemplation that their report would be used by the other companies in the group when deciding to meet the trader's funding requests through S2.[187] Equally, no transactions made by P1 which resulted in the loss of the entire group could be identified as transactions which had been embarked upon in reliance on the audit and which the auditors had in contemplation when they undertook that audit.[188]

**18-79**  This case highlights another issue, causation (but see **18-80**). Even if a duty of care can be established, the alleged breach of duty must be the effective or dominant cause of the claimants' loss as opposed to merely the occasion for the loss. In determining that issue, the court applies its common sense to the issue. In *Galoo Ltd v Bright Grahame Murray*[189] the court struck out a claim for losses arising from continued trading after a negligent audit. It was argued that, had the audit been conducted properly, the companies involved would not have continued to trade and therefore the claim was for the losses arising from the continued trading. The court rejected the claim. The breach of duty gave the companies the opportunity to continue and to incur losses, but it did not 'cause' the loss in the sense that 'cause' is used in law. This point was reinforced in *Haugesund Kommune v Depfa ACS Bank*[190] where the issue was the extent of a law firm's liability for loss in respect of negligent advice given to a bank. The advice resulted in the bank making ultra vires loans to local authorities which could not be recovered. The local authorities were liable in restitution to make full repayment to the bank, but could not do so as they were insolvent. The Court of Appeal ruled that the extent of the lender's loss that falls within the adviser's duty has to depend on the reason for that loss. If it is due to the invalidity of the transactions, the loss plainly falls within the scope of the adviser's duty, but if the loss is due in reality to the impecuniosity of the borrower who cannot meet the restitutionary claim, that loss does not fall within the scope of the adviser's duty.

**18-80**  More recently the authorities have moved away from a focus on causation and *Galoo* is better analysed now in terms of the scope of the duty of care. The overall approach was summed up by Arden LJ in *Johnson v Gore Wood & Co*[191] in the following way:

'Starting with *Caparo v Dickman*, the courts have moved away from characterising questions as to the measure of damages for the tort of negligence as questions of causation and remoteness. The path that once led in that direction now leads in a new direction. The courts now analyse such questions by enquiring whether the duty which the tortfeasor owed was a duty in respect of the kind of loss of which the victim complains. Duty is no longer determined in abstraction from the consequences or vice-versa. The same test

---

[186]  [2002] 2 BCLC 364 at [88].       [187]  [2002] 2 BCLC 364 at [75]–[76].
[188]  [2002] 2 BCLC 364 at [85].
[189]  [1994] 2 BCLC 492. Cf *Sasea Finance Ltd v KPMG* [2000] 1 BCLC 236, where the court accepted that where the auditors failed in breach of duty to 'blow the whistle' on fraudulent and dishonest activities of senior staff, it was arguable that that failure caused continued losses brought about by such frauds.
[190]  [2011] 3 All ER 655.       [191]  [2003] EWCA Civ 1728 at [91].

applies whether the duty of care is contractual or tortious. To determine the scope of the duty the court must examine carefully the purpose for which advice was being given and generally the surrounding circumstances. The determination of the scope of the duty thus involves an intensely fact-sensitive exercise. The final result turns on the facts, and it is likely to be only the general principles rather than the solution in any individual case that are of assistance in later cases.'

**18-81**   Two key points emerge: first, these issues are intensely fact-sensitive and, secondly, the focus is on the scope of the duty in terms of whether there was a duty in respect of the kind of loss of which the victim complains. As Lord Phillips commented in *Stone & Rolls Ltd v Moore Stephens*,[192] it is questionable whether it is sensible in this context to attempt to distinguish between duty, breach, and actionable damage, noting Lord Oliver's comment in *Caparo*[193] that 'it is not a duty to take care in the abstract, but a duty to avoid causing to the particular plaintiff damage of the particular kind which he has in fact sustained'. The position can be illustrated by *MAN Nutzfahrzeuge AG v Freightliner Ltd*[194] where the Court of Appeal dismissed a claim by a parent company for breach of duty by an auditor of a subsidiary company.

**18-82**   Essentially, the facts were that a subsidiary company (S1) was sold by its parent company (P1) to M by way of a share purchase agreement. It later transpired that for some time previously the accounts of S1 had been persistently manipulated by its financial controller, E, who was responsible for a systematic VAT fraud. E had played a prominent role in the negotiations for the sale and made dishonest representations to M as to the accuracy of the accounts. P1 settled a claim in deceit against it by M and the issue before the Court of Appeal was whether P1 could look for a contribution from S1's auditors who accepted that, if the audit had been conducted with due care and skill, the defects in the accounts would have been identified. The auditors were aware of the importance of the accounts in the negotiations with M.

**18-83**   The Court of Appeal accepted that it was within the scope of the auditors' duty of care to protect S1 from the consequences of decisions taken by S1 or by its shareholders in relation to the affairs of S1 on the basis that the accounts were free from material misstatement. Though it was not necessary to decide the point, the court considered that it would also have been within the scope of a special duty of care owed by the auditors to protect P1 from the consequences of representations and warranties made in the share purchase agreement with M. But the auditors could not be held to have assumed responsibility for the fraudulent use which the dishonest employee made of the subsidiary's accounts in the negotiations for the sale of S1 since that would impose on the auditors a liability greater than they could reasonably have thought they were undertaking. P1's losses (its liability in deceit) were the direct result of the dishonesty of S1's employee (which resulted in a vicarious liability for fraudulent misrepresentation) rather than the inaccuracy of the accounts themselves and the auditors did not undertake a special audit duty to P1 in respect of representations made by E as to the accuracy of the accounts. For all those reasons the auditors were not liable for the loss which P1 had suffered.

**18-84**   Auditors also took heart from the decision of the House of Lords in *Stone & Rolls Ltd v Moore Stephens*[195] where, by a 3–2 majority, their Lordships confirmed that auditors sued

---

[192] [2009] 2 BCLC 563 at [81].   [193] [1990] BCLC 273 at 311.   [194] [2008] 2 BCLC 22, CA.
[195] [2009] 2 BCLC 563, aff'g [2008] 2 BCLC 461, CA. See generally Davies, 'Auditors' Liability: No Need to Detect Fraud' (2010) 68 CLJ 505; Halpern, '*Stone & Rolls Ltd v Moore Stephens*: An Unnecessary Tangle' (2010) 73 MLR 487; Watts, '*Stone & Rolls Ltd v Moore Stephens*: Audit Contracts and Turpitude' (2010) 126 LQR 14; Ferran, 'Corporate Attribution and the Directing Mind and Will' (2011) 127 LQR 239.

in negligence by an insolvent audit client, a one-man company under the sole control of S, a fraudster, could rely on the maxim *ex turpi causa non oritur actio* which precludes claims based on the claimant's own illegality. In this case, a company had been used as a vehicle for fraud by S, its beneficial owner. Various defrauded banks had sued the company and S in deceit and obtained judgment, but the company was insolvent and recovery could not be obtained against S. The liquidator of the company then sued the company's auditors in negligence only to be met by the defence *ex turpi causa non oritur actio*. Essentially the auditors argued that the fraudster's conduct was to be attributed to the company such that the company itself was the fraudster and any claim by the company was therefore barred by the *ex turpi causa* principle.[196]

**18-85** The House of Lords divided 3–2 in favour of allowing the auditors' defence. Lords Walker and Brown (of the majority) considered the issue to be one of attribution. S was the sole beneficial owner of the company, he was its embodiment, he was instrumental in carrying out the frauds, his conduct was to be attributed to the company such that the company was the fraudster, and the company's claim could be defeated by reliance on *ex turpi causa*.[197] Lord Phillips, also of the majority, preferred to rest his decision on the narrow ground that the sole person for whose benefit the duty was owed by the auditors was the person who owned and ran the company and who was responsible for the fraud. In those circumstances, *ex turpi causa* provides a defence.[198] He noted what while it might be arguable that the duty of care of auditors should extend to protecting the interest that creditors have in the preservation of the company's assets, that would involve a departure or extension of *Caparo*, something not required by the issue before the court which was the application of the *ex turpi causa* maxim.[199] In the circumstances of this case, to have held the auditors liable, Lord Phillips said, would have required the duty of care undertaken by them to extend to taking reasonable care that the company was not used as a vehicle for fraud and that this duty was owed for the benefit of those that the company might defraud.[200] His verdict on that: 'I see no prospect that such a duty could be established.'[201]

**18-86** Lord Mance (dissenting) did focus particularly on the duty of care owed by auditors[202] and he concluded that they did owe a duty to the company to have detected and reported a fraud by the top management of the company rendering the company increasingly insolvent, i.e. their duty to the company extends beyond the interests of the shareholders in a situation where the company is insolvent at the time of each audit and increasingly so.[203] Such an approach is not inconsistent, in his view, with *Caparo* since a situation of

---

[196]  [2008] 2 BCLC 461 at 493, per Rimer LJ.

[197]  For a discussion of the attribution issues, now resolved by the Supreme Court decision in *Jetivia SA v Bilta (UK) Ltd* [2015] UKSC 23, [2015] 1 BCLC 443, see **4-52** et seq.

[198]  [2009] 2 BCLC 563 at [18], [86]; and see Watts, n 195, 20.

[199]  [2009] 2 BCLC 563 at [85] and see Watts, n 195, 15–16—the audit contract (and therefore any duty of care) extends only to shareholder interests because it is to the shareholders that the auditors' report, otherwise auditors would be exposed to indeterminate liability measured by the extent of the company's creditors.                                                                     [200]  [2009] 2 BCLC 574 at [85].

[201]  [2009] 2 BCLC 574 at [85].

[202]  Lord Scott also dissented; he thought that the majority had in effect pierced the veil in circumstances where it was not established that the wrongdoer was the owner of the company so there was no justification in treating him as the company, and they had applied a rule of public policy (*ex turpi causa*) in circumstances where the beneficiary of the duty owed by the auditors would have been the creditors of an insolvent company, not the wrongdoer, so there was no justification for allowing reliance on *ex turpi causa*, see [2009] 2 BCLC 563 at [116]–[122], but see Davies, n 195. Halpern, n 195, 491 criticises this approach as drawing a dangerous distinction between the position of a company in liquidation and prior to liquidation.

[203]  [2009] 2 BCLC 563 at [265]–[271].

insolvency was not before the court in that case.[204] Lord Mance concluded by stating that the approach taken by the majority in the case would have the effect of weakening the value of an audit and diminishing auditors' exposure in relation to precisely those (one-man) companies most vulnerable to management fraud. It is in relation to exactly such companies that auditors ought to be encouraged to exercise the skill and care anyway due, he thought, rather than to let them feel that the risks of incurring liability to the company for a negligent audit are reduced.[205]

**18-87**  While some have found Lord Mance's reasoning compelling,[206] and certainly the issue in the case would have been better approached in terms of the scope of the duty rather than the contortions indulged in as a result of treating the issue as one of attribution,[207] this approach requires too great a leap from the orthodox position on directors' duties (they have a duty to have regard to creditors' interests if the company is insolvent or doubtfully solvent, see **10-41**) to applying the same reasoning in the quite different context of the scope of auditors' duties.[208] It is also not necessary to make such a dramatic leap, rather the question of duty can be asked in the manner suggested by Lord Oliver in *Caparo* who stated that 'it is not a duty to take care in the abstract, but a duty to avoid causing to the particular plaintiff damage of the particular kind which he has in fact sustained'.[209] If the issue is approached in the pragmatic terms favoured by the courts, see **18-81**, and in the light of the scope of duty identified in *Caparo*, and the question is asked whether an auditor has a duty to avoid causing to a company's creditors damage arising from the fraud of the company's sole shareholder and director, the answer is clearly no,[210] there is no such duty unless the law is expanded to create one.

**18-88**  Of course, many cases where the auditor fails to discover a fraud will fall within the scenario in *Moore Stephens*, i.e. in the context of frauds committed by a sole director and shareholder through the medium of the company and it is easy to agree with Lord Mance that it is unappealing at one level that the auditors in such circumstances should be able to raise the defence of *ex turpi causa*. On the other hand, the answer to fraud in one-man companies probably lies elsewhere than in imposing a duty of care on auditors owed to the creditors of the insolvent, fraudulently run, company. Arguably, it is those who do business with such companies without pursuing their own checks as to the creditworthiness of the company and the integrity of those running it that allow fraudsters to perpetrate frauds in the first place. In any event, as discussed at **4-55**, in *Jetivia SA v Bilta (UK) Ltd*[211] the Supreme Court has resiled from *Moore Stephens v Rolls & Stone* to such a degree that it can be consigned to the sidelines, with Lords Neuberger and Mance noting that the issue as to the extent of the auditors' duties of care to the company's creditors must be left to another day.[212] Lords Toulson and Hodge conceded only that *Moore Stephens* is authority for what it decided, that on the facts of that case, no claim

---

[204] [2009] 2 BCLC 563 at [267]–[268].     [205] [2009] 2 BCLC 563 at [276].

[206] See Ferran, n 195, 253–4.     [207] See Watts, n 195, also Halpern, n 195, and **4-52** et seq.

[208] See Halpern, n 195, 491, who describes Lord Mance's approach as a subversion of *Caparo*, making the point that the much wider duties of directors cannot be simply transposed from directors to auditors.

[209] [1990] BCLC 273 at 311.

[210] A point confirmed in *Jetivia SA v Bilta (UK) Ltd* [2015] UKSC 23, [2015] 1 BCLC 443 at [152], where Lords Toulson and Hodge note that the fundamental proposition which underlay the reasoning of the majority in *Moore Stephens* was that the auditors owed no duty for the benefit of those for whose benefit the claim was brought.     [211] [2015] UKSC 23, [2015] 1 BCLC 443.

[212] [2015] UKSC 23, [2015] 1 BCLC 443 at [28], [50].

lay against the auditors.[213] For Lords Toulson and Hodge, the protection of creditors lies in the enforcement of the directors' duties under CA 2006, s 172(3) to have regard to the interests of the company's creditors where the company is insolvent or bordering on insolvency.[214]

## Limiting auditors' liabilities

**18-89**  Faced with concerns as to the extent of their possible liability for negligent audits, though, as discussed, there are considerable limitations to that liability and it is not as open-ended as auditors would have us believe, the auditing profession has been anxious to secure some safe harbours against liability. The starting point is CA 2006, s 532 which provides (subject to exceptions for indemnities and liability limitation agreements, discussed at **18-90**) that any provision, whether contained in a company's articles or in any contract with the company or otherwise, for exempting an auditor of a company (to any extent) from any liability that would otherwise attach to him in connection with any negligence, default, breach of duty, or breach of trust in relation to the company occurring in the course of the audit of accounts, is void. Despite this restriction, there are a number of ways in which auditors successfully manage or limit their potential liabilities for negligent audits:[215]

(1) Audit firms may incorporate as companies with limited liability or they may register as limited liability partnerships (LLPs) under the Limited Liability Partnerships Act 2000 (see **1-18**). Indeed LLPs were originally conceived as a mechanism to protect auditors from limitless personal liability, but on enactment they were made available to all businesses.[216]

(2) Insurance—auditors may purchase insurance to protect themselves, but insurance is expensive and adequate cover may not be available, at any price. If a claim is for hundreds of millions of pounds, there is likely to be a significant shortfall between the cover (which might be for, say, £50m) and the amount claimed.

(3) Indemnities—a company may indemnify its auditor against any liability incurred by him in defending proceedings (whether civil or criminal) in which judgment is given in his favour or he is acquitted, or in connection with an application under CA 2006, s 1157 in which relief is granted to him by the court (s 533).[217]

(4) Court relief—auditors are amongst those entitled to apply to the court for relief under CA 2006, s 1157 (power of court to grant relief in case of honest and reasonable conduct), see **14-79**.

(5) It is possible for companies and their auditors to enter into liability limitation agreements (LLAs).

---

[213] [2015] UKSC 23, [2015] 1 BCLC 443 at [154].

[214] [2015] UKSC 23, [2015] 1 BCLC 443 at [126]–[131].

[215] More generally, accountants providing services will try to limit their risk by managing the terms of their engagement, see ICAEW, 'Managing the Professional Liability of Accountants' Tech 02/11, though contractual terms are not so effective with respect to the audit engagement where the audit requirements are dictated by statute and professional standards.

[216] For a critical review of this response to auditors' concerns, see Freedman and Finch, 'Limited Liability Partnerships: Have Accountants Sewn up the "Deep Pockets" Debate?' [1997] JBL 387.

[217] CA 2006, s 533. Indemnities are excluded from the application of s 532(1).

## Liability limitation agreements

### Background

**18-90** The background to LLAs is the long-running concern of auditors, already noted, that they risk catastrophic losses in the event of liability in negligence, a concern fuelled by the implosion in 2002 of Arthur Andersen (then one of the world's largest audit firms), following the collapse of the American energy company, Enron, which had been audited by Andersen. The particular concern of auditors is that joint and several liability in English law means that, following a corporate collapse, there is no one left to sue who is worth suing other than the auditors who are treated as the deep pockets to meet the entire losses though the directors and others may also be culpable. As is clear from the case law, the legal position is somewhat more complex with the law limiting the auditor's liability to the company rather than to third parties and with liability in turn limited by the scope of the duty of care imposed. Nevertheless, the auditing profession has been relentless in its pursuit of legal protection against claims.

**18-91** The collapse of Arthur Andersen also increased concerns amongst regulators and national authorities that with the 'Big Five' auditing firms now reduced to the 'Big Four' (PwC, Deloitte, Ernst & Young, KPMG), a further collapse would mean very limited audit choice for the largest companies and indeed a risk that the largest companies would find it very difficult to appoint an auditor at all.

**18-92** This last aspect sufficiently concerned the European Commission that it concluded that unlimited liability for auditors combined with insufficient insurance cover poses significant problems for the development of a competitive audit market. Hence in 2008 it issued a Recommendation to Member States that Member States should take national measures to limit audit firms' liabilities save in the case of an intentional breach of duty by an auditor.[218] The Recommendation suggested three possible limitation methods: a financial cap, a mechanism for proportionate liability, or a contractual limitation approved by the shareholders, and left it to Member States to decide on the appropriate method for limiting liability. The Recommendation also sets out the key principles to be followed by Member States when they select a limitation method, including that a limitation of liability should not apply in the case of an intentional breach of duty by an auditor; and it should not prevent injured parties from being fairly compensated (in other words, only a limitation and not an exemption from liability should be provided), but a limitation should apply to limit claims by the company and by any third party entitled under national law to bring a claim for compensation.[219] In the event, the UK had already made provision for auditor LLAs in the CA 2006, ss 532–538, which came into force on 6 April 2008 and which the Government thought would address the concerns of individual auditors about their liability. It was also thought that the availability of LLAs would help to expand the pool of audit services available (new entrants would be willing to enter the market if they could manage their potential liabilities effectively) and that this would lead to a more competitive market and a reduction in costs.

**18-93** Given the novelty of allowing auditors to limit their liability, the FRC issued guidance on the content of LLAs and the issues which the directors should bear in mind when

---

[218] Commission Recommendation of 5 June 2008 concerning the limitation of the civil liability of statutory auditors and audit firms, OJ L 162/39, 21.6.2008.

[219] The Recommendation follows an earlier consultation on liability, see DG Internal Market Commission Staff Working Paper: *Consultation on Auditors' Liability and its Impact on the European Capital Markets* (January 2007); also London Economics, *Report on Economic Impact of Auditors' Liability Regimes for EC-DG Internal Market and Services* (September 2006); also an earlier study commissioned by the European Commission: *A study on systems of civil liability of statutory auditors in the context of a Single Market for auditing services in the European Union* (2001).

considering an LLA. The FRC Guidance includes specimen clauses and explains the process to be followed to obtain shareholder approval together with specimen shareholder resolutions.[220] While there are concerns (also expressed about the EU Recommendation) that there is an insufficient balance between the protection of auditor interests and shareholder interests, the FRC comments that these concerns must be assessed in the light of the efforts being made to improve audit quality, the need for LLAs to be approved by shareholders, and that, under CA 2006, s 537, the court has the power to disapply the LLA unless it is satisfied that the agreement is fair and reasonable.

### Agreeing a liability limitation agreement

**18-94**  A 'liability limitation agreement' is an agreement that purports to limit the amount of a liability owed to a company by its auditor in respect of any negligence, default, breach of duty or breach of trust, occurring in the course of the audit of accounts, of which the auditor may be guilty in relation to the company (CA 2006, s 534(1)). Each company must negotiate its own LLA and there cannot be group-wide agreements. A liability limitation agreement cannot apply to more than one financial year so, for example, auditors cannot negotiate five-year deals and the agreement must specify the financial year in relation to which it applies (s 535(1)). Shareholder authorisation is required by an ordinary resolution unless the articles require a higher majority.[221] A private company can pass a resolution waiving the need for approval, or pass a resolution before entering into the agreement approving its principal terms,[222] or it can pass a resolution approving the (entire) agreement after the company has entered into it (s 536(2)); likewise for a public company, but a public company cannot waive the need for approval (s 536(3)). Authorisation may be withdrawn by the company passing an ordinary resolution to that effect at any time before the company enters into the agreement, or if the company has already entered into the agreement, before the beginning of the financial year to which the agreement relates (s 536(5)). A company which has made a liability limitation agreement must disclose in a note to the accounts its principal terms and the date of the approval resolution (or resolution waiving the need for approval, in the case of a private company) passed by the company's members.[223]

**18-95**  There are limits to what can be agreed and an auditor cannot limit its liability in an unreasonable way; a significant safeguard imposed is that a liability limitation agreement is not effective to limit the auditor's liability to less than such amount as is fair and reasonable in all the circumstances of the case having regard (in particular) to the auditor's responsibilities under CA 2006, Pt 16, the nature and purpose of the auditor's contractual obligations to the company, and the professional standards expected of him (s 537(1)).[224] A liability limitation agreement that purports to limit the auditor's liability to less than an amount that is fair and reasonable in all the circumstances takes effect as if so limited so the court will simply adjust the limitation downwards when it is set too high (s 537(2)).[225]

---

[220]  See FRC, *Guidance on Auditor Liability Limitation Agreements* (June 2008).

[221]  CA 2006, ss 534(2)(b), 281(3).

[222]  The 'principal terms' of an agreement are terms specifying or relevant to the determination of the kind (or kinds) of acts or omissions covered by the LLA, the financial year to which the LLA relates, or the limit of the auditor's liability: CA 2006, s 535(4).

[223]  CA 2006, s 538; The Companies (Disclosure of Auditor Remuneration and Liability Limitation Agreements) Regulations 2008, SI 2008/489, reg 8.

[224]  The Government has a power by regulations to prescribe specific provisions or to prohibit certain provisions (CA 2006, s 535(2)), but it does not intend to exercise the power at the moment.

[225]  In other words, auditors risk nothing by overreaching in an LLA for the LLA does not become void, but is merely rewritten by the court. This may seem favourable to the auditors but it reflects the fact that all concerned will have made arrangements, such as insurance cover, on the basis of a liability limitation being in place. Note that UCTA 1977, ss 2(2), 3(2) do not apply to LLAs: CA 2006, s 534(2)(b).

In determining what is fair and reasonable in all the circumstances of the case no account is to be taken of matters arising after the loss or damage in question has been incurred, or matters (whenever arising) affecting the possibility of recovering compensation from other persons liable in respect of the same loss or damage (s 537(3)). For example, the fact that the liability is shared with an employee who is not worth suing is ignored.[226]

**18-96** The legislation does not impose a limitation mechanism and, in particular, the limit on the amount of the auditor's liability need not be a sum of money or a formula specified in the agreement (s 535(4)). It is clear that institutional shareholders will only accept agreements providing for proportionate liability (liability based on the auditor's share of the responsibility for the company's loss) or a liability expressed in terms of what is fair and reasonable, and that they will not support fixed caps.[227] For smaller companies, in time, other limitation options will emerge, possibly based on a multiple of the audit fee or other variations.

**18-97** Though these provisions on LLAs came into force in April 2008, there has been only a modest uptake with, it seems, no listed companies entering into an LLA[228] and little evidence of any large companies agreeing them with their auditors. There is no reason for such companies to take the initiative in agreeing something that restricts the ability of the company to recover losses and, at that end of the market, there appears to be little pressure from the audit firms for these agreements, presumably because the audit firm is anxious to retain high value clients (bearing in mind the level of non-audit services which the client may well be purchasing from the auditor). The position may be different lower down the corporate hierarchy with some evidence that LLAs have been agreed in medium and small companies where the audit price seems to have been the leverage used by auditors to secure agreement.[229] In essence, companies seem to have signed up to agreements in order to ensure that they could retain a particular audit firm and/or because they secured the audit at a lower price than would be the case without the agreement.

**18-98** The issue for any directors contemplating entering into an LLA is the need to have regard to their duty to promote the success of the company (s 172, see **10-2**) and to see what the company will get out of the arrangement in terms of assurances that audit quality will be preserved and enhanced by the auditors and that 'other benefits' (not defined) might be secured for the company.[230] The directors will also need to weigh up the fact that the auditors may refuse to act for the company at an acceptable price without an LLA and so the use of an LLA may be necessary to help the company secure the audit firm of choice, a point acknowledged in the FRC Guidance.[231] An alternative point of view is that these changes are too favourable to auditors and too unfavourable to shareholders who pay large fees to auditors in the expectation that they will do a careful and skilful job. Auditors are able to operate through LLPs and manage their liabilities in that way, after all, and the duty of care owed by them is carefully circumscribed by the courts.

---

[226] See *Explanatory Notes to the Companies Act 2006*, para 828.

[227] See Institutional Shareholders' Committee (ISC) Statement on Auditor Liability Limitation Agreements (June 2008)—the ISC is now defunct, but there is nothing to suggest that institutional shareholders have changed their position from that taken in this statement.

[228] It appears that the American Securities and Exchange Commission has indicated that it will not accept the entry into LLAs by UK companies which also have to register with it, a stance which would explain why LLAs are not a realistic option at the listed company level.

[229] The evidence comes from an evaluation conducted on behalf of the Department of Business, Innovation and Skills following the implementation of the CA 2006, see BIS, *Evaluation of the CA 2006* (2010), vol 1, para 6.13.  [230] See ISC Statement, n 227, p 2.

[231] See FRC Guidance, n 220, Section 3 'What Issues Should the Directors Consider?', para 3.6.

# 19

# The unfairly prejudicial remedy and the minority shareholder

## A Introduction

**19-1** The most important shareholder remedy in practice is the ability of a member to petition for relief on the ground that the affairs of the company are being or have been conducted in a manner which is unfairly prejudicial to the interests of members generally or of some part of its members under CA 2006, s 994.

**19-2** Before examining the unfairly prejudicial remedy in detail, it may be useful to draw attention to some background considerations which should be borne in mind.

### Disputes in private companies

**19-3** The vast majority of companies registered under the CA 2006 and its predecessor, the CA 1985, are private companies. These companies typically have only a small number of shareholders,[1] most if not all of whom are also the directors, and many of whom are also employees of the company. Often the shareholders will be members of the same family and, even if they are not, the relationships involved tend to be personal as well as commercial. Disputes too tend to be personal and bitter and settling such cases can be difficult.

**19-4** A typical scenario would involve the initial enthusiastic participation of all the shareholders in the company as directors and employees rapidly followed by disagreements among the participants, perhaps about the direction of the company, or the respective merits of the contributions made by each participant, or the extent to which the parties are benefiting financially from the business, and culminating in the majority shareholder or shareholders voting to remove the minority shareholder from his position as a director and dismissing him as an employee. Voluntary exit by the minority shareholder from the company at this point is the desirable option but it may be difficult to achieve.

**19-5** Finding a purchaser for a minority stake in a private company is not easy and, even if a purchaser is found, the minority shareholder may find that the company's articles of association constrain him as to whom he can sell to. For example, the articles may require him to offer the shares initially to the existing members and may require the price to be determined by the company's auditor and not by the vendor. It is commonly the case that the board of directors has a power in any event to refuse to register any transfer of any shares (see **16-62**). Voluntary exit can be difficult to achieve, therefore, and legal action, or at least the threat of legal action, may be necessary.

---

[1] Research carried out for the Company Law Review showed that 70 per cent of the companies on the register had only one or two shareholders and 90 per cent had fewer than five shareholders: Company Law Review, *Developing the Framework* (2000), para 6.9.

**19-6**   The position of minority shareholders once they are in disagreement with the majority is exacerbated by difficulties in obtaining accurate information about the company's affairs, especially where the shareholder has been removed from the board and no longer has access to management accounts and minutes of board meetings[2] although shareholders are entitled to the annual accounts.[3]

## Disputes in public companies

**19-7**   Disputes in public companies do not have the focus on personal participation in the running of the business which characterises disputes in private companies. Instead there may be complaints about the standard of management and the level of their remuneration. A variety of mechanisms can be deployed to address these issues with litigation and legal redress generally low on the shareholders' range of options. Management underperformance may be addressed by setting contractual targets and linking remuneration to performance and, in quoted companies, shareholders have a right to vote on remuneration payments and policy, see **18-45**. Many of the shareholders in these companies are institutional shareholders who are able to exercise influence by voicing their concerns directly to the board. In the worst cases of mismanagement, a declining share price may mean that the company becomes a target of a takeover and so under-performing management may be replaced through the market for corporate control. Of course, for shareholders with a grievance in a publicly traded company, the best option is often to exit the company by selling their shares, even if that means a loss.

## Majority and minority shareholders

**19-8**   Most disputes necessarily involve minority shareholders seeking redress as the majority can secure redress for themselves through the exercise of their voting power.[4] It should be borne in mind, however, that minority shareholders too can behave in an obstructive and damaging way with a view to forcing the majority to buy them out at an inflated value simply to rid themselves of the nuisance.[5]

## Anticipating and preventing disputes

**19-9**   As Professor Prentice has commented, a feature of shareholder disputes particularly in smaller private companies is the parties' chronic failure to anticipate the nature, extent, and consequences of a breakdown in their relationship.[6] He identified a variety of reasons

---

[2] Shareholders have no right of access to board minutes, only to minutes of general meetings: see CA 2006, s 358; but they can obtain details of directors' service contracts: s 228; and inspect statutory registers such as the register of members, s 116, subject to the company's ability to refuse permission under s 117. As to a petitioner's entitlement to disclosure of company documents, see *CAS (Nominees) Ltd v Nottingham Forest FC plc* [2002] 1 BCLC 613; *Arrow Trading & Investment Est 1920 v Edwardian Group Ltd* [2005] 1 BCLC 696.

[3] The accounts may be quite dated, however, since a private company has nine months from the end of the financial year in which to send the accounts to each member: see CA 2006, ss 423–424, 442.

[4] See *Re Legal Costs Negotiators Ltd* [1999] 2 BCLC 171; *Re Baltic Real Estate Ltd (No 2)* [1993] BCLC 503.

[5] The courts are alert to this possibility, see *Re a Company (No 007623 of 1984)* [1986] BCLC 362 at 367, per Hoffmann J: '... the very width of [the unfairly prejudicial] jurisdiction means that unless carefully controlled, it can become a means of oppression'.

[6] Prentice, 'Protecting Minority Shareholders' Interests' in Feldman and Meisel (eds), *Corporate and Commercial Law: Modern Developments* (1996), p 80.

for this stance including an unwillingness to contemplate breakdown of the relationship at the beginning of the venture; an inability in any event to anticipate all future contingencies; and the fact that the costs of trying to so anticipate may simply not be justified.[7]

**19-10**   These difficulties are compounded by the practice in this jurisdiction whereby a substantial percentage of companies incorporated annually are shelf companies (i.e. purchased from a formation agent as a ready-made company, see **1-10**), with the result that those incorporating in this way are likely to have had minimal, if any, advice and the company's articles of association will simply be a standard version which does not address future breakdown.[8]

## Governing principles

**19-11**   Shareholder remedies were the subject of a detailed review[9] by the Law Commission in 1996–97 and that work was considered and generally adopted by the Company Law Review[10] which did not devote much time to this issue. The Law Commission in its report identified what it considered to be the governing principles appropriate to this area, principles which we encounter throughout our consideration of company law, namely the proper plaintiff rule, the principle of majority rule in matters of internal management, non-interference by the courts in commercial decisions, recognition of the sanctity of contract, and freedom from unnecessary shareholder interference.[11]

**19-12**   The proper plaintiff rule means that normally the company should be the only party entitled to enforce a cause of action belonging to it, reflecting the fact that the company is a separate legal entity. Accordingly, a member should be able to maintain proceedings about wrongs done to the company only in exceptional circumstances. The principle of majority rule reflects the basic mechanism for decision-making in companies which has as its corollary that an individual member should not be able to pursue proceedings on behalf of the company about matters of internal management, that is, matters which the majority are entitled to regulate by ordinary resolution. These two principles are central to the derivative claim which is discussed in Chapter 20.

**19-13**   The importance of the courts having proper regard for the decisions of directors on commercial matters, provided the decision is made in good faith, on proper information and in the light of the relevant considerations, and appears to be a reasonable decision for the directors to have taken, has been a central theme in judgments for a century or more.[12]

**19-14**   The principle of freedom from unnecessary shareholder interference is reflected in the tight judicial control of the derivative claim, discussed in Chapter 20. The intention is that, in keeping with the right of directors to manage the company's affairs, shareholders should not be able to involve the company in litigation without good cause.

---

[7] Prentice, n 6, 89–93.        [8] See Prentice, n 6, 90.

[9] See Law Commission, *Shareholder Remedies* (Law Comm No 246) (Cm 3769, 1997).

[10] Company Law Review, *Developing the Framework* (2000), paras 4.70–4.71; *Completing the Structure* (2000), para 5.106.        [11] See Law Commission Report, n 9, para 1.9.

[12] The courts' reluctance to interfere in commercial decisions is long-standing: see *Carlen v Drury* (1812) 1 Ves & B 154, 35 ER 61 at 63: 'This Court is not to be required on every Occasion to take the Management of every Playhouse and Brewhouse in the Kingdom ...' (per Lord Eldon); also *Burland v Earle* [1902] AC 83 at 93, per Lord Davey; *Hogg v Cramphorn Ltd* [1966] 3 All ER 420 at 428, per Buckley J; and *Shuttleworth v Cox* [1927] 2 KB 9 at 23: 'It is not the business of the court to manage the affairs of the company.'

**19-15**   The principle of sanctity of contract means that a member is taken to have agreed to the terms of the constitution when he became a member, whether or not he appreciated what it contained at the time. In the interests of commercial certainty, the law should continue to treat him as so bound unless he shows that the parties have come to some other agreement or understanding which is not reflected in the constitution. The basis of the parties' relationship, whether it be restricted to the articles or the subject of wider agreements or understandings, is central to the judicial approach to the unfairly prejudicial remedy which is the subject of this chapter.

## B Petitioning on the grounds of unfair prejudice

**19-16**   The most valuable shareholder remedy is that contained in the Companies Act 2006, s 994(1), previously CA 1985, s 459, which provides:

'A member of a company[13] may apply to the court by petition for an order on the ground

(a)   that the company's affairs are being or have been conducted in a manner which is unfairly prejudicial to the interests of members generally or of some part of its members (including at least himself), or

(b)   that an actual or proposed act or omission of the company (including an act or omission on its behalf) is or would be so prejudicial.'[14]

**19-17**   Where the court is satisfied that a petition under s 994 is well founded, it may make such order as it thinks fit for giving relief in respect of the matters complained of (s 996(2)). In practice, relief is most commonly sought in respect of private company disputes where the petitioner has been excluded from participation in the business and the remedy most commonly sought is a purchase order requiring the respondents to purchase the shares of the petitioner at a fair value. To encourage the parties to settle (so saving themselves time and costs and freeing up court time), given that the outcome of these disputes is so predictable (a purchase order), a petition will usually be struck out if, having excluded the petitioner, the respondents made a fair offer for her shares[15] (see **19-72**) which gives her everything which she could reasonably expect to achieve under CA 2006, s 994.

**19-18**   In *Fulham Football Club (1987) Ltd v Richards*[16] the Court of Appeal resolved the uncertainty which had been created by conflicting first instance decisions[17] as to whether it is possible for shareholders to contract out of their right to petition under CA 2006, s 994

---

[13] 'Company' means a company within the meaning of the Act: CA 2006, s 994(3)(a), meaning a company formed and registered under the CA 2006 and its predecessors, see s 1.

[14] See generally Joffe, *Minority Shareholders* (5th edn, 2015), Chs 6, 7; Hollington, *Shareholders' Rights* (8th edn, 2016), Chs 7–9; Payne, 'Sections 459–461 Companies Act 1985 in Flux: The Future of Shareholder Protection' (2005) 64 CLJ 647; Boyle, *Minority Shareholders' Remedies* (2002).

[15] See *O'Neill v Phillips* [1999] 2 BCLC 1.

[16] [2012] 1 All ER 414. See McVea, 'Section 994 of the Companies Act 2006 and the Primacy of Contract' (2012) 75 MLR 1123.

[17] See *Re Vocam Europe Ltd* [1998] BCC 396 (unfair prejudice petition was stayed by the court as a shareholders' agreement provided for disputes to go to arbitration); *Re Exeter City AFC v Football Conference Ltd* [2005] 1 BCLC 238 (shareholders' right to petition was an inalienable right which could not be limited by agreement and an arbitration agreement could not be invoked to require a stay of a petition).

and to agree instead to refer their disputes to arbitration.[18] The court concluded that there is no express or implied statutory preservation of a right of access to the court and nothing in the nature of these disputes which requires the exclusive jurisdiction of the court. Unlike a winding-up order which an arbitrator cannot award, it being a class remedy, s 994 relief cannot be categorised as a class remedy. While orders under the section have some potential to affect third parties, that point has consequences for the remedies which an arbitrator can award but, as Patten LJ put it, these jurisdictional limitations on what an arbitration can achieve are not decisive of the question whether the subject matter of the dispute is arbitral. In the unanimous view of the Court of Appeal, these disputes can be subject to arbitration agreements.[19]

**19-19**  Notwithstanding this ruling, minority shareholders would be ill-advised to give up their right to petition under CA 2006, s 994, given that it is an expansive jurisdiction with flexible remedies which has proved invaluable to shareholders aggrieved at the unfairly prejudicial manner in which a company's affairs are being conducted.

## The petitioner

**19-20**  Only members[20] have a right to petition and the definition of 'member' is extended to include persons to whom shares have been transferred or transmitted by law (CA 2006, s 994(2)) which extends standing to petition to persons such as personal representatives and trustees in bankruptcy.[21] A petition may be brought by a nominee shareholder. In *Atlasview Ltd v Brightview Ltd*[22] the court refused to strike out a petition holding that it was arguable that the 'interests' of a nominee shareholder were capable of including the

---

[18]  See too the decision of the Singapore Court of Appeal in *Tomolugen Holdings Ltd v Silica Investors Ltd* [2015] SGCA 57 at [84] et seq, 26 October 2015, where there is a detailed discussion of *Fulham*. The essence of an unfairly prejudicial petition is to uphold the commercial agreement between the parties found in the constitution, the articles, shareholder agreements, or understandings of the parties; the company is almost always solvent so there is in general no public element to the dispute which makes it unsuitable for arbitration. The remedial deficiencies in arbitration are not so serious as to preclude these matters going to arbitration.

[19]  It is noteworthy that the authorities on the issue, see n 17, had unusual facts; two concerned disputes between football clubs and football bodies (*Exeter City AFC* and *Fulham Football Club*) and the other involved a company where the majority shareholders were Australian companies and the shareholders' agreement provided for arbitration in Melbourne (*Vocam*). None presented the more usual scenario of persons within the jurisdiction engaged in a business venture together.

[20]  In certain circumstances, the Secretary of State may petition on the same grounds under CA 2006, s 995, but this power is never used.

[21]  See *Re McCarthy Surfacing Ltd* [2006] EWHC 832 where the court allowed a petition by two shareholders (who had executed a transfer of their shares) and the transferee (whose request for registration had been refused by the directors), noting that the transferee has to have standing to petition for a period of time after the transfer and before registration, otherwise CA 2006, s 994(2) would have no effect. The court also considered that there was nothing to prevent the three petitioners having concurrent standing as long as care was exercised on any relief being ordered to prevent double recovery. See also *Harris v Jones* [2011] EWHC 1518 at [36], [149] (share transferred by one shareholder to another shareholder to be held on trust, the shareholder trustee executed an undated share transfer form back in favour of the original transferor which made the original transferor a transferee for the purposes of CA 2006, s 994(2) and therefore entitled to petition under s 994(1)).

[22]  [2004] 2 BCLC 191. The court noted with some surprise that this precise point as to the standing of a nominee shareholder had not previously been determined, but it also noted that numerous successful proceedings have been brought by nominee shareholders.

economic and contractual interests of the beneficial owners of the shares.[23] To hold otherwise, the court said, would produce the arbitrary result that the registered shareholder would have standing to petition as a member but no 'interests' for these purposes, while the beneficial owner would have an interest but no standing to present a petition, not being a member. There is nothing to preclude a majority shareholder from petitioning, but the court would normally expect a majority shareholder to exercise his control of the company to bring to an end the conduct complained of.[24]

**19-21**     While there is no requirement that a petitioner should come to the court with clean hands, the conduct of the petitioner may lead the court, depending on the seriousness of the matter and the degree of its relevance, to refuse relief, even if the conditions for the exercise of the discretion in his favour are otherwise satisfied.[25] In *Interactive Technology Corpn Ltd v Ferster*,[26] for example, the court accepted that the respondents had behaved badly, but it concluded that the petitioner's wrongful conduct (he transferred the business and assets of the company to another company owned by the petitioner) was many times more significant than their misconduct and, in the circumstances, it was appropriate to refuse relief.

**19-22**     The respondents commonly include all of the members of the company and the company itself, though it plays no part in the proceedings. If the court would not order relief against a member, because there is no allegation of their involvement in the unfairly prejudicial conduct complained of, the respondent will be struck out of the petition.[27]

### Conduct of the company's affairs, acts or omissions

**19-23**     There are two distinct limbs to s 994(1), (a) that the company's affairs are being or have been conducted in a manner that is unfairly prejudicial to the interests of the members generally, etc, and (b) that an actual or proposed act or omission of the company is or would be so prejudicial. Arden LJ noted in *Graham v Every*[28] that (b) means that the petitioner must identify something which the company does or fails to do whereas (a) does not contain the same stipulation and the petitioner can rely on the actions of some other persons, including his fellow shareholders, as long as those actions amount to the conduct of the company's affairs.

---

[23]   In this instance, the registered shareholder was a company controlled by X. The court ruled that the nominee shareholder was the appropriate petitioner and X had no *locus standi* to be a petitioner.

[24]   See *Re Legal Costs Negotiators Ltd* [1999] 2 BCLC 171 at 199, 201.

[25]   *Richardson v Blackmore* [2006] BCC 276; *Re London School of Electronics Ltd* [1985] BCLC 273; *Re R A Noble & Sons (Clothing) Ltd* [1983] BCLC 273. If the conduct of the petitioner is neither sufficiently serious nor sufficiently closely related to the respondents' unfairly prejudicial conduct, however, it is not appropriate for the court to refuse its discretion to grant relief: *Richardson v Blackmore*; see also *Re BC & G Care Homes Ltd* [2016] BCC 615. And see comments of HHJ David Cooke in *Khoshkhou v Cooper* [2014] EWHC 1087 at [94] that it is normally impossible with hindsight to determine which of the parties in the breakdown of a business relationship was most at fault and the court should not conduct a 'contest of virtue'.

[26]   [2016] EWHC 2896 at [318]–[325].

[27]   *Re Pedersen (Thameside) Ltd* [2018] BCC 58; see also *Crolly v Good* [2011] BCC 105 at [101]; *Shah v Shah* [2010] EWHC 313 at [140]–[141]. In *Re Pedersen (Thameside) Ltd* there was no allegation in the petition of any direct or indirect involvement of the respondent in the unfairly prejudicial conduct alleged or any assistance by him of the other respondent. The relief sought—that the respondent (who held 5 per cent of the share capital) might be required to purchase the shares of the 45.7 per cent petitioner—was manifestly excessive and would never be ordered by the court. The respondent was struck from the petition; see also *Re Little Olympian Eachways Ltd* [1994] 2 BCLC 420 at 429, 432.

[28]   [2015] 1 BCLC 41 at [37], see too at [77].

**19-24**  Shareholders' disputes between themselves in their private capacities are not part of the conduct of the company's affairs and are not within the section. As Harman J noted in *Re Unisoft Group Ltd (No 3)*:[29] '... the vital distinction between acts or conduct of the company and the acts or conduct of the shareholder in his private capacity must be kept clear. The first type of act will found a petition under s 459 [s 994]; the second type of act will not.' For example, in *Re Legal Costs Negotiators Ltd*[30] the complaint was about the failure of a shareholder to sell his shares. The company had been set up by four individuals with equal shareholdings. All the shareholders were directors and employees of the company. Three of the directors fell out with the fourth who was dismissed as an employee and resigned from the board just prior to being removed as a director. Having failed to persuade the fourth member to sell his shareholding to them, the majority shareholders petitioned for an order that he should transfer or sell his shares to them. In essence, they were unhappy with his continued presence as a shareholder in the prosperous business that they were creating. The Court of Appeal rejected the petition for complaint about the respondent's retention of his shares is not a complaint about the conduct of the company's affairs or an act or omission of the company.[31] As David Richards J explained in *Re Coroin Ltd (No 2)*,[32] s 994 'is not directed to the activities of shareholders amongst themselves, unless those activities translate into acts or omissions of the company or the conduct of its affairs'. Non-compliance by a shareholder with pre-emption on transfer provisions in the company's articles or a shareholders' agreement does not amount to conduct of the company's affairs,[33] unless, perhaps, the non-compliance is part of a scheme to exclude a minority from the company.[34] Actions or omissions in compliance or contravention of the articles of association of a company may or may not constitute the conduct of the company's affairs depending on the precise facts.[35]

**19-25**  While the act of individual shareholders exercising their rights to vote are not acts of the company, or part of the conduct of the company's affairs, the resolution consequent on

---

[29] [1994] 1 BCLC 609 at 623. See also *Re Estate Acquisition and Development Ltd* [1995] BCC 338.

[30] [1999] 2 BCLC 171; see also *Re Astec (BSR) plc* [1998] 2 BCLC 556 (statements by the majority shareholder which allegedly depressed the share price could not amount to conduct of the company's affairs since the statements were made on behalf of the shareholder and not on behalf of the company: petition dismissed).

[31] See too *Re Leeds United Holdings plc* [1996] 2 BCLC 545 (disagreement between shareholders as to the manner of the disposal of their shares, petition dismissed, matter did not relate to the conduct of the company's affairs).

[32] [2013] 2 BCLC 583 at [626], Ch D.

[33] *Re Coroin Ltd (No 2)*, *McKillen v Misland (Cyprus) Investments Ltd* [2013] EWCA Civ 781, aff'g [2012] EWHC 2343, [2013] 2 BCLC 583 (Ch D and CA); though a failure by directors to exercise pre-emption powers in the articles if triggered by a shareholder could be an omission of the company and within the section, see at [639].

[34] See *Graham v Every* [2015] 1 BCLC 41. On an appeal on a strike-out application, the Court of Appeal considered it was possible for an allegation of non-compliance with a pre-emption requirement on transfer of shares to amount to conduct of the company's affairs. McCombe and Vos LJJ seemed to consider that the non-compliance was part of a bigger picture of exclusion of the petitioner and dilution of his influence in the management of what was a quasi-partnership and therefore it was part of the conduct of the company's affairs (at [73], [81]–[84]). Arden LJ emphasised that, in this particular company, the directors were remunerated by dividends and therefore a director's shareholding dictated the return for a director's work. Denying the petitioner his pre-emption rights at a time when he was a director arguably therefore was an interference with directors' remuneration which is conduct of the company's affairs (at [40]).

[35] *Re Charterhouse Capital Ltd*, *Arbuthnott v Bonnyman* [2015] 2 BCLC 627 at [45]; *Gross v Rackind* [2005] 1 WLR 3505 at [29]; *McKillen v Misland (Cyprus) Investments Ltd* [2012] EWHC 2343 (Ch) at [626].

the exercise of their voting rights is an act of the company and part of the conduct of the company's affairs.[36]

**19-26**   Likewise, the behaviour of shareholders in another capacity does not amount to conduct of the company's affairs. In *Arrow Nominees Inc v Blackledge*[37] the Court of Appeal dismissed a petition based on allegations against the majority shareholders who were significant lenders and suppliers to the company. The court noted that the complaints against the majority related to the terms of those loan and supply contracts which, even if established, related to the majority's conduct as a lender and supplier to the company and did not relate to the conduct of the company's affairs by the majority. A decision to lend to the company at a certain rate of interest or to supply goods at a particular price could not amount to unfairly prejudicial conduct of the company's affairs. That would only arise if the majority used their position to compel the company to accept the funds/supplies at that rate of interest/price by preventing it securing other, more favourable, funding/suppliers.

**19-27**   Leaving aside these private disputes which fall outside the scope of CA 2006, s 994, the courts do 'not adopt a technical or legalistic approach to what constitutes the affairs of the company but will look to the business realities'.[38] It is frequently stressed that the requirement for the conduct to be of the 'affairs of the company' should be liberally construed for the purposes of the section[39] and may extend to matters which are capable of coming before the board, rather than restricted to matters that actually come before the board.[40] In *Oak Investment Partners XII v Boughtwood*[41] the Court of Appeal endorsed taking an expansive view of whose conduct might amount to the conduct of the company's affairs for this purpose, agreeing with the approach taken by Sales J in the lower court.[42] Sales J had concluded that it is possible for the conduct of a shareholder or director who acts in the carrying out of the company's affairs, but not through any company organ, to attract relief under CA 2006, s 994. In this case, the complaint was that the respondent shareholder (he held a majority of the ordinary shares) and director had persistently failed to adhere to his agreed management role and tried to dictate and ultimately did seize control of the management of the company. This behaviour was in breach of the constitutional arrangements agreed between him and a venture capital firm (the other significant shareholder in the company) as to the conduct of the company's affairs.[43] Sales J held, and the Court of Appeal agreed, that the respondent's conduct did amount to conduct of the company's affairs in an unfairly prejudicial manner, though the conduct was not that of the board or of the directors. Sales J had noted that the jurisdiction under CA 2006, s 994

---

[36] See *Re Unisoft Group Ltd (No 3)* [1994] 1 BCLC 609 at 611. See too *Re Charterhouse Capital Ltd, Arbuthnott v Bonnyman* [2015] 2 BCLC 627 at [48]—an alteration of the company's articles even if legally valid may still constitute in all the circumstances unfairly prejudicial conduct.

[37] [2000] 2 BCLC 167.

[38] *Re Coroin Ltd (No 2)* [2013] 2 BCLC 583 at [628], per David Richards J.

[39] *Hawkes v Cuddy* [2009] 2 BCLC 427 at [50]. See *O'Neill v Phillips* [1999] 2 BCLC 1 at 15; *Gamlestaden Fastigheter AB v Baltic Partners Ltd* [2008] 1 BCLC 468 at [35], PC; *Re Macro (Ipswich) Ltd* [1994] 2 BCLC 354 at 404; *Re Little Olympian Each-Ways Ltd* [1994] 2 BCLC 420 at 429.

[40] It also extends to matters which must go for consideration to the general meeting, rather than the board, see David Richards J in *Re Coroin Ltd (No 2)* [2013] 2 BCLC 583 at [629].

[41] [2010] 2 BCLC 459.        [42] See [2010] 2 BCLC 459 at [120], [122].

[43] The company had been formed as an engineering joint venture with the respondent providing technical expertise and the venture capital firm providing the necessary funding. The respondent subsequently ousted, in effect, the management team which the parties had jointly agreed on and took control of the business when the parties had agreed that he would no longer have overall management control, see [2010] 2 BCLC 459 at [120], [122].

is a broad jurisdiction which allows the court to take into account the myriad ways in which the affairs of a company may in practice be carried on, accepting that the precise distribution of management decision-making authority in any particular company might be a matter of chance.[44] It was difficult to see, Sales J said, why the application of CA 2006, s 994 should turn upon such fortuitous matters. If a significant shareholder, appointed to the management, engages in the course of that role in a way that improperly asserts rights of control over the conduct of the company's affairs, such conduct is capable of being conduct of the company's affairs for the purposes of s 994. In this instance, the destructive conduct of the respondent in overriding the constitutional arrangements (as to board composition and division of management tasks) governing the operation of the business (in effect he seized control of the business) was unfairly prejudicial conduct.[45]

**19-28**  Likewise the courts look to the business realities in the group context. In *Re Citybranch Group Ltd, Gross v Rackind*[46] the Court of Appeal accepted that a shareholder in a holding company may petition for relief though it is the affairs of its wholly-owned subsidiary that are being conducted in an unfairly prejudicial manner, it being possible to regard the conduct of the affairs of the subsidiary as part of the conduct of the affairs of the holding company, especially where the subsidiary is wholly owned and the directors of the holding company are a majority of the directors of the subsidiary. Likewise, in an appropriate case, the conduct of a holding company towards a subsidiary company may constitute the conduct of the affairs of the subsidiary and can be the subject of a complaint by a shareholder in the subsidiary.[47]

**19-29**  A related issue is whether a petitioner when seeking redress against a corporate respondent may seek redress against those who control the corporate respondent, whether they be individuals or a parent company, though they are not members of the company in respect of which the petition is brought. The court can order redress against third parties, i.e. non-members provided they are sufficiently implicated in the unfairly prejudicial conduct such that it would be just to make an award against them, see the discussion at **19-82**. In effect, the allegation becomes one that the non-members have participated in the conduct of the company's affairs in an unfairly prejudicial manner such that it is just that relief be awarded against them too. An interesting illustration can be found in *F & C Alternative Investments (Holdings) Ltd v Barthelemy.*[48] This case involves an LLP, but the case remains useful as the unfairly prejudicial remedy applies to LLPs with appropriate modifications.[49] The court held that the petitioners ('A', minority members of the LLP) were entitled to relief in respect of the conduct of the affairs of the LLP in an unfairly

---

[44]  See [2010] 2 BCLC 459 at [77].

[45]  See too *F & C Alternative Investments (Holdings) Ltd v Barthelemy* [2012] Ch 613 at [1097]—and see **19-29**.

[46]  [2004] 4 All ER 735 at [26]; also *Oak Investment Partners XII v Boughtwood* [2010] 2 BCLC 459 at [8]; *Irvine v Irvine (No 1)* [2007] 1 BCLC 349 at [259]; *Re Ravenhart Service (Holdings) Ltd, Reiner v Gershinson* [2004] 2 BCLC 376 at [104]. See Tan, 'Unfair Prejudice from Beyond: Minority Protection in Corporate Group Structures' (2014) 14 JCLS 367 who considers that the courts are giving effect to the economic reality that these companies are being operated as a single entity; and Goddard and Hirt, 'Section 459 and Corporate Groups' [2005] JBL 247 who criticise the court's failure to respect the separate legal entities involved, noting that this approach gives an unnecessarily wide interpretation to the statutory provision.

[47]  *Scottish Co-operative Wholesale Society Ltd v Meyer* [1959] AC 324, HL (a parent company which stood behind its nominee directors as they ran down the business of the subsidiary to the advantage of the majority and disadvantage of the minority shareholders had conducted the affairs of the subsidiary company in an oppressive manner—the predecessor provision to s 994 required oppression—the parent company was ordered to purchase the shares of the minority).

[48]  [2012] Ch 613 at [1099]–[1104].        [49]  See SI 2009/1804, reg 48.

prejudicial manner by the majority member of the LLP ('B') which was a wholly-owned subsidiary of 'C'. The essence of the unfairly prejudicial conduct was that B had unfairly removed decision-making and control of the LLP's affairs from the minority members and the proper organs of the LLP in breach of agreed governance arrangements. The court found that B was a 'mere cipher' for C in whose interests the representatives of B tended in reality to act and it was to C that the practical benefits of the unfairly prejudicial conduct flowed as it was C which had the ultimate commercial interest in controlling the LLP's affairs. The court found that 'as a matter of business reality, C did not stand aloof from the conduct of the affairs of the LLP, but actively intervened in them'.[50] In those circumstances, it was appropriate to order relief against the majority member, B, and its controller, its parent company C. See further at **19-82**.

**19-30**   Generally, the petitioner's complaints will be of the past conduct of the company's affairs,[51] but proposed acts of the company (such as resolutions of the general meeting) which, if carried out or completed, would be prejudicial to the interests of the petitioner, may be the subject of a petition.[52] The petitioner must not be too hasty, however, in seeking relief. In *Re Astec (BSR) plc*[53] the petition was premature when it was brought at a time when the majority had only made statements as to steps which they would or might take in the future, but they had not taken any of those steps at the time of the petition. A petitioner cannot complain of past conduct if all the members at the material time consented to the conduct, assuming there was no breach of any agreement that the shareholders would not so consent.[54]

### Conduct unfairly prejudicial to the interests of members

**19-31**   The conduct complained of must be conduct which is unfairly prejudicial to the interests of the member as a member as opposed to any other interests which the member might possess,[55] but the courts have emphasised that this requirement must not be too narrowly construed and the courts take a broad view of what may properly be regarded as a petitioner's interests as a member.[56]

---

[50] [2012] Ch 613 at [1102], per Sales J.

[51] Past acts of the company which have been remedied may be the basis of a petition if they are likely to recur but, if they are unlikely to recur, the court would have no scope to give relief. See *Re Kenyon Swansea Ltd* [1987] BCLC 514 at 521; *Re Legal Costs Negotiators Ltd* [1999] 2 BCLC 171 at 198. A member can support his petition by relying on unfairly prejudicial conduct which took place before he became a member: *Lloyd v Casey* [2002] 1 BCLC 454.

[52] See *Re Kenyon Swansea Ltd* [1987] BCLC 514; *Re a Company (No 00314 of 1989), ex p Estate Acquisition and Development Ltd* [1991] BCLC 154.

[53] [1998] 2 BCLC 556; see also *Re a Company (No 005685 of 1988), ex p Schwarcz (No 2)* [1989] BCLC 427 at 451 (concerns about what might happen if the company was re-registered as a private company were premature).

[54] *Re Bateson Hotels Ltd, Bateson v Bateson* [2014] 1 BCLC 507.

[55] *Re a Company (No 004475 of 1982)* [1983] 2 All ER 36 at 44; *Re a Company (No 00314 of 1989), ex p Estate Acquisition & Development Ltd* [1991] BCLC 154 at 160. For example, in *Re J E Cade & Son Ltd* [1992] BCLC 213 the petition was struck out when the petitioner was protecting his interests as a freeholder of a farm rather than his interests as a member of the company running the farm; also *Re Unisoft Group Ltd (No 3)* [1994] 1 BCLC 609 at 626 where the allegations concerned the relationship of the parties as landlord and tenant rather than as members of the company.

[56] See *O'Neill v Phillips* [1999] 2 BCLC 1 at 15: 'the requirement that prejudice must be suffered as a member should not be too narrowly or technically construed', per Lord Hoffmann; *Gamlestaden Fastigheter AB v Baltic Partners Ltd* [2008] 1 BCLC 468 at [35], PC; *Re Tobian Properties, Maidment v Attwood* [2013] 2 BCLC 567 at [12].

**19-32**  In particular, the courts have consistently held that if the terms on which a person became or continues as a member in a small private company include his participation in the management of the company, his removal *as a director* without cause is a prejudice suffered in his capacity as a member[57] entitling him to petition for relief under CA 2006, s 994. This point is important in practice for removal as a director is a common basis for s 994 petitions.

**19-33**  A broad approach to what constitutes the interests of a member as a member may also allow the court to take account of the members' interests as creditors in certain circumstances. In *R & H Electrical Ltd v Haden Bill Electrical Ltd*[58] there were four equal shareholders and directors. The petitioner was one of the shareholders and he provided the company with its working capital through loans from another company wholly owned by him. These loans formed an essential part of the arrangements between him and his fellow shareholders who regarded it as immaterial whether the funding came from the petitioner or through his other company. The relationship between the parties broke down and the others attempted to remove the petitioner from office as a director. He petitioned for relief and the respondents argued that, in so far as he had concerns, they related to his role as a creditor of the company rather than matters affecting his interests as a member. In the circumstances, however, Robert Walker LJ considered the loan arrangements were sufficiently closely associated with his membership of the company[59] to be within the scope of the statutory provision. It was unfairly prejudicial to his interests as a member, therefore, to remove him from management of the company while he was a significant creditor of the company and he was entitled to relief.[60]

**19-34**  That approach was endorsed by the Privy Council in *Gamlestaden Fastigheter AB v Baltic Partners Ltd*[61] (details at **19-83**) where similarly a joint venture company was funded primarily by loans by the petitioner (again via a company associated with the petitioner) and the court considered it would be appropriate to take into account the member's interest as a creditor of the company when considering whether to grant relief. Lord Scott, giving the ruling of the Privy Council, emphasised the importance of the funding arrangements being part of, or in pursuance of, the joint venture arrangements between the parties, as was the case in *R & H Electrical Ltd v Haden Bill Electrical Ltd*. In each of these cases the key element bringing the petitioners within the section was that the company was a joint venture where the intertwining of roles as members and creditors is commonplace, such that it is possible to assert that what has occurred, though it impacts on the petitioners' position as creditors, is unfairly prejudicial to their interests as members.

**19-35**  Finally, the removal of the company's auditor from office on grounds of divergence of opinions on accounting treatments or audit procedures, or on any other improper grounds, is treated as being unfairly prejudicial to the interests of some part of the company's

---

[57]  See *O'Neill v Phillips* [1999] 2 BCLC 1 at 14–15 ('It is the terms, agreement, or understanding on which [the petitioner] became associated as a member which generates the restraint of the power of expulsion', per Lord Hoffmann); see also *R & H Electric Ltd v Haden Bill Electrical Ltd* [1995] 2 BCLC 280 at 292–3.

[58]  [1995] 2 BCLC 280.     [59]  [1995] 2 BCLC 280 at 293–4.

[60]  See also *Re Woven Rugs Ltd* [2010] EWHC 230. The shareholders had funded the company through large-scale, interest-free, subordinated debt. The director and majority shareholder organised a restructuring of the company's finances in a way which left the petitioners as creditors, but the majority shareholder's debt was repaid and replaced by expensive bank loans. The restructuring was unfairly prejudicial to the petitioners' interests as members and as creditors, positions which the court said were in substance indistinguishable, at [96].

[61]  [2008] 1 BCLC 468, PC; noted Walters (2007) 28 Co Law 289; Singla (2007) 123 LQR 542.

members so as to enable a member (not the auditor) to petition for relief in those circumstances (CA 2006, s 994(1A)).[62] This provision gives effect to art 38 of Directive 2006/43/EC on statutory audit[63] which requires Member States to ensure that statutory auditors may only be dismissed on proper grounds and is intended to safeguard the independence of auditors from undue pressure by the company's directors.

### Unfairly prejudicial conduct

**19-36**    Whether the company's affairs are being or have been conducted in a manner which is unfairly prejudicial to the petitioner's interests is an objective, and not a subjective, matter.[64] Commonly, petitions include allegations on numerous grounds, not least because the court will look at the cumulative picture in assessing whether the company's affairs have been conducted in an unfairly prejudicial manner. The prejudice must be real, rather than merely technical or trivial,[65] and the petitioner does not have to show that the persons controlling the company have acted deliberately in bad faith or with a conscious intent to treat him unfairly.[66] The conduct complained of must be prejudicial in the sense of causing prejudice or harm to the relevant interest of the member (usually, but not limited to, financial damage[67]) and also unfairly so (usually connoting some breach of company law or the constitution, but not limited to that) and it is not sufficient if the conduct satisfies only one of these tests.[68] The conduct may be prejudicial but not unfair, for example, if the petitioner has acquiesced in the breaches of which he now complains,[69] or it may be prejudicial to remove a member from his post as a director but not unfairly so if his conduct merited removal.[70] It can be prejudicial not to consult a minority shareholder, but not unfair, if the petitioner has chosen to withdraw from active involvement in the business, as in *Re Metropolis Motorcycles Ltd, Hale v Waldock*.[71] Vice versa, conduct

---

[62] As Judge Purle QC commented in *Re Sunrise Radio Ltd, Kohli v Lit* [2010] 1 BCLC 367 at [9], the effect of this mandatory section is to classify conduct by the board which may have been the result of a good faith genuine disagreement with the auditors as unfairly prejudicial conduct and it is unfairly prejudicial though it may have no necessary impact on the value of the petitioner's shareholding. See *Gray v Braid Group (Holdings) Ltd* [2015] CSOH 146, aff'd [2016] CSIH 68.

[63] OJ L 157/87, 9.6.2006.    [64] *Re Saul D Harrison & Sons plc* [1995] 1 BCLC 14, CA.

[65] *Re Saul D Harrison & Sons plc* [1995] 1 BCLC 14, CA.

[66] See *Re R A Noble & Sons (Clothing) Ltd* [1983] BCLC 273 at 290–1.

[67] While there need not be financial loss which might, for example, be damage to the value of the petitioner's shares or loss of income, '[w]here the acts complained of have no adverse financial consequence, it may be more difficult to establish relevant prejudice', per David Richards J in *Re Coroin Ltd (No 2)* [2013] 2 BCLC 583 (Ch and CA) at [630]–[631]; see too Arden LJ at [16]. See also *Rock Nominees Ltd v RCO (Holdings) plc* [2004] 1 BCLC 439 at [73],[79]; *Re C & MB Holdings Ltd, Hamilton v Brown* [2017] 1 BCLC 269 at [60]–[61].

[68] *Re Saul D Harrison & Sons plc* [1995] 1 BCLC 14 at 31, CA; *Re Sunrise Radio Ltd, Kohli v Lit* [2010] 1 BCLC 367 at [4]; *Re R A Noble (Clothing) Ltd* [1983] BCLC 273.

[69] *Re Batesons Hotels (1958) Ltd, Bateson v Bateson* [2014] 1 BCLC 507. If the shareholders are agreed that the company should be run in disregard of the obligations imposed by the Companies Act, none of them can complain that such conduct by another shareholder is unfair on that ground alone, see *Croly v Good* [2010] 2 BCLC 569 at [94]; also *Hawkes v Cuddy* [2009] 2 BCLC 427 at [72]: a shareholder who had been a party to the other shareholder's unlawful participation in the management of the company (in breach of IA 1986, s 216) could not then found a petition under CA 2006, s 994 on that unlawful conduct. But a shareholder who has agreed or acquiesced for a period of years in the company being run quite informally in disregard of the requirements of the statute and constitution is entitled subsequently, on giving reasonable notice, to revive reliance on her strict entitlements under the articles: see *Fisher v Cadman* [2006] 1 BCLC 499.

[70] See, for example, *Grace v Biagioli* [2006] 2 BCLC 70; *Corran v Butters* [2017] EWHC 2294.

[71] [2007] 1 BCLC 520.

may be unfair but not prejudicial, as in *Irvine v Irvine (No 1)*[72] where the court found that there had been a failure to meet the statutory requirements as to approving the accounts and holding of annual general meetings, but the failures could not be said to have caused the petitioner any material prejudice.[73] In *Re Coroin Ltd (No 2)*[74] David Richards J noted that where there is a breach of duty by directors which has no consequences, no loss to the company, and no profit by the directors, it would be difficult for a member to show prejudice, though the fact of a breach of duty would establish unfairness. It would be, as Jonathan Parker LJ suggested in *Rock Nominees Ltd v RCO (Holdings) plc*,[75] a breach of duty, as it were, in the abstract. The result is that, while financial loss is not a prerequisite, there will be no prejudice if the 'acts or omissions complained of do not in practice result in injury, whether materially or by impairing constitutional and/or equitable rights'.[76]

**19-37**  The difficulties faced by a petitioner of showing conduct which is unfairly prejudicial to his interests as a member where the company is insolvent (so there are no surplus funds in which the shareholders will have an interest) were addressed by the Court of Appeal in *Re Tobian Properties Ltd, Maidment v Attwood*[77] which ruled that, if the company is insolvent, in general, the petitioner must show that his shares would have had a value but for the wrongdoing, while acknowledging that the courts take a wide view of prejudice suffered as a shareholder.[78] Arden LJ noted that the court should not erect technical difficulties to prevent a petitioner from obtaining redress if there is a sufficient prospect that a potential surplus can at some stage be shown and no unfairness to other parties is involved.[79] The Court of Appeal sent the case back to the first instance judge to consider whether the company would have had a surplus if the respondent had not acted as he had (drawing excessive director's remuneration; permitting another business to use the company's trading name without a fee; and selling at an undervalue the company's name and goodwill on the eve of the company's liquidation).[80] If that hearing established that there would have been a surplus if those matters had not occurred, then the petitioner had suffered unfair prejudice as a member of the company in respect of which the court could grant relief.[81]

---

[72]  [2007] 1 BCLC 349. Likewise, in *Oak Investment Partners XII v Boughtwood* [2010] 2 BCLC 459 at [121], there was some evidence of unfair conduct by the petitioners (non-disclosure of information) but it had caused no prejudice; *Watchstone Group plc v Quob Park Estate Ltd* [2017] EWHC 2621 (failure to give petitioner notice of special resolution was unfair, but not prejudicial since the resolution would have been passed in any event).

[73]  See also *Re Sunrise Radio Ltd, Kohli v Lit* [2010] 1 BCLC 367 at [7], [8] (in judging unfair prejudice, isolated trivial complaints, even when in breach of some legal requirement, having no impact on the value of the petitioner's shares or on any realistic objective assessment of the integrity and competence of the board, will be ignored, unless that requirement is an absolute standard imposed by the statute or constitution and, even then, minor inadvertent departures can be ignored as will irregularities which can be set right at any moment).

[74]  [2013] 2 BCLC 583 at [631], [641].        [75]  [2004] 1 BCLC 439 at [79].

[76]  *Re C & MB Holdings Ltd, Hamilton v Brown* [2017] 1 BCLC 269 at [61] and see [159]–[162].

[77]  [2013] 2 BCLC 567, CA, noted Lim (2013) 34 Co Law 115.

[78]  [2013] 2 BCLC 567 at [11]–[12].        [79]  [2013] 2 BCLC 567 at [13].

[80]  [2013] 2 BCLC 567 at [58]. Reflecting the two stages involved, the court usually holds a 'liability hearing' to determine whether a purchase order should be made followed by a 'quantum hearing' to determine the value of the shares; see Arden LJ in *Re Tobian Properties, Maidment v Attwood* [2013] 2 BCLC 567 at [27], who explains that, where the company is insolvent, the court has to reverse the stages and deal with quantum issues first.

[81]  [2013] 2 BCLC 567 at [58].

## C *O'Neill v Phillips* and the boundaries to unfairly prejudicial conduct

**19-38**   The leading authority on the scope of the unfairly prejudicial jurisdiction is *O'Neill v Phillips*,[82] the sole House of Lords authority on the provision, and the speech by Lord Hoffmann is definitive as to the approach to be taken when assessing allegations of unfair prejudicial conduct of the affairs of a company.[83]

**19-39**   The petitioner, O, joined the company as a manual worker in 1983. In 1985, the respondent, P, impressed by O's abilities, gave him 25 per cent of the issued shares and appointed him a director. Between 1985 and 1990, P retired from the board, leaving O as sole director. The company prospered and O was credited with half of the profits. There were discussions with a view to O obtaining a 50 per cent shareholding, but no agreement was concluded. In 1991 P became concerned about the company's financial position and O's management so he resumed personal command and gave O the option of managing, under him, the UK or the German branches of the business. O decided to go to Germany and remained on the board as a director. Later that year P determined that O would no longer receive 50 per cent of the profits but would be paid only his salary and any dividends payable upon his 25 per cent shareholding. O decided to sever his links with the company and petitioned the court claiming that the company's affairs were being conducted in a manner 'unfairly prejudicial' to his interests.

**19-40**   Following a difference of opinion in the lower courts, the matter reached the House of Lords where Lord Hoffmann (who gave the sole speech) concluded that a member will not ordinarily be entitled to complain of unfairness unless there has been:

(1) some breach of the terms on which the member agreed that the affairs of the company should be conducted; or

(2) some use of the rules in a manner which equity would regard as contrary to good faith—i.e. cases in which equitable considerations make it unfair for those conducting the affairs of the company to rely upon their strict legal powers.[84]

In considering the scope of the unfairly prejudicial jurisdiction, Lord Hoffmann emphasised the need to appreciate the business context in which the section operates.[85] Companies are associations of persons for economic purposes where the terms of association are contained in the articles and perhaps in shareholder agreements and the manner in which business is to be conducted is regulated by rules agreed to by the members.[86] It follows that a member is not ordinarily able to complain of unfairness unless there has been some breach of those terms. Additionally, on occasion, equity will restrain the exercise of strict legal rights where equitable considerations make it unfair for those conducting the affairs of the company to rely upon their strict legal powers. Those equitable considerations arise in the context of winding up on the just and equitable ground and

---

[82] [1999] 2 BCLC 1; noted Prentice and Payne, 'Section 459 of the Companies Act 1985—The House of Lords View' (1999) 115 LQR 587; Goddard, 'Taming the Unfair Prejudice Remedy: Sections 459–461 of the Companies Act 1985 in the House of Lords' (1999) 58 CLJ 487; Boyle (2000) 21 Co Law 253.

[83] See *Oak Investment Partners XII v Boughtwood* [2010] 2 BCLC 459 at [118], per Rimer LJ. For a succinct account of Lord Hoffmann's speech, see *Grace v Bialioli* [2006] 2 BCLC 70 at [61].

[84] [1999] 2 BCLC 1 at 8.       [85] [1999] 2 BCLC 1.

[86] See [1999] 2 BCLC 1 at 7; *Re Saul D Harrison & Sons plc* [1995] 1 BCLC 14 at 17–18.

were considered by Lord Wilberforce in *Ebrahimi v Westbourne Galleries Ltd*[87] and Lord Hoffmann considered that a similar approach was applicable to the concept of unfairness in what is now CA 2006, s 994. In his famous speech in *Ebrahimi v Westbourne Galleries Ltd*,[88] Lord Wilberforce considered the nature of a limited company and said that its structure is 'defined by the Companies Act 1948 and by the articles of association by which shareholders agree to be bound'. He went on: '[i]n most companies and in most contexts, this definition is sufficient and exhaustive, equally so whether the company is large or small.'[89]

**19-41**    In some circumstances, however, the exercise of legal rights will be subject to equitable considerations; considerations, that is, of a personal character arising between one individual and another, which may make it unjust, or inequitable, to insist on legal rights, or to exercise them in a particular way. But the fact that a company is a small one, or a private company, is not enough for such considerations to arise, a point worth underscoring. In Lord Wilberforce's view, the superimposition of equitable considerations requires something more, which typically may include one, or probably more, of the following elements:[90]

> (1)  an association formed or continued on the basis of a personal relationship involving mutual confidence;
>
> (2)  an agreement, or understanding, that all or some (for there may be 'sleeping' members) of the shareholders shall participate in the conduct of the business; and
>
> (3)  restrictions on the transfers of shares so that a member cannot take his stake and go elsewhere.

These companies are commonly described as 'quasi-partnerships' though 'it is clear that Lord Wilberforce was not intending to set out an exhaustive list of factors, (but they are very useful starting positions) and that the term quasi-partnership is only intended as a useful shorthand label'.[91] This important point must not be overlooked; the language is merely shorthand for the nature of the relationship which must exist between the parties if broader equitable considerations are to come into play. The point was underlined by Mann J in *Brett v Migration Solutions Holdings Ltd*[92] where he pointed out that the existence of a 'quasi-partnership' is not determinative of the question of whether equitable constraints on the exercise of legal rights apply. As explained in *Corran v Butters*[93] the underlying question is, '… whether the circumstances surrounding the conduct of the affairs of a particular company are such as to give rise to equitable constraints upon the behaviour of other members going beyond the strict rights and obligations set out in the Companies Act and the articles of association'.

---

[87]  [1972] 2 All ER 492 at 500; the case is discussed in detail at **19-103**.
[88]  [1972] 2 All ER 492 at 500.      [89]  [1972] 2 All ER 492 at 500.      [90]  [1972] 2 All ER 492 at 500.
[91]  *Fisher v Cadman* [2006] 1 BCLC 499 at [84]. In this case the court noted that the family relationship between the parties (two brothers and a sister) was as important as the relationship defined by the articles of association and the company was a quasi-partnership though the petitioner had never taken any role in the management of the company and had contributed no capital, having been given or inherited her shares from her parents. The company did not therefore have some of the typical characteristics of a quasi-partnership. See Nourse J in *Re Bird Precision Bellows Ltd* cited by Oliver LJ in CA at [1986] Ch 658 at 667 who noted that Lord Wilberforce did not intend to be exhaustive and stated that, in his view, there may be other typical and important elements, in particular the provision of capital by all or some of the participants (of course, they will have to contribute capital if they are shareholders).
[92]  [2016] EWHC 523.      [93]  [2017] EWHC 2294 at [114].

**19-42**   If the company is of this nature, i.e. something more than a merely commercial association, then equitable considerations enable the court to hold the majority shareholders to the mutual agreements, promises, or understandings which form the basis of the relationship and a petitioner under s 994 can base his petition on breach of these understandings also.

**19-43**   Returning to the facts in *O'Neill v Phillips*,[94] the petitioner could not bring himself within either of the grounds identified by Lord Hoffmann. P had not acted in breach of the terms upon which it was agreed that the affairs of the company should be conducted and there was no ground, consistent with the principles of equity, for any belief, any mutual agreement or understanding, that O was entitled to half the profits and half the shareholding. As O could not bring his claim within either basis for relief, his petition was dismissed. Finally, note that Lord Hoffmann expressly rejected reliance on 'legitimate expectations' as a basis for a petition. This reliance had been a prominent element of the case law prior to this decision with petitions being brought essentially on the basis that a petitioner was aggrieved that (what he perceived to be) his legitimate expectations as to the conduct of the company's affairs had not been met. For example, the petitioner in *O'Neill v Phillips* felt that he had 'legitimate expectations' to 50 per cent of the shares in the company and 50 per cent of the profits although he could establish no entitlement in law or equity to such equality.[95] Lord Hoffmann noted that he himself had used the phrase 'legitimate expectations' in *Re Saul D Harrison & Sons plc*,[96] but he conceded that this use was a mistake.[97]

**19-44**   The key question is whether the relationship between the parties is such as to attract equitable considerations which will restrict the freedom of the majority to act as they wish and enable a petition to be brought on both the grounds identified by Lord Hoffmann. The scenario where the relationship is of that nature is most commonly a quasi-partnership, but *VB Football Assets v Blackpool FC (Properties) Ltd*[98] is a good example of a company which was not a quasi-partnership but equitable considerations nevertheless came into play. Where equitable considerations do not come into play, the petitioner will be limited to allegations of breaches of the statute or the articles or other contractual arrangements governing the shareholders' relationship. In the case of a public company, the expectation generally would be that the entire relationship of the parties is exhaustively determined by the constitution[99] and there is no scope for equitable considerations to arise. This is particularly so if the company is a listed public company, a point made forcibly in *Re Astec (BSR) plc*[100] by Jonathan Parker J:

> 'If the market in a company's shares is to have any credibility members of the public dealing in that market must, it seems to me, be entitled to proceed on the footing that the constitution of the company is as it appears in the company's public documents, unaffected by any extraneous equitable considerations and constraints.'

**19-45**   If the relationship between the parties is spelt out in detailed agreements, especially agreements drafted and advised upon by professional advisers, there is little scope for

---

[94] [1999] 2 BCLC 1.      [95] [1999] 2 BCLC 1 at 12–13.      [96] [1995] 1 BCLC 14.
[97] [1999] 2 BCLC 1 at 11.      [98] [2017] EWHC 2767.
[99] See *Re Saul D Harrison & Sons plc* [1995] 1 BCLC 14; *VB Football Assets Ltd v Blackpool Football Club (Properties) Ltd* [2017] EWHC 2767 at [319].
[100] [1998] 2 BCLC 556 at 589. See also *CAS (Nominees) Ltd v Nottingham Forest FC* [2002] 1 BCLC 613 at 627; *Re Tottenham Hotspur plc* [1994] 1 BCLC 655 (the shareholders are entitled to expect that the entire relationship between the company and the chief executive is set out in his service agreement and the constitution).

arguing that the relationship is other than a purely commercial one,[101] even if there are personal relationships between the participants and even if there are only a small number of participants. In *Moxon v Litchfield*,[102] for example, the court found that, though the company was originally founded on personal relationships (there were just four ordinary shareholders), the parties had chosen to govern the relationships between the shareholders *inter se* and between the shareholders and the company with bespoke and detailed legal agreements, so emphasising the commercial character of the company.[103] In *Re Coroin Ltd (No 2)*[104] the company had a small number of shareholders, but they were highly sophisticated business people purchasing a group of hotels for hundreds of millions of pounds, with lengthy and complex articles of association and shareholders' agreements negotiated between them. David Richards J concluded that he found it hard to image a case where it would be more inappropriate to overlay equitable considerations on the company structure.[105] In *VB Football Assets Ltd v Blackpool FC (Properties) Ltd*[106] the parties (a majority and a minority shareholder essentially) were experienced businessmen who entered into detailed share subscription and loan agreements concerning their relationship as owners of a football club. Nevertheless, the court found that these agreements did not represent the totality of their relationship. There were further important understandings between the parties as to the management of the company on the basis of unanimity and on securing a parity of shareholdings in due course which were not formally recognised (for tax reasons) but which did form the basis of the relationship. Equitable considerations therefore did arise in this instance.

**19-46**    The issue is the nature of the relationship at the time of the unfairly prejudicial conduct, not whether the company was from the outset a commercial association or a quasi-partnership,[107] for the parties' relationship may change over time. A company may start out on a purely commercial footing, but by the time of the conduct complained of, may have become one where equitable considerations come into play, as was the case in *O'Neill v Phillips*.[108] The petitioner initially was an employee of the company, but the relationships within the company changed over the years as he became a shareholder and a director such that the company became a quasi-partnership, a not uncommon scenario. Likewise in *Croly v Good*[109] where the court found that the relationship had changed from being that of employee to that of quasi-partner. The key factors were that the petitioner, who had initially been employed as a salesman, subsequently became a shareholder, participated in management to a significant degree, was held out to outside parties as a principal in the business, and reached agreement with effectively the only other shareholder on an equal division of profits. The court noted that the totality of the arrangements between

---

[101]  See *Re a Company (No 005685 of 1988), ex p Schwarz (No 2)* [1989] BCLC 427; also *Gray v Briad Group (Holdings) Ltd* [2015] CSOH 146, aff'd [2016] CSIH 68 (small number of shareholders, but required to contribute at least £100,000 in share capital, not well acquainted with one another, detailed shareholder agreements); *Wootliff v Rushton-Turner* [2017] EWHC 3129, [2018] 1 BCLC 479 (professionally drafted articles, service agreements, allotments of differing amounts to eight different investors).    [102]  [2013] EWHC 3957.

[103]  On the other hand, in *Oak Investment Partners XII v Boughtwood* [2010] 2 BCLC 459, though the relationship was a joint venture between a large US venture capital firm and an individual entrepreneur and inventor, and therefore it might have been thought that it would be a commercial relationship, there was no dispute that the relationship was of a quasi-partnership nature giving rise to mutual obligations of good faith and trust, see at [119].    [104]  See [2013] 2 BCLC 583 at [636].

[105]  [2013] 2 BCLC 583 at [636].    [106]  [2017] EWHC 2767.

[107]  See *Croly v Good* [2010] 2 BCLC 569 at [88]; *Re Sunrise Radio Ltd, Kohli v Lit* [2010] 1 BCLC 367 at [306].

[108]  [1999] 2 BCLC 1.

[109]  [2010] 2 BCLC 569. See also *Strahan v Wilcock* [2006] 2 BCLC 555 at [19]–[25], another case where an employment relationship developed into participation on a quasi-partnership basis in the company.

the parties must be considered with no single element conclusive either way[110] and, in this instance, the result was a relationship requiring the qualities of trust and confidence found in a quasi-partnership.

**19-47**   Equally, a relationship which begins on a quasi-partnership footing may become a more commercial venture, as in *Re a Company (No 005134 of 1986), ex p Harries*.[111] Here the parties did operate initially as a quasi-partnership but, as the business developed, the petitioner withdrew into the role of a passive shareholder with the result that the relationship moved on to a purely commercial footing. In *Re McCarthy Surfacing Ltd, Hequet v McCarthy*[112] the relationships originally were that of quasi-partners, but the minority shareholders had destroyed that quasi-partnership, the court found, by unfounded legal action some years earlier, after which they ceased to be involved in the running of the company and the position reverted to a formal commercial relationship.[113]

**19-48**   We turn now to consider the two grounds on which a petition may be based in more detail.

### Breach of the terms on which the affairs of the company should be conducted

**19-49**   As noted earlier, Lord Hoffmann in *O'Neill v Phillips* stressed the importance of considering unfair prejudice in the context of a company being a commercial association regulated by rules agreed to by the parties. Arden LJ in *Re Tobian Properties Ltd, Maidment v Attwood*,[114] noted the importance of that point and commented that, while the concept of fairness is flexible and open-textured, it is not unbounded and will be applied in context and an important part of that context is the terms on which the parties agreed to do business together which will include the obligations in the company's articles and the statute. Equally, shareholder agreements may be relevant. As Hildyard J said in *Moxon v Litchfield*,[115] '... neither equity nor the jurisdiction under s 994 sweeps away contractual arrangements; at most, the exercise of contractual rights is subjected to equitable restraint if it would be unconscionable or unfairly prejudicial. If the exercise of the legal right would not be unconscionable, the consequences of its exercise must be permitted to follow.' In *Moxon v Litchfield*[116] the extensive legal agreements which governed the parties' relationships provided that a director who was a 'bad leaver' had to transfer his shares at par value which the court accepted was a potentially 'harsh, even draconian' provision but one to which the director had agreed. Once it was determined that the director was a 'bad leaver' and subject to the proper exercise of the power to require the transfer of his shares, the director could not complain that the application of contractually agreed measures was unfair.[117]

**19-50**   Typically, breaches of the CA 2006 will be central to many petitions, usually involving allegations of breaches of directors' duties (for example, the misappropriation of corporate assets and improper allotments of shares) and breaches of the requirements

---

[110] [2010] 2 BCLC 569 at [89]–[92].     [111] [1989] BCLC 383.

[112] [2009] 1 BCLC 622; see also *Fowler v Gruber* [2010] 1 BCLC 563 where the company started as a quasi-partnership, but became a commercial relationship when the petitioner sold some of his shares and subsequently a local authority also became a shareholder.

[113] [2009] 1 BCLC 622 at [93]–[96].     [114] [2013] 2 BCLC 56 at [21], [31].

[115] [2013] EWHC 3957 at [45].     [116] [2013] EWHC 3957 at [8].

[117] [2013] EWHC 3957 at [44]–[46], [52]–[55]. Especially since the company had distributed profits each year so it was not a case that the director lost all the intermediate benefit of his participation in the company, at [52].

governing disclosure (for example, failures to call meetings or provide accounts).[118] The fact that shareholders have ratified a breach of duty does not necessarily prevent conduct from being unfair for the purposes of this section, if ratification is contrary to the agreed basis as to how the company is to be run, though ratification would preclude a derivative claim.[119]

### Breach of the no-conflict duty

**19-51**    It is a common feature of many of these disputes that, when the majority and minority shareholders fall out, the majority look to use the company's assets as their own and they often appropriate, without authorisation and for their own benefit, opportunities and contracts which properly belong to the company. Typically they extract from the company benefits beyond their strict entitlements and run down the business of the company (so reducing the value of the minority's holding) while transferring business to another entity wholly owned by them. Such clear breaches of the no-conflict duty (CA 2006, s 175, see **12-22**) amount to conduct of the company's affairs in an unfairly prejudicial manner.

**19-52**    Illustrations of such breaches of duty amounting to unfairly prejudicial conduct can be found in the following cases:

- In *Re Little Olympian Each-Ways Ltd (No 3)*[120] the assets of the company were transferred at an undervalue to another company wholly owned by the majority shareholders. The assets were then sold on at their market value to a third party.

- In *Re Full Cup International Trading Ltd*[121] the respondents were found to have stifled the business of the company. They deprived it of its stock and business which was transferred to another entity in which they, but not the petitioner, had an interest.

- In *Re Brenfield Squash Racquets Club Ltd*[122] the majority shareholders and directors caused the company's assets to be used as security for debts of their businesses and transferred to those businesses assets that rightfully belonged to the company.

- In *Lloyd v Casey*[123] a director arranged a variety of transactions for his own ultimate benefit including payments to a company controlled by him and additional contributions to his own pension fund.

- In *Allmark v Burnham*[124] the majority shareholder and director opened a competing business in the same street as the company's main retail outlet, failed to consult the minority shareholder and director on management matters, and doubled his own salary once he had removed the minority shareholder from the board.

- In *Re Baumler (UK) Ltd, Gerrard v Koby*[125] the company was split 49 per cent and 51 per cent between two shareholders who were also the two directors. An opportunity to acquire the company's premises and adjoining land from their landlord was taken up by a third party acting on information provided to him by the 51 per cent

---

[118]  A breach of duty, while unfair, if it has no consequence for the company is not likely to produce any prejudice to a member, see *Re Coroin Ltd (No 2)* [2013] 2 BCLC 583 at [631], [641]–[642].

[119]  See *Re Saul D Harrison & Sons plc* [1995] 1 BCLC 14 at 18: 'Enabling the court in an appropriate case to outflank the rule in *Foss v Harbottle* was one of the purposes of the section', per Hoffmann LJ.

[120]  [1995] 1 BCLC 636.        [121]  [1995] BCC 682.        [122]  [1996] 2 BCLC 184.

[123]  [2002] 1 BCLC 454. See also *Fowler v Gruber* [2010] 1 BCLC 563 (director had the company lend him money to purchase shares from an existing shareholder which purchase made the director the majority shareholder; he had the company write off the loan and awarded himself excessive remuneration as well as making substantial payments to his pension fund).

[124]  [2006] 2 BCLC 437.        [125]  [2005] 1 BCLC 92.

respondent with the expectation of a secret profit. The court found that the under-hand conduct of the respondent in procuring the acquisition of the properties was a breach of duty by him and conduct unfairly prejudicial to the petitioner.

- In *Irvine v Irvine (No 1)*[126] the respondent director in breach of the articles awarded himself excessive and unauthorised remuneration without reference to the board or the minority shareholders. A consequence of this conduct was that the petitioner received less by way of dividend than should have been received consistent with the company's historic policy of maximum profit distribution. Conducting the company's affairs in this manner was unfairly prejudicial to the interests of the petitioner.

- In *Grace v Biagioli*[127] the respondent directors consciously and deliberately failed to pay a dividend which had been declared with the available profits distributed instead in the guise of management fees to the respondents. The non-payment of the declared dividend was unfairly prejudicial conduct.

- In *Re McCarthy Surfacing Ltd, Hequet v McCarthy*[128] a bonus agreement was deliberately designed to benefit the directors (and majority shareholders) and to ensure that none of the profits made on a particular project would be available to the other shareholders. In such circumstances, the making of the bonus agreement was a breach of the duty to act fairly and of the no-conflict rule and was unfairly prejudicial, as was a persistent failure by the board to consider whether or not to declare dividends, as was a failure by the board to have regard to the company's interests when negotiating transactions with the majority shareholder.

- In *Re Woven Rugs Ltd*[129] the respondent director in breach of duty refinanced the company in a way which favoured the interests of the majority shareholders over the interests of the minority shareholders for no purpose other than to benefit the majority at the expense of the company. He was responsible also for the extraction of funds from the company in the form of unauthorised remuneration and management charges. All of these matters amounted to the conduct of the company's affairs in an unfairly prejudicial manner.

- In *VB Football Assets v Blackpool FC (Properties) Ltd*[130] the court found that significant sums of money had been paid away from a company (the football club) to support other companies in the group (all owned by the majority shareholder in the company). The payments were essentially disguised dividends, the court said, from which the other shareholders in the company did not benefit so there was clear discrimination between the interests of the majority shareholder and the interests of the rest of the shareholders. Such conduct was unfairly prejudicial to their interests.

- In *Corran v Butters*[131] it was unfairly prejudicial for the majority shareholders to arrange for the company to make unauthorised pension contributions to them of £64,000 without a proper decision of the company to that effect or the unanimous agreement of the shareholders.

---

[126] [2007] 1 BCLC 349.
[127] [2006] 2 BCLC 70. See also *Re CF Booth Ltd, Booth v Booth* [2017] EWHC 457 where there was a policy not to pay dividends under any circumstances, though the company was profitable. At the same time, the majority enjoyed what the court found to be excessive remuneration. The court found this conduct to be a breach of CA 2006, ss 171, 172, and 173.
[128] [2009] 1 BCLC 622.    [129] [2010] EWHC 230.    [130] [2017] EWHC 2767.
[131] [2017] EWHC 2294.

### Breach of duty to act for a proper purpose and fairly between shareholders

**19-53**    A common ploy in these disputes is for the directors to make an allotment of shares, nominally to raise capital, but really for the purpose of diluting the petitioner's interest in the company, something which is in breach of the directors' duty to act in accordance with the constitution and to exercise their powers for the purposes for which they are conferred (CA 2006, s 171). The ability of directors to manipulate allotments is limited to some extent by the statutory requirement (subject to certain exceptions) for shares to be allotted on a rights basis (i.e. to existing shareholders in proportion to existing holdings, CA 2006, s 561, see **21-34**). Allotting in breach of the rights requirement so diluting the holdings of the minority shareholder is unfairly prejudicial conduct. For example, in *Re Coloursource Ltd, Dalby v Bodilly*[132] an allotment made in breach of the rights requirement by the company's sole director and 50 per cent shareholder had the effect of diluting the other 50 per cent shareholder to a 5 per cent shareholder. There were allegations of other misconduct, but Blackburne J thought it was sufficient to look at the allotment of shares which was the plainest possible breach by the director of his fiduciary duty and unfairly prejudicial conduct.[133]

**19-54**    In some circumstances even a rights issue can be unfairly prejudicial, as in *Re Regional Airports Ltd*[134] where the ulterior motive for a proposed rights issue, the court found, was to enhance the majority's position and to increase pressure on the (now to be diluted) minority to sell their shares at a discounted valuation.[135] Other examples of an improper purpose behind an apparently fair rights issue which would justify a finding of unfairly prejudicial conduct are if it is known that a particular shareholder does not have sufficient funds to take up the rights offer and it is made for that reason, or where a shareholder is engaged in litigation with the majority and the offer is designed to deplete the resources available to him to finance that litigation.[136]

**19-55**    It is even possible for a rights issue which is made for a proper purpose, i.e. genuinely to raise capital, to be unfairly prejudicial if the directors act unfairly when determining the price of the shares. In *Re Sunrise Radio Ltd, Kohli v Lit*[137] the court accepted that a rights issue had been made for the genuine purpose of raising capital though it was made at a time when it was likely that the minority shareholder would not take up the shares and

---

[132] [2005] BCC 627. See also *Re a Company (No 005134 of 1986), ex p Harries* [1989] BCLC 383 (majority shareholder and director made an allotment of shares in breach of the statutory requirements for a rights issue for the purpose of increasing his shareholding and decreasing the petitioner's holding from 40 per cent to 4 per cent). However, where there was a genuine desire to raise capital, a scheme proposed by the directors, although devised so as to avoid the need for a rights issue, was not conduct which was unfairly prejudicial to those shareholders who were thereby denied the possibility of taking up additional shares: see *CAS (Nominees) Ltd v Nottingham Forest FC plc* [2002] 1 BCLC 613 at 627–32.

[133] [2005] BCC 627 at [16]. In the circumstances, it was irrelevant that no dividend had been declared on any of the additional shares and that no use had been made of the additional shareholding. See too *Re Zetnet Ltd, Harris v Jones* [2011] EWHC 1518 at [152] (dilution from 50 per cent to 0.1 per cent shareholding was unfairly prejudicial).    [134] [1999] 2 BCLC 30.

[135] It was obvious to the majority shareholder that the minority shareholders either could not or would not take up the rights issue—it had been made clear to them that their continued presence as investors was not welcome—therefore their holdings were bound to be diluted as a consequence of the issue, see [1999] 2 BCLC 30 at 72–3, 80.

[136] See *Re a Company (No 002612 of 1984)* [1985] BCLC 80 (injunction granted to restrain a proposed rights issue which had followed immediately on the presentation by the minority shareholder of a petition. Had it gone ahead, it would have reduced the petitioner's shareholding in the company from 33 per cent to 0.33 per cent); also *Re a Company (No 007623 of 1984)* [1986] BCLC 362.

[137] [2010] 1 BCLC 367.

therefore faced dilution (from a 15 per cent holding to 8.33 per cent). But the shares had also been issued at par when the evidence was that the shares, which were taken up by the majority shareholder, could have been issued for a significantly higher price, so the minority shareholder suffered a dilution in the value, as well as the size, of her holding. The court held that, even if the directors had acted in accordance with the duty to exercise their powers for a proper purpose (s 171), they were in breach of their duty to act fairly between shareholders (s 172(1)(f)).[138] The court noted that what is the proper price for shares will necessarily fall within a range of possibilities, but the board is required to consider all these matters fairly in the interests of all groups of shareholders and having regard to the foreseeable range of responses from the shareholders to the rights issue. Where it is known or foreseen that the minority may not be able or wish to subscribe, the directors in the interests of even-handedness and fairness must consider the price which can be extracted from those who are willing to subscribe or be in breach of their duties to the company.[139] On the facts, issuing the shares at par without considering any alternative, particularly when the directors (as the majority shareholders) benefited appreciably from the issue at par, was a breach of duty and unfairly prejudicial to the petitioner.[140]

### Breach of duty of care and skill

**19-56**    The courts are reluctant to accept that disagreements over managerial decisions can amount to conduct of the company's affairs in an unfairly prejudicial manner.[141] The judicial view, essentially, is that differences as to commercial judgement are not for the courts to adjudicate upon, especially not with the benefit of hindsight which shows that the decisions were not in the company's interest.[142] After all, the directors are appointed by the shareholders and, if they are disappointed with the quality of the management provided, the remedy lies in the shareholders' power to dismiss the directors. In *Re Elgindata Ltd*,[143] for example, the complaint was a broad complaint where the shareholder was simply disappointed as to the poor quality of the management of the business.[144] That was insufficient, the court said, as a basis for an allegation of unfairly prejudicial conduct.

**19-57**    If the decisions taken cause actual financial loss to the company, the petition is more likely to succeed since, in essence, the allegation then is of a failure to exercise reasonable care, skill and diligence as required by CA 2006, s 174. In *Re Macro (Ipswich) Ltd*,[145] for example, it was possible to point to specific management failures repeated over many years which caused financial loss to the company. The company had a substantial portfolio of properties which had been mismanaged by the sole director who was 83 years of

---

[138] See *Mutual Life Insurance Co of New York v The Rank Organisation* [1985] BCLC 11; also *Re McCarthy Surfacing Ltd, Hequet v McCarthy* [2009] 1 BCLC 622 at [77]–[81] (the directors in adopting a bonus agreement designed to ensure that profits were not available to all the shareholders acted for an improper purpose and contravened their duty to act fairly between the shareholders).

[139] [2010] 1 BCLC 367 at [95].

[140] A subsequent increase in authorised share capital and a disapplication of the rights issue requirement was also unfairly prejudicial, though no shares had been issued pursuant to that authority, when the petitioner had been misled as to the calling of the general meeting where these matters were agreed, see [2010] 1 BCLC 367 at [135].

[141] See *Re Elgindata Ltd* [1991] BCLC 959 at 993–4; *Re Saul D Harrison & Sons plc* [1995] 1 BCLC 14 at 31, CA.        [142] See *Oak Investment Partners XII v Boughtwood* [2010] 2 BCLC 459 at [8].

[143] [1991] BCLC 959.        [144] [1991] BCLC 959 at 993–4.

[145] [1994] 2 BCLC 354. See also *Re C&MB Holdings Ltd, Hamilton v Brown* [2017] 1 BCLC 269 (unfairly prejudicial for the management to include a person who was an undischarged bankrupt who was disqualified from management—petitioners had a right to have the company managed properly and not by disqualified persons).

age and the father of the petitioners in this case. He had failed to institute a proper maintenance system for the properties or to ensure that they were properly let and rents duly paid with the result that the value of these assets had been depleted. Such conduct was unfairly prejudicial conduct. On the other hand, in *Fisher v Cadman*[146] the court rejected complaints from a shareholder about the inactive management of a property company's assets by its directors. It was the practice of the company to hold properties in the hope of realising capital gains without expending large sums of money on repairing and letting the properties. The court thought that the decision to manage the assets in that way was within the range of reasonable business decisions available to the directors as managers and did not amount to mismanagement.

### Breach of statutory rights

**19-58**  A breach of members' statutory rights, for example, repeated failures to hold annual general meetings and to lay accounts before the members (when required to do so[147]) so depriving members of their right to know and consider the state of the company's affairs,[148] may merit a petition, subject to the general qualification that trivial infringements will not found a petition.[149]

### Use of the rules in an inequitable manner

**19-59**  The second basis for a petition under CA 2006, s 994 identified by the House of Lords in *O'Neill v Phillips*[150] is that there has been some use of the rules in a manner which equity would regard as contrary to good faith. As noted at **19-43**, care must be taken in relying on this ground and vague assertions that some legitimate expectations of the petitioner have not been met will be rejected by the court.[151] This ground will be relevant where the company is something more than the usual commercial association and there is a common understanding on all sides that the articles of association do not represent a complete and exhaustive statement of the parties' relationships.[152] In addition to the articles, there are understandings and promises (though not contractually binding) between the parties, typically about matters such as participation in the management of the company, financial returns, and, more broadly, the nature of the venture on which the parties have embarked. While these understandings etc will usually be found at the time of entering into the association, there may be later promises, by words or conduct, which it may be unfair to ignore,[153] given that relationships are not static but evolve over time. As Arden LJ explained in *Strahan v Wilcock*,[154] '[i]n determining what equitable obligations arise between the parties, the court must look at all the circumstances, including the company's constitution, any written agreement between the shareholders and the conduct

---

[146] [2006] 1 BCLC 499.

[147] Only public companies are required to hold annual general meetings or to lay accounts before such meetings: see CA 2006, ss 336, 437.

[148] See *Re a Company (No 00789 of 1987), ex p Shooter* [1990] BCLC 384; *Fisher v Cadman* [2006] 1 BCLC 499.

[149] See *Re Saul D Harrison & Sons plc* [1995] 1 BCLC 14 at 18, CA; also *Irvine v Irvine (No 1)* [2007] 1 BCLC 349. See *Re Sunrise Radio Ltd, Kohli v Lit* [2010] 1 BCLC 367 at [7]–[8] as to trivial infringements, but even a trivial infringement may amount to unfairly prejudicial conduct if the requirement infringed is imposed as an absolute requirement by the statute.   [150] [1999] 2 BCLC 1.

[151] The members must have reached a sufficient degree of agreement that it can be said that there has been a breach of good faith in departing from it: *Khoshkhou v Cooper* [2014] EWHC 1087 at [24].

[152] *Fisher v Cadman* [2006] 1 BCLC 499 at [89].   [153] *O'Neill v Phillips* [1999] 2 BCLC 1 at 10–11.

[154] [2006] 2 BCLC 555 at [27].

of the parties'. Complaints on this ground therefore have to show that the conduct of the company's affairs, while not necessarily a breach of the statute or of the constitution, is a breach of the understandings which form the basis of the association. A useful cross-check, as Lord Hoffmann noted in *O'Neill v Phillips*,[155] is to ask 'whether the exercise of the power in question would be contrary to what the parties, by word or conduct, have actually agreed'.

### Understandings as to participation in management

19-60    Complaints about removal from office are central to most unfairly prejudicial petitions. If the parties in a small private company have come together as members on the basis that all or some of them shall participate in the management of the company, the exclusion of a shareholder from management by removing him without cause as a director (a power open to the majority by ordinary resolution under CA 2006, s 168) is unfairly prejudicial to his interests as a member in the absence of a fair offer by the majority to buy the petitioner's shares or to make some other fair arrangement.[156]

19-61    A typical example is *Brownlow v G H Marshall Ltd*[157] where the company was a family business built up over a long period of time and with the shares now held equally by a brother and two sisters, all of whom were directors. Following various disagreements and the breakdown of the personal relationships involved, an attempt was made to exclude one of the sisters from the board. The court held that attempting to exclude her without a fair offer for her shares amounted to the conduct of the company's affairs in a manner which was unfairly prejudicial to her interests so entitling her to relief.

19-62    An issue which has arisen is whether the fact that the director has a service agreement undermines his case, i.e. by suggesting that the relationship is a commercial one rather than a broader association based on mutual understandings. The courts have been reluctant so to conclude if, when viewed overall, the relationship is broader than a mere commercial association. In *Brownlow v G H Marshall Ltd*,[158] for example, the directors did have service agreements with the company but the court found that there was nothing in the arrangements reached which altered the basis on which the company operated, i.e. that it was a quasi-partnership. The service agreements were not designed, the court thought, to affect the shareholders' position as shareholders or to preclude any potential remedy which a shareholder might have under CA 2006, s 994, but were designed to ensure fair arrangements for the working directors.[159] A similar approach can be found in *Quinlan v Essex Hinge Co Ltd*[160] where the court agreed that the existence of a service agreement between the director and the company did not prevent the company having the characteristics of a quasi-partnership.

---

[155] [1999] 2 BCLC 1 at 10. See *Grace v Biagioli* [2006] 2 BCLC 70 at [61].

[156] *O'Neill v Phillips* [1999] 2 BCLC 1 at 14 ('It is the terms, agreement, or understanding on which [the petitioner] became associated as a member which generates the restraint of the power of expulsion', per Lord Hoffmann). See also *Re BC & G Care Homes Ltd* [2016] BCC 615 (exclusion of petitioner without an offer for his shares in breach of the understanding that he would be a director and employee was unfairly prejudicial to his interests as a member).

[157] [2000] 2 BCLC 655. See also *Shepherd v Williamson* [2010] EWHC 2375 at [131]; *Fowler v Gruber* [2010] 1 BCLC 563 at [129]. See also *VB Football Assets v Blackpool FC (Properties) Ltd* [2017] EWHC 2767, the parties (a 76 per cent shareholder and a 20 per cent shareholder) had an unwritten agreement that the business would be managed on the basis of unanimity, so excluding the minority from significant decision-making which was conducted outside of the board was unfairly prejudicial conduct.

[158] [2000] 2 BCLC 655.        [159] [2000] 2 BCLC 655 at 669.

[160] [1996] 2 BCLC 417.

**19-63**     In the absence of these personal quasi-partnership elements, every director is subject to the possibility of removal and has no right to remain in office.[161] Removal of a director for cause will not merit a petition for, while such removal is prejudicial to the petitioner, it is not unfair.[162] If, as in *O'Neill v Phillips*,[163] and despite a changing relationship between the parties, the respondent chooses to continue to work with the petitioner without attempting to remove him from office, no grounds for complaint exist.

## Understandings as to participation in financial returns

**19-64**     Dividend issues can loom large in disputes in small companies. A common problem is that the company does not declare any dividends while continuing to amass reserves with the majority shareholders rewarded via directors' remuneration.[164] Of course, the mere absence of dividends to shareholders cannot of itself constitute unfairly prejudicial conduct, even if the situation continues for years on end, since the declaration of dividends is a matter within the discretion of the directors. If the directors duly consider that no dividends should be paid for any particular period, even a lengthy period, and do so bona fide in the interests of the company, it is not for the court to second-guess the directors' reasoning or substitute its own view of what the directors ought fairly to have done. But if, as in *Re McCarthy Surfacing Ltd, Hequet v McCarthy*,[165] the board of directors fails even to consider the payment of any dividends,[166] that breach of duty is itself unfairly prejudicial conduct.[167] In *Re a Company (No. 00370 of 1987), ex p Glossop*,[168] having commented that one of the prime purposes of a company is as a vehicle to earn profits which should be distributed by way of dividend to the members, Harman J said:[169]

> 'On that basis, … it is, in my judgment, right to say that directors have a duty to consider how much they can properly distribute to members. They have a duty, as I see it, to remember that the members are the owners of the company, that the profits belong to the members, and that, subject to the proper needs of the company to ensure that it is not trading

---

[161]   *Re Estate Acquisition and Development Ltd* [1995] BCC 338; *Re Tottenham Hotspur plc* [1994] 1 BCLC 655; *Re a Company (No 005134 of 1986), ex p Harries* [1989] BCLC 383; *Re a Company (No 005685 of 1988), ex p Schwarcz (No 2)* [1989] BCLC 427; *Re Blue Arrow plc* [1987] BCLC 585.

[162]   See *Grace v Biagioli* [2006] 2 BCLC 70 (not unfairly prejudicial conduct to remove a director when he had been negotiating secretly to acquire a company dealing in the same line of business as the company and had put himself in a position of actual or potential conflict with his duties as a director). See also *Hussain v Cooke* [2009] EWHC 3690.

[163]   [1999] 2 BCLC 1. See too *Re Coroin Ltd (No 2)* [2013] 2 BCLC 583 at [637]—the majority took no steps to exclude the petitioner who continued to attend (or his alternate did) and participate in board meetings in the usual way.

[164]   See, for example, *Quinlan v Essex Hinge Co Ltd* [1996] 2 BCLC 417 (non-declaration of dividends, despite the company having substantial reserves, with profits distributed by bonus payments to working directors or retained in the company). It is unfairly prejudicial conduct for the majority shareholders and directors to pay themselves remuneration when the understanding of the parties is that remuneration will not be paid, see *Fisher v Cadman* [2006] 1 BCLC 499 where the directors provided only limited services to the company which merely held properties for investment purposes and it was the understanding of all concerned that they would not be paid. It was unfairly prejudicial conduct, therefore, for them to award themselves remuneration in excess of £50,000.

[165]   [2009] 1 BCLC 622.

[166]   In this instance, the directors and majority shareholders were in a long-running dispute with the other shareholders and the majority received remuneration in other ways.

[167]   See also *Re J & J Insurance and Financial Consultants Ltd, Judge v Bahd* [2014] EWHC 2206 at [125] (director's failure to give proper consideration each year to whether a dividend ought to be paid, given past practice was for profits to be shared equally by dividend, and that the petitioner's capital was tied up in the company, was unfairly prejudicial conduct; dividends were stopped once the parties fell out).

[168]   [1988] BCLC 570.        [169]   [1988] BCLC 570 at 576–7.

in a risky manner and that there are adequate reserves for commercial purposes, by and large the trading profits ought to be distributed by way of dividends.'

**19-65**    Even if the circumstances are not quite as blatant as in *Re McCarthy Surfacing Ltd, Hequet v McCarthy*,[170] a failure to declare dividends may be unfairly prejudicial conduct if it can be shown to be contrary to the understandings of the parties as to how the financial rewards are to be shared.[171] In *Croly v Good*[172] the court found that the quasi-partners had an agreed remuneration strategy for an equal division of available funds between them.[173] The intention was that a scheme would be operated whereby each of them would draw money from the company on their directors' loan accounts as required during the year (so giving rise to a debt to the company) and a dividend would be declared at the end of the year which would reduce that debt as much as possible. In fact, no dividends were declared with the result that, when the parties subsequently fell out, and the minority shareholder was excluded from the management of the business, there was a considerable debt due from the petitioner to the company on his loan account which debt would have been reduced had dividends been declared. Given the understanding as to the manner of remuneration, the court found that the failure to declare dividends (when funds were available) with the result that the directors' debts to the company continued to mount was unfairly prejudicial to the petitioner's interests as a member.[174] In *VB Football Assets v Blackpool FC (Properties) Ltd*[175] the court found that significant sums of money had been paid away from the company (the football club) in circumstances which showed the payments were essentially disguised dividends to the majority shareholders and from which the other shareholders in the company did not benefit. The court ruled that, while shareholders have no right to a dividend, disguised payments to enrich the majority and discriminate against the other members is unfairly prejudicial conduct.

**19-66**    If the company's financial situation prevents the company declaring dividends, as in *Re Metropolis Motorcycles Ltd, Hale v Waldock*,[176] the minority shareholder has no grounds for complaint, even if the majority shareholder as a director is able to continue drawing a salary. It would not necessarily be fair for this position to go on forever, however, and the majority would have to recognise, the court said, that the minority could be said to have a legitimate claim to some form of return, see **19-71**. In *Grace v Biagioli*[177] a dividend had been declared, but the respondents (aggrieved by the conduct of the petitioner) then

---

[170]   [2009] 1 BCLC 622.

[171]   See *Irvine v Irvine (No 1)* [2007] 1 BCLC 349; *Quinlan v Essex Hinge Co Ltd* [1996] 2 BCLC 417; *Re a Company (No 004415 of 1996)* [1997] 1 BCLC 479; *Re Sam Weller & Sons Ltd* [1990] BCLC 80. In *Re a Company (No 004415 of 1996)* Sir Richard Scott noted that, if it is established at trial that dividends have been kept at an unreasonably low level, that fact would be reflected in the price which would be set for the petitioner's shares if a purchase order is made under CA 2006, s 996.      [172]   [2010] 2 BCLC 569.

[173]   [2010] 2 BCLC 569 at [65]. The company had a 60/40 shareholding split with the 40 per cent shareholder having moved from being an employee to being a quasi-partner, see **19-46**.

[174]   Further, given the agreement as to equal division of spoils, drawings by the respondent director in excess of that received by the petitioner also amounted to unfairly prejudicial conduct, see [2010] 2 BCLC 569 at [96] and [99]. See too *Sikorski v Sikorski* [2012] EWHC 1613 at [48], [50], [86] where the court found that the parties' bargain required the payment of a certain level of dividend to the minority shareholder so that failure to make those payments was unfairly prejudicial conduct.      [175]   [2017] EWHC 2767.

[176]   [2007] 1 BCLC 520. In this case, the court found that the situation which had occurred—the inability of the company to make payments to the minority shareholder—had not been contemplated by the parties when they had set up the company so, in the absence of anything in the nature of a promise of payments to the minority shareholder, there was no basis for an order that he be bought out.

[177]   [2006] 2 BCLC 70.

deliberately chose not to pay it and instead distributed the available profits as management fees to themselves. This non-payment, the court held, was unfairly prejudicial conduct.

### Understandings as to the basis of the relationship

**19-67**  In *O'Neill v Phillips*[178] Lord Hoffmann also considered that relief will be available under CA 2006, s 994 where some event has occurred which puts an end to the basis on which the parties entered into association with each other, so making it unfair that one shareholder should insist on the continuance of the association (a frustration-type situation).[179] But something more is needed than merely an assertion by the petitioner that the association should be brought to an end. Returning to *O'Neill v Phillips*,[180] it will be recalled that the House of Lords found that there was no unfairly prejudicial conduct. The minority share-holder had not been removed from office and there was no basis for his complaints that he should have received 50 per cent of the shares and of the profits of the company, see **19-43**. It was argued by counsel that, even if nothing unfair had occurred, the trust and confidence between the parties had broken down to such an extent that there had to be a parting of the ways and it would be unfair to leave the petitioner locked into the company as a minority shareholder. Lord Hoffmann noted that the argument essentially was that, in a quasi-partnership company, one partner ought to be entitled at will to require the other partner to buy his shares at a fair value where he considered that trust and confi-dence between the partners had broken down. Lord Hoffmann rejected the argument, noting that he could find no support in the authorities for such a stark right of unilateral withdrawal where the member had not been dismissed or excluded from the company.[181] The purpose of the statutory provision (CA 2006, s 994) is 'to provide relief for sharehold-ers who have been unfairly prejudiced, not to enable a locked-in minority shareholder to require the company to buy him out'.[182]

**19-68**  Mere deadlock between parties who have lost trust and confidence in one another is insufficient then to merit relief under CA 2006, s 994, in the absence of unfairly preju-dicial conduct. In *Re Phoenix Office Supplies Ltd*[183] the court rejected a claim by a share-holder that his co-shareholders and directors were obliged to purchase his shares when he decided (for purely personal reasons) to leave the company. The Court of Appeal ruled that a quasi-partnership company relationship does not give rise to an entitlement to a 'no-fault divorce' enabling one member at will to require the other members to buy his shares at fair value. In *Hawkes v Cuddy*[184] the Court of Appeal confirmed that deadlock alone is insufficient to found a petition under CA 2006, s 994 (though it would suffice for winding up on the just and equitable ground, see **19-95**) even if it shows a breakdown of trust and confidence between the parties which makes it impossible for the company to conduct its affairs as originally contemplated. It is still necessary to establish unfair preju-dice which may lie in the manner in which the other party reacts to the deadlock or the misconduct which created the deadlock and the resulting irrevocable breakdown in trust

---

[178] [1999] 2 BCLC 1.

[179] [1999] 2 BCLC 1 at 11 where Lord Hoffmann noted that the analogy of contractual frustration sug-gested itself.

[180] [1999] 2 BCLC 1.       [181] [1999] 2 BCLC 1 at 13.

[182] *Re a Company* [1983] BCLC 126 at 136. See, for example, *Re Abbington Hotel Ltd, DiGrado v D'Angelo* [2012] 1 BCLC 410 at [105].

[183] [2003] 1 BCLC 76. See also *Re Jayflex Construction Ltd, McKee v O'Reilly* [2004] 2 BCLC 145.

[184] [2009] 2 BCLC 427 at [108].

and confidence between the parties.[185] In *Re Abbington Hotel Ltd, DiGrado v D'Angelo*[186] one of the two effective shareholders tried to sell the business (a hotel) behind the back of the other shareholder in breach of an understanding that they would run the business for some time before selling. That conduct was a breach of the agreed basis on which the business was to be conducted, hence there was fault and unfairly prejudicial conduct. That fault destroyed the essential relationship of trust and confidence between the shareholder resulting in deadlock and relief under s 994, but it was not relief because of deadlock, it was relief as a consequence of the wrongful conduct of the respondent.

**19-69**   Given the clear authority that deadlock and a mere desire to bring to an end the association is not a sufficient basis for a petition, and that unfairly prejudicial conduct is required, it is difficult to see exactly what this category as envisaged by Lord Hoffmann adds to the preceding categories identified as the basis for petitions, i.e. a breach of the statute or the constitution or a use of legal powers in an inequitable way contrary to the understandings which form the basis of the association. Any of these elements would be the 'something more' required in addition to deadlock,[187] but they would in any event found the court's jurisdiction so rendering this 'category' unnecessary.

**19-70**   The nature of Lord Hoffmann's quasi-frustration category was considered by Mann J in *Re Metropolis Motorcycles Ltd, Hale v Waldock*[188] where he noted that:

> 'Lord Hoffmann was demonstrating that unfairness does not arise only out of a failure to comply with prior agreements or to fulfil prior expectations. The relationships between shareholders are more subtle than that, and Lord Hoffmann was recognising that unfairness can come out of a situation *where the game has moved on* [emphasis added] so as to involve a situation not covered by the previous arrangements and understanding. In those circumstances the conduct of the affairs of the company can be unfairly prejudicial within the section notwithstanding the absence of the prior arrangements, and the court can thus intervene. However, for the court to intervene the change in circumstances must be such that it is not reasonable or fair to require the former association to remain as it was, and such that the court's intervention is required to adjust matters. Lord Hoffmann's words have to be borne in mind: "[circumstances] making it unfair that one shareholder should insist upon the continuance of the association".'[189]

**19-71**   The need for the 'game to have moved on' and the 'quasi-frustration' analogy suggest that the change in circumstances which would bring a case within Lord Hoffmann's category would have to be a change which arose independently of the conduct of either

---

[185] [2006] 2 BCLC 70 at [77]. See also *Re Neath Rugby Ltd, Hawkes v Cuddy* [2009] 2 BCLC 427 at [108]; *Oak Investment Partners XII v Boughtwood* [2010] 2 BCLC 459 at [8], [120] (there the parties were deadlocked but misconduct lay in the respondent's underhand, destructive, and unconstitutional usurping of management power within the company which destroyed the relationship between the quasi-partners); *Re Sunrise Radio Ltd, Kohli v Lit* [2010] 1 BCLC 367 at [32] (no-fault divorce is not available, the failure of trust and confidence must be justified by reference to some unfair conduct on the part of those in control—in this case, an improperly priced rights issue).

[186] [2012] 1 BCLC 410. Deadlock can be seen too in *Shepherd v Williamson* [2010] EWHC 2375, but created by the unfairly prejudicial conduct of the respondent in excluding the petitioner from participation in the management of what was a quasi-partnership.

[187] Examples can be seen in *Re Coloursource Ltd, Dalby v Bodilly* [2005] BCC 627 where the court found the trust and confidence between the parties had been destroyed by the willingness of the majority shareholder to make manipulative allotments of shares (so a breach of the statute) and in *Irvine v Irvine (No 1)* [2007] 1 BCLC 349 where the court found a breach of trust and confidence as a result of excessive remuneration awarded to himself by the majority shareholder.

[188] [2007] 1 BCLC 520.        [189] [2007] 1 BCLC 520 at 560.

party (so there would be no breach of the statute, constitution, or understandings), but which would nevertheless render the continuation of the association unfairly prejudicial. Such cases must be rare and, unsurprisingly, in *Re Metropolis Motorcycles Ltd*[190] the court did not feel that the case fell into this 'quasi-frustration' category. The parties had an understanding that only the majority shareholder would be a director. The minority expected to be able to make monthly drawings from the company on account of profits, but the parties failed to anticipate that circumstances might arise which would prevent the minority having any return on his substantial investment in the company. The company fell into financial difficulties and, while the majority shareholder continued to get a financial return as a director, the company was not in a position to declare a dividend to the minority. The court concluded that that was a failure by the parties to anticipate what had occurred rather than a change in the circumstances requiring court intervention to bring the association to an end. Mann J indicated, however, that it might be appropriate for the minority to come back to court at a later date if the majority did not respond to the changed circumstances and make some provision for a financial return to the minority shareholder.[191] In those circumstances, it would then be open to the minority to rely on the frustration analogy and to argue that circumstances were such that it would be unfair for the majority shareholder to insist upon the continuation of the association on a basis that gave a return to him but none to the minority shareholder. Even on that scenario, that would essentially involve an allegation that understandings as to financial participation had not been met, or perhaps a breach of the duty to act fairly between shareholders, something which would found the s 994 jurisdiction in any event. It seems unlikely that this 'quasi-frustration' category is of great significance, particularly given that the just and equitable winding-up jurisdiction will give relief in cases of deadlock in quasi-partnerships, see at **19-101**.

## A fair offer–striking out the petition

**19-72**    As noted, a petition under CA 2006, s 994 may be brought either on the basis of a breach of the terms on which the affairs of the company should be conducted or use of the rules in an inequitable manner, as per *O'Neill v Phillips*.[192] However, while those are the grounds on which a petition may be based, it is not necessarily the case that the petition can proceed for, in some circumstances, the petition may be struck out by the court. Generally, the court will strike out a petition if an offer has been made to the petitioner (whether as required by the articles or otherwise) that gives the petitioner all the relief that he could realistically expect to obtain on the petition and it would therefore be an abuse to continue with the litigation.[193]

**19-73**    As the usual consequence of a successful petition based on the exclusion of the petitioner is an order that the respondents purchase the shares of the petitioner, tactically, it is important for the respondent to consider answering a legitimate complaint by an excluded minority shareholder with a fair offer. Likewise, an excluded petitioner must be careful not to reject a fair offer, for the court will not allow a petition to proceed in those

---

[190] [2007] 1 BCLC 520.    [191] See [2007] 1 BCLC 520 at [91].    [192] [1999] 2 BCLC 1.
[193] *O'Neill v Phillips* [1999] 2 BCLC 1. See also *Wilkinson v West Coast Capital* [2007] BCC 717 at [329]–[331]. Typically the offer will be to buy out the petitioner, but it need not be, see *Music Sales Ltd v Shapiro Bornstein & Co Inc* [2006] 1 BCLC 371. See also *Re a Company (No 007623 of 1984)* [1986] BCLC 362; *Re a Company (No 004377 of 1986)* [1987] BCLC 94; *Re a Company (No 003843 of 1986)* [1987] BCLC 562; *Re a Company (No 006834 of 1988), ex p Kremer* [1989] BCLC 365; *Re Castleburn Ltd* [1991] BCLC 89; *Re a Company (No 00836 of 1995)* [1996] 2 BCLC 192.

circumstances. In effect, the fair offer/strike-out rule is used to force the parties to the negotiating table. The successful petitioner wants to recover his investment in the business and a fair offer will allow him to do that.

**19-74**    In a quasi-partnership, to be a fair offer, the offer typically has to be an offer to purchase the minority shares on a pro-rata basis, see **19-88**, on a valuation made by an independent valuer.[194] The valuer must be independent and, while this does not automatically rule out the company's auditors, the nature of the auditors' relationship with the majority shareholders and their past involvement in matters which will affect the valuation means that in many instances the court will agree that the petitioner need not accept such a valuation and the petition can continue.[195]

**19-75**    Valuable guidance on what is a fair offer such that generally a petition should be struck out was given, obiter, by Lord Hoffmann in *O'Neill v Phillips*[196] as follows and this now provides the basic benchmark for a fair offer rendering pursuit of the petition an abuse of process:

    'i)   the offer must be to purchase the shares at a fair value;

    ii)   the value, if not agreed, should be determined by a competent expert;

    iii)   the offer should be to have the value determined by the expert as an expert. It is not required that the offer should provide for the full machinery of arbitration or the half-way house of an expert who gives reasons. The objective should be economy and expedition, even if this carries the possibility of a rough edge for one side or the other (and both parties in this respect take the same risk) compared with a more elaborate procedure;

    iv)   the offer should provide for equality of arms between the parties. Both should have the same right of access to information about the company which bears upon the value of the shares and both should have the right to make submissions to the expert; and

    v)   when the offer is made after a lengthy period of litigation, it cannot serve as an independent ground for dismissing the petition, on the assumption that it was otherwise well founded, without an offer of costs. But this does not mean that payment of costs need always be offered. If there is a breakdown in relations between the parties, the majority shareholder should be given a reasonable opportunity to make an offer (which may include time to explore the question of how to raise finance) before he becomes obliged to pay costs.'

**19-76**    An example of an offer which did not justify striking out the petition as an abuse of process can be seen in *North Holdings Ltd v Southern Tropics Ltd*[197] concerning alleged misuse by the respondents of the company's assets and goodwill to develop the business of another company in which they were interested. The court thought that valuation of the petitioner's shares in this case raised serious questions of law (as to the extent of the first company's interest in the second company, given the alleged misuse of the first company's assets) which it was not appropriate to leave to a valuer. The offer was not sufficient therefore to remove any potential unfair prejudice and the petition should not be struck out. In

---

[194] See *Re a Company (No 00836 of 1995)* [1996] 2 BCLC 192.

[195] See *North Holdings Ltd v Southern Tropics Ltd* [1999] 2 BCLC 625 at 639; *Re Rotadata Ltd* [2000] 1 BCLC 122 at 132–3; *Re Benfield Greig Group plc* [2002] 1 BCLC 65, CA; also *Re Belfield Furnishings Ltd, Isaacs v Belfield Furnishings Ltd* [2006] 2 BCLC 705 at [38]–[40].

[196] [1999] 2 BCLC 1 at 16.      [197] [1999] 2 BCLC 625.

*Allmark v Burnham*[198] the purported 'offers' were unsatisfactory on a variety of grounds including an absence of equality of arms between the parties with the respondent, but not the petitioner, being allowed to influence the valuation; an absence of detail on matters such as the fair value to be paid (i.e. whether a minority discount would apply) and the date of valuation and the absence of proper accounts in relation to the company. In *Graham v Every*[199] the Court of Appeal agreed that it was not unreasonable to refuse an offer where the petitioner had not been sent a copy of the valuation report at the time of the offer; he was not able to make any submissions to the valuer before the valuation was completed or to have access to the information which was placed before the valuer; he was not offered his costs; and the valuation did not take into account his allegations about financial mismanagement of the business.

**19-77**  The role of 'O'Neill' offers was considered in detail in *Harborne Road Nominees Ltd v Karvaski*[200] where HHJ David Cooke was anxious to stress that the guidance given by Lord Hoffmann does not have the status of legislation.[201] Lord Hoffmann was not prescribing a system whereby someone is protected from a petition, despite behaving in an unfairly prejudicial manner, provided an offer is then made in the specified form. It would be a cardinal error, the court said, to assume that if an offer complied with the guidance, any petition would inevitably be struck out.[202] Also, HHJ Cooke noted that the guidance was given in the context of a majority shareholder buying out a minority, not in the context of equal shareholders where it is not always clear which of the shareholders should exit from the company.[203] In that situation, it would be unjust, he said, if one of them was able to seize control of the company and then effectively force the other to accept an offer.[204] He noted: 'Lord Hoffmann's remarks were not intended to have the effect of establishing a mechanism for seizure and exclusion.'[205]

**19-78**  The question for the court in all cases is whether it is appropriate to strike out the petition because its continued prosecution is an abuse or bound to fail, which will always be highly sensitive to the facts of each case.[206] In particular, the offer must give the petitioner all that he could reasonably achieve at trial[207] and it may be difficult to determine that this is the case where, for example, the petitioner has had limited access to information about the company and so cannot determine whether the offer reflects the true value of his shares.[208] There is also the difficulty that if the petition alleges wrongdoing, such as a diversion of business or misappropriation of assets, the determination of that claim by the court would have a direct bearing on the value of the shares and would be reflected in any order a court might make, but a valuer would only be able to express an opinion as to the impact of the potential claim on the value of the shares.[209] Often the relief sought is wider than a purchase order[210] and so an offer which is limited to an offer to purchase the

---

[198] [2006] 2 BCLC 437 at [97]–[103]. See also *Re Woven Rugs Ltd* [2010] EWHC 230 (offers made did not provide redress for the dissipation of the company's funds which had been found to be unfairly prejudicial conduct); *Rahman v Malik* [2008] 2 BCLC 403 (offers did not make provision for the under-declaration of profits by the company and unpaid dividends); *Hussain v Cooke* [2009] EWHC 3690 at [74] (offer 'subject to affordability' did not meet the requirements of a fair offer); *Shepherd v Williamson* [2010] EWHC 2375 (various defects in the offers made including no equality of arms, no provision for independent valuation, and deferred consideration, all of which meant, the court said, that these were not 'O'Neill' type offers).

[199] [2015] 1 BCLC 41.      [200] [2012] 2 BCLC 420.      [201] [2012] 2 BCLC 420 at [24].

[202] [2012] 2 BCLC 420 at [26].      [203] [2012] 2 BCLC 420 at [27].      [204] [2012] 2 BCLC 420 at [27].

[205] [2012] 2 BCLC 420 at [27].      [206] [2012] 2 BCLC 420 at [26].      [207] [2012] 2 BCLC 420 at [35].

[208] [2012] 2 BCLC 420 at [31].      [209] [2012] 2 BCLC 420 at [30].

[210] [2012] 2 BCLC 420 at [35]. Often the petition will ask for other matters such as adjustments to directors' loan accounts, or provision to be made for any company property which the petitioner used or may seek to keep, see Joffee et al, *Minority Shareholders* (5th edn, 2015), paras 7.128–7.135.

petitioner's shares would not give the petitioner all the relief which he could reasonably expect to achieve from the proceedings and therefore the petition would not be struck out. On the facts in *Harborne Road Nominees Ltd v Karvaski*,[211] there were a number of factors (a failure to resolve all the disputes between the parties, ambiguity as to whether the company would declare certain dividends, and a lack of information about the company's affairs) which meant that the petitioner might well obtain from the court an offer which would be more advantageous to him in material respects than the offer made and so the court declined to strike out the petition.[212]

**19-79**    In *Harborne Road Nominees Ltd v Karvaski*,[213] the court also considered the situation where the petitioner has refused an offer from the respondent so no offer remains on the table and then the court strikes out the petition as an abuse. HHJ Cooke considered that if a fair offer is made which clearly and finally cures the alleged prejudice and it is rejected, the petitioner cannot complain that he is left without an exit mechanism and has to remain as a minority shareholder in an unhappy situation, for he is not entitled to insist on a standing offer that he can accept at any time.[214] This does not mean that he is forever without a remedy, for subsequent unfairly prejudicial conduct may occur which would allow him to petition again.[215]

## D  Court's power to grant relief

**19-80**    Where the court is satisfied that a petition under CA 2006, s 994 is well founded, it may make such order as it thinks fit for giving relief in respect of the matters complained of (CA 2006, s 996(1)).[216] Without prejudice to the generality of that power, the court's order may (s 996(2)):[217]

'(a)  regulate the conduct of the company's affairs in the future;

(b)  require the company—

　(i)  to refrain from doing or continuing an act complained of, or

　(ii)  to do an act that the petitioner has complained it has omitted to do;

(c)  authorise civil proceedings to be brought in the name and on behalf of the company by such person or persons and on such terms as the court may direct;

(d)  require the company not to make any, or any specified, alterations in its articles without the leave of the court;

---

[211] [2012] 2 BCLC 420.    [212] [2012] 2 BCLC 420 at [40], [43]–[47].    [213] [2012] 2 BCLC 420.
[214] [2012] 2 BCLC 420 at [34].

[215] [2012] 2 BCLC 420 at [34]. Also, where the company is a quasi-partnership, the petitioner may be in a position to petition for a winding up on the just and equitable ground on the basis of the breakdown of the relationship of trust and confidence between the parties, see **19-101**.

[216] The court's power extends to granting relief which the petitioner has not sought or agreed to: *Hawkes v Cuddy* [2009] 2 BCLC 427 at [85]–[91], though in practice all petitions specify the relief sought as well as asking for 'such other order as the court thinks fit'. The making of any order is ultimately a discretionary exercise by the court which in a case where there is unfairly prejudicial conduct by both parties (see, for example, *Re Abbington Hotel Ltd, DiGrado v D'Angelo* [2012] 1 BCLC 410) involves a more complicated balancing exercise as to how to exercise the discretion, see *Oak Investment Partners XII v Boughtwood* [2010] 2 BCLC 459 at [119].

[217] In the exceptional case where a member petitions with respect to the improper removal of an auditor under CA 2006, s 994(1A), see **19-35**, presumably any order would relate to the re-appointment of the original auditors, the appointment of new auditors, or any other remedy which the court deems appropriate. See *Gray v Braid Group (Holdings) Ltd* [2015] CSOH 146, aff'd [2016] CSIH 68.

(e) provide for the purchase of the shares of any members of the company by other members or by the company itself and, in the case of a purchase by the company itself, the reduction of the company's capital accordingly.'

The remedy most commonly sought and obtained is a purchase order requiring the respondents to purchase the petitioner's shares at a fair value which normally requires the shares to be valued as if the wrongdoing had not occurred so ensuring that the shareholder recovers any diminution in the value of his shares caused by the wrongdoing.

**19-81** The courts have consistently taken the view that the wording of CA 2006, s 996 ('such order as the court thinks fit') offers the widest possible discretion to grant relief, including interim relief.[218] In making an order under CA 2006, s 996, the court must consider the whole range of possible remedies[219] and it is not limited merely to reversing or putting right the immediate conduct which justifies the order, but it must also look to cure for the future the unfair prejudice suffered by the petitioner[220] so any likelihood of the conduct recurring is a relevant consideration. In determining what is the appropriate remedy, as Patten J noted in *Grace v Biagioli*,[221] the court is 'entitled to look at the realities and practicalities of the overall situation, past, present and future'.[222] In making an order, the court is not restricted to considering the effect on the members of the company, but can take into account the interests of others and the interests of the creditors will often be relevant, though the weight to be given to interests other than those of the shareholders will depend on the circumstances.[223] The relief ordered must be proportionate to the unfair prejudice which has occurred and while, as discussed later, a purchase order is the usual remedy, in the case of relatively modest unfair prejudicial conduct, that remedy may be disproportionate.[224] In *Corran v Butters*[225] the only unfairly prejudicial conduct established was an improper pension payment of £64,000. The court considered that an

---

[218] See *Pringle v Callard* [2008] 2 BCLC 505, where Arden LJ gives useful guidance on the role of interim remedies in this context; also *Re Ravenhart Service (Holdings) Ltd, Reiner v Gershinson* [2004] 2 BCLC 376.

[219] While a purchase order is the common remedy, it is not the only option. See Briggs J in *Sikorski v Sikorski* [2012] EWHC 1613 at [74]–[75] who noted that other solutions may be possible, as long as that other solution 'does not of itself perpetuate an impossible relationship of joint management, or otherwise risk aggravating an existing dispute'. In this case, a purchase order was not the appropriate remedy, rather the court ordered the majority shareholder to adhere to an agreement reached many years previously as to how the company's business was to be run and the financial rewards divided between the two shareholders, at [76] and [86].

[220] *Re Bird Precision Bellows Ltd* [1985] BCLC 493 at 499–500; *Grace v Biagioli* [2006] 2 BCLC 70. See, for example, *Re Woven Rugs Ltd* [2010] EWHC 230 where in addition to the usual purchase order—the majority to purchase the shares of the minority—the court also ordered the majority to repay a loan made by the minority to the (now insolvent) company on the basis that the majority had procured the repayment of their equivalent loan and the loan was inextricably bound up with the shareholders' membership of the company.

[221] [2006] 2 BCLC 70 at [73].

[222] For example, in *Fowler v Gruber* [2010] 1 BCLC 563, the court rejected the successful petitioner's request that he be appointed managing director of the company. Given the level of disagreement between the parties, the court thought that would be neither sensible nor practical and the court ordered instead that the petitioner's shares be purchased by the respondent.

[223] *Re Neath Rugby Ltd (No 2), Hawkes v Cuddy (No 2)* [2009] 2 BCLC 427 at [84], CA; *Fulham Football Club (1987) Ltd v Richards* [2012] 1 BCLC 335 at [46], CA.

[224] See *VB Football Assets v Blackpool FC (Properties Ltd)* [2017] EWHC 2767 at [425]; *Re Neath Rugby Ltd* [2008] BCC 390 at [246]; *Re Phoenix Office Supplies Ltd* [2003] 1 BCLC 76 at [51]. Also, *Re Pedersen (Thameside) Ltd* [2018] BCC 58 (a petitioner who seeks a disproportionate remedy runs the risk of having the claim struck out—the relief sought was a potential order that the respondent (who held 5 per cent of the shares) should purchase the petitioner's 47.5 per cent shareholding—disproportionate).

[225] [2017] EWHC 2294.

order for the purchase of the petitioner's one-third shareholding would be disproportionate. The appropriate relief was to order the repayment of the pension contribution.

**19-82**    The court may make an order against third parties where they are involved, innocently or knowingly, in the prejudicial conduct.[226] In *F & C Alternative Investments (Holdings) Ltd v Barthelemy*[227] Sales J considered that it is appropriate to order relief against a non-member where '… the defendant in a s 994 claim is so connected to the unfairly prejudicial conduct in question that it would be just, in the context of the statutory regime contained in ss 994 to 996, to grant a remedy against that defendant in relation to that conduct'. Orders against non-members can extend to orders against the parties behind a corporate respondent and, while shareholders in corporate respondents should not be joined to a petition as of right,[228] they may be added if they are sufficiently implicated in the unfairly prejudicial conduct such that relief may be ordered against them. In *Apex Global Management Ltd v Fi Call Ltd*[229] Vos J accepted that persons who were the driving forces behind a corporate respondent could be joined as respondents and he agreed that a purchase order may potentially be made against such persons who can be primarily and secondarily liable to buy the petitioner's shares if they are responsible for the unfairly prejudicial conduct.

**19-83**    Orders may be made for the benefit of the company,[230] but if the only purpose of the petitioner is to secure the payment of a sum of money to the company, the petitioner has to show that he will obtain some real financial benefit from the order which, in exceptional cases, need not benefit the petitioner in his capacity as a member. This point derives from *Gamlestaden Fastigheter AB v Baltic Partners Ltd*[231] where the Privy Council considered the Jersey statutory equivalent[232] of CA 2006, s 996. The petitioners in *Gamlestaden* were minority shareholders in a joint venture company and the essence of their allegation was that the directors had negligently allowed the bulk of the company's assets to be lost rendering it insolvent (allegedly the assets were withdrawn from the business for no consideration by the majority shareholders). The minority shareholder had lent the company DM165.5m and an award of damages payable by the majority shareholders to the company, while it would not restore the company to solvency, would at least offer some prospect for the minority as creditors to recover some of these loans.[233] The respondent

---

[226] See, for example, *Clark v Cutland* [2003] 2 BCLC 393 (order addressed to pension fund trustees—the petition was based on unauthorised payments of company money (£145,000) by a director to his pension fund—the court ordered that the company was entitled to a charge over the pension fund cash reserves to secure the sum of £145,000 (set off by £100,000 owed by the company to the pension fund)). See also *Lowe v Fahey* [1996] 1 BCLC 262 at 268; *Re a Company (No 005287)* [1986] BCLC 68 at 71; *Re Little Olympian Each-Ways Ltd* [1994] 2 BCLC 420 at 429.

[227] [2012] 3 WLR 10 at [1096], though an LLP case, CA 2006, s 994 applies to LLP, with appropriate modifications, see SI 2009/1804, reg 48.

[228] *Re Little Olympian Each-Ways Ltd* [1994] 2 BCLC 420.

[229] [2013] EWHC 1652, [2014] BCC 286 at [125]–[130], [135].

[230] See *Clark v Cutland* [2003] 2 BCLC 393; *Bhullar v Bhullar* [2003] 2 BCLC 241; *Anderson v Hogg* [2002] BCC 923, SC, but these cases should be seen as confined to their exceptional facts, see Hannigan, 'Drawing Boundaries between Derivative Claims and Unfairly Prejudicial Petitions' [2009] JBL 606 at 620–6.

[231] [2008] 1 BCLC 468, PC, noted Walters (2007) 28 Co Law 289; Singla (2007) 123 LQR 542 and discussed in detail in Hannigan, n 230, [2009] JBL 606 at 620–6. See also *Atlasview Ltd v Brightview Ltd* [2004] 2 BCLC 191 at [55].        [232] See Companies (Jersey) Law 1991, art 141.

[233] The loans had been provided by the petitioner's parent company, though procured by the petitioner pursuant to its obligations to do so under the joint venture agreement. Their Lordships agreed with Robert Walker J in *R & H Electric Ltd v Haden Bill Electrical Ltd* [1995] 2 BCLC 280 at 294, where there was a similar arrangement, that this feature should not bar the petitioner from relief, see [2008] 1 BCLC 468 at [38] and discussion at **19-33**, though in *Haden Bill* the company was solvent.

directors unsuccessfully applied to have the petition struck out on the basis that relief had to be of benefit to the petitioner in his capacity as a member rather than for the benefit of the creditors. The Privy Council concluded that, given the width of the jurisdiction to give relief under what is now CA 2006, s 996, exceptionally the court may grant relief though the company is insolvent and will remain insolvent, so long as the petitioner derives some real financial benefit from the petition.[234] The exceptional element in *Gamlestaden* was that the company was a joint venture formed on the basis of an agreement between the joint venturers that the company be funded through share and loan capital. These funding arrangements were so closely connected to the petitioner's membership of the joint venture that if the relief sought was of real value to the joint venturer in recovering some part of his investment then, in their Lordships' opinion, he ought not to be precluded from relief on the ground that it would benefit him as a loan creditor and not as a member.[235] It would be inconsistent with the statutory purpose, Lord Scott said, to limit the availability of remedies to cases where the value of the share or shares held by the petitioner would be enhanced by the value of the relief sought.[236] The application to strike out the petition was denied.

**19-84** This issue of corporate relief on an unfairly prejudicial petition requires further consideration in the light of the statutory derivative claim under CA 2006, Pt 11. Where in essence a petitioner is seeking corporate relief for breach of directors' duties, the petition should be dismissed and the petitioner required instead to seek permission to bring a derivative claim (see Chapter 20), other than in the rare case where the petitioner seeks personal and corporate relief and it is convenient and appropriate to deal with the corporate claim on the petition.[237] In a different but still relevant context (unfairly prejudicial conduct of a company's affairs in administration) Millett J in *Re Charnley Davies Ltd (No 2)*,[238] having commented that it is a matter of perspective, explained that there is a distinction between cases where the unlawfulness of the conduct complained of is the whole gist of the complaint and it may be adequately addressed by the remedy provided by the law for that wrong and cases where the burden is of alleging and proving that the acts or omissions complained of evidence or constitute unfairly prejudicial conduct of the company's affairs and wider relief may be sought. In essence, instances of misconduct should be the subject of a derivative claim under CA 2006, Pt 11 while unfairly prejudicial mismanagement of the company's affairs should be the subject of a petition under CA 2006, s 994.

---

[234] [2008] 1 BCLC 468 at [36]. Their Lordships rejected the argument that, as on a winding-up petition, the petitioner under CA 2006, s 994 needs to show a tangible interest in the winding up (essentially that surplus funds would be available for return to the shareholders) on the basis that the public interest considerations which underlie that requirement in winding up do not apply to unfairly prejudicial petitions: see [2008] 1 BCLC 468 at [32]–[33]. There is little difference between a 'real financial benefit' and a tangible interest, but the tangible interest must accrue to the shareholder as such (*Re Rica Gold Washing Co* (1879) 11 Ch D 36) whereas a real financial benefit can arise more broadly as *Gamlestaden* demonstrates.

[235] [2008] 1 BCLC 468 at [36]–[37].   [236] [2008] 1 BCLC 468 at [33].

[237] For a detailed consideration of the issue of corporate relief on an unfairly prejudicial petition, see Hannigan, 'Drawing Boundaries between Derivative Claims and Unfairly Prejudicial Petitions' [2009] JBL 606. The court can give permission under s 996(2)(c) for a derivative claim to be commenced, but if that is the relief which is sought, it was suggested in *Hughes v Weiss* [2012] EWHC 2363 at [67], that the matter should be more appropriately dealt with under s 260 by an application for permission to bring a derivative claim.

[238] [1990] BCLC 760 at 783. This approach was supported by Lord Scott sitting in the HK Court of Final Appeal in *Re Chime Corp* [2004] HKFCAR 546 at [63], discussed in Hannigan, n 237.

### Purchase orders

**19-85**   As noted, in practice, a petitioner usually requests an order under CA 2006, s 996(2)(e), requiring the respondents to purchase the shares held by the petitioner[239] and, as the Court of Appeal commented in *Grace v Biagioli*,[240] in most cases of unfairly prejudicial conduct nothing less than a clean break between the parties is likely to be required. In this case the respondents consciously and deliberately failed to pay a dividend which had been declared and the available profits were distributed instead as management fees to the respondents. At first instance, the trial judge considered that the appropriate relief was to order the company to pay the petitioner the missing dividend plus interest. On appeal, the Court of Appeal concluded that the judge had erred as to the scope of the discretion to order relief, in particular as to the need to cure the problem for the future. In this case, there was some evidence of changes in trading arrangements which would reduce the profits available to be distributed as dividends, a change which the court noted 'does not bode well for future relations between the parties'.[241] Taking everything into account, the Court of Appeal thought that nothing short of a purchase order would provide appropriate protection for the petitioner.[242] A purchase order, the court said, frees the petitioner from the company and enables him to extract his share of the value of the business and assets in return for forgoing any future right to dividends.[243] It also preserves the company and its business for the benefit of the respondents, free from the petitioner's claims, and removes the possibility of future difficulties between the shareholders.[244]

**19-86**   In *Re Coloursource Ltd, Dalby v Bodilly*[245] the unfairly prejudicial conduct was an improper allotment of shares which had the effect of diluting a 50 per cent shareholder to a 5 per cent shareholder. The respondent argued that the appropriate relief was a reversal of the allotment, rectification of the register of members, and an undertaking by him not to make further allotments of shares. The court refused to limit the relief in that way and granted the purchase order sought by the petitioner. A buy-out order was an entirely appropriate order, the court said, when the respondent had conducted himself in such a way as to forfeit the other shareholder's confidence in the respondent's ability to conduct the company's affairs in a proper way.

**19-87**   Once the court determines that a purchase order is the appropriate relief, it is not required to add to the order an 'escape clause', i.e. an order for alternative relief in the event that the respondent is unable to raise the necessary funds to purchase the shares. That approach was rejected as wrong in principle by the Court of Appeal in *Re Cumana Ltd*[246] for a

---

[239] On occasion, the petitioner asks for and obtains an order entitling him to purchase the respondent's shares at a fair value, see, for example, *Re Abbington Hotel Ltd, DiGrado v D'Angelo* [2012] 1 BCLC 410; *Oak Investment Partners XII v Boughtwood* [2010] 2 BCLC 459 at [123]; *Re Hedgehog Golf Co Ltd, Lantsbury v Hauser* [2010] EWHC 390; *Clark v Cutland* [2003] 2 BCLC 393; *Re Brenfield Squash Racquets Club Ltd* [1996] 2 BCLC 184. Where there is an equality of shareholdings, the court may order the persons responsible for the unfairly prejudicial conduct to sell their shares to the petitioner: see *Re Planet Organic Ltd* [2000] 1 BCLC 366.

[240] [2006] 2 BCLC 70.      [241] [2006] 2 BCLC 70 at [82].

[242] [2006] 2 BCLC 70 at [83]. The court also noted that it would not have been appropriate in any event to order the company, as opposed to the respondents, to pay the missing dividend, see at [86].

[243] [2006] 2 BCLC 70 at [75].      [244] [2006] 2 BCLC 70 at [75].

[245] [2005] BCC 627. See also *Irvine v Irvine (No 1)* [2007] 1 BCLC 349; the unfairly prejudicial conduct was the payment of excessive and unauthorised remuneration, but the court considered that the breakdown in trust between the parties had gone too far to be rectified by an order requiring the respondent to repay the excessive amount and fixing the level of his remuneration as to the future. A purchase order requiring him to purchase the minority's shares was the only appropriate remedy.      [246] [1986] BCLC 430.

purchase order is a reflection of the amount of compensation due to the petitioner for the wrong (the unfairly prejudicial conduct) done to him by the respondent and the fact that the respondent is impecunious is no reason for not giving judgment for the amount due to the victim.[247] For the same reason, it is irrelevant that the shares which the respondent is ordered to buy are worthless, as where the company is in administration, for the payment is compensation to the petitioner for the damage caused by the wrongful conduct.[248]

## Valuation issues

**19-88**  The basic approach to the valuation of the shares to be acquired was established in *Re Bird Precision Bellows Ltd*[249] which has been followed in numerous cases. The key considerations are:

(1) The price fixed by the court must be fair,[250] so the valuation must be adjusted to take into account the unfairly prejudicial conduct, for example, any misappropriation of assets or opportunities or use of company funds by the respondents for their personal benefit, etc which will have had the effect of diminishing the value of the shares.[251] The regular practice of the court is to value the shares 'not as they are, but as they would have been if events had followed a different course',[252] i.e. if the unfairly prejudicial conduct had not occurred.

(2) There is no rule that the shares have to be bought on a pro-rata basis, but nor is there a general rule that they have to be bought on a discounted basis to reflect the fact that they are a minority holding. It all depends on the circumstances of the case.

(3) In general, however, the court would distinguish between two types of shareholding in small private companies: (a) where the holding is in what is essentially a quasi-partnership and the sale is being forced on the holder because of the unfairly prejudicial manner in which the majority have conducted the affairs of the company; and (b) where the company is not a quasi-partnership.

(4) Where the sale is of a holding acquired in what is essentially a quasi-partnership and the sale is being forced on the holder because of the unfairly prejudicial manner in which the majority have conducted the affairs of the company then, as a general rule, the correct course would be to fix the price pro rata according to the value of the shares as a whole and without any discount.

---

[247]  [1986] BCLC 430 at 436–7; *Re Scitec Group Ltd, Sethi v Patel* [2011] 1 BCLC 277 at [34].

[248]  *Re Woven Rugs Ltd* [2010] EWHC 230 at [175]. The company going into administration may itself be suspect, see *Re Scitec Group Ltd, Sethi v Patel* [2011] 1 BCLC 277 where the court was suspicious of the fact that the company's value declined rapidly before going into administration whereupon it was sold, by way of a pre-pack, back to the respondent shareholder; likewise in *Shepherd v Williamson* [2010] EWHC 2375, see at [151]–[152].

[249]  [1984] BCLC 195, aff'd [1985] BCLC 493. Often even when there is agreement that a purchase order is appropriate, there is disagreement over the valuation, see, for example, *Re Southern Counties Fresh Foods Ltd* [2010] EWHC 3334 (Ch) where a purchase order was made in January 2009 and in December 2010 the parties were still arguing without an end in sight, the court said, about the proper valuation method to be adopted.

[250]  For example, the valuation of ordinary shares, where there are also preference shares in the company with a priority to a return of capital on a winding up, should reflect that liquidation preference which is an integral feature of the respective rights of the ordinary and preference shares and likely to have an impact on the valuation of the ordinary shares, but the court might have a discretion to order otherwise in the circumstances of a particular case: *Oak Investment Partners XII v Boughtwood* [2010] 2 BCLC 459 at [129].

[251]  See, for example, *Re Scitec Group Ltd, Sethi v Patel* [2011] 1 BCLC 277; *Croly v Good* [2010] 2 BCLC 569; *Re Little Olympian Each-Ways Ltd (No 3)* [1995] 1 BCLC 636.

[252]  *Profinance Trust SA v Gladstone* [2002] 1 BCLC 141 at [31], per Robert Walker LJ. It is not open to the respondent to argue that the shares are valueless if they are so because of his own conduct, see *Croly v Good* [2010] 2 BCLC 569 at [118].

**19-89**    As already explained, the majority of petitions do relate to quasi-partnerships and therefore the general approach is to require a pro-rata valuation. The offer should be on a pro-rata basis because, as Lord Millett explained in *CVC/Opportunity Equity Partners Ltd v Demarco Almeida*,[253] the matter should be approached as a notional sale of the whole business as a going concern to an outside purchaser.[254] In order to be free to manage the company's business without regard to the relationship of trust and confidence which formerly existed between the parties, the majority must buy the whole business, 'part from themselves and part from the minority, thereby achieving the same freedom to manage the business as an outside purchaser would enjoy'.[255]

**19-90**    Classifying a relationship as a quasi-partnership (see **19-40**) will then have a significant impact on valuation. In *Strahan v Wilcock*[256] it was argued that this general rule (pro-rata valuation in a quasi-partnership) should be set aside. In that case the parties' relationship had developed from one of employer/employee into a quasi-partnership, but the acquisition of shares in the business by the petitioner had also been the subject of commercial option agreements. The question was whether such commercial aspects to the relationship meant that a pro-rata basis should be set aside in favour of a discounted value. The Court of Appeal concluded that the relationship overall was correctly classified as a quasi-partnership when the petitioner's employment, his rights under the option agreements (the terms of which did not suggest a purely commercial relationship), and his participation in the management of the business were all taken into account. Given all the circumstances of the relationship, on the petitioner's exclusion from the management of the company, fairness required that his shares be purchased on a non-discounted basis.

**19-91**    Where the company is not a quasi-partnership, different considerations apply and the price fixed will normally be discounted to reflect the fact that it is a minority holding held essentially as an investment. For example, in *Re Elgindata Ltd*[257] a discounted value was appropriate for the shares had been acquired by the petitioners for investment purposes. In *Re McCarthy Surfacing Ltd, Hequet v McCarthy*[258] the relationships originally were those of quasi-partners but, after previous disputes, the position had reverted to a formal commercial relationship so a purchase order on a discounted basis was appropriate.[259] In *Re Planet Organic Ltd*[260] the purchase order related to preference shareholders and

---

[253] [2002] 2 BCLC 108.

[254] [2002] 2 BCLC 108 at [41]. The analogy, Lord Millett said, is between quasi-partnerships and partnerships and on the dissolution of a partnership the court will direct a sale of the partnership business as a going concern with any former partner who wishes to bid for the business able to do so. The valuation is not based on a notional sale of the outgoing partner's share to the continuing partners who, being the only possible purchasers, would offer relatively little. It is based on a notional sale of the business as a whole to an outside purchaser. In valuing the whole of the share capital for this purpose, it is appropriate to take into account the net borrowings of the company, since a willing purchaser would do so when negotiating the price: *Wann v Birkinshaw* [2017] EWCA Civ 84.

[255] [2002] 2 BCLC 108 at [43], per Lord Millett. See also *Re Annacott Holdings Ltd, Attwood v Maidment* [2013] 2 BCLC 46 at [11]; there is no inflexible rule that only in a quasi-partnership case can the court order a valuation on a going concern basis, per Arden LJ.

[256] [2006] 2 BCLC 555, CA.    [257] [1991] BCLC 959.    [258] [2009] 1 BCLC 622.

[259] See also *Fowler v Gruber* [2010] 1 BCLC 563 (company started as a quasi-partnership, but became a commercial relationship when the petitioner sold part of his shares and a local authority became a shareholder—discounted value appropriate); *Re a Company (No 005134 of 1986), ex p Harries* [1989] BCLC 383 (company started as a quasi-partnership but had reverted to a more commercial footing when the petitioner withdrew from the business—discounted value appropriate).    [260] [2000] 1 BCLC 366.

the court concluded that, as they were investors rather than active participants in the running of the company, they should be bought out at a discount. A discounted valuation applies, even if the minority holding is substantial, as in *Irvine v Irvine (No 2)*.[261] In that case, the petitioners tried to persuade the court that their 49.96 per cent shareholding was so substantial that the holding should be valued on a pro-rata, non-discounted basis, though the company was not a quasi-partnership. The court rejected their claim and ruled that a minority shareholding, even where the extent of the minority is slight, is to be valued as a minority shareholding unless a good reason exists (i.e. that the company is a quasi-partnership or some other exceptional circumstance) to attribute to it a pro-rata share of the overall value of the company. In this case, the company was not a quasi-partnership and there was no good reason or exceptional circumstance to order anything other than a discounted valuation. Indeed, in *Strahan v Wilcock*,[262] Arden LJ considered it difficult to conceive of circumstances in which a pro-rata valuation would be appropriate where there was no quasi-partnership relationship.

**19-92** An example can be found, however, in *Re Sunrise Radio Ltd, Kohli v Lit*[263] where the court did order a pro-rata valuation though the company was not a quasi-partnership, noting that there is no inflexible rule of universal application excluding a pro-rata valuation.[264] The unfairly prejudicial conduct in this case (see **19-55**) essentially involved improper allotments of shares at par (when a significant premium might have been obtained) which diluted both the petitioner's shareholding in the company and the value of her shares. In the circumstances, the court thought that there were a variety of reasons why a pro-rata value was appropriate.[265] First, the petitioner was an original shareholder who did not obtain her shares at a discounted value and she was not a willing seller, rather her exit was occasioned by the unfairly prejudicial conduct of the respondents. Secondly, the company had not declared dividends as the strategy was to look for capital growth and, though not in itself a ground for complaint,[266] it was unfair that she would be deprived of any part of the fruits of that capital growth. Thirdly, a solvent winding up of the company would have been open to her on the just and equitable ground (see **19-95**) whereby she would have received a rateable proportion of the realised assets. The court saw no reason why she should be in a worse position under a s 994 petition than she would be under a winding-up petition,[267] given that her choice of remedy kept the company alive for the benefit of the remaining shareholders. Fourthly, the court considered that the particular value of the shares to the respondents might be a very material factor.[268] The company was very successful and was likely to be floated on the stock exchange in the near future, something which the petitioner would have benefited from, had the unfairly prejudicial conduct of the respondents not made her into an unwilling seller of her shares. There was a risk that the respondents would end up unjustly enriched by the acquisition of her shares which had been triggered by their wrongful conduct which was especially unjust if there was reason to suspect that their conduct was influenced by a desire to buy out or worsen the position of the minority.[269] The first three reasons given by the court seem insufficiently compelling to justify a pro-rata valuation and they would be present in many cases so, if they are the determining factors, then the categories of petitioner entitled to a pro-rata valuation would be greatly expanded. The fourth factor, however, appears to be a

---

[261] [2007] 1 BCLC 445.      [262] [2006] 2 BCLC 555 at 561, CA.      [263] [2010] 1 BCLC 367.
[264] [2010] 1 BCLC 367 at [291]–[297].
[265] The reasons are summarised in [2010] 1 BCLC 367 at [308].
[266] See [2010] 1 BCLC 367 at [136]–[142].      [267] [2010] 1 BCLC 367 at [301].
[268] [2010] 1 BCLC 367 at [305].      [269] [2010] 1 BCLC 367 at [305].

genuinely exceptional element which merits a pro-rata valuation though the company was not a quasi-partnership. Exceptionally, fairness did require a different outcome in this case from the normal discount and fairness, as noted in *Re Bird Precision Bellows Ltd*,[270] is the key objective in valuing the shares.

**19-93**    In addition to disputes as to the basis of valuation, it is common for there also to be disagreements as to the appropriate date for valuation for this may have a significant bearing on the outcome. The starting point is that the shares should be valued at the date of the court's order for purchase, as that is the time when the unfairly prejudicial conduct is brought to an end, and an interest in a going concern should be valued at the date when it is ordered to be sold.[271] As the overriding criterion is fairness, in the circumstances of a particular case, fairness may require that the valuation be directed to take place at an earlier date,[272] such as the date of the petition,[273] or the date of improper exclusion from participation in the management of the company if exclusion has been established.[274] In relation to the latter possibility, the court is particularly so disposed to value the shares as at the date of exclusion if, as in *Croly v Good*,[275] the value of the company declines significantly after the exclusion in circumstances which raise suspicions as to how that decline has occurred. A feature of a number of cases is that, by the time of the judgment, the company is in administration, sometimes dubiously so.[276] The fact that the company is in administration is not a bar to making a purchase order, but it does suggest that the valuation date should not be the date of the order.[277] It is possible for the court exceptionally to award interest to the petitioner.[278]

## E  Relationship with other shareholder remedies—winding up on the just and equitable ground

**19-94**    The range of conduct covered and the flexibility of the relief offered means that petitioning for relief under CA 2006, s 994 is almost invariably the most attractive solution for an

---

[270] [1984] BCLC 195, aff'd [1985] BCLC 493.

[271] *Profinance Trust SA v Gladstone* [2002] 1 BCLC 141.

[272] Guidance as to the circumstances in which an earlier valuation might be called for was given by the Court of Appeal in *Profinance Trust SA v Gladstone* [2002] 1 BCLC 141. In determining the date, the Court of Appeal emphasised that the date of valuation may be heavily influenced by the parties' conduct in making and accepting or rejecting 'O'Neill offers' (see **19-72**) either before or during the course of the proceedings. In *Re Scitec Group Ltd, Sethi v Patel* [2011] 1 BCLC 277 the petitioner chose the (earlier) date of his resignation from the company which then worked to his disadvantage when his shares would possibly have been given a higher value at the date of the court order, see at [42].

[273] See, for example, *Re C&F Booth Ltd, Booth v Booth* [2017] EWHC 457.

[274] See *Pinfold v Ansell* [2017] 2 BCLC 489. In this case, the appropriate valuation date was the date of the petitioner's exclusion from the company since thereafter he was subject to a commercial strategy over which he had no input or influence. He had no exit route for no reasonable offer had been made to purchase his shares. See also *Re BC & G Care Homes Ltd* [2016] BCC 615.

[275] [2010] 2 BCLC 569 at [113], [117].

[276] See also *Shepherd v Williamson* [2010] EWHC 2375 (significant decline in value of the company after the petitioner's exclusion followed by the company being placed into administration and sold by way of a pre-pack to persons connected with the original company and therefore with the respondent—the court ordered that the valuation date should be the date of exclusion).

[277] See, for example, *Re Woven Rugs Ltd* [2010] EWHC 230 at [173] (company in administration—earlier date appropriate, a date which preceded the damaging conduct and dissipation of company funds by the majority shareholder); also *Re Cabot Global Ltd* [2016] EWHC 2287.

[278] *Profinance Trust SA v Gladstone* [2002] 1 BCLC 141; *Re Annacott Holdings Ltd, Attwood v Maidment* [2013] 2 BCLC 46.

aggrieved shareholder, but there are other options available, including various statutory rights under the CA 2006, see **20-84**, which may be relevant in some circumstances, and it may be possible to obtain permission to bring a derivative claim on behalf of the company (discussed in Chapter 20). Another option is for a member to petition under IA 1986, s 122(1)(g) for a winding-up order on the just and equitable ground,[279] a provision which has traditionally provided the court with a wide discretionary jurisdiction.[280]

## Winding up on the just and equitable ground

**19-95**    In addition to petitioning for relief under CA 2006, s 994, a petitioner may petition in the alternative for a winding-up order on the just and equitable ground under IA 1986, s 122(1)(g), there being no power to make a winding-up order under CA 2006, s 996. The effect of petitioning under the winding-up jurisdiction is to oblige the company to seek a validation order[281] under IA 1986, s 127 which otherwise avoids dispositions of company property made after the commencement of the winding up (i.e. after the presentation of the petition). The requirement of a validation order under IA 1986, s 127 means that presenting a winding-up petition alongside the unfairly prejudicial petition maximises the pressure that the petitioner can bring to bear on the respondents. The courts are alert to the oppressive possibilities of this tactic, however, and a Practice Direction makes clear that a petitioner should not seek relief under CA 2006, s 994 and winding up unless winding up is the relief which the petitioner prefers or it is thought that it may be the only relief to which he is entitled.[282] In practice, it is unlikely that a petitioner does want a winding-up order. As discussed, the successful petitioner is able under CA 2006, s 996 to obtain a purchase order and exit the company and has no reason to pursue a winding-up order. Moreover, the very availability of relief under s 994 means that the court may refuse to exercise its discretion to make a winding-up order: see IA 1986, s 125(2), discussed at **19-98**. Having said that, there may be circumstances, such as deadlock, in which a claim cannot be brought within CA 2006, s 994 (see **19-68**), but would fall within the just and equitable winding-up jurisdiction. Equally, misconduct by an individual director may not amount to the conduct of the company's affairs in an unfairly prejudicial manner,[283] but may amount to a lack of probity which merits a winding up on the just and equitable ground, see **19-101**. It is possible therefore that the claim for a winding-up order will be instead of or additional to a claim under s 994. We turn therefore to consider the extent of that jurisdiction.

### Procedural matters

**19-96**    An application to the court for a winding-up order may be made by a contributory,[284] defined as every person liable to contribute to the assets of a company in the event of its being wound up.[285] For example, a partly paid-up shareholder who remains liable to

---

[279]  Various other parties (including the directors and creditors) may also petition for a winding up: see **24-28**. Here we deal only with petitioning shareholders.

[280]  See *Re Yenidje Tobacco Co* [1916] 2 Ch 426; *Loch v John Blackwood Ltd* [1924] AC 783; *Ebrahimi v Westbourne Galleries Ltd* [1972] 2 All ER 492; *Re Zinotty Properties Ltd* [1984] 3 All ER 754; *Re A & BC Chewing Gum Ltd* [1975] 1 All ER 1017.

[281]  A validation order permits the company to make dispositions of its property after the commencement of the winding up.

[282]  See CPR, PD 49B which contains a standard form IA 1986, s 127 validation order.

[283]  See *Re Charnley Davies Ltd (No 2)* [1990] BCLC 760 at 783.      [284]  IA 1986, s 124(1).

[285]  IA 1986, s 79(1); every present and past member is included in the definition: s 74(1). In the case of a company limited by shares, no contribution is required from any member exceeding the amount (if any) unpaid on the shares in respect of which he is a liable as a present or past member: s 74(2)(d).

contribute the amount unpaid on his shares in the event of the company being wound up is a contributory, but it is rare now for shareholders to be partly-paid. A fully paid-up member must establish that he has a tangible interest in the winding up, defined as a *prima facie* probability of surplus assets remaining after the creditors have been paid for distribution amongst the shareholders.[286] In other words, in an insolvent company, a fully paid-up member has no *locus standi* to seek a winding up. A further condition is that a contributory is not entitled to present a winding-up petition unless the number of members is reduced below two or the shares held by him, or some of them, either were originally allotted to him, or have been held by him and registered in his name for at least six months during the 18 months before the commencement of the winding up, or have devolved on him through the death of a former holder.[287]

**19-97**    A petitioner seeking a winding-up order on the just and equitable ground must come with clean hands.[288] If the breakdown in the conduct of the company's affairs is a result of the petitioner's own misconduct,[289] or the petitioner has acquiesced in the conduct of which he now complains,[290] the court will refuse the application. If the petitioner can establish sufficient grounds for petitioning, however, the fact that he also has an ulterior, perhaps personal, motive for pursuing the matter does not render those grounds insufficient.[291]

**19-98**    The court has a discretion under IA 1986, s 125(2) to refuse to make a winding-up order where there is some alternative remedy available to the petitioner and he is acting unreasonably in seeking to have the company wound up instead of pursuing that other remedy. An obvious alternative remedy is the ability to petition for relief on the unfairly prejudicial ground under CA 2006, s 994. In *Re a company (No 001363 of 1988), ex p S-P*[292] the court accepted that the availability of relief, possibly wider relief, under the unfairly prejudicial remedy does not of itself make it plainly unreasonable to seek a winding-up order so as to justify striking out the petition. However, winding up is a remedy of last resort and, given the width of the jurisdiction under CA 2006, s 994, generally the courts would expect a petitioner to seek alternative relief under the unfairly prejudicial jurisdiction.[293]

**19-99**    Another option which may be open to the aggrieved shareholder is to exit from the company by selling his shares via a purchase mechanism provided by the articles of association or pursuant to an offer to acquire his shares made by the other shareholders. The courts initially took quite a strict line and regarded a refusal to use such mechanisms as unreasonable and grounds for striking out the winding-up petition.[294] This approach was somewhat harsh, given that in many instances the mechanism in the articles or offer requires the petitioner to accept a valuation of his shares as determined by the company's auditor.

---

[286] *Re Rica Gold Washing Co* (1879) 11 Ch D 36; *Re Expanded Plugs Ltd* [1966] 1 All ER 877; *Re Othery Construction Ltd* [1966] 1 WLR 69; *Re Bellador Silk Ltd* [1965] 1 All ER 667. See also *Re Chesterfield Catering Co Ltd* [1976] 3 All ER 294 at 299 where Oliver J suggested that 'tangible interest' is not limited to surplus assets but could cover where, as a member of the company, the shareholder will achieve some advantage or avoid or minimise some disadvantage which would accrue to him by virtue of his membership of the company.

[287] IA 1986, s 124(2) and subject to sub-s (3), and see **24-29**.

[288] *Ebrahimi v Westbourne Galleries Ltd* [1972] 2 All ER 492 at 507, per Lord Cross.

[289] *Ebrahimi v Westbourne Galleries Ltd* [1972] 2 All ER 492 at 507, per Lord Cross.

[290] *Re Fildes Bros Ltd* [1970] 1 All ER 923.    [291] *Bryanston Finance Ltd v De Vries* [1976] 1 All ER 25.

[292] [1989] BCLC 579.

[293] See, for example, *Re a Company (No 004415 of 1996)* [1997] 1 BCLC 479.

[294] See *Re a Company (No 002567 of 1982)* [1983] 2 All ER 854; *Re a Company (No 004377 of 1986)* [1987] BCLC 94 at 103; *Re a Company (No 003843 of 1986)* [1987] BCLC 562; *Re a Company (No 003096 of 1987)* (1988) 4 BCC 80; *Re a Company (No 005685 of 1988), ex p Schwarcz (No 2)* [1989] BCLC 427 at 452.

Petitioners often feel that such valuations are arbitrary and biased in favour of the majority shareholder, hence their preference for obtaining a winding-up order from the court.

**19-100** The strict position altered with the decision in *Virdi v Abbey Leisure Ltd*[295] which established that there is no hard-and-fast rule that a petitioner who declines to utilise an exit mechanism in the articles or to accept an offer to acquire his shares is necessarily acting unreasonably in pursuing a winding-up order.[296] It depends on the fairness of the purchase mechanism and in *Virdi* the Court of Appeal found that the petitioner's refusal to use the mechanism was not unreasonable, given that the value of his shares might be discounted under that scheme though on the facts a discount was inappropriate.[297] But where a fair offer is available,[298] a petitioner will be acting unreasonably in seeking to have the company wound up rather than pursuing that alternative: he is not entitled to his day or month in court.[299]

## Grounds for the petition

**19-101** The courts have been reluctant to limit the just and equitable jurisdiction by categorising the grounds on which a petition might be brought but certain recognised (and overlapping) categories have developed over the years which centre on quasi-partnerships (see **19-106**, though the jurisdiction is not limited to quasi-partnerships) and on the breakdown in relations between the parties and/or a lack of probity in the conduct of the company's affairs.[300] In *Re Yenidje Tobacco Co Ltd*[301] the relationship between the two shareholders (who were also the directors) had completely broken down. They refused to talk to one another and all communications were through a third party. The court found that the company was in essence a partnership and that there was such a state of animosity between the parties as to preclude all reasonable hope of reconciliation or friendly cooperation.[302] In such circumstances, it is just and equitable that the company be wound up. But the jurisdiction is not limited to situations of deadlock[303] and in looking at a lack of probity in the conduct of the company's affairs, the court looks for conduct 'which substantially impairs those rights and protections to which shareholders, both under statute and contract, are entitled'.[304] In *Loch v John Blackwood Ltd*[305] the directors failed to hold general meetings or submit accounts or recommend a dividend. Instead the majority shareholder treated the business as if it was his own business and ran it down with a view to forcing the minority shareholder to sell out at an undervalue. Though the

---

[295] [1990] BCLC 342, CA.

[296] See *Re a Company (No 00330 of 1991), ex p Holden* [1991] BCLC 597 at 604.

[297] [1990] BCLC 342 at 349. See also *Re a Company (No 001363 of 1988), ex p S-P* [1989] BCLC 579 where the petitioner's refusal to accept an offer for his shares under the articles was not unreasonable when there was a dispute as to the number of shares to which he was actually entitled.

[298] The guidance as to what is a fair offer provided in *O'Neill v Phillips* [1999] 2 BCLC 1 at 16–17, see **19-72**, will be influential on this point.

[299] See *Fuller v Cyracuse Ltd* [2001] 1 BCLC 187 at 193.

[300] See Chesterman, 'The Just and Equitable Winding Up of Small Private Companies' (1973) 36 MLR 129; Prentice, 'Winding Up on the Just and Equitable Ground' (1973) 89 LQR 107.

[301] [1916] 2 Ch 426. See also *Symington v Symington Quarries Ltd* 1906 SC 121; *Re Davis and Collett Ltd* [1935] Ch 693; *Re Wondoflex Textiles Pty Ltd* [1951] VLR 458; *Re Worldhams Park Golf Course Ltd, Re Whidbourne v Troth* [1998] 1 BCLC 554; *Jesner v Jarrad Properties Ltd* [1993] BCLC 1032; *Langley Ward Ltd v Trevor* [2011] EWHC 1893 at [15].

[302] [1916] 2 Ch 426 at 430, per Cozens Hardy MR.

[303] See *Ebrahimi v Westbourne Galleries Ltd* [1972] AC 360 at 376.

[304] *Loch v John Blackwood Ltd* [1924] AC 783 at 788, per Lord Shaw.   [305] [1924] AC 783.

company was not deadlocked, the lack of probity in the conduct of the company's affairs merited a winding-up order.[306]

**19-102**     It was also possible to get a winding-up order if it was or became impossible or illegal to achieve the main objectives for which a company was formed.[307] These loss of substratum cases, as they were known, became less relevant as modern drafting techniques ensured that companies had many and varied objects such that loss of substratum was rarely an issue. Now, companies formed under the CA 2006 have unrestricted objects unless the parties choose to restrict them (see s 31).

### The modern jurisdiction

**19-103**     The landmark modern authority on the just and equitable jurisdiction is the decision of the House of Lords in *Ebrahimi v Westbourne Galleries Ltd*[308] which established that, where a company has the characteristics of a quasi-partnership, as described by Lord Wilberforce, see **19-106**, the court may subject the exercise of legal rights to equitable considerations, i.e. considerations of a personal character arising between one individual and another which may make it unjust or inequitable to insist on strict legal rights or to exercise them in a particular way. It may therefore be just and equitable to wind up a company where the majority have acted in disregard of those equitable considerations.

**19-104**     In this instance, two shareholders (E and N) had formed a company which operated on a quasi-partnership basis including an understanding that both would be involved in the management of the company. N's son later joined the company. The majority shareholders (N and his son) were not entitled in those circumstances subsequently to exercise their undoubted legal power to remove the minority shareholder (E) as a director and, having done so, the House of Lords concluded that the only just and equitable course was to dissolve the association and to grant E a winding-up order under IA 1986, s 122(1)(g).

**19-105**     The House of Lords found that, as a matter of law, the majority shareholders had acted completely within their rights, within the provisions of the articles, and the Companies Act in removing E as a director. But the just and equitable jurisdiction was not limited to proven cases of mala fides and the legal correctness of their conduct did not make it unassailable.

**19-106**     The words 'just and equitable' were:

'a recognition of the fact that a limited company is more than a mere judicial entity, with a personality in law of its own: that there is room in company law for recognition of the fact that behind it, or amongst it, there are individuals, with rights, expectations and obligations inter se which are not necessarily submerged in the company structure. That structure is defined by the Companies Act 1948 and by the articles of association by which shareholders agree to be bound. In most companies and in most contexts, this definition is sufficient and exhaustive, equally so whether the company is large or small. The "just and equitable" provision does not, as the respondents suggest, entitle one party to disregard the obligation he assumes by entering a company, nor the court to dispense him from it. It

---

[306] See also *Re Worldhams Park Golf Course Ltd, Whidbourne v Troth* [1998] 1 BCLC 554; see *Re Sunrise Radio Ltd, Kohli v Lit* [2010] 1 BCLC 367 at [308] (lack of probity indicated by improper allotments of shares would have merited a winding-up order); see also *Re Internet Investment Corporation Ltd* [2010] 1 BCLC 458.

[307] The doctrine originated in *Re Suburban Hotel Co* (1867) 2 Ch App 737. See also *Re Haven Gold Mining Co* (1882) 20 Ch D 151; *Re German Date Coffee Co* (1882) 20 Ch D 169; *Re Red Rock Gold Mining Co Ltd* (1889) 61 LT 785; *Re Baku Consolidated Oilfields Ltd* [1944] 1 All ER 24; *Re Kitson & Co Ltd* [1946] 1 All ER 435.

[308] [1972] 2 All ER 492, HL.

does, as equity always does, enable the court to subject the exercise of legal rights to equitable considerations; considerations, that is, of a personal character arising between one individual and another, which may make it unjust, or inequitable, to insist on legal rights, or to exercise them in a particular way.'[309]

As to when these equitable considerations will arise, Lord Wilberforce noted:

'Certainly the fact that a company is a small one, or a private company, is not enough. There are very many of these where the association is a purely commercial one, of which it can safely be said that the basis of association is adequately and exhaustively laid down in the articles. The superimposition of equitable considerations requires something more, which typically may include one, or probably more, of the following elements: (i) an association formed or continued on the basis of a personal relationship, involving mutual confidence—this element will often be found where a pre-existing partnership has been converted into a limited company; (ii) an agreement, or understanding, that all, or some (for there may be "sleeping" members), of the shareholders shall participate in the conduct of the business; (iii) restriction on the transfer of the members' interest in the company— so that if confidence is lost, or one member is removed from management, he cannot take out his stake and go elsewhere. It is these, and analogous, factors which may bring into play the just and equitable clause, and they do so directly, through the force of the words themselves.'[310]

Lord Wilberforce went on to note that such companies are commonly, if confusingly, called quasi-partnerships, a term which must not obscure the fact that the parties are members in a company.[311]

**19-107**    It has already been noted that this judgment in *Ebrahimi* plays a key role in determining the scope of the unfairly prejudicial jurisdiction, as Lord Hoffmann acknowledged in *O'Neill v Phillips*,[312] see **19-40**. The question is whether there is any role left to be played by the winding-up remedy, given the availability of relief under s 994. The Court of Appeal made clear in *Hawkes v Cuddy*[313] that the winding-up jurisdiction remains an important shareholder remedy in its own right and there are cases where it will be the more appropriate remedy, and possibly the only remedy, available to a shareholder.[314] A situation where relief will be available under IA 1986, s 122(1)(g), but not under the unfairly prejudicial jurisdiction, is where there is deadlock between the parties involving a breakdown in mutual trust (such as *Re Yenidje Ltd*,[315] see **19-101**) where winding up is warranted but where there is no objective unfairness to support a petition under CA 2006, s 994, see **19-68**.

---

[309] [1972] 2 All ER 492 at 500.

[310] [1972] 2 All ER 492 at 500. See also *CVC/Opportunity Equity Partners Ltd v Demarco Almeida* [2002] 2 BCLC 108 at 117.

[311] [1972] 2 All ER 492 at 500. Though Lord Wilberforce cautioned against the use of that term, it has entered common parlance, especially as noted earlier in this chapter in the context of the unfairly prejudicial jurisdiction, and it is too late now to limit its use.    [312] [1999] 2 BCLC 1.

[313] [2009] 2 BCLC 427, overruling a controversial decision by Jonathan Parker J in *Re Guidezone Ltd* [2000] 2 BCLC 321 to the effect that the jurisdiction under IA 1986, s 122(1)(g) was, at the very least, no wider than CA 2006, s 994. The decision was much criticised as a unnecessary conflation of the two jurisdictions, not required by anything said by Lord Hoffmann in *O'Neill v Phillips*, see Boyle, *Minority Shareholders' Remedies* (2002), pp 96–100; Acton, 'Just and Equitable Winding up: The Strange Case of the Disappearing Jurisdiction' (2001) 22 Co Lawyer 134.

[314] As was pointed out in *Re Sunrise Radio Ltd, Kohli v Lit* [2010] 1 BCLC 387 at [303], a winding-up order will often be at break-up value and therefore will not necessarily be advantageous to the petitioning shareholder though it produces a pro-rata distribution of the realised assets for all shareholders.

[315] [1916] 2 Ch 426.

Equally, there may be cases of misconduct which will amount to a breach of probity within the *Lock v John Blackwood*[316] category, see **19-101**, but which do not amount to a carrying on of the company's affairs in an unfairly prejudicial manner. Clearly, winding up on the just and equitable ground remains an option and it may be the desired remedy, depending on the particular circumstances.[317]

### A derivative claim

**19-108**   As is evident from the authorities discussed in this chapter, breaches of directors' duties are classic examples of conduct of the company's affairs in a manner which is unfairly prejudicial to the interests of members generally[318] and therefore within the unfairly prejudicial jurisdiction. But such breaches are primarily wrongs done to the company, of course, in respect of which the company may sue or a derivative claim may lie under CA 2006, Pt 11. Where the derivative claim and the petition raise substantially the same issues, the court may want to look at what is the whole gist of the complaint and the relief sought before determining which proceedings would be most appropriate,[319] see **19-84**. The mere fact that the conduct would merit a derivative claim is not a reason to strike out the petition;[320] equally if a petition would give the petitioner all the relief which he is seeking, the court is likely to refuse permission to continue a derivative claim.[321] If the only substantive relief sought on the petition is a claim on behalf of the company against a third party, however, the court will not necessarily allow the claimant to proceed by petition instead of by derivative claim.[322] The advantage of proceeding by way of a petition under CA 2006, s 994 is that it avoids the procedural obstacles surrounding the derivative claim which require a claimant to obtain the permission of the court to continue the claim. A petition also secures a personal remedy for the petitioner rather than a remedy for the company, as is the case with a derivative claim. On the other hand, a derivative claim may be attractive where the shareholder does not wish to have his shares purchased by the respondents, but wants a remedy for misconduct and the recovery of assets belonging to the company[323] and he wishes to take advantage of the indemnity for costs which is possibly available with respect to a derivative claim.[324]

---

[316]   [1924] AC 783.

[317]   The Singapore Companies Act, s 254(2A) allows the court on a petition for winding up on the just and equitable ground to order the interests in shares of one or more members to be purchased by the company or one or more other members on terms to the satisfaction of the court: see Koh and Tang, 'Towards a "Just and Equitable" Remedy for Companies' (2017) 133 LQR 372.

[318]   See *Atlasview Ltd v Brightview Ltd* [2004] 2 BCLC 191 at [61].

[319]   See *Cooke v Cooke* [1997] 2 BCLC 28; see also *Clark v Cutland* [2003] 2 BCLC 393 at [2], [8].

[320]   See *Re a Company (No 005287)* [1986] BCLC 68; *Lowe v Fahey* [1996] 1 BCLC 262; *Re Little Olympian Each-Ways Ltd (No 3)* [1995] 1 BCLC 636 at 665.

[321]   See *Kleanthous v Paphitis* [2012] BCC 676 (permission refused: evidence suggested that the remedy that the applicant really wanted was to be bought out and he was pursuing the derivative claim because of the availability of a costs indemnity); also *Mission Capital plc v Sinclair* [2010] 1 BCLC 304 (permission refused: the court did not consider that the claimants were seeking anything which could not be recovered by means of an unfair prejudice petition); *Franbar Holdings Ltd v Patel* [2009] 1 BCLC 1 (permission refused: claims by the member for breach of a shareholders' agreement as well as under CA 2006, s 994 should give the applicant all the relief sought).

[322]   *Lowe v Fahey* [1996] 1 BCLC 262.

[323]   See, for example, *Wishart v Castlecroft Securities Ltd* [2009] CSIH 615, [2009] SLT 812, see **20-63**.

[324]   There was some blurring of the lines on this issue in *Clark v Cutland* [2003] 2 BCLC 393 at [35] where it was accepted that where, exceptionally, corporate relief is ordered on a petition, the petitioner is entitled to an indemnity for costs.

# 20

# The derivative claim and the rule in *Foss v Harbottle*

## A Corporate claims for wrongs done to the company

### The rule in *Foss v Harbottle*

**20-1**  At common law shareholders' remedies are dominated by the rule in *Foss v Harbottle*[1] which has two elements: first, the proper plaintiff in respect of a wrong allegedly done to a company is *prima facie* the company; secondly, where the alleged wrong is a transaction which might be made binding on the company by a simple majority of the members, no individual member of the company is allowed to bring a claim in respect of it.[2] As Mellish LJ explained in *MacDougall v Gardiner*:[3] '... if the thing complained of is a thing which in substance the majority of the company are entitled to do ... there can be no use in having a litigation about it, the ultimate end of which is only that a meeting has to be called, and then ultimately the majority gets its wishes'. In *Foss v Harbottle*[4] the court refused to permit two shareholders to bring an action on behalf of the company against the directors and promoters who had allegedly sold property to the company at an inflated value. On the facts, the court was not convinced that there was anything to prevent the company suing in its own name and in its corporate character. In those circumstances, it was not open to individual members to assume to themselves the right of suing in the name of the company. The company was the proper person to sue and while the court acknowledged that the rule could be departed from, it should not be, save for very urgent reasons. Moreover, the alleged transactions were matters which the court considered might be decided by the majority of the shareholders who might elect to adopt them and so render any litigation pointless.

**20-2**  The rule is based then on two fundamental principles of company law, namely respect for the separate legal personality of the company and the principle of majority rule. In addition to reflecting those fundamental principles, the rule has certain practical advantages. It is convenient and efficient that the company should sue in respect of a wrong done to it rather than have a multiplicity of shareholder suits. It eliminates wasteful litigation where the only outcome can be that the majority pass a resolution approving the 'wrongdoing'. It prevents vexatious actions started by troublesome shareholders trying to harass the company. It ensures a process that is for the collective benefit of the shareholders and, where there is any issue as to the solvency of the company, the creditors.

---

[1] (1843) 2 Hare 461.

[2] Classic statements of the rule can be found at *Prudential Assurance Co Ltd v Newman Industries Ltd (No 2)* [1982] 1 All ER 354 at 357–8, CA citing from *Edwards v Halliwell* [1950] 2 All ER 1064 at 1066–7, per Jenkins LJ.

[3] (1875) 1 Ch D 13 at 25.     [4] (1843) 2 Hare 461.

## B The common law derivative claim

**20-3**  Where the wrong done to the company has been committed by a third party, the directors in the exercise of their management powers will decide whether the company should sue.[5] This is not a matter which is within the remit of the shareholders, at least where the company's articles include the standard delegation of all powers of management to the board.[6]

**20-4**  Where the wrong is committed by those in control of the company, it is inappropriate that the first element of the rule in *Foss v Harbottle* (that the company is the proper plaintiff) should prevent an action in respect of that wrongdoing (because the wrongdoer in control will ensure that the company does not claim). Hence the development of an exception to the rule whereby, in limited circumstances consistent with respect for the second element of the rule, a shareholder may sue derivatively, i.e. on behalf of the company to obtain a remedy *for the company*. The circumstances meriting a derivative claim were explained as follows in *Burland v Earle*:[7]

> 'The cases in which the minority can maintain such an action are, therefore, confined to those in which the acts complained of are of a fraudulent character[8] or beyond the powers of the company. A familiar example is where the majority are endeavouring directly or indirectly to appropriate to themselves money, property, or advantages which belong to the company, or in which the other shareholders are entitled to participate, as was alleged in the case of *Menier v. Hooper's Telegraph Works*.[9] It should be added that no mere informality or irregularity which can be remedied by the majority will entitle the minority to sue, if the act when done regularly would be within the powers of the company and the intention of the majority of the shareholders is clear.'

**20-5**  The governing principles at common law, as stated by the Court of Appeal in *Prudential Assurance Co Ltd v Newman Industries Ltd (No 2)*,[10] are that the claimant in a derivative claim must establish:

- a *prima facie* case[11] that the company is entitled to the relief claimed; and
- that the action falls within the proper boundaries of the exception to the rule in *Foss v Harbottle*, namely: (1) that the wrong is a fraud on the minority, in the sense of an unratifiable wrong not capable of 'cure' by the majority; and (2) that wrongdoer control[12] of the company prevents the company itself bringing an action in its own name.[13]

---

[5]  See *Breckland Group Holdings Ltd v London and Suffolk Properties Ltd* [1989] BCLC 100.

[6]  See The Companies (Model Articles) Regulations 2008, SI 2008/3229, art 3 (Ltd); art 3 (Plc), previously SI 1985/805, Table A, reg 70; *Automatic Self-Cleansing Filter Syndicate Ltd v Cunninghame* [1906] 2 Ch 34.

[7]  [1902] AC 83 at 93–4, per Lord Davey.

[8]  i.e deliberate and dishonest breaches of duty, see *Abouraya v Sigmund* [2015] BCC 503 at [18], per David Richard J.      [9] (1874) LR 9 Ch App 350.

[10]  [1982] 1 All ER 354 at 366; and see *Edwards v Halliwell* [1950] 2 All ER 1064 at 1066, per Jenkins LJ; *Daniels v Daniels* [1978] 2 All ER 89 at 91.

[11]  See David Richards J in *Abouraya v Sigmund* [2015] BCC 503 at [53]: 'A prima facie case is a higher test than a seriously arguable case and I take it to mean a case that, in the absence of an answer by the defendant, would entitle the claimant to judgment'; and see Morgan J in *Bhullar v Bhullar* [2016] 1 BCLC 106 at [21]–[26] as to the meaning of 'prima facie' in this context.

[12]  Wrongdoer control will exist if the wrongdoer has a majority of the votes, or the majority has actually approved a fraud on the minority, or the company has otherwise shown that it is not willing to sue: *Russell v Wakefield Waterworks Co* (1875) LR 20 Eq 474 at 482, per Jessel MR; 'wrongdoer control' is satisfied where the aggrieved member and the wrongdoer hold 50/50 shareholdings, see *Re Fort Gilkicker Ltd, UPMS Ltd v Fort Gilkicker* [2013] 3 All ER 546 at [18]; *Abouraya v Sigmund* [2015] BCC 503 at [17].

[13]  *Prudential Assurance Co Ltd v Newman Industries Ltd (No 2)* [1982] 1 All ER 354 at 366; *Smith v Croft (No 2)* [1987] 3 All ER 909 at 945.

**20-6** In *Abouraya v Sigmund*[14] David Richards J reviewed the authorities on fraud on the minority and concluded that:[15]

> 'financial or other loss to the shareholders, albeit normally of a reflective character, is essential to give a claimant shareholder sufficient interest in the proceedings to make the shareholder an appropriate claimant on behalf of the company, whether he is a member of that company or of its holding company. Equally, the authorities require that, in the absence of actual fraud or an ultra vires act, the wrongdoers should themselves have benefitted from the wrongdoing. The significance of this requirement is that their breach of duty cannot be ratified by a majority vote which depends on the votes of the wrongdoers. It is essential to the exception to the rule in *Foss v Harbottle* that the alleged wrongdoing is incapable of lawful ratification ...'

**20-7** In *Abouraya v Sigmund*,[16] the claim was brought by a shareholder in a parent company with respect to alleged breaches of duty by a director of a wholly owned subsidiary (a so-called multiple derivative claim (see **20-16**)). The alleged wrongdoing concerned the transfer of assets and the taking of opportunities of subsidiary A and transferring/giving them to subsidiary B. As both subsidiaries were wholly owned by company C, that parent company suffered no reflective loss, as any loss to the value of its shareholding in subsidiary A was matched by a corresponding gain in value of its shareholding in subsidiary B. There was also no evidence that the director in question benefited personally from the transactions.[17] Unusually, then, the alleged wrongdoing caused no loss to the company and no benefit to the alleged wrongdoers was established. Permission for a derivative claim was refused.

**20-8** In *Harris v Microfusion 2003-2 LLP*[18] the Court of Appeal endorsed the boundaries to the fraud on the minority exception to the rule in *Foss v Harbottle* identified by David Richards J in *Abouraya v Sigmund* as a correct statement of the position.[19] The boundaries are actual fraud in the sense of deliberate and dishonest breaches of duty or wrongdoing which results in a loss to the company and benefit to the wrongdoers.

**20-9** Even when a *prima facie* case exists at common law, the court has a discretion as to whether to grant permission to bring a derivative claim.[20] It must be satisfied that the claimant is a proper person to bring the action and has a legitimate interest in the relief sufficient to justify him in bringing proceedings to obtain it.[21] Further, where a majority of the shareholders who are independent of the wrongdoers, for disinterested reasons, do not wish the proceedings to continue, permission will be refused.[22] The court will

---

[14] [2015] BCC 503.

[15] [2015] BCC 503 at [25]; see his review of the authorities at [16]–[25], including *Daniels v Daniels* [1978] Ch 406 at 414, per Templeman J: 'The principle ... is that a minority shareholder who has no other remedy may sue where directors use their powers, intentionally or unintentionally, fraudulently or negligently, in a manner which benefits themselves at the expense of the company.'

[16] [2015] BCC 503.     [17] [2015] BCC 503 at [6], [52], [56], [57].     [18] [2017] 1 BCLC 305, CA, at [31].

[19] The court rejected counsel's submission that the ambit of the exception had been too narrowly stated by Richards J, see [2017] 1 BCLC 305 at [21], [31].

[20] Elements of the statutory scheme are also being imported into the permission stage at common law. The blurring of the lines can be seen in *Bhullar v Bhullar* [2016] 1 BCLC 106 where, having concluded that fraud on the minority and wrongdoer control were present, the court went on to consider whether a hypothetical board would pursue the matter, whether an alternative remedy under CA 2006, s 994 (unfairly prejudicial) might be appropriate, etc—factors which the courts are required to consider for Part 11 derivative claims.

[21] See *Waddington Ltd v Chan Chun Hoo Thomas* [2009] 2 BCLC 82 at [74]; *Abouraya v Sigmund* [2015] BCC 503 at [25]. See also *Nurcombe v Nurcombe* [1984] BCLC 557 at 562; *Barrett v Duckett* [1995] 1 BCLC 243; *Towers v Africa Tug Co* [1904] 1 Ch 558; Payne, '"Clean Hands" in Derivative Actions' (2002) 61 CLJ 76.

[22] *Smith v Croft (No 2)* [1987] 3 All ER 909.

not allow a derivative claim to proceed if it is being brought for an ulterior motive.[23] For example, in *Abouraya v Sigmund*,[24] discussed earlier, the court considered that the real purpose for the claim was to advance the interests of the claimant as a creditor of subsidiary A. He was concerned as to whether that subsidiary had sufficient assets to meet his claims as a creditor. Refusing permission additionally on this ground (see **20-5**), David Richards J said he did not consider it to be a proper use of the derivative procedure to use it to assist creditors or claimants who happen to be shareholders but who, in that capacity, have no real interest in the outcome of the derivative claim, noting that the law provides other mechanisms to assist creditors.[25]

**20-10**  Common law derivative actions were rare, understandably, given the difficulty in establishing standing to sue and the absence of personal relief, especially when a personal remedy was often available under the generous unfairly prejudicial jurisdiction, now CA 2006, s 994, discussed in Chapter 19.

## C Statutory reform, impact on the common law and on the rule in *Foss v Harbottle*

### Statutory reform

**20-11**  A report on shareholders' remedies by the Law Commission in 1997 concluded that: (1) the rule in *Foss v Harbottle* was complicated and unwieldy; (2) the scope of the exception to the rule (i.e. the circumstances in which a derivative claim could be brought) was uncertain; and (3) the procedural difficulties were such that simply establishing standing to sue could amount to a mini-trial.[26] The Law Commission recommended that the common law action be replaced with a statutory derivative procedure with more modern, flexible, and accessible criteria for determining whether a shareholder may bring a claim.[27] The intention was to put a derivative claim on a clearer and more rational basis which would give the courts flexibility to allow cases to proceed in appropriate circumstances while giving guidance to advisers as to the matters which the court would take into account in deciding whether to grant leave to bring a claim.[28] The Law Commission thought that a statutory procedure would give greater transparency to the requirements for a claim; it would alert interested parties to the availability of a derivative claim; and it would ensure that the Companies Act constituted a more complete code (with the unfairly prejudicial remedy) with regard to shareholders' remedies.[29] The Law Commission also thought that, in an age of international business, it was important to set out the rules in the statute in keeping with other jurisdictions.[30] The Law Commission's recommendations were

---

[23]  *Barrett v Duckett* [1995] 1 BCLC 243.      [24]  [2015] BCC 503.      [25]  [2015] BCC 503 at [60].

[26]  Law Commission, *Shareholder Remedies* (Law Com No 246) (Cm 3769, 1997) ('Law Commission Report'), para 6.4. The Report was preceded by a Consultation Paper of the same name: Con Paper No 142 (1996). For comments on the Law Commission's proposals, see Boyle, *Minority Shareholders' Remedies* (2002), Ch 3; Poole and Roberts, 'Shareholder Remedies—Corporate Wrongs and the Derivative Action' [1999] JBL 99.

[27]  Law Commission Report, n 26, para 6.15.      [28]  Law Commission Report, n 26, para 6.14.

[29]  Law Commission Report, n 26, paras 6.16–6.18.

[30]  Law Commission Report, n 26, para 6.9. See the Canadian Business Corporations Act 1975, s 239, and Cheffins, 'Reforming the Derivative Action: The Canadian Experience and British Prospects' [1997] Company, Financial and Insolvency Law Review 227; the New Zealand Companies Act 1993, ss 165–168, and Watson, 'A Matter of Balance: The Statutory Derivative Action in New Zealand' (1998) 19 Co Law 236; the Australian Corporations Act 2001, ss 236–242, and Ramsay and Saunders, 'Litigation by Shareholders and Directors: An Empirical Study of the Australian Statutory Derivative Action' (2006) 6 JCLS 397.

endorsed by the Company Law Review without much further deliberation[31] and the statutory derivative claim, now CA 2006, Pt 11, is modelled largely on the Law Commission's proposals.[32] Part 11 came into force on 1 October 2007.

**20-12**  Not everyone welcomed the introduction of a statutory derivative claim and, while it has not unleashed the torrent of litigation which its critics feared, it is important to appreciate their concerns since they were influential in shaping the eventual legislation. A particular issue was the juxtaposition of a 'new' shareholder remedy alongside the statutory statement of directors' duties, specifically the obligation in CA 2006, s 172(1) requiring directors to promote the success of the company having regard to the factors set out in that section, see **10-2**. The concern was that shareholder activists might use the combination of the derivative claim and s 172 to challenge business decisions of directors on the basis of an alleged failure to have regard to the factors set out in that section, see **10-35**. There was a perception that the jurisdiction under CA 2006, Pt 11 was very wide, given that the statute swept aside the established common law (high) thresholds requiring fraud on the minority and wrongdoer control and allowed derivative claims in respect of a breach of any duty owed by a director to the company including, for the first time, in respect of alleged negligence by a director (s 260(3)). Furthermore, the CA 2006 rules on ratification require a resolution by independent shareholders. As the critics saw it, the result was more grounds for a derivative claim and less possibility of ratification.

**20-13**  At a practical level, there were concerns that there is more scope for speculative or vexatious litigation for reasons such as the availability of conditional fee agreements[33] and the rise of activist shareholders, sometimes with deep pockets and prepared to litigate.

**20-14**  The Government position throughout the Parliamentary debates was that CA 2006, Pt 11 did not introduce any major change of principle and that there was no reason to expect any significant increase in the number of derivative actions. The Government considered that derivative claims have certain inherent characteristics which limit the potential for speculative litigation, notably that a claim may only be brought on behalf of the company with any sums recovered going to the company and not to the claimant who runs the risk of incurring substantial costs.[34] Nevertheless, in recognition of the concerns, the Government amended the statutory provisions as they were going through Parliament to enhance the protection for directors.[35] This was done by (1) strengthening the judicial controls of derivative claims (discussed shortly), and (2) restating the duty of directors

---

[31] See Company Law Review, *Developing the Framework* (2000), paras 4.112–4.139 for the main discussion of the issues; also *Completing the Structure* (2000), paras 5.82–5.89; and *Final Report* (2001), paras 7.46–7.51.

[32] See *Wishart v Castlecroft Securities Ltd* [2010] BCC 161, decision of Scottish Outer and Inner Houses, where at each level the courts give a detailed consideration of the legislation and its legislative history.

[33] See Reisberg, 'Funding Derivative Actions: A Re-examination of Costs and Fees as Incentives to Commence Litigation' (2004) 4 JCLS 345 at 380; also *Hughes v Weiss* [2012] EWHC 2363 at [55].

[34] See 679 HL Official Report (5th series), cols GC4–5, 27 February 2006; HC Official Report, SC D (Company Law Reform Bill), 13 July 2006, col 665. For an example of the risks, see *Bridge v Daley* [2015] EWCH 2121 at [97]–[99] (the claimant's case, though brought in good faith, was continued past a point when he should have realised the claim was doomed, so when permission to continue was refused, costs were awarded against him on an indemnity basis).

[35] See 681 HL Official Report (5th series), cols 883–4, 9 May 2006.

to act to promote the interests of the company (s 172(1)) to emphasise that the overriding obligation of directors remains to promote the success of the company for the benefit of its members as a whole (see **10-3**). The latter element was intended to curb the scope for allegations of a breach of duty arising from a supposed failure to have regard to one or more of the factors set out in that section. The Government's aim was to strike a balance between protecting directors from vexatious and frivolous claims,[36] so allowing them to take business decisions in good faith, while protecting the rights of shareholders to bring meritorious claims.[37]

### Continued application of the common law

**20-15**   In the absence of an express statutory statement in CA 2006, Pt 11, that all common law derivative claims are abolished, that Part does not displace the common law governing other types of derivative claims.[38] The result is that there is a statutory (ordinary) derivative claim governed by CA 2006, Pt 11 and remnants of a common law jurisdiction covering (i) multiple derivative claims; and (ii) claims in respect of foreign registered companies.

### Ordinary and multiple derivative claims

**20-16**   A derivative claim under CA 2006, Pt 11 is defined as a claim by a member of a company in respect of a cause of action vested in the company and seeking relief on behalf of the company (s 260(1)). It can be described as an ordinary derivative claim. Section 260(2) goes on to provide that a derivative claim may *only* be brought (a) under CA 2006, Pt 11 or (b) in pursuance of an order of the court in unfairly prejudicial proceedings under s 994.[39] A question arose as to whether the wording of s 260(2)(a) meant that the only available derivative claim is one which falls within s 260(1), i.e. a claim by a member of the company in question, so excluding claims by anyone else.

**20-17**   In *Re Fort Gilkicker, Universal Project Management Services Ltd v Fort Gilkicker Ltd,*[40] Briggs J concluded that the correct interpretation is that a derivative claim, as defined by CA 2006, s 260(1), i.e. an ordinary derivative claim brought by a member of the company, may only be brought in accordance with Part 11. In so far as the common law allows multiple derivative claims, where the claim is brought by a member not of the company which has the cause of action, but by a member of its holding company, where the holding company is subject to the same wrongdoer control as the company,

---

[36]   See 679 HL Official Report (5th series), col GC6, 27 February 2006.

[37]   See 681 HL Official Report (5th series), col 883, 9 May 2006.

[38]   See *Re Fort Gilkicker, Universal Project Management Services Ltd v Fort Gilkicker Ltd* [2013] 2 All ER 546. See Lightman, 'Two Aspects of the Statutory Derivative Claim' [2011] LMCLQ 142. See *Waddington Ltd v Chan Chun Hoo Thomas* [2009] 2 BCLC 82 where the HKCFA accepted that, while the HK statute made no provision for a multiple derivative claim, it was possible at common law; noted by Prentice and Reisberg (2009) 125 LQR 209; also Koh, 'Derivative Actions Once Removed' [2010] JBL 101; Goo, 'Multiple Derivative Actions and the Common Law Derivative Action Revisited: A Tale of Two Jurisdictions' (2010) 10 JCLS 255.

[39]   An order under CA 2006, s 996 to commence a derivative claim is unlikely in practice and for the purposes of our discussion can be disregarded. Another type of derivative claim is permitted under CA 2006, s 370 in respect of directors' liability under s 369 for unauthorised political donations and expenditure, but a claim under s 370 must be brought by an authorised group (defined in s 370(3)) and the section regulates a form of group litigation.

[40]   [2013] 2 All ER 546, noted (2013) 129 LQR 337.

such claims remain possible.[41] Briggs J noted that derivative claims are procedural devices designed to prevent a wrong going without a remedy and so, he said, it is unsurprising that the court is willing to extend *locus standi* to permit someone with a sufficient interest to sue as the company's representative claimant for the benefit of all its stakeholders.[42] Usually the claim will be by a member of the company, exceptionally it may be by a member of the parent company where that parent company is under the same wrongdoer control.[43] An ordinary derivative claim is governed by the mandatory provisions of CA 2006, Pt 11 while a multiple derivative claim remains a matter for the common law.

**20-18**   Retaining the common law might not seem desirable as a matter of common sense, Briggs J conceded, but, he said, he did so with some relief, for abolishing multiple derivative claims in a modern context where group structures are commonplace would have the potential to cause real injustice and place the UK out of step with other common law jurisdictions.[44] At common law, as discussed at **20-9**, the claimant must establish a *prima facie* case that the company is entitled to relief and have the permission of the court to proceed on the basis of the exception to the rule in *Foss v Harbottle*. On the facts in *Re Fort Gilkicker Ltd, UPMS Ltd v Fort Gilkicker Ltd*[45] it was accepted that there was a *prima facie* case and Briggs J gave permission for the claim to proceed as it involved an alleged misappropriation of a business opportunity of the company by a director (hence fraud on the minority at common law) and there was wrongdoer control.[46]

**20-19**   The approach taken by Briggs J was endorsed by David Richards J in *Abouraya v Sigmund*[47] where he agreed that a common law multiple derivative claim brought by a shareholder of a parent company in respect of wrongdoing in a wholly owned subsidiary is possible where the parent company is under the same wrongdoer control as the subsidiary company. Therefore, assuming the claimant can meet the common law requirements for a derivative claim, permission for a derivative claim is possible. In *Abouraya v Sigmund*, as discussed at **20-5**, permission was refused as the claimant failed to meet the threshold requirements at common law.

### Derivative claims with respect to foreign companies

**20-20**   To complete the picture, given that CA 2006, Pt 11 does not abolish the common law other than with respect to ordinary derivative claims in respect of companies formed and registered under the CA 2006 and its predecessors,[48] it remains possible to bring a

---

[41]   See [2013] 3 All ER 546 at [21]–[25], where Briggs J identified a number of cases at common law where multiple derivative claims had been brought: *Wallersteiner v Moir (No 2)* [1975] 1 All ER 849; *Halle v Trax BW Ltd* [2000] BCC 1020; *Truman Investment Group v Société Générale SA* [2003] EWHC 1316; *Airey v Cordell* [2007] BCC 785. Briggs J considered that Lord Millett's analysis in *Waddington Ltd v Chan Chun Hoo Thomas* [2009] 2 BCLC 82 HKCFA, see n 38, was equally applicable to English common law.

[42]   [2013] 3 All ER 546 at [24].

[43]   [2013] 3 All ER 546 at [26]. In *Re Fort Gilkicker Ltd*, the parent entity was an LLP, not a company, but Briggs J said that made no difference. The nature of the entity which owns the wronged company's shares is of no legal relevance, provided that it is in wrongdoer control and has some members at least who are interested in seeing the wrong done to the company put right, at [51].

[44]   [2013] 3 All ER 546 at [34], [49].        [45]   [2013] 3 All ER 546.

[46]   [2013] 3 All ER 546 at [53]–[56], [61].

[47]   [2015] BCC 503 at [14]. See too *Bhullar v Bhullar* [2016] 1 BCLC 106, another case where permission was given in a multiple derivative claim.

[48]   Applying CA 2006, ss 1(1) and 260(1).

common law derivative claim with respect to foreign registered companies, to the extent that conflicts of laws would permit such a claim.[49]

## Impact on the rule in *Foss v Harbottle*

**20-21**    Before discussing the statutory derivative claim in detail, it is worth emphasising that the rule in *Foss v Harbottle*[50] has not been swept aside. As noted at **20-1**, there are two elements to the rule: the proper plaintiff element and the majority rule element. Statutory derivative claims, though facilitated by the new procedural mechanism of Part 11, remain subject to those requirements.[51]

**20-22**    As regards the proper plaintiff aspect, the position remains that the proper plaintiff in respect of a wrong allegedly done to a company is *prima facie* the company. If the company is in a position to pursue a claim vested in it, it is for the company to do so, not the shareholders. That fundamental principle has not been discarded, as Roth J made clear in *Cinematic Finance Ltd v Ryder*[52] when refusing permission for a majority shareholder to bring a derivative claim. In those circumstances, there is no reason why the claim cannot be brought in the company's name. Likewise, in *Bamford v Harvey*[53] permission to bring a derivative claim was refused when it became apparent that there was no objection to the claim being brought in the company's name, see **20-57**.

**20-23**    The majority rule element meant that, at common law, a shareholder could not bring a derivative claim in respect of an act which was capable of being confirmed by the majority.[54] As Lord Davey explained in *Burland v Earle*:[55]

> 'This [a derivative claim] … is mere matter of procedure in order to give a remedy for a wrong which would otherwise escape redress, and it is obvious that in such an action the plaintiffs cannot have a larger right to relief than the company itself would have if it were plaintiff, and cannot complain of acts which are valid if done with the approval of the majority of the shareholders, or are capable of being confirmed by the majority.'

Under CA 2006, Pt 11, actual authorisation or ratification is required to bar a claim (s 263(2)(b), (c)), see **20-46**. Otherwise, the possibility of authorisation or ratification is a matter to be taken into account by the court when deciding whether to give permission for a claim to proceed (s 263(3)(c) and (d)), see **20-60**. The position is therefore clearer under the statute in that actual authorisation or ratification is required to bar a claim, but it makes no substantive change to the general principle of majority rule in that, if an independent majority as required by s 239 chooses to authorise or ratify the conduct in question, assuming it is ratifiable, then that ends the matter.

---

[49] *Novatrust Ltd v Kea Investments Ltd* [2014] EWHC 4061; *Konamaneni v Rolls-Royce Industrial Power (India) Ltd* [2002] 1 BCLC 336—it is possible to bring a derivative claim in England with respect to a foreign company, but the law governing the right to bring the claim is the law of the country of incorporation and usually that place of incorporation will also be the most appropriate forum, see generally Mortimore (ed), *Company Directors, Duties, Liabilities and Remedies* (3rd edn, 2017), paras 36.58–36.66; Joffe, *Minority Shareholders* (5th edn, 2015), paras 2.161–2.169. The courts may refuse permission for service out of the jurisdiction.
[50] (1843) 2 Hare 461.    [51] *Burland v Earle* [1902] AC 83 at 93–4.
[52] [2012] BCC 797 at [9]–[14]; and see Roth J at [14], '… only in very exceptional circumstances could it be appropriate to permit a derivative claim brought by a shareholder in control of the company. For my part, I find it difficult to envisage what those exceptional circumstances might be.'
[53] [2013] BCC 311 at [25]–[29], citing *Stimpson v Southern Private Landlords Association* [2010] BCC 387 at [46].
[54] *MacDougall v Gardiner* (1875) 1 Ch D 13 at 25, CA; see **20-1**.    [55] [1902] AC 83 at 93–4.

# D  Derivative claims under CA 2006, Part 11

## General scope of Part II

**20-24**  An ordinary derivative claim may be initiated by a member[56] of the company[57] who requires the permission of the court to continue with it (CA 2006, s 261(1)).[58] The claimant must be a member at the time of the proceedings, but it is immaterial whether the cause of action arose before or after the claimant became a member of the company.[59] No minimum shareholding is required which, in theory, means that litigious parties could purchase one share with a view to bringing a case against the directors, but whether the court would give permission to such a claimant to proceed is another matter.[60] There is little advantage in a person acquiring a single share with a view to bringing a derivative claim since any recovery is for the benefit of the company and the claimant runs the risk that he will be penalised in costs. While the section refers to 'a member', it will be a minority member for, as the court noted in *Cinematic Finance Ltd v Ryder*,[61] only in very exceptional circumstances (which the court thought difficult to envisage) would it be appropriate to permit a shareholder in control of a company to bring a derivative claim, see **20-22**. A controlling shareholder has other options open to him or her, such as appointing a new board of directors. Thereafter, a claim can be brought by the company in the usual way, so respecting the rule in *Foss v Harbottle* (see **20-1**), that a claim vested in the company should be pursued by the company.

**20-25**  A derivative claim may be brought against a director (including a shadow director, **7-22**) or another person or both (CA 2006, s 260(3)). Former directors are included (s 260(5)(a)) and claims against such directors might arise, for example, where directors have resigned in order to exploit an opportunity which came to their attention while they were directors in a situation of a conflict of interest (see **12-33**).

**20-26**  The intention behind permitting derivative claims against 'another person' is to allow a claim to be made on behalf of the company, for example, against a person who has assisted a director in a breach of duty or who is a recipient of corporate assets in circumstances

---

[56] References to a 'member' include a person who is not a member but to whom shares in the company have been transferred or transmitted by operation of law: CA 2006, s 260(5)(c).

[57] As to whether the statute should have allowed for a wider group of applicants than merely members, such as creditors, see Keay, 'The Ultimate Objective of the Company and the Enforcement of the Entity Maximisation and Sustainability Model' (2010) 10 JCLS 35 at 55–63. For example, the Singapore Companies Act, s 216A(1)(c) allows for a derivative claim (for non-listed companies) by any person considered by the court to be a proper person to bring the application.

[58] See CPR 19.9(4), 19.9A(4), and Practice Direction on Derivative Claims; also *Portfolios of Distinction Ltd v Laird* [2004] 2 BCLC 741. It is also possible for a member to apply for permission to continue as a derivative claim a claim commenced by the company or by another member (CA 2006, ss 262(1), (2), 264), but these scenarios are somewhat unlikely.

[59] CA 2006, s 260(4). See Law Commission Report, n 26, para 6.98; 679 HL Official Report (5th series), col GC15, 27 February 2006. The reason being that it is the company's and not the member's substantive right that is being enforced: *Smith v Croft* [1987] 3 All ER 909 at 947; *Seaton v Grant* (1867) LR 2 Ch App 459.

[60] Concerns were raised that shareholder activists would seek to take advantage of the absence of any minimum shareholding: see 679 HL Official Report (5th series), cols GC 11–13, 27 February 2006. But, as Lord Cairns explained in *Seaton v Grant* (1867) LR 2 Ch App 459 at 465, the quantum of the claimant's interest is irrelevant, if the claim is one which should otherwise be brought, for the aggregate interest of all the shareholders is amply sufficient to sustain the claim.

[61] [2012] BCC 797 at [14].

where he knows the director is acting in breach of his duties.[62] The basis for suing them derivatively is their involvement in the director's breach of duty and a derivative claim cannot be brought where the breach of duty etc is solely that of the third party, such as a negligent auditor.[63] As the Law Commission noted, the decision whether to sue a third party (i.e. someone who is not a director and where the claim is not closely connected with a breach of duty by a director) is one for the board.[64]

**20-27**  A derivative claim may be brought only in respect of a cause of action arising from an actual or proposed[65] act or omission involving negligence, default,[66] breach of duty, or breach of trust by a director of the company (s 260(3)).[67] A claim for breach of duty against a number of directors must be particularised with respect to each director.[68] There is no requirement in the statutory claim that the director should have profited or benefited from the breach of duty,[69] though that is an important requirement in the multiple derivative claim at common law, as discussed at **20-6**. The absence of profit or benefit may be something which the court would factor into its deliberations under s 263(3) when considering whether to grant permission.

**20-28**  It is possible to bring a derivative claim in respect of negligence in a change from the common law position,[70] a change recommended by the Law Commission.[71] Of course, while negligence will found a derivative claim, the courts will continue to distinguish between commercial misjudgements and negligent conduct.

**20-29**  Allowing shareholders to pursue a derivative claim for breach of duty by directors enables shareholders to overcome the 'no reflective loss' rule (discussed at **20-73**) which prevents shareholders seeking redress directly for loss suffered by them where their loss is merely

---

[62] See Law Commission Report, n 26, paras 6.35, 6.36; 679 HL Official Report (5th series), cols GC 9–10, 27 February 2006; HC Official Report, SC D (Company Law Reform Bill), 13 July 2006, col 666. See *Konamaneni v Rolls-Royce Industrial Power (India) Ltd* [2002] 1 BCLC 336 where the substance of the proposed derivative claim was to bring an action against a third party who had allegedly bribed a director—permission was refused on a variety of grounds, but the case illustrates the circumstances in which a derivative claim against a third party might be relevant.

[63] See *Iesini v Westrip Holdings Ltd* [2011] 1 BCLC 498 at [75].

[64] See Law Commission Report, n 26, paras 6.34, 6.35. A derivative claim may lie, however, where the board's decision not to pursue a claim against a third party is itself a breach of duty by the directors, subject to difficulties of causation and quantification in such circumstances, see Law Commission Report, n 26, para 6.32.

[65] The ability to bring claims with respect to proposed acts may offer some scope for shareholders to take pre-emptive action, though it would be rare.

[66] 'Default' enables claims to be brought in respect of breaches of statutory obligations imposed by the companies legislation: *Customs and Excise Commissioners v Hedon Alpha Ltd* [1981] 2 All ER 697.

[67] A claim asserting that a third party should make restitution to the company for funds expended by it on a joint venture without any allegation of breach of duty by the directors is not a derivative claim, nor is a claim that assets of the company are held by some third party on trust for the company unless there is a failure by the directors, in breach of duty, to assert or pursue that trust claim against that other person: see *Iesini v Westrip Holdings Ltd* [2011] 1 BCLC 498 at [103]–[109].

[68] See *Bridge v Daley* [2015] EWHC 2121 at [76]; it is not sufficient to claim that 'they are all in it together'.

[69] *Iesini v Westrip Holdings Ltd* [[2011]1 BCLC 498 at [75], per Lewison J, '… it is not a requirement that the delinquent director should have profited or benefited from his misconduct. He may be guilty of no more than negligence in managing the company's affairs.'

[70] At common law, mere negligence from which the director did not benefit personally could not found a derivative claim (it was a ratifiable wrong): *Pavlides v Jensen* [1956] 2 All ER 518. It was necessary to show that the negligence was of the self-serving variety (unratifiable) seen in *Daniels v Daniels* [1978] 2 All ER 89 where the board sold an asset at a gross undervalue to one of the directors.

[71] See Law Commission Report, n 26, para 6.41 (while investors take the risk that those who manage companies may make mistakes, they do not have to accept that directors will fail to comply with their duties); a view endorsed by the Company Law Review, *Developing the Framework* (2000), para 4.127.

reflective of a loss suffered by the company, as is the case where a director breaches his duties to the company. Pursuing the claim derivatively enables a shareholder to force the company to recover the loss which the shareholder would otherwise be barred from recovering directly by the reflective loss principle.

**20-30**   To sum up, a derivative claim under Part 11 may be brought:[72]

- by any member (however few shares he holds and however recently acquired, though not ordinarily by a majority shareholder[73]);

- against any director (including former and shadow directors) and other persons implicated in the breach of duty, etc;[74]

- in respect of negligence, default, breach of duty, and breach of trust by a director of the company.

**20-31**   While it is possible to commence a derivative claim on this basis and therefore Part 11 looks to be a much broader jurisdiction than the common law derivative claim, the statutory claim may not proceed very far, however, for the claimant must obtain the permission of the court to continue the claim.[75]

## Costs of bringing a derivative claim

**20-32**   The CA 2006, Pt 11 makes no specific provision for costs and the position is governed by the Court of Appeal decision in *Wallersteiner v Moir (No 2)*[76] which held that where a shareholder has, in good faith and on reasonable grounds, sued as claimant in a minority shareholder's action, the benefit of which if successful will accrue to the company and only indirectly to the claimant as a member of the company, and which action it would be reasonable for an independent board of directors to bring in the company name, the court may order the company to pay the claimant's costs.[77]

---

[72] As to the statutory derivative claim, see generally Keay, 'Assessing and Rethinking the Statutory Scheme for Derivative Actions' [2016] JCLS 39; Keay, 'Applications to Continue Derivative Proceedings on Behalf of the Company and the Hypothetical Director' [2015] CJQ 346; Mujih, 'The New Statutory Derivative Claim: A Delicate Balancing Act' (2012) 33 Co Law, 66 and 99 (Pts 1 and 2); Lightman, 'Two Aspects of the Statutory Derivative Claim' [2011] LMCLQ 142; Keay and Loughrey, 'Derivative Proceedings in a Brave New World for Company Management and Shareholders' [2010] JBL 151 (an updated version of this paper can be found in Loughrey (ed), *Directors' Duties and Shareholder Litigation in the Wake of the Financial Crisis* (2013), Ch 7, Keay and Loughrey, 'An Assessment of the Present State of Statutory Derivative Proceedings', hereinafter Keay and Loughrey (2013)); Reisberg, 'Derivative Claims under the CA 2006: Much Ado about Nothing' in Armour and Payne (eds), *Rationality in Company Law: Essays in Honour of DD Prentice* (2009); Nessen, Goo, and Low, 'The Statutory Derivative Action: Now Showing Near You' [2008] JBL 627; Keay and Loughrey, 'Something Old, Something New, Something Borrowed: An Analysis of the New Derivative Action under the Companies Act 2006' (2008) 124 LQR 469; Reisberg, *Derivative Actions and Corporate Governance* (2007).          [73] *Cinematic Finance Ltd v Ryder* [2012] BCC 797.

[74] The company is also made a defendant in order that it is bound by the outcome so that, if the claim proceeds and is unsuccessful, the directors are not exposed to the risk of another claim based on the same matter, see *Roberts v Gill & Co* [2010] 4 All ER 367 at [58]–[61].

[75] In *Wilton UK Ltd v Shuttleworth* [2017] EWHC 2195, the court held that, where a claim proceeded without the permission of the court, it was not entirely invalid. Rather, the court has the power to validate with retrospective effect steps taken in the proceedings without consent.          [76] [1975] 1 All ER 849.

[77] [1975] 1 All ER 849 at 868–9, per Buckley LJ; see also CPR 19.9E (the indemnity may cover the costs incurred in obtaining permission to continue and in the claim itself). In *Smith v Croft* [1986] 2 All ER 551, Walton J took a restrictive view of the jurisdiction to make an indemnity order, but this restrictive approach was not followed in *Jaybird v Greenwood Ltd* [1986] BCLC 318. See generally Reisberg, 'Funding Derivative Actions: A Re-examination of Costs and Fees as Incentives to Commence Litigation' (2004) 4 JCLS 345; Quigxiu Bu, 'The Indemnity Order in a Derivative Action' (2006) 27 Co Law 2.

**20-33**    The ability to secure an indemnity from the company is an important consideration for a shareholder contemplating a derivative action[78] and it is common for the claimant to seek permission to bring the derivative claim and immediately to ask for an indemnity for his costs.[79] But the courts are cautious and restrictive in their approach to derivative claim costs. They may refuse to grant an indemnity at the permission stage, leaving it to the trial judge to determine costs once the matter has been determined. On occasion, they have granted only a limited indemnity, either limited in monetary terms or limited to a particular stage of the proceedings.[80] As discussed at **20-55**, the ability of the claimant to fund the proceedings without recourse to an indemnity is a significant consideration for the court when deciding whether to grant permission to continue the claim. The applicant for permission who does not seek costs would seem to have a better chance of securing permission.[81]

**20-34**    The courts are alert to derivative claims being brought in respect of what are essentially shareholder disputes in a small company which might equally have been brought by a s 994 petition where each party is at risk of costs.[82] The concern is that, if permission is given to the claimant to proceed by a derivative claim and he is given an immediate indemnity order, that costs position places him at a considerable advantage over the defendant in terms of the conduct of the litigation and the negotiation of any settlement, as the court explained in *Bhullar v Bhullar*.[83] In those circumstances, if the costs are visited upon the company and the claimant loses, the successful defendant in effect incurs some of the costs and, vice versa, if the claimant wins, the claimant ends up paying some of the costs. In these cases, therefore, the court considers the parties should conduct the litigation at their own risk in the usual way.

## Judicial control of a derivative claim—two stages

**20-35**    The Government was initially reluctant to set any particular permission threshold requirements, preferring to let the matter progress to a hearing when the court would consider the factors set out in s 263(3) so avoiding an expensive and time-consuming preliminary

---

[78] A defendant director may be able to rely on D&O (director and officer) liability insurance, but it will not cover dishonest or fraudulent breaches of duty, nor breaches intended to secure a personal profit by a director. The exclusions are usually quite wide, though cover will apply to a claim in negligence. The company may fund the director's defence costs, but those costs must be refunded if the director loses the case: CA 2006, s 205(1), (2).

[79] Unrealistic concerns were expressed that the very possibility of obtaining an indemnity order would encourage vexatious claims, see 679 HL Official Report (5th series), col GC 13, 27 February 2006. Reisberg, n 77, argues that the only real incentive for shareholders to bring derivative actions would be if the courts could order some element of personal recovery for them when the claim is successful; see also Cheffins, n 30, 256–60.

[80] In *Stainer v Lee* [2011] 1 BCLC 537 at [56], the initial indemnity was limited to £40,000, with permission to apply later for an extension. In *Kiani v Cooper* [2010] 2 BCLC 427 at [48]–[49], an indemnity was awarded but not against any adverse costs order.

[81] In the following cases where permission was granted, no indemnity was sought: *SDI Retail Services Ltd v King and Murray* [2017] EWHC 737; *Hook v Sumner* [2016] BCC 220; *Cullen Investments Ltd v Brown* [2016] 1 BCLC 491.

[82] See *Hughes v Weiss* [2012] EWHC 2363 at [55] (costs refused: 'the substance of the dispute is between the two persons who alone are entitled to the company's assets'); also *Halle v Trax BM Ltd* [2000] BCC 1020 (indemnity refused, in effect asking company to fund dispute between two partners in a joint venture); *Mumbray v Lapper* [2005] BCC 990 (indemnity refused, essentially a partnership break-up). Note also *Watts v Midland Bank plc* [1986] BCLC 15 (no indemnity order where company hopelessly insolvent).

[83] [2016] 1 BCLC 106 at [52]. See also *Hook v Sumner* [2016] BCC 220, court declined to make costs order because it would give the claimant an unfair advantage in the upcoming litigation.

mini-trial.[84] As noted at **20-14**, the Government was persuaded subsequently that the court should have an additional specific power to dismiss unmeritorious cases at an early stage without involving the company. Hence, a *prima facie* threshold was included for that purpose.[85] There are therefore two stages to securing permission.

### The first stage—a *prima facie* case

**20-36**   At the first stage, done entirely on the papers without the company being represented, if it appears to the court that the application and the evidence filed by the applicant in support of it do not disclose a *prima facie* case[86] 'for giving permission' to continue a derivative claim, the court must dismiss the claim (CA 2006, s 261(2)). If the court is satisfied, the case progresses to the second stage. Occasionally, the parties have skipped this paper stage (more by mishap than design, it seems) and gone straight to a permission hearing.[87] In *Langley Ward Ltd v Trevor*,[88] the court criticised such a process and noted that it undermines the statutory scheme which contemplates a preliminary consideration by the court solely on the papers.[89]

**20-37**   In *Iesini v Westrip Holdings Ltd*[90] Lewison J held that this requirement for a *prima facie* case for giving permission necessarily entails a decision by the court that there is a *prima facie* case both that the company has a good cause of action and that the cause of action arises out of a director's default, breach of duty, etc. Lewison J described this as precisely the decision that the Court of Appeal required (at common law) in *Prudential Assurance Co Ltd v Newman Industries Ltd (No 2)*,[91] as to which, see **20-5**.

**20-38**   If the case is not dismissed at this *prima facie* threshold, the court may grant an adjournment, for example, to allow the company to seek authorisation or ratification of the alleged conduct which will then act as a complete bar to the claim proceeding (see CA 2006, s 261(4)) or to enable the company to take some other steps which may have a bearing on whether a derivative claim is needed and appropriate.[92] In effect, there can be a

---

[84]   See 679 HL Official Report (5th series), col GC 22, 27 February 2006; Law Commission Report, n 26, paras 6.4, 6.71.

[85]   The provision was added at Report Stage in the House of Lords, see 681 HL Official Report (5th series), cols 883–4, 9 May 2006. Keay and Loughrey (2013), n 72, 195 make the point that the legislative history to the belated introduction of the first stage might support the view that it was not thought through sufficiently.

[86]   See n 11 as to the meaning of 'prima facie' at common law, per David Richards J in *Abouraya v Sigmund* [2015] BCC 503.

[87]   See *Franbar Holdings Ltd v Patel* [2009] 1 BCLC 1 at [24]; *Mission Capital plc v Sinclair* [2010] 1 BCLC 304 at [36]; *Stimpson v Southern Private Landlords Association* [2010] BCC 387 at [3]; *Bridge v Daley* [2015] EWHC 2121 at [9]; *Brannigan v Style* [2016] EWHC 512 at [3].

[88]   [2011] EWHC 1893 at [6]–[7] and [61]–[63].

[89]   The unfortunate outcome, the court said, was a much greater expenditure of costs and time by the parties when, had the first stage been observed, the claim or at least some of the allegations might have been dismissed, so making any second stage more efficient.    [90]   [2011] 1 BCLC 498 at [78].

[91]   [1982] 1 All ER 354 at 366. Keay and Loughrey have queried (see (2013), n 72, 195) whether, in that case, there is any difference between the first and the second stage, but this may be to over-read what Lewison J said which seems to be little more than noting that the statute requires there to be a *prima facie* case that the company has a cause of action and that it is within the boundaries of 'negligence, default, breach of duty or breach of trust'.

[92]   See *Iesini v Westrip Holdings Ltd* [2011] 1 BCLC 498 (proceedings adjourned to allow the board to consider whether it wished to assert a claim on behalf of the company against third parties in relation to the ownership of certain assets which would obviate the need for a derivative claim against the board for not securing those assets); also *FanmailUK.com Ltd v Cooper* [2008] BCC 877 (proceedings adjourned to allow dispute as to ownership of the company to be determined as a preliminary issue since that would have a bearing on the appropriateness of a derivative claim).

pause in proceedings once the court is satisfied as to a *prima facie* case in order to allow the parties to negotiate a settlement.[93]

### The second stage—factors for judicial consideration

**20-39**   At the second stage, when the company can appear and put in evidence,[94] a variety of factors must be considered, some of which oblige the court to dismiss the claim (s 263(2)), otherwise the court has a broad discretion to give or refuse permission or adjourn the proceedings and give such directions as it thinks fit (s 263(3)).

**20-40**   There is some uncertainty as to the threshold to be applied by the court at this second stage. In *Iesini v Westrip Holdings Ltd*[95] Lewison J agreed that the threshold cannot be a *prima facie* case, since that is the first stage threshold, and 'something more must be needed'.[96] But the courts are also agreed that there is no set threshold test on the merits which must be satisfied before permission to continue will be given.[97] There is no requirement that the claimant show a reasonably arguable case or that the case is likely to succeed. The statute merely requires the court to consider the range of factors set out in section 263(3) and (4). Of course, the merits of the claim are particularly relevant to some of those factors, such as when the court is considering the position of the hypothetical director for the purposes of s 263(2)(a) and s 263(3)(b).[98] The upshot is, as Lewison J said in *Iesini v Westrip Holdings Ltd*,[99] that the court must form a view (provisional though it must be) on the strength of the claim and 'do the best it can on the material before it'.

**20-41**   Uncertainty as to the threshold forces parties, perhaps, to build a more detailed case at this stage than is strictly necessary. There is a risk that practice is veering towards the type of mini-trial at the permission stage[100] which was so criticised when derivative claims were governed solely by the common law, a problem which was meant to have been resolved by the statutory reforms. There may be some judicial unease about how matters are developing as between these stages[101] and, as Keay and Loughrey have noted, there is a risk of substantial costly hearings at both stages which is undesirable and which will deter prospective claimants.[102]

---

[93]   For an example, in the context of a multiple derivative claim, see *Re Fort Gilkicker Ltd* [2013] 3 All ER 546 at [61].

[94]   As can a defendant director, see *Kleanthous v Paphitis* [2012] BCC 676 at [44].

[95]   [2011] 1 BCLC 498.

[96]   [2011] 1 BCLC 498 at [79]; see *Bridge v Daley* [2015] EWHC 2121 at [19]: 'the applicant for permission must show more than a merely arguable case'.

[97]   See *Cullen Investments Ltd v Brown* [2016] 1 BCLC 491 at [33]–[35]; *Hughes v Weiss* [2012] EWHC 2363 at [33]; *Kleanthous v Paphitis* [2012] BCC 676 at [41]–[42]; *Stainer v Lee* [2011] 1 BCLC 537 at [29]; *Brannigan v Style* [2016] EWHC 512 at [43].

[98]   See *Cullen Investments Ltd v Brown* [2016] 1 BCLC 491 at [37].

[99]   [2011] 1 BCLC 498 at [79]. Roth J agreed in *Stainer v Lee* [2011] 1 BCLC 537 at [29]. See also *Hughes v Weiss* [2012] EWHC 2363 at [33]; *Singh v Singh* [2014] 1 BCLC 649 at [17]; *Wishart v Castlecroft Securities Ltd* [2010] BCC 161 at [36]–[40].

[100]   See Vos LJ in *Singh v Singh* [2014] EWCA Civ 103 at [29] who commented that '[t]he conducting of a mini-trial even where the legislation demands something that looks rather like a mini-trial is not desirable even if required'.

[101]   See Vos LJ in *Singh v Singh* [2014] EWCA Civ 103 (hearing an appeal against a refusal of permission) who refers, at [15], to the 'somewhat surprising effects of the CA 2006' and suggests that it would be useful for the Court of Appeal to determine this matter 'for the future benefit of claimants generally', noting that it appears that the court is conducting some sort of mini-trial on the application for permission.

[102]   Keay and Loughrey (2013), n 72, 195.

## Absolute bars to a derivative claim proceeding

**20-42**    Permission to continue a claim must be refused if the court is satisfied that:

(1)  a director acting in accordance with CA 2006, s 172 (duty to promote the success of the company) would not seek to continue the claim; or

(2)  the act or omission has been authorised by the company or ratified by the company (CA 2006, s 263(2)).

### The hypothetical director

**20-43**    The issue under s 263(2)(a) is not what conclusion the court would come to nor what a reasonable director would conclude. The court must ask itself whether a director acting in accordance with his duty under s 172, i.e. acting in the way he considers, in good faith, would be most likely to promote the success of the company, would not seek to continue the claim.[103]

**20-44**    As a director's obligations under s 172 are written in quite expansive terms, see **10-2**, the courts are reluctant to conclude under s 236(2)(a) that a director, faced with a *prima facie* case justifying a derivative claim (which there must be for the application to have reached the second stage) would not seek to continue the claim. Often, a decision either way might be one which a hypothetical director might reach, given the range of factors to which he must have regard under s 172.[104] As a result, a refusal of permission under s 263(2)(a) only occurs if the court is satisfied that no director would seek to continue the claim,[105] as held by Lewison J in *Iesini v Westrip Holdings Ltd*[106] which is much cited and settled law on this point.[107] Lewison J identified the factors that a director would consider in reaching his decision (which will also be relevant to s 263(3)(b)), including:[108]

'... the size of the claim; the strength of the claim; the cost of the proceedings; the company's ability to fund the proceedings; the ability of the potential defendants to satisfy a judgment; the impact on the company if it lost the claim and had to pay not only its own costs but the defendant's as well; any disruption to the company's activities while the claim is pursued; whether the prosecution of the claim would damage the company in other ways (eg by losing the services of a valuable employee or alienating a key supplier or customer) and so on.'

---

[103]  See *Regentcrest plc v Cohen* [2001] 2 BCLC 80 and **10-5**; HC Official Report, SC D (Company Law Reform Bill), 13 July 2006, col 678. As the Law Commission noted, 'this does not mean that the court is bound to accept the views of the director—the existence of a conflict of interest may affect the weight to be given to those views and the court would give no weight to views which no reasonable director could hold': see Law Commission Report, n 26, para 6.79.

[104]  There is an inevitable tendency in the cases to combine the test in s 263(2)(a) and that in s 263(3)(b)— the importance which a hypothetical director would attach to continuing the claim, see *Stimpson v Southern Private Landlords Association* [2010] BCC 387 at [40]; *Iesini v Westrip Holdings Ltd* [2011] 1 BCLC 498 at [86]; *Langley Ward Ltd v Trevor* [2011] EWHC 1893 at [45].

[105]  *Iesini v Westrip Holdings Ltd* [2011] 1 BCLC 498 at [86]. Cases where permission was refused on the basis of s 263(2)(a) include *Zavahir v Shankleman* [2017] BCC 500; *Iesini v Westrip Holdings Ltd*; *Bridge v Daley* [2015] EWHC 2121; *Brannigan v Style* [2016] EWHC 512; *Kleanthous v Paphitis* [2012] BCC 676; *Re Seven Holdings Ltd, Langley Ward Ltd v Trevor* [2011] EWHC 1893.

[106]  [2011] 1 BCLC 498 at [86].

[107]  See, for example, *Cullen Investments Ltd v Brown* [2016] 1 BCLC 491 at [29]; *Hook v Sumner* [2016] BCC 220 at [96]; *Kiani v Cooper* [2010] 2 BCLC 427 at [13]; *Franbar Holdings Ltd v Patel* [2009] 1 BCLC 1 at [30].

[108]  [2011] 1 BCLC 498 at [85].

He went on:

> 'The weighing of all these considerations is essentially a commercial decision, which the court is ill-equipped to take, except in a clear case.'[109]

**20-45**     For example, the courts have considered that no hypothetical director would seek to continue a claim and permission would be refused where the amount potentially recoverable is less than the amount already expended in legal costs,[110] or where it might be extremely difficult to establish and to fund the derivative claim.[111] A hypothetical director might not wish to continue a claim where the amount recovered is likely simply to be returned (circular fashion) to the alleged wrongdoers, given their shareholdings,[112] though that consideration would be a factor in many of the cases, given that the essence of the claim usually is the recovery by the company from the majority shareholders of company assets and profits which they have diverted to themselves.[113] On the other hand, in *Kiani v Cooper*[114] the court considered that a hypothetical director would seek to continue a claim where there was some strong evidence of breach of fiduciary duty by the defendant director involving, *inter alia*, an improper payment of £296,000 to a company controlled by the defendant.[115] In *Hook v Sumner*[116] the court thought that a hypothetical director would consider that the costs were likely to be high, but the potential recoveries were also substantial and the defendants were good to meet the claim and the costs, so he would seek to continue the claim.

### Authorisation and ratification by the company

**20-46**     Actual authorisation or ratification provides a complete defence to a derivative claim (CA 2006, s 263(2)(b)). In an appropriate case, therefore, the court may adjourn proceedings to see if the company wishes to ratify the breach of duty so that the claim is dismissed on this ground. In most cases, there is no evidence of authorisation or ratification, so the courts have not had to consider this defence very often. In *Brannigan v Style*,[117] after the dispute had begun to surface within the company, the shareholders did pass a written resolution ratifying any breach of duty or negligence by the directors. It later turned out that shareholders (trustees of various trusts) connected to three of the four respondent directors (beneficiaries of those trusts) had voted for the ratification, rendering it ineffective under CA 2006, s 239 with respect to those three directors, though the resolution was effective to ratify the conduct of the other unconnected director.

---

[109] [2011] 1 BCLC 498 at [85]. See Keay and Loughrey, 'Derivative Proceedings in a Brave New World for Company Management and Shareholders' [2010] JBL 151 at 161–2, who criticise this dicta, noting that if judges were to follow this thinking, it would render the derivative claim virtually redundant.

[110] See *Zavahir v Shankleman* [2017] BCC 500 at [37]–[39] where the company had few assets, no future prospects, and a wholly successful outcome would yield £136,500 plus interest and costs. At the time of the application for permission, costs had reached £156,000. Permission was refused.

[111] *Brannigan v Style* [2016] EWHC 512 at [84], [90]–[91].

[112] See *Kleanthous v Paphitis* [2012] BCC 676 at [85] where the alleged wrongdoers held 85 per cent of the shares so any recoveries were likely to be returned almost entirely to them.

[113] See *Hook v Sumner* [2016] BCC 220 at [123].     [114] [2010] 2 BCLC 427.

[115] While permission was granted in *Kiani*, the court (using its broad powers under s 261(4)) limited the permission to continue to the point of disclosure only so as to give the defendant director the opportunity to produce the documentation which he said supported the payment.

[116] [2016] BCC 220.

[117] [2016] EWHC 512 at [63]-[65], [70]–[73]. See also *Hook v Sumner* [2016] BCC 220 at [93]—in so far as there was purported ratification of breaches of duty, the court rejected it as ineffective, being by the directors as shareholders.

**20-47**    Authorisation ensures that there is no breach of duty (and is included as a derivative claim lies with respect to proposed acts) while ratification cures any breach that previously existed.[118] The common law governing these matters is preserved by s 180(4)(a) (authorisation) and by s 239(7) (ratification). Authorisation by the company may mean by the shareholders or by the directors or, perhaps, via a provision in the articles. For most purposes, it will be by the shareholders, though by virtue of CA 2006, s 175(4)(b) directors may authorise what would otherwise be a conflict of interest and, by virtue of s 173(2)(b), the articles may authorise what would otherwise be a breach of the duty to exercise independent judgement and otherwise may make provision for dealing with conflicts of interest (s 180(4)(b)). In most cases, the issue will be whether ratification has occurred or is possible.

**20-48**    Ratification is governed by s 239 which provides that a resolution to ratify a breach of duty by a director (including former and shadow directors) is passed at a meeting only if the necessary (simple) majority is obtained disregarding votes in favour of the resolution by the director (if a member of the company) and any member connected with him (as defined in ss 252–255).[119] The limitation on voting in CA 2006, s 239 applies only to ratification of a breach of duty[120] and does not apply to prior authorisation so it might be tempting for the wrongdoer to use his voting power to seek prior authorisation for what would otherwise be a breach of duty, but that too may not be possible. The general position is that a shareholder has a right to vote on any matter though he has a personal interest opposed to or different from the interests of the company, but that right is subject to some ill-defined constraints which preclude its use in what can be described as an oppressive, unfair, and improper manner.[121] In some circumstances, the authorisation sought, if secured by interested voting, may fall foul of those constraints.

**20-49**    At common law, shareholders cannot authorise or ratify acts which are illegal or acts which are ultra vires[122] in the sense of transactions which constitute a return of capital to shareholders other than with the sanction of the court or in accordance with a statutory

---

[118] Permission to bring a derivative claim was refused on grounds of ratification in *Singh v Singh* [2014] 1 BCLC 649 where a claimant complained of the payment (by a solvent company) of dividends and remuneration to a director. The sums paid had been disclosed in the company's accounts each year which had been approved by all of the directors who were also all of the shareholders and so permission was refused (s 263(2)). Refusing permission to appeal in this case, see [2014] EWCA Civ 103, Vos LJ noted that the approval of the accounts provided a complete answer to the question whether the payments had been ratified.

[119] CA 2006, 239(4). The affected director and connected member may attend the meeting, count towards the quorum, and participate in the meeting: s 239(4). Equivalent measures apply where a written resolution is used: s 239(3). Incidentally, s 239 is of general application, it is in CA 2006, Pt 10, not Pt 11.

[120] It is also possible for the shareholders to vote to waive the company's claim rather than to ratify the wrongdoing and that vote is not subject to the restrictions in s 239, but see n 121. See also s 239(6)(b): nothing in this section affects any power of the directors to agree not to sue or to settle or release a claim made by them on behalf of the company.

[121] See *North-West Transportation Co Ltd v Beatty* (1887) 12 App Cas 589, esp at 593–4 (director was able to vote as a shareholder to ratify his own undisclosed conflict of interest in a transaction with the company, but the transaction in that case was fair, the price market-based, and the company benefited from the transaction); *Burland v Earle* [1902] AC 83 at 94, PC; *Cook v Deeks* [1916] AC 554 at 564, PC (majority shareholders by their votes cannot make a present to themselves of an asset belonging in equity to the company). See generally Flannigan, 'Shareholder Fiduciary Accountability' [2014] JBL 1, especially at 17–20, criticising the 'vacuity' of the analysis by the court in *North-West Transportation Co Ltd v Beatty*; see also **12-58**.

[122] Ultra vires is used in another sense to mean transactions beyond the company's objects. For companies with objects clauses (see Chapter 3), a restriction will operate only to limit the authority of the directors (see CA 2006, s 39) and a breach of a restriction is a breach of the duty to act in accordance with the constitution (s 171) which is capable of ratification, see **9-74**.

scheme.[123] Such ultra vires transactions can be described as a fraud on the creditors and are incapable of ratification.[124] It is also not open to the shareholders to authorise or ratify a failure by the directors to have regard to creditors' interests at a time when the company was insolvent or doubtfully solvent,[125] see discussion at **10-41**. These matters are incapable of ratification even by the shareholders unanimously so no question of majority power, interested or disinterested, arises and s 239(7) ensures that these acts do not fall within s 239.[126] Shareholders cannot authorise or ratify by a majority acts in breach of the company's constitution where the matter is a breach of a shareholder's individual, personal, substantive rights which can only be altered by a special resolution, though the extent to which the articles confer substantive rights on a shareholder is problematic and discussed at **5-59** et seq.

**20-50**   At common law, many breaches of duty by directors were ratifiable including non-disclosure of a conflict of interest in a transaction with the company,[127] mere negligence,[128] or the exercise of powers bona fide but for a collateral purpose.[129] But at common law shareholders could not authorise or ratify by their own votes acts which amount to the appropriation to themselves of 'money, property or advantages which belong to the company or in which the other shareholders are entitled to participate', a category usually described as a fraud on the minority.[130] In *Abouraya v Sigmund*[131] David Richards J reviewed the authorities on fraud on the minority and concluded that financial or other loss to the shareholders, albeit normally reflective of loss to the company, and benefit to the wrongdoers is essential to a claim.[132] He went on: 'The significance of this requirement (benefit to the wrongdoers) is that their breach of duty cannot be ratified by a majority vote which depends on the votes of the wrongdoers. It is essential to the exception to the rule in *Foss v Harbottle* that the alleged wrongdoing is incapable of lawful ratification.' In the famous words of Lord Buckmaster in *Cook v Deeks*:[133]

---

[123] *Trevor v Whitworth* (1887) 12 App Cas 409.

[124] *Trevor v Whitworth* (1887) 12 App Cas 409; *Ridge Securities Ltd v IRC* [1964] 1 All ER 275; *Re Halt Garage (1964) Ltd* [1982] 3 All ER 1016; *Aveling Barford Ltd v Perion Ltd* [1989] BCLC 626; also *Barclays Bank plc v British and Commonwealth Holdings plc* [1996] 1 BCLC 1 at 7. See *Rolled Steel Products (Holdings) Ltd v British Steel Corp* [1985] 3 All ER 52 at 86, per Slade LJ.

[125] See CA 2006, s 172(3); *West Mercia Safetywear Ltd v Dodd* [1988] BCLC 250, approving *Kinsela v Russell Kinsela Pty Ltd* (1986) 4 ACLC 215 at 223; *Rolled Steel Products (Holdings) Ltd v British Steel Corp* [1985] 3 All ER 52 at 86, per Slade LJ; *Secretary of State for Business, Innovation and Skills v Doffman* [2011] 2 BCLC 541 at [39]–[45].

[126] CA 2006, s 239(7): This section does not affect any other enactment or rule of law imposing additional requirements for valid ratification or any rule of law as to acts that are incapable of being ratified by the company.

[127] *North-West Transportation Co Ltd v Beatty* (1887) 12 App Cas 589 at 593–4 but see n 121.

[128] As in *Pavlides v Jensen* [1956] 2 All ER 518 (loss to the company, but no benefit to the wrongdoers).

[129] As in *Bamford v Bamford* [1969] 1 All ER 969, see also *Hogg v Cramphorn* [1966] 3 All ER 420; and see **9-73**.

[130] *Burland v Earle* [1902] AC 83 at 93, per Lord Davey, see at **20-4**; *Atwool v Merryweather* (1867) LR 5 Eq 464n; *Menier v Hooper's Telegraph Works* (1874) 9 Ch App 350; *Cook v Deeks* [1916] 1 AC 554; *Daniels v Daniels* [1978] 2 All ER 89; though, as Sealy noted, a fraud on the company would be a more accurate description: Sealy and Worthington, *Cases and Materials in Company Law* (11th edn, 2016), p 670.

[131] [2015] BCC 503.

[132] [2015] BCC 503 at [25]; see his review of the authorities at [16]–[25], including *Daniels v Daniels* [1978] Ch 406 at 414, per Templeman J: 'The principle ... is that a minority shareholder who has no other remedy may sue where directors use their powers, intentionally or unintentionally, fraudulently or negligently, in a manner which benefits themselves at the expense of the company.'

[133] [1916] 1 AC 554 at 564.

'[I]f directors have acquired for themselves property or rights which they must be regarded as holding on behalf of the company, a resolution that the rights of the company should be disregarded in the matter would amount to forfeiting the interest and property of the minority of shareholders in favour of the majority, and that by the votes of those who are interested in securing the property for themselves. Such use of voting power has never been sanctioned by the courts ...'

On this analysis, what matters most is not the nature of the transaction (the misappropriation) but the exercise of voting power to ratify it, a matter which has been the subject of some lengthy debate.[134] The Court of Appeal has endorsed the approach of David Richards J in *Harris v Microfusion 2003-2 LLP*[135] noting that:

'The majority can choose to excuse breaches of duty by directors, provided that the majority have not used their voting powers to confer benefits upon themselves in breach of duty and are not using the self-same powers to prevent the company from recovering the loss caused to it, in effect expropriating the minority in the process.'[136]

**20-51** The position is clarified by CA 2006, s 239 which requires that the votes of the director (if a member of the company) and any member connected with him is disregarded in determining whether the resolution to ratify a breach of duty has been passed. As the foundation of the fraud on the minority category is the abuse of voting power, of wrongdoers voting to approve their own misappropriation of corporate assets etc, as discussed at **20-50**,[137] once wrongdoer voting is no longer possible, the 'fraud on the minority' category falls away.[138] This is a valuable simplification of the law on ratification;[139] all breaches of duty are ratifiable, but only if ratified by disinterested shareholders.

**20-52** A remaining issue is whether a decision of disinterested shareholders in accordance with s 239 is then beyond challenge or whether that decision is in turn subject to those common law constraints suggested in *North-West Transportation Co Ltd v Beatty*,[140] namely that the ratification resolution (though of the independent shareholders) must not itself be brought about by unfair or improper means and must not be illegal or fraudulent or oppressive towards those shareholders who oppose it. It may be that that ratification is carried by the votes of parties allied to the wrongdoers, though not so formally connected with them as to require their votes to be disregarded in accordance with s 239. A further development may be, as Worthington has suggested, that the propriety of any resolution should rest on the bona fides and proper purposes of the decision-making body.[141]

**20-53** To sum up, looking at the absolute bars in s 263(2) to a derivative claim proceeding, it would seem that there is limited scope for dismissing a claim under this provision. As

---

[134] The debate is usefully summarised by Keay and Loughrey (2013), n 72, 202–7. See, in particular, Worthington, 'Corporate Governance: Remedying and Ratifying Directors' Breaches (2000) 116 LQR 638; Payne, 'A Re-examination of Ratification' (1999) 58 CLJ 604.

[135] [2017] 1 BCLC 305.    [136] [2017] 1 BCLC 305 at [33].    [137] [1916] 1 AC 554 at 564.

[138] See Mortimore (ed), *Company Directors: Duties, Liabilities and Remedies* (3rd edn, 2017), para 20.50 et seq; Chivers et al (eds), *The Law of Majority Shareholder Power* (2nd edn, 2017), para 7.19 ('... the fraud on the minority exception ... is now redundant'); Kershaw, *Company Law in Context* (2nd edn, 2012), p 590.

[139] Section 239 is limited to ratification so potentially it is out of step with the common law on authorisation which does not explicitly require independent shareholder authorisation, though the ill-defined constraints on shareholder voting are likely to have a similar consequence. See text to n 121.

[140] *North-West Transportation Co Ltd v Beatty* (1887) 12 App Cas 589 at 593–4.

[141] Worthington, n 134, 646–51. Another possibility, suggested by Payne, n 134, is that a decision should stand (respecting majority rule) unless no reasonable person could regard the decision taken as being in the best interests of the company, see at 623–6.

noted at **20-44**, the courts will only dismiss a claim for permission under s 263(2)(a) if no director would continue the case so a plausible claim cannot be dismissed on this basis. It is also quite likely that there is no evidence of actual authorisation or ratification which would mean the refusal of permission under s 263(2)(b) or (c) for, had there been, the shareholder would not have considered bringing a derivative claim (unless he wishes to dispute whether the matter was capable of authorisation or validly ratified). In many cases, therefore, the court will proceed to consider the matter in the light of the factors set out in CA 2006, s 263(3). Getting to this stage is still no guarantee of getting permission.[142]

### Discretion to allow a claim to proceed

**20-54**  In considering whether to give permission for a claim to proceed, the court must take into account, in particular, a number of factors which are set out in CA 2006, s 263(3) as follows:

(a) whether the member is acting in good faith in seeking to continue the claim;

(b) the importance that a director acting to promote the success of the company would attach to continuing it;

(c) whether the act or omission (still to occur) would be likely to be authorised or ratified by the company; or

(d) where the cause of action arises from an act or omission that has already occurred, whether the act or omission could be, and in the circumstances would be likely to be, ratified by the company;

(e) whether the company has decided not to pursue the claim;

(f) whether the act or omission in respect of which the claim is brought gives rise to a cause of action that the member could pursue in his own right rather than on behalf of the company.

**20-55**  The court is expected to take into account all of the factors together and in no particular order and how important each is in any case is for the court to determine having regard to all the circumstances,[143] but the courts are conscious of the need to avoid a mini-trial at this stage.[144] The factors listed in s 263(3) are not exhaustive and so, while the court must take them into account 'in particular', it can also consider any other matter which it considers to be relevant, such as the position of the company's employees,[145] or the solvency of the company.[146] A derivative claim should not normally be brought on behalf of a company in liquidation or administration for then the liquidator or administrator

---

[142]  See, for example, *Mission Capital plc v Sinclair* [2010] 1 BCLC 304; *Franbar Holdings Ltd v Patel* [2009] 1 BCLC 1 where, in each case, the court quickly concluded that there were no grounds for dismissing the application under the mandatory requirements of CA 2006, s 263(2), but equally quickly dismissed the application under the discretionary jurisdiction in s 263(3) instead.

[143]  See 679 HL Official Report (5th series), col GC 26, 27 February 2006. Boyle, n 26, suggests that the factors are ill-suited to the circumstances likely to arise in public listed companies. Keay and Loughrey, 'Derivative Proceedings in a Brave New World for Company Management and Shareholders' [2010] JBL 151 at 168, criticise the unnecessary proliferation of factors which the courts are considering which only prolong proceedings and create uncertainty as to the basis on which permission is being given or refused.

[144]  *Wishart v Castlecroft Securities Ltd* [2009] CSIH 615, [2009] SLT 812; and see the criticisms expressed in *Langley Ward Ltd v Trevor* [2011] EWHC 1893 at [61].

[145]  *Stimpson v Southern Private Landlords Association* [2010] BCC 387 at [37].

[146]  *Cinematic Finance Ltd v Ryder* [2012] BCC 797.

is in a position to act on behalf of the company.[147] The potential liability of the company for costs is an issue which the court inevitably considers,[148] so it is surprising that it is not listed as a factor in s 263(3). A claimant who does not seek an indemnity for costs removes a significant obstacle to securing permission, not least because the courts consider that to be a factor which would affect how the hypothetical director would view continuation of the claim.[149]

**20-56**   In weighing up the overall position, having regard to all of these factors etc, the court is guided by the purpose of a derivative claim, namely to provide a mechanism to give a remedy for a wrong which would otherwise escape redress.[150] It also has to be borne in mind that the rule in *Foss v Harbottle* remains in place. It follows that if, in fact, there is no wrongdoer control preventing the company from bringing a claim, the court may refuse permission (it is not mandatory to refuse) and require the claim to be brought by the company, respecting the proper plaintiff principle.

**20-57**   In *Bamford v Harvey*[151] the dispute concerned the failure of one director and 50 per cent shareholder (H) to repay a loan made to him by the company. The other director and 50 per cent shareholder (B) sought permission to bring a derivative claim. It emerged that, under the terms of their shareholders' agreement, there was a mechanism whereby B could procure that the company bring proceedings against H.[152] The court ruled that the company is usually the only party entitled to enforce a course of action belonging to it and a member is able to maintain proceedings about wrongs done to the company only in exceptional circumstances. While 'wrongdoer control' (as required at common law) is not an absolute condition for a derivative claim (otherwise it would be a specific provision in the CA 2006, s 263(2)), the court held that where proceedings can clearly be brought in the name of the company and there is no objection raised on that ground, they should be brought in the name of the company.[153] The proper plaintiff principle means that the existence of wrongdoer control remains relevant to the court's consideration of whether it should grant permission for a derivative claim to proceed. In practice, the absence of wrongdoer control may be an 'overwhelming' factor against giving permission for the claim,[154] but, because wrongdoer control is not prescribed as a mandatory threshold, the court has flexibility to consider whether it should still grant permission if the evidence shows that there are real obstacles to a claim by the company.[155]

---

[147] See *Barrett v Duckett* [1995] 1 BCLC 243; *Cinematic Finance Ltd v Ryder* [2012] BCC 797; and this also applies if the company is insolvent, but not in liquidation or administration: *Cinematic Finance Ltd v Ryder* at [22].

[148] See *Iesini v Westrip Holdings Ltd* [2011] 1 BCLC 498 at [126].

[149] See *Cullen Investments Ltd v Brown* [2016] 1 BCLC 491 at [55]—permission granted—the court thought that a hypothetical director would attach considerable importance to continuing a claim where the company could only win and not lose since, if unsuccessful, the costs were to be carried by the claimant. Also *Hughes v Weiss* [2012] EWHC 2363—permission granted, the claimant had accepted that she could not look to the company for an indemnity, at [55].

[150] See *Burland v Earle* [1902] AC 83 at 93–4; *Prudential Assurance Co Ltd v Newman Industries Ltd (No 2)* [1982] 1 All ER 354 at 357–8; *Smith v Croft (No 2)* [1987] 3 All ER 909 at 945 ('... whole doctrine ... is rooted in a procedural expedient and adopted to prevent a wrong going without redress'); *Nurcombe v Nurcombe* [1984] BCLC 557 at 562.

[151] [2013] BCC 311.

[152] This mechanism had simply been overlooked by the parties, see [2013] BCC 311 at [29].

[153] [2013] BCC 311 at [32].

[154] See *Stimpson v Southern Private Landlords Association* [2010] BCC 387 at [46], per Judge Pelling.

[155] See *Bamford v Harvey* [2013] BCC 311 at [29].

### Member acting in good faith–s 263(3)(a)

**20-58**    The motives of the claimant is an important filter and it is for the shareholder seeking permission to establish to the satisfaction of the court that he is a person acting in good faith and that he should be allowed to sue on behalf of the company.[156] Once there is a real purpose in bringing the claim in the company's interest, the court is unlikely to consider the claimant to be in bad faith,[157] even though there may be some collateral benefit or advantage to the claimant.[158] A claimant will not be in good faith, however, if motivated to litigate by personal considerations rather than in the interests of the company.[159] A separate consideration at common law which the court can take account of under Part 11 also, given that the factors listed in s 263(3) are not exhaustive, is whether the claimant is a proper person to bring the claim forward, which he would not be if he had participated in the wrong of which he complains.[160]

### Importance a director would attach to continuing the claim–s 263(3)(b)

**20-59**    Accepting that a director would seek to continue the claim for the purpose of s 263(2)(a) (otherwise the case would not have reached this stage), the court moves on to assessing the importance which a director would attach to continuing it. The court may be as reluctant to refuse permission to continue the claim on this basis as under s 263(2)(a), see **20-44**. The court has to look at the matter from the perspective of the hypothetical director acting in accordance with his duty under s 172[161] and assess the importance he would attach to continuing the claim. That director would look to the same considerations as are relevant to s 263(2)(a) and to which Lewison J drew attention in *Iesini v Westrip Holdings Ltd*,[162] (see at **20-44**), namely, the size and strength of the claim, the time and costs involved, the likelihood of success and recovery and so on.[163] As Roth J noted in *Stainer v Lee*,[164]

---

[156] *Barrett v Duckett* [1995] 1 BCLC 243 at 250. It may be helpful to show that the claimant has the support of other minority shareholders, see *Stainer v Lee* [2011] 1 BCLC 537 at [49] (applicant for permission could show letters of support and a financial contribution from 35 other small shareholders).

[157] See *Mission Capital plc v Sinclair* [2010] 1 BCLC 304 at [42].

[158] *Iesini v Westrip Holdings Ltd* [2011] 1 BCLC 498 at [121]. See *Hughes v Weiss* [2012] EWHC 2363 at [47], if the object of the claim is recovery of moneys for the company, the fact that the claimant would then benefit from an increase in the value of her shareholding does not make the purpose of the litigation an improper purpose; likewise where the claim is for the benefit of the company, but the claimant would also benefit as a creditor, that does not amount to a collateral purpose and lack of good faith: *Parry v Bartlett* [2012] BCC 700 at [86]. See also *Franbar Holdings Ltd v Patel* [2009] 1 BCLC 1 at [33]; Law Commission Report, n 26, para 6.76.

[159] *Barrett v Duckett* [1995] 1 BCLC 243 (claimant not pursuing claim bona fide in the interests of the company, but for personal reasons to do with the divorce of the company's sole director and the claimant's daughter). See also *Abouraya v Sigmund* [2015] BCC 503, a multiple derivative claim—one of the reasons for refusing permission was that the claimant's purpose was to advance his interests as a creditor of the company. See generally Payne, '"Clean Hands" in Derivative Actions' (2002) 61 CLJ 76; Keay and Loughrey, 'Something Old, Something New, Something Borrowed: An Analysis of the New Derivative Action under the Companies Act 2006' (2008) 124 LQR 469 at 485–91.

[160] *Iesini v Westrip Holdings Ltd* [2011] 1 BCLC 498 at [122]; also *Nurcombe v Nurcombe* [1984] BCLC 557 at 562. In *Bridge v Daley* [2015] EWHC 2121 at [84]–[85], [92], the court accepted that the behaviour of the claimant meant it would not be appropriate to allow him to have the conduct of the claim, though the court accepted that he was not acting in bad faith.

[161] 'Success' has to be considered in the context of the company's position and, where the company will be dissolved following the litigation, 'success' may mean ensuring a fair distribution of benefits to the members, so a person acting in accordance with s 172 would attach importance to continuing the proceedings, see *Hughes v Weiss* [2012] EWHC 2363 at [53]–[54].

[162] [2011] 1 BCLC 498 at [86].          [163] *Franbar Holdings Ltd v Patel* [2009] 1 BCLC 1 at [36].

[164] [2011] 1 BCLC 537 at [29], per Roth J; and see *Kleanthous v Paphitis* [2012] BCC 676; *Parry v Bartlett* [2012] BCC 70.

a hypothetical director may consider it appropriate to continue a claim where the case against the director seems very strong, even if the likely level of recovery is not so large, since the claim may provoke a settlement or summary judgment and, likewise, a director may consider it appropriate to continue a claim where the case is less strong, if the amount of potential recovery is very large.[165] A hypothetical director would attach considerable importance to continuing a claim where the claimant has funded it himself without any risk to the company, such that the company's funds cannot be diminished by the litigation, but only enhanced.[166] If the company is no longer trading, the question for the hypothetical director will be whether the funds available for distribution to the members are likely to be increased or diminished by continuing the litigation.[167] A hypothetical director would take into account the views, if they existed, of independent non-executive directors whose conduct is not the subject of the claim and who are legally advised and he would give due consideration to their view that the claim should not be pursued.[168] The fact that the potential claim might more naturally be the subject of a petition for relief under CA 2006, s 994 (unfairly prejudicial conduct) is also something which a hypothetical director would consider. In *Cullen Investments Ltd v Brown*[169] the court noted that the duty under s 172(1)(f) to act fairly as between the members would require the hypothetical director to consider whether the claimant really needs the company to pursue the claim as opposed to the claimant pursing some alternative remedy.

### Authorisation/ratification—s 263(3)(c) and (d)

**20-60**   The position on authorisation and ratification was discussed at **20-46**. The question here is whether an act or omission is likely to be authorised or ratified and this requires the court to consider the factual position within the individual company, bearing in mind that it is always open to the court to adjourn the proceedings (under s 261(4)(c)) to allow a meeting to be called for the purposes of authorisation or ratification.[170]

### Company has decided not to pursue the claim—s 263(3)(e)

**20-61**   Under this heading, the court considers any decision which may have been taken by the company not to pursue the claim (as opposed to authorising or ratifying any breach of duty).[171] If the company has not actually considered the matter, the court may adjourn

---

[165]   Vice versa, a hypothetical director would place little importance on pursuing a claim which would be very difficult to establish, might not be cost effective, and which the company would have difficulty in funding: see *Brannigan v Style* [2016] EWHC 512 at [90]–]91].

[166]   *Cullen Investments Ltd v Brown* [2016] 1 BCLC 491 at [55].

[167]   *Cullen Investments Ltd v Brown* [2016] 1 BCLC 491 at [55].

[168]   See *Kleanthous v Paphitis* [2012] BCC 676. CA 2006, 263(3)(b), provides a mechanism by which the court may have regard to the views of the independent directors while s 263(3)(e) requires the court to have regard to any decision of the company not to pursue the claim and s 263(4) requires the court to have regard to the views of disinterested members. The cumulative effect is to require the court to consider all possible constituencies within the board and the shareholders.

[169]   [2016] 1 BCLC 491 at [58]; also *Franbar Holdings Ltd v Patel* [2009] 1 BCLC 1 at [37]; *Mission Capital plc v Sinclair* [2010] 1 BCLC 304 at [43], [46].

[170]   See 679 HL Official Report (5th series), cols GC 27–8, 27 February 2006; HC Official Report, SC D (Company Law Reform Bill), 13 July 2006, col 679. If it is clear that the breach will be ratified, it is pointless to call a meeting, and the court can simply refuse permission to continue the claim: *Smith v Croft (No 2)* [1987] 3 All ER 909 at 957; see also Law Commission Report, n 26, para 6.84.

[171]   679 HL Official Report (5th series), cols GC 8, 29–30, 27 February 2006. As was noted in *Prudential Assurance Co Ltd v Newman Industries Ltd (No 2)* [1982] 1 All ER 354 at 365, a board might conclude that to pursue the claim would not be to the company's advantage and to allow someone to do so might result in the company being 'killed by kindness'; and see CA 2006, s 239(6)(b).

proceedings so that a properly authorised organ of the company, whether that be the board or the shareholders, can consider the practical desirability of the claim going forward.[172] In *Kleanthous v Paphitis*,[173] refusing permission to continue the claim, the court attached considerable weight to the fact that a committee made up of the two directors (chief executive and the finance director) who were not defendants to the claim, who had taken legal advice and reviewed the matter at the request of the board, was against the claim proceeding. The committee had concluded that it would not be in the company's commercial interests (in terms of management disruption, damage to the company's performance as a result of the loss of experienced and high profile directors, damage to reputation and to the brand[174]) to continue the claim against the company's major shareholders and directors. The court noted that those independent directors were better placed than the court to assess where the company's commercial interests lay.[175] Of course, little weight will attach to a decision taken by the directors where the defendants are in the majority.[176]

### A cause of action that a member could pursue in his own right—s 263(3)(f)

**20-62**    The next question for the court is whether the conduct complained of, etc gives rise to a cause of action that a member could pursue in his own right rather than on behalf of the company.[177] The existence of an alternative personal claim arising from the same act or omission is not a bar to a derivative claim, it is just one of the factors to be considered by the court.[178] In most cases, the issue is whether the potential availability of relief under the broad unfairly prejudicial jurisdiction in CA 2006, s 994 is 'a cause of action' that a member could pursue in his own right[179] so that permission to continue a derivative claim should be refused.[180] The factor which the court needs to consider is the nature of the alleged wrongdoing and whether there are other ways in which it can be addressed effectively rather than by a derivative claim.

---

[172] *Smith v Croft (No 2)* [1987] 3 All ER 909 at 955–6.          [173] [2012] BCC 676.

[174] Factors which would be relevant also to the importance which a director would attach to continuing the claim under s 263(3)(b), see **20-59**.

[175] See [2012] BCC 676 at [75]; see *Bridge v Daley* [2015] EWHC 2121 at [61], [74]—permission refused— an independent board reviewed the allegations, took professional advice, and concluded that continuing the claim was not in the best interests of the company, though they took no formal decision to that effect, deferring to an imminent court hearing in the case.

[176] See *Cullen Investments Ltd v Brown* [2016] 1 BCLC 491 at [57]. The court in *Brannigan v Style* [2016] EWHC 512 at [91] attached little weight to a solicitors' report on the claim commissioned by the board when the solicitors were instructed by the respondent directors.

[177] The wording is quite deliberate for, during the Parliamentary debates, the Government declined to adopt an Opposition amendment which would have required the court to consider specifically the availability of an alternative remedy. It did so on two grounds: (1) that an alternative remedy in the form of an offer to buy the claimant's shares is not an appropriate remedy in the circumstances of a derivative claim; and (2) that this approach might encourage vulture funds to tell companies that they must either buy them out or face a possible derivative claim: see 682 HL Official Report (5th series), cols 726–8 (23 May 2006).

[178] *Iesini v Westrip Holdings Ltd* [2011] 1 BCLC 498; *Kiani v Cooper* [2010] 2 BCLC 427 at [38], [41]; *Franbar Holdings Ltd v Patel* [2009] 1 BCLC 1 at [50].

[179] As was noted in *Langley Ward Ltd v Trevor* [2011] EWHC 1893 at [13], the language of 'cause of action' is not very apt for petitions under CA 2006, s 994, but since the factors listed in s 263(3) are not exhaustive, the court can have regard to the availability of relief under s 994 regardless of whether, strictly speaking, it falls within a 'cause of action' and s 263(3)(f).

[180] See *Jafari-Fini v Skillglass Ltd* [2005] BCC 842, CA, permission to bring a derivative claim at common law refused when, on the same grounds, the claimant could bring and was bringing a claim for breach of contract. The court concluded that it was better for that contractual claim to be determined first than for the company to be put to the cost of funding a derivative claim in respect of the same issues.

**20-63**    Of course, in some situations, a derivative claim may be the most effective remedy (typically resulting in assets being restored to the company) rather than a personal remedy
under s 994 which would typically see the claimant's shares purchased by the respondents
to the petition.[181] For example, a claimant might find that any potential personal claim
would be defeated by the reflective loss principle, so only the company is in a position to
pursue the wrongdoers.[182] Claims for breach of contract or conspiracy may be more difficult to establish by the claimant than by the company, not least because of a lack of access
to corporate information by an individual claimant.[183] In *Hook v Sumner*[184] the real issue
between the warring parties was the extent and terms of a licensing agreement to which the
company was party, so it was more appropriate that the claim be brought in the company's
name. On occasion, the claimant is looking to the potential future value of the business
which he or she can only exploit by remaining in the business, rather than having his or
her shares valued for buy-out purposes on a basis which runs the risk of undervaluing the
potential of the company.[185] In *Wishart v Castlecroft Securities Ltd*[186] a buy-out of shares in
a property company at a time when the property market was depressed was not desirable
whereas recovery by the company of corporate opportunities wrongfully diverted away by
a director via a derivative claim offered the possibility of future value for the shareholders. A further advantage to a derivative claim in this instance was that it would allow the
matter to be pursued against a third party recipient of the opportunities so allowing for
direct relief for the company in respect of that party's knowing assistance in the director's
breach of duty. In *Hook v Sumner*[187] there was significant future earnings potential in the
licensing of the company's assets so it was preferable that the company pursue a claim with
respect to the terms of that licensing.[188] In these cases, a claim by the company is the best
option rather than a buy-out of the claimant which would be the usual consequence of a
s 994 petition. There is also the possibility that the claimant is not able to meet the requirement under s 994 that the company's affairs are being or have been conducted in a manner
which is unfairly prejudicial to the interests of the member or members generally when the
complaint relates to an issue of misconduct by a director,[189] see **19-84**.

[181] See Law Commission Report, n 26, paras 6.10–6.12. See *Airey v Cordell* [2007] BCC 785, a common
law derivative claim was preferable to recover assets improperly diverted away so that the claimant could
participate in the long-term gains to be expected from their exploitation; *Kiani v Cooper* [2010] 2 BCLC 427
at [38], [41], claimant wanted the company to pursue various development projects as planned and wanted
to remain a member of it; *Stainer v Lee* [2011] 1 BCLC 537 at [52], claimant wanted the company to pursue a
claim against two directors for misconduct and an order for restitution to the company, he did not want to
be bought out; also *Hughes v Weiss* [2012] EWHC 2363 at [66], claimant wanted restitution to the company
and did not want her shares to be bought; *Re Fort Gilkicker Ltd, UPMS Ltd v Fort Gilkicker* [2013] 3 All ER
546 (multiple derivative claim, court did not think the theoretical availability of s 994 rendered a derivative
claim inappropriate where neither side wanted a buy-out, at [57]–[58]).

[182] See *Cullen Investments Ltd v Brown* [2016] 1 BCLC 491, claimant had the option of enforcing a joint
venture agreement, but the losses suffered might have been regarded as reflective loss and irrecoverable
other than by the company.

[183] See *Cullen Investments Ltd v Brown* [2016] 1 BCLC 491.          [184] [2016] BCC 220 at [135]–[137].

[185] *Kiani v Cooper* [2010] 2 BCLC 427 (value of future planning developments); *Wishart v Castlecroft
Securities Ltd* [2009] CSIH 615 (company had a property portfolio, value of which could increase in the
future).

[186] [2009] CSIH 615, [2009] SLT 812 (a Scottish decision, but the provisions on derivative claims in
Scotland, set out in CA 2006, Pt 11, Ch 2, are in substance identical to those applicable to the rest of the UK,
though there are procedural differences as the CPR do not apply in Scotland).

[187] [2016] BCC 220.          [188] [2016] BCC 220 at [132].

[189] See *Re Charnley Davies Ltd (No 2)* [1990] BCLC 760, discussed at **19-84**; and *Stainer v Lee* [2011]
1 BCLC 537 at [52]; *Parry v Bartlett* [2012] BCC 700 (not clear that CA 2006, s 994 petition was a realistic
alternative on the facts); also *Cullen Investments Ltd v Brown* [2016] 1 BCLC 491 (the derivative claim was
only brought once it became clear that there might be difficulties in pursuing alternatives, at [61]).

**20-64**   Sometimes liquidation may be the sensible option. In *Langley Ward Ltd v Trevor*[190] the company was deadlocked and its business had run its course and the court thought it was a natural candidate to be wound up on the just and equitable ground under IA 1986, s 122(1)(g), see **19-95**. On balance, a liquidation would be the best forum for the claims to be investigated and the court refused permission for the continuation of a derivative claim. Vice versa, in *Hughes v Weiss*[191] the court thought matters could be more conveniently litigated in a derivative claim than in a liquidation.

**20-65**   In other scenarios, the claim lends itself more naturally to a s 994 petition alleging that the company's affairs are being conducted in an unfairly prejudicial manner, often because the complaint is not so much of breach of duty to the company, but about the way in which the company is being managed.[192] Such complaints are better suited to a petition rather than to a derivative claim. It may be clear also that the claimant just wants to be bought out of the company[193] in which case the court will refuse permission, as the relief which the applicant is seeking is available to him under CA 2006, s 994.[194]

### Views of disinterested shareholders—s 263(4)

**20-66**   In addition to the factors listed in s 263(3), the court is required under s 263(4) to have particular regard to any evidence before it as to the views of members of the company who have no personal interest, direct or indirect, in the matter.[195] This requirement is intended to reflect the position adopted by Knox J in *Smith v Croft (No 2)*[196] as to the weight to be given to the influential views of those shareholders who are independent of the wrongdoers.[197] Knox J was unconvinced that a just result is achieved by a single minority shareholder having the right to involve a company in an action for recovery of compensation for the company if all the other minority shareholders are, for disinterested reasons, satisfied that the proceedings will be productive of more harm than good.[198] In *Iesini v Westrip*

---

[190]   [2011] EWHC 1893.        [191]   [2012] EWHC 2363 at [69].

[192]   See *Bridge v Daley* [2015] EWHC 2121 at [84].

[193]   See *Kleanthous v Paphitis* [2012] BCC 676 (permission refused: evidence suggested that the remedy that the applicant wanted was to be bought out and he was pursuing the derivative claim because of the availability of a costs indemnity, see **20-32**); also *Mission Capital plc v Sinclair* [2010] 1 BCLC 304 (permission refused: the court did not consider that the claimants were seeking anything which could not be recovered by means of an unfair prejudice petition); *Franbar Holdings Ltd v Patel* [2009] 1 BCLC 1 (permission refused: claims by the member for breach of a shareholders' agreement as well as under CA 2006, s 994 should give the applicant all the relief sought).

[194]   In *Iesini v Westrip Holdings Ltd* [2011] 1 BCLC 498 at [82] and [123]–[126]. Lewison J noted that the combination of potential liability for costs and the availability of an alternative remedy under s 994 may justify refusal of permission. In this case, the derivative claim was based essentially on an allegation that the directors have failed to assert the company's rights against a third party and the court thought that, assuming jurisdiction can be established under s 994, the court could order (under s 996) that the company assert that claim, if necessary by litigation. This was one of the earlier cases and the result looks a little odd now. If the essence of the claim was a failure to assert the company's rights against a third party, it would seem to be a clear derivative claim and not something to litigate via s 994.

[195]   The Law Commission had considered this issue in terms of seeking the opinion of an independent organ (see Law Commission Report, n 26, paras 6.88–6.89), a term derived from *Smith v Croft (No 2)* [1987] 3 All ER 909 at 957–60, but it was criticised as being unclear. The formulation in the statute has avoided that problem, but may be difficult to apply in a widely-held company.

[196]   [1987] 3 All ER 909 at 957.

[197]   See 681 HL Official Report (5th series), cols 883–4, 888, 9 May 2006. This provision was one of the amendments made to Part 11 when the Bill was going through Parliament to meet concerns that there were inadequate filters to deter vexatious claims (see **20-14**).

[198]   [1987] 3 All ER 909 at 956.

*Holdings Ltd*[199] Lewison J noted, obiter, that s 263(4) is not easy to understand since, in theory, all shareholders have an obvious interest in any claim brought on the company's behalf as the value of their shareholdings will increase or diminish depending on the outcome. He considered that the provision was probably intended to encompass those members not implicated in the alleged wrongdoing and who do not stand to benefit otherwise than in their capacity as members of the company.[200]

**20-67** It was also suggested in the Parliamentary debates that this provision allows the opinions of shareholders in a major quoted company to be taken into account while acknowledging that it is not practicable or desirable in such companies to ask share-holders formally to approve directors' commercial decisions.[201] Ratification or authori-sation may not have taken place (s 263(3)(c)) and there may not be an actual decision of the company not to continue the claim (s 263(3)(e)), but it may nevertheless be possible to show that the shareholders are content to support the directors in respect of what has occurred.[202]

**20-68** A practical concern is how to evidence the views of the disinterested shareholders for the court. In *Bridge v Daley*[203] the company sent letters to the largest shareholders out-lining the issues being raised by the claimant and none of those consulted supported the claim. The claimant was given an opportunity at the company's annual general meeting to raise his general allegations when asking questions of the board, so the shareholders knew broadly of his concerns. At that same general meeting, the share-holders re-elected the alleged wrongdoers to the board by a 97 per cent majority of votes cast. The court concluded that it was clear that the disinterested shareholders were against the continuation of the action.[204] If the shareholders' views are to be deduced from the manner in which they voted on a resolution at a general meeting, there must be evidence that they were properly informed as to the resolution they were asked to approve.[205]

### The decision on permission

**20-69** Having reviewed all the factors in s 263(3) and considered the views of the disinterested shareholders under s 263(4), the court may grant permission for the claim to proceed, may refuse permission, or may adjourn the proceedings and give such directions as it thinks fit.[206]

**20-70** On occasion, permission has been given on a limited basis, so requiring the applicant to return to the court to determine whether the claim can continue. In *Stainer v Lee*,[207] for

---

[199] [2011] 1 BCLC 498 at [129].

[200] [2011] 1 BCLC 498 at [129]–[130]. In *Iesini* the shareholders who were being held out as having no personal interest in the matter turned out to have an informal understanding with the defendant director which gave them a financial interest in the outcome of the litigation. The court did not consider that they were persons to whom the court had to have particular regard, at [130].

[201] See 681 HL Official Report (5th series), col 884, 9 May 2006.

[202] See 681 HL Official Report (5th series), col 884, 9 May 2006.

[203] [2015] EWHC 2121 at [56]–[58]—the company in this case unusually was a company traded on the Alternative Investment Market (AIM). In *Stimpson v Southern Private Landlords Association* [2010] BCC 387, the company had a large (and fluctuating) number of members and a questionnaire was circulated by order of the court to the members to determine their views on permitting the claim to proceed, but it was an unusual not-for-profit company which was essentially a trade association.

[204] [2015] EWHC 2121 at [73].      [205] *Stainer v Lee* [2011] 1 BCLC 537 at [44]–[46].

[206] Once permission to continue a claim is given, the court may order that the claim cannot be dis-continued, or settled, or compromised without the court's permission, see CPR 19.9F; Practice Direction 19C—Derivative Claims, para 7.      [207] [2011] 1 BCLC 537 at [37], [55].

example, permission was granted to continue the claim just to the conclusion of disclosure which would give a clearer picture of the strength of the case and the quantum of loss.[208]

**20-71**   Overall, few applicants have secured permission and, where they have been successful, it has been on the basis of appropriation of corporate asset/opportunities by the majority for their benefit and to the detriment of the minority.[209] For example, in *SDI Retail Services Ltd v King and Murray*[210] permission was granted where there was a *prima facie* case that the directors in breach of duty had procured the majority (corporate) shareholder to terminate a licensing agreement on which the company's business depended. The directors were also directors of the majority shareholder and its parent company. In *Hook v Sumner*[211] the claim was based on an allegation that the majority were appropriating to themselves the royalties from the company's music catalogue. In *Cullen Investments Ltd v Brown*[212] permission was granted where the director had exploited a conflict of interest to his own benefit without the agreement of the company. In other words, these are all cases which, at common law, would have secured permission. It would seem, then, that Part 11 has not transformed the landscape, has not exposed directors to claims on broader grounds, or indeed opened the floodgates to litigious shareholders.[213] At most, it might be said that it has brought some procedural clarity, but that too is open to debate, given the issues identified earlier around the threshold for the second stage, the myriad factors which the court considers before granting relief and the significant issue of costs.

**20-72**   The position remains that there is no incentive to litigate via a derivative claim. Recovery is for the benefit of the company, not the individual claimant who can only benefit to the extent that benefit to the company is reflected in the value of his shares, Save where a claimant is determined to remain as a member of the company, it continues to be preferable to petition for relief under CA 2006, s 994 (unfairly prejudicial conduct) without the need for permission of the court and with the prospect of personal recovery. All things considered, the mere introduction of the statutory derivative claim has not dramatically increased the litigation risk to directors, nor indeed significantly enhanced the protection of shareholders.

# E  Corporate loss and reflective loss

**20-73**   The decision of the Court of Appeal in *Prudential Assurance Co Ltd v Newman Industries Ltd (No 2)*[214] establishes that a personal claim by a member against another in respect of the diminution in value of his shareholding as a result of a wrong done to the company

---

[208]  See also *Kiani v Cooper* [2010] 2 BCLC 427 at [42]; permission was given to continue down to disclosure which would give the defendant director the opportunity to produce the documentation which he said would refute allegations of improper payments to a company controlled by him. In each case, the applicant must then return to the court to seek further permission to continue the claim.

[209]  Permission was granted in the following cases: *Hughes v Weiss* [2012] EWHC 2363 (concerning alleged misappropriation of company's bank account); *Parry v Bartlett* [2012] BCC 700 (alleged misappropriation of proceeds of sale of company property); *Stainer v Lee* [2011] 1 BCLC 537 (alleged unauthorised, interest free, loans of company money to majority); *Kiani v Cooper* [2010] 2 BCLC 423 (allegations of misappropriation of assets).

[210]  [2017] EWHC 737.    [211]  [2016] BCC 220.    [212]  [2016] 1 BCLC 491.

[213]  This has also been the experience of other jurisdictions which have introduced statutory derivative actions. In Canada, New Zealand, and Australia, the statutory derivative procedures have been used to an insignificant degree and mainly in respect of private companies, not public companies as might have been anticipated: see Ramsay and Saunders, n 30, 420; Cheffins, n 30, 241.

[214]  [1982] 1 All ER 354.

is misconceived and should be struck out, for the shareholder's loss is merely reflective of the loss suffered by the company and that loss will be fully remedied if the company enforces its full rights against the wrongdoer.[215] The wrongdoer may be a director[216] or a third party, such as an auditor or solicitor or other adviser to the company.[217] The *Prudential* principle does not apply where a duty is owed only to the shareholder so that the company has no claim (because it is not a party, for example, to the contract which is the subject of the claim) or where there is a separate duty owed to the shareholder breach of which causes a loss distinct and separate from that suffered by the company and which is not remedied therefore by recovery by the company.[218] But if the substance of the claim is the same, though the cause of action is different, the no reflective loss rule applies.[219] The *Prudential* principle is an exclusionary rule denying the claimant a right to sue and so the onus is on the defendant to establish its applicability.[220] This no reflective loss principle was affirmed by the House of Lords in a complex judgment in *Johnson v Gore Wood & Co*[221] and has been the subject of further analysis by the Court of Appeal, particularly in *Giles v Rhind*[222] and *Gardner v Parker*.[223]

**20-74** The result is that no action lies at the suit of a shareholder suing to make good a diminution in value of his shareholding (including loss of dividends and all other payments which the shareholder might have obtained from the company had it not been deprived of its funds,[224] and whether those payments would have been received in the capacity of shareholder or otherwise[225]) where that claim merely reflects the loss suffered by the company and that loss would have been made good if the company had enforced in full its rights against the defendant wrongdoer. No action by a shareholder lies even if the company acting through its constitutional organs declines or fails to make good that loss,[226] or chooses not to exercise its remedies against the wrongdoers or settles for less than it

---

[215] [1982] 1 All ER 354 at 366–7; see also *Stein v Blake* [1998] 1 All ER 724. It matters not whether the shareholder's claim is for breach of contract, in tort, or for breach of fiduciary duty: *Gardner v Parker* [2004] 2 BCLC 554; *Shaker v Al-Bedrawi* [2003] 1 BCLC 517.

[216] See *Gardner v Parker* [2004] 2 BCLC 554, CA; *Giles v Rhind* [2003] 1 BCLC 1, CA; *Shaker v Al-Bedrawi* [2003] 1 BCLC 517, CA.

[217] See *Johnson v Gore Wood & Co* [2001] 1 BCLC 313, HL; *Day v Cook* [2002] 1 BCLC 1.

[218] *Johnson v Gore Wood & Co* [2001] 1 BCLC 313 at 338, per Lord Bingham; *Giles v Rhind* [2003] 1 BCLC 1 at [30]; *Day v Cook* [2002] 1 BCLC 1 at [41], [79]; and see *Pearce v European Reinsurance Consultants* [2005] 2 BCLC 366 where the shareholder did have a distinct claim; also *Jafari-Fini v Skillglass Ltd* [2005] BCC 842 at [29]. The principle of reflective loss does not prevent a shareholder, as a party to a joint venture agreement, suing for specific performance of that agreement to require the other party to make payments to the company. The action to enforce the contract is not an action open to the company and the recovery is not by the shareholder for the payments are made to the company, hence the no reflective loss principle has no application: *Latin American Investments Limited v Maroil Trading Inc* [2017] EWHC 1254 (appeal pending).

[219] *Gardner v Parker* [2004] 2 BCLC 554 at [49], applying *Shaker v Al-Bedrawi* [2003] 1 BCLC 157.

[220] *Shaker v Al-Bedrawi* [2003] 1 BCLC 517 at [83], per Peter Gibson LJ.

[221] [2001] 1 BCLC 313, HL. See Ferran, 'Litigation by Shareholders and Reflective Loss' (2001) 60 CLJ 245; Watts, 'The Shareholder as Co-promisee' (2001) 117 LQR 388; Shapira, 'Shareholder Personal Action in Respect of a Loss Suffered by the Company (2003) 37 Int'l L 137; Mitchell, 'Shareholders' Claims for Reflective Loss' (2004) 120 LQR 457; also Mukwari, 'The No Reflective Loss Principle' (2005) 26 Co Law 304; Lee Suet Lin, 'Barring Recovery for Diminution in Value of Shares on Reflective Loss Claims' (2007) 66 CLJ 533.

[222] [2003] 1 BCLC 1.

[223] [2004] 2 BCLC 554, affirming the decision of Blackburne J, see [2004] 1 BCLC 417.

[224] See *Johnson v Gore Wood & Co* [2001] 1 BCLC 313 at 370, per Lord Millett.

[225] For example, as a creditor or employee of the company, see *Johnson v Gore Wood & Co* [2001] 1 BCLC 313 at 370, per Lord Millett; *Gardner v Parker* [2004] 2 BCLC 554 at [70], per Neuberger LJ.

[226] See *Johnson v Gore Wood & Co* [2001] 1 BCLC 313 at 337, per Lord Bingham.

might have done.[227] In those situations, the shareholder's claim can be defeated by the no reflective loss principle.[228]

**20-75**   However, if the company has been disabled by the wrongdoer by the very act of which complaint is made from pursuing the loss, as opposed to choosing not to sue or settling the claim disadvantageously,[229] the shareholder can maintain a claim for what is reflective loss, a qualification established by *Giles v Rhind*.[230] That qualification from *Giles v Rhind* was criticised by Lord Millett sitting as a member of the Hong Kong Court of Final Appeal in *Waddington v Chan Chun Hoo Thomas*,[231] who considered that *Giles v Rhind* was wrongly decided and had the effect of allowing recovery by the wrong party to the prejudice of the company and its creditors. Subsequently, in *Webster v Sanderson*,[232] the Court of Appeal robustly rejected that criticism, noting that the decision in *Giles v Rhind* is binding on the Court of Appeal and only the Supreme Court can overrule it, but also noting that the decision was considered in detail and without dissent by the Court of Appeal in *Gardner v Parker*.[233] The critical point in *Giles v Rhind*, the court noted, was that the company was disabled from bringing the claim by the very wrongdoing complained about by the shareholder.[234]

**20-76**   This rule against the recovery of reflective loss is not concerned with barring causes of action as such, but with barring recovery of certain types of loss.[235] The foundation of the rule is the protection of the company and the need to avoid double recovery (and see further at **20-78**).[236] As Lord Millett explained in *Johnson v Gore Wood*: 'If the shareholder is allowed to recover in respect of such loss, then either there will be double recovery at the expense of the defendant or the shareholder will recover at the expense of the company

---

[227] See *Johnson v Gore Wood & Co* [2001] 1 BCLC 313 at 369, per Lord Millett.

[228] In *Sukhoruchkin v Van Bekestein* [2014] EWCA Civ 399, an appeal against the discontinuance of a freezing injunction, the Court of Appeal declined to be drawn, see at [57]–[58], on a distinction suggested by the appellants' counsel (disputed by the respondents) between situations where the company's claim is subject to a procedural bar, such as a limitation defence or a settlement of the claim where the 'no reflective loss' principle applies and a shareholder is barred by it from proceeding, and a situation where the company's claim could be met by a defence (for example, where a claim in misrepresentation inducing a contract is met by a defence of affirmation of the contract) where it was suggested that the no reflective loss principle would not apply (presumably arguing that this latter situation is equivalent to the company not having a cause of action). See *Barings v Coopers & Lybrand (No 1)* [2002] 2 BCLC 364 at [113]–[137] and the obiter comments of Evans-Lombe J on this issue; also *Day v Cook* [2002] 1 BCLC 1 at [38]; *Shaker v Al-Bedrawi* [2003] 1 BCLC 157 at [83]; *Perry v Day* [2004] EWHC 1398, [2005] BCC 375 at [65]. Also De Jong, 'Shareholders' Claims for Reflective Loss: A Comparative Analysis' [2013] EBOR 97.

[229] See *Gardner v Parker* [2004] 2 BCLC 554 at [60], per Neuberger LJ; *Johnson v Gore Wood & Co* [2001] 1 BCLC 313 at 369, per Lord Millett.

[230] [2003] 1 BCLC 1, noted Hirt [2003] JBL 420. As the Court of Appeal noted in this case, it was the defendant director's wrong (essentially he 'stole' the company's business reducing it to insolvency) that had disabled the company from pursuing any claim for damages against him which wrong he then compounded by an application for security for costs against the company when his own breach made it impossible for the company to provide such security: see [2003] 1 BCLC 1 at [66], [74]. The Court of Appeal considered that *Johnson v Gore Wood & Co* [2001] 1 BCLC 313 had no application to that situation which had not been in the contemplation of the House of Lords. See also *Perry v Day* [2005] EWHC 3372, [2005] 2 BCLC 405. See Mitchell, 'Shareholders' Claims for Reflective Loss' (2004) 120 LQR 457 at 471–2.

[231] [2009] 2 BCLC 82 at [81]–[88].      [232] [2009] 2 BCLC 542 at [36].

[233] [2004] 2 BCLC 554.      [234] [2009] 2 BCLC 542 at [38].

[235] *Gardner v Parker* [2004] 2 BCLC 554 at [49], per Neuberger LJ.

[236] *Johnson v Gore Wood & Co* [2001] 1 BCLC 313; *Gardner v Parker* [2004] 2 BCLC 554. Arguably, a claim for specific performance to force defendants to pay sums due to a company in which the claimant holds shares does not breach the reflective loss principle, see *Latin American Investments Ltd v Maroil Trading Inc* [2017] EWHC 1254.

and its creditors and other shareholders. Neither course can be permitted.'[237] He went on: 'Justice to the defendant requires the exclusion of one claim or the other; protection of the interests of the company's creditors requires that it is the company which is allowed to recover to the exclusion of the shareholder.'[238] As Arden LJ put it in *Day v Cook*,[239] '... the company's claim, if it exists, will always trump that of the shareholder', subject now to the 'disability' exception in *Giles v Rhind*.[240] Given that foundation, a claim will be barred even where there is a breach of duty to the company *and* the shareholder and even if the claim is brought in another capacity, for example as a creditor of the company.[241] If the substance of the claim is the same, though the cause of action is different, the no reflective loss rule applies.[242]

**20-77** In *Gardner v Parker*[243] a company had suffered significant losses and gone into administrative receivership as a result of breaches of duty by the company's sole director. Receivers had been appointed to the company and they had settled the company's claims against the director. A claim against the director by the minority shareholder in the company for losses suffered in its capacity as a shareholder in and creditor of the company (the shareholder had made a substantial loan to the company) was rejected for its losses would have been made good if the company had enforced its rights against the defendant. The rule against recovery of reflective loss therefore applied and the claim was dismissed.

**20-78** The position reached on the recovery of reflective loss is clear[244] and it is a position based on a combination of policy and practical considerations which extend beyond preventing double recovery.[245] The principle reflects the first limb of the rule in *Foss v Harbottle*.[246] It looks to company autonomy and ensures that the interests of the company are respected and that a (shareholder) party does not recover compensation for a loss suffered by another (the company).[247] It protects the wrongdoer from double recovery. It protects the interests of the company's creditors and ensures they are not prejudiced by an action by an individual shareholder.[248] At a practical level, it prevents a multitude of cases being brought by shareholders with the courts being required to act as referee between the different

---

[237] [2001] 1 BCLC 313 at 365.     [238] [2001] 1 BCLC 313 at 366.

[239] [2002] 1 BCLC 1 at 15.     [240] [2003] 1 BCLC 1.

[241] See Mitchell, 'Shareholders' Claims for Reflective Loss' (2004) 120 LQR 457 at 473. That is not to say, Neuberger J noted in *Gardner v Parker* [2004] 2 BCLC 554 at [74], that a creditor is without remedies. The creditor may sue the company for repayment if it is solvent (leaving the company to pursue the wrongdoing director) and, if the company is insolvent, the creditor can either fund an action by the liquidator against the director or take an assignment of the company's claim against him; also *Johnson v Gore Wood & Co* [2001] 1 BCLC 313 at 369. In *International Leisure Ltd v First National Trustee Co UK Ltd* [2014] 1 BCLC 128 it was held that where an administrative receiver acted in breach of duty, the person primarily entitled to recover the loss was the debenture holder because he was the person to whom the receiver owed his primary duties and the no reflective loss principle did not debar such a secured creditor from recovering that loss and the company could recover loss only to the extent that it exceeded the amount due under the debenture.

[242] *Gardner v Parker* [2004] 2 BCLC 554 at [49], applying *Shaker v Al-Bedrawi* [2003] 1 BCLC 157.

[243] [2004] 2 BCLC 554.

[244] See Mitchell, 'Shareholders' Claims for Reflective Loss' (2004) 120 LQR 457 at 464–5.

[245] See Koh, 'The Shareholder's Personal Claim, Allowing Recovery for Reflective Losses' (2011) 23 SAcLJ 863 at [13]–[26] criticising the policy justifications relied on by the English courts and arguing for a greater degree of judicial flexibility to avoid the risk of denying the wronged party justice; also Mitchell, n 241, at 463–5 who criticises the courts for not having adopted a more nuanced approach to these issues and who, at 478, concludes that some of the justifications for the principle do not stand up to close analysis. Cf Shapira, n 221, at 150 who considers the policy justifications identified in *Johnson v Gore-Wood* to be compelling.

[246] (1843) 2 Hare 461, see **20-1**.

[247] See *Johnson v Gore Wood & Co* [2002] 1 BCLC 313 at 338, per Lord Bingham; at 365, per Lord Millett.

[248] See *Johnson v Gore Wood & Co* [2002] 1 BCLC 313 at 338, per Lord Bingham; at 366, per Lord Millett.

claimants and with an eye to the need to protect the company's creditors. In the circumstances, it is procedurally efficient to exclude all claims other than those of the company, save where the company has been disabled by the wrongdoer from bringing its claim. It also facilitates settlements of claims for, in the absence of the prohibition of recovery of reflective loss, wrongdoers will be unwilling to compromise or settle claims with the company for fear of being met by a further claim by a shareholder.[249]

**20-79** One question is whether the availability of a statutory derivative claim helps a shareholder get around the no reflective loss principle. If the problem is that the company has not pursued its remedy against the wrongdoer director, the solution may lie in the shareholder pursuing the claim for the company via a derivative claim. Of course, usually the reason the company has not pursued the wrongdoer is that the company is in liquidation and the question is whether a derivative claim can be brought when a company is in liquidation. The common law answer was no,[250] given the proper plaintiff principle which still applies, a view which has been confirmed with respect to the statutory derivative claim.[251] In those circumstances, it is for the liquidator or administrator to sue on the company's behalf and no derivative claim will lie.[252] A derivative avenue to circumventing the no reflective loss principle is not then an option.

**20-80** A breach of a director's duties to the company often forms the basis of a petition under CA 2006, s 994 alleging unfairly prejudicial conduct of the company's affairs and the standard relief for the successful petitioner is a purchase order at a price which reflects the value of his shares as if the unfairly prejudicial conduct had not occurred (see **19-88**). Such a purchase order does in effect allow the petitioner to recover for reflective loss and, while the company is not compensated for the wrong done to it, the diminution in value of the petitioner's shares as a consequence of that wrong is made good.[253] The court in *Atlasview Ltd v Brightview Ltd*[254] was unconcerned about such an outcome, merely noting that the court would be careful to ensure no double recovery by the company and the petitioners.[255]

## F Personal actions at common law

**20-81** It may be that a shareholder wishes to remedy not a wrong done to the company but a wrong done to him personally. Such a personal action is unaffected by the rule in *Foss v Harbottle*.[256] A shareholder may bring a personal claim to obtain an injunction to restrain

---

[249] See *Johnson v Gore Wood & Co* [2002] 1 BCLC 313 at 370, per Lord Millett; *Giles v Rhind* [2003] 1 BCLC 1 at 30, per Chadwick LJ.

[250] See *Fargro v Godfroy* [1986] BCLC 370; *Barrett v Duckett* [1995] 1 BCLC 243, see n 147.

[251] *Cinematic Finance Ltd v Ryder* [2012] BCC 797; cf Keay, 'Can Derivative Proceedings be Commenced when a Company is in Liquidation' (2008) 21 Insolv Int 49.

[252] In *Cinematic Finance Ltd v Ryder* [2012] BCC 797, the court considered this also to be the position if the company is insolvent, though not actually in liquidation or administration, for it can be placed in liquidation or administration and proceedings can be brought on behalf of the company.

[253] See *Re Cumana Ltd* [1986] BCLC 430 at 437. See also Griffin, 'Shareholder Remedies and the No Reflective Loss Principle—Problems Surrounding the Identification of a Membership Interest' [2010] JBL 461 who comments that 'the no reflective loss principle would appear quite irrelevant to the courts' construction of [CA 2006] s 994'.

[254] [2004] 2 BCLC 191 at [60]–[64].

[255] For more detailed discussion of this issue, see Hannigan, 'Drawing Boundaries between Derivative Claims and Unfairly Prejudicial Petitions' [2009] JBL 606 at 615–20. See too Koh, n 245.

[256] (1843) 2 Hare 461.

proposed illegal or ultra vires acts,[257] but this option is of limited significance since it is rare for shareholders to be aware of a proposed illegal or ultra vires act in time to seek an injunction.

**20-82**   When considering the possibility of a personal claim, typically the issues revolve around the enforcement of the articles of association with a shareholder looking either to enforce what he perceives to be his rights under the articles or to prevent breaches by the majority of the articles, or even to prevent the articles from being altered. All these issues are considered in detail in Chapter 5 to which the reader is referred. Trying to enforce particular rights or to prevent the majority from acting in breach of particular provisions is not a straightforward matter with the courts generally taking a restrictive approach to these issues, precisely in order not to undermine the rule in *Foss v Harbottle*, see **5-55** et seq.

**20-83**   In practice, a shareholder aggrieved at difficulties in enforcing his rights under the articles of association, or at non-compliance by the majority with the terms of the articles, is likely to petition for relief under CA 2006, s 994, alleging that the affairs of the company are being conducted in a manner which is unfairly prejudicial to his interests. This general provision is the main remedy used by shareholders in the UK and it is discussed in detail in Chapter 19. On occasion, a shareholder may seek a winding-up order on the just and equitable ground under IA 1986, s 122(1)(g), also discussed in Chapter 19.

## G  Specific statutory rights under the CA 2006

**20-84**   The CA 2006 provides a number of specific statutory rights which shareholders may be able to invoke in an appropriate case. These provisions are designed to enhance shareholders' rights of engagement (e.g. rights of access to information, rights of participation in meetings, right to circulate resolutions etc) and are particularly of interest in larger companies. In each case, the relevant section sets a threshold which needs to be met to exercise the particular right and these vary from provision to provision. A typical requirement would be that the support of holders of not less than 5 per cent of the total voting rights of all the members who have the right to vote is needed. Of particular value are the following rights:

**20-85**   Rights not subject to any minimum shareholding:

- the right to obtain copies of the company's constitutional documents: CA 2006, s 32, see **5-8**;

- the right to inspect the register of members, subject to the company's right to go to court to refuse access: CA 2006, s 117, see **16-79**;

- the right to apply for rectification of the register of members: CA 2006, s 125, see **16-86**;

- the right to copies of the company's accounts and reports: CA 2006, ss 431 and 432, see **18-23**.

---

[257] See *Simpson v Westminster Palace Hotel Co* (1860) 8 HL Cas 712; *Parke v Daily News* [1962] 2 All ER 929; *Smith v Croft (No 2)* [1987] BCLC 206. It had been thought that shareholders could bring a personal action with respect to losses arising from illegal or ultra vires acts, but in *Smith v Croft (No 2)* Knox J took the view that such actions are to recover corporate losses arising from the transaction and, as such, should be the subject of an action by the company, or by the shareholders on a derivative basis, but no personal action will lie.

**20-86**   Rights subject to a minimum shareholding:

- the right to require the holding of a general meeting: CA 2006, s 303; and where the directors fail to call the meeting, the right of shareholders to call it themselves: s 305, see **17-48**;

- the right of members of a private company to require the circulation of a written resolution; CA 2006, s 292, see **17-29**; and, for public companies, the right to require the circulation of resolutions for annual general meetings: s 338, see **17-41**; and, for all companies, the right to require the circulation of statements with respect to proposed resolutions or business to be conducted at a general meeting: s 314, see **17-45**;

- the right of members of a quoted company[258] to require an independent report on any poll taken, or to be taken, at a general meeting of the company: CA 2006, s 342, see **17-15**;

- the right of members of a quoted company to require the company to publish on a website a statement setting out audit concerns that the members propose to raise at the next accounts meeting of the company:[259] CA 2006, s 527, see **18-23**.

**20-87**   Other provisions allow shareholders to object to a particular corporate act, such as the variation of class rights, or to require the company to do something. Some of the statutory provisions set a minimum shareholding threshold for invoking the particular remedy (for example, the holders of not less than 15 per cent of the class who have not agreed to the variation of the class rights: CA 2006, s 633) and possibly a time-limit within which the relief must be sought (for example, within 21 days of the consent to the variation). Examples of these provisions would be:

- the right to object to the re-registration of a public company as a private company: CA 2006, s 98;

- the right to challenge a variation of class rights: CA 2006, s 633, see **16-41**;

- the right to require the company to exercise its powers under CA 2006, s 793 requiring information about the holders of interests in the company's shares: s 803;

- the right of a minority shareholder to be bought out by an offeror where there has been a takeover offer for all the shares in the company: CA 2006, s 983.

**20-88**   Other statutory schemes do not provide a specific shareholder remedy as such, but the ability of the company to proceed with the scheme is dependent on court confirmation, as in the case of a reduction of capital by special resolution confirmed by the court under CA 2006, ss 645–651, see **22-75**, or a scheme of arrangement under CA 2006, s 899, and the protection of the minority in such instances lies in the requirement for court sanction.

**20-89**   Finally, shareholders have the right to remove a director by an ordinary resolution under CA 2006, s 168, although exercise of this power may itself give rise to further problems, see **7-43**. Issues to bear in mind include any entitlement to damages which may arise (see CA 2006, s 168(5)), the possibility that the director in question can command a sufficient majority of votes to prevent his removal, and, most importantly, the possibility that, in certain circumstances, removal (without a fair offer for the dismissed director's shares) may trigger a petition for unfairly prejudicial conduct under CA 2006, s 994: see **19-60**.

---

[258] 'Quoted company' is defined in CA 2006, s 385: see s 361.
[259] 'Accounts meeting' is defined in CA 2006, s 437(3), see **18-23**.

# PART IV

# Corporate Finance– Share and Loan Capital

# 21

# Share capital–capital raising and payment

## A Introduction

**21-1**  This chapter considers the statutory rules governing share capital requirements, especially those relating to the allotment of, and payment for, shares. The share capital measures, while statutory, frequently reflect long-established common law rules.

**21-2**  The general approach is that the capital rules are stricter for public companies than for private companies.[1] This position is a reflection of the general policy that public companies with their greater exposure to investors and creditors should be subject to a more rigorous regime than private companies. More specifically, the stricter capital rules with respect to public companies reflect the requirements of the Second EC Company Law Directive with regard to the establishment and maintenance of share capital in public companies.[2] The requirements of the Directive limited the extent to which amendments could be made in the CA 2006 to the capital rules as they apply to public companies. A feasibility study conducted on behalf of the European Commission on an alternative regime to the capital maintenance regime,[3] published in February 2008, concluded that in fact the Second Directive is flexible in many ways and its requirements do not cause significant operational problems for companies. Subsequently, limited changes were made to the Directive as part of the simplification programme.[4] The Second Company Law Directive has now been codified as Directive 2017/1132.[5]

**21-3**  As far as private companies are concerned, their capital requirements are a domestic matter not subject to Directive 2017/1132 and there is room for a more laissez-faire approach. In fact, most companies on the register are rarely troubled by the statutory requirements.

---

[1]  As 99.8 per cent of the companies on the register are private companies, the stricter rules have limited application, but they may influence the choice of type of company. At 31 March 2017, there were 3,402,554 private companies (99.8 per cent of all companies) on the register and 5,812 public companies (0.2 per cent), figures for England and Wales, see Companies House, *Statistical Tables on Companies Registration Activities 2016–2017*, Tables A2, A3.

[2]  Directive 77/91/EEC, OJ L 26/1, 31.1.1977. See generally Edwards, *EC Company Law* (1999), Ch III. In 2007, the European Commission consulted on possible simplification (including repeal) of a broad sweep of company law, accounting, and audit requirements including the Second Directive, see COM (2007) 394, but respondents favoured simplification rather than outright repeal.

[3]  See KPMG, *Feasibility study on an alternative to the capital maintenance regime established by the Second Company Law Directive 77/91/EEC of 13 December 1976 and an examination of the impact on profit distribution of the new EU accounting regime* (January 2008).

[4]  See Directive 2006/68/EC amending Directive 77/91/EEC, OJ L 264, 25.9.2006, p 32. See Government Response to consultation on implementation of amendments to the Second Company Law Directive (2007), URN 07/1300; also DTI, *Implementation of the Companies Act 2006* (2007), URN 07/666, Ch 6.

[5]  OJ L 169//46, 30.6.2017.

The statistics are no longer provided by Companies House, but, historically, in the region of 80 per cent of all companies on the register of 3 million plus companies have an issued share capital of £100 or less.[6] For those companies with under £100, many of these probably are £2 companies with an issued share capital of two £1 pound shares. In such companies, no share capital is ever issued subsequent to the initial two shares on incorporation and for these companies the rules governing share capital are irrelevant. Given this overall position as to share capital, it is not surprising that the Company Law Review noted that: 'our limited enquiries tend to indicate that creditors and potential creditors do not any longer regard the amount of a company's issued share capital as a significant matter when it comes to deciding whether or not to extend credit'.[7] This absence of significant equity (share) funding means that such companies must fund their activities in other ways, primarily, but not exclusively, through loan capital (typically term loans and bank overdrafts) which may mean that the company is subject to greater economic pressures than would be the case if it had more substantial equity funds. It also means that directors/shareholders in these companies may have to commit themselves to personal guarantees to secure bank lending so reducing the value to them of limited liability. Overall, the absence of significant equity funding acts as a brake on the development of these businesses though obviously many of the micro-businesses are content to remain at that level. For those with an interest in expanding their business, attracting equity funding to smaller companies is a problem. Equally, for many entrepreneurs, the risk of losing control of the company as their holdings are diluted by further issues of shares acts as a deterrent to seeking further equity investment. It is also a form of capital raising which is less familiar to them than debt finance. The question of access to finance—all types of finance—by SMEs is a significant issue, both domestically[8] and across the EU, where the same pattern is evident. The most recent survey by the EU on access to finance found that 'bank-related products remained the most relevant financing source for SMEs vis-à-vis market-based instruments and other sources of finance'.[9] SMEs prefer to use debt instruments such as bank overdraft and bank loans and some form of finance or hire purchase as well as trade credit as their main means of funding.[10]

## B  Share capital requirements

### Nominal value of shares

**21-4**  Shares must have a fixed nominal (or par) value (CA 2006, s 542(1)) and this figure is settled on incorporation (it may change thereafter as and when new classes of shares are created or capital restructuring takes place). As discussed at **1-3**, A and B may form a company with shares with a nominal value of £1, equally they may have shares with a nominal value of 1p. Typically, the figure is set quite low, for example, £1, 25p, and 1p are

---

[6]  See Companies House, *Statistical Tables on Companies Register Activities 2013–14*, Table A6.

[7]  Company Law Review, *Strategic Framework* (1999), para 5.4.3.

[8]  For the difficulties faced by SMEs in accessing finance, see the Breedon Report, commissioned by BIS, *Boosting Finance Options for Business* (March 2012), URN 12/668 and Government Response, URN 12/669; also the Rowlands Review on behalf of BIS and HM Treasury, *The Provision of Growth Capital to UK Small and Medium Sized Enterprises* (2009).

[9]  See European Commission, Survey on the access to finance of enterprises (SAFE) Analytical Report September 2017, p 12.

[10]  See European Commission, Survey on the access to finance of enterprises (SAFE) Analytical Report September 2017, p 12.

quite common nominal values. The relevance of par value to the shareholder is that the company may not issue its shares for less than the par value, see **21-23**. Of course, once the company has been trading for a while and is prospering, A and B will not be willing to sell further shares at £1. They will want a higher figure to reflect the increased value of the company. For example, they might consider that £2 is more appropriate in which case C who buys at £2 is said to contribute £1 of share capital and £1 of share premium, premium being any sum which is obtained above the nominal or par value, see **21-18**.

**21-5** Companies used to have shares of a high par value but today low par values are the norm as they are seen to increase the marketability of the shares and are preferred by investors. Many jurisdictions allow shares of no par value[11] and the issue was considered by the Company Law Review which noted that the requirement of a nominal value is an anachronism which is confusing for the layman. It initially favoured the mandatory introduction of no par shares for all companies while recognising that the requirements of (now) Directive 2017/1132 preclude such a change for public companies.[12] On consultation, a variety of concerns emerged about these proposals, not least regarding the transitional difficulties which would arise given the many contracts and agreements which make express reference to par values. The major obstacle, however, was that par values would have to be retained for public companies so there would be different requirements in this regard for public and private companies. This outcome would make transition from one classification to the other difficult which would be a serious drawback in practice. In the light of these concerns, the Company Law Review reluctantly concluded that the obligation for all companies to have shares with a nominal or par value should be retained,[13] hence CA 2006, s 542(1) requires shares each to have a fixed nominal value.[14]

**21-6** Nominal or par values may be denominated in any currency and different classes of shares may be denominated in different currencies (CA 2006, s 542(3)).

**21-7** On formation, a company with a share capital provides the registrar of companies with a statement of capital and initial holdings (CA 2006, s 9(4)(a)), see **1-25**. That statement of capital contains the following information:

(1) the total number of shares of the company to be taken on formation by the subscribers to the memorandum (see s 8(1));

(2) the aggregate nominal value of those shares;

(3) the aggregate amount, if any, to be unpaid on those shares (whether on account of their nominal value or by way of premium);

(4) for each class of shares,[15] the prescribed particulars of the rights attached to those shares; the total number of shares of that class and their aggregate nominal value (s 10(2)).

---

[11] The Gedge Committee in 1954 (Cmnd 9112) and the Jenkins Committee in 1962 (Cmnd 1749) recommended that no par value shares be permitted in the UK but an attempt to introduce such reforms in the Companies Act 1967 failed.

[12] See Company Law Review, *Strategic Framework* (1999), paras 5.4.26–5.4.33; *Company Formation and Capital Maintenance* (1999), para 3.8; *Capital Maintenance: Other Issues* (2000), paras 8–23.

[13] Company Law Review, *Completing the Structure* (2000), paras 7.2–7.3; *Final Report*, vol I (2001), para 10.7.

[14] An allotment of a share that does not have a fixed nominal value is void: CA 2006, s 542(2); and the company and any officer in default commits an offence: s 542(4), (5).

[15] Most companies have only one type of share, ordinary shares, and a company with only one type of share does not have classes of shares and so this information is not required.

Thereafter, every time the company makes a further allotment of shares, it must deliver to the registrar a return of allotment[16] which includes within it a statement of capital setting out the total capital position of the company[17] so ensuring that the public record always contains an up-to-date statement of the position.

## Issued and allotted share capital

**21-8**  While the terms 'issued' and 'allotted' with respect to shares are often used interchangeably, they refer to distinct processes.[18] For the purposes of the Companies Acts, shares are taken to be allotted when a person acquires the unconditional right to be included in the company's register of members in respect of those shares.[19] An allotment creates an enforceable contract for the issue of the shares and the shares are issued when an application to the company has been followed by allotment and notification to the purchaser and completed by entry on the company's register of members.[20]

## Minimum capital requirements

### Public companies

**21-9**  Public companies are required by the Second Directive now codified as Directive 2017/1132 to have a minimum share capital[21] and the authorised minimum in relation to the nominal value of a public company's allotted share capital is £50,000 or €57,100 (the prescribed euro equivalent),[22] but it cannot be partially in sterling and partially in euros.[23]

**21-10**  A company registered as a public company on its original incorporation may not do business or exercise any borrowing powers unless the registrar of companies has certified under CA 2006, s 761 that he is satisfied that the nominal value of the company's allotted share capital is not less than the authorised minimum.[24] A trading certificate to this effect is conclusive evidence that the company is entitled to do business and exercise any borrowing powers.[25] Once a public company has this trading certificate, it can redenominate the minimum capital into any currency, subject to any prohibition or restriction in the company's articles.[26]

---

[16] See CA 2006, s 555(2); also see The Companies (Shares and Share Capital) Regulations 2009, SI 2009/388, as to the prescribed contents of the return of allotment.

[17] CA 2006, s 555(3); and see s 555(4) as to the prescribed contents of the statement of capital.

[18] See *Clarke's Case* (1878) 8 Ch D 635 at 638, CA; also CA 2006, s 546(1). It would seem that the meaning of 'issue' depends on the context of the enactment in which the word occurs: *National Westminster Bank plc v Inland Revenue Commissioners* [1994] 3 All ER 1, HL.

[19] CA 2006, s 558; see also s 546. The company must maintain a register of its members: s 113, see **16-73**.

[20] *National Westminster Bank plc v Inland Revenue Commissioners* [1994] 3 All ER 1, HL (tax relief to investors in shares was altered in respect of shares 'issued' after 16 March 1993: here shares had been allotted prior to that date but registration took place after the date: held (3–2 majority) shares were 'issued' after 16 March 1993). See *Eckerle v Wickeder* [2013] 3 WLR 1316 at [17]–[18]. See also *Clarke's Case* (1878) 8 Ch D 635 at 638, CA.    [21] OJ L 169/64, 30.6.2017, art 45, requires a minimum of not less than 25,000 euros.

[22] CA 2006, ss 763, 765. See The Companies (Authorised Minimum) Regulations 2009, SI 2009/2425, reg 2. As to the need for it to be paid up, see **21-16**.    [23] CA 2006, ss 763(1), 765(1).

[24] The application for a trading certificate must be accompanied by a statement of compliance that the company meets the requirements for a trading certificate and the registrar may accept that statement as sufficient evidence of the matters stated in it: CA 2006, s 762(2), (3).

[25] CA 2006, s 761(4). A public company registered as such on its original incorporation which has not obtained a trading certificate and more than a year has expired since it was registered as a public company may be wound up by the court: IA 1986, s 122(1)(b).    [26] CA 2006, ss 617(4), 622(1), (7).

**21-11**  If a company does business or exercises any borrowing powers without this trading certificate, the company and any officer in default is liable to a fine (CA 2006, s 767(1)), but the validity of any transaction entered into by the company is not affected (s 767(3)). If a company enters into a transaction in contravention of this requirement and fails to comply with its obligations in that connection within 21 days of being called upon to do so, the directors of the company who were the directors at the time the company entered into the transaction are jointly and severally liable to indemnify the other party to the transaction in respect of any loss or damage suffered by him by reason of the company's failure to comply with those obligations.[27]

**21-12**  This requirement of a trading certificate is of limited practical significance as most companies are formed as private companies and subsequently re-register as public companies (see **1-52**), a process which requires them to have the minimum share capital,[28] but does not require them to obtain a trading certificate.

**21-13**  In addition to requiring public companies to have a minimum allotted share capital, where a public company has suffered a serious loss of subscribed capital so that its net assets are half or less of its called-up share capital, the directors must call a general meeting to consider whether any, and if so what, steps should be taken to deal with the situation (CA 2006, s 656).[29]

### Private companies

**21-14**  There is no minimum share capital required for private companies, hence approximately 78 per cent of all private companies have an issued share capital of £100 or less, as noted at **21-3**. As discussed in Chapter 2, the lack of a minimum share capital for private companies has encouraged businesses in other Member States to incorporate here which has given rise to considerable jurisprudence from the European Court on the freedom of establishment and corporate mobility, see **2-29** et seq.

### Paid-up share capital

**21-15**  Shares may be fully or partly paid up, but any company which adopts the model articles for private companies is restricted to issuing fully-paid shares.[30] This is not likely to be a problem given that the amount of issued share capital in private companies is very small, as noted at **21-3**. Where shares are partly-paid, the company can make calls on the shareholder up to the amount of the share price which has not been paid. For example, a share may be issued at £3.50 of which only £1.50p is paid up on allotment leaving the company later to call up the remaining £2. It is uncommon today to find companies with partly-paid shares as they prefer to obtain from the outset the capital which they have raised and so avoid the administrative burden of making calls on shareholders.

**21-16**  Public companies must not allot a share except as paid up at least as to one-quarter of its nominal value and the whole of any premium, i.e. any amount in excess of the nominal value of the share (CA 2006, s 586(1)).[31] Given the insignificance of the nominal value vis-à-vis

---

[27]  CA 2006, s 767(3), (4), although it would be difficult to establish such loss or damage.

[28]  See CA 2006, ss 90(2)(b), 91(1)(a).       [29]  Directive 2017/1132, OJ L 169/46, 30.6.2017, art 58.

[30]  The Companies (Model Articles) Regulations 2008, SI 2008/3229, reg 3, Sch 1, art 21(1) provides that no share is to be issued for less than the aggregate of its nominal value and any premium to be paid to the company in consideration for its issue.

[31]  In the event of a breach, the allotment is still valid, but the allottee is liable to pay the company the minimum amount which should have been received in respect of the shares less any consideration actually paid: CA 2006, s 586(3).

the market value of shares in most public companies, the effect of this requirement that the whole of the premium be paid up is that shares in public companies are issued fully-paid and, for listed companies, it is a condition of listing that shares be fully paid up.[32]

## C Issuing shares at par, premium, or a discount

**21-17**   A company may issue its shares:

(1) at par, i.e. for the nominal or par value set by the company (nominal value is discussed at **21-4**); or

(2) at a premium, i.e. for a figure in excess of the nominal or par value; but

(3) it must not issue its shares at a discount, i.e. for a figure less than the nominal or par value.

### Issue at a premium

**21-18**   While the initial subscribers to the memorandum may take their shares at the nominal or par value, it is common thereafter for shares to be issued at a premium, i.e. at more than par value. For example, a share with a par value of £1 may be issued for £1.30, £1.50, or any higher figure which the market will bear.

**21-19**   There is no requirement for companies to issue shares at a premium.[33] It depends on the circumstances of each case whether it is prudent or possible to do so and this is a matter for the directors to decide.[34] An example of a situation where the company may forgo some of the available premium is where the company makes a rights issue[35] to raise further capital from its shareholders and does so, as is normally the practice, at a price which is at a discount to the market price. In this instance, the company forgoes the maximum available premium, but the discount ensures (usually) that the shares are taken up and, in some cases, this may mean that the company saves on the expense of having the issue underwritten (see **21-25**). It may also be in the company's commercial interest to issue shares for a lower premium than the market might otherwise bear if the shares are being used to fund the acquisition of an asset which the company particularly wishes to acquire. In other circumstances, however, directors may be in breach of their duties to the company in not obtaining the greatest financial return from an issue of shares.[36] In *Re Sunrise Radio Ltd, Kohli v Lit*,[37] see **19-55**, the court concluded that issuing shares at par in circumstances where they could have been issued for a significant premium, was a breach of duty and unfairly prejudicial to the petitioner.[38]

---

[32]   See Listing Rules, LR 2.2.4(2).

[33]   *Hilder v Dexter* [1902] AC 474; *Lowry v Consolidated African Selection Trust Ltd* [1940] 2 All ER 545.

[34]   *Hilder v Dexter* [1902] AC 474 at 480, per Lord Davey.

[35]   Essentially, an offer of further shares to the company's existing shareholders, see **21-34**.

[36]   *Hilder v Dexter* [1902] AC 474 at 481, per Lord Davey, an allotment at par when a premium is available may be open to challenge as improvident or an abuse or in excess of the powers of management committed to the directors. See also *Lowry v Consolidated African Selection Trust Ltd* [1940] 2 All ER 545 at 565.

[37]   [2010] 1 BCLC 367.

[38]   The directors as the majority shareholders took up the shares and benefited appreciably from the issue at par. A subsequent increase in authorised share capital and a disapplication of the rights issue requirement was also unfairly prejudicial, though no shares had been issued pursuant to that authority, when the petitioner had been misled as to the calling of the general meeting where these matters were agreed, see [2010] 1 BCLC 367 at [135].

**21-20** A premium may arise whether shares are issued for cash or for a non-cash consideration. Shares issued for a consideration other than cash are issued at a premium if the value of the assets in consideration of which they are issued is more than the nominal value of the shares. The point arose in *Henry Head & Co Ltd v Ropner Holdings Ltd*[39] where there was an amalgamation of two shipping companies through the formation of a new holding company. There was a one-for-one exchange of shares by the shareholders of the two companies for shares in the holding company. The assets of the companies were undervalued and were worth £5m more than the nominal value of the shares in the new holding company. The question was whether it was correct for the holding company to transfer £5m to a share premium account. The court found that it was necessary for a transfer to be made to the share premium account and this decision was followed in *Shearer (Inspector of Taxes) v Bercain Ltd*.[40]

**21-21** When a company issues shares at a premium, whether for cash or otherwise, a sum equal to the aggregate amount or value of the premiums on those shares must be transferred to a share premium account (CA 2006, s 610). There are some exceptions to this requirement set out in ss 611–614 which identify certain circumstances when either a share premium account is not required or only a limited amount need be transferred to such an account. These provisions were introduced in response to the decisions in *Henry Head & Co Ltd v Ropner Holdings Ltd*[41] and *Shearer (Inspector of Taxes) v Bercain Ltd*,[42] noted earlier, and the net effect is to allow certain group reconstructions and mergers to take place without a transfer (or only a limited transfer) to a share premium account so releasing certain assets which may be distributed to the members as a dividend.

**21-22** Share premium is treated in most respects as share capital and its use is restricted to writing off any expenses incurred or commission paid on the issue of the shares in respect of which the premium has arisen and to paying up new shares to be allotted to members as fully-paid bonus shares (see **21-56**).[43]

## Prohibition on issue at a discount

**21-23** A company's shares must not be allotted at a discount, i.e. for less than the nominal or par value (CA 2006, s 580(1)). If shares are allotted in contravention of this requirement, the allottee is liable to pay the company an amount equal to the amount of the discount, with interest at the appropriate rate.[44] The company and any officer in default are liable on conviction to a fine (s 590). This statutory rule reflects the long-established common law to this effect laid down in *Ooregum Gold Mining Co of India Ltd v Roper*.[45]

---

[39] [1951] 2 All ER 994.    [40] [1980] 3 All ER 295.    [41] [1951] 2 All ER 994.
[42] [1980] 3 All ER 295.
[43] CA 2006, s 610(2). The CA 2006 tightened the rules on use of share premium. It is no longer possible to use the share premium account to write off (1) the company's preliminary expenses on formation, or (2) the expenses incurred, commission paid, or discount allowed on any issue of debentures or in providing for the premium payable on redemption of debentures of the company, as was the case under CA 1985, s 130.
[44] CA 2006, s 580(2). Directors who allot shares at a discount are guilty of a breach of duty to the company and are liable to pay the amount of the discount and interest to the company if that amount cannot be recovered from the allottee or holder of the shares, as where the shares have passed into the hands of a bona fide purchaser for value from the original allottee: *Hirsche v Sims* [1894] AC 654, PC.
[45] [1892] AC 125, HL. See also *Re Eddystone Marine Insurance Co* [1893] 3 Ch 9; *Welton v Saffery* [1897] AC 299. The rule cannot be evaded by issuing convertible debentures at a discount which are capable of being immediately converted to ordinary shares: *Mosely v Koffyfontein Mines Ltd* [1904] 2 Ch 108.

**21-24**　In this case, a company purported to issue £1 preference shares credited with 15 shillings paid up, leaving only five shillings to be paid on allotment. The House of Lords held that there was no power under the Companies Acts to do this and the allotment was ultra vires with the allottees liable to pay the full amount of £1 on each of their shares.[46] As Lord Macnaghten noted, in a limited liability company shareholders purchase immunity from liability beyond the amount due on their shares, but they do so on the basis that they remain liable up to that limit.[47]

**21-25**　As a limited exception to the no-discount rule, companies are permitted to pay underwriting commissions, provided such payments are authorised by the articles and the amount involved does not exceed specified limits (CA 2006, ss 552–553). Underwriting involves the use of professional intermediaries (such as investment banks and institutional investors) which undertake, in return for a fee, to subscribe or procure subscriptions for shares to the extent that the public or other persons do not subscribe for them. This fee could be prohibited as a discount on the shares were it not for s 553 which permits such payments.

**21-26**　Finally, it should be noted that, while a company may not allot shares at a discount to the nominal value, payment for shares may be in the form of money or money's worth (CA 2006, s 582(1)). Where money's worth is received and the company is a private company, the courts will not inquire into the adequacy of the consideration unless it is illusory or manifestly inadequate.[48] In such circumstances, it is possible that the issue of shares for a non-cash consideration disguises what is, in effect, an issue of shares at a discount, see **21-63**.

## D  Alteration of share capital

**21-27**　A company needs flexibility in dealing with its share capital to enable it to react to changing business circumstances and so the statute allows a company to alter its share capital in the following ways, subject to any prohibition or restriction in the company's articles. Authorisation from the shareholders is also required, usually by an ordinary resolution of the shareholders (a special resolution, if it is a reduction of capital). A company may (CA 2006, s 617):

(1)  increase its share capital by allotting new shares (discussed at **21-29**);

(2)  reduce its share capital (discussed at **22-60**);

(3)  sub-divide or consolidate all or any of its share capital into shares of smaller/larger amount than its existing shares. Sub-division involves dividing a share into a number of new shares (for example, £1 shares can be sub-divided into four 25p shares or ten 10p shares) and may be done to increase the marketability of shares where companies feel the nominal value is too high. It may also be necessary if the company wants to issue new shares at a nominal value lower than the current nominal value since the company cannot issue shares at a discount to the nominal value, as noted at **21-23**. Consolidation involves combining a number of shares into a new share of

---

[46] Allowing the company to allot at a discount is unfair to shareholders who paid the full amount and misleading for creditors who rely on the stated par value as indicating the minimum price at which the company has issued and will issue its shares.

[47] [1892] AC 125 at 145. Equally, the company cannot thereafter increase the member's liability to contribute to the company's share capital without his consent: CA 2006, s 25(1)(b).

[48] *Re Wragg Ltd* [1897] 1 Ch 796.

commensurate nominal value. For example, 10 £1 shares may be consolidated into one £10 share. This process is less common now as investors prefer shares of lower rather than higher nominal value, but it is sometimes used when a capital reorganisation leaves the company with shares of an unwieldy nominal value, for example, 12.5p shares may be consolidated into 50p or £1 shares. This exercise has no financial impact on a shareholder who now holds fewer shares of greater nominal value but representing the same percentage interest in the company as the shareholder held previously;

(4) reconvert any stock into paid-up shares of any denomination. It is rare for UK companies to have stock (which arises from a conversion of fully-paid shares) but this power is retained to allow any company which still has stock to convert it back into shares (CA 2006, s 620). Companies are no longer able to convert shares into stock;

(5) redenominate all or any of its share capital into another currency. The ability to redenominate shares into another currency was introduced by the CA 2006, ss 622–628. It is intended to facilitate companies in changing their capital structures without the need for more complex schemes involving a reduction or purchase of shares followed by the cancellation of those shares and a new allotment in a different currency. It is open to any company, public or private, to redenominate its shares into any currency or into multiple currencies.

**21-28**  Notice of any of these alterations must be given to the registrar of companies typically within one month of the alteration (within 15 days, if a reduction of capital).[49] In each case, the notice must be accompanied by or include a statement of capital.[50] In the event of default in complying with any of these disclosure requirements, the company and any officer in default are liable to a fine.[51]

## E  Allotment of shares

**21-29**  Quite apart from the ability to raise money for the company, the authority granted to the directors to make an allotment of shares is important because an allotment will affect the balance of power within the company, given that shares typically carry one vote per share. An allotment may be used improperly to prejudice minority shareholders by diluting their holdings, or to alter the voting position so as to ensure that the directors cannot be voted out of office, or to guarantee the passing of a particular resolution, or to prevent opponents from being appointed to the board, or to block a takeover of the company. Statutory controls are imposed therefore to restrain directors from acting improperly.

**21-30**  The statutory framework also operates against a backdrop of other constraints which should prevent improper allotments. First, directors are under a duty to exercise their powers for the purpose for which they are conferred, CA 2006, s 171, and a power to allot shares is primarily, though not exclusively, conferred in order that the company may raise capital, see **9-56** et seq. Secondly, the directors must also be mindful of their duty to act to promote the success of the company under s 172(1), having regard (amongst other matters) to the need to act fairly as between the members (s 172(1)(f)), see **10-29** et seq.

---

[49]  CA 2006, s 555(2) (allotment of shares), s 619(1) (sub-division and consolidation), s 621(1) (redenomination). In the case of a reduction of capital, notice must be given within 15 days of the passing of the resolution for reduction: ss 627(1), 644(1).        [50]  CA 2006, ss 555(3), 619(2), 621(2), 625(2), 627(2), 644(1).
[51]  CA 2006, ss 557(1), 619(4), 621(4), 625(4), 627(7), 644(9).

Thirdly, in an appropriate case, minority shareholders may petition for relief under CA 2006, s 994, alleging that the allotment amounts to the conduct of the company's affairs in an unfairly prejudicial manner, see **19-53** et seq.

## Authorisation to allot

**21-31**    As a general rule, directors may exercise the power to allot shares only if authorised to do so by the articles or by an ordinary resolution (CA 2006, s 551(1)).[52] Authorisation may be general or particular, conditional or unconditional, and must specify the maximum number of shares and a date when the authorisation will expire, which must be for no longer than five years from the date of the resolution granting authorisation (s 551(2)–(3)). Public companies typically seek authority to allot at successive annual general meetings and, for premium listed companies, they are mindful of the influential guidelines on share capital management issued by the Investment Association (IA).[53] On allotment, IA members will regard as routine (and therefore as shareholders will usually support) requests by the company for authorisation to allot new shares in an amount up to two-thirds of a company's existing issued share capital, provided that amounts in excess of one-third of the existing issued share capital are applied to rights issues only[54] (rights issues are discussed at **21-34**). This generous leeway for larger companies avoids the expense of having to call a general meeting to seek authorisation.

**21-32**    An important exception to the general rule that authorisation is required is that, in the case of a private company with only one class of shares[55] (and most private companies fall into this category), the directors may allot shares of that class, *without* the need for any express authorisation, *unless* they are prohibited from doing so by the company's articles (CA 2006, s 550). This general permission to allot was introduced by the CA 2006 following a recommendation by the Company Law Review that the requirement for authorisation to allot shares should not apply to private companies.[56] In many private companies, the directors and the shareholders are the same people so the Review considered it an unnecessary complication to require A and B, as shareholders, to authorise A and B, as directors, to allot shares. In so far as there is potential for abuse of this power, it is constrained, as noted at **21-30**, by the requirements of the directors' duties in CA 2006, Pt 10, and the potential for minority relief under s 994. Furthermore, the requirement for authorisation remains if:

(1) the articles prohibit the exercise of the power to allot;

(2) the directors are to allot shares of a different class; or

(3) the private company has more than one class of shares.

**21-33**    A further constraint is that, while the directors have a power to allot, the statutory framework dictates to whom the shares must be allotted. A rights issue is required unless the shareholders choose to exclude or disapply that rights requirement.

---

[52] Allotments must be notified to the registrar of companies within one month of the allotment: CA 2006, s 555; companies must register an allotment in the register of members within two months of the allotment: s 554.

[53] See Investment Association, *Share Capital Management Guidelines* (July 2016).

[54] If the rights issue is in connection with an acquisition, depending on size, a listed company may also need to comply with LR 10.5.1 (class 1 transactions).

[55] See CA 2006, s 629, as to when shares are of one class; and see **16-28**.

[56] Company Law Review, *Developing the Framework* (2000), paras 7.28–7.32; *Completing the Structure* (2000), para 2.16; *Final Report*, vol I (2001), para 4.5.

## Rights issues

**21-34**  A rights issue requires a company to offer a new issue of shares for cash to existing share-holders in proportion to their existing shareholdings. Such pre-emption rights, if taken up, enable the existing shareholders to retain their proportionate shareholdings in the company and prevent the dilution of their holdings which would otherwise occur if a fresh issue of shares was offered to only some of the existing shareholders or to outside investors. As public companies commonly offer a fresh issue of shares at a (usually sub-stantial) discount to the market price, the obligation to offer the shares on a rights basis to the existing shareholders means, not only that they can protect their percentage holding in the company, but also that they, rather than outside investors, get the benefit of any discount to the market price.

**21-35**  The statutory scheme is set out in CA 2006, Pt 17, Ch 3, ss 560 et seq and reference must be made to the precise wording of the somewhat complicated provisions which, as regards public companies, implement the requirements of the Second Directive now codified as Directive 2017/1132.[57] The overall scheme is that a company (including a private com-pany) proposing to make an allotment of shares for cash must do so on a rights basis (i.e. to existing shareholders in proportion to their existing holdings) unless the case falls within one of the exceptions, exclusions, or disapplications permitted by the statute.

**21-36**  A company proposing to allot equity securities[58] (essentially ordinary shares[59] but includ-ing a sale of treasury shares held by the company[60]) for cash must first make an offer to each person who holds ordinary shares in the company to allot to him on the same or more favourable terms a proportion of those shares that is as nearly as practicable equal to the proportion in nominal value held by him of the ordinary share capital of the company (CA 2006, s 561(1)(a)).[61]

**21-37**  The offer may be made in hard copy or electronic form and must state a period of not less than 14 days during which the offer may be accepted[62] and the offer must not be with-drawn before the end of that period.[63] The company cannot allot any of those shares to any person unless the period during which any such offer to the existing holders may be accepted has expired or the company has received notice of the acceptance or refusal of every offer so made (CA 2006, s 561(1)(b)).

**21-38**  In the event of a contravention of the requirement to make an allotment on a rights basis, or of the provisions concerning the communication of pre-emption offers, the

---

[57]  OJ L 169/46, 30.6.2017, art 72. For companies with a premium listing of securities, see LR 9.3.11 which imposes pre-emption requirements, but these too fall away if there is a statutory disapplication under the CA 2006, see LR 9.3.12(1).

[58]  See the definition of 'allotment of equity securities' in CA 2006, s 560(2).

[59]  See CA 2006, s 560(1). 'Equity securities' means ordinary shares in the company or a right to subscribe for, or to convert securities into, ordinary shares in the company; and 'ordinary shares' means shares other than shares that as respects dividends and capital carry a right to participate only up to a specified amount in a distribution.

[60]  CA 2006, s 560(3). A sale of treasury shares for cash by a company is regarded as equivalent to the issuance of new shares by that company under the Pre-emption Group Statement of Principles (2015), part 1, para 4, see **21-53**. See CA 2006, s 724(5) as to when shares are treasury shares; see also **22-41**.

[61]  The right to subscribe in itself has a value which, depending on how the issue is structured, shareholders may be able to sell or have sold for them by the company (known as nil paid rights).

[62]  The period was reduced from 21 days to 14 calendar days amidst concerns that rights issues take too long, especially in volatile market conditions; the Listing Rules state that the offer relating to the rights issue must remain open for acceptance for at least 10 business days, see LR 9.5.6R, and see **21-52**.

[63]  CA 2006, s 562(2), (4)–(5); in certain circumstances, a notice in the *Gazette* suffices: s 562(3).

company, and every officer of it who knowingly authorised or permitted the contravention, are jointly and severally liable to compensate any person to whom an offer should have been made for any loss, damage, costs, or expenses which the person has sustained or incurred by reason of the contravention.[64] A failure to comply with the pre-emption requirement may be grounds for a petition alleging unfairly prejudicial conduct under CA 2006, s 994, see **19-53**.

**21-39**  These requirements are subject to a variety of exceptions and exclusions and may be disapplied by the shareholders in certain circumstances and, for the detail, reference should be made to the wording of the provisions.

## Exceptions

### Allotment of bonus shares

**21-40**  The pre-emption requirement does not apply in relation to an allotment of bonus shares (CA 2006, s 564). Bonus shares are discussed at **21-56**.

### Allotments other than for cash

**21-41**  The pre-emption requirement does not apply to a particular allotment if the shares are, or are to be, wholly or partly paid up otherwise than in cash (CA 2006, s 565). This exception is a common method of avoiding the requirement to have a rights issue.[65]

### Allotments held under an employees' share scheme

**21-42**  The pre-emption requirement does not apply to an allotment that would (apart from any renunciation or assignment) be held under an employees' share scheme (CA 2006, s 566).

## Exclusions

### Exclusion by private companies

**21-43**  All or any of the requirements as to pre-emption (or the provisions governing communication of pre-emption offers to shareholders) may be excluded by a private company by a provision contained in the articles (CA 2006, s 567).[66] As noted earlier, the pre-emption requirements for public companies are mandatory as they are required by Directive 2012/30/EU, art 33.

### Allotments to a class

**21-44**  The pre-emption requirement does not apply where a company is required by its articles to make an allotment on a rights basis to a class of shares in pursuance of a class right to that effect (CA 2006, s 568(1)). If a member of the class (or anyone in whose favour he has renounced his right to the allotment) does not accept the shares offered to him, any subsequent offer of those shares is on a pre-emption basis to the rest of the shareholders rather than to the general public unless, in the case of a private company, the articles exclude the need for a rights issue in this situation[67] or the requirement for a rights issue is disapplied.[68]

---

[64] CA 2006, s 563(1), (2), subject to a two-year limitation period: s 563(3). No provision is made for allotments in breach of these requirements to be set aside, but see *Re Thundercrest Ltd* [1995] 1 BCLC 117 where the court did set aside an allotment by directors in their own favour which was made in breach of the statutory requirements.

[65] See *Siemens AG v Nold: Case C-42/95* [1997] 1 BCLC 291. As to when a share is deemed paid up in cash or allotted for cash, see CA 2006, s 583 and **21-61**.

[66] The pre-emption rights may be excluded generally or in relation to allotments of a particular description: CA 2006, s 567(2); and see s 567(3).     [67] CA 2006, s 568(2), (3).

[68] i.e. under CA 2006, ss 570, 571, or 573.

## Disapplication of pre-emption rights

*Private company with only one class of shares*

**21-45**   The directors of a private company that has only one class of shares may be given power by the articles, or by a special resolution of the company, to allot ordinary shares of that class as if the pre-emption requirement does not apply or applies with such modifications as the directors may determine (CA 2006, s 569(1)).

*Disapplication by other companies*

**21-46**   Any public or private company may disapply the statutory scheme of pre-emption, either by way of a general disapplication or by way of a limited disapplication done with regard to a specified allotment.[69] These provisions are complicated and reference should be made to their precise wording. Their application is linked to the authority to allot shares granted to the directors under CA 2006, s 551 (see **21-31**) and listed companies must have regard to the Pre-emption Group statement which limits the extent of disapplication, see **21-53**.

*A general disapplication*

**21-47**   Where the directors of a company have a general authority to allot shares under CA 2006, s 551, they may be given power by the articles, or by a special resolution of the company, to allot ordinary shares pursuant to that authority as if the requirement for a rights issue does not apply or as if it applies to the allotment with such modifications as the directors may determine (s 570(1)).

*A specific disapplication*

**21-48**   Where the directors of a company have an authority to allot shares under CA 2006, s 551 (whether generally or otherwise), the company may by special resolution resolve either that the rights requirement does not apply to a specified allotment of shares to be made pursuant to that authority or that the rights requirement applies to the allotment with such modifications as may be specified in the resolution (s 571(1)). This special resolution must be recommended by the directors who must circulate to the shareholders a written statement setting out their reasons for making the recommendation, the amount to be paid to the company in respect of the shares to be allotted, and the directors' justification of that amount.[70]

**21-49**   As the disapplication in each case is linked to the authority to allot shares granted to the directors under CA 2006, s 551, the disapplication ceases when that authority under s 551 is revoked or expires, but if the authority to allot is renewed, the disapplication can also be renewed by a special resolution.[71]

*Disapplication on sale of treasury shares*

**21-50**   As noted in **21-36**, the pre-emption requirement applies on a sale of treasury shares (see **22-41**),[72] but this requirement can be the subject of a general or specific disapplication. The directors may be given power by the articles, or by a special resolution of the

---

[69]   A disapplication can be particularly useful to avoid the need to make an offer to overseas shareholders in jurisdictions which may have onerous regulatory requirements with respect to such offers.

[70]   CA 2006, s 571(5)–(6); and see s 572 as to penalties for misleading, false, or deceptive statements. Where the resolution is proposed as a written resolution, the statement must be supplied to every eligible member at or before the time at which the resolution is sent or submitted to him for signature; where the resolution is to be at a meeting, the statement must be circulated with the notice of the meeting: s 571(7).

[71]   CA 2006, ss 570(3), 571(3).        [72]   CA 2006, s 560(2)(b).

company, to sell treasury shares as if the requirement for a rights issue does not apply or as if it applies to the sale with such modifications as the directors may determine (CA 2006, s 573(1)). Alternatively, the company may by special resolution resolve either that the rights requirement does not apply to a specified sale of treasury shares or that the rights requirement applies to a specified sale with such modifications as may be specified in the resolution (s 573(4)).

### Institutional investors and pre-emption rights

**21-51** As noted at **21-34**, pre-emption rights are a protective device ensuring that existing shareholders cannot have their percentage holdings diluted without their having an opportunity to acquire additional shares. Pre-emption rights are also valuable commercially because existing shareholders get the benefit of any discount to market price so that the value of the company is transferred to them and not to outside investors. Pre-emption rights also ensure that long-term shareholders cannot suddenly find control of the company has passed to new investors. It is unsurprising, therefore, that institutional investors (the most significant shareholders in listed public companies) see considerable value in the statutory requirement (reflecting Directive 2017/1132) for rights issues.[73]

**21-52** Equally, on occasion, companies may wish to avoid the administrative burden of a rights issue which can be costly and time-consuming to conduct (a prospectus may be required, see **21-111** et seq), hence the statutory provisions for exceptional cases and the ability to disapply the provisions on a more general basis. There have been concerns that the insistence on pre-emption rights limits the flexibility of smaller listed companies, in particular, and makes it more complicated and expensive for such companies to raise equity capital.[74] In recent years, various changes have been introduced,[75] for example, the offer period during which the rights offer must remain open has been reduced from 21 days to 14 days[76] to speed up the process, and listed companies have been given greater flexibility on authorisation (see **21-31**) by institutional shareholders so reducing the need to call additional general meetings. In 2015, the European Commission consulted on improvements to the Prospectus Directive 2010/73 with the aim of making it easier for companies throughout the EU, especially small and medium-sized entities (SMEs), to raise capital while ensuring effective investor protection.[77] The resulting Prospectus Regulation 2017/1129 exempts an issuer from the need to publish a prospectus for an admission of shares to a regulated market if the shares represent, over a period of 12 months, less than 20 per cent of the number of shares of the same class already admitted to trading on the same regulated market.[78]

**21-53** In addition to adhering to statutory requirements, listed companies are expected to comply with the Statement of Principles on pre-emption drawn up by the Pre-Emption Group

---

[73] See Association of British Insurers (ABI), 'Rights Issues and Capital Raising—An ABI Discussion Paper' (July 2008).

[74] See, for example, the Myners review: DTI, *Pre-emption rights: Final Report* (February 2005), URN 05/679; also HM Treasury, *Smaller Quoted Companies—a Report to the Paymaster General* (November 1998), paras 46–47.

[75] See HM Treasury, *A Report to the Chancellor of the Exchequer by the Rights Issue Review Group* (November 2008).

[76] See FSA, *Rights Issue Subscription Periods*, CP 09/4 (January 2009).

[77] Directive 2010/73, OJ L 327/1, 11.12.2011. See European Commission, 'Consultation Document, Review of the Prospectus Directive', 18.2.2015.          [78] OJ L 168/12, 30.6.2017, art 1(5)(b).

which is made up of representatives of institutional investors and intermediaries.[79] The Statement of Principles primarily relates to issues of equity securities for cash other than on a pre-emptive basis by premium listed companies (wherever incorporated) with a listing on the Main Market of the London Stock Exchange.[80] Companies with a standard listing and companies trading on AIM (see **21-106**) are encouraged to adopt these principles.[81] The Statement reiterates that the overarching principle remains that pre-emption rights are a cornerstone of UK company law and protect shareholders against inappropriate dilution of their investments but it is also accepted that a degree of flexibility is appropriate in circumstances where new issues of shares on a non-pre-emptive basis would be in the interests of companies and their owners.[82] A request for a general disapplication (see **21-47**) is likely to be supported if the company seeks authority to issue shares on a non-rights basis up to no more than 5 per cent of the company's ordinary share capital in any one year and no more than an additional 5 per cent of issued ordinary share capital[83] provided that the company confirms that it intends to use such additional authority only in connection with an acquisition or specified capital investment which is announced contemporaneously with the issue or which has taken place in the preceding six months and is disclosed in the announcement of the issue.[84] Overall, in any rolling three-year period, the company should not issue, on a non-rights basis, equity shares for cash that represent more than 7.5 per cent of the company's ordinary share capital.[85] The Pre-Emption Group confirmed that, despite the relaxation in the Prospectus Regulation, allowing allotments of up to 20 per cent without a prospectus (see **21-52**), the Group continues to support the 10 per cent overall limit in the Statement of Principles.[86]

**21-54** Any discount at which ordinary shares are issued for cash other than to existing shareholders is of concern so companies should restrict the discount to a maximum of the aggregate of 5 per cent of the immediately preceding market price and the expenses of the issue.[87] General disapplication requests which exceed these percentage levels are not ruled out but will be considered by shareholders on a case-by-case basis in the light of a sufficiently strong business case made by the company, as will requests for a specific disapplication (see **21-48**).[88] Following a non-pre-emptive issue of equity pursuant to a general disapplication, the company must set out in the next annual report the actual level of discount achieved, the net proceeds raised, how those net proceeds were used, and

---

[79] Originally introduced in 1987, the latest version is *Disapplying Pre-emption Rights, A Statement of Principles* (2015) which is supported by the Lifetime Savings and Pensions Association and the Investment Association representing owners and investment managers. The Pre-Emption Group was set up in 2005 and reformed in 2015. It is supported by the FRC. In addition to the Statement of Principles, the Group publishes an annual monitoring statement highlighting market practice together with best practice guidance on engagement and disclosure and template resolutions for use by companies.

[80] Statement of Principles (2015), Pt 1, para 1.

[81] As are companies admitted to trading on the High Growth segment (see n 162) of the Main Market, see Statement of Principles (2015), Pt 1, para 1. [82] Statement of Principles (2015), paras 1 and 3.

[83] Treasury shares should not be regarded as forming part of the company's issued share capital, see Statement of Principles (2015), Pt 1, para 4.

[84] Statement of Principles (2015), Pt 2A, para 3. See Pre-Emption Group Monitoring Report 16–17 (May 2017), para 34 on the importance of the additional 5 per cent being linked to a specific acquisition or investment. Template resolutions are provided by the Group for use by companies and these are invariably used now, see Monitoring Report, para 8.

[85] Statement of Principles (2015), Pt 2B, para 1, and see that para as to the calculation of the 7.5 per cent limit, but it is also possible to seek to go above that limit, see para 2.

[86] See Pre-Emption Group Press Release, 5 March 2018.

[87] Statement of Principles (2015), Pt 2B, para 5, and see para 8. There is detailed guidance in the Appendix as to how to calculate the permissible discount. [88] Statement of Principles (2015), Pt 2A, para 5; Pt 3.

the percentage increase in issued share capital due to non-pre-emptive issues for cash over the three-year period preceding the issue.[89]

**21-55**   Reflecting the greater emphasis now on shareholder engagement, the Statement of Principles emphasises the importance of companies signalling their intentions and shareholders and companies engaging in dialogue on these matters and it reminds shareholders that best practice under the Stewardship Code (see **6-56**) is for shareholders to advise the company in advance of their reasons for deciding to abstain or vote against a resolution to disapply pre-emption rights.[90] The statement also notes that companies which do not comply with the principles are likely to find that their shareholders are less inclined to approve subsequent requests for a general disapplication and that this applies to compliance with the letter of the principles and their spirit.[91] To assist with engagement, the Pre-Emption Group has issued best practice guidelines on engagement and disclosure.[92]

### Bonus issues

**21-56**   A bonus issue of shares occurs where a company capitalises profits or revenue reserves or some other permissible fund[93] and applies the proceeds in paying up bonus shares which go to existing members in proportion to their entitlement to dividend so providing the shareholders with additional fully-paid shares in the company.[94] It is essentially an accounting exercise as the company's reserves are reduced but its share capital fund is increased.

**21-57**   From the point of view of the shareholders, calling the issue a bonus issue is somewhat misleading for the company is still worth the same as before the bonus issue and the total value of their shareholding has not altered.[95] All that has happened is that each shareholder holds more shares but each share is worth less than before.

**21-58**   One advantage so far as the company and shareholders are concerned is that a bonus issue is not a distribution[96] for the purposes of the distribution rules in CA 2006, Pt 23, so funds which would not be available for distribution as dividends may be used for this purpose. Distributions are discussed at **22-88** et seq.

## F  Payment for shares

**21-59**   Having considered the requirements as to the issuing of shares, we turn now to the rules concerning payment for share capital and, by way of background, the reader is referred to the discussion of the doctrine of capital maintenance at the beginning of Chapter 22.

---

[89]   Statement of Principles (2015), Pt 2B, para 9.

[90]   Statement of Principles (2015), Overarching Principle 5.

[91]   Statement of Principles (2015), Pt 1, para 5.

[92]   The guidance can be found as an appendix to the Pre-Emption Group Monitoring Report 16–17 (May 2017).

[93]   The company may use its share premium account (CA 2006, s 610(3)), redenomination reserve (s 628(2)), or capital redemption reserve (s 733(5)) to finance a fully-paid bonus issue. See *Re Cleveland Trust plc* [1991] BCLC 424 where a bonus issue was declared void on the ground of common mistake when the directors and shareholders were mistaken as to the availability of profits which could be capitalised; also *EIC Services Ltd v Phipps* [2004] 2 BCLC 589, CA (bonus issue in breach of articles void).

[94]   As this appears to be a case of the company allotting shares without receiving money or money's worth, it would seem to fall foul of CA 2006, s 582(1), but s 582(2)(a) provides that this requirement does not prevent the company from allotting bonus shares.

[95]   Of course, it is not strictly accurate to say that there is no difference in value before and after a bonus issue, for the market may respond favourably to a bonus issue so the shares may gain a little in value but essentially the shareholder's position does not alter.

[96]   CA 2006, s 829(2)(a).

## Payment for shares in money or money's worth

**21-60**    A company cannot make a gratuitous allotment of its shares nor an allotment at a discount.[97] The allottee must pay in full at least the nominal value of the shares and will possibly pay a premium as well. The sum due may be paid up in money or money's worth including goodwill and know-how (CA 2006, s 582).[98]

**21-61**    An extended definition of an allotment for cash is set out in CA 2006, s 583 which provides that a share in a company is deemed paid up (as to its nominal value or any premium on it) in cash or allotted for cash if the consideration received for the allotment or payment up is a cash consideration. A cash consideration for these purposes means (s 583(3)):

(a)  cash received by the company;

(b)  a cheque received by the company in good faith which the directors have no reason for suspecting will not be paid;

(c)  a release of a liability of the company for a liquidated sum;

(d)  an undertaking to pay cash to the company at a future date;[99] or

(e)  payment by any other means giving rise to a present or future entitlement (of the company or person acting on the company's behalf) to payment, or credit equivalent to payment, in cash.[100]

**21-62**    Category (c) requires a little explanation. This provision reflects the decision in *Re Harmony and Montague Tin and Copper Mining Co, Spargo's Case*[101] which illustrates how an allotment which appears to be on a non-cash basis may in fact be regarded as being for cash. It is necessary to regard the transaction as being in two stages: first, an individual sells assets to the company and the company becomes indebted to him for a stated amount (a liquidated sum); secondly, the company allots fully paid shares to him and in return the company is released from the liability to pay the liquidated sum. In *Spargo's Case*, Sir W M James LJ explained that it is not necessary that the formality should be gone through of the money being handed over and taken back again. If the two demands are set off against each other (the demand for payment for the shares and the liability for a liquidated sum), the shares have been paid up in cash.[102]

**21-63**    The possible inconsistency between prohibiting the allotment of shares at a discount (CA 2006, s 580(1)), but allowing payment in money's worth (s 582(1)), which may disguise an allotment at a discount, was noted by Lindley LJ in *Re Wragg Ltd*[103] who accepted that the difference between issuing shares at a discount and issuing them at a price put upon property or services by the vendor and agreed to by the company may not always

---

[97]  CA 2006, s 580; *Re Wragg Ltd* [1897] 1 Ch 796; *Ooregum Gold Mining Co of India Ltd v Roper* [1892] AC 125; *Re Eddystone Marine Insurance Co* [1893] 3 Ch 9.

[98]  Details of any non-cash consideration is given in the return of allotment to the registrar of companies: CA 2006, s 555, and The Companies (Shares and Share Capital) Regulations 2009, SI 2009/388, reg 14(c). Shares taken by a subscriber to the memorandum of a public company in pursuance of an undertaking of his in the memorandum, and any premium on the shares, must be paid up in cash: CA 2006, s 584.

[99]  An assignment of a debt is not an undertaking to pay cash at a future date for these purposes, see *System Control plc v Munro Corporate plc* [1990] BCLC 659.

[100]  Category (e) is intended to clarify uncertainty which had existed as to whether payments within a computerised share settlement system, such as CREST, are a cash consideration. These automated systems provide for assured payment obligations which are to be treated as equivalent to cash: see *Explanatory Notes to the Companies Act 2006*, para 880. The Secretary of State has power to expand category (5) by statutory instrument: CA 2006, s 583(4).                    [101]  (1873) 8 Ch App 407.

[102]  (1873) 8 Ch App 407 at 412.            [103]  [1897] 1 Ch 796.

be very apparent in practice. In the court's opinion, however, the two transactions were essentially different and a company is entitled to issue fully paid-up shares in return for a non-cash consideration provided it does so honestly and not colourably, and provided that it has not been so imposed upon as to be entitled to be relieved from its bargain.[104]

**21-64**    The question whether the consideration is colourable is one of fact in each case[105] and, as Lord Watson noted in *Ooregum Gold Mining Co of India Ltd v Roper*,[106] 'so long as the company honestly regards the consideration given as fairly representing the nominal value of the shares in cash, its estimate ought not to be critically examined'.

**21-65**    It is only where the consideration is illusory or it is manifest on the face of the instrument that the shares are issued at a discount that the court will be prepared to consider the adequacy of the consideration.[107] This judicial attitude is in keeping with the courts' traditional reluctance to interfere in business matters.

## Payment rules applicable to public companies

**21-66**    The common law approach to non-cash consideration, discussed at **21-63**, is rather lax and applied to public companies issuing shares for a non-cash consideration would not be acceptable in view of the general policy to regulate such companies more strictly in the public interest nor would it meet the requirements of Directive 2017/1132[108] which generally requires an independent valuation of any non-cash consideration for the issue of shares by a public company.

### Valuation of non-cash consideration

**21-67**    A public company must not allot shares as fully or partly paid up (as to their nominal value or any premium on them) otherwise than in cash[109] unless:

(1) the consideration for the allotment has been independently valued;[110]

(2) the valuer's report has been made to the company during the six months immediately preceding the allotment of the shares; and

(3) a copy of the report has been sent to the proposed allottee.[111]

**21-68**    If a company allots shares in contravention of these requirements and either the allottee has not received the valuer's report, or there has been some other contravention of

---

[104] Lindley LJ cautioned against being misled by talking of value: 'The value paid to the company is measured by the price at which the company agrees to buy what it thinks it worth its while to acquire. Whilst the transaction is unimpeached, this is the only value to be considered': [1897] 1 Ch 796 at 831. The consideration in this case for the allotment of the shares was the transfer of a business comprising land, stock, and goodwill.            [105] *Re Innes & Co Ltd* [1903] 2 Ch 254 at 262.

[106] [1892] AC 125 at 137.

[107] See *Re White Star Line Ltd* [1938] 1 Ch 458 (certificates, essentially credit notes, equal in nominal amount to the sum due on the shares were accepted which, to the knowledge of all the parties, were always worth less than the nominal value).            [108] OJ L 169/46, 30.6.2017, arts 49 and 51.

[109] See CA 2006, s 583(3) (set out at **21-61**) as to when a share in a company is deemed paid up in cash or allotted for cash.

[110] Detailed rules as to the independent valuation and report are in CA 2006, ss 1150–1153. Any person who knowingly or recklessly makes a statement which is misleading, false, or deceptive in a material particular in connection with the preparation of such report commits an offence: s 1153(2).

[111] CA 2006, s 593(1); bonus issues are not caught by these provisions: s 593(2). These requirements for independent valuation do not apply to an allotment of shares in connection with: (1) a share exchange for all or some of the shares in another company or of a particular class of shares in another company, or (2) a proposed merger of the company with another: ss 594–595.

the requirements as to the independent valuation and report which the allottee knew or ought to have known amounted to a contravention, the allottee is liable to pay the company an amount equal to the aggregate of the nominal value of the shares and the whole of any premium or, if the case so requires, so much of that aggregate as is treated as paid up by the consideration with interest at the appropriate rate.[112]

**21-69** A copy of the valuation report must be filed by the company with the registrar of companies at the same time as it files the return of allotment of those shares by the company.[113]

**21-70** The valuation of the non-cash consideration and the report required thereon must be made by an independent person ('the valuer'), that is to say a person eligible to be the statutory auditor of the company and who meets the independence criteria set out in CA 2006, s 1151.[114]

**21-71** The valuer's report must state:

(1) the nominal value of the shares to be wholly or partly paid for by the consideration in question;

(2) the amount of any premium payable on the shares;

(3) the description of the consideration, the method used to value it and the date of the valuation;

(4) the extent to which the nominal value of the shares and any premium are to be treated as paid up by the consideration or in cash (CA 2006, s 596(2)).

**21-72** The report must also state that:

(1) the method of valuation (and any delegation of responsibility) was reasonable in all the circumstances;

(2) it appears to the valuer that there has been no material change in the value of the consideration since the valuation; and

(3) on the basis of the valuation, the value of the consideration (together with any cash by which the nominal value of the shares or any premium payable on them is to be paid up) is not less than so much of the aggregate of the nominal value and the whole of any such premium as is treated as paid up by the consideration and any such cash (CA 2006, s 596(3)).

**21-73** Directive 2017/1132 allows public companies to allot shares for a non-cash consideration without the need to go through these formalities for independent valuation in cases where there is some other method of valuing the asset in question.[115] The UK decided against

---

[112] CA 1985, s 593(3). The effect is to create an immediate liability as if the allottee had agreed to take up the shares for cash: *Re Bradford Investments Ltd* [1991] BCLC 224 at 233. These penalties can be onerous, see *Re Ossory Estates plc* [1988] BCLC 213; *Re Bradford Investments plc (No 2)* [1991] BCLC 688, but may be mitigated by the court's powers under CA 2006, s 606 to give relief, see **21-87**.

[113] CA 2006, s 597. A return of allotment is required within one month of the allotment: s 555.

[114] CA 2006, s 1150. To be independent, the person must not be an officer or employee of the company or of an associate or a partner or employee of such a person. The company's existing auditor is not included in the categories of excluded persons and so may act as the valuer for these purposes: s 1151. The valuer may also delegate the valuation to another person: s 1150(2).

[115] See art 50, OJ L 169/46, 30.6.2017. For example, where the assets are transferrable shares or money market instruments, the valuation can be taken to be the average market valuation during the relevant period; or where an asset has already been the subject of a fair valuation by an independent expert in the previous six months, that valuation suffices; or where the fair value can be determined from the statutory accounts, duly audited, that valuation suffices. In each case, shareholders holding at least 5 per cent of the company's issued capital may demand a valuation by an independent expert.

taking up this option as permitted by the Directive as there is no deregulatory advantage since another valuation method is required in any event.[116]

### Transfers to public company of non-cash assets

**21-74**    Further controls are imposed on agreements for:

(1) any transfer of non-cash assets[117] to the company (or another) by a subscriber to the memorandum of association of a public company incorporated as such within two years from the date of the company being issued with a trading certificate[118] (CA 2006, s 598);

(2) any such transfers by a member of a private company within two years of the company re-registering as a public company (s 603);

(3) for a consideration equal in value to 10 per cent or more of the company's issued share capital[119] at that time.

**21-75**    In practice, transactions within (1) are unusual and the statutory provisions apply mainly to transactions within (2). Not all agreements within these provisions (ss 598, 603) will involve an allotment of shares but, as many do, it is convenient to consider these matters here.

**21-76**    The company must not enter into the agreements outlined at **21-74** unless the following conditions are met:

(1) the consideration to be received by the company,[120] and any consideration other than cash to be given by the company, must be independently valued by a valuer in the same way[121] as outlined at **21-70** with respect to CA 2006, s 596 (shares allotted for a non-cash consideration) and the valuer's report must be made to the company during the six months immediately preceding the date of the agreement;[122]

(2) the terms of the agreement must be approved by an ordinary resolution of the company;[123] and

(3) copies of the valuer's report must be circulated to the members, where a written resolution is used, at or before the time when the resolution was submitted to the members and, if a meeting is held, the report must be circulated no later than the date on which notice of the meeting is given and the report must be circulated to the other party to the agreement if not then a member of the company.[124]

**21-77**    These requirements do not apply where it is part of the company's ordinary business to acquire such assets as are to be transferred and the agreement is entered into in the ordinary course of business of that company, a potentially wide category (CA 2006, 598(4)).[125]

---

[116] See DTI, *Implementation of the Companies Act 2006* (2007), URN 07/666, Ch 6, esp paras 6.10–6.16, 6.23–6.26.

[117] 'Non-cash asset' is defined in CA 2006, s 1163 as meaning any property or interest in property other than cash; and see s 1163(2) as to the transfer of a non-cash asset.

[118] i.e. a certificate of entitlement to do business required by CA 2006, s 761, see **21-10**. In most cases, this will mean within two years of incorporation.    [119] See definition in CA 2006, s 546.

[120] See CA 2006, ss 599(2), 603.    [121] See CA 2006, ss 600, 603.

[122] CA 2006, ss 599(1)(b), 603. The contents of the report are set out in s 600 and are essentially the same as those required under s 596, outlined at **21-71** et seq.    [123] CA 2006, ss 601, 603.

[124] CA 2006, ss 599(1), 601(3), 603. Copies of the valuer's report and the resolution must be delivered to the registrar of companies within 15 days of passing the resolution: ss 602, 603.

[125] Nor do they apply to agreements entered into as a result of a court order or under court control: CA 2006, s 598(5).

**21-78**  In the event of contravention of these valuation requirements, the company is entitled to recover from the other party any consideration given by it under the agreement, or an amount equal to the value of the consideration at the time of the agreement, and the agreement, so far as not carried out, is void.[126]

**21-79**  There is clearly a degree of overlap between the requirement for a non-cash consideration to be valued before an allotment of shares (CA 2006, s 593), discussed at **21-67**, and these provisions governing the transfer to a public company of non-cash assets in the initial period (ss 598–603), but it is important to appreciate the different scope of the provisions.

**21-80**  Section 593 applies whenever a public company accepts a non-cash consideration from anyone as consideration for an allotment of shares. Section 598 applies to any transfer of a non-cash asset from a subscriber or member to the company whether the consideration for the transfer is an allotment of shares or something else. There are also different exceptions to each provision.

**21-81**  It is possible for the provisions to be applicable in the same instance since the provisions are not mutually exclusive. Any allotment of shares for a non-cash consideration to a subscriber or member within the two-year period is potentially within CA 2006, s 593 and ss 598–603, which is not unduly burdensome as the requirements for an independent valuation and report are similar. The major difference is that ss 598–603 require the relevant agreements to be approved by an ordinary resolution. On the other hand, ss 598–603 do not apply where it is part of the company's ordinary business to acquire such assets as are to be transferred and the agreement is entered into in the ordinary course of that business.[127] The type of transaction which is within ss 598–603 but not within s 593 is where the transaction does not involve an allotment of shares but is simply a transfer of non-cash assets by a subscriber or member within the relevant time-frame to a public company or a company re-registered as a public company.

### Undertakings to do work or perform services

**21-82**  A public company must not accept at any time, in payment up of its shares or any premium on them, an undertaking given by any person that he or another should do work or perform services for the company or any other person (CA 2006, s 585(1)). If a public company accepts such an undertaking, the holder of the shares when they or the premium are treated as paid up (in whole or in part) by the undertaking is liable to pay the company in respect of those shares an amount equal to their nominal value, together with the whole of any premium or, if the case so requires, such proportion of that amount as is treated as paid up by the undertaking, together with interest (s 585(2)). In the event of a contravention, the company and any officer in default is liable on conviction to a fine (s 590). Despite any contravention, any undertaking given by any person to do work or perform services or to do any other thing remains enforceable by the company.[128]

### Restriction on long-term undertakings

**21-83**  A public company must not allot shares as fully or partly-paid (as to their nominal value or any premium on them) otherwise than in cash if the consideration for the allotment is or includes an undertaking which is to be, or may be, performed more than five years after the

---

[126] CA 2006, s 604(1), (2).       [127] CA 2006, ss 598(4), 603.       [128] CA 2006, s 591, subject to s 589.

date of the allotment.[129] In the event of breach, the allottee is liable to pay the company an amount equal to the aggregate of the nominal value and the whole of any premium due.[130]

## Consequences of breach of the payment rules

**21-84**   The consequences of breach of any of the statutory payment and valuation rules are relatively uniform.

**21-85**   As a general rule, the allottee remains liable to pay an amount equal to the nominal amount and any premium due together with interest.[131] Subsequent holders are jointly and severally liable unless they are purchasers for value and did not have actual notice of the contravention or they took from a holder who was not himself liable under these provisions.[132]

**21-86**   These penalties can be quite onerous. In *Re Ossory Estates plc*[133] property was sold to a company and the vendor received as part of the consideration 8m shares in the company. As this was an allotment of shares for a non-cash consideration, an independent valuation and report were required. No such report was ever made with the result that the allottee, despite having transferred his property to the company, was liable to pay the company £1.76m as the price of the shares. Not surprisingly, this was described by Harman J as a somewhat startling conclusion.[134]

**21-87**   It is possible for a person so liable to make an application to the court to be exempted in whole or in part from the liability (CA 2006, ss 589(1), 606(1)). If such liability arises in relation to payment in respect of any shares, the court may exempt the applicant from the liability only if and to the extent that it appears to the court just and equitable to do so having regard to the matters mentioned (CA 2006, ss 589(3), 606(2)). The matters to be taken into account by the court are:

(1)   whether the applicant has paid, or is liable to pay, any amount in respect of any other liability arising in relation to those shares under any of the relevant provisions, or of any liability arising by virtue of any undertaking given in or in connection with payment for those shares;

(2)   whether any person other than the applicant has paid or is likely to pay (whether in pursuance of an order of the court or otherwise) any such amount; and

(3)   whether the applicant or any other person has performed, in whole or in part, or is likely so to perform any such undertaking, or has done or is likely to do any other thing in payment or part payment for the shares.[135]

**21-88**   In determining whether it should exempt the applicant in whole or in part from any liability, the court must have regard to the following overriding principle,[136] namely that

---

[129]  CA 2006, s 587. The provision also applies to a contract which did not originally contravene this provision but is subsequently varied and results in a contravention. In such cases, the variation is void. Equally caught is the situation where an undertaking was to have been performed within five years but was not: s 587(3) and (4).                                    [130]  CA 2006, s 587(2).

[131]  The effect is to create an immediate liability as if the allottee had agreed to take up the shares for cash: see *Re Bradford Investments plc* [1991] BCLC 224 at 233.               [132]  CA 2006, ss 588(1), (2), 605(3).

[133]  [1988] BCLC 213.          [134]  [1988] BCLC 213 at 214.

[135]  CA 2006, s 589(3). See *Re Bradford Investments plc (No 2)* [1991] BCLC 688 at 693 where Hoffmann J thought that, in the light of what is now CA 2006, s 589(5) (see **21-88**), these matters are not intended to be an exhaustive statement of the matters to which the court should or may have regard.

[136]  See *Re Bradford Investments plc (No 2)* [1991] BCLC 688 at 694 where Hoffmann J thought that the designation 'overriding principle' did not oblige the court to refuse relief unless the company had received at least the nominal value of the allotted shares and any premium: had that been the intention, the requirement would have been framed as a rule.

a company which has allotted shares should receive money or money's worth at least equal in value to the aggregate of the nominal value of those shares and the whole of any premium or, if the case so requires, so much of that aggregate as is treated as paid up (CA 2006, ss 589(5), 606(4)).

**21-89**   In *Re Ossory Estates plc*,[137] noted at **21-86**, relief was granted as the company had sold some of the property transferred to it in consideration for the allotment at a substantial profit and had undoubtedly received at least money or money's worth equal in value to, and probably exceeding, the aggregate of the nominal value of the shares and any premium. It was just and equitable that the allottee should be relieved from any further liability.

**21-90**   This outcome can be contrasted with that in *System Control plc v Munro Corporate plc*[138] where the court said there was no prospect of relief being granted when there was absolutely no evidence that the company had received the minimum amount; likewise in *Re Bradford Investments plc (No 2)*[139] where the applicants failed to discharge the burden of showing that the company had received value for its shares.

**21-91**   Where a person is liable under CA 2006, s 604(2) to a company as a result of the transfer to a public company of a non-cash asset in the initial period (see **21-74**), the court may, on application, exempt him in whole or in part from that liability if and to the extent that it appears to the court just and equitable to do so having regard to any benefit accruing to the company by virtue of anything done by him towards the carrying out of the agreement for transfer (s 606(6)).

**21-92**   In addition to the civil consequences, where there is a breach of these provisions, the company and officers in default are also guilty of an offence and liable to a fine.[140] Directors may also be in breach of duty, for example the duty to exercise their powers for a proper purpose (CA 2006, s 171(b)) and to promote the success of the company (s 172), and liable to make good any loss suffered by the company as a result of the breach, see Chapter 14.[141]

## G  Capital raising

### Introduction

**21-93**   The basic function of companies is to provide a vehicle for entrepreneurial activity. Large-scale entrepreneurial activity may require amounts of capital which can only be provided by inviting outside investors to pool their resources and invest in an enterprise over which they may have relatively little control. To persuade such investors to come forward two incentives are needed. One is limited liability and that is provided by the companies legislation.[142] The other is an active stock market to provide a means by which investors can realise their investment. Without such a market investors will require a higher return on their investment to compensate for the lack of liquidity. The existence of a market for shares thus not only makes it possible for companies to raise external funding but makes it cheaper for them to do so as well. A stock market meets these needs of the company and

---

[137] [1988] BCLC 213.      [138] [1990] BCLC 659.      [139] [1991] BCLC 688.
[140] CA 2006, ss 590, 607.      [141] *Hirsche v Sims* [1894] AC 654.
[142] As to the importance of limited liability to investors, see Easterbrook and Fischel, *The Economic Structure of Corporate Law* (1991), Ch 2; Halpern, Trebilcock, and Turnbull, 'An Economic Analysis of Limited Liability in Corporation Law' (1980) 30 Univ of Toronto Law Jo 117.

the investors by providing a primary market through which the company can offer its shares to the public and so raise capital and a secondary market where investors can trade in those shares. For the original owners, admission to a market offers the opportunity to realise their investment in the business and to sell out to new owners. Once admitted to trading, the company may use the stock market to raise further capital in all manner of ways. It may make further public offers of its shares[143] from time to time and, with a broader shareholder base, it may find that a rights issue (i.e. the offer of new shares to existing shareholders in proportion to their existing holdings: see **21-34**) is an appropriate way of raising additional capital. As well as the ability to issue shares to investors to raise capital, traded companies commonly use their shares as consideration for a takeover or in consideration for the acquisition of an asset where the shares are offered, respectively, to the target company's shareholders or to the vendors of the asset (and in some instances immediately resold on their behalf). These offers are described as acquisition or merger issues or vendor consideration or vendor placings. This ability to fund acquisitions and mergers using shares instead of cash is one of the main advantages of being a traded company and it is only available to a public company as a private company is prohibited from offering its shares to the public (CA 2006, s 755), see **21-96**.

**21-94**    In terms of raising capital, the choice typically lies between a public offer (often referred to as an IPO, initial public offer) or a placing (though sometimes companies combine a public offer with a placing) with IPOs being restricted by cost to the larger companies looking to raise significant sums of money while placings are typically used to raise more modest sums.[144] However, IPOs have been in decline across many jurisdictions over the past decade, particularly post the financial crisis and the picture is the same in the UK.[145] Smaller companies, in particular, are deterred by the costs of an IPO.

**21-95**    After an initial raising of capital, subsequent (secondary) issues are typically by rights issues (see **21-34**) or placings. A placing allows the securities to be marketed to specified persons or clients of the sponsor or any securities house assisting in the placing[146] and, as discussed later, an advantage of a placing is that it can usually be structured in such a way as to be exempt from the need to prepare a prospectus (see **21-112**). Where the company itself offers to the public shares not yet in issue or allotted, this is known as an offer for subscription[147] and persons who acquire the shares directly from the company are known as subscribers. Where the offer of shares to the public is not by the company itself, but by a third party holding shares already in issue or allotted (such as an investment bank), it is called an offer for sale and persons who acquire the shares are known as purchasers.[148] The mechanism chosen by a company to raise capital will depend on a variety of factors

---

[143] It is also possible to issue debt securities, typically corporate bonds, to raise loan capital. For large companies, debt securities are a much more important source of funding than equity securities (shares). For example, for the year to December 2017, UK listed companies raised £17bn in equity issues and £79bn in Eurobond issues: see London Stock Exchange, *Main Market, Market Statistics*, Table 3 (December 2017).

[144] For example, in the year to December 2017, (outside of initial offerings), for UK listed companies, there were 199 placings, 119 placings, 21 public offers and placings, and six rights issues: London Stock Exchange, *Main Market, Market Statistics*, Market Summary Table (December 2017). There was one IPO and 50 placings and 12 introductions for new UK companies.

[145] See European Issues, 'EU IPO Report, Rebuilding IPOs in Europe Creating jobs and growth in European capital markets' 23 March 2015. Also see quarterly reporting by PwC on the state of the IPO market in Europe, called IPO Watch Europe.

[146] Listing Rules, App 1.1. Relevant Definitions, see 'placing'.

[147] Listing Rules, App 1.1. Relevant Definitions, see 'offer for subscription'.

[148] Listing Rules, App 1.1. Relevant Definitions, see 'offer for sale'.

including the size of the company, the amount of capital which it needs to raise and the speed with which it needs to raise it, whether shareholder authorisation is needed and whether a rights issue can be disapplied (see **21-47**), and whether the company will be able to avoid or will need to prepare a prospectus (see **21-111**).

## Private companies and public offers

**21-96**  A private company is prohibited from offering to the public any securities (i.e. shares or debentures) of the company (CA 2006, s 755(1), (5)).[149] A company proposing to contravene this prohibition can be restrained by court order (s 757)[150] and, if the contravention has already occurred, on an application being made, the court must require the company to re-register as a public company, save where it is impracticable or undesirable to so order (s 758(2)).[151] If re-registration is not an option, the court may still make a remedial order[152] or a winding-up order or both (s 758(3)).[153] A breach of the prohibition does not affect the validity of any allotment or sale of any securities (s 760).

**21-97**  An offer is not to be regarded as an offer to the public if it can properly be regarded, in all the circumstances:

(1) as not being calculated to result, directly or indirectly, in the shares or debentures becoming available to persons other than those receiving the offer; or

(2) as being a private concern of the person receiving and making it (s 756(3)).

An offer is presumed to be of a private concern of the person making and receiving it if the company offers the shares to its existing members, employees and their families, or an existing debenture holder, or a trustee of a trust where the principal beneficiary of the trust is within these categories, or if the offer is an offer under an employees' share scheme;[154] and, if the offer is renounceable, it is renounceable only to these restricted groups (s 756(4), (5)). The intention with these exceptions is to ensure that a private company may still raise equity capital, but from a limited circle of people.

**21-98**  This prohibition on the offer of shares to the public is not always clearly understood by private companies and they may offer their shares to a wider audience than that permitted which has a number of consequences. First, it is a breach of the prohibition in CA 2006, s 755, as already discussed. Secondly, it is unlawful for a company to offer

---

[149] This prohibition on public offers in CA 2006, s 755 restates the prohibition in CA 1985, s 81, but it removes the criminal sanction which the 1985 Act imposed. The prohibition extends to allotments to third parties with a view to the securities being offered to the public, see CA 2006, s 755(2), and note the presumption that this is the case in certain circumstances. Likewise, a private company may not apply for listing of any of its securities: Financial Services and Markets Act (Official Listing of Securities) Regulations 2001, SI 2001/2956, reg 3(a).

[150] An application can be made by any member, creditor, or the Secretary of State and note the unusual requirement that an order must be made by the court where, in unfairly prejudicial proceedings under CA 2006, Pt 30 (see Chapter 19), it appears to the court that the company is proposing to act in contravention of this prohibition on public offers by private companies: s 757(1).

[151] See CA 2006, s 758(4) for the categories of persons who can apply for an order in this case.

[152] Defined in CA 2006, s 759 as an order for the purpose of putting a person affected by the contravention in the position he would have been in had there not been the contravention.

[153] This power is discretionary because it may be that the prohibition has been breached but the company has not allotted the shares or the company has withdrawn the offer and undertaken not to make a further offer so a remedial order is unnecessary: see *Explanatory Notes to the Companies Act 2006*, para 1061.

[154] Defined CA 2006, s 1166.

transferable securities to the public in the UK without first publishing an approved prospectus (Financial Services and Markets Act 2000 (FSMA 2000), s 85, see **21-111**). Depending on the circumstances, there may also be a breach of the rules governing financial promotion.[155] Each of these provisions applies to different categories of offers and different types of securities and compliance with one set of requirements does not necessarily mean compliance with the others so private companies need to be alert to the various consequences if, inadvertently, they make an offer to the public.

**21-99** The prohibition on public offers by private companies is not an arbitrary barrier, as the CA 2006 makes clear,[156] rather it is the precise point at which the public interest intrudes. Corporate self-interest in raising capital meets the public interest in the protection of investors. A company which wishes to offer shares to the public must submit to the greater regulation imposed on public companies in the interests of investors by the CA 2006 and by the FSMA 2000. The mischief at which CA 2006, s 755 (see **21-96**) is aimed is companies making offers to the public without complying with the range of regulatory requirements (in respect of transparency, capital, and corporate governance requirements) imposed on public companies in the interests of investor protection—hence the leeway allowed to private companies which are technically in breach of s 755 but which are in the process of re-registering and do so re-register (s 755(3)). The presumption in s 758 is therefore that private companies in breach of the prohibition on public offers should be made to re-register as public companies and so be subject to the appropriate level of regulation.

## Publicly traded companies

**21-100** Being a public company is not synonymous with being listed on a stock market nor are all stock markets for listed securities. Technology now allows markets to operate in a much more segmented way than previously which gives rise to a somewhat complex picture as exchanges attempt to meet the demands of investors and issuers (companies looking to raise equity or loan capital). The result is that exchanges are no longer single-tier markets for listed companies but instead offer a variety of markets with differing entry requirements. The law relating to the operation of these markets and the trading of securities is beyond the scope of this work[157] and the discussion here is limited to an overview of the ways in which public companies use the markets and the regulatory requirements which govern them.

**21-101** The questions for public companies are: (a) whether they wish to offer their shares to the public at all (they are not required to do so); (b) whether they wish also to be admitted to

---

[155] Financial promotion is governed by FSMA 2000, s 21 and The Financial Services and Markets Act 2000 (Financial Promotion) Order 2005, SI 2005/1529, as amended. Extensive guidance on the application of s 21 is found in the FCA, *Perimeter Guidance Manual*, PERG 8, Financial Promotion. Essentially, it is a criminal offence for persons other than authorised persons, in the course of business, to communicate an invitation or inducement to engage in investment activity. See *Re UK-Euro Group plc* [2007] 1 BCLC 812 (compulsory winding up on public interest grounds when company raised its share capital in clear breach of FSMA 2000, s 21).

[156] The CA 2006, s 4(4) identifies the two major differences between private and public companies as being those set out in Part 20 of the Act, namely this prohibition on public offers by private companies (s 755) and the requirement for a minimum share capital (s 761, see **21-9**), but it is the former requirement which is the significant difference.

[157] Readers are referred to specialist texts such as Gullifer and Payne, *Corporate Finance Law* (2nd edn, 2015), esp Chs 9, 10; Ferran and Ho, *Principles of Corporate Finance Law* (2nd edn, 2014), esp Chs 13–14; Hudson, *Securities Law* (2nd edn, 2013); also Moloney, *EU Securities and Financial Markets Regulation* (3rd edn, 2015).

trading which usually goes hand in hand with a desire to offer their shares to the public since the public will only be willing to buy the shares if they can then trade them; and (c) the type of market on which they wish to be traded. Essentially, the core markets are regulated markets and multilateral trading facilities (MTFs)—there are other levels but these will suffice for our purposes.[158] Regulated markets have the greatest degree of regulation with admission to trading on a regulated market being the standard threshold for the application of significant EU obligations,[159] such as the Prospectus Regulation and the Transparency Directive, while MTFs were more lightly regulated. In 2011 the European Commission adopted the Directive on Markets in Financial Instruments and the Regulation on Markets in Financial Instruments, commonly referred to as MiFID 2[160] and MiFIR,[161] which bring a greater degree of transparency and oversight to the operation of the markets, especially MTFs, with effect from 3 January 2018.

**21-102**  The usual option in the UK is that larger established public companies look for a listing on a regulated market which means essentially on the Main Market run by the London Stock Exchange (LSE).[162] Smaller, perhaps more speculative, companies look to be admitted to trading on an MTF, usually the Alternative Investment Market (AIM) also run by the LSE, and, under the new MiFID 2 regime, AIM has adopted the label of SME Growth Market[163] which is intended to raise the profile of these markets. The choice of market is not irreversible and companies can move up to the Main Market and down to AIM depending on their circumstances.

### Listed securities admitted to the LSE Main Market

**21-103**  Securities are listed when the security (not the issuer) is admitted to the Official List maintained by the Financial Conduct Authority (FCA) which is the competent authority for these purposes and which, in this context, is known as the UK Listing Authority (UKLA).[164] To be admitted to the Official List, equity securities must be admitted to trading on a regulated market for listed securities operated by a recognised investment exchange[165] which in practice means admitted to trading on the Main Market of the LSE. The Listing Rules drawn up by UKLA govern listing and the LSE's Admission and Disclosure Standards govern admission to trading on the Main Market of the LSE. There are then differing roles for the UKLA and the LSE, but the steps are linked and a simultaneous application is made to UKLA for listing and to the LSE for admission to trading.[166] There are two listing segments,

---

[158] Organised trading facilities (OTFs) are trading platforms for trading in bonds, structured finance products, and derivatives.

[159] The European Securities and Markets Authority (ESMA) maintains on its website the register of regulated markets—there were approximately 110 RMs in Europe and about 146 MTFs (March 2018). The most significant UK regulated market for our purposes is the Main Market of the London Stock Exchange.

[160] Directive 2014/65, OJ L 173/349, 12.6.2014.     [161] Regulation 600/2014, OJ L 173/84, 12.6.2014.

[162] In keeping with the fragmentation of markets, the London Stock Exchange also has a High Growth Segment (HGS) of its Main Market which is for unlisted equity securities and intended for mid-sized European and UK companies. The HGS is a regulated market, however, so companies on it are subject to the London Stock Exchange's HGS Rulebook and existing Admission and Disclosure Standards and, as a regulated market, the relevant Directives, especially the Prospectus Directive and the Transparency Directive apply. In this case, the minimum float is only 10 per cent (compared to 25 per cent for a premium listing) with a value of at least £30 million and the majority of the £30 million must be raised at admission.

[163] Directive 2014/65, art 33, OJ L 173/349, 12.6.2014.     [164] FSMA 2000, s 74(1).

[165] Listing Rules, LR 2.2.3.

[166] In many jurisdictions listing and admission to trading is a single exercise carried out by an exchange, but for historical reasons the UK has a strong and distinct listing regime. The emphasis in EU Directives was originally on admission to listing, but since then the EU has moved to a regulatory threshold of 'admitted to trading on a regulated market'.

Premium and Standard, and companies can migrate between them. Only equity securities are eligible for a premium listing and all other listings of securities are standard listings. Companies with premium listed securities are subject to 'super-equivalence' requirements, i.e. they are subject to the requirements of the EU Directives and other 'super' UK requirements imposed by the Listing Rules, hence this category is synonymous with the highest standards of investor protection. The Listing Rules in respect of a standard listing are based on (though sometimes go beyond) the minimum standards imposed by the EU Directives.

**21-104**   Listing Rule (LR) 2 sets out the basic requirements for admission to listing for all types of securities[167] and LR 14 sets out the additional eligibility and ongoing requirements where a company seeks a standard listing of equity shares.[168] LR 6 sets out additional eligibility requirements where a company seeks a premium listing[169] and LR 7–13 set out a range of additional requirements which apply to a premium listing. LR 9 includes the continuing obligations which apply to a company with a premium listing of equity shares[170] and LR 10 (significant transactions) and LR 11 (related party transactions) are also significant obligations applicable to premium listings. Further requirements are applied to a premium listed company with a controlling shareholding, essentially anyone (whether alone or in concert with others) who controls 30 per cent or more of the voting rights of the company.[171] There are also a series of high-level Listing Principles in LR 7 most of which apply only to a listed company with a premium listing, for example, requiring the company to take reasonable steps to enable its directors to understand their responsibilities and obligations as directors and to act with integrity towards holders and potential holders of its premium listed shares. In the event of any breach of any provision of the Listing Rules, UKLA can impose a penalty of such amount as it considers appropriate or it may publish a statement of censure with respect to the issuer and any director knowingly concerned in the contravention (FSMA 2000, s 91).

**21-105**   The FCA keeps the listing regime under review to make sure 'it appropriately balances the needs of investors and issuers'[172] and, in February 2017, it published a discussion and

---

[167] The requirements for admission to listing include that the issuer is validly incorporated; equity securities are admitted to trading on a regulated market for listed securities operated by a recognised investment exchange; the securities must be freely transferable, fully paid, with an expected market value of at least £700,000; and there must be an approved prospectus: LR 2 and 3.

[168] In particular, a sufficient number (usually at least 25 per cent) of the shares being listed must be distributed to the public and the company must comply with various disclosure obligations under the FCA Disclosure and Transparency Rules (DTR).

[169] Requirements in LR 6 include a requirement for a three-year trading record with published audited accounts over that period; the company must carry on an independent business as its main activity; it must have an independent auditor; an unqualified working capital statement; it must appoint a sponsor; and a sufficient number (usually at least 25 per cent) of the shares being listed must be in the hands of the public; and the securities must be capable of electronic settlement.

[170] The company must comply with the Listing Rules Model Code on directors' dealings, with various obligations with respect to allotments of shares, with disclosure and transparency obligations, especially detailed requirements as to the contents of the annual report and accounts (Disclosure and Transparency Rule (DTR) 4), and with corporate governance obligations (DTR 7) including adherence on a comply or explain basis to the UK Corporate Governance Code.

[171] The company must enter into a relationship agreement with the controlling shareholder (LR 9.2.2A); there are additional requirements with respect to the election or re-election of independent directors which must be approved by a majority of the shareholders as a whole, but also by a majority of the shareholders independent of the controlling shareholder (LR 9.2.2E); and likewise voting limitations apply on a resolution to cancel the company's listing (LR 5.2.5R).

[172] FCA, FS 17/3, *Feedback Statement to DP17/2 Review of Effectiveness of Primary Markets* (October 2017), para 1.8.

a consultation paper on the structure of the UK's primary markets,[173] which led it to propose some mainly technical changes to the wording of some of the Listing Rules.[174] It is also still considering three issues which arose from those discussions, namely the relative positioning of standard versus premium listing, particularly whether there is scope to raise minimum requirements in the standard list (if not constrained by EU Directives); the provision of patient capital to companies that require long-term investment; and retail access to debt markets. Further consultation by the FCA on these matters is awaited at the time of writing.

### Unlisted securities trading on AIM

**21-106**  Of course, a company need not seek a listing and it can be (and most public companies are) unlisted, i.e. its securities are not admitted to the Official List maintained by UKLA, but such a company can still be admitted to trading and unlisted public companies are commonly traded on AIM, the Alternative Investment Market which is an MTF operated by the LSE. Companies trading on AIM are subject to a simpler regime and with more relaxed criteria for entry to the market, set out in the AIM Rules, and generally a prospectus is not required (see **21-111**). Companies are not required to have reached a certain size, or to have a defined percentage of shares in public hands, or to provide a lengthy trading history.[175] All companies must produce an admission document making certain disclosures about such matters as their directors' backgrounds, their promoters, and business activities.[176] Once admitted to AIM, a company has to accept certain ongoing requirements, mainly disclosure requirements with respect to financial matters and company and related party transactions and changes in the business and the management structures.[177]

**21-107**  There were 6,049 UK public companies on the register of companies as at 31 March 2017, just 0.2 per cent of the UK register.[178] As of December 2017, there were 990 UK listed companies and there were 808 UK companies trading on AIM[179] so roughly 30 per cent of public companies are traded on one or other market, but only 16 per cent of public companies are listed public companies. The numbers of companies on the respective markets are a result, in part, of a flight in recent years from regulation and from the high costs

---

[173]  See FCA, DP 17/2, *Review of the Effectiveness of Primary Markets: The UK Primary Markets Landscape* (February 2017); FCA, CP 17/4, *Review of the Effectiveness of Primary Markets: Enhancements to the Listing Regime*. See previously FCA, Policy Statement, Response to CP13/15—*Enhancing the effectiveness of the Listing Regime* (May 2014, PS14/8); CP12/25, *Enhancing the effectiveness of the Listing Regime* (October 2012) and the FCA feedback document of the same title, CP13/15 (November 2013).

[174]  See FCA Feedback Statement 17/3 (October 2017) and FCA Policy Statement 17/22 (October 2017).

[175]  The company must be judged to be appropriate to join AIM by a nominated adviser (a nomad) who must be on a register of nomads maintained by the LSE. The company must retain a nomad at all times and the nomad is responsible for guiding and helping the company to comply with the market rules: AIM Rules, r 1.

[176]  AIM Rules, r 3 and Sch 1.          [177]  AIM Rules, rr 10–36.

[178]  See *Companies Register Activities 2016–17*, Table A3.

[179]  Monthly statistics on Main Market (listed) companies and on AIM companies can be found on the LSE website. Another term commonly but erroneously used as synonymous with listed company is 'quoted company'—this area is bedevilled by confusing terminology. UKLA uses 'quoted company' to describe companies traded on an MTF while, in the CA 2006, the term 'quoted company' has a precise meaning with respect to certain disclosure requirements, for example, with regard to website publication of poll results (CA 2006, s 341); the directors' remuneration report (s 420); website publication of accounts (s 430); and the right of members to require publication of audit concerns on the website (s 527). For the purposes of the CA 2006, s 385, a quoted company is a company whose equity share capital is officially listed in the UK or in an EEA State or is admitted to dealing either on the NYSE or Nasdaq (i.e. the main American stock exchanges), so it is broader than a UK listed company.

of listing. Over the period, there has also been a decline for essentially the same reasons (regulatory burdens and costs) in the numbers of public companies on the register of companies. These market statistics also show that approximately 70 per cent of public companies are not traded on any market. For those businesses, being a public company is about status and credibility with suppliers and customers rather than any need or desire to raise equity or loan capital, but it is also clear that many companies no longer think the benefits justify the burdens and costs associated with public company status, hence the steady percentage decline in the number on the register.

## Public offers of securities

### The EU dimension—the Prospectus Directive

**21-108**  Much of the law relating to securities regulation generally and including public offers of shares derives from EU Directives and Regulations which shape the domestic legislation on these matters. The objectives with respect to EU securities regulation (as broadly reflected in the preambles to the various Directives) would include:

- to establish an equivalent level of securities disclosure and investor protection throughout the EU;

- to contribute to the correct functioning and development of securities markets and to the maintenance of confidence in those markets;

- to facilitate cross-border listings and offers of shares in order to promote greater inter-penetration of national securities markets with a view to ensuring a genuine EU capital market;

- to prevent forum shopping by companies seeking jurisdictions within the EU with the lowest regulatory requirements;

- more recently, an objective would be to facilitate capital raising by SMEs.[180]

**21-109**  A key aspect of this work has been to regulate the use of prospectuses, the document required for public offers of securities or for their admission to trading on a regulated market. The challenge is to strike the appropriate balance between reducing administrative burdens on issuers so making it easier for them to raise capital and effective investor protection. The initial provision was the Prospectus Directive 2003/71/EC[181] which came into force on 1 July 2005. It was amended by Directive 2010/73/EU[182] with effect from July 2012 following a review by the European Commission which noted, in particular, the need to ease the administrative burdens on SMEs, for example, by allowing the introduction, *inter alia*, of a proportionate disclosure regime for SMEs and for rights issues.[183] In February 2015, the European Commission launched a consultation on further amendments to the Prospectus Directive, as part of the Capital Markets Union project, with a view to facilitating the raising of capital across Europe, particularly for smaller firms,

---

[180] See Moloney, *EU Securities and Financial Markets Regulation* (3rd edn, 2015), at II3.3.2 on the 'SME Agenda'.

[181] OJ L 345/64, 31.12.2003; and associated Prospectus Directive Regulation 809/2004/EC, OJ L 149/1, 30.4.2004, much amended, which provided the technical detail as to the content and format of prospectuses. For a detailed analysis of the Directive, see Moloney, *EU Securities and Financial Markets Regulation* (3rd edn, 2015), II.4.          [182] OJ L 327/1, 11.12.2010.

[183] See European Commission, *Study on the Impact of the Prospectus Regime on EU Financial Markets, Final Report* (June 2008), followed by a Commission consultation in 2009 on amending the Prospectus Directive, see COM (2009) 491 final, 23.9.2009.

while maintaining investor protection.[184] The consultation identified several shortcomings with the existing framework, in particular, that drawing up and having a prospectus approved was perceived to be an expensive, complex, and time-consuming exercise, that prospectuses had become overlong documents and somewhat ineffective from an investor protection perspective; and that the proportionate disclosure regime introduced by Directive 2010/73/EU had not been adopted by issuers.[185] The outcome of this review has seen the repeal of the Prospectus Directive and its replacement with the Prospectus Regulation 2017/1129,[186] which comes into force mainly on 21 July 2019, though a small number of provisions are already in force or will come into force ahead of that date. It was decided to proceed by way of a Regulation instead of a Directive because it is directly applicable and ensures uniformity of adoption across the EU. The Prospectus Regulation is a framework Regulation so much of the detail is awaited from ESMA, the European Securities and Markets Authority, which has already consulted on the form and content of the prospectus, the EU Growth prospectus (for SMEs), and the criteria to be applied by national competent authorities when approving and filing prospectuses.[187] ESMA notes that the existing prospectus scheme generally works well and so the aim is to reduce the cost and administrative burden in using a prospectus while also including some additional disclosure requirements that are deemed necessary for investor protection.[188] There remain some practitioner concerns that the changes have not been radical enough and will only make modest improvements to the existing framework. It is expected that, regardless of Brexit, the UK will adopt the provisions of the new Prospectus Regulation, but to date the Treasury has not consulted on its adoption.

### The statutory framework

**1-110**    The governing framework domestically is FSMA 2000, Pt VI (ss 72–103) and the FCA Prospectus Rules (PR) which contain the core rules governing the content and delivery of prospectuses and breach of either Part VI or the PR attracts the penalties specified in FSMA 2000, s 91(1A) and (3), i.e. monetary penalties and public censure.

**1-111**    The basic scheme is that:

(i) It is unlawful for transferable securities[189] to be offered to the public in the UK unless an approved prospectus (approved by UKLA) is available to the public before the offer is made (FSMA 2000, s 85(1)); and,

(ii) it is unlawful to request the admission of transferable securities[190] to trading on a regulated market situated or operating in the UK unless an approved prospectus is publicly available before the request is made (s 85(2)).

---

[184] See European Commission Consultation Document, *Review of the Prospectus Directive*, 18.2.2015; Green Paper, *Building a Capital Markets Union*, COM (2015) 63, 18.2.2015

[185] See Consultation Document in n 184.          [186] OJ L 168/12, 30.6.2017.

[187] See ESMA consultations papers on the Prospectus Regulation, issued July 2017 and subsequent Technical Advice on these three areas, issued April 2018. The technical advice is for consideration and endorsement by the Commission and will form the basis for the delegated acts that will underpin the Regulation.

[188] See ESMA Press Release, 'ESMA proposes simplifications to prospectuses format and content', 3 April 2018.

[189] 'Transferable securities' is defined in FSMA 2000, s 102A(3). The requirement for a prospectus applies for the purposes of this provision to all transferable securities other than those excluded by s 85(5), i.e. those listed in FSMA 2000, Sch 11A or excluded by the Prospectus Rules, see PR 1.2.2R.

[190] 'Transferable securities' is defined in FSMA 2000, s 102A(3). The requirement for a prospectus for the purposes of this provision applies to all transferable securities other than those excluded by s 85(6), i.e. those listed in FSMA 2000, Sch 11A, Pt 1, or excluded by the Prospectus Rules, see PR 1.2.3R.

The consequence of the dual prohibition is that, even though an offer may be exempt from the requirement for a prospectus, if the securities are the subject of a request for admission to a regulated market, an approved prospectus is required,[191] and vice versa. A breach of either prohibition is a criminal offence and attracts civil liability for breach of statutory duty (s 85(3), (4)).

**21-112**    There are exemptions from the requirement to provide a prospectus which vary depending on whether an offer to the public or admission to trading is being sought. If the issues seeks both to make an offer to the public and secure admission to trading, any exemptions relied on must extend to each of those steps. In each case, the requirement for a prospectus is limited by the definition of 'transferable securities' with categories of excluded securities (for example, government and public securities) being set out in FSMA 2000, Sch 11A and the PR, but the categories differ depending on whether the step being taken is an offer to the public or an admission to listing.[192] As to what is an offer to the public, FSMA 2000, s 102B offers the widest possible definition. For these purposes, there is an offer of transferable securities to the public if there is a communication in any form or by any means to any person which presents sufficient information on the transferable securities to be offered and the terms on which they are offered to enable an investor to decide to buy or subscribe for the securities in question (s 102B(1), (3)).[193]

**21-113**    With respect to an offer to the public, the requirement for a prospectus does not apply, for example, to transferable securities included in an offer where the total consideration of the offer is less than €1m, calculated over 12 months, an exemption which is important in practice as it allows companies to raise small but useful sums of money without the need for an approved prospectus.[194] Various categories of exempt offers to the public are set out in s 86, namely offers to qualified investors,[195] to fewer than 150 persons (other than qualified investors) per EEA state, or where the minimum consideration which may be paid by any person is at least €100,000; or the securities are denominated in amounts of at least €100,000; or where the total consideration payable for the securities cannot exceed €8m.[196] In these situations, the investor protection goals which drive the requirement for the publication of a prospectus are of less significance either because of the nature of the securities (low value) or the nature of the would-be purchaser (qualified) or the scale of the would-be purchase (high denomination securities). With respect to the admission to trading of securities, an important exemption is where the securities represent, over a period of 12 months,

---

[191] It was for this reason that the Alternative Investment Market (AIM) altered its status in October 2004 to an exchange regulated market, now an MTF or multilateral trading facility, so that those seeking admission to AIM did not and do not require a prospectus, provided they do not make an offer to the public which they rarely do.          [192] See nn 189 and 190.

[193] Furthermore, to the extent that an offer of transferable securities is made to a person in the UK, it is an offer of transferable securities to the public in the UK: FSMA 2000, s 102B(2), which means it will fall within the requirement in s 85(1) for an approved prospectus, but see the exemption in s 102B(5) for communication in connection with trading on a regulated market or a multilateral trading facility.

[194] FSMA 2000, s 85(1), (5), Sch 11A, para 9, as amended by the Financial Services and Markets Act (Prospectus and Markets in Financial Instruments) Regulations 2018, SI 2018/786, reg 2(6). This exemption does not apply where admission is sought to a regulated market. The Prospectus Regulation 2017/1129 does not apply to offers below a threshold of €1m (art 1(3)).

[195] Qualified investors are as defined in FSMA 2000, s 86(7), essentially professional investors and financial firms. A placing is often directed to these investors so avoiding the need for a prospectus.

[196] FSMA 2000, s 86(1), as amended by the Financial Services and Markets Act (Prospectus and Markets in Financial Instruments) Regulations 2018, SI 2018/786, reg 2(2) and see s 86(1A) for an exemption for so-called 'retail cascades'. There are further exemptions in PR 1.2.2R.

less than 20 per cent of the number of the securities of the same class already admitted to trading on the same regulated market.[197]

## Approval and passporting

**21-114** A prospectus must be submitted to UKLA and be formally approved before publication.[198] The UKLA must be satisfied that it is the home State authority in relation to the issuer, that the prospectus contains the necessary information (see **21-115**), and that all other requirements relating to a prospectus have been complied with.[199] The UKLA merely satisfies itself that these requirements are met by the issuer; it does not investigate or verify the accuracy of the information in the prospectus. A key feature of EU requirements is 'passporting' whereby a document approved in one Member State must be accepted by other Member States without the imposition of any further substantive requirements. UKLA must accept incoming prospectuses approved in EEA States provided they are accompanied by a certificate of approval from the home competent authority and, if requested, a translation of the summary of the prospectus (FSMA 2000, s 87H). UKLA also provides a facility whereby UK companies can request that a prospectus be approved by UKLA so that it may be used in another Member State even though there is to be no public offer or request for admission to trading in the UK.[200] A prospectus must be made available free of charge to the public as soon as possible after approval at various locations including the offices of the relevant exchange or the issuer or any intermediary involved in selling the securities, or it must be published in a newspaper widely circulated in the State where the offer is made, or made available on the issuer's website or the exchange's website.[201]

## Content and form

**21-115** There are detailed requirements with regard to the content and form of the prospectus[202] in keeping with its status as a critically important document intended to ensure that investors are in a position to make an informed decision as to the acquisition of any securities. The necessary information which must be contained in a prospectus if it is to be approved by UKLA is the information necessary to enable an investor to make an informed assessment of the assets and liabilities, financial position, profits and losses, and prospects of the issuer of the securities and of any guarantor and the rights attaching to the securities.[203] In determining whether information is required to be included by virtue of this general duty of disclosure, regard is to be had to the particular nature of the securities and of the issuer (FSMA 2000, s 87A(4)). Essentially, detailed information must be provided as to the business, its performance, its future plans and development, any risks to which

---

[197] PR 1.2.3R(1)—the threshold has been raised from 10 per cent to 20 per cent by the Prospectus Regulation and this provision has already come into force, see FCA, Quarterly Consultation No 16, March 2017, paras 5.4–5.19.     [198] PR 3.1.1R.

[199] FSMA 2000, s 87A(1). 'Home state authority' is defined in s 102C.

[200] As to the passporting process, see FCA, UKLA Procedural Note, PN/905.2, March 2017, *Passporting*. The home authority generally is the authority where the company has its registered office but there are some exceptions to that general principle.     [201] PR 3.2.4R.

[202] As to contents, see PR 2 and Appendix 3 to PR; and n 181.

[203] FSMA 2000, s 87A(2). There are exceptions to the disclosure requirements, for example, on the grounds of public interest, serious detriment to the issuer, and matters of minor importance: see s 87B(1). See *Secretary of State for Business Enterprise and Regulatory Reform v Sullman* [2009] 1 BCLC 397, an interesting disqualification case where the court considered that, whatever the position about a breach of a precise statutory obligation, non-disclosure or partial disclosure to investors is culpable conduct meriting a finding of 'unfitness' and is conduct below the expected standards of commercial probity which the law is entitled to expect.

it might be subject, its financial statements, its working capital position, its directors and management, its major shareholders, and details of the offer being made and the share capital structure together with a summary of the information. The information must be presented in a form which is comprehensible and easy to analyse (FSMA 2000, s 87A(3)). A supplementary prospectus is required where a significant new factor arises or a material mistake or inaccuracy arises in the prospectus (FSMA 2000, s 87G).

**21-116**    There were concerns that the breadth of these disclosure requirements is what contributed to the complexity and length of prospectuses. Hence, under the Prospectus Regulation, the threshold changes, under article 6, to one that a prospectus must contain the necessary information which is material to an investor for making an informed assessment of the assets and liabilities, profits and losses, financial position, and prospects of the issuer and of any guarantor, etc. It also provides that that information may vary depending on any of the following: the nature of the issuer; the type of securities, the circumstances of the issuer; and where relevant, whether the securities are non-equity, high denomination securities offered only to qualified investors. It remains to be seen whether this shift will allow for a more tailored approach to the information disclosed so leading to shorter, clearer, prospectuses.

**21-117**    A prospectus may be made up of one document (including a summary) or several documents and, where there are separate documents, the information must be divided (the so-called 'tripartite regime') between a registration document which concentrates on the issuer, a securities note which concentrates on the securities being offered or listed, and, subject to certain exceptions (notably non-equity traded securities), a summary note.[204] The summary must, briefly and in non-technical language, convey the essential characteristics of, and risks associated with, the issuer, any guarantor, and the transferable securities to which the prospectus relates (FSMA 2000, s 87A(6)). Under the Prospectus Regulation, the summary will be limited to a maximum of seven A4 pages and the risk factors outlined must not exceed 15, a response to concerns that the summary had become too complex for investors. The Prospectus Regulation, article 9, will also introduce a universal registration document (URD), something which is really intended for the largest and most frequent issuers, though it will be available to issuers on either a regulated market or a MTF. This document will need to be approved for two years by the competent authority, but thereafter may be annually updated without prior approval, then a prospectus based on the URD will be eligible for fast-track approval by the competent authority once the issuer decides on an issue. It will also be possible for the URD to be used as a way of meeting the disclosure requirements for annual financial statements under the Transparency Directive, so avoiding the need for duplicated disclosure. The Prospectus Regulation, article 15, also introduces the EU Growth Prospectus for SMEs (subject to certain threshold requirements), other than SMEs admitted to trading on a regulated market, again providing for simplified disclosure for public offers and there is also a simplified disclosure regime, article 14, for those with a listing or trading on a SME Growth Market for at least 18 months, where they make a secondary issue.

**21-118**    Different formats of prospectus reflecting different types of securities, issuers, and investors may be drawn up and it is possible to include information by reference to other previously published documents such as the annual accounts or the company's constitution.[205] Under the Prospectus Regulation, article 16, risk factors will have to be categorized

---

[204] See PR 2.2 and PR 2.1.3R.      [205] See PR 2.4.1R.

according to the type of risk and listed in order of materiality. The prospectus must be in the language of the home Member State and, where it is to be used in other Member States, it must be in the language of that other State or in a language customarily used in international finance although the competent authority of the Member State may require the summary to be translated into its language.[206]

### Responsibility and liability for a misleading prospectus

**1-119**  Compensation is payable by any person responsible for a prospectus when any person has acquired securities to which the prospectus applies[207] and suffered loss in respect of them as a result of any untrue or misleading statements in, or the omission of any required information from, the prospectus (FSMA 2000, s 90),[208] subject to the defences in Sch 10A, see below. The persons responsible for the prospectus where the offer is of equity securities are the issuer (and the offeror, if different), each director,[209] any person who accepts responsibility for all or part of the prospectus, and any person who authorised the contents of the prospectus.[210] There are a number of defences set out in FSMA 2000, Sch 10A, including that it is a defence if a person can satisfy the court (and the burden is on him) that he reasonably believed any statement for which he was responsible to be true and not misleading or that any information omitted was properly omitted.[211] Liability is imposed therefore for negligent or fraudulent false statements. A person is not liable if he satisfies the court that a timely correction was made of any false statements; that the false statement arose from the accurate and fair reproduction of an official statement or document; that the plaintiff was aware of the falsehood or the omitted information; or that he reasonably believed that a change in circumstances was not such as to warrant a supplementary prospectus.[212] This statutory liability under FSMA 2000, s 90(1) does not affect any liability which may otherwise be incurred such as claims for damages for deceit, or damages for untrue or innocent misrepresentation under the Misrepresentation Act 1967.[213] Proceeding under the statute is the most straightforward claim, however, especially as it imposes what Professor Davies has described as a strong version of liability, for it is for the defendant to prove that he was not negligent rather than for the claimant to prove that he was.[214]

---

[206] See PR 4.1.

[207] Relief is not restricted to subscribers, and purchasers in the market can claim compensation.

[208] The measure of compensation is the tort measure rather than the contract measure.

[209] Save in the unlikely situation where the prospectus is published without the director's knowledge or consent and, on becoming aware of its publication, as soon as practicable, he gives reasonable public notice that it was published without his knowledge or consent: PR 5.5.6R.

[210] PR 5.5.3R. The 'persons responsible' for a prospectus are defined in PR 5.5.3R.

[211] This defence applies not only to directors (who basically accept responsibility for the whole prospectus) but also to those experts who have contributed reports etc to the prospectus for which they must accept responsibility but who are able to limit their potential liability in any event to the part for which they accept responsibility. In addition, any person who authorised the inclusion of an expert's statement is not liable for that statement if he reasonably believed that the expert was competent and had consented to the inclusion of the report: FSMA 2000, Sch 10, para 2(2).                    [212] FSMA 2000, Sch 10, paras 3–7.

[213] FSMA 2000, s 90(6). See also *Secretary of State for Business Enterprise and Regulatory Reform v Sullman* [2009] 1 BCLC 397, as to potential disqualification on the grounds of unfitness in a case of non-disclosure or incomplete disclosure.

[214] See Davies, *Review of Issuer Liability, Liability for Misstatements To The Market: A Discussion Paper* by Professor Paul Davies QC (HM Treasury, March 2007), para 28. Prof Davies also noted that it is accepted that the standard of accuracy in prospectuses is high and that this could be attributed in part to the imposition of a negligence standard (see at para 71).

**21-120**   This potential liability under FSMA 2000, s 90 can be contrasted with the 'safe harbours' with respect to untrue or misleading statements in directors' reports, etc,[215] or in periodic or ad hoc disclosures published to the market.[216] In each case, liability arises only in cases of deceit which is unlikely to be established.[217] That this trend to restrict liability has not embraced prospectuses underlines the central role of this document in terms of investor protection. Finally, the Financial Services Act 2012, Pt 7, makes provision for criminal liability with respect to misleading statements and impressions made for the purpose of inducing a person to make an investment decision which would potentially be relevant with respect to a dishonest prospectus, see ss 89 and 90.

---

[215] See CA 2006, s 463 (directors liable only to company and only in deceit with respect to untrue or misleading statements in the directors' report, the strategic report, and the directors' remuneration report), see **18-47**.

[216] See FSMA 2000, s 90A; only the issuer can be liable and only in deceit. See the discussion of s 90A at **18-47**. For the background to the modification of issuer liability under FSMA 2000, s 90A (the scope of the provision was extended in the light of the recommendations of the Davies Review), see HM Treasury, *Extension of the statutory regime for issuer liability* (July 2008); Davies, *Review of Issuer Liability, Final Report* (June 2007) and an earlier discussion paper of the same name (March 2007).

[217] Further, while there is potential for an overlap between liability under FSMA 2000, s 90 and s 90A, it is provided that the application of s 90A does not limit any liability arising under s 90: Sch 10A, para 7(3)(a)(i). This ensures that claims under s 90 are protected and can be pursued rather than have the claimant constrained by the limitations of s 90A.

# 22

# The doctrine of capital maintenance

## A An overview of the doctrine of capital maintenance

**22-1**  With the advent of limited liability in 1855, the courts' concern turned to the protection of creditors. To that end there developed the doctrine of capital maintenance which essentially is a collection of rules designed to ensure, first, that a company obtains the capital which it has purported to raise (hence the rules governing payment for share capital which are discussed in Chapter 21) and, secondly, that that capital is maintained, subject to the exigencies of the business, for the benefit and protection of the company's creditors and the discharge of its liabilities. In particular, the doctrine of capital maintenance precludes the return of capital, directly or indirectly, to the shareholders ahead of a winding up of the company.[1]

**22-2**  The landmark case on the doctrine of capital maintenance is the decision of the House of Lords in *Trevor v Whitworth*[2] which established the fundamental principle that there can be no return of capital to the members other than on a proper reduction of capital duly sanctioned by the courts. At issue in the case was whether a company could purchase its own shares. The House of Lords rejected any such possibility, holding that a company had no such power under the Companies Acts, even if so authorised by its articles of association. Creditors had to be protected from a reduction of capital in this way without the company adhering to the statutory provisions on reduction of capital which required any reduction to be confirmed by the court.[3] Their Lordships noted that creditors took the risk of a company losing its capital in trading, but they also had a right to rely on the company not diminishing its capital by returning any part of it to its shareholders.[4] Lord Watson explained the position as follows:[5]

> 'Paid-up capital may be diminished or lost in the course of the company's trading; that is a result which no legislation can prevent; but persons who deal with, and give credit to a limited company, naturally rely upon the fact that the company is trading with a certain amount of capital already paid, as well as upon the responsibility of its members for the

[1] For an interesting overview of this doctrine, see the judgment of Harman J in *Barclays Bank plc v British & Commonwealth Holdings plc* [1996] 1 BCLC 1 at 6–10, Ch D, aff'd on different grounds [1996] 1 BCLC 27, CA. See also *Aveling Barford Ltd v Perion Ltd* [1989] BCLC 626 at 630–3. Of course, on a winding up of the company, shareholders can retrieve their capital only if all the creditors have been paid.

[2] (1887) 12 App Cas 409. See also *Re Exchange Banking Co, Flitcroft's Case* (1882) 21 Ch D 519 at 533; *Ooregum Gold Mining Co of India Ltd v Roper* [1892] AC 125 at 133, per Lord Halsbury LC, HL. See generally Gullifer and Payne, *Corporate Finance Law* (2nd edn, 2015); Ferran and Ho, *Principles of Corporate Finance Law* (2nd edn, 2014), Chs 7–9; Micheler, 'Disguised Returns of Capital—An Arm's Length Approach' (2010) 69 CLJ 151; Armour, 'Share Capital and Creditor Protection: Efficient Rules for a Modern Company Law' (2000) 63 MLR 355; Ferran, 'Creditors' Interests and "Core" Company Law' (1999) 20 Co Law 314.

[3] See CA 2006, s 641(1). It is possible now for private companies to reduce capital without court approval: see ss 642–644, see **22-69**.

[4] See (1887) 12 App Cas 409 at 415, per Lord Herschell.     [5] (1887) 12 App Cas 409 at 423, 424.

capital remaining at call; and they are entitled to assume that no part of the capital which has been paid into the coffers of the company has been subsequently paid out, except in the legitimate course of its business.'

**22-3** Within the limits then of what the law can achieve, the courts set about developing a set of rules concerning the establishment and maintenance of capital, rules now reflected in the provisions of the CA 2006 governing payment for share capital, the purchase of a company's own shares including financial assistance for such purchases, the reduction of capital, and, crucially, distributions to shareholders. Although in the earliest cases, such as *Trevor v Whitworth*,[6] the term 'return of capital' did mean an actual return of share capital subscribed, over the years the capital maintenance doctrine has broadened into a prohibition on any payment out of or transfer of company assets to a shareholder other than by way of a distribution (typically a dividend) lawfully made, an authorised reduction of capital, or other lawfully authorised procedure.[7]

**22-4** Linked to the prohibition on the return of capital to the members is an equal prohibition on giving away the company's capital to non-members through a gratuitous disposition of the company's assets other than in furtherance of the company's objectives.[8] As Nourse LJ explained in *Brady v Brady*:[9]

'the principle is that a company cannot give away its assets. So stated, it is subject to the qualification that in the realm of theory a memorandum of association may authorise a company to give away all its assets to whomsoever it pleases, including its shareholders. But in the real world of trading companies, charitable or political donations, pensions to widows of ex-employees and the like apart, it is obvious that such a power would never be taken. The principle is only a facet of the wider rule, the corollary of limited liability, that the integrity of a company's assets, except to the extent allowed by its constitution, must be preserved for the benefit of all those who are interested in them, most pertinently its creditors.'

**22-5** Since *Trevor v Whitworth*,[10] the approach of the courts has been consistently to the effect that a company cannot, without the leave of the court or the adoption of a special procedure, return its capital to its shareholders nor give away its capital in the case of dispositions to non-shareholders. Such transactions or dispositions are ultra vires and void and cannot be ratified, not even by the shareholders unanimously.[11]

**22-6** Statutory reinforcement of the protection afforded to creditors by the CA 2006 and the common law can be found in the IA 1986 which allows transactions which prove injurious to creditors to be challenged, for example, on the ground that the transaction is at an undervalue (IA 1986, s 238: see **15-40**) or is a preference (IA 1986, s 239: see **15-55**). As discussed in Chapter 10, directors have a duty in certain circumstances to have regard to creditors' interests in accordance with CA 2006, s 172(3). Directors also run the risk of personal liability for wrongful trading under IA 1986, ss 214 or 246ZB, see **15-18**, if they allow the company to continue trading past a point when they know or ought to know that there is no reasonable prospect of avoiding entering insolvent administration or going into insolvent liquidation. The capital maintenance doctrine and the rules which

---

[6] (1887) 12 App Cas 409.

[7] See Harman J on this point in *Barclays Bank plc v British & Commonwealth plc* [1996] 1 BCLC 1 at 14–15.

[8] *Ridge Securities Ltd v IRC* [1964] 1 All ER 275; and see Hannigan, 'Limitations on a Shareholder's Right to Vote—Effective Ratification Revisited' [2000] JBL 493 at 495–9.

[9] [1988] BCLC 20 at 38; rev'd on other grounds [1988] BCLC 579, HL.

[10] (1887) 12 App Cas 409.    [11] See Hannigan, n 8.

comprise it are broader in application than the provisions of the IA 1986 for there is no requirement that the company actually be insolvent at the time of the transaction or be rendered insolvent by the transaction.[12]

**22-7** It would be fair to say that the doctrine of capital maintenance has its critics. Doubts have been expressed, for example, as to whether the rules on distributions are too restrictive and too costly to apply, whether the rules on financial assistance are part of the doctrine of capital maintenance at all (though this issue is less significant now that the prohibition on financial assistance applies only to public companies[13]), and, more fundamentally, as to whether the rules achieve their aim of creditor protection.

**22-8** There is little doubt that the doctrine of capital maintenance can appear complex, not least because (and despite the statutory interventions) so much of the law has developed from those early cases such as *Trevor v Whitworth*[14] which the courts continue to cite. The result has probably been to obscure (because of the reliance on the language of pre-1900 cases) rather than clarify the modern doctrine. Initially, there was a self-contained and relatively narrow doctrine about the inability of a company to return share capital to its members intended to provide some protection for creditors dealing with companies with limited liability. More than a century later there is a multi-faceted (and therefore untidy) doctrine, still concerned (in part) with the protection of creditors, but also operating to constrain directors and to reinforce their duty to exercise their powers for the purposes for which they are conferred and to act to promote the success of the company (CA 2006, ss 171, 172). In this modern guise, these rules offer protection to creditors, but also to shareholders, against improper conduct by the directors and the unauthorised dissipation of the company's assets. The label 'capital maintenance' may have a dated ring to it, but the mischief at which it is aimed, unauthorised depletion of the company's assets, remains relevant. It is also the case that when an independent review of the capital maintenance doctrine was undertaken for the European Commission (in the context of a review of the Second Company Law Directive, see **21-2**) the result was a finding that the costs arising from the application of the doctrine are not excessive and the doctrine does not unduly hinder companies in the conduct of their affairs.[15] The same is probably true in the domestic context with the notable exception of the rules governing financial assistance which were complex and costly and time-consuming to apply, but which have now been repealed in respect of private companies (99.8 per cent of the register). It is possible that the perception of the costs and complexity of the capital maintenance regime does not quite match the business reality. It is also the case that a change to any new system also would involve costs and uncertainty[16] which may be a reason for continuing the existing settled position which is well understood by company advisers.

---

[12] See *Aveling Barford Ltd v Perion Ltd* [1989] BCLC 626 at 633 where Hoffmann J refutes any such limitation; also *Ridge Securities v IRC* [1964] 1 All ER 275.

[13] See CA 2006, s 678.     [14] (1887) 12 App Cas 409.

[15] KPMG, 'Feasibility Study on an alternative to the capital maintenance regime established by the Second Company Law Directive, etc' (January 2008); and see **2-22**.

[16] See Gullifer and Payne, n 2, who suggest allowing contract law and the IA 1986 to fill any gap in creditor protection arising from abolishing the doctrine of capital maintenance, but that in itself would involve costs for creditors (so far as they would need to adopt new contractual tools or refine their existing ones) and while it would protect the large creditors in a position to use these mechanisms, smaller creditors typically find it difficult to exercise any contractual power. As for reliance on the IA 1986, the relevant creditor protection provisions are currently underused because of problems in their drafting and application and, crucially, the lack of funding for liquidators who have primary responsibility for pursuing these matters, see discussion in Chapter 15.

## B Purchase and redemption of a company's own shares

### Introduction

**22-9**    As noted at **22-2**, the landmark decision of the House of Lords in *Trevor v Whitworth*[17] established the fundamental principle that there can be no return of capital to the members other than one duly sanctioned by the courts. At issue in the case was whether a company could purchase its own shares. The House of Lords rejected any such possibility holding that a company had no such power under the Companies Acts, even if so authorised by its articles of association. Creditors had to be protected from a reduction of capital in this way without the company adhering to the statutory provisions on reduction of capital which required any reduction to be confirmed by the court. The capital maintenance principle established by this case remains a foundation stone of company law but modern business needs have persuaded Parliament that some aspects of the doctrine may be relaxed, in particular with respect to the issue in the case, namely the purchase by a company of its own shares. More recently, the CA 2006 also relaxed the requirement for court confirmation of a reduction of capital.

**22-10**    The relaxation of the prohibition on a company acquiring its own shares came initially in the Companies Act 1981 which permitted companies to issue redeemable shares (i.e. shares redeemable at the option of the company or the shareholder),[18] to purchase back their own shares and, in the case of private companies, to purchase back out of capital, so effecting the very reduction of capital which concerned the House of Lords in *Trevor v Whitworth*.[19]

**22-11**    This statutory change was just one of a series of measures (including tax and other incentives) introduced in the early 1980s designed to make it easier for small companies to raise equity (share) capital. The difficulties which small companies face in trying to raise equity investment are well documented, see **21-3**. Many small businesses are family concerns where the individuals concerned, much as they might welcome an injection of capital, are reluctant to raise it through an issue of shares for fear of losing control of the business to an outsider. Equally, outside investors are reluctant to contribute their capital to an enterprise when the shares are not easily marketable and where they risk being locked in. Any scheme to assist such companies has to be flexible enough to increase the marketability of the shares without necessarily depriving the existing owners of control and without jeopardising the position of the company's creditors.

**22-12**    Allowing a company to have complementary powers to issue redeemable shares and to purchase back its own shares was thought to meet these requirements and give companies the flexible equity capital structure they wanted.[20] A company may issue redeemable shares envisaging from the outset that the shareholder's commitment is to be a short-term one or at least for a definite period. The company has the use of the capital for this period while the investor knows that he is not locked in. The purchase powers, on the other hand, enable the company at some point in the future to buy back shares without having to anticipate that eventuality at the time of issue. As far as investors are concerned, the

---

[17] (1887) 12 App Cas 409.

[18] The power to issue redeemable shares was not new in 1981 as companies had been able from 1929 to issue redeemable preference shares but the power was extended to any type of redeemable shares.

[19] (1887) 12 App Cas 409.

[20] See DTI, *The Purchase by a Company of its Own Shares, A Consultative Document* (Cmnd 7944, 1980).

possibility that the company will purchase the shares reduces the chances of their being locked into the company.

**22-13**  It was thought that these new powers might accommodate family re-arrangements, for example by enabling founding shareholders to resign and realise their investment without the remaining family members being required personally to fund the purchase back of their shares. The provisions might offer a means of dealing with the holdings of deceased members, or buying out discontented shareholders, or buying employee shareholdings when the employment is terminated.

**22-14**  All of these factors pointed towards these powers being of greatest use in private companies, but the powers are also available to public companies and commonly used by them. Indeed, it is standard practice for listed public companies to seek authority from their shareholders each year to purchase back their own shares. Obviously, the use of the powers by such companies is not driven by concerns about any lack of marketability of their shares, rather they see a variety of other advantages in having this flexibility.[21] For example, buy-backs, as purchase schemes are commonly called, may be a means of enhancing earnings per share when market conditions otherwise make this difficult. There may be some scope there for manipulation of directors' remuneration, which is often tied to earnings per share, so BEIS has initiated some research into the motivations for buy-backs.[22] Buy-backs can prove attractive to institutional shareholders who, because of the size of their holdings, find it difficult to offload their holdings in the market in the normal way. In addition, cash-rich companies may want to return capital to shareholders to enable the shareholders to make their individual investment decisions with regard to that capital rather than have the company use it in unsuitable and wasteful ways simply to reduce the company's cash holdings. On occasion, concerns have been voiced that listed companies might use these powers, for example as a defensive mechanism against takeover bids (by buying up shares in the market) or might in effect be insider dealing in their own shares. The general constraints on such conduct (the Takeover Code, the Listing Rules, the criminal law) are sufficient to address any concerns, however, and there is no evidence of any particular abuse of these powers.

**22-15**  A final point to remember is that the exercise of these powers may have tax consequences for both the company and the shareholders involved and that factor weighs heavily in any decision to use these provisions.

## The statutory framework

**22-16**  Given the fundamental shift away from the prohibition on the purchase of a company's own shares as laid down in *Trevor v Whitworth*,[23] Parliament surrounds the exercise of these redemption and purchase powers with stringent procedural requirements designed to ensure that the powers can only be exercised in certain circumstances, using certain funds and in the full glare of publicity. The question is whether such requirements are effective to minimise the erosion of the doctrine of capital maintenance. A broader question, as noted earlier, is whether the doctrine itself is an effective way of protecting creditors.

---

[21]  See Pettet, 'Share Buy-Backs' in Rider (ed), *The Corporate Dimension* (1998).

[22]  See BEIS Press Release, 'Government to research whether companies buy back their own shares to inflate executive pay', 28 January 2018.

[23]  (1887) 12 App Cas 409.

**22-17** The starting point is CA 2006, s 658(1) which, reflecting the rule in *Trevor v Whitworth*,[24] provides that a limited company may not acquire its own shares[25] whether by purchase, subscription, or otherwise[26] except in accordance with the provisions of CA 2006, Pt 18, i.e. redemption in accordance with ss 684–689 or purchase under ss 690–737. This prohibition on a company acquiring its own shares does not apply to:

(1) the acquisition of shares in a reduction of capital duly made (discussed later);

(2) the purchase of shares in pursuance of a court order under certain statutory provisions[27] (which rarely occurs); or

(3) the forfeiture of shares, or the acceptance of shares surrendered in lieu, in pursuance of the articles, for failure to pay any sum payable in respect of the shares (which rarely occurs) (s 659(2)).

**22-18** The statutory provisions on redemption and purchase are complex and the procedures, while similar, are not identical. On points of detail, the precise wording of the statutory provisions should be consulted.

**22-19** Strict adherence to the statutory procedures is required[28] for it is only redemption or purchase in accordance with the statutory provisions which is permissible (CA 2006, s 658(1)). The courts may allow some dispensing with or waiver of some procedural requirements when agreed to informally but unanimously by the members,[29] but not if the provision in question is intended to protect a wider class of persons, in particular the company's creditors rather than merely the current shareholders.[30] In the event of a contravention, the company is liable on conviction to a fine, every officer of the company who is in default is liable to imprisonment or a fine, and the purported acquisition is void.[31]

## Redemption of own shares

**22-20** A private limited company may issue shares that are to be redeemed or are liable to be redeemed, subject to any exclusion or restriction in the company's articles, while a public company may only issue redeemable shares if it is authorised to do so by its articles (CA 2006, s 684(1)–(3)). Redeemable shares cannot be issued unless the company has other shares in issue which are not redeemable (s 684(4)).

---

[24] (1887) 12 App Cas 409.

[25] See also CA 2006, s 136 which generally prohibits a company from being a member of its holding company and ss 660–661 (shares held by company's nominee are treated as held by the nominee on his own account). The prohibition on the acquisition of its own shares does not prevent a company (A) from acquiring the shares of another company (B) in circumstances where the sole asset of the acquired company (B) is shares in the acquiring company (A): *Acatos & Hutcheson plc v Watson* [1995] 1 BCLC 218.

[26] A company may acquire its fully-paid shares other than for valuable consideration: CA 2006, s 659(1).

[27] i.e. under CA 2006, s 98 (objections to resolution for public company to be re-registered as private); s 721(6) (objection to redemption or purchase out of capital); s 759 (breach of prohibition of public offers by private company); or Part 30 (relief on the grounds of unfair prejudice to members): s 659(2).

[28] *Re R W Peak (Kings Lynn) Ltd* [1998] 1 BCLC 193.

[29] *Kinlan v Crimmin* [2007] 2 BCLC 67 at [40]; *Dashfield v Davidson* [2008] BCC 222; *BDG Roof-Bond Ltd v Douglas* [2000] 1 BCLC 401 at 417; *Re Torvale Group Ltd* [1999] 2 BCLC 605, applying the *Duomatic* principle which is discussed at **17-73**.

[30] *Kinlan v Crimmin* [2007] 2 BCLC 67 at [40]; *Dashfield v Davidson* [2008] BCC 222; *BDG Roof-Bond Ltd v Douglas* [2000] 1 BCLC 401 at 417; *Re Torvale Group Ltd* [1999] 2 BCLC 605.

[31] CA 2006, s 658(2), (3); *Trevor v Whitworth* (1887) 12 App Cas 409.

**22-21**  The directors may determine the terms, conditions, and manner of redemption if they are authorised to do so by the articles or by an ordinary resolution of the company,[32] otherwise the terms, conditions, and manner of redemption must be stated in the articles.[33] The directors, if so authorised, must determine those terms etc before the shares are allotted and details of the terms etc must be included in the statement of capital which must be provided to the registrar of companies when the shares are allotted.[34]

**22-22**  Shares to be redeemed must be fully paid up (otherwise the creditors would lose a valuable asset on liquidation, namely uncalled capital) and payment must be made at the time when the shares are redeemed unless the terms of redemption provide for deferred payment[35] by agreement between the company and the holder (CA 2006, s 686). It had been thought that 'payment' had to be in cash, but in *BDG Roof-Bond Ltd v Douglas*[36] the court considered that a non-cash consideration may be agreed—the CA 2006 does not clarify this point. The funds which may be used for payment[37] are restricted to distributable profits[38] and the proceeds of a fresh issue made for the purposes of the redemption (s 687(2)), save in the case of a private company which may redeem out of capital[39] in accordance with Pt 18, Ch 5 (s 687(1)), see **22-45**.

**22-23**  Shares acquired are cancelled on redemption and the company's issued capital is reduced by the nominal value of the shares redeemed (s 688). Because of the requirement to establish a capital redemption reserve (s 733, see **22-37** et seq), a reduction of capital does not occur save in the exceptional case where a private company redeems out of capital. Within one month of the redemption, notice must be given to the registrar of companies specifying the shares redeemed together with a statement of capital (s 689(1), (2)).

**22-24**  If, having agreed to do so, a company fails to redeem shares, the company is not liable in damages in respect of any such failure.[40] Specific performance may still be available but not if the company shows that it is unable to meet the costs of redeeming the shares in question out of distributable profits.[41]

---

[32] CA 2006, s 685(1). Details of the earliest and latest dates on which the company has power to redeem the shares; whether the shares are redeemable in any event or liable to be redeemed at the option of the company or of the shareholder; and whether any (and if so, what) premium is payable on redemption must be included in the notes to the accounts: s 396(3); The Large and Medium-sized Companies and Groups (Accounts and Reports) Regulations 2008, SI 2008/410, Sch 1, Pt 3, para 47(2).

[33] CA 2006, s 685(4); and see *Dashfield v Davidson* [2008] BCC 222 where the contract was contained in the articles.       [34] CA 2006, s 685(3); see also s 555(3)(b).

[35] Allowing for deferred payment is new in the CA 2006, previously deferred payment rendered the transaction void, see *Kinlan v Crimmin* [2007] 2 BCLC 67.       [36] [2000] 1 BCLC 401.

[37] If a premium is payable on redemption, see s 687(3)–(5) as to how the premium is to be funded.

[38] See *Re Finch plc* [2016] 1 BCLC 394 where redemption was invalid as it turned out the company did not have distributable profits at the time.

[39] It would seem that a redemption cannot be made out of cash, as is now permitted for private companies where they purchase small amounts of their own shares, see s 692(1ZA). That section allows for purchase out of capital in accordance with Pt 18, Ch 5 and for purchases out of cash in accordance with s 692. Section 687(1) only allows for redemption in accordance with Pt 18, Ch 5.

[40] CA 2006, s 735(2). The section is concerned with direct claims for damages as a result of a breach by the company of its obligation to redeem or purchase the shares. It does not preclude the recovery of damages claimed by a plaintiff against the company for breach of a financing agreement even though the measure of damages for that breach may well be the equivalent of damages for failure to redeem: *Barclays Bank plc v B & C Holdings plc* [1996] 1 BCLC 1, CA.

[41] CA 2006, s 735(3). As to the redemption when the company goes into winding up, see s 735(4)–(6); also *Pearson v Primeo Fund* [2017] UKPC 19, [2017] BCC 552.

## Purchase of own shares

**22-25**  Any company (public or private) may purchase its own shares (including redeemable shares) in accordance with the statutory scheme, subject to any restrictions or prohibitions in the company's articles, and provided that the company is not left with only redeemable shares or shares held as treasury shares (see **22-41**).[42] Shares to be purchased must be fully paid up and (unlike redemption) payment must be made at the time when the shares are purchased[43] (s 691). The general requirement of payment on purchase is to prevent companies from oppressing shareholders by purchasing their shares so depriving them of their status as members but without actually paying over the proceeds. This requirement also resolves difficulties of timing and valuation. The issue arose in *Dickinson v NAL Realisations Ltd*[44] where a director had the company purchase back some of his shares for £2.5m, but he was content for the company to retain the funds as a loan from him secured by a debenture. In this way, he converted his equity capital into a secured loan (as part of a wider scheme to reduce the company's assets). On a subsequent challenge by the company's liquidator to the validity of the buyback scheme, the court found it to be in breach of the statutory requirement (CA 2006, s 691) that the shares be paid for on purchase. The court held that recognition of the debt which arose between the buyer and the seller by making an entry in the company's books of account did not constitute payment on purchase, but amounted to an agreement for payment at a later date with the result that the terms of the agreement did not comply with the statute.[45] The court considered that, if the company had actually paid the shareholder who then lent the money back, that would have been satisfactory, as long as the company found the funds to make the payment to the shareholder, otherwise the court said the requirement for payment on purchase would be devoid of substance.[46]

**22-26**  It had been thought that 'payment' had to be in cash, but in *BDG Roof-Bond Ltd v Douglas*[47] the court considered that a non-cash consideration may be agreed—the CA 2006 does not clarify this point. Payment may be made from distributable profits or the proceeds of a fresh issue made for the purposes of financing the purchase (s 692(2)). A private limited company has further options and may purchase its own shares out of capital (s 692(1)(a)), see **22-45**, and with cash (if authorised to do so by its articles) up to an amount in a financial year not exceeding the lower of £15,000 or the value of 5 per cent of its share capital, see **22-58**.

**22-27**  On purchase (with the exception of treasury shares, see **22-41**) the shares are cancelled so reducing the company's issued capital by the nominal value of the shares purchased (CA 2006, s 706). Cancellation reduces the impact which purchase schemes can have within the company, for example, by ensuring that directors cannot exercise any voting rights in respect of those shares. Of course, cancellation has an impact on the voting position generally within the company as the percentage voting power of the remaining shareholders is increased. Cancellation should increase the earnings of the remaining shares although this depends on factors such as the market's perception of the wisdom of redemption or purchase, the price paid and whether there has been a fresh issue of shares. Because of the requirement to establish a capital redemption reserve (see **22-37**), a reduction of capital

---

[42]  CA 2006, s 690.

[43]  Unless the company is a private limited company purchasing shares for the purpose of or pursuant to an employees' share scheme: CA 2006, s 691(3).

[44]  [2017] EWHC 28, [2018] 1 BCLC 623.     [45]  [2017] EWHC 28, [2018] 1 BCLC 623, at [84]–[93].

[46]  [2017] EWHC 28, [2018] 1 BCLC 623, at [91].     [47]  [2000] 1 BCLC 401.

does not occur save in the exceptional case where a private limited company purchases out of capital. If, having agreed to do so, a company fails to purchase shares, the company is not liable in damages in respect of any such failure.[48] Specific performance may still be available but not if the company shows that it is unable to meet the costs of purchasing the shares in question out of distributable profits.[49]

### Off-market and market purchases

**22-28**   The scheme of purchase differs depending on whether the share purchases are 'off-market' or 'market' purchases as defined in CA 2006, s 693. A lower level of regulation of market purchases is appropriate in recognition of the fact that the market authorities[50] impose additional regulatory requirements which, coupled with the higher degree of publicity attaching to such purchases, are sufficient to deter any abuses.

**22-29**   A market purchase is made where the purchase is made on a recognised investment exchange (RIE) and subject to a marketing arrangement on the exchange,[51] i.e. where the shares are listed[52] or are capable of being dealt with on the RIE without a requirement for permission for individual transactions.[53] An off-market purchase is where the purchase does not take place on an RIE or the purchase is on an RIE but the company's shares are not listed or traded on the exchange.[54]

**22-30**   As a general rule, private companies and public companies which are not publicly traded make off-market purchases while publicly traded companies normally make market purchases, but in some instances may transact off-market purchases.

**22-31**   Off-market purchases (other than a purchase for the purposes of or pursuant to an employees' share scheme[55]) must be made in pursuance of a contract approved in advance by the company by an ordinary resolution.[56] To give some flexibility to the company, either the terms of the contract must be authorised before the contract is entered into or the contract must provide that no shares may be purchased in pursuance of the contract until its terms have been authorised by a resolution of the company (s 694(2)). In the case of a public company, the resolution must specify a date on which the authority to purchase is to expire and that date must not be later than five years after the date on which the resolution is passed.[57]

---

[48]   CA 2006, s 735(2). See also n 40.

[49]   CA 2006, s 735(3). As to the position where the company goes into winding up, see s 735(4)–(6).

[50]   i.e. the UK Listing Authority, which is part of the FCA, and market operators such as the London Stock Exchange.

[51]   CA 2006, s 693(3). 'Recognised investment exchange' means a body (other than an overseas investment exchange) which is a recognised investment exchange for the purposes of the FSMA 2000, Pt 18: CA 2006, s 693(5). The relevant RIE for this purpose is the London Stock Exchange plc. A list of RIEs is maintained by the FCA on its website.

[52]   i.e. listed by the UKLA, the UK Listing Authority, which maintains the official list of securities, see FSMA 2000, s 74, see **21-103**.

[53]   CA 2006, s 693(3), (4). Purchases of shares in companies traded on AIM (the Alternative Investment Market, see **21-106**) are market purchases therefore.         [54]   CA 2006, s 693(2).

[55]   Such off-market purchases are governed by s 693A and do not require approval of a specific contract, just that the company be authorised to make such purchases by ordinary resolution which must specify the maximum number of shares authorised to be acquired, and determine both the maximum and minimum prices that may be paid for the shares, see s 693A(2)–(5).

[56]   CA 2006, ss 693(1)(a), 694. The authority conferred by the resolution may be varied, revoked, or from time to time renewed by a further resolution: s 694(4). See *Dashfield v Davidson* [2008] BCC 222.

[57]   CA 2006, s 694(5).

**22-32**  Where the resolution is a written resolution, a member who holds shares to which the resolution relates is not an eligible member, i.e. is not entitled to vote, so the resolution must be carried without his support.[58] Where the resolution is to be passed at a meeting, the resolution is not effective if any member of the company holding shares to which the resolution relates exercises the voting rights carried by any of those shares[59] in voting on the resolution and the resolution would not have been passed if he had not done so (CA 2006, s 695(3)). The special resolution is not validly passed where a written resolution is used unless a copy of the contract (if it is in writing) or a memorandum of its terms (if it is not) is circulated to the members at or before the time the resolution is sent or submitted to the members (s 696(2)(a)). The copy or memorandum must give the names of the members holding shares which are to be purchased.[60] Where a meeting is held, the copy or memorandum must be available for inspection by members of the company both at the company's registered office (for not less than 15 days prior to the meeting) and at the meeting itself (s 696(2)(b)).

**22-33**  A company may not make a market purchase unless the purchase has first been authorised by an ordinary resolution (CA 2006, s 701(1)). The authority may be general or limited to the purchase of shares of any particular class or description and may be conditional or unconditional (s 701(1)). The authority must specify the maximum number of shares which may be acquired, determine both the maximum and minimum price which may be paid for the shares,[61] and specify a date on which the authority is to expire which must in any event be not later than five years from the date when the resolution is passed (s 701(5)). Any resolution conferring, varying, revoking, or renewing such an authority to purchase must be sent to the registrar of companies within 15 days after it is passed.[62] No question of disenfranchising any shares arises in this context since the authority is not specifically aimed at any particular shares but is a general authority.

**22-34**  Shareholder approval is sought, whether for a market or off-market purchase because the funding of the purchase comes primarily from distributable profits and these are funds which could otherwise be distributed to all the shareholders as dividend so their approval is needed for a decision to use the funds for the benefit of some shareholders only. This potential disadvantage to all shareholders explains why the Listing Rules require premium listed companies (see **21-103**) which wish to purchase 15 per cent or more of any class of shares to make a tender offer to all the shareholders of that class so that they all have the opportunity to participate, though there need not be a tender offer if the full terms of the buy-back have been specifically approved by the shareholders.[63] The Listing Rules further constrain the manner in which listed companies can conduct share buybacks, in terms of the timing of purchases, the price, and the disclosure required,[64] as do

---

[58]  CA 2006, s 695(2).

[59]  This is less restrictive than the position with respect to a written resolution where the member affected is entirely disenfranchised, whereas on a resolution at a meeting, a member is only restricted from exercising the votes attached to the shares to be acquired.                      [60]  CA 2006, s 696(3), (4).

[61]  CA 2006, s 701(3). The price may be determined either by specifying a particular sum or providing a basis or formula for calculating the price in question without reference to any person's discretion or opinion: s 701(7). This is to ensure that the directors are not in a position to enter into transactions at varying prices depending on their relationship with the vendors.

[62]  CA 2006, ss 701(8), 30(1). This is an exception to the general rule that ordinary resolutions do not have to be delivered to the registrar of companies.

[63]  LR 12.4.2. and 2A. A tender offer is also required by LR 12.4.1R if the price set out in that rule is exceeded by the company.

[64]  See LR 12.2 and LR 12.4. The Takeover Code, rule 9 may also be relevant, see Appendix 1 to the Code.

influential guidelines from the Investment Association (IA) reflecting the expectations of institutional investors as to share capital management.[65] The IA Guidelines make clear that the institutional preference is for regular distributions to shareholders to be by dividend payments rather than share purchases, but they will support purchases where companies decide that share repurchases are in the best interests of their shareholders, but subject to constraints which are more limiting than the statute. The Guidelines suggest that companies should seek authority to purchase their own shares whether on market or off market by special resolution and not simply an ordinary resolution as allowed by the statute and a general authority to purchase shares should be renewed annually rather than taken for up to five years as the statute permits. The investors' expectation is that the company will only exercise an authority for the company to purchase its own shares if it is in the best interests of shareholders generally and normally only if it would result in an increase in earnings per share. The guidelines suggest that companies disclose in their next annual report the justification for any own share purchases made in the previous year, including an explanation of why this method of returning capital to shareholders was decided upon, and the average price paid. Institutional shareholders are unlikely to be concerned about a general authority to purchase back up to 10 per cent of the existing issued ordinary share capital but would take note if authority was sought to purchase between 10 per cent and 15 per cent. As already explained, a purchase beyond 15 per cent has to be carried out by a tender offer, as required by the Listing Rules. As to price, the guidelines endorse the requirement of the Listing Rules that (unless a tender offer is made to all shareholders) purchases of less than 15 per cent of the issued share capital pursuant to a general authority should be at a price which does not exceed the higher of: (a) 5 per cent above the average market value of the company's shares for the five business days before the purchase is made, and (b) the higher of the price of the last independent trade and the highest current independent bid on the market where the purchase is carried out (LR 12.4.1). Finally, the IA guidelines indicate that institutional shareholders discourage share buy-backs that are done off-market unless there is transparency on terms and pricing.

## Financing of redemption and purchase-back schemes

**22-35**   A crucial element in any redemption or purchase-back scheme is the source of the funding to pay for it. The risk to creditors is that capital is returned to the shareholders leaving a corporate shell with inadequate assets to pay off the company's creditors in full. The legislation attempts to prevent that happening by prescribing the funds which may be used. Subject to the ability of private companies to purchase out of capital discussed later, companies must fund redemption or purchase back:

(1) out of distributable profits;[66] or the proceeds of a fresh issue of shares made for the purpose of redemption or financing the purchase; and

---

[65] See Investment Association, *Share Capital Management Guidelines* (July 2016), applicable to premium listed companies. Other companies are encouraged to adopt the guidelines.

[66] i.e. profits out of which the company could make a distribution within the meaning of CA 2006, s 830: s 736. The rules establishing what is a lawful distribution are set out in CA 2006, Pt 23, discussed at **22-88**, and distributable profits must be determined on the basis of the company's accounts properly prepared. See *Re Finch (UK) plc* [2016] 1 BCLC 394, where a redemption was void when it turned out the company did not have distributable profits. The redemption in this case also constituted a preference under IA 1986, s 239, as redemption put the shareholder in a position which, in the event of the company going into insolvent liquidation, would be better than the position he would otherwise have been in.

(2) any premium payable on redemption or purchase must be paid out of distributable profits of the company, subject to certain exceptions.[67]

**22-36** Essentially, the company must use funds (distributable profits) which could have gone to the shareholders anyway (usually in the form of dividends) or it must substitute new capital brought in by a fresh issue of shares for the capital which it is repaying. Neither has any impact on the company's creditors so there is no erosion of the capital maintenance doctrine. Furthermore, to ensure that this is in fact the case, the company must set up a capital redemption reserve fund which is one of the company's undistributable reserves (CA 2006, s 733(1)).

**22-37** Where shares of a company are redeemed or purchased wholly out of the company's profits, the amount by which the company's issued share capital is diminished on cancellation of the shares redeemed or purchased must be transferred to the capital redemption reserve (s 733(2)).

**22-38** If the shares are redeemed or purchased wholly or partly out of the proceeds of a fresh issue and the aggregate amount of those proceeds is less than the aggregate nominal value of the shares redeemed or purchased, the amount of the difference must be transferred to the capital redemption reserve; but this does not apply if the proceeds of the fresh issue are applied by the company in making a redemption or purchase of its own shares in addition to a payment out of capital.[68] Payments out of capital are discussed later.

**22-39** The provisions of the Companies Act relating to the reduction of a company's share capital[69] apply as if the capital redemption reserve were paid-up share capital of the company, except that the reserve may be applied by the company in paying up new shares to be allotted to members of the company as fully-paid bonus shares (CA 2006, s 733(5), (6)). Reduction of capital is discussed at **22-60**.

**22-40** Significantly, however, it is possible for a private limited company to purchase its own shares out of capital in accordance with the detailed requirements of CA 2006, Pt 18, Ch 5 (s 692(1)) and, furthermore, if authorised to do so by its articles, a private limited company may purchase its own shares out of capital, otherwise than in accordance with Pt 18, Ch 5, up to an aggregate purchase price in a financial year of the lower of £15,000 or the nominal value of 5 per cent of its fully paid share capital as at the beginning of the financial year (s 692(1ZA)).[70] Purchase out of capital is discussed at **22-59**.

## Treasury shares

**22-41** Where a limited company purchases its own shares and the purchase is made out of distributable profits, the company may hold those shares, or any of them, 'in treasury' rather than cancel them (CA 2006, ss 724(1), (3), 706).[71]

---

[67] CA 2006, ss 687(2), (3), 692(2); the exceptions are where the shares redeemed or purchased back were originally issued at a premium in which case the proceeds of a fresh issue may be used to pay the premium to a limited extent: see ss 687(4), 692(3).

[68] CA 2006, s 733(3); in the latter case, it is accepted that there will be a reduction of capital.

[69] See CA 2006, ss 641–652.

[70] In these cases, the accounting consequences of the payment out of capital, in terms of impact on the company's capital redemption reserve, are addressed in CA 2006, s 734.

[71] For the background to these provisions which were first introduced in 2003, see Morse, 'The Introduction of Treasury Shares into English Law and Practice' [2004] JBL 303.

**22-42**    Once shares are held in treasury,[72] the voting rights attached to such shares are suspended and the company is prohibited from paying any dividend or making any other distribution to itself[73] as a result of it holding treasury shares (CA 2006, s 726). The holding of treasury shares by nominees is not permitted and the fact that the company is holding the shares as treasury shares will be apparent as the company must be entered in the register of members as the holder of the shares (s 724(4)).

**22-43**    Treasury shares may be sold for cash by the company, transferred for the purposes of or pursuant to any employees' share scheme, or cancelled.[74] The ability to sell the shares for cash gives the company flexibility to raise additional funds without the need for further allotments of shares but, as noted at **21-36**, any sale of treasury shares is subject to the pre-emption requirements. In the case of a public company, details of any shares held as treasury shares must be given in the notes to the company's accounts.[75] Contravention of any of these provisions is an offence by the company and every officer in default (CA 2006, s 732).

## Disclosure requirements

**22-44**    Within 28 days of any shares purchased being delivered to the company, a return must be delivered to the registrar of companies distinguishing between treasury shares and other shares and stating the number and nominal value of the shares and the date on which they were delivered to the company (CA 2006, s 707(1)). In the case of a public company, further details relating to the aggregate amount paid by the company for the shares and the maximum and minimum paid by the company for shares of each class purchased must be included (s 707(4)). A copy of any contract of purchase, or a written memorandum of its terms, must be kept at the company's registered office or other specified place for 10 years from the date of purchase and must be available for inspection by any member of the company and, if it is a public company, by any other person (s 702(2)–(6)). Details of any purchases must also be given in the directors' report.[76]

## Private companies—redemption or purchase out of capital

**22-45**    Subject to any restrictions or prohibitions in its articles, a private limited company may redeem or purchase its own shares otherwise than out of distributable profits or the proceeds of a fresh issue of shares in accordance with the requirements of Pt 18, Ch 5 (CA 2006, s 709(1)).[77] Permitting private companies in certain circumstances to redeem or purchase shares out of capital is something which potentially could have a significant impact on creditors so the statutory provisions surround such purchases with stringent procedural requirements.

---

[72] There is no longer any statutory cap on the percentage of share capital which may be held in treasury. CA 2006, s 725(1), now repealed, imposed a limit of 10 per cent of the nominal value of the company's issued share capital. Institutional shareholders prefer that listed companies hold to the previous 10 per cent limit, see Investment Association guidelines, n 70, para 1.4.4.

[73] An allotment of fully paid bonus shares may be made in respect of treasury shares, see CA 2006, s 726(4), (5).

[74] CA 2006, ss 727(1), 729(1). Treasury shares are commonly used for employees' share schemes.

[75] CA 2006, s 396; The Large and Medium-sized Companies and Groups (Accounts and Reports) Regulations 2008, SI 2008/410, Sch 1, Pt 3, para 47(1)(b).

[76] CA 2006, s 396; The Large and Medium-sized Companies and Groups (Accounts and Reports) Regulations 2008, SI 2008/410, Sch 7, Pt 2, para 9.

[77] CA 2006, Pt 18, Ch 5, is subject to s 692(1ZA) (purchase of own shares up out of capital using cash).

**22-46**  First, to minimise the amount which may be paid out of capital, the company must first use any available distributable profits[78] and the proceeds of any fresh issue made for the purpose of redemption or purchase before resorting to capital with the amount then needed being described as 'the permissible capital payment'.[79] On the other hand, there is no requirement to have any available distributable profits or to have a fresh issue of shares.

**22-47**  Secondly, a payment out of capital is not lawful (CA 2006, s 713(1)) unless the detailed procedural requirements of s 713(1) are met (see later), but s 713(1) does not apply to the purchase out of capital by a private company of its own shares for the purposes of or pursuant to an employees' share scheme which can instead be approved by a special resolution supported by a solvency statement (s 720A) in the manner in which the statute also provides for a private company to make a reduction of capital in this way (s 642), see discussion of the statement at **22-69**. For all other schemes, s 713(1) requires a directors' statement and supporting auditors' report which must be available before the payment is approved by special resolution of the shareholders and public notice of the proposed payment must be given in order to alert creditors who may wish to object to the payment.

**22-48**  The directors' statement[80] must specify the amount of the permissible capital payment for the shares in question and state that, having made full inquiry into the affairs and prospects of the company, they have formed the opinion (see **22-71**):

(1)  as regards its initial situation immediately following the date on which the payment out of capital is proposed to be made, that there will be no grounds on which the company could then be found unable to pay its debts;[81] and

(2)  as regards its prospects for the year immediately following that date that, having regard to:

(a)  their intentions with respect to the management of the company's business during that year; and

(b)  the amount and character of the company's financial resources that will in their view be available to the company during that year,

the company will be able to continue to carry on business as a going concern (and will accordingly be able to pay its debts as they fall due) throughout that year (CA 2006, s 714(3)).

**22-49**  This emphasis on solvency reflects the overriding concern that creditors must be protected from injudicious use of redemption or purchase schemes. Any director who makes this statement without having reasonable grounds for the opinion expressed in it is liable to imprisonment or a fine or both (CA 2006, s 715). More significant, however, is the potential liability where a company is wound up and it has made a payment out of capital and its assets prove insufficient for the payment of its debts and liabilities and the

---

[78] Whether there are available profits is determined in this instance in accordance with CA 2006, s 712 rather than Part 23 which applies generally: s 711(2).

[79] CA 2006, s 710. See s 734(2), (3) as to the necessary transfers to, or reduction of, the capital redemption reserve.

[80] The statement must be in the prescribed form: CA 2006, s 714(5). The requirements are set out in The Companies (Shares and Share Capital) Regulations 2009, SI 2009/388, reg 5: the statement must be in writing, it must indicate that it is the directors' statement, it must be signed by each director, and must state whether the company's business includes that of a banking or insurance company.

[81] CA 2006, s 714(3)(a). In forming their opinion for these purposes, the directors must take into account all of the company's liabilities (including contingent or prospective liabilities): s 714(4).

expenses of winding up.[82] If the winding up commenced within one year of the date on which the relevant payment out of capital was made, then the person whose shares were redeemed or purchased and the directors who signed the statement are, so as to enable the insufficiency to be met, liable to contribute to the company's assets.[83]

**22-50** The person whose shares were so redeemed or purchased is liable to contribute an amount not exceeding so much of the relevant payment as was made by the company in respect of his shares and the directors are jointly and severally liable with that person to contribute that amount.[84] A director will be excused liability if he shows that he had reasonable grounds for forming the opinion set out in the declaration.[85] Presumably he will claim that he was justified in relying on the auditors who, after all, agreed with his opinion because annexed to the directors' statement must be a report by the company's auditor stating that:

(1) he has inquired into the company's state of affairs;[86]

(2) the amount specified in the statement as the permissible capital payment for the shares in question is in his view properly determined in accordance with CA 2006, ss 710–712; and

(3) he is not aware of anything to indicate that the opinion expressed by the directors in their statement as to any of the matters in s 714(3) (set out at **22-48**) is unreasonable in all the circumstances (s 714(6)).

**22-51** Any payment out of capital must be approved by a special resolution.[87] Where a written resolution is used, a member who holds shares to which the resolution relates is not an eligible member, i.e. is not entitled to vote (CA 2006, s 717(2)). Where the resolution is passed at a meeting, the resolution is not effective if any member of the company holding shares to which the resolution relates exercises the voting rights carried by any of those shares in voting on the resolution and the resolution would not have been passed if he had not done so (s 717(3)).

**22-52** The resolution is also ineffective unless the required directors' statement and auditors' report are circulated with or before the written resolution is circulated to the members or the statement and report are available for inspection by members of the company at the meeting at which the resolution is passed (CA 2006, s 718(2), (3)).

**22-53** Various disclosure requirements apply which are aimed at bringing the proposed payment to the attention of creditors who may wish to apply to the court for an order prohibiting payment (see **22-56**). Within the week immediately following the date of the resolution for payment out of capital, the company must cause to be published in the *Gazette* a notice:

(1) stating that the company has approved a payment out of capital for the purpose of acquiring its own shares by redemption or purchase (as the case may be);

---

[82] See IA 1986, s 76(1).    [83] IA 1986, s 76(2).    [84] IA 1986, s 76(3).
[85] IA 1986, s 76(2)(b).
[86] A failure by an auditor to inquire to the extent that an auditor of reasonable competence would do means that the auditor is not in a position to say whether the directors' opinion is reasonable or not and, in consequence, the auditor cannot properly give an opinion for these purposes; if he does give an opinion in such circumstances, he is liable in negligence, see *Cook v Green* [2009] BCC 204 which concerned the equivalent auditor's statement then required for the purposes of financial assistance by a private company.
[87] CA 2006, s 716. The resolution must be passed on or within the week immediately following the date of the directors' statement required by s 714. The actual payment out of capital must be made no more than five and not later than seven weeks after the date of the resolution: s 723(1).

(2) specifying the amount of the permissible capital payment and the date of the resolution;

(3) stating that the directors' statement and the auditors' report are available for inspection; and

(4) stating that any creditor of the company may at any time within the five weeks immediately following the date of the resolution apply to the court for an order prohibiting payment (CA 2006, s 719(1)).

**22-54** A similar notice must be published in a national newspaper or a notice in writing to that effect must be given to each creditor (s 719(2)). A copy of the directors' statement and the auditors' report must also be sent to the registrar of companies at the same time (s 719(4)).

**22-55** In recognition of the potential for abuse when companies are permitted to redeem or purchase back out of capital, provision is made in CA 2006, s 721 for an application by an objecting creditor or member to the court for cancellation of the resolution authorising payment out of capital. No such procedure is available in respect of purchase or redemption in any other instance.

**22-56** An application must be within five weeks of the date on which the resolution was passed and may be made by any member of the company (other than one who consented to or voted in favour of the resolution) or by any creditor of the company.[88] No minimum shareholding or debt is required but the more insignificant the amounts, the less weight is likely to be attached to the objections. The difficulty for those objecting, particularly if they are members, is to persuade the court to set aside something which has been approved by a special resolution and without the votes of any member who holds shares to which the resolution relates. There seems to be little use of this procedure, not least because the courts in similar circumstances have tended to refuse redress, stating that the members know best and that it is not for the court to interfere in what is essentially a difference as to business policy.[89] A similar approach would be likely here.

**22-57** The jurisdiction of the court on any application is open-ended. The court may adjourn the proceedings in order that an arrangement can be made for the purchase of the interests of dissentient members or for the protection of dissentient creditors, as the case may be (CA 2006, s 721(3)). Without prejudice to such powers, the court must make an order on such terms and conditions as it thinks fit either confirming or cancelling the resolution. The court's order may, in particular, provide for the purchase by the company of the shares of any members and for the reduction of the company's capital accordingly.[90]

### Purchase out of capital—use of cash

**22-58** If authorised to do so by its articles, a private limited company may purchase its own shares out of capital, otherwise than in accordance with the procedures in Pt 18, Ch 5 already discussed, up to an aggregate purchase price in a financial year of the lower of £15,000 or the nominal value of 5 per cent of its fully-paid share capital as at the beginning of the financial year (s 692(1ZA)). Shares bought back under this provision may not be held in treasury (see s 724(1)(b)). This cash route was introduced from April 2013 to assist

---

[88] CA 2006, s 721(1), (2); notice of the application must also be given immediately to the registrar of companies: s 722(1).

[89] The position would not be dissimilar to that of shareholders trying to persuade the court not to confirm a reduction of capital sanctioned by special resolution. They have usually been unsuccessful. See **22-82**.

[90] CA 2006, s 721(6). A copy of any order must be delivered to the registrar of companies: s 722(3).

small companies pay modest amounts without having to identify the sum as distributable reserves and without having to comply with all of the procedural requirements of Pt 18, Ch 5, discussed earlier.[91] The Government considered that, given the de minimis amount, it poses no risk to shareholders or creditors and that the requirement for the company to secure authorisation in the articles, so requiring a special resolution to take this authority, is sufficient protection.[92]

### Purchase out of capital/reduction of capital

**22-59**　The Company Law Review recommended the retention generally of the provisions on redemption and purchase of own shares,[93] and it favoured the introduction of a simplified procedure for a reduction of capital on the basis of a special resolution and a declaration of solvency by the directors (see CA 2006, s 641), see **22-69**. The CLR considered that such a procedure would mean that there was no need to retain the procedure allowing for redemption or purchase out of capital.[94] The Government was persuaded, however, that there are sufficient differences between the two regimes to justify the retention of the power to purchase out of capital. The distinct elements of a purchase out of capital include that the directors' statement has to be backed up by an auditors' report, the requirement for publicity in the *Gazette* and a national newspaper, and the ability of a creditor to go to court to challenge the transaction. Those elements may in some circumstances provide greater reassurance for creditors than a reduction of capital on the basis of a solvency statement by the directors under s 641, hence the need for both procedures.

## C  Reduction of capital

### The statutory framework

**22-60**　At the beginning of this chapter, we noted that the House of Lords in *Trevor v Whitworth*[95] had established the fundamental principle that there can be no return of capital by a company to its members other than on a proper reduction of capital duly sanctioned by the courts. The statute now allows for reduction in a number of ways, some of which we have already considered, such as a reduction of capital on a redemption or purchase of its own shares by a private company out of capital.[96] Creditors and members are protected in such cases by the extensive statutory provisions governing such schemes which were discussed

---

[91] See BIS, *Employee Ownership and Share Buy Backs, Simple Guide to the Companies Act 2006 (Amendment of Part 18) Regulations 2013 and 2015* (April 2015), BIS/15/288.

[92] See BIS, *Employee Ownership and Share Buy Backs, Implementation of the Nuttall Review, Government Response* (February 2013), BIS/13/590, paras 41–42; and Simple Guide, n 91, paras 37–38.

[93] Company Law Review, *Final Report*, vol I (2001), para 10.6; *Completing the Structure* (2000), paras 7.16–7.19; *Company Formation and Capital Maintenance* (1999), paras 3.49–3.64 and Annex B.

[94] See *Modernising Company Law* (Cm 5553-I, 2002), para 6.5.

[95] (1887) 12 App Cas 409. The courts are alert to attempts to disguise what is in effect a return of capital to the shareholders, see *Aveling Barford Ltd v Perion Ltd* [1989] BCLC 626 (a sale of an asset, at a gross undervalue, to a company controlled by a shareholder did not hide the true nature of the transaction which was an unauthorised return of capital to that shareholder). See also Harman J in *Barclays Bank plc v British & Commonwealth Holdings plc* [1996] 1 BCLC 1 at 10–11, Ch D, aff'd on different grounds [1996] 1 BCLC 27, CA.

[96] Reduction does not occur in the case of redemption or purchase otherwise than out of capital for, in those instances, an amount equivalent to the amount redeemed or purchased must be transferred to the capital redemption reserve which, for most purposes, is treated as if it were share capital: CA 2006, s 733(6), see **22-36**.

at **22-45**. Reduction can also occur as a consequence of a court order for the purchase by the company of shares held by an objecting member under a variety of provisions[97] or as a result of forfeiture or surrender by members. For example, a public company may provide in its articles that shares may be forfeited for non-payment of calls in respect of sums remaining unpaid on the shares.[98]

**22-61**    In practice, the most important ways in which a limited company may reduce its share capital are set out in CA 2006, s 641(1), namely:

   (1) in the case of a private company limited by shares, by special resolution supported by a solvency statement (ss 642–644);

   (2) in any case, by special resolution confirmed by the court (ss 645–651).

The reserve arising on a reduction, whether on the basis of a solvency statement or a reduction confirmed by the court, is treated as a realised profit and therefore distributable subject to any contrary provision in the court order, the resolution for reduction, or the company's memorandum or articles of association.[99]

**22-62**    The Company Law Review initially favoured the replacement of the procedure for reduction subject to court confirmation with the scheme based on a special resolution supported by a declaration of solvency.[100] Consultations showed that the finality which is given to disputes by a court confirmation is valued highly in practice, however, and so the Review concluded that the court-based procedure should be retained.[101]

**22-63**    These powers to reduce capital are subject to any restriction or prohibition contained in the company's articles[102] (CA 2006, s 641(6)) and, if the reduction of capital amounts to a variation or abrogation of class rights, additionally class consent will be required, see **16-47**. Also, a private company cannot reduce capital by means of a solvency statement if the effect would be to leave the company without any member holding other than redeemable shares (s 641(2)). Otherwise, a company may reduce its share capital in any way,[103] but the

---

[97] For example, under CA 2006, s 98 (proceedings objecting to resolution for public company to be re-registered as private); s 721(6) (objection to redemption or purchase out of capital); s 759 (remedial order in case of breach of prohibition of public offers by private company) or Part 30 (protection of members against unfair prejudice): s 659(2).

[98] See The Companies (Model Articles) Regulations 2008, SI 2008/3229, reg 4, Sch 3, arts 58–61 (public companies) and see CA 2006, ss 662–664. Forfeiture does not fall foul of the prohibition on a company acquiring its own shares: s 659(2)(c). Forfeiture provisions are penal provisions and must be construed strictly: *Johnson v Lyttle's Iron Agency* (1877) 5 Ch D 687, CA. A public company's articles also commonly provide for the surrender of shares in lieu of forfeiture: see SI 2008/3229, reg 4, Sch 3, art 62. A surrender of shares in a public company is governed by the same rules as those applying to forfeiture: CA 2006, s 662(1).

[99] CA 2006, s 654(1) and The Companies (Reduction of Share Capital) Order 2008, SI 2008/1915, art 3(2)–(4).

[100] Company Law Review, *Strategic Framework* (1999), paras 5.4.4–5.4.13; *Company Formation and Capital Maintenance* (1999), paras 3.27–3.35 and Annex B.

[101] Company Law Review, *Completing the Structure* (2000), paras 7.9–7.10; *Final Report*, vol I (2001), para 10.6.

[102] In public companies, the articles typically state that the reduction must not have the effect of reducing the share capital below the authorised minimum, see CA 2006, s 763 and **21-9**. Such a provision does not rule out a reduction by a company which momentarily reduces the company's capital to nil before following it with an increase in capital to above that minimum: *Re MB Group plc* [1989] BCLC 672. When a reduction does result in the capital of a public company falling below the authorised minimum, see CA 2006, ss 650, 651 which allow for expedited re-registration in that case as a private company.

[103] See *British & American Trustee Corpn v Couper* [1894] AC 399 at 410; *Poole v National Bank of China* [1907] AC 229 at 237–8; *Re Thomas de la Rue & Co Ltd* [1911] 2 Ch 361 at 365; *Ex p Westburn Sugar Refineries Ltd* [1951] 1 All ER 881 at 884.

most common methods of reduction are those identified in s 641(4) which provides that a company may:

(1) extinguish or reduce the liability on any of its shares in respect of share capital not paid up; or

(2) either with or without extinguishing or reducing liability on any of its shares,

    (a) cancel any paid-up share capital that is lost or unrepresented by available assets; or

    (b) repay any paid-up share capital in excess of the company's wants.

### Extinction or reduction of liability on shares not paid up

**22-64**  Reduction in this instance appears to involve risk to creditors for it extinguishes a liability (namely the obligation on the part of the holders of partly-paid shares to pay the amount due on those shares) which would be a valuable asset to the creditors in the event of a winding up, assuming that those shareholders were in a position to meet their liability on those shares. This category is of limited significance, however, for it is unusual for shares to be issued as partly-paid so there is rarely any question of there being any unpaid share capital outstanding, see **21-15**.

### Cancellation of share capital lost or unrepresented by available assets

**22-65**  The cancellation of paid-up share capital which is lost or unrepresented by available assets appears to have an impact on creditors for it reduces the minimum level of assets which must be maintained by the company. However, reduction in this instance is usually a necessary exercise to restore reality to the company's accounts. If a company had at one time a paid-up share capital of £200,000 but, following trading losses, its net assets now amount only to £50,000, little is achieved by maintaining the figure of £200,000 in the accounts as the capital yardstick. A reduction of capital in such circumstances will also be crucial to the company's ability to make or resume dividend payments to its shareholders and it is important to appreciate the impact of the distribution rules in CA 2006, Pt 23, see **22-88**, in this context. The need under those distribution rules to have regard to accumulated profits and losses means that it will be necessary for the company to reduce its capital to cancel past losses so as to be in a position to resume the payment of dividends from current profits.

**22-66**  The court must be satisfied that the capital is lost and that that loss is permanent (so far as presently foreseeable) for, if it is not permanently lost, a cancellation of paid-up share capital may prejudice the interests of the creditors. In *Re Jupiter House Investments (Cambridge) Ltd*[104] where the loss could not be proved to be permanent,[105] the court confirmed the reduction subject to an undertaking by the company which ensured that, if the loss of capital was in fact recovered, it would not be distributed to the shareholders as dividends but would be placed to a capital reserve. On the other hand, in *Re Grosvenor Press plc*[106] the court was loath to require such an undertaking, noting that there are already statutory safeguards[107] to protect the interests of future creditors and shareholders and

---

[104] [1985] BCLC 222.

[105] The loss arose from defects in a substantial building which the company owned. The company had been advised that it had more than an even chance of recovering the loss by an action for damages against a third party.    [106] [1985] BCLC 286.

[107] Creditors and shareholders are protected by the publicity requirements surrounding a reduction of capital and the need for the company's accounts to give a true and fair view of the state of its affairs.

there is no need, except in special circumstances, for the court to require a reserve to be set aside indefinitely. It suffices if the reserve is made undistributable as long as any creditor at the time of the reduction remains unpaid.[108]

### Repay share capital in excess of company's wants

**22-67**    The repayment of paid-up share capital in excess of the company's needs poses no risk to creditors[109] and may simply reflect a shrinking of the company's activities. It might be noted that it is only in this instance that capital is actually returned to the shareholders. In the other instances of reduction noted earlier, either the capital has never been received or the capital is lost.

**22-68**    It is not necessary that the shareholders who are being paid off should actually receive cash. Non-cash assets may be used instead[110] and, in that case, there need not be an exact correlation between the capital reduced and the value of the assets transferred.[111] This may appear to offer some opportunity for abuse but the courts have indicated that the important matter is not how much is returned to the shareholders but how much is retained for the protection of creditors.[112] If what is offered to the shareholder is illusory, however, the court will refuse to confirm the reduction.[113]

## Reduction supported by solvency statement

**22-69**    This procedure is only available to private companies and is subject to any restriction or prohibition in the company's articles. In the absence of any restrictions, all that is required is a special resolution and a solvency statement in the prescribed form.[114] Rose J in *BTI 2014 LLC v Sequana SA*[115] noted that Parliament has chosen to enact a new mechanism for reduction without the need for judicial scrutiny and without the protection for creditors provided by the court-based procedure. Under the new procedures, she noted, there is no provision for creditors to be notified of, or to have the opportunity to object to, a proposed reduction.

**22-70**    Where a written resolution is used, a copy of the solvency statement must be sent or submitted to every member at the time when the proposed resolution is sent. If the resolution is passed at a meeting, the solvency statement must be available for inspection by members throughout the meeting. In either case, a failure to comply with this requirement does not affect the validity of the resolution (presumably because of the difficulty of unravelling these transactions if the non-compliance does not come to light for some time), but non-compliance is a criminal offence.[116] A private company cannot reduce capital using this

---

[108] [1985] BCLC 286 at 289.

[109] A reduction of capital by repayment is not a distribution for the purposes of CA 2006, Pt 23: see s 829(2)(b)(ii).

[110] *Ex p Westburn Sugar Refineries Ltd* [1951] 1 All ER 881; *Re Thomas de la Rue & Co Ltd* [1911] 2 Ch 361.

[111] In *Ex p Westburn Sugar Refineries Ltd* [1951] 1 All ER 881 at 885, Lord Reid made the point that this must be the position because in many cases it is impossible to make any exact valuation of the non-cash assets.

[112] See, for example, *Ex p Westburn Sugar Refineries Ltd* [1951] 1 All ER 881 at 884, per Lord Normand.

[113] *Re Thomas de la Rue & Co Ltd* [1911] 2 Ch 361.

[114] The solvency statement must state the date on which it is made and give the name of each director: CA 2006, s 643(3); and it must be in writing, be signed by each director, and indicate that it is a solvency statement for the purposes of s 642: SI 2008/1915, art 2. This type of scheme has been extended to purchases of shares for the purposes of an employees' share scheme (see at **22-47**).

[115] [2017] 1 BCLC 453 at [320].    [116] CA 2006, ss 642(2)–(4), 644(7).

mechanism if the effect would be to leave the company without any member holding other than redeemable shares.[117]

**22-71**   A solvency statement must be to the effect that each of the directors has formed the following two different opinions, namely:[118]

(1) as regards the company's situation at the date of the statement, that there is no ground on which the company could then be found unable to pay (or otherwise discharge) its debts (s 643(1)(a));

(2) and, if it is intended to commence the winding up of the company within 12 months of that date, that the company will be able to pay (or otherwise discharge) its debts in full within 12 months of the commencement of the winding up; or in any other case that the company will be able to pay

(or otherwise discharge) its debts as they fall due during the year immediately following that date (CA 2006, s 643(1)(b)).[119]

In forming those opinions (note the plural) for these purposes, the directors must take into account all of the company's liabilities (including contingent or prospective liabilities):[120] CA 2006, s 643(2).

**22-72**   The basis on which directors should act when making a solvency statement was considered by Rose J in *BTI 2014 LLC v Sequana SA*.[121] In this case, a company had reduced capital and then made a distribution to the shareholders. One of the issues was the validity of the solvency statement and whether the directors had been entitled to make it. The company was the subject of significant outstanding environmental claims in respect of which it had considerable insurance provision, though the final amount of the liabilities was uncertain, with some potential for the figure to be larger than expected. The discussion in the case centred on the requirement in s 643(1)(a)—the directors' opinion that there is no ground at the date of the statement on which the company could be then found unable to pay its debts. Rose J considered, *inter alia*, that:

- The honest opinion (of the directors) alone is insufficient, the directors must have formed the opinion required in fact and they must have applied the correct test in coming to their opinion.[122]

- The section does not require a cross-reference to the considerations which would be relevant to determining whether a company is able to pay its debts for the purposes of IA 1986, s 123 (definition of inability to pay debts in the context of a winding up),[123] nor are the directors required to go through every contingent or prospective

---

[117]   CA 2006, s 641(2).

[118]   As to the requirement of 'each director', this includes de facto directors, which may cause a problem, see *Re In a Flap Envelope Co Ltd* [2004] 1 BCLC 64 (a different context, but still relevant).

[119]   There is no express requirement for the directors to make full inquiry into the affairs and prospects of the company, as is required by CA 2006, s 714(3) in the case of a purchase of own shares out of capital, but such a requirement is probably implicit in any case: see Hannigan and Prentice, *The Companies Act 2006, A Commentary* (2nd edn, 2009), para 8.12; also *Re In a Flap Envelope Co Ltd* [2004] 1 BCLC 64. A director could not have reasonable grounds for his opinion unless he has made such inquiries as he ought to make to enable him to express such an opinion: *Cook v Green* [2009] BCC 204 (concerning an auditors' report on a financial assistance scheme, but relevant in this context also).

[120]   See discussion of taking account of contingencies in *Re a Company* [1986] BCLC 261 at 263; *Re Liberty International Ltd* [2010] 2 BCLC 665 at [15]; also *BNY Corporate Trustee Services Ltd v Eurosail-UK* [2013] 1 BCLC 613, S Ct, aff'g [2011] 2 BCLC 1.          [121]   [2017] 1 BCLC 453.

[122]   [2017] 1 BCLC 453 at [322].          [123]   [2017] 1 BCLC 453 at [325].

liability facing the company, work out what is the worst that can happen, attempt to put a value on the liability in that scenario, and then measure the company's assets against that figure.[124] Rose J noted that such a test would render the solvency statement mechanism unusable in most cases.[125]

- The test is not a technical one, but a straightforward one applying the words of the section. The directors must look at the situation of the company at the date of the statement and, taking into account contingent or prospective liabilities, form an opinion as to whether the company is able to pay its debts.[126]

- 'Taking account' will involve the directors considering the nature of the contingent and prospective liabilities, what assets will be available to meet them and what provision (in a non-technical sense) has been made for that purpose. [127]

On the facts in *Sequana*, Rose J considered that the directors had asked the right questions and the solvency statement could not be challenged. In *LRH Services Ltd v Trew*,[128] on the contrary, the court concluded that the directors had asked themselves the wrong question: they had considered whether companies in the group could discharge the liabilities of the company in respect of which the solvency statement was made. The directors should have asked whether the company could discharge its liabilities.[129] The court agreed with Rose J in *Sequana* that the directors are not obliged to make a worst case assessment, but a realistic commercial one having regard to all the circumstances known to them.[130] The directors must consider all the circumstances relevant to whether a liability will fall on the company, and they must also consider what assets will be available to meet the liabilities, including future liabilities as they fall due over the next 12 months.[131] On the facts,[132] the company could only meet its liabilities if a subsidiary company continued to make rental payments to the company, but the directors were aware that the subsidiary was already in default with respect to its rent obligations. The directors in making the statement on the basis of resources in the group to which the company had no entitlement had applied the wrong test and therefore could not properly hold the opinions expressed in the solvency statement.[133] As the solvency statement was invalid, so the capital reduction and dividend declared on the basis of it was unlawful. The directors were therefore in breach of duty and liable for the full amount of the company's assets (£21m) unlawfully paid away.[134]

**22-73** The solvency statement must be delivered to the registrar of companies within 15 days of the resolution being passed together with a copy of the resolution and a statement of capital (CA 2006, s 644(1)) and the reduction does not take effect until those documents are registered (s 644(4)),[135] see also **22-86**. It is an offence for a director to make a statement and deliver it to the registrar without having reasonable grounds for the opinions expressed in it (s 643(4)).

**22-74** The notable features of this procedure are: the absence of any requirement for an auditors' report to back up the directors' solvency statement; the absence of any publicity

---

[124] [2017] 1 BCLC 453 at [326].   [125] [2017] 1 BCLC 453 at [326].
[126] [2017] 1 BCLC 453 at [327].   [127] [2017] 1 BCLC 453 at [330].   [128] [2018] EWHC 600.
[129] [2018] EWHC 600 at [173], [184].   [130] [2018] EWHC 600 at [27].
[131] [2018] EWHC 600 at [23]–[24].
[132] The company had reduced its capital to £1 and paid a dividend of £21m to its parent company on the basis of a solvency statement.
[133] [2018] EWHC 600 at [178]–[179], [184].   [134] [2018] EWHC 600 at [186].
[135] An error in the statement of capital does not invalidate the reduction: *BTI 2014 LLC v Sequana SA* [2017] 1 BCLC 453 at [344].

to alert creditors either through notification in the *Gazette* or by an advertisement in a national newspaper; and the absence of any mechanism for objections by shareholders or creditors. For these reasons, creditors may be uneasy about the exercise of this power and may choose to protect themselves by making an exercise of these powers a default trigger under loan agreements so in effect preventing the company from using the procedure.[136] Equally, directors may be wary of giving solvency statements, given the civil consequences of an invalid declaration, as well as the criminal sanction which attaches to the giving of a statement without reasonable grounds for the opinions expressed in it.

### Reduction subject to court confirmation

**22-75**  The alternative reduction procedure (and the only option for public companies) is to pass a special resolution (CA 2006, s 641(1)(b)) and seek court confirmation of the reduction (s 645(1)) which order the court may make on such terms and conditions as it thinks fit,[137] subject to the position of the company's creditors having been safeguarded (s 648(1), (2)).

**22-76**  If the proposed reduction of capital involves either (a) diminution of liability in respect of unpaid share capital (which as noted is rare), or (b) the payment to a shareholder of any paid-up share capital (which is sometimes the case), there is a statutory procedure for objecting creditors (s 646) which applies unless the court otherwise directs, which it may do if it thinks it proper to do so (s 645(2), (3)); vice versa, the court can direct that the procedure for objecting creditors applies though the reduction does not fall into these categories (s 645(4)). Every creditor of the company who (a) at the relevant date fixed by the court (for settling the list of creditors) is entitled to any debt or claim that, if that date were the commencement of the winding up of the company, would be admissible in proof against the company[138] and (b) can show that there is a real likelihood that the proposed reduction would result in the company being unable to discharge his debt or claim when it fell due, is entitled to object to the reduction of capital (s 646(1)). Where there are creditors so entitled to object, a list of creditors must be settled (CA 2006, s 646(2)) but the court may, if it thinks fit, dispense with the consent of an undischarged creditor on the company securing payment of his debt or claim (s 646(4)).

**22-77**  What is meant by a 'real likelihood' in this context was considered in *Re Liberty International Ltd*[139] where Norris J held that the section required a creditor to demonstrate a particular present assessment about a future state of affairs.[140] In considering whether such a real likelihood has been shown, the court looks first at the factual—the assessment has to be well grounded in the facts as they are now known—and, while looking to the

---

[136] A prohibition or restriction on the exercise of the power by the company outside of the articles would not be effective: *Russell v Northern Bank Development Corp Ltd* [1992] BCLC 1016, but making an exercise a default event has the same practical effect.

[137] The court can confirm a resolution even if there is a factual error in it, provided that it is so insignificant that no one could be thought to be prejudiced by its correction: *Re Willaire Systems plc* [1987] BCLC 67. See also *Re European Home Products plc* [1988] BCLC 690 where a more significant error occurred but the court reluctantly confirmed the reduction as creditors were not affected and no shareholder regarded the mistake as being of such importance as to seek the court's refusal.

[138] In the absence of an exercise of discretion by the Pensions Regulator (to make a contribution notice or financial support direction against a company), a company was not at present liable to the pension scheme trustees or to the Pension Protection Fund and, in the absence of any liability on the part of the company, there were no pensions claims which were 'admissible in proof' for these purposes and no creditors 'entitled to object' under this provision: *Re Liberty International plc* [2010] 2 BCLC 665.

[139] [2010] 2 BCLC 665.     [140] [2010] 2 BCLC 665 at [17].

future, has to avoid the purely speculative.[141] Secondly, Norris J said, there is a temporal element: in general, the more remote in time the contemplated event that would make payment fall due, the more difficult it must be to establish the likelihood that the return of capital would itself result in inability to discharge the debt.[142] Thirdly, showing a 'real likelihood' requires an objecting creditor to go some way up the probability scale, beyond the merely possible, but short of the probable.[143] On the facts in this case, where there was evidence that the company had working capital for at least 18 months following the transaction, the creditors could not show a real likelihood that the proposed reduction of capital would result in the company being unable to discharge their debts as they fell due.[144] Accordingly, the reduction was confirmed.

**22-78** This limitation of the right to object to creditors who can show (the onus is on the creditor) that the proposed reduction will put at risk the due discharge of their claim is a change brought about from 1 October 2009 by amendments to the Second Company Law Directive, now Directive 2017/1132.[145] Previously all creditors were entitled to object and it was standard practice for the court to dispense with the settling of the list of creditors as invariably the company would have reached an agreement with its creditors who would either have been paid off or have consented to the scheme subject to bank guarantees from the company covering the amounts due to them. In other words, the onus was on the company to reach an accommodation with its creditors. The position under CA 2006, s 646 now puts the onus on the objecting creditor to show to the court how he is at risk from any reduction. There had been concerns that the previous procedures gave creditors a degree of excessive protection[146] and the change is designed to re-balance the position between the company and its creditors. It is not clear that the changes have made much difference in practice. While the section puts the onus on the creditors to establish their entitlement to object (s 646(1)), it may make commercial sense for companies to proceed as before by addressing the concerns of creditors through payment (though the debt is not yet due) or by means of agreements and guarantees (so their claims are secured) so that the court can dispense with their consent under s 646(4), see **22-76**.

**22-79** Where the procedures are followed properly and the necessary special resolution passed, the court's role is little more than to endorse the company's plans which it can do once it is satisfied, as required by s 648(2), that every creditor entitled to object has either consented to the reduction, or his debt or claim has been discharged or has determined, or has been secured. The consent of the creditors having been secured, the shareholders usually have little interest in objecting other than in the context of a variation of class rights (see **16-47**). There are no specific statutory provisions dealing with the position of shareholders who, if they object to the reduction, must persuade the court not to confirm it.

### Role of the court

**22-80** The court has a discretion whether or not to confirm a reduction[147] and the main question for the court is whether the proposed reduction is fair and equitable as between the

---

[141] [2010] 2 BCLC 665 at [18].   [142] [2010] 2 BCLC 665 at [19].
[143] [2010] 2 BCLC 665 at [20].   [144] [2010] 2 BCLC 665 at [21].
[145] OJ L 169/46, 30.6.2017, see art 75.
[146] Company Law Review, *Strategic Framework* (1999), paras 5.4.10–5.4.12; *Company Formation and Capital Maintenance* (1999), para 3.31.
[147] *British & American Trustee Corpn v Couper* [1894] AC 399; *Re Thomas de la Rue Ltd* [1911] 2 Ch 361.

different classes of shareholders,[148] given that the position of the creditors is protected by the procedures outlined at **22-76**.

**22-81**   Speaking generally, a reduction of capital need not be spread equally or rateably over all the shares of the company.[149] If there is nothing unfair or inequitable in the transaction, the shares of one or more shareholders may be extinguished without affecting other shares of the same or a different class.[150] However, a reduction which does not provide for uniform treatment of shareholders whose rights are similar is narrowly scrutinised.[151]

**22-82**   It is rare for there to be any difficulty about securing court confirmation which is seen as a purely routine matter. The scheme in question is always supported by a large majority of the shareholders (necessarily so, for the statute requires a special resolution) and raises issues of internal management and business judgement which are for the company to decide upon and not the courts.[152]

**22-83**   The approach of the courts was explained by Harman J in *Re Ratners Group plc*[153] as follows:

> 'The court has over the years established ... three principles on which the court will require to be satisfied. Those principles are, first, that all shareholders are treated equitably in any reduction. That usually means that they are treated equally, but may mean that they are treated equally save as to some who have consented to their being treated unequally, so that counsel's word "equitably" is the correct word which I adopt and accept. The second principle to be applied is that the shareholders at the general meeting had the proposals properly explained to them so that they could exercise an informed judgment on them. And the third principle is that creditors of the company are safeguarded so that money cannot be applied in any way which would be detrimental to creditors.'

**22-84**   In most instances, the creditors, shareholders, and the company are in complete agreement about the proposed reduction and the court's role is limited to endorsing their plans so even the presence of dissentient shareholders is unlikely to alter the court's willingness to approve a reduction scheme.

---

[148]   *British & American Trustee Corpn v Couper* [1894] AC 399; *Re Thomas de la Rue Ltd* [1911] 2 Ch 361; *Poole v National Bank of China Ltd* [1907] AC 229; *Scottish Insurance Co Ltd v Wilsons & Clyde Coal Co Ltd* 1948 SC 360, aff'd [1949] AC 462, HL; *Ex p Westburn Sugar Refineries Ltd* [1951] 1 All ER 881. As long as creditors and shareholders are not prejudiced, wider public concerns do not influence the court and it is not concerned with any ulterior purpose for the reduction provided it is lawful. Thus reduction schemes for reasons of tax avoidance (as opposed to evasion) or to avoid some of the consequences of nationalisation have in the past been approved: *Ex p Westburn Sugar Refineries Ltd* [1951] 1 All ER 881.

[149]   *Re Agricultural Hotel Co* [1891] 1 Ch 396; *Re Floating Dock Co of St Thomas Ltd* [1895] 1 Ch 691; *Re London and New York Investment Corpn* [1895] 2 Ch 860; *British and American Trustee and Finance Corpn v Couper* [1894] AC 399.

[150]   *British and American Trustee and Finance Corpn v Couper* [1894] AC 399 at 406, 415, 417, HL; *Bannatyne v Direct Spanish Telegraph Co* (1886) 34 Ch D 287, CA; *Re Direct Spanish Telegraph Co* (1886) 34 Ch D 307; *Re Thomas de la Rue & Co Ltd and Reduced* [1911] 2 Ch 361.

[151]   In *Re Robert Stephen Holdings Ltd* [1968] 1 WLR 522, it was stated that the better practice in cases where one part of a class is to be treated differently from another part of the same class (unless all the shareholders consent) is to proceed by way of a scheme of arrangement under what is now CA 2006, Pt 26, as this affords better protection to a non-assenting minority. In this case the court did confirm the reduction despite its affecting shareholders of the same class in different ways but no shareholder appeared to oppose the confirmation.

[152]   See *Poole v National Bank of China Ltd* [1907] AC 229 at 236, per Lord Loreburn '... it is no part of the business of a Court of justice to determine the wisdom of a course adopted by a company in the management of its own affairs'.

[153]   [1988] BCLC 685 at 687. See also *Re Thorn EMI plc* [1989] BCLC 612. The other qualification on the court's discretion noted by Harman J in both of these cases was that the court must not be asked to confirm a reduction which is for no discernible purpose.

**22-85** What has troubled the courts to a slightly greater degree in some of the cases has been a claim by preference shareholders that the effect of a proposed reduction of capital[154] is to vary or abrogate their class rights and so requires their consent before the reduction can be confirmed by the court. That issue is discussed in detail at **16-47**. It suffices to note here that, where the proposed reduction is in accordance with the class rights as they would apply on a winding up of the company, the reduction does not amount to a variation of class rights and the consent of the class to the reduction is not required.[155] Preference shareholders can avoid the danger of a restrictive interpretation of what constitutes a variation of their class rights by the courts by identifying in the terms of issue those matters (such as a reduction of capital) which are deemed to be a variation or abrogation of the rights attached to that class and which therefore are governed by the scheme for variation or abrogation laid down in CA 2006, s 630, see **16-54**. If a scheme of reduction does vary or abrogate class rights, despite the generality of the court's power to confirm (and some suggestions to the contrary in older cases),[156] the court will not confirm a reduction without the appropriate class consent having been obtained.[157]

### Registration of court order

**22-86** The registrar, on production of the court order confirming the reduction and the delivery of a copy of the order and of a statement of capital (approved by the court), registers the order and statement (CA 2006, s 649(1)) whereupon the resolution for the reduction of capital takes effect (s 649(3)(b)), except in the case of a reduction of share capital that forms part of a compromise or arrangement sanctioned by the court under Part 26 (arrangements and reconstructions) in which case the reduction takes effect (1) on delivery of the order and statement of capital to the registrar, or (2) if the court so orders, on the registration of the order and statement of capital (s 649(3)(a)). The registrar certifies the registration of the order and statement of capital and this certificate of registration is conclusive evidence that all the requirements with respect to the reduction of share capital have been complied with and that the company's share capital is as stated in the statement of capital (s 649(5), (6)).

**22-87** Where the court makes an order confirming a reduction of a public company's capital which has the effect of bringing the nominal value of its allotted share capital below the authorised minimum, the registrar of companies must not register the order unless the court so directs, or the company is first re-registered as a private company.[158]

## D Distributions to the members

### Introduction

**22-88** The most common type of distribution is a dividend, expressed as so many pence per share and paid to the shareholders according to the number of shares held by them,[159] but

---

[154] Typically, a proposal for the reduction of capital by paying off the preference shares on the grounds of excessive capital.

[155] *Re Saltdean Estate Co Ltd* [1968] 3 All ER 829; *House of Fraser v ACGE Investments Ltd* [1987] AC 387, HL.

[156] See *Re William Jones & Sons Ltd* [1969] 1 All ER 913.

[157] See *Re Northern Engineering Industries plc* [1994] 2 BCLC 704 at 713, CA.

[158] CA 2006, s 650. The authorised minimum is set at £50,000 or €57,100, the prescribed euro equivalent: s 763, see **21-9**.

[159] It is common for the articles to make provision for dividends to be paid in proportion to the amount paid up on the shares, see CA 2006, s 581(c) and Model Articles, art 70, plc.

the statutory rules on distributions (CA 2006, Pt 23, ss 829–853) are wider and apply to 'every description of distribution of a company's assets to its members, whether in cash or otherwise', subject to a limited number of exceptions (s 829(1)). Furthermore, the wide-ranging common law principle that distributions cannot be paid out of capital is expressly retained by the statute (s 851(1)).[160]

**22-89** The label which the parties give to a transaction is not determinative of whether it is a 'distribution' for these purposes.[161] In *Re Halt Garage (1964) Ltd*[162] the court found that sums paid to a director, at a time when the company was insolvent (and therefore had no distributable profits) and in excess of what the director was entitled to under the articles for holding office as a director, were a disguised gift of capital or payment of dividends in recognition of her co-proprietorship of the business. As such, they were ultra vires and void. In *Aveling Barford Ltd v Perion Ltd*[163] a sale of property by a company (which though solvent had no distributable profits) at a considerable undervalue (sale was at £350,000, independent valuation valued it at £650,000[164]) to another entity controlled by the company's sole beneficial shareholder was an unlawful distribution. As an unauthorised return of capital, it was ultra vires and void. In *Secretary of State for Business, Innovation and Skills v Doffman (No 2)*[165] a company paid £1.2m to an associated company to secure an option to purchase a property from that other company. The court found that the sum was very large for an option which only lasted 18 months; the figure was less a valuation of the option and more the figure of the 'surplus' cash which the purchasing company had. There was no real prospect that the purchasing company would ever exercise the option since there was no evidence of any way in which it could fund the exercise and, in fact, no attempt was ever made to exercise the option. In reality, the court found the payment of £1.2m represented a disguised return of capital to the shareholders at a time when the purchasing company had no distributable profits and the option was merely a device for transferring £1.2m out of the company leaving it with no reserves and no way of meeting its own liabilities. The payment made by the directors was made in breach of their duties and was one of a number in this instance which justified a finding that the directors were unfit and should be disqualified.[166] In each of these cases, the underlying point was that the transactions were attempts to disguise what was an unauthorised return of capital.[167]

**22-90** Whether a transaction amounts to an unlawful return of capital to a shareholder is a matter of substance not of form or labels, requiring the court to enquire into the true purpose and substance of the impugned transaction, as the Supreme Court affirmed in

---

[160] See, generally, Micheler, 'Disguised Returns of Capital—An Arm's Length Approach' (2010) 69 CLJ 151; and see *Progress Property Co Ltd v Moorgarth Group Ltd* [2010] 1 BCLC 1, CA at [22], [31], showing the overlap between the common law and the statute, aff'd [2011] 2 BCLC 332, S Ct.

[161] See *Progress Property Co Ltd v Moorgarth Group Ltd* [2011] 2 BCLC 332, S Ct; *Aveling Barford Ltd v Perion Ltd* [1989] BCLC 626 at 631; *Ridge Securities v IRC* [1964] 1 All ER 275.

[162] [1982] 3 All ER 1016.      [163] [1989] BCLC 626.

[164] The property was sold on six months later for £1,526,000.

[165] [2011] 2 BCLC 541 at [142]–[149].

[166] This case concerned a series of transactions between companies within a group where the directors (the subjects of these disqualification proceedings) transferred assets without regard to the rules prohibiting distributions and without regard to the interests of the separate legal entities; see other unlawful distributions at [97], [207], [213]–[215], involving gratuitous transfers of assets and the waiver of debts at a time when the companies had no distributable profits.

[167] See Mummery LJ in *Progress Property Co Ltd v Moorgarth Group Ltd* [2010] 1 BCLC 1, CA at [27]–[30], aff'd [2011] 2 BCLC 332, S Ct.

*Progress Property Co Ltd v Moorgarth Group Ltd.*[168] In that case, a company (PP) sold an asset (a shareholding in another company) to another company in the group (MG), all of which were controlled by the same investor, for a sum which turned out to be a gross undervalue. The sale price had reflected the fact that, as a term of the sale, PP had been released from substantial liabilities which it was understood by all concerned it had incurred under certain indemnities. Later, it was established that PP had no liability under those indemnities from which it could have been released so the purchase price paid by MG was indeed too low by about £4m. Hence the allegation that the sale was essentially a disguised return of capital by PP to its controlling shareholder via this sale of an asset to MG, also controlled by the same person, whereby MG obtained an asset the value of which greatly exceeded the price paid to PP. The transaction was challenged on a subsequent change of control at PP.[169]

**22-91**     The Supreme Court ruled that, in categorising a transaction, the court must look at the transaction objectively, but not relentlessly objectively, otherwise doubt would be cast on any transaction between a company and a shareholder, even if negotiated in good faith and at arm's length, whenever it was established with hindsight that the company had got significantly the worse of the transaction.[170] The court's task is to inquire into the true purpose and substance of the impugned transaction which means an investigation of all the relevant facts which sometimes include the state of mind of those persons orchestrating the corporate activity.[171] In the case of a commercial transaction, there must be a realistic assessment of all the relevant facts, including the motives and intentions of those involved and not just a retrospective valuation exercise in isolation from all other enquiries (a more sophisticated analysis is required than merely a calculation of what the company gave and what it received).[172] Applying that approach, a commercial transaction may be a genuine transaction, but a bad bargain in which case it stands, the court said, but it may be an improper attempt to extract value by the pretence of an arm's length sale, in which case it will be held unlawful.[173] In the case of unlawful dividend, however, Lord Walker (with whom the rest of their Lordships agreed) considered that an entirely objective analysis to determine whether the distribution is unlawful is possible and appropriate.[174] He said: 'A distribution described as a dividend but actually paid out of capital is unlawful, however technical the error and however well-meaning the directors who paid it.'[175] The same was true, he said, of payments which on analysis are the equivalent of a dividend where it does not matter whether the directors were acting consciously in breach of their duties or just woefully ignorant of their duties. In those cases, as Lord Walker put it, 'what they do is enough by itself to establish the unlawful character of the transaction'.[176] On the facts in *Progress Property Co Ltd v Moorgarth Group Ltd*,[177] looking at the commercial transaction between the parties, the Supreme Court affirmed the Court of Appeal decision that there was no unlawful return of capital, rather an arm's length sale negotiated in good faith, though with hindsight the company had got a bad bargain.[178]

---

[168] [2011] 2 BCLC 332 at [27], per Lord Walker.

[169] The facts are most clearly explained in the Court of Appeal judgments, see [2010] 1 BCLC 1.

[170] [2011] 2 BCLC 332 at [24]. Lord Walker acknowledged (at [26]) an article by Micheler, 'Disguised Returns of Capital—an Arm's Length Approach' (2010) 69 CLJ 151 who argued for an objective approach without regard to the parties' intentions or knowledge, see at 170–5, but Lord Walker did not favour such an approach.

[171] [2011] 2 BCLC 332 at [27].     [172] [2011] 2 BCLC 332 at [29], [31] and see also at [24].

[173] [2011] 2 BCLC 332 at [29].     [174] [2011] 2 BCLC 332 at [28].     [175] [2011] 2 BCLC 332 at [28].

[176] [2011] 2 BCLC 332 at [28].     [177] [2011] 2 BCLC 332.

[178] Lord Mance commented that the suggestion that the transaction be re-categorised as an illegitimate distribution of capital was particularly artificial and unappealing, see [2011] 2 BCLC 332 at [36]; and especially at [48].

**22-92**   The position was summarised succinctly by Popplewell J in *Madoff Securities International Ltd v Raven*:[179]

> 'Whether a transaction infringes the rule is a question of categorisation or characterisation based on substance, not form. The label attached to the transaction by the parties is not decisive. Sometimes the exercise for the court will be a purely objective one in which the subjective intentions of the directors are irrelevant: for example a distribution described as a dividend, but actually paid out of capital, is unlawful, however technical the error and however well-meaning the directors who caused it to be paid. But where what is impugned purports to be a transaction of a different character to a distribution, such as for example a contract for the purchase of assets or services, the intentions of the parties to the transaction are often highly relevant to the categorisation exercise, being one in which the court is inquiring whether the transaction was in substance that which it purported to be.'

**22-93**   The distribution rules, whether statutory or common law, are an important component of the capital maintenance regime. The rules address concerns that, if the directors and shareholders are able to collude in the distribution of the company's assets to the members during the company's lifetime, the creditors will find the company stripped of its assets.[180] On liquidation, the creditors must be paid in full before any capital can be returned to the shareholders and an unlawful distribution of assets ahead of winding up defeats that priority.[181] Equally, the rules protect shareholders against dissipation of the company's assets by the directors for improper purposes in breach of duty.[182] Where a company wishes to return capital to its shareholders, it must do so via a purchase or redemption of shares or reduction of capital in accordance with the statutory schemes discussed earlier in this chapter and not by way of an improper distribution of assets to the members.[183] Where it wishes to make a distribution to its shareholders, it must do so in accordance with the common law and the requirements of CA 2006, Pt 23. In the much cited words of Pennycuick J in *Ridge Securities Ltd v IRC*:[184]

> 'A company can only lawfully deal with its assets in furtherance of its objects. The corporators may take assets out of the company by way of dividend or, with leave of the court, by way of reduction of capital, or in a winding up. They may of course acquire them for full consideration. They cannot take assets out of the company by way of voluntary disposition, however described, and, if they attempt to do so, the disposition is ultra vires the company.'

**22-94**   With regard specifically to dividends, directors have to have regard to broader commercial issues which will vary depending on the size and type of the company. Many private companies are small family concerns where all the shareholders also act as the directors and

---

[179] [2013] EWHC 3147 at [204].

[180] See *It's a Wrap (UK) Ltd v Gula* [2006] 2 BCLC 634 at [18], per Arden LJ, and at [39] where Sedley LJ comments that the ability to recover unlawful dividends from the recipients is 'designed to protect those who have a prior call on a company's funds from the appropriation of them by those who control the company'. A creditor does not have *locus standi* to seek an injunction to prevent an unlawful dividend, however, only a shareholder can do that: *Mills v Northern Railways of Buenos Ayres Ltd* (1870) 5 Ch App 621.

[181] See *It's a Wrap (UK) Ltd v Gula* [2006] 2 BCLC 634 at [18] where Arden LJ notes that any leniency to shareholders in receipt of an improperly paid dividend detracts from the protection available to the creditors.

[182] See *Bairstow v Queens Moat Houses plc* [2001] 2 BCLC 531 at [44], CA.

[183] See *Ridge Securities Ltd v IRC* [1964] 1 All ER 275 at 288; *Re Halt Garage (1964) Ltd* [1982] 3 All ER 1016.

[184] [1964] 1 All ER 275 at 288 (excessive interest on debentures amounted to a gratuitous distribution of the company's assets and was ultra vires and void).

profits may be distributed by way of directors' remuneration instead of by formal declaration of dividends, with tax considerations often dictating how shareholder-directors are to be rewarded. A further point of confusion in small private companies is that directors and shareholders often make withdrawals from the company without identifying clearly whether the payment is: (1) a dividend, (2) a loan from the company, or (3) remuneration.[185] Other difficulties can arise in private companies where profits are distributed by way of remuneration but not all of the shareholders are directors. This practice can be a source of internal tension, particularly if the company has amassed considerable reserves and the directors' remuneration is generous. In such cases, a persistent failure to pay dividends when funds are available, coupled with high levels of directors' remuneration, may amount to unfairly prejudicial conduct meriting relief under CA 2006, s 994, see at **19-64**.

**22-95**    Shareholders in public companies are much less likely to be directors and they expect dividend payments to be made to the shareholders when distributable profits are available. For listed public companies, a failure to maintain an appropriate level of dividend pay-out each year can have an adverse effect on the company's share price and may expose the company to potential takeover bids. It is also likely to be unpopular with the company's institutional investors. Such market pressure for dividend payments is often criticised as contributing to the 'short-termism' problem in British companies. The argument is that it forces management to concentrate excessively on short-term strategies designed to give immediate shareholder returns and maintain the company's share price rather than on long-term planning which would be to the advantage of the company and the economy. Whether there is a short-termism problem as opposed to a perception problem and whether, if there is a problem, it should be attributed to shareholders' attitudes to dividends rather than managerial conduct (given the link between remuneration and short-term targets) continues to be debated, see **6-64**. To some extent, the debate has moved on to a recognition of the need for better engagement between companies and their shareholders which, given their predominance, essentially means between companies and their institutional shareholders, see **6-54**.

### Alternative frameworks—solvency statements

**22-96**    In terms of reform, the Company Law Review favoured only technical amendments to the statutory provisions on distribution rather than wholesale revision.[186] A more fundamental debate subsequently emerged at the European level (though influenced by developments here)[187] as to whether it was time to shift away from a statutory framework on distributions closely tied to the company's accounts and the determination of the existence of available profits under those accounts to a scheme based on directors' declarations

---

[185] See, for example, *Queensway Systems Ltd v Walker* [2007] 2 BCLC 577. Some of the problems are eased somewhat by the relaxation of the prohibitions on loans to directors by CA 2006, ss 197–214. See also *Global Corporate Ltd v Hale* [2017] EWHC 2277 (Ch)—whether payments were salary or dividends—the company had no distributable profits so the distinction mattered—court held payments were remuneration awarded on a *quantum meruit* basis, decision is being appealed to the Court of Appeal; also *Toone v Robbins* [2018] EWHC 569, disagreeing with the approach in *Global Corporate* and upholding a finding that sums had been paid by way of improper dividend and could not be re-characterised as remuneration and that directors cannot claim on a *quantum meruit*, applying *Guinness plc v Saunders* [1990] BCLC 402.

[186] See Company Law Review, *Final Report*, vol I (2001), para 10.6; *Completing the Structure* (2000), paras 7.20–7.23; *Company Formation and Capital Maintenance* (1999), paras 3.65–3.76 and Annex B; also *Capital Maintenance: Other Issues* (2000).

[187] See Rickford (ed), 'Reforming Capital: Report of the Interdisciplinary Group on Capital Maintenance' (2004) 15 EBLR 919.

of solvency whereby, if the directors certify that the company will remain solvent following a distribution, that should suffice. This approach, or variations thereof, is relied upon in other jurisdictions and the accounting profession seemed keen on such reform.[188] The issue arose as part of a broader debate, see **22-8**, as to whether the capital maintenance doctrine is obsolete and serves no practical purpose.

**22-97**  Against that backdrop, the European Commission launched an external assessment of the capital maintenance regime established by the Second Directive which was carried out by KPMG and published in early 2008.[189] KPMG were asked to consider in particular the impact of International Financial Reporting Standards (IFRS, which must be used for consolidated accounts and may be used for individual accounts) on distributions and whether an alternative regime would be better. On the distribution issues, the KPMG study concluded that the requirements of the Second Directive were modest in relation to the cushion required before a distribution might be made, that the use of IFRS as such did not cause companies problems in terms of distributions, and that those jurisdictions which do rely on solvency statements frequently also impose a balance sheet test.[190] In the light of those findings, the Commission announced that 'no follow-up measures or changes to the Second Company Law Directive are foreseen in the immediate future'.[191] Subsequently, the momentum for changes to the rules governing distribution dissipated.

## Statute, common law, and directors' duties

**22-98**  The statutory distribution rules originated in the CA 1980 against a background of a common law principle which prohibits distributions to shareholders out of capital,[192] but the application of which to the payment of dividends was rather lax in some respects.[193] For example, the common law permitted dividends to be paid out of current trading profits without making good losses in fixed capital[194] or trading losses in previous years;[195] allowed dividends to be paid out of an unrealised capital gain resulting from a bona fide revaluation of fixed assets;[196] and did not require companies to provide for depreciation.[197] Many of these legal rules were commercially unwise and contrary to good accounting

---

[188] See FEE Discussion Paper on Alternatives to Capital Maintenance Regimes, September 2007 (FEE, Federation of European Accountants). For the views of a leading British proponent of a move to a solvency regime, see Rickford, 'Legal Approaches to Restricting Distributions to Shareholders: Balance Sheet Tests and Solvency Tests' (2006) 7 EBOR 135.

[189] KPMG, 'Feasibility Study on an alternative to the capital maintenance regime established by the Second Company Law Directive 77/91/EEC of 13 December 1976 and an examination of the impact on profit distribution of the new EU accounting regime', January 2008.

[190] See Schon, 'Balance Sheet Tests or Solvency Tests—or Both?' (2006) 7 EBOR 181, who argues for the dual approach.

[191] Commission statement on the results of the external study on the feasibility of an alternative to the Capital Maintenance Regime of the Second Company Law Directive and the impact of the adoption of IFRS on profit distribution (undated statement on Commission website issued at the time of publication of the results of the external study by KPMG which, though also undated, was published in January 2008).

[192] *Re Exchange Banking Co, Flitcroft's Case* (1882) 21 Ch D 519.

[193] For an interesting account of the historical development of the dividend rules, see Yamey, 'Aspects of the Law relating to Company Dividends' (1941) 4 MLR 273.

[194] *Lee v Neuchatel Asphalte Co* (1889) 41 Ch D 1; *Verner v General & Commercial Investment Trust* [1894] 2 Ch 239.

[195] *Ammonia Soda Co v Chamberlain* [1918] 1 Ch 266; *Re National Bank of Wales Ltd* [1899] 2 Ch 629.

[196] See *Dimbula Valley (Ceylon) Tea Co Ltd v Laurie* [1961] Ch 353 at 371–3.

[197] *Lee v Neuchatel Asphalte Co* (1889) 41 Ch D 1; *Bolton v Natal Land & Colonization Co* [1892] 2 Ch 124.

practice, but the courts were reluctant to interfere with the directors' discretion as men of business.[198]

**22-99** The statutory provisions are particularly useful therefore in constraining dividend abuse though, as noted at **22-88**, they apply more widely to 'any distribution' and operate alongside the common law which is expressly retained by CA 2006, ss 851 and 852. These sections continue the application of any rule of law, any provision in the articles, or in any enactment restricting the sums out of which, or the cases in which, a distribution may be made. The result is the continued application of the common law prohibition on distributions to the members out of capital[199] which has the important consequence that, where a company has distributable profits for the purposes of CA 2006, Pt 23, but those profits have been dissipated subsequent to the preparation of the accounts, the common law rule applies to prevent a distribution out of capital. Mostly, the application of the common law and the statute will give the same result,[200] given that the statute requires distributions to be out of distributable profits, but a distribution which is lawful under the common law could still fall foul of the statute as where the company's accounts are not properly prepared. A distribution to meet the requirements of the statute requires distributable profits, as defined by the statute, determined on the basis of accounts properly prepared as required by the statute. At common law, the question is merely whether, at the time of a distribution, it was made out of capital.[201]

**22-100** The statutory provisions work also within the general framework of the law which imposes other constraints on directors. Directors must exercise their powers for the purposes for which they are conferred (CA 2006, s 171) and have a duty to act to promote the success of the company for the benefit of the members having regard to the factors set out in s 172. That duty is of particular importance in this context because it includes an obligation, in certain circumstances, to have regard to the interests of the company's creditors (s 172(3)), see **10-41**. The directors' duty to exercise care and skill (discussed in Chapter 11) is also relevant. In that regard directors need to consider whether, whatever the position in terms of strict compliance with CA 2006, Pt 23, it is prudent to declare a dividend, given the company's trading position and funding needs.[202] In a situation where the company's position is one of doubtful solvency, or the effect of the dividend would be to render the company insolvent or doubtfully solvent (given the duty to have regard to creditors' interests at that stage), a prudent director exercising care and skill would not recommend the payment of a dividend without ensuring that the company was in a position to meet the claims of its creditors as they fall due.[203] The result is that directors considering distributions need to be alert to their general duties, the requirements of CA 2006, Pt 23, and the common law principle precluding distributions out of capital.

**22-101** Distributions in breach of the common law prohibition or of the statutory requirements or requirements in the articles are ultra vires and void and cannot be ratified by the

---

[198] See *Lee v Neuchatel Asphalte Co* (1889) 41 Ch D 1 at 18, 21.

[199] *Re Exchange Banking Co, Flitcroft's Case* (1882) 21 Ch D 519. See also *Trevor v Whitworth* (1887) 12 App Cas 409.

[200] See *Progress Property Co Ltd v Moorgarth Group Ltd* [2010] 1 BCLC 1, CA at [22], [31], showing the overlap between the common law and the statute, aff'd [2011] 2 BCLC 332, S Ct.

[201] As can be seen in *Progress Property Co Ltd v Moorgarth Group Ltd* [2011] 2 BCLC 332 at [2], S Ct.

[202] See, for example, Tech 02/17BL, n 210, para 2.4 which cautions directors to be prudent when considering a distribution from profits arising from changes in the value of financial instruments considered to be volatile, even if the profits are deemed by accounting principles to be realised profits for these purposes.

[203] See *Re Loquitur Ltd, IRC v Richmond* [2003] 2 BCLC 442 at [240].

company in general meeting.[204] The liabilities of the directors and the shareholder recipients are discussed at **22-122**.

**22-102** The decision in *BTI 2014 LLC v Sequana SA*[205] raises the interesting additional possibility that a distribution may be permissible under CA 2006, Pt 23, but fall foul of IA 1986, s 423 (transactions entered into at an undervalue defrauding creditors). Essentially, a transaction can be challenged under s 423 if a payment is made with the purpose of putting assets beyond the reach of a potential claimant or otherwise prejudicing the interests of such a person. The facts in this case were complicated but concerned a subsidiary company which was exposed to potentially large environmental claims, underwritten by the parent company. The company declared two dividends in a short period of time so facilitating a transfer of value from the company to its parent company—the court found the payments were within Part 23, there being distributable profits and accounts properly prepared as required by Part 23. Nevertheless, the court also considered that a dividend can be a transaction entered into at an undervalue because it is a discretionary payment by the company both as to the amount and as to whether it is paid at all.[206] Further, there was nothing in the wording of IA 1986 s 423 to suggest a blanket exclusion of dividends from the application of that section if a payment is made with the s 423 purpose.[207] Given that the range of claimants and potential court orders under s 423 are broader and more flexible than the remedies available under Part 23, Rose J thought that 'a blanket exclusion of dividend payments from the scope of section 423 will quickly reduce the efficacy of the provision given the many instances where the directors and shareholders of a company are the same or linked individuals'.[208] On the facts, the court found that the second dividend was paid at a time when the intention of the directors was to reduce the risk to the parent company of any environmental liability attaching to it. The dividends were part of a plan to sell the subsidiary to a third party so removing it from the group and ending any potential liability of the parent company. The second dividend was therefore open to challenge under IA 1986, s 423 and relief would be ordered by the court,[209] though the dividend payments were permissible under CA 2006, Part 23. This case opens up another avenue of challenge to improper dividends, especially given that IA 1986, s 423 does not require that the company be insolvent.

## Distributions and distributable profits—CA 2006, Part 23

**22-103** The basic rule is that a company may only make a distribution out of profits available for the purpose, determined by accounts which have been properly prepared in accordance with the Companies Act.[210] In Part 23, a 'distribution' means every description of

---

[204] *Re Exchange Banking Co, Flitcroft's Case* (1882) 21 Ch D 519; *Precision Dippings Ltd v Precision Dippings Marketing Ltd* [1985] BCLC 385; *Aveling Barford v Perion Ltd* [1989] BCLC 626 at 630–1; *Bairstow v Queens Moat Houses plc* [2001] 2 BCLC 531; *Secretary of State for Business, Innovation and Skills v Doffman* [2011] 2 BCLC 541 at [41], CA.   [205] [2017] 1 BCLC 453, and see note by Graham (2017) Co Law 116.

[206] [2017] 1 BCLC 453 at [500].

[207] [2017] 1 BCLC 453 at [501]. Where there is more than one purpose, the prohibited purpose does not need to be the dominant purpose: *JSC BTA Bank v Ablyazov* [2018] EWCA Civ 1176.

[208] [2017] 1 BCLC 453 at [501].

[209] The precise relief to be awarded under IA 1986, s 423, is the subject of ongoing litigation, with an appeal to the Court of Appeal against the judgment on relief at [2017] EWHC 211 which capped relief at the total amount of the May dividend. The position is complicated by the multitude of parties and claims in the environmental litigation which is the back story to the dividend payments.

[210] CA 2006, s 830 and s 836. As discussed at **22-109**, a company's accounts play a crucial role in determining whether a company has profits for distribution for the purposes of CA 2006, Pt 23, and key technical guidance on the accounting issues is provided by the Institute of Chartered Accountants for England and Wales (ICAEW): see ICAEW, Tech 02/17BL, *Guidance on Realised and Distributable Profits under the Companies Act 2006*, hereinafter Tech 02/17BL.

distribution of a company's assets to its members,[211] whether in cash or otherwise, except distributions by way of:

(1) an issue of shares as fully or partly-paid bonus shares;

(2) the reduction of share capital by extinguishing or reducing the liability of any of the members on any of the company's shares in respect of share capital not paid up, or by repaying paid-up share capital;

(3) the redemption or purchase of any of the company's own shares out of capital (including the proceeds of any fresh issue of shares) or out of unrealised profits in accordance with the statutory provisions; and

(4) a distribution of assets to members of the company on its winding up (s 829).

**22-104**   The profits available for distribution are defined as the company's accumulated realised profits, so far as not previously utilised by distribution or capitalisation, less its accumulated realised losses, so far as not previously written off in a reduction or reorganisation of capital duly made (CA 2006, s 830(2)). Whether such sums exist must be determined by reference, essentially, to the company's last annual accounts and to specified items in those accounts,[212] the importance of which is discussed at **22-109**. Primarily the issue of whether there is a realised profit or loss is a matter of the application of accounting principles at the time the accounts are prepared.[213]

**22-105**   It is only *realised* profits or losses which enter the equation, a requirement designed to prevent companies from relying on estimated or expected profits which might never materialise. In accounting terms, profits are treated as realised for these purposes only when 'realised in the form of cash or of other assets, the ultimate cash realisation of which can be assessed with reasonable certainty'.[214] On the other hand, unrealised losses are not taken into account (save to the extent that they are reflected in the accounts) unless the company is a public company and the losses mean that the company's net assets are less than its called-up share capital and undistributable reserves (see **22-107**). Equally important, the amount of *accumulated* realised losses must be deducted before any distribution can be made which abrogates the common law rule that losses made in previous accounting periods did not have to be made good.[215] Accounting periods can no longer be regarded in isolation from one another, hence the need in many cases to write off losses by way of a reduction of capital (see **22-65**) before resuming the payment of dividends.

**22-106**   The decision in *Aveling Barford Ltd v Perion Ltd*,[216] noted at **22-89**, caused problems in practice for reconstructions involving intra-group transfers of assets which were

---

[211] See *Re TXU Europe Group plc* [2012] BCC 363 (a payment proposed by supervisors of a CVA of a subsidiary company to the parent company where the payment was in respect of the parent company's shareholding and was described as an 'equity payment' was a distribution to the company's members for the purposes of CA 2006, Pt 23 and the conditions of Part 23 not being met, the proposed distribution would be unlawful).

[212] CA 2006, s 836(1). In some circumstances, initial or interim accounts may be used instead: see s 836(2).

[213] CA 2006, s 853(4), hence the importance of Tech 02/17BL, see n 210. References to profits and losses, except where the context otherwise requires, are to revenue or capital profits and losses made at any time: s 853(2).

[214] Tech 02/17BL, n 210, para 3.3. See too *In Re Oxford Benefit Building & Investment Society* (1886) 35 Ch D 502 at 510: 'realised profits' must have its ordinary commercial meaning which, if not equivalent to 'reduced to actual cash in hand', must at least be 'rendered tangible for the purpose of division'. Tech 02/17BL, para 3.1, notes that it is apparent that the concept of a realised profit is intended to be dynamic, changing with the development of generally accepted accounting principles, as well as bringing within the definition profits which might not in ordinary language be called realised.

[215] See *Ammonia Soda Co v Chamberlain* [1918] 1 Ch 266; *Re National Bank of Wales Ltd* [1899] 2 Ch 629.

[216] [1989] BCLC 626; see also *Ridge Securities Ltd v IRC* [1964] 1 All ER 275.

commonly done at book value rather than market value. Post-*Aveling Barford* it was thought that such transactions were open to challenge as improper distributions unless the transferring company had distributable profits to cover the gap between the book value and the market value. The issue is addressed by CA 2006, s 845 which deals with distributions consisting of or including, or treated as arising in consequence of, the sale, transfer, or other disposition by the company of a non-cash asset and which applies to distributions under the statute or distributions under the common law (s 851(2)).[217] For companies which have available profits, this provision determines the amount of the distribution (and therefore the amount which needs to be covered by those distributable profits). Where the amount of the consideration received by the company out of the transaction is not less than the book value of the asset, the amount of the distribution is zero (s 845(2)(a)). Where the amount of the consideration received by the company is less than the book value, the company needs distributable profits equal to the difference between the consideration received and the book value (s 845(2)(b)).[218] Where the amount received exceeds the book value of the asset, the profits available for distribution are increased by that amount (s 845(3)). These provisions apply only where the company has available profits; where the company has no distributable profits and makes a distribution of assets at an undervalue, it remains an unlawful distribution, as in *Aveling Barford Ltd v Perion Ltd*.[219]

**2-107**   In addition to having realised profits available for distribution (a requirement which precludes a payment out of capital), a public company must satisfy two further conditions before it makes a distribution.[220] These additional requirements ensure that, not only does a public company not make a distribution out of capital, but a public company must also maintain a cushion of assets sufficient to cover the amount of its share capital and undistributable reserves.[221] This 'cushion' requirement will reduce the funds available for distribution. CA 2006, s 831(1) provides that a public company may only make a distribution:

(1)  if the amount of its net assets is not less than the aggregate of its called-up share capital and undistributable reserves, and

(2)  if, and to the extent that, the distribution does not reduce the amount of those assets to less than that aggregate.[222]

---

[217]  See the *Explanatory Notes to the Companies Act 2006*, paras 1151–1157 on the scope and application of CA 2006, s 845. On the application of s 845, see Tech 02/17BL, n 210, para 2.9B et seq.

[218]  To the extent that the book value represents an unrealised profit, it is treated as realised, for these purposes, see CA 2006, s 846.

[219]  [1989] BCLC 626; see *Explanatory Notes to the Companies Act 2006*, para 1153.

[220]  See CA 2006, s 831. Further requirements are imposed on investment companies, see ss 832–833.

[221]  These additional requirements reflect the Second Company Law Directive, now Directive 2017/1132, OJ L 169/46, 30.6.2017, art 56. In response to criticisms that this requirement is unduly prescriptive, the European Commission pointed out that what is now art 56 does not require non-distributable legal or statutory reserves, rather it recognises them if national law requires them. If there is no national law requirement, art 56 only requires that the net assets cover the amount of the called-up share capital and the Second Directive only requires a minimum share capital of €25,000 (now art 45), which the Commission notes is not a significant amount in this context. See DG Internal Market and Services, Position Paper on Results of External Study on the Feasibility of Alternative to the Capital Maintenance Regime of the Second Company Law Directive (January 2008), pp 10–11.

[222]  CA 2006, s 831(1) (modified for investment companies, see s 832). For this purpose, 'net assets' means the aggregate of the company's assets less the aggregate of its liabilities: s 831(2); and 'called-up share capital' is widely defined to include capital called up but not yet paid and capital to be paid on a specified future date: s 547. The redenomination reserve is treated as if it is paid-up share capital: see s 628(3).

**22-108** A company's undistributable reserves under the CA 2006 are:

(1) its share premium account;

(2) its capital redemption reserve;

(3) the amount by which the company's accumulated unrealised profits (so far as not previously utilised by any capitalisation) exceed its accumulated unrealised losses (so far as not previously written off in a reduction or re-organisation of capital duly made); and

(4) any other reserve which the company is prohibited from distributing by any enactment or by its articles.[223]

### Justification by reference to accounts

**22-109** All of these matters as to distributable profits are determined in accordance with the company's last individual annual accounts[224] circulated to the members in accordance with CA 2006, s 423, properly prepared in accordance with the requirements of the Act[225] and accompanied by an auditors' report unless the company has claimed exemption from audit.[226] The amount of the distribution is to be determined by reference to specified items in the accounts (profits, losses, assets and liabilities, provisions, share capital, and reserves).[227]

**22-110** In some circumstances, initial or interim accounts may be used instead and these accounts generally must be sufficient to enable a reasonable judgement to be made as to whether there are available profits.[228] Where a public company wishes to rely on initial or interim accounts, there are specific requirements as to form and content and the accounts must be delivered to the registrar of companies.[229] Interim accounts are particularly useful when the company's position has improved significantly since the last accounts and it wishes to make a distribution larger than would be possible under those accounts. Contravention of the accounting requirements in CA 2006, ss 837–839 means that the distribution is in contravention of Part 23 (s 836(4)).

**22-111** The central importance of these accounting requirements in determining whether a distribution is lawful was highlighted by the decision in *Bairstow v Queens Moat Houses plc*[230] where the Court of Appeal emphasised that the consequence of the accounts not being properly prepared, or not giving a true and fair view as required, is that the distribution is unlawful. In this case, the accounts gave the misleading impression of significant profits when the company did not have distributable profits. The defendant directors argued that, while the company did not have distributable profits, there were profits available in wholly-owned subsidiary companies which might have been paid up to the parent

---

[223] CA 2006, s 831(4); see s 669(1) for an example of an undistributable reserve.

[224] CA 2006, s 836(1); group accounts are not relevant for this purpose.

[225] CA 2006, s 837(1), or have been properly prepared subject only to matters that are not material for determining (by reference to s 836(1)) whether the distribution would contravene Part 23: s 837(2). Accounts so prepared must only be approved by the directors if they give a true and fair view of the state of the company's affairs: s 393.     [226] CA 2006, s 837(3). As to exemption from audit, see **18-55**.

[227] See CA 2006, s 836(1). See also s 840 which deals with successive distributions on the basis of the same accounts and ensures that other distributions and financial assistance and other relevant payments from available profits already made on the strength of those same accounts are taken into account in determining whether there are sufficient profits for a further distribution.     [228] CA 2006, ss 838(1), 839(1).

[229] See CA 2006, ss 836(2), (3), 838(6), 839(7). For an example of interim accounts being used, see *Re Loquitur Ltd, IRC v Richmond* [2003] 2 BCLC 442.     [230] [2001] 2 BCLC 531, CA.

company and any breach with respect to the accounts of the parent company was purely technical.

**22-112** This argument was emphatically rejected by the Court of Appeal which emphasised that the statutory requirements as to proper accounts are an important part of the protection provided by the Act and are not to be regarded as a mere procedural formality. As the accounts in this case had been drawn up in breach of the statutory requirements, any distribution based upon them was an unlawful distribution and the directors were not entitled to go behind the accounts to argue that the company did have the required distributable profits.[231] The court held that the dividend was an unlawful distribution regardless of whether the company might have had distributable profits had the accounts been properly prepared. The point is clearly made in CA 2006, s 836(4) which provides that, if the accounting requirements are not complied with, 'the accounts may not be relied on for the purposes of this Part and the distribution is accordingly treated as contravening this Part'.

**22-113** In *Allied Carpets Group plc v Nethercott*[232] the court found that the company had declared a dividend on the strength of accounts which did not give a true and fair view. The figures in the accounts for turnover and sales were inflated by a practice known as pre-despatching whereby sales were treated as realised once customers placed an order for carpet although the company's policy was that sales should only be booked to the accounts when the carpet had actually been fitted. Whether the company would have had distributable profits had the accounts been properly prepared was irrelevant and the company was entitled to summary judgment for £227,491 with respect to unlawful dividends received by a director who knew of the pre-despatching practice and knew therefore that the accounts were false.

**22-114** The possibility that the distribution might have been made lawfully (if the accounts had been properly prepared) may influence the court, however, in terms of the remedy which it is willing to grant, for example by allowing relief for the directors under CA 2006, s 1157 (acted honestly and reasonably and ought fairly to be excused, see **14-79**) or by tailoring the remedy which the court is prepared to grant under IA 1986, s 212, see **15-3**, as in *Re Loquitur Ltd*.

**22-115** In *Re Loquitur Ltd, IRC v Richmond*[233] a company failed to make appropriate provision in its accounts for a possible tax liability, though the company knew that the tax relief which the company was seeking was likely to be rejected by the Inland Revenue. A dividend of £5.9m was paid on the strength of those accounts to the company's parent company. On the company going into liquidation, the Inland Revenue successfully challenged the payment of the dividend under IA 1986, s 212 (misfeasance by directors). The court found that the failure to make provision for the possible tax liability meant that the accounts were improperly prepared and therefore the dividend was paid in contravention of the statutory requirements. The directors had acted in breach of their duty to have regard to the interests of their creditors and had failed to exercise appropriate care and skill by not retaining sufficient assets to cover reasonably anticipated liabilities.[234] On that basis, the court did not think that the defendants as directors had acted honestly and reasonably in authorising and procuring payment of the dividend and they could not be granted relief under what is now CA 2006, s 1157. The court declined to order repayment of the entire

---

[231] [2001] 2 BCLC 531 at [35]–[36]; *Inn Spirit Ltd v Burns* [2002] 2 BCLC 780 at [21]–[24].
[232] [2001] BCC 81.     [233] [2003] 2 BCLC 442.     [234] See [2003] 2 BCLC 442 at [240].

amount of the dividend, however, and limited the order to the amount of the outstanding tax liability (exercising its discretion under IA 1986, s 212(3) to make such order for the purposes of s 212 as the court thinks just).[235] The court limited recovery in this way on the basis that, had the accounts been properly drawn up, it is likely that a substantial dividend could have been paid. Crucially, the court also considered that the subsequent insolvency of the company was not caused by the accounting failures, but by a disastrous fire at the company's premises.[236]

**22-116**   Another scenario is where profits are available and the accounts are properly prepared but the company makes an excessive distribution, for example the company has £100,000 available profits for distribution but makes a distribution of £180,000. The question then is whether the distribution is unlawful as to the entire amount or only to the amount in excess of the available profits. In *Re Marini Ltd, Liquidator of Marini Ltd v Dickenson*[237] the court concluded that the prohibition is on making a distribution other than out of profits available for distribution (CA 2006, s 830(1)). To the extent therefore that a distribution is out of such profits, it cannot be unlawful, a conclusion supported by s 847(1) which envisages a shareholder being required to return part of a distribution.

**22-117**   Unless the company has taken advantage of the audit exemption available to small companies (see **18-55**), the auditor must have made his report on the accounts (CA 2006, s 837(3)). If the auditor has qualified his report, he must state in writing (either at the time of his report or subsequently) whether, in his opinion, the substance of the qualification is material for determining whether the proposed distribution would contravene Part 23 and a copy of that statement must have been circulated to the members of a private company and, in the case of a public company, laid before the company in general meeting before the distribution was made (s 837(4)).

**22-118**   The significance of this statement by the auditor was considered by the Court of Appeal in *Precision Dippings Ltd v Precision Dippings Marketing Ltd*.[238] In this case, no auditor's statement had been made although the accounts had been qualified. A dividend of £60,000 was paid by Dippings to its parent company, Marketing. Dippings later went into liquidation. The auditors at that stage (i.e. post-distribution) issued a written declaration to the effect that the qualification in their report did not affect the validity of the dividend payment. The liquidator of Dippings successfully sued to recover the amount of the dividend from Marketing. The court found that the accounting requirements, of which the auditor's statement forms part, are not mere procedural requirements but an important part of the scheme provided by the statutory provisions as a major protection for creditors.[239] The wording of the provision, the 'auditor must have stated' whether the qualification was material to a distribution, now CA 2006, s 837(4)(a), showed that the auditor's statement had to be available to the shareholders before the distribution was made. As it

---

[235] See also *Re Paycheck Services 3 Ltd, Revenue and Customs Commissioners v Holland* [2011] 1 BCLC 141, SC, and the obiter comments therein as to the court's discretion under IA 1986, s 212, see at **15-6**.

[236] See [2003] 2 BCLC 442 at [250]–[251].

[237] [2004] BCC 172. See Ferran and Ho, *Principles of Corporate Finance Law* (2nd edn, 2014), p 224 who note that this decision is not easy to reconcile with the strict approach in other cases. See *LRH Services Ltd v Trew* [2018] EWHC 600 where HH David Cooke made the point that the decision in *Marini* is justifiable because there were properly drawn up accounts in that case which showed how much distributable profits were available. In *LRH Services Ltd*, an improper distribution having been made in circumstances in which there were no properly prepared accounts, the directors were liable for the entire amount unlawfully paid away, see at [186], [187].

[238] [1985] BCLC 385.      [239] [1985] BCLC 385 at 389.

had not been so available, the statutory provisions had been contravened and the payment of the dividend was ultra vires and void.

### Declaration and payment of dividends

**22-119** Assuming that a company does have available profits as determined in accordance with the statutory provisions, the question is whether this automatically entitles the shareholders to a dividend. The position is that it does so only if the articles expressly provide for the payment of a fixed dividend where the company has distributable profits.[240] More commonly, the articles will allow for the declaration of a dividend by ordinary resolution following a recommendation by the directors.[241]

**22-120** Only when a dividend has been declared does it become payable and due to the members.[242] As a rule a dividend must be paid in cash, but the articles may allow for a non-cash distribution to be made,[243] for example, in the form of additional shares. A dividend paid in the form of additional shares is known as a scrip dividend.

### Consequences of unlawful distributions

**22-121** An unlawful distribution, whether unlawful at common law for being out of capital, or unlawful because in breach of the statute (either no available profits and/or some breach of the accounting requirements), is ultra vires and void and cannot be ratified by the company in general meeting;[244] likewise where a dividend is paid in breach of a restriction in the articles[245] or contrary to some other enactment.

**22-122** Where an unlawful distribution has been made, the company may seek to recover the amount distributed under the statute or at common law and the latter option offers the greatest range of possibilities. There are two main targets for any action by the company: (1) the recipient of the unlawful distribution, and (2) the directors who authorised the unlawful distribution.[246] As the shareholder recipients, especially in larger public

---

[240] See *Evling v Israel & Oppenheimer Ltd* [1918] 1 Ch 101. But it seems that a provision which allows for dividends to be paid out of profits available for dividend is subject to the directors' power to transfer profits to a reserve, so dividends are then payable out of the profits left after the directors have exercised their power to create a reserve, see *Bagot Pneumatic Tyre Co v Clipper Pneumatic Tyre Co* [1902] 1 Ch 146 at 158–9; *Long Acre Press Ltd v Odhams Press Ltd* [1930] 2 Ch 196; *Re Buenos Ayres Great Southern Rly Co Ltd* [1947] Ch 384.

[241] See The Companies (Model Articles) Regulations 2008, SI 2008/3229, Sch 1, art 30 (private companies), Sch 3, art 70 (public companies); the resolution may decrease but not increase the amount to be distributed. Informal unanimous assent will suffice, but only if the shareholders know what they are assenting to, see *Queensway Systems Ltd v Walker* [2007] 2 BCLC 577.

[242] The declaration of the dividend creates an immediate debt: *Re Severn and Wye and Severn Bridge Ry Co* [1896] 1 Ch 559, unless it is expressed as payable at a future date, in which case a shareholder has no right to enforce payment until the due date for payment arrives: *Re Kidner, Kidner v Kidner* [1929] 2 Ch 121. In the case of an interim dividend which the board has resolved to pay, it is open to the board at any time before payment to review its decision and resolve not to pay the dividend: *Lagunas Nitrate Co Ltd v Schroeder & Co and Schmidt* (1901) 85 Law Times 22.

[243] See The Companies (Model Articles) Regulations 2008, SI 2008/3229, Sch 1, art 35 (private companies), Sch 3, art 76 (public companies); also *Wood v Odessa Waterworks Co* (1889) 42 Ch D 636.

[244] *Re Exchange Banking Co, Flitcroft's Case* (1882) 21 Ch D 519; *Precision Dippings Ltd v Precision Dippings Marketing Ltd* [1985] BCLC 385; *Aveling Barford v Perion Ltd* [1989] BCLC 626; *Bairstow v Queens Moat Houses plc* [2001] 2 BCLC 531, CA.

[245] *Guinness plc v Saunders* [1990] BCLC 402, HL.

[246] Where the accounts have not been prepared properly and do not give a true and fair view as required, the company may also bring an action for negligence against its auditors.

companies, are frequently unaware of the circumstances surrounding a distribution in the form of a dividend and rely on the directors to act properly, there is little likelihood of successfully pursuing the shareholders to recover unlawful dividends (other than shareholders who are also directors or where the shareholder is a parent company).[247] It is more likely, though still comparatively rare, for the company (usually because a liquidator or new board of directors is in place) to pursue recovery from the directors who authorised the improper payments. Another possibility is that a creditor, such as HM Revenue & Customs, may bring a claim for misfeasance under IA 1986, s 212, see **15-3**, against directors who authorise improper dividends.[248] Disqualification is also a possibility.[249]

### Liability of recipients

**22-123**   Where a distribution, or part of a distribution,[250] is made in contravention of the requirements of CA 2006, Pt 23, any member who, at the time of the distribution, knows or has reasonable grounds for believing that it is so made is liable to repay the distribution (or part of it, as the case may be) to the company.[251] This statutory liability is without prejudice to any obligation imposed apart from the statutory provisions on a member to repay a distribution unlawfully made to him,[252] i.e. as a knowing recipient of trust funds.[253] An illustration of liability based on 'knowing receipt' can be found in *Precision Dippings Ltd v Precision Dippings Marketing Ltd*[254] where a dividend was paid by a company (Dippings) to its parent company (Marketing) and the directors of Dippings were the only directors and shareholders of Marketing. The Court of Appeal held that the payment of the dividend in breach of the statutory provisions was an ultra vires act of the company. Marketing, when it received the money, had notice of the facts and held the £60,000 dividend on constructive trust for the company which was entitled to repayment.[255]

**22-124**   The flexibility to proceed either under the statutory provision or the common law is necessary since, as discussed, it is possible for a distribution to a member to be valid under CA 2006, Pt 23 (there are available profits and the accounting requirements are met) so

---

[247]  See, for example, *Precision Dippings Ltd v Precision Dippings Marketing Ltd* [1985] BCLC 385; *Allied Carpets Group plc v Nethercott* [2001] BCC 81. On occasion, the Serious Fraud Office has recovered dividends paid to parent companies by subsidiaries which were found to have acted corruptly. For an example, see SFO Press Release, 'Shareholder agrees civil recovery by SFO in Mabey & Johnson', 13 January 2012.

[248]  For examples, see *Re Loquitar Ltd, IRC v Richmond* [2003] 2 BCLC 444; *Re Paycheck Services 3 Ltd, Revenue and Customs Commissioners v Holland* [2011] 1 BCLC 141.

[249]  See *Re AG (Manchester) Ltd, Official Receiver v Watson* [2008] 1 BCLC 321 where a director left all financial and strategic decisions to an inner group of directors (including her husband) and was content to take substantial dividends from the company regardless of how and whether they could be paid. The court found her abdication of responsibility in failing to act independently and in the interests of the company justified her disqualification for four years; see also *Secretary of State for Business, Innovation and Skills v Doffman* [2011] 2 BCLC 541 (directors disqualified on the ground of unfitness, most of the evidence of unfitness related to unlawful distributions).

[250]  If the company has available profits and properly prepared accounts, but pays a dividend in excess of that amount, it is only the part in excess of the available profits that is in contravention of the Act and must be repaid to the company: see *Re Marini Ltd, Liquidator of Marini Ltd v Dickenson* [2004] BCC 172.

[251]  CA 2006, s 847(1), (2)(a). Where the distribution is made otherwise than in cash, the statutory liability is to pay to the company a sum equal to the value of the distribution at the time of the distribution: s 847(2)(b), but at common law a proprietary claim may lie against the recipient, see **14-63**.

[252]  CA 2006, s 847(3).

[253]  See *Bank of Credit and Commerce International (Oversea) Ltd v Akindele* [2000] 4 All ER 221, CA and the discussion at **14-63** as to liability on a 'knowing receipt' basis.

[254]  [1985] BCLC 385, CA.

[255]  See [1985] BCLC 385 at 390, per Dillon LJ, applying *Rolled Steel Products (Holdings) Ltd v British Steel Corpn* [1985] 3 All ER 52.

no statutory liability arises, but the payment is in breach of the common law (because, for example, at the time of the payment, the company's position has worsened) or the company's articles. Also the test of liability as a recipient is different under the statute and at common law.[256] Statutory liability arises where the shareholder knows the facts which lead to the conclusion that the distribution is in contravention of the Act, but it is not necessary that the member knows the legal rules and the consequences of those rules when applied to the facts.[257] Liability as a constructive trustee arises where the shareholder knows or ought to know that the distribution is unlawful.[258] Therefore, depending on the facts, one or other route may offer the best chance of recovery.

**22-125** The statutory liability was considered by the Court of Appeal in *It's a Wrap (UK) Ltd v Gula*[259] where the focus was on the meaning of the requirement that the member 'knows or has reasonable grounds for believing' that the distribution is in contravention of the Act (CA 2006, s 847(2)). The company had two members, a husband and wife, who were also the directors. The company made no profits during its brief (four years) existence but the directors each took dividends of £14,000 per annum as a tax-efficient alternative to receiving a salary from the company. On the company going into insolvent liquidation, the liquidator sought to recover £56,000 in total from them, but they were found not liable at first instance on the basis that the section required knowledge of the legal position. The Court of Appeal swiftly overruled the decision and confirmed that it is not necessary to show that the shareholders know the statutory provisions. It is enough that the shareholders know the facts which lead to the conclusion that the distribution does contravene the statutory provisions.[260] The defendants knew the company had no profits, therefore they knew of the contravention for the purpose of the statutory liability and they had to repay the sums which they had received.

### Liability of directors

**22-126** The statute deals with the liability of the recipient of an unlawful dividend, but does not address the liability of the directors for authorising or procuring the payment of the dividend which remains a matter for the common law. Directors are trustees of the company's assets and as such are jointly and severally liable for the full amount of any unlawful distribution of the company's assets to the shareholders, whether the company is solvent or insolvent and whether or not profits could have been available.[261] The classic authority

---

[256] See Arden LJ in *It's a Wrap (UK) Ltd v Gula* [2006] 2 BCLC 634 at [12] who comments that the statutory remedy is more absolute and stringent than that at common law because it is tailor-made to facilitate the recovery of unlawful distributions whereas the remedy under the general law is an adaptation of the law of constructive trusteeship, but the need for some form of actual or constructive knowledge on the part of the shareholder is common to both forms of remedy; see also, at [52], per Chadwick LJ.

[257] *It's a Wrap (UK) Ltd v Gula* [2006] 2 BCLC 634 at [50], per Chadwick LJ.

[258] *Moxham v Grant* [1900] 1 QB 88; see also *Precision Dippings Ltd v Precision Dippings Marketing Ltd* [1985] BCLC 385; *Re Cleveland Trust plc* [1991] BCLC 424; *Allied Carpets Group plc v Nethercott* [2001] BCC 81. See *It's a Wrap (UK) Ltd v Gula* [2006] 2 BCLC 634 at [52] where Chadwick LJ notes that he does not think that the composite phrase 'knows or has reasonable grounds for believing' has the same meaning as 'knows or ought to know'. [259] [2006] 2 BCLC 634, CA.

[260] [2006] 2 BCLC 634 at [50], per Chadwick LJ; see also [27], [35], per Arden LJ; at [39], per Sedley LJ.

[261] *Re Exchange Banking Co, Flitcroft's Case* (1882) 21 Ch D 519; *Re Oxford Benefit Building & Investment Society* (1886) 35 Ch D 502; *Leeds Estate, Building and Investment Company v Shepherd* (1887) 36 Ch D 787; *Re Lands Allotment Co* [1894] 1 Ch 616 at 638; *Re Sharpe, Re Bennett, Masonic and General Life Assurance Co v Sharpe* [1892] 1 Ch 154 at 165–6 (rejecting the contention that, because the directors had acted honestly and openly, they might not be liable to account for the money misapplied); *Belmont Finance Corp Ltd v Williams Furniture Ltd* [1980] 1 All ER 393 at 405; *Bairstow v Queens Moat Houses plc* [2001] 2 BCLC 531 at [44], [50]–[51], CA, aff'g [2000] 1 BCLC 549; *Queensway Systems Ltd v Walker* [2007] 2 BCLC 577 and see the discussion of directors' liabilities in Chapter 14.

is *Re Exchange Banking Co, Flitcroft's Case*[262] where the directors had been in the habit of including among the company's assets a number of debts which they knew to be bad. The effect was to give the appearance of profits when in fact there were none. The directors recommended and the general meeting approved the payment of dividends over a period of several years on the strength of those misleading accounts. On the company going into insolvent liquidation, the court ordered the directors jointly and severally to replace the moneys improperly expended in this way.[263] The potential extent of this liability can be seen in *Bairstow v Queens Moat Houses plc*[264] where the company obtained a judgment for £78m against its former directors who, the court found, had deliberately (and dishonestly in certain cases) made unlawful dividend payments over a period of years based on misleading accounts.[265] The court noted that even if (as was alleged) it could be shown that wholly-owned subsidiaries of the company did have distributable profits which could have been paid up to the company and which would have allowed it to pay a lawful dividend, the fact was that the profits had not been paid up and the distribution made was unlawful and ultra vires, even if the company is still solvent.[266] The directors' heavy and continuing responsibilities for the stewardship of the company's assets meant they were liable for the payment of unlawful dividends out those assets.[267]

**22-127**  To the extent that a distribution is made in excess of available profits as determined by properly prepared accounts, any liability of the directors extends only to the repayment of that part which is unlawful.[268] The feature which distinguishes that situation from *Bairstow v Queens Moat Houses plc*[269] is the availability of distributable profits as determined by the accounts. In *Bairstow* there were no profits in the company and, even if there might have been elsewhere in the group, they had not been paid up into the company.

**22-128**  This issue of the directors' liability for improper dividends was discussed in the Supreme Court in *Re Paycheck Services 3 Ltd, Revenue and Customs Commissioners v Holland*[270] where essentially improper dividends had been paid without appropriate provision for corporation tax. The case revolved around whether a director of a corporate director was a de facto director (see the discussion at **7-16**) with responsibility for having declared the dividends. The Supreme Court found that the defendant was not a de facto director so the question of his liability for the improper dividends fell away, but Lord Hope had some interesting, though obiter, comments on counsel's argument that any liability of a director for the repayment of unlawful dividends was based on negligence rather than a strict liability.

**22-129**  Lord Hope accepted that there were some authorities such as *Kingston Cotton Mill (No 2)*[271] and *Dovey v Cory*[272] which supported a liability based on a duty of care so that a director might be liable only if he knew or ought to have known that a payment or transaction was a misapplication of the company's assets. However, Lord Hope considered that such

---

[262] (1882) 21 Ch D 519.  [263] (1882) 21 Ch D 519 at 534–5.
[264] [2001] 2 BCLC 531, CA; *Re Denham & Co* [1884] LR 25 Ch D 752.
[265] See *JJ Harrison (Properties) Ltd v Harrison* [2002] 1 BCLC 162; *Re Lands Allotment Co* [1894] 1 Ch 616 and authorities in n 261. As to whether the directors might have sought contribution from any shareholder recipients who had knowledge of the unlawful nature of the payments, see [2001] 2 BCLC 531 at [47]; also *Moxham v Grant* [1900] 1 QB 88. Disqualification for permitting unlawful dividends is also possible: see *Re AG (Manchester) Ltd, Official Receiver v Watson* [2008] 1 BCLC 321 at [184]–[187].
[266] [2001] 2 BCLC 531 at [36], [44].
[267] [2001] 2 BCLC 531 at [53], [54]. See also *LRH Services Ltd v Trew* [2018] EWHC 600—improper distribution, directors liable for the entire amount (£21m) unlawfully paid away.
[268] *Re Marini Ltd, Liquidator of Marini Ltd v Dickenson* [2004] BCC 172.
[269] [2001] 2 BCLC 531, CA.  [270] [2011] 1 BCLC 141.  [271] [1896] 1 Ch 331 at 348.
[272] [1901] AC 477.

authorities come to an end with *Dovey v Cory* and that thereafter the authorities, rightly in his view, say that the directors' obligation in respect of improperly paid dividends is to account to the company for the full amount of those dividends.[273] In his opinion, the better view in cases where it is accepted that the payment of the dividends is unlawful is that a director who causes their payment is strictly liable, subject to the possibility of relief under what is now CA 2006, s 1157, or the exercise of the court's discretion in terms of the order it makes under IA 1986, s 212.[274] Once a director is liable, Lord Hope agreed with the Court of Appeal that the remedy is not equitable compensation or damages for loss sustained, but restoration of the money paid out.[275] In this he agreed with Rimer LJ in the court below that the directors' trustee-like duties in respect of the company's assets require the directors to reinstate the full amount of the improper payment of dividends without any inquiry as to the loss said to be suffered by the company.[276]

**22-130**  On the question of the grant of relief under CA 2006, s 1157, as discussed at **14-79**, the courts are unlikely to grant relief in respect of conduct which benefits shareholders to the detriment of creditors and this would be particularly the case where improper dividends or other distributions are involved.[277] The court might be somewhat more generous under IA 1986, s 212 where, on a misfeasance claim, the court can make such order 'as the court thinks just' (s 212(3), discussed at **15-6**). In *Re Locquitar Ltd*,[278] see **22-115**, for example, the court declined to give relief to directors in respect of payment of an unlawful dividend under what is now CA 2006, s 1157, but did limit their liability when making an order under IA 1986 s 212(3) to the amount of corporate tax liability for which provision should have been made in the accounts. It was that failure to make that provision which had made the accounts and therefore the dividend unlawful.

## E  Financial assistance by a company for the acquisition of its own shares

### The problem with financial assistance

**22-131**  Financial assistance given by a company for the purchase of its own shares can arise in many circumstances but the classic abuse relates to the acquisition of a company by a bidder who borrows to fund the acquisition and who then uses the company's assets once

---

[273]  [2011] 1 BCLC 141 at [45]–[46].

[274]  [2011] 1 BCLC 141 at [45]–[46], see discussion of relief under CA 2006, s 1157 and IA 1986, s 212, at **14-79** and **15-3**, respectively. See Ferran (2011) 70 CLJ 321 for critical comment on Lord Hope's views. See too comments of Lord Walker in *Progress Property Co Ltd v Moorgarth Group Ltd* [2011] 2 BCLC 332 at [28]: 'A distribution described as a dividend but actually paid out of capital is unlawful, however technical the error and however well-meaning the directors who paid it. The same is true of a payment which is on analysis the equivalent of a dividend ...' There may be greater scope for argument in non-dividend situations, i.e. the commercial transaction distribution cases, either that the transaction was not a distribution in the first place or, if it was, that the director was not implicated in and did not know of the wrongdoing, see Lord Walker at [32], citing Lord Hamilton in *Clydebank FC Ltd v Steedman* [2002] SLT 109 at [79]; also *Buckley on the Companies Act*, Division 13, para [916].          [275]  [2011] 1 BCLC 141 at [48]–[49].

[276]  [2009] 2 BCLC 309 at [98], per Rimer LJ, with whom Elias LJ agreed, at [125]. There was broad agreement in the Supreme Court with Rimer LJ, see [2011] 1 BCLC 141 at [49], per Lord Hope; at [124], per Lord Walker; at [146], per Lord Clarke.

[277]  See *Inn Spirit Ltd v Burns* [2002] 2 BCLC 780 at [29]–[30]; *Re Loquitur Ltd, IRC v Richmond* [2003] 2 BCLC 442 at [228], [240]–[244]; *Re Marini Ltd, Liquidator of Marini Ltd v Dickenson* [2004] BCC 172 at [57]; *Queensway Systems Ltd v Walker* [2007] 2 BCLC 577 at [66]–[72].

[278]  [2003] 2 BCLC 442 at [247]–[251].

control has been secured to repay the funding. There are legitimate ways of carrying out this manoeuvre, as we shall see, but the concern is that, once the bidder has gained control, an element of asset stripping may occur to the detriment of the creditors.[279] Shareholders who have not had or taken the opportunity to exit from the company may also suffer as a consequence, though the primary concern here is creditor protection which is why these rules are linked to the capital maintenance rules discussed in this chapter. Concerns about the giving of financial assistance by a company for the purchase of its own shares date back to the 1920s. Though the statutory provisions have been restated on a number of occasions since their introduction in the Companies Act 1928, as Arden LJ noted in *Chaston v SWP Group plc*:[280]

'The general mischief, however, remains the same, namely that the resources of the target company and its subsidiaries should not be used directly or indirectly to assist the purchaser financially to make the acquisition. This may prejudice the interests of the creditors of the target or its group and the interests of any shareholders who do not accept the offer to acquire the shares or to whom the offer is not made.'

22-132  The mischief can arise in the context of significant companies with substantial assets, but it may also arise in smaller companies where typically the existing shareholders/directors wish to exit the business but cannot find a purchaser with funds to acquire their shares. The temptation or solution, depending on your viewpoint, is to use the company's assets to assist a possible purchaser. The risk is that the personal determination of shareholders/directors to exit leaves them indifferent or reckless to the consequences of using the company's assets to assist an impecunious purchaser. An example can be seen in *Re In A Flap Envelope Co Ltd*[281] where the directors of a company in financial difficulties sold their shareholding in the company to L. Some months later, when L had still not paid for the shares, it was agreed that the company would lend money to L to enable it to pay for the shares. L then paid the shareholders £355,000, approximately. Twelve months later, the company collapsed owing £3.2m.

### The legislative response

22-133  Financial assistance was first made a criminal offence by the CA 1929. The current prohibition on the giving of financial assistance by companies for the purchase of their own shares is set out in CA 2006, ss 677–683 (previously CA 1985, ss 151–158).[282]

22-134  The provisions on financial assistance are wide-ranging and practitioners frequently complain of the additional expense and complexity involved in ensuring that innocuous transactions linked to the acquisition of companies do not fall foul of the prohibition, particularly given that it is a criminal offence. A further problem is that, while the potential for abuse in funding acquisitions in this way is clear, it is also clear that if this type of funding is not possible, then many perfectly acceptable acquisitions will not occur, giving rise to economic loss and stagnation. Recognising these difficulties, the Companies Act 1981 introduced a 'whitewash' procedure for private companies which enabled such companies to give financial assistance provided certain conditions were met (CA 1985,

---

[279] See Report of the Company Law Committee (the Jenkins Committee) (Cmnd 1749, 1962), para 176; see *Re VGM Holdings Ltd* [1942] 1 All ER 224 at 225.

[280] [2003] 1 BCLC 675 at [31]; for criticism of the view that this mischief requires rules on financial assistance, see Ferran (2004) 63 CLJ 225. [281] [2004] 1 BCLC 64.

[282] For a comprehensive account of the 1985 provisions, see Roberts, *Financial Assistance for the Acquisition of Shares* (2005).

ss 155–158). The whitewash procedure was complicated and costly to execute in that it required a special resolution by the shareholders, a directors' statement (essentially as to the solvency of the company at the time of giving the assistance and for a year thereafter) backed up by an auditor's statement and objecting shareholders could apply to the court to block the assistance. Crucially, the financial assistance could only be given if the company had net assets which were not thereby reduced or, to the extent that they were reduced, the assistance was provided out of distributable profits (CA 1985, s 155(2)).

**2-135**  On a variety of occasions in the early 1990s, the Department of Trade and Industry consulted as to possible reform of the statutory provisions without any progress being made. In due course, the Company Law Review considered the issue and was highly critical of the statutory provisions (CA 1985, ss 151–158).[283] The Review recommended that the provisions on financial assistance should not apply to private companies (so dispensing with the need for the whitewash procedure) and that such abuses as prompted the legislation (asset stripping essentially) should be addressed through directors' duties and the insolvency legislation.[284] Public companies would remain subject to the prohibitions in the light of the Second Company Law Directive, now Directive 2017/1132.[285] These recommendations were adopted in the CA 2006, ss 677–683.

**2-136**  Repealing the prohibition on financial assistance by private companies was one of the main deregulatory measures of the CA 2006. That said, the remaining provisions are complex and wide-ranging and do apply to some extent to private companies (where they are part of a group with public companies) so the position still needs careful consideration. It must also be appreciated that, while the prohibition on the giving of financial assistance by private companies has been repealed, the broader protective rules discussed in this chapter, on distributions and reduction of capital, still apply as does the common law principle (*Trevor v Whitworth*[286]) prohibiting a return of capital to shareholders.[287] Any transaction which involves giving financial assistance needs to be looked at carefully to ensure it does not fall foul of those other rules or principles, for example where it gives rise to a reduction in net assets which cannot be covered by distributable reserves. The possibility that a transaction might be challenged subsequently as a transaction at an undervalue under IA 1986, s 238 also needs to be borne in mind. Directors' fiduciary duties also come into play when the company is giving financial assistance and the

---

[283]  Company Law Review, *Final Report*, vol I (2001), para 2.30: 'These provisions are among the most difficult of the Act, and in many cases it is all but impossible for a company to assess whether a proposed course of action is lawful or not. The provisions are arbitrary in their effect on private companies, and innocuous transactions may be rendered unlawful by criminal law requirements that are often unenforceable and by civil sanctions of wide and damaging effect.'

[284]  See Company Law Review, *Final Report*, vol I (2001), para 10.6; *Completing the Structure* (2000), paras 7.12–7.15; *Company Formation and Capital Maintenance* (1999), paras 3.41–3.48 and Annex B; *Strategic Framework* (1999), paras 5.4.20–5.4.25.

[285]  See n 317.      [286]  (1887) 12 App Cas 409, HL.

[287]  In an attempt to allay concerns as to the extent to which the common law may still be relevant, an obscurely worded saving provision was included in The Companies Act 2006 (Commencement No 5, Transitional Provisions and Savings) Order 2007, SI 2007/3495, art 9, Sch 4, para 52. The intention, apparently, is to ensure that private companies which are now released from the statutory prohibitions on financial assistance should not be subject to any residual common law restriction on financial assistance. The difficulty is that the common law restriction is a broader prohibition on a return of capital so the saving may prove pointless if it was intended to close off challenges on the basis of an improper return of capital. It does close off challenges on the grounds of improper financial assistance, but as the Department of Trade pointed out, that was the consequence of the repeal of the prohibition so far as it applied to private companies in any event. See the Explanatory Memorandum to the Fifth Commencement Order, para 7.

directors need to consider carefully whether they are exercising their powers for a proper purpose (CA 2006, s 171) and to promote the success of the company (s 172). The duty of care and skill is also relevant (s 174) and possibly even the duty to avoid a conflict of interest (under s 175 or even s 177). Removing the prohibition does not therefore open up the way for freewheeling financial assistance of the type which perhaps some of the proponents of abolition envisaged.

**22-137**    The position with respect to public companies was unchanged by the CA 2006 because of the requirements of the Second Company Law Directive, now Directive 2017/1132, which have been modified from an outright prohibition to a position whereby Member States may permit public companies to grant financial assistance up to the limit of the company's distributable reserves.[288] The relaxation is surrounded by onerous procedural requirements, however, including prior shareholder approval based on a detailed report to be presented to the general meeting and the creation of an undistributable reserve equal to the amount of the financial assistance. The UK decided not to implement this option so the prohibition of financial assistance by public companies remains. Public companies can take comfort, however, from evidence of a more pragmatic approach by the courts to financial assistance issues in recent years which respects genuine commercial transactions and seeks to constrain the prohibition to the mischief identified by Parliament, namely the risk to creditors of asset depletion from financial assistance.[289] The courts have emphasised the importance of looking at the overall commercial realities of a situation instead of a narrow focus on whether technically a transaction may be classified as financial assistance, see **22-146**. Further, the courts are minded to limit the scope of the resulting illegality. In *Anglo Petroleum Ltd v TFB (Mortgages) Ltd*,[290] for example, the Court of Appeal noted obiter that, even if it had found illegal financial assistance in respect of the use of funds borrowed by a company, the loan agreement and associated charges and guarantees would not have been illegal. Those agreements did not necessitate any breach of the law, Toulson LJ said, and no reason of public policy required those perfectly ordinary commercial transactions to be struck down.[291] All of these elements show a concern to keep the prohibition within appropriate boundaries.

## The prohibition on financial assistance

**22-138**    There are three prohibitions in all. First, where a person is acquiring or is proposing to acquire any shares in a public company, it is not lawful for the company or a company that is a subsidiary of that company[292] to give financial assistance directly or indirectly for the purpose of that acquisition before or at the same time as the acquisition takes place

---

[288] OJ L 169/46, 30.6.2017, art 64. See criticism by Ferran 'Simplification of European Company Law on Financial Assistance' (2005) 6 EBOR 93.

[289] For example, the courts have been alert to attempts by parties to evade their commercial obligations on the basis of spurious claims of illegal financial assistance, see *Dyment v Boyden* [2005] 1 BCLC 163, CA (tenant tried to have an onerous lease declared void for illegal financial assistance when the reality was that she had made a bad bargain and was paying an extortionate rent, see **22-150**); *Anglo Petroleum Ltd v TFB (Mortgages) Ltd* [2008] 1 BCLC 185, CA (borrower essentially tried to renege on a £15m loan and related guarantee by alleging illegal financial assistance when the reality was that its financial position had worsened and it was finding it difficult to make repayments, see **22-148**).

[290] [2008] 1 BCLC 185, CA.        [291] [2008] 1 BCLC 185 at [83]–[85], CA.

[292] The prohibition applies only to subsidiaries registered in this jurisdiction and a foreign subsidiary of an English parent company can give financial assistance for the acquisition of the latter's shares: *Arab Bank plc v Mercantile Holdings Ltd* [1994] 1 BCLC 330, but see also at 335; *AMG Global Nominees (Private) Ltd v SMM Holdings Ltd* [2008] 1 BCLC 447.

(CA 2006, s 678(1)). The first scenario then is the acquisition of shares in a public company where the financial assistance is given by that (public) company or by a subsidiary company (which may be a private or public company).

**2-139**  Secondly, where a person has acquired shares in a company and a liability has been incurred (by that or any other person) for the purpose of the acquisition, it is not lawful for that company or a company that is a subsidiary of that company[293] to give financial assistance directly or indirectly for the purpose of reducing or discharging the liability[294] if, at the time the assistance is given, the company in which the shares were acquired is a public company (CA 2006, s 678(3)). The second scenario covers the situation where shares have been acquired (whether in a public or private company) provided that at the time the assistance is given (again whether by a public or private company) to reduce or discharge the liability incurred on that purchase, the company in which the shares are acquired is a public company.

**2-140**  Finally, where a person is acquiring or is proposing to acquire shares in a private company, it is not lawful for a public company that is a subsidiary of that company[295] to give financial assistance directly or indirectly for the purpose of that acquisition before or at the same time as the acquisition takes place (CA 2006, s 679(1)) or to give financial assistance directly or indirectly for the purpose of reducing or discharging a liability incurred for the purpose of the acquisition (s 679(3)).[296]

**2-141**  There is no requirement that the assistance be given to the vendor or the purchaser of the shares; it may be given to a subsidiary or associated company or other person nominated by one of the parties, but it will still fall within the prohibitions, provided it is for the purpose of the acquisition.[297]

**2-142**  A breach of these provisions is a criminal offence and the company is liable to a fine and every officer in default is liable to imprisonment or a fine or both (CA 2006, s 680). The civil consequences are not dealt with in the statute and remain a matter for the common law, see **22-159**.

**2-143**  To establish liability, it is necessary to show that financial assistance was given and that it was given for the purpose of the acquisition or the reduction/discharge of a liability, as the case may be.[298]

### The meaning of financial assistance

**2-144**  The legislation is broadly drafted to catch a wide variety of types of financial assistance, for example, financial assistance given by way of gift, guarantee, security or indemnity, release or waiver, or a loan, etc, all of which are listed in CA 2006, s 677(1). The requirement is that the transaction be of the type mentioned (and the terms used, indemnity etc,

---

[293]  See n 292.
[294]  A reference to a company giving financial assistance for the purpose of reducing or discharging a liability incurred by a person for the purpose of the acquisition of shares includes its giving such assistance for the purpose of wholly or partially restoring his financial position to what it was before the acquisition took place: CA 2006, s 683(2)(b).
[295]  See n 292.       [296]  See n 294.
[297]  *Chaston v SWP Group plc* [2003] 1 BCLC 675 at [40], CA. But see criticisms by Ferran, n 280, 237 who argues that there is no need to extend the prohibition beyond assistance of benefit to purchasers, since that is the mischief at which the prohibition is aimed; also Look Chan Ho, 'Financial Assistance after Chaston and MT Realisations' [2003] JIBLR 424.
[298]  *Charterhouse Investment Trust Ltd v Tempest Diesels Ltd* [1986] BCLC 1 at 10, per Hoffmann J.

must be given their normal legal meaning) and also amount to financial assistance.[299] As Arden LJ pointed out in *Chaston v SWP Group plc*,[300] there is no requirement of detriment with regard to these elements, for example, financial assistance via a loan could be on terms which are beneficial to the company.[301] Detriment is only required under CA 2006, s 677(1)(d) which includes 'any other financial assistance given by a company where the net assets[302] of the company are reduced to a material extent[303] by the giving of the assistance, or the company has no net assets'. As Ward LJ noted in *Chaston v SWP Group plc*,[304] these words are 'as wide as can be' and so have the potential to catch the unwary as a transaction which does not appear to be financial assistance in any of the more obvious ways (loans, guarantees etc) may fall foul of this element. On the other hand, CA 2006, s 677(1)(d) is necessary precisely to catch transactions which do not fall into the more obvious categories of financial assistance listed in the section, such as where a company purchases an asset at an overvalue for the purpose of putting the vendor of the asset in funds with which to acquire the company's shares.[305]

**22-145**   Drawing lines can be difficult, however, as noted earlier. For example, the payment of a debt owed by the company cannot be financial assistance for that is a mere discharge of a debt.[306] Likewise the grant of security in respect of a debt cannot amount to financial assistance,[307] but the payment off of a parent company's debt by a subsidiary in order to facilitate an acquisition of the parent company's shares may constitute such assistance.[308] In *Chaston v SWP Group plc*[309] a subsidiary company agreed to pay certain adviser fees with respect to a report on the affairs of its parent company which report was carried out for the purpose of a proposed acquisition of the parent company's shares by another party and that was held by the Court of Appeal to be financial assistance for the purpose of the acquisition of the parent company shares.

**22-146**   The potential scope of the prohibition is wide, but the courts, starting with Hoffmann J in *Charterhouse Investment Trust Ltd v Tempest Diesels Ltd*,[310] have emphasised that, when deciding whether a transaction can properly be described as the giving of financial assistance by the company, the commercial realities of the transaction as a whole must be considered, bearing in mind, as Hoffmann J said, that the section is a penal provision and should not be strained to cover transactions which are not fairly within it.

---

[299]  *Barclays Bank plc v British & Commonwealth Holdings plc* [1996] 1 BCLC 1 at 38, CA.

[300]  [2003] 1 BCLC 675 at [41].

[301]  See Ferran, n 280, 231 who agrees with Arden LJ as a matter of statutory interpretation, but see Look Chan Ho, n 297, who is more critical of this interpretation.

[302]  'Net assets' is defined as the aggregate of the company's assets less the aggregate of its liabilities (CA 2006, s 677(2)), meaning the actual rather than the book value of the assets and liabilities and in this case the liabilities must include provision as required by s 677(3): see *Re Uniq plc* [2012] 1 BCLC 783 at [33], per David Richards J.

[303]  There is no definition of material extent, but in practice a reduction of 1 per cent would be considered material.                                                                       [304]  [2003] 1 BCLC 675 at [58].

[305]  See *Belmont Finance Corpn Ltd v Williams Furniture Ltd* [1980] 1 All ER 393, CA. See *Re Uniq plc* [2012] 1 BCLC 783 at [39] where the court accepted that a payment made by the company to a purchaser of shares in the company in return for the purchaser taking on certain pension responsibilities of the company could not be financial assistance within s 677(1)(d) when the payment made (£79.9m) resulted in the company's release from liabilities for which a provision of £231m was shown in the company's accounts. See Leivesley [2011] JBL 725 on this case.

[306]  *Armour Hick Northern Ltd v Armour Trust Ltd* [1980] 3 All ER 833; and see *Re Uniq plc* [2012] 1 BCLC 783 at [39].                                        [307]  *Anglo Petroleum Ltd v TFB (Mortgages) Ltd* [2008] 1 BCLC 185, CA.

[308]  *Armour Hick Northern Ltd v Armour Trust Ltd* [1980] 3 All ER 833.

[309]  [2003] 1 BCLC 675, CA.          [310]  [1986] BCLC 1 at 10.

That view was endorsed most notably by the Court of Appeal in *Anglo Petroleum Ltd v TFB (Mortgages)*[311] where Toulson LJ crisply summed up the correct approach as follows: 'In cases where its application [the prohibition on financial assistance] is doubtful, it is important to remember its central purpose, to examine the commercial realities and to bear in mind that it is a penal statute.'[312]

**2-147**   In *MT Realisations Ltd v Digital Equipment Co Ltd*,[313] a subsidiary company paid certain sums due under a secured loan to it from its parent company and those sums were used to pay off the liability incurred by the parent company in acquiring the shares in the subsidiary. In fact, for convenience, the sums were paid directly by the subsidiary to the vendor of the shares so it appeared that the subsidiary's funds were being used to pay liabilities arising on the acquisition of shares in the subsidiary. An allegation arose that this was illegal financial assistance. The Court of Appeal found that the commercial reality of this transaction was that (1) the subsidiary was not giving the parent company anything, (2) the parent company was exercising its entitlement as a secured creditor to require certain sums to be paid to it, and (3) as a matter of commercial convenience those sums were paid direct to the vendor rather than from the subsidiary to the parent to the vendor. As a matter of commercial reality and legal principle, the Court of Appeal held, such an agreement did not involve the subsidiary in giving financial assistance for the acquisition of its own shares.

**2-148**   A similarly robust approach is evident in *Anglo Petroleum Ltd v TFB (Mortgages) Ltd*.[314] In this case a company in financial difficulties (it owed £30m, unsecured, to its parent company) negotiated a reduction in that debt to £15m and gave a charge over its assets to secure the repayment of the £15m. At the same time, the parent company sold its entire shareholding in the company to K for £1 and K guaranteed to ensure that the company would repay the outstanding indebtedness. The court rejected a claim that the charge given to secure the repayment of the £15m was financial assistance for the acquisition of the shares by K. The court noted that it is well established that the repayment of a debt which is properly due from a company does not constitute financial assistance. If it is lawful for a company to repay its own indebtedness, the court held, it must also equally be lawful for the company to assist that repayment by providing security. In this case, the commercial reality was a restructuring of debt with a significant reduction in amount achieved in return for security.

**2-149**   K subsequently borrowed £15m from TFB to pay off the outstanding £15m to the original parent company and that TFB borrowing was secured on the company's assets. It was then alleged that this TFB borrowing and charge too was financial assistance since it was done to reduce or discharge a liability incurred in the acquisition by K of the shares. The Court of Appeal did not accept that this could be financial assistance. The issue is not where the money comes from,[315] but the use the company makes of it. The TFB loan and related security was ordinary commercial lending even where, as here, the bank knows the purpose is to repay the original parent company. A bank cannot be expected to investigate whether that repayment might infringe rules of financial assistance. As already noted, the Court of Appeal did not believe that public policy required those perfectly

---

[311] [2008] 1 BCLC 185 at [26]; see also *MT Realisations Ltd v Digital Equipment Co Ltd* [2003] 2 BCLC 117, CA; and *Chaston v SWP Group plc* [2003] 1 BCLC 675, CA.

[312] For criticism of the courts for not adopting a sufficiently commercial approach to the prohibition, see Mercouris, 'The Prohibition on Financial Assistance: The Case for a Commercially Pragmatic Interpretation' (2014) 35(11) Co Law 321.

[313] [2003] 2 BCLC 117.      [314] [2008] 1 BCLC 185, CA.      [315] [2008] 1 BCLC 185 at [50].

ordinary commercial transactions to be struck down,[316] a pragmatic position which gives considerable comfort to parties. This approach is also consistent with the principle that, where an agreement is capable of being performed in alternative ways, one lawful and one in breach of the provisions on financial assistance, it is to be presumed that the parties intend to carry out the agreement in a lawful and not an unlawful manner.[317] A bank is entitled to expect a company to use borrowed funds in a legal and not illegal manner.

### The purpose of the transaction

**22-150**  In addition to the assistance being financial assistance, the assistance must be given for the purpose of the acquisition or to reduce or discharge a liability incurred for the purpose of the acquisition.[318] In *Dyment v Boyden*[319] three individuals had been involved in running a nursing home together. As part of a deal to separate their various interests, A acquired all of the shares of B and C. This acquisition gave A total control of the company which ran the nursing home, but the freehold of the property from which the business was operated was controlled by B and C. They granted the company a lease of the premises at a very high rental. In subsequent proceedings, A tried to argue that the rental payments were linked to her acquisition of B and C's shares in the company and as such amounted to financial assistance given directly or indirectly for the purpose of that acquisition. The Court of Appeal found that the reason why the company entered into the lease was because the company needed the premises from which to conduct its business. The entry into the lease, the court said, could not be linked to A's acquisition of the shares.

**22-151**  In *Chaston v SWP Group plc*,[320] as noted at **22-145**, a subsidiary company paid fees with respect to a report drawn up about its parent company. The purpose of the arrangement was to facilitate the negotiations by a possible purchaser and to enable it to determine whether it wished to acquire the shares. As such, the court held, it was financial assistance given for the purpose of the acquisition of the shares.

**22-152**  Even if the assistance is given for the purpose of the acquisition etc, the prohibition does not apply if the company's principal purpose in giving that assistance is not to give it for the purpose of any such acquisition, or the giving of the assistance for that purpose is but an incidental part of some larger purpose of the company, and the assistance is given in good faith in the interests of the company (CA 2006, s 678(2)). A similar exemption applies where the financial assistance is for the purpose of reducing or discharging a liability incurred in the acquisition of shares (CA 2006, s 678(2)). The scope of this 'principal purpose' etc exception was construed in an unhelpfully narrow way, however, by the House of Lords in *Brady v Brady*.[321] In this case, assistance was given by a company to reduce or discharge a liability incurred for the acquisition of shares in the company in

---

[316] [2008] 1 BCLC 185 at [83]–[85], CA. To the extent that *Re Hill & Tyler Ltd* [2005] 1 BCLC 41 supports striking down a loan and security in these circumstances, it must be considered now to be of doubtful authority.

[317] *Neilson v Stewart* [1991] BCC 713. See also *Brady v Brady* [1988] 2 All ER 617, HL; *Parlett v Guppys (Bridport) Ltd* [1996] 2 BCLC 34.

[318] See *Charterhouse Investment Trust Ltd v Tempest Diesels Ltd* [1986] BCLC 1 at 10, per Hoffmann J.

[319] [2005] 1 BCLC 163.

[320] [2003] 1 BCLC 675. See also *Corporate Development Partners LLC v E-Relationship Marketing Ltd* [2009] BCC 295. See Mercouris, n 312, who is scathing about the judgment in *Chaston*, at 327–9, as being a literal interpretation of the statute without regard to the commercial realities.

[321] [1988] 2 All ER 617, HL. See also *Plaut v Steiner* (1988) 5 BCC 352.

*prima facie* breach of the statutory prohibition. The transaction arose as part of an elaborate scheme for the division of a family business between two brothers. It was argued that this division of the business was the larger purpose, as required by the statute, and the financial assistance was only incidental to it.

**2-153** The House of Lords adopted a restrictive interpretation of the provision, distinguishing between a *purpose* and the *reason* why a purpose is formed. The fact that a company in giving financial assistance has some more important reason for the transaction than the giving of financial assistance, Lord Oliver said, is not the same thing as the company having a 'larger purpose' as envisaged by this provision.[322] The *purpose* of the transaction in *Brady* was to assist in the financing of the acquisition of the shares although the *reason* for the transaction was to facilitate a break-up of the business.[323] The financial assistance in *Brady* was not incidental to a larger purpose, therefore, and was provided in breach of the statute.

**2-154** The approach adopted by the House of Lords in *Brady* was driven by a concern that companies always have a variety of motivations and reasons for transactions and, if financial assistance can be justified as being part of wider corporate schemes, the section could be effectively nullified. The effect of this interpretation has been to limit the scope for applying this exception, but an example can be found in *Re Uniq plc*.[324] In this case, the court was asked to sanction a scheme of arrangement, but an issue arose as to whether the court could sanction it when an element of the scheme appeared to infringe the financial assistance provisions. Essentially, the company, the subject of the scheme, was to pay a significant sum of money, directly or indirectly, to fund Newco which in turn was to acquire shares in the company, hence the immediate appearance of financial assistance. As part of the scheme, the receipt of the moneys by Newco would result in the release of the company from extensive pension liabilities which would instead be assumed by Newco. David Richards J found that the principal purpose of the payments to Newco was to obtain this release which was overwhelmingly in the interests of the company and the payments were made in good faith, hence the case did fall within the exception in s 678(2).

## Exceptions to the prohibition on financial assistance

**2-155** There are two categories of excepted transactions: (1) unconditional exceptions, and (2) conditional exceptions.

### Unconditional exceptions

**2-156** The prohibitions on the giving of financial assistance do not apply (CA 2006, s 681) to:

(1) a distribution of a company's assets by way of dividend lawfully made or a distribution in the course of the company's winding up;

(2) the allotment of bonus shares;

(3) a reduction of capital duly made in accordance with the statutory schemes;

(4) a redemption or purchase of shares made in accordance with the statutory provisions;

---

[322] [1988] 2 All ER 617 at 633, HL.     [323] [1988] 2 All ER 617 at 633, HL.
[324] [2012] 1 BCLC 783; and n 325.

(5) anything done in pursuance of an order of the court under CA 2006, Pt 26 dealing with compromises and arrangements with creditors and members;[325]

(6) anything done under an arrangement made in pursuance of the statutory provisions enabling liquidators in winding up to accept shares as consideration for the sale of property; or

(7) anything done under an arrangement made between a company and its creditors which is binding on the creditors by virtue of the statutory provisions relating to such arrangements when made by a company about to be or in the course of being wound up.

**22-157** As noted, the prohibition of financial assistance is essentially based on the need to protect creditors from the improper depletion of the company's assets.[326] All of the transactions and schemes mentioned in **22-156** are subject to statutory requirements designed to ensure the protection of creditors and prevent the misuse of assets and in a number of cases the schemes require the confirmation of the court. There is no need therefore to subject such transactions to the prohibition on financial assistance.

### Conditional exceptions

**22-158** This category provides exemptions for those companies where the lending of money is part of the ordinary business of the company[327] and exemptions designed to facilitate employees' share schemes.[328] A public company may rely on the exemptions in this category only if the company has net assets that are not thereby reduced by the giving of the assistance, or to the extent that those assets are so reduced, the financial assistance is provided out of distributable profits.[329]

## Consequences of breach of the financial assistance provisions

**22-159** Contravention of the provisions on financial assistance is a criminal offence (CA 2006, s 680) but the statute does not deal with the civil consequences which remain a matter for the common law.

### The status of any agreement

**22-160** An agreement to provide unlawful financial assistance is unenforceable by either party to it.[330] In *Heald v O'Connor*,[331] for example, where the financial assistance consisted of security given by the company for money lent to enable a person to purchase shares in

---

[325] See *Re Uniq plc* [2012] 1 BCLC 783 where David Richards J noted that this power to sanction financial assistance as part of a scheme is not qualified by reference to any particular criteria, at [45], and, on the facts, he would approve the granting of certain indemnities and the payment of costs which would otherwise amount to financial assistance, being granted as they were by a company with respect to the acquisition of the company's shares by a third party as part of the scheme. He noted the restructuring would benefit both the creditors and members of the company and it was appropriate therefore to approve the indemnities etc which were necessary for the restructuring, at [46]. See also n 305. See Mercouris, n 312, who enthusiastically endorses the approach taken by David Richards J in *Re Uniq plc* as commercially sensible and very helpful to 'non-detrimental corporate transactions', at 329–30.

[326] *Wallersteiner v Moir* [1974] 3 All ER 217 at 239, per Denning LJ.

[327] CA 2006, s 682(2)(a); see *Steen v Law* [1963] 3 All ER 770.

[328] CA 2006, s 682(b), (c), (d). For the definition of 'employees' share scheme', see s 1166.

[329] CA 2006, s 682(1)(b), (3)–(4).

[330] *Brady v Brady* [1988] 2 All ER 617, HL; *Plaut v Steiner* (1989) 5 BCC 352.

[331] [1971] 2 All ER 1105.

the company, the court held that that security was unenforceable.[332] The court noted that such a result best furthers the policy of the legislation in that it deters potential lenders from lending money on security which might be held to contravene the statute.

**22-161**   If the illegal element of the transaction can be severed from the agreement, the court will do so.[333] In *Carney v Herbert*[334] the Privy Council took the view that the nature of the illegality in cases of financial assistance is not such as to preclude severance on the grounds of public policy and severance can take place provided that the financial assistance is ancillary to the overall transaction and its elimination would leave unchanged the subject matter of the transaction.[335] In this case, the illegal financial assistance (in the form of mortgages) was severed from an agreement for the sale of shares which could then be enforced between the parties in the ordinary way.

**22-162**   Returning to *Anglo Petroleum Ltd v TFB (Mortgages) Ltd*,[336] see **22-148**, the Court of Appeal said, obiter, that, even if it had found illegal financial assistance in respect of the use of funds borrowed by the company from a third party, the loan agreement and associated charges and guarantees would not have been illegal. Those agreements did not necessitate any breach of the law, Toulson LJ said, and no reason of public policy required those perfectly ordinary commercial transactions to be struck down.[337] This is an important approach which narrows the range of transactions which can be struck down as illegal. The loan and the security are treated as ordinary commercial lending. The use which the company makes of the funds it borrows may amount to financial assistance, but that is a separate matter.

## Breach of fiduciary duty

**22-163**   A director who authorises the giving of financial assistance in breach of the statutory provisions is in breach of his duties to the company.[338] As a trustee of the company's assets, the misapplication by a director of those assets is a breach of trust and the director is obliged to account for the full amount of the improper financial assistance.[339] A shareholder may seek an injunction to restrain the giving of financial assistance in breach of the statutory provisions or he may seek permission to bring a derivative action on behalf of the company to recover the sums expended.[340]

**22-164**   The involvement of third parties such as bankers is often crucial to the carrying out of an illegal financial assistance scheme and they may be liable either on the basis of 'dishonest assistance' in the breach of fiduciary duty by the directors or for 'knowing receipt' of company funds, see Chapter 14.

---

[332] *Victor Battery Co Ltd v Curry's Ltd* [1946] Ch 242 to the contrary effect is generally accepted to be wrongly decided: see *Selangor United Rubber Estates Ltd v Cradock (No 3)* [1968] 2 All ER 1073.

[333] *Herbert Spink (Bournemouth) Ltd v Spink* [1936] 1 All ER 597; *South Western Mineral Water Co Ltd v Ashmore* [1967] 2 All ER 953; *Carney v Herbert* [1985] 1 All ER 438, PC; *Neilson v Stewart* [1991] BCC 713, HL.

[334] [1985] 1 All ER 438, PC.

[335] [1985] 1 All ER 438 at 446, PC.

[336] [2008] 1 BCLC 185, CA. See also *Patel v Mirza* [2016] UKSC 42, [2017] 1 All ER 191.

[337] [2008] 1 BCLC 185 at [83]–[85], CA.

[338] See, for example, *Re In a Flap Envelope Co Ltd* [2004] 1 BCLC 64.

[339] See discussion in Chapter 14 on the liability of directors for breach of trust and see *JJ Harrison (Properties) Ltd v Harrison* [2002] 1 BCLC 162; *Rolled Steel Products (Holdings) Ltd v British Steel Corpn* [1985] 3 All ER 52; *Re Lands Allotment Co* [1894] 1 Ch 616.

[340] See *Smith v Croft* [1987] 3 All ER 909; the derivative action is discussed in detail in Chapter 20.

# 23

# Loan capital–secured creditors and company charges

## A Introduction to company charges

**23-1**   The majority of companies on the register of companies are private companies with very limited amounts of share capital.[1] It follows that if those companies are carrying on business to any significant level, it must be on the basis of other forms of funding and there are many other methods of financing to which companies may resort.[2] For example, they may obtain goods under hire-purchase agreements[3] or conditional sale agreements.[4] They may use invoice factoring[5] and discounting[6] to realise sums due to them by users of their goods or services. For many companies, though, the starting point is usually loan capital, typically in the form of straightforward commercial borrowing from high street banks and financial institutions.

**23-2**   Of course, when lending to a limited liability company, the lender is conscious of the need for security to cover the amount lent, knowing he cannot have recourse to the members to meet any deficiency on insolvency. On occasion, a lender may obtain personal guarantees from the directors, but personal guarantees are a poor substitute for security over tangible assets as the guarantor may not be good for the money when the lender needs to enforce the personal guarantee. The lender/creditor prefers therefore to look to security to protect its position in the event of the insolvency of the company. By security is meant that, in addition to the ability to sue the company for the discharge of the debt, the creditor is able to look to some property in which the company has an interest in order to

---

[1]   Companies House no longer publishes a breakdown of the register by issued share capital, but when it did, typically, 80 per cent of companies would have an issued share capital of up to £100, see, for example, Companies House, *Statistical Tables on Companies Register Activities 2013–14*, Table A6.

[2]   See Law Commission, *Registration of Security Interests: Company Charges and Property other than Land* (Consultation Paper No 164), 2002, Ch 6 where there is a useful account of the other forms of financing which companies use and which the Commission describes as involving a type of quasi-security.

[3]   A hire-purchase agreement is an agreement for the hire of goods under which the hirer is given the option to purchase the goods at a certain point when a certain number of payments have been made.

[4]   A conditional sale agreement is an agreement for the sale of goods under which the property in the goods remains with the seller until payment of the price is completed.

[5]   Factoring involves a factor taking over responsibility for collection of the debts due by customers to a company. The factor pays between 80–90 per cent of the value of those invoices up front to the company, so assisting its cash flow, and pays the balance when the customer pays, in return for a discount charge, typically 3 per cent of the money borrowed, and a fee set as a percentage (usually at least 0.5 per cent) of turnover. Many of the high street banks operate specialist subsidiaries offering factoring services.

[6]   Invoice discounting is very similar to factoring except that the discounter does not take over collection of the company's debts, but provides funds up front (again between 80–90 per cent of the amount) for the company in respect of approved invoices in return for a fee set either as a flat monthly fee or as a percentage of turnover. Many of the high street banks operate specialist subsidiaries providing this service.

enforce the discharge of the company's obligation to the creditor. At the same time as the lender seeks security, the company wants to be able to borrow without having to give such security to the lender that its ability to trade is affected by the constraints imposed by the security.[7] The company therefore wants freedom to trade, the lender wants security for its lending, and the law needs to facilitate both the company and the lender.

## Taking security

**23-3**  Central to the question of security is the issue of priority on insolvency. Obviously, if the company never becomes insolvent, no problem arises and the precise nature of the security obtained never becomes important. It is because the company may become insolvent that security must be sought and the type of security which is sought is dictated by the order of distribution of assets on insolvency. A creditor does not want a form of security which leaves the creditor in the queue behind several other creditors on insolvency. Therefore a creditor requires not just security but a form of security which gives sufficient prior claim to the assets on insolvency so that the creditor has some prospect of recovering the debt.

**23-4**  For our purposes, a broad overview of the order of distribution on winding up will suffice. On liquidation, essentially the assets of the company fall into two categories, those secured to creditors, and the free assets. Those free assets form a common fund which, subject to the expenses of winding up and the rights of a limited class of preferential creditor, are held on a statutory trust for the benefit of the unsecured creditors.[8] The secured creditors who, as we shall see, generally have fixed and floating charges over the company's assets, have rights *in rem* and they look to the secured assets for payment of their debts. They do not need to look to the common fund for repayment of their claims. The precise degree of priority depends on the nature of the security obtained, however, and legislation has established a statutory priority for the payment of the expenses of winding up (and of administration) and the preferential debts which has the effect, as we shall see, of eroding the quality of floating charges held by creditors where the free assets of the company are insufficient to meet these prior claims, as they often are.[9] The two categories of assets overlap in that a deficiency in the 'free' assets must be met by the realisations held by the floating chargeholder to the extent dictated by Parliament. The fixed chargeholder is unaffected by this statutory interference.

**23-5**  The standard devices used by a lender to obtain security are legal mortgages, fixed charges, and floating charges. A mortgage needs no detailed description; it involves the transfer of legal ownership to the lender subject to the mortgagee's equity of redemption. In practice, since the Law of Property Act 1925, the form of legal mortgage of an estate in fee simple has been by a charge by deed expressed to be by way of legal mortgage. For various reasons, the charge by deed has become the standard form of mortgage so that the terms

---

[7] As Nourse LJ noted in *Re New Bullas Trading Ltd* [1994] 1 BCLC 485 at 487: 'He who lends money to a trading company neither wishes nor expects it to become insolvent ... But against an evil day he wants the best security the company can give him consistently with its ability to trade meanwhile.'

[8] See *Ayerst (Inspector of Taxes) v C & K (Construction) Ltd* [1975] 2 All ER 537; *Webb v Whiffin* (1872) LR 5 HL 711 at 721, 724.

[9] As Armour notes, one consequence of carving out a preference for certain claimants on insolvency is that the history of the floating charge (which is subject to these prior claims) is largely the story of the litigation ensuing from attempts by floating chargeholders to draft (at considerable cost) their charges in a way that defeats that statutory priority: see Armour, 'Should We Redistribute in Insolvency?' in Getzler and Payne, *Company Charges: Spectrum and Beyond* (2005).

'mortgage' and 'charge' have become interchangeable.[10] With that statutory exception of a legal charge, all charges, whether fixed or floating, are equitable.

**23-6**     Usually it is clear that the parties have created a charge (though whether it is a fixed or a floating charge may be more problematic) but, in cases of doubt, it is a matter of construction whether the transaction gives rise to a charge. For example, if a contract gives a contracting party the right (on default by the other party) to sell machinery belonging to the other contracting party and to apply the proceeds of sale in discharge of the debts of the other party due under the contract, this provision creates a security interest, a charge, allowing one party to look to a particular asset or class of assets for the discharge of a debt.[11] The essence of an equitable charge, as Millett J explained, is that:[12]

> 'without any conveyance or assignment to the chargee, specific property of the chargor is expressly or constructively appropriated to or made answerable for the payment of a debt, and the chargee is given the right to resort to the property for the purpose of having it realised and applied in or towards payment of the debt.'

**23-7**     On the other hand, a contractual provision which merely allows one contracting party to use a machine belonging to that other party in order to complete works required by the contract does not confer any security interest and is not a charge at all.[13]

**23-8**     As to whether the charge created is a fixed or floating charge, the distinction between them was explained by Lord Macnaghten in *Illingworth v Houldsworth*[14] as follows:

> 'A specific charge ... is one that without more fastens on ascertained and definite property or property capable of being ascertained or defined. A floating charge, on the other hand, is ambulatory and shifting in its nature, hovering over and so to speak floating with the property which it is intended to affect until some event occurs or some act is done which causes it to settle and fasten on the subject of the charge within its reach and grasp.'

**23-9**     A fixed (or specific) charge is typically taken over identified assets not commonly used or dealt with in the day-to-day business of the company. A fixed charge gives the holder of the charge an immediate proprietary interest in the assets subject to the charge which means that a fixed charge is inappropriate for assets which the company needs to deal with in the ordinary course of business.[15]

**23-10**     A floating charge is an equitable invention, first recognised by the Court of Appeal in *Re Panama, New Zealand & Australian Royal Mail Co.*[16] The classic description of the characteristics of a floating charge is that of Romer LJ in *Re Yorkshire Woolcombers Association*,[17] where he stated that a floating charge is:

---

[10] CA 2006, s 859A(7) defines 'charge' for the purpose of Part 25 (Company Charges) as including 'a mortgage'.

[11] See *Re Cosslett (Contractors) Ltd* [1999] 1 BCLC 205 at 216, CA; and sub nom *Smith (Administrator of Cosslett (Contractors) Ltd) v Bridgend County Borough Council* [2002] 1 BCLC 77 at [41], [53], HL.

[12] *Re Charge Card Services Ltd* [1987] BCLC 17 at 40, per Millett J; see also *Re Cosslett (Contractors) Ltd* [1999] 1 BCLC 205 at 215.

[13] See *Re Cosslett (Contractors) Ltd* [1999] 1 BCLC 205 at 215.

[14] [1904] AC 355 at 358.

[15] See *Agnew v IRC (Re Brumark)* [2001] 2 BCLC 188 at [7], PC, per Lord Millett.

[16] (1878) LR 5 Ch App 318; and see *Re Florence Land & Public Works Co, ex p Moor* (1878) 10 Ch D 530. See generally the valuable collection of essays in Getzler and Payne, *Company Charges, Spectrum and Beyond* (2005) (hereinafter Getzler and Payne), also Gough, *Company Charges* (2nd edn, 1996).

[17] [1903] 2 Ch 284 at 295, although Romer LJ did not say that all three elements must be present in order for the charge to be a floating charge.

(1) a charge on a class of assets of a company, present and future;

(2) that class is one which, in the ordinary course of the business of the company, would be changing from time to time; and

(3) by the charge it is contemplated that, until some future step is taken by or on behalf of those interested in the charge, the company may carry on its business in the ordinary way.

**23-11**  A floating charge is typically taken over the entire undertaking of the company,[18] meaning all of the company's assets, both present and future, including assets such as removable plant and equipment, tools, intellectual property rights, stock-in-trade, work in progress and book debts (i.e. sums due to the company by its debtors). These are circulating assets used in the normal course of business and they are constantly changing so they are not amenable to a fixed charge.[19] It is not necessary that, at the time of creation, the company has uncharged assets which would fall within the floating charge. The issue was considered by the Court of Appeal in *SAW(SW)2010 Ltd v Wilson*[20] where Briggs LJ noted that a floating charge may be given at a time when the company does not have assets which are not subject to a prior fixed charge or it may be given at the commencement of business before the company has any significant assets to which the charge can attach. Both as a matter of principle, but also for practical commercial reasons, he said, whether the charge is a floating charge is determined by whether it meets the criteria identified by Romer LJ, above in **23-10**, rather than any consideration of whether the company has assets at the time of creation which fall within it.[21] Arden LJ agreeing, noted that, if there was a requirement that there should be some assets at the time of the creation of the charge, it would be completely unclear what value or amount of assets was required.[22]

**23-12**  The hallmark of the floating charge is the freedom of the company to deal with the assets in the ordinary course of business without the need to obtain the consent of the chargee. The assets in this instance remain under the control of the chargor, not the chargee, so avoiding the 'restricting (and in some cases, paralysing) effect on the use of the assets of the company resulting from a fixed charge'.[23] The charge floats or hovers over the assets until some event occurs causing it to crystallise which can occur in a variety of ways.[24] As

---

[18]  As Lord Millett explained in *Agnew v IRC (Re Brumark)* [2001] 2 BCLC 188 at [6], a charge on the 'undertaking' is taken to mean a charge on all the assets of the company, both present and future, including its circulating assets, i.e. assets that are regularly turned over in the course of trade.

[19]  See *Re Spectrum Plus Ltd* [2005] 2 BCLC 269 at [95], per Lord Scott.

[20]  [2018] 2 WLR 636—the facts are irrelevant but concerned an unsuccessful challenge by some creditors to the appointment of administrators to the company by the holder of a floating charge. One of the issues was whether the charge could be a floating charge if the company had no 'free' assets at the time of creation which would fall within the charge. As noted, the Court of Appeal rejected any such analysis.

[21]  [2018] 2 WLR 636 at [24]–[26], citing Vinelott J in *Re Croftbell Ltd* [1990] BCLC 844.

[22]  [2018] 2 WLR 636 at [48].

[23]  *Re Keenan Bros Ltd* [1986] BCLC 242 at 245, per Walsh J (Irish S Ct).

[24]  The nature of the chargee's interest ahead of crystallisation has been the subject of much debate (possibilities range from no interest, some form of present proprietary interest, which is probably the most generally accepted view, a modified defeasible fixed charge, or a present equitable interest which may be overreached), see Goode, *Legal Problems of Credit and Security* (3rd edn, 2003), Ch 4; Turner, 'Floating Charges—A No Theory Theory' [2004] LMCLQ 319; Nolan, 'Property in a Fund' (2004) 120 LQR 108; also Worthington, 'Floating Charges: The Use and Abuse of Doctrinal Analysis' in Getzler and Payne, n 16, esp at pp 37–44, who admits that the question is of limited practical significance—her view is that it is a modified defeasible form of fixed charge. See too Ferran and Ho, *Principles of Corporate Finance Law* (2nd edn, 2014), who discuss the various theories at pp 321–3 before noting that the lack of certainty on this issue does not appear to cause major practical problems and its significance should not be exaggerated (at p 323).

a matter of law, a floating charge crystallises on the appointment of a receiver or administrator, or when the company goes into liquidation (on a resolution being passed or a compulsory winding up ordered) or there is otherwise a cessation of business on the part of the company, for the effect of these circumstances is to bring to an end the company's freedom to carry on business in the ordinary way.[25] Equally, the charge document may prescribe situations where the charge crystallises which may or may not require the intervention of the chargee. For example, the charge may crystallise on the appointment by the chargee of an administrator under the charge, or on the company exceeding defined financial thresholds, or on the company making a disposition of its assets other than by way of sale in the ordinary course of business, or on the service of a notice by the chargee (a method approved in *Re Brightlife Ltd*).[26] Once the charge has crystallised, the chargor's freedom to deal with the assets comprised in the charge comes to an end and the charge becomes a fixed charge attached to the assets within the scope of the charge. Despite the charge becoming a fixed charge at this point, its priority vis-à-vis other claimants on insolvency is determined by the fact that, *as created*, it was a floating charge.[27]

**23-13**   The freedom of the chargor to deal with the assets in the ordinary course of business includes a freedom to create further fixed charges ranking in priority to the floating charge,[28] though the courts have restricted the ability to create subsequent floating charges. A second floating charge over all of the property comprised in the first charge and ranking *pari passu* with or in priority to that charge is incompatible with the first charge and ranks subject to it.[29] A subsequent floating charge can rank *pari passu* with or in priority to the first floating charge where the first floating charge permits of such a charge and the second charge is over part only of the assets comprised in the original charge.[30]

**23-14**   The possibility that the chargor might grant subsequent charges over the assets within the reach of the floating charge (and so diminish its value) has resulted in the practice of including clauses in the charge document (the debenture), usually described as negative pledges, prohibiting the chargor from creating further fixed or floating charges ranking *pari passu* with or in priority to the current charge. All chargees have constructive notice of prior registered charges as a copy of the charge instrument is available on the public register, see further **23-56**.[31]

**23-15**   Where a high street bank provides funds to a company, therefore, the typical security package which the bank takes is: (1) a legal mortgage over the company's land or buildings; (2) a fixed charge over such of the company's plant, equipment, furniture, and fittings as are not required in the day-to-day conduct of its business (and much ingenuity is expended on drafting charges which fall into this category since, as we shall see, it is the most effective type of charge); and (3) a floating charge over the entire undertaking

---

[25] *Evans v Rival Granite Quarries Ltd* [1910] 2 KB 979; *Re Woodroffes (Musical Instruments) Ltd* [1985] BCLC 227. See also *National Westminster Bank plc v Jones* [2002] 1 BCLC 55, CA.

[26] [1986] BCLC 418.

[27] See IA 1986, s 251. See *Re Beam Tube Products Ltd, Fanshawe v Amav Industries Ltd* [2007] 2 BCLC 732 (floating charge as created was not converted by subsequent conduct of the parties into a fixed charge). The solution is to create a new charge.

[28] *Wheatley v Silkstone Haigh Moor Coal Co* (1885) 29 Ch D 715.

[29] *Re Benjamin Cope & Sons Ltd* [1914] 1 Ch 800.      [30] *Re Automatic Bottle Makers Ltd* [1926] Ch 412.

[31] *Wilson v Kelland* [1910] 2 Ch 306; see *Siebe Gorman & Co Ltd v Barclays Bank Ltd* [1979] 2 Lloyd's Rep 142 at 160, overruled on other grounds; *Re Spectrum Plus Ltd* [2005] 2 BCLC 269, HL. See generally Gough, *Company Charges* (2nd edn, 1996), Ch 23.

of the company, meaning all the assets of the company not otherwise charged. In effect, the floating charge is often used as a catch-all final charge over anything else of value not yet encompassed by another charge. It will be appreciated that once a bank has secured this level of security, there is little security that the company can provide for subsequent creditors since, one way or another, every asset of any value has been appropriated to the payment of the bank borrowings.

**23-16**   In terms of enforcement, if the secured creditor has taken a legal mortgage of the company's property, land, or buildings, the mortgagee is able to sell the property to recover the debts.[32] If the creditor has taken a fixed charge over the company's plant, equipment etc, the creditor has rights *in rem* with respect to those assets which are appropriated to the payment of that creditor's debts and do not fall into the pool of assets for the unsecured creditors. The chargee may take such steps to realise those assets as are permitted by the debenture which invariably provides for their sale to allow the chargee to be repaid. A floating charge, as noted, hovers over the assets within it and only subsequently attaches to those assets when the charge crystallises. Once the charge has crystallised, it becomes a fixed charge and the bank is entitled to realise the assets as provided for by the debenture which will usually provide for the appointment of an administrator: see **23-81**.

**23-17**   Finally, it should be noted that the document setting out the charge taken by a lender is called a debenture, though 'debenture' has many other meanings also. For these purposes, however, it is a document acknowledging an indebtedness which may be (and in this context is) secured by a charge or charges.[33] Hence a lender is often referred to as a debenture holder.

## B  Fixed and floating charges

**23-18**   The attraction of a floating charge for lenders, especially banks, was explained as follows by Lord Millett in *Agnew v IRC (Re Brumark)*:[34]

> 'The floating charge is capable of affording the creditor, by a single instrument, an effective and comprehensive security upon the entire undertaking of the debtor company and its assets from time to time, while at the same time leaving the company free to deal with its assets and pay its trade creditors in the ordinary course of business without reference to the holder of the charge.'

**23-19**   It would seem then that the floating charge meets the two key objectives already noted: security for the lender, the chargee; and flexibility for the company, the chargor. However, the value of a charge lies in the ability of the chargee on insolvency to realise the assets charged to secure repayment of the debt without regard to the insolvency rules governing the distribution of the common fund of unsecured assets. The problem, noted at **23-4**, is

---

[32]   Either under the express terms of the mortgage deed or under the Law of Property Act 1925, s 101.

[33]   See *Levy v Abercorris Slate & Slab Co* (1887) 37 Ch 260 at 264, per Chitty J. See also *Fons HF v Corporal Ltd* [2014] EWCA Civ 304, [2015] 1 BCLC 320 (unsecured loans provided under shareholder loan agreements—the agreements were debentures).

[34]   [2001] 2 BCLC 188 at [8]. While the floating charge has played an important role in corporate financing for many decades, the prevailing academic view (with some support from practitioners) is that the time has come to abolish it and create a modern secured finance regime suitable for domestic purposes and for the role that English law plays in international commerce. See Goode, 'The Case for the Abolition of the Floating Charge' in Getzler and Payne, n 16; also Worthington, n 24, 45–9; Wood, 'A Review of *Brumark* and *Spectrum* in an International Setting' in Getzler and Payne, n 16, 149–50.

that a floating charge is subject to the insolvency rules (priority is given to other claims) in a way that affects the possible recoveries by a floating chargeholder whereas a fixed chargeholder is entitled to the realisations from the assets secured subject only to deduction of the costs of realisation. This is one of the most important distinctions between fixed and floating charges.

**23-20**    A floating charge (but not a fixed charge) is subject to the prior claims of preferential debts (debts accorded statutory priority, though the categories accorded such priority have been reduced[35]) and is subject to the 'prescribed part' provision in IA 1986, s 176A, which ring-fences certain funds in favour of unsecured creditors which would otherwise go to the floating chargeholder.[36] The effect of the latter should be neutral for the chargeholder as the formula used to determine the 'prescribed part' (which must go to the unsecured creditors) is meant to equate to the gain to the floating chargeholder from the reduction of the categories of preferential debts. The application of the prescribed part therefore is not necessarily to the disadvantage of the floating chargeholder, but the floating charge's subordination to the prior claims of the preferential debts is a disadvantage when compared to a fixed charge.

**23-21**    More significantly, a floating charge, but not a fixed charge, is subject, if the company is in liquidation, to the prior claims of the expenses of liquidation[37] and, if the company is in administration, to the prior claims of the expenses of administration.[38] In so far as these claims cannot be met from the unencumbered assets of the company, the deficiency must be made up out of the proceeds of the floating charge.[39] The creditor with a floating charge has security, therefore, in that assets are appropriated to the charge once it crystallises (as discussed at **23-12**), but it is a form of security which is not as comprehensive as a fixed charge because it is subject to these other (usually substantial) claims being met.

**23-22**    One of the major advantages of having a floating charge was that, on crystallisation, the chargeholder could appoint an administrative receiver to realise the assets and pay off the debt. This was an entirely contractual process within the control of the chargeholder and with limited regard being paid to the interests of other creditors. The right to appoint administrative receivers in this way was abolished for the most part (there are some exceptional cases[40]) by the Enterprise Act 2002 (EA 2002) with respect to floating charges

---

[35]  See IA 1986, ss 40, 175, Sch B1, para 65(2); CA 2006, s 754. The priority accorded to preferential debts is not as important an issue as it once was as the preferential status accorded to certain categories of debts (for example, debts to HM Revenue & Customs, Customs and Excise, and social security contributions) was abolished by the Enterprise Act 2002, s 251 with effect from 15 September 2003. The remaining categories of preferential debt are set out in IA 1986, Sch 6, as amended and cover contributions to occupational pension schemes etc; remuneration etc of employees; levies on coal and steel production; deposits covered by the Financial Services Compensation Scheme; and certain other deposits. See Worthington, n 24, at 46, who points out that there is little by way of defensible justification for discriminating between fixed and floating chargeholders in this way. Gullifer and Payne, 'The Characterization of Fixed and Floating Charges' in Getzler and Payne, n 16, suggest the justification lies in the all-embracing nature of a floating charge and the fact that the floating charge enables the company to continue to trade and incur fresh debt: see pp 79–81.

[36]  The prescribed part applies in liquidation, administration, provisional liquidations, and receiverships: IA 1986, s 176A(1); and it is not subject to the expenses of winding up: see IA 1986, s 176ZA(2)(a). The percentage share of the company's assets which must be set aside in this way for unsecured creditors is as prescribed by The IA 1986 (Prescribed Part) Order 2003, SI 2003/2097, art 3.

[37]  To the extent provided for by IA 1986, s 176ZA.

[38]  To the extent provided for by IA 1986, Sch B1, para 99. A floating charge, unlike a fixed charge, is also open to challenge by an administrator or liquidator under IA 1986, s 245 (avoidance of certain floating charges), see discussion at **15-74**.          [39]  See IA 1986, ss 40, 175; Sch B1, para 65(2); CA 2006, s 754.

[40]  See IA 1986, ss 72B–72GA.

created on or after 15 September 2003.[41] For qualifying floating charges (as defined in IA 1986, Sch B1, para 14(2)) created subsequently, the appropriate enforcement mechanism is the appointment of an administrator whose role and functions are statutory and not contractual: see **23-81**. An administrator is an officer of the court (IA 1986, Sch B1, para 5) and has a duty to perform his functions in the interests of the creditors as a whole (IA 1986, Sch B1, para 3(2)). An administrator can also dispose of property subject to a floating charge without the consent of the chargee whereas, if the charge is fixed, the consent of the court is required (IA 1986, Sch B1, paras 70, 71).

**23-23**  It is clear that the fixed charge is the superior charge but there are reasons why it is still worthwhile having a floating charge including:

(1) a qualifying floating charge is required if the lender is to secure valuable rights with respect to the appointment of an administrator and in terms of the choice of administrator.[42] This is very much a prime motivation for obtaining a floating charge;

(2) a floating charge, when coupled with fixed charges, allows one chargee to have comprehensive security over all of the company's assets;

(3) a floating charge gives the chargee a measure of control over the company's business because, while the charge is in existence and especially when coupled with fixed charges, the chargor typically is expected to provide up-to-date accounts to the lender so the lender is well placed to monitor its security;

(4) even if the floating charge is subject to the prior claims of preferential debts and the expenses of winding up/administration, the charge still has priority over the claims of the unsecured creditors (as noted at **23-20**, the position as between the floating chargeholder and the unsecured creditors should be essentially unchanged by the requirements of the prescribed part) and so the lender might as well take a charge for that purpose.

**23-24**  Notwithstanding these advantages, it is still the case that a fixed charge offers greater security than a floating charge and so much of the litigation in this area involves disputes between creditors as to their respective places in the queue to claim the company's assets on insolvency. For example, if Bank A can establish that it has a fixed charge over Asset X, it is able to appropriate that asset to the payment of its debt. On the other hand, if a liquidator or administrator can establish that the charge is a floating charge subject to the expenses of winding up or administration, then the bank's claim is subject to those expenses in the event that the unencumbered assets are otherwise insufficient to meet those expenses. Likewise, if the preferential creditors can establish that a charge is a floating charge, the preferential creditors have a prior claim to the floating charge realisations if the company's assets are otherwise insufficient to meet the preferential claims. For a variety of reasons then the nature of a charge is of real significance and, unsurprisingly, most of the litigation focuses on this issue.

## C The approach to categorisation

**23-25**  In determining the character of a charge, neither the intentions of the parties nor the terms which they use to describe the transaction are necessarily determinative. If the parties describe a charge as fixed when it is in fact floating then, as Millett LJ noted, 'their ill-chosen

---

[41]  See IA 1986, s 72A.   [42]  See IA 1986, Sch B1, paras 14, 35–37.

language must yield to the substance'.[43] Deciding whether a charge is a fixed charge or a floating charge is a two-stage process, as was established by the Privy Council in *Agnew v IRC*[44] (better known as *Re Brumark*). First, the court must construe the instrument of charge and seek to gather the intention of the parties from the language used in order to ascertain the nature of the rights and obligations which the parties intended to grant each other in respect of the charged asset. Once that has been determined, the second stage of the process is one of legal categorisation and it is a matter of law for the courts to determine whether the charge, as created, is fixed or floating. This approach was swiftly endorsed by the House of Lords in *Smith (Administrator of Cosslett (Contractors) Ltd) v Bridgend County Borough Council*[45] (hereinafter *Re Cosslett*). Lord Hoffmann noted that the intentions of the parties are relevant only to establish their mutual rights and obligations: whether such rights and obligations are characterised as a floating charge is a question of law.[46]

**23-26**    In *Re Cosslett* a contractor abandoned a contract for some works with a local council. In accordance with a standard condition contained in the contract, the council then entered the site, seized the contractor's equipment, and obtained another contractor to complete the contract using that equipment. The contract conditions also permitted the council, on a default by the contractor, to sell the contractor's plant and apply the proceeds in discharge of the contractor's debts to the council. The equipment was ultimately sold by the second contractor with the consent of the council.

**23-27**    An initial issue was whether the clause entitling the council to sell the plant and apply the proceeds was a charge. At first instance, the court concluded that the charge was a fixed charge, for there was a further term in the contract which precluded the removal of the equipment from the site until such time as the contract was completed. Jonathan Parker J thought this restriction on the freedom of the chargor was inconsistent with the charge being a floating charge.[47] The Court of Appeal disagreed[48] and pointed out, first, that an unfettered freedom to carry on business is not essential to the existence of a floating charge. After all, floating charges commonly restrict the ability of the company to create further charges (see **23-13**). Secondly, the restriction on removal in this case had nothing to do with the security interest of the council, but was imposed to secure performance of the contract, and therefore did not affect the status of the charge as a floating charge, given that the equipment was not under the control of the chargee. That the charge was a floating charge was confirmed by the House of Lords where the case is reported as *Smith (Administrator of Cosslett (Contractors) Ltd) v Bridgend County Borough Council*,[49] Lord Hoffmann noting:[50]

> 'I do not see how a right to sell an asset belonging to a debtor and appropriate the proceeds to payment of the debt can be anything other than a charge. And because the property ... (constructional plant, temporary works, goods and materials on the site) was a fluctuating body of assets which could be consumed or (subject to the approval of the engineer) removed from the site in the ordinary course of the contractor's business, it was a floating charge.'

---

[43] *Orion Finance Ltd v Crown Financial Management Ltd* [1996] 2 BCLC 78 at 84. See, for example, *Russell-Cooke Trust Co Ltd v Elliott* [2007] 2 BCLC 637 where the charge was described, oddly, as a floating deed, then as a floating charge, and then the document contained restrictions incompatible with a floating charge so leaving it to the court to determine the nature of the charge. In the light of the restrictions, the court decided it was a fixed charge.

[44] [2001] 2 BCLC 188.     [45] [2002] 1 BCLC 77 at [42], per Lord Hoffmann, at [53], per Lord Scott, HL.

[46] [2002] 1 BCLC 77 at [42]; and Lord Scott of Foscote at [53]. See also *Arthur D Little Ltd v Ableco Finance LLC* [2002] 2 BCLC 799 at [31]; *Queens Moat Houses plc v Capita IRG Trustees Ltd* [2005] 2 BCLC 199 at [28]; *Re Beam Tube Products Ltd, Fanshawe v Amav Industries Ltd* [2007] 2 BCLC 732.

[47] See [1996] 1 BCLC 407, Ch D.     [48] [1999] 1 BCLC 205, CA.

[49] [2002] 1 BCLC 77, HL.     [50] [2002] 1 BCLC 77 at [41], HL.

**23-28**    In *Arthur D Little Ltd v Ableco Finance LLC*[51] the court had to determine the nature of a charge created by a company over its shareholding in a subsidiary company where the charge was described as a first fixed charge but the chargor company retained the right to receive dividends and to exercise voting rights with respect to the shares. The chargee asserted that the charge was fixed. The company's administrator argued that it was a floating charge. The court, looking at categorisation as a matter of law, concluded that the charge was fixed. The class of asset involved was not a body of fluctuating assets changing in the ordinary course of business: it was simply the company's shareholding in its subsidiary. There were no dealings in that asset by the chargor company in the ordinary course of business and the shares could not be disposed of, dealt with, or substituted by the chargor company. It followed that the asset was under the control of the chargee not the chargor. The charge was a fixed charge and the ability of the company to receive dividends and exercise voting rights did not alter that characteristic.

**23-29**    Once the court has determined by a process of construction the contractual rights created between the parties, it is then for the law to determine the nature of the security arising. The focus, in particular, is on the third element of the description given by Romer LJ in *Re Yorkshire Woolcombers*,[52] set out at **23-10**, as to whether the chargor has continued freedom to deal with the assets charged in the ordinary course of business. This key issue of the control of the charged assets was central to a series of cases, all concerning book debts, which culminated in the landmark decisions of the Privy Council in *Agnew v IRC (Re Brumark)*,[53] and the House of Lords decision in *Re Spectrum Plus Ltd, National Westminster Bank plc v Spectrum Plus Ltd*.[54] These two cases provide the authoritative statement of the law as to the correct approach to categorisation and the essential characteristics of a floating charge and, more specifically, as to the nature of charges on book debts, an issue which had been the subject of much litigation.

### Re Brumark

**23-30**    Book debts or, to use the modern term, receivables (i.e. sums due to the company and arising from goods or services supplied by the company in the course of its business) are a valuable asset, assuming they are not bad debts, for they represent an income stream for the company and therefore creditors are anxious to obtain security over them.[55] Equally, book debts are precisely the sort of assets where the company is anxious to preserve its freedom to control the assets to the greatest extent possible, given that book debts provide part of the company's cashflow. It is unsurprising therefore that considerable efforts have been expended on drafting charges over book debts in an attempt to meet these conflicting concerns.

---

[51]  [2002] 2 BCLC 799.       [52]  [1903] 2 Ch 284 at 295.

[53]  [2001] 2 BCLC 188, PC.       [54]  [2005] 2 BCLC 269, HL.

[55]  It is accepted that a bank may take a charge over a credit balance in an account maintained by a customer with the bank: *Re BCCI (No 8)* [1998] 1 BCLC 68, so resolving the uncertainty which had arisen on this matter as a result of Millett J's conclusion to the contrary in *Re Charge Card Services Ltd (No 2)* [1987] BCLC 17 which had been affirmed by the Court of Appeal, see [1988] 3 All ER 702, but see Goode (1998) 114 LQR 178. Such a charge is not a charge on book debts: *Northern Bank Ltd v Ross* [1991] BCLC 504; *Re Brightlife Ltd* [1986] BCLC 418; *Re Buildhead (No 2) Ltd* [2006] 1 BCLC 9 at [119]. See also *Re SSSL Realisations (2002) Ltd* [2005] 1 BCLC 1 at [54], a charge over a sum of money once it has been paid to a person is not a charge over the debt or other right by reason of which the sum of money has come to be paid.

**23-31**  In *Agnew v IRC, Re Brumark Investments Ltd*[56] (hereinafter *Re Brumark*) a company created in favour of its bank a fixed charge over all book debts of the company arising in its ordinary course of business. The proceeds of the book debts received by the company were excluded from the fixed charge unless the bank ordered (which it did not do) payment into an account which the company could not operate freely whereupon the proceeds would be treated as being subject to the fixed charge. If the bank did not order the payment of proceeds into such an account, the proceeds were subject to a floating charge in favour of the bank.

**23-32**  A dispute arose between receivers appointed to the company and the preferential creditors as to the nature of the charge on the book debts which were uncollected at the time of the appointment of the receivers.[57] The New Zealand Court of Appeal held that the charge was a floating charge and so subject to the claims of the preferential creditors.[58] The court considered that where the chargor was free to collect the book debts, thus extinguishing them, and was free to deal with the proceeds in the normal course of its business, the charged book debts were not sufficiently under the control of the chargee to make the charge a fixed charge. The Court of Appeal also noted: '... we cannot see how the debate on whether book debts and their collected proceeds constitute separate security interests offers any new aid in determining whether a particular charge is fixed or floating.'[59] The matter was appealed to the Privy Council.

**23-33**  Giving the judgment of the Privy Council, Lord Millett outlined the two-stage process noted at **23-25**. The first step is the ascertainment of the rights which the parties intended to grant each other in respect of the charged assets. Then the court can embark on the categorisation of the charge which is a matter of law and not a matter determined by the description attached to a charge by the parties. If the rights granted are inconsistent with the nature of a fixed charge, the charge cannot be a fixed charge, however the parties choose to describe it. The question, Lord Millett said, is whether the intention is that the company should be free to deal with the charged assets and withdraw them from the security without the consent of the holder of the charge or, to put it another way, whether the charged assets are intended to be under the control of the company or of the chargeholder.[60] The fact that the company may be prohibited from assigning, factoring, or charging the asset to anyone else is not sufficient to make a charge a fixed charge if the company retains the freedom to collect the asset in the ordinary course of business for its own benefit.[61]

**23-34**  As for the fact that different charges were assigned to the debts and the proceeds, Lord Millett stated, and this passage is central to the issues surrounding charges on book debts so it is useful to quote his exact words:[62]

> 'While a debt and its proceeds are two separate assets, however, the latter are merely the traceable proceeds of the former and represent its entire value. A debt is a receivable; it is merely a right to receive payment from the debtor. Such a right cannot be enjoyed in

---

[56] [2001] 2 BCLC 188, PC. See Oditah, 'Fixed Charges over Book Debts after Brumark' (2001) 14 Insolv Int 49; Rumley and Jeffries, 'Brumark: Where Are we Now' (2003) 16 Insolv Int 19; Pennington, 'The Interchangeability of Fixed and Floating Charges' (2003) 24 Co Law 60; Tamlyn and Fennessy, 'Fixed and Floating Charges: Brumark' [2002] Insolv Law 56; Berg, 'Recharacterisation after Enron' [2003] JBL 205.

[57] The dispute arose subsequent to the decision of the English Court of Appeal in *Re New Bullas Trading Ltd* [1994] 1 BCLC 485, CA which had held that it was possible to draft a charge so as to create a floating charge over the proceeds of book debts once collected while retaining a fixed charge over the uncollected proceeds. The debenture in *Brumark* was modelled on that in *New Bullas*.

[58] See [2000] 1 BCLC 353.        [59] See [2000] 1 BCLC 353 at [31].

[60] [2001] 2 BCLC 188 at [32].        [61] [2001] 2 BCLC 188 at [36].        [62] [2001] 2 BCLC 188 at [46].

specie; its value can be exploited only by exercising the right or by assigning it for value to a third party. An assignment or charge of a receivable which does not carry with it the right to the receipt has no value. It is worthless as a security. Any attempt in the present context to separate the ownership of the debts from the ownership of their proceeds (even if conceptually possible) makes no commercial sense.'

**23-35** The issue in the case of a charge on a debt then is who has control of the proceeds and the answer to that question determines the nature of the charge.[63] On the facts in *Re Brumark*,[64] the company's freedom to collect and use the proceeds of the book debts for its own benefit was inconsistent with the nature of a fixed charge. The decision of the New Zealand Court of Appeal that the charge was a floating charge was confirmed.[65]

**23-36** The Privy Council did not deny that a fixed charge might be created over book debts. This might be done where the chargee prohibits the company from realising the debts itself, whether by assignment or collection.[66] Moreover, it is not inconsistent with the fixed nature of a charge on book debts for the holder of the charge to appoint the company as its agent to collect the debts for its account and on its behalf. The Privy Council noted that a fixed charge had been created in *Re Keenan Bros Ltd*[67] by means of a requirement that funds collected by the company be paid into a blocked account with the charge-holder. The prior written consent of the bank was required for each withdrawal from that account. As the debts are not available to the company as a source of its cashflow, such an arrangement is inconsistent with the charge being a floating charge.[68] The Privy Council emphasised, however, that the account must be operated in practice as a blocked account.[69]

**23-37** A decision of the Privy Council while highly persuasive is not binding on the English courts. The banks therefore took what in effect was a test case to the House of Lords in order to secure a definitive statement of the English position which shows how important these issues are to everyday banking arrangements with companies.

### Re Spectrum Plus

**23-38** In *Re Spectrum Plus Ltd, National Westminster Bank plc v Spectrum Plus Ltd*,[70] (hereinafter *Re Spectrum Plus*) the charge in question stated:

'With reference to the book debts and other debts hereby specifically charged the company shall pay into the company's account with the bank all moneys which it may receive in respect of such debts and shall not without the prior consent of the bank sell factor discount or otherwise charge or assign the same in favour of any other person or purport to

---

[63] See also *Re Beam Tube Products Ltd, Fanshawe v Amav Industries Ltd* [2007] 2 BCLC 732 at [38].
[64] [2001] 2 BCLC 188, PC.    [65] [2001] 2 BCLC 188 at [49].    [66] [2001] 2 BCLC 188 at [48].
[67] [1986] BCLC 242 (Irish S Ct).    [68] [2001] 2 BCLC 188 at [48].
[69] [2001] 2 BCLC 188 at [48]. This comment has attracted considerable controversy as to the extent to which post-charge conduct affects the determination of the nature of the charge, see Atherton and Mokal, 'Charges over Chattels: Issues in the Fixed/Floating Jurisprudence' (2005) 26 Co Law 10; Oditah, 'Fixed Charges and the Recycling of Proceeds of Receivables' (2004) 120 LQR 533; also Berg, 'The Cuckoo in the Nest of Corporate Insolvency: Some Aspects of the *Spectrum* Case' [2006] JBL 22 at 33–44. The pragmatic position seems to be that the courts do not have regard to post-agreement conduct when construing the debenture to identify the rights that the parties have agreed to confer on one another, but that the court does look at it in determining the categorisation issue.
[70] [2005] 2 BCLC 269, HL. There are numerous commentaries on the case, see in particular Baird and Sidle, 'Spectrum Plus: House Of Lords Decision—A Cloud With A Silver Lining?' (2005) 18 Insolv Int 113; Hare, 'Charges over Book Debts: The End of an Era' [2005] LMCLQ 440; Berg, n 69.

do so and the company shall if called upon to do so by the bank from time to time execute legal assignments of such book debts and other debts to the bank.'

**23-39** Provided the overdraft limit was not exceeded, the company was free to draw on the account, a current account, for its business purposes. The company duly collected its book debts, paid them into the account and drew on the account as it wished. The company went into voluntary liquidation and the liquidators declined to hand over the collected book debts to the bank. The bank sought a declaration that the proceeds were the subject of a fixed charge in its favour. The issue is different here from in *Re Brumark* (which concerned the existence of two charges, one fixed and one floating) but the court is concerned with the same essential issue, the nature of a charge over the proceeds of a book debt.

**23-40** At first instance, the court held that the charge was a floating rather than a fixed charge over book debts and that *Siebe Gorman & Co Ltd v Barclays Bank Ltd*[71] (where 25 years earlier Slade J held an identically worded charge to be a fixed charge and which wording was adopted by the banks thereafter) had been wrongly decided.[72] The Court of Appeal disagreed and held the charge to be a fixed charge. Lord Phillips considered that there were sufficient restrictions to put the bank in control of the proceeds and therefore the charge was fixed.[73] He also expressed a concern not to upset banking arrangements which have been in place for 25 years and which companies, banks, and individual guarantors of company debts had relied upon.[74]

**23-41** Allowing an appeal, their Lordships held[75] that the debenture, although expressed to grant the bank a fixed charge over the company's book debts, in law granted only a floating charge.[76]

**23-42** As far as book debts are concerned,[77] the main speech is by Lord Scott who agreed with Lord Millett in *Brumark* that it is the third characteristic identified by Romer LJ in *Re Yorkshire Woolcombers Association*[78] (set out at **23-10**) that is the hallmark of the

---

[71] [1979] 2 Lloyd's Rep 142. The restrictions imposed in *Siebe* were a requirement that the chargor pay all moneys received in respect of such book debts into a designated bank account and a prohibition on the charging or assigning of those sums without the prior consent of the chargee. Additionally, and as a matter of construction of the debenture, Slade J considered that, while there was no express prohibition on the use by the company of the proceeds once collected, the debenture did restrict the company's access to those funds without the consent of the bank, see [1979] 2 Lloyd's Rep 142 at 159–60. These restrictions were such that, in Slade J's opinion, the charge was a fixed charge.

[72] See [2004] 1 BCLC 335, Ch D.

[73] [2005] 2 BCLC 30 at [93], [96], CA, and see n 71, as to the restrictions.

[74] [2005] 2 BCLC 30 at [97], CA.

[75] [2005] 2 BCLC 269, HL. As noted, see n 77, the case was heard unusually by seven Law Lords, but on the book debts issues, only Lords Hope, Scott, and Walker expressed a view. Lord Scott's judgment contains a particularly useful account of the development of the floating charge.

[76] The fact that banking practice had relied on it being a fixed charge for a lengthy period was not relevant for, like any first instance decision, *Siebe Gorman* was always open to correction by the higher courts, see [2005] 2 BCLC 269 at [64], HL.

[77] A further issue in the case was whether the House of Lords has power to deliver prospective rulings, applicable only to the future and whether, if so, the power should be exercised in the instant case. The significance of this issue resulted in the case being heard, unusually, by a panel of seven Law Lords. As for prospective overruling, their Lordships held that in a wholly exceptional case the interests of justice might require the House of Lords to declare that its decision was to operate only with prospective effect but the instant case did not fall into such an exceptional category.

[78] [1903] 2 Ch 284 at 295: the third characteristic was that by the charge it is contemplated that, until some future step is taken by or on behalf of those interested in the charge, the company may carry on its business in the ordinary way.

floating charge.[79] The essential characteristic of a floating charge, the characteristic that distinguishes it from a fixed charge, is that the asset subject to the charge is not finally appropriated as a security for the payment of the debt until the occurrence of some future event.[80] In the meantime the chargor is left free to use the charged asset and to remove it from the security. In any case where the chargor is free to remove the charged assets from the security, Lord Scott said, the charge should in principle be categorised as a floating charge for the assets would have the circulating, ambulatory, character distinctive of a floating charge.[81] Lord Walker too agreed that the crucial question is whether the chargor is free to deal with the book debts and withdraw them from the security without the consent of the bank.[82] This approach is entirely consistent with that in *Brumark* as to the issue of categorisation—the issue is whether the chargor has control of the asset such that it can be removed from the security without the consent of the chargee.[83]

**23-43** In this case, the company was free to draw on the account pending notice by the bank terminating the overdraft facility, requiring immediate repayment of the indebtedness and turning the account into a blocked account. Their Lordships were agreed that the restrictions imposed in this case were not sufficient as the chargor remained free to draw on the proceeds of the book debts in the ordinary course of business. So long as the chargor could draw on the account, and whether the account was in credit or debit, the money was available to the chargor and the charge was a floating charge,[84] an outcome entirely consistent with *Brumark*. The decision in *Siebe Gorman & Co Ltd v Barclays Bank Ltd*[85] which had determined commercial practice in this area since 1979 was wrong and overruled.

## Charges on book debts

**23-44** The decisions in *Re Brumark* and *Re Spectrum Plus* end the long-running saga as to the precise nature of charges on book debts. A book debt and its proceeds are indistinguishable as the only value lies in the receipt and the nature of the charge is to be determined therefore by the control of the receipt. As it is practically impossible in most cases to give control to the chargee, charges on book debts will almost invariably be floating charges. The House of Lords did not deny that it is possible to create a fixed charge over book debts,[86] and it is open to the banks to alter their documentation to do so, but essentially to be a fixed charge the proceeds must be placed in a blocked account under the control of the chargee.[87] It will be appreciated that it is difficult to impose the level of control over the proceeds necessary for the charge to be classified as a fixed charge without paralysing the company's activities.[88] In *Re Keenan Bros Ltd*,[89] it will be recalled, the book debts were segregated in a designated account and were unusable by the chargor save with the prior

---

[79] [2005] 2 BCLC 269 at [106]–[107].    [80] See [2005] 2 BCLC 269 at [111].
[81] See [2005] 2 BCLC 269 at [107].    [82] See [2005] 2 BCLC 269 at [154].
[83] See too *Re F2G Realisations Ltd* [2011] 1 BCLC 313 (floating charge where money in the bank account was at the free disposal of the chargor company until certain events of default occurred).
[84] See [2005] 2 BCLC 269 at [117].    [85] [1979] 2 Lloyd's Rep 142.
[86] See Lord Hope on possible methods of creating a fixed charge on book debts, [2005] 2 BCLC 269 at [54].
[87] See *Re Beam Tube Products Ltd, Fanshawe v Amav Industries Ltd* [2007] 2 BCLC 732 (charge on book debts was a floating charge as proceeds were available to company and the fact that the parties did eventually set up a blocked account into which the proceeds were paid did not alter that categorisation).
[88] Although it is not impossible, see *William Gaskell Group Ltd v Highley* [1994] 1 BCLC 197.
[89] [1986] BCLC 242 (Irish S Ct).

written consent of the chargee.[90] Even where the chargee is a clearing bank, the degree of control required over the company's account is commercially impractical and unacceptable for most businesses. As Sir Roy Goode has said, 'for most practical purposes, the fixed charge on book debts is dead'.[91]

**23-45**   At one level, the decision was something of a blow for the banks since they had depended for more than 20 years on obtaining a fixed charge, so defeating the prior claims of the preferential creditors who are the beneficiaries of the *Spectrum Plus* decision.[92] On the other hand, the outcome cannot have been surprising since the lower courts had been signalling for some time that inadequate constraints on the freedom of the chargor would mean that the charge was floating. For example, in *Re Brightlife Ltd*,[93] although there were some restrictions on the debtor company, it retained the freedom to collect in the debts and pay the proceeds into its bank account and to use them in the ordinary course of business and so the charge was a floating charge. In *Royal Trust Bank v National Westminster Bank plc*[94] there was a failure to require and control a designated account and so the charge was a floating charge. In *Re Double S Printers Ltd*[95] the chargee had no control over the debts or the proceeds and so the charge was a floating charge.

**23-46**   In any event, changed circumstances mean that the fixed charge issue is not as significant as it once was. The desire of the banks to have fixed rather than floating charges over book debts was fuelled mainly by a desire to defeat the statutory priority afforded to the preferential debts which were frequently substantial in size (especially the sums due to the HMRC and Customs and Excise). The Enterprise Act 2002 abolished the main categories of preferential debts (including with respect to sums due to HMRC) leaving more limited preferential claims with respect to employees and some other claims: see **24-84**.[96] The result is that whether the charge is fixed or floating with respect to book debts is not as crucial an issue as it was previously.

**23-47**   While the claims of the preferential creditors have been significantly reduced, a floating charge is subject, however, to the prior claims of the expenses of winding up or administration. In view of that priority, a lender's preference would still be for a fixed charge. On

---

[90]   See Berg, n 69, at 44–6, who cautions that there is more to *Re Keenan* than their Lordships seem to have appreciated and therefore merely drafting a charge in the manner of *Re Keenan* will not necessarily guarantee that the charge is a fixed charge.

[91]   See Goode, 'The Case for the Abolition of the Floating Charge' in Getzler and Payne, n 16. See *Re Beam Tube Products Ltd, Fanshawe v Amav Industries Ltd* [2007] 2 BCLC 732 (fixed charge over uncollected and floating charge over proceeds categorised as floating charge over proceeds).

[92]   Indeed the Crown Departments (Inland Revenue, HM Customs and Excise, and the Redundancy Payments Service) were quick to issue a statement reserving the right to challenge any distributions made or proposed to be made to chargeholders after the Privy Council decision based on charges which purport to be fixed charges but which in reality are floating charges. See 'Statement on behalf of HM Revenue & Customs and the DTI Insolvency Service (The Crown Departments) in light of the HL judgment in the case of National Westminster Bank Plc v Spectrum Plus Limited' (2005) 18 Insolv Int 159.

[93]   [1986] BCLC 418; also *Re Pearl Maintenance Services Ltd* [1995] 1 BCLC 449 (no restrictions on the freedom of the chargor to realise the book debts and to use the proceeds in the ordinary course of business: the charge was a floating charge although described as fixed).

[94]   [1996] 2 BCLC 682, CA.

[95]   [1999] 1 BCLC 220. See *Re ASRS Establishment Ltd* [2000] 2 BCLC 631 (charge on escrow account fell within charge on 'debts and other claims' which was designated as a fixed charge but chargor was free to use the proceeds of the escrow account in the ordinary course of business: the charge was a floating charge); see also *Re Chalk v Kahn* [2000] 2 BCLC 361.

[96]   See IA 1986, Sch 6.

the other hand, the holder of a qualifying floating charge has certain valuable rights and privileges with respect to appointing an administrator so there are some advantages in having a charge over book debts even it if is only a floating charge.

**23-48** In any event, banks and other lenders do not rely on one type of security and so, while these decisions effectively prevent lenders from taking fixed charges on book debts, lenders will simply look to increase their protection in other ways, such as by taking fixed charges on other types of assets, or persuading companies to make increased use of factoring and/or invoice discounting which do not involve the creation of charges over the debts,[97] and perhaps, with regard to smaller companies, a greater insistence on personal guarantees from directors in respect of the company's borrowings.

## Charges on other income-generating assets

**23-49** The focus of *Re Brumark* and *Re Spectrum Plus* is clearly book debts so the issue then arises as to the implications, if any, for charges on other income-generating assets.[98] This issue centres to some extent on the decision of the Court of Appeal in *Re New Bullas Trading Ltd*[99] which had held that it was possible to create a floating charge over the proceeds of book debts once collected while retaining a fixed charge over the uncollected proceeds. The decision in *New Bullas* was much criticised on this 'two charges' point[100] and the Privy Council in *Brumark* had no doubt that *New Bullas* was wrongly decided.[101] Lords Scott and Walker in *Re Spectrum Plus* were also in agreement that it was wrongly decided.[102] Applying those decisions (*Brumark* and *Spectrum*) to the facts in *New Bullas*, there was no fixed charge in *New Bullas*, merely a floating charge over the proceeds of the debts. This does not mean that there cannot be fixed charges on income-generating assets. The problem in respect of book debts, as *Re Brumark* and *Re Spectrum Plus* now show and as the dictum from Lord Millett in *Brumark*, noted at **23-34**, makes clear, is that while there are theoretically two assets (debts and proceeds), the debt is worthless as security without the proceeds so in effect the two assets are one asset—the receipt of the money due. Where there are distinct assets (Lord Millett gave the example in *Brumark*[103] of land generating rental income and which would also apply to other assets such as equipment and intellectual property rights which also generate income), then there can be distinct charges secured on the asset and on the income stream derived from the asset. The nature of those charges will be determined by the application of the two-step process already noted (see at **23-25**). There is no legal obstacle to having a fixed charge on the income stream, assuming the requisite control is in place though, as noted, that will often be impracticable and so the charge will be floating, but if the circumstances allow for control by the chargee, the charge can be fixed. In other words, *Re Brumark* and *Re Spectrum Plus*, in dictating that there is only

---

[97] As to factoring and invoice discounting, see nn 5 and 6.

[98] See Frome and Gibbons, 'Spectrum—An End to the Conflict or the Signal for a New Campaign?' in Getzler and Payne, n 16, 111–16 on this issue.

[99] [1994] 1 BCLC 485, CA.

[100] Most of the commentary was hostile, see Goode, 'Charges Over Book Debts: A Missed Opportunity' (1994) 110 LQR 592; Worthington, 'Fixed Charges Over Book Debts and Other Receivables' (1997) 113 LQR 562; Moss, 'Fixed Charges on Book Debts: Puzzles and Perils' (1995) 8 Insolv Int 25; but not all: see Berg, 'Charges Over Book Debts: A Reply' [1995] JBL 433.

[101] [2001] 2 BCLC 188 at 205, PC.

[102] [2005] 2 BCLC 269 at [110], per Lord Scott, [151], per Lord Walker, HL.

[103] [2001] 2 BCLC 188 at 203, PC.

one charge, are limited to charges on book debts and equivalent income streams where the asset and the proceeds of the asset are one and the same thing.[104]

## Categorisation of charges

**23-50**    There is no doubt that there has been a concerted judicial effort to bring some clarity to this area which is of such practical importance to companies and their banks and other lenders. The law is now clearly articulated in *Agnew v IRC (Re Brumark)*, PC[105] and *Re Spectrum Plus Ltd, National Westminster Bank plc v Spectrum Plus Ltd*, HL,[106] which convey a single consistent message. The categorisation of a charge involves a two-step process—determining the parties' rights and categorising those rights as a matter of law. Whether a charge is a fixed or a floating charge depends on whether the intention is that the company should be free to deal with the charged assets and withdraw them from the security without the consent of the holder of the charge or, to put it another way, whether the charged assets are intended to be under the control of the company or of the chargeholder.[107] For most commercial lending to companies, that test can be applied and can provide a clear answer. Of course, there is still uncertainty as to the precise degree of control which makes a charge fixed rather than floating, for example the extent to which 'sweeping' arrangements from a blocked account to an account to which the chargor has access is compatible with a fixed charge[108] and uncertainty as to the precise application of *Brumark* and *Spectrum Plus* to complex securitisations.[109] Nevertheless, these issues do not appear to have given rise to practical difficulties and the position post-*Spectrum* (at

---

[104]    See Worthington, n 24, 37–44; and Wood, n 34, at 147, who makes the point that the decision in *Brumark* (and now *Spectrum*) must be limited to book debts and does not apply to a broad range of income-generating assets since the House of Lords cannot have intended that in all cases charges over such assets should be floating charges. The position taken in *Re Atlantic Computer Systems plc* [1991] BCLC 606 at 625, CA and *Re Atlantic Medical Ltd* [1993] BCLC 386, Ch D (charges over the income from equipment sub-leases where the chargor was allowed continued use of the income were fixed charges) is undermined. They have always been the subject of criticism, see Goode, n 100; Oditah, n 56: 'odd decisions of questionable application'; Moss (1995) 8 Insolv Int 25, unless it is possible to regard the charges over the leases as involving rights greater than merely rights to the income stream, see Frome and Gibbons, n 98, 113–15; *Arthur D Little Ltd v Ableco Finance LLC* [2002] 2 BCLC 799.

[105]    [2001] 2 BCLC 188, PC.        [106]    [2005] 2 BCLC 269, HL.

[107]    [2001] 2 BCLC 188 at [32]. The decision in *Queens Moat Houses plc v Capita IRG Trustees Ltd* [2005] 2 BCLC 199 appears difficult in this regard and must now be read in the light of *Re Spectrum Plus*. The court held that it was not inconsistent with a fixed charge for the chargor to have a contractual right to withdraw property from the charge and distinguished that right from the chargor's freedom to deal with the charged assets in the ordinary course of business which would make a charge a floating charge. But if the feature of the fixed charge, to quote Lord Walker in *Spectrum Plus* [2005] 2 BCLC 269 at [138], is that the asset is permanently appropriated to the payment of the sum charged and that assets can be released from the charge only with the active concurrence of the chargee, then it is difficult to see how the charge here can be a fixed charge if the property subject to it can be altered by the chargor unilaterally.

[108]    A better arrangement may be a sweep from an open access account to a blocked account so the charge is floating on the proceeds paid into the open account but the chargor is required to sweep a certain percentage amount to a blocked account over which the chargee has a fixed charge. Of course, evidence that the chargee sweeps funds back from the blocked account to the open account would raise issues as to whether the accounts were all part of the same arrangement and subject to a single floating charge, but clearly there are permutations here for banks and companies to consider: see Oditah (2004) 120 LQR 533 at 540–1. The uncertainties and practicalities combined may mean that it is cheaper all round to settle for a floating charge.

[109]    See Frome and Gibbons, n 98, at 129, who conclude that the constraints on the SPV (special purpose vehicle) used for securitisation transactions are such that a court would consider the charge is fixed even though the chargor has some rights to use the income stream. But see Ferran and Ho, *Principles of Corporate Finance Law* (2nd edn, 2014), pp 332–3 who note the concerns of rating agencies that the security arrangement might be recharacterised as floating.

least in so far as it can be gauged from the dearth of litigation now on these issues) would suggest that these decisions have brought certainty to a large swathe of the market and have not resulted in the sort of upheaval in lending practices nor the uncertainty in complex transactions such as securitisation which had been predicted.

## D Registration of charges

### Background to registration scheme

**23-51** The Company Law Review (CLR) initially consulted on the option of retaining the core charge registration requirements from the CA 1985 while updating and improving them, though it subsequently put forward a more radical proposal to replace the registration scheme with a system of 'notice filing'.[110] Given that it had not been possible to consult on that more radical proposal, the CLR recommended that the issue of registration be referred for consideration by the Law Commission.[111]

**23-52** The Law Commission duly noted a variety of weaknesses in the statutory registration requirements such as an outdated statutory list of charges which required registration, that the information provided to the registrar of companies was not always reliable or completely accurate with prudent searchers looking to the chargor company for further information, and that registration itself was not a priority point and did not determine priorities. Several consultation papers and a final report making modest proposals for reform duly followed,[112] modest because in part practitioners were not convinced of the need for change, or at least that the disruption of change would be outweighed by the benefits.[113]

**23-53** The Commission's final report concentrated on recommending the introduction of an electronic notice-filing system, akin to the systems in operation in the US and many Commonwealth countries, applying to all charges unless expressly excluded, with priority generally determined by the date of filing. The effect of a failure to register would be invalidity against an administrator or liquidator and a loss of priority against a subsequent secured creditor who filed. While the Government consulted further on whether to

---

[110] See CLR, *Modern Company Law for a Competitive Economy, Final Report*, vol 1 (July 2001), Ch 12; *Modern Company Law for a Competitive Economy, Registration of Company Charges* (October 2000).

[111] The Commission's terms of reference excluded any intrusion into insolvency law, however, a somewhat significant restriction when security issues by their very nature are most acute in the context of insolvency.

[112] The Law Commission published an initial consultation paper on registration of security interests, see Law Commission, *Registration of Security Interests: Company Charges and Property other than Land* (Consultation Paper No 164), 2002; followed by another consultation paper advocating radical reform of personal property security law including the abolition of the floating charge: see Law Commission, *Company Security Interests* (Consultation Paper No 176), 2004, but its final Report in 2005 contained more modest proposals: Law Commission, *Company Security Interests* (Law Comm No 296, Cm 6654). For a detailed account of the process and the proposals by the Law Commissioner with responsibility for the project, see Beale, 'Reform of The Law Of Security Interests Over Personal Property' in Lowry and Mistelis (eds), *Commercial Law: Perspectives and Practice* (2006); also Goode on how the proposals came to move from radical reform to something of a damp squib: see Goode, 'The Case for the Abolition of the Floating Charge' in Getzler and Payne, n 16.

[113] The influential Law Society Committee on Company Law broadly welcomed the proposal for introducing a system of notice filing, but noted that the proposals were potentially very major reforms going well beyond the confines of company law. It also commented that actually the existing system worked relatively well in practice: see Law Society Company Law Committee, *The Registration of Security Interests: Company Charges and Property other than Land* (October 2002), Memo No 448, para 12.2.

implement the Law Commission's recommendations,[114] specifically in terms of the economic benefits of so doing, there was little or no support for change. The upshot was that a power to amend CA 2006, Pt 25 (Company charges) by regulations was included in CA 2006, s 894 and, with effect from 6 April 2013, regulations replaced the original Part 25 of the CA 2006 with a new Part 25 which, while not introducing radical reforms,[115] does provide for an improved, single, UK-wide charge registration scheme applicable to all companies incorporated under the CA 2006 or its predecessors.[116]

### Registering a charge

**23-54**   Whereas previously there was a list of charges which required registration,[117] the requirement to register now applies to every charge[118] granted by a UK-registered company[119] over any of its property (wherever situated, so including over property situated abroad) subject to some limited categories of excluded charges[120] and charges excluded by another Act.[121] This change is a significant improvement as it ends uncertainty over whether certain types of charges require registration. It remains the case that charges may need to be registered in other registries also, such as the Land Registry.

**23-55**   The object of registration is not to provide a comprehensive account of all of a company's charges but to warn unsuspecting creditors that the debtor company has charged its assets.[122] Registration enables creditors taking security to appreciate to what extent the assets are

---

[114] See DTI, *Registration of Companies Security Interests (Company Charges)* (July 2005).

[115] See BIS, *Registration of Company Charges: Issues to be Resolved before Preparation of Draft Regulations* (April 2011), URN 11/862—this useful document gives the background of the new Part 25. The key preceding documents are BIS, *Registration of Charges Created by Companies and Limited Liability Partnerships, Proposals to Amend the Current Scheme and relating to Specialist Registries* (March 2010), URN 10/697; BIS, *Government Response, Consultation on Registration of Charges Created by Companies and Limited Liability Partnerships* (December 2010), URN 10/1319; BIS, *Revised Scheme for Registration of Charges Created by Companies and Limited Liability Partnerships, Proposed Revision of Part 25, CA 2006* (August 2011), URN 11/1108.

[116] See generally Graham, 'Registration of Company Charges' [2014] JBL 175 who at 175–82 gives a detailed account of the various reform proposals and outcomes.

[117] Admittedly a list which included practically all the forms of charges commonly given by companies, covering charges on land, goods, book debts, goodwill, intellectual property, and floating charges over the undertaking. Notwithstanding the scope of the provision, some charges were not registrable, such as a fixed charge on a credit balance at a bank; or a fixed charge on shares; or a fixed charge on an insurance policy (see *Paul & Frank Ltd v Discount Bank (Overseas) Ltd* [1966] 2 All ER 922).

[118] CA 2006, s 859A(1), (6). The company also has the option of registering a charge where it acquires property or an undertaking which is subject to a charge of a kind which if it had been created by the company would have been capable of being registered under s 859A: s 859C. There is no time-limit for registration in this case.

[119] There is no requirement for overseas companies to register charges on property in the UK, see SI 2011/2194, reg 2(3), which revoked the previous requirements with effect from 1 October 2011 with respect to charges created by registered overseas companies over property of the company situated in the United Kingdom. See Graham, n 116, 192–3, who is critical of this change of position.

[120] Excluded are charges on cash deposits in favour of a landlord and charges created by a member of Lloyd's in connection with an underwriting business at Lloyd's: CA 2006, s 859A(6).

[121] Certain security financial collateral arrangements are exempt from registration under the CA 2006, Pt 25, see the Financial Collateral Arrangements (No 2) Regulations 2003, SI 2003/3226, regs 3(1), 4(4), but the exemption requires the collateral taker to have possession or control of the financial collateral and an ordinary floating charge (where necessarily the chargee does not have possession or control of the asset charged) does not fall within the scope of the exemption: *Re F2G Realisations Ltd* [2011] 1 BCLC 313, esp at [52]–[55], [59]–[63]. See BIS, *Registration of Company Charges: Issues to be Resolved before Preparation of Draft Regulations* (April 2011), URN 11/862, pp 7–8.

[122] See *Re Welsh Irish Ferries Ltd* [1985] BCLC 327 at 332. See generally, Castellano, 'Reforming Non-possessory Secured Transactions Laws: a New Strategy? (2015) 78 MLR 611.

already encumbered and assists unsecured creditors also because it allows them to appreciate the extent to which the assets are earmarked for other creditors in the event of insolvency.

**23-56**   If a statement of particulars of the charge and a certified copy of the instrument of charge[123] (where the charge is created by an instrument) are delivered to the registrar of companies within the period allowed, essentially 21 days beginning with the day after the date of creation of the charge,[124] the registrar must register the charge.[125] The brief particulars are as follows: (a) the registered name and number of the company; (b) the date of creation of the charge; (c) where the charge is created by an instrument, the particulars required by s 859D(2) including the name of the person in whose favour the charge has been created, whether the charge contains a floating charge, and, if so, whether it is expressed to cover all the property and undertaking of the company, and whether any of the terms of the charge prohibit or restrict the company from creating further security that will rank equally with or ahead of the charge (i.e. a negative pledge). If there is no instrument creating the charge, in addition to (a) and (b) above, the particulars required are those set out in s 859D(3) which include the name of the person in whose favour the charge is created, the nature of the charge, a short description of the property or undertaking charged, and the obligations secured by the charge (s 859D(1), (3)).

**23-57**   This requirement to file brief prescribed particulars and a certified copy of the charge instrument is a further improvement in the scheme under Part 25, removing the need (as existed under the old scheme) for the registrar's staff to check the accuracy of the particulars against the instrument. They are no longer required to do this since anyone searching the register is able themselves to look at the charge instrument and determine its terms and application. Also a copy of the instrument of charge or an instrument effecting any variation or amendment of a charge must be available at the company's registered office or other specified location for inspection by any creditor or member (CA 2006, s 859P(1)). Further, if the prescribed particulars in s 859D(1) are not contained in the instrument creating the charge, but are instead contained in other documents referred to or otherwise incorporated in the instrument of charge, then the company must also keep available for inspection a copy of those other documents (s 859P(3)).

**23-58**   There is no statutory obligation to register as such,[126] but given that invalidity is a consequence of non-registration, see **23-63**, of course there is a practical obligation to register, but this explains why the statute is not expressed in terms of a duty to register. The power to submit the details for registration lies with the company and any person interested in the charge (CA 2006, s 859A(2)). In practice, because of the consequences of non-delivery, practically all registrations are undertaken by the chargee.[127]

**23-59**   The prescribed particulars and the copy of the instrument of charge must be delivered to the registrar of companies within 21 calendar days after the date of creation,[128] and

---

[123]  Provision is made for the exclusion of certain personal information: see CA 2006, s 859G; and for the replacement of the instrument by court order where that information is included; or the wrong instrument is delivered or the copy delivered is defective: s 859N.

[124]  See s 859B as to the position with respect to charges in a series of debentures.

[125]  CA 2006, s 859A(2), (3). See also s 859M as to rectification of the register by court order where there has been some omission or mis-statement in any statement delivered to the registrar.

[126]  Hence there no longer is a criminal sanction for non-registration.

[127]  A registration fee of £23 is payable, £15 for electronic filing.

[128]  If because of errors in the particulars provided, the registrar is required to return the forms to the presenter for correction, re-submission must occur within the 21-day limit. If the registrar improperly rejects a form, the charge is not invalidated as delivery will have occurred within the 21-day period.

helpfully s 859E determines what is the date of creation. The problem with the 21-day period is that anyone searching the register of charges with respect to the company and finding no charges cannot be sure that there are not charges which have been created but have not yet been registered. Searchers of the register must not rely therefore on the absence of charges and must ask the company to confirm that no other charges have been created which have yet to be registered.

**23-60** It is possible to notify the registrar of amendments or additions to a charge (in accordance with s 859O(2)) where a new term prohibits or restricts the creation of any fixed security or any other charge having priority over, or ranking *pari passu* with, the charge or the new term varies, or otherwise regulates the order of, the ranking of the charge in relation to any fixed security or any other charge: CA 2006, s 859O(1).

**23-61** Once the particulars and copy of the charge are delivered, the registrar must include the documents delivered on the register and give a certificate of registration (CA 2006, s 859I(2)(b), (3)). The certificate is conclusive evidence that the documents required to be delivered were delivered before the end of the relevant period allowed for delivery (s 859I(6)).[129] The statute does not address the question of constructive notice. At common law, anyone dealing with a company is deemed under the doctrine of constructive notice to have notice of its public documents including the articles of association which doctrine was extended, obiter, by *Wilson v Kelland*[130] to give subsequent chargees constructive notice of the existence of a registered charge, though not of any special provisions contained in the charge. It is not clear whether this remains the position under the new scheme or whether the existence of registered particulars, including a statement as to whether the charge contains a negative pledge, means that there would now be constructive notice of the charge and of the registered particulars including the negative pledge,[131] but that would appear to be the position.[132]

**23-62** There is no statutory requirement to notify the registrar of companies of the satisfaction or release of any charge. Companies which want to clear debts off their public record can make a statement under CA 2006, s 859L, however, to the effect either that the debt for which the charge was given has been paid or satisfied in whole or in part, or that part of the property or undertaking charged has been released from the charge or has ceased to form part of the company's property or undertaking. On receipt of that statement, the registrar must enter on the register a statement of satisfaction to this effect (s 859L(5)).

---

[129] This is a change from the previous position which was that the certificate was conclusive evidence that the requirements of the Act as to registration had been satisfied: CA 2006, s 869(6)(b), and it was held to be conclusive even if inaccurate: *Re Mechanisations (Eaglescliffe) Ltd* [1966] Ch 20 (amount secured wrongly stated); even if it showed the wrong date of creation of the charge, so that the charge may not have been delivered within the 21-day period: *Re C L Nye Ltd* [1970] 3 All ER 1061. See Graham, n 116, 188, who notes that it remains to be seen whether the courts will regard this as a significant change in wording.

[130] [1910] 2 Ch 306.

[131] It was BIS's intention that under the new scheme the registration of a charge created by a company should constitute notice of the existence of the charge and, in the case of a floating charge, whether or not it has a negative pledge, see BIS, *Registration of Company Charges: Issues to be Resolved before Preparation of Draft Regulations* (April 2011), URN 11/862, pp 9–10.

[132] See Graham, n 116, 191–2, who suggests that there will continue to be constructive notice of the existence of the charge, but not of all of its terms, other than those disclosed in the registered particulars. To apply constructive notice to all of the terms of the registered charge, because the charge instrument is available on the public record, in his view would be to take the doctrine of constructive notice too far.

## Statutory invalidity for non-registration

**23-63**  The consequence of a failure to deliver the prescribed particulars and copy of the charge within the relevant period allowed for delivery is that the charge is void (so far as any security on the company's property or undertaking is conferred by it) against the liquidator or administrator and any creditor of the company (CA 2006, s 859H(3)), but it is a limited invalidity. The statute 'makes void a security; not the debt, not the cause of action, but the security, and not as against everybody, not as against the company grantor, but against the liquidator, [and now an administrator] and against any creditor'.[133]

**23-64**  The invalidity of the security is without prejudice to any contract or obligation for repayment of the money secured by the charge and the money secured immediately becomes payable (CA 2006, s 859H(4)). This liability to immediate repayment allows a creditor to insist on recovering his money once he has lost his security as a result of the failure to deliver the details to the registrar within the relevant period.

**23-65**  The nature of the statutory invalidity imposed (now) by CA 2006, s 859H(4) was considered by the House of Lords in *Smith (Administrator of Cosslett (Contractors) Ltd) v Bridgend County Borough Council*,[134] which was noted at **23-26**.

**23-66**  A council had contracted with a company (the contractor) to carry out coal washing on a particular site for the council. The terms of the contract allowed the council, in the event of default by the contractor, to enter the site, use the machinery of the contractor to complete the job, and to sell the machinery and apply the proceeds to the liabilities of the contractor under the contract. When the company defaulted on the contract, the council duly entered the site, seized the contractor's machinery, and obtained another contractor to complete the contract using that machinery. The council then permitted the second contractor to remove and sell the machinery. A variety of legal proceedings ensued, part of which concluded, as discussed at **23-27**, that the council's right to sell the machinery and apply the proceeds to the debt due by the contractor to the council amounted to a floating charge which charge was void for non-registration under what is now CA 2006, s 859H.

**23-67**  The administrator brought proceedings claiming damages from the council for conversion of the machinery by allowing the second contractor to remove it from the site. The Court of Appeal allowed an appeal by the council against that liability for conversion, finding that the contractual conditions as to the use of, and power to sell, the machinery etc remained valid as against the company and was the answer, the Court of Appeal said, to the conversion claim.[135]

**23-68**  On appeal to the House of Lords, their Lordships rejected this finding by the Court of Appeal as a narrow and arbitrary construction of what is now CA 2006, s 859H and reversed the decision. The statutory provision does not invalidate a charge against a company while it is a going concern but makes an unregistered but registrable charge void against a company acting by its liquidator or administrator, that is to say void against a company in liquidation or in administration.[136] The council could not therefore rely on its terms against the company or the administrator of the company. As the council's charge was void for non-registration, the council had no proprietary interest in the machinery and therefore allowing the

---

[133] *Re Monolithic Building Company* [1915] 1 Ch 643 at 667, per Phillimore LJ; and see *Re Cosslett Ltd* [2002] 1 BCLC 77 at [21]: it is not void against the company when it is a going concern, but it is void when the company is in liquidation or administration. See also *Re F2G Realisations Ltd* [2011] 1 BCLC 313 (unregistered floating charge). [134] [2002] 1 BCLC 77.

[135] See [2000] 1 BCLC 775, CA. [136] See [2002] 1 BCLC 77 at [21], per Lord Hoffmann.

second contractor to remove the equipment was a violation of the first contractor's right of possession. That was sufficient to amount to a conversion in respect of which the administrator could seek damages. The council's claim for damages for breach of contract by the contractor would have to be pursued in the liquidation of the contractor.[137]

**23-69**    This attempt by the Court of Appeal to ascribe a type of partial invalidity to the unregistered charge was, Lord Hoffmann said, 'a startling and unorthodox approach' to what is now CA 2006, s 859H. He noted that the Court of Appeal may have been influenced in adopting that approach by its perception of the merits of the case. The local council found itself in a position where it had no security for the debts owed to it (which included a large amount advanced by the council to the contractor to enable the contractor to acquire the machinery in the first place) as its floating charge was void for non-registration and it was liable in conversion to the administrator.

### Remedial measures in cases of non-registration

**23-70**    Where the particulars and a copy of the charge have not been delivered to the registrar of companies and the 21-day period has elapsed so attracting the statutory invalidity, there are a number of options open to the company and the chargee. The main option is an application by the company or a person interested to the court for registration out of time under CA 2006, s 859F and this step should be taken without delay once the failure to register is discovered.

**23-71**    Section 859F allows the court to extend the time for registration if satisfied that the omission to register a charge within the time required was accidental, or due to inadvertence or to some other sufficient cause, or is not of a nature to prejudice the position of creditors or shareholders of the company, or that on other grounds it is just and equitable to grant relief.[138] Even if the court's discretion does arise, the court may decide not to exercise it, as where the application is made only after long delay.[139] But in general, the practice of the court is to exercise the power to extend the period for registration, subject to the proviso that registration is without prejudice to any rights acquired between the date of creation of the charge and the date of its actual registration,[140] so as to ensure that intervening creditors are not adversely affected.[141]

---

[137] Counsel for the council attempted to secure some redress by claiming the benefit of some equitable set-off so as to set off the council's breach of contract claim against the administrator's claim for conversion. The House of Lords was robust in rejecting this possibility, Lord Scott noting that, given that the council's security was invalid because of a failure to comply with the statutory provisions as to registration, it was no part of equity to provide, via equitable set-off, an alternative security: see [2002] 1 BCLC 77 at [78].

[138] The final 'just and equitable' category allows for any reason, whether specified in the section or not, to be put forward: *Re Braemar Investments Ltd* [1988] BCLC 556 at 561. See also *Confiance Ltd v Timespan Images Ltd* [2005] 2 BCLC 693. An application can also be made to the court under CA 2006, s 859M, with respect to omissions or mis-statements in the statement of particulars of any charge delivered to the registrar and the court may order the registrar to rectify the register. The application is on the same grounds as s 859F, accidental omission, inadvertence etc.

[139] See *Re Telomatic Ltd* [1994] 1 BCLC 90; *Victoria Housing Estates Ltd v Ashpurton Estates Ltd* [1982] 3 All ER 665.

[140] *Re Joplin Brewery Co Ltd* [1902] 1 Ch 79 (as modified following the decision in *Watson v Duff Morgan & Vermont (Holdings) Ltd* [1974] 1 All ER 794); and see *Victoria Housing Estates Ltd v Ashpurton Estates Ltd* [1982] 3 All ER 665 at 670 for the history of this proviso; and see *Barclays Bank plc v Stuart Landon Ltd* [2001] 2 BCLC 316.

[141] The extension may also be subject to the proviso in *Re L H Charles & Co Ltd* [1935] WN 15 allowing the company, through any liquidator subsequently appointed, to apply within a specified period (for example, 42 days) after the commencement of the winding up to discharge the order granting an extension of time and containing an undertaking by the applicant for late registration to abide by any order which the court may make.

**23-72**   As an alternative to applying to the court, the chargee may attempt to remedy the situation by getting another charge executed by the company and registered before any third party intervenes.[142] This approach is a risky strategy for, if it fails, the court may look unfavourably on an application under CA 2006, s 859F.[143] A further risk with executing a new charge is that if the company goes into insolvent liquidation or administration shortly thereafter, the new charge may be open to challenge as a vulnerable transaction under IA 1986, ss 239 and 245 (discussed in Chapter 15).

**23-73**   Another possibility is that the chargee can seek immediate repayment of the sum secured (see CA 2006, s 859H(4)) and this ability to demand immediate repayment of the entire amount may assist him in obtaining a new charge from the company. If the unregistered chargee succeeds in securing repayment before liquidation or administration, the charge is spent and there is nothing for the statutory invalidity to bite on.[144]

### Priority as between charges

**23-74**   The registration of a charge does not determine priorities as between successive chargees, save to the extent of the statutory invalidity affecting any unregistered charge.

**23-75**   Priority issues are determined at common law with the basic rules being that legal interests prevail over equitable, fixed charges over floating charges, and where the equities are equal, the first in time prevails. The position is then complicated by issues of notice and, in particular, the application of the doctrine of constructive notice, discussed at **23-61**. It means that successive chargees have notice of the preceding charges, assuming they have been registered.

## E   Enforcement of a floating charge

### Receivers, administrative receivers, and administrators

**23-76**   The appointment of a receiver by the Court of Chancery was an ancient equitable remedy available to creditors whether secured or unsecured[145] but, in the modern business context, receiverships are associated particularly with a default by a corporate borrower on a secured loan.[146]

**23-77**   During the nineteenth century conveyancers realised the advantages in terms of costs and speed of providing for the appointment of a receiver as a contractual remedy under a debenture without the necessity of going to court. A *receiver*, strictly speaking, is appointed just to receive the rent or other income from property.[147] Over time,

---

[142]   A process which may be fraught with difficulties: see *Re Telomatic Ltd* [1994] 1 BCLC 90.

[143]   See *Victoria Housing Estates Ltd v Ashpurton Estates Ltd* [1982] 3 All ER 665 at 677 (the court should look askance at a chargee who deliberately defers his application in order to see which way the wind is going to blow).

[144]   *Mercantile Bank of India Ltd v Chartered Bank of India, Australia and China* [1937] 1 All ER 231; *Re Row Dal Construction Pty Ltd* [1966] VR 249 at 258; *NV Slavenburg's Bank NV v Intercontinental Natural Resources Ltd* [1980] 1 All ER 955.

[145]   The power to appoint a receiver is vested in the High Court, see the Senior Courts Act 1981, s 37. For an outline of the development of receivers, see Rigby LJ in *Gaskell v Gosling* [1896] 1 QB 669 at 691–3.

[146]   See generally, *Kerr & Hunter on Receivers and Adminstrators* (20th edn, 2017).

[147]   The powers conferred by the LPA 1925 are limited in this way but they may be varied or extended by the mortgage deed: s 101(3).

appointments of receivers for this purpose became the accepted practice, so much so that the power to appoint a receiver of income is now implied into mortgages by deed unless the parties provided otherwise and such receivers are known as LPA receivers and their powers are usually extended by deed to include powers to sell and manage the property.[148] If it is desirable for the receiver to manage the property or to carry on the debtor's business, the receiver must also be appointed under the terms of the debenture as a manager with appropriate powers and such a person is often referred to as a receiver and manager.[149] Again such powers are commonplace. The result is that the debenture commonly provides for the appointment of receivers with wide power to receive income, to manage the business, and to sell the assets secured for the benefit of the chargee. In addition to receivers, and receivers and managers, the IA 1986, s 29(2) provides for a further category, administrative receivers, defined essentially as receivers appointed under a floating charge over all or substantially all of the company's property. Most appointments of receivers were appointments of administrative receivers, reflecting the prevalence of floating charges over all or substantially all the company's assets. The IA 1986 as amended by the EA 2002 prohibits the appointment of administrative receivers, however, where the floating charge is created on or after 15 September 2003 (IA 1986, s 72A). To understand why this prohibition was imposed, it is necessary to understand how administrative receiverships operated prior to the EA 2002.

**23-78**   Essentially, administrative receivership worked in the following way. A secured creditor (typically a clearing bank with fixed and floating charges over the company and its undertaking) would appoint a receiver following a default by the corporate borrower. Appointment was purely a contractual issue requiring no assistance from the courts and the receiver's primary function was to realise sufficient of the company's assets comprised in the security to discharge the debt due to the secured creditor. The receiver had to decide quite quickly whether to continue the business in order to sell it as a going concern or to sell off the company's assets piecemeal. In theory, once the receiver completed his task of realising sufficient funds to satisfy his appointor, the company could continue trading. In practice, the receiver would commonly not realise sufficient funds even to pay his appointor in full and the company would go into liquidation. Moreover, as the appointment of a receiver did not impose a moratorium on other creditors enforcing their rights, his appointment usually galvanised other creditors into asserting their rights and remedies. For example, creditors might petition the court for a compulsory winding-up order or the members might resolve to put the company into voluntary liquidation.

**23-79**   There were obvious advantages to administrative receiverships, particularly for the appointor, most notably the ease and speed with which an appointment might be made

---

[148] See Law of Property Act 1925, s 101(1)(iii). The use of LPA receivers can be quite effective where the borrower has properties which are generating rental income which the lender would like to secure to repay the mortgage interest at least, especially when it may be difficult to sell the property to recover the capital. The powers of an LPA receiver are usually increased by the terms of the deed and an LPA receiver need not be a qualified insolvency practitioner. For an overview, see UK Finance, Guidance Note, *The Role of LPA Receivers* (14 March 2018).

[149] As to the distinction, see *Re Manchester and Milford Rly Co* (1880) 14 Ch D 645 at 653 where Jessel MR noted that '[a] "receiver" is a term which was well known ... as meaning a person who receives rents or other income paying ascertained outgoings, but who does not ... manage the property in the sense of buying or selling or anything of that kind ... If it was desired to continue the trade at all, it was necessary to appoint a manager, or a receiver and manager as it was generally called.' Where a receiver or manager is appointed, the registrar must be notified within seven days, as he must be notified when that person ceases so to act: CA 2006, s 859K.

once the borrower was in default and the focus on realising sufficient assets to satisfy the debt due to the debenture holder. But receiverships were frequently criticised precisely because of this focus on one secured creditor to the exclusion of other interests, in particular, the interests of unsecured creditors. As a matter of policy, the Government decided their use should not be continued and its preference was for a collective process for the benefit of the creditors as a whole—administration.

**23-80**  The holder of a qualifying floating charge is prohibited then from appointing an administrative receiver of the company where the charge was created on or after 15 September 2003.[150] It is still possible to appoint an administrative receiver under charges created prior to that date but creditors often prefer to appoint an administrator even where they have power to appoint an administrative receiver.[151] The right to appoint an administrative receiver is retained by IA 1986, ss 72B–72GA for specialist areas such as public–private partnership projects, utility projects, and urban regeneration projects[152] but those specialist cases are beyond the scope of this work.

**23-81**  For a floating chargeholder outside of those specialist contexts, the means of enforcement is through the appointment of an administrator under the IA 1986, Sch B1, and it is possible to do so out of court in a manner very similar (in terms of speed and efficiency) to the appointment of an administrative receiver. An administrator is able to realise the assets quickly and to make distributions to secured creditors in a manner which can look very like administrative receivership. The process of enforcement may have changed, but the outcome may be very similar. Readers are referred to works on Insolvency Law for further detail on administrations.[153]

---

[150]  IA 1986, s 72A; SI 2003/2095.

[151]  Figures for the UK show that the number of receiverships in 2012–13 was 1,427 and, in 2016–17, it was only 497 (the figures do not distinguish between administrative receivers and other types, such as receivers appointed under the Law of Property Act 1925); in 2012–13, there were 2,557 administrator appointments which had fallen to 1,818 by 2016–17; total liquidation figures for 2016–17 were 24,327 of which 14,918 were insolvent liquidations; see *Statistical Tables on Companies Registration Activities 2016–17*, Table A10.

[152]  IA 1986, s 72A.

[153]  See Lightman and Moss, *The Law of Administrators and Receivers of Companies* (6th edn, 2017).

# PART V

# Corporate Liquidation

# 24

# Liquidation and dissolution–winding up the insolvent company

## A Introduction

**24-1** Winding up is a term commonly associated with the ending of a company's existence. In fact, winding up or liquidation (the terms are synonymous) is the process by which the assets of the company are collected in and realised, its liabilities discharged, and the net surplus, if there is one, distributed to the persons entitled to it.[1] Only when this has been done is the company's existence finally terminated by a process known as dissolution. A company may be wound up though it is solvent, for example, because a business project has come to an end or because members of a family business wish to retire or, sometimes, because of internal disputes. More commonly a company is wound up because it is insolvent and this chapter concentrates on the winding up of insolvent companies. Prior to winding up, a company may have been in some other insolvency process, for example, it may come to liquidation via administration[2] (and an administration can in some ways look very like a liquidation where there is a distribution to secured creditors followed by speedy dissolution) or via a company voluntary arrangement[3] which has failed. A company may go directly then into liquidation or it may be that winding up is preceded by some other form of insolvency proceeding.

### The legislative framework

**24-2** The core insolvency legislation is the Insolvency Act 1986 while the procedural rules are contained in the Insolvency Rules 2016 (SI 2016/1024) which came into effect on 6 April 2017 and which replace the IR 1986 following a lengthy modernisation project[4] by the Insolvency Service. Most of the changes are clarifications or minor technical changes, improving the clarity of the provisions etc, as well as recognising modern methods of communication. Some substantive changes arising from the reforms were made to the IA 1986 by the Small Business, Enterprise and Employment Act 2015. A significant change is a move from a default position of physical meetings between an insolvency practitioner and creditors (often poorly attended) to one whereby office-holders in insolvency proceedings may only call a physical meeting if it is requested by 10 per cent in value of the creditors or contributories; 10 per cent in number of the creditors or contributories; or 10 creditors or contributories (IA 1986, s 246ZE, 379ZA). Instead of meetings, the

---

[1] See IA 1986, ss 107, 143(1). See, generally, Fletcher, *The Law of Insolvency* (5th edn, 2017); McPherson and Keay's *Law of Company Liquidation* (4th edn, 2017).

[2] Administration is governed by the IA 1986, Sch B1.

[3] CVAs are governed by IA 1986, Pt 1.

[4] See Insolvency Service, *Insolvency Rules 1986—modernisation of rules relating to insolvency law*, Consultation September 2013.

IR 2016, rr 15.2–15.6 allow for qualifying decision-making procedures whereby decisions can be reached using correspondence, electronic voting, virtual meetings etc, subject to the proper provision of information to creditors (see IR 2016, r 15.7). The legislation also allows for deemed consent, where office-holders are able to write to creditors or contributories with a proposal and invoke the deemed consent provision so that, unless objections are received from more than 10 per cent in value of creditors or contributories, the proposal is deemed to be approved (IA 1986, s 246ZF, s 379ZB, and IR 2016, r 15.7). Deemed consent may not be used for approval of an office-holder's remuneration, or where a particular decision is expressly required to be made by way of a decision-making procedure, either in legislation or by the court (IA 1986, 379ZB(1)). Creditors may also opt out of receiving further correspondence from the office-holder, other than notifications of changes of office-holder contact details and notices of distributions (IA 1986, ss 246C, 248A and IR 2016, rr 1.37–1.39). This option reflects the fact that, in many insolvencies, the creditors will receive little or no return and so they do not wish to be bothered with all of the documentation of the insolvency process.[5]

### The common law and modified universalism

**24-3**   Many insolvencies now involve a cross-border element and therefore, as Lord Collins has said, international cooperation in cross-border insolvencies has become a pressing need. The challenge is to reconcile all the different interests in different countries with different laws and, as Lord Collins noted, at the same time provide swift and effective remedies to combat the use of cross-border transfers of assets to evade and defraud creditors.[6] The cross-border problem then raises many issues, the most basic being the need to decide which jurisdiction should govern any insolvency process. Essentially, the choice is between territorialism (each jurisdiction acts with regard to assets within its jurisdiction), universalism (one jurisdiction assumes responsibility for all the assets and liabilities wherever located), or, more pragmatically, a modified universalism which involves identifying the jurisdiction best placed to deal with the insolvent entity while recognising the sovereign right of other jurisdictions to manage aspects of the insolvency process within their territories in respect of assets and liabilities located there. Lord Hoffmann described the principle of modified universalism as '… the golden thread running through English cross-border insolvency law since the 18th century',[7] noting that it requires the English courts, so far as consistent with justice and UK public policy, to co-operate with the courts of the country of the principal liquidation 'to ensure that all the company's assets are distributed to its creditors under a single system of distribution'.[8] As Lord Mance explained in *Singularis Holdings Ltd v PricewaterhouseCoopers*[9] the essence of modified universalism consists in the recognition by the court of the foreign liquidator's power of disposition over the company's assets in the domestic jurisdiction which justifies an order restraining their disposition or seizure inconsistently with that foreign liquidation. But the exact extent of 'modified universalism' in this jurisdiction remains controversial. In

---

[5] See too IR 2016, r 1.45 which allows office-holders to communicate with creditors by email in certain circumstances unless the creditor revokes his consent to email communication. See r 1.50 re communication via websites.   [6] *Rubin v Eurofinance SA* [2012] 2 BCLC 682 at [14], per Lord Collins.
[7] *Re HIH Casualty and General Insurance Ltd; McMahon v McGrath* [2008] 3 All ER 869, [2012] 2 BCLC 655 at [30], HL.
[8] See n 7.   [9] [2014] 2 BCLC 597, PC at [132].

*Rubin v Eurofinance SA*,[10] the Supreme Court (Lord Clarke dissenting), controversially, was seen to step back from it when (overruling the Court of Appeal) it refused a request by receivers of a US company to enforce in the UK a US default judgment. The judgment concerned transactions which were either at an undervalue or a preference in respect of defendants who were neither present in the US nor did they submit to the jurisdiction of the US court. Applying ordinary principles of private international law (the *Dicey* rule), the judgment could not be enforced here in those circumstances and, the court held, the principle of modified universalism did not override those rules to require the English courts to give recognition to judgments in foreign insolvency proceedings.[11] In part, the stepping back was driven, as Lord Collins acknowledged,[12] by an acceptance that 'the law relating to the enforcement of foreign judgments and the law relating to international insolvency are not areas of law which have in recent times been left to be developed by judge made law', noting the lengthy negotiations which preceded both the Insolvency Regulation (EC 1346/2000, now recast as Regulation 2015/848) and the UNCITRAL Model Law (both discussed later).[13] Lord Clarke for his part thought the enforcement of the US order was precisely the sort of evolutionary development of the common law which was necessary to give effect to modified universalism as explained by Lord Hoffmann.[14] These issues, and the divergent views of the senior judiciary, resurfaced in the Privy Council in *Singularis Holdings Ltd v PricewaterhouseCoopers*[15] where by a 3–2 majority the Privy Council rejected an application by liquidators appointed in the Cayman Islands that the courts of Bermuda make an order requiring a company's auditors to disclose information to the liquidators. A further complexity here, in addition to the issue of whether the courts of Bermuda should assist the Cayman liquidators in this way, was that the power of disclosure which the liquidators wanted the Bermuda court to exercise was not a power which existed in the Cayman Islands so this order could not have been obtained

---

[10] [2012] 2 BCLC 682; noted Aitken (2013) 129 LQR 147.

[11] See the trenchant criticism of the court's approach by Kirshner, 'The (False) Conflict between Due Process Rights and Universalism in Cross-Border Insolvency' (2013) 72 CLJ 27 who argues that the Supreme Court could simply have invoked the doctrine of comity which encourages reciprocity among foreign courts and respect for the validity of foreign rules, rather than supporting an outcome which, Kirshner says, subverts efforts to establish a more efficient regime for dealing with multinational insolvencies.

[12] [2012] 2 BCLC 682 at [129]. Lord Collins for the same reasons concluded that *Cambridge Gas Transport Corp v Official Committee of Unsecured Creditors of Navigator Holdings Ltd* [2007] 2 BCLC 141, PC, was wrongly decided, but Lord Mance (at [178]) reserved his position on that decision, and Lord Clarke expressly disagreed (at [192]). Subsequently, in *Singularis Holdings Ltd v PricewaterhouseCoopers* [2014] 2 BCLC 597, the Privy Council by a 3–2 majority (Lords Sumption, Clarke, and Collins of the majority; Lords Mance and Neuberger dissenting) did overrule *Cambridge Gas*. The position on *Cambridge* was summed up by Lord Sumption at [18] as follows: '*Cambridge Gas* marks the furthest that the common law courts have gone in developing the common law powers of the court to assist a foreign liquidation. It has proved to be a controversial decision. So far as it held that the domestic court had jurisdiction over the parties simply by virtue of its power to assist, it was … held by a majority of the Supreme Court to be wrong in *Rubin v Eurofinance SA* [2012] 2 BCLC 682. So far as it held that the domestic court had a common law power to assist the foreign court by doing whatever it could have done in a domestic insolvency, its authority is weakened by the absence of any explanation of whence this common law power came, and by the direct rejection of that proposition by the Judicial Committee in *Al Sabah v Grupo Torras SA* [2014] 2 BCLC 597 at 611 …'

[13] See Anderson, 'Six of the Best: The Record of the Supreme Court in the Insolvency Cases Decided in its First Four Years' [2014] JBL 194 at 203 who says that the decision was not so much a retreat by the court as a recognition of a boundary to its powers.

[14] [2012] 2 BCLC 682 at [199]. But see Anderson, n 13, at 204, who robustly criticises Lord Clarke's position and who, at 206, concludes that for all the criticism, *Rubin* was rightly decided as a matter of principle and gives practitioners considerable certainty.                     [15] [2014] 2 BCLC 597, PC.

by the liquidators in their home jurisdiction. The majority in the Privy Council (Lords Sumption, Clarke, and Collins) held that there was a limited power at common law, under the concept of modified universalism, to assist a foreign court's insolvency jurisdiction by ordering the production of information which was necessary for the administration of the foreign winding up and/or to identify and locate assets of the company, but the power was only exercisable if the requesting court could have made an equivalent order. Moreover, the exercise of the common law power to compel the production of information was subject to the following limitations: (1) it was available only to assist the officers of a foreign court of insolvency jurisdiction or equivalent public officers; (2) it was a power of assistance which existed for the purpose of enabling a foreign court to surmount the problems posed for a world-wide winding up of the company's affairs by the territorial limits of each court's powers, and it was not available to enable the foreign court to do something which it could not do under the law by which it was appointed; (3) it was available only when it was necessary for the performance of the office-holder's functions; and (4) the order had to be consistent with the substantive law and public policy of the assisting court. On the facts, it was not appropriate for a Bermuda court to make an order, analogous to what it could make under its domestic law, to compel disclosure by the auditors to the Cayman liquidators.

## The EC Regulation on Insolvency Proceedings

**24-4**   The European insolvency framework originated in the EC Regulation on Insolvency Proceedings, Regulation 1346/2000.[16] The intention was to improve the efficiency and effectiveness of insolvency proceedings having cross-border effect, but without harmonising insolvency procedures throughout the EU, where generally the applicable law is the national law of the Member State in which proceedings are opened. The main advantage of the Regulation was that it established a clear structure for the commencement and recognition of insolvency proceedings where there is a cross-border element involving business in more than one Member State.[17]

**24-5**   In 2012, the European Commission announced plans to modernise Regulation 1346/2000[18] as part of a review of insolvency matters generally as reflected in a Commission Communication issued at the same time entitled 'A new European approach to business failure and insolvency'.[19] That Communication reflected on: the disparities between national insolvency laws which make it difficult to address the challenges posed by the transnational aspects of the internal market; the importance of insolvency law in supporting economic activity; and on the need to create an efficient system to restore and reorganise businesses in financial difficulty. There were also concerns as to unacceptable

---

[16]   OJ L 160/1, 30.6.2000, which came into effect on 31 May 2002 throughout the EU (with the exception of Denmark); see generally Moss, Fletcher, and Isaacs, *The EC Regulation on Insolvency Proceedings: A Commentary and Annotated Guide* (3rd edn, 2016).

[17]   The EC Regulation also confers jurisdiction on the courts of a Member State to open insolvency proceedings in relation to a company incorporated outside the Community if the centre of the company's main interests is in that Member State: *Re BRAC Rent-a-Car International Inc* [2003] 1 BCLC 470. See the interesting discussion by Mucciarelli, 'Not Just Efficiency: Insolvency Law in the EU and its Political Dimension' (2013) 14 EBOR 175.

[18]   See Proposal for a Regulation amending Council Regulation (EC) No 1346/2000, COM (2012) 744, 12.12.2012; and related report, see COM (2012) 743.

[19]   See COM (2012) 742.

forum shopping, especially in bankruptcy, but also in insolvencies. That Communication was followed by an online consultation exercise[20] and, after lengthy negotiations, the recast EU Insolvency Regulation 2015/848[21] replaced Regulation 1346/2000, with effect from 26 June 2017 (hereinafter the recast Regulation).

**24-6**  Proceedings within the recast Regulation can only be opened in accordance with the Regulation and they enjoy automatic recognition and enforcement in the other Member States. The UK insolvency proceedings within the scope of the recast Regulation are liquidations,[22] voluntary arrangements and administrations (including out of court appointments), and bankruptcy.[23] Receiverships and schemes of arrangement are beyond the scope of the Regulation. There had been some discussion about including schemes within the scope of the Regulation which would bring with it the advantage of recognition of schemes throughout the EU. Given the extensive use of the UK courts by foreign companies, however, the UK decided not to include schemes because of the restricting consequence of such a move. Inclusion would have meant that schemes would then be limited to companies whose centre of main interests (see later) is within the UK, whereas the courts have been willing to sanction schemes by foreign companies on the basis of a much more tenuous, though still sufficient, connection to the UK.

### Main and secondary proceedings

**24-7**  The recast Insolvency Regulation 2015/848 provides, essentially, for main insolvency proceedings, territorial insolvency proceedings, and secondary proceedings (see art 3, recast Regulation). Main proceedings have universal scope and are aimed at encompassing all the debtor's assets (recital 23 to the recast Regulation). Territorial proceedings may be opened in any Member State where the debtor has an establishment and those proceedings are restricted to the assets situated in that Member State. The meaning of 'establishment' for the purposes of the Insolvency Regulation 1346/2000 was considered by the Supreme Court in *Trustees of the Olympic Airlines SA Pension Scheme v Olympic Airlines SA*[24] where the issue was whether Olympic Airlines SA, a company incorporated in Greece, had an 'establishment' in the UK on 20 July 2010 entitling the English court to make a winding-up order under the Insolvency Regulation. If so, a consequence would be that the company's UK employees would benefit from the UK Pension Protection Fund. Regulation 1346/2000 defined an establishment as 'any place of operations where the debtor carries out a non-transitory economic activity with human means and goods'

---

[20]  See also a European Commission Recommendation aimed at encouraging Member States to put in place frameworks which provide for the efficient restructuring of viable enterprises in financial difficulty and (aimed primarily at bankruptcy procedures) give honest entrepreneurs a second chance. See Recommendation on a new approach to business failure and insolvency, C(2014) 1500 final, 12.3.2014; preceded by online Consultation on a new European approach to business failure and insolvency (July to October 2013).

[21]  OJ L 141/19, 5.6.2015. See generally, Moss, Fletcher, and Isaacs, n 16; Fletcher, 'The European Insolvency Regulation Recast: The Main Features of the New Law' (2015) 28 Insolv Int 97; McCormack, 'Something Old, Something New: Recasting the European Insolvency Regulation (2016) 79 MLR 102.

[22]  Meaning winding up by or subject to the supervision of the court and creditors' voluntary winding up with confirmation of the court, see recast Regulation, Annex A. A creditors' voluntary winding up does not require confirmation by the court as a matter of domestic law, but a liquidator in such a winding up may apply to the court for a confirmation order for the purposes of the EC Regulation: see IR 2016, r 21.4. See *Re Marann Brooks CSV Ltd* [2003] BPIR 1159; Patten J thought, obiter, that the Regulation has no application to winding-up petitions brought by the Secretary of State on public interest grounds under IA 1986, s 124A.

[23]  See Regulation 2015/848, art 2(4) and Annex A.     [24]  [2015] UKSC 27, [2015] 1 BCLC 589.

(art 2(h)). In similar fashion, the recast Regulation defines 'establishment' as any place of operations where a debtor carries out or has carried out in the three-month period prior to the request to open main insolvency proceedings a non-transitory economic activity with human means and assets (art 2(10)).

**24-8**    The facts were that, by the relevant date, Olympic Airways had closed all of its offices in the UK except for its head office in London and had ceased all commercial operations. It had terminated the contracts of all remaining UK staff except for the General Manager, the Purchasing Manager, and an accounts clerk, who were retained on short-term ad hoc contracts to implement instructions from the liquidator in Athens, to supervise the disposal of the company's assets in the UK, and to pay bills and conduct other administration relating to the head office building. At first instance, Sir Andrew Morritt held that these activities did constitute 'non-transitory economic activities' and therefore Olympic Airlines did have an 'establishment' in the UK entitling the court to make a winding-up order. The Court of Appeal disagreed and held that the remaining activity consisted only in the winding up of the company's affairs which was not enough to give the court jurisdiction to make the order. The Supreme Court agreed, ruling that the definition of 'establishment' in Regulation 1346/2000, which must be read as a whole, envisages a fixed place of business and business activity carried on there, consisting in dealings with third parties, and not merely acts of internal administration.[25] For example, disposal of stock in trade would clearly satisfy the definition, but mere internal administration of the winding up including administration of remaining premises in the UK would not.[26] Olympic Airlines SA was not carrying on business activity at its head office on 20 July 2010 and did not have an 'establishment' in the UK at that date.[27]

**24-9**    Territorial proceedings may only be commenced prior to the opening of main proceedings and, once the main proceedings are opened, the territorial proceedings become secondary proceedings (art 3(4)). Under Regulation 1346/2000, secondary proceedings had to be winding-up rather than rescue proceedings but that limitation on the nature of secondary proceedings is not retained in the recast Regulation. The recast Regulation allows a court to postpone or refuse the opening of secondary proceedings if such proceedings are not necessary to protect the interests of local creditors because an undertaking has been given in the main proceedings to treat them in the same manner as if secondary proceedings had been opened (arts 36 and 38(2), recast Regulation).[28] The new Regulation also provides for increased cooperation between insolvency practitioners involved in main and secondary proceedings, including exploring possible restructuring of the debtor, and with the courts involved in both sets of proceedings (arts 41–43).

**24-10**    Main proceedings are effective in all Member States as long as no territorial proceedings have been opened (art 20, recast Regulation) and the liquidator appointed in the main proceedings is able immediately to exercise his powers in other Member States in accordance with the general law of that Member State (art 21, recast Regulation) and is required to furnish only a certified copy of his appointment in order so to act (art 22, recast Regulation). Main proceedings extend to actions which derive from the insolvency proceedings and are closely linked to them including avoidance actions such as

---

[25] [2015] UKSC 27, [2015] 1 BCLC 589 at [13].        [26] [2015] UKSC 27, [2015] 1 BCLC 589 at [14].
[27] [2015] UKSC 27, [2015] 1 BCLC 589 at [16].
[28] A practice used and accepted in the UK and now applicable under the new Regulation, see Moss (2013) 26 Insol Intel 55 at 56.

challenges to undervalue transactions and preferences (art 6, recast Regulation and recital 35).[29]

### Centre of main interests

**24-11**　Main proceedings may be opened in the Member State where the debtor has his 'centre of main interests' (comi) which is presumed, in the case of a company, to be the place of the registered office in the absence of proof to the contrary (art 3(1) in each Regulation). That presumption only applies if the registered office has not been moved to another MS within the three-month period prior to the request for the opening of the insolvency proceedings. To rebut the presumption in favour of the registered office, the courts required that there be factors both objective and ascertainable by third parties which establish that the actual position is different.[30] Under the recast Regulation, that case law is reflected in art 3(1) which identifies the centre of main interests as the place where the debtor conducts the administration of its interests on a regular basis and which is ascertainable by third parties. When determining whether the comi is ascertainable by third parties, recital 28 says that special consideration should be given to the creditors and to their perceptions as to where the debtor conducts the administration of its interests. Generally, a number of the recitals to the recast Regulation attempt to clarify the position with respect to comi, reflecting the manner in which the law surrounding it has developed to date. First, it is provided that, before opening insolvency proceedings, the competent court should examine of its own motion whether the debtor's centre of main interests or establishment is actually located within the court's jurisdiction (recital 27). Where the circumstances of the case give rise to doubts about the court's jurisdiction, the court should require the debtor to submit additional evidence to support its assertions and, where appropriate, give the debtor's creditors the opportunity to present their views on the question of jurisdiction (recital 32). Recital 30 clarifies the circumstances in which the presumption that the comi of a company is located at the place of its registered office can be rebutted, reflecting the decision in *Interedil srl v Fallimento Interedil srl*.[31] The recital notes that it should be possible to rebut this presumption where the company's central administration is located in a Member State other than that of its registered office and a comprehensive assessment of all the relevant factors establishes, in a manner that is ascertainable by third parties, that the company's actual centre of management and supervision and of the management of its interests is located in that other Member State. In *Thomas v Frogmore Real Estate Partners GP1 Ltd*[32] the court had to be satisfied that comi was in England if it was to make an order appointing administrators to three Jersey companies. The companies were incorporated to acquire three shopping centres in England, they had borrowed significant sums to do so, and the relevant debentures were governed by English law and had English jurisdiction clauses. The sole shareholder in each case was an English company,

---

[29] This provision is an attempt to address some of the issues which had arisen as to the relationship between the Brussels Regulation on Judgments (Regulation 44/2001) and the Insolvency Regulation 1346/2000 and to reflect the decision of the European Court in *Seagon v Deko Marty Belgium NV* (C-339/07) [2009] ECR-I 767. See McCormack, 'Reconciling European Conflicts and Insolvency Law' (2014) 15 EBOR 209; also *Schmid v Hertel* (C-328/12) [2014] 1 WLR 633, noted by Moss (2015) 28 Insolv Intel 6.

[30] *Interedil Srl v Fallimento Interedil Srl* [2011] BPIR 1639, noted Moss (2011) 24 Insolv Int 126; *Re Eurofood IFSC Ltd* (C-341/04) [2007] 2 BCLC 151. An extensive jurisprudence now exists on the meaning of 'centre of main interests' ('comi') since that determines which Member State has jurisdiction for main proceedings. See Moss, Fletcher, and Isaacs, *The EC Regulation on Insolvency Proceedings: A Commentary and Annotated Guide* (3rd edn, 2016), para 8.85; Wessels, 'Comi, Past, Present and Future' (2011) 24 Insolv Int 17; Mevorach, 'European Insolvency Law in a Global Context' [2011] JBL 666.

[31] [2011] BPIR 1639.　　　[32] [2017] 2 BCLC 101.

the companies had no trading operations in Jersey and no employees there, though board meetings were held there. A management company registered in England provided a wide range of services to the companies. The companies and their directors tried to oppose the appointment of administrators on the basis that the presumption in favour of the registered office had not been rebutted in this instance. The court ruled that the presumption had been rebutted on the basis that the management company provided services akin to the functions expected to be carried out by a head office, the debentures were governed by English law and had English jurisdiction clauses, and day-to-day dealings with third parties were carried out by the management company in London. The fact that board meetings were held in Jersey was of little significance since third parties would not know where board meetings take place, so this would not be information ascertainable by a third party.

**24-12** In keeping with the national and international focus on rescuing businesses in difficulties and recognising the need for resolution of group insolvencies, the recast Regulation provides two distinct routes to assist practitioners: (i) provision for cooperation and communication between those involved in group insolvencies; and (ii) provision for the opening of group coordination proceedings. The obligations with respect to cooperation and communication follow a familiar pattern requiring cooperation and communication between the courts but also between the courts and the insolvency practitioners. Where insolvency proceedings relate to two or more members of a group of companies, an insolvency practitioner appointed in proceedings concerning a member of the group must cooperate with any insolvency practitioner appointed in proceedings concerning another member of the same group to the extent that such cooperation is appropriate to facilitate the effective administration of those proceedings, is not incompatible with the rules applicable to such proceedings, and does not entail any conflict of interest (art 56). In implementing the requirement for cooperation, insolvency practitioners must communicate to one another any relevant information, and consider whether possibilities exist for coordinating the administration and supervision of the affairs of the group members or for restructuring group members which are subject to insolvency proceedings (art 56(2)).

**24-13** To the extent appropriate to facilitate the effective administration of the insolvency proceedings, an insolvency practitioner may be heard or request a stay in any proceedings concerning any other member of the group and he may also apply for the opening of group coordination proceedings (art 60(1)(c)). The request must include a proposal for a nominated person to be appointed as the group coordinator, must outline the proposed group coordination, and must give the reasons why it would facilitate the efficient administration of the proceedings, and give an outline of the estimated costs of the group coordination. It is also provided that any insolvency practitioner appointed to any member company may object to the group coordination plan and then that company is not included within the plan so, in effect, participation is voluntary and any group company can be withdrawn from it. Once appointed, the group coordinator's task and obligations are as set out in art 72, recast Regulation. Essentially, the task is to propose a group coordination plan that identifies, describes, and recommends a comprehensive set of measures appropriate to an integrated approach to the resolution of the group members' insolvencies.

**24-14** Finally, there is provision for greater transparency with Member States required to publish relevant information on cross-border insolvency cases in a publicly accessible electronic insolvency register (for example, information on the parties, the type of proceedings, the date opened, etc, see art 24) and for the interconnection of national insolvency registers via a EU e-Justice portal (art 25). It is important that the courts in each Member State have easy access to this information so as to reduce the risk that conflicting proceedings might be opened in different States, hence provision is made for cooperation and communication between courts in different MS and between the courts and insolvency practitioners (arts 42 and 43).

### UNCITRAL Model Law

**24-15**   The Cross-Border Insolvency Regulations 2006[33] give effect to the UNCITRAL Model Law on Cross-Border Insolvency Proceedings. This Model Law (in the manner of the EU Regulation) does not seek to unify the substantive and procedural law on insolvency of the adopting States. It simply seeks to ease the access of foreign representatives and creditors to the courts and insolvency procedures of Great Britain and is particularly valuable in the context of UK/US insolvencies. The Model Law entitles a foreign representative to apply directly to the courts to commence insolvency proceedings and to participate in such a proceeding once commenced.[34] The Model Law also addresses specific issues such as the recognition of foreign proceedings, coordination of proceedings concerning the same debtor, rights of foreign creditors, the rights and duties of foreign representatives, and co-operation between national authorities. In the event of a conflict between the application of the Model Law and the EU Regulation, the Regulation prevails and when identifying a debtor's comi, the court applies the test promulgated by the Court of Justice of the European Communities, see **24-11**, (not least because it would be absurd to have two differing interpretations of comi) so that, therefore, the presumption is that a debtor's comi is in the State where it has its registered office but that presumption can be rebutted by factors which are both objective and reasonably ascertainable.[35]

## B   Voluntary winding up

### Resolution of the company

**24-16**   In practice, voluntary winding up is the most common form of winding up.[36] The advantage of proceeding in this way is that there is no court involvement so costs and time scales may be reduced and the nomination of the liquidator is a matter for the members and/or the creditors.

**24-17**   A voluntary winding up begins with a resolution passed by the members. Typically, a special resolution is required (IA 1986, s 84(1)(b)), but an ordinary resolution is sufficient in the unusual case where the articles limit the duration of the company (s 84(1)(a)). Five business days' notice of the intention to pass a resolution for voluntary winding up must be given to a floating chargeholder which gives the chargeholder an opportunity to appoint an administrator instead (s 84(2A)).

---

[33]   SI 2006/1030. See generally Mevorach, 'On the Road to Universalism' (2011) 12 EBOR 517; Fletcher, 'The UNCITRAL Model Law in the United Kingdom' (2007) 20 Insolv Int 138; McCormack, 'Comi and Comity in UK and US Insolvency Law' (2012) 128 LQR 140.

[34]   For an example, see *Re Chesterfield United Inc* [2013] 1 BCLC 709.

[35]   *Re Stanford International Bank Ltd* [2011] Ch 33 at [53]–[56].

[36]   In 2016–17, out of 24,327 UK liquidations, 10,739 were creditors' voluntary liquidations (CVLs) and 511 were administrations which converted to CVLs; there were 3,668 compulsory liquidations. There were also 9,409 members' voluntary liquidations: see Companies House, *Statistical Tables on Companies Registration Activities 2016–17*, Table A10.

**24-18**   A copy of the resolution for winding up must be forwarded to the registrar of companies within 15 days of being passed (IA 1986, s 84(3)); and the company must give notice of the resolution by advertisement in the *Gazette* (s 85(1)). A voluntary winding up, whether a members' voluntary or a creditors' voluntary (see later), is deemed to commence at the time of the passing of the resolution for voluntary winding up (s 86). From that commencement, the company ceases to carry on its business, except so far as may be required for its beneficial winding up (s 87(1)).

### Declaration of solvency—members' voluntary winding up

**24-19**   If in the five weeks immediately preceding the date of the resolution to wind up the company, or on the date of the resolution but before it is passed, the directors or a majority of the directors make a statutory declaration of solvency, the winding up is a members' voluntary winding up (IA 1986, ss 89, 90).

**24-20**   The statutory declaration must be to the effect that the directors have made a full enquiry into the affairs of the company and have formed the opinion that the company will be able to pay its debts in full (together with interest) within such period, not exceeding 12 months from the date of the commencement of the winding up (i.e. the date of the passing of the resolution for winding up),[37] as may be specified in the declaration.[38]

**24-21**   The advantage to the directors in making such a declaration is that it enables the appointment of the liquidator by the members. The risk in doing so is that if the declaration is made by a director without reasonable grounds, he commits a criminal offence and, if the debts are not paid in full within the specified time, that raises a rebuttable presumption that the director did not have reasonable grounds for making the declaration.[39]

**24-22**   If it turns out that the declaration is erroneous and the liquidator appointed by the members is of the opinion that the company will be unable to pay its debts in full within the 12-month period, he must draw up a statement of the company's affairs and send it to the creditors within seven days of forming that opinion and the creditors may nominate him or another to act as a liquidator (IA 1986, s 95(1A), (4B), (4C)). As from the day of nomination of a liquidator by the creditors, the situation is treated as if no declaration of solvency was made and the winding up becomes from that date onwards a creditors' voluntary winding up.[40]

### No declaration of solvency—creditors' voluntary winding up

**24-23**   If the directors do not make a statutory declaration of solvency, the winding up is a creditors' voluntary winding up (IA 1986, s 90). In this case, the directors of the company must, before the end of the period of seven days beginning with the day after the day on which the company passes a resolution for voluntary winding up, as outlined at **24-17**, make out a statement in the prescribed form as to the affairs of the company, and send the statement to the company's creditors showing, in particular, the company's assets, debts, and liabilities (s 99(1), (2)).

---

[37] IA 1986, s 86.

[38] IA 1986, s 89(1). The statutory declaration must be delivered to the registrar of companies within 15 days after the resolution for winding up is passed: s 89(3). Failure to do so gives rise to criminal penalties.

[39] IA 1986, s 89(4), (5). See Simmons, 'The Statutory Declaration of Solvency—Voluntary Winding Up of Companies—Members or Creditors' (1996) 9 Insolv Int 33.   [40] IA 1986, s 96(1), (2).

## Appointing a liquidator

**24-24**   Having passed a resolution for voluntary winding up, the members or the creditors proceed to appoint a liquidator. In a members' voluntary winding up, the members at their meeting to pass the resolution for winding up must appoint a liquidator (IA 1986, s 91(1)). In a creditors' voluntary winding up, the creditors may appoint a liquidator using either the deemed consent procedure or a virtual meeting (IR 2016, r 6.14)[41] and they can be invited to consider whether they wish to establish a liquidation committee.[42] In all liquidations (compulsory or voluntary) a liquidator, apart from the official receiver acting in a compulsory liquidation, must be a qualified insolvency practitioner.[43]

**24-25**   Where there is no liquidator appointed for whatever reason, the court may appoint (IA 1986, s 108). In that situation, the directors' powers to deal with the company's assets pending the appointment of a liquidator are essentially restricted to the preservation of the assets.[44] Likewise, in a creditors' voluntary winding up, if the members' meeting has nominated a liquidator prior to the creditors' nomination being made, that liquidator has power only to protect and preserve the company's property or to dispose of perishable items and he otherwise requires the consent of the court to act (s 166(2),(3)).

**24-26**   Once appointed, the liquidator must publish in the *Gazette* and deliver to the registrar of companies a notice of his appointment (IA 1986, s 109). The company ceases to carry on business and all the directors' powers cease[45] although, in a voluntary winding up, they are not automatically removed from office.[46]

## C  Compulsory winding up

**24-27**   A compulsory winding up requires a court order and the court's jurisdiction to make such an order is subject to the recast EC Regulation on Insolvency Proceedings which limits the court's power to open main insolvency proceedings to cases where the debtor's centre of main interests is in the UK and territorial insolvency proceedings to cases where the debtor possesses an establishment within the UK (see **24-7**).[47]

## Petitioners for a winding-up order

**24-28**   The vast majority of petitions for winding up are presented by creditors,[48] but a petition can be presented by, amongst others, the company, its directors, and contributories (essentially members).[49] Equally, provision is made for public interest petitions, for example, by

---

[41] IA 1986, s 100(1); the members' meeting may already have nominated a liquidator but, in the event of a conflict, the creditors' choice prevails: s 100(2). Objectors may apply to the court for an appointment in place of the creditors' choice: s 100(3).

[42] IA 1986, s 101. A liquidation committee essentially oversees the conduct of the liquidation and consists of creditors' (and possibly members') representatives, see IR 2016, rr 17.3–17.27.

[43] IA 1986, ss 230(1)–(5); ss 389–393; and see the Insolvency Practitioners Regulations 2005, SI 2005/524.

[44] IA 1986, s 114; and see *Re a company (No 006341 of 1992), ex p B Ltd* [1994] 1 BCLC 225.

[45] See IA 1986, s 91(2) (members' voluntary winding up), except so far as the company or the liquidator sanctions their continuance; s 103 (creditors' voluntary winding up), except so far as the liquidation committee or the creditors sanction their continuance.

[46] *Madrid Bank Ltd v Bayley* (1866) LR 2 QB 37.        [47] See IA 1986, s 117(7); recast EC Regulation, art 3.

[48] A creditor may petition even though the company is in voluntary winding up: IA 1986, s 116.

[49] IA 1986, s 124(1). 'Contributory' encompasses members of the company as well as others not registered as members but who are liable to contribute to the assets of the company: see IA 1986, s 79.

the official receiver where there are concerns as to the conduct of a voluntary winding up;[50] by the Secretary of State;[51] and by the Financial Conduct Authority.[52] As noted at **24-1**, it is possible that the company has been the subject of some other insolvency process already, hence provision is made for petitions for a winding-up order by a supervisor of a company voluntary arrangement (CVA);[53] by an administrator;[54] and by a liquidator appointed in main proceedings in another Member State under the recast Insolvency Regulation.[55]

**24-29**  A contributory (essentially a member) is not entitled to present a winding-up petition unless either the number of members is reduced below two (except where the company is a single member company)[56] or the shares held by him were originally allotted to him or have been held by him for at least six months during the 18 months before the commencement of the winding up or have devolved to him through the death of a former holder.[57] This provision is designed to prevent individuals from purchasing shares with a view to winding up a company, though a six-month period seems inadequate for this purpose. Additionally, a contributory must establish an interest in the winding up. For example, a partly paid-up shareholder who remains liable to contribute the amount unpaid on his shares in the event of the company being wound up has an interest. For a fully paid-up member to establish that he has a tangible interest in the winding up, he must show a *prima facie* probability of surplus assets remaining after the creditors have been paid.[58]

## Grounds for compulsory winding up

**24-30**  The process of obtaining a winding-up order begins with a petition based on one of the grounds set out in the IA 1986, s 122(1). Some of these grounds are relevant to solvent companies, for example, where a petition is brought for winding up on the just and equitable ground which is essentially a shareholder remedy.[59] For insolvent companies, the ground relied on is that the company is unable to pay its debts (s 122(1)(f)) and, in such cases, the petition is invariably brought by a creditor.[60]

---

[50]  See IA 1986, s 124(5).

[51]  i.e. under IA 1986, ss 122(1)(b), (c) or 124A. As to the exercise of the court's discretion in public interest petitions, see *Secretary of State for Business, Enterprise and Regulatory Reform v Amway (UK) Ltd* [2011] 2 BCLC 716 (in an exceptional case, the court can refuse to make an order and accept undertakings from the company as to its future conduct though the Secretary of State has refused to accept the undertakings); also *Secretary of State v Charter Financial Solutions Ltd* [2011] 2 BCLC 788.

[52]  See Financial Services and Markets Act 2000, s 367.

[53]  IA 1986, s 7(4)(b); Sch A1, para 39(5)(b).        [54]  IA 1986, Sch 1, para 21; Sch B1, para 60.

[55]  IA 1986, s 124(1).        [56]  IA 1986, s 124(2)(a).

[57]  IA 1986, s 124(2)(b). Where the *locus standi* of a contributory to petition is disputed, the court will consider all the circumstances, including the likelihood of damage to the company if the petition is not dismissed, in deciding whether first to require the petitioner to seek the determination of his status outside of the winding-up petition: *Alipour v Ary, Re a company (No 002180 of 1996)* [1997] 1 BCLC 557, CA; and see *Alipour v UOC Corp* [2002] 2 BCLC 770.

[58]  *Re Rica Gold Washing Co* (1879) 11 Ch D 36; *Re Expanded Plugs Ltd* [1966] 1 All ER 877; *Re Othery Construction Ltd* [1966] 1 All ER 145; *Re Bellador Silk Ltd* [1965] 1 All ER 667.

[59]  i.e. under IA 1986, s 122(1)(g): see **19-95**. Other grounds include that the company has resolved by a special resolution to be wound up by the court; that the company is a public company and has not been issued with a trading certificate under CA 2006, s 761; that the company has not commenced business within one year of incorporation or has suspended its business for a whole year: IA 1986, s 122(1)(a), (b), (d).

[60]  Additionally, a creditor (only) may petition for winding up where a company voluntary arrangement with a moratorium comes to an end without a voluntary arrangement being approved: IA 1986, ss 122(1) (fa); 124(3A); the advantage of using this option is that the creditor does not have to establish that the company is unable to pay its debts.

## Company is unable to pay its debts

**24-31**  The circumstances in which a company is deemed to be unable to pay its debts are set out in IA 1986, s 123 and include a failure to meet a statutory demand (s 123(1)(a)), a failure to satisfy a judgment against the company (s 123(1)(b)), and a general ground of being unable to pay its debts as they fall due (s 123(1)(e)). Reliance on a failure to meet a statutory demand is a straightforward way to show that the company is insolvent since it merely requires that the facts about the statutory demand be established, but there must be due compliance with all the procedural requirements of a statutory demand.[61] Section 123(1)(e) allows a creditor, without serving a statutory demand or attempting to enforce a judgment, to satisfy the court by suitable evidence of the company's inability to pay (the cash-flow test). Failure to pay an undisputed debt, despite repeated requests, must *prima facie* mean an inability to pay and a winding-up order may be sought by a creditor.[62] A company is not entitled to have the petition struck out, or prevent it being issued, merely because it is in fact solvent.[63]

**24-32**  If the debt is due and is undisputed, the petition proceeds to hearing and adjudication in the normal way, but it is an abuse of process and the petition will be struck out if the debt is bona fide disputed and the petition is being used as a means of pressurising the company.[64] This long-established approach of dismissing the petition where the debt is bona fide disputed is a rule of practice only, however, and it must give way to exceptional circumstances which make it desirable that the petitioner should proceed.[65] In particular, the court will have regard to whether the petitioner would otherwise be without a remedy, whether injustice would result, whether there is some other sufficient reason for allowing the petition to proceed, or whether there is a likelihood of damage to the company if the petition is not dismissed.[66]

**24-33**  A petition may also be dismissed if the company has a genuine and serious cross-claim for an amount which exceeds the petitioner's debt and which the company has been unable to litigate, subject to the court's residual discretion to consider whether there are any special

---

[61]  A creditor to whom the company is indebted in a sum exceeding £750 then due must have served on the company, by leaving it at the company's registered office, a written demand (in the prescribed form) requiring the company to pay the sum so due and the company must for three weeks thereafter have neglected to pay the sum or to secure or compound for it to the reasonable satisfaction of the creditor. As to the detailed requirements concerning this statutory demand, see IR 2016, rr 7.2–7.3. The demand must be for a liquidated amount. A demand must be for a debt 'then due' and a contingent debt when the contingency has not happened has not fallen due: *JSF Finance & Currency Exchange Co Ltd v Akma Solutions Inc* [2001] 2 BCLC 307.

[62]  *Taylors Industrial Flooring Ltd v M & H Plant Hire (Manchester) Ltd* [1990] BCLC 216, CA; *Cornhill Insurance plc v Improvement Services Ltd* [1986] BCLC 26. The courts will not allow a winding-up petition to enforce what is essentially a small debt and in effect impose a minimum debt of the amount required for a statutory demand: see Fletcher, *The Law of Insolvency* (5th edn, 2017), para 21–009.

[63]  *Cornhill Insurance plc v Improvement Services Ltd* [1986] BCLC 26.

[64]  See *Re MCI WorldCom Ltd* [2003] 1 BCLC 330; *Re a company (No 0012,209 of 1991)* [1992] 2 All ER 797; *Stonegate Securities Ltd v Gregory* [1980] 1 All ER 241; *Mann v Goldstein* [1968] 2 All ER 769. If the debt is disputed, the petitioner may not actually be 'a creditor' and therefore lacks *locus standi* to bring a petition: see *Re Bayoil SA* [1999] 1 BCLC 62 at 66, CA.

[65]  *Re GBI Investments Ltd* [2010] 2 BCLC 624; *Parmalat Capital Finance Ltd v Food Holdings Ltd* [2009] 1 BCLC 274, PC; *Alipour v Ary, Re a company (No 002180 of 1996)* [1997] 1 BCLC 557, CA; *Brinds Ltd v Offshore Oil NL* (1986) 2 BCC 98, 916; *Re Claybridge Shipping Co SA* [1997] 1 BCLC 572, (CA, 1981).

[66]  *Re GBI Investments* Ltd [2010] 2 BCLC 624 at [80]–[90]; *Alipour v Ary, Re a company (No 002180 of 1996)* [1997] 1 BCLC 557, CA; see also *Re Claybridge Shipping Co SA* [1997] 1 BCLC 572, (CA, 1981).

circumstances which might make it inappropriate to dismiss the petition.[67] The fact that the petitioning creditor may have some other purpose behind a petition such as to obtain some collateral advantage from placing a company in winding up (for example as a claimant in ongoing litigation against the company) does not make a petition an abuse of process; as long as a winding-up order is also, objectively, likely to be of substantial advantage to him as a petitioning creditor and to secure such an advantage was the other of his purposes in bringing a petition, it is not necessary that it should have been the principal purpose for presenting the petition.[68] In *Salford Estates (No 2) Ltd v Altomart Ltd*[69] the Court of Appeal held that, where the debt which is the basis of the petition arises out of a contract which makes provision for disputes under the contract to go to arbitration, a petition for winding up will not be automatically stayed, applying the Arbitration Act 1996, s 9, rather the matter will fall within the discretion of the court under Insolvency Act 1986, s 122. However, it is to be expected that the court will exercise its discretion consistently with the legislative policy embodied in the Arbitration Act 1996. Otherwise, it would become a standard tactic for parties to by-pass an arbitration agreement by presenting a winding-up petition.[70]

**24-34**   The three methods of establishing an inability to pay debts (statutory demand, unsatisfied judgment, and inability to pay debts as they fall due, see **24-31**) are based on petitioning creditors who have debts that are immediately due and payable. But petitions may also be brought by contingent or prospective creditors.[71] It might be the case that a creditor has lent money to a company which is not due to be repaid until some date in the future but the creditor is concerned that the present financial position of the company suggests it will not be able to repay the debt when payment is due. Such a creditor may rely on the balance sheet test in IA 1986, s 123(2), to show that the company is insolvent and should be wound up. IA 1986, s 123(2) provides that:

> 'A company is also deemed unable to pay its debts if it is proved to the satisfaction of the court that the value of a company's assets is less than the amount of its liabilities, taking into account[72] its contingent and prospective liabilities.'

---

[67] *Re Bayoil SA* [1999] 1 BCLC 62, CA; *Montgomery v Wanda Modes Ltd* [2002] 1 BCLC 289; *Re VP Developments Ltd* [2005] 2 BCLC 607. The significance of the 'inability to litigate' requirement was doubted in *Montgomery v Wanda Modes Ltd* as not forming part of the ratio of *Bayoil*. Park J noted that there is nothing objectionable in a company which has refrained from pursuing a claim which it believed it has against another party, later deciding to pursue that cross-claim if the other party threatens it with winding-up proceedings; he thought it would be undesirable for companies to be penalised for refraining from litigating a claim or if parties were to be encouraged to litigate possible claims sooner rather than later; see also *Re a debtor (No 87 of 1999)* [2000] BPIR 589 to the same effect and on which Park J relied.

[68] *Ebbvale Ltd v Hosking* [2013] 2 BCLC 204, PC.

[69] [2014] EWCA Civ 1575, [2015] BCC 306.

[70] [2014] EWCA Civ 1575, [2015] BCC 306 at [39]–[40]. On the other hand, where there is a dispute between a company in liquidation and a creditor (each claiming against the other) and the substance of that dispute is subject to an arbitration clause, the court will uphold the arbitration requirement and expect the liquidator to participate in it; the arbitration agreement does not become inoperative following a liquidation or in consequence of the statutory set-off: *Philpott v Lycée Français Charles de Gaulle School* [2016] 1 All ER (Comm) 1.

[71] IA 1986, s 124(1); IR 2016, r 14.1(3).

[72] This does not mean that such contingent or prospective liabilities should be aggregated at their face value with debts presently due, see Morrit C in *BNY v Eurosail-UK* [2011] 2 BCLC 1 at [31], it will involve consideration of the relevant facts, when the prospective liability falls due, whether it is payable in sterling or some other currency, what assets will be available to meet it, and what if any provision is made for the allocation of losses in relation to those assets.

**24-35**   A detailed analysis of that section was central to *BNY Corporate Trustee Services Ltd v Eurosail-UK 2007–3BL plc*[73] which reached the Supreme Court. The case is of particular significance because, in many financial transactions, the balance sheet insolvency test set out in IA 1986, s 123(2) is specified as an event of default. Hence the decision is important, not just in the statutory context of winding-up petitions, but in the commercial context of contractual definitions of acts of default. The facts of the case (a complex bondholder dispute arising out of the collapse of Lehman Brothers) are irrelevant, the general interest lies in the proper approach to the interpretation and application of s 123(2). The Court of Appeal decision attracted a lot of comment because of Lord Neuberger MR's view expressed there that the balance sheet test can only be relied on by a future or contingent creditor of a company which has reached 'the end of the road'.[74] The concern was that this test set the threshold so high that it might be difficult ever to invoke it and trigger enforcement options. Lord Neuberger MR considered that the purpose of s 123(2) and the reason why it is included in addition to s 123(1)(e) (the cash-flow test) is, as Professor Sir Roy Goode had identified, to cover a case where, 'although it could not be said that a company "is [currently] unable to pay its debts as they fall due" (either because it has no debts which are currently payable, or because it has, or can achieve, the cash flow to pay such debts), it is, in practical terms, clear that it will not be able to meet its future or contingent liabilities', having reached the point of no return,[75] '... imprecise, judgement-based and fact-specific as such a test may be'.[76] On the facts in the case, it had not been established that the company at the heart of the dispute had reached the point of no return and therefore it was not insolvent.[77]

**24-36**   In the Supreme Court, Lord Walker gave the main judgment (Lords Mance, Sumption, and Carnwath agreed with Lord Walker) and he noted that a 'cash-flow' test is concerned with debts falling due from time to time in the reasonably near future, as well as debts currently due. What is the reasonably near future, for this purpose, will depend on all the circumstances, but especially on the nature of the company's business. But beyond the reasonably near future, he said, any attempt to apply a cash-flow test becomes completely speculative, and a comparison of present assets with present and future liabilities (discounted for contingencies and deferment) becomes the only sensible test.[78] However, as he acknowledged, that is still very far from an exact test, and the burden of proof has to be on the party which asserts balance sheet insolvency.[79] On the facts, in *Eurosail*, there

---

[73] [2013] 1 BCLC 613; and see Day, 'Taking Balance-sheet Insolvency beyond the Point of no Return' (2013) 72 CLJ 515; Anderson, 'Six of the Best: The Record of the Supreme Court in the Insolvency Cases Decided in its First Four Years' [2014] JBL 194.                                    [74] [2011] 3 All ER 470.

[75] [2011] 2 BCLC 1 at [48]–[49], [115], [121]. See also *Re Cheyne Finance plc* [2008] 1 BCLC 741 at [51]; Goode, *Principles of Corporate Insolvency Law* (4th edn, 2011), para 4–23.

[76] [2011] 2 BCLC 1 at [58], [61], [62]. It is not enough to take the future and contingent liabilities at face amount, a valuation exercise will be needed, at [60], [117]. The starting point would be the company's latest audited accounts, but it would be necessary to take other factors into account and adjust the figures accordingly, at [65], [68].

[77] The court took into account the fact that the company had substantial assets, its liabilities had to be met over a relatively long period of time, and there was potential for significant changes in values since they depended on currency fluctuations, see [2011] 2 BCLC 1 at [80].                       [78] [2013] 1 BCLC 613 at [37].

[79] See Day, n 73, who regrets the failure of Lord Walker to give more guidance on the application of the balance sheet and who wonders how lower courts and legal advisers can be expected to come to consistent and coherent views in the absence of additional guidance; to a degree he thought Lord Neuberger's judgment in the Court of Appeal was more helpful on the application of the balance sheet test. Anderson, n 73, applauds the Supreme Court's more nuanced approach, rejects criticism that the court left open how the test should be applied, while also acknowledging that it has not made advising on these matters any easier.

were three imponderable factors affecting the issuer company—currency movements, interest rates, and the UK economy and housing market—and the final redemption date for all the notes issued by the company was not until 2045. The movements of currencies and interest rates in the meantime, if not entirely speculative, were incapable of prediction with any confidence. The court could not be satisfied, therefore, that there would eventually be a deficiency. The company was not balance sheet insolvent so as to have triggered the enforcement provisions and the appeal was dismissed. In so concluding the Supreme Court expressly rejected the approach favoured by Lord Neuberger in the Court of Appeal. Lord Walker noted that, in the Court of Appeal, while Toulson LJ had agreed with Lord Neuberger, he had expressed himself in a more guarded way.[80] Toulson LJ had agreed that Professor Sir Roy Goode's reference (which Lord Neuberger had relied on particularly) to a company having 'reached the point of no return because of an incurable deficiency in its assets' illuminated the purpose of IA 1986, s 123(2) but did not purport to be a paraphrase of it. Toulson LJ had continued:[81]

> 'Essentially, section 123(2) requires the court to make a judgment whether it has been established that, looking at the company's assets and making proper allowance for its prospective and contingent liabilities, it cannot reasonably be expected to be able to meet those liabilities. If so, it will be deemed insolvent although it is currently able to pay its debts as they fall due. The more distant the liabilities, the harder this will be to establish.'

Lord Walker went on:[82] 'I agree with what Toulson LJ said here, and with great respect to Lord Neuberger MR, I consider that "the point of no return" should not pass into common usage as a paraphrase of the effect of s 123(2).'[83] The decision in *Eurosail* is generally considered to provide insufficient practical guidance as to how to determine when a company is balance sheet insolvent, since the period of futurity required may be difficult to determine, and complex valuation issues may need to be resolved (for example, with respect to contingent claims) especially in the context of a trading entity.[84]

**24-37** The application of *Eurosail* was considered by the Court of Appeal in *Re Casa Estates (UK) Ltd, Carman v Bucci*.[85] A company had entered into a transaction at an undervalue with a connected person (see **15-54**) and so the presumption in IA 1986, s 240(2) arose, namely that the transaction was at a time when the company was unable to pay its debts within the meaning of IA 1986, s 123. The question for the Court of Appeal was whether, if it could be shown that a company was cash-flow solvent at the relevant time, the presumption was rebutted, or whether it was necessary also to consider whether the company was balance sheet solvent at that time. The Court of Appeal held that the balance sheet test in IA 1986, s 123 is not excluded merely because a company is, for the time being, in fact paying its debts as they fall due. The tests of cash-flow insolvency and balance sheet insolvency feature as part of a single exercise, namely to determine whether a company is unable to pay its debts as they fall due. It is not enough merely to ask whether the company is, for the time being, paying its debts as they fall due, the court must go on to inquire how

---

[80] [2013] 1 BCLC 613 at [42].    [81] [2011] 2 BCLC 1 at [119].    [82] [2013] 1 BCLC 613 at [42].

[83] See Day, n 73, who thinks there is considerable merit in Lord Neuberger's approach while acknowledging Lord Walker's criticism of it and conceding that Lord Neuberger may have overstated the position.

[84] See generally Day, 'Taking Balance-sheet Insolvency beyond the Point of no Return' (2013) 72 CLJ 515; Anderson, 'Six of the Best: The record of the Supreme Court in the Insolvency Cases Decided in its first Four Years' [2014] JBL 194. Also Meng Seng Wee, 'Misconceptions about the "Unable to Pay its Debts" Ground of Winding Up' (2014) 130 LQR 648 who argues that the decision makes it more difficult for trade creditors to rely on cash-flow insolvency and unhelpfully blurs the line between the cash-flow test and the balance sheet test, as *Re Casa Estates* [2014] 2 BCLC 49 would seem to confirm.    [85] [2014] 2 BCLC 49.

it is managing to do so. On the facts in the case, the company was only able to pay its debts by taking new deposits from customers, each deposit resulted in a liability to that depositor, but the judge had not asked how those liabilities were to be satisfied. The company could not properly have used the new moneys received to pay the old debts and therefore it was cash-flow insolvent at that time.[86] It was also balance sheet insolvent at the material time as a relevant asset, a loan to a connected company, had no value. The presumption that, at the relevant time, the company was unable to pay its debts had not been rebutted. Lewison LJ took the opportunity to provide a valuable summation of the position reached in *Eurosail* as follows (references omitted):[87]

(i) The tests of insolvency in s 123(1)(e) and 123(2) were not intended to make a significant change in the law as it existed before the IA 1986.

(ii) The cash-flow test looks to the future as well as to the present. The future in question is the reasonably near future; and what is the reasonably near future will depend on all the circumstances, especially the nature of the company's business. The test is flexible and fact-sensitive.

(iii) The cash-flow test and the balance sheet test stand side by side. The balance sheet test, especially when applied to contingent and prospective liabilities, is not a mechanical test. The express reference to assets and liabilities is a practical recognition that, once the court has to move beyond the reasonably near future, any attempt to apply a cash-flow test will become completely speculative and a comparison of present assets with present and future liabilities (discounted for contingencies and deferment) becomes the only sensible test.

(iv) But it is very far from an exact test. Whether the balance sheet test is satisfied depends on the available evidence as to the circumstances of the particular case. It requires the court to make a judgment whether it has been established that, looking at the company's assets and making proper allowance for its prospective and contingent liabilities, it cannot reasonably be expected to meet those liabilities. If so, it will be deemed insolvent even though it is currently able to pay its debts as they fall due.

Lewison LJ also noted[88] the approval in *Eurosail* of the judgment of Briggs J in *Re Cheyne Finance plc*[89] and drew attention to two of the points made by Briggs J, namely that:

(i) Cash-flow solvency or insolvency is not to be ascertained by a blinkered focus on debts due at the relevant date. Such an approach will in some cases fail to see that a momentary inability to pay is only the result of temporary illiquidity. In other cases it will fail to see that an endemic shortage of working capital means that a company is on any commercial view insolvent, even though it may continue to pay its debts for the next few days, weeks, or even months.

(ii) Even if a company is not cash-flow insolvent, the alternative balance sheet test will afford a petitioner for winding up a convenient alternative means of proof of a deemed insolvency.

---

[86] See also *BHS Group Ltd v Retail Acquisitions Ltd* [2017] 2 BCLC 472 at [28]— company was cash flow insolvent given there was an 'endemic shortage of working capital'.

[87] [2014] 2 BCLC 49 at [27]. See Fennell, case comment (2014) 27 Insolv Intel 121.

[88] [2014] 2 BCLC 49 at [28].        [89] [2008] 1 BCLC 741.

Finally, it is settled law that, in valuing assets for the purposes of IA 1986, s 123, contingent assets may not be taken into account. IA 1986, s 123(2) explicitly refers to contingent and prospective liabilities, but it does not refer to contingent or prospective assets.[90] The issue was addressed in *Evans v Jones*[91] where various claims made against directors of a company turned on whether the company was insolvent at the time of various transactions (alleged preferences contrary to IA 1986, s 239). The company was balance sheet insolvent at the time, but there were potentially some unlawful dividend payments (£75,000) which, if treated as a company asset (being unlawful, they were held on trust for the company), would have rendered the company solvent. There was then a potential or contingent asset available to the company which would alter the position from insolvency to solvency and so render the various transactions immune from challenge. The court at first instance accepted that the contingent asset altered the picture. On appeal, the Court of Appeal reaffirmed that contingent assets should not be taken into account. Moreover, the court said, the test in s 123 must be applied in a way that has regard to commercial reality. To count the dividend payment of £75,000 as an asset would involve assuming that the unlawfulness would be discovered, the dividend would be reclaimed, the recipients would concede the claim, and the money would be recovered, none of which accorded with commercial reality.

### The court's discretion to make a winding-up order

**24-38**   Having grounds for the presentation of a petition does not necessarily entitle the creditor to a winding-up order, though if the creditor has standing and the court is satisfied that the company is unable to pay its debts, a winding-up order should follow unless there is some special reason why it should not be made.[92] Winding up is a collective or class remedy, however, and an order may be refused if the petitioner is merely seeking to obtain some private advantage;[93] but if the purpose of the petition is legitimate, it does not matter that the motive of the petitioner is malicious.[94]

**24-39**   There may well be differences of opinion among the creditors as to whether a compulsory winding up is appropriate in which case the court can direct, so as to ascertain the creditors' wishes, that qualifying decision procedures be instigated or the deemed consent procedure be used, in accordance with any directions given by the court, and the result be reported to the court (IA 1986, s 195). A particular aspect of this clash of opinions is where a company is already in voluntary winding up and the court is asked to substitute a compulsory winding-up order for that voluntary process. The court takes account of the wishes of the majority of the creditors and, where the majority oppose the making of a compulsory winding-up order, the onus is on those seeking the order to show good reason why it should be granted.[95] The court looks carefully at the quality of the creditors on either side as well as the quantity and, where some of the creditors are also shareholders

---

[90] A claim in a liquidation of a company is a present asset consisting of a chose in action which can be given a value and what it fetches in the market is good evidence of that value, see Lewison LJ in *Evans v Jones* [2017] 1 BCLC 184 at [20], citing Morrit C in *BNY v Eurosail* [2011] 2 BCLC 1 at [30].

[91] [2017] 1 BCLC 184, CA.

[92] See *Re Demaglass Holdings Ltd* [2001] 2 BCLC 633; *Re Lummus Agricultural Services Ltd* [2001] BCLC 137. But see *Re Minrealm Ltd* [2008] 2 BCLC 141 where the court adjourned the petition to await the resolution of unfairly prejudicial proceedings.          [93] *Re a Company (No 001573 of 1983)* [1983] BCLC 492.

[94] *Bryanston Finance Ltd v De Vries (No 2)* [1976] 1 All ER 25, CA; *Re a Company (No 001573 of 1983)* [1983] BCLC 492.

[95] *Re JD Swain Ltd* [1965] 2 All ER 761; *Re Gordon and Breach Science Publishers Ltd* [1995] 2 BCLC 189. It may be more appropriate in some cases simply to apply under IA 1986, s 171 for the appointment of a different liquidator: see *Re Inside Sport Ltd* [2000] 1 BCLC 302.

or directors of the company or their associates, their views may be given less weight or disregarded altogether.[96] Principles of fairness and commercial morality are taken into account and may require that the creditors secure the independent scrutiny of the company's affairs which is a consequence of a compulsory winding-up order.[97]

**24-40**  On the making of the winding-up order and by virtue of his office, the official receiver becomes the liquidator.[98] At any time when he is the liquidator, or if 25 per cent in value of creditors request it, the official receiver may seek nominations from the creditors and the members for a person to be the liquidator of the company in his place.[99] In the event of different nominations, the creditors' nominee is appointed.[100] If no nominations are made, the official receiver remains as liquidator.[101]

## D  Consequences of winding-up order

**24-41**  In the case of a compulsory winding up, the winding up is deemed to commence at the time of the presentation of the petition, unless the company had passed a resolution for voluntary winding up prior to the presentation of the petition, in which case the winding up is deemed to commence at the date of the passing of the resolution.[102] In a compulsory winding up, the directors are automatically dismissed from office on the making of the order,[103] the employment of all employees is terminated, and the liquidator takes the company's property into his custody and control (IA 1986, s 144).[104]

### Dispositions of the company's property

**24-42**  A compulsory winding up commences with the presentation of the petition but there is a risk that property which should be available to the creditors may be disposed of in the period (which may be quite lengthy) between the presentation of the petition and the making of the winding-up order. To preserve such property for the creditors, any disposition of the company's property and any transfer of shares or alteration in the status of the company's members after the commencement of a compulsory winding up is void, unless the court otherwise orders (IA 1986, s 127).[105] The value of this provision is that it enables

---

[96]  *Re Demaglass Holdings Ltd* [2001] 2 BCLC 633; *Re Lummus Agricultural Services Ltd* [2001] BCLC 137; *Re Falcon (R J) Developments Ltd* [1987] BCLC 437.

[97]  *Re Lowerstoft Traffic Services Ltd* [1986] BCLC 81; *Re Palmer Marine Surveys Ltd* [1986] BCLC 106; *Re Gordon and Breach Science Publishers Ltd* [1995] 2 BCLC 189.

[98]  IA 1986, s 136(1), (2). The court also has power to appoint a provisional liquidator prior to the making of the winding-up order: see s 135. Three copies of the winding-up order are sent to the official receiver; one copy is served by him on the company at its registered office and one copy is sent to the registrar of companies and the order is notified in the *Gazette* and advertised in a local paper: IR 2016, r 7.22.

[99]  IA 1986, s 136(4), (5)(c).       [100]  IA 1986, s 139(2), (3).

[101]  The Secretary of State may appoint a replacement liquidator on the application of the official receiver or following the failure of the meetings to appoint: IA 1986, s 137(1)–(3).

[102]  IA 1986, s 129. Presentation of the petition takes place when the petition is delivered to the court for issue, not when it is issued: *Re Blights Builders Ltd* [2008] 1 BCLC 245.

[103]  *Measures v Measures* [1910] 2 Ch 248.

[104]  Note also IA 1986, s 132 which provides that where a winding-up order is made by the court, it is the duty of the official receiver to investigate the causes of the failure (if the company has failed) and, generally, the promotion, formation, business dealings, and affairs of the company, and to make such report (if any) to the court as he thinks fit.

[105]  See IA 1986, s 88 (which applies in a voluntary winding up) to similar effect, but it is limited in application to transfers of shares and alterations in the status of the company's members.

liquidators subsequently to challenge certain dispositions with a view to recovering assets for the benefit of the creditors generally. Equally, the court's discretion to validate transactions offers some relief for those dealing with a company in this situation. The application of s 127 is therefore of considerable practical importance (its application is limited to compulsory winding up).

**24-43**  In exercising this discretion to validate dispositions, the court looks to see if the disposition was made bona fide to assist the company,[106] such as the repayment of or the grant of security for loans made to the company after the commencement of winding up.[107] But the court generally refuses to validate payments which have the effect of preferring pre-insolvency creditors[108] unless the payment confers a benefit on creditors generally.[109] It is open to the company or any creditor to apply to the court to validate a transaction in advance of it taking place and this is particularly useful where the company carries on business in the period between the presentation of a winding-up petition and the making of a winding-up order. In such circumstances, the court adopts the same general approach and takes into account the benefit to the creditors generally of keeping the business going with a view to selling it as a going concern.

**24-44**  The application of IA 1986, s 127 is limited to where there is 'a disposition of the company's property'. In *Hollicourt (Contracts) Ltd v Bank of Ireland*[110] the Court of Appeal considered the position regarding payments out of a company's bank account. In this case, after the presentation of a petition for the winding up of the company, the bank continued to operate the company's bank account for a period of three months, having overlooked the advertisement of the petition. The bank debited the company's account, which was in credit throughout, with payments in favour of third parties totalling £156,200. The liquidator commenced proceedings against the bank seeking repayment by the bank of the moneys paid out on the basis that the payments were 'dispositions' of the company's property within IA 1986, s 127 and void.

**24-45**  The Court of Appeal held that IA 1986, s 127 only invalidated dispositions by the company of its property to the payees of the cheques. It enabled the company to recover the amounts disposed of from the payees but not from the bank. The purpose of s 127, the court said, is to prevent the directors of a company, when liquidation is imminent, from disposing of the company's assets to the prejudice of its creditors and to preserve those assets for the benefit of the general body of creditors. The policy promoted by s 127 is not aimed at imposing on a bank restitutionary liability to a company in respect of payments made by cheque in favour of creditors in addition to the unquestioned liability of the payees of the cheques. The section impinged on the end result of the process of payment initiated by the company, i.e. the point of ultimate receipt of the company's property in consequence of a disposition by the company. The statutory purpose is accomplished, the court said, without any need for the section to impinge on the legal validity of intermediate steps, such as banking transactions, which are merely part of the process by which dispositions of the company's property are made.[111]

---

[106] *Re J Leslie Engineering Co Ltd* [1976] 2 All ER 85.
[107] *Re Steane's (Bournemouth) Ltd* [1950] 1 All ER 21; *Re Clifton Place Garage Ltd* [1970] 1 All ER 353, CA.
[108] *Re Civil Service and General Store Ltd* (1887) 57 LJ Ch 119.
[109] *Re A I Levy (Holdings) Ltd* [1963] 2 All ER 556.
[110] [2001] 1 BCLC 233, CA; see Hare, 'Banker's Liability for Post-Petition Dispositions' (2001) 60 CLJ 468.
[111] [2001] 1 BCLC 233 at 239.

**24-46** Though not necessary to its decision (the account in *Hollicourt* was in credit throughout), the Court of Appeal made the point that, even if the payments had been made out of an overdrawn account (as in *Coutts v Stock*[112]), the outcome would have been the same in respect of a claim for recovery against the bank. The court thought that this result had the very real practical advantage of not requiring what could be a complex analysis of whether payments were made out of an account which was in debit or in credit.[113] This approach also avoids the risk that the banks are the deep pockets pursued by liquidators rather than the payees in respect of whom the liquidators had an undoubted claim.

**24-47** These cases concerned payments *out* of a company's bank account. Payments by a company *into* an overdrawn account with its bank with the resulting reduction in its indebtedness to the bank are dispositions requiring consent[114] while a payment into an account which is in credit simply results in an adjustment of the records between the company and its bank and is not a disposition of the company's property for these purposes.[115] Where a bank seeks a validation order with respect to payments into an overdrawn account, the essential question is whether the payments into the account are in the ordinary course of business and whether they are likely to be for the benefit of the creditors generally, but where there is no real benefit to the creditors generally, merely a reduction in the amount owed to the bank, a validation order will not be made.[116] To do so would breach the *pari passu* principle and result in the bank's pre-liquidation debt being repaid to the detriment of the other creditors.[117]

## Control of legal proceedings and enforcement of remedies

**24-48** When a winding-up order is made, all pending proceedings are automatically halted and no new proceedings may be commenced except by the leave of the court under IA 1986, s 130(2).[118] In practice, the court allows the enforcement of rights by secured creditors[119] (since such proceedings cannot adversely affect the position of unsecured creditors), but in relation to other matters the court must decide whether there is any sensible point in allowing the proceedings to continue and what is right and fair in the circumstances of the particular case.[120] The purpose of the provisions of s 130(2) and equivalent provisions on administration or bankruptcy is not so much to protect creditors as to ensure that

---

[112] [2000] 1 BCLC 183.       [113] [2001] 1 BCLC 233 at 242.

[114] *Re Gray's Inn Construction Co Ltd* [1980] 1 All ER 814, CA. Although this case was much criticised in *Hollicourt (Contracts) Ltd v Bank of Ireland* [2001] 1 BCLC 233, CA, on this point it remains valid; see also *Re Tain Construction Ltd* [2003] 2 BCLC 374.       [115] *Re Barn Crown Ltd* [1994] 4 All ER 42.

[116] *Re Tain Construction Ltd* [2003] 2 BCLC 374.       [117] *Re Tain Construction Ltd* [2003] 2 BCLC 374.

[118] Distress is defined as including use of the procedures in Schedule 12 to the Tribunals, Courts and Enforcement Act 2007: IA 1986, s 436, and distress is an 'action or proceeding' within s 130(2) and requires court consent: *Re Memco Engineering Ltd* [1985] BCLC 424; *Herbert Berry Associates Ltd v IRC* [1978] 1 All ER 161, HL.

[119] *Re David Lloyd & Co, Lloyd v David Lloyd & Co* (1877) 6 Ch D 339, CA and *Re Aro Co Ltd* [1980] 1 All ER 1067, CA (secured creditors enforcing security); *Re Coregrange Ltd* [1984] BCLC 453 (creditor suing for specific performance). A freezing order over assets, without more, does not constitute a security for these purposes, for it does not impose an obligation to satisfy any judgment debt out of those frozen assets: *Flightline Ltd v Edwards* [2003] 1 BCLC 427, CA.

[120] *New Cap Reinsurance Corp Ltd v HIH Casualty & General Insurance* Ltd [2002] 2 BCLC 228, CA; see also *Bourne v Charit-Email Technology Partnership LLP* [2010] 1 BCLC 210. Leave will not be given if the issues can conveniently be decided in the winding up: *Craven v Blackpool Greyhound Stadium and Racecourse Ltd* [1936] 3 All ER 513, CA; *Re Exchange Securities and Commodities Ltd* [1983] BCLC 186; but will be given if the issues are better decided by an action: *Currie v Consolidated Kent Collieries Corpn Ltd* [1906] 1 KB 134, CA.

when an order has been made all proceedings having any bearing upon the administration or winding up of the company or the bankruptcy, as the case might be, remain under the supervision and control of the court which had made the order. On that basis, proceedings brought without permission are not a nullity and retrospective permission may be given for their commencement.[121]

**24-49**   Where provisional liquidators were appointed in England in respect of a Luxembourg company whose centre of main interests was in England, so opening main proceedings under the Insolvency Regulation 1346/2000/EC (see **24-4**), the effect is to make English law the applicable law determining the conduct of the proceedings and, applying s 130(2), this means that any action or proceedings against the company requires permission. Hence liquidation proceedings commenced against the company in Luxembourg were stayed by the application of IA 1986, s 130(2).[122] Once a winding-up order has been made, IA 1986, s 128(1) appears to render void any enforcement of a remedy (attachment, sequestration, distress, or execution) after the commencement of the winding up.[123] It is invariably treated, however, as also subject to the court's discretion under s 130(2) to allow the enforcement to continue.[124] The court has a broad and unfettered discretion to do what is right and fair in the circumstances of the particular case, but it must not allow the individual creditor the benefit of enforcing the judgment if this will prejudice the equal treatment of creditors generally.[125] On the other hand, the court has allowed an individual creditor to succeed where the debtor forced,[126] tricked,[127] or persuaded[128] the creditor to abstain from enforcing a judgment sometime before the winding up commenced.

## E  The role and powers of a liquidator

**24-50**   Duties owed by liquidators are owed to the company and not to individual contributories or creditors.[129] When carrying out his functions, the liquidator acts as an agent of the company.[130] Any contracts entered into by him are entered into by the company

---

[121]  *Governor and Company of the Bank of Ireland v Colliers International UK plc* [2013] Ch 422.

[122]  *Re ARM Asset Backed Securities SA* [2014] 2 BCLC 364. The relevant proceedings were not secondary proceedings within Regulation 1346/2000 and not stayed under it.

[123]  This provision is limited to compulsory winding up and there is no directly equivalent provision with respect to voluntary winding up, but the liquidator would apply to the court for directions under IA 1986, s 112 with a view to the court exercising its discretion as to whether to permit execution following the commencement of the winding up. If proceedings have already resulted in a judgment against the company, but enforcement of that judgment has not been completed prior to the commencement of the winding up, the proceeds of an execution etc cannot be retained by the creditor against the liquidator unless the court orders otherwise, see IA 1986, s 183, which applies to compulsory and voluntary winding up.

[124]  *Re Lancashire Cotton Spinning Co, ex p Carnelly* (1887) 35 Ch D 656, CA. If distress is in progress at the commencement of the winding up but not completed, the courts will allow it to continue unless there is something inequitable in allowing the distraining party to have the fruits of the distress. See *Re Memco Engineering Ltd* [1985] BCLC 424; *Herbert Berry Associates Ltd v IRC* [1978] 1 All ER 161, HL; *Re Bellaglade Ltd* [1977] 1 All ER 319. The Tribunals, Courts and Enforcement Act 2007, s 71 abolished the common law right to distrain for arrears of rent with effect from 6 April 2014, instead there is a limited right for the recovery of rent arrears due under a lease of commercial premises only, see s 72.

[125]  *New Cap Reinsurance Corp Ltd v HIH Casualty & General Insurance Ltd* [2002] 2 BCLC 228, CA; *Re Aro Co Ltd* [1980] 1 All ER 1067, CA; *Roberts Petroleum Ltd v Bernard Kenny Ltd* [1983] 1 All ER 564, HL; *Re Grosvenor Metal Co Ltd* [1950] Ch 63.       [126]  *Re London Cotton Co* (1866) LR 2 Eq 53.

[127]  *Armorduct Manufacturing Co Ltd v General Incandescent Co Ltd* [1911] 2 KB 143, CA.

[128]  *Re Grosvenor Metal Co Ltd* [1950] Ch 63; *Re Suidair International Airways Ltd* [1950] 2 All ER 920; *Re Redman (Builders) Ltd* [1964] 1 All ER 851.       [129]  See *Lomax Leisure Ltd v Miller* [2008] 1 BCLC 262.

[130]  A liquidator in a compulsory winding up is an officer of the court: IA 1986, s 160.

and the liquidator incurs no personal liability unless the terms of the contract show that he is undertaking a personal liability.[131] Title to the company's assets is not automatically vested in the liquidator but remains vested in the company unless, exceptionally, the court so orders (IA 1986, s 145).

**24-51**  The basic duty of the liquidator in all types of liquidation is to wind up the company's affairs, to collect in and realise the company's assets, and to make distributions to the creditors in accordance with the statutory scheme with any surplus being returned to the shareholders.[132] To assist in these tasks, an extensive array of powers are conferred on a liquidator by IA 1986, Sch 4, including the power to pay any class of creditors in full; to reach any compromise with any creditors; to bring any legal proceedings under certain provisions of the IA 1986;[133] to bring or defend any action or other legal proceeding in the name and on behalf of the company; to carry on the business of the company so far as may be necessary for its beneficial winding up; to sell any of the company's property; and including the power to do all such other things as may be necessary for winding up the company's affairs and distributing its assets.[134]

**24-52**  A liquidator also has extensive statutory powers to assign causes of action (including the proceeds of a cause of action) arising from the avoidance provisions of the IA 1986, hence a liquidator can assign claims for wrongful and fraudulent trading, for undervalues and preferences, and for extortionate credit bargains, see IA 1986 s 246ZD.[135]

**24-53**  A particularly useful power which a liquidator has is the power of disclaimer. Disclaimer is a means by which a liquidator can terminate certain future obligations of the company or disclaim ownership of unsaleable assets and he can exercise the power to disclaim onerous property notwithstanding that he has taken possession of the property, endeavoured to sell it, or otherwise exercised rights of ownership in relation to it.[136] Any person sustaining loss or damage as a consequence of the operation of a disclaimer has a statutory right to compensation (s 178(6)).[137]

---

[131] *Stewart v Engel* [2000] 2 BCLC 528; *Stead, Hazel & Co v Cooper* [1933] 1 KB 840; *Re Anglo-Moravian Hungarian Junction Rly Co, ex p Watkin* (1875) 1 Ch D 130, CA.

[132] IA 1986, ss 91(1), 100(1), 107 (voluntary winding up); s 143(1) (compulsory winding up).

[133] i.e. IA 1986, ss 213, 214, 238, 239, 242, 243, or 423 (provisions allowing actions to be brought to recover assets or seek contributions to the company's assets), see Chapter 15.

[134] Previously, to exercise some of these powers, the sanction of the court or the liquidation committee, or a special resolution of members, was required. The requirement for sanction was removed in all cases by the Small Business, Enterprise and Employment Act 2015, s 120, with effect from 26 May 2015. See *Explanatory Notes to the Small Business, Enterprise and Employment Act 2015*, para 717. As to the operation of the new regime, see *Re Longmeade Ltd* [2017] 1 BCLC 605, where, despite not needing the sanction of the court, the liquidators sought directions from the court under IA 1986, s 168(2), as to whether to bring a claim on behalf of the company when bringing it was opposed by two of the largest creditors for their own individual reasons.

[135] Inserted by Small Business, Enterprise and Employment Act 2015, s 118.

[136] IA 1986, s 178(2). 'Onerous property' is defined as: (1) any unprofitable contract; and (2) any other property of the company which is unsaleable or not readily saleable or is such that it may give rise to a liability to pay money or perform any other onerous act: s 178(3). It is a necessary feature of an 'unprofitable contract' that it imposes future obligations (i.e. obligations yet to be performed), the performance of which might be detrimental to creditors by prejudicing the liquidator's obligation to realise the company's property and pay a dividend to the creditors within a reasonable time: *Re SSSL Realisations (2002) Ltd* [2007] 1 BCLC 29, CA. 'Property' is defined in IA 1986, 436 and extends to a waste disposal licence under the Environmental Protection Act 1990 which may be disclaimed by a liquidator: *Re Celtic Extraction Ltd* [1999] 2 BCLC 555, CA.

[137] See *Re Park Air Services plc* [1999] 1 BCLC 155, HL.

**24-54**  Disclaimer is effected by the liquidator serving a notice[138] and the effect of a disclaimer is to terminate, as from the date of the disclaimer, the rights and liabilities of the company in the property disclaimed (IA 1986, s 178(4)(a)). But, it does not, except so far as is necessary for the purposes of releasing the company from any liability, affect the rights or liabilities of any other person.[139] There is no time-limit within which the liquidator must decide whether to disclaim property, but any person with an interest in the property can serve a notice on the liquidator requiring the liquidator to disclaim within 28 days or lose the right to do so (s 178(5)). The court can interfere with a disclaimer only if it is exercised in bad faith or the liquidator's decision is perverse.[140]

**24-55**  To assist liquidators to get a complete picture of the company's affairs, liquidators have extensive powers to inquire into the company's dealings and to seek the court's assistance by summoning persons to appear before it, or requiring persons to submit affidavits or produce books, documents, or other records relating to the company (ss 235, 236). In a compulsory winding up, the liquidator may seek a decision on any matter from the company's creditors or contributories; and must seek a decision on a matter (a) from the company's creditors, if requested to do so by one-tenth in value of the creditors; (b) from the company's contributories, if requested to do so by one-tenth in value of the contributories (s 168(1), (2)). He may also apply to the court for directions in relation to any particular matter arising in the winding up.[141]

**24-56**  In a compulsory liquidation, individual contributories or creditors may apply to the court to control the exercise or proposed exercise of any of the liquidator's powers (IA 1986, s 167(3)). There is no equivalent provision with respect to voluntary liquidation, but an application to the court may be made under IA 1986, s 112(1) by any contributory or any creditor to determine any question arising in the winding up. Furthermore, in a compulsory winding up, any person aggrieved by an act or decision of the liquidator may apply to the court under s 168(5) which may confirm, reverse, or modify the act or decision complained of and may make such order as it thinks fit.[142] The court will not interfere with the business decisions of a liquidator, however, and it is necessary to establish that the liquidator has acted mala fide or in a way in which no reasonable liquidator would have acted.[143]

**24-57**  Individual contributories or creditors may use the summary misfeasance procedure under IA 1986, s 212 to ask the court to compel the liquidator to restore property to the company or compensate it for breach of duty. The power to make such an application continues after the winding up is completed and notwithstanding the release of the liquidator from all liability connected with the liquidation,[144] but any application in these circumstances requires the court's consent (s 212(4)).

---

[138]  For the rules as to the notice, see IR 2016, rr 19.2–19.6.

[139]  IA 1986, s 178(4)(b); and see *Hindcastle Ltd v Barbara Attenborough Associates Ltd* [1996] 2 BCLC 234, HL; *Capital Prime Properties plc v Worthgate Ltd* [2000] 1 BCLC 647.

[140]  *Re Hans Place Ltd* [1993] BCLC 768.

[141]  IA 1986, s 168(3) (compulsory winding up); s 112 (voluntary winding up).

[142]  Applications under IA 1986, s 168(5) may be brought by creditors or contributories or persons directly affected by the exercise of a power given specifically to a liquidator and who otherwise would not be able to challenge the exercise of that power: *Mahomed v Morris* [2000] 2 BCLC 526, CA.

[143]  See *Re Greenhaven Motors Ltd* [1997] 1 BCLC 739; *Re Edennote Ltd, Tottenham Hotspur plc v Ryman* [1996] 2 BCLC 389, CA.

[144]  IA 1986, ss 173(4), 174(6).

## F  The anti-deprivation rule, proof of debts, and set-off

### Overview

**24-58**  On liquidation all the assets of the company form a common fund which, subject to the expenses of the winding up and the rights of the preferential creditors, is subject to a statutory trust for the benefit of all the unsecured creditors.[145] Secured creditors look not to the statutory trust but to their security for payment of the sums due to them but, if that security takes the form of a floating charge, the sums realised by that charge are subject to the prior claims of the expenses of winding up (so far as the general assets are insufficient to meet those expenses), the claims of the preferential creditors, and the need to set aside the 'prescribed part' (a percentage of the realisations of the floating charge set aside for the general body of creditors), all of which are discussed later. Unsecured creditors are restricted to claiming against any 'free' assets of the company, i.e. assets not appropriated to any security, (and only after the expenses of winding up and the claims of the preferential creditors have been met) and that pool of assets must be distributed *pari passu* (a fundamental principle of insolvency law)[146] which requires that all creditors participate in the pooled assets in proportion to the size of their claim and where the assets are insufficient to meet all the claims, they abate proportionately.[147] For example, if there are three unsecured creditors who are owed £100,000 (A), £200,000 (B), and £300,000 (C) and £240,000 remains available for distribution by the liquidator, A gets £40,000, B gets £80,000, and C £120,000. While the *pari passu* principle is the fundamental basis for the distribution of assets on insolvency, its application is limited to unsecured creditors (and preferential creditors in the event of a deficiency in meeting their claims) and it is precisely in order to avoid its application that creditors look for security and other mechanisms to remove themselves from the common pool.[148] In an attempt to limit the scope for defeating the *pari passu* distribution rule which applies to the common fund, there are some rules affecting the composition of the fund and the claims which can be made against it which need to be considered.

### Establishing the estate—the anti-deprivation rule

**24-59**  Clearly it is important that an insolvent company should not be able to remove or permit the removal of assets from its estate at the point of insolvency so leaving the creditors to claim against a smaller estate.[149] This rule is known now as the anti-deprivation rule and its origins can be traced to the nineteenth century. Often cited in this regard is the dictum of Cotton LJ in *Ex p Jay, re Harrison*[150] that 'there cannot be a valid contract that a man's property shall remain his until his bankruptcy, and on the happening of that event shall go over to someone else, and be taken away from his creditors'. The anti-deprivation

---

[145]  See *Ayerst (Inspector of Taxes) v C & K (Construction) Ltd* [1975] 2 All ER 537; *Webb v Whiffin* (1872) LR 5 HL 711 at 721, 724.

[146]  See *Re HIH Casualty and General Insurance Ltd; McMahon v McGrath* [2008] 3 All ER 869, HL.

[147]  IA 1986, s 107; IR 2016, r 14.12.

[148]  See, generally, Fletcher, *The Law of Insolvency* (5th edn, 2017), para 24–053 et seq; *McPherson and Keay's Law of Company Liquidation* (4th edn, 2017), para 13–022 et seq.

[149]  There is an overlap with the rule of *pari passu* distribution (discussed at **24-58**), see *Belmont Park Investments Pty Ltd v BNY Corporate Trustee Services Ltd* [2012] 1 All ER 505 at [1], [9], [14].

[150]  (1880) 14 Ch D 19 at 26.

rule was the subject of lengthy consideration by the Supreme Court in *Belmont Park Investments Pty Ltd v BNY Corporate Trustee Services Ltd*.[151]

**24-60**   The case arose out of the collapse of Lehman Brothers and the facts are complex but, in essence, the issue was that various investors (noteholders) claimed certain assets held as security by a trustee in circumstances where the investors' claim to the assets was in competition with a claim to the assets by a related insolvent swap counterparty (LBSF, one of the Lehman companies). The terms of the investment agreement provided that, on an event of default, the prior claim of LBSF to the assets would flip so as to give the investors prior claim to the assets. LBSF argued that the effect of 'the flip' was to deprive it (an insolvent company) of valuable assets on insolvency and so it infringed the anti-deprivation rule, a view rejected by the High Court and the Court of Appeal, each of which held that the anti-deprivation rule was not infringed in these circumstances. The Supreme Court affirmed the lower court decisions with five of their Lordships endorsing the judgment of Lord Collins who provided a detailed analysis of the development and scope of the rule.[152] The key points made by Lord Collins were that:

- The policy behind the anti-deprivation rule is clear: the parties cannot, on bankruptcy, deprive the bankrupt of property which would otherwise be available for creditors, but the rule is not triggered by deprivation for reasons other than insolvency.[153]

- The anti-deprivation rule is too well established to be discarded[154] despite the detailed provisions set out in modern insolvency legislation, all of which should be taken to have been enacted against the background of the rule.[155]

- Despite statutory inroads, party autonomy is at the heart of English commercial law, particularly in the case of complex financial instruments.[156] It is desirable that, so far as possible, the courts give effect to the contractual terms which parties have agreed. In line with that approach, it is possible to give the policy behind the anti-deprivation rule a common sense application which prevents its application to bona fide commercial transactions which do not have as their predominant purpose, or one of their main purposes, the deprivation of the property of one of the parties on bankruptcy.[157] Lord Collins noted that there is an impressive body of authority that, in the case of the anti-deprivation rule, a deliberate intention to evade the insolvency

---

[151] [2012] 1 All ER 505, aff'g the ruling of the Court of Appeal which is reported as *Perpetual Trustee Co Ltd v BNY Corporate Trustee Services Ltd* [2010] 1 BCLC 747, aff'g [2009] 2 BCLC 400. On the Supreme Court ruling, see Fletcher (2012) 25 Insolv Int 25; Worthington (2012) 75 MLR 78; on the Court of Appeal ruling, see Goode (2011) 127 LQR 1. See also *Money Markets International Stockbrokers Ltd v London Stock Exchange Ltd* [2001] 2 BCLC 347; *Lomas v JFB Firth Rixson* [2013] 1 BCLC 27 at [80]–[100].

[152] Lord Mance agreed with the conclusion but not with the analysis put forward by Lord Collins.

[153] [2012] 1 All ER 505 at [104].

[154] In the Court of Appeal Patten LJ had queried whether the rule was needed any longer in the light of the IA 1986, see [2010] 1 BCLC 747 at [171]–[172].

[155] [2012] 1 All ER 505 at [101]. See Fletcher, n 151, who notes the judicial determination not to deliver any game-changing pronouncements in this eagerly awaited judgment and the insistence that it is now for the legislature to change this rule. He also noted that realistically the prospect of any such reform must be considered very remote, at 27.                                                [156] [2012] 1 All ER 505 at [103].

[157] [2012] 1 All ER 505 at [104]. See Bridge and Braithwaite, 'Private Law and Financial Crises' (2013) 13(2) JCLS 361 at 371–5 for robust criticism of the difficulty of determining with any certainty whether a transaction will be of this commercial character so as to escape the application of the principle; the result, they say, is to leave 'a huge range of commercial transactions vulnerable to the uncertainty of a "case-by case" test' (at 398).

laws is required, though not in the sense of finding a subjective intention.[158] Finally, the source of the asset—who funded its acquisition (which the High Court and Lord Neuberger in the Court of Appeal thought important)—is an important and sometimes decisive factor when concluding that a transaction is a commercial one entered into in good faith and outside the scope of the anti-deprivation rule.[159]

**24-61**   In the instant case, the court had to look at the substance of the matter which was that LBSF had had a security interest, the content and extent of which had altered by an act of default (insolvency proceedings in the US). The transaction in question had been a complex commercial transaction. There had never been any suggestion that those provisions had deliberately been intended to evade insolvency law. That was obvious in any event from the wide range of non-insolvency circumstances capable of constituting an event of default under the swap agreement. The fact that, in certain circumstances, the change in priority would lead to a (possibly unanticipated) benefit to the investors and to the loss of LBSF's security rights in the assets did not alter the position. The anti-deprivation principle is essentially directed to intentional or inevitable evasion of the principle that the debtor's property is part of the insolvent estate and, applying the principle in a commercially sensitive manner, taking into account the policy of party autonomy and the upholding of proper commercial bargains, these 'flip' provisions did not infringe the principle.[160] Overall, the approach of the Supreme Court is to endorse the rule while offering commercial parties considerable freedom to contract around it, as long as there is a commercial purpose to the transaction and the parties are not starting from a position of a deliberate intention to contract out of the insolvency legislation.[161]

**24-62**   A more routine application of the anti-deprivation rule can be seen in *Folgate London Market Ltd v Chaucer Insurance plc*.[162] In this case, a truck company commenced proceedings against a broker in negligence after it transpired that the company did not have insurance coverage in respect of an accident involving a third party. The company and the broker entered into a settlement agreement whereby the broker agreed to pay 85 per cent of any claim which the company had to pay to the third party, but the broker would be released from its obligations under the settlement on the insolvency of the company. The truck company went into administration and the administrators assigned all interest in the settlement agreement to the company's insurers (the claimant) which sought and obtained an order striking down these settlement provisions as offending the anti-deprivation rule. On appeal, the Court of Appeal held that the commercial objective of this provision in the settlement agreement, properly construed, was an attempt to provide that, while the company's right to payment and the broker's obligation to pay would survive so long as the payment accrued exclusively to the benefit of the company, they were to be extinguished if such payment would instead be available for the company's creditors generally in the event of its insolvency. It was settled law, the court said, that a purported contracting out of insolvency legislation is contrary to public policy and therefore this

---

[158] [2012] 1 All ER 505 at [78]–[79]. See Anderson, 'Six of the Best: The Record of the Supreme Court in the Insolvency Cases Decided in its First Four Years' [2014] JBL 194 at 199 who makes the point that the practical effect of this emphasis on intention is to marginalise the anti-deprivation rule as liquidators will not usually be able to establish any such intention in relation to arm's length commercial transactions.
[159] [2012] 1 All ER 505 at [98].          [160] [2012] 1 All ER 505 at [106], [108]–[114].
[161] Worthington, n 151, at 121, criticises the focus on intention and comments that the ruling 'effectively eliminates the insolvency-triggered deprivation limb of the anti-deprivation principle, certainly for complex financial deals involving sophisticated parties'.
[162] [2011] BCC 675, aff'g [2010] 2 BCLC 440 where the case is reported as *Mayhew v King*.

provision was void. As Lord Collins noted in *Belmont Park Investments*,[163] this case was a blatant attempt to deprive a party of property in the event of liquidation.

**24-63**    A further rule which was thought to raise anti-deprivation issues was the so-called football creditors' rule, the details of which we can gloss over; suffice it to say that in effect it meant that where a football club was insolvent, particular classes of creditors, such as other clubs in the Football League (FL), the insolvent club's players, managers, other employees, and the FL itself, were paid in full in priority to any other creditors with the result that, often, the main unpaid creditor in a football insolvency is HMRC.

**24-64**    In *Revenue and Customs Commissioners v Football League Ltd*[164] HMRC unsuccessfully sought a declaration that the football creditors' rule contravenes the *pari passu* (see **24-58**) and anti-deprivation principles. There is a very useful judgment in this case by David Richards J where he reviewed the operation of these principles, and carefully distinguished between them,[165] before concluding on the facts that there was no breach. The key points made by him were:

(1)    The *pari passu* principle applies whenever the effect of a contractual or other provision is to apply an asset belonging to the debtor at or following the commencement of the insolvency procedure in a non-*pari passu* way. Contracts conflicting with the *pari passu* principle are void without any need to show that their purpose was to avoid a *pari passu* distribution. Because of that (void) consequence, the *pari passu* principle only comes into play if the purpose of the insolvency proceedings is to effect a distribution, as is the case when a company enters liquidation.

(2)    The anti-deprivation rule is aimed at attempts to withdraw an asset thereby reducing the value of the insolvent estate to the detriment of creditors. While there is some overlap with the *pari passu* principle, it is distinct from it and aimed at a different mischief. The anti-deprivation rule applies only if the deprivation is triggered by the insolvency proceedings, and the deprivation has to be of an asset of the debtor which would otherwise be available to creditors.

(3)    Accordingly, if a transaction has the effect of depriving a company of an asset in order to distribute it among some only of the creditors otherwise eligible to participate in the distribution, it offends both the *pari passu* and the anti-deprivation principles.

Applying those principles, in most circumstances in which the relevant football creditors' rule would operate, they would not be rendered void by the anti-deprivation rule or the *pari passu* principle. On the facts, the football clubs had no legal entitlement to any money until completion of all their fixtures so no asset arises until then and payments by the Football League to football creditors during the season out of sums held by the League to

[163] [2012] 1 All ER 505 at [104].

[164] [2013] 1 BCLC 285, and see the valuable commentary by Fletcher, 'Kicked into Touch? The Anti-Deprivation Rule and the Football Creditor Rule Judicially Considered' (2013) 25 Insolv Intel 49.

[165] See Bridge and Braithwaite, 'Private Law and Financial Crises' (2013) 13(2) JCLS 361 at 368–9 emphasising that the application of the anti-deprivation rule may depend on the exercise of a judicial discretion as to whether a transaction has been concluded for bona fide commercial reasons whereas the *pari passu* rule is of mandatory application and indifferent to commercial motivation. See *Belmont Park Investments Pty Ltd v BNY Corporate Trustee Services Ltd* [2012] 1 All ER 505 at [1], [9], [14]. But see Anderson, 'Six of the Best: The Record of the Supreme Court in the Insolvency Cases Decided in its First Four Years' [2014] JBL 194 at 198–9 who considers that the only real objection to deprivation provisions is that they interfere with *pari passu* distribution.

be paid to the clubs at the end of the season do not deprive the company of any asset, they merely reduce the balance to which the club would eventually have a legal entitlement. The court therefore declined to make the declarations sought by the Revenue and also noted that the overall approach of the Revenue seemed at times to be to treat the anti-deprivation rule as a general anti-avoidance principle when in fact the anti-deprivation rule is specific in what it prohibits. Broader or different restrictions would require statutory intervention, as has occurred in the cases covered by IA 1986, ss 238 to 245 (transactions at an undervalue, preferences etc).

**24-65**    One area where the anti-deprivation rule is not engaged is in the context of licences and leases which determine on insolvency. Rather than viewing these transactions as a contracting out contrary to the anti-deprivation rule, the position is better viewed as one whereby the company has a determinable interest in an asset which determines on insolvency in accordance with the terms of its grant.[166] The termination does not remove from the insolvent estate property in which the company ever had an unfettered interest, the company's interest always was limited by the terms on which it was granted and therefore the rule has no application.[167]

**24-66**    The result of the anti-deprivation rule and its invalidation of any removal of assets from the pool on insolvency is that creditors go to great lengths prior to this point to ensure that assets are available to meet their claims outside of the common fund. Indeed, in many cases, these devices ensure that there are no unencumbered assets available to the unsecured creditors. The mechanisms involved include, for example, taking security over the assets (even if a floating charge is subject to some prior claims) or retaining title to the goods so that those assets never become part of the company's assets on liquidation and are not swept into the common fund for *pari passu* distribution. A clause in a sale of goods contract preventing property in the goods passing to the purchaser until payment of debts due to the supplier ensures that such goods remain in the ownership of the supplier pending payment and do not form part of the assets of the company available to any unsecured creditors in a winding up.[168]

**24-67**    Another useful mechanism for some creditors is a trust. It is only property to which the company is beneficially entitled that is available to its creditors so, if the company holds property on trust for others, that property is not available to the company's creditors.[169] This has led to the use of the trust as a means of protecting unsecured creditors, especially where customers make advance payments to a company when the company is already in some financial difficulty.[170] By holding such customer sums on trust, they are protected from the claims of the creditors of the company in the event of insolvency. The use of such trusts is relatively common now and disputes tend to centre on whether the three

---

[166] While this carve-out for licences and leases is criticised, it is too well established now, as Professor Sir Roy Goode notes, to be dislodged other than by legislation, see Goode (2011) 127 LQR 1 at 8. See discussion in *Butters v BBC Worldwide Ltd* which is reported as a joined appeal in *Perpetual Trustee Co Ltd v BNY Corporate Trustee Services Ltd* [2010] 1 BCLC 747 at [84]–[88].

[167] See *Perpetual Trustee Co Ltd v BNY Corporate Trustee Services Ltd* [2010] 1 BCLC 747 at [146], per Patten LJ.

[168] See *Aluminium Industries Vaassen v Romalpa Ltd* [1976] 2 All ER 552; *Clough Mill Ltd v Martin* [1985] BCLC 64.

[169] See *Barclays Bank Ltd v Quistclose Investments Ltd* [1968] 3 All ER 651, HL; also *Carreras Rothmans Ltd v Freeman Matthew's Treasure Ltd* [1985] 1 All ER 155.

[170] For a valuable account of the advantages and disadvantages of using trusts in this way, see Ellis and Verrill, 'Twilight Trusts' (2007) 20 Insolv Int 151.

certainties (of intention, subject matter, and objects) required of any trust are present.[171] As these trusts are often hastily constructed as financial problems mount, it is not unusual for there to be issues as to whether they have been correctly constituted and disputes as to whether moneys have been properly assigned to the trust fund.[172] Another way in which unsecured creditors may escape from the pool is if they are in a position to benefit from the doctrine of set-off which is discussed at **24-72**.

### Establishing the liabilities–proof of debts and set-off

**24-68**   Contrary to what might be supposed, the administration of an insolvent debtor's estate does not involve the payment and discharge of all the debts owing by the debtor. Instead, it is only those debts which are provable in the insolvency and which are proved which will receive any payment.

### Submission of proofs

**24-69**   The rules specifying which debts are provable and the procedure to be followed in establishing a claim are contained in the Insolvency Rules 2016.[173] All claims by creditors are provable as debts against the company whether they are present or future, certain or contingent, ascertained or sounding only in damages (IR 2016, r 14.2). The debt may be a debt to which the company is subject at the date on which the company goes into liquidation[174] or it may be a debt which arises after the company goes into liquidation provided that it is in respect of an obligation incurred before that date.[175] Thus a contractual promise, entered into before going into liquidation, to pay a sum of money at a date occurring after the company has gone into liquidation gives rise to a provable debt. Any liability in tort is a debt provable in the winding up if either (1) the cause of action has accrued at the date on which the company goes into liquidation; or (2) all the elements necessary to establish the cause of action exist at that date except for actionable damage.[176] The liquidator is given power to estimate the value of contingent liabilities or debts of an uncertain amount.[177]

---

[171] See *Re Kayford Ltd* [1975] 1 All ER 604; *Re Lewis's of Leicester Ltd* [1995] 1 BCLC 428; *Re Holiday Promotions (Europe) Ltd* [1996] 2 BCLC 618; *Re Fleet Disposal Services Ltd, Spratt v AT & T Automotive Services Ltd* [1995] 1 BCLC 345; *Re Sendo International Ltd* [2007] 1 BCLC 141; *Re Farepak Food & Gifts Ltd* [2007] 2 BCLC 1. *Re BA Peters plc* [2010] 1 BCLC 142.

[172] For an example of the value of having customer funds held on trust, see *Re Lehman Brothers International (Europe) (No 2)* [2011] 2 BCLC 184 (court found statutory trust in that case imposed in respect of client money immediately the money was received from or on behalf of the client regardless of when it was segregated in a client account).                                                    [173] IR 2016, rr 14.3–14.11.

[174] IR 2016, r 14.1(3)(a). A company goes into liquidation if it passes a resolution for voluntary winding up or an order for its winding up is made by the court at a time when it has not already gone into liquidation by passing such a resolution: IA 1986, s 247(2).                                    [175] IR 2016, r 14.1(3)(b).

[176] IR 2016, r 14.1(4). This rule was substituted by SI 2006/1272 to redress the problems created by the decision in *Re T & N Ltd* [2005] EWHC 2870, [2006] 2 BCLC 374 where the court held that future asbestos claims were not provable debts for the purposes of winding up because the cause of action had not accrued by the liquidation date. See Toube, 'Future Contingent Claims' (2008) 21 Insolv Int 12 for the background to the change.

[177] IR 2016, r 14.14; and see *Re Danka Business Systems plc* [2013] 2 BCLC 313, CA, as to the liquidator's obligation to value contingent claims and to complete the liquidation by making a distribution on the basis of the value assigned to those contingent claims, even though that might result in unfairness to claimants whose claims are not readily quantifiable. In cases of difficulty, application may be made to the court for assistance: IA 1986, s 168(3), (5). See *Revenue and Customs Commissioners v Maxwell* [2011] 2 BCLC 301 as to how estimates might be made—in that case in the context of an administration and determining the value of a debt for voting purposes, but useful also in this context of a liquidator estimating the amount of a debt.

**24-70**  In a compulsory winding up, creditors are required to submit their claim and the document by which a creditor seeks to establish his claim is known as his 'proof'.[178] In a voluntary winding up, it is for the liquidator to decide whether he requires written proofs[179] and in practice he will require the submission of proofs. The liquidator examines the proof and may admit all or part of the debt or may reject it.[180] Parties aggrieved by his decision may apply to the court.[181] The liquidator has two months from the last date for proving to declare a dividend which he must do, provided he has sufficient funds (IR 2016, r 14.34), unless he has cause to postpone or cancel the dividend (r 14.33). But the liquidator is not personally liable in respect of a dividend and there is no relationship of debtor and creditor between the liquidator and any creditor.[182] If a liquidator fails to pay a declared dividend, an aggrieved creditor can apply to the court for an order directing payment.[183]

**24-71**  In the case of secured creditors, if they are content to rely solely on their security they do not submit a proof of debt at all. Alternatively, they may realise their security and prove for any unsecured balance, or surrender their security and prove for the whole amount.[184]

### Set-off

**24-72**  A further restriction on the amount for which creditors may prove arises from the application of the set-off rule in IR 2016, r 14.25 where, before the company goes into liquidation, there have been mutual credits, mutual debts, or other mutual dealings (subject to certain exclusions, r 14.25(6)) between the company and any creditor of the company proving or claiming to prove for a debt in the liquidation.[185] In that case, an account must be taken of what is due from each party to the other in respect of the mutual dealings and the sums due from one party must be set off against the sums due from the other (r 14.25(2)). Set-off is mandatory and creditors are not allowed to contract out of their right of set-off.[186] Set-off is automatic and self-executing as at the date of the winding-up order[187] with the original claims extinguished and only a net balance remaining.[188]

**24-73**  The provisions on insolvency set-off are intended 'to promote speedy and efficient administration of the assets so as to enable a distribution to be made to creditors as soon as possible and in a manner which achieves substantial justice between the parties to the set-off and, so far as practicable, equality in the treatment of creditors'.[189] In practice, set-off benefits creditors for, instead of having to prove with other unsecured creditors for the whole of their debt (i.e. having to claim against the pooled assets and possibly risk not being paid at all), creditors can set off debts which they owe to the company and

---

[178] IR 2016, r 1.2 (definitions) and r 14.3. Small debts of less than £1,000 may be treated as proved, see IR 2016, r 14.31.

[179] IR 2016, r 14.3.          [180] IR 2016, r 14.7.          [181] IR 2016, r 14.8.

[182] *Lomax Leisure v Miller* [2008] 1 BCLC 262.          [183] See *Lomax Leisure v Miller* [2008] 1 BCLC 262.

[184] IR 2016, r 14.19. As to the liquidator's right to redeem the security at the creditor's valuation, see r 14.17.

[185] IR 2016, r 14.24 sets out the equivalent set-off rule in administration which applies if the administrator gives notice that he intends to make a distribution to creditors.

[186] *National Westminster Bank Ltd v Halesowen Presswork and Assemblies Ltd* [1972] 1 All ER 641, HL; *Stein v Blake* [1995] 2 All ER 961, HL, noted Berg [1997] LMCLQ 49; *MS Fashions Ltd v Bank of Credit and Commerce International SA (No 2)* [1993] 3 All ER 769, Ch D, CA.

[187] *MS Fashions Ltd v Bank of Credit and Commerce International SA (No 2)* [1993] 3 All ER 769 at 775.

[188] *Re Bank of Credit and Commerce International SA (No 8)* [1997] 4 All ER 568, HL, aff'g [1996] 2 All ER 121, CA; *Stein v Blake* [1995] 2 All ER 961, HL. Any balance can be assigned by the party entitled to it: *Stein v Blake*.

[189] *Re Kaupthing Singer & Friedlander Ltd (No 2)* [2011] 1 BCLC 12 at [32], per Etherton LJ.

prove or pay only the balance.[190] Creditors will therefore seek to acquire rights of set-off, but there must be mutual credits, mutual debts, or other mutual dealings giving rise to set-off which must have occurred before the company went into liquidation (IR 2016, r 14.25(1), (6)). 'Mutual debts' does not in itself require anything more than commensurable cross-obligations between the same people in the same capacity and the origin of the debt (whether contract, statute, tort, voluntarily or by compulsion) is immaterial.[191] 'Mutual dealings' merely requires that there should be 'dealings' (in an extended sense which includes the commission of a tort or the imposition of a statutory obligation) giving rise to commensurable cross-claims.[192]

**24-74**  Set-off is strictly limited to mutual claims existing at the time of liquidation[193] and there can be no set-off of claims by third parties, even with their consent. The issue of third party claims was considered in several banking cases where companies had borrowed from and therefore were debtors of an insolvent bank and their controlling shareholders and directors were also depositors with the bank. The question was whether the depositors' claims against the bank could be set off against the banks' claims against the companies. Without set-osff, the bank liquidators were entitled to claim the entire debt from the companies while the depositors would have to prove in the liquidation for their deposits with little hope of recovery. In *MS Fashions Ltd v Bank of Credit and Commerce International SA (No 2)*[194] the bank advanced money to a company and repayment was guaranteed by a director who had a deposit account with the bank. As between himself and the bank, the director was expressed to be a principal debtor. It was held that the company director, as a principal debtor, could rely on the right of set-off to reduce or extinguish the debt owed to the bank by him and his company by the amount standing to his credit in his own deposit account with the bank. The key point, however, was that under the terms of this particular loan, the director was deemed to be the principal debtor.

**24-75**  In *Re Bank of Credit and Commerce International SA (No 8)*[195] the House of Lords considered this issue of third party deposits.[196] In this case the bank had lent money to a company on the security of a deposit made with the bank by the company's controlling shareholder. A charge was granted over the deposit but the charge did not contain any promise by the shareholder to pay what might be due from the company to the bank. The liquidators sought directions as to whether the bank could claim repayment of the loan from the company and leave the depositor to prove in the liquidation or whether it was obliged to set off the loan against the deposit and treat the company as discharged to that extent. The House of Lords held that set-off was limited to mutual claims existing at

---

[190] See *Stein v Blake* [1995] 2 All ER 961, HL. This is a bankruptcy case, but the principles are essentially common to winding up and bankruptcy. Any balance due to the company is not discounted to its current value in the way that a future debt is discounted for the purpose of set-off, see *Re Kaupthing Singer & Friedlander Ltd (No 2)* [2011] 1 BCLC 12 (administration case, but the equivalent rule applies in liquidation).

[191] *Re West End Networks Ltd, Secretary of State for Trade and Industry v Frid* [2004] 2 BCLC 1, HL. The mutual debts must have existed before the company went into liquidation and the company cannot seek to create a set-off after that date: see *Hague v Nam Tai Electronics Inc* [2007] 2 BCLC 194 at 198, PC.

[192] *Re West End Networks Ltd, Secretary of State for Trade and Industry v Frid* [2004] 2 BCLC 1, HL (there was mutuality and therefore set-off was permissible when a company had a claim against Customs & Excise for a VAT credit and there was a claim against the company by the Secretary of State with respect to redundancy payments). See also *Manson v Smith* [1997] 2 BCLC 161, CA; *Re a company (No 1641 of 2003)* [2004] 1 BCLC 210; *Smith (Administrator of Cosslett Contractors Ltd) v Bridgend County BC* [2002] 1 BCLC 77 at [35].

[193] The time of liquidation is defined in IA 1986, s 247(2), see n 174.     [194] [1993] 3 All ER 769.

[195] [1997] 4 All ER 568, HL, aff'g [1996] 2 All ER 121, CA; see Calnan (1998) 114 LQR 174; Goode (1998) 114 LQR 178. See also *Tam Wing Chuen v Bank of Credit and Commerce Hong Kong Ltd* [1996] 2 BCLC 69, PC.

[196] The third parties were the beneficial owners of the companies.

the date of the winding-up order and there could be no set-off of claims by third parties, even with their consent, as to do so would be to allow parties by agreement to subvert the fundamental principle of *pari passu* distribution of an insolvent company's assets.[197] There was no mutuality between the depositor and the bank which would permit the sum owed by the bank to the depositor (i.e. the amount of the deposit and interest) to be set off against the amount owed by the company to the bank. The depositor did not owe anything to the bank (not having taken on any personal liability for the borrower's debt) but had simply created an effective charge over the deposit in favour of the bank.[198] *MS Fashions Ltd v Bank of Credit and Commerce International SA (No 2)* was distinguishable on the basis of the very unusual security documents executed by the depositor in that case which resulted in the depositor being personally liable to the bank and so the bank's liability to the depositor and the depositor's liability to the bank in that case did constitute mutual dealings falling to be set off under IR 2016, r 14.25.[199] Here there was no such mutuality.

## G The order of distribution

**24-76** On winding up, secured creditors look to realise their security outside of the liquidation[200] while the fund available for distribution in the liquidation is disbursed in the following order: (1) the expenses of liquidation; (2) the preferential debts; (3) the claims of the floating chargeholder from which must be deducted the prescribed part if the charge was created on or after 15 September 2003 and the floating chargeholder may not have recourse to recoveries under avoidance provisions and for wrongful and fraudulent trading (see s 176ZB); (4) the unsecured creditors on a *pari passu* basis (and their fund is swelled by the amount set aside under the prescribed part).

### The expenses of winding up

**24-77** Section 115 of the IA 1986 provides that all expenses properly claimed in the winding up, including the remuneration of the liquidator, are payable out of the company's assets in priority to all other claims.[201] Section 176ZA further provides that the expenses of winding up, including the remuneration of the liquidator, have priority over any claims to property comprised in or subject to any floating charge and must be paid out of such property to the extent that the assets of the company available for payment of general creditors (excluding any sum set aside under the prescribed part provisions: see **24-85**) are insufficient to meet the expenses of winding up.[202]

**24-78** Obviously, given the priority accorded to expenses of the winding up, if extensive costs can be recovered as expenses, less will be available to pay the floating chargeholder and

---

[197] [1997] 4 All ER 568 at 573.      [198] [1997] 4 All ER 568 at 574, 576, 577.

[199] See [1997] 4 All ER 568 at 574.

[200] As a practical matter the secured creditor may ask the liquidator to realise the assets and charge the costs of realisation against those assets.

[201] The company's assets for this purpose include the proceeds of any legal action taken by a liquidator in his own name or on behalf of the company or arising from any arbitration or other dispute resolution procedure: IR 2016, r 6.42(2)(a)(i) and (ii); r 7.108(2)(a)(i) and (ii).

[202] Inserted by CA 2006, s 1282, overruling *Re Leyland Daf, Buchler v Talbot* [2004] 1 BCLC 281, HL, and applicable to liquidations post 6 April 2008, subject to certain transitional provisions; see Fletcher, 'CA 2006, Reversal of *Leyland Daf*' (2007) 20 Insolv Int 30.

ultimately the general unsecured creditors. Creditors have an interest therefore in what is an expense of the winding up, both in terms of whether they can bring their claim within that category and secure priority and, vice versa, whether they can prevent undue depletion of such funds as are available by challenging whether a particular cost is indeed an expense of the winding up.

**24-79**   The issue of what amounts to an 'expense of the winding up' was for many years a hotly disputed matter, both as to what constituted an 'expense' and as to the order of priority to be accorded *inter se*. The position was clarified initially by the decision of the House of Lords in *Re Toshoku Finance UK plc*.[203] The key provisions now are IR 2016, r 6.42 (creditors' voluntary winding up) and r. 7.108 (winding up by the court) which identify 18 classes of debts as expenses of the winding up and set out the order of priority in which they must be paid.

**24-80**   In *Re Toshoku Finance UK plc*[204] the House of Lords reviewed the operation of IR 1986, r 4.218, now IR 2016, r 6.42, r. 7.108, and concluded that the rule is a definitive statement of what counts as an expense of the liquidation. It is a complete statement of liquidation expenses, subject only to the qualifications contained in the rules themselves and subject to the principle, described by Lord Hoffmann as the principle in the *Lundy Granite* case,[205] which allows liabilities incurred before the liquidation in respect of property afterwards retained by the liquidator for the benefit of the insolvent estate to be treated as expenses in the winding up (such as liabilities arising under a pre-existing lease). To that limited extent, benefit of the estate is a relevant issue, but it is irrelevant to the payment of an item expressly provided for by IR 2016, r 6.42, r 7.108.[206] The only power reserved to the court is that conferred by IA 1986, s 156 which gives the court in a compulsory winding up a discretion to rearrange the priorities of the listed expenses *inter se*.[207]

**24-81**   The result is that IA 1986, s 115 determines the priority of expenses of winding up as against other claims and IR 2016, r 6.42 and r 7.108, respectively, determine both what is an expense and the order of priority of expenses *inter se*.[208] Two of the most important categories of debts identified therein are:

- expenses properly chargeable or incurred by the official receiver or the liquidator in preserving, realising, or getting in any of the assets of the company or otherwise in the preparation or conduct of any legal proceedings, arbitration, or other dispute resolution procedures which he has power to bring or defend whether in his own name or the name of the company or relating to the settlement or compromise of any action or dispute to which the proceedings or procedures relate (r 6.42(4)(a), r 7.108(4)(a)(ii)); and

- any necessary disbursements by the liquidator in the course of his administration (r. 6.42(4)(m), r 7.108(4)(m)).

**24-82**   In relation to IR 2016, r 6.42(4)(a), r 7.108(4)(a)(ii), the issue of legal costs had been controversial with creditors concerned that such realisations as the liquidator might have in hand should not be 'wasted' on litigation by the liquidator against the former directors

---

[203] [2002] 1 BCLC 598, HL.      [204] [2002] 1 BCLC 598, HL.
[205] *Re Lundy Granite Co* (1871) 6 Ch App 462.
[206] In reaching this conclusion the House of Lords rejected the so-called liquidation expenses principles as expressed in *Re Atlantic Computers plc* [1992] Ch 505 at 519–23 to the effect that all expenses incurred post liquidation were payable provided they were incurred for the benefit of the insolvent estate.
[207] See also IR 2016, r 6.43, r 7.110.      [208] *Re Toshoku Finance UK plc* [2002] 1 BCLC 598.

on grounds such as wrongful trading (IA 1986, s 214: see **15-18**) or transactions at an undervalue or preferences (IA 1986, ss 238, 239: see **15-46**, **15-60**). Liquidators for their part were anxious to pursue possible claims, but not if the costs were not permissible as an expense in the winding up, as the courts in fact confirmed.[209] The issue is resolved by IR 2016, rr 6.44–6.48 and rr 7.111–7.116 which expressly allows litigation costs to be recoverable as an expense in the winding up, but litigation expenses which exceed £5,000 are only recoverable out of floating charge realisations where approval or authorisation of such litigation expenses has been granted by the preferential creditor or chargeholder with a claim to the realisations or by the court.

**24-83**   In *Re Nortel GmbH*,[210] the Supreme Court concluded that sums due under certain directions and notices issued by the Pensions Regulator under the Pensions Act 2004 against companies in administration[211] (equally applicable to companies in liquidation) gave rise to a provable debt in the administration (or liquidation), but did not amount to an expense of the administration (or liquidation) as these are liabilities under an enactment arising by reason of obligations incurred before the administration or liquidation. The Supreme Court also noted that there is nothing in the IA 1986 or the IR 1986 (now IR 2016) which was intended to give the court a roving commission to vary the clear statutory ranking of liabilities in an administration or liquidation, citing *Re Toshoku Finance UK plc*.[212]

## Preferential debts

**24-84**   Preferential debts are debts (sometimes described as Crown debts) which Parliament has decided should be paid in priority to all other debts other than the expenses of winding up (IA 1986, s 175). The now quite limited categories of debts which qualify as preferential debts are set out in IA 1986, Sch 6.[213] Preferential debts rank equally amongst themselves and must be paid in full unless the assets are insufficient to meet them in which case they abate in equal proportions.[214] In so far as the assets available for payment of general creditors are insufficient for the payment of the preferential debts, the preferential debts have priority over the claims of and must be paid out of the property subject to the floating charge.[215]

---

[209]   See *Re Floor Fourteen Ltd, Lewis v IRC* [2001] 2 BCLC 392, CA; *Re R S & M Engineering Ltd, Mond v Suddards* [1999] 2 BCLC 485; *Re M C Bacon Ltd (No 2)* [1999] 2 BCLC 485.

[210]   [2013] 2 BCLC 135.

[211]   Essentially notices or directions requiring these companies to make payments to an employer's under-funded pension scheme—the employer usually being other companies in the same group.

[212]   [2002] 1 BCLC 598, HL.

[213]   The Enterprise Act 2002, s 251 removed the preference afforded to categories of claims payable to the Inland Revenue, Customs & Excise, and certain social security contributions. The remaining categories are contributions to occupational pension schemes (category 4); remuneration etc of employees (category 5); levies on coal and steel production (category 6); and a new category 7 with effect from 31 December 2014, deposits covered by the Financial Services Compensation Scheme (protecting to a limited extent depositors in financial institutions). A further sub-category of secondary preferential debts has also been created, see category 8, other deposits.

[214]   A creditor owed preferential and non-preferential debts must exercise any right of set-off proportionately against each class of debt: *Re Unit 2 Windows Ltd* [1985] 3 All ER 647.

[215]   See IA 1986, s 175(2)(b), see also s 176ZA(2)(b). 'Floating charge' is defined in s 251. Note also that in a compulsory winding up where distress is levied in the three months before a winding-up order, the preferential debts constitute a first charge on the proceeds of the distress: s 176(2), (3). This does not apply in a voluntary winding up: *Herbert Berry Associates Ltd v IRC* [1978] 1 All ER 161, HL.

### The floating chargeholder and the prescribed part

**24-85** As noted, to the extent that the assets of the company are insufficient to meet the expenses of winding up and the preferential debts, they must come out of the property subject to the floating charge (IA 1986, s 176ZA), so this is a vulnerability for the floating charge-holder. A further limitation is that recoveries by a liquidator from claims for fraudulent or wrongful trading, transactions at an undervalue, preferences or extortionate credit transactions, or from the assignment of such claims, do not fall within the grasp of any floating charge for they arise post the commencement of the winding up as a result of the exercise of a statutory power by a liquidator (s 176ZB), though such recoveries are subject to the prior claims of the expenses of the winding up[216] and the preferential debts[217] and to that extent improve the position of the floating chargeholder.

**24-86** As also noted, the categories of preferential debts have been reduced with the intention of releasing funds to benefit unsecured creditors and so hopefully save such creditors from insolvency themselves. To ensure this outcome, it was necessary to provide a mechanism whereby the sums released from Crown preference did not merely increase the returns to the floating chargeholder but would percolate down to the unsecured creditor. The mechanism used is the 'prescribed part' imposed by IA 1986, s 176A, which is that part of the estate of a company which must be set aside for unsecured creditors out of sums which would otherwise be available to the holders of a floating charge.[218] The percentage share of the company's assets which must be set aside in this way for unsecured creditors is:[219]

(1) where the company's net property does not exceed £10,000 in value, 50 per cent of that property;

(2) where the company's net property exceeds £10,000 in value, 50 per cent of the first £10,000 in value; and 20 per cent of that part of the company's net property which exceeds £10,000 in value, subject to a maximum of £600,000.

**24-87** The prescribed part only applies to floating charges created on or after 15 September 2003 (IA 1986, s 176A(9)). It is possible to disapply the requirement to set aside the prescribed part if the net property amounts to less than £10,000 and the office-holder thinks that the cost of making a distribution to the unsecured creditors would be disproportionate to the benefits (s 176A(3)). It is also possible for the prescribed part to be disapplied as part of a company voluntary arrangement or a scheme of arrangement (s 176A(4)) or by court order (s 176A(5)) where costs are disproportionate to the benefits.[220] In *Re International Sections Ltd*[221] the court suggested that disapplication orders should be exceptional for, in these sorts of situations, small dividends will often be the case irrespective of the costs of making any distribution. Here a significant, albeit relatively small, sum would remain

---

[216] IA 1986, s 115.      [217] IA 1986, s 175(2).

[218] The prescribed part applies in liquidations, administrations, provisional liquidations, and receiverships: IA 1986, s 176A(1); and it is not subject to the expenses of winding up: see IA 1986, s 176ZA(2)(a).

[219] See The IA 1986 (Prescribed Part) Order 2003, SI 2003/2097, art 3. See generally Keay, 'The Prescribed Part: Sharing around the Company's Funds' (2011) 24 Insolv Int 81. The Insolvency Service found no support for any amendment of the level of the prescribed part, see Ministerial Statement, 20 December 2011.

[220] The power to disapply the prescribed part is a power to disapply it in its entirety or not at all: *Re Courts plc* [2009] 2 BCLC 363 (court refused to disapply the prescribed part in a way which would have allowed the 37 largest creditors (with claims in excess of £28,000) to take the prescribed part in its entirety while leaving the remaining 260 creditors (claims below that amount) to receive nothing). See also *Re Hydroserve Ltd* [2008] BCC 175.                                    [221] [2009] 1 BCLC 580.

for distribution once the costs were catered for and the court refused to make a disapplication order saying that it would not be right to deprive the unsecured creditors of what
remained.[222]

**24-88**   A fixed or floating chargeholder with a shortfall in their security cannot be classed as an
unsecured creditor so as to participate in the prescribed part which is held for the benefit
of unsecured creditors alone. In *Re Airbase (UK Ltd), Thorniley v Revenue and Customs
Comrs*[223] and in *Re Permacell Finesse Ltd*[224] the courts rejected such claims concluding
that, as a matter of construction of IA 1986, s 176A and as a matter of policy, secured creditors are precluded from participation in the prescribed part with respect to a shortfall.
But there is no policy reason and nothing in the statute to prevent a floating chargeholder
surrendering totally their security and then participating as an unsecured creditor in the
prescribed part carved out of realisations of chargeholders with priority to them.[225] The
relevant time for determining the matter is when the claim is made against the prescribed
part and a floating chargeholder who surrenders his entire security after the commencement of the winding up may participate in the prescribed part.[226]

## Unsecured creditors—the *pari passu* principle

**24-89**   As noted, unsecured creditors must be paid in accordance with the principle of *pari passu*
distribution that all creditors participate in the pooled assets in proportion to the size of
their claim and, where the assets are insufficient to meet all the claims, then they abate
proportionately.[227] The *pari passu* rule is designed to ensure equal treatment applies but,
as Professor Milman has noted, the application of the rule may simply secure an equality
of misery,[228] given the widespread use of various mechanisms (i.e. security, trusts, and
retention of title clauses) which mean that the pooled assets will usually be insubstantial
and quite inadequate to meet the claims of the unsecured creditors. After all, they will
have been depleted by the payment of the expenses of winding up and the preferential
creditors. The position is alleviated somewhat by the prescribed part, as discussed at **24-
85**. Also, a liquidator may be able to swell the assets available to the unsecured creditors by
challenging transactions entered into by the company prior to winding up on the grounds
(or by assigning such claims), for example, that they were transactions at an undervalue or
preferences or by seeking a contribution from the company's directors alleging wrongful
trading: all these issues are discussed in Chapter 15.

**24-90**   There is nothing to prevent an unsecured creditor with a claim against the pooled assets
from agreeing as a matter of contract to subordinate his claim until such time as all other
unsecured creditors are paid, for such an agreement does not have the effect of shrinking

---

[222] The company had 66 known unsecured creditors to whom £230,613 was owed. The prescribed part
amounted to £6,731.09, with the estimated costs amounting to £3,332, leaving a maximum balance of
£3,409.09 available for distribution which would result in each of the unsecured creditors receiving a dividend of 1.48 pence in the pound.
   [223] [2008] 1 BCLC 437.          [224] [2008] BCC 208.
   [225] *Re PAL SC Realisations 2007 Ltd, Kelly v Inflexion Fund Ltd* [2011] BCC 93. The chargeholder was third
behind two other chargeholders and their claims would wipe out all the available assets so the chargeholder
would recover nothing; the chargeholder once it had surrendered its security would be able to claim against
the prescribed part and given the level of its claim would gain about 73 per cent of the prescribed part which
was estimated to be in the region of £317,000. In those circumstances, it made sense to surrender the security.
   [226] [2011] BCC 93 at [44].          [227] IA 1986, s 107; IR 2016, r 14.12.
   [228] See Milman, 'Priority Rights on Corporate Insolvency' in Clarke (ed), *Current Issues in Insolvency
Law* (1991), p 77.

the pool of assets available to the creditors.[229] In *Re SSSL Realisations (2002) Ltd*[230] the Court of Appeal concluded that if a group of companies enters into a subordination agreement (that no group company will prove for an inter-company debt in the liquidation of any group company until a principal creditor is paid in full), it is commercially important that the group companies be held to that agreement when the very circumstances which it addressed (insolvent group companies) arise.[231]

### Deferred debts

**24-91**   Certain debts are deferred by statute until all the other debts of the company have been paid. Thus interest on all proved debts, whether or not the debt was an interest-bearing debt, from the company going into liquidation until the date of actual payment, is deferred until the payment of all debts, but any surplus then remaining must be applied in paying interest before being applied for any other purpose.[232] Another deferred debt is where a company has contracted to redeem or purchase some of its own shares (see Chapter 22) and the company has not completed the transaction by the time of the commencement of the winding up. The company may be compelled to complete the bargain but only after all other debts and liabilities of the company (other than any due to members in their character as such) have been paid, see **22-24**.[233] A further deferred payment is any debt or liability due to a member in his character of a member whether by way of dividends, profits, or otherwise (IA 1986, s 74(2)(f)). A sum is due to a member of a company 'in his character of a member' if the right to receive it is based on a cause of action founded on the statutory contract between the members and the company imposed by CA 2006, s 33 and such other provisions of the Act as confer rights or impose liabilities on members.[234] A member having a cause of action independent of the statutory contract is then in no worse a position than any other creditor. Debts due to members in other capacities such as trade creditors or lenders rank, therefore, alongside similar debts due to non-members. Finally, the courts have a power to defer payment of debts due from the company to persons found liable for fraudulent or wrongful trading in relation to it until all other debts owed by the company (and interest) have been paid (IA 1986, s 215(4)).

### Shareholders

**24-92**   It is only on a solvent winding up that there can be any return of capital or surplus to the shareholders and the priorities as amongst the shareholders and classes of shareholders are discussed in Chapter 16, see **16-22**. On an insolvent liquidation, there will be insufficient funds to pay the creditors in full and therefore there will be no funds remaining for the shareholders who lose their capital, but their losses are limited to that amount and they bear no responsibility for payments to creditors (assuming they have not given personal guarantees to any creditor), hence the attraction of limited liability.

---

[229] See *Re Maxwell Communications Corp plc (No 2)* [1994] 1 BCLC 1; Nolan, 'Less Equal than Others: *Maxwell* and Subordinated Unsecured Obligations' [1995] JBL 485; also *Re British & Commonwealth Holdings (No 3) plc* [1992] BCLC 322.

[230] [2007] 1 BCLC 29, CA.          [231] [2007] 1 BCLC 29 at 59, CA.

[232] IA 1986, s 189(1), (2); for the purposes of interest under this provision, all debts rank *pari passu* and it makes no difference, for example, whether the debt was preferential: s 189(3).

[233] CA 2006, s 735(4)–(6).

[234] *Soden v British and Commonwealth Holdings plc* [1997] 2 BCLC 501, HL.

## H  Dissolution of the company

### Dissolution after winding up

**24-93**  After completion of the winding-up process, the company is removed from the register of companies, a process known as dissolution, and it ceases to exist. In both compulsory and voluntary liquidation, dissolution occurs automatically three months after the registration by the registrar of companies of the liquidator's final account and statement at Companies House.[235] An official receiver acting as the liquidator in a compulsory liquidation may apply to the registrar for early dissolution of the company where the realisable assets are insufficient to cover the expenses of winding up and the affairs of the company do not warrant further investigation. In that case, the company is dissolved three months after the application for early dissolution.[236] On being dissolved, any property of the company is deemed to be *bona vacantia* and vests in the Crown (CA 2006, s 1012).

### Striking companies off the register of companies

**24-94**  In practice, the majority of companies that are dissolved in England and Wales each year are not formally wound up at all. Instead, they cease to exist when the registrar of companies strikes them off the register as defunct. The registrar has power to do this where the registrar has reasonable cause to believe that a company is not carrying on business or is not in operation (CA 2006, s 1000(1)).[237] Many of the companies targeted will have failed to file confirmation statements and annual accounts which may suggest that the company has ceased trading.

**24-95**  Alternatively, any company may apply to be struck off the register on payment of the appropriate fee (currently £10). This procedure is governed by CA 2006, s 1003–1011 and is designed to enable companies quickly and inexpensively to be dissolved and removed from the register. The application for striking off must be made by the company's directors or a majority of them (s 1003(2)). Elaborate provision is made for notifying members, creditors, and interested parties (via the *Gazette* and otherwise) of the application to be struck off (ss 1003(3), 1006).

### Restoration to the register

**24-96**  An application may be made to the court for an order restoring a company to the register where the company has been dissolved or deemed dissolved on liquidation or administration or has been struck off either by the registrar of companies or following an application for striking off (CA 2006, s 1029(1), (2)). The registrar of companies is able also to restore companies to the register when they have been struck off as defunct by the registrar, see CA 2006, ss 1024–1028.

---

[235]  IA 1986, s 201(1), (2) (voluntary winding up); s 205(1), (2) (compulsory winding up).
[236]  IA 1986, s 202(2), (5).
[237]  The registrar may also strike off a company under this procedure where the company has gone into liquidation but no liquidator is acting or the final returns have not been delivered: see CA 2006, s 1001.

# Index